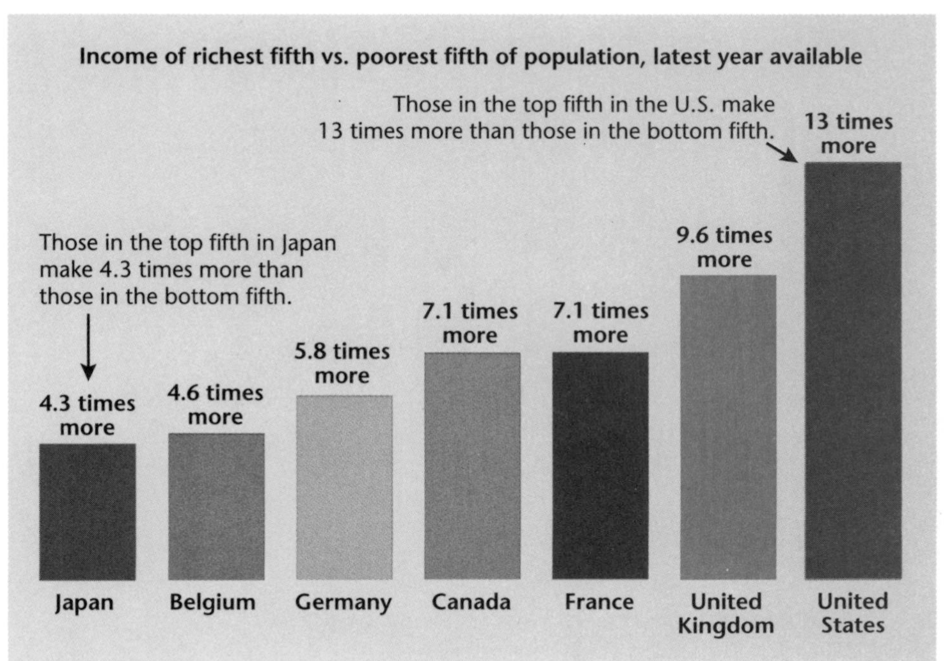

Income Gap:
United States Leads Industrialized Nations

Sources: Clarifying Issues '96, 1996. New York: Public Agenda, p. 9; The World Bank; U.S. Bureau of the Census. 2000 *Current Population Reports* P-60, 210. Washington, DC: U.S. Government Printing Office.

Distribution of HIV/AIDS, 2000

Region	*Number of People with HIV/AIDS*
Sub-Saharan Africa	25,300,000
South and Southeast Asia	5,800,000
Latin America/Caribbean	1,790,000
United States/Canada	920,000
Western Europe	540,000
East Asia/Pacific	640,000
Eastern Europe/Central Asia	700,000
North Africa/Middle East	400,000
Australia/New Zealand	15,000
Total	36,100,000

Source: United Nations, World Health Organization. 2001. "Report on the Global HIV/AIDS Epidemic." New York: Joint United Nations Programme on HIV/AIDS.

SOCIAL PROBLEMS

Ninth Edition

D. Stanley Eitzen
Colorado State University
Maxine Baca Zinn
Michigan State University

Boston New York San Francisco
Mexico City Montreal Toronto London Madrid Munich Paris
Hong Kong Singapore Tokyo Cape Town Sydney

Editor-in-Chief: Karen Hanson
Series Editor: Jeff Lasser
Senior Developmental Editor: Ellen Darion
Series Editorial Assistant: Andrea Christie
Marketing Manager: Jude Hall
Production Administrators: Joe Sweeney and Annette Pagliaro
Editorial Production: WordCrafters Editorial Services, Inc.
Composition Buyer: Linda Cox
Manufacturing Buyer: Megan Cochran
Cover Administrator: Linda Knowles
Photo Researcher: Sarah Evertson, Image Quest
Text Design and Composition: Glenna Collett

Library of Congress Cataloging-in-Publication Data

Social problems / D. Stanley Eitzen, Maxine Baca Zinn.— 9th ed.
p. cm.
Includes bibliographical references and index.
ISBN 0-205-33721-X
1. Social problems. 2. Social problems—United States. 3. Social structure—United States. 4. United States—Social conditions—1945– I. Zinn, Maxine Baca, 1942–

HN17.5 .E37 2003
361.1—dc21 2002023643

Printed in the United States of America
10 9 8 7 6 5 4 3 2 1 RRD-OH 08 07 06 04 03 02

Photo Credits
Chapter 1: p. 1, AP/Wide World Photos; p. 8, © Steven Rubin/The Image Works; p. 9. © Jim Richardson/CORBIS; p. 15, AP/Wide World Photos.
Chapter 2: p. 22, AP/Wide World Photos; p. 31,AP/Wide World Photos; p. 37, © Reuters/Getty News Images.
Photo credits continue on page 622, which should be considered an extension of the copyright page.

Brief Contents

Contents

Boxes

Chapter 15

Chapter 16

Chapter 17

Chapter 18

Chapter 19

Preface

Social Problems, Ninth Edition, examines subjects such as crime, corporate crime, racism, sexism, urban decay, poverty, the politics of drugs, and terrorism. These topics are inherently interesting. The typical book on social problems describes these phenomena separately, using a variety of explanations. Students exposed to such a melange of approaches might retain their interest in these problems, but they probably would complete the book with little grasp of how social problems are interrelated and of society's role in their creation and perpetuation. This book is different. The approach is consistently sociological. There is a coherent framework from which to analyze and understand society's social problems.

Our overarching goal in *Social Problems,* Ninth Edition, is to capture the imagination of our readers. We want them not only to be interested in the topics, but also to become enthusiastic about exploring the intricacies and mysteries of social life. We want them, moreover, to incorporate the sociological perspective into their explanatory repertoire. The sociological perspective requires, at a minimum, accepting two fundamental assumptions. The first is that individuals are products of their social environment. Who they are, what they believe, what they strive for, and how they feel about themselves are all dependent on other people and on the society in which they live. The incorporation of the sociological perspective requires that we examine the structure of society in order to understand such social problems as racism, poverty, and crime. This method, however, runs counter to the typical explanations people offer for social ills. The choice is seen in an example supplied by Thomas Szasz:

> Suppose that a person wishes to study slavery. How would he go about doing so? First, he might study slaves. He would then find that such persons are generally brutish, poor, and uneducated, and he might conclude that slavery is their "natural" or appropriate social status. . . . Another student "biased" by contempt for the institution of slavery might proceed differently. He would maintain that there can be no slave without a master holding him in bondage; and he would accordingly consider slavery a type of human relationship and, more generally, a social institution supported by custom, law, religion, and force. From this point of view, the study of masters is at least as relevant to the study of slavery as is the study of slaves. (Szasz, 1970:123–124)

Most of us, intuitively, would make the first type of study and reach a conclusion. This book, however, emphasizes the second type of study: looking at masters as well as slaves. An observer cannot gain an adequate understanding of racism, crime, poverty, or other social problems by studying only bigots, criminals, and the affluent. Therefore, we focus on the social structure to determine the underlying features of the social world in an effort to understand social problems.

Because our emphasis is on social structure, the reader is required to accept another fundamental assumption of the sociological perspective (see Eitzen and Baca Zinn, 2001). We are referring to adopting a critical stance toward all social forms. Sociologists must ask these questions: How does the social system really work? Who has the power? Who benefits under the existing social arrangements and who does not? We should also ask questions such as: Is the law neutral? Why are some drugs illegal and others, which are known to be harmful, legal? Why are so few organizations in the United States—which is characterized as a democracy—democratic? Is U.S. society a meritocratic one in which talent and effort combine to stratify people fairly? Questions such as these call into question existing myths, stereotypes, and official dogma. The critical examination of society can demystify and demythologize. It sensitizes the individual to the inconsistencies present in society. But, most important, a critical stance toward social arrangements allows us to see their role in perpetuating social problems. In conclusion, the reader should be aware that we are not dispassionate observers of social problems. Unlike the chemist, who can observe the reaction of chemical compounds in a test tube objectively, we are participants in the social life we seek to study and understand. As we examine riots in Cincinnati, child abuse, poverty, urban blight, or the terrorist attack on the World Trade Center and the Pentagon, we cannot escape our feelings and values. The choice of topics, the order in which they are presented, and even the tone of the discourse in the book reveal our values. We cannot, however, let our values and our feelings render the analyses invalid. All pertinent findings—not only those that support our point of view—must be reported. In other words, we must be as scientific as possible, which requires a recognition of our biases so that the findings will not be invalidated.

Let us, then, briefly make our values more explicit. We oppose social arrangements that prevent people from developing to their full potential. That is, we reject political and social repression, educational elitism, institutional barriers to racial and sexual equality, economic exploitation, and official indifference to human suffering. Stating these feelings positively, we favor equality of opportunity, the right to dissent, social justice, an economic system that minimizes inequality, and a political system that maximizes citizen input in decisions and provides for an adequate health care system and acceptable living conditions for all people. Obviously, we believe that U.S. society as currently organized falls short of what we consider to be a good society. The problem areas of U.S. society are the subjects of *Social Problems*, Ninth Edition. So, too, are structural arrangements around the globe that harm people.

In 2001 the Colorado Commission on Higher Education (a state oversight commission appointed by the governor) commissioned a conservative watchdog group to evaluate teacher education programs in the state universities of Colorado. The report criticized the University of Colorado's school of education for pushing an agenda that "indoctrinates" students in issues of race, class, gender, and sexual orientation. David Saxe, the principal investigator of the report, said, "More than any other reviewed institution, CU's teacher education programs are the most politically correct and stridently committed to the social justice model" (quoted in Curtin, 2001:1B). Suffice it to say that our approach to social problems would also be castigated by Mr. Saxe, for we are absolutely committed to social justice; and this means, among other things, an understanding of how many social problems of U.S. society are rooted in the hierarchical arrangements based on class, race, gender, and sexuality.

Ordinarily, when revising a book for the ninth time, the task is rather routine: updating and making other cosmetic changes with, perhaps, a new chapter. Since the last edition was published, several important trends have intensified, making a significant revision necessary. For example:

- The possibility of nuclear war among the superpowers is remote, but terrorism is a reality.
- The magnitude of domestic and global environmental problems has accelerated.
- Racial and ethnic tensions throughout the world and within the United States have escalated.
- The pace of immigration continues to increase the diversity of U.S. society.
- The world has added three hundred million people, most of whom are poor.
- We are reminded daily of the cozy relationship between money and politics.
- Although some large cities in the United States are showing signs of vigor, most are troubled with growing dependent populations, shrinking job markets, increasing racial tensions, and declining economic resources to meet their problems.
- The economy continues its massive transformation, adding workers in some areas and displacing them in others. Among other consequences, the middle class continues its decline in numbers, and the gap between the affluent and the poor and near poor widens.
- A Republican president and a middle- to right-of-center Congress have altered the way government seeks to solve social problems.
- The health care delivery system in the United States has two major problems: 43 million are left out of it, and those included are now typically in managed care systems, which are motivated to provide the least expensive treatments.

This ninth edition of *Social Problems* considers each of these important trends and events, as well as others. A chapter on the disabled as a minority group has been added, making this edition the only social problems text with such a chapter. The chapter on national security has been completely revised and reorganized to incorporate international terrorism. Other chapters have been reorganized to include new data, current research, and new interpretations.

Features of This Book

Five types of panels are included (usually three per chapter). First, "Voices" panels provide the personal views of those affected by a social problem. Second, "A Closer Look" elaborates on a topic in detail. Third, "Social Problems in Global Perspec-

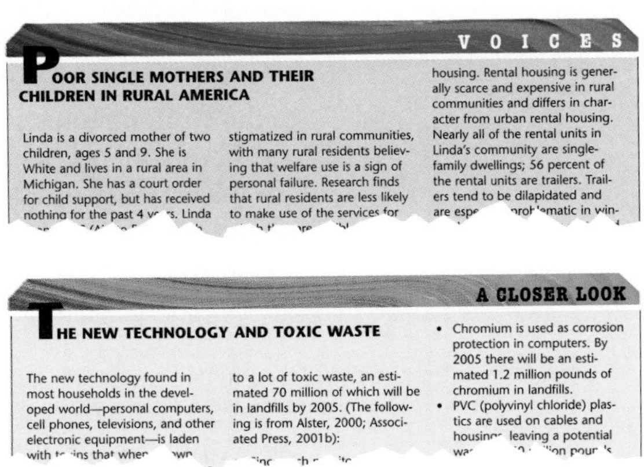
VOICES

POOR SINGLE MOTHERS AND THEIR CHILDREN IN RURAL AMERICA

Linda is a divorced mother of two children, ages 5 and 9. She is White and lives in a rural area in Michigan. She has a court order for child support, but has received nothing for the past 4 ye...s. Linda ... stigmatized in rural communities, with many rural residents believing that welfare use is a sign of personal failure. Research finds that rural residents are less likely to make use of the services for ... housing. Rental housing is generally scarce and expensive in rural communities and differs in character from urban rental housing. Nearly all of the rental units in Linda's community are single-family dwellings; 56 percent of the rental units are trailers. Trailers tend to be dilapidated and are espe... problematic in win-...

A CLOSER LOOK

THE NEW TECHNOLOGY AND TOXIC WASTE

The new technology found in most households in the developed world—personal computers, cell phones, televisions, and other electronic equipment—is laden with t...ins that when ... to a lot of toxic waste, an estimated 70 million of which will be in landfills by 2005. (The following is from Alster, 2000; Associated Press, 2001b):

- Chromium is used as corrosion protection in computers. By 2005 there will be an estimated 1.2 million pounds of chromium in landfills.
- PVC (polyvinyl chloride) plastics are used on cables and housing... leaving a potential wa... ...ion pour...

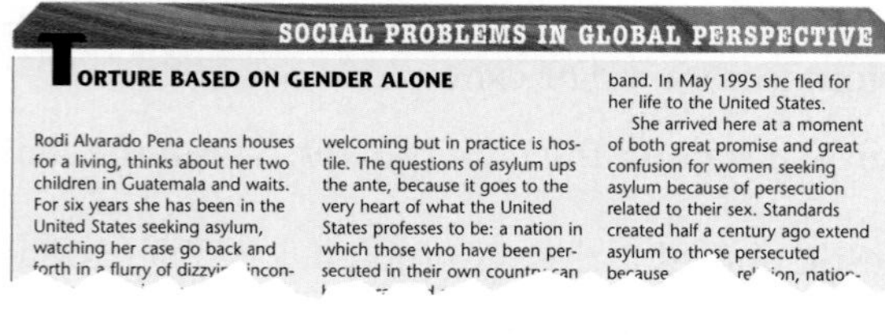

SOCIAL PROBLEMS IN GLOBAL PERSPECTIVE

TORTURE BASED ON GENDER ALONE

Rodi Alvarado Pena cleans houses for a living, thinks about her two children in Guatemala and waits. For six years she has been in the United States seeking asylum, watching her case go back and forth in a flurry of dizzy-

welcoming but in practice is hostile. The questions of asylum ups the ante, because it goes to the very heart of what the United States professes to be: a nation in which those who have been persecuted in their own countr-

band. In May 1995 she fled for her life to the United States.

She arrived here at a moment of both great promise and great confusion for women seeking asylum because of persecution related to their sex. Standards created half a century ago extend asylum to those persecuted

SOCIAL POLICY

REFORMS TO INCLUDE DISABLED PERSONS IN THE WORKFORCE

The ADA has not "leveled the playing field"—the goal of most civil rights legislation—by eliminating economic discrimination. In liberal capitalist economies,

• *Remove Discriminatory Insurance Language:* William Robb, an advocate from South Carolina, points out that "employers see disabled workers as a liability rather than as an asset, and

Work Incentives Improvement Act of 1999 (WIIA), a subsidy that will allow disabled workers to retain their public health care by permitting them to buy into Medicare and Medicaid. But typical of most reforms, this measure falls way short. For example, it is not mandatory that states adopt

tive" illustrate how other societies deal with a particular social problem. This global emphasis is also evident in panels and tables that compare the United States with other nations on such topics as crime/incarceration, medical care, and education. Two variations of social policy panels are included: One looks at policy issues and the other illustrates a social policy that works to alleviate a social problem. Finally, "Looking Toward the Future" panels examine the trends concerning the social problem under consideration at the beginning of a new millennium. At the conclusion of each chapter are a chapter review, key terms, and websites for further reference.

In summary, this ninth edition of *Social Problems* improves on the earlier editions by focusing more deliberately on five themes: (1) the structural sources of social problems; (2) the role of the United States in global social problems; (3) the centrality of class, race, gender, sexuality, and disability as sources of division, inequality, and injustice; (4) the critical examination of society; and (5) solutions to social problems.

NOTE ON LANGUAGE USAGE

In writing this book we have been especially sensitive to our use of language. Language is used to reflect and maintain the secondary status of social groups by defining them, diminishing them, trivializing them, or excluding them. For example, traditional English uses masculine words (*man, mankind, he*) to refer to people in general. Even the ordering of *masculine* and *feminine,* or of *Whites* and *Blacks,* within the discussion or the reference to one category consistently preceding its counterpart subtly conveys the message that the one listed first is superior to the other. In short, our goal is to use language so that it does not create the impression that one social class, race, or gender is superior to any other.

The terms of reference for racial and ethnic categories are changing. Blacks increasingly use the term *African American,* and Hispanics often refer to themselves as *Latinos*. In *Social Problems,* Ninth Edition, we use each of these terms for each social category because they often are used interchangeably in popular and scholarly discourse.

Also, we try to avoid the use of *America* or *American society* when referring to the United States. *America* should be used only in reference to the entire western hemisphere: North, Central, and South America (and then, in the plural, *Americas*). Its use as a reference to only the United States implies that the other nations of the western hemisphere have no place in our frame of reference.

ACKNOWLEDGMENTS

We want to thank the following reviewers for their helpful comments: Larry R. Ridener, James Madison University; Nita L. Bryant, Virginia Commonwealth

University; Lutz Kaelber, University of Vermont; Charles W. Jarrett, Ohio University Southern Campus; Alberto Restrepo, University of San Diego; Dean G. Rojek, University of Georgia; and Woody Doane, University of Hartford. For reviewing the disability chapter, we want to thank Rosalyn Benjamin Darling, Indiana University of Pennsylvania; Lynn Schlesinger, Plattsburgh SUNY; Greg Olsen, University of Wisconsin-Oshkosh; and Horton and Elsie Flaming.

Thanks also to Angela Y. H. Pok for her research assistance, Heather Dillaway for compiling a list of websites for each chapter, and Janice Johnston and Dan Derezinski for their computer assistance.

Focusing on the poor and ignoring the system of power, privilege, and profit which makes them poor, is a little like blaming the corpse for murder.

—Michael Parenti

1

PART ONE
POLITICAL ECONOMY OF SOCIAL PROBLEMS

Sociological Approach to Social Problems

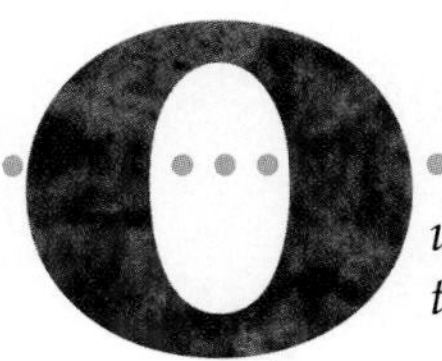

ur most serious problems are social problems for which there are no technical solutions, only human solutions.

—George E. Brown, Jr., Chairman of the House Committee on Science, Space, and Technology

At the beginning of the new millennium, there were reasons for optimism among Americans concerning social problems. Fueling this optimism were these facts: African American and Latino poverty rates were down; infant mortality was down; violent crime rates were falling; the number of people on welfare had decreased dramatically; and the United States was the world's most powerful nation by far, no longer challenged by the specter of Communism. Has the United States turned the corner? Are we in a new era where social problems are diminishing? While there are indications that some social problems are lessening in intensity, many are not and remain serious. Consider these facts (see Table 1.1 for how the United States ranks compared to other industrialized nations on a number of dimensions):

- One in eight Americans is poor.
- Emergency food requests and people seeking emergency shelter are increasing.
- Inequality (the gap between the rich and the poor) is at record levels.
- Forty-three million Americans are without health insurance, including one in five workers.
- Two million Americans are in jail or prison.
- On an average day 135,000 children take guns to school.

TABLE 1.1

How the United States Stands Among Industrialized Countries

The United States ranks:

1st	In military technology
1st	In military exports
1st	In Gross Domestic Product
1st	In the number of millionaires and billionaires
1st	In health technology
1st	In defense expenditures
10th	In eighth-grade science scores
11th	In the proportion of children in poverty
16th	In living standards among our poorest one-fifth of children
17th	In low-birth-weight rates
18th	In the gap between rich and poor children
21st	In eighth-grade math scores
23rd	In infant mortality
Last	In protecting our children against gun violence

Source: Children's Defense Fund. 2001. *The State of America's Children: 2001 Yearbook.* Washington, DC: Children's Defense Fund, p. xxii.

"Where did we go wrong?"

- Among all nations, the United States is number one in cocaine and heroin use.
- Annually, 5,000 children are killed by their parents and 30,000 are left permanently disabled from abuse and neglect.
- In international comparisons, eighth graders in the United States are behind their peers in other industrial nations.
- The United States, while 5 percent of the world's population, uses one-fourth of the world's resources and is the largest contributor to global warming through the use of petroleum products.

Since 1970 two social scientists, Marc and Marque-Luisa Miringoff (1999), have tabulated an annual index—"The Index of Social Health"—for the United States. This index includes measurements on sixteen major social problems, among them unemployment, percent of children in poverty, the gap between the rich and the poor, average weekly earnings, levels of child abuse, and health insurance coverage. This barometer of social problems, which works something like the Dow Jones Industrial Average (the higher the score, the better), has declined from an index score of 72 to the low 40s now. There have been improvements in infant mortality, high school dropouts, poverty among the elderly, and life expectancy; but, in general, the trend is down, our problems are worsening. For example, during the past three decades rates for social indicators such as child abuse, child poverty, youth suicide, health care coverage, inequality, wages, and violent crime have deteriorated. Why are our social problems continuing to decline? Is the answer to recapture traditional family values, as some assert, or are there social arrangements within society that exacerbate human misery? (See the panel titled "Looking toward the Future.")

Sociologists have always been intrigued with the causes, consequences, solutions, and changing definitions of social problems. The following historical sketch of how sociologists have approached social problems provides a useful background to the focus of this book.

LOOKING TOWARD THE FUTURE

INDICATORS OF DECLINE

It's not so much being able to forecast change as to recognize it as it occurs.
—Anonymous

Societies, like economies, have "leading indicators" that give great insight into the future. While these are never infallible predictors, they are almost always helpful in judging direction. They are not always right, but they are usually close. They do not predict, but they forecast. They may be wrong, but we ignore them at our peril. These leading indicators are the status of a nation's human resources, values, political system, social systems, and economic competitiveness.

It is my thesis that America's leading indicators have turned negative and are flashing warning signs. America is heading for multiple crises and relative decline. I set forth this case knowing that the world is a complex place and that history is fond of playing tricks on all civilizations—particularly great civilizations. Every great nation had false prophets of doom. Yet, no great nation in history has survived the ravages of time. All great civilizations believed their greatness to be permanent. In Spain, God was on the side of the King and would never let Spain decline because it was specially blessed. England knew that Britain would forever rule the waves and that "the sun would never set on the British empire." But history teaches us that nations rise and nations fall.

Where is America in this cycle? We judge at our peril. The optimists have so far prevailed. True, America has many tangible strengths, but a nation's wealth and status are like starlight: What you see is not what is, but what was. Just as the light we see from a distant star started its journey thousands of years ago, so is the nation's current success due principally to past actions. Great nations have great momentum; past investments in education and productivity continue to give benefits even after those good traits deteriorate. To a large degree, one generation benefits from the seeds planted by their fathers and mothers. We, in turn, plant seeds that will be reaped by our children. They reap what we sow.

There are always forces of decline and forces of renewal at work within societies, and it is difficult to know which are in the ascendancy. I clearly recognize that my theory may be wrong. Schopenhauer warns us that "every man confuses the limits of his mind for the limits of the world." That said, I believe our current problems and trends are nation-threatening and perhaps irreversible. I believe they likely will lead to a decline in power, prestige, and our standard of living. Most likely, this will lead to social and political turmoil.

My argument is that the chances (70–30) are that America has entered into a cycle of decline. It is not irreversible, but, to some degree, it is inevitable. Our kids will live in a far different and more chaotic America—an America that doesn't have nearly the wealth or the opportunities that our generation had. Decline, like fog, creeps up on civilizations on little cat's feet, and America's decline began in the recent past. Tomorrow's futurist will wonder how we were so myopic.

In my mind, we have seriously compromised our future. We have overconsumed and underinvested. We have not adequately maintained our wealth-creating potential. A society that spends more government money than it raises in taxes, that consumes more than it produces, that borrows more than it saves, that imports more than it exports is a society on its way to second-class status.

A nation whose students are at the bottom of all international comparisons in education, whose cities are battlefields, who has a disproportionate number of functional illiterates and the world's highest crime rate should beware of chauvinistic reassurances. We face nation-threatening problems that are getting, not better, but worse.

There is a story about a sailor on the *Titanic,* just before it sailed on its fatal voyage, telling a newspaper that "God almighty couldn't sink this ship." We may find a way to solve our problems and go on to a brighter future, but we are fighting history. Every once-great nation in history thought itself immune from decline, and, up to now, none of them has been right.

Source: Richard D. Lamm. 1993. "Indicators of Decline." *The Futurist* 27 (July/August):60.

HISTORY OF SOCIAL PROBLEMS THEORY

Typically, social problems have been thought of as social situations that a large number of observers felt were inappropriate and needed remedying. Early U.S. sociologists applied a medical model to the analysis of society in order to assess whether some pathology was present. Using what were presumed to be universal criteria of normality, sociologists commonly assumed that social problems resulted from "bad" people—maladjusted people who were abnormal because of mental deficiency, mental disorder, lack of education, or incomplete socialization. These social pathologists, because they assumed that the basic norms of society are universally held, viewed social problems as behaviors or social arrangements that disturb the moral order. For them, the moral order of U.S. society obviously defined such behaviors as homosexuality, alcoholism, suicide, theft, and murder as social problems. But this approach did not take into account the complexity inherent in a diverse society.

In a variation of the absolutist approach, sociologists in the 1920s and 1930s focused on the conditions of society that fostered problems. Societies undergoing rapid change from the processes of migration, urbanization, and industrialization were thought to have pockets of social disorganization. Certain areas of the cities undergoing the most rapid change, for example, were found to have disproportionately high rates of vice, crime, family breakdowns, and mental disorders.

In the past few decades many sociologists have returned to a study of problem individuals—deviants who violate the expectations of society. The modern study of deviance has developed in two directions. The first sought the sources of deviation within the social structure. Sociologists saw deviance as the result of conflict between the culturally prescribed goals of society (such as material success) and the obstacles to obtaining them that some groups of people face. The other, of relatively recent origin, has focused on the role of society in creating and sustaining deviance through labeling those people viewed as abnormal. Societal reactions are viewed as the key in determining what a social problem is and who is deviant.

Most recently, some sociologists have tried to alert others to the problematic nature of social problems themselves (see Spector and Kitsuse, 1987). These theorists emphasize the **subjective nature of social problems.** They say that what is defined as a social problem differs by audience and by time. Pollution, for example, has not always been considered a social problem. This perspective also examines how particular phenomena come to be defined as social problems, focusing on how groups of people actively influence those definitions.

This brief description reveals several issues that must be addressed in looking at social problems. First, sociologists have difficulty agreeing on an adequate definition of social problems. Second, there is continuing debate over the unit of analysis: Is the focus of inquiry individuals or social systems? Related to the latter is the issue of numbers: How many people have to be affected before something is a social problem? In this regard C. Wright Mills (1962) made an important distinction. If a situation such as unemployment is a problem for an individual or for scattered individuals, it is a "private trouble." But if unemployment is widespread, affecting large numbers of people in a region or the society, it is a "public issue" or a "social problem."

TOWARD A DEFINITION OF SOCIAL PROBLEMS

There is an **objective reality to social problems:** There *are* conditions in society (such as poverty and institutional racism) that induce material or psychic suffering for certain segments of the population; there *are* sociocultural phenomena that prevent a significant number of societal participants from developing and using their full potential; there *are* discrepancies between what the United States is supposed to stand for (equality of opportunity, justice, democracy) and the actual conditions in which many of its people live; and people *are* fouling their own nest through pollution and the indiscriminate use of natural resources (Eitzen, 1984). This normative approach assumes that some kinds of actions are likely to be judged deleterious in any context. Therefore, one goal of this book is to identify, describe, and explain situations that are objective social problems.

There are several dangers, however, in defining social problems objectively. The most obvious is that subjectivity is always present. To identify a phenomenon as a problem implies that it falls short of some standard. But what standards are to be used? Will the standards of society suffice? In a pluralistic society such as the United States, there is no uniform set of guidelines. People from different social strata and other social locations (such as region, occupation, race, and age) differ in their perceptions of what a social problem is and, once defined, how it should be solved. Is marijuana use a social problem? Is pornography? Is the relatively high rate of military spending a social problem? Is abortion a social problem? There is little consensus in U.S. society on these and other issues. All social observers, then, must be aware of differing viewpoints and respect the perspectives of the social actors involved.

Even sociologists and other social scientists do not agree among themselves on the definition of social problems and on what types of phenomena should be included under that rubric. Nor can they escape making value judgments as they pursue their work. It is impossible to do research that is uncontaminated by personal and political sympathies (Becker, 1967). The values of the scholar-researcher affect both the choice of questions and the answers. In the study of poverty, for example, should the social scientist examine the poor people or the system that tends to perpetuate poverty among a certain segment of society? In the study of the problems of youth, should the major question be why some youth are troublesome for adults, or why adults make so much trouble for youth? These quite different questions will yield very different results.

We should recognize, then, that the study of social problems cannot be value free and that the type of problems researched and the strategies used tend either to support or to undermine existing societal arrangements. Seen in this way, both types of social research are political. Yet there is a tendency to label as political only the research that challenges the system. Research that finds fault with the social system on behalf of the powerless implies that the system is being questioned, and the charge typically arises that such research is biased. Becker has described the logic of this situation:

> When do we accuse ourselves and our fellow sociologists of bias? I think an inspection of representative instances would show that the accusation arises, in one important class of cases, when the research gives credence, in any serious way, to the perspective of the subordinate group in some hierarchical

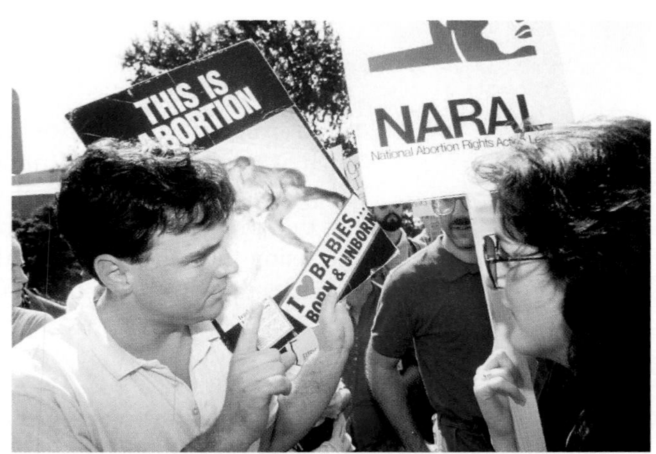

There is widespread disagreement as to whether abortion is a social problem.

> relationship. In the case of deviance, the hierarchical relationship is a moral one. The superordinate parties in the relationship are those who represent the forces of approved and official morality; the subordinate parties are those who, it is alleged, have violated that morality. . . .
>
> It is odd that, when we perceive bias, we usually see it in these circumstances. It is odd because it is easily ascertained that a great many more studies are biased in the direction of the interests of responsible officials than the other way around. (Becker, 1967:240, 242)

In looking for objective social problems, we must also guard against the tendency to accept the definitions of social problems provided by those in power. Because the powerful—the agencies of government and business—provide the statistical data (such as crime rates), they may define social reality in a way that manipulates public opinion, thereby controlling behaviors that threaten the status quo (and their power). The congruence of official biases and public opinion can be seen in several historical examples. Slavery, for instance, was not considered a social problem by the powerful in the South, but slave revolts were. In colonial New England the persecution of witches was not a social problem, but the witches were (Szasz, 1970). Likewise, racism was not a social problem of the Jim Crow South, but "pushy" Blacks were. From the standpoint of U.S. public opinion, dispossessing Native Americans of their lands was not a social problem, but the Native Americans who resisted were.

Thus, to consider as social problems only those occurrences so defined by the public is fraught with several related dangers. First, to do so may mean overlooking conditions that are detrimental to a relatively powerless segment of the society. In other words, deplorable conditions heaped on minority groups will tend to be ignored as social problems by the people at large. If sociologists accept this definition of social problems as their sole criterion, they have clearly taken a position that supports existing inequities for minority groups.

Second, defining social problems exclusively through public opinion diverts attention from what may constitute the most important social problem: the existing social order (Liazos, 1972). If defined only through public opinion, social problems will be limited to behaviors and actions that disrupt the existing social order. From this perspective, social problems are manifestations of

Are families to blame for their poverty, or are the institutions of society to blame for their plight by not providing jobs, adequate wages, and health care?

the behaviors of abnormal people, not of society; the inadequacies and inequalities perpetuated by the existing system are not questioned. The distribution of power, the system of justice, how children are educated—to name but a few aspects of the existing social order—are assumed to be proper by most of the public, when they may be social problems themselves. As Skolnick and Currie have noted:

> Conventional social problems writing invariably returns to the symptoms of social ills, rather than the source; to criminals, rather than the law; to the mentally ill, rather than the quality of life; to the culture of the poor, rather than the predations of the rich; to the "pathology" of students, rather than the crisis of education. (Skolnick and Currie, 1973:13)

By overlooking institutions as a source of social problems (and as problems themselves), observers disregard the role of the powerful in society. To focus exclusively on those who deviate—the prostitute, the delinquent, the drug addict, the criminal—is to exclude the unethical, illegal, and destructive actions of powerful individuals, groups, and institutions in U.S. society and to ignore the covert institutional violence brought about by racist and sexist policies, unjust tax laws, inequitable systems of health care and justice, and exploitation by the corporate world (Liazos, 1972).

TYPES OF SOCIAL PROBLEMS

This book examines two main types of social problems: (1) acts and conditions that violate the norms and values present in society and (2) societally induced conditions that cause psychic and material suffering for any segment of the population.

Norm Violations

Sociologists are interested in the discrepancy between social standards and reality for several reasons. First, this traditional approach directs attention to society's failures: the criminals, the mentally ill, the school dropouts, and the poor. Sociologists have many insights that explain the processes by which individuals experience differing pressures to engage in certain forms of deviant behavior because of their location in the social structure (social class, occupation, age, race, and role) and in space (region, size of community, and type of neighborhood). A guiding assumption of our inquiry here, however, is that norm violators are symptoms of social problems, not the disease itself. In other words, most deviants are victims and should not be blamed entirely by society for their deviance; rather, the system they live in should be blamed. A description of the situations affecting deviants (such as the barriers to success faced by minority group members) helps explain why some categories of persons participate disproportionately in deviant behavior.

Another reason for the traditional focus on norm violation is that deviance is culturally defined and socially labeled. The sociologist is vitally interested in the social and cultural processes that label some acts and persons as deviant and others as normal. Because by definition some social problems are whatever the public determines, social problems are inherently relative. Certain behaviors are labeled as social problems, whereas other activities (which by some other criteria would be a social problem) are not. People on welfare, for example, are generally considered to constitute a social problem, but slum lords are not; people who hear God talking to them are considered schizophrenic, but people who talk to God are believed perfectly sane; murder is a social problem, but killing the enemy during wartime is rewarded with medals; a prostitute is punished, but the client is not; aliens entering the country illegally constitute a social problem and are punished, but their U.S. employers are not. The important insight here is that "deviance is not a property *inherent* in certain forms of behavior; it is a property *conferred upon* these forms by the audiences which directly or indirectly witness them" (Schur, 1971:12). The members of society, especially the most powerful members, determine what is a social problem and what is not.

Powerful people play an important role in determining who gets the negative label and who does not. Because there is no absolute standard that informs citizens of what is deviant and what is not, our definition of deviance depends on what behaviors the law singles out for punishment. Because the law is an instrument of those in power, acts that are labeled deviant are so labeled because they conflict with the interests of those in power. Thus, to comprehend the labeling process, we must understand not only the norms and values of the society but also what interest groups hold the power (Quinney, 1970).

Social Conditions

The second type of social problem emphasized in this text involves conditions that cause psychic and material suffering for some category of people in the United States. Here, the focus is on how the society operates and who benefits and who does not under existing arrangements. In other words, what is the bias of the system? How are societal rewards distributed? Do some categories of persons suffer or profit because of how schools are organized or juries selected, because of the seniority system used by industries, or because of how health care is delivered? These questions direct attention away from individuals who violate norms and toward society's institutions as the generators of social problems.

Social problems of this type generate individual psychic and material suffering. Thus, societal arrangements can be organized in such a way as to be unresponsive to many human needs. As a benchmark, let us assume, with Abraham Maslow, that all human beings have a set of basic needs in common: the fundamental needs for shelter and sustenance, security, group support, esteem, respect, and **self-actualization** (the need for creative and constructive involvement in productive, significant activity) (Maslow, 1954). When these needs are thwarted,

> individuals will be hostile to society and its norms. Their frustration will be expressed in withdrawal, alcohol or other drugs, or in the violence of crime, terrorism, and aggression. People will take up lives outside of the pale of social control and normative structure; in so doing they will destroy themselves and others. They will rightly be condemned as "bad" people, *but this is so because they have lived in bad societies.* [Italics added.] (Doyle and Schindler, 1974:6)

When health care is maldistributed, when poverty persists for millions, when tax laws permit a business to write off 50 percent of a $100 luncheon but prohibit a truck driver from writing off a bologna sandwich, when government is run by the few for the benefit of the few, when businesses supposedly in competition fix prices to gouge the consumer, when the criminal justice system is biased against the poor and people of color, then society is permitting what is called **institutionalized deviance** (Doyle and Schindler, 1974:13). Such a condition exists when the society and its formal organizations are not meeting the needs of individuals. But these conditions often escape criticism and are rarely identified as social problems. Instead, the focus has often been on individuals who vent their frustration in socially unacceptable ways. A major intent of this book is to view individual deviance as a consequence of institutionalized deviance.

In summary, here we consider **social problems** to be (1) societally induced conditions that cause psychic and material suffering for any segment of the population and (2) acts and conditions that violate the norms and values found in society. The distribution of power in society is the key to understanding these social problems. The powerless, because they are dominated by the powerful, are likely to be thwarted in achieving their basic needs (sustenance, security, self-esteem, and productivity). In contrast, the interests of the powerful are served because they control the mechanisms and institutions by which the perceptions of the public are shaped. By affecting public policy through reaffirming customs and through shaping the law and its enforcement, powerful interest groups are instrumental in designating (labeling) who is a problem (deviant) and who must be controlled. Our focus, then, is on the structure of society—especially on how power is distributed—rather than on "problem" individuals. Individual deviants are a manifestation of society's failure to meet their needs; the sources of crime, poverty, drug addiction, and racism are found in the laws and customs, the quality of life, the distribution of wealth and power, and the accepted practices of schools, governmental units, and corporations. As the primary source of social problems, society, not the individual

SOCIAL PROBLEMS IN GLOBAL PERSPECTIVE

SOCIAL WELFARE STATES: A Mixture of Capitalism and Socialism

The nations of Western Europe, Scandinavia, and Canada have generous welfare policies for their citizens, certainly much more generous than found in the United States (the description here is general, characterizing all of the nations to a degree, although there are variations among them). These nations are capitalistic, permitting private property and privately owned businesses. To a much greater degree than in the United States, these nations have publicly owned enterprises and some nationalization of industry, typically transportation, mineral resources, and utilities.

Most important, these nations provide an array of social services to meet the needs of their citizens that is much greater than in the United States. These include a greater subsidy to the arts (symphony orchestras, art exhibitions, artists, auditoriums), more public spaces (parks, public squares, recreation facilities), more resources for public libraries, universal preschool education, free public education through college, universal health insurance, housing subsidies to help low-income families, paid leave for new parents (mother and father), the provision of safe government child care facilities, extended unemployment benefits, paid vacations, and excellent retirement benefits including paid long-term care if necessary.

These services are expensive, resulting in relatively high taxes, almost double the rate in the United States. But as Joe R. and Clairece Booher Feagin point out:

> If we were to add the cost of the private medical insurance carried by many Americans . . . as well as the cost of medical care not covered by insurance and the cost of private social services such as day care centers, [the taxes of the social welfare states] and U.S. "taxes" are much more nearly equal. Much of what [they] pay for through the tax system, we in the United States buy, if at all, from private enterprise—and we often get less adequate (or no) health care, child care, and other services as a result. Indeed, Americans may pay more, everything considered, for all services than do [those in the social welfare states]—and receive less. (Feagin and Feagin, 1997:469)

As a result of these extensive social services, the people in the social welfare states have several advantages over those living in the United States: longer life expectancy, lower infant and maternal mortality, greater literacy, less poverty and homelessness, lower rates of violent crime, a lower proportion of single-parent households, and, proportionately, a larger middle class.

Are the people in these countries less free than Americans? There is freedom of speech and freedom of the press in each of the nations. The governments in these countries, for the most part, permit greater individual freedom than is found in the United States for personal behaviors (greater acceptance of homosexuality, legalization of prostitution, few restrictions on abortion, and the like).

Is there a downside? These countries are not immune to economic problems such as recessions, high unemployment, and citizen unrest over high taxes. In the past few years, the governments in these countries have reduced some of their social programs, but they are still much more generous than the social programs in the United States (which has also curbed its more meager welfare programs). Typically, government leaders in each of these countries have argued that more austere programs are needed to stimulate the economy and permit the government to pay its bills. These measures have been met with citizen protest, particularly from the labor unions, which are much stronger than in the United States. It will be interesting to see how this plays out. If the austerity measures hold, will the countries follow the U.S. example and become more unequal, have more social unrest, with life itself more problematic? Or, as conservatives argue, will the substitution of more capitalism for socialism make these nations more efficient and more prosperous?

deviant, must be restructured if social problems are to be solved. (See the panel titled "Social Problems in Global Perspective," which compares the United States with other nations on social problems, and the panel titled "Social Policy," which shows how societies can be designed to minimize social problems.)

SOCIAL POLICY

SOCIAL PROBLEMS AND SOCIAL POLICY

The political-social-economic system of a society does not simply evolve from random events and aimless choices. The powerful in societies craft policies to accomplish certain ends, within the context of historical events, budgetary constraints, and the like. Addressing the issue of inequality, Claude Fischer and his colleagues from the sociology department at the University of California-Berkeley say:

> The answer to the question of why societies vary in their structure of rewards is more political. In significant measure, societies choose the height and breadth of their "ladders." By loosening markets or regulating them, by providing services to all citizens or rationing them according to income, by subsidizing some groups more than others, societies, through their politics, build their ladders. To be sure, historical and external constraints deny full freedom of action, but a substantial freedom of action remains. . . . In a democracy, this means that the inequality Americans have is, in significant measure, the historical result of policy choices of Americans—or, at least, Americans' representatives. In the United States, the result is a society that is distinctly unequal. Our ladder is, by the standards of affluent democracies and even by the standards of recent American history, unusually extended and narrow—and becoming more so. (Fischer et al., 1996:8)

In other words, America's level of inequality is by design (Fischer et al., 1996:125).

Social policy is about design, about setting goals and determining the means to achieve them. Do we want to regulate and protect more, as the well-developed welfare states do, or should we do less? Should we create and invest in policies and programs that protect citizens from poverty, unemployment, and the high cost of health care, or should the market economy sort people into winners, players, and losers based on their abilities and efforts? Decision makers in the United States have opted to reduce the welfare state. Are they on the right track? Can those policies that the generous welfare states have adopted be modified to reduce the United States' social problems? If societies are designed, should the United States change its design?

Source: D. Stanley Eitzen and Craig S. Leedham. 2001. "U.S. Social Problems in Comparative Perspective." In D. Stanley Eitzen and Craig S. Leedham (Eds.), *Solutions to Social Problems: Lessons from Other Societies,* 2nd ed. Boston: Allyn & Bacon, pp. 10–11.

SOCIAL STRUCTURE AS THE BASIC UNIT OF ANALYSIS

There is a very strong tendency for individuals—lay people, police officers, judges, lawmakers, and social scientists alike—to perceive social problems and prescribe remedies from an individualistic perspective. For example, they blame the individual for being poor, with no reference to the maldistribution of wealth and other socially perpetuated disadvantages that blight many families generation after generation; they blame African Americans for their aggressive behavior, with no understanding of the limits placed on social mobility for African Americans by the social system; they blame dropouts for leaving school prematurely, with no understanding that the educational system fails to meet their needs. This type of thinking helps explain the reluctance of people in authority to provide adequate welfare, health care, and compensatory programs to help the disadvantaged.

The fundamental issue is whether social problems emanate from the pathologies of individuals (**person-blame**) or from the situations in which deviants are involved (**system-blame**); that is, whether deviants are the problem itself or only victims of it. The answer no doubt lies somewhere between the two extremes, but since the individual- or victim-blamers have held sway, we should examine their reasoning (Ryan, 1976).

Person-Blame Approach versus System-Blame Approach

Let us begin by considering some victims, such as the children in a slum school who constantly fail. Why do they fail? The victim-blamer points to their **cultural deprivation.*** They do not do well in school because their families speak different dialects, because their parents are uneducated, because they have not been exposed to the educational benefits available to middle-class children (such as visits to the zoo, computers in the home, extensive travel, attendance at cultural events, exposure to books). In other words, the defect is in the children and their families. System-blamers look elsewhere for the sources of failure. They ask, What is there about the schools that make slum children more likely to fail? The answer is found in the irrelevant curriculum, class-biased IQ tests, the tracking system, overcrowded classrooms, differential allocation of resources within the school district, and insensitive teachers whose low expectations for poor children create a self-fulfilling prophecy.

Ex-convicts constitute another set of victims. Why is their **recidivism** rate (reinvolvement in crime) so high? The victim-blamer points to the faults of individual criminals: their greed, their feelings of aggression, their weak control of impulse, their lack of conscience. The system-blamer directs attention to very different sources: the penal system, the scarcity of employment for ex-criminals, and even the schools. For example, 20 to 30 percent of inmates are functionally illiterate; that is, they cannot meet minimum reading and writing demands in U.S. society, such as filling out job applications. Yet these people are expected to leave prison, find a job, and stay out of trouble. Illiterate ex-criminals face unemployment or at best the most menial jobs, with low wages, no job security, and no fringe benefits. System-blamers argue that first the schools and later penal institutions have failed to provide these people with the minimum requirements for full participation in society. Moreover, lack of employment and the unwillingness of potential employers to train functional illiterates force many to return to crime in order to survive.

The inner-city poor are another set of victims. The conditions of the ghetto poor, especially African Americans, have deteriorated since the mid-1960s. Some observers believe that this deterioration is the result of the transplantation of a southern sharecropper culture (Lemann, 1986), welfare programs (Murray, 1984), and laziness. The more compelling system-blame argument, however, is made by William J. Wilson (1987). He claims that the ghetto poor endure because of the disappearance of hundreds of thousands of low-skill jobs, those mainly involving physical labor, in the past 30 years or so. Wilson's contention, supported by research, is that the pathologies of the ghetto (such as teenage pregnancy, illegitimacy, welfare dependency, and crime) are fundamentally the consequence of too few jobs.

The strong tendency to blame social problems on individuals rather than on the social system lies in how people tend to look at social problems. Most

*Cultural deprivation is a loaded ethnocentric term applied by members of the majority to the culture of the minority group. It implies that the culture of the group in question is not only inferior but also deficient. The concept does remind us, however, that people can and do make invidious distinctions about cultures and subcultures. Furthermore, people act on these distinctions as if they were valid.

people define a social problem as behavior that deviates from the norms and standards of society. Because people do not ordinarily examine critically the way things are done in society, they tend to question the exceptions. The system not only is taken for granted but also has, for most people, an aura of sacredness because of the traditions and customs with which they associate it. Logically, then, those who deviate are the source of trouble. The obvious question observers ask is, Why do these people deviate from norms? Because most people view themselves as law-abiding, they feel that those who deviate do so because of some kind of unusual circumstance, such as accident, illness, personal defect, character flaw, or maladjustment (Ryan, 1976:10–18). The flaw, then, is a function of the deviant, not of societal arrangements.

Interpreting social problems solely within a person-blame framework has serious consequences. First, it frees the government, the economy, the system of stratification, the system of justice, and the educational system from any blame:

> [B]laming the poor [for example] is still easier than fixing what's really wrong with America: segregated schools, unjust wages, inadequate health care, and other such complicated matters. (Vogel, 1994:31)

This protection of the established order against criticism increases the difficulty of trying to change the dominant economic, social, and political institutions. A good example is the strategy social scientists use in studying the origins of poverty. Because the person-blamer studies the poor rather than the nonpoor, the system of inequality (buttressed by tax laws, welfare rules, and employment practices) goes unchallenged. A related consequence of the person-blame approach, then, is that the relatively well-off segments of society retain their advantages.

A social control function of the person-blame approach is that troublesome individuals and groups are controlled in a publicly acceptable manner. Deviants—whether they are criminals, mentally ill, or social protesters—are

Deviance is not a property inherent in certain forms of behavior; it is a property conferred upon these forms by the audiences that directly or indirectly witness them. Thus, the poor living in slums are generally considered a social problem, but slum lords are not.

incarcerated in prisons or mental hospitals and administered drugs or other forms of therapy. This approach not only directs blame at individuals and away from the system, but it also eliminates the problems (individuals).

A related consequence is how the problem is treated. A person-blame approach demands a person-change treatment program. If the cause of delinquency, for example, is defined as the result of personal pathology, then the solution must clearly lie in counseling, behavior modification, psychotherapy, drugs, or some other technique aimed at changing the individual deviant. The person-blame interpretation of social problems provides and legitimates the right to initiate person-change rather than system-change treatment programs. Under such a scheme, norms that are racist, sexist, or homophobic, for example, will go unchallenged.

The person-blame ideology invites not only person-change treatment programs but also programs for person-control. The system-blamer would argue that this emphasis, too, treats the symptom rather than the disease.

A final consequence of a person-blame interpretation is that it reinforces social myths about the degree of control individuals have over their fate. It provides justification for a form of **Social Darwinism:** that the placement of people in the stratification system is a function of their ability and effort. By this logic the poor are poor because they are the dregs of society. In short, they deserve their fate, as do the successful in society. Thus, in this viewpoint there is little sympathy for government programs to increase welfare to the poor. (See the insert on William Graham Sumner for an example of this ideology.)

Reasons for Focusing on the System-Blame Approach

We emphasize the system-blame approach in this book. We should recognize, however, that the system-blame orientation has dangers. First, it is only part of the truth. Social problems are highly complex phenomena that have both indi-

William Graham Sumner and Social Darwinism

William Graham Sumner (1840–1910), the sociologist who originated the concepts of folkways and mores, was a proponent of Social Darwinism. This doctrine, widely accepted among elites during the late nineteenth and early twentieth centuries, was a distorted version of Charles Darwin's theory of natural selection. From this viewpoint, success is the result of being superior. The rich are rich because they deserve to be. By this logic the poor also deserve their fate because they are biological and social failures and therefore unable to succeed in the competitive struggle.

Social Darwinism justified not only ruthless competition but also the perpetuation of the status quo. Superior classes, it was believed, should dominate because their members were unusually intelligent and moral. The lower classes, on the other hand, were considered inferior and defective. Their pathology was manifested in suicide, madness, crime, and various forms of vice.

On the basis of this philosophy, Sumner opposed social reforms such as welfare to the poor because they rewarded the unfit and penalized the competent. Such reforms, he argued, would interfere with the normal workings of society, halting progress and perhaps even contributing to a regression to an earlier evolutionary stage.

vidual and systemic origins. Individuals, obviously, can be malicious and aggressive for purely psychological reasons. Clearly, society needs to be protected from some individuals. Moreover, some people require particular forms of therapy, remedial help, or special programs on an individual basis if they are to function normally. But much behavior that is labeled deviant is the end product of social conditions.

A second danger of a dogmatic system-blame orientation is that it presents a rigidly deterministic explanation of social problems. Taken too far, this position views individuals as robots controlled totally by their social environment. A balanced view acknowledges that human beings may choose between alternative courses of action. This issue raises the related question of the degree to which people are responsible for their behavior. An extreme system-blame approach absolves individuals from responsibility for their actions. To take such a stance would be to argue that society should never restrict deviants; this view invites anarchy.

Despite these problems with the system-blame approach, it is the guiding perspective of this book for three reasons. First, because average citizens, police officers, legislators, social scientists, and judges tend to interpret social problems from an individualistic perspective, a balance is needed. Moreover, as noted earlier, a strict person-blame perspective has many negative consequences, and citizens must recognize these negative effects of their ideology.

A second reason for using the society-blaming perspective is that the subject matter of sociology is not the individual—who is the special province of psychology—but society. Because sociologists focus on the social determinants of behavior, they must make a critical analysis of the social structure. An important ingredient of the sociological perspective is the development of a critical stance toward social arrangements. Thus, the sociologist looks behind the facades to determine the positive and negative consequences of social arrangements. The sociologist's persistent questions must be, Who benefits under these arrangements, and who does not? For this reason, there should be a close fit between the sociological approach and the society-blaming perspective.

A final reason for the use of the system-blame approach is that the institutional framework of society is the source of many social problems (such as racism, pollution, unequal distribution of health care, poverty, and war). An exclusive focus on the individual ignores the strains caused by the inequities of the system and its fundamental intransigence to change. A guiding assumption of this book is that because institutions are made by human beings (and therefore are not sacred), they should be changed whenever they do not meet the needs of the people they were created to serve. As Skolnick and Currie have stated:

> Democratic conceptions of society have always held that institutions exist to serve people, and not vice versa. Institutions therefore are to be accountable to the people whose lives they affect. Where an institution—any institution, even the most "socially valued"—is found to conflict with human needs, democratic thought holds that it ought to be changed or abolished. (Skolnick and Currie, 1973:15)

One goal of this book is to help the reader understand the social nature of social problems. Accepting the system-blame perspective is a necessary first step in efforts to restructure society along more humane lines. The job of social scientists in this endeavor should be to provide alternative social structures (based on theory and research) for those about which we complain. To do this job, social scientists must ask very different research questions from those posed in the past, and they must study not only the powerless but also the powerful.

ORGANIZATION OF THE BOOK

The organizing theme of this book is that many aspects of social problems are conditions resulting from cultural and social arrangements. It therefore begins by examining the fundamental organization of U.S. society. The remainder of Part I elaborates on the political economy of social problems, emphasizing the political and economic organization of society and its impact on social problems. The focus is on power because the powerful, by making and enforcing the laws, create and define deviance. They determine which behaviors will be rewarded and which ones punished. The powerful influence public opinion, and they can attempt to solve social problems or ignore them. Through policies for taxation and subsidies, the powerful determine the degree to which wealth is distributed in society. They also determine which group interests will be advanced and at whose expense.

The economy is equally important. The particular form of the economy establishes a distribution process, not only for wealth but also for goods and services. In many important ways Karl Marx was correct: The economy is the force that determines the form and substance of all other institutions—the church, school, family, and polity.

Critical scrutiny of the polity and the economy provides clues for the bias of society. It helps explain the upside-down qualities of society whereby the few benefit at the expense of the many; how reality gets defined in contested issues; how political and economic processes affect what is currently being done about social problems; and thus, why so many social policies fail.

Part II focuses on the context of social problems in the United States. Chapter 3 examines world population and global inequality. Chapter 4 looks at environmental degradation globally and domestically. Chapter 5 focuses on two major population changes in the United States—the browning and the graying of America. The final chapter in Part II provides a useful overview to social problems by focusing on the problems of cities. This is important because social problems are concentrated in cities.

Part III examines a crucial element of U.S. social structure: the various manifestations of social inequality. It describes inequality based on wealth, race/ethnicity, gender, sexual orientation, and disability.

Part IV examines the impact of social structure on individuals. **Deviant behavior** is activity that violates the norms of an organization, community, or society. Consequently, deviance is culturally defined and socially labeled. Certain behaviors are also labeled as deviant because they conflict with the interests of the powerful in society. Public policy, then, reflects the values and interests of those in power and is codified into law. Members of society are also taught how to respond to deviants. The law and these structured responses to deviants are societal reactions that establish deviance in social roles; paradoxically, the degraded status that results from societal reactions reinforces the deviance that society seeks to control. Deviance, then, is fundamentally the result of social structure. We examine these processes in relation to two types of deviance: crime and drug use.

Part V describes problems found within five representative institutions. The initial chapter in Part V addresses the allocation and remuneration of jobs. The number and types of jobs are undergoing a major shift as society deindustrializes and moves toward a service economy. While the resulting changes bring many opportunities, they also bring many problems, such as the widening gap between the haves and the have-nots and the emergence of a new form of poverty. The chapter on families looks at the family-related problems of single-parent families, child care, violence, and divorce. The chapter on education illustrates how this institution of society, while necessary as the source for transmitting the necessary skills and shared understandings to each generation, is also a generator of social problems. Thus, it shows once again how social problems (in this case, inequality) originate in the basic structure of society. The chapter on health care focuses on the reasons for the high cost of health care in the United States and on the unequal delivery of health care. National security, especially the threat of terrorism, is the final topic of Part V.

The book concludes with a chapter that answers the question: What do we do about social problems? The solutions come from the bottom up—that is, people organize through human agency to change social structures. Solutions also come from the top down—social policies determined by the powerful. Both of these forces and the interaction between the top and the bottom are the topics of the concluding chapter.

CHAPTER REVIEW

1. Historically, U.S. sociologists have viewed social problems in terms of social pathology: "Bad" people were assumed to be the sources of social problems because they disturbed the prevailing moral order in society.
2. In the 1920s and 1930s, sociologists focused on the conditions of society, such as the rapid changes accompanying urbanization and industrialization, as the sources of social problems.
3. More recently, many sociologists have returned to a study of problem individuals—deviants who violate the expectations of society. The modern study of deviance has developed in two directions. The first sought the sources of deviation within the social structure. The other, of relatively recent origin, has focused on the role of society in creating and sustaining deviance through labeling those viewed as abnormal. In this view, societal reactions are assumed to determine what a social problem is and who is deviant.
4. There is an objective reality to social problems; some conditions or situations do induce material and psychic suffering. There are several dangers, however, in defining social problems objectively. Subjectivity cannot be removed from the process. A standard must be selected, but in a pluralistic society there are many standards. Moreover, social scientists not only disagree on what a social problem is, but also cannot escape their own values in the study of social problems. Most important, the objective approach to social problems entails acceptance of the definitions provided by the powerful. The acceptance of these definitions diverts attention away from the powerful and toward those the powerful wish to label negatively, thus deflecting observations away from what may constitute the most important social problem—the existing social order.
5. This book examines two types of social problems: (a) acts and conditions that violate the norms and values of society and (b) societally induced conditions that cause psychic and material suffering for any segment of the population. The key to understanding both types of social problems is the distribution of power.
6. The focus is on the structure of society rather than on "problem" individuals. A guiding assumption of our inquiry is that norm violators are symptoms of social problems. These deviants are for the most part victims and should not be blamed entirely for their deviance; the system in which they live should also be blamed.
7. The person-blame approach, which we do not use, has serious consequences: (a) It frees the institutions of society from any blame and efforts to change them; (b) it controls "problem" people

in ways that reinforce negative stereotypes; (c) it legitimates person-control programs; and (d) it justifies the logic of Social Darwinism, which holds that people are rich or poor because of their ability and effort or lack thereof.

8. The system-blame orientation also has dangers. Taken dogmatically, it presents a rigidly deterministic explanation for social problems, suggesting that people are merely robots controlled by their social environment.

KEY TERMS

Subjective nature of social problems. What is and what is not a social problem is a matter of definition. Thus, social problems vary by time and place.

Objective reality of social problems. There are societal conditions that harm certain segments of the population and, therefore, are social problems.

Self-actualization. The assumed need (by Maslow) of individuals for creative and constructive involvement in productive, significant activity.

Institutionalized deviance. When a society is organized in such a way as to disadvantage some of its members.

Social problems. Societally induced conditions that harm any segment of the population, and acts and conditions that violate the norms and values found in society.

Person-blame. The assumption that social problems result from the pathologies of individuals.

System-blame. The assumption that social problems result from social conditions.

Cultural deprivation. The assumption by the members of a group that the culture of some other group is not only inferior but also deficient. This term is usually applied by members of the majority to the culture of a minority group.

Recidivism. Reinvolvement in crime.

Social Darwinism. The belief that the place of people in the stratification system is a function of their ability and effort.

Deviant behavior. Activity that violates the norms of a social organization.

WEBSITES FOR FURTHER REFERENCE

http://www.asanet.org/
The American Sociological Association (ASA), founded in 1905, is a nonprofit membership association dedicated to advancing sociology as a scientific discipline and profession serving the public good. With approximately 13,000 members, ASA encompasses sociologists who are faculty members at colleges and universities, researchers, practitioners, and students. About 20 percent of the members work in government, business, or nonprofit organizations. The ASA aims to articulate policy and implement programs likely to have the broadest possible impact for sociology now and in the future.

http://www.ucm.es/info/isa/
The goal of the International Sociological Association (ISA) is to represent sociologists everywhere, regardless of their school of thought, scientific approaches, or ideological opinion; and to advance sociological knowledge throughout the world. To this end "the ISA undertakes activities: (i) to secure and develop personal contacts between sociologists throughout the world; (ii) to encourage the international dissemination and exchange of information on significant developments in sociological knowledge; (iii) to facilitate and promote international sociological research."

http://www.ssrn.com/home_bd.html
Social Science Research Network (SSRN) is devoted to the rapid worldwide dissemination of social science research and is composed of a number of specialized research networks in each of the social sciences.

http://www.socioweb.com/~markbl/socioweb/
The SocioWeb is an independent guide to the sociological resources available on the Internet and is founded on the belief that the Internet can help to unite the sociological community in ways never before possible.

http://www.unesco.org/most/
The Management of Social Transformations Programme (MOST) is a research program designed by UNESCO to promote international comparative social science research. Its primary emphasis is to support large-scale, long-term autonomous research and to transfer the relevant findings and data to decision-makers. MOST also publishes state-of-the-art reports that assess existing information on specific topics. The overall long-term objective of MOST is to establish sustainable links between the scientific and policy com-

munities and to emphasize the relevance of social science research for policy formulation. Available in English, French, and Spanish.

http://www.americaslibrary.gov
America's Library: Welcome to America's Story from America's Library! This website is brought to you from the Library of Congress in Washington, D.C., the largest library in the world and the nation's library. It represents "one of the most comprehensive historical research sites available to students and researchers."

http://www.siris.si.edu/
Smithsonian Institution Research Information Services: The Smithsonian Institution Research Information System (SIRIS) is the online catalog of resources held by the Institution's libraries, archives, and other specialized research centers.

http://www.alternet.org
AlterNet.org is a project of the Independent Media Institute, a nonprofit organization dedicated to strengthening and supporting independent and alternative journalism. First launched in 1998, AlterNet's online magazine provides a mix of news, opinion, and investigative journalism on subjects ranging from the environment, the drug war, national security (including features on recent terrorism), technology, and cultural trends to policy debate, sexual politics, and health issues. The AlterNet article database includes more than 7,000 stories from over 200 sources.

2

Wealth and Power

The Bias of the System

We can have a democratic society or we can have the concentration of great wealth in the hands of a few. We cannot have both.

—Justice Louis Brandeis

The thesis of this book is that the problems of U.S. society result from the distribution of power and the form of the economy. This chapter begins the analysis of U.S. social problems by looking at the political and economic realities of interest groups and also at power, powerlessness, and domination. As we discuss, the state is not a neutral agent of the people but is biased in favor of those with wealth—the upper social classes and the largest corporations. As we analyze the bias of the system, we begin to see that, contrary to popular belief, the U.S. system does not produce a society that is democratic, just, and equal in opportunity. Rather, we find that the United States is an upside-down society, with the few benefiting at the expense of the many. Finally, we see how our society itself is the source of social problems.

The study of social problems requires the critical examination of the structure of society. Some readers will find this approach uncomfortable, even unpatriotic. In this regard, introducing his critical analysis of the United States, Michael Parenti has said:

> If the picture that emerges in the pages ahead is not pretty, this should not be taken as an attack on the United States, for this country and the American people are greater than the abuses perpetrated upon them by those who live for power and profit. To expose these abuses is not to denigrate the nation that is a victim of them. The greatness of a country is to be measured by something more than its rulers, its military budget, its instruments of dominance and destruction, and its profiteering giant corporations. A nation's greatness can be measured by its ability to create a society free of poverty, racism, sexism, imperialism, and social and environmental devastation, and by the democratic nature of its institutions. Albert Camus once said, "I would like to love my country and justice too." In fact, there is no better way to love one's country, no better way to strive for the fulfillment of its greatness, than to entertain critical ideas and engage in the pursuit of social justice at home and abroad. (Parenti, 1995b:6)

This chapter is divided into four sections. The first section describes the two polar types of economic systems, capitalism and socialism. The second describes the U.S. economy, with its concentration of corporate and private wealth. The third examines the political system and its linkages to the economic elites. The final section shows how the politicoeconomic system is biased in favor of those who are already advantaged.

Capitalism and Socialism

Industrialized societies organize their economic activities according to one of two fundamental forms: capitalism or socialism. Although no society has a purely capitalist or socialist economy, the ideal types provide opposite extremes on a scale that helps us measure the U.S. economy more accurately.

Capitalism

Three conditions must be present for pure **capitalism** to exist—private ownership of property, personal profit, and competition. These necessary conditions constitute the underlying principles of a pure capitalist system. The first is private ownership of property. Individuals are encouraged to own not only private possessions but, most important, also the capital necessary to produce and distribute goods and services. In a purely capitalist society, there would be no public ownership of any potentially profitable activity.

The pursuit of maximum profit, the second essential principle, implies that individuals are free to maximize their personal gains. Most important, the proponents of capitalism (see the inserts on Adam Smith and Milton Friedman) argue that profit seeking by individuals has positive consequences for society. Thus, seeking individual gain through personal profit is considered morally acceptable and socially desirable.

Competition, the third ingredient, is the mechanism for determining what is produced and at what price. The market forces of supply and demand ensure that capitalists produce the goods and services wanted by the public, that the goods and services are high in quality, and that they are sold at the lowest possible price. Moreover, competition is the mechanism that keeps individual profit seeking in check. Potential abuses such as fraud, faulty products, and exorbitant prices are negated by the existence of competitors who soon take

Adam Smith

Adam Smith (1723–1790), a Scottish economist, is the godfather of laissez-faire capitalism. His *Inquiry into the Nature and Causes of the Wealth of Nations,* written in 1776, presented a logical vision of how society was bound inextricably by the private decisions of entrepreneurs and consumers alike.

Of the many issues that Smith addressed, one is paramount for our concerns: How does society hang together when everyone is pursuing his or her self-interest? For Smith the answer is in the laws of the marketplace; the needs of society and its citizens are met by each person producing what will bring a profit. According to Smith, someone will provide whatever is needed because demand increases the likelihood of profit. But if all entrepreneurs are profit-hungry, what will prevent them from taking unfair advantage of their consumers? The answer, simply, is competition. The existence of competition will keep prices fair and product quality high.

The market also regulates the incomes of those who produce the goods. If wages are too high in one kind of work, other workers will rush to that type of job, bringing down the exorbitant wages. Similarly, if wages are too low, then workers will change to better-paying jobs. The marketplace also reduces the possibility of surpluses because entrepreneurs, foreseeing the problem, will move to more profitable arenas where the demand and profits are high. Thus, the laws of the marketplace provide an "invisible hand" that regulates the economy without government intervention. The government is not needed to fix prices, to set minimum wages, or to protect against consumer fraud. All that is needed is a free and competitive marketplace.

The question, of course, is whether the nature of the marketplace in a world of huge multinational corporations, multimillion-member labor unions, and conglomerates is the same as it was in the eighteenth century.

Milton Friedman

Milton Friedman (b. 1912), a Nobel laureate in economics, is the leading contemporary advocate of a free market economy to solve society's ills. He is fundamentally opposed to central planning on the grounds that such a system is coercive. Rather, people should be free to work and produce whatever they feel will bring a fair price. According to Friedman, price is the key. If the price is high for a certain product because of demand, individuals will be attracted to producing it; if the price is low, many producers will turn to other, more profitable activities. The result of such a system, Friedman has argued, is peaceful cooperation among millions of persons in societies and among societies. More important, because such a system is based on freedom of choice, it promotes political, human, and religious freedom as well.

Freidman maintains that government intervention interferes with the natural mechanism of the free market. Thus, for him the basic problem of U.S. society today is too much government, not too little. He is especially fearful of the move toward socialism. Friedman characterizes capitalist societies as voluntarily cooperative, whereas the essential notion of a socialist society is force. Either the individual is master or the government is. In the former case freedom reigns, and the dignity and the individuality of people are respected. In a socialist society, on the other hand, individuals must be coerced to work for what the government considers the common good. Thus, for Friedman capitalism tends to give freer reign to the more humane values by fostering a climate of individual responsibility and achievement:

> I am only saying that a set of social institutions that stresses individual responsibility, that treats the individual—given the kind of person he is, the kind of society in which he operates—as responsible for and to himself, will lead to a higher and more desirable moral climate than a set of institutions that stresses the lack of responsibility of the individual for what happens to him and relieves him of blame or credit for what he does to his fellowmen. (Friedman, 1978:11)

business away from those who violate good business judgment. So, too, economic inefficiency is minimized as market forces cause the inept to fail and the efficient to succeed.

These three principles—private property, personal profit, and competition—require a fourth condition if true capitalism is to work: a government policy of laissez-faire, allowing the marketplace to operate unhindered. Capitalists argue that any government intervention in the marketplace distorts the economy by negatively affecting incentives and freedom of individual choice. If left unhindered by government, the profit motive, private ownership, and competition will achieve the greatest good for the greatest number in the form of individual self-fulfillment and the general material progress of society.

Critics argue that capitalism promotes inequality and a host of social problems because the object is profit, not enhancing the human condition. Consider this critique by Jesse Jackson:

> The operation of free markets is a wondrous and mighty thing. To allocate goods and services, to adjust supply with demand, the market has no equal. But the market sets the price—not the value—of things. It counts consumers, not citizens. . . . The market has no opinion on the distribution of income, wealth and opportunity in society. . . . The market does not care if kids in Appalachia or Brooklyn go to school in buildings that are dangerous to their

> health. The market has no opinion on whether opportunity is open to the many, or limited to the few. The market does not care that 45 million Americans go to bed every night without health insurance. . . . The market does not care if the economy is swimming in speculative capital, but large segments of the country are effectively red-lined [a banking practice of not loaning money within certain boundaries, most typically where the poor and racial minorities are located] as banks merge. The market does not care if the shows our children watch on television are filled with sex, violence, and racial stereotyping. The market measures TV shows by the price of their advertising. On the values they impart, the market has no opinion. (Jackson, 1998b:19)

As political observer Molly Ivins has observed: "Capitalism. . . is a dandy system for creating wealth, but it doesn't do squat for social justice. No reason to expect it to—that's not its job" (Ivins, 2000:22).

The economy of the United States is not purely capitalistic. Taxes are levied on the population to raise monies for the common good, such as the federal interstate highway system, the air traffic control system and the subsidizing of airports, flood control projects, the defense establishment, the postal system, and the like. In many ways the government interferes with the market by monitoring the safety of food and drugs, prohibiting the sale of certain products, regulating the environment, insisting on health and safety regulations in workplaces, issuing licenses, protecting the civil rights of women and minorities, taxing income, subsidizing certain business activities, overseeing the banking and insurance industries, and preventing monopolies.

Moreover, while U.S. social programs are less generous than those found in the social welfare states (see the panel titled "Social Problems in Global Perspective"), there is nonetheless minimal help for victims of natural disasters, preschool training for children of the poor, low-interest student loans, Medicare, and Medicaid.

Socialism

The five principles of **socialism** are democratism, egalitarianism, community, public ownership of the means of production, and planning for common purposes. True socialism must be democratic. Representatives of a socialist state must be answerable and responsive to the wishes of the public they serve. Nations that claim to be socialist but are totalitarian violate this fundamental aspect of socialism. The key to differentiating between authentic and spurious socialism is to determine who is making the decisions and whose interests are being served. Thus, it is a fallacy to equate true socialism with the politicoeconomic systems found in Cuba or the People's Republic of China. These societies are socialistic in some respects; that is, their material benefits are more evenly distributed than those in the United States. But their economies and governments are controlled by a single political party in an inflexible and authoritarian manner. Although these countries claim to have democratic elections, in fact the citizens have no electoral choice but to rubber-stamp the candidates of the ruling party. The people are denied civil liberties and freedoms that should be the hallmark of a socialist society. In a pure socialist society democratic relations must operate throughout the social structure: in government, at work, at school, and in the community.

The second principle of socialism is egalitarianism: equality of opportunity for the self-fulfillment of all, equality rather than hierarchy in decision making,

SOCIAL PROBLEMS IN GLOBAL PERSPECTIVE

COMPARING THE UNITED STATES WITH OTHER INDUSTRIALIZED NATIONS ON SELECTED SOCIAL PROBLEMS

When the United States is compared to its counterparts of Europe, Scandinavia, Japan, Canada, and Australia, it ranks first on a number of social problems indicators: murder rate, reported rapes, robbery rate, incarceration rate, number of drunken driving fatalities, cocaine use, greenhouse gas emissions, oil consumption per capita, forest depletion, hazardous waste per capita, garbage per capita, use of cars rather than public transportation, proportion of children and elderly in poverty, homelessness, inequality in wealth distribution, single-parent families, reported cases of AIDS, infant mortality rate, death of children younger than five, and teenage pregnancy.

Also, among these nations, the United States ranks *last* in spending on the poor; fully immunizing preschoolers against polio, DTP (diptheria–tetanus–pertussis), and measles; giving humanitarian aid to developing countries; in the percentage of people with health insurance; and providing paid maternity leave. In addition, although the United States was not last, it ranked fifteenth in women's wages as a percentage of men's, fifteenth in life expectancy, and ninth in early childhood education.

Some additional facts underscore the depth of social problems in the United States relative to its peers:

- Compared to its industrialized counterparts, the United States (1) has the highest incidence of poverty; (2) experiences the longest periods of people being in poverty; and (3) provides the least amount of income security to the poor and the most meager forms of welfare to help the needy.
- The United States is the only industrialized nation without some form of universal health care.
- The United States has the most unequal distribution of wealth and income in the industrialized world.
- U.S. cities, compared to those in other industrialized nations, have more concentrated poverty and racial and ethnic segregation; they have more deteriorated infrastructures (streets, buildings); and they have the worst public transportation.
- Compared to its peers, the United States ranks first on a number of crime and criminal justice dimensions: (1) the percentage of the population who have been victims of crime, (2) the murder rate, (3) reported rapes, and (4) the incarceration rate.
- The United States provides the least generous child benefit packages of housing, health, education, welfare allowances, and tax benefits.

Source: D. Stanley Eitzen and Craig S. Leedham. 2001. "U.S. Social Problems in Comparative Perspective." In D. Stanley Eitzen and Craig S. Leedham (Eds.), *Solutions to Social Problems: Lessons from Other Societies,* 2nd ed. Boston: Allyn & Bacon, pp. 4–5.

and equality in sharing the benefits of society. For some socialists the goal is absolute equality. For most, though, equality means a limit to inequality, with some acceptable disparities in living standards. This more realistic goal of socialism requires a fundamental commitment to achieving a rough parity by leveling out gross inequities in income, property, and opportunities. The key is a leveling of advantages so that all citizens receive the necessities (food, clothing, medical care, living wages, sick pay, retirement benefits, and shelter).

The third feature of socialism is community, which is the "idea that social relations should be characterized by cooperation and a sense of collective belonging rather than by conflict and competition" (Miller, 1991:406).

The fourth characteristic of socialism is the public ownership of the means of production. The people own the basic industries, financial institutions, utilities, transportation, and communication companies. The goal is serving the public, not making profit.

The fifth principle of socialism is planning. The society must direct social activities to meet common goals. This means that socialists oppose the heart of capitalism, which is to let individuals acting in their own interests in the marketplace determine overall outcomes. For socialists, these uncoordinated activities invite chaos and, while possibly helping some people in the society, will do damage to others. Thus, a purely socialist government requires societal planning to provide, at the least possible individual and collective cost, the best conditions to meet the material needs of its citizens. Planning also aims to achieve societal goals such as protecting the environment, combating pollution, saving natural resources, and developing new technologies. Public policy is decided through the rational assessment of the needs of society and how the economy might best be organized to achieve them. In this situation the economy must be regulated by the government, which acts as the agent of the people. The government sets prices and wages; important industries are run at a loss if necessary. Dislocations such as surpluses or shortages or unemployment are minimized by central planning. The goal is to run the economy for the good of the society.

Critics of democratic socialism argue that it minimizes individual freedom and choice. Government monopoly is inefficient because of a centralized bureaucracy making "one size fits all" decisions. Taxes are high to pay for the social programs. And, the argument goes, the "cradle to grave" social programs for individuals and families reduce their motivation to succeed, an attitude that, when held by many, limits creativity, economic productivity, and growth.

U.S. ECONOMY: CONCENTRATION OF CORPORATE WEALTH

The U.S. economy has always been based on the principles of capitalism; however, the present economy is far removed from a free enterprise system. The major discrepancy between the ideal system and the real one is that the U.S. economy is no longer based on competition among more or less equal private capitalists. It is now dominated by huge corporations that, contrary to classical economic theory, control demand rather than respond to the demands of the market. However well the economic system might once have worked, the increasing size and power of corporations disrupt it. This development calls into question what the appropriate economic form is for a modern industrialized society.

Monopolistic Capitalism

Karl Marx, more than 120 years ago, when bigness was the exception, predicted that capitalism was doomed by several inherent contradictions that would produce a class of people bent on destroying it (see the insert on Karl Marx and "self-destruct" capitalism). The most significant of these contradictions for our purposes is the inevitability of monopolies. Marx hypothesized that free enterprise would result in some firms becoming bigger and bigger as they eliminate their opposition or absorb smaller competing firms. The ultimate result of this process is the existence of a monopoly in each of the various sectors of the economy. Monopolies, of course, are antithetical to the free enterprise system because they, not supply and demand, determine the price and the quality of the product.

Karl Marx and Self-Destruct Capitalism

Karl Marx (1818–1883) was one of history's greatest social theorists. His ideas have fueled revolutionaries and revolutions. His writings have had an enormous impact on each of the social sciences. His intellectual contributions to sociology include (1) elaboration of the conflict model of society, (2) the theory of social change based on antagonisms between the social classes, (3) the insight that power originates primarily in economic production, and (4) concern with the social origins of alienation.

Marx believed that the basis of social order in every society is the production of economic goods. What is produced, how it is produced, and how it is exchanged determine the differences in people's wealth, power, and social status. Marx argued that because human beings must organize their activities in order to clothe, feed, and house themselves, every society is built on an economic base. The exact form this organization takes varies from society to society and from era to era. The form that people chose to solve their basic economic problems would, according to Marx, eventually determine virtually everything in the social structure, including polity, family structure, education, and religion. In Marx's view all these social institutions depend on the basic economy, and an analysis of society will always reveal its underlying economic arrangements.

Because it owns the means of production, the social class in power uses the noneconomic institutions to uphold its position. Thus, Marx believed that religion, the government, and the educational system are used by the powerful to maintain the status quo.

Marx argued that every economic system except socialism produces forces that eventually lead to a new economic form. In the feudal system, for example, the market and factory emerged but were incompatible with the feudal way of life. The market created a professional merchant class, and the factory created a proletariat. Thus, new inventions create a tension with the old institutions, and new social classes threaten to displace old ones. Conflict results, and society is rearranged with a new class structure and an alteration in the division of wealth and power based on a new economic form. Feudalism was replaced by capitalism; land ownership was replaced by factories and the ownership of capital.

Capitalism, Marx maintained, also carries the seeds of its own destruction. Capitalism will produce a class of oppressed people (the proletariat) bent on destroying it. The contradictions inherent in capitalism are (1) the inevitability of monopolies, which eliminate competition and gouge consumers and workers; (2) lack of centralized planning, which results in overproduction of some goods and underproduction of others, encouraging economic crises such as inflation, slumps, and depressions; (3) demands for labor-saving machinery, which force unemployment and a more hostile proletariat; and (4) control of the state by the wealthy, the effect of which is passage of laws favoring themselves and thereby incurring more wrath from the proletariat. All these factors increase the probability that the proletariat will build class consciousness, which is the condition necessary to class conflict and the ushering in of a new economic system.

Sources: Robert J. Werlin. 1972. "Marxist Political Analysis." *Sociological Inquiry* 42 (Nos. 3–4): 157–181; Karl Marx. 1976. *Karl Marx: Selected Writings in Sociology and Social Philosophy* (T. B. Bottomore, Trans.). New York: McGraw-Hill, pp. 127–212. See also Michael Harrington. 1976. *The Twilight of Capitalism.* New York: Simon & Schuster.

For the most part, the evidence in U.S. society upholds Marx's prediction. Less than 1 percent of all corporations produce over 80 percent of the private sector output. Most sectors of the U.S. economy are dominated by a few corporations. Instead of one corporation controlling an industry, the typical situation is domination by a small number of large firms. When four or fewer firms supply 50 percent or more of a particular market, a **shared monopoly** results, which performs much as a monopoly or cartel would. Most economists agree that above this level of concentration—a four-firm ratio of 50 percent—the economic costs of shared monopoly are most manifest. Government data show that a number of industries are highly concentrated (e.g., each of the following industries has four or fewer firms controlling at least 60 percent: light bulbs, breakfast cereals, turbines/generators, aluminum, cigarettes, beer, chocolate/cocoa, photography equipment, brewing, guided missiles, and roasted coffee).

This trend toward ever-greater concentration among the largest U.S. business concerns has accelerated because of two activities—mergers and interlocking directorates.

Megamergers. There are thousands of mergers each year, as giant corporations become even larger. In 1999 the value of mergers and acquisitions was $3.48 trillion (Valdmanis, 2000). The ten largest mergers in U.S. history have occurred in the past fifteen years (e.g., Time, Inc., and AOL joining with Warner Communications; Disney merging with Capital Cities/ABC; the combining of Wells Fargo and First Interstate Banks; the merger of NationsBank and BankAmerica; Philip Morris taking over Miller Brewing; the AT&T buyout of Tele-Communications, Inc.; Citicorp merging with Travelers Group; Texaco buying out Getty Oil, Exxon merging with Mobil Oil, and MCI World-Com's acquiring of Sprint). The federal government encouraged these mergers by relaxing antitrust law enforcement on the grounds that efficient firms should not be hobbled.

This trend toward megamergers has at least five negative consequences: (1) it increases the centralization of capital, which reduces competition and raises prices for consumers; (2) as corporations become fewer and larger, they have increased power over workers, unions, and governments; (3) it reduces the number of jobs as the merged companies eliminate redundant positions; (4) it increases corporate debt (currently, U.S. corporations spend about half their earnings on interest payments); and (5) it is nonproductive. Elaborating on this last point, mergers and takeovers do not create new plants, products, or jobs. Rather, they create profits for chief executive officers, lawyers, accountants, brokers, bankers, and big investors. The amount of money these people make is incredible. For example, the chief executive officer of U.S. Bancorp, Gerry Cameron, put together a deal in which his bank was taken over by First Bank Systems. As a result, 4,000 of his employees lost their jobs, but he received a $12.4 million payment tax free (First Bank agreed to pay all taxes that he would owe on the deal); he also received an annual paycheck of $1.6 million, as chairman of the Portland division of the new company (Hightower, 1997).

Defenders of a free and competitive enterprise system should attack the existence of monopolies and shared monopolies as un-American. There should be strong support of governmental efforts to break up the largest and most powerful corporations.

Interlocking Directorates. Another mechanism for the ever-greater concentration of the size and power of the largest corporations is **interlocking directorates,** the linkage between corporations that results when an individual serves on the board of directors of two companies (a **direct interlock**) or when two companies each have a director on the board of a third company (an **indirect interlock**). Such arrangements have great potential to benefit the interlocked companies by reducing competition through the sharing of information and the coordination of policies.

In 1914 the Clayton Act made it illegal for a person to serve simultaneously on corporate boards of two companies that were in direct competition with each other. Financial institutions and indirect interlocks, however, were exempt. Moreover, the government has had difficulty in determining what constitutes "direct competition." The result is that, despite the prohibition, over 90 percent of large U.S. corporations have some interlocking directors with other corporations. When directors are linked directly or indirectly, there is the potential for cohesiveness, common action, and unified power. Clearly, the principles of capitalism are compromised when this phenomenon occurs.

Despite the relative noncompetitiveness among the large corporations, many of them devote considerable efforts to convincing the public that the U.S. economy is competitive. Many advertisements depict the economy as an Adam Smith–style free market with competition among innumerable small competitors. This, however, is a myth. Competition does exist among the mom-and-pop stores, but they control only a minute portion of the nation's assets. The largest assets are located among the very large corporations, and competition there is minimal.

Multinational Corporations

The thesis of the previous section is that there is a trend for corporations to increase in size, resulting eventually in huge enterprises that join with other large companies to form effective monopolies. This process of economic concentration provides the largest companies with enormous economic and political power. If, for example, we compare government budgets with gross corporate revenues, the world's largest entities include 66 corporations and only 34

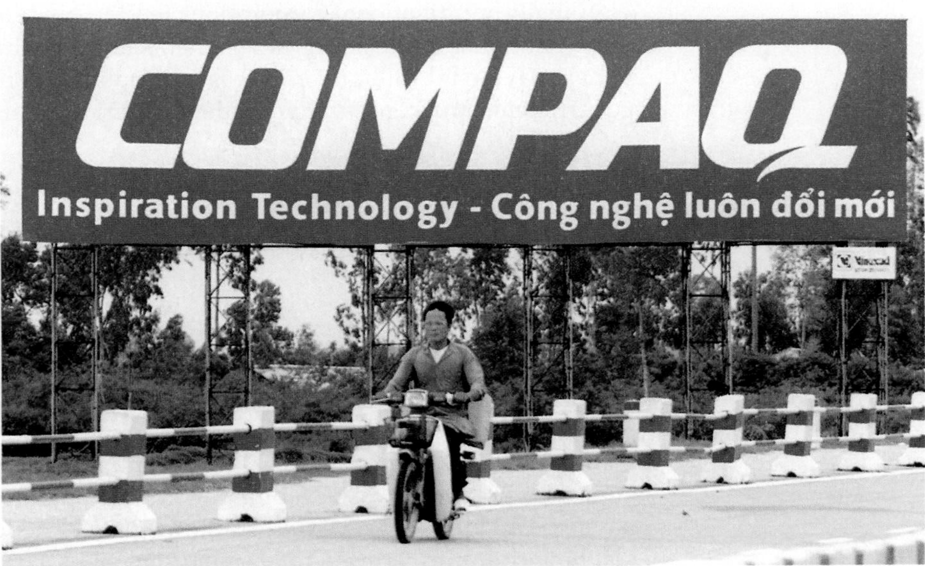

U.S. corporations often locate in countries where labor costs are cheap.

national governments. Each of the top three giant corporations, each a U.S. multinational—Exxon Mobil, General Motors, and Ford—has more annual revenue than all but 7 of the 191 national governments of the world (C. Gray, 1999) (see Figure 2.1).

Within the United States, the globalization of its largest corporations makes their power all the greater. This fact of international economic life has very important implications for social problems, both domestically and abroad.

A number of U.S. corporations have substantial assets overseas, with the trend to increase these investments rapidly. In 1999, for example, Exxon Mobil was the largest U.S. multinational with $115.5 billion in foreign revenues, followed by IBM with $50.4 billion in foreign revenues (Zajac, 2000). Why are U.S. corporations shifting more and more of their total assets outside the United States? The obvious answer is that the rate of profit tends to be higher abroad. Resources necessary for manufacture and production tend to be cheaper in many other nations. Most significant, U.S. corporations increase their profits by moving their production facilities from high-wage situations to low-wage nonunion countries. Moreover, foreign production costs are lower because labor safety laws and environmental protection laws are much more lax than in the United States.

The consequences of this shift in production from the United States to other countries are significant. Most important is the reduction or even drying up of many semiskilled and unskilled jobs in the United States. The effects of increased unemployment are twofold: increased welfare costs and increased discontent among people in the working class. We return to this problem of domestic job losses through overseas capital investments in Chapter 12, where deindustrialization is discussed.

Another result of the twin processes of concentration and internationalization of corporations is the enormous power wielded by gigantic multinational corporations. In essence, the largest corporations control the world economy. Their decisions to build or not to build, to relocate a plant, or to start a new product or scrap an old one have tremendous impacts on the lives of ordinary citizens in the countries they operate from and invest in. See the "Social Problems in Global Perspective" panel on page 34.

Finally, multinational corporations tend to meddle in the internal affairs of other nations to protect their investments and maximize profits. The multinationals have paid millions in bribes and political contributions to reactionary governments and conservative leaders in various countries.

Concentration of Wealth

The other discrepancy between free enterprise in its real and ideal states is the undue concentration of wealth among a few individuals and corporations. This imbalance makes a mockery of claims that capitalism rewards the efforts of all enterprising individuals.

Concentration of Corporate Wealth. Wealth in the business community is centralized in a relatively few major corporations, and this concentration is increasing. In 2000, for example, the minimum revenue to be in among the 500 largest corporations was $2.9 billion with the top corporation—Exxon Mobil—having $210 billion in revenues (Clifford, 2001). The following examples show just how concentrated wealth is among the major U.S. corporations:

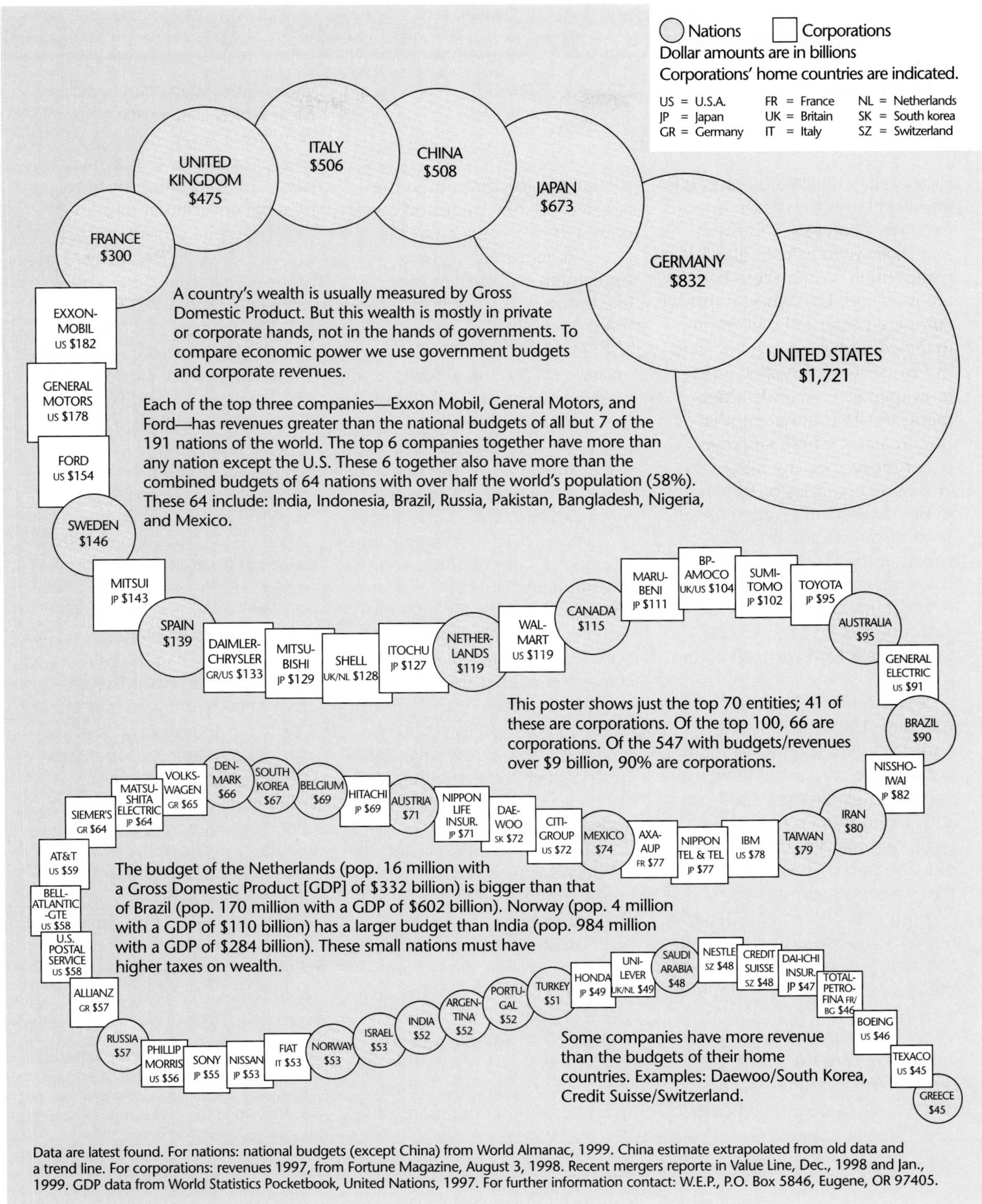
Nations
Corporations
Dollar amounts are in billions
Corporations' home countries are indicated.
US = U.S.A.
JP = Japan
GR = Germany
FR = France
UK = Britain
IT = Italy
NL = Netherlands
SK = South korea
SZ = Switzerland
FRANCE $300
UNITED KINGDOM $475
ITALY $506
CHINA $508
JAPAN $673
GERMANY $832
UNITED STATES $1,721
A country's wealth is usually measured by Gross Domestic Product. But this wealth is mostly in private or corporate hands, not in the hands of governments. To compare economic power we use government budgets and corporate revenues.
EXXON-MOBIL US $182
GENERAL MOTORS US $178
FORD US $154
Each of the top three companies—Exxon Mobil, General Motors, and Ford—has revenues greater than the national budgets of all but 7 of the 191 nations of the world. The top 6 companies together have more than any nation except the U.S. These 6 together also have more than the combined budgets of 64 nations with over half the world's population (58%). These 64 include: India, Indonesia, Brazil, Russia, Pakistan, Bangladesh, Nigeria, and Mexico.
SWEDEN $146
MITSUI JP $143
SPAIN $139
DAIMLER-CHRYSLER GR/US $133
MITSU-BISHI JP $129
SHELL UK/NL $128
ITOCHU JP $127
NETHER-LANDS $119
WAL-MART US $119
CANADA $115
MARU-BENI JP $111
BP-AMOCO UK/US $104
SUMI-TOMO JP $102
TOYOTA JP $95
AUSTRALIA $95
GENERAL ELECTRIC US $91
This poster shows just the top 70 entities; 41 of these are corporations. Of the top 100, 66 are corporations. Of the 547 with budgets/revenues over $9 billion, 90% are corporations.
BRAZIL $90
NISSHO-IWAI JP $82
IRAN $80
TAIWAN $79
IBM US $78
NIPPON TEL & TEL JP $77
AXA-AUP FR $77
MEXICO $74
CITI-GROUP US $72
DAE-WOO SK $72
NIPPON LIFE INSUR. JP $71
AUSTRIA $71
HITACHI JP $69
BELGIUM $69
SOUTH KOREA $67
DEN-MARK $66
VOLKS-WAGEN GR $65
MATSU-SHITA ELECTRIC JP $64
SIEMER'S GR $64
AT&T US $59
The budget of the Netherlands (pop. 16 million with a Gross Domestic Product [GDP] of $332 billion) is bigger than that of Brazil (pop. 170 million with a GDP of $602 billion). Norway (pop. 4 million with a GDP of $110 billion) has a larger budget than India (pop. 984 million with a GDP of $284 billion). These small nations must have higher taxes on wealth.
BELL-ATLANTIC-GTE US $58
U.S. POSTAL SERVICE US $58
ALLIANZ GR $57
RUSSIA $57
PHILLIP MORRIS US $56
SONY JP $55
NISSAN JP $53
FIAT IT $53
NORWAY $53
ISRAEL $53
INDIA $52
ARGEN-TINA $52
PORTU-GAL $52
TURKEY $51
HONDA JP $49
UNI-LEVER UK/NL $49
SAUDI ARABIA $48
NESTLE SZ $48
CREDIT SUISSE SZ $48
DAI-ICHI INSUR. JP $47
TOTAL-PETRO-FINA FR/BG $46
BOEING US $46
TEXACO US $45
GREECE $45
Some companies have more revenue than the budgets of their home countries. Examples: Daewoo/South Korea, Credit Suisse/Switzerland.
Data are latest found. For nations: national budgets (except China) from World Almanac, 1999. China estimate extrapolated from old data and a trend line. For corporations: revenues 1997, from Fortune Magazine, August 3, 1998. Recent mergers reporte in Value Line, Dec., 1998 and Jan., 1999. GDP data from World Statistics Pocketbook, United Nations, 1997. For further information contact: W.E.P., P.O. Box 5846, Eugene, OR 97405.

FIGURE 2.1

Corporate Cash: Few Nations Can Top It

Source: C. Gray, 1999. "Corporate Goliaths," *Multinational Monitor* 20 (June):27.

SOCIAL PROBLEMS IN GLOBAL PERSPECTIVE

THE PROBLEMS WITH GLOBAL TRADE AGREEMENTS

Historically, the United States has imposed tariffs on certain imports to protect domestic industries and their workers from global competition. When these barriers are removed, U.S. workers cannot compete because the wages in many countries are very low and the workers are not allowed to form unions. Free trade agreements create a climate in the United States where employers either move their operations to low-wage countries or threaten to do so to extract wage concessions or discourage unionization efforts in the U.S. plants. The consequence of these actions is what Chuck Collins and Felice Yeskel term a "race to the bottom" where workers in all countries lose.

The solution is to raise global standards by expanding the right to organize, establishing a bottom-line core set of labor standards, eliminating child labor, and raising human rights and environmental standards. Instead of being pitted against each other, workers, consumers, and communities should be allied in raising standards and improving the quality of life for everyone on the planet. This is the opposite of a race to the bottom.

Global trade and investment agreements are the primary mechanisms through which U.S. workers are forced to compete in the race to the bottom. In the last decade, free trade and investment agreements such as the North American Free Trade Agreement (NAFTA) and the expansion of the General Agreement on Tariffs and Trades (GATT) into a World Trade Organization (WTO) have reflected the biased and narrow interests of the worldwide governing corporate elite. These agreements spell out in careful terms the rights for global corporations and investment capital—while remaining shockingly silent on the concerns of workers, communities, and the environment. The WTO, for instance, has intricate legal protections for "intellectual property rights," which are the rights of ownership related to patents, inventions, research, and artistic materials. WTO rules carefully spell out how a corporation like Time Warner could sue the government of India if they allow an underground market in compact discs by Michael Jackson. Yet, the WTO says virtually nothing about human rights, conditions for workers, the right to organize labor unions, minimum wage standards, worker safety conditions, or protections for the environment.

Because of agreements like NAFTA and the WTO, owners of capital can quickly move their investments and operations offshore with minimal constraints. Meanwhile, U.S. workers have very little bargaining power against countries that allow slave labor, outlaw unions, or have minimal environmental standards. Despite promises of job growth, the U.S. Department of Labor certified that, between 1993 and February 2000, 263,596 workers had lost their jobs directly as a result of NAFTA. These workers only include those who qualified for NAFTA Transitional Adjustment Assistance (NAFTA-TAA), special job training benefits for production workers who lose their jobs because their employer shifted production to Canada or Mexico. In actuality, these job losses are just a small fraction of the total number of jobs lost under NAFTA. Service workers are ineligible for NAFTA-TAA and many eligible workers do not even apply for the program because they do not know it exists or choose to seek other forms of assistance. Proponents of NAFTA claim that over 200,000 jobs have been created by the agreement, yet they are unable to produce evidence. A survey of companies that pledged to expand jobs after the passage of NAFTA found that 89 percent admitted that they had failed to do so. Many had relocated jobs to Mexico.

Source: Chuck Collins and Felice Yeskel. 2000. *Economic Apartheid in America: A Primer on Economic Inequality and Insecurity.* New York: New Press, pp. 94–95.

- Less than 1 percent of all corporations account for over 80 percent of the total output of the private sector.
- Of the 15,000 commercial U.S. banks, the largest 50 hold more than one-third of all assets.
- One percent of all food corporations control 80 percent of all the industry's assets and about 90 percent of the profits.

- Six multinational corporations ship 90 percent of the grain in the world market.
- Nine massive conglomerates dominate the U.S. media landscape, supplying virtually all the television programs, movies, videos, radio shows, music, and books (McChesney, 1999a, b).

Concentration of Private Wealth and Income. Capitalism generates inequality. Wealth is concentrated not only in the largest corporations but also among individuals and families. For example, in 1999, according to *Forbes,* there were 298 billionaires in the Unites States. The two richest were Bill Gates, head of software giant Microsoft, with an estimated fortune of $63 billion and Larry Ellison, founder of Oracle, with $58 billion. The total net worth of the 400 richest Americans was $1.2 trillion (*Forbes,* 2000). At the other extreme, 32.3 million Americans were living below the poverty line in 1999 (see Chapter 7).

The concentration of wealth is greatly skewed. Consider the following facts:

- The top 1 percent of wealth holders controlled 38.1 percent of total household wealth (up from 34 percent in 1983) (Henwood, 2001).
- Considering just the ownership of financial stocks, the richest 1 percent of households own 42 percent of the value of all stock owned in the United States; the top 5 percent accounts for about two thirds (Wolff, 2001; Collins, 1999).
- Personal wealth is badly skewed by race. In 1995 White households had a median net worth of $49,030, about seven times that of Latino households ($7,255) and African American households ($7,073) (*Population Today,* 2001). At the lower end of the economic strata (incomes less than $15,000 a year), the median African American family has a net worth of zero, while the equivalent White family's net worth is $10,000 (Conley, 2001:20).
- The richest 2.7 million Americans, the top 1 percent, have as many after-tax dollars to spend as the bottom 100 million, a ratio that has more than doubled since 1977 (Johnston, 1999).

The data on wealth always show more concentration than do income statistics, but the convergence of money among the few is still very dramatic when considering income. The share of the national income of the richest 20 percent of households was 49.4 percent, while the bottom 20 percent received only 3.6 percent of the nation's income in 1999. The data in Table 2.1 (p. 36) show that income inequality is increasing in U.S. society. Especially noteworthy is the sharp gain in the Gini index, which measures the magnitude of income concentration from 1970 to 1999. The Gini index of 0.394 is the highest (indicating the greatest degree of inequality) of any other rich country. Great Britain's is 0.346, Germany's 0.300, Canada's 0.286, and Sweden's 0.222 (Murphy, 2000). (See Figure 2.2.)

Another measure of this increasing gap is the difference in earnings between the heads of corporations and the workers in those corporations. In 1980 the average chief executive officer (CEO) of a corporation was paid 42 times more than the average worker. In 1990 the CEOs made 96 times as much. By 2000 the average CEO was paid 458 times more than the average production and nonsupervisory worker (Sklar, 2001). Put another way, had U.S. workers enjoyed the same 535 percent pay raise as the nation's top corporate executives

TABLE 2.1

Share of Aggregate Income by Each Fifth of Households, 1970, 1980, 1990, 1999

	Percentage Distribution of Aggregate Income					
Year	*Lowest Fifth*	*Second Fifth*	*Third Fifth*	*Fourth Fifth*	*Highest Fifth*	*Gini* Index*
1999	3.6	8.9	14.9	23.2	49.4	.457
1990	3.9	9.6	15.9	24.0	46.6	.448
1980	4.2	10.2	16.8	24.8	44.1	.403
1970	4.1	10.8	17.4	24.5	43.3	.394

*The income inequality of a population group is commonly measured using the Gini index. The Gini index ranges from 0, indicating perfect equality (i.e., all persons having equal shares of the aggregate income), to 1, indicating perfect inequality (i.e., where all of the income is received by only one recipient or one group of recipients and the rest have none). The increase in the Gini index for household income between 1970 and 1999 indicates a significant increase in income inequality.

Source: U.S. Bureau of the Census, *Current Population Surveys.* Online. Available: http://www.census.gov/hhes/ www/incineq.html.

during the decade of the 1990s, the minimum wage would be $24.13 an hour, instead of $5.15, and the average worker would make $114,035 rather than the $23,753 the worker actually makes (Deibel, 2000).

Between 1977 and 1999 the average after-tax income of the wealthiest 1 percent of Americans increased 115 percent, after adjustment for inflation, while the average income of the highest-earning 20 percent of families increased by 43 percent. In sharp contrast, the middle fifth in income gained 8 percent, the second fifth stagnated at 1 percent, while the income of the poorest fifth shrank 9 percent (Shapiro and Greenstein, 1999). The inequality gap has risen dramatically for a number of reasons. The gain at the top reflects the increased tax benefits received by the affluent from changing tax laws during the 1980s and 1990s.

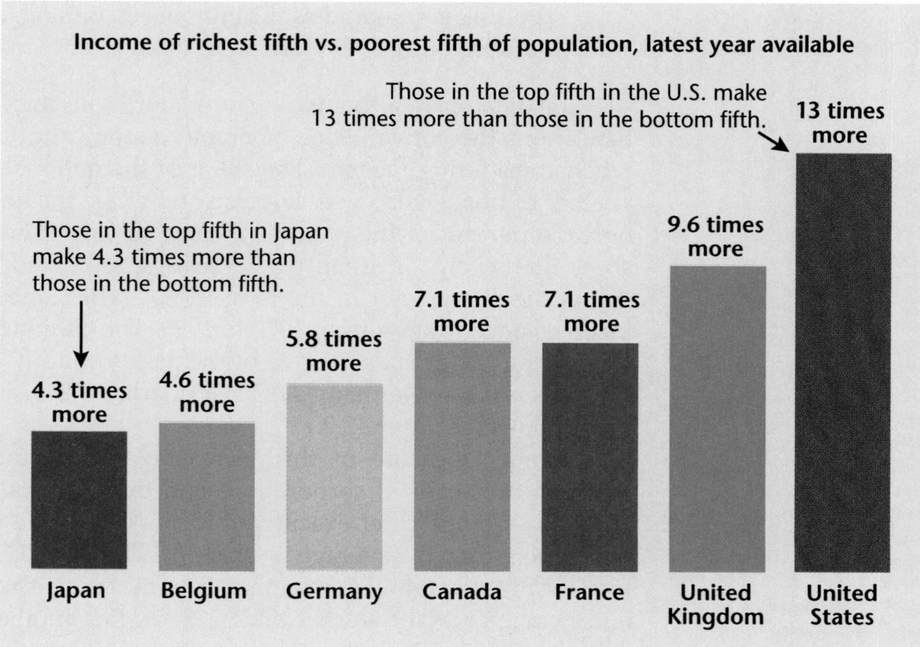

FIGURE 2.2

Income Gap: United States Leads Industrialized Nations

Sources: Clarifying Issues '96, 1996. New York: Public Agenda, p. 9; The World Bank; U.S. Bureau of the Census. 2000 *Current Population Reports* P-60, 210. Washington, DC: U.S. Government Printing Office.

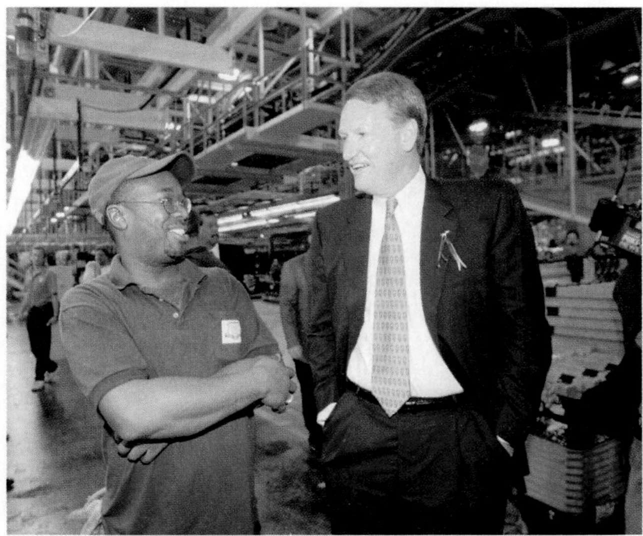

In 2000 the average Chief Executive Officer of a corporation was paid 458 times more than the average production and nonsupervisory worker.

Another factor explaining this inequality gap is the changing job structure as the economy shifts from manufacturing to service and as U.S. jobs are exported. At the upper end, corporate executives added handsomely to their incomes while downsizing their corporations. Congress has increased this upper-class feast by reducing capital gains taxes (taxes on the profits from the sale of property) and by allowing the affluent to place as much of their income as they wish in special tax-deferred pay plans not available to the less well-to-do. In 2001 President Bush signed a ten-year tax cut that included many benefits to the wealthy, thus exacerbating the inequality gap (see the "Social Policy" panel). Some of these provisions are:

- Repeal of the estate tax, the only federal tax on wealth (a tax that raises $30 billion a year). Only about 1.9 percent of deaths triggered estate taxes under the previous law, thus the repeal adds to the wealth of the already wealthy.
- A tax rebate in 2001 of $300 per adult that skips people with incomes below $25,000.
- There is a tax reduction of some $1.35 trillion over 10 years. Somewhere between 40 and 45 percent of the total cut goes to the richest 1 percent of Americans.
- The huge tax cut will have the effect of reducing government spending for programs that help the less fortunate, and it will weaken public institutions that benefit society (see the panel on tax relief and social problems).

POLITICAL SYSTEM: LINKS BETWEEN WEALTH AND POWER

In many ways the U.S. government represents the privileged few rather than the majority. Although the government appears democratic, with elections, political parties, and the right to dissent, the influence of wealth prevails. This influence is seen in the disproportionate rewards the few receive from the politicoeconomic system and in government decisions that consistently benefit

SOCIAL POLICY

TAX RELIEF AND SOCIAL PROBLEMS

The 2001 tax relief package passed by Congress was the primary priority of the new Bush administration. By reducing taxes, government waste would be eliminated and the people would have more money to spend and invest, thus improving the economy. The federal budget needs restructuring to increase efficiency. But is reducing federal activities the answer to society's problems? Given the projected budget surpluses (that will be lost through tax relief), we could address a number of social problems. Consider what we could do.

> We could truly address the disgraceful truth that in this rich nation one in six children is raised in poverty and deprived of the healthy, fair start vital to equal opportunity. Now we have the resources to rebuild an aging and overburdened infrastructure—witnessed daily in the power blackouts, collapsing sewers and aged water systems, overburdened airports, deferred toxic waste cleanups. Now we can redress the growing shortage of affordable housing and insure that every American has access to healthcare. (Borosage, 2001:5)

All of these actions are within our reach but the decision makers have ruled them out, making the reduction of taxes paramount. Consequently, these social problems will continue to fester.

Moreover, the inequality gap, already the most unequal by far among the industrialized nations of the world, continues to widen. The 2001 tax rebate checks (of $300 per adult) will not go to the bottom 40 percent of the population—34 million adults and another 17 million will get only a partial rebate. The affluent, by paying less in taxes, will, in effect, withdraw their support from programs that help those who are poor, those who do not have health insurance, and those who cannot afford decent housing. Former Secretary of Labor Robert Reich argues that what is really at issue here is the sorting of America, where our society is becoming more rigidly stratified. Reich says:

> There's only one way to reverse the sorting mechanism. . . . We have to rededicate ourselves to strong public institutions that are indubitably public because they work well for everyone. Of course this means more money and higher performance standards. But it also requires a renewed public spiritedness—a we're-all-in-this-together patriotism that says it's good for Americans to transcend class, race, education, health, and fortune, and to participate together. (Reich, 2000b:64)

them. Bernard Sanders, the only Independent in the House of Representatives, argues that the United States is, increasingly, an oligarchy. An **oligarchy** is a government ruled by the few. In Sanders's words, "Oligarchy refers . . . to the fact that the decisions that shape our consciousness and affect our lives are made by a very small and powerful group of people" (Sanders, 1994:B1).

Government by Interest Groups

Democracy may be defined as a political system in which the majority will prevail, in which there is equality before the law, and in which decisions are made to maximize the common good. The U.S. principle of majority rule is violated by the special interests, which by deals, propaganda, and the financial support of political candidates attempt to deflect the political process for their own benefit. Individuals, families, corporations, unions, and various organizations use a variety of means to obtain tax breaks, favors, subsidies, favorable rulings, and the like from Congress and its committees, regulatory agencies, and executive bureaucracies. Among the means used to accomplish their goals are the following:

> [A]long with the slick brochures, expert testimony, and technical reports, corporate lobbyists still have the succulent campaign contributions, the secret slush funds, the "volunteer" campaign workers, the fat lecture fees, the stock awards and insider stock market tips, the easy-term loans, the high-paying corporate directorship upon retirement from office, the lavish parties and accommodating female escorts, the prepaid vacation jaunts, the luxury hotels and private jets, the free housing and meals, and the many other hustling enticements of money. (Parenti, 1995b:208)

In 1998 special interests spent $1.4 billion on federal lobbying, including $25.1 million by British American Tobacco, $23.0 million by Philip Morris, $21.2 million by Bell Atlantic, and $16.8 million by the American Medical Association. Cities and public agencies spent $34 million of the taxpayers money to lobby the federal government. For example, the Commonwealth of Puerto Rico spent $4.0 million, the City and County of Denver spent $840,000, and the Metro Transit Authority of Harris County of Texas spent $420,000 in 1998 (Schouten and Weiser, 1999).

The existence of lobbyists does not ensure that the national interest will be served or that the concerns of all groups will be heard. Who, for example, speaks for the interests of minority groups, the poor, the mentally retarded, children, renters, migrant workers—in short, who speaks for the relatively powerless? And if there is a voice for these people, does it match the clout of lobbyists backed by immense financial resources?

Financing of Political Campaigns

Perhaps one of the most undemocratic features (at least in its consequences) of the U.S. political system is how political campaigns are financed. Campaigns are becoming more and more expensive, with money needed to pay for staff, direct-mail operations, phone banks, computers, consultants, and advertising. The campaigns for Congress and the presidency in 2000 cost $3.5 billion overall (up from $2.2 billion in 1996), including monies from the federal government (each major presidential candidate received about $75 million in public funds), individuals, political parties, and political action committees (PACs). The median expenditure on a Senate seat in 2000 was $4 million, up from $610,000 in 1976, and a House seat cost $891,000. The candidates for the Senate seat in New York—Hillary Rodham Clinton and Rick Lazio—spent a combined $68.6 million, making it the most expensive Senate race in the nation's history.

These expensive campaigns are funded by the candidates' personal wealth, individual contributions, and (in the case of congressional candidates) money donated from special-interest groups through PACs. The increasingly higher sums given to congressional candidates gives the distinct impression that we have "the best Congress money can buy." PACs are formed to represent interests such as labor unions, doctors, real estate agents, auto dealers, teachers, and corporations. Each PAC may give up to $5,000 to any candidate in a primary and another $5,000 in a general election.

In addition to PACs, there are three other legal ways for individuals and special interests to funnel money to the candidate or party of their choice. First, each individual can give $1,000 to a candidate. A common tactic is for the executives of a corporation to "bundle" their $1,000 contributions so that a sizable gift is given to a political candidate. In 2000 the Republicans raised $391 million and the Democrats $250 million in these $1,000 or less donations. A second legal way to contribute is through what is called "soft money." Here any amount can be given by individuals, corporations, unions, and other organizations to political parties at the national, state, and local levels, or to other private organizations that are technically independent of the candidates. These gifts are not covered by the federal election laws, and thus the amounts can be unlimited. This loophole is used by wealthy persons to contribute to the Republican and Democratic national parties (and indirectly to the presidential candidates). In 2000 the two parties raised $430 million in soft money (up from $263 million in 1996). The third method to raise money is through contributions to a "foundation" sponsored by a candidate. Through this loophole, donors can give *unlimited* contributions to a candidate with their identities *hidden* from the public record. A fourth source of money is the contributions to the political conventions. In 2000 the cost of the Republican convention in Philadelphia was underwritten by, among others, contributions of $1 million or more by Microsoft, AT&T, General Motors, United Parcel Service, Bell Atlantic, Comcast, Motorola, and Peco Energy (Lacayo, 2000).

In addition to the legal ways to influence campaigns with money, there are the contributions made outside the federal law. Fred Wertheimer, former president of Common Cause, who has investigated campaign abuses for 20 years, puts it this way:

> When you add it all up—the illegality, the cheating, the evasion, as well as the arrogance and cynicism—what we have is a collapse of the system on a scale we simply haven't seen before. . . . Put simply, we've seen that the attitude of our national leaders when it comes to campaign laws is no different than that of tax evaders, deadbeat dads and welfare cheats. (Wertheimer, 1996:29)

What do contributors of large sums receive for their donations? Obviously, they have access to the politician, perhaps even influence. It is difficult to prove

Drawing by M. Wuerker

conclusively that receiving campaign contributions from a special interest buys a vote, but there is some indirect evidence that such contributors do gain advantage:

- PACs often give to candidates who are running unopposed.
- Some PACs give money to both sides in an election. Other PACs contribute after the election to the candidate they opposed but who won anyway.
- Some corporations work both sides of the street by giving soft money to both parties.
- PACs overwhelmingly support incumbents. By giving to the incumbent, the giver is almost assured of giving to the winner.
- PAC money disproportionately goes to the most powerful members of the House and Senate (those in leadership roles).

Money presents a fundamental obstacle to democracy because only the interests of the wealthy tend to be served. It takes money—and lots of it—to be a successful politician. The candidate must be either rich or willing to accept contributions from others. In either case, the political leaders will be part of or beholden to the wealthy.

Candidate Selection Process

Closely related to the financing of campaigns is the process by which political candidates are nominated. Being wealthy or having access to wealth is essential for victory because of the enormous cost of the race. Thus, the candidates tend to represent a limited constituency—the wealthy.

The two-party system also works to limit choices among candidates to a rather narrow range. Each party is financed by the special interests—especially business. As William Domhoff puts it:

> When all of these direct and indirect gifts (donations provided directly to candidates or through numerous political action committees of specific corporations and general business organizations) are combined, the power elite can be seen to provide the great bulk of the financial support to both parties at the national level, far outspending the unions and middle status liberals within the Democrats, and the melange of physicians, dentists, engineers, real-estate operators and other white-collar conservatives within the right wing of the Republican Party. (Domhoff, 1978:148)

Affluent individuals and the largest corporations influence candidate selection by giving financial aid to those candidates sympathetic with their views and withholding support from those who differ. The parties, then, are constrained to choose candidates with views congruent with the monied interests.

BIAS OF THE POLITICAL SYSTEM

Most people think of the machinery of government as a beneficial force promoting the common good. But although the government can be organized for the benefit of the majority, it is not always neutral (Parenti, 1978). The state regulates; it stifles opposition; it makes and enforces the law; it funnels information; it makes war on so-called enemies (foreign and domestic); and its policies determine how resources are apportioned. In all of these areas the government is generally biased toward policies that benefit the wealthy, especially the business community. In short, power in the United States is concentrated in a **power elite,** and this elite uses its power for its own advantage.

Power in the United States is concentrated among people who control the government and the largest corporations. This assertion is based on the assumption that power is not an attribute of individuals but rather of social organization. The elite in U.S. society are those people who occupy the power roles in society. The great political decisions are made by the president, the president's advisers, cabinet members, members of regulatory agencies, the Federal Reserve Board, key members of Congress, and the Supreme Court. Individuals in these government command posts have the authority to make war, raise or lower interest rates, levy taxes, dam rivers, and institute or withhold national health insurance.

Formerly, economic activity was the result of many decisions made by individual entrepreneurs and the heads of small businesses. Now, a handful of companies have virtual control over the marketplace. Decisions made by the boards of directors and the managers of these huge corporations determine employment and production, consumption patterns, wages and prices, the extent of foreign trade, the rate at which natural resources are depleted, and the like.

The few thousand people who form this power elite tend to come from backgrounds of privilege and wealth. It would be a mistake, however, to equate personal wealth with power. Great power is manifested only through decision making in the very large corporations or in government. We have seen that this elite exercises great power. Decisions are made by the powerful, and these decisions tend to benefit the wealthy disproportionately. But the power elite is not formally organized; there is no conspiracy per se. The interests of the powerful (and the wealthy) are served, nevertheless, through the way in which society is structured. This bias occurs in three ways: by the elite's influence over elected and appointed government officials at all levels, by the structure of the system, and by ideological control of the masses.

As noted earlier, the wealthy receive favorable treatment either by actually occupying positions of power or by exerting direct influence over those who do. Laws, court decisions, and administrative decisions tend to give them the advantage.

More subtly, the power elite can get its way without actually being mobilized at all. The choices of decision makers are often limited by what are called **systemic imperatives;** that is, the institutions of society are patterned to produce prearranged results regardless of the personalities of the decision makers. In other words, there is a bias that pressures the government to do certain things and not to do other things. Inevitably, this bias favors the status quo, allowing people with power to continue to exercise it. No change is easier than change. The current political and economic systems have worked and generally are not subject to questions, let alone change. In this way, the laws, customs, and institutions of society resist change. Thus, the propertied and the wealthy benefit, while the propertyless and the poor remain disadvantaged. As Parenti has argued:

> The law does not exist as an abstraction. It gathers shape and substance from a context of power, within a real-life social structure. Like other institutions, the legal system is class-bound. The question is not whether the law should or should not be neutral, for as a product of its society, it cannot be neutral in purpose or effect. (Parenti, 1978:188)

In addition to the inertia of institutions, there are other systemic imperatives that benefit the power elite and the wealthy. One such imperative is for the government to strive to provide an adequate defense against our enemies, which stifles any external threat to the status quo. Thus, Congress, the president, and the general public tend to support large appropriations for defense, which in turn provide extraordinary profit to many corporations. In addition, the government will protect U.S. multinational companies in their overseas operations, so that they enjoy a healthy and profitable business climate. Domestic government policy also is shaped by the systemic imperative for stability. The government promotes domestic tranquility by squelching dissidents.

Power is the ability to get what one wants from someone else, by force, authority, manipulation, or persuasion. In Parenti's words, "The ability to control the definition of interests is the ability to define the agenda of issues, a capacity tantamount to winning battles without having to fight them" (Parenti, 1978:41). U.S. schools, churches, and families possess this power. The schools, for instance, consciously teach youth that capitalism is the only correct economic system. This indoctrination to conservative values achieves a consensus among the citizenry concerning the status quo. Each of us comes to accept the present arrangements in society because they seem to be the only options that make sense. Thus, there is general agreement on what is right and wrong. In sum, the dominance of the wealthy is legitimized. Parenti observes, "The interests of an economically dominant class never stand naked. They are enshrouded in the flag, fortified by the law, protected by the police, nurtured by the media, taught by the schools, and blessed by the church" (Parenti, 1978:84).

Finally, popular belief in democracy works to the advantage of the power elite, as Parenti has noted:

> As now constituted, elections serve as a great asset in consolidating the existing social order by propagating the appearances of popular rule. History demonstrates that the people might be moved to overthrow a tyrant who shows himself provocatively indifferent to their woes, but they are far less inclined to make war upon a state, even one dominated by the propertied class, if it preserves what Madison called "the spirit and form of popular government." Elections legitimate the rule of the propertied class by investing it with the moral authority of popular consent. By the magic of the ballot, class dominance becomes "democratic" governance. (Parenti, 1978:201)

Consequences of Concentrated Power

Who benefits from how power is concentrated in U.S. society? At times, almost everyone does; but for the most part, the decisions made tend to benefit the wealthy. Whenever the interests of the wealthy clash with those of other groups or even of the public at large, the interests of the former are served. Consider how the president and Congress deal with the problems of energy shortages, inflation, or deflation. Who is asked to make the sacrifices? Where is the budget cut—are military expenditures reduced or are funds for food stamps slashed? When Congress considers tax reform, after the clouds of rhetoric recede, which groups benefit from the new legislation or from the laws that are left unchanged? When a corporation is found guilty of fraud, violation of antitrust laws, or bribery, what are the penalties? How do they compare with the penalties for crimes committed by poor individuals? When there is an oil spill or other ecological disaster caused by a huge enterprise, what are the penalties?

Who pays for the cleanup and the restoration of the environment? The answers to these questions are obvious: The wealthy benefit at the expense of the less well-to-do. In short, the government is an institution made up of people—the rich and powerful or their agents—who seek to maintain their advantageous positions in society.

Two journalists, Donald Barlett and James Steele, have argued that there are two ways to get favorable treatment by Congress and the White House: contribute generously to the right people and spend lavishly on lobbying.

> If you do both of these things success will maul you like groupies at a rock concert. If you do neither—and this is the case with about 200 million individuals of voting age and several million corporations—those people in Washington will treat you accordingly. In essence, campaign spending in America has divided all of us into two groups—first- and second-class citizens. This is what happens if you are in the latter group:
>
> You pick up a disproportionate share of America's tax bill.
>
> You pay higher prices for a broad range of products. . .
>
> You pay taxes that others in a similar situation have been excused from paying.
>
> You are compelled to abide by laws while others are granted immunity from them.
>
> You must pay debts that you incur while others do not.
>
> You are barred from writing off on your tax return some of the money spent on necessities while others deduct the cost of their entertainment.
>
> You must run your business by one set of rules while the government creates another set for your competitors.
>
> In contrast, first-class citizens—the fortunate few who contribute to the right politicians and hire the right lobbyists—enjoy all the benefits of their special status. Among them:
>
> If they make a bad business decision, the government bails them out.
>
> If they want to hire workers at below-market wage rates, the government provides the means to do so.
>
> If they want more time to pay their debts, the governments gives them an extension.
>
> If they want immunity from certain laws, the government gives it.
>
> If they want to ignore rules their competitors must comply with, the governments gives its approval.
>
> If they want to kill legislation that is intended for the public good, it gets killed.
>
> Call it government for the few at the expense of the many. (Barlett and Steele, 2000:40–42)

The bias of the system today is nothing new. Since the nation's founding, the government's policy has primarily favored the needs of the corporate system. The founding fathers were upper-class holders of wealth. The Constitution they wrote gave the power to people like themselves—White, male property owners.

This bias continued throughout the nineteenth century as bankers, railroad entrepreneurs, and manufacturers joined the landed gentry as the power elite. The shift from local business to large-scale manufacturing during the last half of the nineteenth century saw a concomitant increase in governmental activity in the economy. Business was protected from competition by tariffs, public subsidies, price regulation, patents, and trademarks. When there was unrest by troubled miners, farmers, and laborers, the government invariably sided with the strong against the weak. Militia and federal troops were used to crush railroad strikes. Antitrust laws, though not used to stop the monopolistic practices of business, were invoked against labor unions.

During this time approximately 1 billion acres of land in the public domain (almost half the present size of the United States) were given to private individuals and corporations. The railroads in particular were given huge tracts of land as a subsidy. These lands were and continue to be very rich in timber and natural resources. This active intervention by the government in the nation's economy during the nineteenth century was almost solely on the behalf of business. Parenti notes, "The government remained laissez-faire in regard to the needs of the common people, giving little attention to poverty, unemployment, unsafe work conditions, child labor, and the spoliation of natural resources" (Parenti, 1995b:66).

The early twentieth century was a time of great government activity in the economy, which gave the appearance of restraining big business. However, the actual result of federal regulation of business was to increase the power of the largest corporations. The Interstate Commerce Commission, for instance, helped the railroads by establishing common rates instead of ruinous competition. Federal regulations in meat packing, drug manufacturing, banking, and mining weeded out the weaker cost-cutting competitors, leaving a few to control the markets at higher prices and higher profits. Even the actions of that great trustbuster, Teddy Roosevelt, were largely ceremonial. His major legislative proposals reflected the desires of corporation interests. Like other presidents before and since, he enjoyed close relations with big businessmen and invited them into his administration (Parenti, 1995b:67–68).

World War II intensified the government bias on behalf of business. Industry was converted to war production. Corporate interests became more actively involved in the councils of government. Government actions clearly favored business in labor disputes. The police and military were used against rebellious workers; strikes were treated as efforts to weaken the war effort and therefore as treasonous.

The New Deal is typically assumed to be a time when the needs of people impoverished by the Great Depression were paramount in government policies. But as Parenti has argued, "the central dedication of the Franklin Roosevelt administration was to business recovery rather than social reform" (Parenti, 1980:74). Business was subsidized by credits, price supports, bank guarantees, stimulation of the housing industry, and the like. Welfare programs were instituted to prevent widespread starvation, but even these humanitarian programs also worked to the benefit of the big business community. The government's provision of jobs, minimum wages, unemployment compensation, and retirement benefits obviously aided people in dire economic straits. But these programs were actually promoted by the business community because of the benefits to them. The government and business favored social programs not because millions were in misery but because violent political and social unrest posed a real threat.

Two social scientists, Piven and Cloward, in a historical assessment of government welfare programs, have determined that the government institutes massive aid to the poor only when the poor constitute a threat (Piven and Cloward, 1971). When large numbers of people are suddenly barred from their traditional occupations, they may begin to question the legitimacy of the system itself. Crime, riots, looting, and social movements aimed at changing existing social, political, and economic arrangements become more widespread. Under this threat the government initiates or expands relief programs in order to defuse the social unrest. During the Great Depression, Piven and Cloward contend, the government remained aloof from the needs of the unemployed until there was a surge of political disorder. Added proof for Piven and Cloward's thesis is the contraction or even abolition of public assistance programs when stability is restored.

The historical trend for government to favor business over less powerful interests continues in current public policy. This bias is perhaps best seen in the aphorism enunciated by President Calvin Coolidge and repeated by subsequent presidents: "The business of America is business."

Subsidies to Big Business

There is a general principle that applies to the government's relationship to big business: Business can conduct its affairs either undisturbed by or encouraged by government, whichever is of greater benefit to the business community. The following are examples of governmental decisions that were beneficial to business.

- State and local governments woo corporations with various subsidies including tax breaks, low-interest lows, infrastructure improvements, and relatively cheap land. In 1985, for example, the government offered Mitsubishi and Chrysler $115 million in incentives to build a joint plant. When the city of Toledo was faced with the threat of the local Jeep plant closing, it showered a $281 million local, state, and federal subsidy package to keep the plant. In 2001, Chicago beat out the offers by Denver and Dallas, by offering $50 million in incentives to encourage Boeing to move its headquarters from Seattle. To keep the New York Stock Exchange in New York City, the city and state of New York have offered an incentive package worth more than $1 billion. To which Ralph Nader replies: "It would be hard to script a more brazen and shameless corporate giveaway than a billion-dollar donation to the emblem of global capitalism from a city where nearly one in three children lives in poverty, and public investment necessities go begging" (Nader, 2001a:26).
- In 1996 Congress gave broadcasters spectrum rights to broadcast one channel of super-high-resolution digital programs or several channels that could be used for digital interactive services or TV programs of high, but not superhigh resolution. To which the *New York Times* editorialized: "By giving the new spectrum away instead of auctioning it off to the highest bidders, Congress deprived the treasury, and thus taxpayers, of tens of billions of dollars" (*New York Times,* 2000e:1).
- The government often funds research and develops new technologies at public expense and turns them over to private corporations for their profit. This transfer occurs routinely with nuclear energy, synthetics, space communications, and pharmaceuticals. Although the pharmaceutical industry, for example, argues that it must charge high prices on

drugs to recoup its costly research, the Joint Economic Committee of Congress found that *public* research led to 15 of the 21 drugs considered to have the highest therapeutic value introduced between 1965 and 1992 (reported in Goozner, 2000). Three of those drugs—Capoten, Prozac, and Zovirax—have sales of more than $1 billion each.

- Congress subsidizes the timber industry by building roads for logging. Under an 1872 law, mining companies need not pay for the $2 billion worth of minerals they extract from *public* lands (Scher, 2000). The government subsidizes corn growers and its processors by mandating the use of ethanol (a corn-based fuel product) in gasoline. The Department of Agriculture subsidizes crop insurance even on marginal lands at a cost of $1.5 billion a year.
- Multinational corporations move operations overseas to set up tax havens to make various intracompany transactions from a unit in one foreign country to another, thus legally sheltering them from U.S. taxes. This practice adds up to $1.8 billion in lost tax revenue (Hunt and Murray, 1999).
- In 1994 the Clinton administration and the Republican Congress passed a $20 billion package to help Mexico during its financial crisis. In reality, most of this money was to help Mexico pay off its debts to U.S. banks. In 1998 Congress gave $18 billion to the International Monetary Fund to help in the Asian economic crisis. Most of this money went to six U.S. banks with large amounts of bad loans in this region: Citicorp, J. P. Morgan, Bankers Trust, Bank of America, the Bank of New York, and Chase Manhattan (Sanders, 1998a).
- Two decisions in 1994 and 1995 by Congress and the president—NAFTA and GATT—helped make multinational corporations more profitable by encouraging investments where wages are lowest; by reducing the tax burden, and by lowering safety, consumer, and environmental protections.

Perhaps the best illustration of how business benefits from government policies is the system of legal loopholes allowed on federal income taxes. Corporations legally escape much of the tax burden through such devices as the investment tax credit, accelerated depreciation, and capital gains. Some corporations escape taxes altogether even when they are profitable because of these tax subsidies.

> Forty-one companies [such as Texaco, Chevron, PepsiCo, General Motors, and J. P. Morgan] actually paid less than zero in federal income taxes for at least one year from 1996 to 1998. They reported a total of $25.8 billion in pretax profits. Rather than paying $9 billion in federal income taxes at the 35 percent rate, the companies enjoyed so many excess tax breaks that they received $3.2 billion in rebate checks from the U.S. Treasury. In other words, they made more money *after* taxes than before! (McIntyre, 2000:12; see also McIntyre, 2001)

Trickle-Down Solutions

Periodically, the government is faced with finding a way to stimulate the economy during an economic downturn. One solution is to spend federal monies through unemployment insurance, government jobs, and housing subsidies. In this way, the funds go directly to the people most hurt by shortages, unemployment, inadequate housing, and the like. Opponents of such plans contend that the subsidies should go directly to business, which would help the economy by encouraging companies to hire more workers, add to their inventories, and build new plants. Subsidizing business in this way, the advocates argue, benefits everyone. To provide subsidies to businesses rather than directly to needy individuals is based on the assumption that private profit maximizes the public good. In effect, proponents argue, because the government provides direct benefits to businesses and investors, the economic benefits indirectly trickle down to all.

Opponents of "trickle-down" economics argue that this is an inefficient way to help the less-than-affluent.

> One way to understand "trickle-down" economics is to use a more graphic metaphor: horse-and-sparrow economics—that is, if you feed the horse well, some will pass on through and be there on the ground for the sparrow. There is no doubt that sparrows can be nourished in this manner; and the more the horses get fed, the more there will be on the ground for the sparrows to pick through. It is, however, probably not a very pleasant way for sparrows to get their sustenance, and if one's primary goal is to feed the sparrows, it is a pretty silly—and inefficient—way to do the job. . . . Why waste the money on the horses when it might go directly to the sparrows? (MacEwan, 2001:40)

There are at least two reasons government officials tend to opt for these trickle-down solutions. First, because they tend to come from the business class, government officials believe in the conservative ideology that says that what is good for business is good for the United States. The second reason for the probusiness choice is that government officials are more likely to hear arguments from the powerful. Because the weak, by definition, are not organized, their voice is not heard or, if heard, not taken seriously in decision-making circles.

Although the government most often opts for trickle-down solutions, such plans are not very effective in fulfilling the promise that benefits will trickle down to the poor. The higher corporate profits generated by tax credits and other tax incentives do not necessarily mean that companies will increase wages or hire more workers. What is more likely is that corporations will increase dividends to the stockholders, which further increases the inequality gap. Job creation is also not guaranteed because companies may use their newly acquired wealth to purchase labor-saving devices. If so, then the government programs will actually have widened the gulf between the haves and the have-nots.

The Powerless Bear the Burden

Robert Hutchins, in his critique of U.S. governmental policy, characterized the basic principle guiding internal affairs as follows: "Domestic policy is conducted according to one infallible rule: the costs and burdens of whatever is done must be borne by those least able to bear them" (Hutchins, 1976:4). Let us review several examples of this statement.

When threatened by war, the government institutes a military draft. A careful analysis of the draft reveals that it is really a tax on the poor. During the height of the Vietnam War, for instance, only 10 percent of men in college were drafted, although 40 percent of draft-age men were in college. Even for those educated young men who ended up in the armed services, there was a greater likelihood of their serving in noncombat jobs than for the non-college-educated. Thus, the chances of getting killed while in the service were about three times greater for the less educated than for the college educated (Zeitlin, Lutterman, and Russell, 1977). Even more blatant was the practice that occurred legally during the Civil War. The law at that time allowed the affluent who were drafted to hire someone to take their place in the service.

The poor, being powerless, can be made to absorb the costs of societal changes. In the nineteenth century the poor did the backbreaking work that built the railroads and the cities. Today, they are the ones pushed out of their homes by urban renewal and the building of expressways, parks, and stadiums.

The government's attempts to solve economic problems generally obey the principle that the poor must bear the burden. A common solution for runaway inflation, for example, is to increase the amount of unemployment. Of course, the poor, especially minorities (whose rate of unemployment is consistently twice the rate for Whites), are the ones who make the sacrifice for the economy. This solution, aside from being socially cruel, is economically ineffective because it ignores the real sources of inflation—excessive military spending, excessive profits by energy companies (foreign and domestic), and administered prices set by shared monopolies, which, contrary to classical economic theory, do not decline during economic downturns (Harrington, 1979).

More fundamentally, a certain level of unemployment is maintained continuously, not just during economic downturns. Genuine full employment for all job seekers is a myth. But why is it a myth, since all political candidates extol the work ethic and it is declared national policy to have full employment? Economist Robert Lekachman (1979) has argued that it is no accident that we tolerate millions of unemployed persons. The reason is that a "moderate" unemployment rate is beneficial to the affluent. These benefits include the following: (1) People are willing to work at humble tasks for low wages; (2) the children of the middle and upper classes avoid the draft as the unemployed join the volunteer army; (3) the unions are less demanding; (4) workers are less likely to demand costly safety equipment; (5) corporations do not have to pay their share of taxes because local and state governments give them concessions to lure them to their area; and (6) the existing wide differentials between White males and the various powerless categories such as females, Latinos, and African Americans are retained.

Foreign Policy for Corporate Benefit

The operant principle here is that "foreign policy seems to be carried on in the light of the needs of the munitions makers, the Pentagon, the CIA, and the multinational corporations" (Hutchins, 1976:4). For example, military goods are sold overseas for the profit of the arms merchants. Sometimes, arms are sold to both sides in a potential conflict, the argument being that if we did not sell them the arms, then someone else would, so we might as well make the profits.

The government has supported foreign governments that are supportive of U.S. multinational companies regardless of how tyrannical these governments might be. The Reza Shah's government in Iran (Risen, 2000), Chiang's regime in China, Chung Hee Park's dictatorship in South Korea, and Ferdinand Marcos's rule in the Philippines are four examples from the last half of the twentieth century of this tendency.

The U.S. government has directly intervened in the domestic affairs of foreign governments to protect U.S. corporate interests. In Latin America, for example, the United States has intervened militarily since 1950 in Guatemala, the Dominican Republic, Chile, Uruguay, Nicaragua, Haiti, Grenada, and Panama. As Parenti has characterized it:

> Sometimes the sword has rushed in to protect the dollar, and sometimes the dollar has rushed in to enjoy the advantages won by the sword. To make the world safe for capitalism, the United States government has embarked on a global counter-revolutionary strategy, suppressing insurgent peasant and worker movements throughout Asia, Africa, and Latin America. But the interests of the corporate elites never stand naked; rather they are wrapped in the flag and coated with patriotic appearances. (Parenti, 1988:94)

In sum, the current politicoeconomic system is biased. It works for the benefit of the few at the expense of the many. Because the distribution of power and the organization of the economy give shape and impetus to the persistent social problems of U.S. society, the analysis of these problems requires a politico-economic approach.

CHAPTER REVIEW

1. The state is not a neutral agent of the people but is biased in favor of the upper social classes and the largest corporations.
2. There are two fundamental ways in which society can organize its economic activities: capitalism and socialism.
3. Capitalism in its pure form involves (a) private ownership of property, (b) the pursuit of personal profit, (c) competition, and (d) a government policy of allowing the marketplace to function unhindered.
4. Socialism in its pure form involves (a) democracy throughout the social structure; (b) equality of opportunity, equality rather than hierarchy in decision making, and equality in sharing the benefits of society; (c) public ownership of the means of production; (d) community; and (e) planning for common purposes.
5. Marx's prediction that capitalism will result in an economy dominated by monopolies has been fulfilled in the United States. But rather than a single corporation dominating a sector of the economy, the United States has shared monopolies, whereby four or fewer corporations supply 50 percent or more of a particular market.
6. Economic power is concentrated in a few major corporations and banks. This concentration has been accomplished through mergers and interlocking directorates.
7. Private wealth is also highly concentrated. Poverty, on the other hand, is officially dispersed among 32.3 million people; many more millions are not so designated by the government but are poor nonetheless.
8. The government tends to serve the interests of the wealthy because of the influence of interest groups and how political campaigns are financed.
9. An obvious undemocratic feature of the United States is the exclusion of minorities from economic and political power.
10. The powerful in society (those who control the government and the largest corporations) tend to come from backgrounds of privilege and wealth. Their decisions tend to benefit the wealthy disproportionately. The power elite is not organized and conspiratorial, but the interests of the wealthy are served, nevertheless, by the way in which society is organized. This bias occurs through influence over elected and appointed officials, systemic imperatives, and ideological control of the masses.
11. The government supports the bias of the system through its strategies to solve economic problems. The typical two-pronged approach is, on the one hand, to use trickle-down solutions, which give the business community and the wealthy extraordinary advantages; and, on the other hand, to make the powerless bear the burden and consequently become even more disadvantaged.
12. Finally, business benefits from governmental actions through foreign policy decisions, which typically are used to protect and promote U.S. economic interests abroad.

KEY TERMS

Capitalism. The economic system based on private ownership of property, guided by the seeking of maximum profits.

Socialism. The economic system in which the means of production are owned by the people for their collective benefit.

Shared monopoly. When four or fewer companies control 50 percent or more of an industry.

Interlocking directorate. The linkage between corporations that results when an individual serves on the board of directors of two companies (a direct interlock) or when two companies each have a director on the board of a third company (an indirect interlock).

Oligarchy. A political system that is ruled by a few.

Democracy. A political system in which the majority rules, there is equality before the law, and decisions are made to maximize the common good.

Power elite. People who occupy the power roles in society. They either are wealthy or represent the wealthy.

Systemic imperatives. The economic and social constraints on political decision makers that promote the status quo.

Power. The ability to get what one wants from someone else.

WEBSITES FOR FURTHER REFERENCE

http://factfinder.census.gov/
American Factfinder: In 1996, the U.S. Census Bureau undertook a comprehensive multiyear development effort to build a data dissemination system. In order to expand public access to demographic and economic information, the Bureau wanted to provide access to its data through the Internet. American Factfinder was created in 1999 to help disseminate Census Bureau data to the larger public.

http://inequality.org/
Inequality.Org provides data and essays on various aspects of inequality in the United States.

http://www.cbpp.org
The Center on Budget and Policy Priorities is a nonpartisan research organization and policy institute that conducts research on a range of government policies and programs, with an emphasis affecting low-income and middle-income people.

http://www.census.gov/statab/www/
The Statistical Abstract of the United States. Acting as "Uncle Sam's Reference Book," this online volume contains a collection of statistics on social and economic conditions in the United States. Selected international data are also included.

http://www.brook.edu/
The Brookings Institution functions as an independent analyst and critic, committed to publishing its findings for the information of the public. In its conferences and activities, it serves as a bridge between scholarship and public policy, bringing new knowledge to the attention of decision makers and affording scholars a better insight into public policy issues. Much of this institution's research focuses on inequalities that exist in the United States.

http://globetrotter.berkeley.edu/macarthur/inequality/
The MacArthur Foundation's Network on the Effects of Inequality on Economic Performance. Housed at University of California–Berkeley. "What is the relationship between inequality and the economic success of nations, firms, and local communities? This question is the central focus of a research network based at the University of California, Berkeley. The establishment of the network was motivated by recent developments in economics that challenge two views long held by most economists: Inequality goes hand in hand with a nation's economic success; and reducing economic inequalities inevitably compromises efficiency."

http://www.capitalism.org/
Capitalism.org is the "website for the *moral* social system: laissez-faire capitalism." All you need or want to know about capitalism can be found online at this web address. The "Capitalism Visual Tour" is the most popular feature of this site; it is a quick review of the basic foundations and ideals of capitalism. This site also features a library on capitalism, *Capitalism Magazine,* and information on how capitalists view certain issues or problems of our world today.

http://www.sharedcapitalism.org/
The mission of the Shared Capitalism Institute is to "catalyze critically needed progress at the local, regional, national, and global levels toward a more equitable and sustainable form of free enterprise." To

further that mission, the Institute seeks to "enhance the level of public debate about a long-neglected cause of fast-widening economic disparities both within and among nations: noninclusive patterns of ownership." Through a combination of research, education, communication and advocacy, the Institute is challenging the prevailing "agnosticism" that surrounds the issue of ownership patterning in modern political economies.

http://socialism.org/
The Socialism.org website is a not-for-profit research project initiated by Wyith Limited. The vision of this project is to "form an online rendezvous for nonviolent socialists sharing similar visions, building in all conscience a peaceful and ordered socialist society, regardless of race and nation." While Socialism.org holds no interests nor special aim in politics, they "aim to spread the good name of socialism to every corner of the world because there have been many false impressions that socialism is too radical or too advanced in opinions and policies."

http://home.vicnet.net.au/~dmcm/
This is the socialism website. The discussion of socialism on this site aims to examine its nature, looking particularly at the change in the system of ownership and how this impacts on life and society as a whole; show how it is superior to capitalism both as a society and as an economic system; defend it from its detractors; show how social and economic developments are creating the conditions it needs to thrive; and assess its future prospects.

http://www.marxists.org/
The Marxist Writers Archive is a nonpolitical, nonprofit organization dedicated to offering the complete written works of Marxists online. This archive includes the full works of many Marxists free to the public. It also includes some biographies and other secondary sources, but its focus is on primary sources. The site also houses *The Encyclopedia of Marxism* which "contains factual material, which also employs quotes and direct links to Marxist analysis in the Writers Archive and, when necessary, provides a foundation of Marxist analysis to make facts comprehensible and to ensure a contemporary rendering."

http://www.fec.gov/
The Federal Electoral Commission. In 1975, Congress created the Federal Election Commission (FEC) to administer and enforce the Federal Election Campaign Act (FECA), the statute that governs the financing of federal elections. The duties of the FEC, which is an independent regulatory agency, are to disclose campaign finance information, to enforce the provisions of the law such as the limits and prohibitions on contributions, and to oversee the public funding of presidential elections.

http://www.american.edu/spa/ccps/
The Center for Congressional and Presidential Studies (CCPS) is located in the nation's capital at American University. Under the sponsorship of the School of Public Affairs, CCPS provides an integrated teaching, research, and study program focusing on Congress and the presidency and the interactions of these two basic American institutions. Established in 1979, the Center provides a scholarly organization uniquely able to draw on its Washington, D.C., location in the very heart of the events shaping Congress and the presidency.

http://www.bls.gov/
The Bureau of Labor Statistics provides a comprehensive picture of the U.S. economy at any given moment in time. The Bureau of Labor Statistics is the principal fact-finding agency for the federal government in the broad field of labor economics and statistics.

http://www.opensecrets.org/
The Center for Responsive Politics is a nonpartisan, nonprofit research group based in Washington, D.C., that tracks money in politics and its effect on elections and public policy. This Center hosts a website called OpenSecrets.Org that researches issues that citizens want to know more about.

PART TWO
PROBLEMS OF PEOPLE, THE ENVIRONMENT, AND LOCATION

3

World Population and Global Inequality

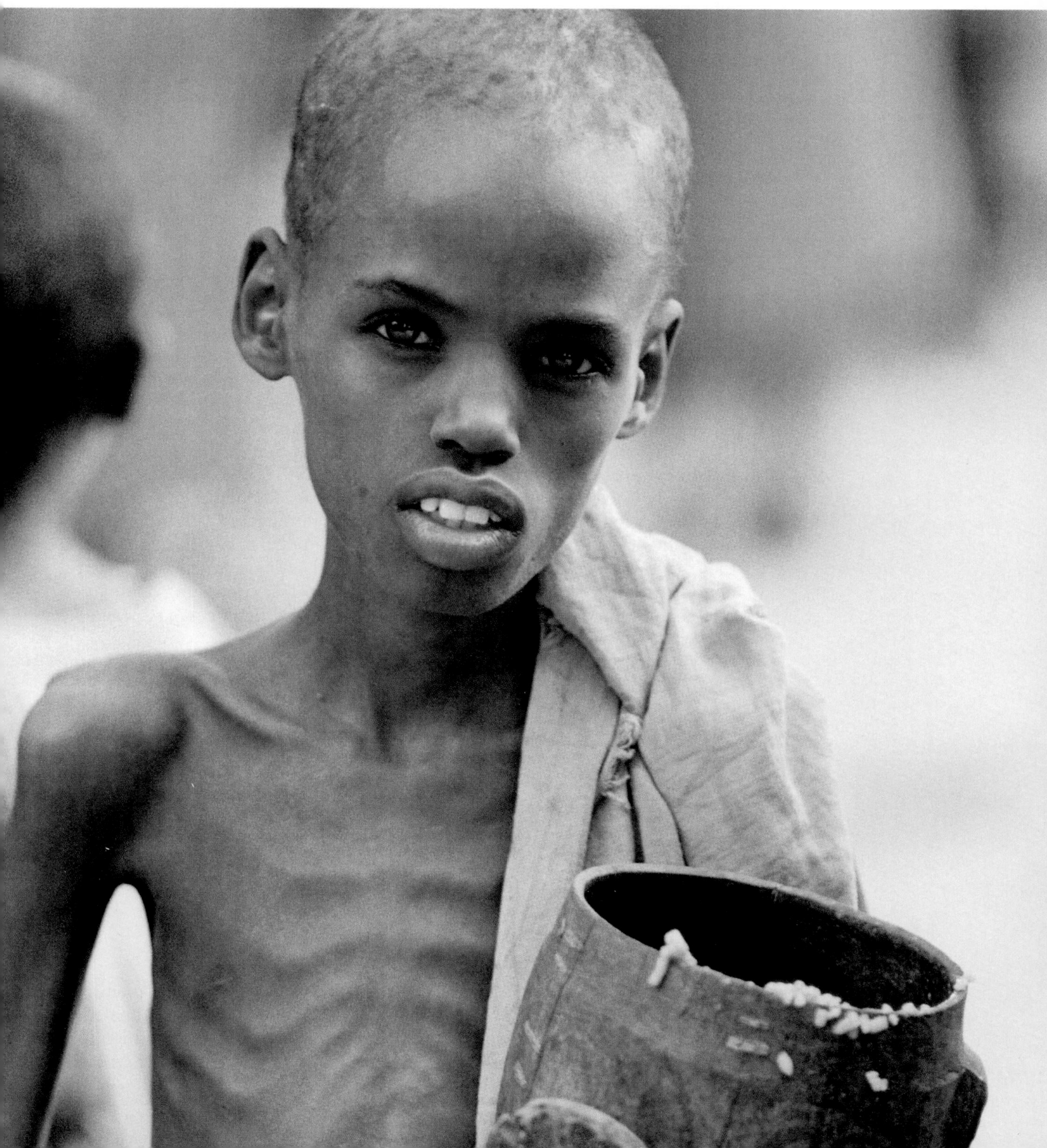

If the global village were reduced to 1,000 who proportionately represent the world's population, 584 would be Asians, 124 Africans, 84 Latin Americans, 95 eastern/western Europeans, 55 from the former Soviet Union, 52 North Americans, four Australians and two would be from New Zealand. . . . Rich folks call the shots in the global village. One-fifth of the people control three-quarters of the wealth. Another fifth of the population receive only 2 percent of the wealth. Only 70 people own automobiles. Only one-third of the population have access to clean drinking water. Fewer than 20 have a college education.

—Brigada (reported in Amole, 1999)

Today more than one-fourth of the world's 6 billion people are between the ages of 10 and 24, making this the largest group ever to enter adulthood. The actions of these young people—86 percent of whom live in less developed countries—will shape the size, health, and prosperity of the world's future population.

—Population Reference Bureau (2000)

The countries of the world vary widely in levels of material conditions. Some nations are disproportionately poor with rampant hunger, disease, and illiteracy. Other nations are exceptionally well off, with ample resources. Table 3.1, using an index based on life expectancy, educational attainment, and real per capita gross domestic product, ranks the world's nations. Notice that the bottom twenty-four countries are all in sub-Saharan Africa. Hidden in these data is that more than three-fourths of the world's population live in countries in which the per capita gross national product (GNP) is below $700.

The reasons for such global inequality include, as one might suspect, the degree of geographic isolation, climate, and natural resources. Another key determinant is the effect of power. The poor are poor, as we discuss, because they have been and continue to be dominated and exploited by powerful nations that have extracted their wealth and labor. This continuing domination by the powerful of the weak has resulted in an ever-widening gap between the rich and poor nations.

This chapter examines the plight of the poorest countries and the role of the richest—especially the United States—in maintaining global inequality. The first section focuses on world population growth, examining in particular the variables affecting why some nations have high growth while others do not. The second part examines poverty throughout the world and the social problems generated by impoverishment such as hunger, unhealthy living conditions, and economic/social chaos. The third part explores the relationship of the United States with the poor nations, historically through colonialism, and currently through the impact of multinational corporations and official government policies.

World Population Growth

The number of people on this planet constitutes both a major problem and potential future calamity. The world population in mid-2001 was estimated to be 6.123 billion, and at its current rate of growth, the net addition annually is about 78 million people (the equivalent of adding a city the size of San Fran-

TABLE 3.1

The Ranking of Countries by the 2000 Human Development Index*

1. Canada
2. Norway
3. USA
4. Australia
5. Iceland
6. Sweden
7. Belgium
8. Netherlands
9. Japan
10. Britain
11. Finland
12. France
13. Switzerland
14. Germany
15. Denmark
16. Austria
17. Luxembourg
18. Ireland
19. Italy
20. New Zealand
21. Spain
22. Cyprus
23. Israel
24. Singapore
25. Greece
26. Hong Kong
27. Malta
28. Portugal
29. Slovenia
30. Barbados
31. South Korea
32. Brunei
33. Bahamas
34. Czech Republic
35. Argentina
36. Kuwait
37. Antigua/Barbuda
38. Chile
39. Uruguay
40. Slovakia
41. Bahrain
42. Qatar
43. Hungary
44. Poland
45. United Arab Emirates
46. Estonia
47. St. Kitts and Nevis
48. Costa Rica
49. Croatia
50. Trinidad and Tobago
51. Dominica
52. Lithuania
53. Seychelles
54. Grenada
55. Mexico
56. Cuba
57. Belarus
58. Belize
59. Panama
60. Bulgaria
61. Malaysia
62. Russia
63. Latvia
64. Romania
65. Venezuela
66. Fiji
67. Suriname
68. Colombia
69. Macedonia
70. Georgia
71. Mauritius
72. Libya
73. Kazakstan
74. Brazil
75. Saudi Arabia
76. Thailand
77. Philippines
78. Ukraine
79. St. Vincent/Grenadines
80. Peru
81. Paraguay
82. Lebanon
83. Jamaica
84. Sri Lanka
85. Turkey
86. Oman
87. Dominican Republic
88. St. Lucia
89. Maldives
90. Azerbaijan
91. Ecuador
92. Jordan
93. Armenia
94. Albania
95. Western Samoa
96. Guyana
97. Iran
98. Kyrgyzstan
99. China
100. Turkmenistan
101. Tunisia
102. Moldova
103. South Africa
104. El Salvador
105. Cape Verde
106. Uzbekistan
107. Algeria
108. Vietnam
109. Indonesia
110. Tajikistan
111. Syria
112. Swaziland
113. Honduras
114. Bolivia
115. Namibia
116. Nicaragua
117. Mongolia
118. Vanuatu
119. Egypt
120. Guatemala
121. Solomon Islands
122. Botswana
123. Gabon
124. Morocco
125. Myanmar
126. Iraq
127. Lesotho
128. India
129. Ghana
130. Zimbabwe
131. Equatorial Guinea
132. Sao Tome/Principe
133. Papua New Guinea
134. Cameroon
135. Pakistan
136. Cambodia
137. Comoros
138. Kenya
139. Republic of Congo
140. Laos
141. Madagascar
142. Bhutan
143. Sudan
144. Nepal
145. Togo
146. Bangladesh
147. Mauritania
148. Yemen
149. Djibouti
150. Haiti
151. Nigeria
152. Congo
153. Zambia
154. Ivory Coast
155. Senegal
156. Tanzania
157. Benin
158. Uganda
159. Eritrea
160. Angola
161. Gambia
162. Guinea
163. Malawi
164. Rwanda
165. Mali
166. Cent. African Rep.
167. Chad
168. Mozambique
169. Guinea-Bissau
170. Burundi
171. Ethiopia
172. Burkina Faso
173. Niger
174. Sierra Leone

*The Human Development Index is a measure based on life expectancy at birth, educational attainment (based on adult literacy and school enrollment levels), and real per capita GDP.

Source: United Nations. 2000. *Human Development Report.* New York: Oxford University Press.

cisco every three days, or a New York City every month, or the combined populations of France, Greece, and Sweden every year). According to the United Nations Population Division, the world's population will increase by 50 percent to 9.3 billion in 2050, with nearly nine of every ten people living in a developing country (reported in Lee, 2001).

> The jump from six billion to nine billion is the equivalent of the impact of adding 33 more Mexicos to the world. And 33 additional Mexicos is the appropriate metaphor, because essentially all of the projected increase will occur in developing nations, the very places that strain to accommodate those already present. (Easterbrook, 1999:23)

To put the population growth curve in perspective, it took all of human history until about 1830 to reach the first billion. The next billion took 100 years (1930); the third billion, 30 years (1960); the fourth billion, 15 years (1975); the fifth billion, 12 years (1987); the sixth billion, 12 years (1999), and with the current slowing trend, the next billion will take about 14 years. (For future population growth scenarios, see Figure 3.1.)

Most significant, 98 percent of the current population growth occurs in the less developed nations where poverty, hunger, and infectious disease are already rampant. Table 3.2 contrasts the population data for Third World countries with data for much more affluent nations. The data reveal, most obviously, that there is a strong inverse relationship between per capita GNP and population growth rates—the lower the per capita GNP, the higher the population growth. For example, the Third World countries, on average, double in population in 40 years (with Ethiopia doubling every 28 years), compared with an average doubling time of 548 years in the developed countries (with some nations not growing in population size at all). To illustrate the population consequences of this differential fertility, let us compare sub-Saharan Africa with western and northern Europe. In 1950 Africa's population was half of Europe's, by 1985 it had drawn level, and by 2025 it is expected to be almost four times greater than Europe's (1.07 billion versus 283 million). These differences in fertility rates reveal a future world population that will be overwhelmingly from the developing countries (see Figure 3.2, p. 58).

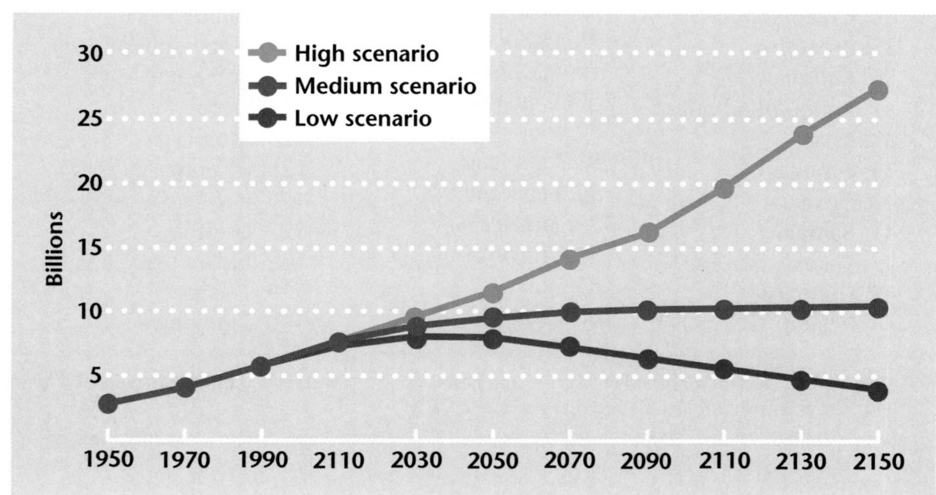

FIGURE 3.1

Three Possible Futures for World Population

Source: Population Reference Bureau, 1998. *1998 World Population Data Sheet.* Washington, DC: Population Reference Bureau, p. 1.

TABLE 3.2

Population Data for the Richest and Poorest Countries, 2001

	Gross National Income per Capita (U.S.$)	Percent of U.S.	Population Size Mid-2001 in Millions	Projected Population in Millions		Infant Mortality Rate	Total Fertility Rate
				2025	2050		
World	6,650	20.8	6,137	7,818	9,036	56	2.8
More developed	20,520	64.3	1,193	1,248	1,242	8	1.6
Less developed	3,300	10.3	4,944	6,570	7,794	61	3.2
Richest Ten							
Luxembourg	41,230	129.2	0.4	0.6	0.6	4.7	1.7
United States	31,910	100.0	284.5	346.0	413.5	7.1	2.1
Switzerland	28,760	90.1	7.2	7.6	7.4	4.6	1.5
Norway	28,140	88.2	4.5	5.0	5.2	3.9	1.8
Iceland	27,210	85.5	0.3	0.3	0.3	2.4	2.0
Belgium	25,710	80.6	10.3	10.3	10.0	5.3	1.6
Denmark	25,600	80.2	5.4	5.8	6.2	4.2	1.7
Canada	25,440	79.7	31.0	36.0	36.6	5.5	1.4
Japan	25,170	78.9	127.1	120.9	100.5	3.4	1.3
Austria	24,600	77.1	8.1	8.3	8.2	4.8	1.3
Poorest Ten							
Nigeria	770	2.4	126.6	204.5	303.6	75.0	5.8
Niger	740	2.3	10.4	18.8	28.5	123.0	7.5
Mali	740	2.3	11.0	21.6	36.4	123.0	7.0
Guinea-Bissau	630	2.0	1.2	2.2	3.3	131.0	5.8
Ethiopia	620	1.9	65.4	117.6	172.7	97.0	5.9
Burundi	570	1.8	6.2	10.5	16.1	75.0	6.5
Malawi	570	1.8	10.5	17.1	22.2	104.0	6.4
Congo	540	1.7	3.1	6.3	10.7	105.0	6.3
Tanzania	500	1.6	36.2	59.8	88.3	99.0	5.6
Sierra Leone	440	1.4	5.4	9.9	15.7	153.0	6.3

Source: Popultion Reference Bureau. 2001. *2001 World Population Data Sheet.* Washington, DC: Population Reference Bureau.

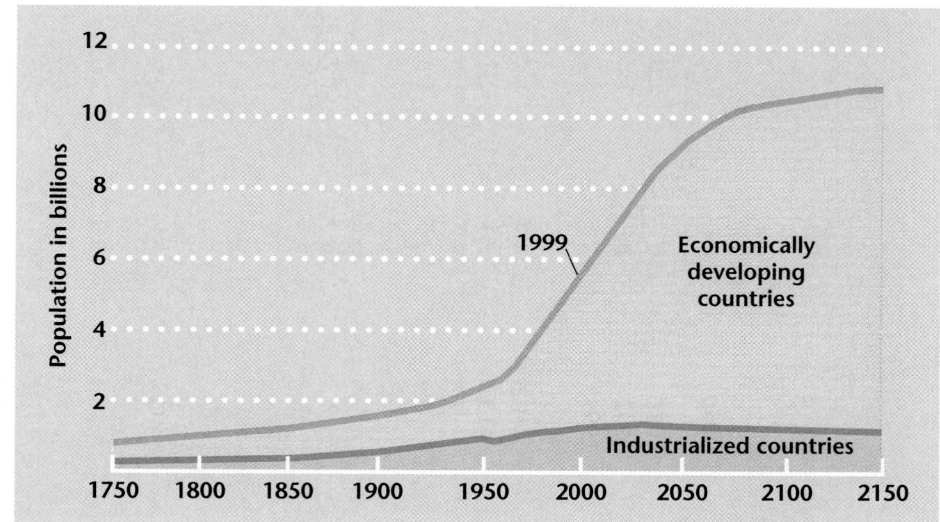

FIGURE 3.2

World Population Growth, 1750–2150

Source: Population Reference Bureau, "The World of Child 6 Billion," Washington, DC: Population Reference Bureau, no date, p. 5.

The population growth rates in the poor countries make it difficult to provide the bare necessities of housing, fuel, food, and medical attention. Ironically, there is a relationship between poverty and fertility: The greater the proportion of a given population living in poverty, the higher is the fertility of that population. This relationship is not as irrational as it first appears. Poor parents want many children so that the children will help them economically and take care of them in their old age. Because so many children die, the parents must have a large number to ensure several surviving children. Large families make good economic sense to the poor because children are a major source of labor and income. As Murdoch has put it: "That poor people are breeding themselves into poverty out of ignorance, religious superstition, poor economic judgment or lack of handy contraception is a persistent, but a false notion. Poor parents have large families because they are poor—they are not poor because they have large families" (Murdoch, 1981:3).

How can the nations of the world deal with the problems of expanding population? Basically, there are three ways to reduce fertility—through economic development, family-planning programs, and social change.

Demographic Transition

Historically, as nations have become more urban, industrialized, and modernized, their population growth has slowed appreciably. Countries appear to go through three stages in this process, which is known as the **modern demographic transition.** In the agricultural stage, both birth and death rates are high, resulting in a low population growth rate. In the transition stage, birth rates remain high but the death rates decrease markedly due to access to more effective medicines, improved hygiene, safer water, and better diets. Many nations are presently in this stage, and the result for them is a population explosion. Much later in the process, as societies become more urban and traditional customs have less of a hold, birth rates decline, slowing the population growth and eventually stopping it altogether (as is now occurring in many nations of Europe and Japan). Figure 3.3 shows the population pyramids for the less

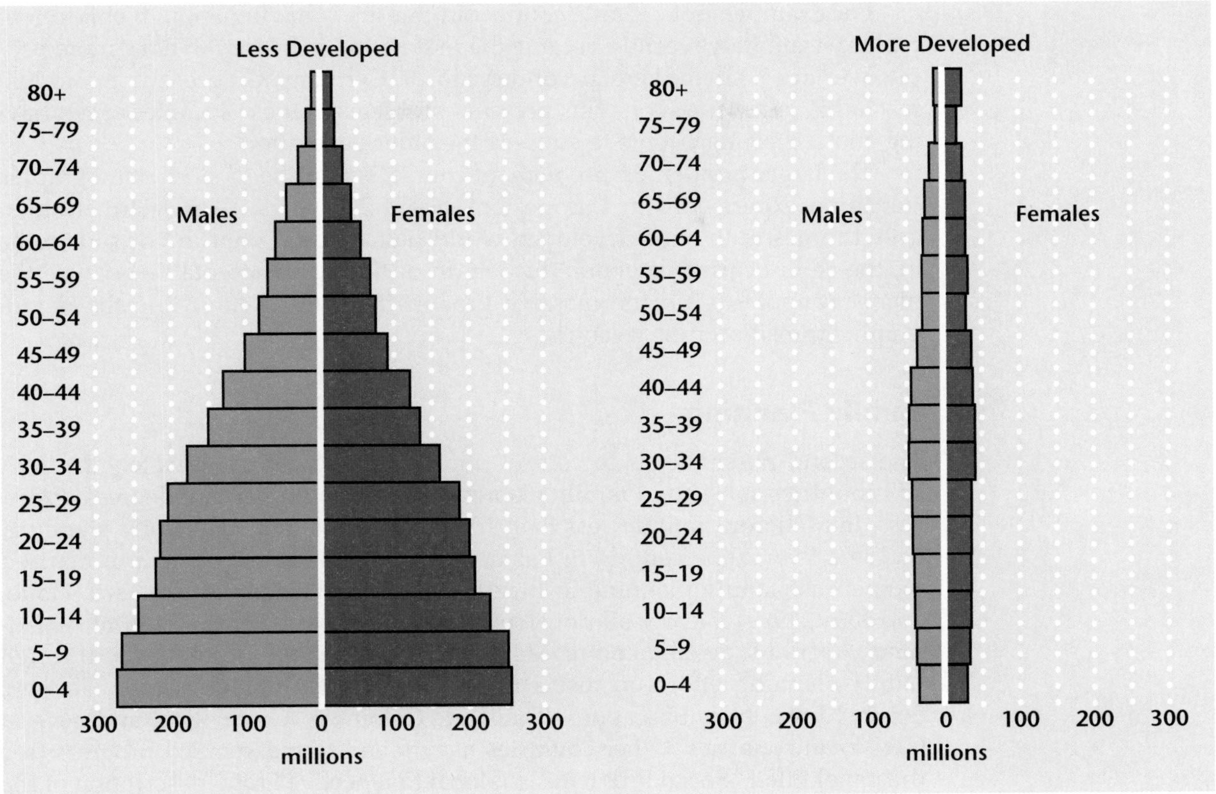

FIGURE 3.3

Population Pyramids for the World's Less and More Developed Countries, 1998

Source: Population Reference Bureau. 1998. *1998 World Population Data Sheet.* Washington, DC: Population Reference Bureau, p. 1.

developed countries, where population growth is booming, and the more developed countries, where population growth is extremely slow. Figure 3.3 includes the "critical cohort" of those under age 20 in the less developed countries. These 2 billion young people will soon become parents (400 million are already between 15 and 19). What will be the fertility of this critical cohort? Figure 3.1 shows the three possibilities. If the low or medium scenarios occur, the demographic transition with its accompanying urbanization, medical advances, and the liberation of women from traditional gender roles will have worked.

The concept of a demographic transition is supported empirically (Lutz, 1994). As a result, birthrates in the developed world are down dramatically. Spector summarizes the situation:

> [We are witnessing] one of the fundamental social revolutions of this century. Driven largely by prosperity and freedom, millions of women throughout the developed world are having fewer children than ever before. They stay in school longer, put more emphasis on work and marry later. As a result, birthrates in many countries are now in rapid, sustained decline. Never before—except in times of plague, war and deep economic depression—have birthrates fallen so low, for so long. (Spector, 1998:40A)

For example, not a single country in Europe is having enough children to replace itself. Italy recently became the first nation in history to have more people over age 60 than there are under age 20. Germany, Greece, and Spain will reach this milestone soon. This presents problems in these societies of not having enough young people to support the older generation.

The larger population problem, of course, is that the modern demographic transition experienced in Europe took about 200 years. With relatively high growth rates in the less developed world plus a huge cohort in, or soon to be in, the child-bearing category, this length of time is unacceptable because the planet cannot sustain the massive growth that will occur while the demographic transition runs its course.

Family Planning

The second possibility is to control population growth immediately. In 1997, 155 countries subsidized family planning services with varying degrees of success. In Mali, for example, less than 10 percent of women use family planning, and less than 20 percent do in Pakistan. But more than 60 percent of married women use family planning in Brazil, Mexico, and Thailand (Gelbard, Haub, and Kent, 1999). Nearly all developing countries have instituted family-planning programs. Several countries have reduced fertility dramatically through family-planning efforts in just a few decades, most notably China, Taiwan, South Korea, Iran, Singapore, Thailand, Colombia, Costa Rica, and several Caribbean countries. Other countries have failed to make much progress (see the panel titled "Social Problems in Global Perspective" for a description of the mildly successful family-planning effort in India). The United Nations estimates that half of the married women in developing countries do not want more children but do not have access to effective methods of birth control. The World Bank estimates that it would take $8 billion to make birth control readily available on a global basis. Such availability would reduce the projected world population from 10 billion to 8 billion during the next 60 years. The important point is that family-planning programs do work. Beginning in the late 1960s, the United States and the United Nations began funding such programs. The results:

- The average number of children born to a woman in the less developed nations has fallen from six to four.
- The number of married women using contraception has risen from under 10 to 54 percent.
- Annual population growth has dropped from 2.1 to 1.3 percent.

These gains were made despite the major reductions in family-planning assistance under the Reagan and Bush administrations (1980–1992). Because of their opposition to abortion and the use of the drug RU-486 (a pill that induces a relatively safe miscarriage in the early stages of pregnancy), the United States withdrew aid from the United Nations Population Fund and the International Planned Parenthood Federation. President Clinton reversed these policies, but this was later overturned by President George W. Bush.

Societal Changes

The third strategy to reduce population growth involves societal changes. Ingrained cultural values about the familial role of women and about children

SOCIAL PROBLEMS IN GLOBAL PERSPECTIVE

POPULATION GROWTH IN INDIA

More than one-third of the world's population live in either China or India. In 2001 China's population was 1.3 billion and India's 1.03 billion (Sharma, 2001). If current growth rates continue, India will surpass China as the country with the world's largest population between 2030 and 2035 with a projected 1.5 billion people. China has reduced its population growth significantly by placing limits on family size (one child per urban couple while rural residents may have two children). India's population policy is to encourage small family size through family planning (48 percent of married women use contraceptives), female literacy programs, and sterilization, which has reduced the birthrate over the past 50 years from six births for each woman of childbearing age to 3.1. Still India grows by 48,000 every day.

While India has had birth control programs since the early 1950s and public education at virtually no cost, the population continues to grow, especially in poor rural areas.

> In poor rural areas—such as Bihar state, where women's literacy rates are lowest and family sizes are largest—girls are often married by the age of 15 and pressured to produce children quickly—especially sons who will one day provide for their elders and light their father's funeral pyre, a ritual central to Hinduism.
>
> "Many women do not want large families anymore, but this is still a patriarchal society, where men make the decisions on reproduction," says Saroj Pachauri, who heads the local branch of the Population Council, an international nonprofit group. "Ask a woman in Bihar if she wants more children, and she will say no. Ask her if she is using [birth control], and she will also say no."
>
> Another obstacle is the popular notion, especially in the countryside, that more children mean more hands to work—rather than mouths to feed—and that larger clans mean mightier defenses. (Constable, 1999:16).

India, roughly one-third the geographical size of the United States, has almost four times as many people. Half of its population is illiterate. More than 320 million are so poor that they have but the equivalent of $1 a day for food, clothing, and shelter. About 50 million children do not go to school (Crossette, 1999). Resources such as arable land and water are strained to the limit. That is the situation now. What will it be like when they add another 500,000 million in the next half century?

as evidence of the father's virility or as a hedge against poverty in old age must be changed.

Religious beliefs, such as the resistance of the Roman Catholic hierarchy to the use of contraceptives and fundamentalist Muslim regimes such as in Saudi Arabia, are a great obstacle to population control. However, religion is not an insurmountable barrier. Despite the Catholic hierarchy's resistance to family planning, some nations with overwhelming Catholic majorities have extremely low birthrates. Italy, for example, has an average of fewer than 1.2 children per adult woman (a rate of 2.11 is needed to sustain the stable population), the lowest figure ever recorded. And some Muslim countries have instituted successful family planning. For example, Iran, with a strong commitment to limiting population, has seen its fertility rate drop almost in half.

Perhaps the most significant social change needed to reduce fertility is to change the role of women. When women are isolated from activities outside the home, their worth depends largely on their ability to bear and rear children. Conversely, fertility rates drop when women gain opportunities and a voice in society (Sen, 2000). Women need to be included in the formal education process. Research has shown that increasing education is one of the most effective ways to reduce birthrates. Educated women are more likely to use effective

Drawing by Danzinger. The Christian Science Monitor/Los Angeles Times Syndicate.

methods of family planning than uneducated women (Gelbard, Haub, and Kent, 1999:21).

Unplanned social change, such as economic hard times, also affects birthrates. Recent data show that economic difficulties for individual families in less developed countries can cause couples to delay marriage and to be more likely to use contraceptives. When enough families are affected negatively by an economic downturn, the fertility rate can fall for a nation. This is opposite the usual relationship of declining birthrates accompanying long-term economic success (the demographic transition).

Poverty

There is a huge inequality gap worldwide. Here are the facts:

- In 1900, people in the ten richest nations earned nine times as much per capita as did people in the ten poorest nations. This gap increased to thirty to one in 1960 and to seventy-two to one in 2001 (Gergen, 2001a).
- The top fifth of nations possess 86 percent of the world's gross domestic product, 68 percent of direct foreign investment, and 74 percent of the world's telephone lines (Street, 2001b).
- The richest 20 percent of the world's people receive at least 150 times more income than the poorest 20 percent (Street, 2001b).
- The top 20 percent consume 86 percent of the world's goods and services, while the poorest fifth consumes but 1 percent (Thad Williamson, 2000).

- About half of the world's people live on less than $2 a day, the World Bank's definition of poverty (Gergen, 2001a).
- The three richest people on Earth have wealth that exceeds the combined economic output of the 47 least-developed countries (Thad Williamson, 2000). The world's richest 200 people together have more money than the combined income of the lowest 40 percent of the world's population, or about 2.4 billion people (Geewax, 1999).
- Each day 40,000 children die from malnuitrion and disease (Gergen, 2000).
- Girls and women are disproportionately disadvantaged. Women represent two-thirds of the world's illiterate people and three-fifths of its poor. Stemming from cultural practices, lean rations at home are often given to father and sons before mother and daughters, resulting in a greater likelihood of malnourishment and disease (Gardner and Halweil, 2000).
- In annual spending for education, the developed countries spend $4,636 per child, compared to $165 in developing countries, and $49 in sub-Saharan Africa (Briscoe, 1999).
- In terms of consumption, the Human Development Report of the United Nations reports that in 1998 the richest 20 percent used 17 times as much energy as the bottom 20 percent. The richest fifth consume more than 45 percent of all meat and fish, while the poorest fifth a mere 5 percent (reported in Weissman, 1998).

Overpopulation and rapid population growth occur in the **Third World,** which refers to the underdeveloped and developing nations in which poverty, hunger, and misery abound. They are also characterized by relative powerlessness because most of them were colonies and remain economically dependent on developed nations, especially those of North America and Europe. Third World nations are also characterized by rapid population growth, high infant mortality, unsanitary living conditions, and high illiteracy. This section documents the poverty, hunger, squalor, and marginality of life in these countries.

Those considered in **absolute poverty** (extreme poverty) throughout the world make less than $1 a day. More than three in ten of the world's people (1.3 billion) are trapped in this condition, living typically in the rural areas and the shanty towns in Third World cities. Poverty translates into hunger, unsanitary living conditions, high infant mortality, high rates of infectious diseases, low life expectancy, and high illiteracy rates.

There is a striking maldistribution in life chances—the chances for life, health, and education—between the developed and developing nations. The significance of worldwide poverty and its concentration in the Third World nations cannot be overstated. The gap between the rich and poor countries is increasing, and the gap between the rich and poor in the poor countries is increasing. Those in absolute poverty suffer from disease, malnutrition, squalor, stigma, illiteracy, unemployment, and hopelessness. These deplorable conditions will likely lead to extreme solutions such as terrorist movements and government policies of military expansion.

Food and Hunger

The world's agriculture produces enough food for the world's 6 billion people. Actually, if everyone adopted a vegetarian diet and no food were wasted, current production would feed 10 billion people, more than the projected population for 2050 (Bender and Smith, 1997:5). This food production, however, is unevenly distributed, resulting in 1.1 billion people being undernourished and underweight (Brown, 2001), about one in every three of the world's inhabitants being food insecure, and some 18 million people dying of starvation each year (Andersen, 1997). How can we explain these chilling figures?

An obvious source of the problem is rapid population growth, which distorts the distribution system and strains the productive capacity of the various nations. The annual increase of 78 million people requires an enormous increase in grain production just to keep up. A number of factors are shrinking the productive land throughout the world, in rich and poor countries alike. The earth loses 24 billion tons of topsoil each year. Overgrazing of the grassland areas is slowly converting the marginal areas to desert. Irrigation systems that tap underground reserves are dropping water tables to dangerously low levels in many areas, causing the land to revert to dry-land farming. Air pollution and toxic chemicals have damaged some crops and water sources. The rising concentration of greenhouse gases (see Chapter 4) is changing the climates negatively. And, finally, each year millions of acres of productive land are paved over or built on. As Lester Brown of the Worldwatch Institute has summarized:

> In the mid-nineties, evidence that the world is on an economic path that is environmentally unsustainable can be seen in shrinking fish catches, falling water tables, declining bird populations, record heat waves, and dwindling grain stocks, to name a few. (Brown, 1995:3–4)

Most significant, of course, is that almost all of the population increase is occurring in regions and countries that are already poor. Because of low levels of economic development, the various levels of government, farmers, and others in these countries lack adequate money and credit for the machinery, fertilizer, pesticides, and technology necessary to increase crop production to meet the always increasing demand. The high cost of oil has an especially devastating effect on food production in poor nations. Food production in Third World nations is also more adversely affected by natural disasters (floods and droughts) than it is in more affluent nations because these countries are less likely to have adequate flood control, irrigation systems, and storage facilities. As a result,

> Most of the world's hungry [are] concentrated in two regions: the Indian subcontinent and sub-Saharan Africa. In India, with more than a billion people, 53 percent of all children are undernourished. In Bangladesh, the share is 56 percent. And in Pakistan, it is 38 percent. . . . In Ethiopia, 48 percent of all children are underweight. In Nigeria, the most populous country in Africa, the figure is 39 percent. (Brown, 2001:44)

Another way to explain the food problem is to view it as a poverty problem. Food supplies are adequate, but people must have the resources to afford them. Because the poor cannot afford the available food, they go hungry. While this view of poverty is correct, it has the effect of blaming the victims for their plight. To do so ignores the political and economic conditions that keep prices too high, make jobs difficult to obtain and poorly paid, and force too many people to compete for too few resources.

The major problem with food shortages is not food production, although that is exceedingly important, but the political economy of the world and of the individual nations. Economic and political structures thwart and distort the production and distribution of agricultural resources. [The following discussion is adapted from Lappe and Collins (1979, 1986), and Murdoch (1980).] The primary problem is inequality of control over productive resources. In each country in which hunger is a basic problem, most of the land is controlled by a small elite, and the rest of the population is squeezed onto small plots or marginal land or is landless. For example, although colonial rule ended in southern Africa decades ago, the small White minority still controls most of the arable land. In Zimbabwe Whites are only 0.6 percent of the population but they own 70 percent of the land (Jeter, 2000). The evidence is that when the few control most of the agriculture, production is less effective than when land is more equally apportioned among farmers. Yields per acre are less, land is underused, wealth produced is not reinvested but drained off for conspicuous consumption by the wealthy, and credit is monopolized. Most important, monopoly control of agricultural land is typically put into cash crops that have value as exports but neglect basic local needs.

Agriculture controlled by a few landowners and agribusiness interests results in investment decisions made on the basis of current profitability. If prices are good, producers breed livestock or plant crops to take advantage of the prices. This approach results in cycles of shortages and gluts. Small farmers, on the other hand, plant crops based on local needs, not world prices.

The way food surpluses are handled in a world in which more than a billion people are chronically hungry is especially instructive. The grain surplus is handled by feeding more than a third of the world's production to animals. Crops are allowed to rot or plowed under to keep prices high. Surplus milk is fed to pigs or even dumped to keep the price high. The notion of food scarcity is an obvious distortion when the major headaches of many agricultural experts around the world are how to reduce mountains of surplus and keep prices high.

From this view, then, the problem of food scarcity lies in the social organization of food production and distribution. The solution to hunger is to construct new forms of social organization capable of meeting the needs of the masses. The problem, though, goes beyond the boundaries of individual countries. The policies of the rich nations and multinational corporations are also responsible for the conditions that perpetuate poverty in the Third World. The United States, for example, supports the very conditions that promote hunger and poverty. The last section of this chapter documents this role.

Sickness and Disease

Chronic malnutrition, an obvious correlate of greater numbers of people and poverty, results in shorter life expectancies and a stunting of physical and mental capacities.

> Malnutrition takes its heaviest toll on children, and the health damage can begin before birth. Pregnant women who receive inadequate nourishment are likely to have underweight babies, who are especially vulnerable to infections and parasites that can lead to early death. Children who survive but receive inadequate food in the first five years of life are susceptible to the permanent stunting of their physical growth. Incredibly, 60 percent of children in South Asia have stunted growth, as do 39 percent of children in sub-saharan Africa,

> and 33 percent in East and Southeast Asia. . . . The percent of children underweight in developing nations ranges from 12 percent in Latin America and the Caribbean to 58 percent in South Asia. (Bender and Smith, 1997:6)

We know, for example, that "one in ten babies born in [poor] countries will not make it to its first birthday" (Ehrlich and Ehrlich, 1990:67). We also know that protein deficiency in infancy results in permanent brain damage. "When protein is not available in the diet to supply the amino acids from which brain proteins are synthesized, the brain stops growing. Apparently it can never regain the lost time. Not only is head size reduced in a malnourished youngster, but the brain does not fill the cranium" (Ehrlich and Ehrlich, 1972:92).

Vitamin deficiencies, of course, cause a number of diseases such as rickets, goiter, and anemia. Iron deficiency is a special problem for hungry children: Some 25 percent of men and 45 percent of women (60 percent for pregnant women) in developing countries are anemic, a condition of iron deficiency (Gardner and Halweil, 2000).

Vitamin deficiencies make the individual more susceptible to influenza and other infectious diseases. Health in overpopulated areas is also affected by such problems as polluted water and air and inadequate sewage treatment.

Malnourishment also causes a low level of energy. Not only lack of food but also intestinal disorders commonly associated with poverty cause general lassitude in the afflicted.*

Disease along with malnourishment threatens the world's poor. Polluted water, contaminated food, exposure to disease-carrying insects and animals, and unsanitary living conditions make the world's poor highly vulnerable to among other diseases, chronic diarrhea, tuberculosis, malaria, Ebola, dengue, hepatitis, cholera, and parasites. More than half of the annual deaths in sub-Saharan Africa are caused by infectious and parasitic diseases (Goliber, 1997). In addition to these diseases, one has emerged in the last two decades with devastating effects—HIV/AIDS.

HIV, the virus that causes AIDS, is transmitted through the exchange of bodily fluids, usually through sex, but also from contaminated needles, contact with tainted blood, or during birth for an infant born of an infected mother. Since the start of the AIDS **pandemic** (a worldwide epidemic), some two decades ago, some 60 million people have been stricken with AIDS worldwide with 22 million deaths. Currently more than 36 million are infected, with 14,500 newly infected with HIV every day (including 1,800 babies born infected daily), or more than 5 million new cases each year, making HIV/AIDS one of the greatest epidemics in human history (the Black Death that ravaged Europe in 1348 killed approximately 25 million, a number soon to be surpassed by AIDS). Seventy percent of those infected with HIV worldwide live in sub-Saharan Africa, where AIDS is the leading cause of death. In seven African countries, more than 20 percent of the 15- to 49-year-old population is infected with HIV (the highest rate is in Botswana with 36 percent). It is estimated that within 10 years, there will be 40 million AIDS orphans in Africa (Begley, 2001). There are expensive drugs ($10,000 to $15,000 cost per year) available to keep HIV in check, but because of the expense some 95 percent of HIV-infected people in poor nations will die within 2 years (Fischer, 2000). (See Table 3.3 for the worldwide distribution of HIV/AIDS.)

*Although low energy levels are a result of poverty, many persons have blamed poverty on a lack of energy, or "drive," in the poor—a classic example of blaming the victim.

TABLE 3.3
Distribution of HIV/AIDS, 2000

Region	*Number of People with HIV/AIDS*
Sub-Saharan Africa	25,300,000
South and Southeast Asia	5,800,000
Latin America/Caribbean	1,790,000
United States/Canada	920,000
Western Europe	540,000
East Asia/Pacific	640,000
Eastern Europe/Central Asia	700,000
North Africa/Middle East	400,000
Australia/New Zealand	15,000
Total	36,100,000

Source: United Nations, World Health Organization. 2001. "Report on the Global HIV/AIDS Epidemic." New York: Joint United Nations Programme on HIV/AIDS.

The New Slavery

"In almost every culture and society there has been, at one time or another, slavery" [Bales, 2000:xiii; this section is dependent largely on Bales (1999, 2000)]. Typically, slaves were captured by the powerful to work the rest of their lives for the benefit of their captors. Often slavery was legalized with people bought and sold as property to work at the whim of their owners.

By conservative estimate, there are 27 million slaves in the world today, and the number is growing (*New York Times*, 2000c). Slavery today (the **new slavery**), just as slavery in other times, means the loss of freedom, the exploitation of people for profit, and the control of slaves through violence or its threat. But today's forms of slavery also differ from the past. Typically, slavery is no longer a lifelong condition, as the slave is freed after he or she is no longer useful (e.g., a prostitute who has AIDS). Second, sometimes individuals and families become slaves by choice—a choice forced by extreme poverty. The population explosion in the poorest nations has created a vast supply of potential workers who are desperate and vulnerable, conditions that sometimes translate into enslavement. Often the poor must place themselves in bondage to pay off a debt. Faced with a crisis (crop failure, illness) an individual borrows money, but having no other possessions uses his or his family's lives as collateral. The slave must work for the slaveholder until the slaveholder decides the debt is repaid. This is problematic since many slaveholders use false accounting or charge very high interest, making repayment forever out of reach. This sometimes means that the debt can be passed to subsequent generations, thus enslaving offspring. Debt bondage is most common in South Asia.

Impoverishment may also lead desperate parents to sell their children (often told that the children will have good jobs) to brokers who in turn sell them to slaveholders. This practice is common in Thailand as the conduit for young girls to end up as prostitutes in brothels against their will. The United Nations Children's Fund estimates that 200,000 children in West and Central Africa are sold into slavery by their parents. Most come from the poorest countries, such as Benin, Burkina Faso, or Mali, where up to 70 percent of the people live on less than $1 a day. Faced with grinding poverty, parents may sell

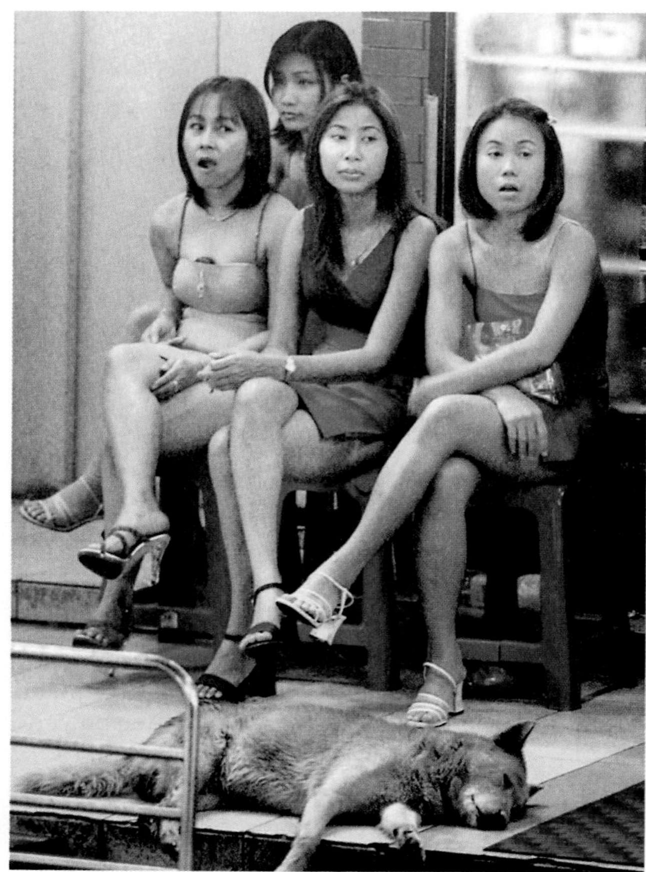

Impoverishment sometimes leads desperate parents to sell their children to brokers, who in turn sell them to slaveholders. This practice is common in Thailand as the conduit for young girls to end up as prostitutes in brothels against their will.

their children to traders for as little as $15, in the hope that the children will find a better life. Girls end up as domestic workers or prostitutes while boys are forced to work on coffee or cocoa plantations or as fishermen (Robinson and Palus, 2001). Sometimes poor young people with little prospect for success may deal directly with a broker who promises legitimate jobs, but once they are away from their homes violence is used to take control of their lives.

There is an international traffic in slavery, involving forced migration, the smuggling of illegal immigrants, and criminal networks. These migrants who end up as slaves come from Asia, Africa, Latin America, Eastern Europe, and the nations of the former Soviet Union, where as many as two-thirds of women live in poverty. The antitrafficking program at Johns Hopkins University estimates that 1 million undocumented immigrants are currently trapped in the United States in slavelike conditions (France, 2000). The State Department estimates that as many as 50,000 women and children (and a smaller number of men) are smuggled into the United States. each year to be forced into prostitution (about 40,000), domestic service, or as bonded labor in factories and sweatshops. Immigrants pay as much as $50,000 (in debt bondage) to get smuggled into the United States with false promises of decent jobs. Once in this country, most find their passports are stolen, and they are forced to work as prostitutes or maids, on farms or in sweatshops. They may be locked up, but even if not they are trapped because they fear violence by the slaveholders, they fear the police because they are illegals, and because they are strangers in a strange land.

Concentration of Misery in Cities

Although the majority of the poor in the Third World are landless and near-landless rural peasants, the greatest growth in poverty and other problems is occurring in cities. Whereas the population is doubling in less developed countries about every 40 years, it is doubling in Third World cities every 13.5 years. In 1950 only one Third World city, Shanghai, had a population of more than 5 million. By 2000 seven Third World cities had populations of 12.1 million or more. In 1950, for example, the Nigerian capital of Lagos had a population of 290,000. By 2015 it is projected to have a population of 23.2 million (Brockerhoff, 2000). The Ehrlichs describe the unlikely prospect of these cities being able to meet the needs of their poor inhabitants:

> The prospects for these gigantic agglomerations are not bright. They have grown so fast that they have far outstripped their ability to care for their inhabitants. Lack of sewage systems, inadequate water supplies laced with pathogens, air pollution, and gigantic garbage dumps (often occupied and "mined" by the poorest of the poor) plague these overgrown metropolises. (Ehrlich and Ehrlich, 1990:154)

A major problem of these cities is providing employment for their citizens. The special problem is to find employment for new immigrants to the cities, the farmers pushed off the land because of high rural density and the resulting poverty. The people who are pushed into the cities are, for the most part, unprepared for life and work there. They do not possess mechanical skills; they are illiterate; they are steeped in tradition. The cities, too, are unprepared for them. Aside from the obvious problems of housing and sanitation, the cities of the Third World do not have the industries that employ many workers. Because their citizens are usually poor, these countries are not good markets for products, so there is little internal demand for manufactured goods.

Another massive problem of the Third World cities is the mushrooming of squatter settlements. In the next 30 years some 3 billion people will be added to the world population. About 60 percent of that number (1.8 billion) will be added to the cities of Asia, Africa, and Latin America, which in many cases are already bursting at the seams. The sources of this growth are urban fertility and immigration of people from rural areas. Most of these people have merely exchanged the squalor of rural poverty for that of urban poverty. They have neither money nor skills that are useful in an urban setting.

The immediate question for these immigrants is where to live. They have little choice but to create houses out of scraps (tin, plywood, paper) on land that does not belong to them (in streets, alleys, or ravines or on hillsides). Shantytowns are the fastest growing sections of Third World cities. For example, 25 percent of the citizens of Seoul are illegal homesteaders, as are 67 percent of those in Ankara.

How do squatters react to their deplorable situation? They are unemployed or work at the most menial of tasks. They are hungry. Their children remain illiterate. They suffer the indignities of being social outcasts. Will they revolt? Some observers believe that for those experiencing abject poverty, the struggle is for the next meal, not for a redistribution of power. Others see the growing squatter settlements as breeding grounds for riots and radical political movements.

The prospects for the cities of the developing countries are bleak. Their growth continues unabated. Unbelievable poverty and hunger are common.

Jobs are scarce. Resources are limited and becoming more scarce as the number of inhabitants increases. The capital necessary for extensive economic development or for providing needed services is difficult to raise.

In sum, the high growth rates of cities, combined with the high concentration of people who are poor, unemployed, angry, hungry, and miserable, magnifies and intensifies other problems (such as racial and religious animosities, resource shortages, and pollution).

PRIORITIES OF THIRD WORLD NATIONS: MILITARY SECURITY OR ECONOMIC SECURITY?

Third World governments, anxious to protect themselves from outside threats (and from internal insurgents), have usually opted for spending the bulk of their meager resources on military strength. The fears leading to these decisions may be realistic given their relative weakness, the imperialistic schemes by other nations, and border disputes. The priorities of the ruling elites in these countries have been for guns rather than education, health care, agricultural development, and other desperately needed social programs that would enhance the social and economic well-being of their citizens and society. As a result, the developing nations (1) increase their military expenditures faster than their living standards; (2) seek more military foreign aid than humanitarian aid; (3) go into debt to purchase military supplies; and (4) employ a disproportionate number of their citizens as soldiers.

There are at least three major consequences of the disparate spending for military goods over social expenditures in the developing countries. First, military expenditures impede social development by reducing the monies that could have been spent on education and health care. Many of these nations have massive debts to foreign governments and banks, which means that monies that could go for social programs must go to pay off these debts and the interest. And extravagant military expenditures must be added to rapidly growing population, inefficient land use, and the like as major reasons for the increased poverty, illiteracy, disease, and high infant mortality in the Third World.

A second result of overexpenditures for the military in the Third World is that poor countries have become poorer and more dependent on industrialized nations because of the increased debt to finance the military.

Finally, the overreliance on military expenditures is a major source for the likelihood of military personnel holding major positions of power in the poor countries. These military-controlled governments are not democratic and have a strong tendency to use force against the people, including torture, brutality, disappearances, and political killings.

U.S. RELATIONS WITH THE THIRD WORLD

There is a huge gap between the rich and poor nations of the world. About 75 percent of the world's people live in the overpopulated and poverty-afflicted Third World, yet these nations produce only one-tenth of the world's industrial output and one-twelfth of its electric power output.

The nations of the Third World are underdeveloped for a number of reasons, including geography, climate, lack of arable land and minerals, and a history of continuous warfare; but the rich nations are also responsible. The Third World economies are largely the result of a history of colonialism and of economic domination by the developed nations in the postcolonial era.

As recently as 1914, approximately 70 percent of the world's population lived in colonies (in those areas now designated as the Third World). As colonies of superpowers, their resources and labors were exploited. Leadership was imposed from outside. The local people were treated as primitive and backward. Crops were planted for the colonizer's benefit, not for the needs of the indigenous population. Raw materials were extracted for exports. The wealth thus created was concentrated in the hands of local elites and the colonizers. Population growth was encouraged because the colonizer needed a continuous supply of low-cost labor. Colonialism destroyed the cultural patterns of production and exchange by which these societies once met the needs of their peoples. Thriving industries that once served indigenous markets were destroyed. The capital generated by the natural wealth in these countries was not used to develop local factories, schools, sanitation systems, agricultural processing plants, or irrigation systems. Colonialism also promoted a two-class society by increasing land holdings among the few and landlessness among the many.

Although the process began centuries ago and ended, for the most part, in the 1960s and 1970s, the legacy of colonialism continues to promote poverty today. In short, the heritage of colonialism that systematically promoted the self-interest of the colonizers and robbed and degraded the resources and the lives of the colonized continues to do so today. Vestigial attitudes, both within and outside these countries, and the continued dependency of Third World nations on the industrialized superpowers exacerbate their problems. As a result, the gap between the Third World and the industrial nations continues to widen.

This section explores the relationship of the United States to the Third World, focusing on the economic mechanisms that maintain Third World dependency and the political policies that promote problems within these countries.

Multinational Corporations

Gigantic **multinational corporations,** the majority of which are U.S.-based, control the world economy. Their decisions to build or not to build, to relocate a plant, to begin marketing a new product, or to scrap an old one have a tremendous impact on the lives of ordinary citizens in the countries in which they operate and in which they invest.

In their desire to tap low-wage workers, the multinational corporations have tended to locate in poor countries. Although the poor countries should have benefited from this new industry (by, say, gaining a higher standard of living and access to modern technology), they have not. One reason is that the profits generated in these countries tend to be channeled back to the United States. Second, global companies do not have a great impact in easing the unemployment of the poor nations because they use advanced technology whenever feasible, which reduces the demand for jobs.

The global corporations have enormous advantages over local competition when they move into an underdeveloped country. Foremost, they have access to the latest technology, whether it be computers, machinery, or genetic engineering. Second, they receive better terms than local businesses when they borrow money. They are preferred customers because their credit is backed by their worldwide financial resources. Moreover, global banks and global corporations are, as noted in Chapter 2, closely tied through interlocking directorates and shared ownership. Thus, it is in the interest of these banks to give credit under favorable conditions to their corporate friends. Finally, the global corporations have an enormous advantage over local companies through their manipulation of the market, influence over local government officials, and their control of workers.

An important source of the Third World countries' current dependency on the United States and on other industrialized countries is their growing public and private debt. This debt, which is more than half the collective GNP of these countries, is so large for some nations that they cannot spend for needed public works, education, and other social services. Available monies must be spent, rather, on servicing the debt. Thus, the debt treadmill stifles progress. This situation is further exacerbated by the toll on the natural resources of the developing countries. "Forests have been recklessly logged, mineral deposits carelessly mined, and fisheries overexploited, all to pay foreign creditors" (Durning, 1990:144).

The United States, as a lender nation, is also negatively influenced. First, the United States is encouraged to buy imports and reduce exports, which eliminates domestic jobs. Second, to the degree that foreign governments default on their loans, the U.S. banks that made the bad loans are subsidized by American taxpayers, ensuring the banks' profit. This occurred most recently in Mexico's 1995 financial crisis, and the 1998 financial crisis in a number of Asian nations. While this money shored up a teetering economy, in reality it protected the assets of U.S. banks that were in danger of losing their investments in Mexico and Asia.

Two activities by multinationals are highly controversial because they have negative costs worldwide and especially to the inhabitants of Third World nations—arms sales and the sale of products known to be harmful.

Arms Sales. The wealthy nations sell or give armaments to the poorer nations. Since the end of the Cold War, the United States has sold well over $100 billion worth of weapons abroad. In 2000, for the eighth straight year, the United States was the number one seller of arms abroad. In that year it had contracts for $18.6 billion, with more than two-thirds going to developing nations. Russia was next with $7.7 in arms sales, followed by France, $4.1 billion, and Germany, $1.1 billion (Jensen, 2001). The United States is actively engaged in promoting and financing weapons exports through 6,500 full-time government employees in the Defense, Commerce, and State Departments. These sales efforts are motivated by what was deemed to be in the national interests of the countries involved and by the profit to the manufacturers (in the United States the multinationals most involved are Lockheed Martin, General Motors/Hughes, Northrop Grumman, General Electric, and Boeing). Not incidentally, the top ten arms-exporting companies give millions in political contributions (political action committees and soft money) during federal election campaigns.

There are several important negative consequences of these arms sales. First, they fan the flames of war, rather than promoting stability in already tense regions. Second, and related to the first, the Third World has become a life-threatening place even for civilians. Consider the use of land mines, which the rich countries sell to Third World nations:

> Of approximately 1 million persons who have been killed or maimed by land mines since 1975, the majority—some 80 percent—were civilians. Estimates of the number of mines scattered in some 62 countries range from 65 million to more than 100 million, or one mine for every 50–85 people on earth. In the 12 countries with an extremely severe problem . . . there is one mine for every 3–5 people. And the mines continue to be laid far faster than they are being removed: each year, even as governments struggle to remove roughly 80,000 mines, about 2 million new ones are put in place. More than 250 million land mines have been produced during the past 25 years, and 10–30 million are still made annually. (Renner, 1995:156–157)

A third consequence is that arms sales can boomerang; that is, they can come back to haunt the seller—for example, the United States has sold armaments to Iran, Iraq, Somalia, and the freedom fighters in Afghanistan, only to have these armaments used against it in subsequent conflicts.

Fourth, the United States, in its zeal to contain or defeat regimes unfriendly to its interests, has sold arms to countries that are undemocratic and that violate human rights.

Corporate Sales That Endanger Life. **Corporate dumping,** the exporting of goods that have either been banned or not approved for sale in the United States because they are dangerous, is a relatively common practice. Most often the greatest market for such unsafe products is among the poor in the Third World. These countries often do not bar hazardous products, and many of their poor citizens are illiterate and therefore tend to be unaware of the hazards involved with the use of such products.

The United States and other industrialized nations continue to use the Third World as a source of profits as nations purchase these unhealthy products. For example, the Dalkon Shield intrauterine device was sold overseas in 42 nations after the manufacturer, A. H. Robins, withdrew it from the U.S. market because of its danger to women. Similarly, after the Consumer Product Safety Commission forced children's garments with the fire retardant called tris phosphate off the domestic market because it was found to be carcinogenic, the manufacturer shipped several million garments overseas for sale.

Chemical pesticides pollute water, degrade the soil, and destroy native wildlife and vegetation. The use of the most potent pesticides is banned in the United States This ban, however, does not pertain to foreign sales, as 25 percent of the pesticides exported by the United States are restricted or banned by the Environmental Protection Agency for domestic use.

Another form of corporate dumping, in the literal sense of the word, is the practice of shipping toxic wastes produced in the United States to the Third World for disposal. This practice is attractive to U.S. corporations because the Environmental Protection Agency requires expensive disposal facilities, whereas the materials can be dumped in Third World nations for a fraction of the cost. The host nations engage in such potentially dangerous transactions because they need the money.

Some companies dump workplace hazards as well as hazardous products and waste materials in poor nations. Governmental regulations often require U.S. corporations to provide a reasonably safe environment for their workers. These requirements, such as not exposing workers to asbestos, lead, or other toxic substances, are often expensive to meet. Thus, many corporations move their manufacture (and unsafe working conditions) to a country with few or no

Some multinational corporations "dump" hazardous working conditions and pollution on the workers and inhabitants of poor nations.

restrictions. This move saves the companies money and increases their profits, but it disregards the health and safety of workers outside the United States.

Corporate dumping is undesirable for three reasons. First, and most obvious, it poses serious health hazards to the poor and uninformed consumers of the Third World. Second, the disregard of U.S. multinational corporations for their workers and their consumers in foreign lands contributes to anti-U.S. feelings in the host countries. Third, many types of corporate dumping have a boomerang effect; that is, some of the hazardous products sold abroad by U.S. companies are often returned to the United States and other developed nations, negatively affecting the health of the people in those countries. For example, the United States imports about one-fourth of its fruits and vegetables, and some of this produce is tainted with toxic chemical residues.

United States in the Global Village

In the global economy, the fate of the world's poorest nations and the poor within these nations are of crucial importance to all nations and the people within them. Huge gaps in income, education, and other measures of the quality of life make the world less safe. And, as the population growth surges in the Third World, the inequality gap will widen and the world will become less stable. Unless wealthy nations do more to help the poor nations catch up, the twenty-first century will witness Earth split into two very different planets, one inhabited by the fortunate few, and the other by poverty-stricken, desperate masses.

What can the wealthy nations do to help the impoverished nations? First, the affluent nations can pledge more resources targeted for development aid. At present, less than 1 percent of the U.S. federal budget goes for economic aid to poor countries (about $29 per American, whereas the typical developed country gives about $70 per person—Denmark, for example, contributes ten times more per capita than the United States). During the 2000 presidential election campaign, columnist David Gergen asked the candidates to consider the following:

> When John Kennedy and Richard Nixon ran against each other, your country regularly sent about 0.6 percent of your GDP to help foreign nations out of the mire. Today you send about one fifth of that, which makes you one of the world's stingiest nations, spending less than half, per capita, what major industrialized countries spend on foreign aid. With those whopping surpluses, shouldn't you loosen the purse strings? (Gergen, 2000:76)

According to the chief economist of the World Bank, Nicholas Stern, "if the rich nations increased aid to 0.7 percent of their economic output, it would add $100 billion a year in assistance" (quoted in Memmott, 2001:3B). What could be accomplished with an additional $100 billion?

- The global relief agency Oxfam argues that about $8 billion more each year is needed in spending for education in the world's poorest countries to fulfill a pledge by 155 nations that every child on earth have a basic level of literacy by 2015 (Briscoe, 1999).
- The world's poor countries owe the rich ones $2.5 trillion (Henwood, 1999). The annual interest owed on this debt exceeds the amount spent on health and education in the poor countries. Some poor countries spend 40 percent of their income for interest on a foreign debt that will never be repaid (much like the contract debt that enslaves poor individuals). The rich countries must provide debt relief to the poor countries. Currently, there is a partial debt relief plan where the Unitd States pays 4 percent of the wealthy nation's total, or $920 million over 4 years. Each dollar contributed to this plan produces $20 in debt relief (*New York Times,* 2000d).
- There could be a frontal assault by the World Health Organization and the developed countries to reduce the incidence and spread of infectious diseases such as tuberculosis, malaria, and meningitis. Eradication of diseases for which the technology is already available (poliomyelitis, leprosy, tetanus, Chagas' disease, and dracunculiasis) and the disorder of iodine deficiency could be reached. Education programs need to be instituted to warn about sexually transmitted diseases and how to protect against them.
- The 1997 *Human Development Report* by the United Nations noted that for just $40 billion a year, basic health and nutrition, basic education, reproductive health, and family-planning services could be extended to the entire world's population (reported in Thad Williamson, 2000:42).
- Kofi Annan, Secretary-General of the United Nations, has argued that an annual expenditure of $7 billion to $10 billion (five times the current expenditure) sustained for many years is needed to defeat AIDS in the developing world. Specifically, the money would be used for prevention through education, providing medicines to prevent the transmission from mother to child, care and treatment of those infected, and protection of those left most vulnerable (widows and orphans) (Annan, 2001).

The wealthy nations can provide humanitarian aid to the developing nations with three provisos: (1) that it is truly humanitarian (such as technology, medical supplies, food, inoculation programs, family planning, agricultural equipment, sewage treatment systems, water treatment) and not military aid; (2) that the aid reaches the intended targets (those in need) not the well-off elites; and

(3) that the governments in the impoverished nations have sensible plans for using the new resources such as spending on health (e.g., the vaccination of children) and education, especially for women (Sen, 1999).

How much commitment should the United States make to bringing poor nations up to a minimum standard? Many citizens, corporations, and politicians are indifferent to the plight of the poor far away. Many have misgivings about helping corrupt governments. Others are opposed to our support of family planning and the funding of abortion (U.S. policy under recent Republican presidents has prevented the United States from funding family-planning services offered by overseas providers that perform abortions with non-U.S. funding).

The ultimate interest of the United States is best served if there is peace and stability in the Third World. These goals can be accomplished only if population growth is slowed significantly, hunger and poverty alleviated, and the extremes of inequality reduced.

If the United States and other developed nations do not take appropriate steps, human misery, acts of terrorism against affluent nations, tensions among neighbors, and the possibility of war—even nuclear war—will increase. The last factor becomes especially relevant given the knowledge that the following Third World nations have nuclear bomb capabilities: China, India, Pakistan, North Korea, Syria, Libya, Iran, Iraq, and Algeria. Moreover, a number of Third World countries have been alleged to have used chemical weapons (Burma, Iraq, Ethiopia, the Philippines, Sudan, Egypt, South Africa, Thailand, and Vietnam). The ultimate question is whether the way these steps are implemented will help the Third World reduce its dependence on the more developed nations, the hunger and misery within their countries, and, in the process, international tensions. We ignore the poor of the Third World at our peril.

CHAPTER REVIEW

1. The term *Third World* refers to the underdeveloped and developing nations where poverty, hunger, and misery are found disproportionately. These nations also are characterized by relative powerlessness, rapid population growth, high infant mortality, unsanitary living conditions, and high rates of illiteracy.
2. In mid-2001 the world population exceeded 6.1 billion and was increasing by about 78 million annually. About 90 percent of the population growth occurs in the Third World, where food, housing, health care, and employment are inadequate to meet present needs.
3. While world population is growing rapidly, the amount of productive land is shrinking in rich and poor countries alike because of the loss of topsoil, the lowering of water tables from irrigation and overgrazing, and pollution.
4. Within the nations experiencing the most rapid population growth, cities are growing much faster than are rural areas. The problems of survival for individuals and families are increased dramatically in cities: Food is too expensive, jobs are scarce and poorly paid, and sanitation problems increase the likelihood of disease. The concentration of the poor in the limited space of cities increases tensions and the probability of hostility.
5. There are three ways to reduce high fertility in the Third World: (a) economic development (modern demographic transition), (b) family-planning programs, and (c) social change, especially through the changing of traditional women's roles.
6. Poverty is a special problem of the underdeveloped nations of the Third World: 1.3 billion people have inadequate diets, high infant mortality, low life expectancy, and high rates of illiteracy. Poverty also contributes to high fertility.
7. Hunger is a worldwide problem, especially in the Third World, but even there food production is adequate to meet the needs of all of the people. The problem of hunger results from high prices, unequal distribution of food, overre-

liance on cash crops, and concentration of land ownership among very few people—all the consequences of the political economy in these nations and the world.

8. The ruling elites of the poor countries have typically used their meager resources to arm themselves rather than to upgrade education and agriculture, improve health care, and provide better housing and sanitation. This emphasis on military spending has resulted in (a) the inequality gap in these poor countries increasing, (b) increased overall impoverishment of these countries and their greater dependence on industrialized nations because of higher debts, and (c) a strong tendency for the military to control these countries.
9. The Third World is underdeveloped for a number of reasons, the most important of which is a heritage of colonialism. Colonialism destroyed local industries and self-sufficient crop-growing patterns, drained off resources for the benefit of the colonizers, and promoted local elites through concentration of land ownership among the few. In the postcolonial era the dependency of the Third World and its control by outside forces continue.
10. A huge worldwide problem, especially among the poor in the Third World is HIV/AIDS. In just two decades, 60 million have contracted this disease worldwide, with 22 million deaths.
11. It is estimated that there are 27 million slaves in the world. The new slavery is a consequence of the population explosion in the poorest countries.
12. The world economy is controlled by multinational corporations, the majority of which are based in the United States. Their power in the underdeveloped nations perpetuates the dependency of many Third World nations on the United States.
13. Multinationals add to the tensions in Third World countries through arms sales, corporate dumping of products known to be dangerous, and intervention in the domestic affairs of host countries.
14. The developed nations must work to alleviate the problems faced by the developing nations by increasing their financial commitment, by providing debt relief, and by working with international agencies to promote education and health programs. To do so is in our national interest.

KEY TERMS

Modern demographic transition. A three-stage pattern of population change occurring as societies industrialize and urbanize, resulting ultimately in a low and stable population growth rate.

Third World. The underdeveloped and developing nations in which poverty, hunger, and misery abound.

Absolute poverty. A condition of life so degraded by disease, illiteracy, malnutrition, and squalor as to deny its victims the basic necessities. Statistically, those making less than $1 a day are in this category.

Pandemic. A worldwide epidemic.

New slavery. The new slavery differs from traditional slavery in that it is, for the most part, not a lifelong condition and sometimes individuals and families become slaves by choice—a choice forced by extreme poverty.

Colony. A territory controlled by a powerful country that exploits the land and the people for its own benefit.

Multinational corporation. A profit-oriented company engaged in business activities in more than one nation.

Corporate dumping. The exporting of goods by a business that have either been banned or not approved for sale in the United States because they are dangerous.

WEBSITES FOR FURTHER REFERENCE

http://www.worldbank.org/poverty/wdrpoverty/report/index.htm

This is the online version of the *2001–2002 World Development Report: Attacking Poverty*. The new study—"the World Bank's most detailed-ever investigation of global poverty"—adds that "economic growth is crucial but often not sufficient to create conditions in which the world's poorest people can improve their lives." More than two years in the making, the *World Development Report 2000–2001* draws on a large volume of research, including a background study, *Voices of the Poor,* which systematically sought the personal accounts of more than 60,000 men and women living in poverty in 60 countries.

http://www.iris.umd.edu/
The Center for Institutional Reform and the Informal Sector (IRIS) at the University of Maryland, College Park, was founded on the premise that countries with healthy institutions have correspondingly healthy economies. Thus, IRIS offers a virtually unique perspective on economic development. IRIS researchers and consultants "assist fledgling democracies and newly industrializing countries to build robust democratic, legal, and economic institutions which provide both a foundation and a guiding hand for future broad-based, stable economic growth." IRIS is working with The World Bank's Initiative on Defining, Monitoring and Measuring Social Capital.

http://www.popnet.org
PopNet is a resource for global population information. It offers various links to other population resources as well.

http://www.prb.org
The Population Reference Bureau is the leader in providing timely and objective information on U.S. and international population trends and their implications. PRB informs policymakers, educators, the media, and concerned citizens working in the public interest around the world through a broad range of activities, including publications, information services, seminars and workshops, and technical support.

http://www.populationconcern.org.uk/
Population Concern works for the right to reproductive health care worldwide. Its website provides news and feature articles, information about the organization and its work, and links to other organizations.

http://www.uscommittee.org
The U.S. Committee for UN Population Fund works to strengthen American moral, political, and financial support for the UN Population Fund, the world's largest internationally funded source of population assistance to developing countries. The website contains news, topical information, statistics, personal stories, a D.C. update, and links.

http://www.essential.org/clearinghouse/clearinghouse.html
The Multinational Resource Center was created by an activist association called Essential.Org. "Southern countries increasingly find themselves exploited by the worst abuses of multinational corporations' rampant pollution, oppressive labor practices, exploitative trading arrangements, and more. Yet Southern residents often have limited access to even basic information such as who owns local factories and what is their labor and environmental history, what are the laws that regulate specific industries in the North, and what are cleaner alternative waste management methods." The Multinationals Resource Center (MRC) helps redress this situation by providing valuable information, free of charge, to Southern activists, environmental and consumer groups, and journalists.

http://www.cgiar.org/
Created in 1971, CGIAR is an association of public and private members supporting a system of 16 Future Harvest Centers that work in more than 100 countries to mobilize cutting-edge science to reduce hunger and poverty, improve human nutrition and health, and protect the environment. The CGIAR promotes sustainable agricultural development based on the environmentally sound management of natural resources. It contributes to food security and poverty eradication in developing countries through research, partnership, capacity building, and policy support.

Threats to the Environment

We did not make the planet; we do not own the planet; and we have no right to wreck the planet.

—Monsignor Bruce Kent

Human societies have always altered their physical environments. They have used fire, cleared forests, tilled the soil, mined for mineral deposits, damned rivers, polluted streams, overgrazed grasslands, and the like. In the twentieth century, especially since 1950, the pace and magnitude of the negative environmental impacts of human activities have magnified and intensified. Especially significant are the extraordinary use of fossil fuels, the deforestation of the rain forests, the pumping of billions of tons of greenhouse gases into the air, the pollution of water by fertilizers, pesticides, and animal wastes, emission of toxic chemicals, and the rapid erosion of top soil. In effect, we human beings are fundamentally changing the planet in ways that are diminishing the planet's ability to sustain life.

The Worldwatch Institute concluded its annual State of the World report in 2000 saying:

> Species are disappearing, temperatures are rising, reefs are dying, forests are shrinking, storms are raging, water tables are falling: Almost every ecological indicator shows a world in decline. And with the global population expected to hit 9 billion in the next 50 years, those indicators are liken to worsen. (quoted in Braile, 2000:16a)

As environmental problems are examined in this chapter, the discussion is guided by three facts. First, while some environmental problems are beyond human control (volcanoes, earthquakes, solar flares), most are social in origin. As demographers Leon Bouvier and Lindsey Grant summarize it:

> *Homo sapiens* is a very recent, very talented and thoroughly disruptive species. We are perhaps the principal source of change to the Earth's ecosystem—most of it unintentional—and the pace of our disruption is increasing. The rate at which the species is altering the Earth has accelerated geometrically. Arguably, the most important fact about this century is the intertwined growth of human populations and human technology and the resultant changes to the Earth and to human society. (Bouvier and Grant, 1994:11)

Second, the magnitude of environmental problems has become so great that the ultimate survival of the human species is in question. Third, while environmental problems may originate within a nation's borders, they usually have global consequences. Thus, this chapter examines human-made environmental problems at both the domestic and international levels. The first section describes the nature of these problems and their consequences. The second focuses on the U.S. case. The third section examines the social sources of these problems and alternative solutions. The final section describes the long-range international implications of environmental problems.

WORLDWIDE ENVIRONMENTAL PROBLEMS

Earth's **biosphere** (the surface layer of the planet and the surrounding atmosphere) provides the land, air, water, and energy necessary to sustain life. This life-support system is a complex, interdependent one in which energy from the sun is converted into food:

> The mechanisms that supply [human beings with the essentials for life] are **ecosystems**—plants, animals, and microorganisms interacting with each other and their physical environments. The energy that flows through these ecosystems and the oxygen, nitrogen, carbon, and other materials they recycle are the essence of the life-support system within which [6.1] billion people are inextricably embedded. Ecosystems supply civilization with public services both free and irreplaceable. They include regulation of climate and the makeup of the atmosphere, generation and maintenance of soils, control of potential crop pests and carriers of human diseases, pollination of many crops, and provision of food from the sea. Ecosystems supply the nutrients without which we could not survive, and in the process they dispose of our wastes. (Ehrlich and Ehrlich, 1988:916)

These ecosystems are being disturbed profoundly by three *social* forces. First, the tremendous increase in population increases the demand for food, energy, minerals, and other products. With the world's population (6.1 billion in 2001) increasing by 78 million a year (in effect, adding the population of Sweden every month), the stresses on the environment mount. The environmental problem, however, is not just the increasing number of people, although that is clearly a problem. Postel says:

> The environmental impact of the world's population. . . has been vastly multiplied by economic and social systems that strongly favor growth and ever-rising consumption over equity and poverty alleviation; that fail to give women equal rights, education, and economic opportunity, and thereby perpetuate the conditions under which poverty and rapid population growth persist; and that do not discriminate between the means of production that are environmentally sound and those that are not. (Postel, 1994:5)

The second driving force contributing to the pressures on Earth's natural systems is growing inequality in income between the rich and poor (as discussed in the previous chapter). The richest 20 percent of the world's population absorb about 86 percent of the world's goods and services, while the poorest 20 percent subsist on 1 percent (Thad Williamson, 2000). This inequality (and the gap is growing) is a major source of environmental decline. This is because those at the top overconsume energy, raw materials, and manufactured goods, and the poor must cut down trees, grow crops, fish, or graze livestock in ways that are harmful to the planet merely to survive (Postel, 1994).

> Since 1950 the richest fifth of humankind has doubled its per capita consumption of energy, meat [see the panel on meat consumption], timber, steel, and copper, and quadrupled its car ownership, greatly increasing global emissions of CFCs and greenhouse gases, accelerating tropical deforestation, and intensifying other environmental impacts. The poorest fifth of humankind has increased its per capita consumption hardly at all. (Ehrlich et al., 1997:104)

These consumption patterns apply to nations as well. Consider the consumption patterns in the United States, with but 4.6 percent of the world's population:

- The United States consumes 25 percent of the world's fossil fuel, 20 percent of its metals, and 33 percent of its paper, and produces 72 percent of the world's hazardous waste (Crews and Stauffer, 1997).

A CLOSER LOOK

THE NEGATIVE IMPACTS OF MEAT ON THE ENVIRONMENT

Since 1950 the per capita consumption of meat worldwide has more than doubled. This reliance on meat has many negative effects on the environment. First, eating meat is an inefficient source of meeting dietary demands. It takes 7 pounds of grain to produce 1 pound of feedlot beef. In the United States 70 percent of all wheat, corn, and other grains is diverted from human consumption to the feeding of livestock.

Second, consider the impact on water. It takes 7,000 pounds of water to produce 1 pound of feedlot beef (compared to 1,000 pounds of water to produce 1 pound of grain). "Pass up one hamburger, and you'll save as much water as you save by taking 40 showers with a low-flow nozzle" (Ayers, 1999:106). Groundwater is also polluted by animal wastes, causing fish kills and outbreaks of such diseases as pfiesteria, which causes memory loss, confusion, and acute skin burning in people exposed to contaminated water (Ayers, 1999:107).

> Much of the nitrogen-containing waste from livestock is converted into ammonia and into nitrates, which leach into the groundwater beneath the soil or run directly into surface water, contributing to high nitrate levels in the rural wells which tap the groundwater. In streams and lakes, high levels of waste runoff contribute to oxygen depletion and algae overgrowth. American livestock contribute five times more harmful organic waste to water pollution than do people, and twice that of industry. (Lappe, 1999:118)

Third, livestock produce 130 times as much waste as people do. The meat industry in the United States has been transformed into huge megafarms where cattle, hogs, turkeys, and chickens are mass produced. In two enormous feedlots owned by ConAgra in Greeley, Colorado, each holding up to 100,000 head of cattle, the process works this way:

> These cattle don't eat blue grama and buffalo grass off the prairie. During the three months before slaughter, they eat grain dumped into long concrete troughs that resemble highway dividers. The grain fattens the cattle quickly, aided by anabolic steroids implanted in their ear. A typical steer will consume more than three thousand pounds of grain during its stay at a feedlot, just to gain four hundred pounds of weight. . . . Each steer deposits about fifty pounds of urine and manure every day. Unlike human waste, the manure is not sent to a treatment plant. It is dumped into pits, huge pools of excrement that the industry calls "lagoons." The amount of waste left by the cattle to pass through Weld County is staggering. The two Monfort [owned by ConAgra] feedlots outside Greeley produce more excrement than the cities of Denver, Boston, Atlanta, and St. Louis—combined. (Scholosser, 2001:150)

Fourth, the tropical rain forest is being burned down and uprooted to make room for more and more cattle. "Agriculture is the world's biggest cause of deforestation, and increasing demand for meat is the biggest force in the expansion of agriculture" (Ayers, 1999:107).

Finally, the factory nature of the meat and poultry industries has significant downsides for consumer health. The incidents of *E. coli* contamination and salmonella poisoning have increased concomitantly with the greater industry concentration. Health risks to humans have also increased with the use of chemicals, hormones, and antibiotics given to animals in factory farming to speed up growth and prevent diseases in the animals (Cooper, Rosset, and Bryson, 1999).

- Americans waste more food than most people eat in sub-Saharan Africa. Forty-eight million tons of food suitable for human consumption are wasted each year in the United States (*Harper's,* 2001).
- Two percent of the United States is paved, an area the size of Georgia (Crenson, 2001).

Although it composes only 4.6 percent of the world's population, the United States consumes 25 percent of the world's fossil fuel, 20 percent of its metals, and 33 percent of its paper, and produces 72 percent of the world's hazardous waste.

- There are three automobiles for every four people in the United States.
- The United States produces one-fourth of the world's greenhouse gas emissions. Emissions from U.S. power plants alone exceed the total emissions of 146 other nations combined, which represent 75 percent of the world's population (Gergen, 2001c).
- The United States produces 22 percent of the world's gross domestic product (GDP), but uses 25 percent of the world's energy—and in doing so produces 25 percent of the global emissions of carbon dioxide. In contrast, the European Union accounts for 20 percent of world GDP, while consuming only 16 percent of the world's energy. "What these figures boil down to is that for every dollar's worth of goods and services the United States produces, it consumes 40 percent more energy than other industrialized nations" (Walter, 2001:1).

> While developing countries severely tax their environments, clearly the populations of rich countries leave a vastly disproportionate mark on the planet. *The birth of a baby in the United States imposes more than a hundred times the stress on the world's resources as a birth in, say, Bangladesh.* Babies from Bangladesh do not grow up to own automobiles and air conditioners or to eat grain-fed beef. Their life-styles do not require huge quantities of minerals and energy, nor do their activities seriously undermine the life-support capability of the entire planet [italics added]. (Ehrlich and Ehrlich, 1988:917)

The third driving force behind the environmental degradation of the planet is economic growth. Since 1950 the global economy has expanded fivefold. This expansion, while important for the jobs created and the products produced, has an environmental downside. Economic growth is powered by the accelerated extraction and consumption of fossil fuels, mining, irrigation, water use, and timber. In turn, environmental damage increased proportionately.

"And may we continue to be worthy of consuming a disproportionate share of this planet's resources."

Degradation of the Land

A thin layer of topsoil provides food crops for 6.1 billion people and grazing for about 4 billion domesticated animals. This topsoil, the source of food, fiber, and wood, is degraded by erosion and desertification caused by overuse and misuse. This topsoil is being depleted or lost because of careless husbandry and urbanization. Farmland is lost because of plowing marginal lands, leading to wind and water erosion. The fertility of farmland is lost because it is exhausted by overuse. It is also lost due to irrigation practices that poison the land with salt, a process called salinization. The overuse of irrigation drains rivers and taxes aquifers. The use of chemical fertilizers and pesticides kill helpful creatures, taint groundwater, and create dead zones in the oceans (e.g., where the Mississippi River drains into the Gulf of Mexico). In a special issue on the "State of Planet," *Time* summarizes the United Nations assessment of Earth's ecosystems. With respect to the situation for agricultural lands:

> One-third of global land has been converted to food production, but three-quarters of this area has poor soil. So far, harvests outpace population growth, but the future is clouded by the loss of land to urban development, soil degradation, and water scarcity. . . . More than 40 percent of agricultural land has been badly degraded [through] erosion, nutrient depletion and water stress. (Linden, 2000:20)

In addition to the degradation and loss of topsoil, productive land is lost through the growth of cities and urban sprawl, the building of roads, and the damming of rivers. In the United States, for example, more area than the entire state of Georgia is now under pavement.

Environmental Pollution and Degradation

The following description of the various forms of pollution present in industrial societies, especially the United States, presents a glimpse of how humanity is fouling its nest.

Chemical Pollution. More than 75,000 chemicals have been released into the environment (Hazen, 2001). These chemicals are found in food. They are used in detergents, fertilizers, pesticides, plastics, clothing, insulation, and almost everything else. Consumers are exposed to the often toxic substances in what they buy, but the danger is more acute for the workers involved in the manufacture of these chemicals.

The manufacture of chemicals requires disposing of the waste. Waste disposal, especially safe disposal of toxic chemicals, is a huge problem. These toxic chemicals are released into the air, water, land, underground, and public sewage either by accident or deliberately. "Each year American industries belch, pump and dump more than 2.5 billion pounds of really nasty stuff—like lead compounds, chromium, ammonia and organic solvents—into the air, water, and ground" (Amato, 1999:115). Typically, corporations choose the cheapest means of disposal, which is to release the waste products into the air and waterways and to bury the materials in dump sites. In one infamous instance, the Hooker Chemical and Plastics Corporation over a number of years dumped 43.6 million pounds of 82 different chemical substances into Love Canal, New York, near Niagara Falls. Among the chemicals dumped were 200 tons of trichlorophenol, which contained an estimated 130 pounds of one of the most toxic and carcinogenic substances known—dioxin. Three ounces of this substance can kill more than a million people. (A variant of dioxin—Agent Orange—was used in the Vietnam War with extremely adverse results to vegetation and human life.) As a result of exposure to the various chemicals dumped at Love Canal, nearby residents had an unusual number of serious illnesses, a high incidence of miscarriages, and an unusual number of children born with birth defects.

The Love Canal dump site is only one of many dangerous locations in the United States. Of the nearly 50,000 dump sites nationwide, some 2,000 have been labeled as potentially dangerous by the federal government and 350 have been documented as sure sources of toxic wastes.

There is a movement known as **"environmental justice"** that works for improving environments for communities and is especially keen to the injustices that occur when a particular segment of the population, such as the poor or minority groups, bears a disproportionate share of exposure to environmental hazards (Pellow, 2000). This movement is a reaction against the overwhelming likelihood that toxic-producing plants and toxic waste dumps are located where poor people, especially people of color, live (when this pattern occurs it is called **"environmental racism"**). In Mississippi, for example, people of color represent 64 percent of residents near toxic facilities—but just 37 percent of the state population (Dervarics, 2000). Robert Bullard, the expert on environmental racism, says that "Blacks and other economically disadvantaged groups are often concentrated in areas that expose them to high levels of toxic pollution: namely, urban industrial communities with elevated air and water pollution problems or rural areas with high levels of exposure to farm pesticides" (Bullard, 2000:6–7).

There is an overwhelming likelihood that toxic-producing plants and toxic waste dumps are located where poor people, especially people of color, live.

U.S. corporations are also involved in global chemical pollution. They not only dump wastes into the oceans and the air, which, of course, can affect the people in other countries, but they also sell to other countries chemicals (such as pesticides) that are illegal to sell here because they are toxic. In addition, U.S. corporations have used other countries as dump sites for their hazardous substances, because the U.S. government outlawed indiscriminate dumping of toxic wastes in this country in 1975.

The nations of western Europe and North America have relatively strict environmental laws, which is good for their inhabitants. These countries, however, transport roughly 2 million tons of toxic waste annually to poor nations that desperately need the cash:

> This "trash imperialism," whereby the richer countries can push off their problems onto the poorer countries, has been banned by most African and Pacific island nations and has shifted to Central America. Although some Central American countries have also passed bans on waste imports, the laws can be circumvented by mislabeling waste or exporting it for "recycling," which is often not completely accomplished. . . . Some shippers have even tried to *sell* toxic ash to Third World countries as landfill, claiming the ash was nontoxic and nonhazardous. (Feagin and Feagin, 1994:376).

Toxic wastes are also exported when U.S. multinational corporations move operations to countries with less stringent environmental laws. For example, the 2000 foreign-owned (mostly by the United States) factories along the United States–Mexico border in Mexico (*maquiladoras*) have created environmental hazards on both sides of the border.

Another problem with toxic wastes is accidental spills from tankers, trucks, and trains as the wastes are transported. These spills number about 400 a year in the United States alone. When these incidents occur, the air is polluted, as is the groundwater, and the oceans. Fires sometimes occur along with explosions. The result is that people, animals, and plant life are endangered.

Solid Waste Pollution. People throw away enormous amounts of old food, glass, plastics, metals, textiles, rubber, wood, and paper. On average, each American produces 4.4 pounds of garbage a day (up from 2.7 pounds in 1960), for an annual total of 217 million tons (up from 88 million tons in 1960), most of which is placed in landfills.

The United States is the largest producer of solid waste among the industrialized nations, both in absolute and per capita terms. The European nations, because they are much better at recycling waste, generate only about half the amount per capita as the United States (Livernash and Rodenburg, 1998:16):

> In 1995 . . . Germany recycled 75 pecent of its glass waste and 67 percent of its cardboard and paper waste, a substantial increase over 1980 numbers. Recycling has increased more slowly in the United States. Americans recycled about 23 percent of glass and 35 percent of paper and cardboard in 1995, similar to recycling levels in the United Kingdom. (Livernash and Rodenburg, 1998:17)

The problem of what to do with solid waste is compounded by the increased amounts of waste that are contaminated with compounds and chemicals that do not appear in nature. These wastes pose new and unknown threats to human, animal, and plant life. All landfills leak, seeping toxic residues into the groundwater. Many communities have contaminated drinking water and crops as a result. With the problem clearly becoming serious, some experimentation is now being conducted with landfills that have impermeable linings to prevent such pollution. See the panel on personal computers and toxic waste.

A CLOSER LOOK

THE NEW TECHNOLOGY AND TOXIC WASTE

The new technology found in most households in the developed world—personal computers, cell phones, televisions, and other electronic equipment—is laden with toxins that when thrown away will leach into groundwater or produce dioxins and other carcinogens when burned (Alster, 2000). Let us consider computers.

The computer revolution changes quickly with each new generation having much more memory and being infinitely faster, yet available at a cheaper price than the original. As a result, many junk their old computers for the latest version, an estimated 33 million in 2000 (Holstein, 2000). That amounts to a lot of toxic waste, an estimated 70 million of which will be in landfills by 2005. (The following is from Alster, 2000; Associated Press, 2001b):

- Since each monitor has at least 5 pounds of lead, the landfills will have a total of 350 million pounds of lead from obsolete computers.
- Printed circuit boards and semiconductors contain cadmium. By 2005, a total of more than 2 million pounds of cadmium will exist in discarded computers.
- The batteries and switches contain mercury, leaving 400,000 pounds nationwide in 2005.
- Chromium is used as corrosion protection in computers. By 2005 there will be an estimated 1.2 million pounds of chromium in landfills.
- PVC (polyvinyl chloride) plastics are used on cables and housings, leaving a potential waste of 250 million pounds per year.
- With the increased use of flat-panel monitors, it is estimated that 500 million defunct monitors will be discarded by 2007, each of which contains phosphorous and 4 to 8 pounds of lead.

The problem is that only 10 percent of computers are recycled. The rest threaten the environment.

There are several alternatives to dumping trash in landfills. One option has been to dump rubbish in the ocean. This has polluted beaches, poisoned fish, and hurt fisheries. As a result, international agreements and domestic legislation within various countries have curtailed this alternative. The environmentally preferred solutions are for the trash to be reprocessed to its original uses (paper, glass containers, metals), or converted into new products such as insulation.

The alternative most commonly selected is to incinerate the garbage (which disposes of 16 percent of the country's total waste). The burning of trash has two major benefits. It reduces the volume of garbage by almost 90 percent, and it can generate steam and electricity. The downside of burning trash, however, is significant. The incinerating of plastics and other garbage releases toxic chemicals, including deadly dioxins and heavy-metal emissions, into the air. The residue (ash) is contaminated with lead and cadmium.

About one-fourth of solid waste is currently recycled, a positive environmental step. So, too, is the transforming of organic waste—paper, food scraps, and lawn clippings into compost, a product that invigorates agricultural soils. European countries are leading the way with composting (Brown et al., 1999:141). If we could sort trash into recyclables, compostables, and disposables, we could "keep 60 to 70 percent of what was trash out of our landfills and incinerators" (Gavzer, 1999:6).

Water Pollution. The major sources of water pollution are industries, which pour into rivers, lakes, and oceans a vast array of contaminants such as lead, asbestos, detergents, solvents, acid, and ammonia; farmers, whose pesticides, herbicides, fertilizers, and animal wastes drain into streams and lakes; cities, which dispose of their wastes including sewage into rivers to end up downstream in another city's drinking water; and oil spills, caused by tanker accidents and leaks in offshore drilling. These are problems throughout the world.

Water pollution is a most immediate problem in the less developed countries. In China, for example, a nation undergoing rapid economic growth, an estimated 80 percent of the country's industrial and domestic waste is discharged, untreated, into rivers (Zimmermann, Lawrence, and Palmer, 1996). Contaminated water in poor countries results in high death rates from cholera, typhoid, dysentery, and diarrhea. According to the latest data, 1.2 billion people do not have enough safe drinking water. Nearly 3 billion people are at risk of contaminated water because of improper sanitation. More than 5 million die each year of easily preventable waterborne diseases such as diarrhea, dysentery, and cholera (Leslie, 2000).

In the United States, the Mississippi River provides an example of the seriousness of water pollution. Greenpeace USA, the environmental organization, surveyed pollution in the Mississippi River and found that industries and municipalities along the river discharged billions of pounds of heavy metals and toxic chemicals into it. This occurs along the 2,300 miles of the river; the worst pollution is concentrated along 150 miles in Louisiana, where 25 percent of the nation's chemical industry is located.

A serious threat to drinking water comes from the chemicals that farmers put on their fields to increase yields, kill pests (pesticides), and destroy weeds (herbicides). The chemicals applied seep into wells and drain into streams and rivers. A study of the Mississippi River Basin (including the Mississippi, Missouri, and Ohio Rivers) found that 14 million Americans were drinking herbicide-laced water. Testing more than 15,000 water samples in 12 states, the researchers found that the most common cancer-causing herbicide in the drinking water supply was atrazine:

> High levels of atrazine cause cancer in laboratory animals, and the federal government has set a maximum level for humans of three parts per billion. At that level, there is a lifetime risk of one extra cancer case for every million individuals drinking the water. . . . [The report] said that 14 million Americans had drinking water that exceeded that threshold, including 3.5 million people whose water had more than 10 times the federal standard. Those 3.5 million include populations of Kansas City (both Missouri and Kansas); Indianapolis; Fort Wayne, Ind.; Columbus, Ohio; and Omaha. (Webb, 1994:8A)

The Environmental Protection Agency (EPA) has a list of large toxic sites to be cleaned up with funds supplied by Congress. The largest of these Superfund sites is a 200-mile stretch of the upper Hudson River, where General Electric has dumped polychlorinated biphenyls (PCBs) into the river over a 30-year period (this section is from Pollak, 2001). PCBs cause cancer in laboratory animals, and they are linked to premature births and developmental disorders. General Electric stopped the practice in 1977 when the federal government banned PCB use. More than two decades later the New York State Health Department continues to advise women of childbearing age and children under age 15 not to eat any fish from the Hudson River and urges no one eat any fish from the upper Hudson, where the cancer risk from such consumption is 700 times the EPA protection level. The problem is that some 100,000 pounds of PCBs remain in the sediment of the Hudson and continue to poison fish, wildlife, and humans.

In 1997 the United States used 20 million tons of fertilizer (this amount ranked second to China's use of 33 million tons). While this increases agricultural output, it presents health concerns from the nitrates that run off into the streams and underground water supplies (Brown, Renner, and Flavin, 1998:44).

Pollution of the oceans occurs from wastes dumped into rivers. Thus, industrial wastes, fertilizers, and pesticides flow into the oceans. Winds carry pollutants from cities and factories to the oceans. And oceans have been used as dumping grounds for ages. The result is that coastal regions, home for 85 percent of the world's fish, are especially polluted:

> The global supply of fish and the viability of the oceans are being threatened by viruses and bacteria that attack marine life. Harmful blooms of algae, often referred to as "red tides," are increasing in incidence, duration, and geographic extent. In red tides, a powerful toxin accumulates in the shellfish that feed on the algae and can produce serious illness in humans. . . . The Marine Conservation Biology Institute claims that dozens of diseases—including yellow blotch, white pox, white plague, and rapid wasting disease—are affecting reef corals. . . . The epidemic [that killed 18,000 harbor seals in the Baltic Sea] was caused by a virus related to canine distemper and measles, which had not previously attacked harbor seals. . . . Though the underlying causes of these new diseases have not been established, scientists suspect that pollution is responsible. Pollution makes marine species vulnerable to disease by weakening their immune systems. (Livernash and Rodenburg, 1998:21–22)

Radiation Pollution. Human beings cannot escape radiation from natural sources such as cosmic rays and radioactive substances in Earth's crust. Technology has added greatly to these natural sources through the extensive use of

X rays for medical and dental uses, fallout from nuclear weapons testing and from nuclear accidents, and the use of nuclear energy as a source of energy.

The dangers of radiation are evidenced in the extreme in the physical effects on the survivors of the atomic bombs at the end of World War II. These victims experienced physical disfigurement, stillbirths, infertility, and extremely high rates of cancer. In 1986 the most serious nuclear accident to date occurred at Chernobyl in the Soviet Union. The full consequences of this accident will not be known for years, but so far there have been numerous deaths in Russia and widespread contamination of food and livestock as far away as Scandinavia and western Europe. The most serious nuclear accident in the United States occurred with the near meltdown in Pennsylvania at Three Mile Island in 1979.

Less dramatic than nuclear accidents but lethal just the same have been the exposures to radiation by workers in nuclear plants and those living nearby. The Hanford nuclear weapons plant in Washington State provides an example. For more than 40 years, the U.S. government ran this facility, monitoring nuclear emissions but not notifying the workers or the 270,000 residents in the surrounding area of the dangers:

> From 1944 to 1947 alone, the Hanford plant spewed 400,000 curies of radioactive iodine into the atmosphere. The bodily absorption of 50 millionths of a single curie is sufficient to raise the risk of thyroid cancer. For years thereafter, Hanford poured radioactive water into the Columbia River and leaked millions of gallons of radioactive waste from damaged tanks into the groundwater. . . . Some 13,700 persons absorbed an estimated dose of 33 rads to their thyroid glands [equivalent to about 1,650 chest X rays] some time during the last 40 years. . . . There was no diagnostic or therapeutic purpose. No one told them; there was no informed consent. Some have called this situation a "creeping Chernobyl" but there is a difference. Chernobyl was an accident. Hanford was deliberate. Chernobyl was a singular event, the product of faulty reactor design and human error. Hanford was a chronic event, the product of obsessive secrecy and callous indifference to public health. (Geiger, 1990:E19)

Similar situations occurred at the weapons factories at Rocky Flats near Denver, Fernald near Cincinnati, and Savannah River in South Carolina, and at the testing sites for weapons in Nevada and other areas in the Southwest.

Utility companies in 31 states operate 103 commercial nuclear reactions, providing about 20 percent of the nation's electricity (second only to coal) (Gugliotta, 2001). Unlike coal, the electricity generated by nuclear energy does not produce carbon dioxide and other greenhouse gases. The problem involves the safe storage of nuclear waste. The generation of nuclear power creates radioactive by-products such as uranium mill tailings, used reactors, and the atomic waste itself. The safe storage of these materials is an enormous and perhaps impossible task since some remain radioactive for as long as 250,000 years. Neither the nuclear industry nor the government has a long-term technology for safe nuclear waste disposal.

The Russian Parliament, however, by a vote of 320 to 30, will make Russia the world's nuclear dumping ground (St. Clair, 2001). Over the next 50 years, Russia will accept around 20,000 tons of radioactive waste from the United States, Europe, and Asia to be added to Russia's own total of 14,000 tons of radioactive waste. In return, Russia will receive about $20 billion, much of it used to build a new generation of nuclear plants.

Air Pollution. Air pollution is a major source of health problems such as respiratory ailments (asthma, bronchitis, and emphysema), cancer, impaired central nervous functioning, and cirrhosis of the liver. These problems are especially acute among people who work in or live near industrial plants in which waste chemicals are released into the air and among people who live in metropolitan areas where conditions such as temperature and topography tend to trap the pollutants near the ground (e.g., cities such as Mexico City, Los Angeles, and Denver). The pollutants emitted into the air have extremely serious consequences for the environment; the greenhouse effect and the loss of ozone protection are topics discussed later in this chapter.

The two major sources of air pollution are emissions from automobiles and from industrial plants (lesser but nonetheless serious sources are toxic waste dumps, burning trash, wood burning, and aerosols). (See Table 4.1.) Automobiles emit five gases implicated in global warming: carbon monoxide, carbon dioxide, nitrous oxide, chlorofluorocarbons, and ozone smog. Currently, automobile-generated air pollution is a problem of the wealthier nations. The United States has 561 cars per 1,000 people; the other industrialized nations average 366 cars per 1,000 people, while there are only 68 cars per 1,000 Latin Americans, 14 per 1,000 Africans, and 2 per 1,000 Chinese (Livernash and Rodenburg, 1998:17).

> Simply put, "cars have bad breath," as one environmental biologist observed. The airborne emissions are deadly, Charles Levy of Boston University goes on to say. "The agencies looking at studies of toxins, many on animals, cite acute toxicities—lungs, respiratory, eyes, nasal passages." Such chronic poisons ingested through the lungs and penetrating into the body through the respiratory system, or even through the skin, hit the stomach and bloodstream. Together, they interact, increasing the probability of disease years down the road—cancer, lung diseases like asthma and bronchitis, possible cardiovascular conditions. (Kay, 1997:111)

TABLE 4.1

Air Pollutant Emissions, by Pollutant and Source, 1997 (in thousands of tons)

Source	*Particulates*	*Sulfur Dioxide*	*Nitrogen Oxides*	*Volatile Organic Compounds*	*Carbon Monoxide*	*Lead*
Fuel consumption, stationary sources	1,101	17,259	10,724	860	4,817	496
Industrial processes	861	1,664	804	1,527	4,779	2,251
Waste disposal and recycling	296	50	103	449	1,242	646
Highway vehicles	268	320	7,035	5,230	50,257	19
Miscellaneous*	30,469	13	346	858	9,568	(NA)

*Includes emissions such as from forest fires and other kinds of burning, various agricultural activities, fugitive dust from paved and unpaved roads and other construction and mining activities, and natural sources.

Source: U.S. Bureau of the Census. 1999. *Statistical Abstract of the United States, 1999,* 119th ed. Washington, DC: U.S. Government Printing Office, Table 406, p. 246.

Industrial emissions are the second major source of air pollution in the United States. Industrial plants and factories release several billion pounds of poisonous chemicals annually, and hundreds of industrial plants are cited annually by the EPA as posing the greatest risks to human health.

GLOBAL ENVIRONMENTAL CRISES

Each form of pollution just described threatens human life. This section focuses on environmental threats to Earth itself. The discussion is limited to three interrelated threats: dependence on fossil fuels for energy, destruction of the tropical rain forests, and global warming.

Fossil Fuel Dependence, Waste, and Environmental Degradation

The Industrial Revolution involved, most fundamentally, the replacement of human and animal muscle by engines driven by fossil fuels. These fuels (coal, oil, natural gas) are also used for heating, cooking, and lighting. Considering just oil, the world consumes 27.7 billion barrels of oil annually (76 million barrels a day), and it is expected that the global oil consumption by 2020 will be 42 billion barrels annually (Drozdiak, 2000). The United States is the greatest consumer of oil products, using 7.1 billion barrels of oil annually (19.5 million barrels a day) (*Nation,* 2001c). Carbon dioxide emissions from fossil fuels, the main villain among the greenhouse gases, has gone from almost nothing a hundred years ago to more than a ton of carbon per person each year. Each person in the United States, by the way, produces 20 times that much. The United States, for example, with 4.6 of the world's population, has one-third of the world's cars and drives 50 percent of the total world mileage. To provide for this extravagance, the United States imports more than 10 million barrels of oil a day, over half of the 19.5 million barrels used daily. (See the panel titled "Social Policy" on automobiles and fossil fuels.)

The worldwide demand for energy will rise sharply as the developing nations, where 90 percent of the world's population growth is taking place, industrialize and urbanize. China, for example, expects to add 170 million cars by 2020 (Zagorin, 2000). People in these countries will be replacing traditional fuels such as wood and other organic wastes with electricity, coal, and oil. This likely trend has important consequences for the world and its inhabitants. First, the demand for fossil fuels has given extraordinary wealth to the nations in the Persian Gulf area, where two-thirds of the world's estimated petroleum reserves are located. The primary reason the United States, with the backing of the United Nations, sent troops to Saudi Arabia in 1991 to stop Iraq's attempts to control Kuwait and other oil-rich nations was to keep the oil from the Persian Gulf flowing to the industrialized nations. In short, the maldistribution of the world's energy supply heightens world tensions.

Second, because most nations need to import oil, vast amounts are carried across the world's oceans in about 2,600 tankers. Along with offshore drilling, these voyages increase the probability of accidents that damage aquatic life, birds, and coastal habitats. Three examples of large-scale spills are the wreck of the *Amoco Cadiz* off the coast of France in 1978, spilling 68 million gallons of crude oil; the blowout of the Ixtoc I oil well, which poured 140 million gallons

SOCIAL POLICY

AMERICA'S DEPENDENCE ON THE AUTOMOBILE AND FOSSIL FUELS

There are more than 200 million automobiles in the United States. "The automobile is not just a moving vehicle but also a 'mobile source of pollution.' . . . In a single second America's cars and trucks [travel] another 60,000 miles, [use] up 3,000 gallons of petroleum products, and [add] 60,000 pounds of carbon dioxide to the atmosphere" (Kay, 1997: 80). When gas unites with oxygen during the process of combustion, carbon dioxide is created—more than 3 pounds from burning 1 pound of gas (Volti, 1995:88). In addition to fossil fuel vehicles creating two-thirds of the carbon dioxide emissions in the United States, they also generate one-fourth of its chlorofluorocarbons, 40 percent of its nitrogen oxides, more than 50 percent of its methane, and most of the carbon monoxide (Kay, 1997:81). Other forms of environmental degradation from automobiles are the 20 million cars and the 250 million tires discarded each year, the millions of tons of corrosive, polluting salt spread on roadways to combat icy road conditions, and the 38.4 million acres of roads and parking lots that are covered with asphalt or concrete. The United States uses over 16 million barrels of oil a day, over half of which is imported, to provide fuel for its cars (and other uses such as heating oil and natural gas). Our insatiable appetite for oil has additional environmental consequences: degrading local environments drilling for oil, oozings from pipelines, leaky underground tanks, oil spills from shipping accidents, the routine flushing of tankers, and leaks and accidents from deep-sea drilling.

What can be done to reduce oil consumption? There are several strategies, each of which is currently not in political favor: (1) High taxes could reduce usage, which is what occurs in western Europe and Japan. France, for example, taxes gas at $2.84 a gallon, compared to an average of 38 cents in the United States. (2) The automobile industry could increase the fuel efficiency of vehicles, which it did after the 1973–1979 crisis, increasing the average miles per gallon for new cars from 15.3 in 1975 to 24.9 in 1995. (3) There could be a greater effort by the automobile industry and the government to produce electric cars. (4) Instead of subsidizing federal highways, which led to the development of suburbs where people must drive to work, play, and shop, mass transit could be subsidized to a much greater degree, as well as increasing population density in urban areas. The U.S. Department of Transportation estimates that by 2000, 89.5 percent of people will commute to work in private vehicles and only 4.7 percent will travel by public transit (*Newsweek,* 1997). (5) Alternative and affordable sources of energy need to be developed for transportation, heating, cooling, and the like. Included among these possibilities are fuel cell, solar, wind, tidal, and geothermal sources. There is a huge roadblock to these needed changes, however, in the form of powerful corporations.

Ultimately, transforming transportation to meet twenty-first-century environmental goals means moving beyond combustion and beyond petroleum. That requires major changes in the country's biggest business; half of the top ten Fortune 500 companies are either auto or oil companies. General Motors, Ford, and Exxon are the three largest U.S. companies, together raking in nearly half a trillion dollars in annual revenues. Such concentrated economic power leads to great political clout. And the technological cartel forged over the past century between the internal combustion engine and petroleum is not easily beaten (Mark, 1998:19).

of oil into the Gulf of Mexico in 1979; and the grounding of the *Exxon Valdez* in Alaska's Prince William Sound in 1989, which released 11 million gallons of crude oil into an ecologically sensitive region, contaminating 1,000 miles of coastline and destroying extraordinary amounts of fish and wildlife.

Finally, and most important, the combustion of fossil fuels results in the emission of carbon dioxide, which appears to be related to climate change. The consequences of the present level of carbon dioxide emissions, plus the

The Exxon Valdez, *a huge oil tanker, went aground in Alaska's Prince William Sound in 1989, releasing 11 million gallons of crude oil into an ecologically sensitive region, contaminating 1,000 miles of coastline, and destroying extraordinary amounts of fish and wildlife.*

expected increase in the near future, may have disastrous consequences for Earth in the form of global warming, as discussed later in this section.

Destruction of the Tropical Rain Forests

Tropical rain forests cover about 6 percent of Earth's land surface (about the same area as the 48 contiguous United States). About 1.9 billion acres of these forests remain in equatorial countries in the Caribbean, West Africa, Southeast Asia, and Latin America. These rich forests are losing an area about half the size of Florida each year (Wilson, 2000). This massive destruction continues to occur because of economics, from the greed of developers to the desperation of poor peasants.

Lumber and mining companies build roads into the jungles to extract their products and transport them to markets. Governments encourage the poor people to settle in these regions by building roads and offering land to settlers, who must clear it for farming. Cattle ranchers require vast expanses for their herds (5 acres of pasture for each head). Land speculators clear huge areas for expected profits. The recovered land, however, is fragile, which leads to a cycle of further deforestation.

The sources of deforestation are not just local. The poverty of these nations (often the result of their colonial heritage), their indebtedness to wealthy nations, and the products needed by the wealthy nations are also responsible for the destruction of the tropical forests.

U.S. corporations are directly and indirectly involved in various aspects of rain forest destruction. These involve the timber companies such as Georgia–Pacific and Weyerhaeuser, mining companies such as Alcoa and Freeport McMoRan, oil companies such as Amoco, Arco, Chevron, Exxon-Mobil, Occidental, Texaco, and Unocal, paper companies such as Kimberly–Clark, and agricultural companies such as Castle & Cooke and Chiquita.

The two major environmental consequences of this deforestation are climate change and the vanishing of species. The climate is affected in several related ways. As hundreds of thousands of forest acres are destroyed, rain patterns change. Huge areas once covered with plants, which give off moisture, are replaced by exposed, sandy soils. Also, the massive burning required to clear the land creates clouds of smoke that block the sun and lead to weather change. Thus, lush, green areas often become near deserts. The tropical forest in Brazil (the world's largest) has so much rainfall that it provides 20 percent of Earth's freshwater supply. What will be the long-range effects as this water supply dwindles? Just as important, forests absorb huge quantities of carbon dioxide through photosynthesis. Thus, as forests are diminished so, too, is Earth's capacity to absorb the gas most responsible for global warming. This diminished capacity to process carbon dioxide, changing it into oxygen, leads to changes in the climate and to desertification.

The second critical environmental consequence of deforestation is the loss of animal and plant species. The eminent expert on biodiversity E. O. Wilson describes the contemporary threat:

> [Biologists] generally agree that the rate of species extinction is now 100 to 1,000 times as great as it was before the coming of humanity. Throughout most of geological time, individual species and their immediate descendants lived an average of about 1 million years. They disappeared naturally at the rate of about one species per million per year, and newly evolved species replaced them at the same rate, maintaining a rough equilibrium. No longer. Not only has the extinction rate soared, but also the birthrate of new species has declined as the natural environment is destroyed. (Wilson, 2000:30)

Wherever humans destroy their habitat, species are eliminated. Although these tropical forests cover only 6 percent of Earth's land surface, they are Earth's richest factory of life, containing more than half of the world's species of plants, insects, birds, and other animals. As the forests are cleared and burned, species become extinct.

Humanity benefits from nature's diversity in many ways. One important aspect is that exotic plants and animals are major sources of pharmaceuticals. For example, Squibb used the venom of the Brazilian pit viper to develop Capoten, a drug to lower high blood pressure. The yew, which grows in the Pacific Northwest, produces a potent chemical, taxol, which shows promise for curing certain forms of lung, breast, and ovarian cancer. Biotechnology provides the potential to improve agricultural crops by transferring genes from wild plants to domestic crops so that they can be drought resistant, repel insects, or create their own fertilizers naturally. By destroying the forests we may be eliminating future solutions to disease and famine.

Global Warming

As noted, the burning of fossil fuels and the destruction of the tropical forests contribute to the greenhouse effect. The **greenhouse effect** occurs when harmful gases (carbon dioxide, nitrous oxide, chlorofluorocarbons, and methane)—all products of diverse human activities—accumulate in the atmosphere and act like the glass roof of a greenhouse. Sunlight reaches Earth's surface, and the gases trap the heat radiating from the ground. The results, according to the theory, are a warming of Earth, the melting of the polar ice caps, a significant changing of climate, megastorms, and the rapid spread of tropical diseases such as malaria, dengue fever, cholera, and encephalitis.

Before the Industrial Revolution, forest fires, plant decomposition, and ordinary evaporation released carbon dioxide into the atmosphere, but in small enough amounts to be absorbed by growing plants and by the oceans without noticeable environmental effect. But in the past century or so, human activities—especially the reliance on fossil fuels for internal combustion engines and in smokestack industries, and the use of chlorofluorocarbons to make plastic foam and as coolants in refrigerators and air conditioners, coupled with the destruction of the tropical rain forests—have increased the prevalence of dangerous gases beyond Earth's capacity to absorb them; hence, a gradual warming. The United States, for example, while only 4.6 percent of the world's population, accounts for roughly one-fourth of all greenhouse gas emissions. (See Table 4.2.)

Earth is now the warmest it has been in the past 6,000 years or so. The decade of the 1990s was very likely the hottest of the last millennium. The average global temperature rose 1.1 degree over the past 100 years. As a result

> The oceans are rising, mountain glaciers are shrinking, low-lying coastal areas are eroding, and the very timing of the seasons is changing, with spring coming as much as a week earlier in parts of the Northern Hemisphere. And

TABLE 4.2

Total Carbon Dioxide Emissions, 1950–2000 and Ecological Footprint, 1999

Country	*Total Carbon Dioxide Emissions (in Billions of Tons)*	*Percent of World's Population*	*Footprint* Acres/Capita*
United States	186.1	4.6	24
European Union	127.8	4.6	12
Russia	68.4	2.5	11
China	57.6	20.9	4
Japan	31.2	2.1	10
Ukraine	21.7	0.8	—
India	15.5	16.6	2
Canada	14.9	0.5	18
Poland	14.4	0.3	10
Kazakhstan	10.1	0.8	—
South Africa	8.5	0.7	7
Mexico	7.8	2.0	6
Australia	7.6	0.3	23

*The ecological footprint measures what we consume of nature. It shows how much productive land and water we occupy to produce all the resources we consume and to take in all the waste we make. For example, the average American uses 24 acres to support his or her current lifestyle. In comparison, the average Canadian lives on 25 percent less, the average Japanese on 60 percent less.

Sources: World Resources, Population Reference Bureau. 2000–2001. *World Population Data Sheet; Redefining Progress, "The Ecological Footprint."* Online. Available: http://d6b.cas.psu.edu/footprint_acres. htm.

> all indications are that the warming of the earth in the 21st century will be significantly greater than it was in the 20th (Herbert, 2000:1)

In 2001 a panel of scientists sponsored by the United Nations reported that the average surface temperature of Earth could rise 2.6 to 10.4°F from 1990 to 2100. Should Earth's temperature increase 10 degrees, sea level would rise 35 inches (it rose 9 inches in the twentieth century), there would be violent storms and persistent droughts. The panel also said that it is likely that most of the warming since the 1950s is "due to the increase in greenhouse gas concentrations" (reported in Watson, 2001).

Scientists do not debate that Earth is warmer or that carbon dioxide is emitted into the air in ever-increasing amounts, but they do differ on the relationship between the two facts. Some scientists are cautious, arguing that recent warming and dramatic climatic events are random and part of the natural year-to-year variations in weather. Their caution is countered by the majority of scientists who are convinced that the magnitude of the greenhouse effect is great and accelerating (see Figure 4.1, p. 98):

> "Under business as usual, we'll reach carbon dioxide concentrations that haven't been seen on this planet in the past 50 million years," Harvard professor and Nobel Laureate John Holdren told a recent White House conference on global warming. "We will have achieved that in the geological blink of an eye, exposing, as we do it, natural systems to a rate of temperature change faster than at any time in the last 10,000 years." (Hoagland, 1997:6)

SOURCES OF U.S. ENVIRONMENTAL PROBLEMS

The United States has been blessed with an abundance of rich and varied resources (land, minerals, and water). Until recently, people in the United States were unconcerned with conservation because there seemed to be so vast a storehouse of resources that waste was not considered a problem. And as a result, Americans have disproportionately consumed the world' resources. For example, although they constitute 4.6 percent of the world's population, people in the United States use 25 percent of the world's oil output each year. This is because we own 200 million cars and trucks and drive some 1.6 trillion miles annually, almost as much as all the rest of the world. See the panel on sports utility vehicles.

Although the perception of abundance may explain a tendency to be wasteful, it is only a partial and superficial answer. The underlying sources of our present environmental problems can be located in the culture and structure of U.S. society.

Cultural Sources

Culture refers to the knowledge that the members of a social organization—in this case, a society—share. Shared ideas, values, beliefs, and understandings shape the behaviors, perceptions, and interpretations of the members of society. The dominant ideologies of U.S. society have tended to legitimize or at least account for the wastefulness of Americans and their acceptance of pollution.

Cornucopia View of Nature. Most Americans conceive of nature as a vast storehouse waiting only to be used by people. They regard the natural world as

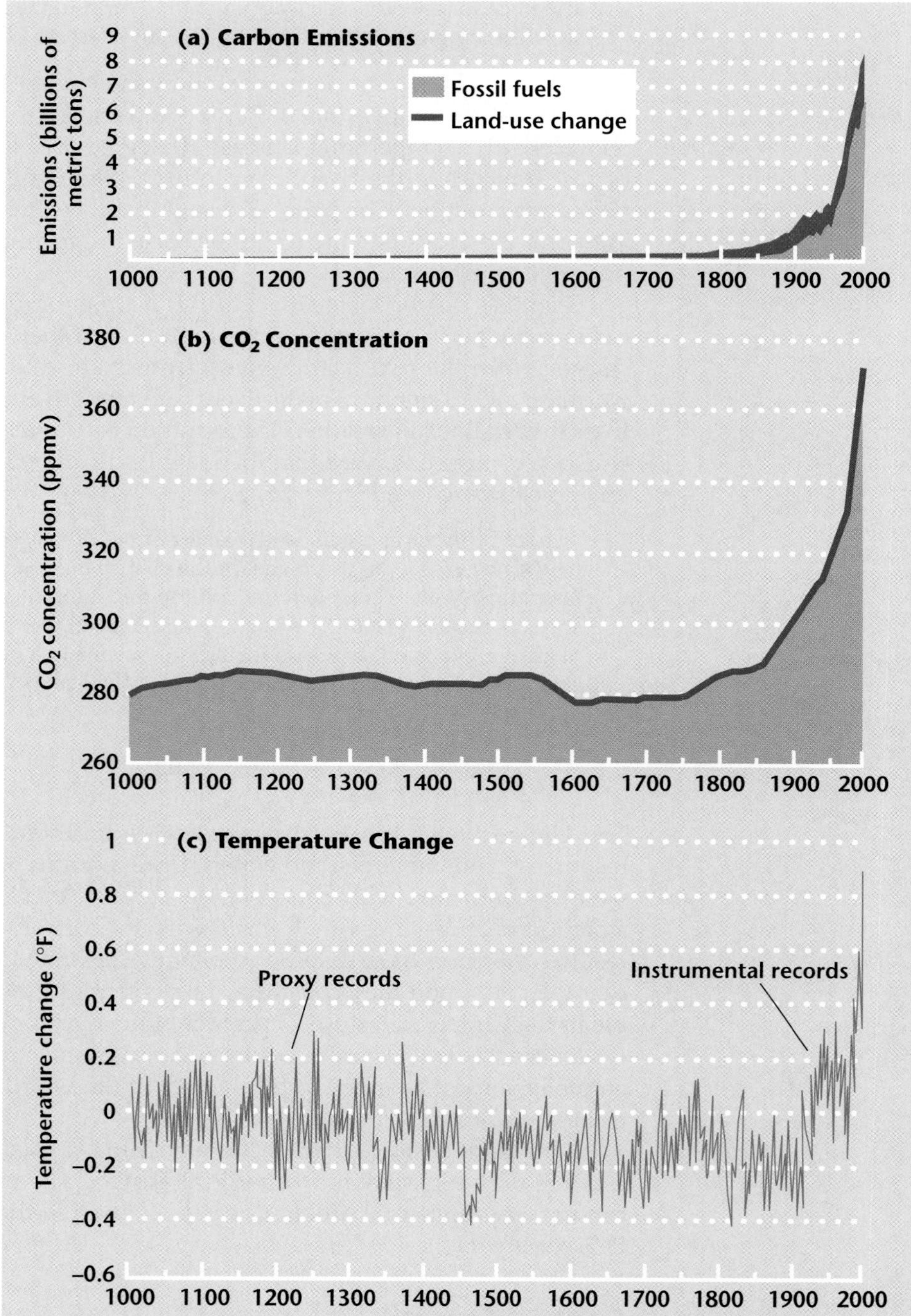

FIGURE 4.1

1000 Years of Global CO_2 and Temperature Change

Source: National Assessment Synthesis Team. 2001. *Climate Change Impacts on the United States: The Potential Consequences of Climate Variability and Change.* Report for the U.S. Global Change Research Program. Cambridge: Cambridge University Press, p. 22.

a bountiful preserve available to serve human needs. In this view nature is something to be used; it is free and inexhaustible. This **cornucopia view of nature** is widespread and will likely persist as a justification for continuing abuse of the environment even in an age of ecological consciousness. Jonathan Turner believes that to turn events around,

A CLOSER LOOK

SPORTS UTILITY VEHICLES AND THE ENVIRONMENT

Ten Facts About SUVs

- Americans bought 2.8 million SUVs as of November 2000—17 percent of all vehicles sold last year.
- The Ford Excursion, at 7,600 pounds, seats nine, gets 12.5 miles per gallon, and weighs the equivalent of three Honda Civics. In its lifetime, a Honda Civic emits 40 tons of carbon dioxide. A Ford Excursion 134 tons.
- Crashes between a car and an SUV killed 5,447 people last year. That's over 1,000 more people killed than in crashes involving two cars, despite the fact that car-to-car accidents are more common than car-to-SUV accidents and that there are twice as many cars as SUVs on the road.
- The fuel-economy average for both cars and trucks is at its lowest point since 1980.
- Federal law allows SUVs, which are classified as light trucks, to emit 30 percent more carbon monoxide and hydrocarbons and 75 percent more nitrogen oxides than passenger cars.
- Federal law permits SUVs to waste 31 percent more gasoline than passenger cars.
- SUVs spew out 43 percent more global-warming pollutants and 47 percent more air pollution than an average car.
- Cars and light trucks are a major source of global warming, as each gallon of gasoline pumps 28 pounds of carbon dioxide into the atmosphere.
- Driving an SUV that gets 13 miles per gallon rather than an average car for a year wastes more energy than leaving your bathroom light burning for 30 years or your color television turned on for 28 years.
- America's cars and light trucks produce nearly 20 percent of U.S. carbon dioxide pollution—more carbon dioxide than all but four countries worldwide.

Source: "10 Facts About SUV's." *In These Times* (April 30, 2001):18.

> it will cost the public money to visualize nature as a common good: Industries will have to pay for their pollution, which in turn will mean that they will raise prices; the federal government will have to engage in expensive monitoring and control of pollution emitted by industries, with the result that federal taxes will be raised; and local communities will have to increase taxes to pay for their pollution and to expand their sewage and garbage treatment facilities. Thus, the belief that nature is a free good may persist for some time as an ideology for keeping prices and taxes down. (Turner, 1977:408–409)

Faith in Technology. There are three basic ways in which human beings can relate to nature. They can view it as a controlling force, thereby submitting to the environment in a fatalistic manner. They can strive to attain harmony with it: People need nature and nature needs people. Finally, they can try to attain mastery over nature.

Most Americans regard human beings as having mastery over nature. Rather than accepting the environment as given, they have sought to change and conquer it. Damming rivers, cutting down timber, digging tunnels, plowing up prairie land, conquering space, and seeding clouds with silver nitrate are a few examples of this orientation to overcoming nature's obstacles rather than acquiescing to them. Most Americans, then, view nature as something to be subdued and used.

From this logic proceeds a faith in technology; a proper application of scientific knowledge can meet any challenge. If the air and water are polluted and if we are rapidly running out of petroleum, science will save us. We will find a substitute for the internal combustion engine, create plants that will "scrub" the air by using carbon dioxide as food, find new sources of energy, develop new methods of extracting minerals, or create new synthetics. While this faith may yet be vindicated, we are beginning to realize that technology may not be the solution and may even be the source of the problem.

Scientific breakthroughs and new technology have solved some problems and do aid in saving labor. But often, new technology creates unanticipated problems. Automobiles, for example, provide numerous benefits, but they also pollute the air and kill about 50,000 Americans each year. It is difficult to imagine life without electricity, but the generation of electricity pollutes the air (over half of the carbon emissions in the United States come from coal-burning electrical plants), and causes the thermal pollution of rivers. Insecticides and chemical fertilizers have performed miracles in agriculture but have polluted food and streams (and even "killed" some lakes). Obviously, the slogan of the DuPont Corporation—"Better living through chemistry"—is not entirely correct. Jet planes, while helping us in many ways, cause air pollution (one jet taking off emits the same amount of hydrocarbon as the exhausts from 10,000 automobiles) and noise pollution near busy airports.

- **Growth Ethic.** Americans place a premium on progress; they dislike the status quo. They tend never to be entirely satisfied. Something better is always attainable. This desire (which is encouraged by corporations and their advertisers) causes people to discard items that are still usable and to purchase new things. Thus, industry continues to turn out more products and to use up natural resources.

  The presumed value of progress has had a negative effect on contemporary U.S. life. Progress is typically defined to mean either growth or new technology. Community leaders typically want their cities to grow. Chambers of commerce want more industry and more people (and, incidentally, more consumers). The logic of capitalism is that every company needs to increase its profits from year to year. Thus, we all benefit if the gross national product increases each year. For all these things to grow as people wish, there must be a concomitant increase in population, products (and use of natural resources), electricity, highways, and waste. Continued growth will inevitably throw the tight ecological system out of balance, for there are limited supplies of air, water, and places to dump waste materials, and these supplies diminish as the population increases.

- **Materialism.** The U.S. belief in progress is translated at the individual level into consumption of material things as evidence of one's success. The U.S. economic system is predicated on the growth (progress?) of private enterprises, which depend on increased demand for their products. If the population is more or less stable, then growth can be accomplished only through increased consumption by individuals. The function of the advertising industry is to create a need in individuals to buy a product that they would not buy otherwise. Consumption is also increased if products must be thrown away (such as nonreturnable bottles) or if they do not last very long. The policy of **planned obsolescence** by many U.S. companies accomplishes this goal of consumption very well, but it overlooks the problems of disposal as well as the unnecessary waste of materials.

- **Belief in Individualism.** Most people in the United States place great stress on personal achievement. They believe that hard work and initiative will bring success. There is a tendency to sacrifice present gains for future rewards (*deferred gratification*). Many people will sacrifice by working days and going to school at night in order to get a better job. Parents may make great sacrifices so that their children will have the opportunity for a college education or other advantages they never received. In this manner, success is accomplished vicariously through the achievements of one's children.

This self-orientation (as opposed to a collective orientation) forms the basis for a number of the value configurations of work, activity, and success mentioned previously. The individual is successful through his or her own initiative and hard work. The stress on individualism is, of course, related to capitalism. Through personal efforts, business acumen, and luck, the individual can (if successful) own property and see multiplying profits. Most Americans share this goal of great monetary success—the "American dream"—and believe that anyone can make it, if he or she works hard enough. Curiously, people who are not successful commonly do not reject capitalism. Instead, they wait in the hope that their lot will improve or that their children will prosper under the system.

The belief that private property and capitalism should not be restricted has led to several social problems: (1) unfair competition (monopolies, interlocking directorates, price fixing); (2) an entrepreneurial philosophy of caveat emptor ("let the buyer beware"), whose aim is profit with total disregard for the welfare of the consumer; and (3) the current environmental crisis, which is due in great measure to the standard policy of many people and most corporations to do whatever is profitable while ignoring conservation of natural resources. Industrial pollution of air and water with refuse and agricultural spraying with pesticides that harm animal and human life are two examples of how individuals and corporations look out for themselves with little or no regard for the short- and long-range effects of their actions on life.

As long as people hold a narrow self-orientation rather than a group orientation, this crisis will steadily worsen. The use people make of their land, the water running through it, and the air above it has traditionally been theirs to decide because of the belief in the sanctity of private property. This belief has meant in effect that individuals have had the right to pave a pasture for a parking lot, to tear up a lemon grove for a housing development, to put down artificial turf for a football field, and to dump waste products into the ground, air, and water. Consequently, individual decisions have had the collective effect of taking millions of acres of arable land out of production permanently, polluting the air and water, and covering land where vegetation once grew with asphalt, concrete buildings, and Astroturf, even though green plants are the only source of oxygen.

In summary, traditional values of U.S. citizens lie at the heart of environmental problems. Americans want to conquer nature. They want to use nature for the good life, and this endeavor is never satisfied. Moreover, they want the freedom to do as they please.

Our individualistic and acquisitive values lead us to resist group-centered programs and humanitarian concerns. Will an energy crisis or continued global warming change our values? Will we vote for politicians who argue for societal planning and sacrifice to reduce environmental perils, or will we opt for politicians who favor the traditional values?

Structural Sources

The structural arrangements in U.S. society buttress the belief system that reinforces the misuse of resources and abuses the ecosystem. The following discussion is adapted from Turner (1977:410–429).

Capitalist Economy. The U.S. economic system of capitalism depends on profits. The quest for profits is never satisfied: Companies must grow; more assets and more sales translate into more profits. To maximize profits, owners must minimize costs. Among other things, this search for profits results in abusing the environment (such as strip mining and the disposal of harmful wastes into the air or waterways), resisting government efforts to curb such abuse, and using corporate and advertising skills to increase the consumption of products, including built-in obsolescence.

This last point needs elaboration. Profits require consumers; growing profits require overconsumption. Corporations use several mechanisms to generate the desire to purchase unnecessary products. Advertising generates hyperconsumerism by creating demand for products that potential consumers did not know they needed. Innovative packaging designs also help to sell products; the size, shape, and colors of the package and its display affect choices. Another common tactic is product differentiation, where existing products (such as an automobile) are given cosmetic changes and presented to consumers as new. This planned obsolescence creates consumer demand as purchasers trade or throw away the "old" product for the "new."

The increased production that results from greater levels of consumption has three detrimental consequences for the environment: more pollution of air and water, depletion of resources, and a swelling of waste products (sewage, scrap, and junk).

Because the profit motive supersedes the concern for the environment, there is an unwillingness of corporations to comply with government regulations and to pay damages for ecological disasters such as oil spills. In addition, the possibility of solving environmental problems is further minimized under a capitalist system because jobs depend on business profits. Economic prosperity and growth mean jobs. Thus, most observers see only a narrow alternative between a safe environment or relatively full employment. The fate of many workers depends on whether companies are profitable. Solving environmental problems appears to be incompatible with capitalism unless ecological disasters occur.

Polity. As discussed in Chapter 2, political decisions are fundamentally influenced by powerful interest groups. This bias of the political system is readily seen in government's relatively cozy relationship with large polluters: corporations. Consumer advocate Ralph Nader has provided several illustrations of this upside-down effect (i.e., the benefits accrue to the wealthy few). The following examples are adapted from Nader (1970, 1977).

- Those who define violence are those who perpetuate most of it. The government focuses its attention on the violence that occurs from street crimes but tends to ignore the violence that emerges from the chemical assault on the environment. Much more is lost in money and health through pollution, yet only tangible physical assaults are defined officially as violence.

- Before the liberalization of marijuana laws, an individual in some states could get a jail sentence exceeding 10 years for smoking pot, yet industrialists knowingly causing smog in a city could be fined just a few hundred dollars a day while they continued to endanger public safety.
- A person who throws a banana peel out of a car window in Yosemite will be fined $25; yet the oil companies responsible for the oil spill in Santa Barbara paid nothing for its cleanup or for restoring the beaches.
- It is a crime for individuals to relieve themselves in Puget Sound but legal for a corporation to do it 24 hours a day.
- The size of a business enterprise legitimizes its right to pollute the environment. Suppose you own a fifteen-room house and rent out rooms to six tenants. You employ several people, such as a cook, gardener, and janitor; to keep costs down, you throw all your garbage and trash into the street. The city officials do not permit this wanton disregard for the welfare of the city and its citizens. You argue, however, that you must keep your costs down in order to contribute to the employment of some of the city's inhabitants. If you are forced to pay for garbage collection or recycling of waste materials, your profits will be reduced and you will have to close down, throwing your few employees out of work. Faced with your threat, the city orders you to desist. The problem is that your operation is not big enough. If you employed thousands of employees, the city would allow you to continue polluting the environment lest thousands be added to the city's unemployed—a clear case of industrial extortion.

These examples illustrate the bias of the law. Moreover, the efforts of the administrative agencies operating under the regulatory laws have been superficial at best. Typically, government intervention has had the effect of adminis-

"IT'S THE SAME AGE-OLD QUESTION: IS THE LAKE HALF-POLLUTED, OR HALF-PRISTINE?"

Kirk Anderson

tering a symbolic slap on the wrist, and pollution of the environment has continued virtually unabated. The government apparently will not or cannot push the largest and most powerful corporations to do something unprofitable. Not only are these corporations the largest polluters, but they also have a vested interest in the status quo. General Motors and Ford, for example, resist congressional attempts to legislate stricter standards for reducing pollution because the necessary devices add to the cost of automobiles and might curb sales. The government has achieved gradual change, but the powerful automobile industry has consistently responded more slowly than the environmental lobby wanted. Thus, the existing laws to curb pollution are largely meek and ineffective.

The government could take a much firmer stance if it chose to do so. Suppose, as Henslin and Reynolds have suggested, that the situation were reversed: "Can you possibly reverse this situation and imagine the poor polluting the streams used by the rich, and then not only getting away with it and avoiding arrest, but also being paid by the rich through the government to clean up their own pollution?" (Henslin and Reynolds, 1976:220–221). In such a case, how would the poor be treated? The answer is obvious. The powerful would punish them severely and would immediately curb their illegal behaviors. The implication is that whoever has the power can use it for their own benefit, disregarding both nature and other people.

- **Demographic Patterns.** The population of the United States is generally concentrated in large metropolitan areas. Wherever people are concentrated, the problems of pollution are increased through the concentration of wastes. Where people are centralized, so too will be the emission of automobile exhausts, the effluence of factories, and the dumps for garbage and other human refuse.

The location of cities is another source of environmental problems. Typically, cities have evolved where commerce would benefit the most. Because industry needs plentiful water for production and waste disposal, cities tend to be located along lakes, rivers, and ocean bays. Industry's long-established pattern of using available water to dispose of its waste materials has caused rivers, such as the Missouri, Mississippi, and Ohio, lakes, such as Erie and Michigan, and bays like Chesapeake and New York to be badly polluted.

The ready availability of the automobile and the interstate highway system resulted in the development of suburbs. The growth of suburbs not only strained the already-burdened sewage facilities but also increased air pollution through increased use of the automobile. The greater the urban sprawl, the greater the smog is.

- **System of Stratification.** One major focus of this book (and of Chapter 7, in particular) is how U.S. society victimizes the poor. Because of where they live and work, poor people and racial minorities are more susceptible than are the well-to-do to the dangers of pollution, whether it takes the form of excessive noise, foul air, or toxic chemicals such as lead poisoning. These probabilities are called **environmental classism** and environmental racism. Another inequity is that the poor will have to pay disproportionately for efforts to eliminate pollution. That is, their jobs may be eliminated, their neighborhoods abandoned, and a greater proportion of their taxes required (through regressive taxes) to pay for environmental cleanups.

The bitter irony of the poor having to sacrifice the most to abate environmental problems is that they are not the polluters—the affluent are. The affluent drive excessively; travel in jet planes; have air-conditioned, large homes; consume large quantities of resources (conspicuous consumption); and have the most waste to dispose. Their demand increases economic demand and, concomitantly, industrial pollution.

In summary, the United States is a wasteful, inefficient, and vulnerable energy-centered economy. The natural environment is being destroyed by pollution and waste, for several reasons: First, the economic system exploits people and resources. The emphasis on profit requires growth and consumption. Thus, meeting short-term goals supersedes planning to prevent detrimental long-term consequences. Second, we depend on technology that is wasteful. Third, most people believe in capitalism, growth, and consumption. Finally, population growth increases the demand for products, energy, and other resources.

SOLUTIONS TO THE ENVIRONMENTAL CRISES

Probusiness Voluntaristic Approach

The solution advocated by conservatives is based on the premise that if left alone, mechanisms in the marketplace will operate to solve environmental problems. When cleaning up pollution becomes profitable enough, entrepreneurs will provide the services to clean the air, treat the water, and recycle waste. There is a contradiction here, though: The free market approach will not eliminate pollution, pollution controls reduce profits, and the goal of companies is to maximize profits. A possible compromise is for the government to provide incentives to industries to curb their polluting activities. These incentives could take the form of tax breaks for the purchase and use of pollution controls or outright grants for the use of effective controls.

The probusiness approach, exemplified by the George W. Bush administration, sought to unleash the energy industry to produce more by drilling aggressively for more oil and gas even in marginal areas (Alaska, offshore), burning more coal (of which there is an abundance), and building more nuclear plants. At the same time, efforts at conservation, to quote Vice President Cheney "may be a sign of personal virtue but not the basis for a sound, comprehensive energy policy" (quoted in Moberg, 2001:14). It should be noted that the oil and gas industry during the 2000 election cycle gave Bush $1.86 million and Republicans $24.4 million, compared to $6.6 million to Democrats) (D. Z. Jackson, 2001). Moreover, President Bush and Vice President Cheney were both executives in the oil industry before their stint in politics.

Egalitarian/Authoritarian Plan

According to its opponents, the business-oriented plan just described has a basic flaw: It lacks overall provision for the whole society. To allow individuals and companies free choice in what to consume, how much to consume, what to produce, and in what quantities is a luxury that society cannot afford in a time of scarcity and ecological crises. Let us look at the two main authoritarian alternatives to solving the problem of pollution.

The government must operate on the premise that pollution is a crime against society and will not be tolerated. This approach entails the enactment of comprehensive laws carrying severe criminal and civil penalties for harming the environment. At the corporate level it means rigorous inspections of companies and prosecution of violators. Moreover, if penalized, these companies must not be allowed to pass the fines on to consumers through higher prices. At the individual level it means inspection of vehicles and homes to enforce compliance with accepted standards.

One obstacle to a comprehensive plan to curb pollution is our federal system of government, in which states and communities are free to set their own standards. In principle this system makes sense because the people in an area should be the most knowledgeable about their situation. However, mining operations along Lake Superior cannot be allowed to dump tailings in the lake on the rationale that having to pay for recycling would reduce local employment levels. Similarly, air pollution is never limited to one locality; wind currents carry the pollutants beyond local borders and add to the cumulative effect on an entire region. Therefore, it seems imperative that the federal government establish and enforce minimum standards for the entire country. Localities could make the standards stricter if they wish. For example, because of its high altitude, Denver has special problems with air pollution. Denver is susceptible to temperature inversions that trap pollutants near the land surface, and automobiles at high altitude emit more pollutants than they would at lower elevations. The city of Denver may therefore want to impose very strict automobile emission standards, just as California has to meet the unusual conditions of its geography.

But while it is easy to list what the government should do, it is also easy to see that the implementation of a centralized, authoritarian plan will meet many obstacles and considerable opposition. Industries, corporations, and communities will resist what will be commonly interpreted as arbitrary and heavy-handed tactics by bureaucrats who do not understand the necessity of profits for maintaining employment and a good local tax base. More fundamentally, the concept of free enterprise means, for many, the freedom to use one's property as one wishes. Will Congress, faced with these pressures, institute a national antipollution program with the necessary clout to be effective? Unless people and their representatives take a more realistic view of the ecological dangers that now exist, Congress will not act.

Control of Resource Use

To start any effective system of resource use, the government must begin by gathering correct information about the extent of natural resource reserves. Currently, government data depend largely on information provided by private firms. Data must also be gathered about the use of the various resources. How much actual waste is there? Can the waste be recycled? What is the turnaround time for renewable resources? Are there alternatives to existing resources? Once authoritative answers to these questions are determined, the government can plan rationally to eliminate waste, develop alternatives, and limit use to appropriate levels.

A rational plan to conserve energy, for example, could include government insistence that new-car fuel economy average 40 miles per gallon (which would reduce U.S. oil consumption by 2.8 million barrels a day by the year 2005); universal daylight saving time (it could even be extended to a 2-hour difference, rather than one); strict enforcement of a relatively low speed limit; the use of governors on automobiles and thermostats; banning neon signs and other energy used in advertising; minimal use of outdoor lighting; and a reversal of the current policy that reduces rates for electricity and natural gas as the volume increases. These steps are important, but the key ingredient to conservation is mandatory rationing, which would reduce consumption in an equitable fashion.

Regardless of the plan that is eventually chosen, most people would agree that the waste of energy must be curtailed. Conserving energy will require not only individual alterations of life-styles but also changes in the economic system. Under the current private enterprise system based on profits, corporations seek the profitable alternative rather than the conserving one. In the search for greater profits, we have shifted from railroads and mass transit (the most energy-efficient means of moving people and freight on land) to energy-inefficient cars, trucks, and planes. Instead of using energy-sparing and renewable resources such as wood, cotton, wool, and soap, companies have switched to synthetic fibers, plastics, and detergents made from petroleum.

Can the United States continue to operate on an economic system that allows decisions about what to produce and how to produce it to be governed by profit rather than the common good? The heart of the capitalists' argument, going back to Adam Smith more than 200 years ago, is that decisions made on the basis of the entrepreneur's self-interest will also accomplish the needs of society most efficiently. This fundamental precept of capitalism is now challenged by the environmental crisis, the energy crisis, and the problems related to them. Can capitalism be amended to incorporate central planning regarding societal needs of a safe environment and plentiful resources?

The exact form that the economy should take in an energy-short and polluted world is a source of controversy. At one extreme are people who believe that capitalism is the solution, not the problem. Others would demand a socialistic system as the only answer. At a minimum, it would seem that (1) there must be central planning; (2) pollution must be controlled and such control tightly enforced; (3) the monopoly structure of the energy industry must be broken up (currently, the largest oil companies control the production, refining, transportation, and retail distribution of oil and are the largest owners of coal, uranium, and geothermal energy); (4) there must be mandatory conservation measures; and (5) the government must subsidize efforts to obtain alternative, nonpolluting sources of energy, and the resulting structures should be publicly owned so that the public good, not profit, is the primary aim.

A final problem is that an energy-short world will not continue to tolerate America's disproportionate use of energy and other resources. The possibility of war increases with the growing resentment of have-not nations toward the haves. Noted economist Robert Heilbroner has used a train analogy to make this point:

> [The peoples] of the underdeveloped world are aware of the ghastly resemblance of the world's present economic condition to an immense train, in which a few passengers, mainly in the advanced capitalist world, ride in first-class coaches, in conditions of comfort unimaginable to the enormously greater numbers crammed into the cattle cars that make up the bulk of the train's carriages. To the governments of revolutionary regimes, however, the passengers in the first-class coaches not only ride at their ease but have

> decorated their compartments and enriched their lives using the work and appropriating the resources of the masses who ride behind them. Such governments are not likely to view the vast differences between first class and cattle class with the forgiving eyes of the predecessors. (Heilbroner, 1974:39–40)

At the international level, the United States along with other developed nations must seek solutions to the environmental crises facing the planet. This means mandating that the developed countries reduce the production of materials that pollute the air, water, and land. The United States must also develop for itself and for other countries environmentally appropriate technologies that will sustain economic progress and be substituted for the ecologically destructive technologies currently in use. As the United States makes trade agreements such as the ones encouraging free trade with Mexico and Canada, agreements must include standard environmental protections. Similarly, loan agreements must contain environmental protections as a condition to receive monies. Finally, the wealthy nations can help themselves and help the debtor nations by engaging in "debt-for-nature" exchanges. Many of the poor nations are hopelessly in debt to the rich nations. Presently, many pay the interest (rarely the principal) by cutting down their forests or by farming marginal lands. The creditor nations could reduce debt in exchange for enforceable agreements by the debtor nation to protect vulnerable parts of their environment.

INTERNATIONAL IMPLICATIONS OF ENVIRONMENTAL PROBLEMS

Environmental problems are not confined within political borders. The oceans, rivers, lakes, and air are shared by the world's inhabitants. If a corporation or a nation pollutes, the world's citizens are the victims. If the tropical forests are destroyed, we are all affected. If a country wastes finite resources or uses more than its proportionate share, the other nations are shortchanged.

What will the world be like in 50 years or so? In all likelihood, its population will have leveled off at about 9 billion. The planet will be crowded; the production of enough food and its fair distribution will be extremely problematic. Fresh water will be scarce. Oil will have been replaced by some other energy source. Unless dramatic changes are instituted, the quality of air and water, especially in the less developed, rapidly growing nations, will have deteriorated greatly and the climate will have been altered. Global warming will have altered climates and flooded low-lying regions.

What should the nations of the world do about environmental crises? One school of thought is pessimistic: The cupboard is almost bare and there is no hope; we must therefor prepare for a world of subsistence living and chaos. At the other extreme, optimists assert that science has always found a solution and will save us again. We cannot foresee now the discovery of new sources of energy, new synthetics, and new processes of recycling wastes. Throughout history skeptics have looked at existing technology and foreseen shortages of items currently in demand. But the future for us may be different, in the sense that we and the next few generations face a future in which the limits of space and resources are reached. Will something yet save us?

The safe prediction is that nations that are now affluent will undergo dramatic changes. Expanding technology will have to be limited because of its demands on precious resources, its generation of harmful heat, and other negative ecological effects. People's freedom to order life as they please—to pave a vacant lot, to irrigate land, to have as many children as they want, to acquire things, to consume fuel on a pleasure trip—will be controlled. The needs of the group, community, society, and perhaps even the world will take precedence over those of the individual. Other values people in the United States hold dear—such as growth and progress, capitalism, and the conquest of nature—will no longer be salient in a world of less space, endangered ecology, energy shortages, and hunger. These values will die hard, especially the choice of individual freedom. No doubt there will be a great deal of social upheaval during the period of transition from growth to stability, from affluence to subsistence. But these changes must occur or we will perish.

The dangers posed by the future require solutions at two levels. At the physical level efforts must be directed to finding, for instance, new sources of energy (e.g., fuel cells, solar, wind), methods to increase the amount of arable land, new types of food, better contraceptives, and relatively inexpensive ways to desalt seawater. At the social level there must be changes in the structural conditions responsible for poverty, wasted resources, pollution, and the like. One such target would be to determine ways of overcoming the cultural habits (customs, values, beliefs) that reinforce high fertility, people's refusal to eat certain foods or to accept central planning, and the dependence on growth and technology. New forms of social organization, such as regional councils and world bodies, may be required to deal with social upheavals, economic dislocations, resource allocation, and pollution on a global scale. These new organizations will require great innovative thinking, for it is likely that the dominant modes of the present age not only are unworkable for the demands of an overpopulated planet but also are in large measure responsible for many of our present and future difficulties.

One complicating factor is that, currently, nations tend to focus on national problems rather than on transnational cooperative efforts. Moreover, they direct their efforts to physical rather than social solutions. They seek answers in technological and developmental wizardry. These solutions are important and should not be neglected, but massive efforts should also be directed to finding ethical, legal, religious, and social solutions.

CHAPTER REVIEW

1. Earth's biosphere is disturbed profoundly by three social forces: population growth, the concentration of people in urban areas, and modern technology.
2. While population growth, which occurs mostly in the developing countries, has adverse effects on the environment, the populations of rich countries are much more wasteful of Earth's resources and generate much more pollution.
3. Chemicals, solid waste disposal, and radiation pollute the land, water, and air.
4. The three major interrelated environmental crises that Earth faces are the burning of fossil fuels, the destruction of the tropical forests, and global warming.
5. The United States, while only 4.6 percent of the world's population, consumes roughly one-fourth of the world's resources and accounts for one-fourth of all greenhouse gas emissions.
6. The cultural bases of the wasteful and environmentally destructive U.S. society are the dominant ideologies of (a) the cornucopia view of nature, (b) faith in technology, (c) the growth ethic, (d) materialism, and (e) the belief in individualism.
7. The structural bases for the misuse and abuse of the U.S. environment and resources are (a) urbanization, (b) the system of stratification, (c) capitalism, and (d) the bias of the political system.

8. The probusiness voluntaristic solution to the environmental crises is to rely on the marketplace rather than on the government. If energy sources are in short supply, prices will rise and two beneficial results will occur: (a) Consumption will be reduced among those who cannot afford the high prices, and (b) corporations and individuals will be motivated to search for new sources.
9. The egalitarian/authoritarian solution is based on government planning and control to reduce problems and promote conservation. This solution shares the burdens throughout the social strata. Moreover, it controls consumption to meet societal goals.
10. The worldwide problems of pollution and resource depletion will become more acute in the future because of population growth, urbanization, expanding technology, and the lack of planning by nations individually and collectively.
11. The dangers posed by these critical problems require solutions at two levels: (a) At the physical level we need discoveries and inventions of nonpolluting technologies and renewable resources; and (b) at the social level we need changes in the structural conditions responsible for these problems and the creation of new forms of transnational social organizations.

KEY TERMS

Biosphere. The surface layer of the planet and the surrounding atmosphere.

Ecosystems. The mechanisms (plants, animals, and microorganisms) that supply people with the essentials of life.

Environmental justice. A movement to improve community environments by eliminating toxic hazards.

Environmental racism. The overwhelming likelihood that toxic-producing plants and toxic waste dumps are located where poor people, especially people of color, live.

Greenhouse effect. When gases accumulate in Earth's atmosphere and act like the glass roof of a greenhouse, allowing sunlight in but trapping the heat that is generated.

Culture. The knowledge (ideas, values, beliefs) that the members of a social organization share.

Cornucopia view of nature. The belief that nature is a vast and bountiful storehouse to be used by human beings.

Planned obsolescence. Existing products are given superficial changes and marketed as new, making the previous product out of date.

Environmental classism. The poor, because of dangerous jobs and residential segregation, are more exposed than the more well-to-do to environmental dangers.

WEBSITES FOR FURTHER REFERENCE

http://www.worldwatch.org/
The Worldwatch Institute Online: "your internet source for cross-disciplinary, global environmental information." The Worldwatch Institute is dedicated to "fostering the evolution of an environmentally sustainable society—one in which human needs are met in ways that do not threaten the health of the natural environment or the prospects of future generations." The Institute seeks to achieve this goal through the conduct of interdisciplinary nonpartisan research on emerging global environmental issues, the results of which are widely disseminated throughout the world.

http://www.populationenvironmentresearch.org
The Population-Environment Research Network seeks to advance academic research on population and the environment by promoting online scientific exchange among researchers from social and natural science disciplines worldwide. Its website provides an online research database, a cyber seminar series, highlights of new material, upcoming events and opportunities, and membership information. Links to related sites are provided.

http://www.rprogress.org
Redefining Progress is a nonprofit public policy and research organization that develops policies and tools to reorient the economy so it will "value people and nature first."

http://www.iclei.org/
The International Council for Local Environmental Initiatives (ICLEI) is the international environmental agency for local governments. ICLEI's mission is to

"build and serve a worldwide movement of local governments to achieve tangible improvements in global environmental and sustainable development conditions through cumulative local actions."

http://www.rca-info.org/
The mission of the Resource Conservation Alliance (RCA) is to protect natural forests and other ecological systems through market- and commodity-based conservation strategies. These strategies include reduced consumption and increased recycling, redesign, and resource diversification. RCA encourages consumers to conserve forests by reducing their consumption of paper and building products overall and by replacing virgin wood products with products made from recycled fibers, straw, kenaf, hemp, etc.

http://www.epa.gov/superfund/action/community/index.htm
The "Superfund Community Involvement Page" of the EPA's Superfund Program, this site is for individuals or community groups who want to help clean up Superfund sites and/or learn more about them. This page provides links to community activities and programs, such as community services, grants, hazardous sites in your community, technical assistance, job training, and other resources.

http://www.epa.gov/projectxl/file2.htm
Project XL, which stands for "eXcellence and Leadership," is a national pilot program that allows state and local governments, businesses, and federal facilities to develop with EPA innovative strategies to test better or more cost-effective ways of achieving environmental and public health protection.

http://www.nrcs.usda.gov/
The Natural Resources Conservation Service works in partnership with the American people to conserve and sustain natural resources on private lands.

http://www.un.org/esa/sustdev/
This is the site for the UN's Commission on Sustainable Development (CSD). Its goal is to ensure that sustainable development issues are made public at world meetings. It also keeps updated information on sustainable development resources and conferences around the world.

5 Demographic Changes in the United States

The Browning and Graying of Society

The United States of 2050 will differ considerably from the United States of today. Its population will be older; it will be ethnically more diverse.

—Leon F. Bouvier and Lindsay Grant

Two population shifts are transforming U.S. society—one with external sources and the other internal. The first is the "new immigration." The racial landscape and rate of population growth are greatly affected as approximately 1 million immigrants annually, mostly Latino and Asian, set up permanent residence in the United States. The second population change is internal—the age of the population has risen rapidly during the twentieth century. In 15 years or so this change will become even more dramatic as the baby boomers reach age 65. Both of these demographic transitions have profound implications for social problems, creating some and exacerbating others. The facts, myths, and consequences of these two demographic changes are the subjects of this chapter. We begin, though, with a brief demographic overview of the United States.

PROFILE OF THE U.S. POPULATION

As of April 1, 2000, the population of the United States was 281,421,906, the third highest in the world (behind China and India, each over 1 billion), and above Indonesia (214 million) and Brazil (170 million). Unlike other developed nations, the United States continues to increase (a rate of 1.0 percent a year) primarily because of the large influx of immigrants. The United Nations population office estimates that the United States will have a population of 357 million by 2050 (Hampson, 2001). Some additional facts:

- Life expectancy for men born in 1997 is 74 years, compared to 79 years for women born in that year.
- Over three-quarters of Americans live in cities. Nine cities exceed 1 million (New York, Los Angeles, Chicago, Philadelphia, Houston, San Diego, Phoenix, San Antonio, and Dallas).
- The total fertility rate (the number of children a woman bears in her child-bearing years) is 2.075, below the replacement rate of 2.1 children. This rate varies by race/ethnicity: Whites (1.85), Asian Americans (1.90), African Americans (2.21), Puerto Ricans (2.38), and Mexican Americans (3.18) (Wattenberg, 2001).
- The baby boom generation, roughly 76 million Americans born from 1946 to 1964, is the largest generation in U.S. history (at the crest of the boom, the total fertility rate was 3.8 children per woman). In 2000 they were 36 to 54 years old and, as they have done from the beginning, they are having an enormous impact on U.S. society.
- One in five householders is aged 65 or older.
- Twelve percent of Americans live in California. Slightly less than 50 percent of Californians are White. Nonwhites in Texas are projected to surpass Whites in that state by 2004.
- The number of Latinos in the United States is greater than the population of Canada.
- Almost one in three Americans is nonwhite, compared to one in five in 1980.

NEW IMMIGRATION AND THE CHANGING RACIAL LANDSCAPE

There is a societal upheaval that is shaking up society: massive immigration. This change is occurring in numbers (see Figure 5.1) and in diversity. *Newsweek's* special issue anticipating the new millennium describes it this way:

> Immigration's vital to understanding the United States today. Americans now aged around 50 built their suburban dreams in places like the San Fernando Valley, the heartland of support for California's Proposition 187 [the successful 1994 vote initiative that opposed education, welfare, and health services for illegal immigrants]. The world of their youth was one in which immigration was rare. . . . Now the Valley's 40 percent Latino and Asian . . . and it isn't just southern California that's been changed. . . . Just like their predecessors a century ago, today's immigrants will struggle with the twin urges to assimilate and to remember their roots. Just like their forebears, they will be accused of Balkanizing the country and stealing jobs from "real" Americans. (Elliott, 1994/1995:131)

This demographic force—the new immigration—is challenging the cultural hegemony of the White European tradition; creating incredible diversity in race, ethnicity, language, and culture; rapidly changing the racial landscape; and leading, often, to division and hostility.

Historically, immigration has been a major source of population growth and ethnic diversity in the United States. Immigration waves from northern and southern Europe, especially from 1850 to 1920, brought many millions of people, mostly Europeans, to America. In the 1920s, the United States placed limits on the number of immigrants it would accept, the operating principle being that the new immigrants should resemble the old ones. The "national origins" rules were designed to limit severely the immigration of Eastern Europeans and to deny the entry of Asians.

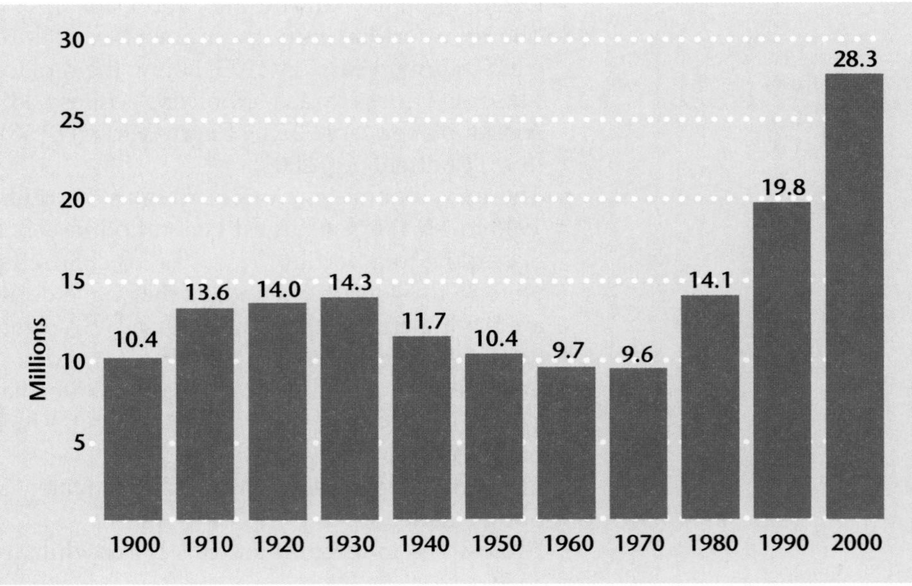

FIGURE 5.1

Foreign-Born Population: 1900 to 2000 (millions)

Sources: U.S. Bureau of the Census. 1993. *We the Americans . . . Foreign Born.* (September):2; G. C. Armas. 2000. "Foreign-Born Population in U.S. Passes 28.3," Associated Press (January 3).

The Immigration Act amendments of 1965 abandoned the quota system that had preserved the European character of the United States for nearly half a century. The new law encouraged a new wave of immigrants, only this time the migrants arrived not from northern Europe but from the Third World, especially Asia and Latin America. Put another way, 100 years ago Europeans were 90 percent of immigrants to the United States; now 90 percent of immigrants are from non-European countries. The result, obviously, is a dramatic alteration of the ethnic composition of the U.S. population (see Figure 5.2). And the size of the contemporary immigrant wave has resulted in a visible and significant number of U.S. residents who are foreign born (28.3 million people or 10.4 percent of the total population in 2000, up from 8 percent in 1990) (Armas, 2000a).

About 1 million immigrants enter the United States legally each year [the following data are from Martin and Midgley (1999); and Population Reference Bureau (1999)]. Another estimated 300,000 unauthorized aliens enter and stay (an estimated 1.5 million to 2.5 million people enter the United States illegally each year, but most return to their native countries either voluntarily or by force if caught by the Immigration and Naturalization Service) for a net gain of about 1.2 million annually. Although the number who enter clandestinely is impossible to determine, it is estimated that somewhere between 6 million and 11 million undocumented aliens live in the United States. Roughly 60 percent of these undocumented immigrants are Latino (and two-thirds of these are Mexicans).

The settlement patterns of this new migration differ from previous flows into the United States. Whereas previous immigrants settled primarily in the industrial states of the Northeast and Middle Atlantic region, or in the farming areas of the Midwest, recent immigrants have tended to locate on the two coasts and in the Southwest. Asians have tended to settle on the West Coast; Mexicans tend to settle in the Southwest, with other Latinos scattered (e.g., Cubans in Florida and Puerto Ricans in New York).

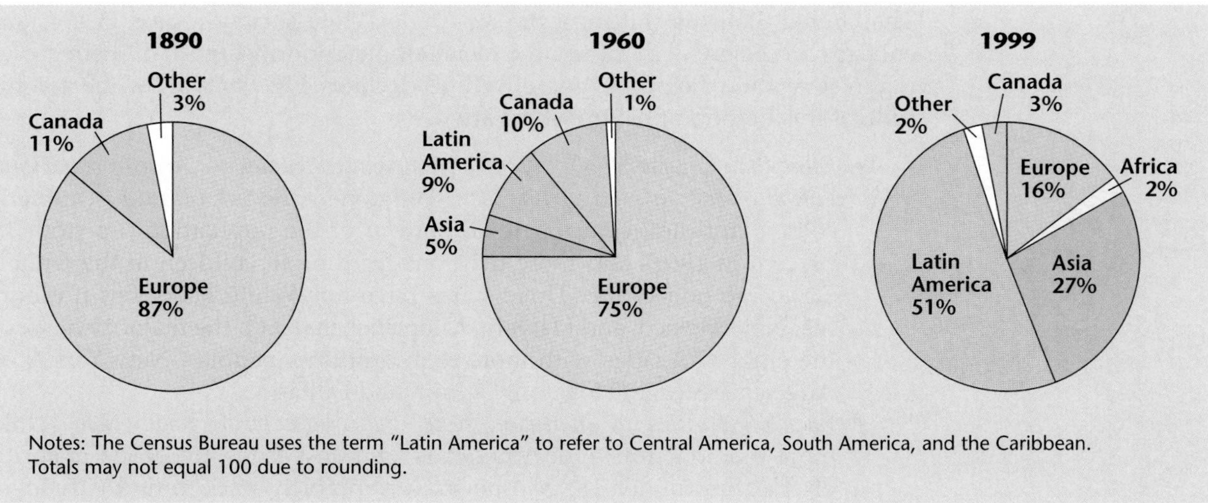

Notes: The Census Bureau uses the term "Latin America" to refer to Central America, South America, and the Caribbean. Totals may not equal 100 due to rounding.

FIGURE 5.2

Composition of the U.S. Foreign-Born Population, by Regions or Country of Birth

Source: Foreign-Born Population. June 30, 2001. Online. Available: http://ameristat.org.

California is a harbinger of the demographic future of the United States. As recently as 1970 California was 80 percent White, but since then it has been uniquely affected by immigration. The result is that Whites now are a numerical minority (47 percent in 2000, with 32 percent being Latino, 11 percent Asian, and 7 percent African American) (Werner, 2001), and by 2025 only one-third of California's population will be White (Chideya, 1999). Less than 38 percent of California's public school students are White (Verdin, 2000). Los Angeles has the largest population of Koreans outside of Korea, the biggest concentration of Iranians in the Western world, and a huge Mexican population. The diverse population of southern California speaks 88 languages and dialects. Greater Los Angeles has more than 50 foreign-language newspapers and television shows that broadcast in Spanish, Mandarin, Armenian, Japanese, Korean, and Vietnamese (Fletcher, 1998). For all this diversity, though, California, especially southern California, is becoming more and more Latino. California holds nearly half of the U.S. Latino population and well over half of the Mexican-origin population. Latinos are expected to surpass Whites in total California population by 2025 and become an absolute majority by 2040 (Purdum, 2000).

Latinos are also concentrated and growing rapidly in Arizona and Texas. Historian David Kennedy argues that there is no precedent in U.S. history for one immigrant group to have the size and concentration that the Mexican immigrant group has in the Southwest today:

> If we seek historical guidance, the closest example we have in hand is the diagonally opposite corner of the North American continent, in Quebec. The possibility looms that in the next generation or so we will see a kind of Chicano Quebec take shape in the American Southwest, as a group emerges with strong cultural cohesiveness and sufficient economic and political strength to insist on changes in the overall society's ways of organizing itself and conducting its affairs. (Kennedy, 1996:68)

Immigration and Increasing Diversity

The United States is shifting from an Anglo-White society rooted in Western culture to a society with three large racial-ethnic minorities, each of them growing in size while the proportion of Whites declines. Five facts show the magnitude of this demographic transformation.

- *More than one-fourth of the people in the United States are African American, Latino, Asian, or Native American.* The non-White population is numerically significant, comprising 28 percent of the population (up from 15 percent in 1960), and more than one-third of all children in the United States are non-White. Three states have non-White majorities (California, New Mexico, and Hawaii). Minorities make up the majority in six of the eight U.S. cities with more than a million people—New York, Los Angeles, Chicago, Houston, Detroit, and Dallas.
- *Racial minorities are increasing faster than the majority population.* While more than one-fourth of Americans are non-Whites, by 2030 a majority of children (under 18) will be from a minority background (Chideya, 1999:37), and between 2050 and 2060 minorities will surpass in size the White population (Riche, 2000). (See Figure 5.3.)
- *African Americans have lost their position as the most numerous racial minority.* In 1990, for the first time, African Americans were less than half of all

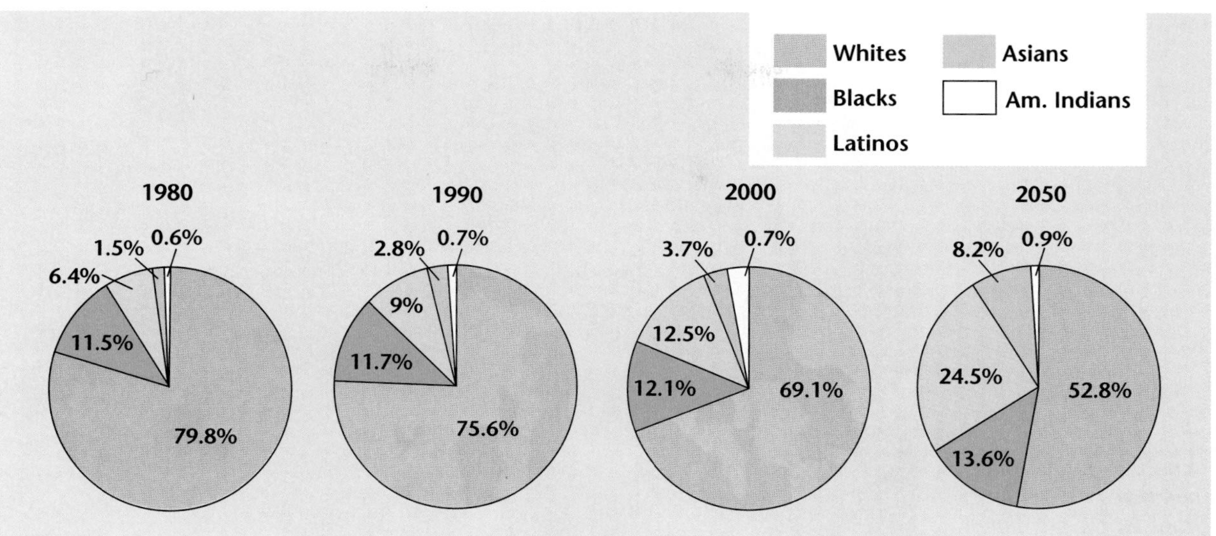

FIGURE 5.3

U.S. Population by Race, 1980, 1990, 2000, and Projected 2050

Source: U.S. Bureau of the Census. 1996. *Current Population Reports,* Series P25-1130. Washington, DC: U.S. Government Printing Office.

minorities. By 2000 Latinos outnumbered Blacks 35.3 million to 34.6 million in the official census (however, if those who identified themselves as Black and some other racial category are included in the Black category, the total is 36.4 million). By 2050 Latinos are estimated to comprise about one-fourth of the U.S. population with African Americans at about 14 percent.

- *Immigration now accounts for a large share of the nation's population growth.* Today slightly more than one in ten (10.4 percent) current U.S. residents are foreign born. Since 1970 the number of foreign-born people has almost tripled from 9.6 million to 28.3 million. This growth far outpaces the growth of the native-born population. Immigration accounts for over a third of the current population growth directly and adds more indirectly as first- and second-generation Americans have more children on average than the rest of the population (Chideya, 1999).
- *New patterns of immigration are changing the racial composition of society.* Among the expanded population of first-generation immigrants, the Asian born now outnumber the European born and those from Latin America, especially Mexicans, outnumber both. This contrasts sharply with what occurred as recently as the 1950s, when two-thirds of legal immigrants were from Europe and Canada.

These trends signal a transformation from a White majority to a multiracial/multicultural society:

> Around the year 2050, Whites will become a "minority." This is unchartered territory in this country, and this demographic change will affect everything. Alliances between the races are bound to shift. Political and social power will be reapportioned. Our neighborhoods, our schools and workplaces, even racial categories themselves will be altered. (Chideya, 1999:35)

In 2000 Latinos outnumbered African Americans for the first time. By 2050 Latinos will make up about one-fourth of the U.S. population.

The pace of these changes is quickening. During the 1990s the Latino population increased by 53 percent (from 22.4 million to 35.3 million in 2000) (Parker, 2001), the Asian population grew by 58 percent, the African American population by 12 percent, and the White population by only 2 percent.

Consequences of the New Immigration

The new immigration raises a number of questions. We consider three: (1) Do immigrants take jobs away from Americans? (2) Are immigrants a drain on society's resources? (3) Will the increasing proportion of non-Whites, fueled by immigration, lead to a blurring of racial lines or a heightening of tensions among the races/ethnic groups? (Much of the following is taken from a major report by the National Academy of Sciences/National Research Council, reported by Cassidy, 1997.)

Do Immigrants Take Jobs from U.S. Citizens? Immigrants do not have negative effects on the wages of most Americans, but they do for the low-wage/poorly skilled segment of workers. The wages of the lowest 15 percent of the workforce (typically, those with less than a high school degree) receive about 5 percent less in their paychecks because of competition from a large number of immigrants who are relatively uneducated, unskilled, and eager to work. This problem will increase in the future as the federal and state governments no longer provide welfare benefits to legal immigrants, and most non-immigrant welfare recipients are required to leave welfare and find work, adding several million workers to compete for relatively few jobs at the low end of the occupational scale.

On the positive side, immigrants are more likely than the rest of the population to be self-employed and start their own businesses, which in turn creates jobs and adds strength to local economies. For example, 5 years after the 1992

Los Angeles riots there was an unexpected rebirth in some of the riot-torn areas, led largely by Asian and Latino entrepreneurs, many of whom were first-generation immigrants. These people invested locally and hired locals who spent much of the wages locally. Similar patterns of a migrant-based economy led by entrepreneurs from Jamaica, Mexico, Korea, Taiwan, and India have led to a resurgence in parts of Brooklyn and Queens in New York City and in Houston (Kotkin, 1997).

Are Immigrants a Drain on Society's Resources? There are two reasons why immigrants require more resources from the state than nonimmigrant families. First, they have relatively large families, and these children go to public schools. Second, they pay less in taxes because they tend to earn low wages and have relatively little discretionary income.

Immigration policies are federal policies, yet the cost of providing services to immigrants (education, health care) is typically the responsibility of the individual states. This places an unfair burden on states such as California, New York, Texas, and Florida, which have the largest immigrant populations. In California, for example, households headed by U.S.-born persons paid, on average, $2,700 more in federal taxes than they received in federal benefits in 1996. In contrast, immigrant households received $2,700 more in federal benefits than they paid in federal taxes. "This deficit accrued largely because immigrant households had below-average incomes and thus paid lower taxes than the average household, but they had more children attending public schools than households headed by U.S.-born Californians" (Martin and Midgley, 1999:31). The deficit is less in states with few immigrants. Using the entire U.S. population, households headed by a U.S.-born person paid an extra $200 each in 1996 to cover the gap between taxes paid and services used by immigrant-headed households (Martin and Midgley, 1999:31).

During the 1990s the Asian population in the U.S. grew by 58 percent.

In the long run, however, immigrants are a good investment for society. The Academy of Sciences study (Cassidy, 1997) found that by the time a typical immigrant with a family dies, that immigrant and his or her children will have paid $80,000 more in taxes than they received in government benefits. The evidence is that immigrants are a fiscal burden for two decades or so, mainly because of educational costs. After that the society benefits monetarily.

Research also shows that legal and illegal immigration add $1 billion to $10 billion per year to the U.S. gross domestic product, "largely because immigration holds down wages for some jobs, and thus prices, and increases the efficiency of the economy" (Martin and Midgley, 1999:24).

There is also a global dimension to the economic benefits derived from immigrants. Most undocumented immigrants (i.e., those who entered the country illegally) are young, male, and Mexican. They leave their families in Mexico and work for months at a time as manual laborers in the United States. Typically, they send some of their earnings back to their families in Mexico—an aggregate of $22 million a day. "As a source of foreign capital [to Mexico], migrant remittances trail only oil, tourism, and illegal drugs. They provide basic support for nearly 1.2 million Mexican households, about 5 percent of the total, according to Mexico's National Population Council" (E. B. Smith, 2001:9A).

Will the Increasing Proportion of Non-Whites Fueled by Immigration Lead to a Blurring of Racial Lines or a Heightening of Tensions among the Races/Ethnic Groups? The latest wave of immigration has taken place in a historical context that includes the restructuring of the U.S. economy (see Chapter 12) and an increasingly conservative political climate. New immigrants have always been seen as a threat to those already in place. The typical belief is that immigrants, because they will work for lower wages, drive down wages and take jobs away from those already settled here. These fears increase during economic hard times, when businesses downsize, pay lower wages, and replace workers with technology as they adapt to the economic transformation. The hostility toward immigrants is also the result of the common belief that the new immigrants increase taxes because they require services (education, health care, and welfare) that cost much more than the taxes they produce.

Previous immigration waves were White, coming mostly from Ireland, England, Germany, Italy, and Eastern Europe. Today's immigrants, in sharp contrast, are coming from Latin America and Asia. They are non-White and have distinctly non-European cultures. When these racial and ethnic differences are added to economic fears, the mix is very volatile.

The situation is worsened further by where the new immigrants locate. Typically, they move where immigrants like themselves are already established. For example, 20 percent of the 90,000 Hmong in the United States live in Minnesota, mostly around Minneapolis-St. Paul. One in twelve Asian Indians lives in Illinois, primarily in the Chicago area. Approximately 40 percent of all Asian Americans live in California. This tendency of migrants to cluster geographically by race/ethnicity provides them with a network of friends and relatives who provide them with support. This pattern of clustering in certain areas also tends to increase the fear of nonimmigrants toward them. They fear that wages will be depressed and taxes will be greater because their new neighbors are relatively poor, tend to have children with special needs in school, and likely do not have health insurance.

A second tendency is for new immigrants to locate where other poor people live for the obvious advantage of cheaper housing. A problem often arises when poor Whites live side by side with one or more racial minorities. Despite their common condition, tensions in such a situation are heightened as groups disadvantaged by society often fight each other for relative advantage. The tensions between African Americans and Asian immigrants were evidenced, for example, during the South Los Angeles riots in 1992, when roughly 2,000 Korean-owned business were looted or damaged by fire.

The result of these factors is commonly an anti-immigrant backlash. Opinion polls taken over the past 50 years report consistently that Americans want to reduce immigration. Typically, these polls report that Americans believe that immigration in the past was a good thing for the country but that it no longer is.

The states with the most immigrants have the highest levels of anti-immigrant feeling. Several states have filed suit against the federal government seeking reimbursement for the services provided to immigrants. Some twenty-two states have made English the official state language. The voters in California have passed two propositions recently that indicate anti-immigrant feelings. In 1994 they denied public welfare such as nonemergency medical care, prenatal clinics, and public schools to undocumented immigrants. Californians in 1998 also passed a proposition eliminating bilingual education in public schools.

If present immigration patterns continue, by 2050 some one-third of the U.S. population will be post-1970 immigrants and their descendants. As noted earlier, by then neither Whites nor non-Whites will be the numerical majority. Under these circumstances of racial diversity, will the social meaning of ethnic and racial lines become increasingly blurred or more starkly defined? Will the people be pulling together or pulling apart? Will the gulf between affluent Whites and the disproportionately poor non-Whites be narrowed or widened? Will there be a de facto segregation as Whites who once lived and worked

Ed Stein. Reprinted courtesy of Rocky Mountain News.

together with non-Whites move to White enclaves? Demographer William Frey has noted a "White flight" from high-immigration areas, a trend he fears may lead to the Balkanization of America (cited in Cassidy, 1997:43). Is this our future? (For one scenario for the future, see the panel titled "Looking toward the Future.")

Immigration and Agency

Immigration can be forced (e.g., the slave trade) or freely chosen. Immigration in this latter sense is clearly an act of **human agency** (rather than passively accepting structural constraints, people cope with, adapt to, and change their social situations to meet their needs). Most people in developing countries do not move. Others move, breaking with their extended family and leaving neighborhood and community ties, mostly to improve their economic situations or to flee repression.

Typically, new immigrants face hostility from their hosts, who, as we have seen, fear them as competitors or hate them because they are "different." Moreover, they face language barriers as they seek jobs. Often, most especially for undocumented immigrants, their initial jobs are demeaning, poorly paid, and without benefits. How do they adapt to these often very difficult circumstances? Most commonly, immigrants move to a destination area where there is already a network of friends and relatives. These networks connect new immigrants with housing (often doubling up in very crowded, but inexpensive, conditions), jobs, and an informal welfare system (health care, pooling resources in difficult times). These mutual aid efforts by immigrant communities have been used by immigrant networks throughout U.S. history, whether by Swedish settlers in Minnesota, Mennonite settlers in Kansas, Irish settlers in Boston, or Mexican or Vietnamese settlers now (Martin and Midgley, 1999).

To overcome low wages, all able family members may work in the family enterprise or at different jobs by combining family resources. To overcome various manifestations of hostility by others, the immigrant community may become closer (the pejorative word is "clannish"), having as little interaction with outsiders as possible. Some may become involved in gangs for protection. Still others may move to assimilate as quickly as possible.

Effects of Immigration on Immigrants: Ethnic Identity or Assimilation?

Martin and Midgley sum up the universal dilemma for immigrants:

> There is always a tension between the newcomers' desires to keep alive the culture and language of the community they left behind, and their need and wish to adapt to new surroundings and a different society. (Martin and Midgley, 1999:35–36)

A principal indicator of assimilation is language. In the 1990 census, about 80 percent of newcomers spoke a language other than English at home, compared with about 8 percent of the native-born population. For earlier immigrants to the United States the shift to English usage took three generations—from almost exclusive use by newcomers of their traditional language, to their children being bilingual, and their children's children being monolingual English speakers (Martin and Midgley, 1999).

LOOKING TOWARD THE FUTURE

LOS ANGELES TODAY AS A HARBINGER OF FUTURE RACE RELATIONS

In 1960 four out of five people in [Los Angeles County] were white. But a wave of immigration has transformed the jurisdiction into one where no ethnic or racial group holds the majority. The county's population of 9.5 million is now 41 percent Hispanic, 37 percent white, 11 percent Asian and 10 percent black. The Latino and Asian populations each have more than doubled in the past 20 years, dramatically altering the dynamics of race here.

Just over a decade ago, the broad swath of the county popularly known as South Central was synonymous with black Los Angeles. But now middle-class African Americans are leaving, often dispersing to communities that once were all white. Asian Americans, who once congregated in enclaves near downtown, are moving into suburban communities that ring L. A. Meanwhile, many non-Hispanic whites are often relocating to even more distant suburbs or leaving California altogether.

What is happening here represents the leading edge of racial and ethnic changes affecting communities across America. Demographers predict that by the middle of the next century the nation as a whole will look much like Los Angeles does now: a rich tapestry of people whose sheer diversity makes once-familiar notions of racial interaction obsolete.

"Politicians like to say that diversity is our greatest strength," says Ron Wakabayashi, executive director of the Los Angeles County Commission on Human Relations. "That is b.s. Diversity simply is. The core question is how do we extract its assets while minimizing its liabilities?"

To be sure, the new immigrants have renewed old neighborhoods, created new businesses and enriched the culture of Los Angeles. But the exploding diversity also has changed the nature of racial conflict and drawn new groups into battles that once were waged almost exclusively between blacks and whites. Here, black and Latino civil servants square off over public jobs. Black activists and Asian store owners fight over control of local businesses. And Latino and Asian gangs battle for control of their turf.

This new reality fuels the racial isolation evident in many walks of life here. Researchers have found deep racial divisions in the Los Angeles job market—partly the result of discrimination but reinforced because people typically find jobs through personal connections that most often do not cross racial or ethnic lines. Many of the furniture factories in South Central have only Latino workers. The toy factories near downtown employ mainly Chinese. Many of the small grocery stores are owned and run by Koreans. And African Americans disproportionately work in government jobs, where they are desperately trying to hold their place in the face of fierce competition from Latinos who want in. . . .

Rather than prompting people to come together, the more common reality of the new diversity is people living separate lives in often vibrant but segregated communities. . . . [But] when people from diverse backgrounds find themselves thrust together in the same neighborhoods, the same jobs or the same schools, the result can often be conflict.

Source: Michael A. Fletcher. 1998. "All Fighting for a Piece of the Dream: Immigration Has Transformed the Racial Dynamic of South Central Los Angeles." *Washington Post National Weekly Edition* (May 18):8–9.

If the past is a guide, the new immigrants will assimilate. "Our society exerts tremendous pressure to conform, and cultural separatism rarely survives more than a generation" (Cole, 1994:412). But conditions now are different.

An argument countering the assumption that the new immigrants will assimilate as did previous generations of immigrants is that the new immigrants are racial/ethnics, not Whites. As such, they face individual and institutional racism that excludes them from full participation, just as it has excluded African Americans and Native Americans (O'Hare, 1993:2). The current political mood is to eliminate affirmative action (as did California with Proposition

209, which took effect in 1997), a policy aimed at leveling the playing field so that minorities would have a fair chance to succeed. Should these efforts succeed, then the new immigrants will find it more difficult than their predecessors did to assimilate, should they wish to do so.

Another factor facing this generation of immigrants is that they enter the United States during a critical economic transformation, in which the middle class is shrinking and the working class faces difficult economic hurdles. A possible result is that the new immigrants, different in physical characteristics, language, and culture, will be used as scapegoats for the difficulties that so many face. Moreover, their opportunities for advancement will be limited by the new economic realities. Sociologist Herbert Gans (1990) argues, for example, that the second generation of post-1965 immigrants likely will experience downward mobility compared to their parents because of the changing opportunity structure in the U.S. economy.

The issue of immigrant adaptation to the host society is complex, depending on a number of variables. Zhou (1997) describes a number of these critical variables, including the immigrant generation (i.e., first or second), their level in the ethnic hierarchy at the point of arrival, what stratum of U.S. society absorbs them, the degree to which they are part of a family network, and the like.

Immigrants who move to the United States permanently have four options regarding assimilation. Many try to blend into the United States as quickly as possible. Others resist the new ways, by either developing an adversarial stance toward the dominant society or resisting acculturation by focusing more intensely on the social capital (i.e., social networks) created through ethnic ties (Portes and Zhou, 1993). The fourth alternative is to move toward a bicultural pattern (Buriel and De Ment, 1997). That is, immigrants adopt some patterns similar to those found in the host society and retain some from their heritage. While this concept of a bicultural pattern appears to focus on culture, the retention or abandonment of the ethnic ways depends on structural variables (Kibria, 1997:207). These variables include the socioeconomic resources of the ethnic community, the extent of continued immigration from the sending society, the linkages between the ethnic community and the sending society, and the obstacles to obtaining equal opportunity in the new society.

In sum, the new immigration, occurring at a time of economic uncertainty and reduced governmental services, is having three pronounced effects that will accelerate in the foreseeable future: (1) an increased bifurcation between the haves and the have-nots, (2) increased racial diversity, and (3) a heightened tension among the races.

THE AGING SOCIETY

During the twentieth century the population of the United States experienced a pronounced change—it became older and is on the verge of becoming much older. In 1900 about one in twenty-five residents of the United States was 65 years and older. By 1950 it was about one in twelve. In 2000, one in eight was 65 and older and by 2030 it will likely be around one in five, with more people over 65 than under age 18. In effect, by 2030, when most of today's college students will be around 50, there will be more grandparents than grandchildren. "The Senior Boom is coming, and it will transform our homes, our schools, our politics, our lives and our deaths. And not just for older people. For everybody"

(Peyser, 1999:50). This trend will continue until the middle of the next century, with dramatic effects on public policies and social problems. This section is divided into two parts: (1) a demographic (**demography** is the study of population) description of the aged category now and in the future and (2) the implications of an aging society for social problems.

Demographic Trend

Until the twentieth century high **fertility** (birthrate) and high **mortality** (death rate) kept the United States a youthful nation. During this century, however, the birthrate has fallen (except for the post-World War II period, which was an anomaly), resulting in fewer children as a proportion of the total population. Most important, greater longevity because of advances in medical technology (everything from beta blockers for reducing hypertension to organ transplants) has increased the life expectancy of Americans. The average life expectancy in 1900 was 49.0 years, and in 2000 it was 77 (74 for men and 79 for women). In 1900, for example, 4.1 percent of the U.S. population was age 65 and older (we will use this customary but arbitrary age to divide the old from the nonold); by 1950 this had almost doubled to 8.1 percent; and by 2000 the elderly constituted 13 percent of the population. Put another way, in 100 years the elderly segment of the population had gone from one out of twenty Americans to one out of eight Americans. In terms of raw numbers, there were 3.1 million Americans age 65 and older in 1900 and 35 million in 2000—more than a tenfold increase. In effect, then, this age category of 65 and older constitutes the fastest growing segment of the U.S. population, increasing twice as fast as the population as a whole.

But this is only half the story. The Census Bureau estimates (using middle assumptions concerning fertility, mortality, and immigration) that the elderly population will be 20.1 percent of the population (one out of five) by 2030. So, essentially in 130 years people age 65 and older will have shifted from one out of twenty Americans to one out of five. The surge in the number of elderly during the next few decades is the consequence of three demographic forces: a continued low fertility rate, ever-greater life expectancy rates, and the **baby boom generation** (the 75 million born from 1946 to 1964, representing 70 percent more people than were born during the preceding two decades) reaching old age, beginning in 2011 and ending in 2030. [See Figure 5.4, p. 126, showing the population pyramids for 1900 (characteristic of a young population), 1980, 2000, and 2020. The latter three show the changing age structure as the baby boom group moves toward old age.]

Hidden within these statistics is another important fact about the old—they are getting older: The relatively vigorous "young old" (ages 65 to 74) will continue to make up the majority of older Americans until about 2030. After that time, people age 75 or older (the "old-old") will account for more than half of all elderly. By the middle of the twenty-first century, most of the projected growth of older Americans will occur because of increases in the population age 85 and older. In 1950, there were 600,000 in this category of 85 and older compared to 4,300,000 in 2000, a sevenfold increase. In 2030 there will be 8,500,000 age 85 and over (see Figure 5.5, p. 127). In 2000 some 72,000 Americans were at least 100 years old. Because of the continued advances in medicine and nutrition, it is expected that the number of centenarians will increase to about 1 million by the middle of the twenty-first century.

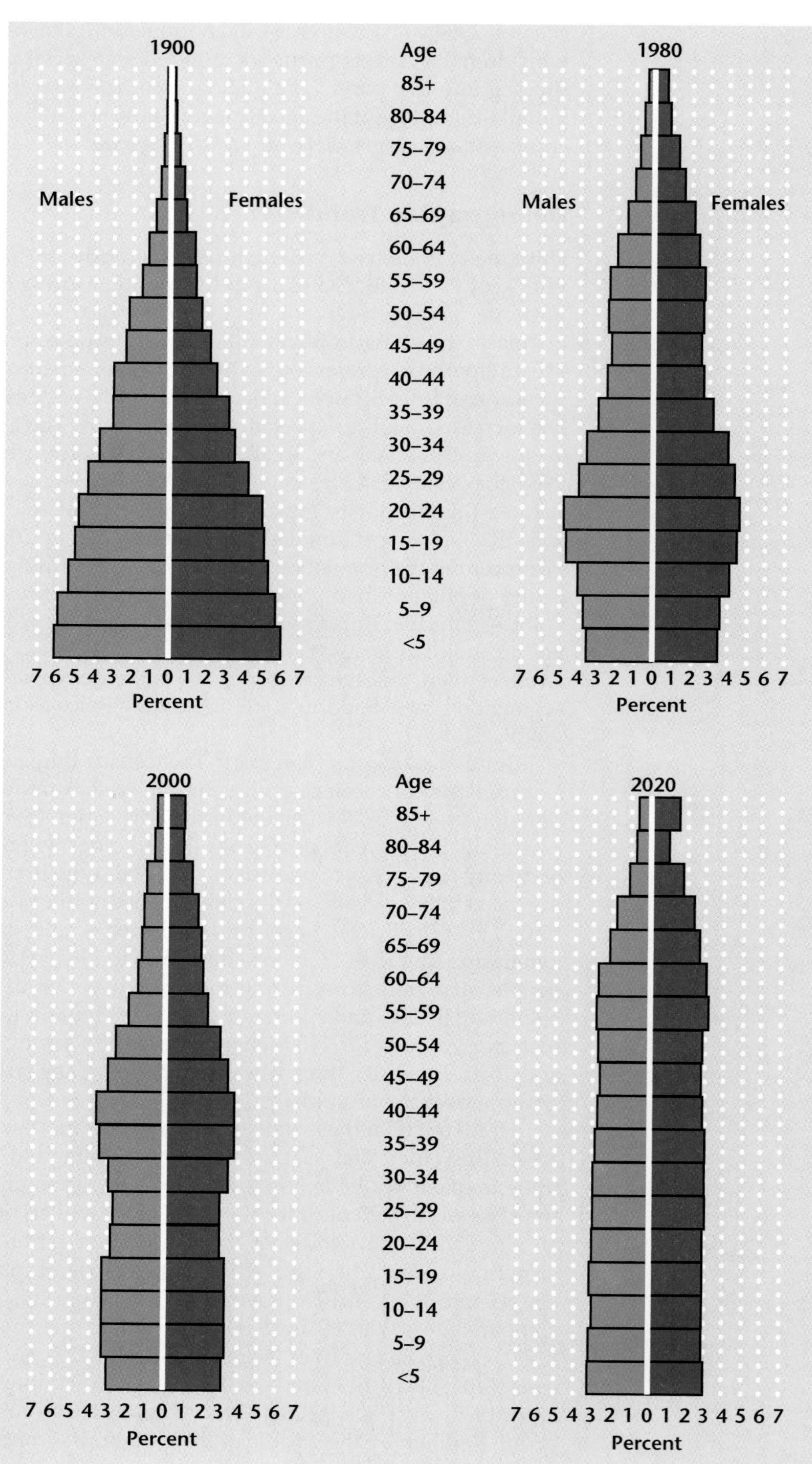

FIGURE 5.4

U.S. Population by Age and Sex, 1900, 1980, 2000, and Projections for 2020

Source: Martha Farnsworth Riche. 2000. "America's Diversity and Growth: Signposts for the 21st Century." *Population Bulletin* 54 (June):20–21.

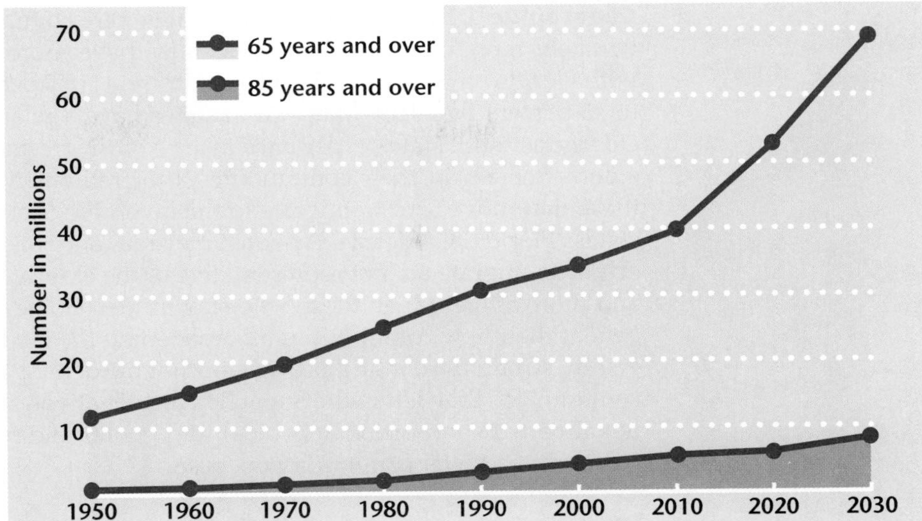

FIGURE 5.5

Population 65 Years of Age and Over: United States, 1950–2030

Source: U.S. Department of Health and Human Services. 1999. *Health, United States, 1999*. Hyattsville, MD: National Center for Health Statistics, p. 23.

Demographic Portrait of the Current Elderly Population

- **Sex Ratio.** In 2000 the elderly constituted 13 percent of the population (35 million). Older women outnumber older men by a ratio of 3 to 2. As age increases, the disparity becomes greater—for those age 85 and older, there are about five women to every two men.

  A combination of biological advantages for women and social reasons explains this difference. The secondary status of women in U.S. society has provided them with extra longevity. Traditional gender roles have demanded that men be engaged in the more stressful, demanding, and dangerous occupations. It will be interesting to note whether there are any effects on female longevity as women receive a more equal share of all types of jobs. Meanwhile, though, the current situation creates problems for the majority of elderly women, who are often widows and have low incomes. Elderly women are more likely than men to live alone as widows. This is the result of two factors: the greater longevity of women and the social norm for men to marry younger women. Thus, to the extent that isolation is a problem of the aged, it is overwhelmingly a problem for the female elderly.

- **Racial Composition.** Because racial minorities have a lower life expectancy than do Whites (African Americans, e.g., live about 6 years less), they form a smaller proportion of the elderly category than of other age groups. The trend is for the elderly population to become more racially diverse (by 2050 it is expected that non-Whites will be one-third of the elderly population, with Latinos being the largest minority after 2020).

- **Longevity.** At the founding of the United States, life expectancy at birth was about 35 years. By 1900, life expectancy had increased to 47 years. Now it is about 77 years. This average masks some differences: (1) women live longer than men (their life expectancy is 79, compared to 74 for men), and (2) there are racial gaps that show little sign of closing. For instance, the life expectancy for White females is 80 and for White males it is 73 years; for Black females it is 74 and for Black males it is 65.

- **Geographic Distribution.** Some states and communities have disproportionately more older residents. Six states have more than 15 percent elderly, with Florida having the highest concentration (18.5 percent and expected to rise to 25 percent by 2010). Many rural states have a relatively high proportion of elderly, as these states experience a large outmigration of young people. Most elderly remain in their communities after retirement ("aging in place"), but those that move tend to migrate to the favorable climate found in the Sun Belt states (Florida, California, Arizona, Nevada, and Texas) (Frey, 1999). The elderly who migrate are not representative of the elderly. They tend to be younger and more affluent than those who stay in their home communities. Thus, they benefit their new communities by broadening the tax base through home ownership, strong purchasing power, and not burdening the local job market. The communities they left in the Snow Belt are negatively affected. The elderly who remain are disproportionately older and poorer and require more public assistance from a lower community tax base.

- **Wealth, Income, and Cumulative Advantage or Disadvantage.** In general, recent retirees have personal resources—education, income, and assets—unknown to previous cohorts. Many have benefited from a sharp rise in the stock market during the 1990s and extraordinary gains in real estate markets over the last three decades, that ultimately they will pass on to their fortunate heirs. Yet, many elderly missed out on the boom. They did not own a home or have enough assets to invest. In 1999, for example, the median net worth for older White families was $181,000, while it was less than $13,000 for older African American families (Federal Interagency Forum on Aging-Related Statistics, reported in Newman, 2000).

  Home equity is most significant in having a reasonable net worth. In this regard, those who are currently in the old category had an advantage because their home purchases in the 1950s and 1960s were much cheaper in interest and mortgage payments relative to wages than were homes bought in the 1970s, 1980s, and 1990s. Subsequent generations, as they become old, will be much less likely to own their homes and thus will have substantially lower net worth than those who are old now.

  The elderly who are members of a racial or ethnic minority are disproportionately poor. In 1997, for example, African American elderly were 2.9 times as likely and Latino were 2.7 times as likely to live in poverty as White elderly persons (U.S. Department of Health and Human Services, 1999:28). This relative lack of resources for racial minorities translates into a reduced likelihood, compared to Whites, of their receiving adequate health care and, when needed, living in nursing homes with full-time skilled nursing care under a physician's supervision.

  Elderly married couples tend to have greater net worth than elderly singles. Households maintained by unmarried elderly males have a greater net worth than households maintained by unmarried elderly women. Similarly, White married-couple households with a householder age 65 or older will likely have higher family incomes than racial minority married couples.

  Personal income is usually reduced by one-third to one-half after retirement. In 1999 the median income for White households was $44,400, compared to $30,700 for Latinos and $27,900 for African Americans. The important point is that those groups with advantage before becoming old maintain their economic advantage in old age.

Typically, we assume that economic inequality narrows after age 65, when benefit programs replace work as principal income sources. This, however, is not the case; the inequalities from income and privilege tend to be magnified among elderly people. People who are initially advantaged, for example, are more likely than their less fortunate counterparts to receive good educations and obtain good jobs with better health and pension benefits, which lead to higher savings and better postretirement benefit incomes. Crystal and Shea (1990) present data to support this contention:

- For every $1 the bottom 20 percent receive in Social Security income, the top 20 percent receive $1.72.
- For every $1 the bottom 20 percent receive in pension income, the top 20 percent receive almost $16.
- For every $1 the bottom 20 percent receive in dividend income, the top 20 percent receive almost $90.

Most noteworthy, the government is partly responsible for these skewed advantages to the affluent. The relatively affluent are encouraged by the government, because of tax incentives, to invest in retirement income programs such as IRAs (individual retirement accounts), Keogh plans, or other tax-deferred programs. Thus, the already advantaged are given preferential tax treatment, which amounts to tax subsidization, thereby increasing their economic advantage over the disadvantaged after age 65.

In 1999, 9.7 percent of people age 65 and older were poor. This proportion is relatively low (the overall poverty rate in 1999 was 11.8 percent) because Social Security benefits are indexed for inflation. This poverty rate, slightly below the poverty rate for the nation as a whole, is perceived typically as a success. However, 3.3 million elderly were poor, and another 30 percent of the elderly were in the "economically vulnerable" category—that is, they had incomes above the poverty line but below 150 percent of the official poverty rate.

The elderly spend about 20 percent of their income on health care, with the poor elderly spending about 35 percent of their incomes on health care (Findlay, 1998). Roughly half of the incomes of the poor elderly go for food. Thus, they are especially affected by inflation at the grocery store. The only recourse for the poor in inflationary times, when their incomes do not increase with spiraling costs, is either to eat less or to eat cheaper, less nutritious food.

The elderly poor spend about 20 percent of their incomes on energy for heat and electricity, both of which increase with inflation. Those on fixed incomes are likewise negatively affected by inflationary increases in the cost of rents, taxes, and health care. The last is a special burden for the old who are poor. Health costs for the elderly are almost four times those for people under age 65. The result is that the elderly poor tend to live in substandard housing, receive inadequate medical care, and have improper diets.

If the poor and the old are doubly cursed, then the elderly poor who are members of a racial or ethnic minority group experience a triple disadvantage. Individual and institutional sources of discrimination coalesce to make these people's lives especially miserable and problematic. Twenty-two percent of the Black elderly and 20 percent of the Latino elderly, for example, were poor in 1999, compared to only 8 percent of Whites age 65 and older. The higher probability of older African Americans being poor is a direct consequence of their relatively low status throughout life. With average incomes only about 60 percent those of Whites, they have little chance of building a nest egg to supplement their pension incomes. African Americans are also more likely than Whites to have worked at jobs that do not qualify for Social Security (prior to 1974, e.g., only 80 percent of elderly Blacks received some Social Security benefits, compared with 90 percent of older Whites). If they have worked at jobs qualifying for Social Security, minority members usually are eligible only for lower benefits because of their lower wages.

These related problems reflect the discrimination in the job market and unfair legislation. Clearly, equity in Social Security benefits will not occur until racial minorities and Whites experience similar work careers and compensation.

After a lifetime of lower earnings and receiving small or no pensions, elderly minorities must live in substandard housing. They are much more likely than elderly Whites to live in deteriorated housing with inadequate plumbing, heating, and sewage disposal. Similarly, the minority elderly suffer more health problems than do the majority elderly. For instance, among all minority elderly the prevalence of chronic disabilities is twice as high as among the White elderly.

PROBLEMS OF AN AGING SOCIETY

We focus on three problems inherent in our aging society: (1) inadequate income from pensions or Social Security, (2) the high cost of elderly health care, and (3) abuse of the elderly.

Social Security

Social Security is the only source of income for about half of retired people and a major source of income for 80 percent of the elderly in the United States. Since the introduction of Social Security in the 1930s, this program has been a significant aid to the elderly. Social Security has reduced poverty significantly among the elderly—from 35.2 percent in 1959 to 9.7 percent in 1999. "Without Social Security income, 54 percent of America's elderly would live in poverty" (Wellstone, 1998a:5). Social Security also provides life insurance benefits to the survivors in cases of the death of a breadwinner and disability payments when a wage earner is unable to work. Most fundamentally, Social Security expresses the belief in society taking responsibility for the welfare of all its citizens. In the words of economist Robert Kuttner:

> Social Security serves, and reinforces, a kind of collective solidarity rarely articulated explicitly in the ordinary idiom of American politics. But it has precisely expressed the modern liberal view of social entitlement—the collectivity taking responsibility for unearned misfortune, not by singling out (and thus stigmatizing) the certifiably needy, but within a universal system. This approach offers a logic that is both moral and political, both redistributive and inclusive. It cultivates a politics of social empathy and, in turn, an astonishing level of political support for a surprisingly social concept in a fiercely capitalistic society. (Kuttner, 1998a:30)

Despite its considerable strengths, the Social Security program has several serious problems that place a disproportionate burden on certain categories of the elderly and on some portions of the workers paying into the program.

An immediate problem is that not all workers are covered by Social Security. Some groups of workers are unable to participate because they work for states with alternative retirement programs. Other workers, however, are covered by neither Social Security nor other pension programs. Legislation has specifically exempted certain occupations (such as agricultural workers) from the Social Security program.

For workers who are eligible for Social Security, there are wide disparities in the benefits received. The amount of benefits depends on the length of time workers have paid into the Social Security program and the amount of wages on which they paid a Social Security tax. In other words, low-paid workers receive low benefits at retirement. Thirty percent of the elderly who depend almost exclusively on Social Security benefits are still below the poverty line despite these benefits. These elderly typically are people who have been relatively poor during their working years or are widows.

The Social Security system is also biased against women. Let us examine some of the specific provisions of Social Security benefits that disadvantage women.

- Social Security recognizes only paid work. The benefits for nonworking spouses (typically wives) are 50 percent of the working spouse's benefits.
- Social Security benefits are based on the number of years worked and wages earned during the highest 35 years. Since women are in the workforce fewer years than men (mostly because they take time off to bear and care for children), and because women generally earn less than men, working women will receive smaller retirement benefits than working men (Hinden, 2001).
- A divorced woman receives half of her former husband's benefit if they had been married at least 10 years. If the divorce occurs before being married 10 years, then she receives nothing.
- Where wife and husband are both employed, the wife will receive Social Security benefits for her work only if her benefits exceed those earned by her husband. If she collects a benefit based on her own wages, she loses the 50 percent spouse's payment for which her husband's payroll taxes paid.
- A woman who is widowed will not receive any Social Security benefits until age 60 unless she has a child under 16 or an older disabled child or if she herself is disabled.
- Retired female workers receive lower monthly Social Security benefits than retired male workers. This is because women are usually paid less than men and they spend more time out of the workforce—an average of 11 years—usually to care for children.

Criticizing Social Security, a publication by the Older Women's League, stated:

> Social Security and pension systems benefit male work patterns. Designed when lifestyles were dramatically different, Social Security best serves "traditional" families that consist of a lifelong breadwinner, a lifelong homemaker, and two children. Less than 10 percent of American families fit that definition today; even fewer will fit in the future. . . . As long as women continue to assume greater child and elder care responsibilities, are paid less than men, and live longer, these biases will take an enormous toll on women's retirement income. (Crooks, 1991:284)

The Social Security system is financed through taxes on wages and salaries. From a payroll tax of 2 percent on the first $3,000 of earnings when it began in the 1930s, the rate has increased substantially over the years. The 2000 rate was 15 percent on the first $68,400 of earnings, with the cost being split between the worker and the employer, but most economists agree that the burden of the tax is on the employee because employers finance their share by paying their employees that much less.

The method of financing Social Security is not equitable, because it disproportionately disadvantages lower-income wage earners. In other words, the tax is **regressive:** It takes a larger percentage from people with the lowest incomes. The Social Security tax has the following negative features:

- It is levied at a constant rate (everyone, rich and poor, pays the same rate).
- It starts with the first dollar of earned income, offering no allowances or exemptions for the very poor.
- It applies only to wages and salaries, thus exempting income typical for the wealthy, such as interest, dividends, rents, and capital gains from the sale of property.
- It is imposed up to a ceiling ($68,400 in 2000). Thus, in effect, in 2000 a worker making $68,400 and an executive or a ballplayer making a $5,000,000 salary paid exactly the same Social Security tax.

There is an overarching problem facing Social Security—how to finance it in the future. Three demographic factors make financing the program problematic. The first is that more people are living to age 65, and people live much longer after reaching 65 than in earlier generations. Average life spans are 14 years longer than they were when Social Security was created in 1935. The obvious consequence of this greater longevity is that the Social Security system pays out more and more to an ever-expanding pool of elderly who live longer and longer.

The third demographic factor working against the system is a skewed **dependency ratio** (the proportion of the population who are workers compared to the proportion not working). Social Security is financed by a tax on workers and their employers. In 1950 there were 16 workers for each person on Social Security; in 1970 there were 3.7 workers; in 2000 there will be 3.2; and in 2030 there will be 2.1 workers for each person receiving benefits. At present, the Social Security Administration collects more in taxes than it pays out, with the surplus going into a trust fund. But as people live longer and the baby boomers reach retirement, this system will fail. Estimates vary, but sometime around 2015 the system will begin paying out more than it collects, and after 2037 it will be able to pay out only about 70 cents of each dollar of promised benefits (Zuckerman, 2000b). See the "Social Problems in Global Perspective" panel for the problems facing the developed nations as they become disproportionately old.

To deal with this pending crisis in funding Social Security, Congress will have to either raise Social Security taxes, use other revenues, or cut benefits. Other options include raising the age of eligibility (starting in 2000 and continuing to 2022, the age for receiving full benefits will gradually rise from 65 to 67). Raising the eligibility age is unfair to certain groups: African American males, for example, live nearly 8 years less than White males, meaning that relatively few would receive benefits if the retirement age were raised to 70. Blue-collar workers also die earlier than professionals. A worker in a mine has only a 50–50 chance of reaching age 65 alive (*USA Today*, 1998b). Another plan is the reduction or elimination of the cost of living adjustment (COLA), which allows the payments to keep pace with inflation. This proposal hurts the poor most because it is regressive. Another strategy is to tax Social Security benefits as income, which would protect the poor because they pay little, if any, federal income tax. Another solution that is popular with the Republican Party is to privatize Social Security. Generally, this would allow each individual to invest part of his or her Social Security taxes in the stock market. This plan would be

SOCIAL PROBLEMS IN GLOBAL PERSPECTIVE

THE DEVELOPED WORLD TURNS GRAY

Over the next several decades the nations in the developed world will experience an unprecedented growth in the number of their elderly and an unprecedented decline in the number of their youths. Peter Peterson, author of *Gray Dawn: How the Coming Age Wave Will Transform America and the World,* calls this demographic transformation the "Floridization of the Developed World" (Peterson, 1999). In effect, today's Florida with its concentration of seniors (19 percent) is a demographic benchmark that every developed nation will soon pass—Italy in 2003, Japan in 2005, Germany in 2006, France and Britain in 2016, the United States in 2021, and Canada in 2023. In today's developed world the elderly population is 14 percent but by the year 2030 it will reach 25 percent.

This demographic shift has several consequences. First, as the proportion of the elderly population grows beyond 20 percent in a society, coupled with a corresponding fertility rate that does not replace itself (below 2.11), the working-age population will shrink. Japan, for example, will suffer a 25 percent decline over the next ten years in the number of workers under 30 (Longman, 1999).

Second, the shrinking of the working-age population, means that productivity will decline and taxes and/or debts will rise to pay for the enormous burden of pensions and health care for the elderly. Or, alternatively, governments will have to reduce benefits to the elderly significantly, causing political upheavals.

Third, unless their fertility rates turn up, the total populations of western Europe and Japan will shrink to about one-half of their current size by the end of the twenty-first century. The Third World will continue to grow rapidly until leveling off around 2050, resulting in an ever-enlarging population gap between the developed and developing worlds and increasing resentment by the latter over the disproportionate resource use by an ever-smaller developed world.

Fourth, worker shortages will increase the demand for immigrant laborers, bringing diversity in religion, language, and customs. This diversity increases the possibility of racial and ethnic conflicts. Moreover, there will be an increasing inequality gap between the new immigrants who arrive at the bottom of society's stratification system and those who are privileged. Thus, the possibility of clashes between the "haves" and the "have-nots."

beneficial when the stock market goes up, but it also makes retirement savings vulnerable to stock market declines.

> Social Security is far more than a pension system, and its payouts are government guaranteed. It is also deliberately redistributive. More than three-fifths of retired Americans derive at least half their income from Social Security; without it, half would live in poverty. Dedicating some of the payroll tax to a private account system would divert that much revenue into a system that is neither redistributive nor government guaranteed. (Kuttner, 1998a:34)

Paying for Health Care

Most older people are in reasonably good health. Of all age groups, however, the elderly are the most affected by ill health. Health problems occur especially from age 75 onward, as the degenerative processes of aging accelerate. In addition to physical disorders, mental conditions disproportionately affect the elderly. Alzheimer's disease, the leading cause of dementia in old age, affects more than 4 million Americans. The disease rises sharply with advancing age—from less than 3 percent of those age 65 and doubling every 5 years of age between 65 and 85 so that for those 85 and older, the rate is almost half (47 percent) (Neergaard, 2000). Since the old-old are growing so rapidly, it is expected that the number of those afflicted with Alzheimer's will triple by the year 2050.

Here are some additional facts:

- Although the elderly made up 13 percent of the population, they consume more than one-third of all health care in the United States.
- Elderly people make more than twice as many doctor visits, on average, than younger people age 15 to 44.
- The elderly are four times as likely as the nonold to be hospitalized. When hospitalized, they stay longer (on average about 3 days longer) than the nonold.
- The medical expenses of the old are three times greater than those of middle-aged adults, yet their incomes are typically much less.
- Although only 13 percent of the population, the elderly account for more than one-third of all spending for prescription drugs. Moreover, the cost of prescription drugs rises much faster than inflation (e.g., up 17 percent from 1999 to 2000), placing an increased burden on the elderly living on fixed incomes.
- Average health care takes 19 percent of income for people age 65 and older. The poor spend 35 percent of their income on health care (Findlay, 1998).
- The cost of long-term care is prohibitive, with the average yearly cost in 1999 for nursing home care at $46,000. Since Medicare does not pay for most long-term care, long-term care insurance is expense, and Medicaid will help only after the patient's resources are exhausted, the result is that many elderly will end their lives impoverished. (*USA Today,* 1999a)

Medicare is the health insurance program begun in 1965 for almost everyone age 65 and older. Everyone is automatically entitled to hospital insurance, home health care, and hospice care through this program (known as Medicare Part A). The supplemental medical insurance program (known as Medicare Part B) helps pay for doctor bills, outpatient services, diagnostic tests, physical therapy, and medical supplies. People may enroll in this program by paying a relatively modest monthly fee. Overall, Medicare is financed by payroll taxes, premiums paid by recipients, and a government subsidy.

There are three major problems with Medicare. First, it is insufficiently financed by the government. Second, from the perspective of the elderly, only about half of their health care bills are paid through the program, leaving many with substantial costs. The affluent elderly are not hurt because they can purchase supplemental health insurance. The poor are not hurt because they are also covered by Medicaid, a separate program financed by federal and state taxes that pays for the health care of indigent persons. The near poor, however, do not qualify for Medicaid, and they cannot afford additional health insurance.

A third problem with Medicare is that physicians feel that the program pays them too little for their services. As a result many physicians limit the number of Medicare patients they will serve, some even refusing to serve any Medicare patients. Thus, some elderly have difficulty in finding a physician.

Elderly Abuse

Problems of the Institutionalized Elderly. An estimated 1.8 million patients resided in 17,000 nursing homes in 2000. By 2020 it will be almost a million more. The data indicate that at any one time, between 4 and 5 percent of people age 65 and older are confined to nursing homes and other extended-care facilities. This low figure is misleading, however. It does not mean that only 4 to 5 percent of the aged ever will be confined to a nursing home. At age 65 a person may have no need for such a facility, but at 85 it may be a necessity.

The residents of nursing homes are typically age 75 and older (87 percent), female (75 percent), and White (89 percent) (Curran and Renzetti, 2000:287). Conspicuously absent are racial minorities, as Curran and Renzetti note:

> The small number of elderly people of color in nursing homes is the result of several factors. First, the states with the highest numbers of people of color are in areas of the country—the South and the Southwest, for example—that have low overall nursing care institutionalization rates. Second, many racial and ethnic minority grroups have cultural norms that include respect and veneration of the elderly, so members of these groups often care for their elderly themselves rather [than] using institutional care. However, a third reason for the small number of people of color in nursing homes is discrimination in nursing home admissions. Research indicates that African American and other minority elderly are sometimes channeled into other types of institutions, such as state mental hospitals, or they are admitted to nursing homes that have low quality-of-care ratings. (Curran and Renzetti, 2000:287)

The economically advantaged elderly are not as likely as their less-wealthy age cohorts to be institutionalized, and if institutionalized, they are apt to be in private nursing homes and to receive better care. Kosberg (1976) compared nursing homes for private residents with those for welfare recipients and found the former decidedly superior in staffing, freedom, pleasantness of surroundings, cleanliness, patient communication, and meals. Kosberg found that homes for the affluent old tend to provide **therapeutic care** (the approach that focuses on meeting the needs of patients and treatment), whereas homes housing welfare recipients tend to provide **custodial care** (the approach in a health facility that focuses on meeting the needs of the institution, rather than those of the residents). This distinction is an important attitudinal difference; custodial "residents are conceived of in stereotyped terms as categorically different from 'normal' people, as totally irrational, insensitive to others, unpredictable, and dangerous. . . . Custodialism is saturated with pessimism, impersonalness, and watchful mistrust" (Kosberg, 1976:427–428). This finding has implications for the federal law stating that nursing home residents must use all of their savings before receiving Medicaid. Because nursing home care costs can be as high as $50,000 a year, and less than 8 percent of Americans have private insurance for lengthy care, long-term care results in many residents' spending themselves into poverty, where Medicaid will take over the financial payments. Previous research indicates that the shift to Medicaid results in a change from therapeutic care to custodial care.

There are two extreme points of view concerning the functions of nursing homes. One view is that such homes are necessary places for the elderly who need extensive health care. Obviously, such facilities are needed for people who have Alzheimer's disease and for people who have been paralyzed by strokes or are bedridden. The opposing view sees nursing homes as dumping grounds or repositories for getting rid of people who represent what we do not want to be or see. Whatever one's views on these institutions, one fact is pertinent: Although many nursing homes provide good environments for their residents, there are serious problems in others. There are no federal standards that nursing homes must meet for the health and safety of their residents. The standards are left to the individual states, and they vary in their standards and rigor in enforcing them.

Government studies of nursing homes (reported in Thompson, 1998; McQueen, 2001b) found the following:

- Nearly one in three of the nation's nursing homes has been cited by state inspectors for abusing patients.
- Problems will likely increase as the rapidly increasing elderly population puts even greater pressure on the nation's nursing homes.
- Nursing homes have become dangerous places largely because they are understaffed and underregulated.
- A review of nursing home deaths in California suggests that, if the same percentages hold elsewhere, as many as 20,000 U.S. nursing home residents die prematurely or are in unnecessary pain, or both.

Common problems in nursing homes with a custodial style are the overuse and misuse of drugs. Drugs can be used for a host of therapeutic reasons, but one common use is not healthful—drugging an individual to control behavior. The use of tranquilizers, for example, keeps people from complaining and from asking for service. This procedure minimizes disturbances, thereby requiring fewer personnel and thus increasing profits. Of course, the quality of life for the residents is diminished, and even their lives may be broken:

> The scenario is all too familiar. An elderly woman goes into a nursing home suffering from a broken hip, but is otherwise alert and continent. A few months later, she is depressed, drooling, incontinent, unable to remember things or follow simple conversation. When her children ask what happened, they discover their mother has been placed on psychoactive drugs. They ask why and are told that she was "agitated." She withdraws still further and spends her remaining months of life effectively warehoused, an empty, broken shell of a person. (Beck, 1990:77)

The nursing home business is big business ($87 billion in 1999). Two factors make the profit potential especially great: (1) The elderly population is growing at a 2 percent annual rate, and (2) the government pays for much of the care (75 percent). One consequence of these factors is the proliferation of private nursing homes (about 75 percent are private) organized to generate profits. Many of these facilities provide excellent care for their clients, but others have shown that their interest in profit exceeds their interest in clients.

Not all nursing homes are unnecessary, and not all owners and personnel are greedy and uncaring. Many older people benefit from a sheltered environment, and doubtless many of the 17,000 nursing homes in the United States are resident oriented and provide adequate—perhaps even superior—services to their clients. But we must also acknowledge that there are widespread abuses in U.S. nursing homes. The danger, of course, is the profit motive—the less money that nursing homes spend on care such as living space, good food, adequate heat in the winter and air conditioning in the summer, and recreational equipment, the more profit for the company and its shareholders (Bates, 1999).

What is the effect of institutionalization on the residents? Obviously, it will vary according to the facilities and treatment philosophy of a particular nursing home. But all institutions (including prisons, mental hospitals, and nursing homes) must be wary of depersonalizing individual clients. In the name of efficiency, people eat the same food at the same time, wear the same type of clothing, perform the same chores in the prescribed manner, watch the movies provided them, and live in rooms with identical dimensions and decor. The widespread use of tranquilizers compounds this depersonalization. The result is that docility and similarity abound, which makes management happy but obviously overlooks the individual needs of the elderly residents.

- **Noninstitutionalized Care of the Elderly by Their Children.** Two demographic trends mentioned earlier—the decline in fertility and an increased life expectancy—affect the patterns of taking care of the elderly by family members [the following is from Bengtson, Rosenthal, and Burton (1990) and Bengtson, Marti, and Roberts (1991)]. First, new multigeneration kinship patterns have emerged, such as the **beanpole family structure,** where the number of living generations within linkages increases, but there is an intragenerational contraction in the number of members within each generation:

> In the decades to come, individuals will grow older having more vertical than horizontal linkages in the family. For example, vertically, a four-generation family structure has three tiers of parent–child relationships, two sets of grandparent–grandchild ties, and one great-grandparent–great-grandchild linkage. Within generations of this same family, horizontally, aging individuals will have fewer brothers and sisters. In addition, at the level of extended kin, family members will have fewer cousins, aunts, uncles, nieces, and nephews. (Bengtson, Rosenthal, and Burton, 1990:264)

Second, family members will spend more time occupying intergenerational family roles than ever before. In other words, people will spend more years both as parents and as children of aging parents than any earlier generation.

Third, there is an increased likelihood that family members will be involved in longer periods of elder caregiving. At the extreme, this means that the young-old (those around age 65) will care for their parents who are old-old (those age 85 and older).

Fourth, because there are fewer siblings in families, the caretaker responsibilities in a particular family will be concentrated among a few (usually daughters or daughters-in-law) rather than shared among many. This is significant because an estimated 5 million people provide care for elderly family members.

Finally, with more and more children assuming a caretaker role of their elderly parents, there is an increased likelihood of elder abuse. This abuse can take the following forms:

- Physical abuse: hitting, slapping, shoving, and use of physical restraints, as well as the withholding of personal care, food, medicine, adequate medical attention, and the like.
- Psychological abuse: verbal assaults, threats, fear, and isolation.
- Drug abuse: encouragement by doctors and families to take too many drugs, which serves the families by keeping the elderly manageable.
- Financial exploitation: theft or misuse of money and other personal property owned by the elderly.
- Violation of rights: forcing a parent into a nursing home, for instance.

A government study revealed that 11 percent of all murder victims age 60 and older were killed by a son or daughter (Dawson and Langan, 1994). For the most part, though, accurate information on how many elderly people are subjected to these abusive acts is impossible to obtain. The elderly victims are in a double-bind situation that traps them in an abusive situation in which they feel that they cannot notify the authorities.

> [T]he abuser is providing financial and other resources necessary for the victim's survival. Thus, the [elderly victim recognizes his or her dependency on the] abusing caretaker. These battered parents, whose attacks cover an even wider range of abuse than that perpetrated upon children, often refuse to report the abuse for fear of retaliation, lack of alternative shelter, and the shame and stigma of having to admit that they reared such a child. Paralleling the battered wife, these abused old people prefer the known, even when

> it includes physical abuse, to the unknown, if they seek to leave the situation. (Steinmetz, 1978:55)

As a result, as many as five out of six cases of elder abuse go unreported (National Center on Elder Abuse, 1998). This is because, in addition to the reasons just mentioned, many mistreated elders are homebound and isolated, and thus are unlikely to be seen at banks, senior centers, hospitals, health programs, and police stations (Wolf, 2000:8).

Despite these problems with underreporting, Rosalie Wolf (2000) summarizing the findings from community surveys, found that 4 to 6 percent of older adults report experiencing incidents of domestic elder abuse, neglect, and financial exploitation. With about 35 million Americans 65 and older, a middle estimate of 5 percent yields an estimated 1,750,000 who are victims of some form of abuse.

The problem seems to occur in situations in which adult children are overwhelmed by the role of taking care of their parent or parents. The emotional, physical, and financial costs of caregiving can be enormous. Hospital and other medical costs are extremely expensive for the elderly because they are more prone to illness. There are obvious additional food and housekeeping costs. Furthermore, the timing of the additional financial burdens may be especially difficult for caretakers because it is likely to coincide with higher expenses for their children (college, wedding, helping them buy their first home).

Parents living with their adult children cause stress and resentment in a number of other ways as well. The household is more crowded, causing different sleeping arrangements, overcrowded bathrooms, shortages of hot water, and the like. The caretaking responsibility is likely to be assumed by the wife, and she may resent the elders' presence because of the extra work, the intrusion into her privacy, and the excessive demands on her time. Of course, as parents age and disabilities become more pronounced, the care they need can become overwhelming. The wife may be especially hostile to the parents because she is losing the freedom she expected to have once her children were gone—freedom to travel, go back to school, or take a job. But with elderly parents to restrain her, she is back to the parental role.

Parents living with an adult child can cause special problems when they have not resolved their problems from an earlier time. The parents may continue to treat their adult child as a child, taking over or trying to take over the decision-making role. Or the hostile feelings generated when the child was an adolescent return to haunt both parties. Clearly, there is tension when the behaviors and values of the adult child do not coincide with those of the elderly parent. They may differ on political issues, religious issues, how the grandchildren should be raised, and what television programs to watch.

The adult child may also resent parents living in his or her home because the adult child feels forced into the situation. Perhaps the other siblings live in different communities, and so the parents, no longer able to live alone, move in with the child living in their community. The hostile feelings increase if the adult child feels that other relatives are not sharing the burden, at least financially.

This emphasis on the elderly causing stress among caregivers blames the victim. In the words of Karl Pillemer, a major researcher in the field:

> In the same way that some writers held that "spoiled" children were more likely to be abused, or that nagging, demanding wives were more likely to be battered, the elderly themselves have been cited as the cause of abuse. Focusing on caregiver stress normalizes the problem: it relieves the abuser of much

of the blame because, after all, the elderly are demanding, hard to care for, and sometimes even downright unpleasant. (Pillemer, 1993:246–247)

Despite this disclaimer, the stress generated between the elderly and their caregivers is a major source of abuse. Stresses and tensions between the generations are inevitable. For some families, such a situation results in actual physical and mental abuse of the elderly. The psychological and social factors related to child and spouse abuse are also pertinent for the abuse of the elderly. One additional catalyst that must be considered is the **ageism** prevalent in society. This provides an atmosphere in which the elderly are devalued, negatively stereotyped, and discriminated against. To the extent that older people accept these negative definitions of the aged, they may view abusive treatment as deserved or at least unavoidable. Similarly, if their children accept tenets of ageism, they are likely to assume that the elderly deserve their mistreatment.

RESPONSES BY THE ELDERLY: HUMAN AGENCY

Being old is a difficult stage in life for many. People who were once attractive, active, and powerful may no longer be so. They must live on restricted incomes that become more constricted by inflation. They must face chronic health problems, pain, and impending death. Many are isolated because they lost a spouse and their children live at a distance. Some elderly, especially the poor and those in many nursing homes, live lives of desperation and hopelessness. What are the characteristic coping responses of the elderly to these psychological and social conditions?

After studying the elderly for 15 years, Bernice Neugarten and her associates have found that four major personality types prevail among people age 70 and over; these types are essentially extensions of the middle-age coping patterns. (The following material is adapted from Neugarten, 1980.) The majority of elderly people retain *integrated* personalities. They function well, are intellectually able, and have competent egos. Another category, the *defended,* are achievement-oriented people who continue working hard. They fight the aging process by not giving in to it and by remaining very active. *Passive-dependent* people, in contrast, have essentially given in to the inevitability of aging. They become inactive and depend on others. Finally, a relatively small proportion are the *disinterested* (disorganized) elderly. These people have experienced a deterioration of their thought processes. They may be confused, disoriented, forgetful, childish, and paranoid.

These personality types reflect responses to being old, a devalued status in U.S. society. Being considered old by society and by oneself is a catalyst that provokes the individual to respond in characteristic ways. But—and this is the crucial sociological point—the elderly are reacting to socially structured inequalities and socially constructed definitions, not to age as such. In a different cultural setting in which status increases with age, observers might find different personality types and responses.

Some researchers have argued that senior citizens respond to the aging process by retreating from relationships, organizations, and society (called **disengagement**). This behavior is considered normal and even satisfying for the individual because withdrawal brings a release from societal pressures to compete and conform. Other researchers have quarreled with disengagement theory, arguing that many elderly people are involved in a wide range of activities.

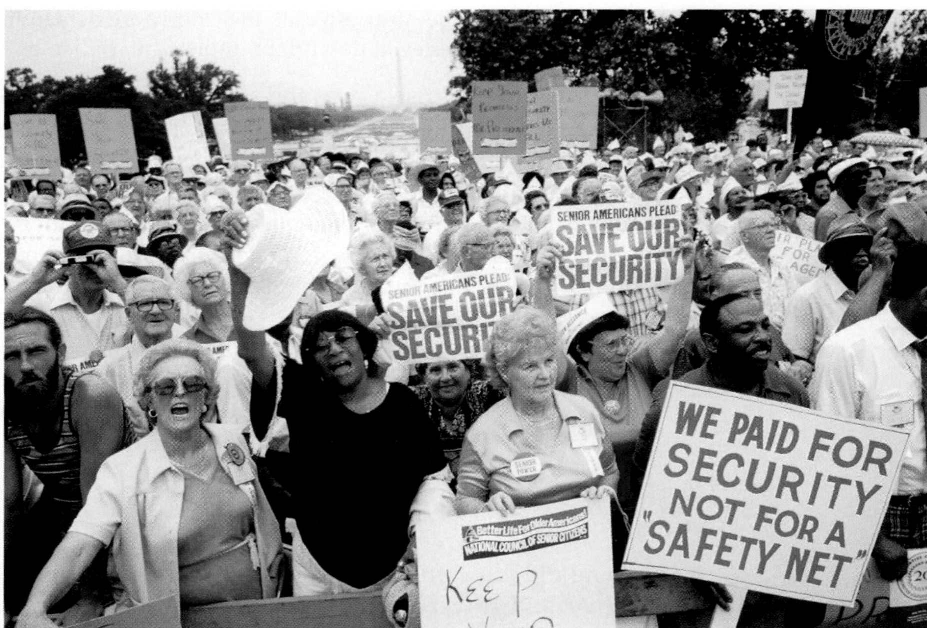

A striking number of elderly people are politically active, often joining with others in collective attempts to make changes beneficial to them.

The majority of the elderly do remain active until health problems curtail their mobility. A striking number of them are becoming more politically active in an attempt to change some of the social conditions especially damaging for them. More senior citizens are more likely to vote than young people. Faced with common problems, many are joining in a collective effort. Several national organizations are dedicated to political action that will benefit the elderly, including the American Association for Retired Persons (AARP), the nation's largest special-interest organization; the National Committee to Preserve Social Security and Medicare; the National Council of Senior Citizens; the National Council on Aging (a confederation of some 1,400 public and private social welfare agencies); the National Caucus on Black Aged; and the Gerontological Society. Collectively, these organizations have many millions of members. They work through lobbyists, mailing campaigns, advertising, and other processes to improve the lot of the elderly in U.S. society.

Just how effective these organizations are or will be is unknown. But as the elderly continue to increase in numbers, their sphere of influence is likely to increase as well. Because they now account for more than 15 percent of the voting public, elderly citizens could be a significant voting bloc if they developed an age consciousness and voted alike. Politicians from states with a high concentration of elderly people are increasingly aware of their potential voting power, and legislation more sympathetic to the needs of the elderly may be forthcoming. It is probably only a matter of time before the elderly focus their concerns and become an effective pressure group that demands equity.

CHAPTER REVIEW

1. A major demographic force in U.S. society is massive immigration. This immigration (adding about 1 million immigrants annually) differs from previous waves because the immigrants come primarily from Latin America and Asia rather than Europe.

2. Racial and ethnic diversity ("the browning of America") is increasing, with the influx of immigrants and differential fertility (i.e., immigrant groups having a higher fertility rate than other groups).
3. The two fastest growing minorities are Latinos and Asian Americans.
4. The reaction of Americans to the new immigrants is typically negative. This is based on two myths: (a) immigrants take jobs away from those already here, and (b) immigrants are a drain on society's resources.
5. Immigrants face a dilemma: Do they fit into their new society or do they retain the traditions of the society they left? Immigrants in the past, for the most part, assimilated. But conditions are different for the new immigrants: (a) They are racial/ethnics, not Whites; (b) the current political mood is to eliminate affirmative action programs and welfare programs; and (c) they have entered during difficult economic times brought about by the economic transformation.
6. The second major demographic shift is toward an aging society ("the graying of America").
7. The proportion of the U.S. population age 65 and older is growing. In this category, women outnumber men and minorities are underrepresented. Although the elderly as a category are not disproportionately poor, the elderly who are women, minorities, or who live alone are disproportionately poor.
8. The Social Security program is the only source of income for about one-half of retired people and a major source of income for 80 percent of the elderly. The key problem is how this program will be financed in the future.
9. The Social Security program is biased in several ways: (a) Some workers are not included, (b) people with low career earnings receive fewer benefits, (c) women (homemakers, divorced, and widowed) are disadvantaged, and (d) the tax is regressive.
10. Medicare is the health insurance program for almost everyone age 65 and older. The program is insufficiently financed: (a) From the perspective of the elderly, the program does not pay enough of the medical expenses, and (b) the program is too expensive for the government to finance adequately.
11. At any one time, only about 5 percent of people age 65 and older are confined in nursing homes. These homes have important functions for those needing their services, but abuses are associated with some of these operations: Residents are given custodial care, drugged, and provided with inadequate nutrition.
12. As many as 1.5 million elderly people in the United States are physically abused by relatives annually. Most commonly, abuse occurs when adult children are overwhelmed by the role of taking care of their parents. Elder abuse also occurs in about one-third of the nation's nursing homes, according to government studies.
13. The elderly may respond to their devalued status in several characteristic ways. They may withdraw from social relationships; they may continue to act as they have throughout their adult lives; or they may become politically active to change the laws, customs, and social structures that disadvantage them.
14. The numbers and proportion of the elderly in the U.S. population will increase. This aging population will create a difficult burden for the young, who, through taxes, will be required to finance pension plans and other assistance for the elderly. If the gap between the needs of the elderly and the benefits they receive widens, political activity and age consciousness among older people are likely to increase.

KEY TERMS

Human agency. People are agents and actors who cope with, adapt to, and change social structures to meet their needs.

Demography. The study of population.

Fertility. Birthrate.

Mortality. Death rate.

Baby boom generation. The term referring to people born in the 15-year period following World War II, when an extraordinary number of babies were born in the United States.

Regressive tax. Taxing at a set percentage, which takes a larger proportion of the wealth from the poor than from the nonpoor.

Dependency ratio. The proportion of the population who work compared to the proportion who do not work.

Therapeutic care. The approach in a health facility that focuses on meeting the needs of residents.

Custodial care. The approach in a health facility that focuses on meeting the needs of the institution, resulting in poor-quality care for the patients.

Beanpole family structure. A family structure in which the number of living generations within linkages increases, but there is an intragenerational contraction in the number of members within each generation.

Ageism. The devaluation of and the discrimination against the elderly.

Disengagement. The response by some people to the aging process of retreating from relationships, organizations, and society.

WEBSITES FOR FURTHER REFERENCE

http://ameristat.org/
Ameristat.Org is a website developed by the Population Reference bureau in partnership with the Social Science Data Analysis Network. It provides the latest statistics on marriage, family, children, fertility, foreign-born populations, income and poverty, and the elderly.

http://www.aarp.org/indexes/legislative.html
American Association of Retired Persons (AARP): This organization is specifically for individuals over 50 years old, but the website is available to all. This site includes articles and discussion groups on current events, as well as issues pertinent to older individuals; it offers a unique perspectives on mainstream issues.

http://www.nih.gov/nia/
The National Institute on Aging (NIA), one of the 25 institutes and centers of the National Institutes of Health, leads a broad scientific effort to understand the nature of aging and to extend the healthy, active years of life. In 1974, Congress granted authority to form the National Institute on Aging to provide leadership in aging research, training, health information dissemination, and other programs relevant to aging and older people. The NIA's mission is to improve the health and well-being of older Americans through research.

http://www.immigration.about.com/
About Immigration provides a long list of features—some practical, some scholarly—from a variety of sources.

http://www.cis.org/
The Center for Immigration Studies (Washington, D.C.) is a nonprofit organization founded in 1985 devoted to research and policy concerning the impact of immigration on the United States. It is the Center's mission to expand the base of public knowledge and understanding of the need for an immigration policy that gives first concern to the broad national interest.

http://www.umn.edu/ihrc/profiles.htm
The Immigration History and Research Center locates, collects, preserves, and makes available for research the records of 24 ethnic groups that originated in eastern, central, and southern Europe and the Near East. In addition, the IHRC's General Collection documents the response to immigration by organizations and individuals who provided services, worked for government policy reform, and educated Americans about immigrant needs and problems.

http://www.ins.usdoj.gov/graphics/aboutins/statistics/gbpage.htm
The Immigration and Naturalization Services statistics page will help you locate information about foreign nationals who enter or attempt to enter the United States for temporary or permanent residence through a variety of status categories (e.g., immigrant, refugee, asylee, etc.), as well as subsequent INS actions such as apprehension, removal, or naturalization.

http://www.ins.usdoj.gov/graphics/aboutins/history/chinese.html
Chinese Immigrant Files: This INS website gives visitors access to information regarding Chinese immigration into the United States, as well as access to public records. Responsibility for enforcement of U.S. Chinese Exclusion law transferred to the Immigration and Naturalization Service in 1903, and continued until repeal of the Chinese Exclusion Act in 1943. The old Chinese Service transferred into INS along with its records, which INS maintained as a separate set until 1908. Those files on Chinese matters, kept separate from general immigration files at Washington, D.C., until 1908, are referred to as Segregated Chinese Files, and are today found at the National Archives in Washington, D.C. INS continued to file records of Chinese in separate file series at major ports of entry and district offices, and those files are today found at Regional Archives across the country.

http://opr.princeton.edu/
The Office of Population Research at Princeton University is the oldest population research center in the country.

6

Urban Problems
in the United States

The serious problems of the cities are largely insoluble now and will be for the foreseeable future.

—Edward C. Banfield

The modern city is the most unlovely and artificial sight this planet affords. The ultimate solution is to abandon it. We shall solve the city problem by leaving it.

—Henry Ford

The city is not obsolete; it's the center of our civilization.

—Edward Logue

The United States is an urban nation, with four out of five Americans living in metropolitan areas. Almost three out of ten Americans (28 percent) live in eight metropolitan areas with populations of 5 million or more (U.S. Bureau of the Census, 2001a). Some observers (e.g., Magnet, 2000) have argued that while American cities in the past had problems, they are on the rebound as neighborhoods are revitalized, formerly abandoned downtowns are being rebuilt with financial services and other businesses moving back, and it is becoming fashionable to live in the urban core. But while there are successes, the cities of the United States are in trouble. Baltimore provides a good example of a city that appears revitalized but has serious problems. On the surface, Baltimore is a revitalized city with a popular major league baseball team in a unique stadium, a National Football League Super Bowl champion in a new stadium, a lively waterfront district, and a rejuvenated downtown. However, this glitter "has blinded a lot of people to the urban rot that festers just blocks from the much-ballyhooed Inner Harbor" (Wickham, 2001:A6). Baltimore has lost 11.5 percent of its population during the 1990s while the surrounding suburbs have grown steadily. Although the city is but 13 percent of Maryland's population, it has 56 percent of the state's welfare caseload. Only about one-fourth of its public high school students graduate in 4 years. In 2000, 262 homicides were recorded in Baltimore (Katz and Bradley, 1999; Wickham, 2001).

> And Baltimore is not unique. The image of America's cities has improved greatly over the past few years, thanks to shiny new downtowns dotted with vast convention centers, luxury hotels, and impressive office towers, but these acres of concrete and faux marble hide a reality that is in many cases grim. (Katz and Bradley, 1999:26)

The focus of this chapter is on the grim reality of cities in the United States.

No other industrial nation has allowed the kind of decline and deterioration facing U.S. urban centers. Most of the social and economic problems discussed in this book are primarily concentrated and have their severest consequences in the city, particularly the largest cities. It is in this locale, more than any other, that many of these problems are expanding and intensifying. In this sense, place is crucial to understanding U.S. social problems.

Urban poverty is especially acute and contributes to and is associated with a host of other city problems. These include a decaying infrastructure, a shortage of affordable housing, homelessness, inadequate public transit, pollution,

*Doug A. Timmer, ACORN of Chicago, is the co-author of this chapter.

lack of health care, failing public school systems, drugs, gangs, and crime. These problems are discussed in the four parts of this chapter: the mugging of U.S. cities, the declining quality of urban life, urban unrest, and urban public policy.

Mugging of U.S. Cities

Many people in the United States fear being mugged in the city. But individuals are not the only ones who have been mugged. The cities also have been victimized and abandoned since World War II by suburbanization and sprawl (metropolitan deconcentration), job flight, disinvestment, and the federal government. The mugging of the city is an apt metaphor for urban America.

Suburbanization and Sprawl

For nearly 50 years there has been a dramatic population shift in the United States—people moving from cities to the suburbs. Although this shift had begun in some metropolitan areas at the turn of the century or even earlier, it accelerated and became the dominant demographic trend in almost every major U.S. metropolitan area after World War II. The result is that in 1999, for the first time, half of the country lived in suburbia (for the remainder, 30 percent lived in central cities and 20 percent in rural areas and small towns). The shift toward the suburbs continues as within metropolitan areas, central cities increased 4 percent in population from 1990 to 1999, compared to a 14 percent growth in suburban areas (U.S. Bureau of the Census, 2001). As a result, within metropolitan areas, 38 percent live in central cities and 62 percent in suburban areas, and the gap increases.

Those who move to the suburbs are predominantly upper-middle-class, middle-class, and to a lesser extent working-class Whites. This process of **"White flight"** has increased and continues to increase both class and race segregation. As suburbs grow and became essentially middle class and White, shrinking central cities are left with a greater proportion of their remaining population who were poor and minority, a trend heightened by the huge number of immigrants, mostly Latino and Asian, moving to U.S. cities (El Nasser, 2001a). The suburbanization of the United States has meant the geographic separation of classes and races, particularly of middle-class Whites from poor Blacks. Today, very high levels of racial segregation persist in most major U.S. metropolitan areas. Even when Blacks leave the city, they are often resegregated in Black suburbs or in Black neighborhoods in White suburbs.

Middle-class Whites move to the suburbs for a better place to raise their children, better schools, and less crime. Race plays a part in these motives. "A better place to raise children" often meant a neighborhood with few or no African Americans or Latinos. "Better schools" often meant virtually all-White schools not under court order to desegregate. And "crime" was synonymous with inner-city Blacks for many suburbanites. Those people moving to the suburbs were also attracted to the open space and the prospect of an unattached, single-family dwelling with a yard. This prospect was made more attainable by generally lower real estate costs and lower property tax rates outside of the city.

The exodus to the suburbs was not limited to people. Property taxes moved with them. That broad segment of the population most likely to own property and most likely to pay taxes left the city for the suburbs. And with it went the city's ability to raise revenue for and provide for schools, infrastructure, and other essential city services. The suburbs now had this revenue for their own schools, streets, parks, sanitation, sewers, police, and fire protection as well as for other municipal services.

Business and industry, too, along with the jobs they generate, moved to the suburbs, further reducing the property tax base of cities. There, they could sidestep inner-city minorities, equal employment opportunity, and affirmative action mandates. Land was cheaper, as were property taxes and utility rates. Also, unions were sometimes fewer and weaker in the suburbs. The suburbs also provided a workplace and living environment perceived to be safe. Suburbanites found themselves surrounded by skilled white-collar and high-tech workers living in the other nearby "pink ghettos." In the end, as the White middle class, business, industry, and jobs fled, suburbanization left the central cities with a poorer population and a reduced tax base to provide the schools, infrastructure, other services, and jobs this population needs. Under these circumstances, inequality between the cities and their suburbs increased. There are some estimates that class segregation may have increased more than 25 percent between 1970 and 1990—much of it between city and suburb (Morin, 1998). Indeed, by the summer of 1998, in spite of the much heralded 1990s "economic boom" in the United States, the inequalities between cities and suburbs had grown more pronounced than ever (Wyly, Glickman, and Lahr, 1998).

Suburbanization and the resulting inequality, segregation, and other problems it caused for the central cities were not naturally occurring phenomena. They were encouraged, supported, and directly subsidized by the federal government, and they profited large developers and corporations. The history of suburbanization in the United States, as Kenneth Jackson (1985), Peter Dreier (2000), and Daniel Lazare (2001) make clear, shows that federal government policies and spending shaped consumer choices that pushed people out of the cities and pulled them into the suburbs. The federal government financed the construction of the interstate highway and expressway system, which opened the suburbs to speculation and development and connected them to the city, where many suburbanites still worked. Housing policies implemented by the FHA (Federal Housing Authority) and VA (Veterans Administration) that offered low-cost government-insured mortgages—reserved, for the most part, for Whites and the suburbs—facilitated the population shift. The government subsidizes home ownership by permitting taxes and mortgage interest to be tax deductible (a savings to homeowners of $53.7 billion in 1998) (Collins, Leondar-Wright, and Sklar, 1999:38). Housing policies that allow local suburban governments to refuse public and subsidized housing in their communities have also encouraged the White middle class to reside where there is less affordable housing and few poor and minority residents. Low fuel taxes (such taxes are five to ten times higher in Europe than in the United States) have supported both suburbanization and the extreme dependency of American metropolitan areas on automobiles (discussed later). Also, policies set by Congress earmark these taxes to be spent on road building rather than mass transit. And, local governments have set more favorable property tax rates to lure people, businesses, and jobs to the suburbs.

More than one-fourth of all cities with a population of between 100,000 and 400,000 are suburbs. The rapid growth of the suburbs, particularly swift in the 1990s, has led to a new city form called "boomburgs." A **boomburg** is defined as a suburban city that has at least 100,000 people and has experienced double-digit growth every decade since it became defined by the Census Bureau as urban (2,500 or more). The 2000 Census found that there are 53 boomburgs, four of which exceed 300,000. That is bigger than Miami or St. Louis.

> These cities, built in the late 20th century, feature all the elements of sprawl: office parks, "big-box" retailers such as Home Depot, strip developments and subdivisions of large, single-family homes. They have now coalesced into suburban super cities that have all the functions of a traditional city but are built for a drive-through society. (El Nasser, 2001b)

The kind of dispersal and sprawl of population, retail business, and jobs that suburbanization brings continues unabated. The population of the Los Angeles metropolitan area increased more than fourfold during the past 50 years, but its geographic size increased 20 times. Metropolitan Chicago's population increased only 4 percent over the past two decades, but its geographic area grew by 46 percent. But now the spreading out and deconcentration of metropolitan areas over more land are becoming more extreme. The deconcentration of U.S. metropolitan areas is proceeding beyond the suburbs to what are being called "urban villages" or "edge cities" even more remote from the central cities, sometimes as much as 40 miles from the central business district.

The addition of new highways and beltways around and through metropolitan areas typically opens up new land for development of tract homes and strip malls. Such **urban sprawl** (low-density, automobile-dependent development) absorbs farmland at a rate of some 50 acres an hour in the United States, an area the size of Connecticut and Rhode Island every 10 years (*USA Today,* 1999b). Another way to express this growth is that the rate of land development in the United States is 0.7 percent, which means "that over the lifetime of a child born today, the developed area of the nation will more than double" (Pedersen, Smith, and Adler, 1999:24). It also results in slow commutes, traffic congestion, polluted air, overcrowded schools, automobile dependency, and visual blight (a similar look whether on the outskirts of Phoenix, Omaha, or Detroit composed of fast-food franchises, Wal-marts, drive-through banks, tract housing architecture, and the like), that one observer has called a new kind of "postindustrial ugliness that has overspread the landscape" (Lazare, 2001:276–277).

Some facts associated with sprawl (Pedersen, Smith, and Adler, 1999):

- Farmland around Denver is falling to sprawl at a rate of 90,000 acres a year.
- There are more cars than people in Seattle, Washington, with the number of automobile trips each day per household twice the number in 1990.
- Atlantans drive 36.5 daily miles round trip to work, more than Dallas's 29.5 and Los Angeles's 20.5.

The effects of suburbanization and sprawl are enormous. First, there are environmental effects such as the disruption of wildlife habitats, the altering of rivers and streams, and of course pollution (a topic considered later in this chapter).

A second consequence of suburbanization is "the draining of the center while flooding the edges" (Katz and Bradley, 1999:30). As mentioned earlier, as the more affluent leave cities for the suburbs, they take their spending and their taxes with them, leaving businesses less profitable and city governments strapped for the funds to provide adequate services. This is exacerbated by con-

Urban sprawl absorbs farmland at a rate of 50 acres an hour in the United States.

centrating poverty in the cities—the homeless, new immigrants, the working poor, the elderly, and people with disabilities.

The third consequence is the loss of jobs in the central cities, the topic of the next section.

Urban Job Loss

About one-third of the jobs in major U.S. metropolitan areas are with corporations that export goods and services outside the metro area. These are the highest paying jobs with the best benefit packages, in such industries as aerospace, defense, international trade, oil refining, computer software and hardware development, pharmaceuticals, and entertainment. These export jobs create a second type of employment in metropolitan areas—regional-serving jobs. About a quarter of jobs in most metropolitan areas are regional serving—in finance, real estate, utilities, media, and other professional services. These jobs generally pay less than export jobs but still represent good employment opportunities. The remainder of jobs in metropolitan areas serve the local area. The best of these include schoolteachers, police officers, firefighters, other municipal employees, and neighborhood doctors and lawyers. The worst include low-wage, insecure, temporary, part-time, dead-end work with few or no benefits in retail, clerical, custodial, food service, and private security work. The "good" jobs are leaving, or in the case of business expansion and new jobs, not locating in the central city or in the older, closer suburbs; thus they are farther and farther away from the growing proportion of poor and minority people in the city.

Symbolizing the relocation of U.S. business and industry, by 1992, only General Motors of the Big Three U.S. automakers had a Detroit address. Ford Motor Company's headquarters was in suburban Dearborn, and Chrysler's was Auburn Hills, some 40 miles north of the Motor City.

Race and class, as well as the fear of crime, play into the corporate motivation to move to the fringes of urban areas. The perception of many corporations and their employees is that not just the central city, but close suburbs as well, are now unsafe and have a large minority workforce. Sears and Roebuck's relocation from the Sears Tower in downtown Chicago to Hoffman Estates, 37 miles to the northwest, is a prime example of this perception. Hoffman Estates cannot be reached by public transit, and a number of prominent local real estate agents have said privately that Sears wants to get rid of its predominantly Black workforce from Chicago's Southside. The move will allow Sears to hire more highly educated workers, mostly White, who live near the 1.9-million-square-foot campus-style complex. The state of Illinois used taxpayer dollars to subsidize Sears's relocation with lowered land costs, infrastructure and expressway improvements, and tax abatements.

Unstopped, this kind of metropolitan deconcentration to the extreme urban fringe will continue and accelerate the post–World War II middle-class exodus from the central cities and will encourage the same sort of movement out of the older, closer suburbs. The results will be fewer jobs and poorer residents in both the city and the older suburbs.

Also, the economic costs of all this suburbanization, deconcentration, and sprawl are extremely high. Each time metropolitan areas spread out, new highways, streets, bridges, sewers, police and fire stations, and schools must be built. Much of this cost is covered by government with the public's tax dollars. Meanwhile, taxpayers in the cities and older suburbs watch their infrastructures, public transit, and schools deteriorate even though it is almost always less costly to repair and maintain old infrastructure than to build new.

In addition to the jobs that cities have lost to the suburbs and now to the edge cities, there has been a net loss of good-paying and well-benefited jobs in the wider U.S. economy. Over the past three decades, deindustrialization, the shift from manufacturing to services, and corporations moving their operations outside the United States have devastated the domestic economy in general, worsened the decline of the cities, and devastated millions of workers (see the panel titled "Voices," pp. 150–151). These economic changes and their impact on U.S. society are discussed in detail in Chapter 14.

Particularly as the business of the old industrial cities of the Northeastern and Midwestern United States shifted from manufacturing to legal, financial, real estate, and the other service work discussed earlier, the worst of the local-serving jobs, the jobs of low-skill workers, were hit hard. Especially impacted were people of color in the inner city. As a result of the exodus of jobs away from the city and the deindustrialization of the economy, unemployment is high in the central cities. In 1998, for example, 17 percent of central cities had unemployment rates at least 50 percent higher than the national average (Brockerhoff, 2000).

According to the U.S. Census Bureau, nearly one-fifth of all full-time jobs in the U.S. economy are low-wage jobs, not making enough to lift an urban family of four above the government's poverty line. As low-wage employment proliferates throughout the U.S. economy, it is increasingly the only kind of employment available to less skilled central-city workers.

VOICES

UNEMPLOYED STEEL WORKERS

Before 1980 Chicago's Southeast Side was a booming area. Then during a 3-year period Wisconsin Steel shut down and U.S. Steel's South Works all but closed, leaving a total of more than 15,000 former employees without work. Here are the stories of two of these former steel workers.

Mary Morgan, Black Female, Early 50s

I started in at South Works in 1973. I had two kids still at home and was just separated from my husband. He died a few month later.

I really liked that job. By me being a widow, I could support myself. I didn't have to go out and ask somebody for money. I didn't have to go on Aid. I could support my own self. That's very important to me.

I've been off work since January of '82. I haven't been able to find anything else. And all my benefits is ran out, even my little savings. My children help a little. I have six—all grown now. They're all unemployed. Three of them worked at one company that was sort of like the mill. It's all but closed down now. They had been going on unemployment and trying to find a job, but that has ran out now. I have my youngest son, my oldest daughter, and one little grandchild living with me. Altogether I have ten grandchildren. That's what makes it rough.

I've been looking for other jobs. I've been to Sweetheart, Tootsie Roll, Sure-Plus, Libby's, Soft Sheen. I've been to places to find something in the line of what maybe I could do. Cause, you see, some of these jobs you can't apply for them if you don't have the ability or education. Most of them just say they're not hiring. It gets discouraging. . . .

I have very little hope—very, very little. I'm praying that I can find me a job somewhere. But if they don't open up something where peoples can get a job, it don't look very good at all. I guess they just want us all to dig a hole and get in it.

But often, not even low-wage employment is available. For growing numbers of people in the city, there are no jobs. Microchip technology and the electronics revolution have fueled the development of a global economy in which large corporations have little or no loyalty to any particular locale or country; they are footloose multinational corporations. Since the early 1970s, many high-wage industries have fled U.S. cities to relocate in places with a more advantageous business climate—lower wages, weak or nonexistent unions, and lax environmental regulations. Sometimes these places have been suburbs, the urban fringe, or sprawling new metropolitan areas in the Sun Belt states; often they have been Third World countries, as when General Motors moved assembly plants to Mexico and Ford moved to Brazil. This corporate flight has been promoted in the United States by tax policies that encourage businesses to relocate to new sites rather than to modernize and expand their old plants in the cities. And with the U.S. government entering into international agreements that eliminate tariffs and other protections against free and unfettered trade—agreements such as GATT (General Agreement on Tariffs and Trade) and NAFTA (North American Free Trade Agreement)—American business will only find more reasons to relocate outside the United States.

Disinvestment

Systematic patterns of investment and disinvestment have also mugged U.S. cities. Banks, savings and loans, and insurance companies have redlined cities and metropolitan areas—literally drawing red lines on the map and making

Victor Gonzalez, Hispanic Male, Early 50s

I spent most of my life at Wisconsin Steel. I thought I was set. In four more years, I'd have had my thirty years and got my pension.

I'm a carpenter. I've tried everything to get a job. But you don't have the opportunity to prove to anyone what you can do. When you tell people you're a former steelworker, they won't hire you. I went down to the Job Service [Illinois Bureau of Employment Security] and they were going to send me out for an interview. But when I told the guy I'd worked for Wisconsin, he said, "Forget it, they won't want you."

Then I went to Florida to look for work because my wife's mother lives there. I got a job in the fields trimming trees for $2 an hour. Then I got into construction; I was hauling cement bricks for $4 an hour. The boss really liked me, but the job ended and there wasn't any more work. So we came back up here.

We had just moved from South Chicago to Dolton [a nearby suburb] the year before the mill closed. The mortgage payments were $310 a month and we couldn't handle them on top of all our other bills. Our unemployment ran out. We lost the house—and our car too. We went to live with our daughter in South Chicago. But that's hard. You feel like you're intruding. You wish you had a place of your own.

Our children are hurting too. Out of six, only one has a regular job. One daughter worked at South Works, another at Wisconsin; our son was at Wisconsin; one son-in-law was there, another at South Works. So it's the whole family.

So many people that I know, they just gave up. But I'm not giving up. Right now, I'm trying to get into construction. It's hard, though. I feel like I've been robbed—robbed of twenty-five, twenty-six years of my life really.

Source: Excerpted from David Bensman and Roberta Lynch. 1987. *Rusted Dreams.* New York: McGraw-Hill, pp. 94–96.

loans and providing insurance on one side of the line and not on the other. **Redlining** refers to the practice of not providing loans, or insurance, in what are deemed undesirable areas. These areas are almost always made up of high concentrations of poor minorities and located in the central cities. They are the communities that suffer the consequences of the disinvestment that denies loans to homebuyers, small business entrepreneurs, and neighborhood real estate developers.

For the most part, the federal government has allowed redlining, even though in 1977, Congress passed the Community Reinvestment Act (CRA) requiring local institutions to make a fair proportion of their loans in poor neighborhoods and communities in decline. Another federal law, the Mortgage Disclosure Act (MDA), mandated lending institutions to document and make available to the federal government, as well as to their customers, their record regarding investment in poor and decaying areas. But assisted by little or no enforcement of these laws by federal bank regulators, most banks and savings and loans have not responded to the financial needs of these communities. The panel titled "Social Policy" on the South Shore Bank, p. 152, provides an example of an exception—a bank that has made community development its primary activity.

The patterns of disinvestment and investment that have resulted from redlining in U.S. metropolitan areas have discriminated by both race and place.

- **Race.** The most significant factor determining the flow of mortgage credit in U.S. cities is the racial composition of a neighborhood. In fourteen metropoli-

SOCIAL POLICY

INVESTING IN INNER-CITY NEIGHBORHOODS: South Shore Bank

Twenty-five years ago, the South Shore neighborhood in Chicago, an inner-city bedroom community of approximately 80,000 working-class Blacks, was headed for economic disaster. A downward spiral of redlining, housing deterioration, and slumlording had devastated the once prosperous community, which in 1960 had been completely White and middle class.

Into this demoralized climate stepped four idealistic bankers—three White and one Black—who managed to pull off the seemingly impossible. The neighborhood's downward spiral has been reversed to one of growth, without displacing the African American residents of the community. And perhaps most significantly, the process of urban decay was halted while South Shore Bank simultaneously made a profit.

The founders of South Shore Bank call it a combination of "radical values and conservative principles" (Grzywinski, 1991:87). Their conviction was an old-fashioned one—that banks had geographical market areas to which they owed services. Banks, they believed, had a social responsibility to invest in their local communities, even though that investment might entail a slightly higher risk or smaller profit margin. Following through on this principle, residents in capital-starved South Shore were given priority access to credit and loans by the local bank, fostering a shared social and economic stake in the community. This infusion of capital was not granted without standards, but through prudent loaning practices that rewarded hard work and careful planning but did not unduly and stereotypically penalize those with no credit history or a lack of business experience.

Most of South Shore Bank's loans were made for multifamily dwelling rehabilitation in the neighborhood, since the primary small business in the community was and continues to be residential housing. The targeting of the South Shore neighborhood resulted in the concentration of housing upgrades, so that improved properties fed upon each other, collectively improving each project's chances for success.

Where did the money for these loans come from? In most poorer communities, there is a net capital outflow. That is, residents deposit their relatively meager savings in the local bank, but the bank makes loans in other, more affluent communities. At South Shore Bank, the opposite is the case. A net capital inflow results from money outside the service area coming into the bank, which is then invested locally. "Development Deposits," as South Shore Bank terms them, are marketed nationally (and even internationally) to non–South Shore residents who know how their money is being used and can support the bank's social goals without risk by investing in federally insured deposits paying regular interest rates. Currently, 30 percent of South Shore Bank's deposit dollars come from outside the city of Chicago.

The neighborhood of South Shore is thriving. Other Chicago banks compete to make loans there. South Shore Bank has recently doubled in size, and is now targeting the Austin neighborhood on Chicago's far west side for community development efforts. South Shore Bank has successfully lent over $400 million to more than 11,000 inner-city businesses and individuals in its 25-year history, and has been profitable every year since 1975. Its loan default rate remains well below the national average (South Shore Bank, 1998).

Source: This essay was written expressly for *Social Problems* in 1999 by Kathryn D. Talley, Office of Institutional Research, Olive-Harvey College, Chicago, IL.

tan areas nationwide, in a 1-year period, banks and savings and loans made on the average three times more loans in White census tracts than in minority census tracts. In a recent 7-year period in Atlanta, five times as many mortgages in predominantly White areas of the city were approved by local banks and savings and loans as were mortgages in Black neighborhoods with the same income level. Another study found that the lending ratio in Detroit, a city that is three-fourths Black, was 3 to 1 in favor of White neighborhoods. Nationwide,

Black home mortgage applicants are rejected at savings and loan institutions twice as often as Whites, even when their income level and other indicators of credit are similar. In fact, a study of Atlanta indicated that the home lending rate disparity between Blacks and Whites was greatest in areas where Blacks had the highest incomes. A study conducted by ACORN (the Association of Community Organizations for Reform Now), using statistics available from the Home Mortgage Disclosure Act found that African Americans in the Denver metropolitan area were 1.86 times as likely to be denied for conventional loans and Latinos 2.06 times as likely to be rejected as White applicants. Moreover, Latinos and African Americans earning more than $74,259 a year were more likely to be turned down than Whites who made between $49,000 and $62,100 (Arellano, 2000). Another ACORN study, this time for Chicago, found that 30.2 percent of all first mortgage applications by African Americans were made by subprime lenders, while only 3.1 percent of such applications by Whites were from subprime lenders. To be assigned a subprime loan rather than a conventional loan means paying interest rates as much as 4 percentage points higher (Tammy Williamson, 2000). Similar problems have occurred with securing car loans and even when purchasing homeowners insurance.

Place. Patterns of lending also discriminate with regard to location. Suburbs receive a much greater and disproportionate share of loans compared to the central city. This discrimination, of course, is clearly related to the patterns of disinvestment and investment based on race described previously, since suburban areas are predominantly White, while inner-city neighborhoods are often Black or Latino. Moreover, research on 4,600 small businesses found that Black-owned businesses were twice as likely to be denied a loan from a bank or financial institution as similar White-owned businesses (Koretz, 1998b).

City dollars, central city capital, regularly go to the suburbs. Bank deposits made by inner-city residents in city banks are more likely to be used for home and business loans in the suburbs than in the cities where the need for capital is so apparent.

This sort of redlining, discrimination, and disinvestment ultimately leads to a self-fulfilling prophecy of decline in inner-city neighborhoods. When banks disinvest in a neighborhood, residents and small businesses cannot maintain their homes and property. Without loans, small businesses often fail, and the jobs, goods, and services they provide are lost to the neighborhood. Indeed, often the banks themselves are among the businesses that physically leave the community. Disinvestment by banks, savings and loans, and insurance companies also discourages other private investors and government agencies from investing in poor and minority neighborhoods.

The racist myth in the United States is that Black inner-city neighborhoods are run down because Blacks lack pride and other middle-class values. In reality, they lack capital, not pride and good values. This capital is denied to them and to their communities by primarily White-controlled financial institutions.

The inability of poor and minority residents and communities to acquire loans and capital from the private sector of the economy has become even more critical to the decline and decay in the central city over the past 25 or so years. This is because, beginning in the late 1970s, the federal government, as discussed in the next section, began to curtail drastically its investment in cities in general and in inner-city neighborhoods in particular.

Federal Abandonment

We have seen how federal government policies have supported and encouraged suburbanization, metropolitan deconcentration, corporate and job flight, and disinvestment patterns that have contributed to the decline of U.S. cities. Over the past two decades the federal government has also made huge cuts in dollars and services for the central cities.

Federal aid to cities was cut drastically under the Reagan and Bush administrations by more than half. The Reagan administration eliminated the existing federal revenue sharing program with the cities. Welfare, medical, and other essential social services were reduced dramatically. Successful urban programs—for public works, economic development, job training, housing, schools, and health and nutrition—were slashed by more than 70 percent (Dreier, 1992:22). In fact, if all of these federal programs are figured in, America's cities lost approximately $770 billion between 1980 and 1995 (Prell, 1995). In addition, forty states made cuts in various forms of public assistance to the poor between 1980 and 1995, and the federal welfare legislation of 1996, so-called welfare reform, meant even fewer federal dollars flowing to cities and their poorest residents.

Facing their fiscal crisis alone and with a shrinking tax base, cities have had to cut services or raise taxes, with most doing both. Raising taxes while closing schools, hospitals, and police and fire stations, laying off municipal employees, neglecting health and housing codes, cutting public transit, and postponing infrastructure maintenance and improvements had the effect of encouraging more business, industry, jobs, and middle-class residents to leave the city. This movement, of course, only deepens the budgetary crisis of the downward-spiraling cities. And as urban government downsizes, the poor and working-class residents of the city are left to compete for the dwindling resources and services still available. Douglas Massey compares the financial situation in the suburbs with that of the central city:

> The concentration of affluence in certain suburbs generates high real estate values that allow the affluent to tax themselves at low rates while offering generous, even lavish municipal services. The concentration of poverty in central cities and some inner suburbs generates a high demand for services but yields low property values; thus, higher tax rates are required to support generally inferior services. The end result is a vicious cycle whereby city taxes are raised to maintain deficient services; consequently families with means are driven out; property values then decline further; the result is more tax increases and additional middle-class flight, which further exacerbate the concentration of poverty. (Massey, 1996b:406)

As the central cities lose population, jobs, and businesses, they also lose political clout in state legislatures. As the suburbs and edge cities gain these things, they also gain power. With half of the U.S. population now living in the suburbs, politicians are more likely to make policies favorable to the suburbs than to the central cities where only 30 percent of Americans live and relatively few of them vote.

And at the beginning of the twenty-first century, American cities are "going it alone" more than at any time in the last half century. Abandoned by the federal government, cities in the United States are more dependent on their own resources and the health of their own local economies than at any time since World War II (Wyly, Glickman, and Lahr, 1998).

DECLINING QUALITY OF URBAN LIFE

Urban Poverty

In the past 50 years poverty has shifted from a primarily rural to an urban phenomenon. In 1959, 27 percent of America's poor lived in central cities. In 1999, 41 percent of the nation's poor lived in central cities. In that year, 16.4 percent of all central city residents were living in households with incomes below the federal poverty line, as compared to 8.3 percent of suburban residents and 14.3 percent of those living outside metropolitan areas (U.S. Bureau of the Census, 2000d). This increasing urban poverty is even more concentrated in the nation's largest cities.

Poverty is even further concentrated in particular urban neighborhoods. There has been not only an increase in poverty in central cities but an increase in poverty in central city **"poverty areas"** (neighborhoods in which at least one in five households live below the poverty line are designated by the federal government as poverty areas). There has also been an increase in the poverty concentrated in **"high-poverty areas"** in U.S. cities—areas where at least two in five households, or 40 percent of households, fall below the official poverty line. Urban public housing developments are most likely to fall into this category.

Child poverty is also concentrated in U.S. cities. In Chicago, for example, during the 5-year period from 1990 to 1994, 48 percent of children age 6 and under lived below the poverty line and 29 percent lived in extreme poverty—in a household with income below half the official poverty line (Pitt, 1996).

Urban Poverty and Race. For many people, the words *cities* and *urban* have become metaphors or euphemisms for race. The media, for example, have increasingly equated cities with poor Blacks and Latinos. This, of course, is not the whole truth.

Not all Blacks and Latinos live in cities. Not all Blacks and Latinos are poor. Neither are all Whites middle class and living in the suburbs. Some are poor and living in the central city. Nevertheless, people of color are more likely to be affected by poverty in U.S. cities. For example, about three in five poor Blacks and poor Latinos live in central cities, whereas only one in three poor Whites reside there.

People of color are also more likely to be concentrated in poverty areas in the city and much more likely to be among the poorest of the poor. The increase over the past decade in the proportion of poor people who fell into the "poorest of the poor" category hit Black children particularly hard.

Urban Poverty, Race, and Segregation. Not only are poor Blacks and Latinos highly concentrated in poverty and high-poverty areas, but they also make up a large proportion of the urban poor. Throughout the 1990s, at least one-third of all Blacks living in central cities were poor.

Matching the high rates of Black central city poverty are high rates of residential segregation. High proportions of Blacks live in overwhelmingly racially segregated neighborhoods. Analysis of 2000 census data found that about 30 percent of Whites live in central cities, but they typically live in urban neighborhoods that are about 72 percent White. More than 60 percent of African Americans live in cities, in neighborhoods that are 76 percent minority, in which 60 percent of the residents are Black. The most segregated cities (by neighborhood) in 2000 were Detroit, Milwaukee, Chicago, Cleveland, Cincinnati, St. Louis, Miami, New York, and Newark (Schmitt, 2001). See Figure 6.1 for a regional breakdown of racial segregation.

In reality, even the extremely high levels of segregation reflected in census-tract data underestimate racial separation and isolation. Racial segregation is even more severe when smaller units, such as immediate neighborhoods and blocks, are analyzed. High levels of segregation in housing also lead to segregation in schools, churches, and other neighborhood institutions.

This means that not only are the urban poor a growing proportion of all poor people in the United States, but also that a growing proportion of the urban poor are racially segregated in poverty and high-poverty areas in the central city. Racial segregation contributes to and perpetuates poverty because

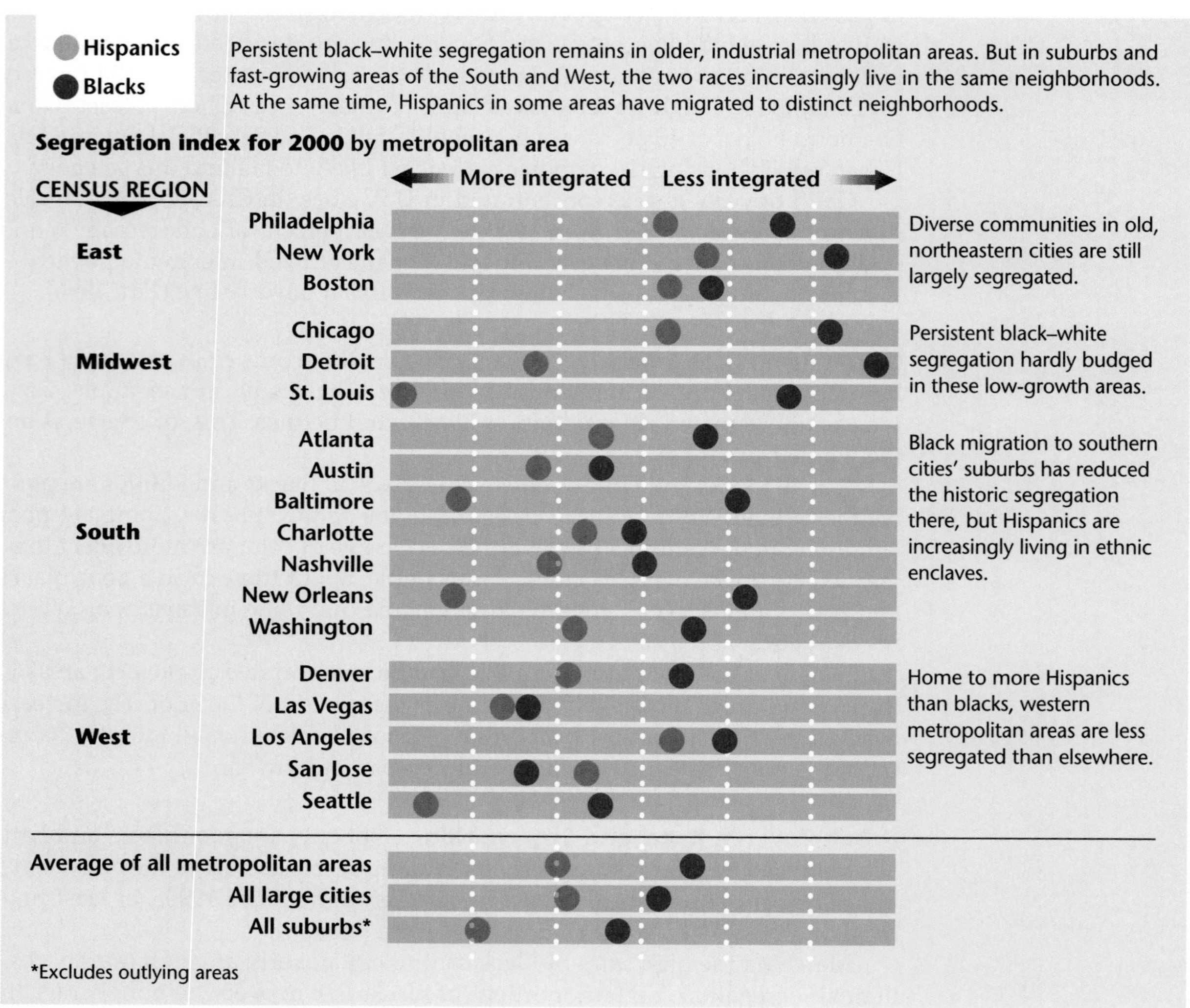

FIGURE 6.1

Residential Segregation by Race and Ethnicity in Selected Metropolitan Areas, 2000

Source: Washington Post National Weekly Edition (April 9–15, 2001):6.

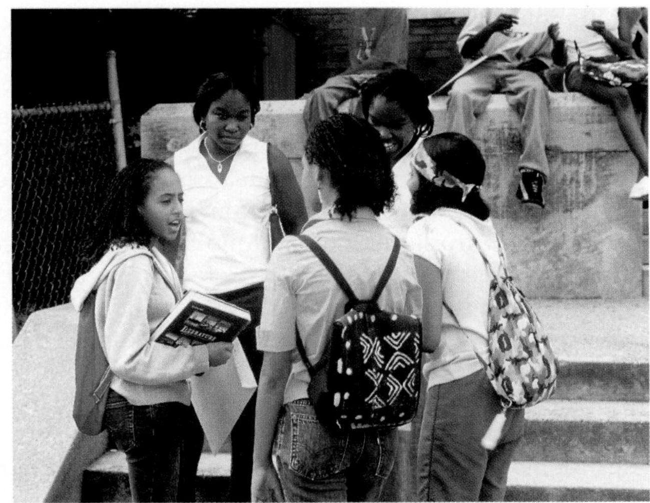

Racial segregation is pronounced in urban neighborhoods, a fact that is reflected in segregated schools, churches, and other neighborhood institutions.

it isolates poor people from the educational and economic opportunities they need. The schools in racially segregated, poor Black communities in the inner city are separate but not equal. The poor people living in the poorest, racially segregated, central city neighborhoods are disconnected—both socially and physically—from urban labor markets. As a consequence of this "American apartheid," urban African Americans and Latinos are disproportionately unemployed and uneducated. Also, as poverty is more concentrated in inner cities, crime and violence proliferate. The poor may adopt violence as a survival strategy. This escalates violence even further (Massey, 1996a). The structural analysis employed in our analysis focuses on social conditions, not immoral people. This allows us to understand that social conditions and policies of abandonment create racial impoverishment in U.S. inner cities.

Urban Housing Crisis

The demand for low-income and affordable housing in U.S. cities far exceeds the supply. In 1995, for example, there were only 6.1 million low-rent units for the nation's 10.5 million low-income households, a shortfall of 4.4 million units. Census data indicate that there are 5.3 million families with "worst case housing needs," that is, these families live in substandard housing or pay over half their income in rent (Collins, Leondar-Wright, and Sklar, 1999:38). The government, by the way, defines housing as "unaffordable" if it costs more than 30 percent of a family's monthly income (Barry, 1998). The sources of this shrinkage include trends in the urban housing market that affect both the affordability of existing housing and the number of low-income units.

One trend is that urban rental housing is increasingly controlled by a decreasing number of large owners who cooperate in and through landlord management firms as well as formal and informal professional associations and groups. In such groups, they are able to reduce competition and ensure rising and higher rents. In this way urban housing affordability is negatively affected, particularly for the poor and working class.

Another factor reducing housing affordability and the supply of low-income housing units in urban areas is that private developers and builders, throughout the 1970s, 1980s, and 1990s, tended to invest only in middle-class and luxury housing, where the market provided the highest margins. In many cities, this exclusively middle-class/luxury focus led to considerable overbuilding of this kind of housing. Relatively high vacancy rates, however, do not solve the housing problems of the people who simply cannot afford middle-class or luxury rents and prices. Nevertheless, developers and owners often profited more, because of higher margins, from less-than-full upscale middle-class developments than from full low- and moderate-income ventures. This private real estate investment included both condo conversion and gentrification.

Condominium conversion involves taking rental units and turning them into apartments for sale. This process often displaces people who cannot afford a down payment and do not qualify for a home mortgage with more affluent residents who can and do. **Gentrification** typically includes buying older, often rundown properties in poor and working-class neighborhoods and rehabilitating them into middle-class condominiums, townhouses, single-family dwellings, and upscale lofts and apartments. Often, the original residents are displaced because they are unable to afford the increased rents, purchase prices, and property taxes based on the neighborhoods' rising property values.

The redevelopment of the downtown areas in many U.S. cities during the past two decades has also led to the loss of significant numbers of low-income housing units. As the economy moved from manufacturing to services, many big-city downtowns were remade as financial, real estate, legal, and retail centers. Building often boomed on the fringes of the old downtown areas and in the process destroyed most of the SROs (single-room occupancy hotels) in many cities. SROs had historically provided housing for economically marginal single persons in the city. Although apartments were small, and occupants often had to share a bathroom or a kitchen or both, the units were affordable and available for this part of the urban population. Now the SRO is becoming a thing of the past. Since 1973, Chicago has lost 70 percent of its SRO units. The figures are comparable for New York, and the losses have been significant in other large cities.

Slumlords have also contributed to the housing shortage in the inner city. **Slumlording** occurs when landlords buy properties in poor neighborhoods and have no intention of investing in their upkeep and maintenance. Slumlords often fail to pay utility and property tax bills as well. Over time, serious housing code violations develop, roofs leak, stairways deteriorate, plumbing fails, and electrical wiring becomes dangerous. Often the utilities are turned off and tenants are left without water, gas, electricity, and heat. Finally, the city must condemn the building, evict the residents, and take it over for nonpayment of taxes. With few city funds available for rehabilitation or demolition, the building stands vacant and is boarded up. All along the way, of course, slumlords collect as much rent as they can from their poor tenants.

Another urban housing market phenomenon that adds to the housing crisis in some cities is **warehousing.** Here urban real estate speculators withhold apartments from the housing market. Speculators purchase buildings and gradually empty them by not renting the units. They hold the property until developers on the edges of gentrifying areas become interested and purchase them for considerably more than their original cost. Developers are especially attracted to warehoused apartments, which spare them the trouble of getting rid of poor and working-class tenants who will not be able to afford the newly gentrified property.

Moreover, less than 10 percent of all new housing construction in the United States is presently taking place in cities. Thus, it is clear why the urban housing market is not adequately providing for all city residents (Barry, 1998).

Failed Housing Policies. All the forces in the urban housing market that have led to the shrinking supply of affordable and low-income housing have been met with, or encouraged by, failing government housing policies.

As early as the 1960s, federally financed urban renewal projects were bulldozing low-income housing in poor and working-class neighborhoods. In theory, federal urban renewal funds were meant for the rehabilitation and redevelopment of decaying urban neighborhoods. In practice, what usually happened was quite different. Cities applied for the federal funds and, when they received them, used their legal powers of eminent domain and other powers granted them under both federal and state urban renewal legislation to declare an area to be blighted. Once so designated, all structures in the area were eliminated. Often, this was done to facilitate the development of large public projects such as airports, colleges or universities, medical centers, or even private commercial projects on the now available land. The second phase of federal urban renewal was to include replacement housing for people who lost their homes or apartments and neighborhood. For the most part, however, funds were never appropriated for this phase, and urban renewal projects continued to reduce the supply of low-income housing throughout the 1970s. Much of the housing stock lost was in fact blighted, but for many people, it was at least an affordable place to live.

The budget cutbacks during the Reagan and Bush administrations slashed federal housing funds by 70 percent. New construction of low-income housing by the Department of Housing and Urban Development (HUD), the federal agency responsible for the creation and maintenance of low-income housing in American cities, decreased by 90 percent. Congress and the Clinton administration decreased the HUD budget again in 1995—this time by 25 percent. For the first time in 20 years, funding for the construction of new public housing units was cut. For the first time there was no increase in the number of available Section 8 certificates (certificates that subsidize eligible low-income tenants renting from private landlords). Congress and the president also slashed funds for the maintenance and rehabilitaion of existing public housing, thereby ensuring its further deterioration. They also repealed the long-standing federal one-for-one replacement rule, which required that a new unit of public housing be built before any old unit could be demolished. The Republican Congress and President Clinton endorsed these changes in public and subsidized housing at a time when the housing needs of the poorest households in U.S. cities were at an all-time high. And they made these cuts at a time when government subsidies were providing 75 percent of affordable housing units for low-income Americans (Barry, 1998).

These recent cutbacks in public housing in the United States come on top of an already meager public housing sector. When compared to the industrial democracies of Europe, for example, U.S. public housing makes up a small share of the total housing stock. In Germany, France, the Netherlands, and the Scandinavian countries, urban public housing often accounts for as much as 40 percent or more of all housing. In the United States, only 1.3 percent of the housing stock is publicly owned. Throughout Europe there has been a more widespread recognition that the private housing market—housing for profit—

will not adequately house all parts of the population. Therefore, a larger share of the housing stock, as compared to the United States, has been provided by the not-for-profit or public sector. In European social democracies, public housing has been for middle-class as well as for poor and working-class residents. In U.S. cities, public housing has been the housing of last resort for the poorest of the poor only. No more than a third of U.S. households who qualify for low-income housing assistance get it from the government (Barry, 1998). In some large cities such as Chicago, the figure is barely half that. And only one-fifth of the poor live in government-subsidized housing of any kind, be it public housing run by local government, privately owned developments subsidized by HUD, or private apartments where tenants pay rent with government vouchers. Hence, with only the poorest of the poor inhabiting it, public housing has remained low on the U.S. political agenda and is presently sinking even lower.

No federal program has ever reached more than a fraction of the urban households in the United States that need housing assistance. Government expenditures have never provided the decent, safe, and sanitary housing guaranteed all Americans by the Housing Act of 1949. Instead, government housing policy and funds were designed to make the provision of low- and moderate-income housing profitable for private developers, builders, and landlords. The government could have chosen, as was done in much of Europe, to provide this affordable housing by building, owning, and managing it itself. Rather than do this, U.S. housing policy has relied on subsidizing the private sector to provide low- and moderate-income housing that the market was not otherwise providing. This approach has proven to be inefficient, ineffective, costly, and a contributing factor in the dwindling supply of low-income housing in U.S. cities.

When subsidizing private developers is the mechanism relied on for low- and moderate-income housing, a permanent, public, not-for-profit stock of affordable units is not developed. The running out, buying out, and corruption of federal HUD mortgages to private builders and developers illustrate this. Typically, HUD makes something like a 20-year low-interest loan available to private interests to build or rehabilitate low-income apartments. For the duration of the loan, the owners are required to rent a percentage of their units at below-market rates to low- or moderate-income households. The problem with this arrangement became apparent in the 1980s, when a number of these developments built in the 1960s now were able to rent all units to middle-class households at market rates because the mortgages were paid off. In this way, federal dollars spent to provide low-income or affordable housing now could claim fewer units. HUD mortgages run out in this way.

Some developers buy out their loans early, with the same effect. Instead of taking 20 years to repay the loan, developers may pay them off in 5 or 10 years, thus freeing their units to be rented at market rates to the middle class even earlier. In this way, private real estate ventures may use low-interest government loans to develop housing without any real commitment to long-term affordable shelter for poor or working-class households. This situation is made worse by the high potential for corruption whenever public monies are used to subsidize the private housing market. For example, already meager HUD dollars for low-income housing assistance were often diverted to politically connected real estate firms that were given an exemption from the federal law requiring a percentage of their units be rented to low-income renters, or federal dollars were simply used to develop middle-class townhouses and even golf courses and country clubs.

In addition to this, by 2002 HUD will have the contracts on nearly 3 million government-subsidized Section 8 apartments (contracts HUD has with private landlords to provide these apartments to low-income renters) come up for renewal. It will cost between $17 and $20 billion to renew them. This would require nearly a doubling of the current HUD budget at a time when Congress and the George W. Bush administration have been cutting that budget. HUD secretary under President Clinton, Andrew Cuomo, has called this threat to these Section 8 renewals the "greatest crisis in HUD's history" (Barry, 1998).

Another problem is that government housing policy in the United States is heavily biased toward the middle class and above. About 80 percent of all federal housing subsidies currently go to the homeowning middle and upper middle class. Most of this subsidy comes in the form of tax shelters: local property tax deductions and home mortgage interest payment deductions. About 58 percent of these tax shelters go to U.S. families in the top 20 percent income bracket and only 15 percent flow to the bottom 20 percent of households (Lazare, 2001). In 1997, the mortgage deduction added up to a $53.7 billion subsidy to the middle and upper classes ($23 billion more than the total 1998 fedeal spending by HUD) (Collins, Leondar-Wright, and Sklar, 1999:38). Canada does not allow this kind of subsidy for middle- and upper-class homeowners and, not coincidentally, does a much better job of housing low-income residents in its cities.

U.S. housing policies have also contributed to the **jobs/housing mismatch.** What little affordable low-income housing there is in U.S. metropolitan areas is kept out of the suburbs and urban fringe. Suburbs and edge cities have used legal, political, and economic means to prevent this kind of housing from being built in their communities. The problem with this is that job growth, as we have seen, is occurring on the remotest edges of metropolitan areas. Thus, people who need the jobs the most, the poor in the central city, are the farthest from them. The jobs are located where the inner-city poor cannot afford to live, or discrimination prevents their living there. The poor are also the least likely to be able to afford to own a car, and public transit systems rarely extend to the urban fringe.

Before job growth became concentrated in the urban fringe, it was centered in the closer suburbs. Although low-income residents of the central city were unable to afford housing in these communities as well, their proximity allowed more of them to hold jobs in these locations. This has changed dramatically with more and more metropolitan deconcentration. Many ex-urban areas and edge cities are experiencing a labor shortage, particularly in the low-wage service sector, while growing numbers of central city residents go without jobs.

The jobs/housing mismatch is a form of **spatial apartheid.** Jobs and job growth occur in one place, populated by relatively affluent Whites, while poor Blacks and Latinos are restricted to another place.

In short, because they increase the property tax base—and hence, revenues—city, state, and federal approaches to housing and economic development have tended to support and encourage both market trends and public policies that favor middle-class residential and commercial development at the expense of low-income and affordable housing.

Consequences of the Urban Housing Crisis. Trends in the urban housing market together with failed housing policies have had, and continue to have, predictable consequences for a growing number of urban households.

sprawl (sprôl) *n.* The haphazard result of letting the market direct housing development patterns.

Kirk Anderson

One consequence is that more and more households are experiencing a rent squeeze. More than half of all tenants pay rents that exceed the federal government's definition of affordable housing—not more than 30 percent of household income. More than one-quarter of all renters now devote more than half their income to rent. When the demand for low-cost housing exceeds the supply, the cost of low-cost rents rises; so, too, when gentrification upscales areas that once housed the poor and the near poor. When urban residents, particularly poor urban residents, have to pay more for housing, they have less money available for food, transportation, education, and health care.

When so much of an economically marginal family's budget is devoted to housing, a crisis such as a medical emergency or sudden unemployment often means that they are evicted from their homes, resulting in homelessness:

> The affordable housing crisis is taking an increasing toll. On any given night, some 750,000 people are homeless; many more are "hidden homeless," missed in varied counts. Over the course of a year, some 2 million people experience homelessness for some period of time. More than one-third of the homeless are families with children. (Collins, Leondar-Wright, and Sklar, 1999:38)

Homelessness is most concentrated in big cities—now, each year, there are probably more than 100,000 homeless people in New York City, 90,000 in Los Angeles, and as many as 75,000 in Chicago.

Decaying Infrastructure

The fiscal crisis of the cities has also affected them physically. The urban infrastructure is crumbling. Old water mains regularly erupt in the winter. Streets are marred with potholes. Clogged and overburdened expressways deteriorate. Sewer systems are decaying and overstressed. Public transit stations, subway tunnels, and rail and trolley tracks all make mass transportation less efficient as years go by without needed maintenance. The U.S. Department of Transportation has rated 40 percent of all U.S. bridges, many in the oldest cities, as structurally deficient or functionally obsolete.

Spending on infrastructure is only about 2.5 percent of the federal budget. Governments in countries such as Germany, Japan, and the Netherlands invest public dollars in the urban infrastructure at a rate three to four times that of the United States. As a result of the U.S. government's failure to spend adequately on the infrastructure of the nation's cities, people are increasing endangered because of inadequate waste treatment, tainted water, leaking gas lines, structurally unsound bridges, and the like.

There is a strong link between declining infrastructure and declining economic growth and productivity in the U.S. economy. Overburdened and deteriorating expressways, closed bridges, moratoriums on new connections to sewer systems, congested airports—all have real economic costs. Studies by economist David Aschauer indicate that a pattern of less spending on public works in cities leads to declines in economic growth. Aschauer has found that the current low levels of public infrastructure spending in the United States first occurred around 1968, just before the persistent pattern of slow economic growth and declines in productivity began. Furthermore, Aschauer believes that as much as half of the drop in productivity growth in the U.S. economy can be attributed to deterioration of the infrastructure, much of it in the cities. He also estimates that each dollar invested in public infrastructure today improves national economic productivity about four times as much as a dollar invested in new plants or equipment by private companies (cited in Dorning, 1992).

Many economists now believe that investing public dollars in a job creation program to rebuild the nation's infrastructure and a much needed and expanded mass transit system are the best ways to spur economic growth and productivity.

Transportation, Pollution, and the Environment

The urban transportation system in the United States, again in contrast to most European cities, is dominated by the private automobile. In 1946, public mass transit in the United States peaked as Americans took 23.4 billion trips on trains, buses, and trolleys. By 1960, that figure had dropped to 9.3 billion trips and bottomed out at 6.5 billion trips in 1972. The number of trips remained low until 1995 when it began to climb, with 1999 showing 9 billion trips, which is still lower than in 1960 (Layton, 2000). Moreover, the 9 billion mass-transit trips compare to *over one trillion trips taken by car and truck every year* (Layton, 2001). The consequences of this attachment to the automobile are enormous:

- Traffic jams are getting much worse. Americans spent three times as many hours stalled in traffic in 1999 as they did in 1982 (Frank, 2001).
- Since 1982, while the U.S. population has risen by 20 percent, the time Americans spend in traffic has grown by 236 percent (Longman, 2001).
- Traffic congestion costs Americans $78 billion a year in wasted fuel and lost time (Longman, 2001).
- On a typical day, the average married mother with school-age children spends 66 minutes driving—taking more than five trips and covering 29 miles (Longman, 2001).
- Long commutes are a significant reason for Americans' decreasing involvement in community affairs (PTA, church, recreational clubs) (Putnam, 2000).
- San Diego is expected to grow by 1 million by 2020, which translates into an additional 685,000 cars (by current patterns). To find sufficient parking

spaces for these added cars will require an additional 37 square miles of parking lots (Longman, 2001).

- People making long commutes are at a higher risk for high blood pressure, sleep deprivation, and depression (Longman, 2001). They have more frequent disputes with their co-workers and families. They suffer more frequent and more serious illnesses, and they are more likely to experience premature deaths (Frank, 2001).
- The United States produces twice as much carbon dioxide per capita as Germany, Japan, and Great Britain, eight times as much as China, and twenty-three times as much as India (Lazare, 2001:264).

To a large extent, the dependency of U.S. cities on automobiles was created by powerful oil and auto lobbies. These corporate interests sometimes literally bought up and tore up city mass-transit systems and shaped federal, state, and local legislation to develop the highway system instead of railroads and subways. By 1949, General Motors Corporation had replaced more than one hundred electric trolley and train transit systems in forty-five cities with gas-driven buses. In April 1949, a federal jury in Chicago convicted General Motors of conspiring with Standard Oil of California and Firestone Tire to replace electric transportation with gas- and diesel-powered buses and to monopolize the sale of buses and related products (gas, oil, and tires) to local transit authorities. In most instances, these corporations accomplished this by creating a holding company and buying up the electric transportation systems. General Motors was fined $5,000. H. C. Grossman, treasurer of General Motors and chief engineer of the campaign, was fined $1. General Motors continued the practice into the 1950s (Liazos, 1982).

Between 1936 and 1955, the number of operating trolley cars in U.S. cities dropped from 40,000 to 5,000. People found the buses dirtier, less efficient, and less reliable and began to move away from using public transit and toward the private automobile, benefiting the same corporate interests busy tearing down the existent transit system. Between 1945 and 1970, cities, states, and the federal government spent $156 billion constructing hundreds of thousand of miles of roads, but only 16 miles of subway were built in the entire country during the same time period (Liazos, 1982). This subsidization of the automobile by the government continues, as more than 80 percent of federal transportation funds go to highways (Kay, 1998).

Consequences of Auto Dependency. The development of the auto-dependent urban transportation system contributes to the suburbanization and deconcentration of metropolitan areas. Highways, interstates, expressways, and cars helped to gut the central cities, taking away middle-class taxpayers, jobs, business, and retail and commercial activity. As auto dependency sprawls and decentralizes urban areas, a vicious cycle of more cars and highways sets in. The auto-reliant transportation system that has aided the deconcentration of U.S. cities has contributed to lower population densities in suburban and urban fringe areas. These lower densities remove many of the energy, environmental, and cost advantages of urban mass transit and lead to the construction of more and bigger highways with yet more cars, further decentralizing metropolitan areas.

The reliance on the private automobile at the expense of mass public transportation also further disadvantages the urban poor. Unable to afford owning and operating a car, they must rely on an underfunded and often undependable public transit system with limited service. Since most jobs are amid the malls, office parks, and construction in the suburbs, inner-city residents have difficulty finding the transportation to work there. "Instead of springing up where they are needed, jobs are being created where they are not" (Lazare, 2001:x). Unlike the suburbs, compact and walkable cities are efficient.

> It is estimated . . . that a nickel trolley fare in turn-of-the-century Chicago brought a typical worker within reach of an estimated forty-eight thousand jobs. A century or so later, that same worker would have to invest thousands of dollars in a car, drive through endless miles of suburban sprawl, consume hundreds of gallons of gasoline, and generate dangerous levels of pollution and carbon dioxide in order to gain access to a fraction of that number. (Lazare, 2001:203)

The decentralization that comes with auto transportation has destroyed the landscape and encouraged the spread of commercial strips, shopping malls, and multilane roads and streets. The shopping areas are spread out so that suburban residents cannot walk to a store, as is possible in high-density cities. Instead they must use an automobile. As a result "each home in a typical new development generates an average of 7.5 car trips per day" (Lazare, 2001:225).

Thus, urban sprawl, with its reliance on the automobile, has also led to environomental pollution and a waste of natural resources.

> "One one-thousand," environmentalist David Burwell counted, clocking an instant in the polluting life of the automobile. In that single second America's cars and trucks traveled another 60,000 miles, used up 3,000 gallons of petroleum products, and added 60,000 pounds of carbon dioxide to the atmosphere. . . . Our fossil fuel vehicles . . . not only consume more than one-third of all U.S. energy but [they also exhale] two-thirds of its carbon dioxide emissions, one-quarter of its chlorofluorocarbons (CFCs), more than 50 percent of its methane, and 40 percent of its nitrogen oxides, plus most of the carbon monoxide. (Kay, 1997:80–81).

Other Environmental Threats in the Central City. The air is not the only source of the environmental pollution concentrated in urban areas. Illegal or "fly" dumping, lead paint poisoning, and abandoned hazardous waste sites also plague the central city. Research shows that communites that are low-income neighborhoods, especially those populated by people of color, bear a disproportionate burden of environmental hazards (Pellow, 2000; Bullard, 2000). This pattern suggests a perception among corporate polluters that poor minority residents will be less likely to have the organized political clout to resist the environmental degradation of their neighborhood; that they either won't, or can't, fight back. "Polluting corporations have lobbyists who represent their interests with government officials, but the poor lack this representation, thus they have a diminished ability to ensure clean air and water for their families" (Burnett, 2001:1).

Evidence of **environmental racism** abounds in American metropolitan areas. For example, the Center for Policy Alternatives analyzed toxic release information by ZIP code and found that people of color were 47 percent more likely than Whites to live near toxic waste sites (reported in Dervarics, 2000).

As poor minority communities are illegally dumped on and find themselves on top of more and more toxic and hazardous wastes, waste management corporations scramble to locate their incinerators and disposal facilities in these neighborhoods. This often places these impoverished communities in the position of choosing between at least some kind of economic development and their collective health. Recently, for example, poor Black suburbs south of Chicago, some of the very poorest suburbs in the country, have had to choose between jobs that come with incinerators and/or toxic waste dumps and their residents' own health and well-being.

Health and Health Care

Health and health care problems in U.S. society are discussed at length in Chapter 17. But here, these problems in urban locations deserve special attention because some health and health care problems are more concentrated in large cities.

Because poverty is concentrated in the central city, so are the diseases that go with it. Poor people in the city get tuberculosis and other diseases almost unheard of among the suburban middle class. Poor city dwellers are much more likely to die of cancer. Low birthweights plague poor children in the inner city and reduce their chances for survival. Chronic conditions such as diabetes often go untreated. Many of the urban poor, without health insurance of any kind, cannot afford to burden their families with the huge debt that life-saving technologies would bring.

Infant mortality rates are highest in poor minority neighborhoods in the inner city and are as high as or higher than in many Third World countries. African American infants are four times more likely to die from low birthweight than White infants. Many poor inner-city children who survive their first year are then threatened by such diseases as measles, tetanus, polio, tuberculosis, diphtheria, and whooping cough because they have not received adequate inoculations. In 1999, 80 percent of 2-year-olds were fully immunized, a 40 percent increase from 1992 (Children's Defense Fund, 2001:35). The United States still falls short of the Western democracies, however. In virtually all of northern and western Europe, inoculation rates against all of those childhood diseases is 100 percent.

Perhaps more than any other disease, tuberculosis is associated with poor living and working conditions and thus is a good indicator of the overall level of urban health. During the 1970s, tuberculosis rates steadily declined, continuing the trend of several decades. But in the 1980s, this trend reversed. Tuberculosis began to resurge, particularly in poor minority neighborhoods in New York City, Los Angeles, and Chicago. Making the situation worse was increasing evidence that in these cities strains of tuberculosis were developing that are resistant to the antibiotic drugs historically used to control the disease.

Another health problem adding to the burden of public hospitals is AIDS. The Centers for Disease Control and Prevention (CDC) in Atlanta has confirmed that the incidence of AIDS and the costs of caring for people with AIDS are highest and most concentrated in central cities, where gay men and intravenous drug users are overrepresented. But AIDS is increasingly an epidemic of the poor and minorities. According to the CDC, Blacks, who comprise only 13 percent of the nation's population, now account for 54 percent of all new HIV infections (reported in Stolberg, 2001b), with the disease concentrated in inner-city neighborhoods (Herbert, 2001a). For example, AIDS has killed 75,000 New Yorkers, nearly 20 percent of the Americans who have died from that disease (Steinhauer, 2001). Again, a disproportionate share of the cost has been passed on to the urban public hospital. The annual and lifetime cost of treating a person with AIDS is higher in the United States than anywhere else in the world—$38,000 a year, $102,000 over the life span. In addition, there are the treatment costs for HIV-infected people who have not yet developed AIDS. Many people with AIDS and HIV who come to urban public hospitals, of course, are not paying patients.

Many poor and working-class central city residents have seen their small neighborhood or community hospitals close under the pressure of rising costs. For many of these hospitals, the number of indigent nonpaying patients became too high a proportion of their total number. This has happened in at least six Chicago communities over the past 10 years, for example. Other city hospitals have begun to turn away patients who are uninsured and/or cannot pay the prevailing charge for medical treatment they require. More than one in ten U.S. hospitals are now routinely refusing to treat these people.

This means that more and more central city residents are unable to find any medical care in private for-profit or private not-for-profit hospitals and clinics. Increasingly, they have only one alternative—the large, underfunded, understaffed, underequipped public hospital that cannot legally deny them care. The problem is threefold (Orenstein, 2001). First, the number of patient visits is rising (in 1988, there were 81 million visits to emergency rooms; in 1998, there were 100.4 million). Second, the number of emergency departments fell from 5,200 to just over 4,000 in that decade. For those remaining emergency rooms, the average annual patient volume rose from 15,500 to 24,800—an increase of over 50 percent. Third, and related to the second, the number of hospital beds was reduced from 927,000 in 5,384 community hospitals to 829,000 in 4,956 such hospitals—at a time when the nation's population had grown by 10 percent. The closing of public hospitals in cities leaves the poor in increasing jeopardy. But that has happened in Chicago, St. Louis, and in Washington, D.C., when the federal control board privatized the only public hospital in the nation's capital (Stolberg, 2001a).

Thus, facilities are being overwhelmed by the number of patients and the cost of treating them. Because they are unable to afford doctor visits or are unable to find doctors who will accept the lower fees of Medicaid (the state and federal government's insurance program for the poor), patients are coming to the emergency room sicker and in need of more costly care. But the urban public hospitals are less and less able to provide adequate care.

Urban public hospitals are forced to practice **triage**—treating the most urgent emergencies first. Other patients must wait for treatment, sometimes for days. As Wesley Fields, chairman of the American College of Emergency Physicians Safety Net Task Force, put it:

> Crowded as we are, if you walk in the door, you'll be treated whether you can pay or not. Just get in line and take a number with everyone else. I don't like this any more than my dissatisfied, frustrated patients do. I tell them that it's like rush hour on nearby Interstate 66—too many bodies packed into a space built ages ago for a much smaller population. (Quoted in Orenstein, 2001:21)

Many private hospitals that have remained open have done so by cutting high-cost services. Many have closed emergency rooms and trauma units. Trauma networks, for example, have collapsed in Chicago, Detroit, Los Angeles, Miami, St. Louis, and San Diego. In Chicago, ten hospitals have left the city's trauma network in the last 10 years, leaving only two private hospitals with trauma centers in the third largest city in the country. High-risk obstetrical care, as well as drug and alcohol abuse treatment programs, also have been shut down. As private hospitals in the city abdicate these high-cost services, more of them must be taken over by public hospitals, increasing their burden with more patients and higher costs.

In short, the increasing number of uninsured and underinsured people seeking health care in the emergency rooms of public hospitals, the lack of federal government support for these hospitals, and the inability of city governments caught in a budgetary crisis to fund them, all ensure that without major reforms urban health and health care can only deteriorate further.

Urban Schools

Public schools in the United States are separate and unequal. The more affluent middle class has moved to the suburbs, where their children attend virtually all White schools; or if they have remained in the city and can afford it, they send their children to private schools. The less affluent and racial minorities are left in the city's public schools.

Urban schools are class segregated. With poverty becoming more geographically concentrated, poor children will typically go to school with other poor children. Most significant, the amount of money spent on the education of the children attending city schools pales in comparison to what is spent on each student in the more affluent suburbs. This results from the heavy reliance on local property taxes to finance public schooling in the United States. As suburbanization robbed the city's tax base, the city became less able to adequately fund public education. Consequently, suburban schools, when compared to inner-city schools, are more likely to have smaller class sizes, more computers, a better library, more likely to have special programs for the gifted and the disabled, and more likely to have state-of-the-art equipment and facilities. In effect, the children of the urban poor are "educated in schools that are woefully inadequate on most measures of quality and funding" (Noguera and Akom, 2000:29). Chapter 16 provides the details and the consequences of these severe inequities. As a preview, we note that the results of all of this are predictable: lower standardized test scores and high dropout rates in many urban school districts. Already disadvantaged inner-city students are further disadvantaged.

Crime, Drugs, and Gangs

The problems of crime and drugs in the United States are discussed in Chapters 12 and 13. These problems also have a special relation to urban areas. In the United States, *crime* has become a euphemism for *cities*. More specifically, there is a media and popular identification of crime, and the drugs and gangs assumed to be related to it, with the inner city. And because crime is also a code word for race, it comes to be associated in both media and popular accounts primarily with young African American males in the inner city.

Admittedly, the FBI's *Uniform Crime Report* and the U.S. Justice Department's *National Crime Survey* have shown for some time that poor minority males in the inner city have the highest arrest rates for serious felony offenses and are, along with other members of poor minority inner-city communities, the most likely to be victims of this sort of crime in the United States. Why is this so?

Throughout this chapter, we have seen how suburbanization and metropolitan deconcentration have gutted the cities, taking away jobs, businesses, and industries. Criminologists have documented how the investment patterns of American business and industry are related to street crime. When business and industry disinvest in the central city, deindustrialization occurs, jobs are lost, and street crime rates rise (F. Hagan, 1994). Beyond this, private lending institutions have disinvested in our cities, and the federal government and its policies have encouraged growth and affluence in the suburbs and the urban fringe while promoting decay and decline in the central cities. Cities have increasing and concentrating poverty, rising unemployment and low-wage employment, a dwindling supply of decent and affordable housing, a crumbling infrastructure, and an inadequate public transportation system unable to connect central city residents with the job growth on the edges of the metropolitan area. More central city residents are becoming sicker, unable to gain access to adequate health care. Underfunded urban school systems are ill-prepared to ready students for the current metropolitan labor market. Again, all these socioeconomic conditions lead to crime, drug use, and gangs in the cities.

Official crime statistics have shown for several decades that there is more property crime, or economic crime, in the United States than violent crime, often ten times as much. And many violent offenses, such as robberies, have an economic dimension. The transition of many U.S. cities from manufacturing centers to service economies has severely limited the ability of many low- and semiskilled workers to find jobs with livable wages and benefits. Because migration to the suburbs has been extremely limited for low-income and minority populations, poor Black, Latino, and immigrant neighborhoods in the inner city have become fertile ground for the development of an alternate or **informal economy** (alternative economic activities) to ensure their survival. An important part of this informal economy is criminal (Hagedorn, 1998). Over the past 25 years, participation of minority teenagers in the legal labor market has declined significantly. Workforce participation rates for 18- to 24-year-olds have dropped precipitously, especially for minority young adults. When work and survival are not forthcoming from the legal or formal economy, young people in the inner city become more susceptible to and attracted to opportunities in the criminal economy. Street crime becomes their work (Hagedorn, 1998). Participation in drug rings can spell money, status, and survival. That the socioeconomic conditions in the inner city make it an ideal location for the illegal drug economy has not been lost on the people who control international drug trafficking. The gangs that provide members with meaningful social relationships and status in the barren, isolated inner city and with protection from other sources of violence in their communities can also ensure survival with specialized stolen property, drug, and weapons sales (Hagedorn, 1998).

Official U.S. drug policy has deleterious effects on inner-city communities as well. By criminalizing them, the official strategy is to eliminate drugs and their negative consequences by arresting, prosecuting, convicting, and imprisoning drug users, buyers, and sellers. This "war on drugs" actually escalates drug selling, use, and addiction and magnifies the negative consequences that go with them (see Chapter 13). Criminalization increases drug prices and profits, thus making the drug trade more attractive. Sellers thus work to recruit more users and addicts. Because their drugs are illegal and expensive, users and addicts may have to steal or sell drugs themselves to afford their own habits.

Intravenous (IV) drug users and addicts are pushed underground to avoid detection and criminal sanction. They share contaminated needles, giving the United States the highest proportion of people with AIDS who have contracted the disease through intravenous drug use anywhere in the world. By contrast, many European countries and cities are decriminalizing drug use and curbing the illegal drug trade by reducing its profitability, thus lowering drug use and addiction rates. They are also controlling the spread of AIDS among IV drug users and addicts with clean-needle exchange programs used because they are free of stigma and legal punishment. In Dutch cities, for example, where drugs are treated as a public health problem instead of a criminal one, de facto decriminalization of drugs and harm reduction policies and programs have produced the lowest proportion of people with AIDS who use IV drugs in the industrialized world.

Besides failing as a drug control strategy, the war on drugs is not being waged fairly. Although the official claim is one of zero tolerance, pursuing all users, buyers, and sellers no matter who or where they are, the war is racist and focused on young African American males in poor inner-city neighborhoods (see Chapter 12). The National Council on Crime and Delinquency attributes this to the war on drugs, which is not a zero-tolerance war on drugs, but a war on the poor and Black in U.S. inner cities (see Timmer, 1991). One in three Black males is now under the supervision of the criminal justice system—on probation or parole, in jail or prison, or under pretrial release (a rate eight times higher than for White men). In many cities, and in many inner-city neighborhoods, this proportion is much higher. This only serves to marginalize further the already highly marginal poor Black inner-city residents, with ripple effects throughout Black families, schools, and communities.

- **Fear of Crime in the City.** Fear of crime is often exaggerated in comparison to the reality of, or actual potential for, criminal victimization. Often the fear is not of crime at all. What people identify as a fear of crime is often a fear of people of cultural and racial groups different than their own. Nonetheless, such misdirected fear of crime is often a significant factor in central city decline. If people, corporations, retailers, and small businesses will not stay in or move to the city because they believe it is not safe, then the process of urban decline cannot be turned around. A self-fulfilling prophecy of central city decline sets in. Because of the belief that the city is crime ridden and unsafe, people, businesses, and jobs leave the city, thereby helping make it more crime prone and unsafe and further removing the possibility that the businesses and jobs that could begin to change the socioeconomic conditions that produce crime will go there in the future. And even though over the past 5 years, official murder and other violent crime rates have declined some in most American cities—most precipitously in New York City—fear of crime has shown few signs of abating.

URBAN POLICY: REBUILDING U.S. CITIES

Why Save the Cities?

There are moral and political reasons to rebuild U.S. cities and improve the quality of life for all urban residents. Cities, after all, are home to a lot of people. More than one in eighteen Americans live in just three central cities—New York, Los Angeles, and Chicago. About one in eight reside in just the three largest metropolitan areas (central cities and their suburbs). Large cities have also been the cultural, educational, and intellectual centers of American life and should thrive once again on those grounds. They are also the sites of much "immobile capital," enormous investments made in the past that cannot be easily moved—stock exchanges and other financial institutions and districts, huge medical complexes, great and vast universities, and even many private businesses.

Cities are also potentially cheaper, greener, and cleaner than adding more suburban sprawl and deconcentration. It is "cheaper" to repair and maintain the existing urban infrastructure than to continually build anew for deconcentrating and sparse suburban and fringe populations. Cities are "greener" because high-density urban development takes less land and damages the natural ecology and environment less. Urban growth boundaries set around cities can ensure that this happens. High population densities in cities also make mass transit more efficient and effective, creating the potential for "cleaner," less polluted metropolitan areas.

But perhaps the most compelling argument for saving U.S. cities is economic. Few people would allow the decay of their cities if they believed it would limit economic growth in general and their own economic opportunity in particular.

Research indicates that declining cities lead to declining suburbs. If economic growth and job opportunities decline in the central city, the entire metropolitan area fares worse economically when compared to areas where growth and opportunities are sustained in the central city. These studies have also found that the lower the income inequality between cities and their suburbs, the higher the job growth and expansion of other economic opportunities in the entire metropolitan region.

As capital moves farther and farther from the central city, many older, closer suburbs begin to share many of the same social, economic, and fiscal problems facing the central cities. Not even the bedroom suburbs on the urban fringe can isolate themselves and escape all the economic and social problems created by a troubled economy, widening income inequality, and rising urban poverty. If large sections of big cities are left to rot, entire metropolitan areas and U.S. society as a whole, not just the local residents, will ultimately pay a heavy price.

Unfortunately, the future for cities is bleak, according to a survey of leading urban historians, planners, and architects. In essence, those polled predicted that suburbs will continue to thrive and inner cities will continue to deteriorate (El Nasser, 1999). See the "Looking toward the Future" panel, p. 172, for the most important past and future influences on metropolitan areas, as noted by those in this poll.

Policy Alternatives

Three broad policy alternatives exist for rebuilding cities: moral exhortation, the market, and a Marshall Plan.

Moral Exhortation. This view blames the problems in our cities on urban residents, particularly poor Blacks in the inner city. The poor themselves, their families, their culture, and their neighborhoods produce values and behavior that are the essential cause of poverty and of all the urban problems connected to it. From this perspective, the values and behavior of the poor and Black in the inner city must be brought up to middle-class standards. The poor must be shown the error of their ways. President Clinton's "urban initiative" is an example of this approach. The "Value-Based Violence Prevention Initiative" would funnel federal dollars to churches and other community organizations in sixteen large cities to instill better "values" in troubled inner-city youth (Simon, 1998).

This approach assumes that the values and behavior of poor people are different from the values and behavior of the White middle and upper middle

LOOKING TOWARD THE FUTURE

THE FACTORS INFLUENCING THE FUTURE OF CITIES

A survey conducted by Rutgers University professor Robert Fishman of leading urban historians, planners, and architects revealed the ten most likely influences on cities for the next 50 years. The consensus was that suburbs will continue to thrive and inner cities will continue to deteriorate. The key to the future of cities is the growing gap between the wealthy who live in the suburbs and the poor who live in the inner cities. The following factors will influence the future of cities, in the rank order established by the survey:

1. Growing disparities of wealth
2. Suburban political majority
3. Aging of baby boomers
4. Perpetual "underclass" in central and close-in suburbs
5. Environmental and planning initiatives to limit sprawl
6. Internet
7. Deterioration of post-1945 suburbs closest to cities
8. Shrinking household size
9. Expanding superhighway system to serve new cities on the edge of old cities
10. Racial integration

Source: Haya El Nasser. 1999. "Urban Experts Pick Top Factors Influencing Future." *USA Today* (September 27):4A.

classes (see Chapters 7 and 8 for an elaboration and critique of this approach). A growing body of evidence suggests that this is not true, that poor racial minorities in the city and affluent White people outside of it display similar behavior under similar socioeconomic conditions and circumstances. By focusing on the behavior of the poor, this approach fails because it ignores the social, economic, and political sources of urban decline. Urban anthropologist Micaela di Leonardo delivers the fatal blow to policy rooted in this perspective:

> I'll say it one last time. Of course we have to love, control and enlighten all our children. Street crime and drug addiction are terrible things. Early childbearing isn't great. People, including poor people, ought to be kindly and sensitive to one another in public and private. But prior to all these considerations are public policies that have created and maintained poverty and racial stratification. (di Leonardo, 1992:186)

- **The Market.** This policy position is shared by most conservatives and liberals and by both major political parties, and was shared by both the Republican and Democratic candidates for president in 1996 and 2000. It holds that if government provides the proper subsidies and incentives to business, the private sector will redevelop urban areas and the benefits will ultimately trickle down to all urban residents. To promote economic development, this approach advocates government financial assistance for new businesses in the city and urban enterprise zones.

  In the first case, city and federal low-interest loans, loan guarantees, and sometimes outright subsidies have been used to prod private developers and corporations to participate in urban redevelopment projects. The problems with this approach have been twofold. First, public monies are most often used for upscale development—office towers, middle-class residential complexes, exclusive retail shopping, luxury hotels, and sports arenas. Normally the economic benefits do not trickle down to poor and working-class city residents. And second, many times the loans sour. The private sector reneges on its financial commitments to government when its projects fail to turn a profit and the businesses involved would just as soon have the property turned over to the city or federal government.

The logic of urban enterprise zones is that tax incentives and credits will encourage businesses to locate or relocate in depressed inner-city areas, thereby creating the jobs that will lead to the redevelopment of these neighborhoods. The Clinton administration, for example, designated "empowerment zones" in nine large cities, making $100 million available to each to use in conjunction with tax incentives and credits for business. The hope was that the $100 million in federal money would leverage more investment from local private lenders and developers to revitalize these neighborhoods.

However, the evaluation of existing enterprise zones shows that this approach is not encouraging. For the most part, businesses relocate jobs to urban enterprise zones for tax advantages, but this does not create significant numbers of new jobs. Moreover, the jobs that do come to the inner city generally do not go to inner-city residents. Studies show that there are high inner-city unemployment rates even in areas close to enterprise zones (Kasinitz and Rosenberg, 1996). Evidence also suggests that the tax revenues lost in urban enterprise zones could have been used to create education and training programs, employment programs, better police protection, and subsidized housing construction that would create more jobs and thus improve the quality of life in these poor neighborhoods more than the enterprise zone does.

Currently, one of the favorite strategies of those employing a market approach to rebuilding our cities is tax increment financing (TIFs). TIF districts involve declaring an area "blighted" and then indirectly (through publicly funded infrastructure improvements) and directly subsidizing private business and developers with city dollars to redevelop the area. The city subsidies come from the future tax dollars the redeveloped area will produce. Critics of TIFs point out that they often are not blighted areas at all—the vital Loop in Chicago is a TIF district—and that although they may benefit a few dominant economic interests, they do not benefit the city nor its residents in general because they limit the spending of new tax revenue to the TIF district only. In this way, the general property tax base is actually robbed of the revenues that could be used for all sorts of education, transit, and other infrastructure improvements across the entire city (Shiller, 1997).

Critics of this urban policy perspective point to the irony in offering the market as the solution to urban problems. For them, the market has caused the problems. What but the market, they ask, has taken decent jobs farther from the central city? What, more than the market, has influenced the decline of our cities?

Marshall Plan for the Cities. From this perspective, massive intervention by both regional and federal governments is required. There must be a government plan for rebuilding urban areas that rivals the Marshall Plan that rebuilt Europe after World War II. Public investment in U.S. cities needs to proceed on a level never seen before.

Regional government should be encouraged. Here, more affluent suburbs and edge cities share tax revenues and services with less affluent cities, improving the quality of life throughout the metropolitan area. This will, of course, be opposed by many suburbanites who do not see it as serving their interest. There is some precedent for it, however. Louisville, Kentucky, and its suburbs have come to such an agreement. Portland, Oregon, has an elected regional or "metro area" government. This is similar to the much more widespread practice in Canada and Europe, where provincial and national governments, unlike in the United States, often have the authority to set city, suburb, and tax district boundaries (Glazer, 1996). In Minneapolis–St. Paul, any county in the metropolitan area that exceeds the average growth rate by 40 percent or more shares the excess tax revenue with the rest of the area, including the central city.

Advocates of regional government also favor inclusionary zoning—a policy whereby all new housing development in a metropolitan area must provide some legislated percentage of affordable and low-income housing. This has worked with some success, for example, in suburban Montgomery County, Maryland.

The rationale for the urban region approach is that the central core cannot be separated from its suburbs. Cities and suburbs are related, rather than antithetical, making up a single social and economic reality. To drain the center while flooding the edges makes no sense.

> People work in one municipality, live in another, go to church or the doctor's office or the movies in yet another, and all these different places are somehow independent. Newspaper city desks have been replaced by the staffs of metro sections. Labor and housing markets are area-wide. Morning traffic reports describe pileups and traffic jams that stretch across a metropolitan area. Opera companies and baseball teams pull people from throughout a region. Air or water pollution affects an entire region, because pollutants, carbon monoxide, and runoff recognize no city or suburban or county boundaries. (Katz and Bradley, 1999: 28,30)

For its part, the federal government must stop underwriting the deconcentration of metropolitan areas with its policies and subsidies. It must enforce prohibitions against disinvestment in the city. On the positive side, it must fund a public works job creation program modeled after those of the Great Depression and the New Deal era. This public works program could be used to rebuild the decaying urban infrastructure. The federal government's urban policy ought to increase public assistance and welfare payments, build more affordable public housing, develop an adequate public mass-transit system, and fund the cleanup of toxic and hazardous waste, particularly in poor and minority neighborhoods. The federal government must provide health insurance to all people, including inner-city residents, and increase financial assistance for urban public hospitals. It must also, along with state government, take on a greater share of the funding of public schools. This will help remove the educational inequalities between suburban and urban schools that result from the reliance on local property taxes.

These changes in the federal government's urban policy will not come easy. Presently, urban residents are not viewed as a constituency by either major political party. Compared to the past, fewer members of Congress represent cities. The suburbs, on the other hand, include half of all Americans and are a political force. More congressional districts incorporate cities and suburbs. Members of Congress, even those from the cities, are now more loyal to national political action committees (see Chapter 2) than they are to local urban political machines and organizations. The long-range tax cut package passed by Congress and signed by President George W. Bush in 2001 combined with increased military spending and a slumping economy ensured that social spending programs, including any that might help the cities, by the federal government will be meager and inadequate to meet their crucial needs.

Meanwhile, city governments, city employees, and poor and working-class residents lose ground as cities cope with the myriad of problems by raising local taxes, cutting services, and, through the process of privatization, turning as many city functions as possible over to the profit-making private sector. This latter process, privatization, is a source of yet more decline in the city. As city hall replaces unionized public employees who receive decent wages and benefits and turns to private contractors using nonunion, low-wage labor, more city residents and their neighborhoods slide into poverty (Spielman, 1997).

AMERICAN CITIES AT THE BEGINNING OF A NEW CENTURY

Recent media attention has celebrated the revitalization of the cities with new office buildings, new areas of consumer and recreational activities. The metamorphosis of old warehouses and decrepit hotels into restaurants and lofts for the affluent are clear evidence of the new urban renaissance. So, too, is the return of some suburban residents to the once decaying central city.

Much of this is myth. Much of the benefit of downtown and financial district revitalization accrues to white-collar and professional workers who most often live in affluent suburbs. Significant gentrification and upscale development is occurring, to be sure. But much of it is limited to cities that have established themselves as financial centers in the new "global," high-tech service economy—New York City, San Francisco, Miami, Boston, Chicago, and so on. And even in these cities, neighborhood gentrification is selective and spotty. On the whole, there remains as much ghettoization as gentrification in most of America's central cities. As for the return to the city, it simply isn't so. Most large American cities continue to lose population to their sprawling metropolitan areas. Across the board for every suburbanite returning to the city, three more people leave the city for the suburbs or urban fringe (Wyly, Glickman, and Lahr, 1998). And more and more, both inside and outside the city, the affluent choose to isolate themselves both physically and politically from the less affluent in "gated communities" (Diamond, 1997).

Cleveland, for example, has been lauded as the "comeback city" of the 1990s. Two new downtown state-of-the-art professional sports facilities, the Rock and Roll Hall of Fame, and an assortment of residential and commercial real estate ventures in its center have supposedly transformed this once gritty, old, deindustrialized and decaying city into a thriving and vibrant urban place. But is this the reality for most residents of Cleveland? Hardly:

> While Cleveland has been lauded by the media as a classic comeback town, life is no better for the city's population, which continues to shrink. The huge projected tax revenues [from the downtown redevelopment] that were to go for hospitals, housing for the homeless and help for the elderly never materialized. The percentage of Clevelanders in poverty rose from 17 percent in 1970 to more than 40 percent by the mid-nineties. The city school system, drained of property taxes, is a shambles—only 38 percent of students graduate from high school, with only 7 percent testing at a twelfth grade level—and was placed in state receivership in 1995 . . . the public school system [has been described by] Superintendent Richard Boyd . . . as "in the worst financial shape of any school district in the country." (Cagan and deMause, 1998:24)

As we embark on a new century, disparities between cities and suburbs are growing more pronounced than ever before. The Center for Urban Policy Research's "State of the Nation's Cities" database indicates that the processes currently driving U.S. economic growth—including job and stock market growth—are continuing to build and reinforce the inequalities between cities and their suburbs (see Wyly, Glickman, and Lahr, 1998).

Indeed, contrary to the myth, the reality of the American city and metropolitan area at the dawn of the century is increasing inequality—more deconcentration, gentrification, and ghettoization.

CHAPTER REVIEW

1. Many social problems in the United States, including poverty, homelessness, decaying infrastructure, inadequate public transit, pollution, failure to deliver health services to all social classes, failing public schools, drugs, gangs, racism, and crime, are concentrated in large cities.
2. Through the process of suburbanization and metropolitan deconcentration, the central cities have lost people, jobs, industry, business, and their tax base. Central cities have also lost jobs in the transformation from a manufacturing to a service economy. Central city jobs, particularly in the Midwest and Northeast, have been lost to the Third World, the Sun Belt, and also the suburbs. Federal transportation, housing, economic, and tax policies have encouraged this gutting or mugging of the cities.
3. Race and class have played an important role in suburbanization and metropolitan deconcentration. The middle class and Whites tend to move to the suburbs and urban fringe; the poor and minorities remain in the city. As a result, over the past 40 years, many large cities have lost population, even in growing metropolitan areas. They have also become poorer and seen their proportion of minority residents increase.
4. Beginning in the 1950s, U.S. business and financial and lending institutions have tended (a) to disinvest in cities and invest in suburbs and edge cities and (b) to disinvest in Black and Latino neighborhoods and invest in White communities. This pattern of disinvestment is directly responsible for urban neighborhood and central city decline.
5. Suburbanization, metropolitan deconcentration, disinvestment, and the federal policies that have encouraged them, along with cuts in federal funds for programs that assist poor and working-class city residents that began in the late 1970s, have led to a declining quality of life in U.S. cities.
6. The declining quality of life in U.S. big cities is reflected in increasing and intensifying poverty, the lack of affordable housing, homelessness, decaying infrastructure, inadequate public transit, pollution, health problems and the lack of access to adequate health care, underfunded and failing schools, crime, drugs, and gangs.
7. Urban poverty has been increasing and becoming more concentrated in particular areas in the central city. The poor have also been getting poorer, especially the minority poor. African Americans and Latinos are more likely than Whites in the city to be poor, and Blacks are much more likely to live in highly segregated neighborhoods that are also high-poverty areas.
8. Both the urban housing market and government-subsidized and public housing have failed to provide enough decent and affordable shelter in U.S. cities. The results are a dwindling supply of low-income housing and increasing urban homelessness.
9. The lack of public investment in the urban infrastructure has begun to significantly limit growth and productivity in the U.S. economy.
10. An automobile-dependent transportation system has polluted U.S. cities and prevented the development of public mass transit. Inadequate public transit affects the poor in the central city who cannot afford to own and operate a car and are thus unable to reach jobs in the suburbs and urban fringe.
11. Poor and minority communities in the inner city are the site of a disproportionate amount of illegal dumping and toxic and hazardous waste (environmental classism and environmental racism).
12. Poor and minority inner-city neighborhoods have the highest rates of many health problems—infant mortality, asthma, sexually transmitted diseases, lead poisoning, tuberculosis, and AIDS. Residents of these same places suffer most from lack of access to adequate health care as private hospitals in cities close their doors to under- and uninsured patients. The emergency rooms of underfunded, ill-equipped, and understaffed urban public hospitals become their only alternative.
13. Because U.S. public education is funded primarily with local property taxes, gross inequalities exist between suburban and city schools. Urban schools are increasingly characterized by crumbling facilities, textbook and teacher shortages,

outdated equipment and technologies, few extracurricular activities and special programs, low standardized test scores, and high dropout rates.

14. When opportunities in the formal and legal economy are not forthcoming, young minority males turn to the informal economy for survival. Much of the informal economy is illegal, involving property crime, drug trafficking, and certain gang activities.
15. Fear of crime contributes to urban decay as it works against the people, business, and jobs that could increase economic development and discourage crime from remaining in, or relocating to, the city.
16. By criminalizing drugs, drug users, and addicts, the war on drugs makes the drug trade in the cities more attractive and profitable and then further marginalizes already marginal poor Black inner-city neighborhoods.
17. One can make a very pragmatic and economic argument for rebuilding U.S. cities; research shows that declining cities lead to declining suburbs and metropolitan areas.
18. There are three broad policy positions on rebuilding U.S. cities. One position blames urban decay on the culture, values, and behavior of the minority poor; urban redevelopment will occur only when these things change. A second position relies on the market. Government should provide incentives to businesses to develop and locate in the central city. Urban enterprise zones will begin the rebirth of cities. A third view argues that the first two approaches misdiagnose the source of urban ills and fail to redevelop the central city. What is needed is massive public intervention and investment in our cities on the part of both regional and federal governments.

KEY TERMS

White flight. The movement of predominantly upper-middle-class, middle-class, and working-class Whites from the central cities to the suburbs.

Boomburg. A suburban city of at least 100,000 that has experienced double-digit growth each decade since it became urban.

Urban sprawl. Low-density, automobile-dependent development outside the central city.

Redlining. When banks, savings and loans, government agencies, and insurance companies refuse to make home and small-business loans and insure property in poor and minority neighborhoods.

Poverty areas. Neighborhoods in which at least one in five households live below the poverty line.

High-poverty areas. Neighborhoods where at least two in five households live below the poverty line.

Gentrification. The redevelopment of poor and working-class urban neighborhoods into middle- and upper-middle-class enclaves; often involves displacement of original residents.

Slumlording. Landlords buy properties in poor neighborhoods for rent income. They do not maintain these properties because to do so would lower their profits.

Warehousing. The withholding of apartments from the housing market by speculators who hope to sell them at a profit to developers.

Jobs/housing mismatch. The inability of central city residents most in need of decent jobs to reach them on the urban fringe because (1) they cannot afford to operate a private auto, and (2) the public transportation system is inadequate; moving to the urban fringe is not an option because of housing costs and racial segregation. To the extent that jobs and job growth occur in one place—affluent and White—and poor Blacks or Latinos are restricted to another, this "mismatch" is a form of spatial apartheid.

Environmental racism. The tendency for poor and minority areas in cities and metropolitan areas to be the targets of a disproportionate share of illegal dumping and the sites where most toxic and hazardous waste is disposed; these communities also suffer, as compared to more affluent White communities, from lax enforcement of environmental regulations and laws.

Triage. The practice in understaffed and underfinanced public hospitals of treating the most urgent emergencies first, thereby delaying the treatment of other cases.

Informal economy. When opportunities are not present in the regular legal economy, people in poor inner-city neighborhoods often turn to this alternate economic exchange and activity for survival; much of the informal economy is illegal activity involving crime and drug trafficking.

Regional government. A single metropolitan governmental unit, encompassing the central city and its suburbs.

WEBSITES FOR FURTHER REFERENCE

http://www.urban.org

The Urban Institute is a nonpartisan economic and social policy research organization that investigates social and economic problems. Its research is relevant to families and welfare, immigration, violence, crime, and health care.

http://www.citiesalliance.org/citiesalliance/citiesalliancehomepage.nsf/?Open

Cities Alliance: Cities Without Slums was launched in 1999 by the World Bank and Habitat International and is creating a "coalition of community-based organizations involved in slum upgrading in partnership with existing networks of local authorities, private sector agencies, and national and international development organizations to provide affordable community-based solutions to urban poverty." It is committed to improving the living conditions of the urban poor through action in two key areas: (1) city development strategies that reflect a shared vision for the city's future and local priorities for action to reduce urban poverty; and (2) citywide and nationwide slum upgrading—moving upgrading to scale.

http://www.iir.com/nygc/

The proliferation of gang problems in large and small cities, suburbs, and even rural areas over the last two decades led to the development of a comprehensive, coordinated response to America's gang problem by the Office of Juvenile Justice and Delinquency Prevention (OJJDP). The OJJDP response involves five major components, one of which is the implementation and operation of the National Youth Gang Center (NYGC). The purpose of the NYGC is to "expand and maintain the body of critical knowledge about youth gangs and effective responses to them." The Center assists state and local jurisdictions in the collection, analysis, and exchange of information on gang-related demographics, legislation, literature, research, and promising program strategies, and coordinates activities of the OJJDP Youth Gang Consortium, a group of federal agencies, gang program representatives, and other service providers.

http://www.unchs.org/guo/

The Global Urban Observatory (GUO) has been established by the United Nations Commission on Human Settlements, which called for a mechanism to monitor global progress in implementing the Habitat Agenda and to monitor and evaluate global urban conditions and trends. Its purpose is to "address the urgent need to improve the worldwide base of urban knowledge by helping governments, local authorities, and organizations of the civil society develop and apply policy-oriented urban indicators, statistics, and other urban information."

http://www.hud.gov/

U.S. Department of Housing and Urban Development (HUD). HUD's mission is to "help secure a decent, safe, and sanitary home and suitable living environment for every American." Its services include: creating opportunities for homeownership; providing housing assistance for low-income persons; working to create, rehabilitate, and maintain the nation's affordable housing; enforcing the nation's fair housing laws; helping the homeless; spurring economic growth in distressed neighborhoods; and helping local communities meet their development needs. HUD was born in 1965, but its history extends back to the National Housing Act of 1934. Learn more about HUD's mission and its rich past.

http://www.urbanlawinstitute.org/

The Urban Law and Public Policy Institute's mission of public interest law and policy is to try to equalize, as much as possible, the imbalance of power and knowledge in impoverished urban communities. The Institute's objective is to ensure that the promises of public participation and transparency of government decision-making are in fact fulfilled, especially for lower income people and other too-often excluded groups. This, along with "appropriate enforcement of those laws that are supposed to benefit and/or protect low- and moderate-income communities and consumers," is the mission of the Institute.

http://www.nul.org/

The Urban League is the nation's oldest and largest community-based movement devoted to empowering African Americans to enter the economic and social mainstream. The mission of the Urban League movement is to "enable African Americans to secure economic self-reliance, parity, and power and civil rights."

http://www.edc.org/urban/

The mission of the National Institute for Urban School Improvement is to "support inclusive urban communities, schools, and families to build their capacity for sustainable, successful urban education." The National Institute will accomplish this mission through dialogue, networking, technology, action research, information systems, and alliance and consensus building.

PART THREE
PROBLEMS OF INEQUALITY

Poverty

The other America, the America of poverty, is hidden today in a way that it never was before. Its millions are socially invisible to the rest of us.

—Michael Harrington

The United States is envied by most peoples of the world. It is blessed with great natural resources, the most advanced technology known, and a very high standard of living. Despite these facts, a significant portion of U.S. residents live in a condition of **poverty** (with a standard of living below the minimum needed for the maintenance of adequate diet, health, and shelter). Many millions are ill-fed, ill-clothed, and ill-housed. These same millions are discriminated against in the schools, in the courts, in the job market, and in the marketplace, and discrimination has the effect of trapping many of the poor in that condition. The so-called American dream is just that for millions of people—a dream that will not be realized. Moreover, when compared to other Western industrial democracies, the United States has the highest proportion of its population living in poverty (Smeeding and Gottschalk, 1998).

This chapter is descriptive, theoretical, and practical. On the descriptive level we examine the facts of poverty—who the poor are, how many there are, where they are located, and what it means to be poor. Theoretically, we look at the various explanations for poverty—individual, cultural, and structural. On the practical level we explore what might be done to eliminate extreme poverty.

There are two underlying themes in this chapter. The first theme is that most of the poor are impoverished for structural reasons, not personal ones as is commonly believed. That is, the essence of poverty is inequality—in money and in opportunity. The second theme is important when we take up the possible solutions to this social problem: The United States has the resources to eliminate poverty if it would give that problem a high enough priority.

EXTENT OF POVERTY

What separates the poor from the nonpoor? In a continuum there is no absolute standard for poverty. The line separating the poor from the nonpoor is necessarily arbitrary. The Social Security Administration (SSA) sets the **official poverty line** based on what it considers the minimal amount of money required for a subsistence level of life. To determine the poverty line, the SSA computes the cost of a basic nutritionally adequate diet and multiplies that figure by 3. This multiplier is based on a government research finding that in 1955 poor people spent one-third of their income on food. Since then the poverty level has been readjusted annually by the Consumer Price Index to account for inflation. Using this official standard ($8,667 for one person under age 65, $13,032 for a family of three, and $17,184 for a family of four), 11.8 percent of Americans (32.3 million) were poor in 1999 (the statistics for this section are taken largely from U.S. Bureau of the Census, 2000a). See Figure 7.1 for the poverty rate data over time.

In this chapter, we consider the poor as people below this arbitrary line. However, not only is the government procedure arbitrary, it also minimizes the extent of poverty in the United States. Critics of the measure point out that the

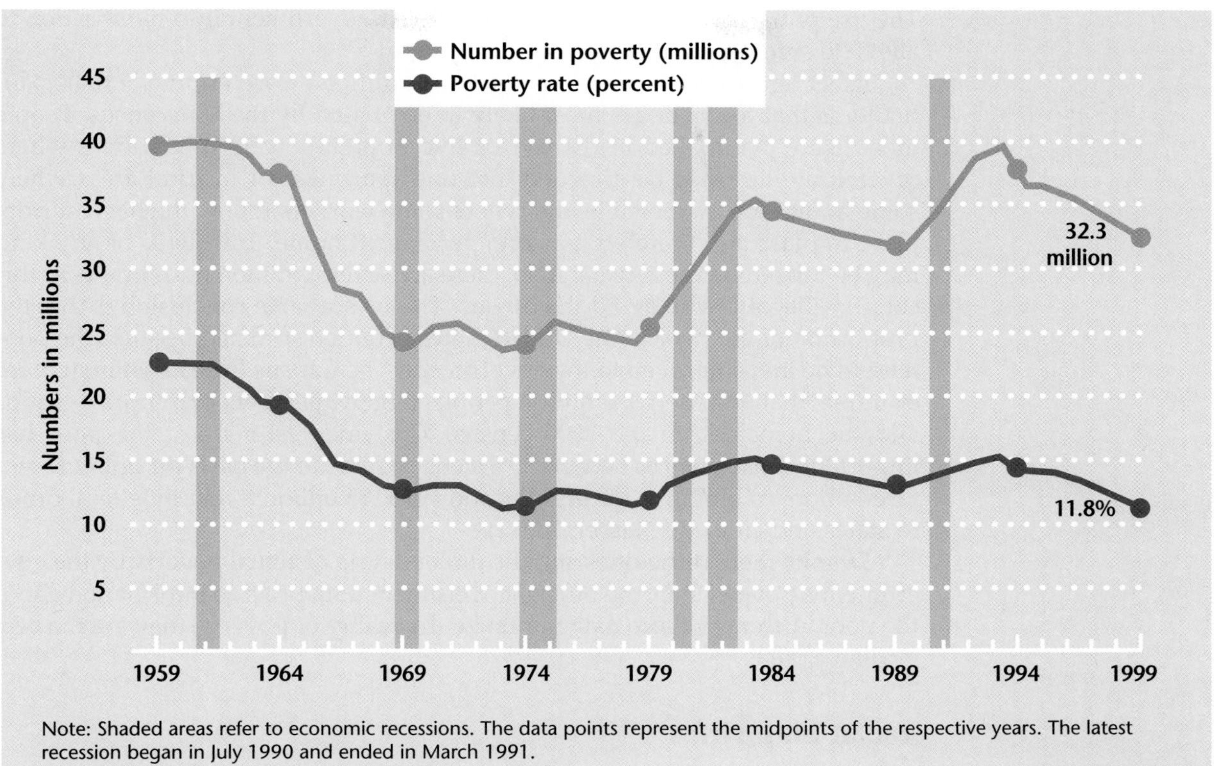

Note: Shaded areas refer to economic recessions. The data points represent the midpoints of the respective years. The latest recession began in July 1990 and ended in March 1991.

FIGURE 7.1

Number of Poor and Poverty Rate: 1959 to 1999

Source: U.S. Bureau of the Census. 2000. "Poverty in the United States, 1999." *Current Population Reports*. Series P60-210. Washington, DC: U.S. Government Printing Office, p. vii.

government measure does not keep up with inflation, that housing costs now take up a much larger portion of the family budget than food, that there is a wide variation in the cost of living by locality, and that the poverty line ignores differences in health insurance coverage and the medical care needs of individual families (Schwarz and Volgy, 1993; Burtless, Corbett, and Primus, 1997; Institute for Research on Poverty, 1998). Schwartz and Volgy, for example, argue that the poverty threshold should be at least 50 percent more than the current measure. Were such a realistic poverty line used, the number of people below it would be about 52 million (17.8 percent of the population), not the 32.3 million officially counted as poor. The Economic Policy Institute provides another measure of poverty. It looks at what it really costs to live in the United States. Its research shows that it takes about $28,000 for a family of three and $36,000 for a family of four.

> That means that the real number of Americans in economic trouble is something like two and a half times the number characterized as "poor." That is something on the order of 80 million people, or 30 percent of the population. These are people who typically report problems affording enough food, paying the rent or the mortgage, paying the phone bill, or paying for health care or child care. (Edelman, 2001:2)

The use of this measurement might shock the government into more action to alleviate suffering in this country.

Exact figures on the number of poor are difficult to determine. A major difficulty is that the poor are most likely to be missed by the U.S. census. People most likely overlooked in the census live in high-density urban areas where several families may be crowded into one apartment or in rural areas where some homes are inaccessible and where some workers follow the harvest from place to place and therefore have no permanent home. Transients of any kind may be missed by the census. Also, there are several million immigrants in this country illegally who avoid the census. The inescapable conclusion is that the proportion of the poor in the United States is underestimated because the poor tend to be invisible, even to the government. The Census Bureau estimated, for example, that it missed 3.4 million people, largely members of minority groups and the homeless, in the 2000 census. This underestimate of the poor has important consequences because U.S. census data are the basis for political representation in Congress, for the allocation of $185 billion a year in federal funds to states and cities (El Nasser, 2001a).

Despite these difficulties and the understating of actual poverty by the government's poverty line, the official government data provide information about the poor. Although these data minimize the reality of poverty, they are the best available data.

Racial Minorities

Income in the United States is maldistributed by race (for data on race and other social characteristics, see Table 7.1). In 1999, the median family income for Asian American households was $51,205, compared with $44,366 for White households, $30,784 for American Indian and Alaska Native households, $30,735 for Latino households, and $27,910 for African American households. Not surprisingly, then, 7.7 percent of Whites were officially poor, compared with 10.7 percent of Asian Americans, 22.8 percent of Latinos, 23.6 percent of African Americans, and 25.9 percent of Native American and Alaska Natives.

These summary statistics mask the differences within each racial/ethnic category. For example, Americans of Cuban descent, many of whom were middle-class professionals in Cuba, have relatively low poverty rates, while Puerto Ricans, Mexicans, and Central Americans have disproportionately high poverty rates. Similarly, Japanese Americans are much less likely to be poor than Asians from Cambodia, Laos, and Vietnam.

Native Americans have about the same poverty rate as African Americans and Latinos. As with other racial categories, though, there is a wide variation among Native Americans, with some in the middle class, some poor, and some extremely poor. In the latter category are the 25 percent of Native Americans who live on reservations. There, poverty rates and unemployment tend to be very high, health problems rampant, and educational attainment comparatively low.

Nativity

In 1999, 4.8 million of the foreign-born individuals in the United States (16.8 percent of the foreign born) were poor. Of these poor foreign born, 1.0 million were naturalized citizens and 3.8 million were noncitizens, for poverty rates of

TABLE 7.1

Population of the Poverty Population, 1970, 1980, and 1999

	Percentage of Poor		
	1970	*1980*	*1999*
All people	12.6%	13.0%	11.8%
Race/ethnicity			
White	9.9	10.2	9.8
African American	33.5	32.5	23.6
Latino	24.3	25.7	22.8
Asian or Pacific Islander	—	17.2	10.7
Nativity			
Native	—	—	11.2
Foreign born	—	—	16.8
Family structure			
In all families	10.9	11.5	9.3
In families, female householder, no spouse	38.1	36.7	27.8
Age			
Children under age 18	14.9	17.9	16.9
Adults age 65 and older	24.5	15.7	9.7
Residence			
Central cities	14.3	17.2	16.4
Suburbs	7.1	8.2	8.3
Outside metropolitan areas	17.0	15.4	14.3

Sources: U.S. Bureau of the Census. 1995. "Income, Poverty, and Valuation of Noncash Benefits: 1993." *Current Population Reports.* Series P60-188 (February). Washington, DC: U.S. Government Printing Office, p. xvi; U.S. Bureau of the Census. 2000. "Poverty in the United States, 1999." Series P60-210 (September). Washington, DC: U.S. Government Printing Office, p. vi.

9.1 and 21.3 percent, respectively. These official statistics do not include the 6 to 10 million undocumented workers and their families who enter the United States illegally.

Gender

Women are more likely to be poor than men (13.2 percent compared to 10.3 percent). This is a consequence of the prevailing institutional sexism in society. There is a dual labor market with women found disproportionately in lower paying jobs with fewer benefits. Thus, the female-to-male earnings ratio was 0.72 in 1999 (i.e., women earned 72 cents for every dollar earned by men). The relatively high frequency of divorce and the large number of never-married women with children, coupled with the cost of child care, housing, and medical care, have resulted in high numbers of poor female headed families (with no husband present) being poor (27.8 percent, compared to 4.8 percent for two-parent families). This trend, termed the **feminization of poverty,** implies that the relatively large proportion of poor women is a new phenomenon in U.S. society. Thus, the term obscures the fact that women have always been more economically vulnerable than men, especially older women and women of color. But when women's poverty was mainly limited to these groups, their economic deprivation was mostly invisible. The plight of women's poverty became a visible problem when the numbers of White women in poverty increased rapidly in the past decade or so with rising marital disruption. Even with the growing numbers of poor White women, the term *feminization of poverty* implies that all women are at risk, when actually the probability of economic deprivation is much greater for certain categories of women. The issue, then, is not only gender but class and race as well.

Race and gender contribute independently to the poverty equation. An African American woman is almost two and a half times more likely to be poor than is a White woman (26.6 percent compared to 10.9). And, a Latino woman is almost twice as likely as a White woman to be poor (20.1 percent in contrast to 10.9 percent).

Age

The nation's poverty rate was 11.8 percent in 1999, but the rate was 16.9 percent for children under age 18 (see previous Table 7.1). The younger the child, the greater the probability of living in poverty, with the rate being 18.0 percent for children under age 6. Related children under age 6 living in families with a female head of household, no husband present, had a poverty rate of 50.3 percent, a rate more than five times that for their counterparts in married-couple families (9.0 percent). Although there are more White children in poverty, children of color are disproportionately poor. In 1999 the rate for White children under age 18 was 13.5 percent, compared to 30.3 percent for Latino children, and 33.1 percent for African American children.

To put a finer point on the magnitude of children's poverty in the United States: In 1972 there were 3.4 million children living below the poverty line; in 1999, with a poverty line that understates the real extent of poverty, there were 12.1 million children under age 18 living in poverty.

Contrary to popular belief, the elderly as a category have a much lower poverty rate (9.7 percent in 1999) than the general population (11.8 percent). In fact, there are more than four times as many children as elderly people living in poverty in the United States. This seeming anomaly is the result of government programs for the elderly being indexed for inflation, whereas many welfare programs targeted for the young were reduced or eliminated, especially since 1980 (see Figure 7.2). This disparity between the young and old in poverty differs from the pattern found in other industrial nations. "In most industrial nations, poverty among youth and adults has been experienced as a 'shared fate.' In Western Europe, child and adult poverty rates are similar, and considerably lower than in the United States" (Males, 1994:18).

While the elderly are underrepresented in the poverty population, it is important to note that a higher proportion of the elderly than nonelderly hovered just above the poverty line. In other words, the elderly are overrepresented among the near poor. Moreover, elderly women are much more likely than elderly men to be living in poverty. This gender gap increases with the age category. For those age 75 and older, 1 in 5 women is poor compared to only 1 in 10 men. Gender and race combine to make the situation especially difficult for elderly African American and Latino women.

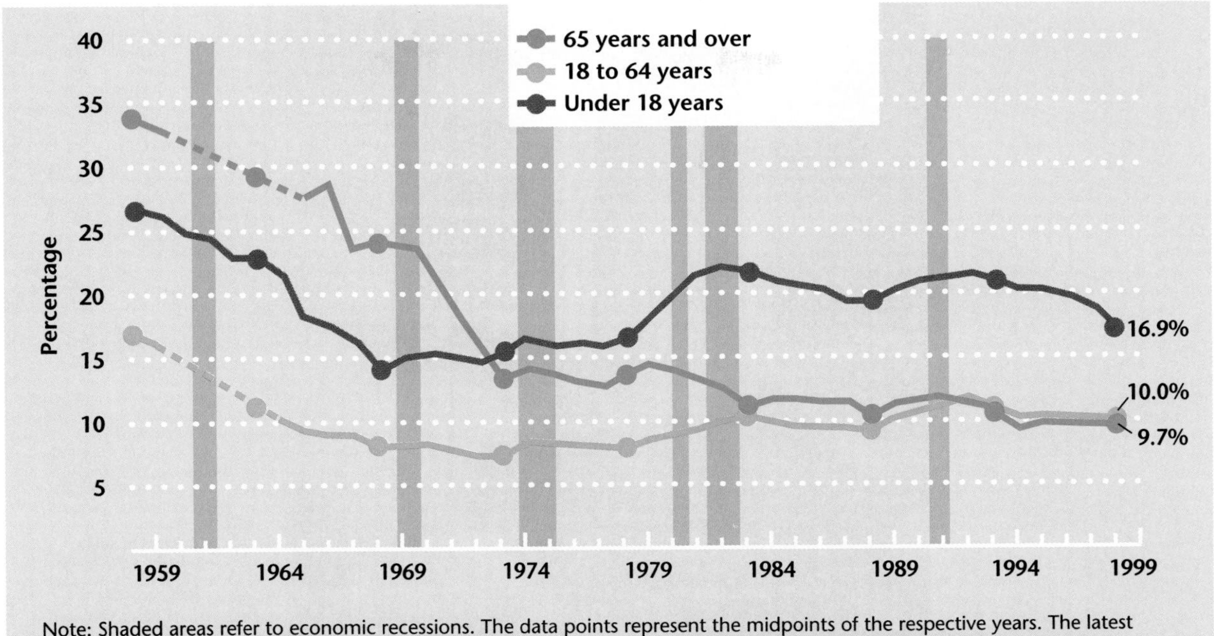

FIGURE 7.2

Poverty Rates by Age: 1959 to 1999

Source: U.S. Bureau of the Census. 2000. "Poverty in the United States, 1999." *Current Population Reports.* Series P60-210 (September). Washington, DC: U.S. Government Printing Office, p. ix.

Place

Poverty is not randomly distributed geographically; it tends to cluster in certain places. Regionally, the area with the highest poverty in 1999 was the South (13.1 percent), compared to 12.6 percent in the West, 10.9 percent in the Northeast, and 9.8 percent in the Midwest. The higher poverty rate in the South and West reflects their large minority populations and the relatively large number of recent immigrants. The three states with the highest average poverty rates from 1997 to 1999 were New Mexico (20.8 percent), Louisiana (18.2 percent), and Mississippi (16.8 percent). Each of these states has a disproportionate number of racial minorities and has a higher rural than urban population. The states with the lowest poverty rates were Maryland (7.6 percent), Utah (7.9 percent), and Indiana (8.3 percent).

There are 25 counties in the United States with more than 45 percent of their people living below the poverty line, with two counties exceeding 60 percent (Shannon in South Dakota, where the Pine Ridge reservation is located, and Starr in Texas, which is predominantly Latino).

In metropolitan areas the poverty rate in 1999 was higher in the central cities (16.4 percent) than in suburban areas (8.3 percent). For those living outside of metropolitan areas, the poverty rate was 14.3 percent. Two trends are significant: The proportion who are poor is increasing in the central cities, and,

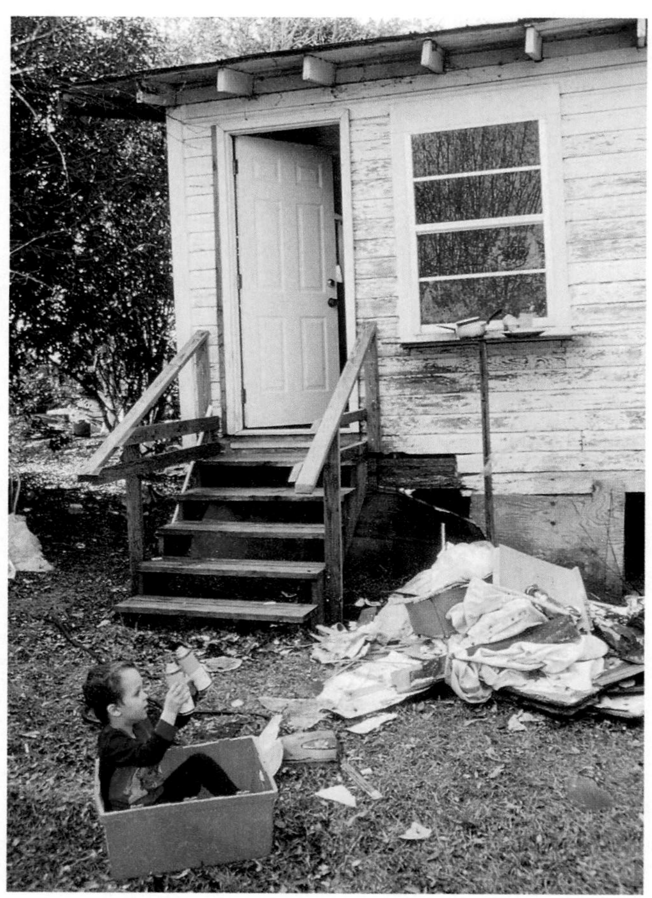

There is a concentration of poverty in the Appalachian mountain region.

increasingly, the poverty is more and more concentrated [i.e., the poor are more and more likely to be living in already poor neighborhoods (Massey, 1996b)]. This spatial concentration of poverty means that the poor have poor neighbors, the area has a low tax base to finance public schools, and the number of businesses dwindles as they tend to move to areas where the local residents have more discretionary income. This means a reduction in services and the elimination of local jobs. Moreover,

> Just as poverty is concentrated spatially, anything correlated with poverty is also concentrated. Therefore, as the density of poverty increases in cities . . . so will the density of joblessness, crime, family dissolution, drug abuse, alcoholism, disease, and violence. Not only will the poor have to grapple with the manifold problems due to their own lack of income; increasingly they also will have to confront the social effects of living in an environment where most of their neighbors are also poor. (Massey, 1996b:407)

Although poverty generally is more concentrated in cities, the highest concentration of U.S. poverty exists in four nonmetropolitan pockets: the Appalachian mountain region, where the poor are predominantly White; the old Southern cotton belt from the Carolinas to the Louisiana delta, where the poor are mostly African American; the Rio Grande Valley/Texas Gulf Coast, where the poor are largely Latino; and the Native American reservations of the Southwest, where poverty is nearly all Native American:

> Rural poverty is not necessarily the result of laziness and personal failure. Half the rural poor work, and one-quarter of rural poor families have two family members who work; yet the families remain poor. High-paying, high-skill jobs tend not to be found in rural areas, where schools are often bad and educational levels low. Low-wage, unskilled jobs flow into such counties and therefore tend to perpetuate indigence. (Flynt, 1996:33)

There are important differences between the rural and the urban poor. The rural poor have some advantages (low-cost housing, raising their own food) and many disadvantages (low-paid work, higher prices for most products, fewer social services, fewer welfare benefits) over the urban poor.

Poverty is greatest among those who do not have an established residence. People in this classification are typically the homeless and migrant workers. Currently, an estimated 1 million Americans are homeless at some time during the year, with about 760,000 homeless on any given night (enough to create a city the size of Seattle). In twenty-nine major cities, the homeless outnumber the number of beds in temporary shelters forcing many to literally spend the night in cars, in doorways, under bridges, or in the streets.

The other category, migrant workers, are believed to be about 3 million adults and children who are seasonal farm laborers working for low wages and no benefits. It is estimated that about 50 percent of all farm workers live below the official poverty line and that this percentage has not changed since the 1960s. Latinos are overrepresented in this occupation.

Finally, the United States, when compared to other major industrialized democracies, has more poverty, has more severe poverty, and supports its poor people least. See the "Social Problems in Global Perspective" panel.

SOCIAL PROBLEMS IN GLOBAL PERSPECTIVE

POVERTY IN THE UNITED STATES RELATIVE TO OTHER WESTERN DEMOCRACIES

The United States does not fare well when compared to other western democracies on various dimensions of poverty. Consider these facts:

- Among the industrialized nations, the United States has the highest rate of child poverty (one in six). Nearly 11 million children have no health insurance and 500,000 children are homeless (Pollitt, 2001).
- Comparing the United States with Canada and the nations of Western Europe and Scandinavia, the United States eliminates much less poverty than any of the other fourteen nations through welfare subsidies (Solow, 2000).
- The average annual exit rate from poverty is lower in the United States and the United Kingdom (where 29 percent move above the poverty line annually) than in Sweden (36 percent), Germany (37 percent), Canada (42 percent), and the Netherlands (where 44 percent leave poverty status) (Economic Policy Institute, 2000).
- America's well-to-do children are richer than the wealthy kids of any of the other nations. But its poor children have less to live on—$10,923 per average family—than those in all but Ireland and Israel. Most of the countries would have double-digit child poverty rates—like America's—were it not for government programs that lift millions out of poverty. All offer broader child tax credits than does the United States. Many guarantee day care, health care, and child support when fathers won't pay (Rainwater and Smeeding, 1995).

The New Poor

Millions of blue-collar workers have lost their jobs as plants have closed and as companies have moved in search of cheaper labor, or when they were replaced by robots or other forms of automation (see Chapter 14). Many of these displaced workers find other work, but 65 percent end up in jobs that pay less than did their previous jobs. They are poorer but not poor. Many others, though, especially those over 40, find employment difficult because their skills are no longer needed and they are considered too old to retrain.

These **new poor** are quite different from the old poor. The **old poor**—that is, the poor of other generations—had hopes of breaking out of poverty; if they did not break out themselves, at least they believed their children would. This hope was based on a rapidly expanding economy. There were jobs for immigrants, farmers, and high school dropouts because of the needs of mass production. The new poor, however, are much more trapped in poverty (Harrington, 1984). A generation ago, those who were unskilled and uneducated could usually find work and could even do quite well financially if the workplace was unionized. But now these people are displaced or misplaced. Hard physical labor is rarely needed in a high-tech society. This phenomenon undercuts the efforts of the working class, especially African Americans, Latinos, and other minorities who face the additional burden of institutional racism.

Tens of millions of Americans have lost their jobs in the past two decades or so because of plant closings and layoffs. Almost half of these newly unemployed were longtime workers (workers who had held their previous jobs at least 3 years), and seven out of ten of them found new jobs. Of those reemployed full time, slightly less than half make less money than before. These workers are downwardly mobile but likely not poor. About 15 percent, however, did not find employment and they constitute the new poor.

The Working Poor

Having a job is not necessarily a path out of poverty. National data that includes poor adults 16 years and older, and excludes poor adults who are ill, disabled, retired, or in school found that: (1) 43 percent worked at some time during the year; and (2) one-seventh of all poor people work full time for the entire year (summarized in Miller, 2000). Put another way, about 3 percent of all full-time workers are below the poverty line, with non-White full-time workers one and one-half times more likely to be poor than White full-time workers (Barrington, 2000). Expanding this to the poor and the near poor, Congressman Bernard Sanders of Vermont has said: "30 percent of American workers earn poverty or near-poverty wages" (Sanders, 2000:3). Despite working, these people remain poor because they hold menial, deadend jobs that have no benefits and pay the minimum wage or below. About 10 million workers (70 percent of whom are adults) work for the minimum wage, yet this wage does not support a family. The federal minimum wage of $5.15 an hour adds up to only $10,712 for full-time work (it takes $8.20 an hour for a full-time worker to earn the poverty level for a family of four). Just above the minimum wage, there are more than 2 million Americans working in nursing homes earning, on average, between $7 and $8 an hour. The median wage of the estimated 2.3 million child care workers is $6.60 an hour, usually without benefits. Workers in other occupations, such as janitors, health care aides, hospital orderlies, funeral attendants, and retail sales clerks typically make similarly low wages (Reich, 2000a).

Those working at poverty wages are disproportionately women and racial/ethnic minorities. One in three women earned poverty-level wages in 1999, compared to one out of five men. Mishel, Bernstein, and Schmitt (2000) found that in 1999, one in three African American men, two out of five Black women and Latino men, and slightly more than half of Latino women were in jobs that paid poverty wages. Compounding the economic woes of the poor is that only three out of ten workers whose wages place them in the bottom fifth have employer-provided health insurance (Mishel, Bernstein, and Schmitt, 2000).

The lot of the **working poor** is similar to that of the nonworking poor on some dimensions and worse on others (Newman, 1996). They do society's dirty work for low pay and little if any benefits. Like the poor, they live in substandard housing and their children go to underfinanced public schools. They are poor but, unlike the poor, they are not eligible for many government supports such as subsidized housing, medical care (Medicaid), and food stamps.

The Near Poor

The **near poor** are people with family incomes at or above their poverty threshold but below 125 percent of their threshold (i.e., with the official poverty line at $13,032 for a family of three, 125 percent of that number is $16,030. In 1999 some 12.0 million Americans were near poor, including 9.1 million Whites, 2.2 million African Americans, and 2.8 million Latinos.

The Severely Poor

Use of the official poverty line designates all people below it as poor whether they are a few dollars short or far below that threshold. In reality, most impoverished individuals and families have incomes considerably below the poverty threshold. In 1999, for example, the average dollar amount needed to raise a poor family out of poverty was $6,687 (i.e., the average family needed $6,687 *additional* income to reach the poverty threshold). The per capita income deficit among poor people in families was $1,908. For poor individuals not in families, the average income deficit was $4,206 in 1999.

In 1999 some 39 percent of the poor population (12.7 million Americans) were **severely poor** (i.e., those people living at or below half the poverty line). Some facts about these people who are the poorest of the poor are:

- Of these 12.7 million, 4.9 million (94 percent) are children under 18.
- In this category, 3.58 million are African Americans (31 percent), and 3.03 million are Latinos (21 percent).
- Typically, the severely poor must use at least 50 percent of their meager income for housing.

This category of the poor-poor has increased by half since 1979. This upsurge in the truly destitute occurred because (1) many of the poor-poor live in rural areas that have prospered less than other regions; (2) a decline in marriage resulted in a substantial increase in single mothers and unattached men; and (3) public assistance benefits, especially in the South, have steadily declined since 1980. We return to the explanations for poverty later in this chapter.

Myths About Poverty

What should be the government's role in caring for its less fortunate citizens? Much of the debate on this important issue among politicians and citizens is based on erroneous assumptions and misperceptions. Those myths are refuted in this section.

Refusal to Work

Several facts belie the faulty assumption that poor people refuse to work. First, 78 percent of poor children live in families where somebody worked all or part of the time in 1999 (Children's Defense Fund, 2001:xv). Overall, there are about 30 million Americans who are poor or near poor who work. They hold menial, dead-end jobs that have no benefits and pay the minimum wage (some actually less than the minimum wage). Low wages are the source of the problem: Today about 3.7 million workers make the minimum wage, yet a full-time minimum-wage worker earns only 82 percent of the poverty level for a family of three (in 1968 a family of three with one minimum-wage earner had a standard of living 17 percent above the poverty line). Second, many of the poor who do not work are too young (under age 18), too old (age 65 and older), or have a work disability (O'Hare, 1996:11). Third, the main increase in the number of poor since 1979 has been among the working poor. This increase is the result of declining wages, the increase in working women who head households, and a very low minimum hourly wage of $5.15.

Economist Marlene Kim analyzed census data on a sample of 57,000 U.S. households and concluded:

> Most of the working poor would remain poor even if they worked 40 hours a week, 52 weeks a year. In addition, of those who could climb out of poverty if they worked such hours, two out of five are either disabled or elderly or unable to find full-time or full-year employment. Thus it appears that most of the working poor are doing all they can to support themselves (Kim, 1998:97).

For those poor not officially in the labor force, many work (either for money or for the exchange of goods or services) in the informal economy by cleaning, painting, providing child care, repairing automobiles or appliances, or other activities. Clearly, these people are workers, they just are not in the official economy.

Welfare Dependency

In 1996 Congress passed the Personal Responsibility and Work Opportunity Conciliation Act, which reformed the welfare system [the following is from Eitzen and Baca Zinn (1998b)]. This new law shifted welfare programs from the federal government to the states, mandated that welfare recipients find work within 2 years, limited welfare assistance to 5 years, and cut various federal assistance programs targeted for the poor by $54.5 billion over 6 years. Thus, this law made assistance to the poor temporary and cut monies to supplemental programs as food stamps and child nutrition. The assumption by policymakers was that welfare was too generous, making it easier to stay on welfare than leave for work, and welfare was believed to encourage unmarried women to have children.

We should recognize some facts about government welfare before the 1996 welfare reform (O'Hare, 1996:11). First, welfare accounted for about one-fourth of the income of poor adults; nearly half of the income received by poor adults comes from some form of work activity. Second, about three-fourths of the poor received some form of noncash benefit (Medicaid, food stamps, or housing assistance); but only about 40 percent received cash welfare payments. Third, the welfare population changes—that is, people move in and out of poverty every year. The average welfare recipient stays on welfare less than 2 years (Sklar, 1992:10). Only 12 percent of the poor remain poor for 5 or more consecutive years (O'Hare, 1996). Fourth, although the prereform welfare system was much more generous than now, it was inadequate to meet the needs of the poor, falling far short. The average poor family of three on welfare had an annual income much below the poverty line:

> Many poor families manage by cutting back on food, jeopardizing their health and the development of their children, or by living in substandard and sometimes dangerous housing. Some do without heat, electricity, telephone service, or plumbing for months or years. Many do without health insurance, health care, safe child care, or reliable transportation to take them to or from work. (Children's Defense Fund, cited in Sklar, 1992:10)

Fifth, contrary to the common assertion that welfare mothers keep having babies to get more welfare benefits and thereby escape working, research from a number of studies shows that most welfare recipients bring in extra money from various activities such as house cleaning, laundry, repairing clothing, child care, and selling items they have made. For example, sociologist Kathleen Harris, summarizing her findings from a nationally representative sample of single mothers who received welfare, says:

> I found exclusive dependence on welfare to be rare. More than half of the single mothers whom I studied worked while they were on welfare, and two-thirds left the welfare rolls when they could support themselves with jobs.

Drawing by M. Wuerker

> However, more than half (57 percent) of the women who worked their way off public assistance later returned because their jobs ended or they still could not make ends meet. (Harris, 1996:B7)

Concerning the larger picture about government welfare programs, there is a fundamental misunderstanding by the U.S. public about where most governmental benefits are directed. We tend to assume that government monies and services go mostly to the poor (**welfare**), when in fact the greatest amount of government aid goes to the nonpoor (**wealthfare**). Most (about three-fourths) of the federal outlays for human resources go to the nonpoor, such as to all children in public education programs and to most of the elderly through Social Security Retirement and Medicare.

The upside-down welfare system, with aid mainly helping the already affluent, is also accomplished by two hidden welfare systems. The first is through tax loopholes (called **tax expenditures**). Through these legal mechanisms the government officially permits certain individuals and corporations to pay lower taxes or no taxes at all. For illustration, one of the biggest tax expenditure programs is the money that homeowners deduct from their taxes for real estate taxes and interest on their mortgages (mortgage interest is deductible on mortgages up to $1 million). In a telling irony, the government tax breaks to homeowners (over $53.7 billion in 1998) are $23 billion more than the Department of Housing and Urban Development's 1998 budget for low-income housing (Collins, Leondar-Wright, and Sklar, 1999:38). Put another way, while fewer than one-fourth of low-income Americans receive federal housing subsidies, more than three-quarters of Americans, many living in mansions, get housing aid from Washington.

The second hidden welfare system to the nonpoor is in the form of direct subsidies and credit to assist corporations, banks, agribusiness, defense industries, and the like. Some examples (from Zepezauer and Naiman, 1996; Goodgame, 1993; Glassman, 1997; *Multinational Monitor,* 1997a) are the following:

- The savings and loan bailout ($37 billion, every year for 30 years)
- Agribusiness subsidies ($18 billion a year)
- Media subsidies ($8 billion a year; in 1997 the Federal Communications Commission (FCC) gave broadcast licenses for digital television to existing broadcasters at no cost. The FCC itself estimated the value of these licenses to be worth $20 billion to $70 billion)
- Timber subsidies ($427 million a year, not counting tax breaks)
- Business meals and entertainment ($5.5 billion a year)
- Aviation subsidies ($5.5 billion a year)
- Mining subsidies ($3.5 billion a year)
- Tax avoidance by transnational corporations ($12 billion annually)

These subsidy programs to wealthy and corporate interests amount to many times over the welfare to the poor. Ironically, when Congress passed the sweeping welfare reforms of 1996, it did not consider the welfare programs for the nonpoor.

Finally, an assessment of the 1996 welfare reform 5 years after it was passed reveals premature, mixed, and uncertain results. Positively, the number of people on welfare has fallen by half to 6 million. Many of the former recipients, including single mothers, have found at least part-time employment. The transition from welfare to work, however, has not always been successful. Research by sociologists William Julius Wilson and Andrew J. Cherlin in Boston,

Chicago, and San Antonio reveals that while work has improved sense of self for former welfare recipients, three-fourths of the women who had been off welfare for 2 years or less had incomes *below* the federal poverty line (Wilson and Cherlin, 2001). They were meeting basic expenses with government help such as food stamps. The longer these women had been off welfare, the less likely they were to have health insurance for themselves and their children. The women facing the greatest difficulties after welfare were those with less education, poorer health, and younger children.

The first five years were extraordinary, with historically low unemployment, low inflation, and a booming economy. The real test of the 1996 Welfare Reform will be to assess what happens to those pushed off welfare for jobs during a prolonged economic slowdown, as has occurred since late 1999. In 2001 two powerful forces—a severe economic downturn and the September 11 attacks on the World Trade Center and the Pentagon—combined to wreak havoc on the poor, especially those who had left welfare for work, as the 1996 Welfare Reform dictated. Rising unemployment rates in 2001 hit former welfare recipients because, as recently hired employees, they were the most likely to be fired when the companies they worked for reduced their workforces. Moreover, the service sector of the economy, especially hotel, restaurant, travel, tourism, and retail, where former welfare recipients were most likely to find jobs, was hit hardest by the September 11 fallout. This recession was the first since the 1930s in which the "safety net" was virtually nonexistent. As a result, the number of people seeking emergency food aid and the number without shelter rose significantly. If these trends continue, will the Congress reassess its reform of welfare and find ways to increase the safety net for the impoverished?

The Poor Get Special Advantages

The common belief is that the poor get a number of handouts for which other Americans have to work—food stamps, Medicaid, housing subsidies, and the like. As we have seen, these subsidies amount to much less than the more affluent receive, and recent legislation has reduced them more and more. Most significant, *the poor pay more than the nonpoor for many services*. This, along with earning low wages and paying a large proportion of their income for housing, helps to explain why some have such difficulty getting out of poverty.

The urban poor find that their money does not go as far in the inner city. Food and commodities, for example, cost more since supermarkets, discount stores, outlet malls, and warehouse clubs have bypassed inner-city neighborhoods. Since many inner-city residents do not have transportation to get to the supermarkets and warehouse stores, they must buy from nearby stores, giving those businesses monopoly powers. As a result, the poor pay more. The New York City Department of Consumer Affairs found that groceries cost 8.8 percent more in poor neighborhoods than in middle-class areas. Similarly, a survey in Chicago found that the poor paid 18 percent more (see Timmer, Eitzen, and Talley, 1994:94–95).

Many companies—including some of the largest, such as Citibank and American Express—provide financial services to approximately 60 million poor and near poor who are shut out of banks and other conventional merchants. Thus, they provide a needed service but at an extremely high cost—230 percent interest from a rent-to-own company, 240 percent interest for a loan from a pawnbroker, 300 percent for a finance company loan, and as high as

2,000 percent for a quick "payday" loan from a check-cashing outlet (Hudson, 1996; Freedman, 1993; Pascale, 1995; Berenson, 1996). A study by the National Association of Insurance Commissioners in 1994 concluded that poor people and minorities across the country have a harder time obtaining insurance and pay higher premiums than other customers.

The conclusion is obvious: The poor pay more for commodities and services in absolute terms, and they pay a much larger proportion of their incomes than the nonpoor for comparable items. Similarly, when the poor pay sales taxes on the items they purchase, the tax takes more of their resources than it does from the nonpoor, making it a **regressive tax.** Thus, efforts to move federal programs to the states will cost the poor more, since state and local taxes tend to be regressive.

Welfare Is an African American and Latino Program

The myth is that most welfare monies go primarily to African Americans and Latinos. While poverty rates are higher for African Americans and Latinos than for other racial/ethnic groups, they do not make up a majority of the poor. Non-Hispanic Whites are the most numerous group (48 percent of the poor are White) among the poverty population, compared to 27 percent for African Americans and 22 percent for Latinos (O'Hare, 1996:11). Thus, Whites take the majority of the welfare budget. Barbara Ehrenreich states:

> [W]hite folks have been gobbling up the welfare budget while blaming someone else. But it's worse than that. If we look at Social Security, which is another form of welfare, although it is often mistaken for an individual insurance program, then whites are the ones who are crowding the trough. We receive almost twice as much per capita, for an aggregate advantage to our race of $10 billion a year—much more than the $3.9 billion advantage African Americans gain from their disproportionate share of welfare. One sad reason: whites live an average of six years longer than African Americans, meaning that young African American workers help subsidize a huge and growing "overclass" of white retirees. (Ehrenreich, 1991:84)

Costs of Poverty

Some 32.3 million people in the United States were officially poor in 1999. These people and those just above the poverty line generally receive inferior educations, live in substandard housing, are disproportionately exposed to toxic chemicals, are malnourished, and have health problems. Here are a few examples of the conditions of the poor. Some of these items are discussed in more detail at other points in the text.

- About 43 million people (including some 10.8 million children) have no private or public health insurance. About 1 million families a year are refused medical care for financial reasons.
- The infant mortality rate in some poor urban neighborhoods exceeds the rate in Third World countries. The United States has a higher infant mortality rate than most other industrialized countries. Reflecting the disproportionate number of African American and Native Americans in poverty, their infant mortality rates were 13.7 and 8.7, respectively, in 1997, compared to 6.0 for Whites (Children's Defense Fund, 2000:36).

Over five million families with low incomes pay more than 50 percent of their meager incomes for rent.

- In 1999 the Department of Agriculture estimated that 27 million people, including 11 million children, were hungry or at least food insecure (Brasher, 2000). The elderly, especially older single women, are at risk for hunger. The National Policy and Resource Center on Nutrition and Aging estimates that 60 percent of those 65 and older are at high to moderate nutritional risk (reported in Weaver, 2000).
- In 1998 the Department of Housing and Urban Development (HUD) estimated that a record 5.3 million U.S. families (12.5 million people) with low incomes faced a crisis of unaffordable rent because they pay more than 50 percent of their incomes for rent (Havemann, 1998). Their options are to live on the street, seek homeless shelters, double up with friends or relatives, move into substandard housing, or continue to spend 50 percent or more of their incomes for housing.

Summarizing the research on poor children, Robert Solow (Children's Defense Fund, 1995:19) notes that poor children in the United States are:

- Two times more likely than other children to die from birth defects
- Three times more likely to die from all causes combined
- Four times more likely to die from fires
- Five times more likely to die from infectious diseases and parasites
- Six times more likely to die from other diseases

The research also documents that poor children are two or more times as likely as other children to suffer from such problems as stunted growth, severe physical or mental disabilities, severe asthma, iron deficiency, and fatal accidental injuries (Children's Defense Fund, 1995:19). (See Table 7.2, p. 196.)

The psychological consequences of being poor are many. The poor are rejected and despised by others in the society, looked down on as lazy, shiftless, dirty, and immoral. Being poor is therefore degrading. The poor are not wanted

TABLE 7.2

Poor Outcomes for Poor Children

Outcome	*Poor Children's Risk Relative to Nonpoor Children*
Health	
Death in childhood	1.5 to 3 times more likely
Stunted growth	2.7 times more likely
Iron deficiency in preschool years	3 to 4 times more likely
Partial or complete deafness	1.5 to 2 times more likely
Partial or complete blindness	1.2 to 1.8 times more likely
Serious physical or mental disabilities	About 2 times more likely
Fatal accidental injuries	2 to 3 times more likely
Pneumonia	1.6 times more likely
Education	
Average IQ score at age 5	9 points lower
Average achievement scores at age 3 and above	11 to 25 percentiles lower
Learning disabilities	1.3 times more likely
Placement in special education	2 or 3 percentage points more likely
Below usual grade for child's age	2 percentage points more likely for each year of childhood spent in poverty
Dropping out between ages 16 and 24	2 times more likely than middle-income youths; 11 times more likely than wealthy youths

Source: Children's Defense Fund. 1998. *The State of America's Children: Yearbook 1998.* Washington, DC: Children's Defense Fund, p. xiv. Copyright 1998 by the Children's Defense Fund. Used with permission.

by the more well-to-do as neighbors, friends, mates, or colleagues. Thus, many of the poor define themselves as failures. They are the rejects of society, and they feel it.

Being poor also engenders hopelessness and, thus, apathy. The poor have virtually no power. They cannot afford lawyers or lobbyists. They cannot afford to go on strike against low wages or high rent. Consequently, they tend to feel that their fates are in the hands of powerful others.

There is also a great deal of anger among the poor. They pay higher interest rates; they are the last to be hired and the first to be fired; they must live in poor housing and often filthy conditions. They also live in fear, as their neighborhoods are unsafe and they are the most likely to be the victims of street crime. One of the most important sources of anger is that they see affluence all about them but, no matter how hard they try, are unable to share in it.

Given the propensity for alienation, hostility, and lack of ego strength among the poor, there are three ways in which the individual poor cope with the conditions in which they find themselves: put up with the aversive situation, withdraw from it, or fight it.

What are the consequences for society if a significant proportion of the populace is poor? In economic terms the cost is very high. For example, the poor constitute a relatively unproductive mass of people. These people are wasted, their work output is marginal, and they pay few or no taxes (usually only sales tax, since they have little property and low incomes). The cost to other taxpayers is quite large, in the form of welfare programs and crime prevention. If poverty were eliminated through more better-paying jobs and more adequate monetary assistance to the permanently disabled or elderly, the entire society would prosper from the increased purchasing power and the larger tax base:

> Every year of child poverty at current levels will cost the economy between $36 billion and $177 billion in lower future productivity and employment among those who grow up poor. These costs, moreover, do not include the billions of additional dollars that will be spent on special education, crime, foster care, and teenage childbearing resulting from child poverty. (Children's Defense Fund, 1995:19)

But economic considerations, though important, are not as crucial as humanitarian ones. A nation that can afford it must, if it calls itself civilized, eliminate the physical and psychological misery associated with poverty.

CAUSES OF POVERTY

Who or what is to blame for poverty? There are two very different answers to this question. One is that the poor are in that condition because of some deficiency: Either they are biologically inferior or their culture fails them by promoting character traits that impede their progress in society. The other response places the blame on the structure of society: Some people are poor because society has failed to provide equality in educational opportunity, because institutions discriminate against minorities, because private industry has failed to provide enough jobs, because automation has made some jobs obsolete, and so forth. In this view, society has worked in such a way as to trap certain people and their offspring in a condition of poverty.

Deficiency Theory I: Innate Inferiority

In 1882 the British philosopher and sociologist Herbert Spencer came to the United States to promote a theory later known as **Social Darwinism** (see Chapter 1). He argued that the poor were poor because they were unfit. Poverty was nature's way of:

> excreting . . . unhealthy, imbecile, slow, vacillating, faithless members of society in order to make room for the "fit," who were duly entitled to the rewards of wealth. Spencer preached that the poor should not be helped through state or private charity, because such acts would interfere with nature's way of getting rid of the weak. (quoted in *Progressive*, 1980:8)

Social Darwinism has generally lacked support in the scientific community for 50 years, although it has continued to provide a rationale for the thinking of many individuals. In the last 25 years the concept has resurfaced in the work of three scientists. They suggest that the poor are in that condition because they do not measure up to the more well-to-do in intellectual endowment.

Arthur Jensen, professor of educational psychology at the University of California, has argued that there is a strong possibility that African Americans are less well endowed mentally than Whites. From his review of the research on IQ, he found that approximately 80 percent of IQ is inherited, while the remaining 20 percent is attributable to environment. Because African Americans differ significantly from Whites in achievement on IQ tests and in school, Jensen claimed that it is reasonable to hypothesize that the sources of these differences are genetic as well as environmental (Jensen, 1969, 1980).

The late Richard Herrnstein, a Harvard psychologist, agreed with Jensen that intelligence is largely inherited. He goes one step further, positing the formation of hereditary castes based on intelligence (Herrnstein, 1971, 1973). For Herrnstein, social stratification by inborn differences occurs because (1) mental ability is inherited and (2) success (prestige of job and earnings) depends on mental ability. Thus, a meritocracy (social classification by ability) develops through the sorting process. This reasoning assumes that people who are close in mental ability are more likely to marry and reproduce, thereby ensuring castes by level of intelligence. According to this thesis, "in times to come, as technology advances, the tendency to be unemployed may run in the genes of a family about as certainly as bad teeth do now" (Herrnstein, 1971:63). This is another way of saying that the bright people are in the upper classes and the dregs are at the bottom. Inequality is justified just as it was years ago by the Social Darwinists.

Charles Murray, along with Herrnstein, wrote *The Bell Curve* (Herrnstein and Murray, 1994), the latest major revival of Social Darwinism. Their claim, an update of Herrnstein's earlier work, is that the economic and social hierarchies reflect a single dimension—cognitive ability, as measured by IQ tests.

Notwithstanding the flaws in the logic and in the evidence used by Jensen, Herrnstein, and Murray (for excellent critiques of the Herrnstein and Murray work, see Gould, 1994; Herman, 1994; Reed, 1994; and *Contemporary Sociology,* 1995), we must consider the implications of their biological determinism for dealing with the problem of poverty.

First, biological determinism is a classic example of blaming the victim. The individual poor person is blamed instead of inferior schools, culturally biased IQ tests, low wages, corporate downsizing, or social barriers of race, religion, or nationality. By blaming the victim, this thesis claims a relationship between lack of success and lack of intelligence. This relationship is spurious because it ignores the advantages and disadvantages of ascribed status. According to William Ryan, "Arthur Jensen and Richard Herrnstein confirm regretfully that black folks and poor folks are born stupid, that little rich kids grow up rich adults, not because they inherited Daddy's stock portfolio, but rather because they inherited his brains" (W. Ryan, 1972:54).

The Jensen–Herrnstein–Murray thesis divides people in the United States by appealing to bigots. It provides "scientific justification" for their beliefs in the racial superiority of some groups and the inferiority of others. By implication, it legitimates segregation and unequal treatment of so-called inferiors. The goal of integration and the fragile principle of egalitarianism are seriously threatened to the degree that members of the scientific community give this thesis credence or prominence.

Another serious implication of the biological determinism argument is the explicit validation of the IQ test as a legitimate measure of intelligence. The IQ test attempts to measure innate potential, but this measurement is impossible because the testing process must inevitably reflect some of the skills that develop during the individual's lifetime. For the most part, intelligence tests measure educability—that is, the prediction of conventional school achievement. Achievement in school is, of course, also associated with a cluster of other social and motivational factors, as Joanne Ryan observes:

> The test as a whole is usually validated, if at all, against the external criterion of school performance. It therefore comes as no surprise to find that IQ scores do in fact correlate highly with educational success. IQ scores are also found to correlate positively with socio-economic status, those in the upper social classes tending to have the highest IQs. Since social class, and all that this implies, is both an important determinant and also an important consequence of educational performance, this association is to be expected. (J. Ryan, 1972:54)

Thus, the Jensen–Herrnstein–Murray thesis overlooks the important contribution of social class to achievement on IQ tests. This oversight is crucial because most social scientists feel that these tests are biased in favor of those who have had a middle- and upper-class environment and experience. IQ tests discriminate against the poor in many ways. They discriminate obviously in the language that is used, in the instructions that are given, and in the experiences they assume the subjects have had. The discrimination can also be more subtle. For minority examinees, the race of the person administering the test influences the results. Another, less well-known fact about IQ tests is that in many cases they provide a **self-fulfilling prophecy,** as Joanne Ryan notes:

> IQ scores obtained at one age often determine how an individual is subsequently treated, and, in particular, what kind of education he receives as a consequence of IQ testing will in turn contribute to his future IQ, and it is notorious that those of low and high IQ do not get equally good education. (J. Ryan, 1972:44)

Another implication is the belief that poverty is inevitable. The survival-of-the-fittest capitalist ideology is reinforced, justifying both discrimination against the poor and continued privilege for the advantaged. Inequality is rationalized so that little will be done to aid its victims. Herrnstein and Murray in *The Bell Curve* argue that public policies to ameliorate poverty are a waste of time and resources. "Programs designed to alter the natural dominance of the 'cognitive elite' are useless, the book argues, because the genes of the subordinate castes invariably doom them to failure" (Muwakkil, 1994:22). The acceptance of this thesis, then, has obvious consequences for what policy decisions will be made or not made in dealing with poverty. If their view prevails, then welfare programs will be abolished, as will programs such as Head Start.

This raises the serious question: Is intelligence immutable or is there the possibility of boosting cognitive development? A number of studies have shown that programs such as Head Start raise scores among poor children by as much as 9 points. These results, however, fade out entirely by the sixth grade. Yet this rise and fall of IQ scores makes the case for the role of environmental factors in cognitive development (see the panel titled "Social Policy," pp. 200–201). As Maschinot has argued:

> [The critics of Head Start] ignore the obvious fact that once they leave Head Start, poor students typically attend substandard schools from the first grade onward. The fact that IQ scores drop again after this experience should lead one logically to conclude that intelligence as defined by IQ tests is highly reponsive to environmental manipulations, not the reverse. (Maschinot, 1995:33)

Research on programs other than Head Start makes the same point. The Abecedarian Project conducted at the University of North Carolina studied high-risk children from 120 families. The conclusion:

> The most important policy implication of these findings is that early educational intervention for impoverished children can have long-lasting benefits,

SOCIAL POLICY

EARLY CHILDHOOD PROGRAMS PAY OFF

Early intervention programs such as high-quality preschools and nurses visiting first-time mothers at home save society more money than they cost, a Rand study released Wednesday concludes.

The study, "Investing in Our Children: What We Know and Don't Know about the Costs and Benefits of Early Childhood Interventions," was launched in 1997 with the encouragement of actor/director Rob Reiner and his "I Am Your Child" campaign.

"This new research does point to the wisdom of investing in the development of our youngest children," Reiner said.

Key findings:

- Some early intervention efforts yield improvements for children in several areas, including emotional development, educational achievement, health, higher earnings and lower arrest rates.
- Some programs also racked up long-term savings far exceeding the government's original investment. "They do this by diverting participants from welfare and crime, by reducing their need for special education and health services, and by generating higher tax revenues from increased earnings," the study said.
- The best interventions target children who most need the services. That makes it more likely that savings to government and society will exceed costs.

The Rand study focused on nine model programs and assessed developmental indicators, educational achievement, economic well-being and health for participants.

One of the nine programs was the Perry Preschool, which during the mid-1960s enrolled 123 disadvantaged African-American children in Ypsilanti, Mich. The program also included weekly home visits by the teacher.

Among the positive effects the Rand study found was that 27 years later participants' earnings

> in terms of improved cognitive performance. This underscores the critical importance of good early environments and suggests that the focus of debate should now be shifted from whether government should play a role in encouraging good early environments to how these environments can be assured. (Campbell and Ramey, 1994:694–695)

Another study, by the Robert Wood Johnson foundation, of low-birth-weight infants, followed their development for 3 years. The researchers found that the infants who had a stimulating day care environment had, on average, a 13-point-higher IQ score than the babies who did not have those experiences (Richmond, 1994).

In another study, high-risk African American children in Ypsilanti, Michigan, were randomly divided into two groups. One group received a high-quality active learning program as 3- and 4-year-olds. The other group received no preschool education. The two groups were compared when they were age 27, with these results:

> By age 27, those who had received the preschool education had half as many arrests as the comparison group. Four times as many were earning $2,000 or more a month. Three times as many owned their own homes. One-third more had graduated from high school on schedule. One-fourth fewer of them needed welfare as adults. And they had one-third fewer children born out of wedlock. (Beck, 1995:7B)

As a final example, researchers at the University of Wisconsin studied 989 poor children all born in 1980, who enrolled in the Chicago Child Parent Cenwere 60 percent greater than those in control groups and savings were more than twice the program's costs.

Another program studied was the Prenatal/Early Infancy Project in Elmira, N.Y., which from 1978 to 1982 involved 400 disadvantaged, primarily nonminority families who received home visits by nurses trained in parent education. Mothers also received an average of 32 visits from the fourth month of pregnancy through the child's second year.

Fifteen years later, high-risk families yielded savings four times greater than the program's costs, the study found. The Elmira project is being replicated at other sites around the country.

But many questions remain, the Rand researchers said, including:

- How will welfare reform alter the intervention environment?
- Which programs yield the largest benefit per investment dollar?
- Can model programs be expanded without losing their effectiveness?

"There is still widespread opposition to any new initiatives for early childhood intervention programs," said Jess Cook, a Rand spokesman.

"Many have argued that public programs of this sort have consistently failed."

Nevertheless, politicians and other policymakers, including groups such as the National Governors' Association, have become motiviated by strong public support for initiatives targeting children and are seeking ways to direct public-sector resources toward the period of earliest child development.

The Rand study does have a message for those policymakers: proceed with caution; replicate those programs that have demonstrated their value; evaluate results rigorously; and conduct more coordinated and comprehensive research.

Among other programs studied included preschool programs in Houston, Chicago, Syracuse and North Carolina and a multisite experiment to prepare children born at low birth weights to enter school.

Source: Alvin Peabody. 1998. "Early Childhood Programs Pay Off." Gannett News Service. Reprinted in the *Fort Collins Coloradoan* (April 23):C1.

ter Program no later than age 4, and were taught an average of 2.5 hours a day for 18 months (reported in Steinberg, 2001). The students were tracked until age 20. Comparing these students with 550 other poor children from the same neighborhoods, few of who attended any preschool, researchers found: (1) fewer graduates of the Chicago program had been arrested for juvenile crimes; (2) more graduates of the program also graduated from high school; and (3) the Chicago program children were much less likely to be assigned to special education classes or to repeat a grade.

The Jensen–Herrnstein–Murray thesis also provides justification for unequal schooling. Why should school boards allot comparable sums of money for similar programs in middle-class schools and lower-class schools if the natural endowments of children in each type of school are so radically different? Why should teachers expect the same performance from poor children as from children of the more well-to-do? The result of such beliefs is, of course, a self-fulfilling prophecy. Low expectations beget low achievement.

Finally, the biological determinism thesis encourages policymakers either to ignore poverty or to attack its effects rather than its causes in the structure of society itself.

Deficiency Theory II: Cultural Inferiority

One prominent explanation of poverty, called the **culture-of-poverty** hypothesis, contends that the poor are qualitatively different in values and life-styles from the rest of society and that these cultural differences explain continued poverty. In other words, the poor, in adapting to their deprived condition, are found to be more permissive in raising their children, less verbal, more fatalistic, less likely to defer gratification, and less likely to be interested in formal education than the well-to-do. Most important is the contention that this deviant cultural pattern is transmitted from generation to generation. Thus, there is a strong implication that poverty is perpetuated by defects in the lifeways of the poor. If poverty itself were to be eliminated, the former poor would probably continue to prefer instant gratification, be immoral by middle-class standards, and so on. This reasoning **blames the victim.** From this view, the poor have a subculture with values that differ radically from values of the other social classes.

Edward Banfield, an eminent political scientist, has argued that the difference between the poor and the nonpoor is cultural—the poor have a present-time orientation while the nonpoor have a future-time orientation (Banfield, 1977). He does not see the present-time orientation of the poor as a function of the hopelessness of their situation. Yet it seems highly unlikely that the poor see little reason to complain about their slums: What about the filth, the rats, the overcrowded living conditions, the high infant mortality? What about the lack of jobs and opportunity for upward mobility? This feeling of being trapped seems to be the primary cause of a hedonistic present-time orientation. If the structure were changed so that the poor could see that hard work and deferred gratification really paid off, they could adopt a future-time orientation. Needless to say, there have been many severe criticisms of Banfield's position (see Ryan, 1970).

Critics of the culture-of-poverty hypothesis argue that the poor are an integral part of U.S. society; they do not abandon the dominant values of the society but, rather, retain them while simultaneously holding an alternative set of values. This alternative set is a result of adaptation to the conditions of poverty. Elliot Liebow, in his classic study of lower-class African American men, took this view. For him, street-corner men strive to live by society's values but are continually frustrated by externally imposed failure:

> From this perspective, the street corner man does not appear as a carrier of an independent cultural tradition. His behavior appears not so much as a way of realizing the distinctive goals and values of his own subculture, or of conforming to its models, but rather as his way of trying to achieve many of the goals and values of the larger society, of failing to do this, and of concealing his failure from others and from himself as best he can. (Liebow, 1967:222)

Most Americans believe that poverty is a combination of biological and cultural factors. Judith Chafel reviewed a number of studies on the beliefs of Americans and found that they "view economic privation as a self-inflicted condition, emanating more from personal factors (e.g., effort, ability) than external-structural ones (e.g., an unfavorable labor market, racism). Poverty is seen as inevitable, necessary, and just" (Chafel, 1997:434).

Structural Theories

In contrast to blaming the biological or cultural deficiencies of the poor, the structural theory states that how society is organized creates poverty and makes certain kinds of people especially vulnerable to being poor.

Institutional Discrimination. Michael Harrington, whose book *The Other America* was instrumental in sparking the federal government's war on poverty, has said, "The real explanation of why the poor are where they are is that they made the mistake of being born to the wrong parents, in the wrong section of the country, in the wrong industry, or in the wrong racial or ethnic groups" (Harrington, 1963:21). This is another way of saying that the structural conditions of society are to blame for poverty, not the poor. When the customary ways of doing things, prevailing attitudes and expectations, and accepted structural arrangements work to the disadvantage of the poor, it is called **institutional discrimination.** Let us look at several examples of how the poor are trapped by this type of discrimination.

Most good jobs require a college degree, but the poor cannot afford to send their children to college. Scholarships go to the best-performing students. Children of the poor most often do not perform well in school. This underperformance by poor children results from the lack of enriched preschool programs for them, low expectations for them among teachers and administrators. This attitude is reflected in the system of tracking by ability as measured on class-biased examinations. Problems in learning and test-taking may also arise because English is their second language. Because poverty is often concentrated geographically and schools are funded primarily by the wealth of their district, children of the poor typically attend inadequately financed schools. All these acts result in a self-fulfilling prophecy—the poor are not expected to do well in school, and they do not. Because they are failures as measured by objective indicators (such as the disproportionately high number of dropouts and discipline problems and the small proportion who desire to go to college), the school feels justified in its discrimination toward the children of the poor.

Another job-related trap for the poor is the way low-end jobs are paid. Peter Edelman argues that:

> The basic problem is the way our economy is structured. There are too many jobs that don't pay enough to let workers get by. Everybody knows that many high-paying manufacturing jobs have disappeared to automation, to other countries, and that those opportunities have been replaced by lower-paying service jobs. But not everybody seems to know what that has done to the income of millions of Americans. They do the best they can every day but don't earn enough to make ends meet. (Edelman, 2001:1–2)

The poor are also trapped because they get sick more often and stay sick longer than the well-to-do. The reasons, of course, are that they cannot afford preventive medicine, proper diets, and proper medical attention when ill. The high incidence of sickness among the poor means either that they will be fired from their jobs or that they will not receive money for the days missed from work (unlike the well-to-do, who usually have jobs with such fringe benefits as sick leave and paid medical insurance). Not receiving a paycheck for extended periods means that the poor will have even less money for proper health care, thereby ensuring an even higher incidence of sickness. Thus, there is a vicious cycle of poverty. The poor will tend to remain poor, and their children will tend to perpetuate the cycle.

The traditional organization of schools and jobs in U.S. society has limited the opportunities of racial minorities and women. The next two chapters describe at length how these two groups are systematically disadvantaged by the prevailing laws, customs, and expectations of society, so we will only summarize the structural barriers that they face. Racial minorities are deprived of equal opportunities for education, jobs, and income. As a result African Americans, for example, are half as likely to be wealthy and twice as likely to be poor as Whites. They are also twice as likely as Whites to be unemployed. Structuralists argue that these differences are not the result of flaws in African Americans but result rather from historical and current discrimination in communities, schools, banks, and the work world. Similarly, women typically work at less prestigious jobs than do men and, when working at equal-status jobs, receive less pay and have fewer chances for advancement. These differences are not the result of gender differences but because of personal, social, and societal barriers to equality based on gender.

- **Political Economy of Society.** The basic tenet of capitalism—who gets what is determined by private profit rather than collective need—explains the persistence of poverty. The primacy of maximizing profit works to promote poverty in several ways. First, employers are constrained to pay their workers the least possible in wages and benefits. Only a portion of the wealth created by the laborers is distributed to them; the rest goes to the owners for investment and profit. Therefore, employers must keep wages low. That they are successful is demonstrated by the millions of people *who worked full-time but were below the poverty line.*

A second way that the primacy of profit promotes poverty is by maintaining a surplus of laborers because a surplus depresses wages. Especially important for employers is to have a supply of undereducated and desperate people who will work for very low wages. A large supply of these marginal people (such as minorities, women, and undocumented workers) aids the ownership class by depressing the wages for all workers in good times and provides the obvious category of people to be laid off from work in economic downturns.

A third impact of the primacy of profits in capitalism is that employers make investment decisions without regard for their employees (potential or actual). If costs can be reduced, employers will purchase new technologies to replace workers (such as robots to replace assembly line workers and word processors to replace secretaries). Similarly, owners may shut down a plant and shift their operations to a foreign country where wages are significantly lower.

In sum, the fundamental assumption of capitalism is individual gain without regard for what the resulting behaviors may mean for other people. The capitalist system, then, should not be accepted as a neutral framework within which goods are produced and distributed, but rather as an economic system that perpetuates inequality.

A number of political factors complement the workings of the economy to perpetuate poverty. Political decisions made to fight inflation with high interest rates, for example, hurt several industries, particularly automobiles and home construction, causing high unemployment.

The powerful in society also use their political clout to keep society unequal. Clearly, the affluent in a capitalist society will resist efforts to redistribute their wealth to the disadvantaged. Their political efforts are, rather, to increase their benefits at the expense of the poor and the powerless.

In summary, the structural explanation of poverty rests on the assumption that the way society is organized perpetuates poverty, not the characteristics of poor people. In the words of Claude Fischer and his colleagues: "Inequality is not fated by nature, nor even by the 'invisible hand' of the market; it is a social construction, a result of our historical acts. *Americans have created the extent and type of inequality we have, and Americans maintain it*" (Fischer et al., 1996:7).

ELIMINATION OF POVERTY

As we have discussed, about 32.3 million people in the United States are officially poor. Probably another 30 million or so hover just above the poverty line. Must some portion of U.S. society live in poverty? Is there a way to get everyone above the poverty level to a level at which they are not deprived of the basics of adequate nutrition, health care, and housing? The remainder of this chapter enumerates some assumptions that appear basic to achieving such a goal and some general programs that adoption of these assumptions requires.

Assumption 1: Poverty is a social problem and the source of other social problems; therefore, it must be eliminated. By way of summary, let's examine four consequences of poverty to reinforce the magnitude of this social problem.

The United States, by far, has the highest rates of violent crimes of any industrialized nation. The reasons for this high rate are complex, with many sources, but two stand out—the extraordinarily high rate of poverty in the United States and the very high degree of inequality in the United States (i.e., the gap between the rich and the poor). To buttress the argument, those industrial societies with the greater commitment to the welfare state—that is, those that "have done the most to blunt the inequalities produced by the market system—have low rates of crime, particularly when compared to the one major industrial society that has done the least: the United States" (Currie, 1998).

Poverty leads to personal pathologies. A high unemployment rate, for example, leads to higher rates of property crimes, homicide rates, and drug/alcohol abuse (Currie, 1998). The poor and especially minority poor are disproportionately in prison.

Poverty damages families. Poor couples are twice as likely to divorce as more affluent couples. Jobless people are three to four times less likely to marry than those with jobs. Teenagers living in areas of high unemployment, poverty, and inferior schools are six to seven times more likely to become unwed parents than are the more fortunate teens (Coontz, 1994).

Poverty damages children. Infant mortality is twice as high among the poor than among the more affluent. Persistent poverty during the first 5 years of life leaves children with an IQ deficit, regardless of family structure. Children exposed to lead are seven times less likely to graduate from high school and six times more likely to have a reading disability than are other children (Coontz, 1994).

Assumption 2: Poverty can be eliminated in the United States. Michael Harrington has argued forcefully that poverty must be eliminated because the United States has the resources: "In a nation with a technology that could provide every citizen with a decent life, it is an outrage and a scandal that there should be such social misery" (Harrington, 1963:24).

With the breakup of the Soviet Union and the lessening of global tensions, the United States could reduce its defense budget ($328 billion for fiscal 2002) by many billions of dollars without threatening national security. The United States spends more than the next ten biggest defense spenders *combined* (see Chapter 8). We could spend $100 billion less a year and still be number one militarily. The resulting savings, called the Peace Dividend, could be committed to bringing all people in the United States above the poverty line.

Similarly, we could make a commitment to help children living in poverty, with a commitment like the one we make to meet a national emergency. In the words of the late Albert Shanker, president of the American Federation of Teachers:

> When a great disaster, like a hurricane or an earthquake, strikes people in our country, the president often declares a state of emergency. This mobilizes resources; it cuts through red tape; and it focuses attention on the people who are in danger so they get the help they need—and get it right away. . . . Victims of floods and earthquakes didn't bring their misfortunes on themselves, and we give them help in rebuilding their lives. How can we deny poor children the chance to build theirs? (Shanker, 1992a:E9)

Or sometimes the government makes a huge financial commitment to bolster a sagging part of the economy. If, for example, the government can agree to bail out the deregulated, imprudent, and sometimes fraudulent savings and loan industry for an estimated $500 billion (prorated over a number of years), then surely the government is able to spend one-tenth of that amount to lift 32.3 million people out of poverty.

Assumption 3: Poverty is caused by a lack of resources, not a deviant value system. Basic to a program designed to eliminate poverty is the identification of what keeps some people in a condition of poverty. Is it lack of money and power or the maintenance of deviant values and life-styles? This question is fundamental because the answer determines the method for eliminating poverty. The culture-of-poverty proponents would address non-middle-class traits. The target would be the poor themselves and making them more socially acceptable. Developing the social competence of the poor—not changing the system—would bring an end to poverty. This approach treats the symptom, not the disease. The disease can be cured only by attacking its sources within the society—the structural arrangements that maintain inequality. Thus, the attack must be directed at the structural changes that will enable lower-class people to earn a living wage to support their families adequately and to help their children succeed in school.

Assumption 4: Poverty is not simply a matter of deficient income; it results from other inequities in the society as well. Poverty involves a reinforcing pattern of restricted opportunities, deficient community services, powerful predators who profit from the poor, institutional racism and sexism (see Chapters 8 and 9), and unequal distribution of resources. These problems can be eliminated through structural changes, including (1) the enforcement of the laws regarding equal opportunity for jobs, advancement, and schooling; and (2) the redistribution of power on the local and national levels. The present system works to keep the poor powerless. What is needed, rather, is the organization of the poor into groups with power to determine, or, at least, to shape, policy in local communities. The poor need to have some power over school policies. They need to have a voice in the decisions about the distribution of resources within the community (such as money for parks and recreation, fire protection, street maintenance, and refuse collection). The U.S. system of representative democracy is one of "winner take all" and is therefore to blame for the powerlessness of all minorities. A system of proportional representation would guarantee a degree of power. A third structural change involves an increasing reliance on planning and action at the national level to alleviate the causes of poverty.

Assumption 5: Poverty cannot be eliminated by the efforts of the poor themselves. The poor have neither the power nor the resources to bring about the structural changes necessary to eliminate poverty. Some poor people escape poverty by their own efforts, but most will remain poor unless the people and groups with the power and the resources change the system. This is not to say that the poor cannot have some effect. They can, but usually only indirectly through influential people or groups who become concerned about their plight.

Assumption 6: Poverty cannot be eliminated by the private sector of the economy. Assuming that private enterprises will not engage in unprofitable activities, we can assume also that private enterprise efforts will never by themselves eliminate poverty. In other words, private profit will tend to subvert the human needs that are of public concern; businesses will not provide jobs that they consider unnecessary or not immediately profitable, nor will they voluntarily stop activities that are profitable (e.g., renting deteriorated housing because the unimproved land may increase in value, or charging exorbitant interest rates to the poor, or lobbying to keep certain occupational categories outside minimum-wage restrictions, or moving their operations to another state or nation where wages are lower).

Conventional wisdom, however, suggests that private business is the answer because it will generate new and better-paying jobs. This solution simply will not work because the new poor, as noted earlier, differ dramatically from the old poor. Some of the new poor are workers who have been displaced by robots, word processors, and other labor-saving devices. The jobs of others have moved—from the urban core to the suburbs, to other regions of the country, or to other countries. The jobs were lost because of rational business decisions. In short, the private sector, with its emphasis on profit (and therefore efficiency), will not generate the new jobs needed to eliminate poverty.

Assumption 7: Poverty will not be eliminated by a rising economy. A common assumption is that a growing economy will help everyone—"a rising tide lifts all boats." This assumption has some validity, as evidenced by the very robust economy of the late 1990s, where unemployment dipped to 4.0 percent, jobs were plentiful, and wages for the bottom segment of the population shifted upward. But even in this halcyon economic time, the lot of the poor did not improve much. Actually, affordable housing became even more of a problem because much low-cost housing was gentrified (refurbished for upscale renters) or demolished for office buildings or other uses irrelevant to the poor. Even in the best of times, the conditions of poverty limit and deny. Cities with low tax bases do not provide the needed social services such as pre- and postnatal health care and good schools. During the boom times of the 1990s, the federal goverment cut programs for the poor such as Head Start, food stamps, and Aid to Families with Dependent Children (AFDC). Employers do not have jobs with decent wages and benefits, even in good times, for those with inadequate education and training. In the words of George Will, a conservative who usually argues for market-based solutions: "A rising tide does not raise all boats . . . those stuck in the mud have unique problems and a uniquely powerful claim on our help" (Will, 1991:115).

Assumption 8: Poverty will not be eliminated by volunteer help from well-meaning individuals, groups, and organizations. In 1988 presidential candidate George H. W. Bush called for "a thousand points of light" as the solution to social problems such as poverty. By this Bush meant that charities and volunteers are the answers, not big government. At one level, this makes good sense. That is, churches, private organizations, and the like can and do provide food for the hungry, shelters for the homeless, and emergency care for the victims of natural disasters. In Fort Collins, Colorado, for example, a retired physician began a health clinic for indigent children. With volunteer help and donations, this clinic provides free medical and dental care for thousands of poor youth each year. This wonderful program provides services not provided by the city, county, state, and federal governments. It is also rarely found in other localities.

There are two problems with leaving poverty to charities. The first is that since 1980 the money received by charities and the number of adults volunteering their services to charities have declined. These declines occurred at a time of increasing need by the poor. The second problem is that since this plan is voluntary, the poor in many communities will be denied adequate food, clothing, health care, and shelter. Only a national program will ensure that the needs of all poor will be met.

In 2001 President George W. Bush proposed a variation on his father's "thousand points of light." This was for the federal government to provide funds to religious organizations that help the needy ("faith-based initiative"). In effect, the plan proposes to allow religious charities that serve the poor to compete for $8 billion annually in government funds (Benedetto, 2001). While laudable in many respects given the important contributions by religious charities such as Catholic Charities and the Salvation Army, there are several problems with the plan. First, there is the danger that the churches will use federal resources to try and win converts to their religion, clearly an unconstitutional activity. Second, the government may bypass religious organizations that are not Christian or otherwise mainstream (e.g., Moslems, Buddhists, Scientologists) thereby missing important clusters of poor people. A third objection is that the White House might funnel funds on a political basis rather than according to need, such as to Catholic organizations to win the Catholic vote. Finally, this plan misses the essence of a federal plan to solve the poverty crisis across the United States (J. Jackson, 2001). The federal government needs to spread its resources to make sure that all of those in need are covered. The federal government needs to increase the minimum wage so that every full-time workers can lift his or her family from poverty. The federal government needs to guarantee universal, affordable health care. The federal government needs to make low-cost housing available to all who qualify. The federal government needs to provide every child a fair and healthy start, with adequate nutrition, universal inoculation to prevent diseases, and universal preschool. While President Bush pushes his faith-based initiative to fight poverty, he neglects these other structural elements.

Assumption 9: Poverty will not be eliminated by the efforts of state and local governments. A basic tenet of political conservatism is decentralization of government. Indeed, that was the cornerstone of the 1996 welfare reform. Relatively small and locally based governmental units are believed to be best suited for understanding and meeting the needs of the people. This theory, though logical, has not always worked in practice. In fact, it has increased the problems of some localities.

A good deal of money is gathered and dispensed at the city, county, and state levels for the purpose of alleviating the misery associated with poverty. Some federal programs function only through local units of government. The basic problem is that these local units differ dramatically in their willingness and resources to attack poverty. For example, there are vast differences among states in levels of welfare assistance. In 1990, for example, Idaho spent 24 cents per child to help low-income parents with either child care or preschool programs. At the other extreme, Massachusetts spent $152.04 per child (Gannett News Service, 1992). In 1997 the states ranged in AFDC payments from monthly payments of $164 (14.8 percent of the poverty line) for a family of three in Alabama to $639 in Vermont (57.5 percent of the poverty line). The average for all states was $377 (33.9 percent of the poverty line) (Children's Defense Fund, 1998:110).

Because many politicians believe that relatively high welfare benefits attract poor people from other states and because many states are in a fiscal crisis, there is a current trend to reduce welfare benefits at the state level. Many state legislatures also reflect the current mood to reduce government, beginning with taxes and welfare. In Arizona, for example, where a higher percentage of its people are in poverty than in 31 other states and its welfare benefits are below the national average, the 1994-1995 legislature and governor cut taxes, killed a plan to bring 150,000 of the working poor into the state's health plan for the disadvantaged, and eliminated $1 million from the Women, Infants, and Children (WIC) nutrition program that purchased food for 10,000 extra people each month (Meacham, 1995).

Assumption 10: Poverty is a national problem and must be attacked with massive, nationwide programs financed largely and organized by the federal government. Poverty must be addressed at the federal level to assure that the poor throughout the nation will receive equal benefits and services. Poverty must be attacked nationally to deal with the structural problems that cause poverty (e.g., the changing economy that results in too few jobs, declining real wages for all but the top 20 percent, uneven resources for education, and a health care delivery system that misses or overlooks so many). Poverty must be handled at the national level to ensure that the programs are funded uniformly.

Poverty can be eliminated through the massive infusion of money and compensatory programs, coupled with federal mandates and state cooperation. A federal program funded by taxes (which, by definition, will mean some states will underpay and others will overpay) is a form of socialism because it redistributes resources and therefore is suspect to many. Government control and government subsidies are not new phenomena in the United States, yet it is a curious fact that subsidies for the poor are generally decried while other subsidies go unnoticed or even praised. The federal government has subsidized, for example, defense industries (loans), the oil industry (oil depletion allowance), all corporations (tax write-offs), students (government scholarships and interest-free loans), professors (research grants), homeowners (the interest on mortgages and home taxes is deductible), churches (no property tax or income tax), and farmers (farm subsidies).

What can the federal government do to achieve the goal of getting all people permanently above the poverty line? Three quite different programs are needed because there are three kinds of poor people: (1) those who are unemployed (or employed at low-wage jobs); (2) those who cannot work because they are too old, are physically or mentally handicapped, or are mothers with dependent children; and (3) the children of the poor.

The able-bodied poor need three things: (1) adequate training, (2) guaranteed employment, and (3) a guaranteed minimum income that provides the necessities of food, clothing, shelter, and medical care. The minimum wage needs to be raised significantly. New jobs and even new occupational categories must be created. These new jobs may involve working as "indigenous" neighborhood social workers, teacher's aides, child care providers, community organizers, or research assistants. These new opportunities would be in the service sector of the economy rather than in the goods-producing sector, where automation occurs. Other jobs could be in such public works areas as highway construction, mass transit, improving the nation's infrastructure, recycling waste materials, and park maintenance. An important component of such jobs is social usefulness. Jobs with high social productivity would also have some beneficial by-products (latent consequences) in the form of less estrangement of workers from their jobs and overall improvements for the society itself.

For poor parents in the workforce, at least three things are needed: (1) subsidized child care that is safe and nurturing; (2) if their employer does not pay a living wage, then the workers require a subsidy that brings their wages up to the minimum standard; and (3) a guarantee of health insurance.

All segments of society benefit under full employment. If the poor are paid adequately and therefore have more money to purchase products, the private sector of the economy will be stimulated by increased demand for goods and services. At the same time, full employment and decent pay will give power to the poor. The greater their resources are, the greater is their likelihood to organize for political and social power, to vote their interests, and to become respected by others.

The disabled and incapacitated who cannot or should not be employed require government subsidies to rise above the poverty line. These subsidies may be in the form of money, food, housing, recreational facilities, or special-care centers for the physically and mentally challenged. An important need is adequate low-cost housing since most of the poor currently live in deteriorated housing units. Whatever the cost, there must be a nationwide commitment to provide a decent standard of living for these people.

About 40 percent of the poor in the United States are children. Their economic disadvantage translates into educational disadvantages. Many drop out of school for dead-end jobs, criminal activities, or just hanging out because they have lost hope. How can this cycle of disadvantage be broken? One clear need is for compensatory programs. In the words of Michael Harrington:

> The poor, so to speak, cannot be given the same voucher as everyone else. Having been systematically deprived for so long, they require the use of federal power to make the schooling market more favorable to them than to the children of the affluent. (Harrington, 1968:34)

Head Start is one federally funded program that has documented positive effects for economically disadvantaged children. Lisbeth Schorr has summarized what is known about this excellent program:

> The basic Head Start model has proved to be sound. When three- to five-year-old children are systematically helped to think, reason, and speak clearly; when they are provided hot meals, social services, health evaluations, and health care; when families become partners in their children's learning experiences, are helped toward self-sufficiency, and gain greater confidence in themselves as parents and as contributing members of the community, the results are measurable and dramatic. (Schorr, 1988:192)

The problem with Head Start is that it is underfunded, with only four in ten eligible children able to be included.

Michael Harrington has suggested a more comprehensive program than just Head Start for disadvantaged youth:

> We should have a GI bill in the war against poverty and pay people to go to school, pay for their tuition, their books, and give them an additional living allowance if they have a family. The GI bill was one of the most successful social experiments this society ever had. Why does it require a shooting war for us to be so smart? Why can't we in the war on poverty say that the most productive thing a young person between ages 16 and 21 can do is go to school, and that this is an investment in the Great Society? (Harrington, 1965:xii–xiii)

The positive consequences of this plan would be, first, that a significant segment of potential workers would be kept out of the labor force for a time, thereby reducing the number of jobs needed. Second, individuals would learn the skills needed in an automated society. Third, the educated workers could command greater wages and therefore pay more in taxes. The lifetime earnings for veterans who took advantage of the GI bill were significantly greater than for those who chose to bypass the plan—so much so that they will pay back to the government in taxes approximately six times the amount the government invested in their education. A similar approach could work for the poor.

The problem with this emphasis on education (and with alleviating poverty in general) is the difficulty of providing enough socially useful jobs with a decent U.S. standard of pay. The creation of jobs, then, is the key to eliminating poverty. Because most of these jobs will no doubt be in the public sector of the economy, the government must divert its best minds to tackling this immense problem.

Universal programs such as these are necessary if the United States is to get everyone above the absolute minimum level of economic security. This goal is attainable because the productive capacity of the United States is great enough to make it possible without too much sacrifice. If implemented, they will eliminate the human suffering associated with extreme deprivation.

CHAPTER REVIEW

1. According to the government's arbitrary dividing line, which minimizes the actual extent of poverty, 11.8 percent of the U.S. population (1999) is officially poor. Disproportionately represented in this category are African Americans, Latinos, Native Americans, children, women (especially female heads of families), and people living in central cities and rural areas.
2. The poor are not poor because they refuse to work. Most adult poor either work at low wages, cannot find work, work part-time, are homemakers, are ill or disabled, or are in school.
3. Government assistance to the poor is not sufficient to eliminate their economic deprivation. Less than half of the poor actually receive any federal assistance. When compared to the nonpoor, the poor have a higher incidence of health problems, malnutrition, social pathologies, and homelessness.
4. Most governmental assistance is targeted to the affluent rather than the poor. The nonpoor receive three-fourths of the federal monies allocated to human services. Tax expenditures and other subsidies provide enormous benefits to the already affluent, which further redistributes the nation's wealth upward.
5. One explanation for poverty is that the poor themselves are to blame. The culture-of-poverty hypothesis, for example, contends that the poor are qualitatively different in values and life-styles from the affluent and that these differences explain their poverty and the poverty of their children.
6. Another position that blames the poor for their condition is the innate inferiority hypothesis. This theory, a variant of Social Darwinism promoted by Arthur Jensen and Richard Herrnstein, holds that certain categories of people are disadvantaged because they are less well endowed mentally.
7. Critics of the culture-of-poverty and the innate inferiority hypotheses charge that in blaming the victim, both theories ignore how social conditions trap individuals and groups in poverty.

8. The elimination of poverty requires (a) a commitment to accomplish that goal; (b) a program based on the assumption that poverty results from a lack of resources rather than from a deviant value system; (c) a program based on the assumption that poverty results from inequities in the society; (d) recognition that poverty cannot be eliminated by the efforts of the poor themselves, by the private sector of the economy, by charitable individuals or groups, or by the efforts of state and local governments alone; and (e) recognition that poverty is a national problem and must be attacked by massive, nationwide programs largely financed and organized by the federal government.
9. Three quite different programs are needed because there are three kinds of poverty. The unemployed or underpaid need adequate training, guaranteed employment, and a guaranteed minimal income that is adequate to provide the necessities. The disabled and incapacitated require government subsidies to meet their needs. Finally, the children of the poor need education and opportunities to break the poverty cycle.

KEY TERMS

Poverty. Standard of living below the minimum needed for the maintenance of adequate diet, health, and shelter.

Official poverty line. Arbitrary line computed by multiplying the cost of a basic nutritionally adequate diet by 3.

Feminization of poverty. Viewed erroneously as a trend for contemporary women to be more economically vulnerable than men. This view obscures the fact that women have always been poorer than men, especially older women and women of color.

Old poor. Poor of an earlier generation, who had hopes of breaking out of poverty because unskilled and semiskilled jobs were plentiful.

New poor. Poor who are displaced by new technologies or whose jobs have moved away to the suburbs, to other regions of the country, or out of the country. They have less hope of escaping poverty than did the old poor.

Working poor. People who work but remain below their poverty threshold.

Near poor. People whose incomes are above the poverty threshold but below 125 percent of that threshold.

Severely poor. People whose cash incomes are at half the poverty line or less.

Welfare. Government monies and services provided to the poor.

Wealthfare. Government subsidies to the nonpoor.

Tax expenditures. Legal tax loopholes that allow the affluent to escape paying certain taxes and therefore to receive a subsidy (e.g., the tax deduction to homeowners).

Regressive tax. Tax rate that remains the same for all people, rich or poor. The result is that poor people pay a larger proportion of their wealth than do affluent people.

Social Darwinism. Belief that the place of people in the stratification is a function of their ability and effort.

Self-fulfilling prophecy. Event that occurs because it is predicted. That is, the prophecy is fulfilled because people alter their behavior to conform to the prediction.

Culture of poverty. View that the poor are qualitatively different in values and life-styles from the rest of society and that these cultural differences explain continued poverty.

Blaming the victim. Belief that some individuals are poor, criminals, or school dropouts because they have a flaw within them, which ignores the social factors affecting their behaviors.

Institutional discrimination. When the social arrangements and accepted ways of doing things in society disadvantage minority groups.

WEBSITES FOR FURTHER REFERENCE

http://www.ssc.wisc.edu/irp/
The Institute for Research on Poverty at the University of Wisconsin is a national, university-based center for research into the causes and consequences of poverty and social inequality in the United States. It is one of the two centers designated as a National Poverty Re-

search Center by the U.S. Department of Health and Human Services.

http://www.jcpr.org/
The Joint Center for Poverty Research. Sponsored by Northwestern University and the University of Chicago, the Joint Center for Poverty Research is a national and interdisciplinary academic research center that seeks to advance our understanding of what it means to be poor in America.

http://cpmcnet.columbia.edu/dept/nccp/
The National Center for Children in Poverty identifies and promotes strategies that reduce the number of young children living in poverty in the United States, and that improve the life chances of the millions of children under six who are growing up poor.

http://www.clasp.org
Center for Law and Social Policy (CLASP) is a "national nonprofit organization with expertise in both law and policy affecting the poor. Through education, policy research, and advocacy, CLASP seeks to improve the economic security of low-income families with children and secure access for low-income persons to our civil justice system."

http://www.libertynet.org/~kwru
The Poor People's Summit, held in Philadelphia October 9–11th, 1999, brought together poor and homeless leaders from across the country. The Summit was sponsored the North-South Dialogue and hosted by the Kensington Welfare Rights Union and the Temple University School of Social Work. Over 300 people came to Philadelphia, representing poor people's organizations from around the country and over 60 schools of social work and other allied organizations. The Poor People's Summit is a part of the Economic Human Rights Campaign, where poor people are documenting and organizing against the human rights violations occurring because of welfare reform, downsizing, and poverty.

http://www.welfareinfo.org
The Welfare Information Network "provides information on policy choices, promising practices, program and financial data, funding sources, federal and state legislation and plans, program and management tools, and technical assistance. WIN's website provides one-stop access to over 9,000 links on more than 400 websites."

http://epinet.org/
The Economic Policy Institute: This website provides information and data on various policy alternatives.

http://arc.org/
The Applied Research Center: This website focuses on the consequences of welfare reform.

http://inequality.org/
Inequality.Org provides data and essays on various aspects of inequality in the United States.

http://www.isr.umich.edu/src/psid/
The Panel Study of Income Dynamics is a longitudinal survey of a representative sample of U.S. individuals and the families in which they reside. It has been ongoing since 1968. The data are collected annually, and the data files contain the full span of information collected over the course of the study. PSID data can be used for cross-sectional, longitudinal, and intergenerational analysis and for studying both individuals and families.

Racial and Ethnic Inequality

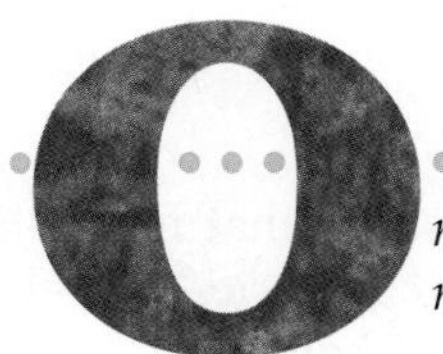

ne can accurately describe the United States as a "total racist society" in which every major aspect of life is shaped to some degree by the core racist realities.

—Joe R. Feagin

Dramatic racial transformations of the past two decades have shattered the hope that civil rights victories would end racial injustice. Instead, the United States now faces serious new racial problems. These problems include the increasing isolation of minorities in central cities, growing minority unemployment, and other forms of economic dislocation. As the proportion of racial minorities in the United States increases, the problems they face become more and more the problems of the entire society. This chapter focuses on how structured racial inequality produces social problems.

HOW TO THINK ABOUT RACIAL AND ETHNIC INEQUALITY

Different racial and ethnic groups are unequal in power, resources, and prestige. Why are some groups dominant and others subordinate? The basic reason is power—power derived from superior numbers, technology, weapons, property, or economic resources. Those holding superior power in a society—the **majority group**—establish a system of inequality by dominating less-powerful groups. This system of inequality is then maintained and perpetuated through social forces. The terms *majority* and *minority* describe power differences.

Like the class and gender hierarchies, racial and ethnic inequalities are deeply embedded in U.S. society. Such inequalities operate as a structure of opportunity and oppression through its unequal distribution of privilege. Racial privilege reaches far back into America's past. The racial hierarchy, with White groups of European origin at the top and people of color at the bottom, serves important functions for society and for certain categories of people. It ensures, for example, that some people are available to do society's dirty work at low wages. The racial hierarchy has positive consequences for the status quo: It enables the powerful to retain their control and their advantages. **Racial stratification** also offers better occupational opportunities, income, and education to White people. These advantages constitute racial privilege. This chapter examines racial inequality from several vantage points. First, we outline the important features of racial and ethnic groups. We then profile four racial minority groups: African Americans, Latinos, Asian Americans, and Native Americans. Next, we examine explanations of racial inequality, followed by a look at its effect on Blacks and Hispanics in terms of income, jobs, education, and health. Finally, the chapter turns to contemporary trends in racial and ethnic relations.

The theme of the chapter is that racial problems have structural foundations. This framework challenges common misperceptions about race and race relations. Many people believe that discrimination has disappeared and that minorities are no longer disadvantaged. We show that minorities lag significantly behind Whites in employment, income, education, and access to health care. Old forms of discrimination thrive alongside new patterns of inequality. Racial minorities are not responsible for inequality. Instead, the problems lie in social institutions, which prevent people of color from achieving economic and social parity. This framework also helps us to understand that minorities are not always passive victims of racial oppression. Their histories reveal varied strategies of struggle and resistance in the face of overwhelming odds. Nevertheless, racial divisions continue to limit the opportunities of people of color.

Racial and Ethnic Minorities

Race is a social category that serves as a basis of power relations and group position. Because race relations are power relations, conflict (or at least the potential for conflict) is always present. Overt conflict is most likely when subordinate groups attempt to change the distribution of power. Size is not crucial in determining whether a group is the most powerful. A numerical minority may in fact have more political representation than the majority, as was the case in South Africa. Thus, the most important characteristic of a **minority group** is that it is dominated by a more powerful group.

Determining who is a minority is largely a matter of history, politics, and judgment—both social and political. Population characteristics other than race and ethnicity—such as age, gender, or religious preference—are sometimes used to designate minority status. However, race and ethnicity are the characteristics used most often to define the minority and majority populations in contemporary U.S. society (O'Hare, 1992:5).

The different experiences of racial groups are structurally embedded in society even though races, per se, do not exist. What does exist is the *idea* that races are distinct groups. Social scientists increasingly reject race as a valid way to divide human groups. Scientific examination of the human genome finds no genetic differences between the so-called races. DNA shows that humans are all one race, evolved in the last 100,000 years from the same small number of tribes that migrated out of Africa and colonized the world (Angier, 2000). Although there is no such thing as biological race, races are real insofar as they are *socially defined*. In other words, racial categories *operate* as if they are real.

Racial classification in the United States is based on a Black/White dichotomy; that is, the construction of two opposing categories into which all people fit. However, social definitions of race change over time and vary in different regions of the country. In the Southwest the divide has been between Anglos and Latinos; in part of the West Coast it is between Asians and Whites (Rosenblum and Tavris, 1966:15). Arab Americans confront discrimination whenever a Mideast crisis occurs. Since the terrorist attacks on the World Trade Center and the Pentagon, Arab Americans, Muslims, and people of Middle-Eastern descent (viewed by many as a single entity) are stereotyped as different and dangerous. (See the "Voices" panel "I'm Not the Enemy.")

Racial Categories

In Chapter 5, we discussed current immigration patterns that are profoundly reshaping the U.S. racial landscape. Sociologists Michael Omi and Howard Winant (1994:55) call this **racial formation,** meaning that society is continually creating and transforming racial categories. Groups previously self-defined in terms of specific ethnic background (such as Mexican Americans and Japanese Americans) have become racialized as "Hispanics" and "Asian Americans." Even the U.S. Census Bureau, which measures race on the basis of self-identification,

VOICES

I'M NOT THE ENEMY

The horror is unspeakable. Like every American, I am paralyzed by the carnage on the news, on our streets. My head pounds, thinking of the grief engulfing thousands of families whose loved ones were killed or injured on Sept. 11. When I close my eyes, I see bodies tumbling from the windows of skyscrapers.

As the attack unfolded, I panicked, racing through what until this moment had felt like a safe, suburban neighborhood to find my son and his babysitter, who were playing, as usual, at a nearby park. I begged my husband, who was at work in a prominent Washington, D.C., building, to come home. With the phone lines going in and out, I felt sure that it just wasn't over.

Like every American, I am afraid. Wondering what this means for us. Wondering whether it's over, or when and where the next attack will take place. It's the first time I've felt the kind of fear I imagine that people in other countries feel when they are at war.

Like every American, I am outraged. And I want justice. But perhaps unlike many other Americans, I'm feeling something else too. A different kind of fear. I'm feeling what my 6 million fellow American Muslims are feeling—the fear that we, too, will be considered guilty in the eyes of America, if it turns out that the madmen behind this terrorism were Muslim.

I feel as though I've suddenly become the enemy of two groups—those who wish to hurt Americans, and those Americans who wish to strike back. It's a frightening corner to be in. In the past, when lone Muslims have committed acts of terrorism—or have been mistakenly assumed to be guilty, as in Oklahoma City—hate crimes have abounded against American Muslims who look like they're from "that part of the world," against American mosques, against American children in Muslim schools who pray to the same peace-loving God as Jews and Christians.

I am now not just afraid, as we all are, for our safety as Americans. I am also afraid for the safety of my sisters-in-law, who wear head scarves in public, and I implore them not to walk alone in the streets of our hometown. I am afraid for my brother, a civil rights lawyer who defends Muslims in high-profile discrimination cases. I am afraid to hear people openly state that Muslim blood is worthless and deserves to be spilled, as I heard when I was in college during the Persian Gulf War. I am afraid that my son won't understand why strangers aren't smiling at him the way they used to. I am afraid that we will be dehumanized because of our skin color, or features, or clothing. My heart aches each time a friend or relative calls, CNN blaring in the background, and sadly reminds me, "It's over for us now. Muslims are done for."

I was briefly heartened to hear author Tom Clancy, interviewed on CNN, explaining that Islam is a peaceful religion and that we as Americans must not let go of our ideals of religious tolerance, because it's the way our country behaves when it's been hurt that really reflects who we are.

Still, I'm afraid that Americans might view the televised images of a few misguided and deeply wounded people overseas celebrating the pain that America is now feeling, and will assume that I too must share that anti-American sentiment, that I, or my family, or my community, or my religion, could be part of the problem. In fact, every major American Muslim organization has decried this violence against us all. In fact, Islam forbids such acts of violence. In fact, all the Muslims I know cringe at the idea of our faith being used, abuse, in the name of political agendas.

And though I, like other Americans, want the perpetrators brought to justice, I shudder to think of the innocent lives that may be unnecessarily lost overseas in that pursuit. Children like ours. Mothers like us.

Every time I hear of an act of terrorism, I have two prayers. My first is for the victims and their families. My second is, please don't let it be a Muslim. Because unlike when an act of terrorism is committed by a Christian or a Jew, when it is a Muslim it's not considered an isolated act perpetrated by an isolated group of madmen. The entire faith is characterized as barbaric, as inhuman. And, my fellow Americans, I stand before you, as broken as you are, to tell you that it's not. That we are not. That we Muslims love our country as you do, and that we are bleeding and grieving alongside you.

Source: Reshma Memon Yaqub. 2001. "I'm Not the Enemy." *Washington Post National Weekly Edition* (September 17–23):26.

revised its racial categories for the 2000 census. For the first time, people could identify themselves as members of more than one racial group on census and other federal forms (see Figure 8.1). Of the U.S. population 2.4 percent, or 7 million people, identified themselves as multiracial, reporting that they were of two races. The option of choosing more than one race provides a more accurate, if complex, portrait of racial composition in the United States. Multiracial categories may grow faster than the total population as interracial marriages increase and more people acknowledge their diverse backgrounds. "Already, children are much more likely to identify themselves as multiracial than adults. Four percent of the population under age 18 were identified in more than one racial category in the 2000 census, twice the percentage for adults" (Kent et al., 2001:6).

Although the 2000 census has begun to capture the complex mix of racial groups present in the United States, it uses a confusing classification for Hispanics. According to the U.S. census guidelines, Hispanics are an ethnic group, not a racial group. Despite the census terminology, Hispanics *are* racialized in the United States. This is the Hispanic population paradox. Hispanics are classified as an ethnic category, yet "Hispanic" encompasses heterogeneous ethnic groups. At the same time, although Hispanics are not officially defined as a race, they are socially defined in racial terms. In other words, Hispanics are treated as a racial group and many identify themselves as belonging to a distinctive racial category (Baca Zinn and Pok, 2002).

Despite the past and present racialization of people of color, we tend to view race as either Black or White. At the same time, Whites as the dominant

→ **NOTE: Please answer BOTH Questions 5 and 6.**

5 **Is this person Spanish/Hispanic/Latino?** *Mark* ☒ *the* **"No"** *box if* **not** *Spanish/Hispanic/Latino*

- ☐ **No,** not Spanish/Hispanic/Latino
- ☐ Yes, Mexican, Mexican Am., Chicano
- ☐ Yes, other Spanish/Hispanic/Latino — *Print group*
- ☐ Yes, Puerto Rican
- ☐ Yes, Cuban

6 **What is this person' race? Mark** ☒ **one or more races** *to indicate what this person considers himself/herself to be*

- ☐ White
- ☐ Black, African Am., or Negro
- ☐ American Indian or Alaska Native — *Print name of enrolled or principal tribe*
- ☐ Asian Indian
- ☐ Chinese
- ☐ Filipino
- ☐ Other Asian — *Print race*
- ☐ Japanese
- ☐ Korean
- ☐ Vietnamese
- ☐ Native Hawaiian
- ☐ Guamanian or Chamorro
- ☐ Samoan
- ☐ Other Pacific Islander — *Print race*
- ☐ Some other race — *Print race*

FIGURE 8.1

Reproduction of Questions on Race and Hispanic Origin from Census 2000

Source: Elizabeth M. Grieco and Rachel C. Cassiday. 2000. "Overview of Race and Hispanic Origin." U.S. Bureau of the Census. *Census 2000 Brief.* (March):1. Washington, DC: U.S. Government Printing Office.

group are usually seen as raceless. Being White is not defined as having a racial status (Andersen, in press), and most Whites do not think of themselves in racial terms because they are not people of color (McIntosh, 1992:79). Race is treated as something possessed by people of color and as something affecting *them,* whereas Whites are depicted as unaffected by race. In this view Whiteness is the normal or natural condition. It is racially unmarked and immune to investigation. This is a false picture of race. In reality, the racial order shapes the lives of all people, even Whites who are advantaged by the system. Just as social classes exist in relation to each other, "races" are defined, compared, and judged *in relation to other races.* "Black" is meaningful only insofar as it is set apart from, and in distinction to, "White." This point is particularly obvious when people are referred to as "non-White," a word that ignores the differences in experiences among people of color (Lucal, 1996:246). Race should not be seen simply as a matter of two opposite categories but as power relations between dominant and subordinate groups (Weber, 2001).

Whereas race is used for socially marking groups based on physical differences, **ethnicity** allows for a broader range of affiliation. Ethnic groups are distinctive on the basis of national origin, language, religion, and culture. Today's world is replete with examples of socially constructed ethnicities. In the United States, people started to affiliate along ethnic lines such as Italian American or German American much more frequently after the civil rights movement. In Europe, as the Western countries move toward economic and political integration, there is a proliferation of regional identification—people may no longer identify as Italian, but as Lombardians, Sicilians, or Romans, as these regions lose economic resources to a larger entity: the European community (Wali, 1992:6). Despite the globalization of national economies, regional and parochial divisions reflect ethnic boundaries and conflicts. "During the last decade of the century, ethnic and religious differences have lead to massacres of ethnic Tutsis by Hutus in Rwanda; full-scale war involving Serb, Bosnian, Albanian, and other ethnic groups in the Balkans; and violence against ethnic Chinese in Indonesia (Pollard and O'Hare, 1999:5).

In the United States, race and ethnicity both serve to mark groups as different. Groups labeled as *races* by the wider society are bound together by their common social and economic conditions. As a result, they develop distinctive cultural or ethnic characteristics. Today, we often refer to them as **racial-ethnic groups** (or racially defined ethnic groups). The term *racial-ethnic group* refers to groups that are socially subordinated and remain culturally distinct within U.S. society. It is meant to include (1) the systematic discrimination of socially constructed racial groups and (2) their distinctive cultural arrangements. The categories of African American, Latino, Asian American, and Native American have been constructed as both racially and culturally distinct. Each group has a distinctive culture, shares a common heritage, and has developed a common identity within a larger society that subordinates it. The racial characteristics of these groups have become meaningful in a society that continues to change (Baca Zinn and Dill, 1994).

Terms of reference are also changing, and the changes are contested both within groups as well as between them. For example, *Blacks* continue to debate the merits of the term *African American,* while *Latinos* disagree on the label *Hispanic.* In this chapter we use such terms interchangeably because they are currently used in both popular and scholarly discourse.

Differences among Ethnic Groups

Both race and ethnicity are historical bases for inequality, although they have differed in how they incorporated groups into society. Race was the social construction that set people of color apart from European immigrant groups (Takaki, 1993:10). Groups identified as races came into contact with the dominant majority through force and state-sanctioned discrimination in work that was unfree, and offered little opportunity for upward mobility. In contrast, European ethnics emigrated to the United States voluntarily, to enhance their status or to market their skills in a land of opportunity. They came with hope and sometimes with resources to provide a foundation for their upward mobility. Unlike racial groups, most had the option of returning if they found the conditions here unsatisfactory. The voluntary immigrants came to the United States and suffered discrimination in employment, housing, and other areas. Clashes between Germans, Irish, Italians, Poles, and other European groups during the nineteenth and early twentieth centuries are well documented. But most European immigrants and their descendants—who accounted for four-fifths of the U.S. population in 1900—eventually achieved full participation in U.S. society (Pollard and O'Hare, 1999:5).

While European ethnics have moved into the mainstream of society, racially defined peoples have remained in a subordinate status. Native Americans, African Americans, Latinos, and Asians have not been assimilated. Continuing racial discrimination sets them apart from others. (See Figure 8.2 for percent of the U.S. population by race in selected years.)

African Americans. By 2000, African Americans (34 million) were 12.3 percent of the total population (U.S. Bureau of the Census, 2001c:3). Virtually all African Americans descend from people who were brought involuntarily to the

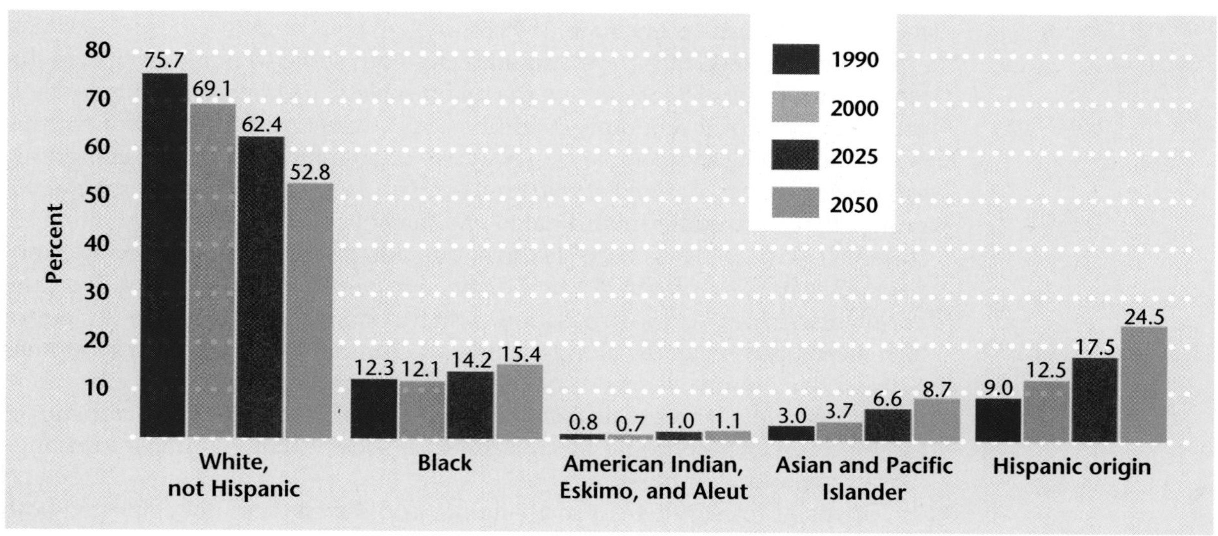

FIGURE 8.2

Percent of the Population, by Race and Hispanic Origin: 1990, 2000, 2025, and 2050 (middle-series projection)

Sources: U.S. Bureau of the Census. 1997. "Population Profile of the United States: 1997." *Current Population Reports.* Series P23-194. Washington, DC: U.S. Government Printing Office, p. 9, U.S. Bureau of the Census accessed online at www.census.gov/population/www/cen2000.

United States before the slave trade ended in the nineteenth century. They entered the Southern states to provide free labor to plantations, and as late as 1890, 90 percent of all Blacks lived in the South, 80 percent as rural dwellers. In the South, they endured harsh and violent conditions under slavery, an institution that would have consequences for centuries to come. During the nineteenth century, the political storm over slavery almost destroyed the nation. Although Blacks left the South in large numbers after 1890, within northern cities they also encountered prejudice, discrimination, and segregation that exposed them to unusually high concentrations of poverty and other social problems (Massey, 1993:7; Takaki, 1993:7). African Americans have a distinctive history of slavery and oppression. "Black" is more than skin color or physical appearance; it is a shared memory and a set of common experiences. The term *Black* denotes a meaningful social category that exists apart from the rubric used by statisticians to identify people of African ancestry (Massey, 1993:7).

Latinos. As we saw in Chapter 5, the U.S. Latino population has edged past the African American population, several years earlier than predicted. In 2000, Hispanics or Latinos numbered 35 million, or 12.5 percent of the total U.S. population. Two-thirds (66 percent) of all Hispanic Americans are Chicanos or Mexican Americans, 9 percent are Puerto Ricans, 4 percent are Cubans, 14 percent are Central American and South American, and 6 percent are "other Hispanic" (U.S. Bureau of the Census, 2001c:1).

The category *Hispanic* was created by federal statisticians to provide data on people of Mexican, Cuban, Puerto Rican, and other Hispanic origins in the United States. The term was chosen as a label that could be applied to all people from the Spanish-speaking countries of Latin America and from Spain. There is no precise definition of group membership, and Latinos do not agree among themselves on a group label. While many prefer the term Latino, they use it interchangeably to self-identify (Romero, 1997). The national origins of Latinos are diverse, and so is the timing of their arrival in the United States. As a result, Mexicans, Puerto Ricans, Cubans, and other Latino groups have varied histories that set them apart from each other. Cubans arrived largely in the period between 1960 and 1980; Mexicans indigenous to the Southwest were forcibly annexed into the United States in 1848, while others have been migrating continuously since 1890. Puerto Ricans came under U.S. control in 1898 and obtained citizenship in 1917; Salvadorans and Guatemalans have been migrating to the United States in substantial numbers during the past two decades.

As a result of these varied histories, Hispanics are found in many legal and social statuses—from fifth-generation Americans to new immigrants, from affluent and well-educated to poor and unschooled. Such diversity means that there is no "Hispanic" population in the sense that there is a Black population. Hispanics neither have a common history nor do they compose a single, coherent community. Rather they are a disparate collection of national-origin groups with heterogeneous experiences of settlement, immigration, political participation, and economic incorporation into the United States. Saying that someone is "Hispanic" or "Latino" reveals little about attitudes, behaviors, beliefs, race, religion, class, or legal situation in the United States (Massey, 1993).

Despite these differences, Latinos in the United States have a long history of discrimination by governments controlled by non-Hispanic Whites. Mexican Americans in the Southwest lost property and political rights as Anglos moved into the region in the 1800s. As late as the 1940s, local ordinances in some Texas

The history, social class, and politics of the American Latino and Asian populations vary widely.

cities blocked Mexican Americans from owning real estate or voting. Also, Mexican Americans were required to attend segregated public schools in many jurisdictions before 1950 (Pollard and O'Hare, 1999:6).

Asian Americans. Asian Americans are another rapidly growing minority group in the country. In 2000, Asian Americans accounted for 3.7 percent of the U.S. population (U.S. Bureau of the Census, 2001c). The nation's 10.6 million Asians now make up 25 percent of the nation's immigrants (U.S. Bureau of the Census, 2001b:3).

Like the Latino population, the Asian population in the United States is extremely diverse, giving rise to the term *Pan-Asian,* which encompasses immigrants from Asian and Pacific Island countries and native-born citizens descended from those ethnic groups (Lott and Felt, 1991:6). Until recently, immigrants who arrived in the United States from Asian countries did not think of themselves as "Asians," or even as Chinese, Japanese, Korean, and so forth, but rather as people from Toisan, Hoeping, or some other district in Guangdong Province in China or from Hiroshima, Yamaguchik, or some other locale. It was not until the late 1960s, with the advent of the Asian American movement, that a Pan-Asian consciousness was formed (Espiritu, 1996:51).

The largest Asian American groups in the United States are Chinese (24 percent), Filipinos (21 percent), Japanese (10 percent), Vietnamese (11 percent), Korean (10 percent), and Asian Indian (13 percent). There also are Laotians, Kampucheans, Thais, Pakistanis, Indonesians, Hmong, and Samoans (Lee, 1998:15).

The characteristics of Asians vary widely according to their national origins and time of entry in the United States. Most come from recent immigrant families, but many Asian Americans can trace their family's American history back more than 150 years. Much of this period was marked by anti-Asian laws and discrimination. The 1879 California Constitution barred the hiring of Chinese workers, and the federal Chinese Exclusion Act of 1882 halted the entry of most Chinese immigrants until 1943. Americans of Japanese ancestry were interned in camps during World War II by an executive order signed by President Franklin D. Roosevelt. Not until 1952 were Japanese immigrants granted the right to become naturalized U.S. citizens (Pollard and O'Hare, 1999:6–7).

Whereas most of the pre–World War II Asian immigrants were peasants, recent immigrants vary considerably by education and social class. On the one hand, many arrived as educated middle-class professionals with highly valued skills and some knowledge of English. Others, such as the Indochinese, arrived as uneducated, impoverished refugees. These differences are reflected in the differences in income and poverty level by ethnic category. Asian Americans taken together have higher average incomes than do other groups in the United States. Although a large segment of this population is financially well off, many are poor. Given this diversity in social classes among the immigrants, most Asian American leaders say the "model minority" label is misleading. Even the term *Asian American* masks great diversity.

Native Americans. Once thought to be destined for extinction, the Native American or American Indian population today is larger than it has been for centuries. Now at about 1 percent of the total U.S. population (Kent et al., 2001:6), Native Americans have more autonomy and are more self-sufficient than at any time since the last century (Snipp, 1996:390). Nevertheless, the population remains one of the most destitute in society.

The tribes located in North America were and are extremely heterogeneous, with major differences in physical characteristics, language, and social organization. As many as 7 million indigenous people lived in North American when the Europeans arrived. However, disease, warfare, and in some cases genocide reduced the Indian population to less than 250,000 by 1890. In the first half of the nineteenth century, the U.S. government forced Indians from their homelands. Those forced migrations accelerated after President Andrew Jackson signed the Indian Removal Act of 1830. Many tribes then lived on marginal land that was reserved for them (Pollard and O'Hare, 1999:6).

The current political and economic status of Native Americans is the result of the process by which they were incorporated into U.S. society. "This amounts to a long history of efforts aimed at subordinating an otherwise self-governing and self-sufficient people that eventually culminated in widespread economic dependency (Snipp, 1996:390).

Important changes have occurred in the social and economic well-being of the Native American population from 1960 to the present. At the time of the 1970 census, Native Americans were the poorest group in the United States, with incomes well below those of the Black population. By 1980, despite poverty rates as high as 60 percent on many Indian reservations, poverty among Native Americans had declined. At the end of the twentieth century, Native Americans were better off than they were in the 1900s. However, in some respects, little has changed. Native Peoples ranked at the bottom of most U.S. socioeconomic indicators, with the lowest levels of life expectancy, per capita income, employment, and education (Thornton, 1996; Harjo, 1996; Pollard and O'Hare, 1999).

Despite the arrival of gambling facilities on reservations, which has enriched a handful of tribes, 25 percent of Native Americans live below the poverty line. On the reservations, half of all children under age 6 live in poverty; one in five Native American homes lack both a telephone and an indoor toilet (Biema, 1995:49).

Although Third World conditions prevail on many reservations, a renaissance has occurred in Native American communities. In cities, modern pan-Indian organizations have been successful in making the presence of Native Americans known to the larger community and have mobilized to meet the needs of their people (Snipp, 1996:390). A college-educated Native American middle class has emerged, Native American business ownership has increased, and some tribes are creating good jobs for their members (Fost, 1991:26).

To summarize this section, the combined population of the four racial minority groups now accounts for 29 percent of the total U.S. population (U.S. Bureau of the Census, 2001c:3). New waves of immigration from non-European countries, high birthrates among these groups, and a relatively young age structure account for the rapid increase in minorities. By the middle of the twenty-first century, today's minorities will comprise nearly one-half of the U.S. population. (See Figure 8.2 for population projections through 2050.) African Americans, Latinos, Asian Americans, and Native Americans are different in many respects. Each group encounters different forms of exclusion. Nevertheless, as racial minorities they remain at the lowest rungs of society.

EXPLANATIONS OF RACIAL AND ETHNIC INEQUALITY

Why have some racial and ethnic groups been consistently disadvantaged? Some ethnic groups, such as the Irish and the Jews, have experienced discrimination but managed to overcome their initial disadvantages. However, African Americans, Latinos, Asian Americans, and Native Americans have not been able to cast off their secondary status. Three types of theories have been used to explain why some groups are treated differently: deficiency theories, bias theories, and structural discrimination theories.

Deficiency Theories

A number of analysts have argued that some groups are disadvantaged because they *are* inferior. That is, when compared with the majority, they are deficient in some important way. There are two variations of **deficiency theories.**

- **Biological Deficiency.** This classical explanation for racial inferiority maintains that group inferiority is the result of flawed genetic traits. This is the position of Arthur Jensen, Richard Herrnstein, and Charles Murray (as discussed in Chapter 7). *The Bell Curve* (Herrnstein and Murray, 1994) is the latest in a long series of works claiming that Blacks are mentally inferior to Whites and that genetic inferiority cannot be altered by environmental changes (Gould, 1994). Despite the media attention given the work of these and other theorists, there is no definitive evidence for the thesis that racial groups differ in intelligence. Biological deficiency theories are generally not accepted in the scientific community (see *Contemporary Sociology,* 1995).

- **Cultural Deficiency.** Many explanations of racial subordination center on group-specific cultural characteristics presumed to be handed down from generation to generation. Supposedly deficient characteristics of the groups themselves (including motivation, moral background, and family forms) are the reason some groups remain at the bottom. Cultural explanations argue that flawed minority life-styles are responsible for each group's secondary status.

From this perspective, minorities are disadvantaged because of their group-specific heritage and customs. Cultural deficiency was the basis of Daniel Patrick Moynihan's famous 1967 report, which charged that the "tangle of pathology" within Black ghettos was rooted in the deterioration of the Negro family (U.S. Department of Labor, 1965). High rates of marital dissolution, female-headed households, out-of-wedlock births, and welfare dependency were said to be the residuals of slavery and discrimination, a complex web of pathological patterns passed down through the generations. The Moynihan report was widely criticized for being a classic case of "blaming the victim." It locates the problem within Blacks, not in the structure of society.

Cultural deficiency theorists ignore the social opportunities that affect groups in different ways. Many social scientists have long opposed cultural explanations. Nevertheless, this approach is still found in scholarship and popular thought. Today, much of the public discussion about race and poverty rests on false assumptions about deficient minorities (Reed, 1990; di Leonardo, 1992). We return to this theme in the last section of this chapter.

Bias Theories

The deficiency theories discussed above blame minorities for their plight. **Bias theories,** on the other hand, blame the members of the majority. They blame individuals who hold *prejudiced attitudes* toward minorities. Gunnar Myrdal, for example, argued in his classic book *An American Dilemma* that prejudiced attitudes toward an entire group of people are the problem (Myrdal, 1944). This reduces racism to a set of ideas or beliefs that induce individuals to discriminate (Bonilla-Silva, 1996:466).

David Wellman has made an extensive critique of bias theories and presented an alternative (Wellman, 1977). He challenged the notion that the hostile attitudes of White Americans, especially lower-class Whites, are the major cause of racism. Instead, he shows that prejudiced beliefs do not explain the

Institutional racism is more injurious than individual racism, but it is not recognized by the dominant-group members as racist.

behaviors of unprejudiced Whites who defend social arrangements that negatively affect minorities. Unbiased people fight to preserve the status quo by favoring, for example, the seniority system in occupations, or they oppose affirmative action, quota systems, busing to achieve racial balance, and open enrollment in higher education. As Wellman has argued:

> The terms in which middle-class professionals defend traditional institutional arrangements are, strictly speaking, not examples of racial prejudice. They are neither overtly racial nor, given these people's interests, misrepresentations of facts. However, while the sentiments may not be prejudiced, they justify arrangements that in effect, if not in intent, maintain the status quo and thereby keep Blacks in subordinate positions. (Wellman, 1977:8)

To focus strictly on prejudice is to take too narrow a view. This view is inaccurate because it concentrates on the bigots and ignores the structural foundation of racism. The determining feature of majority–minority relations is not prejudice but differential systems of privilege and disadvantage. "The subordination of people of color is functional to the operation of American society as we know it and the color of one's skin is a primary determinant of people's position in the social structure" (Wellman, 1977:35). Thus, institutional and individual racism generate privilege for Whites. Discrimination provides the privileged with disproportionate advantages in the social, economic, and political spheres. Racist acts, in this view, not only are based on hatred, stereotyped conceptions, or prejudgment but also are rational responses to the struggle over scarce resources by individuals acting to preserve their own advantage.

Structural Discrimination Theories

Deficiency and bias theories focus, incorrectly, on individuals: the first on minority flaws, and the second on the flawed attitudes of the majority. Both kinds of theory ignore the social system that oppresses minorities. Parenti has criticized those who ignore the system as victim blamers. "Focusing on the poor and ignoring the system of power, privilege, and profit which makes them poor, is a little like blaming the corpse for the murder" (Parenti, 1978:24). The alternative view is that racial inequality is not fundamentally a matter of what is in people's heads, not a matter of their private individual intentions, but rather a matter of public institutions and practices that create or perpetuate racism. **Structural discrimination theories** move away from thinking about "racism-in-the-head" toward understanding "racism-in-the-world" (Lichtenberg, 1992:5).

Many sociologists have examined how race is structural, permeating every aspect of life. Sociologists who use this framework make a distinction between *individual racism* and *institutional racism* (Carmichael and Hamilton, 1967). Individual racism is related to prejudice. It consists of overt acts by individuals that harm other individuals or their property. Institutional racism is structural. It refers to social processes that, intentionally, or not, protect the advantages of the dominant group while maintaining the unequal position of the subordinate group (Miles, 1989:50). Institutional racism views inequality as part of society's structure. Therefore, individuals and groups discriminate whether they are bigots or not. These individuals and groups operate within a social milieu that ensures racial dominance. The social milieu includes laws, customs, religious beliefs, and the stable arrangements and practices through which things get done in society. Joe R. Feagin (2000) has synthesized structural perspectives in a theory called systemic racism. *Systemic racism* includes a diverse assortment of racist practices; the unjustly gained economic and political power of Whites; the continuing resource inequalities; and the White-racist ideologies, attitudes, and institutions created to preserve White advantages and power. Systemic racism is both structural and interpersonal. "At the macrolevel, large-scale institutions . . . routinely perpetuate racial subordination and inequalities. These institutions are created and recreated by routine actions at the microlevel by individuals" (Feagin, 2000:16).

Social institutions have great power to reward and penalize. Therefore, the term **institutional discrimination** is a useful one for understanding racial inequality. There are four basic themes of institutional discrimination (Benokraitis and Feagin, 1974). First is the importance of history in determining present conditions and affecting resistance to change. The United States was founded and its institutions established when Blacks were slaves, uneducated, and different culturally from the dominant Whites. From the beginning, Blacks were considered inferior (the original Constitution, for example, counted a slave as three-fifths of a person). Religious beliefs buttressed this notion of the inferiority of Blacks and justified the differential allocation of privileges and sanctions in society.

The second theme of institutional discrimination is that discrimination can occur without conscious bigotry. Everyday practices reinforce racial discrimination and deprivation. Although actions by the Ku Klux Klan have an unmistakably racial tone, many other actions (choosing to live in a suburban neighborhood, sending one's children to a private school, or opposing government intervention in hiring policies) also maintain racial dominance (Bonilla-Silva, 1996:475). With or without malicious intent, racial discrimination is the "normal" outcome of the system. Even if "racism-in-the-head" disappeared, "racism-in-the-world" would not because it is the system that disadvantages (Lichtenberg, 1992).

Finally, institutional discrimination is reinforced because institutions are interrelated. The exclusion of minorities from the upper levels of education, for example, is likely to affect their opportunities in other institutions (type of job, level of remuneration). Similarly, poor children will probably receive an inferior education, be propertyless, suffer from bad health, and be treated unjustly by the criminal justice system. These inequities are cumulative.

Institutional derogation occurs when minority groups and their members are made to seem inferior or to possess negative stereotypes through legitimate means by the powerful in society. The portrayal of minority group members in the media (movies, television, newspapers, and magazines) is often derogatory. A study of prime-time network programming by the advocacy group Children Now found that minorities are still shortchanged. In 2000, Blacks made up 17 percent of prime-time television characters while Latinos made up 2 percent, Asians Americans made up 3 percent, and Native Americans made up 0.2 percent (Fall Colors, 2000). According to another study, Black men are also depicted disproportionately as drug users, criminals, lower-class, and "pathological" (Muwakkil, 1998b:18). If we based our perceptions of minority populations on media images, we would have considerably skewed views.

Why is U.S. society organized along racial lines? Sociologists have a longstanding debate over the relative importance of race and class in shaping systems of racial privilege and disadvantage. Many scholars argue that modern race relations are produced by world capitalism. Using the labor of non-White peoples began as a means for White owners to accumulate profits. This perspective contends that capitalism as a system of class exploitation has shaped race and racism in the United States and the world (Bonacich, 1992).

Other structural theories are based on the interplay between the U.S. economy and racially stratified labor systems. For example, **colonial theory** incorporates class and race to address the question of why some ethnic groups have overcome their disadvantaged status, whereas others have not. This is important because it challenges the myth that the United States is a melting pot. Colonial theory argues that there are fundamental differences between the experiences of racial ethnics and European ethnics. Racial ethnics have been much like colonial subjects in the United States, while Europeans immigrated to this society. Using this framework, we can see that despite certain similarities (such as poverty and discrimination), the experiences of racial minorities contrasted sharply with those of European immigrants.

A key feature of the colonial model is the labor that people of color did when they were brought into the United States. European ethnics began work mostly in industry, or at least in industrial sectors of the economy, where they could move about as families or individuals in response to the needs of an industrializing economy. In contrast, Blacks and Hispanics were forced into other preindustrial work in the least advanced sectors of the economy and the most industrially backward regions of the nation. This placement of non-White groups, however, imposed barrier upon barrier on their social mobility (Blauner, 1972:62).

Some contemporary theories point to race itself as a primary shaper of the social structure. The racial formation perspective is the most current explanation of how racial inequalities are supported through institutional practices (Omi and Winant, 1986, 1994). This theory proposes that the United States is organized along racial lines from top to bottom—a racial state, composed of institutions and policies to support and justify racial stratification (Omi and Winant, 1986).

DISCRIMINATION AGAINST AFRICAN AMERICANS AND LATINOS: CONTINUITY AND CHANGE

The treatment of Blacks and Hispanics has been disgraceful throughout American history. Through public policies and everyday practices, they have been denied the opportunities that should be open to all people. Since World War II, however, under pressure from civil rights advocates, the government has led the way in breaking down these discriminatory practices. The 1960 civil rights movement overturned segregation laws, opened voting booths, created new job opportunities, and renewed hope for racial equality. By the close of the twentieth century, many well-educated people of color had climbed into the middle class. In 1999, 28 percent of African Americans and 25 percent of Latino families had incomes of $50,000 or more (U.S. Bureau of the Census, 2000a: 43–46). They have taken advantage of fair-housing legislation and moved to the suburbs looking for better schools, safer streets, and better services (del Pinal and Singer, 1997:39). Yet having "made it" in the United States does not shield people of color from discrimination. Studies of public accommodation have found that in stores, bars, restaurants, and theaters, middle-class Blacks are ignored or treated with hostility (Feagin and Sykes, 1994). No matter how affluent or influential, Black people are vulnerable to "microinsults" such as being followed around in stores or ticketed for "driving while Black" (Muwakkil, 1998a:11).

The minority middle class has not erased the problem of segregation. A class divide now characterizes minority communities across the country. As some successful people of color have become richer, many more unsuccessful ones have been marginalized. As much as some things have changed, others have stayed the same. The present segregation of African Americans cannot be dismissed as wrongs committed in the past. U.S. neighborhoods were sharply segregated in the 1990s (Massey and Denton, 1993). Today, they are just as segregated. The 2000 census data show high levels of racial segregation in residential areas. Whites tend to live in neighborhoods that are overwhelmingly White, while minorities live in neighborhoods with other minorities. The average Black person lives in a neighborhood that is 33 percent White and 51 percent Black. Compared with 1990, Blacks were more likely to have Hispanic and Asian neighbors, but they were no more likely to have White neighbors. Asian and Hispanic populations—which include large numbers of recent immigrants—were somewhat more isolated from other racial groups in 2000 than they were in 1990 (Kent et al., 2001:24). (See Figure 8.3 on the segregation of Asians, Blacks, and Hispanics.)

Separation of Asians

Of the 50 metropolitan areas with the largest percentage of Asians, here are the 10 areas where Asians and whites are most segregated:

Area name	*2000 rank*	*1990 rank*
New York	**1**	7
Stockton, Calif.	**2**	1
Houston	**3**	8
Sacramento	**4**	6
San Francisco	**5**	4
Los Angeles	**6**	15
Vallejo, Calif.	**7**	16
San Diego	**8**	10
Detroit	**9**	9
Atlanta	**10**	17

. . . and of blacks

Of the 50 metropolitan areas with the largest percentage of blacks, here are the 10 areas where blacks and whites are most segregated:

Area name	*2000 rank*	*1990 rank*
Detroit	**1**	1
Milwaukee-Waukesha, Wisc.	**2**	4
New York	**3**	7
Chicago	**4**	2
Newark, N.J.	**5**	3
Cleveland	**6**	5
Cincinnati	**7**	6
Nassau-Suffolk, N.Y.	**8**	9
St. Louis	**9**	8
Miami	**10**	15

. . . and of Hispanics

Of the 50 metropolitan areas with the largest percentage of Hispanics, here are the 10 areas where Hispanics and non-Hispanic whites are most segregated:

Area name	*2000 rank*	*1990 rank*
New York	**1**	2
Newark, N.J.	**2**	1
Los Angeles-Long Beach	**3**	5
Chicago	**4**	4
Philadelphia	**5**	3
Salinas, Calif.	**6**	7
Boston	**7**	8
Bergen, N.J.	**8**	6
Ventura, Calif.	**9**	11
Orange County, Calif.	**10**	14

For the complete segregation report, go to www.albany.edu/mumford/census.

FIGURE 8.3

Segregation Still Touches Minorities Where They Live

Source: Haya El Nasser. 2001. "Segregation Still Touches Miniorities Where They Live." *USA Today.* (April 4):2A.

Income

The average income for White families is greater than the average income for Black and Hispanic families. Racial income disparities have remained unchanged over time. In 1999, the median income of Black families was $29,404, the median income of White families was $49,023, and the median income of Hispanics was $29,608 (U.S. Bureau of the Census, 2000d). Even though the median family income for Blacks is still below that of Hispanics, per-person income for Hispanics is actually lower because Hispanics tend to have larger families.

Although the racial income gap is wide, the racial wealth gap is even wider. White families generally have greater net worth than Black or Latino families (Collins et al., 1999). In their book, *White Wealth/Black Wealth,* Melvin Oliver and Thomas Shapiro (1995) define wealth as the command over financial resources that a family actually has accumulated over its lifetime, along with those resources that have been inherited across generations. White families generally have greater resources for their children and bequeath them as assets at death. Oliver and Shapiro call this "the cost of being Black." One important indicator of a family's wealth is home ownership. Paying off a home mortgage is the way most people build net worth over their lifetimes. More minorities are buying homes, but because of discrimination in employment, housing, and insurance, they are still less likely than Whites to own the homes in which they live. In 1995, the home ownership rate was 47 percent for African Americans and 44 percent for Latinos, about two-thirds the rate for White households (Collins et al., 1999).

Poverty rates for all minority groups are higher than those of Whites. The percentage of Blacks, Hispanics, and Native Americans in poverty is about three times that of Whites. Even Asian Americans, who have a higher average income than Whites, are more likely to live in families with incomes below the poverty line (O'Hare, 1992:37). Although most poor people are White, Blacks and Hispanics are disproportionately poor. In 1999, the poverty rate for Whites was 10 percent, compared with 26 percent for Blacks and 25 percent for Hispanics (U.S. Bureau of the Census, 2000a). In recent years, the poverty rate of Hispanics rose more rapidly than that of Whites or Blacks. However, poverty rates differ greatly among Hispanic groups. Puerto Rican and Mexican families are most likely to be poor, while Cubans are least likely (del Pinal and Singer, 1997:39). Economic conditions in some areas where Hispanics are concentrated account for the difference. Puerto Ricans are concentrated in major cities of the eastern end of the Snow Belt, where larger economic changes have affected unskilled workers (Aponte, 1991).

The growing poverty rate among minority children is one of the nation's most ominous social problems (Harris and Bennett, 1995:196). In 1999, 13 percent of White children lived in poverty, compared with 30 percent of Latino children and 33 percent of Black children (U.S. Bureau of the Census, 2000a). The situation is even worse in families headed by women. Black and Hispanic women maintaining families have lower labor force participation rates and higher unemployment rates than do White women maintaining families. This gives one explanation for the high poverty rates in families maintained by women. The "feminization of poverty" explains some kinds of poverty, but it does not explain the income inequality in minority families with a man and a woman present. A two-parent family is no guarantee against poverty for racial minorities. Many young children in married-couple homes are in the lowest income tier—two in ten White children, three in ten Black children, and four in ten Hispanic children (Ahlburg and De Vita, 1992:38).

Many factors explain the difference in White and minority incomes. Racial ethnics are concentrated in the South and Southwest, where incomes are lower for everyone. Another part of the explanation is the differing age structure of minorities. They are younger, on average, than the White population. A group with a higher proportion of young people of working age will have a lower average earning level, higher rates of unemployment, and lower rates of labor force participation.

Looking at racial inequalities by age reveals another disturbing pattern. The degree of inequality increases after the teenage years. Racial disparities become greater in peak earning years. This suggests that another part of the explanation for racial inequalities in earnings lies in the lack of education and skill levels required to move out of poor-paying jobs. All these explanations leave a substantial amount of inequality unexplained. Current racial discrimination in the labor force means that minorities at all levels of employment and education still earn less than do Whites, as we see in Chapter 14.

Education

In 1954, the Supreme Court outlawed segregation in the schools. Since then, more U.S. residents have completed high school and college. By 1995, when minorities made up one-third of public school students, they still had lower levels of educational completion than Whites (see Figure 8.4).

Among young adults, Hispanics have the lowest levels of educational completion while Whites and Asians have the highest. High school graduation rates for Whites are 88 percent compared with 85 percent for Asian Americans, 77 percent for African Americans, and 56 percent for Hispanics (U.S. Bureau of

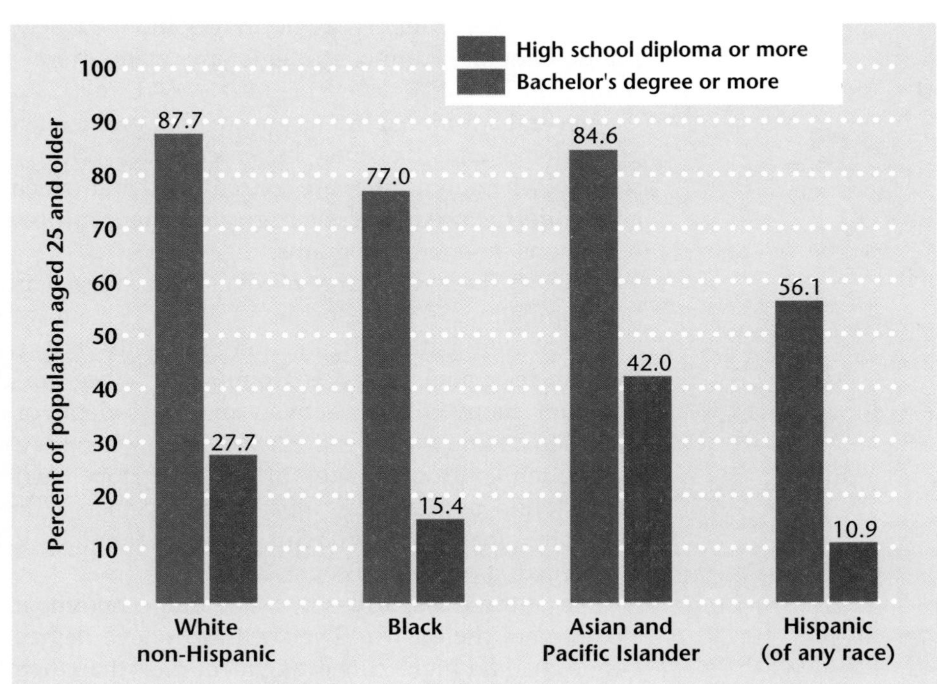

FIGURE 8.4

High School and College Graduates by Race and Hispanic Origin: 1999 (percent of the population aged 25 and older)

Source: U.S. Bureau of the Census. 2001. "Population Profile of the United States, 1999." *Current Population Reports.* Series P23-205. Washington, DC: U.S. Government Printing Office, p. 64.

Decreased public support of education poses a greater burden on inner-city schools.

the Census, 2000c). This is a growing problem, since most new jobs in the new century will require education beyond high school (Pollard and O'Hare, 1999c:30).

The minority education gap is caused by several factors, including language differences, different educational opportunities, and lack of family support for education. Yet many of the problems have less to do with minority students themselves and more to do with the failure of schools to retain minority students and provide them with a marketable education. Segregation in schools is due largely to the residential segregation that exists throughout the country. Minority students attend schools with mostly minority students (Sidel, 1994:67). Black students are no longer the most segregated group. In today's public schools, Latino students are even more segregated (Tienda and Simonelli, 2001).

Several additional trends are creating problems for minority students. The general movement against increased taxes hurts public schools. Inner-city schools, where minorities are concentrated and which are already understaffed and underfinanced, face even greater financial pressures because of current reductions in federal programs.

In 1999, there were large racial gaps in college enrollment. Of the total campus population, 70 percent were White, 11 percent were African American, and 8 percent were Latino (Tienda and Simonelli, 2001) (see the "Looking Toward the Future" panel, "Who Is Coming to College in the Coming Decades?"). Although many colleges actively recruit students of color, many factors contribute to having low retention rates. Even when they reach college, students of color often confront a range of discriminatory barriers. Studies have consistently found that they are more alienated than White students and drop out more often than White students. Discrimination by Whites on and off campus is a recurring problem (Feagin, 2000:170).

All of these disparities translate into economic inequalities. Yet education alone is not the answer. Even with a college degree, African Americans and Latinos had far higher unemployment rates than their White counterparts (Fol-

LOOKING TOWARD THE FUTURE

WHO IS COMING TO COLLEGE IN THE COMING DECADES?

College campuses will clearly be much more racially and ethnically diverse in the coming decades. This report reminds us, however, that the highest levels of racial/ethnic diversity at colleges and universities will be clustered in particular regions of the country. More than half of the overall increase in undergraduates will occur in just five states—California, Texas, Florida, New York, and Arizona. Minority undergraduates will outnumber White students on campus in 2015 in the District of Columbia and in Hawaii, California, and New Mexico. Texas will be about evenly split between minority and White undergraduates in 2015, with minorities as a group becoming a majority soon after. Minority enrollment will exceed 40 percent of undergraduates in 2015 in six other states—New York, Maryland, Florida, New Jersey, Louisiana, and Mississippi.

Minority student enrollment will rise both in absolute number of students—up about 2 million—and in percentage terms, growing from 29.4 percent of overall undergraduate enrollment in 1995 to 37.2 percent in 2015. The report defines "minority" as African American, Hispanic, and Asian/Pacific Islander.

Hispanic students will register the largest absolute gains. There will be an additional 1.0 million undergraduate Hispanic students. This group will grow from 10.6 percent of the nation's campus population in 1995 to 15.4 percent in 2015. ETS projects that Hispanic undergraduates will become the nation's second largest student group by race/ethnicity, surpassing the enrollment of African American undergraduates, in 2006. Four states—California, Texas, Florida, and New York—will account for two-thirds of the increase in Hispanic students.

In percentage terms, Asian-Pacific Islanders on campus are the fastest growing minority. The report suggests that the Asian/Pacific Islander undergraduate population will swell by 600,000 students between 1995 and 2015, an 86 percent increase. This group will grow from 5.4 percent to 8.4 percent of all U.S. college students. The increase projected by ETS for African American undergraduates will be about 400,000 students, concentrated in Texas, Georgia, Florida, Maryland, and North Carolina. The percentage of African American undergraduates will remain steady, however, at about 13 percent.

The number of White college students will also be rising in the coming decades, but they will make up a declining portion of the undergraduate population. The share of White students on campuses nationwide will decline to 62.8 percent in 2015, a drop of 7.8 percent over 1995 levels. The absolute numbers of White undergraduates will fall in ten states, led by New York, Ohio, and Pennsylvania.

* * *

Simply assembling a more diverse population of students doesn't mean a campus has achieved a meaningfully inclusive learning environment. Colleges and universities, for instance, still have a long way to go before they will achieve a diversity of their faculty and administrative ranks comparable to the diversity of their student bodies. In addition, creating an effective learning environment for all students on a diverse campus is still a significant challenge. Reports of differential experiences of acceptance and instances of overt and covert acts of discrimination on college campuses still abound.

Source: Debra Humphries. 2000. "Achieving Equity as Generation Y Goes to College: New Data." *Diversity Digest* 4 (3) (Spring/Summer):6–7.

bre, 1995:4–8). This is compounded by the reality that education does not pay equally. Minority members, regardless of their level of education, are underpaid compared with Whites of similar education. For example, in the nineties, Hispanic women with bachelor's degrees earned less than White men with high school diplomas. African American women with bachelor's degrees earned just $600 per year more than White men with high school diplomas (Outtz, 1995:68). (See Table 8.1, p. 234, on the disparities in median income by race.)

TABLE 8.1

Median Income in 1999 by Educational Attainment for Full-Time Workers Age 25 and Older by Race/Ethnicity

	Not High School Graduate	*High School Graduate*	*Some College*	*Bachelor's Degree or More*
White				
Male	$23,004	$34,765	$40,341	$60,984
Female	16,445	23,719	28,562	42,344
Black				
Male	21,745	27,906	33,141	45,415
Female	16,069	20,945	25,795	37,646
Latino				
Male	19,193	25,362	31,830	45,502
Female	14,239	20,366	25,187	36,234

Source: U.S. Bureau of the Census. 2000. "Educational Attainment in the United States," *Current Population Reports.* Series P20-536. Washington, DC: U.S. Government Printing Office.

Unemployment

African Americans and Latinos are more likely than Whites to be unemployed. For the last three decades, unemployment among Black workers has been twice that of White workers, with Latinos in between. Unemployment among Latinos is now almost as pervasive as among Blacks. In 2000, the unemployment rate for Latinos was 5.7 percent, compared with 7.6 percent for African Americans and 3.5 percent for Whites (U.S. Department of Labor, 2001). Minority teenagers had an even harder time. The unemployment rate among Black teens was 24 percent; for Latinos, it was 16 percent, and for Whites it was 11 percent.

These government rates are misleading because they count as employed the almost 6 million people who work part time because they cannot find full-time jobs, and these rates also do not count as unemployed the discouraged workers, numbering more than 1 million, who have given up their search for work.

Type of Employment

African Americans and Latinos have always been an important component of the U.S. labor force. However, their job prospects are different from those of other people in the United States. Not only are they twice as likely as Whites to be unemployed, they are more likely to work in low-skilled occupations and less likely to work in managerial or professional occupations (see Table 8.2).

Although Blacks, Hispanics, and Native Americans are in the least rewarding jobs, and many face discrimination in hiring and promotion, the occupational status of minorities improved slowly during the last decade. Between 1990 and 1998, the percentage of Blacks in managerial and professional occupations increased from 17 to 20 percent, while the percentage increased from 13 to 15 percent for Hispanics and from 16 to 20 percent for American Indians (Pollard and O'Hare, 1999:33). Despite these gains, however, a huge gap remains. As more minorities enter high-status work, they are confronting new forms of discrimination in the form of "job ceilings" that keep them out of executive suites and boardrooms (Higginbotham, 1994).

Economic restructuring of the U.S. economy is affecting minority employment patterns in communities across the country. The job crisis in minority communities is linked to the widening division of the U.S. economy and van-

TABLE 8.2

Selected Labor Force Characteristics by Race and Ethnicity, 2000

		Race/Ethnic Group			
	Total	*Black*	*Hispanic*	*Asian*	*White*
Percent in civilian labor force					
Women	60.7	63.9	56.6	59.3	60.8
Men	74.2	68.1	80.4	74.0	74.3
Percent unemployed					
Women	4.3	7.4	7.7	3.6	3.3
Men	4.4	8.1	6.2	4.1	3.6
By occupation					
Women					
Professional, administrative, sales	48.3	38.9	32.5	54.9	51.4
Service, skilled/unskilled labor	26.6	36.8	42.4	28.5	22.8
Men					
Professional, administrative, sales	42.9	27.6	20.9	56.8	47.7
Service, skilled/unskilled labor	48.1	62.0	65.4	34.9	44.3

Source: U.S. Census Bureau. 2000. *Current Population Reports* (March). Racial Statistics Branch and Ethnic and Hispanic Statistics Branch, Population Division. Washington, DC: U.S. Government Printing Office, Tables 9.0, 9.1, 9.2, 10, 10.5, 10.6, and 12.

ishing jobs for unskilled, poorly educated workers. The new economy will be increasingly made up of people of color. If they continue to be denied equal access to higher paying jobs, the entire society will be at risk for poverty and other problems associated with economic inequality.

Health

The health of the U.S. population is distributed unevenly across race. Hispanics are the most likely to be without health coverage. 33 percent of Hispanics, 21 percent of African Americans, 21 percent of Asian Americans, and 11 percent of Whites were not covered by private or government medical insurance in 1999 (U.S. Bureau of the Census, 2001a:58). Hispanics born outside the United States were almost twice as likely to lack health insurance as their U.S.-born counterparts. Many are unfamiliar with the U.S. health care system, and a few are illegal immigrants who are afraid to seek medical assistance (del Pinal and Singer, 1997:37: Folbre and the Center for Popular Economics, 2000).

Racial discrimination affects health in other ways as well. **Environmental racism** is the disproportionate exposure of some racial groups to environmental toxic substances. Race is the strongest predictor of hazardous waste facilities in the country, even after adjustment for social class. On virtually every measure of health, African Americans and Latinos are disadvantaged, as revealed in the following selected facts:

- Compared to the general population, Blacks and Hispanics are less likely to have a consistent source of medical care and more likely to use emergency rooms as a primary source of care. Compared to Whites, Hispanics had a 700 percent higher rate of visits to community health centers, but a 35 percent lower rate of visits to physicians' offices. Compared to Whites, Blacks had a 550 percent higher rate of visits to community health center, but a 48 percent lower rate of visits to physicians' offices (Forest and Whelan, 2000).

- Death rates for African Americans from all causes are 1.6 times higher than for White Americans (Goode, 1999).
- White men live approximately 7 years longer than Black men, and White women live about 5 years longer than Black women (Kockaneck et al., 2001).
- Due to lower socioeconomic status and more limited access to health care, less than 72 percent of African Americans, 68 percent of American Indians, and 74 percent of Hispanic women reported receiving prenatal care during their first trimester of pregnancy in 1997 (Pollard and O'Hare, 1999:18).
- Black babies are nearly twice as likely as White babies to die within their first year (Pollard and O'Hare, 1999:18). They are much more likely to be born prematurely and to have low birth weight. Low birth weight is associated a lower chance of surviving the first year of life and with many long-term health and developmental problems (Pollard and O'Hare, 1999:18).

CONTEMPORARY TRENDS AND ISSUES IN U.S. RACIAL AND ETHNIC RELATIONS

Racial diversity presents a host of new social problems that reflect differences in group power and access to social resources. Three major trends reveal new forms of racial inequality: growing racial strife, the economic polarization of minorities, and a national shift in U.S. racial policies. These trends are occurring in a global context, closely associated with macro social forces at work around the world.

Growing Racial Strife

Together with racial impoverishment, the growing immigrant and minority presence is adding tensions in society. Social scientists use the term **nativism** to denote hostility toward immigrants. Here, and in other countries, racial diversity is marked by growing conflicts. Some cities are like racially divided societies where minorities seldom meet Whites as neighbors or classmates in public schools (Harris and Bennett, 1995:158). Racial tensions often erupt in violence between Whites and minorities and among minorities themselves as individuals compete for a shrinking number of jobs and other opportunities. In 1992, racial rivalries between neighborhoods in Los Angeles erupted in violence.

Racial violence is often associated with uncertain economic conditions. Lack of jobs, housing, and other resources can add to fear and minority scapegoating on the part of Whites. In Florida and many parts of the West and Southwest, perceptions that Cubans, Mexicans, and other Hispanics are taking jobs from Anglos have touched off racial tensions.

Hate crimes against Hispanics increased during the 1990s. The number of anti-Hispanic incidents increased steadily during the decade. The perception that Latinos are "foreign" or "unAmerican" often translates into hate-related activity. One effect of the increasing anti-immigrant sentiment in the nation is the surge in incidents of vigilantism—unauthorized attempts to enforce immigration laws by ordinary citizens. Some private citizens are increasingly taking the law into their own hands to stem the perceived "flood" of illegal immigrants into the country (National Council of La Raza, 1999). Certain forms of racial strife are on the rise.

- **More Racially Based Groups and Activities.** The Southern Poverty Law Center documented 602 hate groups in 48 states and the District of Columbia in 2000, up from 457 the year before (*SPLC Report,* 2001:3). Hate groups include White supremacist groups with such diverse elements as the Ku Klux Klan, neo-Confederate groups (those describing southern culture as fundamentally White), Nazi-identified parties, and skinheads. Many groups use the Internet to spread their literature to young people. As a result, more than half of all hate crimes are now committed by young people, ages 15 to 24. In addition to racist websites, cyber extremism flourishes on e-mail, and in discussion groups and chat rooms (*Intelligence Report,* 2001:47). Violence is the driving force of racist music, which is rapidly spreading around the world.

- **Native Americans Hit Hard by Violent Crime.** Native Americans are far more likely to be victims of violent crimes than members of other racial groups according to the first comprehensive study of crimes involving Indians, released in 1999 by the U.S. Department of Justice (*SPLC Report,* 1999:1).

- **Profiling and Maltreatment.** Numerous reports testify to the widespread police practice of systematically stopping (and sometimes savagely beating) Black and Latino drivers (Herman, 1996:38). Some state troopers illegally target minority drivers (Wilgoren, 1999:1,5). In other cases, Arab Americans, Muslims, and other Middle-Easterners are targets of threats, gunshots, firebombs, and other forms of vigilante violence. Fear of terrorism has provoked a rash of hate crimes and a national debate about the official use of *profiling*—that is, the use of race and ethnicity as clues to criminality and potential terrorism.

- **Campus Racial Tensions.** Recent headlines about racism on college campuses have surprised many people because educational institutions are formally integrated. Yet we are witnessing a growing "balkanization" among students of different racial and ethnic backgrounds and a parallel increase in racial conflict and tension (Winant, 1994:58). Campus racism is widespread. From MIT to the University of California—Berkeley, and on campuses across the nation, racial attacks on Blacks, Hispanics, and Asians are revealing an extensive problem of intolerance. These problems are not isolated or unusual events. Instead, they reflect what is occurring in the wider society (Feagin, 2000; Sidel, 1994).

Economic Polarization in U.S. Inner Cities

The notion of a troubled "underclass," locked in U.S. inner cities by a deficient culture, is commonly used to explain racial poverty. According to this reasoning, broken families and bad life-styles prevent minorities from taking advantage of the opportunities created by antidiscrimination laws. However, like the older cultural deficiency models we discussed earlier, this explanation is wrong on many counts. It relies too heavily on behavioral traits to explain poverty. It falls back on blaming the victim to explain patterns that are actually rooted in social structure. Economic and technological changes in society have removed jobs and other opportunities from inner-city residents. This is a better explanation of poverty among African Americans.

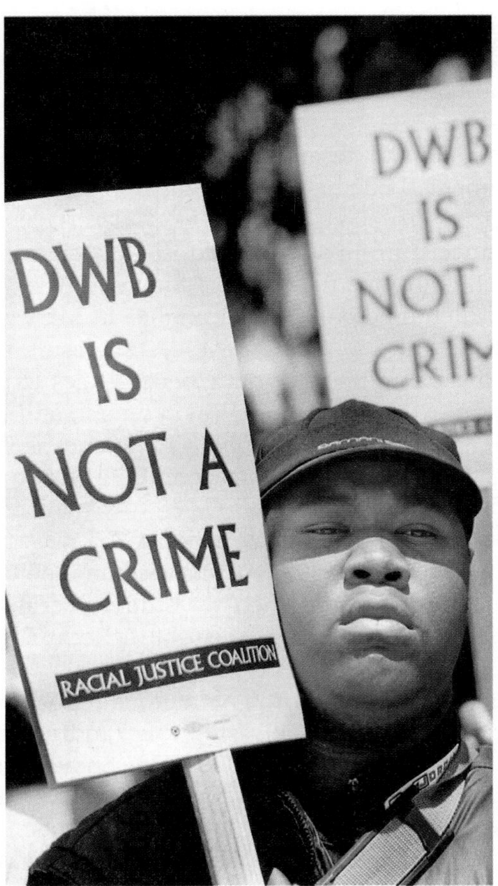

The use of race and ethnicity profiling as clues to criminality and political terrorism has provoked a national debate.

This explanation is detailed in two works by sociologist William J. Wilson. In his compelling book *The Truly Disadvantaged* (1987), he argues that the social problems of the inner city are due to transformations of the larger economy and to the class structure of ghetto neighborhoods. The movement of middle-class Black professionals from the inner city has left behind a concentration of the most disadvantaged segments of the Black urban population. In his more recent book *When Work Disappears* (1996), he shows how crime, family dissolution, and welfare are connected to the structural removal of work from the inner city.

Wilson (1987) examines the relationship between work and marriage, finding that men with higher incomes are more likely to be married than are men with lower incomes. He proposes that inner-city male joblessness encourages nonmarital childbearing and undermines the foundation of Black families. Structural conditions require that many Black women leave their marriages or forgo marriage altogether. Adaptations to structural conditions leave Black women disproportionately divorced and solely responsible for their children. The Black inner city is not destroying itself by its own culture; rather, it is being destroyed by economic forces.

Rising poverty rates among Latinos have led many policymakers and media analysts to conclude that Latinos have joined inner-city African Americans to form a hopeless "underclass." This is not an accurate view of minority impoverishment. Although changes in the U.S. economy have hit Latinos hard because of their low educational attainment and their labor market position, structural unemployment has different effects on the many diverse Latino barrios across the nation (Moore and Pinderhughes, 1994). The loss of jobs in Rust Belt cities has left many Puerto Ricans living in a bleak ghetto economy. Mexicans living in the Southwest, where low-paying jobs remain, have not suffered the same degree of economic dislocation. Despite high levels of poverty, Latino communities do not fit the conventional portrait of the underclass.

A structural analysis of concentrated poverty does not deny that inner cities are beset with a disproportionate share of social problems. As poverty is more concentrated in inner cities, crime and violence proliferate. The poor may adopt violence as a survival strategy. This escalates violence even further (Massey, 1996a). A structural analysis, however, focuses on social conditions, not immoral people. This helps us understand that social conditions and social policies create racial impoverishment in U.S. inner cities.

Racial Policies at the Millennium

The 1960s civil rights movement legalized remedies to end racial bias. Government policies based on race overturned segregation laws, opened voting booths, created new job opportunities, and brought hopes of racial justice for people of color. As long as it appeared that conditions were improving, government policies to end racial injustice remained in place.

But by the 1980s, the United States had become a very different society from the one in which civil rights legislation was enacted. Economic restructuring brought new dislocations to both Whites and minorities. As racial minorities became an ever larger share of the U.S. population, racial matters have grown more politicized. Many Whites began to feel uncomfortable with race-conscious policies in schools and the workplace. The social climate fostered an imaginary White disadvantage, said to be caused by affirmative action and other racial reforms (Winant, 1997). There is no empirical evidence for White disadvantage. Nevertheless, some politicians have resorted to race-baiting strategies in their political campaigns. This has exacerbated racial tensions. Heated debates about the fairness of racial policies are now in the political arena.

Ironically, just as the United States is becoming a multiracial society, we are witnessing a backlash against civil rights reforms. Despite continued racial discrimination in all arenas of public life, racial equality is being downsized through policies related to affirmative action, school desegregation, and voting rights. Growing racial populations are controlled through many different forms of discrimination including employment practices, neighborhood and school segregation, and other inequalities discussed in this chapter. In addition, international systems of dominance (global capitalism and geopolitical relations) together with new forms of racism now shape public perceptions and behavior. For example, "model minority" and "illegal aliens" along with new racialized standards in education and the workplace (e.g., Asian quotas) pit Asians and Latinos against Blacks (Allen and Chung, 2000:802).

Despite the new racial climate, the struggle against racism continues. Rich historical traditions of resistance and creative adaptations that exist today demonstrate the tremendous ingenuity and resourcefulness of people of color. Since the country was founded, antiracist activities have sought to end discrimination. Multiracial organizations composed of racial ethnic *and* White antiracist activists continue to work at national and local levels to fight and eradicate racist prejudices and institutional racism.

CHAPTER REVIEW

1. Racial and ethnic stratification are basic features of U.S. society. These forms of inequality are built into normal practices. They exclude people from full and equal participation in society's institutions. Racial and ethnic stratification exist because they benefit certain segments of society.
2. The concept of race is socially rather than biologically significant. Racial groups are set apart and singled out for unequal treatment.
3. An ethnic group is culturally distinct in race, religion, or national origin. The group has a distinctive culture. Some ethnic groups such as Jews, Poles, and Italians have distinguishing cultural characteristics that stem from religion and national origin. Because racial groups also have distinctive cultural characteristics, they are referred to as *racial-ethnics*.
4. Minority racial and ethnic groups are systematically disadvantaged by society's institutions. Both race and ethnicity are traditional bases for social inequality, although there are historical and contemporary differences in the societal placement of racial-ethnics and White ethnics in this society.
5. Racial-ethnic groups are socially subordinated and remain culturally distinct within U.S. society. African Americans, Latinos, Asian Americans, and Native Americans are constructed as both racially and culturally distinct. Each group has a distinctive culture, shares a common history, and has developed a common identity within a larger society that subordinates them.
6. Deficiency theories view minority groups as unequal because they lack some important feature common among the majority. These deficiencies may be biological (such as low intelligence) or cultural (such as the culture of poverty).
7. Bias theories place the blame for inequality on the prejudiced attitudes of the members of the dominant group. These theories, however, do not explain the discriminatory acts of the unprejudiced, which are aimed at preserving privilege.
8. Structural theories view inequality as the result of external social conditions rather than group-specific cultural factors. There are four main features of institutional discrimination: (a) The forces of history shape present conditions; (b) discrimination can occur without conscious bigotry; (c) this type of discrimination is less visible than are individual acts of discrimination; and (d) discrimination is reinforced by the interrelationships among the institutions of society.
9. Civil rights legislation improved the status of some racial-ethnics, yet the overall position of Blacks and Latinos relative to Whites has not improved. Large gaps remain in work, earnings, and education. Economic transformations have contributed to the persistent poverty in U.S. urban centers.
10. The racial demography of the United States is changing dramatically. Immigration and high birthrates among minorities are making the United States a multiracial, multicultural society. These trends are also creating new forms of racial segregation and racial conflict.
11. Public policy has shifted from race-conscious remedies to a color-blind climate that is dismantling historic civil rights reforms.

KEY TERMS

Majority group. Dominant group in society.

Racial stratification. System of inequality in which race is the major criterion for rank and rewards.

Minority group. Subordinate group in society.

Racial formation. Sociohistorical process by which races are continually being shaped and transformed.

Ethnicity. Culturally distinctive characteristics based on race, religion, or national origin.

Racial-ethnic group. Group labeled as a "race" by the wider society and bound together by their common social and economic conditions, resulting in distinctive cultural and ethnic characteristics.

Deficiency theories. Explanations that view the secondary status of minorities as the result of their own behaviors and cultural traits.

Bias theories. Explanations that blame the prejudiced attitudes of majority members for the secondary status of minorities.

Structural discrimination theories. Explanations that focus on the institutionalized patterns of discrimination as the sources of the secondary status of minorities.

Institutional discrimination. Established and customary social arrangements that exclude on the basis of race.

Individual racism. Overt acts by individuals that harm members of another race.

Colonial theory. Argues that race was used by the dominant group in society to oppress a racial minority.

Environmental racism. The disproportionate exposure of some racial groups to toxic substances.

Nativism. Hostility toward immigrants, and efforts to restrict their rights.

WEBSITES FOR FURTHER REFERENCE

http://www.pbs.org/wgbh/aia

The Africans in America—PBS Online website is a companion to "Africans in America," a six-hour public television series. The website chronicles the history of racial slavery in the United States—from the start of the Atlantic slave trade in the sixteenth century to the end of the American Civil War in 1865—and "explores the central paradox that is at the heart of the American story: a democracy that declared all men equal but enslaved and oppressed one people to provide independence and prosperity to another." Africans in America examines the economic and intellectual foundations of slavery in America and the global economy that prospered from it. And it reveals how the presence of African people and their struggle for freedom transformed America.

http://www.naacp.org/links

NAACP List of Recommended Links: The NAACP (National Association for the Advancement of Colored People) is the oldest, largest, and strongest civil rights organization in the United States. The principal objective of the NAACP is to "ensure the political, educational, social, and economic equality of minority group citizens of the United States." This website provides a list of links to other Internet resources supported by NAACP. Most links concern specific racial or ethnic groups, women, and other groups that have historically been disadvantaged.

http://www.census.gov/pubinfo/www/hotlinks.html

U.S. Census Bureau—Minority Links provides some quick and easy links to the latest data on racial and ethnic populations in the United States.

http://www.latinoweb.com

Latino Web: a homepage for Latinos on the Internet.

http://www.hsph.harvard.edu/grhf/WoC/

Women of Color Web explores the intersection of gender and race. It provides material on Blacks as well as Chicanas. This website includes research, other Internet resources, and articles.

http://www.coombs.anu.edu.au/WWWVL-AsianStudies.html

Asian Studies WWW Virtual Library represents a conglomerate of research publications and archives on Asian peoples in every country/region in the world. This research tool is produced by the Internet Publications Bureau, Research School of Pacific and Asian Studies at The Australian National University (ANU), Canberra, and is updated regularly.

http://www.nativeweb.org/

The NativeWeb provides resources for indigent peoples and cultures around the world. NativeWeb is "an international, nonprofit, educational organization dedicated to using telecommunications including computer technology and the Internet to disseminate information from and about indigenous nations, peoples, and organizations around the world; to foster communication between native and non-native peoples; to conduct research involving indigenous peoples' usage of technology and the Internet; and to provide resources, mentoring, and services to facilitate indigenous peoples' use of this technology."

http://www.aaiusa.org/arabamericans/

The Arab American Institute was organized in 1985 to represent Arab American interests in government and politics. The institute serves as a clearinghouse for Arab American participation in national, state, and local politics and government; research on the Arab American constituency; and a forum for consensus positions on pressing domestic and foreign policy matters. In light of increased interest in the Arab American community following the September 11 attacks, AAI has also put together a packet of resources on Arab Americans, the Middle East, and Islam; these resources can be accessed from this website.

http://www.webcom.com/~intvoice

Interracial Voice (IV) is an independent, information-oriented, networking newsjournal, serving the mixed-race/interracial community in cyberspace. This electronic publication advocates "universal recognition of mixed-race individuals" as constituting a separate "racial" entity and wholeheartedly supported the initiative to establish a multiracial category on the 2000 census.

http://www.census.gov/apsd/www/wepeople.html

A link to a series of U.S. Census groups on various groups in the Unites States, this series is called "We the Americans" and profiles racial and ethnic groups, women, the elderly, and immigrants, to name a few.

9 Gender Inequality

ore than ever, it is time to take stock of current experiences with and perceptions of sexism. We are living at a particularly crucial historical moment for examining the problem of sexism.

—Carol Rambo Ronai, Barbara A. Zsembik, and Joe R. Feagin

Every society treats women and men differently. Today, there is no nation where women and men are equals. Worldwide, women perform an estimated 60 percent of the work, yet they earn only 10 percent of the income and own only 10 percent of the land. Two-thirds of the world's illiterate are women. Despite massive political changes and economic progress in countries throughout the world, women continue to be the victims of abuse and discrimination. Even where women have made important strides in politics and the professions, women's overall progress remains uneven.

The United States falls short of ensuring equality of women in employment, education, and health care. This chapter examines the structural arrangements and social interactions that make women and men unequal and create problems for society at large. The gender system organizes society in such a way that women and men are treated differently. From the macro level of the societal economy, through the institutions of society, to interpersonal relations, gender is the basis for assigning roles, dividing labor, and allocating social opportunities.

Gender is the patterning of difference and domination through distinctions between women and men (Acker, 1992). Almost everything social is gendered. **Gendered** refers to distinguishing and differentially evaluating males and females. Until recently, differences between women and men seemed natural. However, new research shows that gender is not natural at all, but is socially constructed. Gender differences are a means of organizing the social world.

Gender casts males and females as opposites and places them into two mutually exclusive categories. The distinction between women and men is a central organizing principle of social life. In fact, the point of gender differentiation is "to justify the exploitation of an identifiable group—women" (Lorber, 1994:5).

Gender is often invisible to men. Many think of themselves as "genderless," as if gender applied only to women. Yet, from birth through old age, men's worlds are deeply gendered (Kimmel and Messner, 1998). (See the "Voices" panel titled "Making Masculinity Visible," p. 244) In the big picture, gender divisions make women and men unequal. Still, we cannot understand the gender system, nor women's and men's experiences, by looking at gender alone. Gender intersects with other inequalities such as race, class, and sexual orientation. These complex, intersecting inequalities mean that different groups of men exhibit varying degrees of power, while different groups of women exhibit varying levels of inequality. Nevertheless, the gender system denies women and men the full range of human and social possibilities. Gender inequalities produce social problems. This chapter examines gender stratification in U.S. society at both structural and interpersonal levels of social organization. Taking a **feminist approach** (one in support of women's equality), the theme of this chapter is that social rather than individual conditions are responsible for women's inequality and its problems.

VOICES

MAKING MASCULINITY VISIBLE

American men have come to think of ourselves as genderless, in part because we can afford that luxury of ignoring the centrality of gender. So we treat our male military, political, scientific, or literary figures as if their gender, their masculinity, had nothing to do with their military exploits, policy decisions, scientific experiments, or writing styles and subjects. And those whom we disenfranchise and oppress are those whose manhood we come to believe is not equal to ours.

Even when we do acknowledge gender, we often endow manhood with a transcendental, almost mythic set of properties that still keep it invisible. We think of manhood as eternal, a timeless essence that resides deep in the heart of every man. We think of manhood as innate, residing in the particular anatomical organization of the human male.

I think we must start to think and teach about manhood in a different way—as neither static nor timeless, but historical. Not as some inner essence, but as a social construction, much like how feminist scholars have analyzed femininity for years. What we know from the social and behavioral sciences is that masculinity means different things to different people at different times. Some cultures encourage manly stoicism and constant demonstration of power, authority and strength; others prescribe a more relaxed definition based on civic participation, emotional responsiveness, and the collective provision for the community's needs. What it meant to be a man in 17th century France, or among Aboriginal peoples in the Australian outback today, are very different things.

And within our society there are also multiple meanings of manhood. Just because we bring gender to the center of our analysis ought not mean that we ignore those other categories of difference—race, class, age, ethnicity, sexuality, able-bodiedness, region of the country. Each of these modifies the others. What it means to be a 71-year-old black, gay man in Cleveland is probably radically different from what it means to a 19-year-old white, heterosexual farm boy in Iowa.

Thus we cannot speak of masculinity in the singular, but of masculinities, in recognition of the different definitions of manhood that we construct. By pluralizing the term, we acknowledge that masculinity means different things to different groups of men at different times. But, at the same time, we can't forget that all masculinities are not created equal. All American men must also contend with a singular vision of masculinity, a particular definition that is held up as the model against which we all measure ourselves. We thus come to know what it means to be a man in our culture by setting our definitions in opposition to a set of "others"—racial minorities, sexual minorities, and, above all, women. Our integration of men into the curriculum must acknowledge these masculinities, and, at the same time, take note of the way this one particular version of what masculinity means was installed as the normative one.

To fully integrate gender, it seems to me, we have to see both women and men as gendered, to take both masculinity and femininity seriously. I see many schools that take women seriously, but I see only a handful that take women seriously in the presence of men. And I see precious few, if any, that take men and masculinity seriously. As gender inequality is reduced, the real differences among people—based on race, class, ethnicity, age, sexuality, as well as gender—will emerge in a context in which each of us can be appreciated for our uniqueness as well as our commonality.

Source: Michael Kimmel. 1999. "Educating Men and Women Equally." *On Campus with Women* 28 (3) (Spring):3, 15.

WOMEN AND MEN ARE DIFFERENTIATED AND RANKED

Females and males are constructed dichotomously and they are ranked. **Gender stratification** refers to the ranking of the sexes in such a way that women are unequal in power, resources, and opportunities. Women's and men's roles are not the same throughout the world. Nevertheless, every society has certain ideas about what women and men should be like as well as ways of producing people who are much like these expectations. To emphasize the point that gender is socially constructed, sociologists distinguish between *sex* and *gender*. **Sex** refers to the biological distinctions between male and female. **Gender** refers to the social characteristics attributed to women and men. Like race, however, gender cannot be understood at the individual level alone (Andersen and Collins, 2001:84).

Scientists have competing explanations for gender differences. Biological models argue that innate biological differences between males and females program different social behaviors. Anthropological models look at masculinity and femininity cross culturally, stressing the variations in women's and men's roles. Sociologists have tended to argue that gender differences are explained by differential learning (Kimmel and Messner, 1998).

Is Gender Biological or Social?

We know that there are biological differences between the two sexes. The key question is whether these unlearned differences in the sexes contribute to the gender differences found in societies. To answer this question, let us first review the evidence for each position.

Biological Bases for Gender Roles. Males and females are different from the moment of conception. Chromosomal and hormonal differences make males and females physically different. Hormonal differences in the sexes are also significant. The male hormones (androgens) and female hormones (estrogens) direct the process of sex differentiation from about 6 weeks after conception throughout life. They make males taller, heavier, and more muscular. At puberty they trigger the production of secondary sexual characteristics. In males, these include body and facial hair, a deeper voice, broader shoulders, and a muscular body. In females, puberty brings pubic hair, menstruation, the ability to lactate, prominent breasts, and relatively broad hips. Actually, males and females have both sets of hormones. The relative proportion of androgens and estrogens gives a person masculine or feminine physical traits.

These hormonal differences may explain in part why males tend to be more active, aggressive, and dominant than females. However, there are only slight differences in the levels of hormones between girls and boys in childhood. Yet, researchers find differences in aggression between young girls and boys (Fausto-Sterling, 1992).

Biological differences that do exist between women and men are only averages. They are often influenced by other factors. For example, although men are on the average larger than women, body size is influenced by diet and physical activity, which in turn may be influenced by culture, class, and race. The all-or-none categorizing of gender traits is misleading because there is considerable overlap in the distribution of traits possessed by women and men. Although most men are stronger than most women, some men are weaker than some women, and vice versa. And although males are on the average more aggressive than females, greater difference may be found among males than among males and females (Basow, 1996:81). Furthermore, gender is constantly changing. Femininity and masculinity are not uniformly shaped from genetic makeup. Instead, they are molded differently (1) from one culture to another, (2) within any one culture over time, (3) over the course of all women's and men's lives, and (4) between and among different groups of women and men, depending upon class, race, ethnicity, and sexuality (Kimmel, 1992:166).

- **Social Bases for Gender Roles.** Every society transforms biological females and males into socially interacting women and men. Cross-cultural evidence shows a wide variation of behaviors for the sexes. Table 9.1 provides some interesting cross-cultural data from 224 societies on the division of labor by sex. This table shows that for the majority of activities, societies are not uniform in their gendered division of labor. Even activities requiring strength, presumably a male trait, are not strictly apportioned to males. In fact, activities such as burden-bearing and water-carrying are done by females more than by males. Even an activity such as house-building is not exclusively male. Although there is a wide variety in the social roles assigned to women and men, their roles seldom vary "randomly" (O'Kelly, 1980:41). In most societies, domestic and family settings are women's worlds, while public and political settings are men's worlds.

TABLE 9.1

Gender Allocation in Selected Technological Activities in 224 Societies

	Number of Societies in Which the Activity is Performed by:					
Activity	*Males Exclusively*	*Males Usually*	*Both Sexes Equally*	*Females Usually*	*Females Exclusively*	*Percent Male*
Smelting of ores	37	0	0	0	0	100.0
Hunting	139	5	0	0	0	99.3
Boat building	84	3	3	0	1	96.6
Mining and quarrying	31	1	2	0	1	93.7
Land clearing	95	34	6	3	1	90.5
Fishing	83	45	8	5	2	86.7
Herding	54	24	14	3	3	82.4
House building	105	30	14	9	20	77.4
Generation of fire	40	6	16	4	20	62.3
Preparation of skins	39	4	2	5	31	54.6
Crop planting	27	35	33	26	20	54.4
Manufacture of leather products	35	3	2	5	29	53.2
Crop tending	22	23	24	30	32	44.6
Milking	15	2	8	2	21	43.8
Carrying	18	12	46	34	36	39.3
Loom weaving	24	0	6	8	50	32.5
Fuel gathering	25	12	12	23	94	27.2
Manufacture of clothing	16	4	11	13	78	22.4
Pottery making	14	5	6	6	74	21.1
Dairy production	4	0	0	0	24	14.3
Cooking	0	2	2	63	117	8.3
Preparation of vegetables	3	1	4	21	145	5.7

Source: Adapted from George P. Murdock and Caterina Provost. 1973. "Factors in the Division of Labor by Sex. A Cross-Cultural Analysis." *Ethnology* 12 (April):207. Reprinted by permission of the publisher.

Gender and Power

Gender is about power. Social institutions and gender relations reveal men's power over women. Everywhere we look—politics, corporate life, family life—men are in power. But men are not uniformly dominant. Some men have great power over other men. In fact, most men do not *feel* powerful; most feel powerless, trapped in stifling old roles and unable to changes their lives in ways they want (Kimmel, 1992:171). Nevertheless, socially defined differences between women and men legitimate **male dominance,** which refers to the beliefs, meanings, and placement that value men over women and that institutionalize male control of socially valued resources. *Patriarchy* is the term used for forms of social organization in which men are dominant over women.

Structured gender inequality interacts with other inequalities such as race, class, and sexuality to sort women and men differently. These inequalities also work together to produce differences *among women* and differences *among men.* Some women derive benefits from their race and their class while they are simultaneously restricted by gender. Such women are subordinated by gender, yet race and class intersect to create for them privileged opportunities and ways of living (Baca Zinn, Hondagneu-Sotelo, and Messner, 2000). Men are encouraged to behave in "masculine" fashion to prove that they are not gay (Connell, 1992). In defining masculinity as the negation of homosexuality, **compulsory heterosexuality** is an important component of the gender system. Compulsory heterosexuality imposes negative sanctions on those who are homosexual or bisexual. This system of sexuality shapes the gender order by discouraging attachment with members of the same sex. This enforces the dichotomy of "opposite" sexes. *Sexuality* is also a form of inequality in its own right because it systematically grants privileges to those in heterosexual relationships. Like race, class, and gender, sexual identities are socially constructed categories. **Sexuality** is a way of organizing the social world based on sexual identity and is a key linking process in the matrix of domination structured along the lines of race, class, and gender (Messner, 1996:223).

Gender scholars have debated the question of universal male dominance, that is, whether it is found in all societies across time and space. Many scholars once adopted this position, claiming that all societies exhibit some forms of **patriarchy** in marriage and family forms, in division of labor, and in society at large (Ortner, 1974; Rosaldo, 1974). More recently, however, scholars have challenged the universality of patriarchy by producing cases that serve as counterexamples (Shapiro, 1981). Current thought tends to follow the latter course. Sexual differentiation, it seems, is found in all societies, but it does not always indicate low female status (Rogers, 1978). Male dominance and female subordination are not constants. Gender and power vary from society to society.

We should keep in mind that although gender stratification makes women subordinate to men, they are not simply the victims of patriarchy. Like other oppressed groups, women find ways to resist discrimination. Through personal and political struggles, they often change the structures that subordinate them.

What Causes Gender Inequality?

To explain gender and power, sociologists turn to the systems that shape our social worlds. Structural thinking treats gender inequality as the outcome of male control over socially valued resources and opportunities. There are several models of gender inequality. Most of them focus on the divisions of labor and power between women and men, and the different value placed on their work. This idea originated in the work of Friedrich Engels and Karl Marx. They wrote that industrialism and the shift to a capitalist economy widened the gap between the power and value of men and women. As production moved out of the home, the gendered division of labor left men with the greater share of economic and other forms of power (Chafetz, 1997; Sapiro, 1999:67).

Macro structural theories explain gender inequality as an outcome of how women and men are tied to the economic structure of society (Neilson, 1990:215). These theories say that women's economic role in society is a primary determinant of their overall status (Dunn, 1996). The division between domestic and public spheres of activity is constraining to women and advantageous to men. Women's reproductive roles and their responsibilities for domestic labor limit their association with the resources that are highly valued (Rosaldo, 1980). Men are freed from these responsibilities. Their economic obligations in the public sphere assure them control of highly valued resources and give rise to male privilege.

In capitalist societies the domestic–public split is even more significant because highly valued goods and services are exchanged in the public, not the domestic, sphere. Women's domestic labor, although important for survival, ranks low in prestige and power because it does not produce exchangeable commodities (Sacks, 1974). Because of the connections between the class relations of production (capitalism) and the hierarchical gender relations of its society (patriarchy) (Eisenstein, 1979a, b), the United States is a **capitalist patriarchy** where male supremacy keeps women in subordinate roles at work and in the home.

Socialization versus Structure: Two Approaches to Gender Inequality

To understand gender inequality, we must distinguish between (1) a gender roles approach and (2) a gender structure approach. The **gender roles approach** emphasizes characteristics that individuals acquire during the course of socialization, such as independent or dependent behaviors and ways of relating. The **gender structure approach** emphasizes factors that are external to individuals, such as the social structures and social interactions that reward women and men differently. These approaches differ in how they view the sexes, in how they explain the causes and effects of sexism, and in the solutions they suggest for ending inequality. Both the individual and the structural approaches are needed for a complete understanding of sexism. This chapter places primary emphasis on social structure as the cause of inequality. Sociologists have moved from studying gender at the individual level to the study of **gendered institutions.** As Joan Acker explains, "the term 'gendered institutions' means that gender is present in the processes, practices, images, and ideologies, and distributions of power in the various sectors of social life. Taken more or less as functioning wholes, the institutional structures of the United States and other societies are organized along lines of gender" (Acker, 1992:567). Although gender roles are learned by individuals, gender stratification is maintained by societal forces.

LEARNING GENDER

The most complex, demanding, and all-involving role that a member of society must learn to play is that of female or male. "Casting" for one's gender role:

> takes place immediately at birth, after a quick biological inspection; and the role of "female" or "male" is assigned. It is an assignment that will last one's entire lifetime and affect virtually everything one ever does. A large part of the next 20 years or so will be spent gradually learning and perfecting one's assigned sex role; slowly memorizing what a "young lady" should do and should not do, how a "little man" should react in each of a million frightening situations—practicing, practicing, playing house, playing cowboys, practicing—and often crying in confusion and frustration at the baffling and seemingly endless task. (David and Brannon, 1980:117)

From infancy through early childhood and beyond, children learn what is expected of boys and girls, and they learn to behave according to those expectations.

The traits associated with conventional gender roles are those valued by the dominant society. Keep in mind that gender is not the same in all classes and races. However, most research on gender socialization reflects primarily the experience of White middle-class people—those who are most often the research subjects of these studies. How gender is learned depends on a variety of social conditions affecting the socialization practices of girls and boys. Still, society molds boys and girls along different lines.

Children at Home

Girls and boys are perceived and treated differently from the moment of birth. Parents and "congratulations" greeting cards describe newborn daughters as "sweet," "soft," and decorative and girls are usually pictured as sleeping, whereas boys are immediately described as "bigger," "active," "angry," "more alert," "better coordinated," "strong," and "hardy." Cards sent to parents depict frills, ribbons, hearts, and flowers for girls, but mobiles, toys, rattles, sports equipment, and vehicles for boys. The most striking difference in cards, however, is that expressions of happiness or joy are more often found on cards for boys. People, in a sense, expect parents to be happier about the birth of a boy than about the birth of a girl. Newborn greeting cards thus project an early gender scheme that introduces two "classes" of babies: one decorative, the other physically active and bringing greater joy (Valian, 1998:19–20).

Children learn at a very early age what it means to be a boy or girl in our society. One of the strongest influences on gender role development in children occurs within the family setting, with parents passing on both overtly and covertly their own beliefs about gender (Witt, 1997:254). From the time their children are babies, parents treat sons and daughters differently, dressing infants in gender-specific colors, giving them gender-differentiated toys, and expecting different behaviors from boys and girls (Thorne, 1993; Witt, 1997). While both mothers and fathers contribute to the gender stereotyping of their children, fathers have been found to reinforce gender stereotyping more often than mothers (Valian, 1998; Campenni, 1999; Witt, 1997; Itle, Wood, and Desmarias, 1993).

In addition to the parents' active role in reinforcing society's gender demands, a subtler message is emitted from picture books for preschool children. A classic sociological study of eighteen award-winning children's books from 1967 to 1971 found the following characteristics (Weitzman et al., 1972):

- Females were virtually invisible. The ratio of male pictures to female pictures was 11:1. The ratio of male to female animals was 95:1.
- The activities of boys and girls varied greatly. Boys were active in outdoor activities, while girls were passive and most often found indoors. The activity of the girls typically was that of some service for boys.
- Adult men and women (role models) were very different. Men led, women followed. Females were passive and males active. Not one woman in these books had a job or profession; they were always mothers and wives.

We have seen improvements in how girls and women are portrayed. Females are no longer invisible, they are as likely as males to be included in the books, and they have roles beyond their family roles. In many respects, however, female storybook characters remain in conventional activities. An update of the classic Weitzman study found that no behavior was shared by a majority of the females, whereas all males were portrayed as independent and active. Girls expressed no career goals, and there were no adult female role models to provide ambition. The researchers found that only one woman in the entire 1980s collection of twenty-four books had an occupation outside of the home, and she worked "as a waitress at the Blue Tile Diner" (Williams et al., 1987:155). Crabb and Bielawski (1994) also found that Caldecott Award–winning children's books were still portraying females in traditional roles, with the large majority of female characters using household artifacts and most male characters using nondomestic production-oriented tools and objects. These researchers found little change over the past two decades. Other studies, however, have documented a trend toward more egalitarian depiction of both gender roles. A more recent replication of the Weitzman study (surveying approximately 800 children's books) showed that female characters are portrayed in more egalitarian ways than they were in the 1960s and 1970s (Clark, Lennon, and Morris, 1993). Such conflicting reports over how female characters are portrayed suggest that this topic must be studied further.

Gendered socialization is found even where gender roles are changing and socialization is becoming more flexible or androgynous. **Androgyny** refers to the combination of feminine and masculine characteristics in the same individual. Jeanne Brooks-Gunn at the Educational Testing Service in Princeton, New Jersey, conducted a study of masculine, feminine, and androgynous mothers. The androgynous mothers were both self-reliant and tender, affectionate and assertive. While they encouraged nurturing and independent behavior in their daughters, they did not promote nurturing in their sons. We can speculate that in the next generation, some women will be androgynous, but men will still be socialized in conventional ways (Shreve, 1984:43). Some research has found that while girls are more likely than boys to experience depression during adolescence, girls raised in more egalitarian households had significantly lower depression rates than those raised in more gender-traditional households (Obeidallah, McHale, and Silberisen, 1996). Witt (1997) found that parents who foster androgynous attitudes and behaviors in their children ultimately cause their girls and boys to have high self-esteem and self-worth.

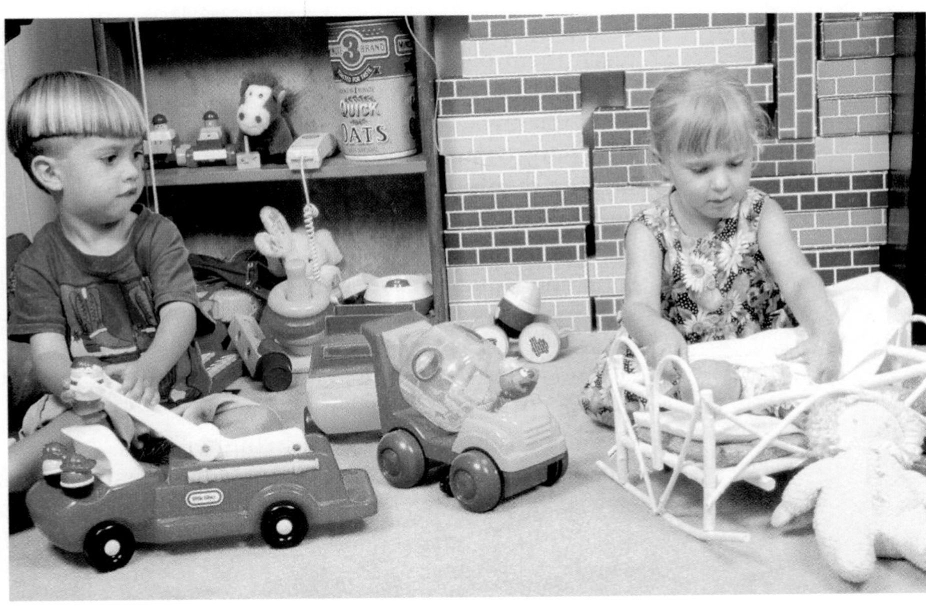

Toys model society's gender norms.

Children at Play

Children teach each other to behave according to cultural expectations. Same-sex peers exert a profound influence on how gender is learned. In a classic study of children's play groups, Janet Lever discovered how children stress particular social skills and capabilities for boys and others for girls. Her research among fifth graders (most of whom were White and middle class) found that boys, more than girls, (1) played outdoors, (2) played in larger groups, (3) played in age-heterogeneous groups, (4) were less likely to play in games dominated by the opposite sex, (5) played more competitive games, and (6) played in games that lasted longer (Lever, 1976).

Barrie Thorne's study of gender play in multiracial school settings (1993) found that boys control more space, more often violate girls' activities, and treat girls as contaminating. According to Thorne, these common ritualized interactions reflect larger structures of male dominance. In reality, the fun and games of everyday schoolchildren are *power play,* a complex social process involving both gender separation and togetherness. Children's power play changes with age, ethnicity, race, class, and social context. In her analysis of how children themselves construct gender in their daily play, Thorne shifts the focus from individuals to social relations:

> The social construction of gender is an active and ongoing process. . . . Gender categories, gender identities, gender divisions, gender-based groups, gender meanings—all are produced actively and collaboratively, in everyday life. When kids maneuver to form same-gender groups on the play ground or organize a kickball game as "boys-against-the girls," they produce a sense of gender as dichotomy and opposition. And when girls and boys work cooperatively on a classroom project, they actively undermine a sense of gender as opposition. This emphasis on action and activity, and on everyday social interactions that are sometimes contradictory, provides an antidote to the view of children as passively socialized. Gender is not something one passively "is" or "has." (Thorne, 1993:4–5)

Toys play a major part in gender socialization. Toys entertain children; they also teach them particular skills and encourage them to explore a variety of roles they may one day occupy as adults. Today, most toys for sale are gender linked. Toys for boys tend to encourage exploration, manipulation, invention, construction, competition, and aggression. In contrast, girls' toys typically rate high on manipulability, creativity, nurturance, and attractiveness. Playing with gendered toys may encourage different skills in girls and boys (Renzetti and Curran, 1999:74–75). As noted in previous sections, parents encourage their sons and daughters to play with gendered toys including dolls and housekeeping equipment for girls and trucks and sporting equipment for boys. This is reinforced by the resurgence of gender-specific toy marketing. Some Toys R Us outlets have recently inaugurated separate "Boys World" and "Girls World" sections (Bannon, 2000:7D).

In a study of parents and children in a day care setting, children eagerly accepted most of the toys presented to them by their parents and discarded other available toys in favor of their parents' choices (Idle, Wood, and Desmarias, 1993). When parents discouraged their sons from playing with cross-gender toys, their sons learned and adopted this behavior. Campenni (1999) found that adults were most likely to choose gender-specific toys for their children. Toys that adults deemed most appropriate for girls included items pertaining to domestic tasks (such as a vacuum cleaner or kitchen center), child rearing (dollhouse, cradle stroller), or beauty enhancement (makeup kits, jewelry items). Toys rated "appropriate" for boys included sports gear, male action figures, building items, plastic bugs, and attire for traditional male occupations. Like other researchers, the Campenni study found that girls are often involved in cross-gender or neutral toy behavior. While girls are encouraged by both parents to branch out and play with neutral toys some of the time, boys tend not to be given this same encouragement (Campenni, 1999). While we may be seeing some breakdown of traditional play patterns and socialization of girls, the same does not appear true for boys.

Although girls are now encouraged to engage in activities such as playing video games, traditional gender stereotypes still underlie this new pastime. A popular video game among girls today is the "Barbie Fashion Designer" game, which made its debut in 1996 (Hafner, 1998). Subsequently, Mattel has produced twenty-nine more "girl games," each holding Barbie's name. Other companies are following suit with make over and jewelry software. Feminine toys are certainly not out—in fact, these pink- and purple-gendered games are doing well with little girls all over the world.

Dichotomous gender experiences may be more characteristic of White middle-class children than of children of other races. An important study on Black adolescent girls by Joyce Ladner has shown that Black girls develop in a more independent fashion (Ladner, 1971). Other research has also found that among African Americans, both girls and boys are expected to be nurturant and expressive emotionally as well as independent, confident, and assertive (McAdoo, 1988; Stack, 1990).

Formal Education

In 1972 Congress outlawed gender discrimination in public schools through Title IX of the Educational Amendments Act. Three decades later, girls and boys in the United States are still not receiving the same education. A major report

Many forms of gender bias exist in education. For example, girls' "good" behavior results in less attention from the teacher.

by the American Association of University Women (AAUW, 1992) offers compelling evidence that discrimination remains pervasive. Schools shortchange girls in every significant dimension of education. Let us examine the following areas: course offerings, textbooks, teacher–student interactions, sports, female role models, and counseling.

Curriculum. Schools are charged with the responsibility of equipping students to study subjects (e.g., reading, writing, mathematics, and history) known collectively as the formal curriculum. But schools also teach students particular social, political, and economic values that constitute the so-called hidden curriculum operating alongside the more formal one. Both formal and informal curricula are powerful shapers of gender (Renzetti and Curran, 1999:82). The *AAUW Report* offers the following findings (AAUW, 1992):

- Differences between girls and boys in math achievement are small and declining. Yet in high school, girls are still less likely than boys to take the most advanced courses and to be in the top-scoring math groups.
- The gender gap in science is not decreasing and may, in fact, be increasing. One-fourth of boys take physics in high school, in contrast to 15 percent of girls.
- Schools ignore topics that matter in students' lives. The *evaded curriculum* is a term coined in the *AAUW Report* to refer to matters central to the lives of students that are touched on only briefly, if at all, in most schools. Students receive inadequate education on sexuality, teen pregnancy, the AIDS crisis, and the increase of sexually transmitted diseases among adolescents.

Although cultural conservatives have trivialized the *AAUW Report* (Barlow, 1999; Lewin, 1998), new research provides evidence that inequality still exists (the following is based on Sadker, 1999).

- The majority of females major in English, French, Spanish, music, drama, and dance, whereas males populate computer science, physics, and engineering programs.
- More boys drop out of school overall, but if girls drop out, they are less likely to return and complete school than boys.
- In early grades, equal numbers of girls and boys are selected for "gifted" programs. Yet, by tenth grade, girls begin to drop out of these programs at a much higher rate than do boys.
- Gender bias also affects males. Three out of four boys currently report that they were the targets of sexual harassment in schools—usually of taunts challenging their masculinity. In addition, while girls receive lower test grades, boys often receive lower overall course grades. Boys are less likely to have friends and more likely to endure alienation and loneliness throughout life. These negative effects on males all partially begin in educational institutions.

- **Textbooks.** The content of textbooks transmits messages to readers about society, about children, and about what adults are supposed to do. For this reason, individuals and groups concerned about gender bias in schools have looked carefully at how males and females are portrayed in textbooks assigned to students. Their findings provide a consistent message: Textbooks commonly used in U.S. schools are both overtly and covertly sexist. Sexism has become a recent concern of publishers, and a number have instituted guidelines for creating inclusive images in educational materials.

  Despite these efforts, the AAUW study (1992) reports that the contributions of minorities and women are still marginalized or ignored in many textbooks used in our nations's schools. Regardless of the subject—English, history, reading, science—minorities and women continue to be underrepresented. When women are mentioned, it is usually in terms of traditional feminine roles, such as women who were married to famous men (Renzetti and Curran, 1999:91).

- **Teacher–Student Interactions.** Even when girls and boys are in the same classrooms, boys are given preferential treatment. Girls receive less attention and different types of attention from classroom teachers.

  In one study conducted by Myra and David Sadker, boys in elementary and middle school called out answers eight times more often than girls. When boys called out, teachers listened. But when girls called out, they were told to "raise your hand if you want to speak" (AAUW, 1992). Even when boys do not volunteer, teachers are more likely to encourage them to give an answer or an opinion than they are to encourage girls (Sadker and Sadker, 1994).

  Teachers are now advised to encourage cooperative cross-sex learning, to monitor their own (teacher) behavior, to be sure that they reward male and female students equally, and to actively familiarize students with gender-atypical roles by assigning them specific duties as leaders, recording secretary, and so on (Lockheed, 1985; cited in Giele, 1988).

- **Sports.** Sports in U.S. high schools and colleges have historically been almost exclusively a male preserve (this section is dependent on Eitzen and Sage, 2003). The truth of this observation is clearly evident if one compares by sex the number of participants, facilities, support of school administrations, and financial support.

Such disparities have been based on the traditional assumptions that competitive sport is basically a masculine activity and that the proper roles of girls and women are as spectators and cheerleaders. What is the impact on a society that encourages its boys and young men to participate in sports while expecting its girls and young women to be spectators and cheerleaders? Sports reinforce societal expectations for males and females. Males are to be dominant and aggressive—the doers—while females are expected to be passive supporters of men, attaining status through the efforts of their menfolk.

An important consequence of this traditional view is that approximately half of the population has been denied access to all that sport has to offer (physical conditioning, enjoyment, teamwork, goal attainment, ego enhancement, social status, and competitiveness). School administrators, school boards, and citizens of local communities have long assumed that sports participation has general educational value. If so, then girls and women should also be allowed to receive the benefits.

In 1972 passage of Title IX of the Educational Amendments Act required that schools receiving federal funds must provide equal opportunities for males and females. Despite considerable opposition by school administrators, athletic directors, and school boards, major changes occurred over time because of this federal legislation. More monies were spent on women's sports; better facilities and equipment were provided; and women were gradually accepted as athletes. The most significant result was an increase in female participation. The number of high school girls participating in interscholastic sports increased from 300,000 in 1971 to 2.7 million in 2001. By 2002, 41 percent of all high school participants were female, and the number of sports available to them was more than twice the number available in 1970. Similar growth patterns occurred in colleges and universities.

On the positive side, budgets for women's sports improved dramatically, from less than 1 percent of the men's budgets in 1970 at the college level to approximately 33 percent of the men's budgets in 1999. On the negative side, budgets for women's sports will stay at about the same level because football is both expensive and exempt from the equation (*USA Today,* 2002). Thus, women's sports remain and will remain unequal to men's sports. This inequality is reinforced by unequal media attention, the scheduling of games (men's games are always the featured games), and the increasing lack of women in positions of power. One ironic consequence of Title IX has been that as opportunities for female athletes increased and programs expanded, many of the coaching and administration positions formerly held by women are being filled by men. In the early 1970s most coaches of women's intercollegiate teams were women. But by 2002 the percentage had decined to 45.6, the lowest level in the history of intercollegiate athletics. This trend is also true at the high school level. Also, whereas women's athletic associations at the high school and college levels were once controlled by women, they have now been subsumed under male-dominated organizations. Thus, females who aspire to coaching and athletic administration have fewer opportunities; girls and women see fewer women as role models in such positions; and patriarchy is reinforced as women are dominated by males in positions of power. Thus, even with federal legislation mandating gender equality, male dominance is maintained.

Despite many obstacles to gender equity in sports, there are many signs of progress. More television time and newspaper space are now devoted to women's sports. Professional female tennis players are at least as popular with crowds as men and they compete for significant payoffs. The Tennessee–Connecticut women's basketball game was attended by over 26,000 fans in 2002. U.S. female athletes have been incredibly successful in international competition. In the 2000 Olympics, U.S. women captured 40 medals, more than women from any other nation. U.S. women also took first place in the 1999 Soccer World Cup before more than 90,000 fans. This last event appears to indicate a sea change. In the words of former professional basketball player Mariah Burton Nelson:

> American sports fans' fascination with female athletes has shifted from skirted skaters . . . and tiny teenage tumblers . . . to rough muscular women in their 20s and 30s, who grunt, grimace and heave each other aside with their hips. (Nelson, 1999)

- **Female Role Models.** The work that women and men do in the schools supports gender inequality. The pattern is the familiar one found in hospitals, business offices, and throughout the work world: Women occupy the bottom rungs while men have the more powerful positions. Women make up a large percentage of the nation's classroom teachers but a much smaller percentage of school district superintendents. In 1999, women comprised 83 percent of all elementary school teachers, more than half of all secondary school teachers (54 percent), and 62 percent of all school administrators (U.S. Bureau of the Census, 2000d:415–418).

  As the level of education increases, the proportion of women teachers declines. In the 2000–2001 academic year (25 years after the Office of Civil Rights issued guidelines spelling out the obligations of colleges and universities in recruiting and hiring), women represented only 35 percent of full-time faculty. Furthermore, they remained overwhelmingly in the lower faculty ranks, where faculty are much less likely to hold tenure. In 2001, women comprised 21 percent of full professors, 36 percent of associate professors, 46 percent of assistant professors, and 55 percent of instructors/lecturers (*Academe*, 2001). At mid-decade, women made up only 16 percent of all college presidents, more than half of them at private institutions. Of the 453 female college presidents in 1995, 15 percent were women of color. Thirty-nine female college presidents were African American women. Other minority female college presidents included fourteen Latinas, seven American Indians, and two Asians (Monthly Forum for Women in Higher Education, 1995:9).

- **Counseling.** A fundamental task of school guidance personnel is to aid students in their choice of a career. The guidance that students receive on career choice tends to be biased. High school guidance counselors may channel male and female students into different (i.e., gender-stereotyped) fields and activities. There is evidence that gender stereotyping is common among counselors and that they often steer females away from certain college preparatory courses, especially in mathematics and the sciences (Renzetti and Curran, 1999:98).

  In the past, aptitude tests have themselves been sex-biased, listing occupations as either female or male. Despite changes in testing, counselors may inadvertently channel students into traditional gendered choices.

Socialization as Blaming the Victim

The discussion so far demonstrates that gender differences are learned. This does not mean that socialization alone explains women's place in society. In fact, a socialization approach can be misused in such a way that it blames women themselves for sex inequality. This is the critique offered by Linda Peterson and Elaine Enarson. They argue that socialization diverts attention from *structured inequality:*

> Misuse of the concept of socialization plays directly into the Blaming the Victim ideology; by focusing on the victim, responsibility for "the woman problem" rests not in the social system with its sex-structured distribution of inequality, but in socialized sex differences and sex roles. (Peterson and Enarson, 1974:8)

Not only is the cause of the problem displaced, but so are the solutions.

> Rather than directing efforts toward radical social change, the solution seems to be to change women themselves, perhaps through exhortation ("If we want to be liberated, we'll have to act more aggressive . . .") or, for example, changing children's literature and mothers' child rearing practice. (Peterson and Enarson, 1974:8)

This issue raises a critical question: If the socialization perspective is limited and perhaps biased, what is a better way of analyzing gender inequality? To answer this question, let us look at how male dominance affects our society.

REINFORCING MALE DOMINANCE

Male dominance is both a socializing and a structural force. It exists at all levels of society, from interpersonal relations to institutional structures. This section describes the interpersonal and institutional reinforcement of gender inequality.

Language

Language perpetuates male dominance by ignoring, trivializing, and sexualizing women. Use of the pronoun *he* when the sex of the person is unspecified and of the generic term *mankind* to refer to humanity in general are obvious examples of how the English language ignores women. Common sayings such as "that's women's work" (as opposed to "that's men's work!"), jokes about women drivers, and phrases such as "women and children first" or "wine, women, and song" are trivializing. Women, more than men, are commonly referred to in terms that have sexual connotations. Terms referring to men (*studs, jocks*) that do have sexual meanings imply power and success, whereas terms applied to women (*broads, bimbos, chicks*) imply promiscuity or being dominated. In fact, the term *promiscuous* is usually applied only to women, although its literal meaning applies to either sex (Richmond-Abbott, 1992:93). Research shows that there are many derogatory or at least disrespectful generic terms for women, but there are few for men generically (Sapiro, 1999:329). Terms such as *broads, bimbos,* and *chicks* tell us a great deal about how women are regarded by society.

Interpersonal Behavior

Gender is reproduced in the day-to-day interaction that occurs between women and men. For example, the way women and men speak and interact reveals power differences. According to sociolinguist Deborah Tannen (1990), women and men have different styles of communication and different communication goals. Women and men speak different "genderlects." Like cultural dialects, these differences sometimes lead to miscommunication and misunderstanding based on how girls and boys learn to use language differently in their separate-sex peer groups:

> Typically, a girl has a best friend with whom she sits and talks, frequently telling secrets. It's the telling of secrets, the fact and the way that they talk to each other, that makes them best friends. For boys, activities are central: Their best friends are the ones they do things with. Boys also tend to play in larger groups that are hierarchical. High-status boys give orders and push low-status boys around. So boys are expected to use language to seize center stage: by exhibiting their skill, displaying their knowledge, and challenging and resisting challenges. (Tannen, 1991:B3)

Despite the stereotype that women are more talkative, research shows that in conversations, men are more direct, interrupt more, and talk more. Men also have greater control over what is discussed (Parlee, 1979). Another marker of women's lower status lies in the work they do to keep conversations going. Pamela Fishman (1978) studied male–female conversations and found that women work harder in conversations, even though they have less control over the subject matter.

Power is also sustained by various forms of nonverbal communication. Men take up more space than do women and also touch women without permission more than women touch men. Women, on the other hand, engage in more eye contact, smile more, and generally exhibit behavior associated with low status. These behaviors show how gender is continually being created in various kinds of social interaction. Candace West and Don Zimmerman (1987) call this *doing gender*. It involves following the rules and behaviors expected of us as males or females. We "do gender," because if we do not, we are judged incompetent as men and women. Gender is something we create in interaction, not something we are (Risman, 1998:6).

Mass Communications Media

Much of the information we receive about the world around us comes not from direct experience but from the mass media of communication (radio, television, newspapers, and magazines). Although the media are often blamed for the problems of modern society, they are not monolithic and do not present us with a simple message. The media have tremendous power. They can distort women's images and they can bring about change as well (Sapiro, 1999:224). In the print media, women's influence has not matched their larger presence in the field. At U.S. newspapers, one-third of the workforce is female, but women hold only 15 percent of the executive positions. In magazines, women's portrayal has become less monolithic since the 1980s. With the rise of feminism, many magazines devoted attention to women's achievements. Alongside these magazines for the new woman, many "ladies'" magazines continue to define the lives of women in terms of men—husbands or lovers.

Women are 52 percent of the population, but you would not know it by watching network news. Although they fare better on local newscasts than national ones, they are still under represented in television newsrooms. In 1998, women reported only 19 percent of all stories on network evening news programs (Albinak, 1998; Messina-Boyer, 1999).

Studies have continually demonstrated that highly stereotyped behavior characterizes both children's and adult programming as well as commercials. Male role models are provided in greater numbers than are female, with the exception of daytime soap operas, in which men and women are equally represented. Prime-time television is distorted. Although men represent 49 percent of the U.S. population, they represented 62 percent of prime-time television characters in 2000. And while women represent 52 percent of the population, they represented only 38 percent of prime-time television characters. Racial-ethnic women are even more under represented. Of the female prime-time characters, 81 percent were White, 13 percent were African American, 3 percent were Asian American, and 2 percent were Latina (*Fall Colors,* 2000:13). Such imbalance has also been found with respect to occupations of men and women. Males are represented as occupying a disproportionately high percentage of the workforce, a greater diversity of occupations, and higher-status jobs (*USA Today,* 1997a:3A).

Images of women on entertainment television have changed greatly in recent decades. A report by The National Commission on Working Women has found increasing diversity of characters portraying working women as television's most significant improvement. In many serials, women do play strong and intelligent roles, but in just as many shows, men are still the major characters and women are cast as glamorous objects, scheming villains, or servants. And for every contemporary show that includes positive images of women, there are numerous other shows in which women are sidekicks to men, sexual objects, or helpless imbeciles (Andersen, 2000:56).

Television commercials have long presented the sexes in stereotyped ways. Women appear less frequently in ads than men, are much more likely to be seen in the home rather than in work settings, and are much more likely to appear in ads for food, home, and beauty/clothing products (Andersen, 2000:56). In the past decade, however, the potential buying power of working women has caused the advertising industry to modify women's image. Working women have become targets of advertising campaigns. But most advertising aimed at career women sends the message that they should be superwomen—managing multiple roles of wife, mother, and career woman, and being glamorous as well. Such multifarious expectations are not imposed on men. The advertising aimed at "the new woman" places additional stresses on women and at the same time upholds male privilege. Television commercials that show women breezing in from their jobs to sort the laundry or pop dinner in the oven reinforce the notion that it is all right for a woman to pursue a career as long as she can still handle the housework.

Religion

Most U.S. religions follow a typical pattern. The clergy is male, while the vast majority of worshipers are women (Paulson, 2000). Despite important differences in religious doctrines, there are common views about gender. Among these are the beliefs that (1) women and men have different missions and different standards of behavior, and (2) although women and men are equal in the eyes of the deity, women are to some degree subordinated to men (Sapiro, 1999:219). Limiting discussion to the Judeo-Christian heritage, let us examine some teachings from the Old and New Testaments regarding the place of women. The Old Testament established male supremacy in many ways. Images of God are male. Females were second to males because Eve was created from

Adam's rib. According to the Scriptures, only a male could divorce a spouse. A woman who was not a virgin at marriage could be stoned to death. Girls could be purchased for marriage. Employers were enjoined to pay women only three-fifths the wages of men: "If a male from 20 to 60 years of age, the equivalent is 50 shekels of silver by the sanctuary weight; if it is a female, the equivalent is 30 shekels" (Leviticus 27:3–4). As Gilman notes:

> The Old Testament devotes inordinate space to the listing of long lines of male descent to the point where it would seem that for centuries women "begat" nothing but male offspring. Although there are heroines in the Old Testament—Judith, Esther and the like—it's clear that they functioned like the heroines of Greek drama and later of French: as counterweights in the imaginations of certain sensitive men to the degraded position of women in actual life. The true spirit of the tradition was unabashedly revealed in the prayer men recited every day in the synagogue: "Blessed art Thou, O Lord . . . for not making me a woman." (Gilman, 1971:51)

The New Testament retained the tradition of male dominance. Jesus was the son of a male God, not of Mary, who remained a virgin. All the disciples were male. The great leader of the early church, the Apostle Paul, was especially adamant in arguing for the primacy of males over females. According to Paul, "the husband is supreme over his wife," "woman was created for man's sake," and "women should not teach nor usurp authority over the man, but to be silent."

Contemporary religious thought reflects this heritage. In 1998, the Southern Baptist Convention, the nation's biggest Protestant denomination, amended its statement of beliefs to include a declaration that "a woman shall submit herself graciously to her husband's leadership and a husband should provide for, protect and lead his family." Some denominations limit or even forbid women from decision making. Others allow women to vote but limit their participation in leadership roles.

There are, however, many indications of change (see Figure 9.1). Throughout the west, women are more involved in churches and religious life (Paulson, 2000). The National Council of Churches seeks to end sexist language and to

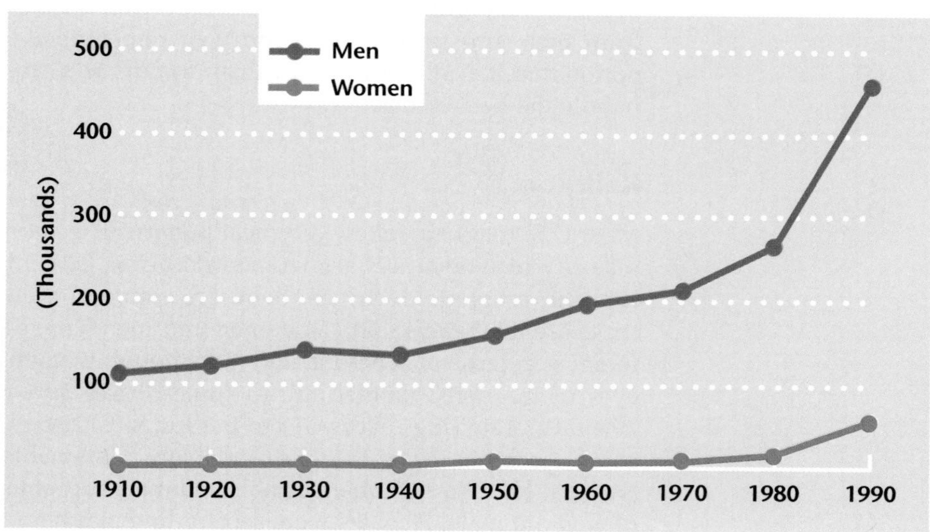

FIGURE 9.1

Male and Female Clergy, 1910–1990

Source: Barbara Brown Zikmund, A. T. Lummis, and P. M. Y. Chang. 1998. *Clergy Women: An Uphill Calling.* Louisville, KY: Westminster John Knox Press, p. 5.

use "inclusive language" in the Revised Standard Version of the Bible. Terms such as *man, mankind, brothers, sons, churchmen,* and *laymen* would be replaced by neutral terms that include reference to female gender. Across the United States, women clergy are struggling for equal rights, bumping up against what many call a "stained glass ceiling." Today, half of all religious denominations in the U.S. ordain women. At the same time, the formal rules and practices discriminate against women. In denominations that ordain women and those that do not, women often fill the same jobs: leading small churches, directing special church programs, preaching, and evangelizing (Sharn, 1997).

In 2000, only 13 percent of the clergy were women; 10 percent were Black and 5 percent were Hispanic (U.S. Department of Labor, Women's Bureau, 2001). In the 1990s, 10 to 20 percent of all Protestant clergy were female (Simon, Scanlan, and Madell, 1993:115). Within Judaism, the Reform and Conservative branches ordain female rabbis. The Orthodox branch does not. Since the first female rabbi was ordained in the United States in 1972, their numbers grew to approximately 4 percent of an estimated 3,500 rabbis in the 1990s. (Simon, Scanlan, and Madell, 1993). A new study of American Jews finds that women are more likely than men to be studying traditional Jewish texts (Paulson, 2000). Within the Black church, African American women have also made progress. Some notable firsts were the election in 1984 of Rev. Leontine T. C. Kelly as bishop by the United Methodist Church, and in 1989, the Most Rev. Barbara Harris was also made the first female bishop within the Episcopal church (*Ebony,* 1995:94). In 1995, the Roman Catholic Church through the Vatican declared the ban on ordaining women to be infallible. Nevertheless, Catholic women are involved in all administrative activities and most ministerial functions except exercising the sacramental power of celebrating mass and hearing confession (Henle, 1994). Thus, despite the continued opposition of organized religion, many women are making advances in status within established churches and leaving their mark on the ministerial profession.

The Law

That the law has been discriminatory against women is beyond dispute. We need only recall that women were denied the right to vote prior to the passage of the Nineteenth Amendment.

During the past four decades, legal reforms and public policy changes have attempted to place women and men on more equal footing. Some laws that focus on employment include the 1963 Equal Pay Act, Title VII of the 1964 Civil Rights Act, and the 1978 Pregnancy Discrimination Act. The 1974 Educational Amendments Act calls for gender equality in education. Other reforms have provided the framework for important institutional changes. For example, sexist discrimination in the granting of credit has been ruled illegal, and discrimination against pregnant women in the workforce is now prohibited by the law. Affirmative action (which is now under assault) remedied some kinds of gender discrimination in employment. Sexist discrimination in housing is prohibited, and the gendered requirements in the airline industry have been eliminated. The force of these new laws, however, depends on their enforcement as well as on the interpretation of the courts when they are disputed.

Legal discrimination remains in a number of areas. There are still hundreds of sections of the U.S. legal code and of state laws that are riddled with sex bias or sex-based terminology, in conflict with the ideal of equal rights for women

(Benokraitis and Feagin, 1995:24). State laws vary considerably concerning property ownership by spouses, welfare benefits, and the legal status of homemakers.

Today, many legal reforms are threatened by recent Supreme Court decisions in the areas of abortion and affirmative action. In 1989 and 1992, the Supreme Court narrowed its 1973 landmark *Roe v. Wade* decision, which established the right to abortion. *Roe v. Wade* was a major breakthrough for women, giving them the right to control their bodies. The 1989 and 1992 decisions made it easier for the states to restrict women's reproductive freedoms at any stage of pregnancy, including the first 3 months. These decisions have placed limits on abortion. By moving the battleground to state legislatures, the Supreme Court returned the nation to a pre-*Roe* patchwork of laws and conditions that make it more difficult for women to obtain abortions (Leonard, 1997).

Politics

Women's political participation has always been different from that of men. Women received the right to vote in 1920, when the Nineteenth Amendment was ratified. Although women make up a very small percentage of officeholders, 1992 was a turning point for women in politics. Controversies such as Anita Hill's harassment allegations, the abortion rights battle, and the lack of representation at all levels of politics propelled women into the political arena. In 1992 Congress experienced its biggest influx of women (and minorities) in history. Subsequent elections have increased the number of women in our national legislature. As of 2001, thirteen U.S. senators are women, and fifty-nine women are in the House of Representatives (see Table 9.2).

Despite this progress, the gender gap in our nation's capital is scandalous. In Washington D.C.'s less visible workforce of professional staff employees, women hold 60 percent of the jobs, but they are nowhere equal to men. Congress has two classes of personal staff employees: highly paid men who hold most of the power, and lower-paid women who are relegated to clerical and support staff. Many answer the phones and write letters to constituents, invisible labor that is crucial to their boss's reelection. A recent study of congressional staff workers conducted by Gannett News Service found the following:

- House members pay women about 22 percent less than men.
- Senate members pay women about 24 percent less than men.
- The pay gap exists for female workers no matter who they work for: male or female; Republican or Democrat; Black, White, or Hispanic; newcomer or veteran (Brogan, 1994).

This discrimination is legal because Congress exempts itself from federal sex discrimination laws that it passes for the rest of the nation!

Compared to other industrialized nations, the United States ranks low in terms of women's representation in national government (see Table 9.2). Across the world, many nations have higher percentages of female lawmakers in their top legislative bodies. The United States has just over 13 percent female lawmakers in Congress. Countries with higher percentages of women are Sweden (34 percent), Cuba (24 percent), Canada (20 percent), and China (21 percent). (Inter-Parliamentary Union, 2001). In the 200-year history of the United States, there has never been a female president or vice-president. Before 1993, there was only one female justice on the Supreme Court.

The gender gap refers to measurable differences in the way women and men vote and view political issues. Voting studies of national elections since 1980 demonstrate that women often vote differently from men, especially on issues of economics, social welfare, and war and peace (Renzetti and Curran, 1999:279).

STRUCTURED GENDER INEQUALITY

In this section of the chapter, we focus on the contemporary workplace because it is a key arena for making women unequal to men. The workplace produces gender stratification by placing women and men in different settings, assigning them different duties, and rewarding them unequally (Reskin and Padavic, 1994:31).

Occupational Distribution

The shifting economy discussed in Chapter 14 has changed both women's and men's employment rates. Increasingly, it is viewed as "normal" for adult women and men, regardless of parental status, to be employed (Bianchi, 1995:110). Yet men's labor force participation rates have decreased slightly while women's have increased dramatically. In 2000, 74 percent of all men were in the labor force, compared with 60 percent of all women. Today, women make up nearly half of the workforce. African American women have had a long history of high workforce participation rates. Today, they have edged ahead of other women participating in the labor force at a rate of 63 percent; 59 percent of White women were in the labor force in 2000, compared with 56 percent of Hispanic women (U.S. Department of Labor, 2001) (see Table 9.3, page 266).

Today's working woman may be any age. She may be any race. She may be a nurse or a secretary or a factory worker or a department store clerk or a public schoolteacher. Or she may be—though it is much less common—a physician or the president of a corporation or the head of a school system. Hers may be the familiar face seen daily behind the counter at the neighborhood coffee shop, or she may work virtually unseen, mopping floors at midnight in an empty office building. The typical female worker is a wage earner in clerical, service, manufacturing, or some technical jobs that pay poorly, give her little possibility for advancement, and often little control over her work. More women work as sales workers, secretaries, and cashiers than in any other line of work. The largest share of women (40 percent), however, work in technical sales and administrative support occupations (U.S. Department of Labor, Women's Bureau, 2000a).

Massive economic changes have shifted the gender distribution of many occupations. Since 1980, women have taken 80 percent of the new jobs created in the economy. But the overall degree of gender stratification has not changed much since 1900. Women and men are still concentrated in different occupations (Herz and Wootton, 1996:56). **Gender segregation** refers to the pattern whereby women and men are situated in different jobs throughout the labor force (Andersen, 2000:119).

In 2000, the six most prevalent occupations for women were, in order of magnitude, sales workers, secretaries, managers and administrators, cashiers, sales supervisors, and registered nurses (U.S. Department of Labor, Women's

TABLE 9.2

World Classification: Women in National Parliaments 2001

The data in the table below has been compiled by the Inter-Parliamentary Union *on the basis of information provided by National Parliaments. 178 countries are classified by descending order of the percentage of women in the lower or single House. You can use the PARLINE database to view detailed results of parliamentary elections by country.*

		Lower or Single House				*Upper House or Senate*			
Rank	*Country*	*Elections*	*Seats*	*Women*	*Percent Women*	*Elections*	*Seats*	*Women*	*Percent Women*
1	Sweden	09 1998	349	149	42.7	—	—	—	—
2	Denmark	03 1998	179	67	37.4	—	—	—	—
3	Finland	03 1999	200	73	36.5	—	—	—	—
4	Norway	09 1997	165	60	36.4	—	—	—	—
5	Netherlands	05 1998	150	54	36.0	05 1999	75	20	26.7
6	Iceland	05 1999	63	22	34.9	—	—	—	—
7	Germany	09 1998	669	207	30.9	N.A.	69	17	24.6
8	New Zealand	11 1999	120	37	30.8	—	—	—	—
9	Mozambique	12 1999	250	75	30.0	—	—	—	—
10	South Africa	16 1999	399	119	29.8	06 1999	89	17	31.5*
11	Spain	03 2000	350	99	28.3	03 2000	259	63	24.3
12	Cuba	01 1998	601	166	27.6	—	—	—	—
13	Austria	10 1999	183	49	26.8	N.A.	64	13	20.3
14	Grenada	01 1999	15	4	26.7	01 1999	13	1	7.7
15	Argentina	10 1999	257	68	26.5	12 1998	72	2	2.8
16	Turkmenistan	12 1999	50	13	26.0	—	—	—	—
"	Vietnam	07 1997	450	117	26.0	—	—	—	—
17	Rwanda	11 1994	74	19	25.7	—	—	—	—
18	Namibia	11 1999	74	19	25.0	11 1998	26	2	7.7
19	Seychelles	03 1998	34	8	23.5	—	—	—	—
20	Belgium	06 1999	150	35	23.3	06 1999	71	20	28.2
21	Australia	10 1998	148	34	23.0	10 1998	76	23	30.3
"	Switzerland	10 1999	200	46	23.0	10 1999	46	9	19.6
22	Tanzania	10 2000	274	61	22.3	—	—	—	—
23	Monaco	02 1998	18	4	22.2	—	—	—	—
24	China	1997–98	2984	650	21.8	—	—	—	—
25	Lao People's Democratic Rep.	12 1997	99	21	21.2	—	—	—	—
26	Canada	11 2000	301	62	20.6	N.A.	105	34	32.4
27	Croatia	01 2000	151	31	20.5	04 1997	65	4	6.2

Bureau, 2000a) (see Table 9.4, page 267). The phenomenal growth of service work in the new economy would appear to benefit women. But most of the newly created jobs are in the low-wage sectors of the workforce with limited opportunities for advancement.

Media reports of women's gains in new kinds of jobs are often misleading. In blue-collar work, for example, gains look dramatic at first glance, with the number of women in blue-collar jobs rising by 80 percent in the 1970s. But the increase was so high because women had been virtually excluded from these

TABLE 9.2, continued

		Lower or Single House				Upper House or Senate			
Rank	Country	Elections	Seats	Women	Percent Women	Elections	Seats	Women	Percent Women
28	Dem. People's Rep. of Korea	07 1998	687	138	20.1	—	—	—	—
29	Costa Rica	02 1998	57	11	19.3	—	—	—	—
30	Dominica	01 2000	32	6	18.8	—	—	—	—
31	Portugal	10 1999	230	43	18.7	—	—	—	—
32	Guyana	12 1997	65	12	18.5	—	—	—	—
33	United Kingdom	06 2001	659	118	17.9	N.A.	666	104	15.6
34	Estonia	03 1999	101	18	17.8	—	—	—	—
35	Suriname	05 2000	51	9	17.6	—	—	—	—
36	Peru	04 2001	120	21	17.5	—	—	—	—
37	Botswana	10 1999	47	8	17.0				
"	Latvia	10 1998	100	17	17.0	—	—	—	—
38	Luxembourg	06 1999	60	10	16.7	—	—	—	—
"	San Marino	05 1998	60	10	16.7	—	—	—	—
"	Senegal	04 2001	120	20	16.7	—	—	—	—
39	Dominican Rep.	05 1998	149	24	16.1	05 1998	30	2	6.7
40	Mexico	07 2000	500	80	16.0	07 2000	128	20	15.6
41	Angola	09 1992	220	34	15.5	—	—	—	—
42	Bahamas	03 1997	40	6	15.0	03 1997	16	5	31.3
"	Czech Republic	06 1998	200	30	15.0	11 2000	81	10	12.3
43	Eritrea	02 1994	150	22	14.7	—	—	—	—
44	Ecuador	05 1998	123	18	14.6	—	—	—	—
45	Burundi	06 1993	118	17	14.4	—	—	—	—
46	Andorra	03 2001	28	4	14.3	—	—	—	—
47	Slovakia	09 1998	150	21	14.0	—	—	—	—
"	United States	11 2000	435	61	14.0	11 2000	100	13	13.0
48	Israel	05 1999	120	16	13.3	—	—	—	—
"	Jamaica	12 1997	60	8	13.3	12 1997	21	5	23.8
"	St. Kitts & Nevis	03 2000	15	2	13.3	—	—	—	—
49	Poland	09 1997	460	60	13.0	09 1997	100	11	11.0
50	Rep. of Moldova	02 2001	101	13	12.9	—	—	—	—

Source: Inter-Parliamentary Union. 2001. *PARLINE database,* pp. 1–2. Online. Available: http://www.ipu.org/wmn-e/classif.htm. Retrieved July 18, 2001.

occupations until then. Women's entry into skilled blue-collar work such as construction and automaking was limited by the very slow growth in those jobs (Amott, 1993:76). In 2000, only 3 percent of mechanics, 2 percent of construction workers, and 2 percent of tool and die makers were women. However, some women made inroads into prestige jobs in the highly paid primary sector. The years 1970 to 1990 found more women in the fields of law, medicine, journalism, and higher education. Today, women fill 40 percent of all management positions (up from 19 percent in 1972). Still, there are fewer women in prestige

TABLE 9.3

Projected Civilian Labor Force and Participation Rates of Women, by Race

	In Labor Force (in thousands)		*Change, 1998–2008*		*Participation Rate*	
Women	*1998*	*2008*	*Numerical*	*Percent*	*1988*	*2008*
All races	63,714	73,444	9,729	15.3	59.8	61.9
Hispanic origin	5,746	8,552	2,806	48.8	55.6	57.9
White	52,380	59,001	6,621	12.6	59.4	61.5
Black	8,441	10,224	1,783	21.1	62.8	64.6
Asian and other	2,895	4,219	1,323	45.7	59.2	60.5

Source: U.S. Department of Labor, Women's Bureau. 2000. *Facts on Working Women: Women of Hispanic Origin in the Labor Force,* No. 00-04 (April, 2000 p. 3). Online. Available: http://www.dol.gov/dol/wb/public/wb–pubs/hispwom2.htm. Retrieved September 3, 2000.

jobs than men. In 1999, only 29 percent of lawyers, 24 percent of doctors, and 42 percent of university or college teachers were women (U.S. Bureau of the Census, 2000d:416–417. Although women have made inroads in the high-paying and high-prestige professions, not all have fared equally. White women were the major beneficiaries of the new opportunities. There has been an occupational "trickle down" effect, as White women improved their occupational status by moving into male-dominated professions such as law and medicine, while African American women moved into the *female-dominated* jobs, such as social work and teaching, vacated by White women. This improvement for White women was related to federal civil rights legislation, particularly the requirement that firms receiving federal contracts comply with affirmative action guidelines (Amott, 1993:76).

As women continue moving into jobs that were once considered "men's work," men are still rare in traditionally defined "women's work." Lower pay and attitudes about men's work discourage men from entering jobs associated with women (Zaldivar, 1997).

Earnings Gap

Although women's labor force participation rates have risen, the gap between women's and men's earnings has remained relatively constant for three decades. Women workers do not approach earning parity with men even when they work in similar occupations and have the same levels of education.

The gender wage gap has narrowed (see Table 9.5). In 2001, women earned 76 cents for every dollar men earned (up from 71 cents in 1995). Closing the wage gap has been slow, amounting to less than half a cent per year. For women of color, earning discrimination is even greater. Women's incomes are lower than men's in every racial group. Among women and men working year-round and full-time in 1999, White women earned 76 percent of White men's earnings; Black women earned 83 percent of Black men's earnings but only 64 percent of White men's earnings; Hispanic women earned 85 percent of Hispanic men's earnings, but only 54 percent of White men's earnings (U.S. Bureau of the Census, 2000d). The earnings gap affects the well-being of women and their families. It adds up to over $8,000 per year and more than $250,000 over a

TABLE 9.4

Twenty Leading Occupations of Employed Women (2000 National Averages)

Occupations	Total Employed (thousands) Women	Total Employed (thousands) Men and Women	Percent Women	Women's Median Usual Weekly Earnings*	Ratio Women's Earnings to Men's Earnings
Total, 16 years and over	62,915	135,208	46.5	$491	76.0
Sales workers, retail and personal services	4,306	6,782	63.5	301	55.8
Secretaries	2,594	2,623	98.9	450	N.A.
Managers and administrators†	2,418	7,797	31.0	733	66.3
Cashiers	2,277	2,939	77.5	276	88.2
Sales supervisors and proprietors	1,989	4,937	40.3	485	69.8
Registered nurses	1,959	2,111	97.8	782	87.9
Elementary school teachers	1,814	2,177	83.3	701	81.5
Nursing aides, orderlies, and attendants	1,784	1,983	90.0	333	88.1
Receptionists	984	1,017	96.8	388	N.A.
Bookkeepers, accounting, and auditing clerks	1,584	1,719	92.1	478	88.7
Sales workers, other commodities‡	949	1,428	66.5	319	69.3
Accountants and auditors	903	1,592	56.7	690	72.4
Cooks	899	2,076	43.3	290	89.5
Investigators ad adjusters, excluding insurance	833	1,097	75.9	459	82.6
Janitors and cleaners	811	2,233	36.3	309	83.1
Secondary school teachers	764	1,319	57.9	741	88.6
Hairdressers and cosmetologists	748	820	91.2	339	N.A.
General office clerks	722	864	83.6	430	91.3
Managers, food serving and lodging establishments	677	1,466	46.8	475	73.0
Teachers' aides	646	710	91.0	338	N.A.

*Wage and salary for full-time workers.

†Not elsewhere classified.

‡Included in sales workers, personal and retail workers.

Source: U.S. Department of Labor. 2000. *Twenty Leading Occupations of Employed Women, 2000 Annual Averages.* Online. Available: http://www.dol.gov/dol/wb/public/wb_pubs/20lead2000.htm. Retrieved July 24, 2001.

lifetime for the average woman—earnings that could have bought a home, educated children, and been set aside for retirement (Greim, 1998; Love, 1998). The earnings gap persists for several reasons:

- Women are concentrated in lower-paying occupations.
- Women enter the labor force at different and lower-paying levels than men.
- Women as a group have less education and experience than men; therefore, they are paid less.
- Women work less overtime than men.

These conditions explain only part of the earnings gap between women and men. They do not explain why female workers earn less than male workers with the same educational level, work histories, skills, and work experience. Female doctors make 76 percent of what male doctors make, and female nurses make 94 percent of what their male counterparts make (U.S. Bureau of the Census, 1999:211, 213–218). Several studies have found that if women were men with the same credentials, they would earn substantially more. Research on the income gap has found that women's and men's credentials explain some differences, but experience accounts for only one-third of the wage gap. The largest part of the wage gap is caused by sex discrimination in the labor market that blocks women's access to the better-paying jobs through hiring, promotion, and simply paying women less than men in any job (*ISR Newsletter*, 1982; Dunn, 1996; Leinwand, 1999).

Intersection of Race and Gender in the Workplace

There are important racial differences in the occupational concentration of women and men (see Table 9.5). Women of color make up over 10 percent of the U.S. workforce (Jackson, 1999). They are the most segregated group in the

TABLE 9.5

Women's Earnings as Percent of Men's, 1979–2000

	Ratio of Women's Earnings to Men's Earnings		
Year	*Hourly*	*Weekly*	*Annual*
1979	64.1	62.5	57.9
1980	64.8	64.4	60.2
1981	65.1	64.6	59.2
1982	67.3	65.4	61.7
1983	69.4	66.7	63.6
1984	69.8	67.8	63.7
1985	70.0	68.2	64.6
1986	70.2	69.2	64.3
1987	72.1	70.0	65.2
1988	73.8	70.2	66.0
1989	75.4	70.1	68.7
1990	77.9	71.9	71.6
1991	78.6	74.2	69.9
1992	80.3	75.8	70.8
1993	80.4	77.1	71.5
1994	80.6	76.4	72.0
1995	80.8	75.5	71.4
1996	81.2	75.0	73.8
1997	80.8	74.4	74.2
1998	81.8	76.3	73.2
1999	83.8	76.5	72.2
2000	83.2	76.0	

Source: U.S. Department of Labor. 2000. *Women's Earnings as a Percentage of Men's.* Online. Available: http://www.dol.gov/dol/wb/public/wb_pubs/2000.htm. Retrieved July 24, 2001.

workplace—concentrated at the bottom of the work hierarchy, in low-paying jobs with few fringe benefits, poor working conditions, high turnover, and little chance of advancement. Latinas, for example, are concentrated in service jobs such as housekeeping and kitchen work. Both Black women and Latinas are more likely than their White counterparts to work in service occupations or as machine operators or laborers. A much larger share of White women (30 percent) than Black women (21 percent) or Latinas (17 percent) hold managerial and professional specialty jobs (Herz and Wootton, 1996:58–59).

The economic well-being of women and their children suffers from the concentration of minority women in low-wage sectors of the labor market. Earnings for all workers are lowest in those areas of the labor market where women of color predominate. The higher the concentration of women in a given occupational category, the worse the pay (Dill, Cannon, and Vanneman, 1987). In the mid-1990s, White men who worked full time earned the most of any group, followed by White women and Black men. Black women and Hispanic men and women had the lowest earnings (Herz and Wooton, 1996:67).

Pay Equity

Women's low earnings create serious problems for women themselves, for their families, and for their children. Increasingly, families need the incomes of both spouses, and many working women are the sole providers for their children. Given these trends, equal pay is a top concern of women.

The Equal Pay Act, passed in 1963, made it illegal to pay women less for doing the same work as men. In most cases, however, they do not do the same work. For example, to be a secretary (usually a woman) requires as much education and takes as much responsibility as being a carpenter (usually a man), but the secretarial job is paid far less. This makes the law difficult to enforce (Folbre and the Center for Popular Economics, 1995).

In the early 1980s, a number of state and local governments began addressing the pay-gap issue by instituting pay-equity policies in the public sector. Pay-equity policies are designed to bring the pay levels of women in closer alignment with those of men. Because pay equity calls for jobs of comparable value to be paid the same, it is also called comparable worth (Sociologists for Women in Society, 1986). Since 1980, 20 states have implemented pay-equity programs that reduced the gender wage gap. Minnesota, Oregon, and Washington were among the most successful (Folbre, 1995:3.7). **Pay equity** struggles are difficult. Yet, in recent years, women willing to fight for their rights have won multimillion-dollar pay equity settlements from corporations such as Home Depot, Eastman Kodak, and Merrill Lynch (Leinwand, 1999).

How Workplace Inequality Operates

Common explanations for gender differentials in the workplace rest on individual or group-level traits. Women's psychology and socialization—in other words, their own behaviors, aspirations, and choices—are said to produce gender divisions in the workplace. But sociological research shows that organizational structure of work, not socialization, is responsible for gender differences in the quality of work life (Martin, 1998). Let us examine the organization of the labor force that assigns better jobs and greater rewards to men and positions of less responsibility with lower earnings to women.

The labor market is divided into two separate segments, with different characteristics, different roles, and different rewards. The primary segment is characterized by stability, high wages, promotion ladders, opportunities for advancement, good working conditions, and provisions for job security. The secondary market is characterized by low wages, fewer or no promotion ladders, poor working conditions, and little provision for job security. Women's work tends to fall in the secondary segment. For example, clerical work, the largest single occupation for women, has many of the characteristics associated with the secondary segment.

To understand women's disadvantages, we must look at structural arrangements that women confront in the workplace. A classic study by Rosabeth Kanter (1977), *Men and Women of the Corporation,* found that organizational location is more important than gender in shaping workers' behavior. Although women and men behave differently at work, Kanter demonstrated that the differences were created by organizational locations. Workers in low-mobility or blocked situations (regardless of their sex) tended to limit their aspirations, seek satisfactions in activities outside of work, dream of escape, and create sociable peer groups in which interpersonal relationships take over other aspects of work. Kanter argued that "when women seem to be less motivated or committed, it is probably because their jobs carry less opportunity" (Kanter, 1977:159).

Many organizational features block women's advancement. In the white-collar workforce, the well-documented phenomenon of women going just so far—and no further—in their occupations and professions is called the **glass ceiling.** This refers to the invisible barriers that limit women's mobility despite their motivation and capacity for positions of power and prestige (Lorber, 1994:227). The movement of women into highly skilled blue-collar work has been limited by the steady decline of manufacturing jobs.

Those women who do enter blue-collar work often confront blatant resistance from male co-workers. Even the movement of women into "male" jobs does not always bring about integration. Sociologists Barbara Reskin and Patricia Roos (1990) studied eleven once male-dominated fields that had become integrated between 1970 and 1988: book editing, pharmacy, public relations, bank management, systems analysis, insurance sales, real estate sales, insurance adjusting and examining, bartending, baking, and typesetting and composition. Reskin and Roos found that women gained entry into these fields only *after* earnings and upward mobility in each of these fields declined; that is, salaries had gone down, prestige had diminished, or work had become more like "women's work" (Kroeger, 1994:50). Furthermore, in each of these occupations, women specialized in lower-status specialties, in different and less desirable work settings, and in lower paid industries. Reskin and Roos call this process *ghettoization*. Some occupations changed their sex typing completely while some became resegregated by race as well as gender (Reskin and Roos, 1990; Amott, 1993:80).

Many fields that have opened up to women no longer have the economic or social status they once possessed. Their structures now have two tiers: (a) higher-paying, higher-ranking jobs with more authority and (b) lower-paying, more routinized jobs with less authority. Women are concentrated in the new, more routinized sectors of professional employment, but the upper tier of relatively autonomous work continues to be male dominated, with only token increases in female employment (Carter and Carter, 1981). For example, women's entry into three prestige professions—medicine, college teaching, and

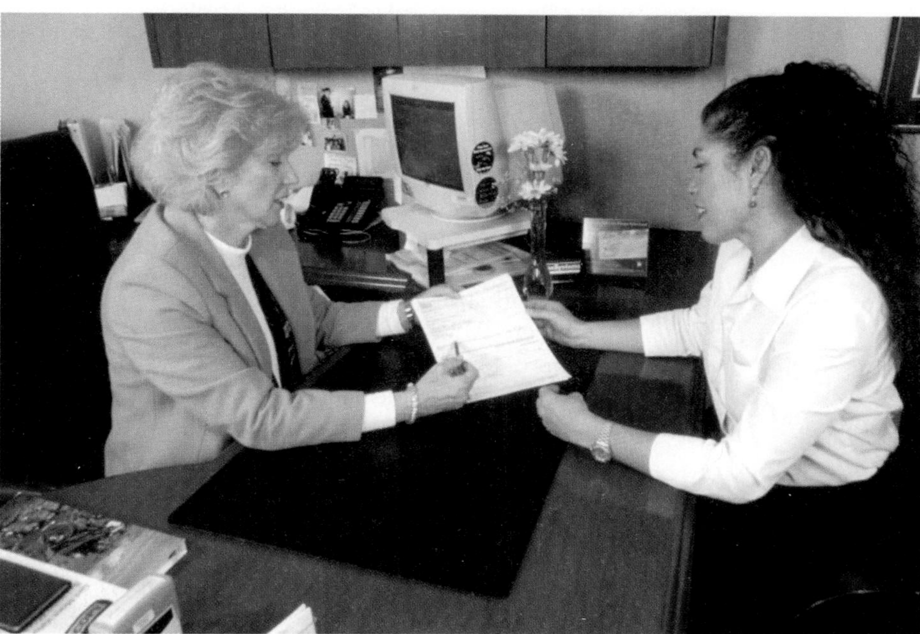

Women gained entry into many types of work only after pay, prestige, and mobility dropped.

law—has been accompanied by organizational changes. In medicine, hospital-based practice has grown as more women have entered the profession. Women doctors are more likely than men to be found in hospital-based practice, which provides less autonomy than the more traditional office-based practice. In college teaching, many women are employed in 2-year colleges, where heavy teaching loads leave little time or energy for writing and publishing—the keys to academic career advancement. And in law, women's advancement to prestigious positions is being eroded by the growth of the legal clinic, where much legal work is routinized.

Many of the old discriminatory patterns are difficult to change. In the professions, for example, sponsor–protégé systems and informal interactions among colleagues limit women's mobility. Sponsorship is important in training personnel and ensuring leadership continuity. Women are less likely to be acceptable as proteges. Furthermore, their sex status limits or excludes their involvement in the buddy system or the old-boy network (Epstein, 1970). These informal interactions create alliances that can further chances for social mobility, but they are systematically blocked for women.

Women and Men in Families

Women's status in the family parallels their status in other social institutions. The gender-structured family assigns maintenance work (work with no identifiable product) to women. In the role of wife and mother, a woman earns no money for her household chores of cleaning, cooking, and caring for the needs of the household members (see Chapter 14). Like most women throughout the world, U.S. women spend as much time as men, or more, working when unpaid labor is taken into account. Today, men are doing more shopping and housework, but only because women are making them change. Although many wife–husband relationships are becoming more equal, men continue to exercise greater power in families.

COSTS AND CONSEQUENCES OF SEXISM

Who Benefits?

Clearly, gender inequality enters all aspects of social life in the United States. This inequality is profitable to certain segments of the economy, and it also gives privileges to individual men. Capitalists derive extra profits from paying women less than men. Women's segregation in low-paying jobs produces higher profits for some economic sectors—namely, those where most workers are women. Women who are sole breadwinners and those who are in the workforce on a temporary basis have always been a source of exploitable labor. These women provide a significant proportion of the marginal labor force capitalists need to draw on during upswings in the business cycle and to release during downswings (Edwards, Reich, and Weisskopf, 1978:333).

Gender inequality is suited to the needs of the economy in other ways as well. The U.S. economy must accumulate capital and maintain labor power. This requires that all workers be physically and emotionally maintained. Who provides the daily maintenance that enables workers to be part of the labor force? Women! They maintain workers through the unpaid work they do inside the home. This keeps the economy going and it also provides privileges for individual men at women's expense.

Social and Individual Costs

Gender inequality benefits certain segments of society. Nevertheless, society at large and individual women and men pay a high price for inequality. Sexism diminishes the quality of life for all people. Our society is deprived of half of its resources when women are denied full and equal participation in its institutions. If women are systematically kept from jobs requiring leadership, creativity, and productivity, the economy suffers. The pool of talent consisting of half the population will continue to be underutilized and underproductive.

Sexism also produces suffering for millions of people. We have seen that individual women pay a heavy price for economic discrimination. Their children pay as well. The poverty caused by gender inequality is one of the most pressing social problems facing the United States as we enter the new century. Adult women's chances of living in poverty are still higher than men's at every age. Black and Latina women fare the worst, with poverty rates around 30 percent (Bianchi and Spain, 1996). As we saw in Chapter 7, this phenomenon is called the feminization of poverty (Pearce, 1978). Economist Nancy Folbre points out that the highest risk of poverty comes from being female and having children—which helps explain the high rates of both female and child poverty in the United States. Folbre calls this trend the "pauperization of motherhood" (Folbre, 1985; cited in Albelda and Tilly, 1997:23). Of course, sexism produces suffering around the world. Some women are persecuted simply *because* they are women. (See the panel "Social Problems in Global Perspective" titled "Torture Based on Gender Alone.")

Women's economic problems can be compounded by divorce and widowhood. But sexism's price is not only economic. The psychological costs of sexism are also deep. Society's devaluation of women often creates identity problems, low self-esteem, and a general sense of inadequacy.

Sexism also denies men the potential for full human development. Gender segregation denies employment opportunities to men who wish to enter such fields as nursing, grade-school teaching, or secretarial work. Eradicating sexism would benefit such males. It would benefit all males who have been forced into stereotypic male behavioral modes. In learning to be men, boys express their masculinity through physical courage, toughness, competitiveness, and aggression. Expressions typically associated with femininity, such as gentleness, expressiveness, and responsiveness, are seen as undesirable for males. In rigidly adhering to gender expectations, males pay a price for their masculinity. As Pleck puts it:

> The conventional expectations of what it means to be a man are difficult to live up to for all but the lucky few and lead to unnecessary self-deprivation in the rest when they do not measure up. Even for those who do, there is a price: they may be forced, for example, to inhibit the expression of many emotions. (Pleck, 1981:69)

Male inexpressiveness can hinder communication between husbands and wives, between fathers and children; it has been called "a tragedy of American society" (Balswick and Peck, 1971). Certainly, it is a tragedy for the man himself, crippled by an inability to show the best part of a human being—his warm and tender feelings for other people (Balswick and Collier, 1976:59).

Feminist Movements in the United States

Gender inequality in this society has led to feminist social movements. Three stages of feminism have been aimed at overcoming sex discrimination. The first stage grew out of the abolition movement of the 1830s. Working to abolish slavery, women found that they could not function as equals with their male abolitionist friends, and they became convinced that women's freedom was as important as freedom from slavery. In July 1848 the first convention in history devoted to issues of women's position and rights was held at Seneca Falls, New York. Participants in the Seneca Falls convention approved a declaration of independence, asserting that men and women are created equal and that they are endowed with certain inalienable rights.

During the Civil War, feminists for the most part turned their attention to the emancipation of Blacks. After the war and the ratification of the Thirteenth Amendment abolishing slavery, feminists were divided between those seeking far-ranging economic, religious, and social reforms and those seeking voting rights for women. The second stage of feminism gave priority to women's suffrage. The women's suffrage amendment, introduced into every session of Congress from 1878 on, was ratified on August 26, 1920, nearly three-quarters of a century after the demand for women's suffrage had been made at the Seneca Falls convention. From 1920 until the 1960s, feminism was dormant. "So much energy had been expended in achieving the right to vote that the women's movement virtually collapsed from exhaustion" (Hole and Levine, 1979:554).

Feminism was reawakened in the 1960s. Social movements aimed at inequalities gave rise to an important branch of contemporary feminism. The civil rights movement and other protest movements of the 1960s spread the ide-

SOCIAL PROBLEMS IN GLOBAL PERSPECTIVE

TORTURE BASED ON GENDER ALONE

Rodi Alvarado Pena cleans houses for a living, thinks about her two children in Guatemala and waits. For six years she has been in the United States seeking asylum, watching her case go back and forth in a flurry of dizzying inconsistency. One judge granted her the right to stay in this country; a panel of other judges reversed that decision. The U.S. attorney general herself vacated that ruling and said the case should be decided in light of soon-to-be-released regulations. But administrations changed, the new regulations have not appeared, and Rodi cleans and worries and waits some more.

The question of immigration in America is like one of those ill-fated science experiments in school that blow up with a boom. It combines a passive element, the great unyielding bureaucracy of the Immigration and Naturalization Service, with an active one, the hot-button issue of allowing foreigners residency in a land that in theory is welcoming but in practice is hostile. The questions of asylum ups the ante, because it goes to the very heart of what the United States professes to be: a nation in which those who have been persecuted in their own country can be guaranteed succor and a second home.

But the issue of asylum for women as women raises the stakes even higher, because it shines unwelcome light on the violence that has long been inflicted on one part of the population by another as a matter of course. Rodi Alvarado says that during a decade of marriage her husband, a member of the Guatemalan military, raped her, tried to abort one of their children by kicking her, and hit her until she lost consciousness in front of those children. And she says that as a matter of policy the government of her country looked the other way, that a judge told her domestic violence was a private matter, that the police would not arrest her husband. In May 1995 she fled for her life to the United States.

She arrived here at a moment of both great promise and great confusion for women seeking asylum because of persecution related to their sex. Standards created half a century ago extend asylum to those persecuted because of race, religion, nationality, membership in a social group or political opinions. One category is glaringly missing from that list, of course, and it is gender. Asylum standards have remained frozen in the amber of a time when silence about gender politics prevailed and asylum was understood as a remedy for unpopular views, not devalued human status.

As a result, women who seek asylum because of sex-based persecution seek it under the rubric of membership in a social group, as though gender were somehow less definitive than race, religion or nationality instead of more so. And they have made some progress. Karen Musalo, the director of the Center for Gender and Refugee Studies at the University of California's Hastings

ology of equality. But like the early feminists, women involved in political protest movements found that male dominance characterized even movements seeking social equality. Discovering injustice in freedom movements, they broadened their protest to such far-reaching concerns as health care, family life, and relationships between the sexes. Another strand of contemporary feminism emerged among professional women who discovered sex discrimination in earnings and advancement. Formal organizations, such as the National Organization of Women, evolved, seeking legislation to overcome sex discrimination (Freeman, 1979).

These two branches of contemporary feminism gave rise to a feminist consciousness among millions of U.S. women. As a consequence, during the 1960s and early 1970s many changes occurred in the roles of women and men. However, periods of recession, high unemployment, and inflation in the late 1970s fed a backlash against feminism. The contemporary women's movement may be the first in U.S. history to face the opposition of an organized antifeminist

College of Law, who is representing Rodi Alvarado, was responsible for a major victory in 1996 in the successful asylum claim of an African woman who would have faced traditional genital mutilation had she returned home. But results in cases involving domestic violence have been more equivocal, perhaps because the United States has no history of female genital mutilation but, until recently, a somewhat spotty record of protecting women beaten and even killed in their own homes.

Musalo is also keeping tabs on the case of Rosalba Aguirre-Cervantes, who claimed asylum based on a lifetime of beatings by her father. A federal appeals court ordered immigration authorities not to deport her, and the panel lambasted her native country, Mexico, for its "tacit approval of a certain measure of abuse." But an immigration judge in Chicago recently denied an asylum claim by an Indian woman who says her abusive husband, after beating her so severely that she needed to have a hysterectomy, was let go by police because of the intervention of her own father, who had arranged the marriage.

Opposition to this sort of asylum claim relies on the old floodgates argument that has been used over the years to try to curtail admission of everyone from the Irish to the Vietnamese. But it also covertly minimizes societally permissible persecution of women. One anti-immigration activist in California, Barbara Coe, charmingly describes these asylum claims as "You get a punch in the mouth, and you're home free." (Perhaps that quote should be paired with the one from a father in Istanbul who killed his 13-year-old daughter: "I fulfilled my duty. We killed her for going out with boys.") Ms. Coe is not only glib but, by the numbers, wrong. Only about 1,100 of the 55,000 asylum claims in 1999 were from women claiming gender bias.

The numbers in Canada are similar, which is significant because the Canadian Immigration and Refugee Board has adopted progressive guidelines for asylum claims that urge officials to consider the "subordinate status" of women in many countries. Asylum standards, according to the board, were based on "the experiences of male claimants" and ignored the special conditions of women around the world, ranging from compulsory sterilization to honor killings. Canada was in an excellent position to do the right thing, both politically and legally; unlike the United States, it has a Constitution that expressly prohibits discrimination on the basis of gender.

This situation cries out for the simple common-sensical remedy of adding gender to the list of categories that constitute reasonable asylum claims. Countries that permit the abuse, sexual assault, even murder of women as a matter of commission or omission are as guilty of a form of systemic persecution as those that make life unlivable for members of a hated religion or political movement.

Source: Anna Quindlen. 2001. "Torture Based on Sex Alone." *Newsweek* (September 10):76.

social movement. From the mid-1970s a coalition of groups calling themselves *profamily* and *prolife* emerged. These groups, drawn from right-wing political organizations and religious organizations, oppose feminist gains in reproductive, family, and antidiscrimination policies. In addition, many gains have been set back by opposition to affirmative action programs and other equal rights policies. Political, legal, and media opposition to feminism continues to undermine women's equality (Faludi, 1991).

Women's Struggles in the Twenty-First Century

As we enter a new century, the women's movement is not over. "Quite the contrary, the women's movement remains one of the most influential sources of social change, even though there is not a single organization that is identified as representing feminism" (Andersen, 2000:320). Not only do mainstream feminist organizations persist, but the struggle for women's rights continues.

Today, many feminist activities occur at the grass-roots level where issues of race, class, and sexuality are important. In communities across the country women *and* men fight:

> against the abuse of women, against corporate poisoning of their neighborhoods, against homophobia and racism, and for people-centered economic development, immigrants' rights, educational equity, and adequate wages. Many have been engaged in such struggles for most of their lives and continue despite the decline in the wider society's support for a progressive social agenda. (Naples, 1998:1)

Whether or not they call themselves feminists, activists across the country are using their community-based organizing to fight for social justice. Instead of responding passively to the outside world, women are forging new agendas and strategies to shape their own lives.

CHAPTER REVIEW

1. U.S. society, like other societies, ranks and rewards women and men unequally.
2. Gender differences are not natural but are, instead, socially constructed. Although gender divisions make women unequal to men, different groups of men exhibit varying degrees of power, and different groups of women exhibit varying levels of inequality.
3. Men as well as women are gendered beings.
4. Gender works with the inequalities of race, class, and sexuality to produce different experiences for all women and men.
5. Many sociologists have viewed women's inequality as the consequences of behavior learned by individual women and men. More recently, sociologists have moved from studying gender as the individual traits of women and men to the study of gender as social structure.
6. Gender inequality is reinforced through language, interpersonal behavior, mass communication, religion, the law, and politics.
7. The segregation of women in a few gendered occupations contrasts with that of men, who are distributed throughout the occupational hierarchy; and women, even with the same amount of education and when doing the same work, earn less than men in all occupations.
8. Gender segregation is the basic source of women's inequality in the labor force. Work opportunities for women tend to concentrate in a secondary market that has few advancement opportunities, fewer job benefits, and lower pay.
9. The combined effects of gender and racial segregation in the labor force keep women of color at the bottom of the work hierarchy, where working conditions are harsh and earnings are low.
10. The position of women in families parallels their status in the labor force. Their responsibility for domestic maintenance and child care frees individual men from such duties and supports the capitalist economy.
11. Gender inequality deprives society of the potential contributions of half its members, creates poverty among families headed by women, and limits the capacities of all women and men.
12. Feminist movements aimed at eliminating inequality have created significant changes at all levels of society. Despite a backlash against feminism, women and men across the country continue to work for women's rights.

KEY TERMS

Gendered. Differentiation of women's and men's behaviors, activities, and worth.

Gender polarization. Males and females are considered "opposites" and placed in mutually exclusive categories.

Feminist approach. View that supports equal relations between women and men.

Gender stratification. Differential ranking and rewarding of women's and men's roles.

Sex. Biological fact of femaleness and maleness.

Gender. Cultural and social definition of feminine and masculine.

Male dominance. Beliefs, meanings, and placement that value men over women and that institutionalize male control of socially valued resources.

Compulsory heterosexuality. The system of sexuality that imposes negative sanctions on those who are homosexual or bisexual.

Sexuality. A way of organizing the social world based on sexual identity.

Patriarchy. Forms of social organization in which men are dominant over women.

Capitalist patriarchy. Condition of capitalism in which male supremacy keeps women in subordinate roles at work and in the home.

Gender roles approach. Males and females differ because of socialization. The assumption is that males and females learn to be different.

Gender structure approach. Males and females differ because of factors external to them.

Gendered institutions. All social institutions are organized by gender.

Androgyny. The integration of traditional feminine and masculine characteristics.

Gender segregation. Pattern whereby women and men are situated in different jobs throughout the labor force.

Pay equity. Raising pay scales according to the worth of the job instead of the personal characteristics of the workers.

Glass ceiling. An invisible barrier that limits women's upward occupational mobility.

WEBSITES FOR FURTHER REFERENCE

http://www.iwpr.org

"The Institute for Women's Policy Research (IWPR) is an independent, non-profit, scientific research organization incorporated in the District of Columbia, established in 1987 to rectify the limited availability of policy relevant research on women's lives and to inform and stimulate debate on issues of critical importance for women. The Institute also works in affiliation with the graduate programs in public policy and women's studies at The George Washington University."

http://www.nowldef.org/

In its 29th year, the NOW Legal Defense and Education Fund (NOW LDEF) continues to be at the center of every major social and economic justice concern on the women's rights agenda, defining the issues and bringing them to public attention. NOW LDEF pursues equality for women and girls in the workplace, the schools, the family, and the courts, through litigation, education, and public information programs.

http://www.feminist.com

Feminist.com is a grassroots, interactive community by, for, and about women. Its aim is to "facilitate information-sharing among women and encourage mobilization around political issues." Feminist.com promotes women's business development, supports women-friendly organizations, expands civic participation, and encourages women's self-sufficiency.

http://www.oxygen.com

Oxygen Media is an integrated media company designed to serve active women through entertainment and information. "What does that mean? Oxygen is comprised of a 24-hour cable television network and a website, designed by women for women. Founded in 1998 by Geraldine Laybourne, Marcy Carsey, Tom Werner, Caryn Mandabach, and Oprah Winfrey, Oxygen is a wholly original blend of talk, health, comedy, movies, sports, and advocacy."

http://www.ivillage.com

The Women's Network: "busy women sharing solutions and advice" on a whole range of topics.

http://members.aol.com/aawon1/welcome.htm

It is the vision of Women of the Net to create an informative and entertaining website. It will address the concerns of most women, particularly the interests of women of color, so often neglected through media. Additionally, while fostering a positive image of all women, "it is the intent of the organization to provide links to other sites (external resources) and to create an information center (internal resources) on topics most often affecting women, including but not limited to the following: Health Care and Child Development, Adult and Child Education, Career and Employment Opportunities, Feminism and Gender Issues, Beauty and Fashion, Ecology, Business, and the Arts."

http://www.aauw.org

The American Association of University Women is a national organization that promotes education and equity for all women and girls.

http://www.agi-usa.org/

The mission of The Alan Guttmacher Institute (AGI) is to "protect the reproductive choices of all women and men—in the United States and throughout the world." To fulfill this mission, AGI seeks to inform individual decision-making, encourage scientific inquiry and enlightened public debate, and promote the formation of sound public- and private-sector programs and policies. The aims of AGI's domestic and international projects and activities are to (1) foster sexual and reproductive health and rights; (2) promote the prevention of unintended pregnancies; (3) guarantee the freedom of women to terminate unwanted pregnancies; (4) achieve healthy pregnancies and births; (5) secure societal support for parenthood and parenting; and (6) promote gender equality within sexual, familial, and social relationships.

http://www.nwhp.org/index.html
The National Women's History Project is a nonprofit organization dedicated to recognizing and celebrating the diverse and historic accomplishments of women by providing information and educational material and programs.

http://www.mtsu.edu/~kmiddlet/history/women/wh-manu.html
American Women's History: A Research Guide to Archival Collections: A definitive guide to searching archives: resources, finding aids, and directories of archives.

http://www.ifge.org/
The International Foundation for Gender Education (IFGE), founded in 1987, is a leading advocate and educational organization for promoting the self-definition and free expression of individual gender identity. "IFGE is not a support group, it is an information provider and clearinghouse for referrals about all things which are transgressive of established social gender norms. IFGE maintains the most complete bookstore on the subject of transgenderism available anywhere. It also publishes the leading magazine providing reasoned discussion of issues of gender expression and identity, including crossdressing, transsexualism, female-to-male and male-to-female issues spanning health, family, medical, legal, workplace issues and more."

http://www.hsph.harvard.edu/grhf/WoC/
Women of Color Web explores the intersection of gender and race. It provides material on Blacks as well as Chicanas. This website includes research, other Internet resources, and articles.

http://www.sagepub.co.uk/frame.html?http://www.sagepub.co.uk/journals/details/j0244.html
The new journal, *Men and Masculinities,* is a Sage publication that is currently available electronically as well as in print. It is "a refereed journal publishing the most recent gender studies research on men and masculinities. It presents empirical and theoretical articles that use both interdisciplinary and multidisciplinary approaches, employ diverse methods, and are grounded in current theoretical perspectives within gender studies, including feminism, queer theory, and multiculturalism." Michael Kimmel, a leading gender scholar, is the current editor.

http://www.vix.com/men/
The Men's Issues Page seeks to cover several men's movements encyclopedically. Its specific goals are to: (1) maintain comprehensive reference lists of mens movement organizations, books, periodicals, web links, and other related resources; (2) serve as an online reference source for statistics, studies, and bibliographies of interest to the men's movements; (3) provide writers, researchers, legislators, activists, and litigants with accurate information and links toward original sources; and (4) particularly, address topics of special need in the areas of fathering and fatherlessness, false accusations, single dads (child-support, custody, visitation), and battered men.

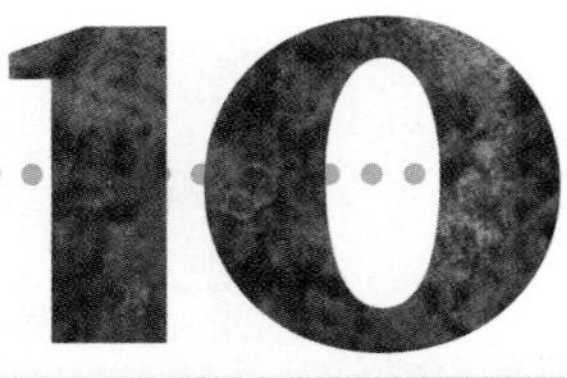

10 Sexual Orientation

omophobia—the fear and loathing of homosexuality and homosexuals—is the last acceptable prejudice.

—Bryne Fone

The University of Southern California marching band repeatedly taunts their rivals by simply playing the notes F A and G, over and over. Jason Mangan, the USC band manager, admits that this is standard for the band, "but it's not homophobic."

—*Los Angeles Times* (November 17, 2000)

What has changed the climate in America is the long experience of gay struggle, the necessary means having been, first, coming out, and second, making a scene. Sometimes it is personal witness, other times political action, and overall it is the creation of a cultural community based on sexual identity.

—Andrew Kopkind

The previous three chapters examined categories of people designated as minorities in society because of their impoverishment, race/ethnicity, or gender. The members of these social categories suffer from powerlessness, negative stereotypes, and discrimination. This chapter looks at another type of minority group. Unlike the other minorities, which are disadvantaged because of economic circumstances or obvious ascribed characteristics, the minority group examined in this chapter—gay men and lesbian women—is the object of discrimination because it is defined by the majority as different and, therefore, deviant. It is important to underscore a crucial point—*homosexuality is not inherently deviant but it is defined and labeled as deviant*. In other words, the deviance ascribed to gays and lesbians is a social construction.

This chapter is divided into four sections. The first section examines the concept of deviance and its implications. The next section presents what is known about homosexuals. The third section describes the various forms of discrimination faced by gay men and lesbian women in the United States. The final section describes the coping strategies of gays and their political activities aimed at changing the societal structures unfair to them.

SOCIAL DEVIANCE

Most of us conform to the norms of society most of the time. Similarly, most of us on occasion violate minor social norms, and these violations are usually tolerated or even ignored. An occasional breach of etiquette, participation in a riotous celebration after an important sports victory, or loud chatter in a theater may bring some minor social disapproval to the violators but no serious punishment. The social deviance that most interests sociologists concerns offenses that are seriously disapproved of by many people and therefore evoke serious social consequences for the violators. The following discussion examines some important principles that help us understand social deviance in general and a sexual orientation that is defined as deviant in particular.

Because **deviance** is behavior that does not conform to social expectations, *it is socially created* (Becker, 1963:8–9). Societies create right and wrong by originating norms and saying that failure to follow the rules constitutes deviance.

Whether an act is deviant depends on how other people react to it. As Kai Erikson has put it: "Deviance is not a property *inherent* in any particular kind of behavior; it is a property *conferred upon* that behavior by the people who come into direct or indirect contact with it" (Erikson, 1966:6).

Even though sexuality has a biological base, it is also a social construction. Society impinges on this intensely private form of intimacy to shape our ideas about what is erotic, to define what is taboo, and to determine who are appropriate sexual partners. The social context of parents, peers, community, church, school, media, and government thus condition, constrain, and socially define sexual behavior (Ross and Rapp, 1983:53). In contemporary U.S. society **heterosexuality** (opposite-sex eroticism) is the expected—actually, demanded—sexual orientation. Thus, the term **compulsory heterosexuality** applies; that is, within U.S. society the beliefs and practices of the majority enforce heterosexual behavior as normal, while stigmatizing other forms of sexual expression. In fact, most people in the United States believe that **homosexuality** (sexual preference for someone of the same sex) or **bisexuality** (attraction to both sexes) is evidence of moral weakness or pathology. Thus, society has created homosexuality as deviance.

Because deviance is not a property inherent in any particular kind of behavior, *deviance is a relative, not an absolute, notion*. Evidence for its relativeness is found in the wide variation of definitions of deviance from society to society and from one historical period to another. Homosexuality is deviant in the United States, but is not a universally deviant form of sexuality. One anthropological study of 190 societies found that two-thirds of them accept homosexuality for certain individuals or for specific occasions. Among the 225 Native American tribes, more than half accepted male homosexuality and 17 percent accepted female homosexuality (Pomeroy, 1965). In ancient Greece homosexual relationships between men were considered the supreme intellectual and spiritual expression of love (Crooks and Baur, 1987:310). Men in ancient Greece and Rome were regarded as naturally bisexual, as Lawrence Stone notes:

> No distinction was made between the love of boys and the love of women. This was simply a question of taste, about as significant as preferring coffee or tea for breakfast. The crucial distinction in law and morality was between those who took the active roles and those who took the passive roles—the penetrators as opposed to the penetrated. This concept effectively degraded submissive boys, women, and slaves of both sexes, and elevated active men, regardless of their gender preference. (Stone, 1985:27; see also Clausen, 1996)

Stone, in his review essay of twenty-six books and articles on the history of sexuality in Western civilization, concluded:

> What is absolutely certain . . . is that over the long history of Western civilization, there has been no such thing as "normal sexuality." Sexuality is a cultural artifact that has undergone constant and sometimes dramatic changes over time, and there is every reason to suppose that there are still more surprising transformations in store for us in the not too distant future. (Stone, 1985:37)

Historical and cross-cultural data support strongly that sexuality is a social construction. As Baca Zinn and Eitzen argue:

> Although grounded in the body, the physical does not by itself define human sexuality. If this were true, we would expect to find uniformity across the world's cultures. Yet the sexual diversity we see is startling. Activities con-

> demned in one society are encouraged in another; and ideas about what is attractive or erotic or sexually satisfying, or even sexually possible, vary a great deal. Even deeply felt personal identities (for example masculinity/femininity or heterosexuality/homosexuality/bisexuality) are not privately or solely the product of biology but are created by social, economic, and political forces that change over time. (Baca Zinn and Eitzen, 1999:224)

Kai Erikson has summarized the relative nature of the concept of deviance:

> Definitions of deviance vary widely as we range over the various classes found in a single society or across the various cultures into which mankind is divided, and it soon becomes apparent that there are no objective properties which all deviant acts can be said to share in common—even within the confines of a given group. *Behavior which qualifies one man for prison may qualify another for sainthood, since the quality of the act itself depends so much on the circumstances under which it was performed and the temper of the audience which witnessed it.* [Italics added.] (Erikson, 1966:5–6)

Deviance is an integral part of all societies. According to Emile Durkheim, deviant behavior actually has positive consequences for society because it gives the nondeviants a sense of solidarity. By punishing the deviant, the group expresses its collective indignation and reaffirms its commitment to the rules. Durkheim explains:

> We have only to notice what happens, particularly in a small town, when some moral scandal has just been committed. They stop each other on the street, they visit each other, they seek to come together to talk of the event and to wax indignant in common. From all the similar expressions which are exchanged, for all the temper that gets itself expressed, there emerges a unique temper . . . which is everybody's without being anybody's in particular. That is the public temper. (Durkheim, 1960:102)

Thus, when individuals in an organization condemn a homosexual colleague, they are reaffirming that their sexuality—heterosexuality—is the only legitimate option. The negative sanctions applied to the deviant (gossip, avoidance, exclusion) serve to enforce conformity in the group by restraining other people from deviating, and thus reaffirming compulsory heterosexuality.

Whoever holds the power determines who or what is deviant. Power is a crucial element in deciding who or what is deviant. Certain social groups have relatively greater power and resources than others in getting their definitions of deviance to prevail. The major religious bodies in the United States, for example, have taken a strong position against homosexuality, and their opposition has influenced the laws and community norms. And occasionally, even deviants can mobilize power to change a discriminatory situation. As we discuss later in this chapter, homosexual activists were able to mobilize enough political power to persuade the psychiatric community to no longer consider homosexuality as a mental disorder.

The status of a person is an identification. An individual has many statuses—male, student, adolescent, sociology major, Latino, athlete, son, and brother. When one status dominates the others in an interaction, it is called a **master status.** The status that defines one as a minority (race/ethnicity, gender, deviance) tends to be a master status because it is the one that determines how you are evaluated and treated by other people. As Edwin Schur has said, "Sex is one of the several 'master status-determining traits.' Sexual orientation goes to the very heart of social and personal identity" (Schur, 1965:98). A male physician, for example, who is known to be gay, will find that his status of gay male supersedes his other statuses in the eyes and behaviors of other people in straight society.

This discussion leads to a final insight about deviance—that *violators of important social norms are* ***stigmatized.*** That is, deviants are not only believed to be different from so-called normals, but they are also set apart by being socially disgraced. The society—through the church, the medical community, and the law—stigmatizes gays as sick, sinful, criminal, and despicable . In the community they are pejoratively labeled as "queers," "dykes," "faggots," and "fairies." This societal/community reaction to gays has several consequences for them that are considered later in this chapter. The extremely negative reaction to gays may keep many of them invisible, will drive those open about their sexuality into gay ghettos, and may cause extreme personal distress. In the latter instance, gays experiencing the disgust that so-called normals have toward them may accept society's negative label and consider themselves as sinners, criminals, and sick, therefore, in need of help. The opposite may also occur: People labeled as outsiders may reject the dominant rules and regard those who judge them so harshly and unfairly as the problem.

GAY AND LESBIAN COMMUNITY: AN OVERVIEW

Defining Homosexuality

Homosexuality has become more visible in U.S. society in the past 25 years or so. This emergence of homosexuality into the mainstream of society has generated new questions about how homosexuality should be labeled and defined. The terms *sexual preference* and *sexual orientation* are both used to denote one's sexuality. The implications of each are important. **Sexual preference** implies a sense of choice regarding the sex of people to whom one is attracted, while **sexual orientation** implies a deterministic view of sexual proclivities. Heterosexuals tend to assume that homosexuality is a matter of sexual preference, while gays and lesbians tend to define their sexuality in terms of sexual orientation.

Roots of Homosexuality

Central to the issue just considered is the debate on whether homosexuality has genetic or social origins. There is a growing scientific literature that provides evidence for a biological basis for homosexuality (for a summary, see Thompson, 1995). If biology is destiny and homosexuality is genetic, then it is natural, rather than an aberration that results from selection, socialization, or seduction. Such a finding has profound implications. On the positive side for gays, such a finding supports the contention that gays deserve legal protection similar to laws that prohibit racial discrimination. And "when people understand that being gay or lesbian is an integral characteristic, they are more open-minded about equality for gay Americans" (Thompson, 1995:61).

Although most gays and lesbians assume that the biological argument is conclusive, there are at least two negative implications to consider. If homosexuality is largely a biological phenomenon, it will be seen by some as a physical illness in need of a cure. Brain surgery, gene splicing, or some other technique might be used to change the "deviant." Or prenatal testing might be used to identify homosexual fetuses for abortion.

So far, however, the scientific evidence is inconclusive (*Chronicle of Higher Education,* 1999). Some researchers are convinced that an area of the brain, the hypothalamus, is responsible. Others find that the size of the anterior commissure of the brain makes the difference. Other researchers remain unconvinced, given the complexity of biology and environmental factors on individual behavior. This ambiguity is expressed by John D'Emilio, a historian of sexuality:

> There's a tremendous amount of evidence in history and cross-cultural studies to suggest that human sexual behavior and desire are enormously malleable, not just from culture to culture or from time period to time period, but in an individual's life. I'm not willing to say that there isn't a biological component, but there's too much else we haven't explored. (quoted in Wheeler, 1992:A9)

The biological argument, while important, is still far from fully persuasive. For example, while identical twins are more likely than other pairs of siblings to have the same sexual orientation, not every identical twin of a gay man or lesbian woman is homosexual. There are probably multiple genetic factors interacting with multiple environmental factors that lead to becoming homosexual.

Whatever its origins, there are two important sociological points. The first is that sexualities are malleable, shaped differently across time and location. Homosexuality is a social role as well as a sexual orientation. Homosexual desire is one thing; the lived homosexual life-style is quite another. The homosexual life-style is not merely a matter of same-sex genital activity. It is a culture with identifiable norms and values about sexuality and intimacy (Fowlkes, 1994:171). And, second, the issue of whether homosexuality has biological or social roots is immaterial. The real issue is one of social justice not origins (Davis, 2000).

Numbers: How Many Gays and Lesbians?

The numbers of gay men and lesbian women are unknown and probably unknowable because many never reveal their sexual orientation, living lives that appear heterosexually oriented. Moreover, the number of gays and lesbians willing to identify themselves as homosexuals to survey researchers is probably less than the real number. There are also problems of definition, as Hess, Markson, and Stein note:

> Is homosexuality to be defined strictly in terms of behavior, or is self-definition the key? Many people who are attracted to persons of their own sex do not act on these feelings. Conversely, many people who have had homosexual relations continue to define themselves as basically heterosexual. (Hess, Markson, and Stein, 1988:306)

There have been several major studies on homosexuals by social scientists. Pioneering research by Alfred Kinsey and his associates—first on men, in 1948, and then on women, in 1953—made it clear that homosexuality was much more common than anyone had suspected, as high as 10 percent of the population. A more recent study (Laumann et al., 1994) found that the incidence rate of homosexual desire was 7.7 percent for men and 7.5 percent for women, while the rate at which men identify themselves as gay was 2.8 percent, and the rate for which women identify themselves as lesbians was 1.4 percent. The most definitive study with data from six studies, using four definitions of homosexuality, found that:

> 4.7% of men in the combined samples have had at least one same-sex experience since age 18, but only 2.5% of men have engaged in exclusively same-sex sex over the year preceding the survey. Similarly, 3.5% of women have had at least one same-sex sexual experience, but only 1.4% have had exclusively same-sex sex over the year preceding the survey. (Black et al., 2000:141)

The numbers debate has repercussions. Gay activists accept the higher numbers because it makes violence and discrimination against them more of an outrage, politicians will have to take them seriously, and there is a greater chance for public acceptance. The antigay right, on the other hand, argues for the lower numbers because it undercuts the gay movement for equality. Perhaps the best response to the numbers issue was given by Congressman Henry Waxman: "One percent, 10%, discrimination is discrimination" (quoted in Cole and Gorman, 1993:29).

Interpersonal Relationships and Domestic Arrangements among Gays and Lesbians

Social scientists have studied "gay life-styles." Their conclusions about sexual relationships point to a number of similarities and differences between homosexuals and heterosexuals and between gay men and lesbian women, some of which contradict the prevailing stereotypes. Alan Bell and Martin Weinberg (1978) studied 979 Black and White, male and female homosexuals. On the basis of interviews and questionnaires, they formulated five categories of homosexuals:

1. *Closed couples.* These homosexual couples were "closely bound together" and looked to each other rather than to outsiders for sexual and interpersonal satisfaction. They described themselves as "happily married."
2. *Open couples.* These couples were living with a special sexual partner but were "not happy with their circumstances" and tended to seek satisfaction with people outside their partnership.
3. *Functionals.* These men and women tended to organize their lives around their sexual experiences. They engaged in a wide variety of sexual activity.
4. *Dysfunctionals.* This group conformed to the stereotype of the "tormented homosexual." They reported many problems due to their homosexual orientation.
5. *Asexuals.* These women and men were lonely, were less overt about their sexual orientation, and had few friends.

The Bell and Weinberg study (1978) is also the best source on homosexuality among African Americans. In general, they found that Black male homosexuals were younger, had less education, and were employed at a lower occupational level than White male homosexuals. Black homosexuals do not find a high degree of acceptance in the Black community (Staples, 1982:93). More recent studies have confirmed this finding, reporting that combined racism and homophobia make minority lesbian women and gay men a "minority within a minority" (Morales, 1990).

Gays are similar to heterosexuals in their desire for an intimate relationship with one special person. Because homosexuals are denied marriage by law, homosexual couples must turn to cohabitation relationships. Research has found that long-lived partnerships between gay men are not uncommon, but neither are they typical. Lesbians, on the other hand, tend to attach a high priority to domestic partnerships (Bell and Weinberg, 1978). More lesbians than gay men (close to 75 percent) are in committed relationships at any given time (Fowlkes, 1994).

Blumstein and Schwartz (1983) found that lesbian couples and gay male couples faced many of the same issues confronting heterosexual couples who live together, married or not. They must work out issues related to the division of household labor, power and authority, and emotional obligations. But homosexual couples face additional problems. Because of the general antipathy toward homosexuality in U.S. society, gay men and lesbian women are not encouraged to be open about their sexual orientation and their relationships. Hence, they may feel restricted in showing public affection toward their lovers. They are seldom extended such commonplace courtesies as having a partner invited to an office party or to a retirement banquet. Even heterosexuals who might like to welcome a gay friend's partner may not know how to go about doing so. Blumstein and Schwartz contend that the "couple" status of homosexuals is always in jeopardy:

> The problem with gay male culture is that much of it is organized around singlehood or maintaining one's sexual marketability. Meeting places like bars and baths promote casual sex rather than couple activities. The problem with the lesbian world is quite different. Women are often in tight-knit friendship groups where friends and acquaintances spend so much intimate time together that, it seems to us, opportunities arise for respect and companionship to turn into love and a meaningful affair. (Blumstein and Schwartz, 1983:322–323)

Differences among lesbians and gay men have given rise to popular stereotypes. For example, lesbians are commonly depicted as masculine women, while gay men are assumed to be effeminate. In reality, homosexuals are not inverts of heterosexuals. Lesbians and heterosexual women are more alike than different, as are gay and heterosexual men. In effect, "men are like men, and women are like women despite differences in sexual orientation" (Fowlkes, 1994:172).

According to Letitia Peplau, the fact of being a man or a woman often exerts greater influence on relationships than does sexual orientation. Gay men in Peplau's study (1981) were much more likely than lesbians to have sex with someone other than their steady partners. This issue of sexual exclusivity is often a major source of tension in male homosexual relationships. Charles Silverstein has suggested that "at some point in the life of every gay couple, the monogamy battle will be fought" (Silverstein, 1981:140). The tendency for gay men to be less sexually exclusive than lesbian women parallels the difference in heterosexual males and females. And this difference is related to gender-role socialization in society, where "males are socialized to engage in sexual behaviors both with and without affection while women are expected to combine the two" (Harry, 1983:226).

In a major departure from the heterosexual pattern, homosexual couples tend to be egalitarian. Heterosexual couples, whether in cohabitation or marriage relationships, tend to accept the traditional gender roles for men and women. In contrast, homosexual couples are much more likely to share in the decision making and in all the household duties. There are three likely reasons for this difference from the heterosexual pattern. One is the conscious effort by homosexuals to reject the dominant marriage model that prescribes specific and unequal roles. Another reason is that in same-sex relationships the partners have received the same gender role socialization. Another source of equality in gay relationships is that there tends to be little income difference between the partners, a condition rare in heterosexual relationships. Most gay and lesbian couples are dual-income units. And because both partners in a homosexual relationship are of the same sex, they are subject to the same degree of sex discrimination in jobs and income (Harry, 1983:219).

An important implication of the equality found in homosexual relationships is that, contrary to the stereotype, the partners do not take the role of either "husband" or "wife." The prevailing assumption is that one person takes the masculine role and is dominant in sexual activities and decision making, while the other does the "feminine" household tasks and is submissive. Research consistently refutes this so-called butch/femme notion, noting that only a small minority of couples reflect the stereotype. Those relatively few couples who conform to the stereotype generally are composed of individuals who are older, from lower socioeconomic levels, newcomers to the homosexual community, and male (Bell and Weinberg, 1978; Peplau, 1981).

A final stereotype about gays and lesbians is that their homosexuality is a master status for them. That is, there is the widespread belief that being homosexual is such a powerful identity that it overrides every other aspect of a person. But according to Hess, Markson, and Stein:

> This is not necessarily the case. Just as heterosexuality does not obsess most men and women, coloring their every thought and act, the homosexual's choice of sex partner is only one part of a complex social person. The problems of daily life—work, leisure, comfort and safety, companionship, death, and taxes—beset the gay as well as the straight, and in many ways, they are harder for the homosexual to resolve because of discrimination and stigmatization. (Hess, Markson, and Stein, 1988:308)

Gays and lesbians, like other minorities, tend to cluster in certain cities and neighborhoods within those cities (e.g., the Castro district in San Francisco and Greenwich Village in New York City). The research by Black and his associates (2000) found several patterns concerning the geographic concentration of gays:

- Almost 60 percent of gay couples and 45 percent of lesbian couples are concentrated in twenty cities that house 26 percent of the U.S. population. The highest concentration of gay male couples is found in San Francisco, followed by New York, Los Angeles, Washington, D.C., and Chicago. The highest concentration of lesbian couples is in New York, Los Angeles, San Francisco, Minneapolis, and Washington, D.C.
- Lesbians are less geographically concentrated than gays.
- Gays and lesbians in smaller cities (200,000 to 700,000) are found disproportionately where there is a major university (e.g., Ann Arbor, Michigan, and Madison, Wisconsin).

DISCRIMINATION

Variance from the societal norm of heterosexuality is not a social problem; *the societal response to it is.* Society has defined what is appropriate sexual behavior and orientation. Consequently, people who differ from the approved orientation are objects of derision and contempt by members of society and are discriminated against by individuals and by the normal way that the institutions of society operate. In short, their different sexual orientation makes homosexuals a minority group. Gays confront three types of oppression: (1) ideological, in which their behaviors are defined and stigmatized as immoral; (2) legal, where their activities are defined as illegal or they are treated unfairly by the courts and other agents of control; and (3) occupational, where jobs, advancement, and income are restricted or denied. This section examines each of these manifestations of institutional discrimination that homosexuals experience.

Ideological Oppression

Homophobia is fear and loathing of homosexuality and homosexuals. It shares many of the same roots with other prejudices. Like racism and anti-Semitism, homophobia includes "an intolerance toward otherness; a fear of lives, perspectives, and practices that one doesn't understand; and a visceral desire for a social hierarchy that puts some people on the rungs below you" (Angier, 1993:4E). There is a long tradition of homophobia in Western society. Gays are considered by the majority as outsiders. Homosexuals are targets of ridicule, restricted from social interaction, and stigmatized. A national *Newsweek* poll in 2000 found that (reported in Leland, 2000):

- 46 percent believed homosexuality to be a sin.
- 57 percent were opposed to gay marriage.

VOICES

HOMOPHOBIA IN SCHOOLS AND ITS CONSEQUENCES

Adolescence is a difficult time of emotional, physical, and sexual changes. It is also a stage when peer approval is especially crucial for a positive sense of self. The American Academy of Pediatrics worries about gay and lesbian youths because they are subjected to abuse and isolation at a time when acceptance and peer approval is crucial to their development. Homosexual youths "are severely hindered by societal stigmatization and prejudice, limited knowledge of human sexuality, a need for secrecy, a lack of opportunities for open socialization. . . . Peers may engage in cruel name-calling [and] ostracize or even physically abuse the identified individual. School and other community figures may resort to ridicule or open taunting, or they may fail to provide support" (quoted in Carman, 2001:lB). Thus, for the 2 million or so school-age children who are lesbian, gay, or bisexual school is an extremely difficult place to be (Human Rights Watch, 2001). If they are "out" as gay or lesbian or suspected of being homosexual, students face a barrage of verbal assaults, threats, and physical harassment. A study by the Massachusetts Department of Education (2000) found that lesbian, gay, and bisexual youth were nearly three times as likely as their heterosexual peers to have been assaulted, three times as likely to be have been threatened or injured with a weapon at school, and nearly four times as likely to skip school because they felt unsafe. Here are some comments from lesbian or gay students surveyed by Human Rights Watch (2001):

- "Relentless verbal abuse and other forms of harassment are all part of the normal daily routine" (Dylan N.).
- When students discovered he was gay they harassed him daily. "They'd come up to me and say, 'I'll pray for you tonight.' Or [they'd] just call me 'faggot'" (Casey G.).
- "People will start rumors about me because I'm the

- 50 percent were opposed to gay couples adopting a child.
- 36 percent said that gays should not teach in elementary school.

The categories of people most intolerant of gays are the poor, African Americans, people over age 50, and non-high-school graduates (Goldberg, 1998).

For many people, the homosexual individual is an outcast. Gays are seen as an aberration, perhaps even a dangerous deviation, from so-called normal sexuality. When people believe that gays are immoral, they belittle their lifestyle; tell jokes about "queers"; deny their rights to housing, jobs, and memberships in organizations; and even engage in hostile acts (verbal and physical assaults) such as gay bashing by adolescent males (see the "Voices" panel). These homophobic attitudes and behaviors cause many homosexuals to have personal problems with self-concept and other adjustment problems. As Long and Sulton have argued: "We wish to suggest that many of the problems of adjustment that may be experienced by some homosexuals do not result directly from being homosexual, but are created by the way society views homosexuality" (Long and Sulton, 1987:227). The way that society views homosexuality is shaped significantly by our religious heritage and the views of the medical community.

Religion. The Judeo-Christian tradition considers homosexual behavior a heinous sin. The Old Testament approves of sexual intercourse only within marriage and for the purpose of procreation. Homosexuality has, therefore, been expressly forbidden. Crooks and Baur comment:

only gay person who's out in the whole school. The worst was when people were saying that I had AIDS" (Miguel S.).

- Gina T. said that she received threatening calls at home, making her "hate every minute of school."
- One of Ron T.'s classmates vandalized the school theater, scrawling messages such as "[Ron] is a faggot" and "All gays must die."
- Dylan N. reported that his classmates passed fake love letters to other boys with his name signed at the bottom.
- Erin B., an eighth grader, told of the verbal abuse that one of her classmates receives. "Taylor is the only openly gay male student at school. He gets teased so badly every five seconds."
- Alex M. said that he missed fifty-six days of school the previous semester. "I'm not proud of that. I know I should've done better. I just couldn't deal with it anymore."

These attacks on lesbian, gay, and bisexual students creates a hostile climate that can be unbearable for them. It can undermine their confidence, and lead to feelings of isolation. It can interfere with their school performance. Some switch schools to escape. Some drop out of school altogether. They are more likely than their heterosexual peers to use alcohol or other drugs. The Massachusetts Youth Risk Behavior Survey (Massachusetts Department of Education 2000, Chapter 4) found that they had higher lifetime rates of marijuana use (70 percent compared to 49 percent of all other youth), cocaine (29 percent compared to 7 percent), and injected drugs (18 percent compared to 2 percent). Similarly gay, lesbian, and bisexual youth are more likely than heterosexual youth to engage in risky sexual behaviors, to run away from home (and to be thrown out by the parents), and to consider, attempt, or complete suicide. The Massachusetts study (2000) found that they were more than three times as likely as other students to report a suicide attempt. A national study in 1998 found that youth who are lesbian or gay were more than twice as likely as their heterosexual counterparts to attempt suicide (Russell and Joyner, 1998).

> Many religious scholars believe that the condemnation of homosexuality stems from a reformation movement beginning in the seventh century B.C., through which Jewish religious leaders wanted to develop a distinct, closed community that was different from others of the time. Homosexual activities were a part of the religious services of many groups of people, including the Jewish people, in that era. Rejecting religious rituals involving homosexual activities that had previously been considered sacred was one way of establishing the uniqueness of a religion. Homosexual behaviors were then condemned as a form of pagan worship. Strong prohibitive biblical scriptures were written: "You shall not lie with a man as one lies with a female, it is an abomination" (Leviticus 18:22). (Crooks and Baur, 1987:308)

The New Testament continued this tradition. The early Christians strived for human perfection unencumbered by the desires of the flesh—celibate religious leaders, sexual intercourse only within marriage, and condemnation of homosexuality. Speaking of homosexuality, the apostle Paul, for example, considered lustful behavior between men and between women as "vile passions . . . against nature" (Romans 1:26). Paul in Corinthians also wrote that homosexuals, along with fornicators, idolaters, adulterers, and thieves, would never inherit the kingdom of God. Summarizing the Judeo-Christian theology condemning nonprocreative sex, Meredith Gould has said:

> The Scriptures are a powerful body of myth, legend, and divine law which have significantly shaped the ideology of Western Civilization. The portion of the code regulating sexuality is firmly entrenched in the assumption, indeed the prescription, that sexual intercourse is for procreation; only through reproduction can sexual activity of any sort be condoned. Consequently, mas-

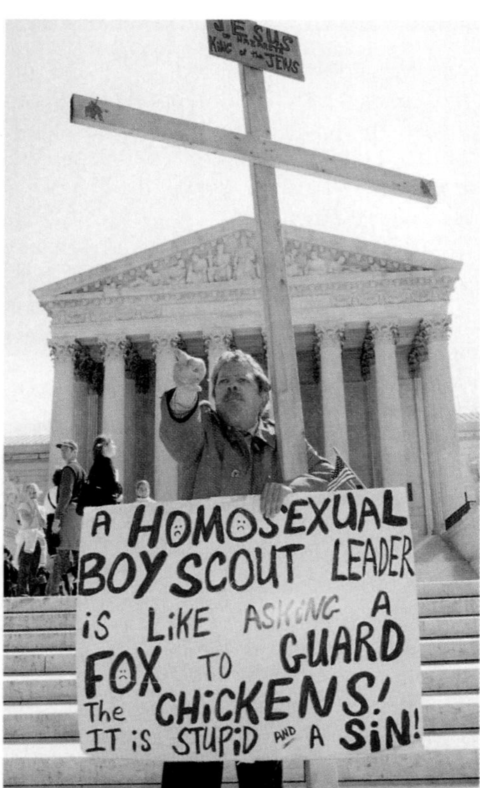

Some religious groups believe that homosexuality is a sin.

> turbation, cunnilingus, fellatio, and anal intercourse are fundamentally heretical, threatening the natural order established by a stern, moralistic God. Anything other than penis-vagina coitus is condemned as sinful and morally rank according to the Christian church. (Gould, 1979:51–52)

Contemporary Christian churches and denominations have varied in their response to the homosexual issue. Some, perhaps the majority, reject homosexuality and consider it a sin. This position is consistent with Christian history, where for centuries the church ostracized homosexual people and gave its blessing to civil persecutions. The current expression of this position continues the heritage of moral condemnation and punitiveness toward gays. The Reverend Jerry Falwell, fundamentalist preacher and founder of the Moral Majority, for example, called the outbreak of AIDS among homosexuals a "form of judgment of God upon a society" (Crooks and Baur, 1987:312). The Reverend Pat Robertson, television evangelist, said in 1998 that the widespread practice of homosexuality will bring God's wrath: "[It] will bring about terrorist bombs, it'll bring earthquakes, tornadoes and possibly a meteor" (Wharton, 1998:14A). Another extreme example of fundamentalist thinking on homosexuality, Pastor Peter J. Peters asserts, "The truth is, the Bible advocates discrimination against, intolerance of and the death penalty for homosexuals" (Peters, 1992:1). In 1996 the Southern Baptist Convention voted to boycott Disney parks, movies, and products, for Disney's "promotion of homosexuality" because it provides the same health care benefits for the live-in mates of gay employees as it does for the spouses of straight workers and it allowed gay groups to organize an event at Disney World (Means, 1996).

In 1986 the Vatican's doctrinal congregation issued a directive, approved by Pope John Paul II, to all Roman Catholic bishops around the world. This directive ordered all bishops to withdraw support from any organization opposing the church's teaching that homosexual behavior is sinful. This meant that gay liberation groups and organizations such as Dignity, which is an explicitly gay organization for Catholics, would no longer be able to meet in Catholic churches or schools. In 1992 the Vatican issued a document that condoned the discrimination against homosexuals in employment, housing, and the adoption of children:

> Sexual orientation does not constitute a quality comparable to race, ethnic background, etc. in respect to non-discrimination. Unlike these, homosexual orientation is an objective disorder. There are areas in which it is not unjust discrimination to take sexual orientation into account, for example, in the placement of children for adoption or foster care, in employment of teachers or athletic coaches and in military recruitment. (*Rocky Mountain News*, 1992:3)

While affirming Catholic doctrine that sexual activity between same-sex partners is immoral, U.S. Catholic bishops released a pastoral letter in 1997 that departed from the Vatican's position: The letter said that homosexual orientation is not freely chosen and that parents must not reject their gay children in a society full of rejection and discrimination (Briggs, 1997).

In 1999 the Vatican ordered a Maryland-based priest and a nun to end their 22-year ministry to lesbians and gays because they refused to condemn homosexuality as intrinsically evil (Associated Press, 1999).

Many congregations and denominations are more accepting of homosexuality. Some maintain that homosexuality must be condemned but, because of God's grace, homosexuals must *not* be condemned. Others are even more

Kirk Anderson

accepting, ranging from the acceptance of gay Christians as members to the ordination of gays as ministers. "Currently, a mere handful of the nation's 375,000 religious congregations call themselves 'welcoming and affirming' or 'reconciling.' Such phrases signify that gay, lesbian, bisexual and transgendered people are accepted in the church with the same rights, responsibilities and opportunities as heterosexuals" (Grossman, 2001a:D2). The Quakers, for example, have adopted a full acceptance of gays:

> One should no more deplore homosexuality than left-handedness. . . . Homosexual affection can be as selfless as heterosexual affection, and therefore we cannot see that it is in some way morally worse. (Crooks and Baur, 1987:310)

But the full acceptance of homosexuals in churches is relatively rare. While the United Church of Christ, the Unitarian-Universalist Association, Evangelical Lutheran Church in America (only if abstinent), and the Reform or liberal branch of Judaism allow the ordination of gays, Orthodox Jews, Roman Catholics, Eastern Orthodox Christians, Mormons, and fundamentalist Christian groups do not even discuss the issue. More liberal groups (such as the Presbyterians, Methodists, and Episcopalians) discuss this and other issues, then reject them.

Thorny theological questions surround the church's definition and treatment of homosexuals. Wilfrid Sheed ruminates on some:

> Until recently, homosexuality was considered largely voluntary, a series of perverse choices by a free will. But as it becomes likelier that homosexuality is a physical predisposition, presumably God-given, the next kind of question has to be, What might God have had in mind, and is it significant that Christ never mentioned the subject? And the question after that: What injustices may have been done to homosexuals under the old understanding, and what can be done to avoid more of them? (Sheed, 1996:44)

Medicine. The beliefs that people in the United States have about homosexuals have been shaped by religion, as we have seen, and also by the prevailing views of the medical community. Whereas religious ideology tends to view homosexuality as a sin, psychiatric theory, until 1973, considered homosexuality as an illness. As an illness, it was assumed to be curable, and many techniques were tried, including prefrontal lobotomies, crude forms of conditioning (such as drugs that induce a sensation of suffocation or emetics to induce vomiting), and even castration. These and more moderate strategies of psychoanalysis were singularly unsuccessful in treating this so-called malady.

The American Psychiatric Association publishes the *Diagnostic and Statistical Manual,* which defines officially the conditions considered mental illnesses. In the first edition, homosexuality was labeled as a mental illness. Some mental health professionals held the minority view that this label was wrong. Dr. Robert Spitzer, for example, said:

> With the exception of homosexuality, all other disorders were associated with impairment in general, occupational or social functioning, or inherently caused some distress. . . . The argument the gay activists were making was that any distress was a reaction to social pressure. (Mach, 1987:44)

In 1973, after years of lobbying by gay activists and the efforts of other people, the American Psychiatric Association by a majority vote of its membership declassified homosexuality as a mental disorder; homosexual behavior was henceforth to be regarded simply as a manifestation of a preference, not as mad or bad. Although this enlightened view is not universally held in the psychiatric community, it does prevail officially.

Many gays and lesbians do have problems, but their problems do "not result directly from being homosexual, but are created by the way society views homosexuality" (Long and Sulton, 1987:227). Homosexuals are more likely than other people to have problems with guilt, anger, and self-esteem owing to prevailing religious views, occupational discrimination, and the rejection they experience because they differ from the sexual norms of society.

Legal Oppression: The Law, the Courts, and the Police

In fourteenth-century Europe the common punishment for homosexuality was burning at the stake. The Puritans in the colonies continued the death penalty for this "crime." Around the time of the American Revolution, Thomas Jefferson and some liberal reformers of the day proposed changing Virginia law, replacing the death penalty for homosexuality with castration (Tivnan, 1987).

The legal status of homosexuals has progressed considerably since the days of death and castration, but they are still not treated equally. For example, the marriage of homosexuals is not recognized by the state. In addition to losing the symbolic importance of having a union legitimated by the state, gays experience other negative consequences. Gould elaborates:

> While heterosexuals enjoy many rights and privileges by virtue of marriage, homosexuals in similar long-term relationships forfeit legal and financial protection such as community property rights, inheritance, tax breaks, and insurance premium reductions. (Gould, 1979:63)

This section begins by surveying the major developments in the law in three areas of great concern to the gay community: sodomy laws, discrimination against gays by the military, and family rights for homosexuals.

Sodomy Laws. Prohibitions against **sodomy** (oral or anal sex) were universal in the United States until 1961, when Illinois became the first state to repeal its

Drawing by M. Wuerker

sodomy law. Other states followed, but twenty-three states still have sodomy laws. In 1986 there was a constitutional challenge to sodomy laws. The argument in this challenge was that sexual activity between consenting adults in private is not questioned, let alone regulated, even in states with laws prohibiting sodomy, *provided the adults are heterosexual*. In short, sodomy laws are used to harass homosexuals, especially gay men, because women in general and lesbians in particular are socially invisible in society. Gould notes, "Homosexual men, in contrast, routinely encounter blatant and humiliating invasions of privacy and freedom which lesbians have been spared—such is the bitter irony of a sexist society" (Gould, 1979:53).

In *Bowers v. Hardwick* (1986) the Supreme Court reversed the U.S. Court of Appeals decision, ruling by a five-to-four vote that states had the right to prohibit sodomy. Justice Byron White's opinion "characterized as 'facetious' the argument that gay people have a 'fundamental right' to engage in consensual sex" (Leonard, 1990:12).

The Military. The armed forces have always discriminated against gays and lesbians. From 1982 to 1992 about 14,000 people were dishonorably discharged from the military as homosexuals. According to Defense Department statistics, women are three times more likely to be removed for homosexuality than are men, "with 16 of every 10,000 women on active duty expelled compared to 5 of every 10,000 men" (Atkins, 1989:16). These discharges have led to many law suits. The decisions consistently reaffirm the military's right to purge homosexuals from its ranks. In 1990 the Supreme Court refused to hear two challenges to the Pentagon regulation that homosexuality is incompatible with military service. In doing so, the Supreme Court upheld this rule, although by not hearing the case, the court did not set a precedent affecting future cases.

In 1993 newly elected President Clinton vowed to change the regulations so that homosexuals would not be discriminated against in the military. This proposal was resisted by many citizens, politicians, military leaders, and military personnel. The result was a compromise—the "don't ask, don't tell" rule. This meant that the military was not to ask its personnel about their sexuality, and to prosecute only if gay and lesbian service members were blatant about their sexual orientation. In short, as long as homosexual service members "stayed in the closet," they were allowed to be in the military. In 1997, some 997 gays in the military were discharged under this "don't ask, don't tell" rule (a rate of 7 per 10,000 troops), an increase from the 730 discharged in 1992 (Priest, 1998).

In 1995, President Clinton ended 50 years of official federal discrimination against homosexuals by ordering that gays and lesbians are no longer considered security risks. This ruling meant that gays and lesbians in government would be granted access to classified government documents on the same basis as other federal employees.

Family Rights. No U.S. state permits marriage between members of the same sex. Vermont in 2000 became the first state to offer legal status to same-sex couples, a civil union, something short of marriage but, according to the Vermont Supreme Court, the couples have the same rights and responsibilities as heterosexual couples in the matters of insurance, inheritance, child custody, and taxes. One year after the civil-union law was passed, 2,000 gay licenses have been granted, 80 percent to out-of-state residents (Drummond, 2001). Thirty-four (as of 2001) other states have passed various forms of the federal Defense of Marriage Act, which defines marriage as the exclusive union of a man and a woman (Bayles, 2001). Thus, most state law affirms homophobia because it formally condemns the living arrangements among homosexual couples. Laws banning same-sex marriages convey a message of intolerance, saying in effect that those couples are neither legitimate nor respected (Delgado and Yun, 1997). (See the panel titled "Voices," p. 296.)

Although forty-nine states do not recognize same-sex marriages, several counties and cities do recognize "legal domestic partners," including San Francisco, New York City, Seattle, Santa Cruz (California), West Hollywood, Boulder (Colorado), and Madison (Wisconsin). This status of "domestic partners" permits partners to receive limited spousal benefits. In New York City, for example, a gay or lesbian may inherit an apartment lease if a partner dies. These domestic arrangements, however, continue to carry minimal legal weight because same-sex marriages are only recognized by one state. In 1997 the first state—Hawaii—allowed same-sex couples to qualify for health and other benefits reserved for married couples. In 2000 the justices of the Vermont Supreme Court in *Baker v. State* granted equal marriage rights for same-sex couples. But these rights are currently denied in the other states and at the federal level.

Parenthood has become the newest battleground for lesbian and gay rights. The legality of homosexual parenthood varies from state to state, and the interpretation of the law often varies from judge to judge. Consider the case of adoption: In some states, homosexual couples can adopt children. In 1994 the Massachusetts Supreme Court ruled that there was nothing in the state law to prohibit adoption by a gay or lesbian couple even though the state does not recognize same-sex marriages. In other states, it is illegal. As a result, there are only a few hundred documented cases of adoption by openly homosexual couples. Of course, many adoptions occur where a single person seeks the adoption while concealing her or his homosexuality.

VOICES

A PLEA FOR THE LEGALIZATION OF SAME-SEX MARRIAGES

The following letter was sent to the well-known newspaper advisor Ann Landers:

> Dear Ann Landers:
>
> Last year, I married the woman of my dreams. She is funny, intelligent, loving, caring, exciting, and gentle. Ours is a full and rewarding life together. We have traveled to several states for both business and pleasure. We go to church, get together with friends and relatives, and share the household chores. We have known good times and bad, and our commitment to one another is stronger now than ever.
>
> So why am I writing to you? Because I hope you will help educate a few million people today. Our marriage, blessed by a minister and approved by many friends and family members, is not legal in the United States. And if Congress has anything to say about it, we may never have a chance to make it legal. You see, Ann, I am also a woman.
>
> My wife and I are hard-working professionals who pay our taxes and vote regularly. We pay our bills on time and are law-abiding citizens. However, we are not accorded all the civil rights that most Americans assume to be their privilege.
>
> Because we are not legally married, we have none of the legal rights married couples enjoy, such as gaining immediate access to a loved one in case of an emergency, sharing insurance policies at reduced rates, holding property together, filing joint returns and so on.
>
> We are not seeking "special rights." We simply want the same rights every other American couple has: the right to be free from discrimination in housing and employment, the right to legal protection from harassment and, most importantly, the right to marry whomever we choose and to enjoy the benefits of marriage. (Landers, 1996:12D)

Landers, by the way, although supportive of the gay rights movement and the rights of same-sex couples, does not support same-sex marriage, because, for her, marriage is a union between a man and a woman.

Source: Permission granted by Ann Landers/Creators Syndicate.

Another situation is custody of children following a heterosexual marriage. In such a situation judges routinely give custody to the heterosexual parent, assuming that this arrangement is better for the child. In 1994 a Virginia judge ruled that the biological mother could not have custody of her child because she was now in a lesbian relationship and therefore an unfit parent.

Some lesbians achieve parenthood through artificial insemination. The trick with this arrangement is for the partner of the mother to achieve legal status through adoption. Presently only eight states permit a lesbian to adopt her lover's child and become a second parent.

A final extreme example shows the negative feelings that some have about gay parents. In Pensacola, Florida, a judge ruled that custody of a young girl should go to the father and not the mother. He made this ruling despite the father's failure to make child support payments and his history of having served 8 years in prison for murdering his first wife. The judge ruled that this father could provide a better environment for the child because the child's mother is a lesbian and single:

> Notwithstanding the studies proving that people don't "become" homosexual because of their parent's orientation, and despite incontrovertible evidence that gay and lesbian parents can provide love and nurturance, and

> despite dozens of studies showing that it is heterosexual men who commit 97 percent of the child molesting in this country, "family values" means heterosexuality at all costs. (Townsend, 1996:12)

Police Action. Although the rate and kind of harassment vary from jurisdiction to jurisdiction, the police often use a variety of techniques to harass homosexuals. They may use questionable means to apprehend and arrest homosexuals (e.g., filming sexual interactions through one-way mirrors installed in public restrooms, wiretapping telephones, and using decoys to entrap). Bars where homosexuals gather are frequently raided for suspected violation of the sodomy laws. Patrons in these raids may be photographed and fingerprinted, which is particularly frightening to people who wish to keep their sexual orientation private. The owners of these establishments are harassed by public authorities who may, for example, revoke their liquor license or issue citations for inconsequential or even nonexistent building code violations. In effect, the agents of social control in many communities have an unofficial policy that encourages the harassment of deviant groups, of which homosexuals are considered by many to be the most abhorrent.

A third police action, actually inaction, that negatively affects gays is police response to gays as victims of violence. There is evidence that homosexuals are the most frequent victims of hate-motivated violence (assault, verbal intimidation, and vandalism), more so than African Americans, Latinos, Southeast Asians, or other minority groups. Only a few police and sheriff's departments have made bias crime a priority, however, and even fewer have expanded their jurisdiction to include antigay violence (San Francisco, Boston, and New York City are three prominent exceptions). The majority, however, reveal a bias against gays by their selective inattention to crimes against gays and lessbians.

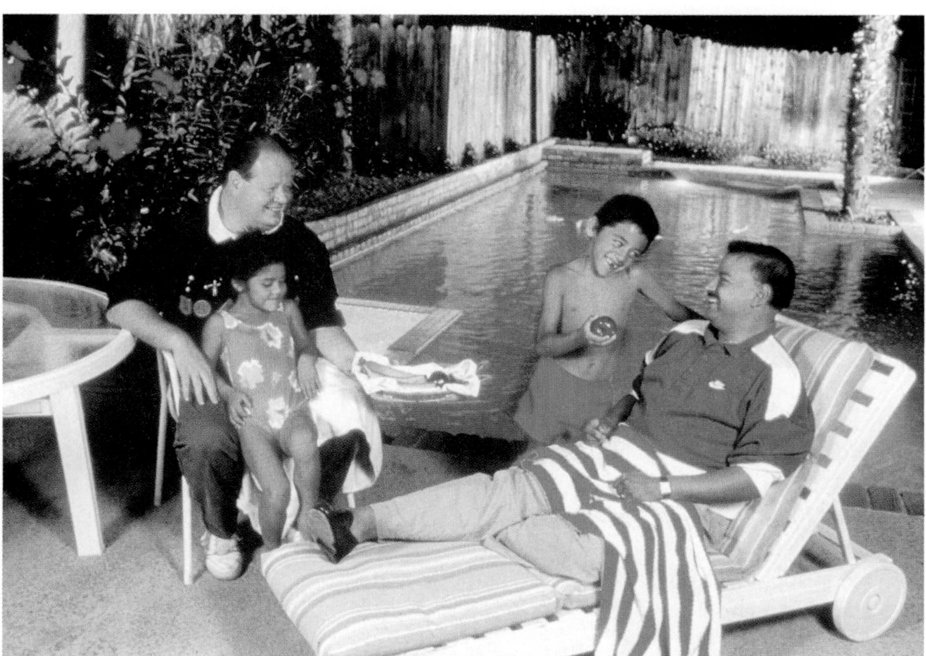

The legality of homosexual parenthood varies from state to state and the interpretations of the law often vary from judge to judge.

Occupational Discrimination

The exact amount of job discrimination against homosexuals is unknown, primarily because the government does not provide gay employment discrimination statistics, as it does for women, African Americans, and other minorities. The two elements of discrimination that confront gays and lesbians in the workplace are anticipated discrimination and actual discrimination.

Many homosexuals fear that they will lose their jobs if their sexual orientation is revealed. Or, if not fired, they may experience other forms of discrimination, such as being passed over for deserved promotions, being given relatively low salary raises, and being harassed.

These fears are likely based on reality. The New York State Health Code includes a section, for example, that states that employees can be fired for moral turpitude (which includes homosexuality as such a case). Because few legal protections are available to homosexuals, especially in the private sector, and because homophobic attitudes are common, homosexuals have little choice in many cases but to hide their sexual orientation (see Table 10.1).

After employment, the hidden homosexual, knowing that retention and promotion depend on keeping the secret, uses a number of ploys to appear heterosexual. The strategies include bringing someone of the opposite sex to company social events, telling appropriate sexual jokes, and wearing appropriate clothing. But as Levine observes, "Needless to say, passing causes psychological problems, feelings of being on stage, anxiety over exposure and subsequent sanctions, strain from artificial behavior and talk" (Levine, 1979:156).

Actual discrimination against known homosexuals occurs frequently in the workplace. Many employers, personnel directors, school boards, and other people involved in hiring do not hire homosexuals. They may not hire gays and lesbians because they are bigoted or because they feel the community or clients may object. Or, they may feel that the exclusion of gays is justified because they believe that homosexuals are neurotic, morally degenerate, sexually dangerous to youth, and a medical danger because of AIDS.

TABLE 10.1

Hiring of Homosexuals in Selected Occupations

Do you think homosexuals should or should not be hired for each of the following occupations? First, . . . Next . . . (RANDOM ORDER)

	Hired in Following Occupations?—Trend (percent saying "yes")							
	1977	*1982*	*1985*	*1987*	*1989*	*1992*	*1996*	*1999*
Salespersons	68%	70%	71%	72%	79%	82%	90%	90%
As a member of the president's cabinet	NA	NA	NA	NA	NA	54	71	74
Doctors	44	50	52	49	56	53	59	75
Armed forces	51	52	55	55	60	57	65	70
Clergy	36	38	41	42	44	43	60	54
High school teachers	NA	NA	NA	NA	47	47	60	61
Elementary school teachers	27	32	36	33	42	41	55	54

Source: Gallup Poll Monthly, No. 375 (December 1996):13; No. 402 (March 1999):28.

The process of applying for a job is more problematic for lesbians and gays than it is for other people. The application form may ask if the applicant has ever been arrested, and if so, why. Because the laws criminalize homosexuality in many jurisdictions, lesbians and gays are more likely than heterosexuals to have a police record. Gays and lesbians are thus caught in a double bind. If, on the one hand, they disclose their arrest for homosexual behavior, they will be denied a job. On the other hand, if they conceal this fact, they will be fired for lying because most companies check information on application forms against official records. A similar situation occurs when the form asks about one's military service. Known homosexuals will have been dishonorably discharged, which is an obvious excuse for not hiring them. Finally, if applicants voluntarily disclose their homosexuality on the application, they are not likely to be hired.

About 300 occupations require that practitioners be certified by a government agency or board of professionals (e.g., architect, teacher, doctor, and barber). Applicants who possess a criminal record—which, as noted previously, is a relatively high probability for gays and lesbians—will not receive the license. Nor will they if there is evidence of supposedly bad moral character. Similarly, some jobs in government and private industry require a security clearance because of access to classified information. Homosexuals until 1995 were typically denied this clearance because it is assumed that they are susceptible to blackmail. In 1995, President Clinton by executive order decreed that homosexuals would no longer be denied clearance because of their sexuality.

A few employers are taking the lead in breaking down discrimination in the workplace. As of August 2000, over 3,500 employers offered domestic partner health insurance to their employees. Coors Brewing Company, for example, offers all family benefits to gay and lesbian employees and their partners. Thus, gay employees of Coors and their partners receive medical and dental care, vision and hearing coverage, bereavement leave, and coverage for natural or adopted children, or children of whom one partner has legal custody. Other large corporations that provide same-sex partner benefits include Microsoft, IBM, Walt Disney Company, Boeing, General Motors, Ford, Daimler Chrysler, Prudential, Motorola, General Mills, Honeywell, and Xerox. However, of the 500 largest companies only 102 provide such benefits (Gates, 2001).

Among large companies of 5,000 or more employees, 23 percent offer such benefits (Jones, 1997a). San Francisco passed an ordinance in 1997 requiring companies doing business with the city to offer benefits to gay and unmarried couples, thus putting pressure on such large corporations as United Airlines. Some progressive corporations (e.g., Microsoft, AT&T, Xerox, Apple Computer, and Pacific Gas and Electric) provide diversity training to demystify homosexuality and to encourage gay and lesbian groups within the organizations.

FIGHTING THE SYSTEM: HUMAN AGENCY

The chapter to this point has documented the hostility, anger, and abhorrence aimed at homosexuals in U.S. society. These reactions occur at the societal level through court actions that discriminate and in punitive religious ideology that condemns homosexuals' immorality. At the personal level, hostility occurs with looks, taunts, ostracism, and even violence. The objects of this assault—individual lesbian women and gay men—experience great personal stress as a result. According to Patton:

> [T]he stress of being a lesbian [woman] or gay man is enormous. Worrying about self and friends, and constructing elaborate shields against discovery and persecution occupy a great deal of time for the individual lesbian [woman] or gay man. There are virtually no local or social remedies for the organized and systematic attacks on individuals and the community by police, ministers, doctors, politicians, and the average citizen and his/her rude comments and [hostile] methods. (Patton, 1985:14)

Gays use two basic strategies for living in a society hostile to their sexual orientation. One is to conceal their sexual orientation from straights to avoid stigmatization, harassment, and discrimination. These **secret gays** segregate their lives into gay and straight activities. When in the straight world, they conceal their sexual orientation from family, friends, co-workers, and other associates. Those most likely to stay in the closet are from the working class. The structural and personal pressures against coming out are much greater for them than for those from the middle and upper classes.

Gay activists, on the other hand, identify themselves openly as homosexuals. Rather than evade the efforts of straights to stigmatize them, they challenge society in an effort to transform it. The gay men and lesbian women who confront society are the focus of this section.

The negative sanctions from society, employers, friends, and family have kept lesbians and gays for most periods of U.S. history from organizing to change a repressive situation. Political activist Emma Goldman in 1915 became the first person to speak publicly in favor of gay and lesbian rights. A few homosexual organizations were formed (the first, the Chicago Society for Human Rights in 1924, and the first modern gay rights organization, the Mattachine Society in 1950) for mutual support, but only a relatively few homosexuals were willing at the time to declare publicly their deviance from the norm of heterosexuality.

The 1960s provided a better climate for change when youths, African Americans, women, pacifists, and other groups questioned the norms and ideologies of the dominant society. This decade clearly was one of heightened awareness among the oppressed of their oppression and of the possibility that through collective efforts they could change what had seemed to be unchangeable.

The precipitating event for gay and lesbian unity occurred at 3 a.m. on June 28, 1969, when police raided the Stonewall Inn of New York's Greenwich Village. Instead of dispersing, as gays had always done in similar situations, the 200 patrons threw objects at the police and set fire to the bar. The riot lasted only 45 minutes, but it gave impetus to a number of collective efforts by gays to publicize police harassment of the gay community, job discrimination, and other indignities they faced. In effect, the Stonewall resistance came to symbolize the birth of the modern gay rights movement (Duberman, 1993).

Following Stonewall, gay liberation groups emerged in many cities and on university campuses. Many neighborhoods in major cities became openly homosexual—most notably the Castro district in San Francisco, New Town in Chicago, and Greenwich Village in New York City. These communities included gay churches, associations of professionals, health clinics, and networks of gay-owned businesses to supply the gay community's needs. The proliferation of these organizations for lesbians and gays provided a supportive climate, allowing many of them to come out of the closet.

The increased numbers of public gays and lesbians have provided the political base for changing the various forms of oppression that homosexuals routinely experience. The Gay Media Task Force promotes accurate and positive images of gays in television, films, and advertising; the Gay Rights National Lobby promotes favorable legislation; the Gay Men's Health Crisis helps gays deal with the reality of AIDS; and the National Gay Task Force serves to further gay interests by attacking the minority-group status of homosexuals in a variety of political and ideological arenas.

Two countervailing forces in the 1980s affected the gay rights movement. The election of Ronald Reagan and his conservative agenda, along with the surge of Christian fundamentalism, inhibited the movement's momentum in the first part of the decade. The AIDS epidemic acted to propel the movement in the late 1980s. As it became clear that AIDS endangered the lives of more and more gay males, the sense of a shared danger and the realization that they needed to push the government into action quickly inspired unity. More organizations formed, some directed specifically at the health needs of people with AIDS and others aimed at lobbying Congress and state governments for legislation important to gays.

On October 11, 1987, the largest gay rights demonstration occurred when approximately 250,000 lesbians, gay men, and their supporters marched in Washington, D.C. They held a parade, had a huge marriage ceremony to mock the laws forbidding the marriage of gays, mourned their comrades who had died of AIDS, staged a mass civil disobedience action at the U.S. Supreme Court to protest the 1986 decision upholding state sodomy laws (840 people were arrested), and joined with other activist groups. The Rev. Jesse Jackson spoke at the rally:

> We are together today to say we insist on legal protection under the law of every American . . . for workers' rights, for civil rights, for the rights of religious freedom, the rights of individual privacy, for the rights of sexual preference. We come together for the rights of the American people. (Quoted in Freiberg, 1987a:15)

By 2000, 31 years after Stonewall, many positive changes had occurred for the gay community:

- At the time of Stonewall, 48 states had sodomy laws meant to outlaw homosexual sex. Now 23 states have such laws.
- In 1969 no state or local government had a law protecting the civil rights of homosexuals. Iin 1996 the Supreme Court in *Romer v. Evans* ruled that states and municipalities had the right to protect gays from discrimination. Many observers feel that this ruling marked a turning point in the generation-long battle for gay rights. The majority opinion stated that gay people are a distinct class who do not receive the same protections as other people without specific legal protections. This ruling struck down a constitutional amendment passed by Colorado voters that denied civil rights protections to homosexuals. In doing so, the Supreme Court overturned efforts by states to treat gays as second-class citizens.
- In another ground-breaking decision, the Supreme Court in 1998 ruled unanimously that sexual discrimination in the workplace applies to harassment between workers of the same sex. This ruling gives civil rights protections to all employees, male or female, homosexual or heterosexual, something unheard of in 1969.
- When Del Martin and Phyllis Lyons wrote the groundbreaking *Lesbian/Woman* in 1972, not one woman mentioned in the book allowed her name to be used. In the twentieth-anniversary edition, not a single pseudonym was used.

- In 1994 more than 11,000 athletes from forty-four countries competed in Gay Games IV in New York City, an event beyond imagination in 1969.
- In 2000 there were gay and lesbian clubs meeting in more than 600 high schools, up from just 100 two years earlier (Ritter, 2000).
- In 1998 the AFL–CIO recognized Pride at Work, the national organization for gay, lesbian, bisexual, and transgender labor, as an official constituency affiliate.
- Public opinion polls show a gradual acceptance of gays and lesbians (refer back to Table 10.1).

In addition, homosexuals have made some modest gains through court decisions, laws by progressive legislatures and city commissions, and acceptance of gays and lesbians by some religious leaders and a few congregations. But huge obstacles remain. The religious right (e.g., James Dobson's Focus on the Family, Gary Bauer's Family Research Council, and Pat Robertson's Christian Broadcasting Network) refuses to yield on gay rights, making opposition to gay rights a defining issue (Lacayo,1998). Gay issues such as the ordination of gay pastors and priests and the sanctification of same-sex unions continue to divide religious denominations and local churches. Many localities have voted down efforts to ban discrimination against gays in housing and employment. In 1998 President Clinton signed an executive order to protect homosexual federal workers from job discrimination. This sparked strategies by Republican conservatives to place amendments on spending bills that would prohibit the government from spending money to carry out Clinton's order. This is consistent with efforts by conservatives to roll back some or all of the gains of the last 30 years. The Republican Party during the 1992, 1994, 1996, 1998, and 2000 election campaigns made thinly veiled attacks on homosexuals in their "family values" rhetoric (another form of "gay bashing"). In short, homosexuals still remain a target. As Brownworth notes:

> [G]ay men and lesbians are the only minority in the country . . . that it is still safe to scapegoat. . . . In Philadelphia, where a gay rights bill was adopted more than nine years ago, a recent study . . . found that a majority of gays and lesbians felt the law did not protect them or that they had no recourse against discrimination. A recent report by the National Gay and Lesbian Task Force, citing several university-based studies, finds that anti-gay violence is on the rise, and that gay men and women are four to seven times as likely to be victims of violence as any other group. . . . Rampant discrimination and the lack of legal recourse remain compelling reasons for many to stay in the closet, reaffirming homophobia. (Brownworth, 1989:5–6)

CHAPTER REVIEW

1. Homosexuals are a minority group in U.S. society. They are relatively powerless and the objects of negative stereotypes and discrimination.
2. Unlike the status of most minorities, the minority status of homosexuals is based on deviance from society's norms rather than on ascribed characteristics. There are several important characteristics of social deviance: (a) it is socially created; (b) it is a relative, not an absolute, concept; (c) it is found universally in societies; (d) it serves society by reaffirming the rules; (e) it allows the powerful to determine who or what is deviant; and (f) it creates an atmosphere in which deviants can be stigmatized for their disreputable behavior.
3. The response to homosexuals varies by society and historical period. Although homosexuality is considered deviant behavior in contemporary U.S. society, it was not so considered in ancient Greece and Rome. Nor is it deviant among some Native American tribes.

4. The identification as homosexual is a master status superseding other characteristics for most heterosexuals. Because this status is stigmatized, the accomplishments of gays do not negate their powerful but negative master status in the opinions of other people.
5. Although the proportion of the population that is homosexual is not known and is probably unknowable, the best estimate is 10 percent. About three-fourths of lesbian couples live together, as do about half of gay male couples. Gay men are more likely than lesbian women to have sex with someone other than their steady partners, a similarity shared with heterosexual males. Homosexual couples are much more likely than heterosexual couples to be egalitarian. Contrary to the common stereotype, homosexual couples are not composed of a "male" partner and a "female" partner. Finally, being a homosexual is not necessarily a master status for the person involved.
6. Variance from the societal norm of heterosexuality is not a social problem; the societal response to it is. Gays confront three types of oppression: (a) ideological, stemming from traditional homophobic beliefs, especially religious and medical; (b) legal, stemming from the law, court decisions, and behaviors by society's social control agents; and (c) occupational, where jobs, advancement, and income are restricted or denied.
7. Homosexuals use two basic strategies to cope with living in a society hostile to their sexual orientation. One is to conceal their homosexuality from heterosexuals. The other is to identify openly as a homosexual. Gay activists, of course, are in this latter category. Rather than evade the efforts of straights to stigmatize them, they challenge society in an effort to transform it.
8. The challenge to change society's oppression of homosexuals began with the Stonewall Inn riot in 1969. Since then, homosexuals have organized communities, organized protests, and formed self-help and political lobbying organizations.

KEY TERMS

Deviance. Behavior that does not conform to social expectations.

Heterosexuality. Sexual orientation toward someone of the opposite sex.

Compulsory heterosexuality. Beliefs and practices that enforce heterosexual behavior as normal while stigmatizing other forms of sexual expression.

Homosexuality. Sexual orientation toward someone of the same sex.

Bisexuality. Sexual orientation toward or attraction to both sexes.

Master status. Position so important that it dominates all other statuses.

Stigma. Powerful negative social label that affects a person's social identity and self-concept.

Sexual preference. Person's choice regarding the sex of people to whom he or she is attracted.

Sexual orientation. Sexual attraction to the same or opposite sex is not a matter of choice but is determined by genetic or environmental factors.

Homophobia. Fear or loathing of homosexuality and homosexuals.

Sodomy. Oral or anal sex.

Secret gays. Homosexuals who conceal their sexual orientation.

Gay activists. Homosexuals who openly identify themselves as such and challenge society in an effort to eliminate the stigma and discrimination they face.

WEBSITES FOR FURTHER REFERENCE

http://www.indiana.edu/~kinsey/SSRC/sexreas.html
Sexuality Research: This website was created by the Social Science Research Council and represents a summary of a report done on why sexuality should be researched in the United States. This summary comes from a more comprehensive report, done by the Social Science Research Council: *Sexuality Research in the United States: An Assessment of the Social and Behavioral Sciences*.

http://www.sexuality.org/
The Society for Human Sexuality is an all-volunteer social and educational organization devoted to the

appreciation of the myriad consensual forms of human relationships and sexual expression. The site is packed with great resources and information.

http://www.biresource.org/
Bisexual Resource Center: A resource of information about bisexuality from the creators of the *Bisexual Resource Guide.* Contains pamphlets on bisexuality available for download; sells bi books, music, and products; and lists online resources.

http://www.hrw.org/reports/2001/uslgbt
HumanRightsWatch.Org dedicates itself to "defending human rights worldwide." Currently it features a report called "Hatred in the Hallways." This report outlines violence against gays, lesbians, bisexuals, and transgendered people in schools, and discusses ways to combat against this hatred. The full report is also available online.

http://www.datalounge.net/lha/
Lesbian Herstory Archives: A guide to a wide-ranging collection of resources, including many primary resources—books, manuscripts, magazines, and photographs.

http://www.lambdalegal.org/cgi-bin/iowa/index.html
The Lamda Legal Defense and Education Fund is the nation's oldest and largest legal organization dedicated to the civil rights of lesbians, gay men, and people with HIV/AIDS.

http://www.glsen.org/
The Gay, Lesbian and Straight Education Network (GLSEN) strives to assure that each member of every school community is valued and respected regardless of sexual orientation or gender identity/expression. GLSEN is the leading national organization fighting to end antigay bias in K–12 schools.

http://www.ngltf.org/
The National Gay and Lesbian Task Force (NGLTF) is the national progressive organization working for the civil rights of gay, lesbian, bisexual, and transgendered people, with the vision and commitment to building a powerful political movement

http://www.glaad.org
The Gay and Lesbian Alliance Against Defamation (GLAAD) was formed in New York in 1985 and began by protesting *The New York Post*'s blatantly offensive and sensationalized stories about AIDS. Its mission was to improve the public's attitudes toward homosexuality and to put an end to violence and discrimination against lesbians and gay men. "GLAAD's impact on the media is far-reaching. Not only has GLAAD changed the way that gays and lesbians are portrayed on the screen and in the news, GLAAD has also become a major source of information for decision makers in both the entertainment and news media. In 1992, Entertainment Weekly named GLAAD as one of Hollywood's most powerful entities and *The Los Angeles Times* described the group as possibly the most successful organizations lobbying the media for inclusion. GLAAD has not only reached industry insiders, but has also impacted millions through newspapers, magazines, motion pictures, television, and visibility campaigns."

http://www.outproud.org/
The website for OutProud, The National Coalition for Gay, Lesbian, Bisexual, and Transgender Youth invites you "to take advantage of the wide range of resources available for youth and educators by clicking on any icon to get to the related subject area."

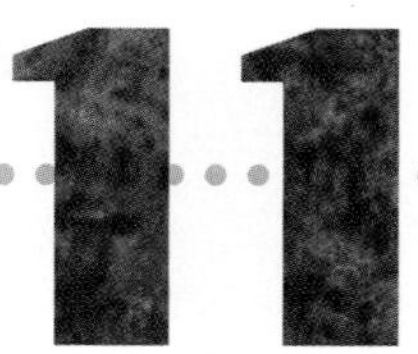

11 Disability and Ableism

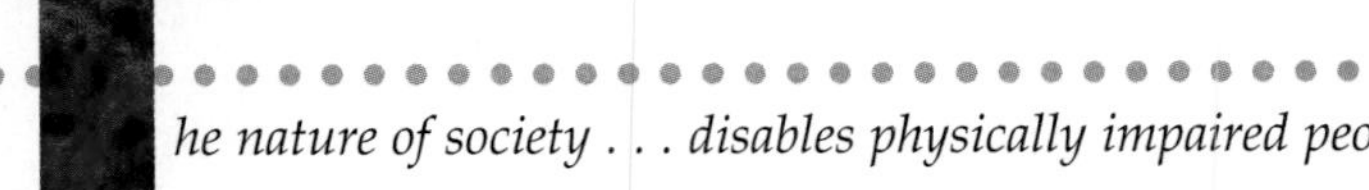

he nature of society . . . disables physically impaired people.

—Victor Finkelstein

This section of the book has been devoted to various forms of inequality, examining categories of people experiencing discrimination, negative stereotypes, and powerlessness because of their being different from the dominant category in economic resources (the impoverished), racial classification (people of color), gender (females), and sexual orientation (gays and lesbians). This chapter turns our attention to another category of people defined as different and who constitute a minority group—those with physical, sensory, or cognitive impairments. This category is the largest minority group in the United States. People with disabilities, however, while sharing the characteristics of a minority group in most ways, differ in one significant way—it is a category in which most of us will eventually be included.

> It is a category whose constituency is contingency itself. Any of us who identify as "nondisabled" must know that our self-designation is inevitably temporary, and that a car crash, a virus, a degenerative genetic disease, or a precedent-setting legal decision could change our status in ways over which we have no control whatsoever. (Berube, 1998:viii)

The facts are these: 20 percent of people in the United States have some form of impairment (55 million in 2000). About 15 percent of people with a disability were born with it, 85 percent will experience a disabling condition in the course of their lives, usually from accidents, disease, environmental hazards, or criminal victimization (Russell, 2000). The probability of disability increases with age (approximately half of those 80 and older, for example, have Alzheimer's, a disease of the brain that erases memory and judgment). Since the population 65 and older is the fastest growing segment of the U.S. population, the proportion of the disabled will continue to increase. For example, in 1950, 600,000 Americans were 85 and older; in 2000, there were 4.3 million in this category, and in 2030 there will be 8.5 million.

Social scientists, until recently, have largely ignored people with disabilities because their impairments were considered physical and psychic shortcomings, having little to do with the social. That is a false assumption. The very definition of who is able and who is disabled is a social construction; the stereotypes and fears about people who are disabled are social constructions; and society creates financial, physical, and discriminatory barriers for people who are disabled.

Definitions

The definition of disability influences how people relate to people who they perceive to be disabled, and how people who are disabled think of themselves. Because of the way disability is typically defined, disabled people may be feared, distrusted, pitied, overprotected, and patronized (Barton, 1996:8).

Individual Model of Disability

The individual approach to disability (also known as the medical model of disability) defines disability in terms of some physiological impairment due to

Eighty-five percent of people will experience a disabling condition in the course of their lives.

genetic heritage, accident, or disease. "As a form of biological determinism, the focus of disability is on physical, behavioural, psychological, cognitive, and sensory tragedy. Thus the problem to be addressed by disability services is situated within the disabled individual (Gilson and Depoy, 2000:208). This view is commonly held. The federal government, for example, defines *disability* as any physical or mental condition that substantially limits one or more major life activities and *disabled* as anyone who is regarded as having such an impairment. A person who is disabled might have difficulty performing activities such as personal care, walking, seeing, hearing, speaking, learning, or working (Taub and Fanflik, 2000:13). The problem with focusing on the physical or mental impairment of people is that individuals are defined as deficient, inferior, and incomplete since they do not conform to what the majority in society define as "normal." While some people with disabilities internalize these negative attitudes about themselves, others reject being defined as abnormal and thus dismiss the medical model as the dominant model of disability (Llewellyn and Hogan, 2000).

Because the focus is on the individual, the goal of rehabilitation is for health practitioners to overcome, or at least minimize, the negative consequences of an individual's disability by addressing the person's special needs and personal difficulties. If possible, these health professionals would like to return disabled individuals to the "normal" condition of being able-bodied. While these goals seem appropriate, they make people with disabilities dependent on a vast army of allied professionals who dominate their lives (Barnes, Mercer, and Shakespeare, 1999:25). Moreover, adaptation to the environment is stressed, rather than changing the social arrangements that make life difficult for people with disabilities. Because of the emphasis on the individual, "courage, independence, will-power are all lauded when a disabled person proves that overcoming disability is a matter of individual effort" (Llewellyn and Hogan, 2000:158). The concentration on the biology of disability also defines people by only one dimension, ignoring their other qualities. To counteract this problem, we use the phrase "person with a disability" rather than "a disabled person," thereby reorienting our social construction so that it puts the human being first and the impairment second rather than making the impairment the defining characteristic (Linton, 1998:13).*

Finally, a note of caution. People with disabilities are a heterogeneous category. Where most have visible impairments, others have invisible disabilities such as chronic pain or dyslexia. Those who cannot hear face different societally induced problems than those who cannot see or those people who must use wheelchairs. Thus, as we discuss people with disabilities, we must remember that the people involved are complex, varying by type of disability and their other social locations (e.g., gender, race, social class, sexual orientation).

Social Model of Disability

The social model, while acknowledging the biological conditions of disability, challenges the notion that disability is primarily a medical category. From this perspective, the real problem with physical and mental impairment is *not* physical but social: It is the way people with able bodies view people with disabilities and the institutionalization of these views that are the genuine handicaps (Duncan, 2001; Oliver, 1996b). For adherents of the social model, the consequence of the power to define the identity of the disabled by professionals results in the disempowerment, marginalization, and dependency of people with disabilities (Barton, 1996:9). It is the limited physical access, limited access to resources, and negative attitudes that create barriers that interfere with the potential of people with disabilities to actualize their desired roles (Gilson and Depoy, 2000). Furthermore, it is the way that people with disabilities are oppressed by societal views of normality. In effect, then, society disables people. Consider, for example, the argument by a man with a disability:

> [We] are disabled by buildings that are not designed to admit us, and this in turn leads to a whole range of further disablements, regarding our education, our chances for gaining employment, our social lives and so on. However this argument is usually rejected, precisely because to accept it involves recognizing the extent to which we are not merely unfortunate, but are directly oppressed by a hostile social environment. (Brisenden, 1986:176)

With the incredible medical, technological, and manufacturing advances available, many people made dysfunctional by infection, injury, or deleterious genes "need not remain so if appropriate social arrangements are in place to address these deficits. . . . in this sense, then, when disadvantage attendant on disability goes unremedied, its persistence is a social rather than a biological phenomenon" (Silvers, 1998:16).

*The naming of people with disabilities is a complicated issue. On the one hand, many people with disabilities have wanted to keep disability as a characteristic of the individual as opposed to the defining characteristic. Yet beginning in the early 1990s the term "disabled people" became popular among disability rights activists. Rather than keeping disability as a secondary characteristic, *disabled* became a marker of identity that they wanted to highlight as they protested for social change (Linton, 1998:13).

Congruent with this perspective, the Union of Physically Impaired Against Segregation (UPIAS) in the United Kingdom promotes this definition of disability: "*Disability* is the disadvantage or restriction of activity caused by a contemporary social organization which takes no or little account of people who have physical impairments and thus excludes them from participation in the mainstream of social activities" (UPIAS, 1976:3–4). The social model of disability redirects attention away from the individual and places the problem back on to the collective responsibility of society (Llewellyn and Hogan, 2000:159). The social model focuses on the experience of disability. It considers a wide range of social, economic, and political factors and conditions such as family circumstances, financial support, education, employment, housing, transportation, the built environment, disabling barriers and attitudes in society, and the impact of government policies and welfare support systems (Barnes, Mercer, and Shakespeare, 1999:31).

Adherents of the social model see the goal of rehabilitation much different from the individual model.

> A social model of disability is socially constructed. This lens views the locus of the "problem" to be addressed by services and supports within the social context in which individuals interact. Rather than attempting to change or fix the person with the disability, a social model of disability sets service goals as removal of social and environmental barriers to full social, physical, career and spiritual participation. (Gilson and Depoy, 2000:208)

But it is more than the removal of architectural or other physical barriers.

> The social model is not about showing that every dysfunction in our bodies can be compensated for by a gadget, or good design, so that everybody can work an 8-hour day and play badminton in the evenings. It's a way of demonstrating that everyone—even someone who has no movement, no sensory function and who is going to die tomorrow—has the right to a certain standard of living and to be treated with respect. (Vasey, 1992:44).

Toward a More Complete Definition of Disability

The assumptions of both the medical and social models of disability are contradictory. Taken alone, each of these perspectives fosters a one-sided and, therefore, incomplete and faulty perception and interpretation on disability and people with disabilities. A synthesis that combines the best of each model will aid our understanding and allow for an acceptable definition.

The individual (medical) model is correct in that there is an **ontological truth** (a universal and undeniable reality) to the claim that disabilities result from some physiological or mental impairment. It follows, then, that disabled people do need medical support at specific points in their lives (Barton, 1996:9). But this emphasis on locating problems and solutions within the disabled person is only half of the equation because it overlooks the role of society in defining and creating barriers for people with disabilities. The social model points to the very real (ontological) social barriers for most people with disabilities.

The definition of disability that we use combines the insights of the individual and social models: **Disability,** then, refers to a reduced ability to perform tasks one would normally do at a given stage of life that are exacerbated by the individual and institutional discrimination that people with disabilities encounter.

People with Disabilities as a Minority Group

Disability shares a number of characteristics common to the social constructions of race, sex and gender, and sexual orientation, thus making it a minority group as are they.* These are: (1) being defined as different, (2) derogatory names, (3), their "differentness" is a master status, (4) categorization, stigma, and stereotypes, (5) exclusion and segregation, (6) the matrix of domination, and (7) discrimination.

Defined as Different

Minority groups are socially constructed categories. Which categories have minority status varies from society to society and over time within a society. Society assigns some categories of people—in the United States, the categories are races other than Caucasian, certain ethnic groups, women, homosexuals, and people with disabilities—to minority status. The minority is composed of people with similar characteristics that are defined as significantly different from the dominant group. These characteristics are salient: they are visible, though not necessarily physical, and they make a difference. Whites dominate Blacks, Whites dominate Latinos, men dominate women, heterosexuals dominate homosexuals, and the able-bodied dominate people with disabilities.

Naming

Naming is not a neutral process; the names given to the members of minority groups by the majority have enormous symbolic significance that contributes to and perpetuates the dominance of the majority (Hall, 1985; Eitzen and Baca Zinn, 1989b). These pejorative names belittle, trivialize, exclude, diminish, deprecate, and demean. In essence, pejorative names not only put the minority "down" but they also separate and segregate. Just as "boy" can be blatantly offensive to minority men, so "girl" can have comparable patronizing and demeaning implications for women" (Miller and Swift, 1980:71). Gays and lesbians are called "queers" and "faggots," terms that clearly separate them from the heterosexual majority.

Consider the implications of names for people with disabilities such as "invalid," "cripple," "freak," "gimp," "vegetable," "dumb," "deformed," "handicapped," and "retard." These labels imply not only impairment but also a lack of worth, marginality, and their dependence on the "able" (Barton, 1996). The images that these names evoke are opposite the notion that "disability stems from the failure of a structured social environment to adjust to the needs and aspirations of citizens with disabilities *rather* than from the inability of a disabled individual to adapt to the demands of society" (Hahn, 1986:128).

*There are several ways to view people with disabilities. We use the minority groups model because of its: (1) emphasis on social and economic discrimination, (2) consistency with our structural emphasis that explains systematic exclusion on the basis of gender, class, race, and sexual orientation, and (3) emphasis on social factors rather than biological and cultural ones (Block, Balcazar, and Keys, 2000).

Minority as a Master Status

Although people have many statuses simultaneously, typically one of these is dominant. This is known as a **master status.** This master status may be imposed by others, or it can also be internalized by the individual with exceptional significance for social identity. The master status of minority group members is (are) the characteristic(s) that distinguish them from the majority. That is, African Americans or gays or homeless families are known and identified by others foremost by their race, sexual orientation, or impoverishment. Disability can be and often is a master status, as people frequently perceive those with disabilities first in terms of their disability and only second as individuals. That is, an impairment such as blindness or using a wheelchair is seen as the most salient part of a person's identity, and therefore trumps all other statuses such as occupation, educational attainment, and income level.

Categorization, Stigma, and Stereotypes

Not only are minority members singled out by their master status, they encounter the negative stereotypes and beliefs that accompany their defining characteristics. In other words, being a minority is not only a master status but it is a master status with a stigma. A **stigma** is an attribute that is socially devalued and disgraced. Sociologist Erving Goffman describes it this way:

> While the stranger is present before us, evidence can arise of his possessing an attribute that makes him different from others in the category of persons available for him to be, and of a less desirable kind—in the extreme, a person who is quite thoroughly bad, or dangerous, or weak. He is thus reduced in our minds from a whole and usual person to a tainted, discounted one. Such an attribute is a stigma, especially when its discrediting effect is very extensive; sometimes it is also called a failing, a shortcoming, a handicap. (Goffman, 1963:3)

People with stigmas have what Goffman called a spoiled identity, and this spoiled identity has negative consequences.

> By definition, of course, we believe the person with a stigma is not quite human. On this assumption we exercise varieties of discrimination, through which we effectively, if often unthinkingly, reduce his life chances. We construct a stigma-theory, an ideology to explain his inferiority and account for the danger he represents, sometimes rationalizing an animosity based on other differences such as those of social class. We use specific stigma terms such as cripple, bastard, moron in our daily discourse as a source of metaphor and imagery, typically without giving thought to the original meaning. We tend to impute a wide range of imperfections on the basis of the original one, and at the same time to impute some desirable but undesired attributes, often of a supernatural cast, such as "sixth sense," or "understanding." (Goffman, 1963:5)

Minority group members are stigmatized. The majority defines certain characteristics as different and abnormal and then discriminates against those in the category defined as inferior. Thus, some people are "in" while others are defined as "out" or they are either "us" or "them." In effect, the minority is defined as "other" because they have characteristics that differ from the majority. The definition is simplified by making the distinctions binary. "'Race' becomes Black or White, 'gender' becomes male or female, 'sexual orientation' becomes gay or straight, and people are either disabled or normal" (Gordon and Rosenblum, 2001:12). In each instance, the side defined as "other" is considered not only different but deficient. Their characteristics are stigmatized. For example, people with disabilities face the negative evaluations given their identity by society.

> Whatever the physically impaired person may think of [themselves], [they are] given a negative identity by society, and much of social life is a struggle against this imposed image. It is for this reason that we can say that stigmatization is less a by-product of disability than its substance. The greatest impediment to a [disabled] person's taking full part in society is . . . the tissue of myths, fears, and misunderstandings that society attaches to them. (Murphy, 1995:140)

The disabled confront the dichotomous comparison with the able-bodied where they always come up short in one of two ways. Many internalize the inadequacy society regularly ascribes to them, thinking of themselves as incomplete or broken. Others reject the dichotomy dictated by society. "Although they certainly have greater physical challenges to overcome, they discover authenticity in them, not embarrassment or shame" (Tingus, 2000:10B).

The dominant members of society perceive disability as a medical matter, associating disability with physiological, anatomical, or mental "defects." Viewed in this way, those with physical and mental impairments seem like they are not only different but that they lack the "normal" interests and concerns that occupy others of their social class, race, gender, age, and gender orientation. In short, their "otherness" moves them to the margins of society as "inferiors."

The disabled, therefore, confront not only the challenges of living with their conditions but the challenges of inequality characterizied by **ableism.** The short definition of ableism is discrimination in favor of the able-bodied (Tullock, 1993). Similar to racism and sexism, ableism also includes "the idea that a person's abilities or characteristics are determined by disability or that people with disabilities as a group are inferior to nondisabled people" (Linton, 1998:9). As an example, research shows that those who murder children with disabilities are punished less severely by the criminal justice system than those who murder able children (Unnithan, 1994).

A longer and more inclusive definition illuminates further:

> Ableism is that set of often contradictory stereotypes about people with disabilities that acts as a barrier to keep them from achieving their full potential as equal citizens of society. Among these are the beliefs that people with disabilities are inherently unable to manage their own lives, that they are embittered and malevolent, and that they are, by reason of their disability, morally, intellectually, and spiritually inferior to temporarily able-bodied people, or, conversely, that people with disabilities are saintlike, ever cheerful, asexual, childlike, and unusually heroic. Ultimately, it is the belief that people with disabilities are different from normal people, and that their lives are inherently less worthwhile than those of people without disabilities. It is the "ism" at the root of discrimination against people with disabilities on the job, in school, and in the community. (Pelka, 1997:3)

Implicit in the ideology of ableism that permeates U.S. society is the belief that disability is an *individual* problem, susceptible to individual solutions. This frees the nondisabled to ignore or minimize social issues of accessibility, accommodation, and personhood (Duncan, 2001).

Exclusion and Segregation

Stigmatized race, sex/gender, and sexual orientation categories have traditionally been excluded from full participation in society by institutional barriers or custom. Historically, racial minorities have been excluded through Jim Crow segregation, Supreme Court rulings (e.g., *Plessy v. Ferguson,* which gave "separate but equal" facilities legal authority), and legislation that denied voting and other civil rights. Although recent laws have outlawed blatant discrimination by race, there is still de facto segregation in residential housing, in schools, and in private clubs. Women were once property of their husbands. Their "imputed physical and mental frailty . . . became the grounds for refusing her any civil or legal rights" (Miles, 1988:187). Women today are underrepresented in the professions and in leadership positions in government, business, and religious organizations. Gays are not allowed as leaders in the Boy Scouts. Same-sex marriages are illegal, and the rights of gays and lesbians to adopt is difficult and in some states impossible because of legal barriers.

Historically, people with disabilities were often separated by segregated housing, sheltered workshops, and, occasionally, in attics and basements to hide a family's shame. They have also been separated in nursing homes, asylums, and hospitals for "incurables." In the past, children with disabilities were separated from their "able" classmates in separate "special education" classrooms.

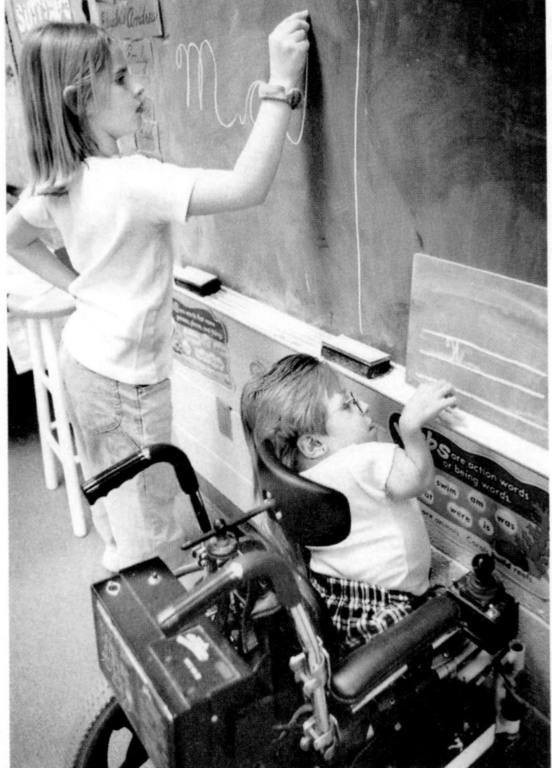

The Disabilities Education Act has been interpreted to mean that children with disabilities should be included in classrooms with typically developing children.

However, the Individuals with Disabilities Education Act (IDEA), originally passed as the Education for All Handicapped Children Act in 1975, now requires that children be educated in the "least restrictive environment." This requirement generally has been interpreted to mean that children with disabilities should be included in classrooms with typically developing children. Although inclusion is required by law, many children continue to be segregated in special education classes. Sometimes, of course, "special education" is reasonable, allowing educators to be more responsive to the "special" needs of children who cannot see, hear, think, or move as well as others. There are drawbacks, however, as those segregated as "different" are sometimes objects of abuse by other students. "Special education" teachers may be either more attentive to the conditions of their students than to their scholarship and/or they may have reduced expectations for them, resulting in a negative self-fulfilling prophecy. The evidence is that children with disabilities who have been in segregated schooling are, in general, less well prepared than other children to exercise the skills and knowledge in the basic subjects of English, math, and science (Silvers, 1998:24).

Despite the Americans with Disabilities Act, which requires the elimination of architectural barriers, many still remain and thus people with disabilities are often separated from mainstream society by the lack of access to public transportation or by architectural barriers.

> The present forms of architectural structures and social institutions exist because statutes, ordinances, and codes either required or permitted them to be constructed in that manner. These public policies imply values, expectations and assumptions about the physical and behavioral attributes that people ought to possess in order to survive or to participate in community life. Many everyday activities, such as the distance people walk, the steps they climb, the materials they read, and the messages they receive impose stringent requirements on persons with different levels of functional skills. (Hahn, 1988:40)

It does not matter if policymakers intend their policies to discriminate, what matters are the consequences of their actions. "Stairs, curbs, or small-print signs hung over doorways make admission nearly impossible. They may lack discriminatory intent, but they have the effect nonetheless" (Gordon and Rosenblum, 2001:12).

Matrix of Domination

The hierarchies of stratification—class, race, gender, and sexual orientation—place socially constructed groups, and the individuals and families assigned to those groups, in different social locations (this section is taken from Baca Zinn and Eitzen, 1999:135–136). Placement in these hierarchies determines to what extent one will have or not have the rewards and resources of society. These are also systems of power and domination, as those from dominant race, class, gender, and sexuality groups play a part in and benefit from the oppression of subordinates.

These stratification hierarchies are interrelated. People of color and women, for example, have fewer occupational choices than do White males. People of color and women typically earn less income for the work they do, resulting in advantage for White males. Thus, these systems of inequality intersect to form a **matrix of domination** in which each of us exists (Collins, 1990). These intersections of oppression have important implications.

> First, people experience race, class, gender, and sexuality differently depending on their social location in these structures of inequality. For example, people of the same race will experience race differently depending on their location in the class structure as poor, working class, professional/managerial class, or unemployed and their location in the gender structure as male or female and in the sexuality system as heterosexual or homosexual.
>
> Second, class, race, and gender are components of both social structure and social interaction. As a result, individuals because of their social locations experience different forms of privilege and subordination. In short, these intersecting forms of inequality produce both oppression and opportunity.
>
> A third implication of the inequality matrix has to do with the relational nature of dominance and subordination. Power is embedded in each system of stratification, determining whether one is dominant or subordinate. The intersectional nature of hierarchies means that power differentials are linked in systematic ways, reinforcing power differentials across hierarchies. (Eitzen and Baca Zinn, 2001:238–239; see also Baca Zinn and Dill, 1996)

An important insight from this matrix of domination approach is that discrimination is more than additive. To be a disabled African American lesbian, for example, is to be marginalized and discriminated against in simultaneous and multiple ways. As one woman put it: "As a black disabled woman, I cannot compartmentalize or separate aspects of my identity in this way. The collective experience of my race, disability and gender are what shape and inform my life" (Hill, 1994:7). Thus, we cannot study classism, racism, sexism, homophobia, or ablism or any other oppression in isolation from each other (Oliver, 1996b:37; Block, Balcazar, and Keys, 2001).

Discrimination

By definition, minority group members experience discrimination. They are the last to be hired and the first to be fired (e.g., the unemployment rate for African Americans is typically twice that for Whites). Racial minorities experience problems involving fairness in the criminal justice system, in obtaining loans, in housing, in schools, and other institutions. So, too, do people with disabilities find discrimination throughout their lives. Some examples (from Russell, 1998, 2000):

- Forty-seven percent of applicants genetically screened for insurance are denied health insurance because of "defects."
- Thirty-four percent of adults with disabilities live in households with an annual income of less than $15,000, compared to 12 percent of those without disabilities.
- Seventy percent of working-age disabled people are unemployed and 79 percent report that they want a job. In addition, for those who are employed many are underemployed in low-level, low-paying jobs.
- On average, workers with a disability make 85 percent (for men) and 70 percent (for women) of what their co-workers without disabilities earn. When people who are disabled are also Latino, African American, or Native American, there is an increased chance for unemployment and, for those who are employed, an even greater difference in wages than for their nondisabled co-workers (Kendall, 2001).

The discrimination that people with disabilities experience is related to how they are perceived by the rest of society. If society is convinced that disabled people cannot have good lives, then there is no reason to invest in equal education, equal access, and equal opportunity for them (see the "Voices" panel).

ISSUES OF GENDER, SEXUAL BEHAVIOR, AND FERTILITY

Although people with disabilities deal with a number of social barriers, our discussion here is limited to sexual relationships and related issues. We focus on sexuality because it demonstrates so clearly how social factors often negatively affect people with disabilities.

Gender Stereotyping

The foregoing section showed that people with disabilities are marginalized and stigmatized in U.S. society. This occurs, in part, because women and men with disabilities do not measure up to the cultural beliefs for each gender (this section is dependent on Gerschick and Miller, 2001). For the physically disabled, their bodies are perceived as unattractive. The bodies of physically disabled men do not allow them to demonstrate the socially valuable characteristics of toughness, competitiveness, and ability (Messner, 1992). Anthropologist Robert Murphy writes of his own experiences with disability: "Paralytic disability constitutes emasculation of a more direct and total nature. For the male, the weakening and atrophy of the body threaten all the cultural values of masculinity: strength, activeness, speed, virility, stamina, and fortitude" (Murphy, 1990:94). **Hegemonic** (the dominant belief system) masculinity privileges men who are strong, aggressive, independent, and self-reliant. But men who are physically disabled are perceived to have polar opposite traits, as they are treated as weak, passive, pitiful, and dependent. Men with physical disabilities may cope with the fundamental incongruity by constructing their own sense of masculinity (Gerschick and Miller, 2001). They may do all they can to meet society's definition of masculinity by becoming as athletic and competitive as possible (e.g., lifting weights, playing wheelchair basketball, participating in the paralympics). Others may redefine masculinity to fit their own unique characteristics (e.g., achieving a sense of independence by controlling those around them; redefining gender in terms of emotional relations rather than the emphasis on the physical). Still others may reject society's standards by either denying masculinity's importance in life or by creating alternative masculine identities and subcultures that provide them with a supportive environment. For example, a man who no longer can be sexually active might reject the importance of fathering through sexual intercourse. Consider this rationale by an informant:

> There's no reason why we (his fiancee and himself) couldn't use artificial insemination or adoption. Parenting doesn't necessary involve being the male sire. It involves being a good parent. . . . Parenting doesn't mean that it's your physical child. It involves responsibility and an emotional role as well. I don't think the link between parenthood is the primary link with sexuality. (Quoted in Gerschick and Miller, 2001:323–324)

As difficult as dealing with disability is for men, it is as burdensome if not more so for women. Women with physical disabilities, similar to men, do not measure up to the cultural ideals of what it is to be a woman. Consequently,

VOICES

YOUR FEARS, MY REALITIES

Most of us are morally certain that we're not prejudiced against people with disabilities. Don't we root for Christopher Reeve and Jerry's Kids with our hearts and minds and checkbooks? (Many disabled people think we shouldn't, but that's another matter.)

Didn't we cheer for Jeannie VanVelkinburgh when she was shot and paralyzed by Nathan Thill? Aren't we genuine admirers of Stephen Hawking and Muhammad Ali? How could we discriminate?

To understand disability discrimination, look close to home. Its most transparent feature is that it is caused by fear. We are the living proof that minds and bodies can go haywire and that it can happen to anyone at any time. Some people aren't ready for that news, so they react to us with overt anxiety or hostility.

But it's more subtle forms of discrimination that harm us the most. To cite one ubiquitous example, every family newspaper in the country runs occasional profiles of people with disabilities. They're usually found in the Living section, and they're usually fawning.

They marvel that we can keep our faith in the face of adversity, graduate from college, raise kids or maintain a generous attitude. If we appear to overcome our disabilities—something that's not really feasible for most of us—so much the better. Then we're brave, we're true, we inspire.

The trouble with these feel-good stories is that they become archetypal. By celebrating a single achiever as newsworthy and remarkable, they confirm society's low expectations for all other people with disabilities. Doesn't the exception prove the rule? And aren't we brave because we live lives that readers think they couldn't or wouldn't live themselves? Don't we inspire because we make them feel grateful that they're not like us?

The reading public loves our imagined triumphs of mind over matter, but not our real issues.

It loves us when we're docile, asexual and childlike, but not when we vent our anger that the deck is stacked against us. It loved VanVelkinburgh's courage at the crime scene and her readiness to move on with her life, but loved her less after a court appearance when she proved herself to be a real, mercurial person rather than patience on a monument. Real people are harder to deal with than idealized fictions.

After my injury in 1968, my business partner told me he would have killed himself under similar circumstances. Even my mother briefly toyed with the idea that I might be better off dead than disabled. "If I were paralyzed," people still tell me, "I couldn't handle it."

"Nonsense," I say, "you'd cope with it fine." But you seldom believe me. You think I'm still being brave, painting a happy face on the unspeakable. Disability discrimination is about your fears, not my realities.

Discrimination deepens when an entire nation takes this view of disability. If society is convinced that we can't have good lives, it's slow to invest in equal education, equal access and equal opportunity. And even though most people know at heart that sooner or later they're likely to become disabled themselves, they're slow to act on readily achievable solutions because they're scared to death of disability's stigma. This is disability discrimination, and it's largely unconscious.

The result of this attitude—as successive Harris polls since the early '80s have consistently shown—is that people with disabilities are the poorest minority in America. We have less money, less employment, less education, less transportation, less recreation, less of almost anything you can think of. We're the have-nots of this country.

It's not because people hate us. It's because they assume that our lives are so terrible that any effort to level the playing field is futile. And it's not because disability is so tough. It's because our cultural bias perpetuates the inequities.

Source: Barry Corbet. 2000. "Your Fears, My Realities." *Denver Post* (August 23):11B.

many think of themselves as asexual or unattractive. Many of these women feel undermined by a society that defines a woman's sexual attractiveness in terms of physical fitness and physical beauty, characteristics that are impossible for many of them to reach. Nancy Mairs writes about her physicality in this light:

> My shoulders droop and my pelvis thrusts forward as I try to balance myself upright, throwing my frame into a bony S. As a result of contractures, one shoulder is higher than the other and I carry one arm bent in front of me, the fingers curled into a claw. My left arm and leg have wasted into pipe stems, and I try always to keep them covered. When I think about how my body must look to others, especially to men, to whom I have been trained to display myself, I feel ludicrous, even loathsome. (Mairs, 1992:63)

Women with disabilities are disadvantaged over men with impairments when it comes to occupying traditional roles. Men with disabilities are more likely to be employed than women with disabilities, even filling socially powerful male roles such as President Franklin D. Roosevelt (use of a wheelchair and crutches because of polio) or Representative James Langevin of Rhode Island, who in 2000 became the first quadriplegic elected to Congress, or Senator Max Cleland of Georgia who is missing both legs and an arm. Disabled women, on the other hand, are often even denied access to tradititonal female roles as ableist and sexist stereotypes combine in much of the public, making it difficult even for the friends and relatives of disabled women to envision them as functional wives and mothers (Hanna and Rogovsky, 1991).

In heterosexual relationships, men with disabilities are more likely to maintain their relationships while women with disabilities are more likely to be abandoned (Shakespeare, 1996:202). At least one fourth "of all married women who become disabled eventually are separated or divorced, nearly twice the rate for similarly situated nondisabled women and for disabled men" (Silvers, 1998:37).

Sexual Relationships

Increasingly, more and more people with disabilities have positive and fulfilled sexual lives. Many form strong and happy relationships with other people with disabilities or with nondisabled partners. The growing Disability Rights Movement (a topic discussed further at the end of this chapter), with its emphases on removing social barriers and social oppression is important in this regard because it has helped provide people with disabilities a positive identity by working together to achieve common goals. The resulting activism has opened up many possibilities as disabled people end their isolation, engage in political acts, and make friends with others in the movement. But sexual problems remain, not because of individual incapacity but because of prejudice, discrimination, and structural barriers (this section is taken primarily from Shakespeare, 1996:192–209).

- **Assumptions about People with Disabilities: Asexual, Unlovely, and Undesirable.** Among the beliefs of non-disabled people about people with disabilities are a number that center on sexual difference:

> That we are asexual, or at best inadequate.
>
> That we cannot ovulate, menstruate, conceive or give birth, have orgasms, erections, ejaculations or impregnate.
>
> That if we are not married or in a long-term relationship it is because no one wants us and not through our personal choice to remain single or live alone.
>
> That if we do not have a child it must be the cause of abject sorrow to us and likewise never through choice.

> That any able-bodied person who marries us must have done so for one of the following suspicious motives and never through love: desire to hide his/her own inadequacies in the disabled partner's obvious ones; an altruistic and saintly desire to sacrifice their lives to our care; neurosis of some sort, or plain old fashioned fortune-hunting.
>
> That if we have a partner who is also disabled, we chose each other for no other reason, and not for any other qualities we might possess. When we choose "our own kind" in this way the able-bodied world feels relieved, until of course we wish to have children; then we're seen as irresponsible. (Morris, 1991:20ff)

Add to this list the assumptions discussed earlier that disabled people do not meet the societal standards for beauty and physical attractiveness. Also, "just as public displays of same-sex love are strongly discouraged, so two disabled people being intimate in public will experience social disapproval" (Shakespeare, 1996:193).

- **Denial of Sex.** People with disabilities are often not welcome in nightclubs and other social venues where sex is on the agenda. They may not be admitted to a gay or straight facility because they are defined as "not sexy" and are believed to detract from the sexuality of the scene (i.e., their impairment was alienating to other patrons). Clubs designed for sexual interaction are often not designed for the disabled. They may be basements or other inaccessible buildings with steps, narrow hallways, flashing lights, and loud noise, which act as barriers for the disabled. Many gay men meet in saunas or in public restrooms, which are typically inaccessible for disabled people. So, too, for lesbians with disabilities who find it difficult to meet with other lesbians because they often meet in inaccessible outdoor or sporting activities.

  People who live in day centers, group homes, adult foster care homes, or other residential environments for people with disabilities may encounter policies and staff members who often deny their patients the right to form emotional or sexual relationships.

- **Difficulty in Finding Partners.** People with disabilities often face barriers to access the environments where nondisabled people make contacts that lead to sexual encounters or romantic relationships. They may be blocked by inaccessible public transport, inadequate income, and inaccessible pubs and clubs, making it difficult to interact with potential partners. The workplace is a likely place for such encounters but many disabled people lack access to paid employment. People with disabilities may also find churches, another common place for meeting potential partners, inaccessible because of physical or attitudinal barriers.

  Computer chat rooms or advertisements in lonely hearts newspaper columns provide an option to those with physical mobility difficulties. But these options are not usually accessible to people with visual impairments (the exception is software that "talks"). Moreover, the language used in these venues emphasizes one's physical attractiveness, thus disqualifying people with disabilities if they are honest about their impairments. This problem is minimized in the personal advertisements section of disability-related publications. Here honesty is expected and the chances for rejection, so common in nondisabled settings, are reduced significantly.

People who become disabled later in life often find that impairment interrupts their social networks and personal relationships, leaving them isolated. This is more true for women with disabilities than for men with disabilities.

Physical and Sexual Abuse

The evidence is clear that people with disabilities, both children and adults, are more likely to be abused physically and sexually than those without disabilities (Mitchell and Buchele-Ash, 2000). Because of the social context, and the social opportunity, people with disabilities may experience quantitatively more abuse than the nondisabled (Shakespeare, 1996:203).

> There are the ones who are chosen because they cannot speak of the horror. There are the ones who are chosen because they cannot run away, and there is nowhere to run. There are the ones who are chosen because their very lives depend on not fighting back. There are the ones who are chosen because there is no one for them to tell. There are the ones who are chosen because no one has even taught them the words. There are the ones who are chosen because society chooses to believe that, after all, they don't really have any sexuality, so it can't hurt them. (Cross, 1994:165)

Those most vulnerable to physical and sexual abuse are deaf people who cannot speak and people with learning difficulties who may be lured into situations without understanding the consequences (for a chilling account of sexual assault of a girl with learning difficulties by athletes from her high school, see Lefkowitz, 1998). The abuse may occur in institutional settings where staff members or other patients may take advantage of the vulnerable. In these settings, patients lack communication with the outside world, and the youngest or the most impaired are the most likely victims of those who have institutional power or personal power over them. Abuse can take other forms in institutions that are more like warehouses than welcoming environments. In such instances, the goal of profit surpasses patient care, resulting in savings through such activities as the overuse of drugs to control patients, inadequate health care, thermostats too low in the winter and too high in the summer, cheap food, and other forms of neglect (Press and Washburn, 2000; K. Thomas, 2001).

Abortion Issue

The primary rationale for prenatal testing is to determine whether the fetus is "normal" or will result in a child with a disability. When the test affirms that possibility, the prospective parents have the choice and the legal right to terminate the pregnancy if they wish. But this issue is a thorny one for those who favor a woman's right to choose (and we are among them), if we examine the ramifications of aborting "disabled" fetuses *from the perspective of people with disabilities* (these arguments are primarily from Hershey, 2000).

Foremost, when a woman chooses to abort a fetus rather than to give birth to a disabled child she accepts society's negative views about people with disabilities:

> She is making a statement about the desirability or the relative worth of such a child. Abortion based on disability results from, and in turn strengthens, certain beliefs: children with disabilities (and by implication adults with disabilities) are a burden to family and society; life with a disability is scarcely

> worth living; preventing the birth is an act of kindness; women who bear disabled children have failed. (Hershey, 2000:558)

In short, the choice to abort a disabled fetus is a rejection of children and adults who have disabilities.

Second, most people with disabilities, despite the manifold medical and social difficulties associated with their conditions, affirm that their lives are meaningful and worthwhile. Laura Hershey, for example, has a rare neuromuscular condition. She must rely on a motorized wheelchair for mobility, a voice-activated computer for writing, and the assistance of Medicaid-funded attendants for daily needs such as dressing, bathing, eating, and going to the bathroom. She also has a house, a career, a partner, and a community of friends with and without disabilities. She says:

> My life of disability has not been easy or carefree. But in measuring the quality of my life, other factors—education, friends, and meaningful work, for example—have been decisive. If I were asked for an opinion on whether to bring a child into the world, knowing she would have the same limitations and opportunities I have had, I would not hesitate to say, "Yes." I know that many women do not have the resources my parents had. Many lack education, are poor, or are without the support of friends and family. The problems created by these circumstances are intensified with a child who is disabled. No woman should have a child she can't handle or doesn't want. Having said that, I must also say that all kinds of women raise healthy, self-respecting children with disabilities, without unduly compromising their own lives. (Hershey, 2000:559)

Third, in addition to traditional genetic testing, the Human Genome Project, which maps DNA, can predict hundreds, perhaps thousands, of disorders before birth and, in doing so, has the potential to eliminate hereditary diseases in a generation. It also presents a danger. Many in the disabled community fear that the widespread use of these genetic tools and abortion for the purpose of eliminating disability could inaugurate a new eugenics movement. Two examples from the twentieth century show how governments have viewed the lives of people with disabilities to have little value and should be extinguished (Silvers, 1998):

- A 1939 German decree authorized physicians to put to death impaired persons who could not be cured. In the following two years about 200,000 physically and mentally impaired children and adults were killed because they were judged to have "lives unworthy of life."
- As late as the 1930s, over half of the states in the United States had laws encouraging sterilization of people with disabilities, typically those with developmental disabilities, epilepsy, the blind, and the deaf.

Abortion, then, presents a major quandary for feminists who defend the right for women to choose, a right that can conflict with efforts to promote acceptance, equality, and respect for people with disabilities. Such is the dilemma of Laura Hershey, cited earlier, a prochoice feminist who is also disabled. She offers this solution to a highly complex issue:

> I wouldn't deny any woman the right to choose abortion. But I would issue a challenge to all women making a decision whether to give birth to a child who may have disabilities. The challenge is this: consider all the relevant information, not just the medical facts. More important than a particular

> diagnosis are the conditions awaiting a child—community acceptance, access to buildings and transportation, civil rights protection, and opportunities for education and employment. Where these things are lacking or inadequate, consider joining the movement to change them. In many communities, adults with disabilities and parents of disabled children have developed powerful advocacy coalitions. I recognize that, having weighed all the factors, some will decide they cannot give birth to a child with disabilities. It pains me, but I acknowledge their right and their choice. (Hershey, 2000:563)

People with disabilities have always had to accommodate to environments and social settings that were designed for the able-bodied. As we have seen, they experience discrimination in housing, education, and work. Equal access is frequently denied because of transportation and architectural barriers in streets and buildings. Added to these structural barriers to equality are the stings of widespread stereotypes that demean them as inferior, unattractive, asexual, and pitiful. Their frustration with unequal access and discrimination has led many people with disabilities to become active in the Disability Rights Movement. In joining with others, their feelings of isolation became feelings of a common bond and empowerment. This section focuses on their collective efforts and the results.

Disability Rights Movement

A **social movement** is a group that develops an organization and tactics to promote or resist social change. Its members share a belief system that defines common grievances and goals and group identity. The disability rights movement is comprised of a wide variety of individuals as well as local and national organizations with a common goal—equal rights for disabled people. It is a loose structure of organizations since many focus exclusively on people with particular disabilities (e.g., the National Federation of the Blind, the Disabled American Veterans, the National Association of the Deaf). But this network, while seemingly lacking unity, is united by the overarching objectives of empowerment and collective rights—human, civil, and legal—for people with disabilities.

The civil rights struggles by African Americans in the 1950s and 1960s and, to some extent, the antiwar protests of the 1960s and the student movement served as catalysts for oppressed groups such as women, gays/lesbians, and people with disabilities. Social movements capture the imagination of potential adherents when social conditions are right. "A disability rights movement was much more likely to occur at a historical moment when protests were legitimate, widespread, and focused not only along lines of established economic conflicts but also around issues of identity and social roles" (Scotch, 1989:386). Under the right conditions, people who once were resigned to living their lives in isolation came to believe that in joining with others they could make a difference as they saw protests and heard leaders argue that disability was not their fault, but rather the failure of the political system to acknowledge their rights as human beings and to be equal in society.

The disability rights movement began in the late 1960s with local organizing by Ed Roberts at the University of California at Berkeley and Judy

Heumann in New York City, both of whom were postpolio quadriplegics. Roberts was instrumental in getting the Berkeley campus to provide students with disabilities peer counseling and support to gain access to university programs and housing. By 1972 Roberts and others founded the Berkeley Center for Independent Living in an apartment, which was the forerunner to the Independent Living Movement and its unofficial newspaper for the disability rights movement—the *Disability Rag* (now called *Ragged Edge*). Meanwhile Judy Heumann filed a law suit when she was denied teaching certification because of her disability. Beginning with this action, others joined to form an organization called Disabled in Action (DIA), which had the goal to break down barriers to disabled people's full societal participation. In 1972 DIA, with 1,500 members organized protests targeted at inaccessible public buildings, the Jerry Lewis telethon (which they believed perpetuated demeaning stereotypes of disabled people), and media organizations that either neglected or provided prejudicial coverage of disability issues. This group also blocked traffic in front of Richard Nixon's 1972 New York campaign headquarters to protest his veto of the Rehabilitation Act.

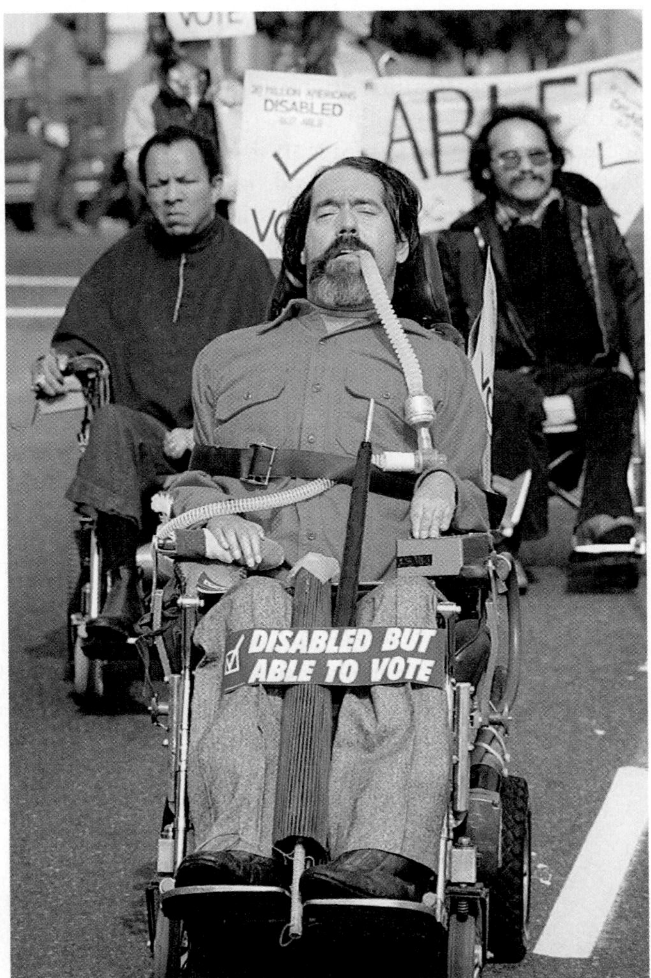

People with disabilities have organized protests to make their case to the public and policymakers.

Congruent with the politics of the times (i.e., the War on Poverty, passage of the voting rights act), policymakers became more receptive to the civil rights of people with disabilities. Congress, for example, passed the Rehabilitation Act of 1973, which prohibited government agencies and contractors from discriminating against people with disabilities. In 1975 Congress passed the Education for All Handicapped Children Act (legislation that Judy Heumann had worked on as a legislative intern), which required a free and appropriate public education and related services to all children with disabilities. Also, the Developmental Disabilities Amendments of 1975 expanded services for people with such impairments as mental retardation and cerebral palsy and mandated a network of state protection agencies to monitor and protect their rights. In 1977 the Department of Health and Human Services (HHS) issued regulations that required all recipients of HHS funds to provide equal access (through ramps and elevators) to employment or services or lose their subsidies. It is crucial to note that HHS made these progressive changes only after sit-ins occurred in federal offices across the United States to protest the inaction by HHS on these issues.

Following the election of Ronald Reagan in 1980 the political climate changed for disability rights activists. The 1980s were characterized, in general, by weakened federal requirements, reduced budgets, deregulation, and judicial decisions that threatened previously established guarantees for the disabled. There were occasional victories such as success in organizing opposition to the Reagan administration attempts to weaken several previously passed laws, including the Education for All Handicapped Children Act. They were defeated, however, when Reagan rescinded a Carter administration requirement that all new transit systems and newly acquired buses be wheelchair accessible. An organization within the disability rights movement, American Disabled for Accessible Public Transit (ADAPT), organized demonstrations in a number of cities to publicize the lack of access for many people with disabilities with only limited success during the chilly politically conservative climate of the 1980s. Despite these setbacks, major progressive legislation was about to be enacted, the Americans with Disabilities Act of 1990.

Americans with Disabilities Act

When President George H. W. Bush signed the Americans with Disabilities Act of 1990 (ADA), it was called by some the most far-reaching civil rights legislation since the Civil Rights Act of 1964. The ADA was intended to eradicate discrimination against people with disabilities:

- Prohibited discrimination in employment against qualified individuals. This meant that people with disabilities could participate with equal opportunity in the application process, have an equal chance to perform essential functions, be provided with reasonable accommodations because of one's disability, and have equal benefits and privileges of employment. This applies to all employers with fifteen or more employees.
- Prohibited discrimination in programs run by public entities such as state and local governments, including public transportation.
- Mandated that private businesses open to the public must make sure

sively deteriorates the spinal cord and the brain causing loss of muscle control and, typically, death in 3 years, must pay for their expensive care, drawing down their families' resources, requiring them in some cases to raid their children's college funds or sell their homes. Currently, there are about 30,000 people in the United States with ALS, 17,000 of whom are ineligible for Medicare services (King, 2000).

- In 1999 the U.S. Supreme Court narrowed the Americans with Disabilities Act, ruling that people with physical impairments that can be treated with medication or devices such as eyeglasses or hearing aids are not protected.
- In 2001, by a five to four majority, the U.S. Supreme Court held that state employees could not collect damages from their states for offenses under the federal Americans with Disabilities Act (Rosenbaum, 2001). An organizer in the Denver disabled community, Joe Ehman, said of this ruling: "That basically says that if you're a state employee that you have no rights. Once again, we're second-class citizens, according to the Supreme Court" (quoted in Kirksey, 2001:49A).

have their personal assistance services, SSI/SSDI and Medicaid share of cost recalculated every month they earn income, something these systems are not efficient enough to do without delays and shortfalls for the recipient. Los Angeles activist Nancy Becker Kennedy, says, "It would be inadvisable for any disabled individual to work at part time or sporadic employment because they run the highly probable risk of throwing these very sluggish benefit systems into confusion." Experience shows that this often results in one losing their health care, living allowance, and money to pay their attendant for months or even years while Social Security Administration and other agencies sort it out (and hopefully get it right when they do).

• *Enforce Minimum Wage Standards:* Other dubious subsidies already exist. Section 504 of the Rehabilitation Act of 1973 provides that federally financed institutions are required to pay a "fair" or "commensurate" wage to disabled workers, but they are not required to meet even minimum wage standards. The traditional sheltered workshop is the prototype for justifying below-minimum wages for disabled people, based on the theory that such workers are not able to keep up with the average widget sorter. Any nonprofit employer is allowed to pay subminimum wage to disabled employees under federal law, if the employer can show that the disabled worker has "reduced productive capacity." About 6,300 such U.S. workshops employ more than 391,000 disabled workers, some paying 20% to 30% of the minimum wage; others paying as little as $11 per week (*Washington Post,* Dec. 12, 1999). In reality, workers with disabilities in these workshops know that they are sometimes paid less, not because they lack productive capacity, but because of the nature of segregated employment.

• *Subsidize Accommodations:* Government could pay for disabled workers' reasonable accommodations. Perhaps that would remove the added cost from the employer's bottom line and stop some employers from fighting disabled employees' much needed accommodations in court.

• *Mandate Affirmative Action for Disabled Workers.* Unlike the Civil Rights Act of 1964, the ADA was not followed up with an affirmative action program. While the Labor Department can mandate affirmative action for women and minorities, it only urges employers to hire disabled workers.

Source: Marta Russell. 2000. "The Political Economy of Disablement." *Dollars & Sense,* No. 231 (September/October): 15, 48.

Most significant, more than a decade after the passage of the Americans with Disabilities Act and other legislation favorable to people with disabilities, the evidence is that the disabled unemployment and poverty rates remain the highest for any minority group (Russell, 2000).

Despite legislative and judicial setbacks, the Disabilities Movement perseveres and continues to make a difference. In 2000, for example, a class action suit, the first of its kind in the United States was filed against Kaiser Permanente, a health maintenance organization (HMO) on behalf of all its California members with disabilities. The law suit argued that Kaiser discriminated against disabled patients by having inaccessible medical equipment (e.g., mamography machines that cannot be used by people in wheelchairs). The next year (2001) Kaiser agreed to a far-reaching settlement that included not only installing accessible medical equipment but also removing architectural barriers and instituting training programs, handbooks, and a complaint system to meet the needs of the disabled. Sid Wolinksy of Disability Rights Advocates said, "We believe this will be revolutionary in terms of its impact on health care for people with disabilities. The agreement with Kaiser provides a comprehensive blueprint that . . . we intend to use as a template . . . for other major healthcare providers" (quoted in Lewin, 2001:2).

To provide equal rights and opportunities for people with disabilities requires long-term solutions such as universal health care and a living wage. These are difficult to achieve in the current conservative political climate. There are some more readily achievable short-term goals that will help the cause immeasurably. These are government actions to strengthen the Americans with Disabilities Act and other federal laws (see the "Social Policy" panel, pp. 326–327, for a suggested list of such reforms).

Conclusion

A fundamental progressive goal for society is social justice. The chapters in this inequality section show vividly that we are far from achieving that goal for racial/ethnic minorities, women, gays, and people with disabilities. In the words of Gail Schoettler, former lieutenant governor and treasurer of Colorado:

> The Civil Rights Movement made great strides. Yet as long as any person in America is denied a job or housing or simple courtesy because of her or his personal characteristics, whether they be disabilities or skin color or beliefs or sexuality, we have not affirmed the basic equal opportunity promised by our Constitution. (Schoettler, 2000:2L)

Chapter Review

1. About 20 percent of the U.S. population have some form of impairment. Approximately 15 percent of people with disabilities were born with the condition; 85 percent will experience a disabling condition in the course of their lives.
2. The individual approach (the medical model) defines disability in physiological terms, a physical or mental condition caused by the genes, accident, or disease. The goal is to return people with disabilities back to "normal," and if this is not possible, to get them to adapt to their environment.
3. The social model, while acknowledging the biological basis of disability, focuses on the ways that

social factors "disable" those with impairments. Some of these social factors are barriers to physical access, limited access to resources, and negative stereotypes.

4. People with disabilities constitute a minority group. Their marginality in society occurs because: (a) they are defined as different (b) the names given to them by society demean, diminish, trivialize, and deprecate, (c) the fact of disability establishes a master status, by which people are categorized, (d) they are stigmatized, (e) they are excluded, (f) disability combines with other stratification hierarchies to form a matrix of oppression, and (g) they experience discrimination.
5. People with disabilities face a number of social barriers in the related areas of gender and sexuality. Women and men who are physically disabled are perceived as unattractive, asexual, and undesirable. While both sexes are disadvantaged by the cultural expectations for what it takes to be feminine or masculine, women are more disadvantaged than men.
6. People with disabilities, both children and adults, are more likely to be abused physically and sexually than those without disabilities. Deaf people who cannot speak and people with learning disabilities are the most vulnerable to both types of abuse.
7. To counter their secondary status in society, many people with disabilities have taken an active part in the Disability Rights Movement, a social movement with the goal of achieving empowerment and collective human, civil, and legal rights. Through the use of demonstrations and protest, this movement has succeeded, in part, to achieve favoring legislation that attempts to eliminate discrimination in housing, schooling, the workplace, as well as the removal of architectural and other barriers to access to buildings and transportation. Most significant was the passage of the Americans with Disabilities Act of 1990, which while flawed in its details and in its enforcement, advanced the cause of equality for people with disabilities.

KEY TERMS

Individual approach to disability (also known as the medical model). Disability is defined in terms of some physiological impairment due to genetics, accident, or disease.

Social model of disability. The real problem with physical and mental impairment is not physical but social—the way people with able bodies view people with disabilities and the institutionalization of these views in limited physical access and other social barriers that interfere with the potential of people with disabilities.

Ontological truth. Universal and undeniable reality.

Disability. Reduced ability to perform tasks one would normally do at a given stage of life that are exacerbated by the individual and institutional discrimination encountered.

Master status. Status that has exceptional importance for social identity, overshadowing other statuses. Being defined as a member of a minority group is a master status.

Stigma. Attribute that is socially devalued and disgraced.

Ableism. Set of often contradictory stereotypes about people with disabilities that act as a barrier to keep them from achieving their full potential.

Matrix of domination. Intersections of the hierarchies of class, race, gender, sexuality, and disability in which each of us exists.

Hegemony. Dominant belief system, which privileges the group in power.

Social movement. Group that develops an organization and tactics to promote or resist social change in society.

WEBSITES FOR FURTHER REFERENCE

http://www.usdoj.gov/crt/ada/adahom1.htm
The home page of the U.S. Department of Justice's Americans with Disabilities Act not only lays out the specific components of this landmark act, but it also serves as an informational resource on the latest court cases on disability, mandates for disability training and certification, and the ways in which the Department of Justice attempts to enforce this law. The website also

includes current discussions about the Americans with Disabilities Act.

http://www.dredf.org/
Founded in 1979 by people with disabilities and parents of children with disabilities, the Disability Rights Education and Defense Fund, Inc. (DREDF) is "a national law and policy center dedicated to protecting and advancing the civil rights of people with disabilities through legislation, litigation, advocacy, technical assistance, and education and training of attorneys, advocates, persons with disabilities, and parents of children with disabilities." This website provides up-to-date details on recent legal cases, conferences, and current events that are pertinent for people with disabilities. DREDF also keeps track of international efforts and laws for disabled individuals.

http://www.disabledwomen.net/
Disabled Women on the Web (DWOW) was established by the Disabled Women's Alliance to provide information, resources, and support for women with disabilities to continue to "change the world!" Resources on this website include contact information and descriptions of businesses owned by disabled women, women working on disability issues, and disabled women projects. Links to other websites for women and the disabled are also available on this website. Eventually this website will contain oral histories of disabled women, audio and video resources, links to articles on disabled women, and information on the history of disabilities.

http://www.jik.com/
This website offers "cutting-edge disability resources." June Isaacson Kailes works as a consultant and a disability rights advocate, and is one of the original and recognized national leaders in the "independent living movement." Her web page describes many of the social movements undertaken to secure rights for disabled people, many disabilities that people have today, and some of the problems that disabled people face. The website also explains disability access issues, focusing on issues such as disabled people's access to everyday technology or how building designs can discriminate against disabled persons. Current mandates for disability diversity training are also detailed. This website holds a wide range of information, resources and links; it is perfect for individuals unfamiliar with some aspect of disabilities and/or ableism.

http://www.dav.org/
Home page of the Disabled American Veterans (DAV). "Formed in 1920 and chartered by Congress in 1932, the million-member DAV is the official voice of America's service-connected disabled veterans—a strong, insistent voice that represents all of America's 2.1 million disabled veterans, their families and survivors." DAV is not a political association. Its members reflect all shades of American political opinion and rely on the DAV to advocate their needs as disabled veterans. DAV offers employment and service programs directly to disabled veterans; its legislative lobbying component continues to secure rights for this contingent of the U.S. population.

http://www.nad.org/
The National Association of the Deaf (NAD), established in 1880, is the "oldest and largest constituency organization safeguarding the accessibility and civil rights of 28 million deaf and hard of hearing Americans in education, employment, health care, and telecommunications." Its many programs and activities include grassroots advocacy and empowerment, captioned media, certification of American Sign Language professionals, certification of sign language interpreters, deafness-related information and publications, legal assistance, policy development and research, public awareness, and youth leadership development. This website includes a link to important questions and answers about the legal rights of deaf individuals, difficulties in seeking medical treatment, educational issues, and incidences of prejudice and discrimination.

http://www.nfb.org/
Founded in 1940, the National Federation of the Blind (NFB) is the nation's largest and most influential membership organization of blind persons. "The purpose of the National Federation of the Blind is twofold: to help blind persons achieve self-confidence and self-respect and to act as a vehicle for collective self-expression by the blind. By providing public education about blindness; information and referral services; scholarships, literature and publications about blindness; aids and appliances and other adaptive equipment for the blind; advocacy services and protection of civil rights; job opportunities for the blind; development and evaluation of technology; and support for blind persons and their families, members of the NFB strive to educate the public that the blind are normal individuals who can compete on terms of equality."

http://www.mdri.org/
Mental Disability Rights International (MRDI) is a non-governmental advocacy organization dedicated to the recognition and enforcement of the rights of people with mental disabilities. "Established in 1993 as a joint project of the Bazelon Center for Mental Health Law and American University's Center for Human Rights and Humanitarian Law, MDRI documents conditions, publishes reports on human rights enforcement, and promotes international oversight of the rights of people with mental disabilities."

http://www.aoa.gov/factsheets/disabilities.html
The Administration on Aging (AOA) produces convenient fact sheets on older and younger people with dis-

abilities. Its goal in disseminating this information is to improve chronic care across the lifespan. With a current life expectancy of 75 years, today's newborns can expect to experience an average of 13 years with an activity limitation. Furthermore, with many people living past age 75 in recent years, many of us can expect to spend over 20 years of our lives limited by physical disabilities. Thus, the AOA pays particular attention to elderly disabilities and considers disability and chronic care issues to be important health concerns in the near future.

http://www.modimes.org/

For more than 63 years, March of Dimes programs and research have saved millions of babies from death and disability. According to this website, "four major problems threaten the health of America's babies: birth defects, infant mortality, low birth weight, and lack of prenatal care." While many of the March of Dimes' programs are geared toward preventing birth defects and disabilities, much of their effort goes toward identifying the numerous causes of birth defects; the organization is best known for these efforts.

http://www.easter-seals.org/

Easter Seals provides services to children and adults with disabilities and other special needs and support to their families. Some of Easter Seals' programs include summer camps for disabled children and adults, training programs for family members of disabled children and adults, job training, and medical rehabilitation programs. This website not only covers Easter Seals' extensive services in depth, but also keeps track of contemporary disabilities issues.

http://www.disabilityworld.org/11-12_01/women/genderreport.shtml

Disability World is a bimonthly "webzine" of international disability news and views. The first issue, released in 2002, detailed survey results on gender, disability, and development. This survey was the "first attempt to systematically document the extent to which U.S.-based international development organizations include people with disabilities, particularly women and girls, in policies, employment, programs, and services. One hundred four members of InterAction, a coalition of international relief, development, environmental and refugee agencies based in the U.S., participated in the research project, which was sponsored by the United States Agency for International Development (USAID) Office of Women in Development." This online magazine clearly covers the breaking news on disabilities worldwide.

12

PART FOUR
SOCIAL STRUCTURE AND INDIVIDUAL DEVIANCE

Crime and Justice

 *think the first duty of society is justice.*

—Alexander Hamilton

There can be no equal justice where the kind of trial a man gets depends on the money he has.

—Supreme Court Justice Hugo Black

Equal justice cannot be achieved in an unequal society. The justice system in American society merely reinforces those inequalities.

—Randall G. Shelden

This chapter examines the nature of crime and how society reacts to criminal behavior in the processing of criminals. These topics are important because they help us understand the role of the powerful in regulating social behavior and the bias of the system against the powerless.

CRIME IN SOCIETY

The people of society are naturally concerned with crime for two obvious reasons: If left unchecked, crime destroys the stability necessary for the maintenance of an orderly society, and the people are the potential victims of criminal activities. Though legitimate, these concerns direct attention away from the deviance that results from the orderly working of society and from crimes that are much more costly than street crimes (which we tend to think are overwhelmingly the greatest criminal danger). These ironies will become apparent as we examine four aspects of crime: its definition, the incidence of crime, the kinds of people arrested, and the various types of criminal behavior.

What Is Crime?

Groups and individuals within society differ in their definition of crime. Some people equate crime with all antisocial behavior. Others argue that crimes are acts such as racism, sexism, and imperialism that violate basic human rights. Similarly, some people use moral rather than legal criteria to define what is or is not a crime. For example, Martin Luther King Jr. and his followers believed that the laws enforcing racial segregation were morally wrong, so to violate them was not a crime but a virtue. Antiabortion activists believe that abortion is a crime regardless of what the formal law decrees.

Although there is no universally accepted definition of **crime,** the most common one—the breaking of a law—officially labels people and separates society into criminal and noncriminal categories. In other words, criminality is a social status determined by how an individual is perceived, evaluated, and treated by legal authorities. Generally, the law designates as criminal any behaviors that violate the strongly held norms of society. There is common agreement in the United States, for example, that the law should protect property from theft and vandalism. There is also universal agreement that society must protect its citizens from bodily harm (rape, assault, and murder). But although there may be consensus in society on certain laws, the political nature of the lawmaking and enforcement process has important negative implications for the individuals caught up in them.

Because law is an inherently political phenomenon, a violation of law means that the crime is ultimately an expression of group conflict and interest (Quinney, 1970). Individuals and groups in power determine what behaviors violate these interests and thus are criminal. As Pearl observes:

> [If] the original colonists had failed in their revolution, they would have been branded criminals and their valor, ritualized for subsequent generations, would instead be denounced. Their motives would have been base, etc. The trade-off between crime and revolution in oppressive societies is vital for political stability. This is not to say that there is no such thing as criminal behavior, but ruling forces' description of all opposition as criminal makes it almost impossible to consider the nature of "true" crime. (Pearl, 1977:50)

Consider, for example, how antiwar protesters were treated by local and federal authorities during the late 1960s and early 1970s. Their behavior was considered criminal because it threatened the power structure. What the powerful consider criminal depends, in fact, on what they perceive to be the intent of the individuals they observe. In the United States, society does not always forbid or condemn some acts of force that injure people or destroy property. Property damage during football games, Halloween, or Mardi Gras is often overlooked or trivialized. Even 10,000 beer-drinking, noisy, and sometimes destructive college students on the beaches of Florida during spring break are allowed to go on such a binge because "kids will be kids." But if the same 10,000 college students were to destroy the same amount of property in a demonstration whose goal was to change the system, the acts would be defined as criminal and the police called to restore order by force if necessary. Thus, violence is condoned or condemned through political pressures and decisions. The basic criterion is whether the act supports or threatens existing social and political arrangements. (See the panel on Emile Durkheim.) If they are not supportive, then by definition the acts are to be condemned and punished.

A related implication of the political nature of crime is that the design of laws is influenced by a class bias. "The law and the legal order especially favor the very wealthy, but they favor enough of the rest of the population to appear to be equal. Yet the law clearly has never done a good job supporting the most marginalized sectors of the population: the poor in general, and African Americans, and other minorities" (Shelden, 2001:15). That is the interpretation by notable historian of law and criminal justice, Lawrence Friedman:

> Law is a fabric of norms and practices in a particular society; the norms and practices are social judgments made concrete: the living, breathing embodiment of society's attitudes, prejudices, and values. Inevitably, and invariably, these are slanted in favor of the haves; the top riders, the comfortable, respectable, well-to-do people. After all, articulate, powerful people *make* the laws; and even with the best will in the world, they do not feel moved to give themselves disadvantage.
>
> Rules thus tend to favor people who own property, entrepreneurs, people with good position in society. The lash of criminal justice, conversely, tends to fall on the poor, the badly dressed, the maladroit, the deviant, the misunderstood, the shiftless, the unpopular. (Friedman, 1993:101)

This view pervades the criminal justice system, as discussed in a later section of this chapter.

Emile Durkheim and the Social Functions of Crime

Three nineteenth-century social thinkers—Karl Marx, Max Weber, and Emile Durkheim—have had an enormous impact on contemporary thinking about society and social problems. Of these three, Emile Durkheim (1858–1917) was an especially important influence on people who call themselves functionalists (also called order theorists). The whole of Durkheim's scholarly work centered on the question of what holds society together. For him, even crime plays a vital role in achieving social solidarity.

Durkheim argued that society is based on a common moral order. One indicator of morality, though an imperfect one, is the laws of a society. Criminal laws, for example, express the common will because they provide for the punishment of those who disobey. When a crime is committed, there is a widespread sense of public outrage. This outrage at the criminal and his or her deviant behavior reaffirms the underlying principles of the society—morality, order, and protection—all of which promote social solidarity. In this way, Durkheim argued, crime serves a positive function of society by holding it together.

Durkheim's notion is rather easy to grasp when the crime is murder, theft, rape, or treason. But what of lesser crimes such as (depending on the society) public nudism, eating forbidden foods, or irreverent behavior in the presence of a sacred object? These crimes are not physically harmful to society, so why are they labeled as deviant? Such logic misses Durkheim's point: Many laws may appear unrelated to social survival, but upholding them is essential because they are addressed to the moral force of the society. As Durkheim put it:

> We must not say that an action shocks the common conscience because it is criminal, but rather that it is criminal because it shocks the common conscience. We do not reprove it because it is a crime, but it is a crime because we reprove it. (Durkheim, 1960:81)

Because the law defines crime, then what is a crime depends on the current law. As society changes and as new interest groups become powerful, the laws and interpretations of the laws regarding criminal behavior may also change. Many behaviors once considered criminal no longer are, such as missing church on Sunday, harboring a runaway slave, or selling liquor.

Finally, because crime is defined by the powerful in society, the organization and priorities of society are never regarded as harmful to human life (and therefore a moral crime). Yet the order of society itself can be very destructive to some categories of people, as Carmichael and Hamilton (1967) showed in their book *Black Power*. They noted that when White terrorists bombed a Black church in Birmingham, Alabama, and killed five children, the act was deplored by most elements of U.S. society. But when hundreds of Black babies die each year in Birmingham because of the effects of racism, no one in the power structure gets upset and calls this violence. Although high infant mortality and rates of preventable disease, which are perpetuated through discrimination, take many more lives than civil disorder or street crimes, the term **violence** is not applied to these crimes (Carmichael and Hamilton, 1967:4). Thus, violence is defined as an act of force perceived by the powerful as threatening to the status quo.

Crime Rates

The innately political nature of crime is clearly evident when one examines the official crime rates, which emphasize certain types of crimes (those of the powerless) while minimizing or ignoring others. These discrepancies have profound implications because they mean, in effect, that some categories of people are disproportionately labeled as criminals.

The basic source of crime statistics is the *Uniform Crime Reports,* published yearly by the FBI (see Figure 12.1). The primary problem with these statistics is that they focus on traditional crimes and omit white-collar crimes, corporate crime, organized crime, and political crimes. The FBI statistics (called index crimes) emphasize burglary, larceny, auto theft, robbery, rape, assault, and murder. This focus has the effect of directing public attention almost exclusively to crimes involving violence and property, in which the poor and minorities are thought to be the major perpetrators, and away from the crimes of the affluent.

The other obvious problem with the official crime statistics is that they underreport the actual extent of crime because they list only known crimes (the arrest figures supplied by 17,000 local police agencies). Victimization surveys (the government's annual survey of nearly 160,000 people in 86,000 households about their personal experiences with crime) reveal that about seven in ten crimes go unreported to police.

Official crime rates are also misleading because they imply that the amount of crime varies a good deal from year to year or from region to region. These changes may occur, but the official statistics make real variations difficult to determine. In some cases the actual incidence of crime may not change, but the accuracy of reports or the ability of law enforcement officials to prosecute crim-

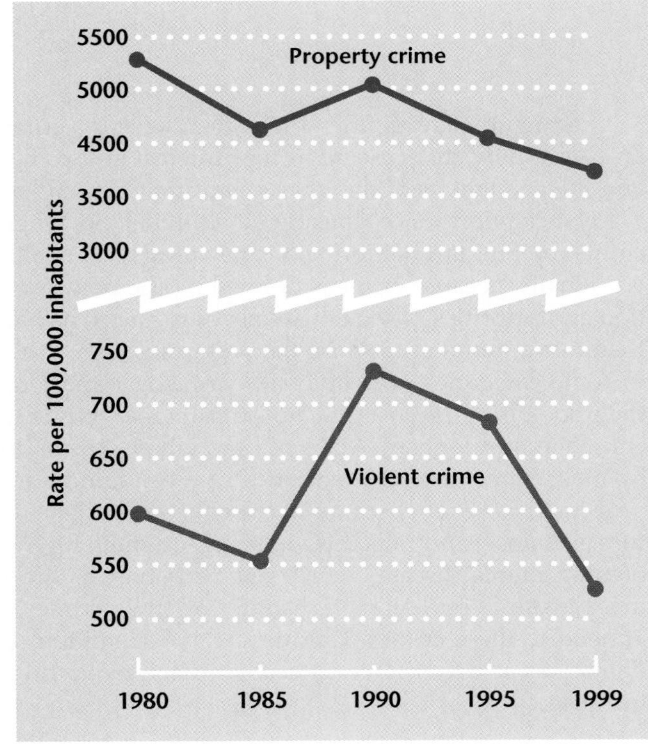

FIGURE 12.1

Crime Rates for Property and Violent Crimes, 1980–1999

Source: Federal Bureau of Investigation. 2000. *Uniform Crime Reports 2000*. Washington, DC: U.S. Government Printing Office, p. 64.

inals may change. For example, in 1997 Philadelphia was ranked as the fourth safest among America's ten largest cities. However, a new police commissioner found that about 10 percent of Philadelphia's major crimes (assaults, rapes, and robberies) had systematically been downgraded to minor crimes or not crimes at all (Cox, 1998), calling into question whether Philadelphia was actually the fourth safest among the largest U.S. cities.

Despite these problems of accuracy, the official statistics do reflect the actual degree of labeling that occurs, as Hartjen has argued perceptively:

> If crime is defined as a label imposed upon behavior, then crime rates reflect the labeling activity of official agencies. In this respect, crime rates are a perfectly accurate measure of the amount of social labeling produced by a population and are not indicative of the number of crimes, in the sense of illegal acts, taking place. (Hartjen, 1978:187)

The official crime rates have declined steadily since 1990, from a total crime index of 1091.1 arrests per 100,000 in 1990 to 880.0 in 1999. The murder rate, for example, of 5.7 per 100,000 was the lowest in 30 years and almost half the rate in 1974. There are several possible reasons for this decline. First, the decade of the 1990s was a time of general prosperity and low unemployment and greater job opportunities for racial minorities, teenagers, and high school dropouts. A large social scientific literature shows that as the economy expands unemployment is reduced, crime falls (Currie, 1998:141–147). Second, there have been demographic changes, most notably a drop in the numbers of young people who have traditionally committed a disproportionate number of crimes. Third, for whatever reason, the crack epidemic has declined in many parts of the country. "Rates of serious violence, including homicide, went up during the rise of the crack epidemic and have been dropping with the decline" (Blumstein and Rosenfeld, 1998:10). A fourth reason for the decline in crime is the incarceration (imprisonment) boom (over 2 million). A fifth reason is greater efforts to reduce crime at the community level (increased expenditures for the police, after-school programs to keep the young off the streets, and neighborhood watch programs). Finally, there has been a concerted crackdown on guns, particularly efforts aimed at taking them out of the hands of juveniles. Whether the crime rate will continue downward is an empirical question depending on a number of social, economic, and demographic factors. There are signs that the rates are bottoming and in some localities on the rise (e.g., murders in the largest cities). Noted criminologist James Alan Fox says that these increases are inevitable. "It's Newton's Law of Criminology. If he had studied criminology, he would've said what goes up, must come down. And what comes down, must go up" (quoted in Locy, 2000:3A).

Realizing that the official statistics are misleading and that they represent the degree of official labeling in society, let us look at what kinds of people are arrested and labeled for criminal behavior in U.S. society.

Demographic Characteristics of People Arrested for Crimes

The data from official sources clearly indicate that people from certain social categories are more likely than others to be arrested for criminal activities. We examine these categories of sex, age, social class, and race.

Sex. Street crime as measured by the FBI's *Uniform Crime Reports* has shown a consistently low level of female arrests and, if arrested, a greater likelihood of receiving lighter sentences than males. As Frank Hagan notes:

> The traditional handmaiden of sexism has been paternalism, a sort of noblesse oblige in which males felt that they were responsible for protecting the dependent female. This policy is reflected in the law and its administration, since females generally receive much lighter sentences for the same offense, are viewed more favorably by judges and juries, and seldom receive the death penalty. (F. Hagan, 1994:85)

The arrest rates by types of crimes committed vary by sex (see Table 12.1). About 22 percent of all arrests are of women, with juvenile females arrested nearly twice as often as the adult female rate. Seventeen percent of all those arrested for violent crimes are women and about 30 percent of those arrested for property crimes are women (Greenfeld and Snell, 1999). The number of women in prison has risen recently (the incarceration rate for women was 66 per 100,000 in 2000, compared to a rate of 32 per 100,000 in 1900). Even so, women, who make up more than half the general population, constituted only 6.7 percent of the nation's total prison population in 2000 (Beck, 2001:3). The differences by sex raise two questions: (1) Why is there such an apparent difference in criminal behavior by gender? (2) Why are women committing more property crimes now?

Explaining the Gender Gap. There are three reasons for greater likelihood of male involvement in crime. First, there are biological differences, such as levels of testosterone, which explain why males are more aggressive than females.

TABLE 12.1

Arrests by offense Charged and Sex, 1999

Offense Charged	*Male*	*Female*
Murder and manslaughter	88.6%	11.4%
Forcible rape	98.7	1.3
Robbery	89.9	10.1
Aggravated assault	80.3	19.7
Burglary	87.1	12.9
Larceny-theft	64.5	35.5
Motor vehicle theft	84.4	15.6
Arson	85.6	14.4
Violent crime	**83.0**	**17.0**
Property crime	**70.4**	**29.6**
Noncrime Index Crimes		
Forgery and counterfeiting	61.6%	38.4%
Fraud	56.4	43.6
Embezzlement	50.8	49.2
Vandalism	84.7	15.3
Prostitution and vice	39.2	60.8
Drug abuse violations	82.4	17.6
Driving under the influence	84.1	15.9
Drunkenness	87.3	12.7
Disorderly conduct	77.0	23.0
Vagrancy	81.6	18.4
Curfew and loitering violations	69.5	30.5
Runaways	40.8	59.2

Source: U.S. Department of Justice. 2000. *Sourcebook of Criminal Justice Statistics.* Washington, DC: U.S. Government Printing Office, Table 4.8.

Women constitute only 6.7 percent of the nation's total prison population.

Second, the gender gap is the result of differences in socialization for males and females. Boys are taught to be aggressive and risk takers, while girls are not. Sons are given more freedom by parents, while daughters are typically subject to greater social control.

The third explanation for gender differences in criminal behavior involves structural barriers that limit the possibilities for lawlessness by women. Women, for example, have fewer opportunities than men in employment to embezzle from their employers or to swindle customers. Also, patriarchy among criminals gives women few opportunities in organized crime, neighborhood gangs, and narcotics networks. "In sum, females' social experiences and social opportunities, legitimate and illegitimate, are likely to limit their criminal involvement" (Sykes and Cullen, 1992:108).

Explaining the Rise in Female Criminality. The number of women arrested and incarcerated is growing faster than that for men. One possible reason for this is that the women's movement for social, political, and economic equality has not only increased gender role equality of women in legitimate ways but has also opened up new opportunities, traditionally reserved for criminal males, in illegitimate and illegal activities. Others argue that the impact of the women's movement on female crime, though real, is less direct. Perhaps, for example, law enforcement agencies have paid more attention to women in general and their criminal activities in particular since the advent of the women's movement. Or possibly, because the present increase in female crime is primarily property crime, their increased participation in the labor force has moved many women closer to opportunities to commit certain crimes. More significant, though, is the link between female criminality and their greater economic marginality:

> Many criminal justice scholars attribute the rise in female crime rates more to the growing poverty among young, unattached mothers and the new ways

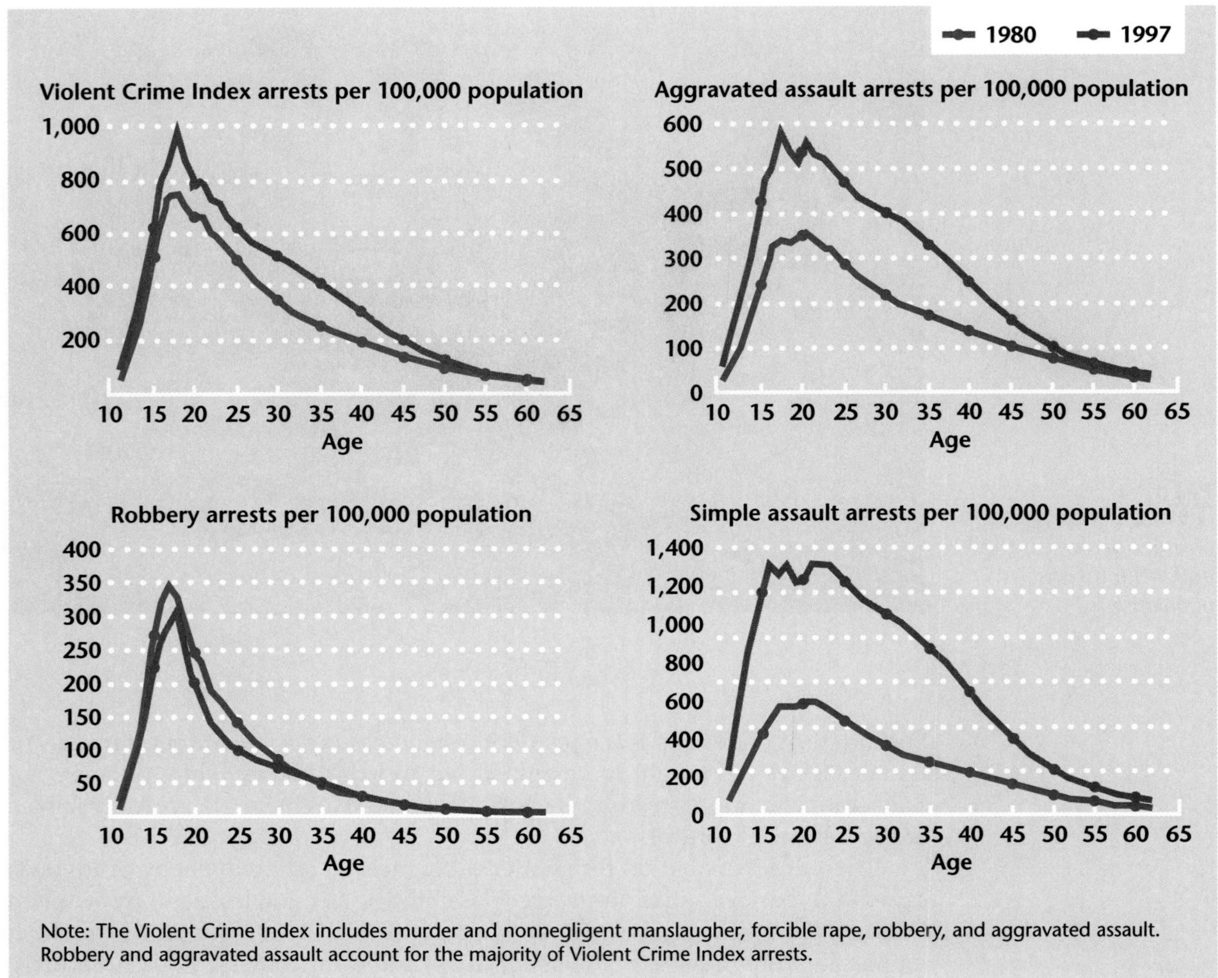

FIGURE 12.2

The Increase in Violent Crime Arrests between 1980 and 1997 Was Common across All Age Groups and Linked to Large Increases in Arrests for Aggravated Assaults

Source: U.S. Department of Justice. 2000. "Challenging the Myths." 1999 National Report Series. *Juvenile Justice Bulletin* (February):23.

> society treats women than to the wider opportunities they have. More men are abandoning their families, leaving women with the burdens of children, and with the temptations to commit crimes to care for them. (Krauss, 1994:E3)

- **Age.** A disproportionate amount of street crime in the United States is committed by relatively young people, with those under 25 accounting for half of all violent crime arrests and three-fifths of all property crime arrests. "The peak arrest age for property crime is sixteen, while age eighteen is the highest for violent crime" (F. Hagan, 1994:80) (see Figure 12.2).

  Why are young people more likely than adults to engage in street crimes? There are at least four plausible explanations for this tendency. First, young people are increasingly disengaged from their parents and more greatly influenced by their peers. Youths also want to impress their peers and this is sometimes done by acts of daring, some of which may involve breaking the laws. Related to this, adolescents (in groups) seek pleasure, experiment with drugs and alcohol, and engage in reckless behaviors. Second, adolescents often feel they need more money than their part-time jobs or parents' largesse provide for their desired life-style. Third, adolescence is a time of rebellion, a time of challenging authority. Contrast this with adulthood when individuals acquire full-time jobs, marry, and have children. Adults are much more likely than adolescents to feel tied to and have a stake in the community. This "maturation leads to less crime" phenomenon occurs across White, African American, and Latino populations.

Trend data show that violent crimes by juveniles (age 10 to 17) increased dramatically from 1987 to a high in 1994 and have since dropped to the still-high 1991 level. Although predictions are always tricky, some facts suggest that there is a ticking demographic time bomb. From 1985 to 1994 the arrest rate of youths age 14 to 17 increased by more than 250 percent (from 7.0 to 19.1 per 100,000). By the year 2005, the number of teens in that age category is projected to increase by 20 percent. Criminologist James Alan Fox concludes:

> Even if the per capita rate of teen homicide remains the same, the number of 14- to 17-year-olds who will commit murder could increase from 4,000 per year to nearly 5,000 annually by 2005 because of changing demographics alone. But the causes of increasing youth violence go beyond demographics. More dangerous drugs, more deadly weapons, and an apparently more casual attitude toward violence make this generation of youth more violent than previous generations. If offending rates continue to rise because of worsening conditions for our nation's youth, the number of teen killings could increase even more. (Fox, 1996:5)

Social Class. The bulk of the people processed by the criminal justice system for committing street crimes are the undereducated, the poor, the unemployed, or those working at low-level, alienating jobs. There are several explanations for this relationship. First, the kinds of crimes listed by the FBI are those of the lower classes (white-collar and corporate crimes, e.g., are omitted). Second, the police and others in the criminal justice system assume that lower-class people are more likely to be criminals. Thus, they place more personnel in lower-class neighborhoods, which ensures that they will find more criminal activity. Third, economic deprivation may induce people to turn to crime to ease their situations. The evidence is clear that direct interpersonal types of crime (robbery, larceny, assault) are committed disproportionately by members of the poor. In the words of criminologist Elliott Currie:

> [B]rutal conditions breed brutal behavior. To believe otherwise requires us to argue that the experience of being confined to the mean and precarious depths of the American economy has no serious consequences for personal character or social behavior. But this not only misreads the evidence; it also trivializes the genuine social disaster wrought by the extremes of economic inequality we have tolerated in the United States. (Currie, 1985:160)

Or, as the President's Commission on Law Enforcement and the Administration of Justice put it: "Crime flourishes where the conditions of life are the worst" (Currie, 1998:110).

Social class is also significant in the upper strata of the stratification system. White-collar crimes are committed by those in lofty occupational and political roles. Embezzlement, computer crimes, bribery, manipulation of the stock market, land swindles, and the like involve people at the other end of the social hierarchy. The irony is that while white-collar, political, and corporate crimes do much more harm than do the crimes by the poor, crimes by the poor are seen as the crime problem.

- **Race.** People labeled as criminals in the United States are disproportionately people of color—African Americans, Latinos, and Native Americans (see Table 12.2). For example, while Blacks are 13 percent of the U.S. population, they constitute 38.8 percent of all those arrested for violent offenses in 1999. Even more disproportionate, Native Americans, while only 0.7 percent of the population, represented 14.1 percent of the arrests for violent crimes (Greenfeld and Smith, 1999).

  Although racial minorities have more contact with the criminal justice system than Whites do, this statistic does not mean that race causes crime. Many crimes on the street are committed by racial minorities because the social conditions of unemployment, poverty, and racism fall more heavily on them. Especially in urban centers, there are more and more African Americans living in poverty, jobless, and without hope—"a tangle of social circumstances conducive to high rates of violence" (Sykes and Cullen, 1992:111). Moreover, we should remember that the official statistics reflect arrest rates and are not necessarily a true indication of actual rates. The bias of the system against the poor, and especially poor minorities, makes the likelihood of their arrest and conviction greater than for well-to-do Whites, as we see in the section on the criminal justice system.

  In terms of victims by race, Native Americans are the most likely to be victims, followed in order by African Americans, Whites, and Asian Americans (see Figure 12.3).

TABLE 12.2

Persons Arrested by Federal Agencies, by Race and Type of Offense, 1999

		Percent of Suspects Arrested for:								
				Property Offenses			Public-order Offenses			
	Number Arrested	All Offenses	Violent Offenses	Fraudulent	Other	Drug Offenses	Regulatory	Other	Supervision Violations	Material Witness
All arrestees	109,857	100%	3.9%	12.1%	3.2%	29.1%	0.7%	33.1%	14.3%	3.7%
White	77,599	70.6	43.7	63.6	60.5	67.2	85.5	82.3	59.8	93.3
Black	27,052	24.6	38.8	31.0	31.9	30.8	7.3	12.9	34.7	2.2
Native American	1,875	1.7	14.1	0.7	4.4	0.4	1.6	0.9	3.5	0.3
Asian/Pacific Islander	2,549	2.3	3.0	4.0	2.5	1.0	4.1	3.0	1.4	3.5
Other	769	0.7	0.5	0.7	0.8	0.5	1.5	0.9	0.5	0.7

Source: U.S. Department of Justice, Bureau of Justice Statistics. 1999. *Compendium of Federal Justice Statistics.* NCJ 186179. Washington, DC: U.S. Department of Justice, p. 17.

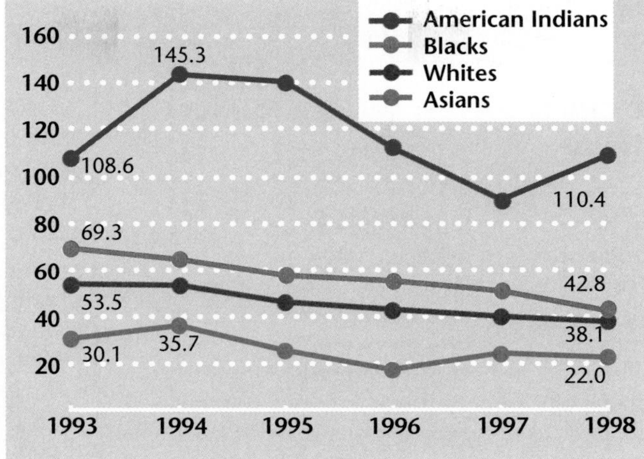

FIGURE 12.3

Victims of Violent Crimes per 1,000 People over Age 12

Source: U.S. News and World Report (April 2, 2001): 10.

Categories of Crime

The *Uniform Crime Reports* of the FBI focus on traditional types of crime, which tend to be concentrated among the young and the poor. The focus on traditional crime ignores other types that may actually be more costly to society in terms of lives and property—organized, white-collar, corporate, and political crime. Another type of crime—moral order crime—is significant in enforcement costs but not necessarily in human costs.

- **Traditional Street Crimes.** These are the crimes emphasized by the police, the government, and the media. They are the FBI's index crimes of burglary, larceny, auto theft, robbery, rape, assault, and murder. These are serious crimes against property or violence against people that many people consider to be the whole of crime. People accused of these crimes are ones who typically clog the courts and prisons.

The perpetrators of these types of crimes are disproportionately people on the economic margins of society—the poor, the uneducated, the unemployed, the homeless, and racial minorities (see the "Social Policy" panel titled "Comparative Crime Rates," pp. 344–345).

In evaluating this type of crime, we need to consider two types of offenders. One type is habitual offenders, who, for whatever reason, continue their criminal patterns. For all seven major traditional crime categories, the majority of those arrested are repeaters. Obviously, the career criminal must be converted to a new way of life, to a legitimate career that offers all the gratifications received through criminality, if rehabilitation is to be successful.

The other type is one-time-only criminals (accidental or incidental criminals). Progressives maintain that such people should not be punished harshly, for that would be counterproductive. As Pearl puts it:

> The act is idiosyncratic to a life and regardless of the heinousness of the act, there is little to be gained from either punishment or treatment of the offender. Social policy should provide for restitution, if appropriate. Social policy must not encourage accidental criminals to careers in crime (which often happens when such a criminal is stigmatized, forced to associate with career criminals, and is prevented from returning to noncriminal ways). (Pearl, 1977:50)

SOCIAL POLICY

COMPARATIVE CRIME RATES: We Are Number One in Violent Crimes!

International comparisons of crime data, while inexact, do provide rough approximations of how crime is patterned geographically. What is accepted is that among the industrialized nations there is not too much difference in burglaries, bicycle thefts, and other property crimes. What is striking, however, is that among these nations, the United States has much higher rates of violent crimes (robberies, assaults, murders, and rapes). "For at least a century and probably longer we have been the most murderous 'developed' society on earth" (Harwood, 1997:27). To support this assertion, consider the following representative facts:

- Holland's murder rate is one-sixth the U.S. rate. The U.S. national homicide rate ranges from about three to four to more than twenty times that of other industrialized nations. If the United States brought its homicide rate down to the level of Germany or France, it would save more than 15,000 lives every year.
- The 1995 murder rate with guns was 5.25 per 100,000 people in the United States, compared to 0.116 in Great Britain.
- In 1994 an American male age 15 to 24 was ninety-two times more likely to die by violence as his Austrian counterpart. Similarly, he was thirty-seven times as likely to die by deliberate violence as a Brit, twelve times as likely as a young Canadian, twenty times as likely as a Swede, 26 times as likely as a French youth, and over sixty times as likely as a Japanese.
- Compared to the British, Americans are far more likely to commit robbery, more likely to use a gun in the course of a robbery, and more likely to inflict deadly force on their victim, whether or not they use a gun.

Criminologists are in general agreement that the extraordinary high rate of violent crime in the United States is the result of the confluence of at least four major forces. First, countries where there is a wide gap between rich and poor have the highest levels of violent crime. The United States has the greatest inequality gap between the affluent and the poor.

Second, the greater the proportion of the population living in poverty, the higher the rate of violent crime. The United States differs from the other industrialized nations "in having an underclass that is not merely poor, but has few chances of escaping poverty" (Rubenstein, 1995:20). Currie says, "[We] know that the links between disadvantage and violence are strongest for the poorest and the most neglected of the poor. . . . [The] people locked into the most permanent

Conservatives, on the other hand, argue for swift and severe punishment to deter the person from a life of crime and to reinforce the notion in the rest of society that crime does not pay. Again, to quote Pearl:

> [C]onservatives are moralists with pessimistic notions about other human beings. They want criminals to be punished for transgressions. In essence, conservatives propose more support for local police and certain and severe punishment for law violators. Conservatives believe that crime prospers because we are encouraged to commit crime by the shackles put on police by lenient judges, by "bleeding-heart liberal" parole and probation officers, etc. Conservatives believe most people need laws to deter them from misdeeds. Conservative policy, then, is coercive policy. (Pearl, 1977:48)

- **Crimes against the Moral Order.** To enforce the morality of the majority, legislation makes criminal certain acts deemed offensive. Violations of these laws are **moral order crimes.** Examples of this type of crime are gambling, recreational drug use, and sex between consenting adults. Sometimes these acts forms of economic marginality in the most impoverished and disrupted communities [have] the highest concentrations of serious violent crime" (Currie,1998:127).

Third, violent crime is worse in those societies with weak "safety nets" for the poor. The United States provides few if any social supports (health care, education, child care, and other forms of welfare) for those in the lower social classes. As Elliott Currie has put it: "[The United States,] though generally quite wealthy, is also far more unequal and far less committed to including the vulnerable into a common level of social life than any other developed nation" (Currie, 1998:120). In fact, the current trend in the United States is to reduce the meager benefits to the poor even more. The other industrialized nations are also reducing social spending, but their social budgets are still high compared to the United States.

Finally, the greater the availability of guns in a society, the higher the level of violent crime. Without question, the United States has more guns per capita than in any other industrialized nation—an estimated 235 million guns in a population of 281 million. The 1995 rate of gun ownership per capita in Great Britain is 0.006, compared to 0.853 in the United States. This huge arsenal makes gun access relatively easy in the United States, resulting in crimes of rage using guns rather than fists or knives or thrown objects. As Harwood has said, "Eliminating handguns would not eliminate rage or conflict but certainly would lower the life-threatening consequences of these encounters" (Harwood, 1997:27).

Thus, by examining crime rates and social policies in other industrialized nations, we have a good sociological handle on what fosters violent crimes. If this understanding guided social policy—that is, if the inequality gap and poverty were reduced by increasing taxes on the affluent while providing greater social supports, more employment opportunities, and better wages to the economically disadvantaged, plus strict controls on handguns and automatic/semi-automatic weapons—then violent crime and the human and social costs accompanying violent crime would be reduced significantly. Such a plan, however, flies in the face of the conservative ideology that guides current political leaders. They, in fact, have decided to move in the opposite direction—less of a safety net for the poor, increasing tax benefits and other subsidies to the wealthy, perpetuation of a "winner–loser society," incarcerating more of the economically marginal, and rejecting efforts to control handguns.

Sources: Elliott Currie. 1998. *Crime and Punishment in America.* New York: Metropolitan Books, pp. 15, 24–25, 116–126, 148–160; Stryker McGuire. 1996. "The Dunblane Effect." *Newsweek* (October 28):46; Richard Harwood. 1997. "America's Unchecked Epidemic." *Washington Post National Weekly Edition* (December 8):27; Ed Rubenstein. 1995. "The Economics of Crime." *Vital Speeches of the Day* (October 15):19–21.

that violate the moral order are called **victimless crimes** because even though they may offend the majority, they do not harm other people. The argument for such laws is that the state has a right to preserve the morals of its citizens in the interest of promoting social stability and consensus.

Should an individual have the right to choose among alternative forms of behavior without fear of social sanction if that behavior does not harm other people? The answer to this question is not as unqualified as it may seem; many so-called victimless crimes in fact hurt other people, at least indirectly. The family members of an alcoholic, drug addict, or compulsive gambler are affected both materially and emotionally by his or her habit. Overindulgence in alcohol or drugs increases the probability of automobile accidents. Prostitution is a victimless crime, except that some people are unwillingly forced to become prostitutes and to live in servitude to a pimp.

A fundamental problem with legislating morality, aside from putting limitations on individual freedoms, is that it labels people as "criminals" on the basis of the tastes of those in power. Thus, **secondary deviance** (deviant behavior that is a consequence of the self-fulfilling prophecy of a negative label) may result, not because someone harmed another but because his or her act was presumed by powerful others to be harmful to them.

The detection, arrest, and prosecution of victimless criminals is an enormous and expensive task. More than half the arrests and roughly 80 percent of the police work in the United States are related to the regulation of private morals (alcohol abuse, homosexuality, pornography, juvenile runaways, drug use, prostitution, gambling, and the like). About half of the jail and prison populations are there for drug offenses. If these private acts were legalized, then the police, the courts, and the prisons would be free for other, more important duties. Formerly illicit activities could become legitimate businesses providing tax revenues to local and state governments. Most important, organized crime, which now acquires most of its income from providing illegal goods and services, would no longer be able to hide its investments and profits. Thus, laws against victimless crimes are indirectly responsible for maintaining organized crime.

Moral order crimes also contribute to the corruption of the police and courts. Although many police officers are unwilling to accept bribes from murderers and thieves, they may accept them from the perpetrators of victimless crimes, using the justification that they believe these crimes are harmless and impossible to control anyway. This rationale opens the way for people involved in organized crime to buy protection for their illicit activities.

Organized Crime. **Organized crime** is a business syndicate that seeks profit by supplying illegal goods and services such as drugs, prostitution, pornography, gambling, loan sharking, the sale of stolen goods, money laundering, cigarette bootlegging, and even disposal of hazardous wastes. In short, people can and do organize to provide what others want even if it is illegal. In fact, the illegality of what people want ensures that someone will supply the goods or service because the profits are so high.

Several characteristics of organized crime serve to perpetuate it. First, organized crime supplies illegal goods and services that are in great demand. So, one reason for the continued existence of organized crime is that it fills a need. If moral order crimes were decriminalized, organized crime would be left with products and services that could be easily and cheaply supplied by legitimate sources, and its profits and existence might be eliminated.

A second characteristic of organized crime is that it depends on the corruption of police and government officials for survival and continued profitability. Bribery, campaign contributions, delivery of votes, and other favors are used to influence police personnel, government attorneys, judges, media personnel, city council members, and legislators.

Another characteristic of organized crime is its use of violence to enforce conformity with the organization. There are strict rules for conduct and means of enforcing those rules. Individuals who cheat or fail to meet their obligations are disciplined severely. Violence is also used to eliminate competition. When rival organizations vie for the monopoly of a geographic territory or the distribution of a particular service or product, the struggle is often extremely violent.

Finally, organized crime is structured to ensure efficiency. This organization is not composed just of members of a criminal society. There are criminals, of course, but many of these people are linked with legitimate members of society as well. Together, the criminal and legitimate elements combine to form networks within cities, regions, and even nations. William Chambliss's field study of organized crime in Seattle led him to conclude the following:

> [T]here is . . . a loose affiliation of businessmen, politicians, union leaders, and law enforcement officials who cooperate to coordinate the production and distribution of illegal goods and services, for which there is a substantial consumer demand. (Chambliss, 1978:151)

These crime networks that we know as organized crime are often controlled by a racial or ethnic group. The stereotype is that they are dominated by Italians. The President's Commission on Organized Crime found, however, that various crime networks were controlled by Chinese, African Americans, Mexicans, Italians, Vietnamese, Japanese, Cubans, Colombians, Irish, Russians, Canadians, and a variety of others (Beirne and Messerschmidt, 1995:261).

White-Collar Crime. The public, influenced by the media and the FBI reports, focuses its fears on traditional street crimes such as assault and robbery. Even though these are legitimate concerns, crime of the street variety (typically by the young, poor minority person) is much less significant in cost and social disruption than are **white-collar crimes**—those committed by middle-class and upper-middle-class people in their business and social activities (such as theft of company goods, embezzlement, bankruptcy fraud, swindles, tax evasion, forgery, theft of property by computer, passing bad checks, illicit copying of computer software, movies, and music, and fraudulent use of credit cards, automatic teller machines, and telephones). Some examples of the magnitude of white-collar crimes include:

- Telephone marketing swindlers cheat U.S. consumers out of an estimated $15 billion annually.
- The underground economy (i.e., people providing goods and services for cash) avoids paying some $300 billion yearly in taxes.
- Retail stores lose $29 billion a year to vanishing inventory. One-third is lost to shoplifting and 45 percent is stolen by employees, with the average loss of $1,004.35 per crooked worker in 1999 (Farrell, 2000).
- Time theft by employees (e.g., faked illness, excessive breaks, and long lunches) costs U.S. businesses as much as $200 billion annually.
- Seven percent of college students who take out student loans fail to repay them (Nakashima, 2000).
- Surveys by the Internal Revenue Service consistently find that three out of ten people cheat on their income taxes.
- Otherwise law-abiding citizens routinely copy computer software, videos, and photocopy copyrighted sheet music, even though these activities are against the law.
- The nation's largest cash cop is marijuana. The Justice Department's Drug Enforcement Agency (DEA) estimates the number of commercial growers at 90,000 to 150,000, with another million people growing marijuana for their personal use.

Although we know that white-collar crimes are expensive and extensive, we do not know by how much. The statistics just noted understate the actual amount because many of them are so difficult to detect. Moreover, the victims are often embarrassed at their naiveté in having been bilked. Whatever the numbers, the losses are huge. Suffice it to say that the criminal activities of the relatively well-to-do are widespread and expensive. What is remarkable, however, is how lenient U.S. society is to such wrongdoers when they are caught. Moreover, for the relatively few who are sentenced to prison (compared to street criminals), they serve relatively light sentences.

> A final and crucial point about white collar crime—it is much more costly than street crime. The FBI estimates, for example that burglary and robbery—street crimes—cost the United States $3.8 billion a year. Compare this to the billions of dollars stolen as a result of corporate and white-collar fraud. Health care fraud alone costs U.S. citizens $100 billion to $400 billion a year. The savings and loan fraud—which former Attorney General Dick Thornburgh called "The biggest white-collar swindle in history"—cost anywhere from $300 billion to $500 billion. And then there are lesser frauds: auto repair fraud, $40 billion a year, securities fraud, $15 billion a year—and on down the list. (Mokhiber, 1999:10)

Corporate Crime. Business enterprises can also be guilty of crimes, which are known as **corporate crimes.** The list of illegal acts committed in the name of corporate good includes fraudulent advertising, unfair labor practices, noncompliance with government regulations regarding employee safety and pollution controls, price-fixing agreements, stock manipulation, copyright infringement, theft of industrial secrets, marketing of adulterated or mislabeled food or drugs, bribery, swindles, and selling faulty merchandise. The magnitude of such crimes far surpasses the human and economic costs from other types of crime manyfold. Some recent examples:

- The National Highway and Traffic Safety Administration has recorded 203 deaths and more than 700 injuries, amid thousands of complaints involving rollover-prone Ford Explorers that crashed following sudden tread separation on factory-installed Firestone tires. Internal corporate memos at the two corporations reveal that Ford and Firestone "willfully and knowingly kept unsafe products on the market" (Milchen and Power, 2001:9).
- In 2000, the world's largest auction houses, Sotheby's and Christie's, agreed to pay $512 million to settle claims that they cheated buyers and sellers in a price-fixing scheme dating back to 1992.
- In recent years Exxon, International Paper, United Technologies, Weyerhaeuser, Pillsbury, Ashland Oil, Texaco, Nabisco, and Ralston-Purina have been convicted of environmental crimes.
- Cosco did not tell the Consumer Product Safety Commission of the more than 200 children who had been injured by its tandem stroller injuries and did not recall the stroller until more than a year after it began receiving what turned out to be 3,000 complaints. "This is a pervasive problem in a wide range of products used by children. . . . Product manufacturers frequently conduct internal investigations but remain publicly silent as complaints about alleged defects pile up. In the past three years, 75% of the most dangerous problems that led to recalls were never voluntarily reported to the government" (O'Donnell, 2000:1B).
- Archer Daniels Midland (ADM) pled guilty and was fined $100 million (the company had revenues of $13.6 billion) for its role in conspiracies to fix prices and eliminate competition and allocate sales in the lysine and citric acid markets worldwide. In return for its guilty plea, ADM was granted immunity against charges of price fixing on other products.

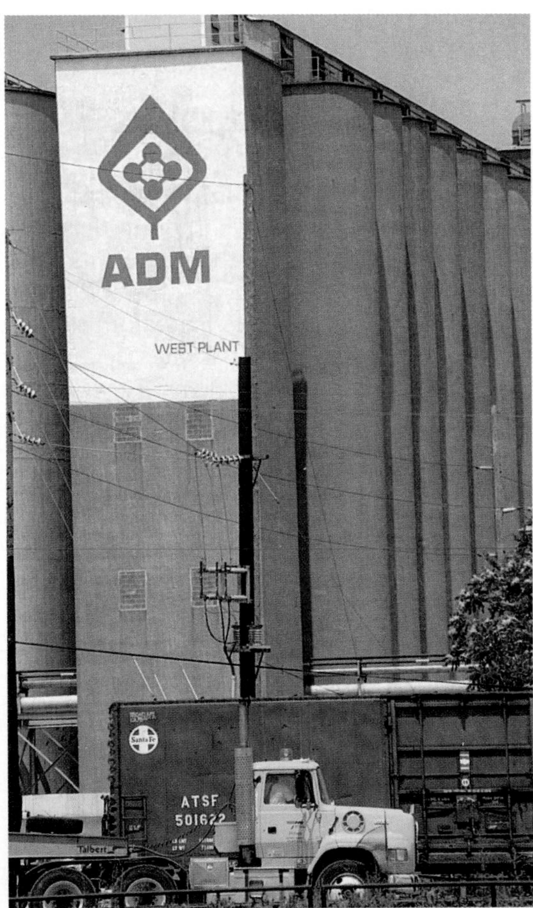

Archer Daniels Midland, the world's largest grain processor, pleaded guilty to conspiring to fix prices on two products. The company was fined $100 million (the company had revenues of $13.6 billion).

- Royal Carribbean Cruises pled guilty to twenty-one felony counts and agreed to pay an $18 million criminal fine for dumping waste oil and hazardous materials and lying to the U.S. Coast Guard.
- United Technology Electronics used phony computer-controlled measurements to allow defective bolts in missiles sold to the Pentagon to pass inspection.
- McDonnell Douglas was fined $500,000 for misleading the Pentagon on a $6.6 billion contract.
- It is estimated that as many as 3 million workers are paid less than the federally mandated minimum wage. Garment makers are the worst offenders (43 percent pay illegally low wages) followed by trucking companies, restaurants, and construction firms.
- Costain Coal pled guilty to twenty-nine counts and no contest to three counts of misconduct at a Kentucky mine shaft site where an explosion killed ten workers. These counts included violations of the Mine Safety Act's mandatory health and safety standards and false statements on records filed by the company.
- Texaco, Astra USA, WMX Technologies, Monsanto, and Mitsubishi Motors, among others were found guilty of discrimination (involving age, disability, whistleblowing, race, and sex).

- In compiling a list of the 100 corporate criminals of the 1990s, Russell Mokhiber noted that six corporations were criminal recidivist (repeat offenders) corporations: Exxon, Royal Caribbean, Rockwell International, Warner-Lambert, Teledyne, and United Technologies each pled guilty to more than one crime during the 1990s (Mokhiber, 1999).

These examples make two points. First, the goal of profit is so central to capitalistic enterprises that many corporate decisions are made without consideration for the consequences to their customers and employees. But not only are entrepreneurs indifferent to people; society is also essentially indifferent to certain offenders. The punishments meted out to individual white-collar criminals, and especially to corporate officials, are incommensurate with their misdeeds. Moreover, criminal corporations are treated much more gently than criminal individuals. For instance, states commonly have "three strikes and you're out" laws (i.e., if found guilty for three felonies, you go to prison for life), but these do not apply to corporations. Consider the case for General Electric Corporation (GE), which, from 1990 to 2001 had a rap sheet involving forty-two situations where the company was fined or ordered by the federal government to make restitution for crimes involving environmental violations, defense contracting fraud, consumer fraud, workplace safety, and employment discrimination [see the special issue of the *Multinational Monitor* (2001) devoted to General Electric].

Finally, the companies that are criminally prosecuted represent only a fraction of corporate wrongdoing:

> For every company convicted of health care fraud, there are hundreds of others who get away with ripping off Medicare and Medicaid, or face only mild slap-on-the-wrist fines and civil penalties when caught.
>
> For every company convicted of polluting the nation's waterways, there are many others who are not prosecuted because their corporate defense lawyers are able to offer up a low-level employee to go to jail in exchange for a promise from prosecutors not to touch the company or high-level executives.
>
> For every corporation convicted of bribery or of giving money directly to a public official in violation of federal law, there are thousands who launder money legally through political action committees to candidates and political parties [see Chapter 2]. They profit from a system that effectively has legalized bribery. (Mokhiber and Weissman, 1999:20)

Political Crime. Typically, a **political crime** is seen as any illegal act intended to influence the political system. The operant word in this definition is *illegal*. Is it illegal to disobey unjust laws such as laws supporting racial segregation? Is it illegal to oppose tyranny? If the answer to these questions is yes, then Martin Luther King, Jr., and George Washington must be considered political criminals. The definition given here assumes that the political system is always right and that any attempt to change it is wrong. Though antithetical to the heritage of the early American colonists and the Declaration of Independence, such thinking is typical of how those in power interpret any attempt to change the existing political system.

Another way to conceive of political crime is to concentrate on the deviance of the people in power. One example of this type of political crime is the imprisonment or harassment by the powerful of those who act against established authority. Such acts include the jailing of Martin Luther King, Jr., the

FBI's infiltration of dissident groups, the Internal Revenue Service's intimidation of people on President Nixon's "enemies list," and the punishment of people involved in providing housing, transportation, and jobs to refugees escaping political repression in Guatemala and El Salvador (the Sanctuary Movement).

Government itself can be engaged in illicit activities. Some examples are the involvement in covert actions to overthrow legitimate governments, such as the Reagan administration's policy to aid the contra effort in Nicaragua, the U.S. attack on Panama in order to capture its leader, Manuel Noriega, the suppression of popular revolts in countries favorable to the United States, the use of secrecy, lying, and deceit, the use of people as unwilling and unknowing guinea pigs in medical experiments, and war crimes (for an elaboration on each of these types, see Simon and Eitzen, 1993:251–286).

- The government revealed in 1995 that the Department of Energy conducted 435 human radiation experiments involving 16,000 people during the Cold War. Included among these experiments was one in which 18 people were injected with plutonium without their knowledge or consent (Eisler, 2000).
- From 1932 to 1972 the U.S. Public Health Service followed 400 African American men with syphilis without treating them. The purpose of the research was to determine the natural course of syphilis. In 1947, when penicillin was found to be an effected treatment for syphilis, it too was withheld.

We have seen that there are a number of different types of crimes and criminals. However, the laws and their enforcement apparatus selectively focus on traditional street crimes. The social reaction to these crimes is the subject of the remainder of this chapter.

UNJUST SYSTEM OF JUSTICE

Justice refers to the use of authority to uphold what is lawful in a completely impartial and fair manner. Even though fairness is the goal of the U.S. system of justice, it is far from realized. The law itself, the administration of the law by the police and judges, and the prisons all express bias against certain categories of people. To document this assertion, we will examine the criminal justice system from the labeling perspective, which focuses on the societal reactions to deviation.

This perspective has two emphases: (1) the social processes that create norms, thereby labeling those who behave contrary to the norms as deviants and (2) the negative reactions (the stigma and segregation) directed at these people, which in turn generate further deviance. From this perspective, deviance is created and sustained at three levels. (The following discussion is adapted from Schur, 1971, 1973.) The first level is that of collective rule making. The rules of society create deviance. As noted in Chapter 10, what is deviant varies from society to society and from one period to another within a society. Deviance is therefore not inherent in an act itself but only in an act that violates a rule. To assess the fairness of a judicial system, we must know whether its rules are fair. Most important is the question, To what extent do powerful interest groups impose their will in the creation of the laws?

The second level of creating and sustaining deviance is that of interpersonal relations. Howard Becker has suggested that deviance is not a characteristic of individuals but rather is a status conferred on the person by an audience or series of audiences (Becker, 1963:9). In a number of studies, researchers have determined that many people at various times are involved in serious acts of deviance, yet only a relatively small proportion are labeled deviant. In other words, something other than the commission of the deviant act must differentiate the deviant(s) and those who consistently work to disadvantage certain categories of people. Or is the process impersonal?

Finally, the third level is the formal organizational processing of deviants. Here, the focus is on the public and private agencies that process the wayward—the courts, prisons, and mental hospitals. With reference to those accused of criminal behavior, we need to determine how attorneys are assigned, bail set, juries selected, sentences imposed, and parole granted. Is there a bias at each of these levels that works to the disadvantage of certain types of people? What are the consequences of being legally processed as a criminal? Does the process itself promote the deviance it is created to suppress?

This section, then, examines all phases of the system of criminal justice. Are all people accorded equal treatment under the law? Are the police fair? Are the procedures commonly used in the courts free of bias? As a nation, the United States has always pledged equal and therefore fair treatment to all its residents. This section documents that the reality is far removed from the ideal. There is a systematic bias in the criminal justice system that disproportionately labels the powerless as deviants.

Laws

Of all the requirements for a just system, the most fundamental is a body of nondiscriminatory laws. Many criminal laws are the result of public consensus as to what kinds of behaviors are a menace and should be punished (such as murder, rape, and theft). The laws devised to make these acts illegal and to specify the extent of punishment for violators are nondiscriminatory because they do not single out a particular social category as the target. Although these laws in themselves are not discriminatory, the remainder of this chapter demonstrates that the administration of them often is.

Other laws, however, do discriminate because they result from the exertions of special interests to translate their objectives into public policy. In contrast, some segments of society (such as the poor, minorities, youth, renters, and debtors) rarely have access to the lawmaking process and therefore often find the laws unfairly aimed at them. Vagrancy, for example, is really a crime that only the poor can commit.

One example of this interest group approach to the law is the pre–Civil War and Jim Crow legislation in the South. The majority created laws to keep the races separate and unequal. Here are a few specific examples of the historical bias of the law against Blacks (Burns, 1973:156–166):

- The law played a critical role in defining and sanctioning slavery. For instance, the law made slavery hereditary and a lifetime condition.
- The slave codes denied Blacks the rights to bring law suits or to testify against a White person.
- Jim Crow laws codified the customs and uses of segregation.

- After Reconstruction, the grandfather clause, the literacy test, and the poll tax were legal devices designed to keep Blacks from voting.
- In the nineteenth century the law allowed only White men to sit on juries.

Not only is the formation of the law political, so, too, is its administration. At every stage in the processing of criminals, authorities make choices based on personal bias, pressures from the powerful, and the constraints of the status quo. Examples of the political character of law administration include attempts by the powerful to coerce other people to their view of morality, resulting in laws against homosexuality, pornography, drug use, and gambling; pressure exerted by the powerful on the authorities to crack down on certain kinds of violators, especially individuals and groups who are disruptive (protesters); pressure exerted to keep certain crimes from public view (embezzlement, stock fraud, the Iran–Contra scandal); pressure to protect the party in power, elected officials, and even the police department; and any effort to protect and preserve the status quo. Hartjen has explained why we must conclude that the administration of justice is inherently political:

> Unless one is willing to assume that law-enforcement agents can apply some magic formula to gauge the opinions of the public they serve, unless one is willing to assume that citizens unanimously agree on what laws are to be enforced and how enforcement is to be carried out, unless one is willing to assume that blacks, the poor, urbanites, and the young are actually more criminalistic than everyone else, it must be concluded, at least, that discriminatory law enforcement is a result of differences in power and that actual decisions as to which and whose behavior is criminal are expressions of this power. One need only ask himself why some laws, such as those protecting the consumer from fraud, go largely unenforced while the drug addict, for example, is pursued with a paranoiac passion. (Hartjen, 1978:13)

Police

Formal law enforcement policy begins with the police. They decide whether a law has been broken. They interpret and judge what behavior is "disorderly," how much noise constitutes a "public nuisance," when a quarrel becomes a "criminal assault," when protest becomes illegitimate, and what constitutes "public drunkenness." Their authority to interpret these questions suggests that the police have great decisional latitude. Unlike other agencies in the criminal justice process, the police in their work often deal with their clients in isolation. Their decisions are rarely subject to review by higher authorities. As Jerome Skolnick has said, "police work constitutes the most secluded part of an already secluded system and therefore offers the greatest opportunity for arbitrary behavior" (Skolnick, 1966:14).

Given the great discretionary powers of the individual police, one must determine whether police officers as a group tend to hold particular biases that affect their perceptions and actions. Several characteristics of the job and the types of people attracted to it suggest that certain biases may prevail among this occupational category.

The job itself causes police personnel to develop a distinctive way of perceiving the world. Foremost is that they are given the authority to enforce the law. They have power, even the ultimate power of legitimate force, at their disposal to uphold the law. As authorities sworn to uphold the law, police support the status quo. Naturally, then, they find people who defile the flag or otherwise protest against the system abhorrent.

Second, the danger inherent in their occupation promotes a particular worldview among the police. The element of danger tends to make them suspicious of behavior that is nonconforming or otherwise unusual. In the interests of self-defense, they tend to assume the worst of people they believe to be dangerous (minorities, protesters, drug users).

The police also tend to be socially isolated. Because they have actual power to punish other citizens, police personnel are the objects of hostility for many, but especially for minority group members. This hostility is manifested in epithets ("pigs"), abusive language, spitting, and other forms of harassment. The result, of course, is that the police, even those relatively free of prejudice toward minorities, tend to become hostile toward members of certain social categories over time. The harassment directed toward the police also increases the threat of danger to them. The result is a self-fulfilling prophecy: The police, harassed by victimized categories in societies, in turn harass their tormentors, which leads to charges of police brutality and the justification to be hostile toward them.

This characterization presupposes that the police are relatively free of prejudice, at least at the beginning of their career. This assumption, however, is not always true. Police tend to be recruited from the lower-middle and upper-lower social classes of the community. Research shows that police recruits tend to hold attitudes typical of their working-class origins (respect for authority, belief in the status quo, and hostility toward certain racial and ethnic groups).

Racial profiling (the practice of targeting citizens for police encounters on the basis of race) is common. DWB (driving while Black) is not a crime but because of racial profiling by the police, there is the assumption of criminal behavior (Lamberth, 1998). For example, a study of Maryland State troopers and the searches they made of motorists on Interstate 95 in 1995 found that while Black motorists constituted 17 percent of all motorists and 17.5 percent of

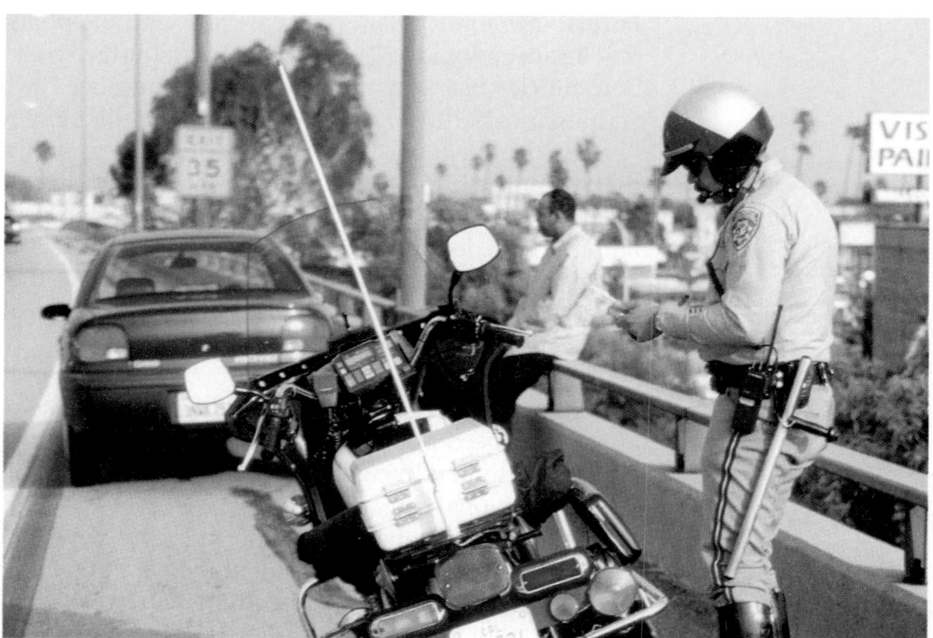

Black motorists are stopped more often by the police than are White motorists because of racial profiling.

the speeders, Black motorists were subject to 409 of the 533 searches (77 percent) made by the police looking for contraband (Stone, 1999). Similarly, over 80 percent of the automobile searches by the New Jersey State police on the New Jersey turnpike during the 1990s were conducted on vehicles driven by African Americans and Latinos (Kocieniewski and Hanley, 2000). A report of Missouri police found that they stop Black motorists at a rate 30 percent higher than White drivers, and search them 70 percent more often (Associated Press, 2001a). This targeting of racial minorities by the police is based on the assumption that racial minorities are more likely than Whites to commit crime. However,

> race is a particularly bad basis for suspicion, since most black people, like most whites, don't commit any crime. Annually at least 90 percent of African Americans are not arrested for anything. On any given day, the percentage of innocent African Americans is even higher. Thus racial profiles necessarily sweep in a large number of innocents. In addition, when officers target minorities they miss white criminals. (Cole, 1999:13)

The police engage in racial profiling also in ways other than in traffic encounters. For example, the police are much more likely to engage in a crackdown on the use of crack than on the use of drugs on a middle-class college campus, even though the level of drug use may be higher on campus. The result is a greater proportion of African Americans arrested for drug charges than middle-class Whites, thereby reinforcing the stereotypes and the rationale for further use of racial profiling (Kalet, 2000).

In sum, the pressures on the police and the type of people attracted to that role ensure that the incumbents tend to be politically conservative. Their task is to defend the status quo. They are the first line of defense against crime. Social innovators, therefore, would not find police work compatible with their goals. Moreover, police personnel may harbor negative attitudes toward minorities or be ignorant of the social bases for the hostility of minorities toward themselves and other authorities.

Judicial Process

How fair is the process by which lawbreakers are prosecuted, tried, convicted, and sentenced? Given that the courts deal only with those whom the police arrest, clearly the process begins with a bias. The question is, Do the courts increase the degree of unfairness or not? A related question involves the operation of the principle that individuals brought before the courts are presumed to be innocent: How great is the gap between principle and practice?

To answer these questions, let us examine the formal procedures of the system of justice for the commission of a serious crime. The police arrest the probable offender and bring him or her before a magistrate. The magistrate examines the evidence and decides whether to allow the alleged offender to be free on bail. The case is then turned over to a prosecuting attorney, who formally charges the defendant. This charge is subject to review by a judge at a preliminary hearing or by a grand jury. If the defendant pleads not guilty, then he or she comes to trial, where the facts of the case are argued by the prosecuting and defense attorneys before a judge and jury. If the jury finds the defendant guilty, he or she is sentenced by the judge to a term in prison or to a term of probation.

Magistrate and the Setting of Bail. The primary functions of the magistrate are to inform defendants of their right to counsel, to assign them counsel if so requested, to set a date for a preliminary hearing, and to set bail. In the last procedure the magistrate exercises considerable discretion.

Bail is the posting of money by the accused to guarantee that he or she will be present at the time of trial. The Constitution provides the right to bail in noncapital cases. Bail allows accused people to stay out of jail, thereby retaining their family, community, and work responsibilities; most important, it allows them a chance to investigate and prepare their cases.

Several practices in setting bail, however, undermine the principle of treating all people fairly. The primary problem is that the amount of bail to be posted is left to the discretion of the magistrate, who may set high bail to "teach the accused a lesson" or to "protect the community." Magistrates have often taken such an approach when the defendants have been political protestors and minority group members. This practice violates the Eighth Amendment, which specifically forbids the setting of excessive bail; moreover, the concept of preventive detention contradicts the presumption of innocence that is supposed to be at the heart of the judicial process.

The setting of bail is also unfair because magistrates tend to determine the amount of bail by the type of crime alleged instead of by the accused's ability to pay. Moreover, the accused or their families typically obtain bail money from professional bondspersons, who receive 5 to 10 percent of the total as their fee. If the bail were set at $10,000 for everyone accused of a felony and the accused had to pay a bondsperson a fee of $1,000, clearly the accused who were poor would suffer the greatest hardship.

The obvious result of the system of setting bail is that the poor remain in jail and the wealthy are released, either because the latter have their own money or bail or because bail bondspersons consider them better risks. This result highlights another problem: the power of bail bondspersons to decide whom they will bond and whom they will not. Of course, the poor are considered more risky. Moreover, bondspersons may refuse to grant bail as a "favor" to the police.

Thus, the biggest problem with the bail-setting practice as it now operates is that it tends to imprison the poor. Time spent in jail before trial varies by locality and by the backlog of pending cases. In some jurisdictions defendants who cannot make bail spend as long as 18 months in jail awaiting trial. Clearly, this situation violates the principle that the accused person is presumed innocent until proven guilty, for it provides punishment before conviction. And the difference between those who languish in jail before their trial and those who are free is money.

Plea Bargaining. Less than 10 percent of the people charged with crimes ever go to trial. The thousands of cases that bypass the trial process do so because either the charges are dropped or the people accused plead guilty to the original or lesser charges. The latter event is called **plea bargaining** because the defendants bargain away their right to a trial in return for their guilty plea and a more lenient punishment than if they were found guilty of the original charge. Plea bargaining has become the rule, not the exception, in the disposition of criminal cases in the United States.

There are many pressures on defendants, lawyers, prosecutors, and judges to encourage plea bargaining. Foremost is the overwhelming caseload facing police, prosecutors, and judges. Without guilty pleas to speed defendants through the system, the criminal justice process could not function because of impossibly crowded courts. One obvious solution is for judges to encourage guilty pleas by implementing the agreements negotiated by prosecutors and defense counsel. Similarly, prosecutors encourage plea bargaining because of their large caseloads. In addition, prosecutors must have a high conviction rate, and plea bargaining achieves this goal at relatively little expense.

Defendants are pressured in several ways to plea bargain. People who are assigned as defense counsel typically encourage their clients to "cop a plea." One reason they encourage plea bargaining is that assigned counsel receive little compensation, and they would rather return quickly to their more lucrative private practice. Counsel may also feel that plea bargaining is in the best interests of the client because it will reduce time spent in jail awaiting trial. District attorneys often force plea bargaining on defendants by charging them with more serious crimes (carrying heavier penalties). Compelling defendants to plea bargain has the effect of reducing caseloads. A defendant who refuses faces the possibility of serving a longer sentence and for a more serious offense. Public defenders also encourage plea bargaining to reduce the burden of their large caseloads on their small investigative staffs. They would rather concentrate their efforts on capital crimes.

There are special pressures on defendants who are poor or of moderate means to plead guilty. They will be unable to bear the expense of a lengthy trial. Moreover, those unable to make bail must await trial in jail. These factors deter poor defendants from insisting on their rights. Although overcrowding in the courts may make it a necessity, plea bargaining subverts the basic foundations of the system of criminal justice. Contrary to the Bill of Rights, the practice operates on an implicit assumption of guilt. It fails to distinguish between the innocent and the guilty, thus penalizing the innocent and rewarding the guilty. Moreover, because it reduces sentences, plea bargaining erodes the elements of deterrence on which criminal sanctions are based. The procedure especially discriminates against the poor. The poor defendant, already in jail, is pressured by court-appointed counsel to bargain from a position of weakness. In a plea-bargaining situation the need for competent and conscientious counsel outweighs all other factors. Yet it is inevitable that a lawyer receiving a handsome fee for his or her services will be more interested in a client's welfare than will an overburdened and undercompensated court-appointed one.

Adversary System. An intrinsic feature of the U.S. criminal justice system is the concept of adversary roles. In the **adversary system,** the state and the accused engage in a public battle to argue and provide evidence before an impartial judge or jury. For this principle to work, the adversaries must be relatively equal in ability, incentive, and resources. But this is not usually the case. The state has enormous resources (police, crime labs, detectives) with which to build its case. The accused, if wealthy, can match the resources and expertise of the state. In the famous O. J. Simpson case, for example, the defendant spent between $5 million and $6 million for a team of lawyers, jury selection experts, DNA authorities, and other specialists. In what would have been a speedy trial and probably an open-and-shut case of guilty for a poor defendant, the Simpson team was able to contest every piece of evidence by the prosecution, present countertheories, and raise a reasonable doubt among the jurors:

> The Simpson case has demonstrated perhaps more starkly than ever before that in the American justice system, as in so much else in this country, *money changes everything—and huge amounts of money change things almost beyond recognition.* [Emphasis added.] (Gleick, 1995:41)

"Not guilty."

But the Simpson case was an anomaly. Of all felony defendants in the United States, 80 to 90 percent are too poor to hire their own lawyer and are represented by court-appointed attorneys. These poor defendants are especially disadvantaged by the adversary system. Obviously, they cannot pay for detective work, hire expert witnesses, and do the other things necessary to build their case. States vary in the resources they commit to such cases. In Alabama, for example, the state will pay no more than $1,000 for out-of-court fees for defending a death-penalty case, whereas Indiana averages $53,000 on capital cases. The caseload for public defenders is huge, typically resulting in "assembly-line justice that often is not justice at all" (Gleick, 1995:44).

Trial by Jury. Fundamental to a fair system of criminal justice is the right to a trial by a jury consisting of a representative body of citizens. In practice, however, certain categories of people are underrepresented on juries: minorities, people not registered to vote, students, and low-prestige occupational groups. The result is that the poor, especially the poor from minority groups, are typically not judged by a jury of their peers.

The failure of juries to reflect communities is significant because the people least represented are those most likely to challenge community norms. This situation puts a special burden on defendants accused of political crimes (such as antiwar and civil rights protest).

In selecting a jury, the attorneys for the state and the accused attempt to choose jurors who are likely to favor their particular side. The selection process tends to be unfair, however. The state, with enormous investigatory and financial resources at its disposal, may use the police and the FBI to investigate minute details about each prospective juror. Unless the accused is very wealthy, the defense usually decides on the bases of intuition and superficial data.

Trial outcomes are also affected to some extent by whether the case is heard by a jury or a trial judge. The research suggests that juries tend to be more lenient than are judges. This points to another inequity of the judicial system: Because jury trials increase the probability of acquittal for defendants, they should be equally available to all people.

African Americans do not fare as well as Whites in civil trials. Verdicts go against African Americans more often than against Whites, both as plaintiffs and defendants. Not only do Blacks lose more often than Whites, but when Blacks do win, they win smaller awards than do White plaintiffs.

Judicial Sentencing. Until the 1970s judges were given considerable latitude in determining the exact punishment for convicted criminals. The discretion of the judges was almost without limits, and sometimes the results were very inconsistent from judge to judge and even by a particular judge. This discretionary sentencing permitted individualized justice. In other words, the judge could take into account the peculiar factors of the case in her or his decision. Although this ideal is a worthy one, the procedure resulted in a kind of courtroom roulette, depending on the law in the jurisdiction, the ideology of the judge, media attention, and other factors. Most telling among these other factors are the social class and racial characteristics of the defendants, with a strong tendency for middle- and upper-class Whites to receive lighter sentences than do lower-class Whites and non-Whites.

Beginning in the 1970s there was a movement to curb the discretionary power of judges with the passage of mandatory and determinate sentencing laws. **Mandatory sentencing** forced judges to incarcerate violent and habitual criminals. **Determinate sentencing** means that for a given offense, the judge must impose a sentence (sometimes a fixed sentence and sometimes a range, depending on the state), within the guidelines of the law, depending on the crime and the offender's past record. Typically, a sentencing commission would be appointed in a state to determine these penalties.

The leading example of mandatory sentencing is the "three strikes and you're out" law passed by the federal government (1994) and many state legislatures. The essence of this law is that someone found guilty of three serious crimes would be locked up for life with no hope for parole (serious is defined differently by the various states, with some accepting only violent crimes in this category, while others may include low-level property crimes and drug offenses). This provision is popular because it is punitive on so-called habitual criminals and, thus, will lower the crime rate. There are several problems with this get-tough policy, however (the following is from Skolnick, 1994, and Currie, 1998). First, despite the highest imprisonment rates (other than Russia) in the industrialized world, U.S. crime rates remain the highest. Second, the vast majority of violent offenses are committed by teenagers and young men:

> Serious violent offenses . . . peak at age 17. The rate is half as much at age 24 and declines significantly as offenders mature into their thirties. If we impose life sentences on serious violent offenders on their third conviction . . . we will generally do so in the twilight of their criminal careers. Three-strikes laws will eventually fill our prisons with geriatric offenders, whose care will be increasingly expensive when their propensities to commit crimes are at the lowest. (Skolnick, 1994:31)

Third, this mandatory provision increases the demand on limited prison space. This has two negative implications: increased cost to build and maintain prisons (about $80,000 to build a cell and $16,000 to $25,000 annually to house a prisoner) and overcrowded prisons that will force the early release of other violent prisoners to make room.

Fourth, the prisons are increasingly populated by lower-level offenders (small-time thieves, repeat property criminals, and drug offenders). Inmates in federal prisons convicted of violent crimes, for example, were 17 percent in 1990 but 12 percent in 1998. Meanwhile, those in federal prisons for drug offenses increased from 53 to 59 percent. Similarly, those in federal prisons for public-order offenses increased from 15 percent of all prisoners in 1990 to 20 percent in 1999 (Beck, 2000:12).

Consequences of a Biased Judicial Process. The facts make the case that the judicial system is biased against racial minorities.

- African Americans are three times more likely than Whites to be arrested but seven times more likely to end up in jail (Kalet, 2000).
- Of Black males born in the United States 28.5 percent go to state or federal prison for a sentence of more than one year. The corresponding chance for Latino males was 16 percent, and for White males, 4.4 percent (Stone, 1999).
- A study by the U.S. Department of Justice concluded: Minority youths, particularly African Americans, are treated significantly worse than Whites at every stage of the judicial process: "They are more likely to be locked up prior to trial, more likely to be tried as adults, more likely to be given hard time and less likely, at any step, to be given a break" (cited in Cose, 2000:17A).
- Federal prison sentences overall are almost 50 percent longer for African Americans than for Whites (*Population Today*, 2000).
- While five times as many Whites use drugs as Blacks, 62 percent of drug offenders admitted to state prisons are Black (Lowenstein, 2001).
- More than 90 percent of those on death row are poor (*Z Magazine*, 2000).

Criminologist Randall Shelden summarizes the situation:

> Our modern system of justice takes place within a society that is highly stratified by race, class, and gender. It is my contention that *equal justice cannot be achieved in an unequal society*. The justice system in America merely reinforces these inequalities.
>
> . . .
>
> One result of social inequality is vast differences in the probabilities of having one's behaviors labeled "criminal." Evidence for this is found throughout the social science literature during the last half century or more. Therefore, the legal system responds accordingly and, more often than not, tends to focus its attention on those from the less privileged sectors of society: the poor, racial, and ethnic minorities and [especially] women of color, who more often than not are also poor. (Shelden, 2001:3,18)

Correctional System

U.S. citizens constitute 5 percent of the world's population, yet the number of U.S. prison inmates amount to 25 percent of the world's prisoners, with a higher proportion of its citizens jailed than any other country in history (*Z Magazine*, 2000). The United States incarcerates its citizens at a rate six times higher than Canada, England, and France, seven times higher than Switzerland and Holland, and ten times Sweden and Finland (Street, 2001a).

Not only does the United States have a very high rate of incarceration, the prison population is unrepresentative of the general population, being disproportionately racial and ethnic minorities, the poor, and the uneducated. The facts support the thesis of this chapter that the criminal justice system in the United States is biased against the powerless (the following are from various annual reports by the Department of Justice, most notably Beck, 2001):

- At midyear 2000, there were 1,931,859 persons incarcerated in the nation's federal and state prisons and local jails. This is a fourfold increase since 1975 (see Figure 12.4 for the growth in the past 10 years).
- From 1990 to 2000, the rate of incarceration in prison (federal and state) and jail (local) increased from 1 in every 218 residents to 1 in every 142.
- There were 110 female inmates per 100,000 women in the United States, compared to 1,297 male inmates per 100,000 men.
- There is a wide variation by state in incarceration rates. For example, Louisiana had 793 prisoners per 100,000 residents (Black inmates in Louisiana outnumber Whites 3 to 1, yet Blacks account for only a third of the state's population), Texas (779), and Oklahoma (681), while at the low end, Minnesota had 129, Maine 130, and North Dakota 146.
- Whites were 37.4 percent of the male inmates in federal or state prisons and local jails, while African Americans were 44.8 percent, and Latinos 16.4 percent. In other words, non-Whites who were 28 percent of the population were disproportionately represented in prison (62.6 percent).
- When total incarceration rates are shown by race and age, young Black males are vastly overrepresented. Expressed in percentages, 13.1 percent of all Black males age 25 to 29 were in prison or jail in midyear 2000, compared to 4.1 percent of Latino males, and 1.7 percent of White males in this age group.
- In the United States 1.5 million children have a parent in prison. These children are at risk since estimates are that they are as much as five times

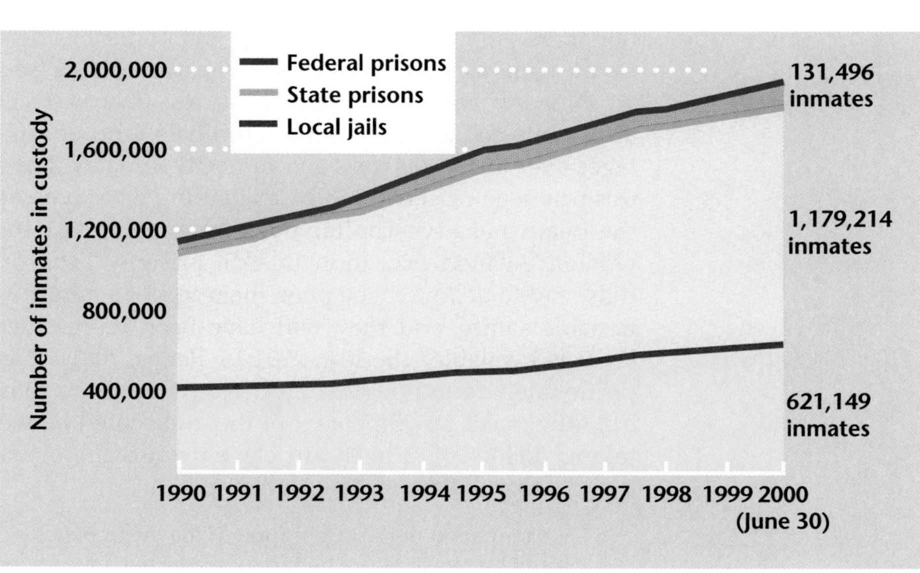

FIGURE 12.4

Prison and Jail Inmates, 1990 to Midyear 2000

Source: U.S. Deprtment of Justice. 2001. "Prison and Jail Inmates at Midyear 2000" NCJ185989. *Bureau of Justice Statistics Bulletin* (March):1.

more likely to end up in prison themselves as children whose parents are not in prison. These children of the imprisoned, most likely, come from disadvantaged circumstances. The stings of stigma, family disruption, and living in poverty put these children at increased risk for doing badly in school, as well as for early pregnancy, drug abuse, and delinquency (Lowenstein, 2001).

- The median income for both male and female inmates did not exceed the government's poverty level during the year before arrest.
- The median income for both male and female inmates did not exceed the government's poverty level during the year arrested.
- The highest incarceration rate among males age 16 to 64 was among those who were unemployed prior to arrest. Of those inmates who were working prior to arrest, 30 percent were employed outside what they considered their normal occupation. This suggests, very likely, that they were **underemployed** (i.e., employed at a level below that for which they had been trained).
- The proportion of blue-collar workers in prison was more than double that found in the U.S. population. The reverse was true of white-collar workers, who constituted less than one-third of their proportion in the population.
- Over 40 percent of all jail and prison inmates were high school dropouts, compared to 11 percent of the U.S. population of males age 20 to 29.

There are three major reasons for this relationship. First, the crimes defined by official sources as the most important (the FBI's *Uniform Crime Index*) are the ones most likely to be committed by members of the lower classes. As has already been mentioned, these official data on crimes are biased, and they bias the public, police, juries, and the courts. Because of the official emphasis, we view these crimes as the most threatening, yet in reality the crimes by the powerful (the well-to-do, the corporations, and organized crime) do more harm to people and their property. Second, as we have seen, the criminal justice system is not just. Economic resources make a crucial difference at every stage. And finally, society continues to be racist. Institutional discrimination works to keep racial minorities disproportionately poor, unemployed, and despised. Institutional discrimination has also kept the minorities disproportionately *underrepresented* among police, lawyers, judges, and juries (see Miller, 1996).

Not only are the more well-to-do less likely to receive a prison sentence, but also white-collar and wealthy criminals who are imprisoned receive advantages over the lower-class and minority inmates. The most extreme example of this privilege can be found by examining what type of person actually receives the death penalty—**capital punishment.** In 2001 more than 3,700 men and women awaited execution in U.S. prisons. "The overwhelming number of those put to death will be poor, members of a minority, uneducated, or of questionable sanity, and they will have been represented by some of the worst lawyers available" (Berlow, 2001:16; Benac, 2001). Racial minorities are disproportionately found on death row (e.g., Blacks are 12 percent of the population, but they make up 35 percent of those executed between 1976 and 2001). Most telling, killers of Whites are eleven times more likely to receive the death penalty than killers of African Americans:

> Discrimination in the application of the death penalty can be seen most vividly by focusing on the race of the *victim*. Prosecutors nationwide—more than nine out of ten of whom are white—tend to seek the death penalty more

> often if the victim is white. To take one typical example, Georgia prosecutors sought the death penalty in 70 percent of the cases where the perpetrator was African-American and the victim was White. When there was a White killer and an African-American victim, the same prosecutors sought the death penalty in only 15 percent of the cases. (Donziger, 1996:114)

Who gets parole is another indicator of a bias in the system. **Parole** is a conditional release from prison that allows a prisoner to return to his or her community under the supervision of a parole officer before completion of the maximum sentence. Typically, parole is granted by a board established for each correctional institution or for the state. Often, the parole board members are political appointees without training or experience in criminal justice issues. The parole board reviews the prisoner's social history, past offenses, and behavior in prison and makes a judgment about release. The board's decision is rarely subject to review and can be made arbitrarily or discriminatorily.

The bias that disadvantages minorities and the poor throughout the system of justice continues as parole board members, corrections officers, and others make judgments that often reflect stereotyped notions. What type of prisoner represents the safest risk, a non-White or a White? An uneducated or educated person? A white-collar worker or a chronically unemployed, unskilled worker? Research shows, consistently, that decision makers in these situations typically give preferential treatment to people with the social characteristics more valued in society.

That the members of the disadvantaged in society (the poor and the minorities) are disproportionately represented in the prison population reinforces negative stereotypes already prevalent among the majority of the population. The large number of African Americans and the poor in prison is taken as proof that those groups have criminal tendencies. Moreover, the high **recidivism** (the return to crime by ex-prisoners) **rate** (70 percent of inmates in U.S. prisons or jails are not there for the first time) is viewed as further proof of the criminality of the poor, the uneducated, and minority groups.

Criminologist Jeffrey Reiman states that "prison produces more criminals than it cures" (Reiman, 2001:34). At least four factors related to prison experiences operate to fulfill the expectation that the poor and African Americans will be prone to criminal behavior—and a high recidivism rate. The first is that the disadvantaged view the entire criminal justice system as unjust. There is a growing belief among prisoners that because the system is biased against them, all prisoners are in fact political. This perception increases their bitterness and anger.

A second reason for the high rate of crime among the people processed through the system of criminal justice is the accepted fact that prison is a brutal, degrading, and altogether dehumanizing experience. Mistreatment by guards, sexual assaults by fellow prisoners, overcrowding, and unsanitary conditions are commonplace in U.S. prisons. Prisoners cannot escape humiliation, anger, and frustration. Combined with the knowledge that the entire system of justice is unjustly directed at certain categories of people, these feelings create a desire for revenge in many ex-convicts.

A third factor is that prisons provide learning experiences in the art of crime. Through interaction with other inmates, individuals learn the techniques of crime from experts and develop contacts that can be used later.

Finally, ex-convicts face the problems of adjusting to life without regimentation. More important, because well-paying jobs are difficult for anyone to find, particularly in times of economic recession, ex-convicts, who are automatically assumed to be untrustworthy, must choose between unemployment or jobs nobody else will take.

Nonacceptance by society causes many ex-convicts to return to crime. On the average, previous offenders are arrested for crime within 6 weeks of leaving prison. This fact, of course, justifies the beliefs of police, judges, parole boards, and other authorities that certain categories of people should receive punishment but others should not.

UNJUST IMPOSITION OF THE LABEL "CRIMINAL"

The evidence presented in this chapter strongly suggests that the powerless in society (the poor and the minorities) are disadvantaged throughout the criminal justice process. Although the bulk of research has been limited to the poor and African Americans, similar results are found for treatment of other minority groups in the criminal justice system.

That there is a bias is beyond dispute because the studies compare defendants by socioeconomic status or race, controlling for type of crime, number of previous arrests, type of counsel, and the like. These studies, however, do not answer the question so often asked: *Are the poor and minorities more prone toward crime, as the differential arrest rates and composition of the prison population appear to indicate?*

This question is difficult to answer definitively because the crime rate is a function of police activities and does not reflect unreported crimes or activities that are overlooked by the authorities. The actual amount of crime is unknown and probably unknowable. We do know, however, that criminal behavior is found throughout the social structure—by rich and poor, by Whites and African Americans, by ruralites, urbanites, and suburbanites. Businesspeople, for example, are sometimes involved in forms of lawbreaking, such as fraud, misleading advertising, restraint of trade, income tax evasion, bribery, and the like. Studies that ask respondents to report, under the assurance of anonymity, the type and frequency of their criminal acts show that (1) a huge proportion of crimes go undetected, (2) adults and juveniles, regardless of social class, tend to have committed numerous acts for which they could have been adjudicated and imprisoned, if caught, and (3) there is no substantial difference in the amount of criminal behavior of middle-class and lower-class respondents.

If criminal activities are common throughout the social structure, then how do certain groups of people avoid the criminal label while others do not? The data show that the administration of criminal law consistently works to the disadvantage of the poor, minority groups, and others who are powerless. The fact that the system operates with this bias, however, is not proof that there is a conscious attempt to control and punish just certain segments of the population. A number of factors that work to the disadvantage of the powerless help to explain the bias. There is the widespread assumption that the poor and powerless are less trustworthy than the more well-to-do. Thus, their behavior is subject to greater scrutiny, and there is a greater presumption of guilt for them than for the more advantaged in society. This assumption is based on the predominance of the economically deprived in the official crime statistics and in the composition of prison populations and on their high recidivism rate. Thus, the bias of the system creates a self-fulfilling prophecy and a rationale for citizens, police personnel, judges, jurors, and corrections officers to assume the worst about these types of people.

"Proof" that these people are more crime prone is also found in the greater likelihood of their making crime a career. This tendency is the result of crime being a realistic means for a poor person to achieve material success because attainment through conventional means is virtually impossible for many. Just as important a factor is secondary deviance, the criminal behavior that results from being labeled a criminal. Upon release, the ex-convict returns to a community that is apprehensive and distrustful. Jobs are unavailable or, if available, degrading. The individual is likely to be rejected socially because of the stigma of being a criminal. As Erikson has put it:

> [I]f a returned deviant encounters this feeling of distrust often enough, it is understandable that he too may begin to wonder if the original verdict or diagnosis is still in effect—and respond to this uncertainty by resuming deviant activity. In some respects, this solution may be the only way for the individual and his community to agree on what forms of behavior are appropriate for him. (Erikson, 1962:312)

Thus, if the powerless of society are disproportionately singled out for the criminal label, the subsequent stigmatization and segregation they face results in a tendency toward further deviance—thereby justifying society's original negative response to them. This tendency toward secondary deviance is especially strong when the imposition of the label is accompanied by a sense of injustice. Lemert argued that a stronger commitment to a deviant identity is greatest when the individual believes the label (stigma) to be inconsistently applied by society (Lemert, 1967). The research findings presented in this chapter clearly substantiate the existence of such an inconsistency.

Thus, if the powerless do engage in more deviance than do people from the middle and upper classes, they do so largely in response to society's differential treatment, demonstrated at every phase in the process of criminal justice. An excellent statement by Clayton Hartjen summarizes the thesis of this chapter:

> Criminal sanctions are supposedly directed toward a person's behavior—what he does, not what kind of person he is. Yet, the research on the administration of criminal justice . . . reveals that just the opposite occurs. A person is likely to acquire a social identity as a criminal precisely because of what he is—because of the kind of personal or social characteristics he has the misfortune to possess. Being black, poor, migrant, uneducated, and the like increases a person's chances of being defined as a criminal. . . . What I am suggesting here is that the very structure and operation of the judicial system, which was created to deal with the problem called crime, are not only grounded in an unstated image of the criminal but also—merely because the system exists—serve to produce and perpetuate the "thing" it was created to handle. That is to say, the criminal court (and especially the juvenile court) does not exist in its present form because the people it deals with are what they are. Rather, the criminals and delinquents become the way they are characterized by others as being because the court (and the world view it embodies) exists in the form that it does. *The criminal, thus, is a "product" of the structural and procedural characteristics of the judicial system.* (Hartjen, 1978:143–144)

CHAPTER REVIEW

1. Criminality is a social status determined by how an individual is perceived, evaluated, and treated by legal authorities. What is a crime depends on the law, which is created by the powerful. Crime, then, is innately political.
2. Official crime statistics (the FBI's *Uniform Crime*

Reports) focus on street crimes against people and property. They omit white-collar crimes, corporate crimes, political crime, and organized crime.
3. According to the official crime statistics: (a) More males than females commit crimes, (b) juveniles and young adults have the highest crime rates, and (c) members of the lower classes and racial minorities are more likely to be criminals.
4. Victimless crimes are private acts designated as criminal by powerful interest groups that are able to legislate morality. Making these acts criminal creates several problems: (a) They are impossible to enforce; (b) they are costly to enforce, and, if legal, they would bring in significant tax revenues; (c) they make organized crime profitable; and (d) they contribute to the corruption of the police and courts. Moreover, so-called victimless crimes are rarely victimless—they do harm people.
5. Losses resulting from individual white-collar crime amount to ten times the monetary loss from street crimes. Yet official agencies do not devote as much attention to white-collar crimes, and the few criminals that are apprehended receive relatively light sentences.
6. Corporate crimes are the most dangerous and expensive to society because they involve unsafe working conditions, pollution of the environment, unsafe products, and fraud.
7. Political crimes are of two types: (a) acts that threaten the power structure and (b) illegal acts by those in power.
8. Organized crime is the second most lucrative business in the United States. Organized crime thrives because of (a) the demand for illegal goods and services, (b) corruption among the police and government officials, (c) violence and intimidation, and (d) its well-organized operation at all levels—locally, regionally, nationally, and internationally.
9. The system of justice is fundamentally unjust. The laws favor the powerful. The Crime Index channels police activities toward certain criminal acts and away from others. The poor are disadvantaged at every stage of the judicial process because lawyers, bail, and an adequate defense are costly. Thus, for similar offenses the powerless are more likely than the powerful to be found guilty, to be sentenced far more harshly, to wait longer for parole, and if sentenced to die, actually to be executed.

KEY TERMS

Crime. An act that breaks the law.

Violence. An act of force perceived by the powerful as threatening to the status quo.

Moral order crimes. Acts that violate laws that enforce the morality of the majority.

Victimless crimes. Acts that violate moral order crimes; they may offend the majority but they do not harm other people.

Secondary deviance. Deviant behavior that is a consequence of the self-fulfilling prophecy of a negative label.

Organized crime. A business operation that seeks profit by supplying illegal goods and services.

White-collar crimes. Illicit acts committed by middle-class and upper-middle-class people in their business and social activities.

Corporate crimes. Illegal acts by business enterprises.

Political crimes. Illegal acts intended to influence the political system. Also, the abuse of authority by those in power. Finally, actions by governments that are illegal or immoral.

Racial profiling. The practice of targeting citizens for police encounters on the basis of race.

Bail. Posting of money by the accused to guarantee that he or she will be present at the trial.

Plea bargaining. Arrangement between the prosecution and the accused where the latter pleads guilty in return for a reduced charge.

Adversary system. The U.S. system of justice, whereby the state and the accused engage in a public battle to argue and provide evidence before an impartial judge or jury.

Mandatory sentencing. By law, judges must incarcerate certain types of criminals.

Determinate sentencing. For a given offense, a judge must impose a sentence that is within the guidelines of the law.

Underemployed. Employed at a level below that for which one has been trained.

Capital punishment. Killing of a criminal by the state.

Parole. Conditional release from prison in which the former prisoner remains under the supervision of a parole office.

Recidivism rate. Percentage of offenders who, after their treatment or punishment has ended, are arrested and convicted of new offenses.

WEBSITES FOR FURTHER REFERENCE

http://ojjdp.ncjrs.org/
The Office of Juvenile Justice and Delinquency Prevention (OJJDP) provides national leadership, coordination, and resources to prevent and respond to juvenile delinquency and victimization. OJJDP accomplishes this by supporting states and local communities in their efforts to develop and implement effective and coordinated prevention and intervention programs and improve the juvenile justice system so that it "protects the public safety, holds offenders accountable, and provides treatment and rehabilitative services tailored to the needs of families and each individual juvenile."

http://www.uscourts.gov/
Article III of the United States Constitution establishes the judicial branch as one of the three separate and distinct branches of the federal government. The other two are the legislative and executive branches. The federal courts often are called the guardians of the Constitution because their rulings protect rights and liberties guaranteed by the Constitution. Through fair and impartial judgments, the federal courts interpret and apply the law to resolve disputes. This is USCourts.Gov, the official website of the Federal Judiciary. Users of this site will find general information on federal courts, with links to individual court sites provided. Also featured are a newsroom with news stories and postings of recent press releases, and resources for teachers.

http://www.ncjrs.org/
The National Criminal Justice Reference Service (NCJRS) is a federally sponsored information clearinghouse for people around the country and the world involved with research, policy, and practice related to criminal and juvenile justice and drug control. NCJRS services and resources are available to policymakers, criminal and juvenile justice practitioners, educators, community leaders, and the general public. Anyone interested in the fields of criminal and juvenile justice and drug policy can use or request NCJRS services and assistance.

http://www.ojp.usdoj.gov/bjs/
The Bureau of Justice Statistics (BJS) was first established on December 27, 1979, under the Justice Systems Improvement Act of 1979, Public Law 96-157 (the 1979 Amendment to the Omnibus Crime Control and Safe Streets Act of 1968, Public Law 90-351). The Bureau of Justice Statistics (BJS) is a component of the Office of Justice Programs in the U.S. Department of Justice. BJS's mission is to "collect, analyze, publish, and disseminate information on crime, criminal offenders, victims of crime, and the operation of justice systems at all levels of government. These data are critical to federal, state, and local policymakers in combating crime and ensuring that justice is both efficient and evenhanded."

http://www.uncjin.org/
The United Nations Crime and Justice Information Network (UNCJIN). This electronic clearinghouse represents the culmination of several years of incremental efforts coordinated by the United Nations Centre for International Crime Prevention, Vienna. This site holds statistics on international crime, laws regarding crime, and crime prevention.

http://www.crimelibrary.com/
The Crime Library is the only place on the web to find in-depth, factual information on the most notorious crimes of all time, worldwide crime news, reports on criminal profiling and forensics, as well as crime fiction by leading writers.

http://www.ycwa.org/
The Youth Crime Watch of America (YCWA) brings youth of all backgrounds together to identify and correct problems unique to their schools and communities. The program empowers youth to take an active role in addressing the problems around them. Its goal is to "provide crime-free, drug-free environments through a youth-led movement."

http://www.crimespider.com/
Crime Spider searches for the best crime and law enforcement sites, then categorizes topics so you don't have to sort through hundreds of sites to find the one that fits the bill. "You can easily find the information you want at Crime Spider. Whether you are doing research on criminalistics, forensic anthropology, FBI, unsolved murders, homicide investigation techniques, child abuse, domestic violence, the death penalty, terrorism, law and courts, behavioral profiling, gang violence, juvenile crime, missing persons, serial killers or mass murderers, criminals, local police, or other cop or crime topics, we can help you find the information you want."

13 Drugs

There is a contradiction so common that few people even notice it—the idea that altering the body and mind is morally wrong when done with some substances and salutary when done with others.

—Joshua Wolf Shenk

A **drug** is any substance that directly affects the brain or nervous system when ingested. This broad definition includes such substances as aspirin, caffeine, nicotine, heroin, and alcohol. Every society accepts some drugs as appropriate and regards others as unacceptable. Some drugs are considered dangerous, and others are harmless. But the definitions vary from society to society, and within U.S. society they are inconsistent and often ambiguous. As Szasz has said:

> There is probably one thing, and one thing only, on which the leaders of all modern states agree; on which Catholics, Protestants, Jews, Mohammedans, and atheists agree; on which Democrats, Republicans, Socialists, Communists, Liberals, and Conservatives agree; on which medical and scientific authorities throughout the world agree; and on which the views, as expressed through opinion polls and voting records, of the large majority of individuals in all civilized countries agree. That thing is the "scientific fact" that certain substances which people like to ingest or inject are "dangerous" both to those who use them and to others; and that the use of such substances constitutes "drug abuse" or "drug addiction"—a disease whose control and eradication are the duty of the combined forces of the medical profession and the state. However, there is little agreement—from people to people, country to country, even decade to decade—on which substances are acceptable and their use therefore considered a popular pastime, and which substances are unacceptable and their use therefore considered "drug abuse" and "drug addiction." (Szasz, 1975:ix)

Many in the United States are concerned about the drug problem. But what is meant by "the drug problem"? Is drug use equated with abuse? Why are alcohol and tobacco legal drugs when they are addictive, physically harmful, and socially disruptive? Put another way, why is the use of alcohol accepted by U.S. society, whereas the use of marijuana is not? Is drug use a medical or a criminal problem? Joshua Wolf Shenk highlights inconsistent views of drugs:

> We take more drugs and reward those who supply them. We punish more people for taking drugs and especially punish those who supply them. One kind of drugs is *medicine,* righting wrongs, restoring the ill to a proper, natural state. These drugs have the sheen of corporate logos and men in white coats. They are kept in the room where we wash grime from our skin and do the same for our souls. Our conception of illegal drugs is a warped reflection of this picture. Offered up from the dirty underworld, they are hedonistic, not curative. They induce artificial pleasure, not health. They harm rather than help, enslave rather than liberate. . . . We say, "The good is in that Prozac power," or "The evil is in that cocaine powder." But evil and good are not attributes of molecules. (Shenk, 1999a:38–39; 42)

Three points should be made at the outset of this discussion. First, definitions concerning drugs and drug-related behaviors are **socially constructed.** That is, definitions about drugs are not based on some **ontological truth** (a universal and undeniable reality) but rather on meanings that people in groups have imputed to certain substances and behaviors. Second, because definitions concerning drugs are socially constructed, members of different societies or groups (e.g., religious and political) within societies will often differ in their social constructions about this phenomenon. Third, the definition of drugs by the most powerful interest groups in a society will become part of the law and be enforced on others. Thus, the labeling of some drugs as licit and others as illicit involves politics. Therefore, in examining such topics as drug use and abuse, types of drugs, the history of drug laws, and the consequences of official drug policies, this chapter continually refers to the **politics of drugs.**

DRUGS IN SOCIETY

Drugs are used worldwide for conviviality, pleasure, and medicinal purposes. The average U.S. family has about thirty different drugs in its medicine cabinet and numerous alcoholic beverages in its liquor cabinet. In 2000 U.S. pharmacies filled 2.9 billion prescriptions at a cost of $131.9 billion (Pear, 2001). More than 80 percent of the people in the United States are regular caffeine users, two-thirds of adults consume alcoholic beverages, and 47 million use nicotine regularly. A 1999 University of Michigan survey found that 25.9 percent of high school seniors had used some illicit drug during the previous 30 days (see Fig-

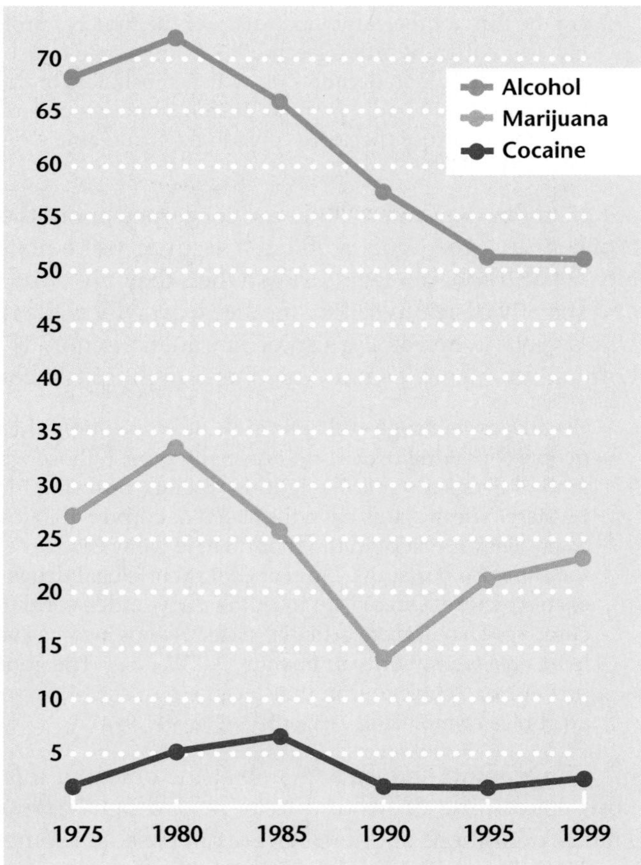

FIGURE 13.1

Percent of High School Seniors Reporting Use of Alcohol, Marijuana, and Cocaine in Past 30 Days

Source: University of Michigan, Institute for Social Research Study. 2000. "Monitoring the Future." Ann Arbor, MI.

ure 13.1). More than 1.5 million people are arrested on drug charges in each year, and more than 460,000 are now in prison for drug offenses (a tenfold increase over 1980). In short, psychoactive drugs, legal and illegal, are important to a significant portion of Americans.

Commonly Abused Illegal Drugs

Marijuana. Very much like alcohol, marijuana is a social drug, used as a social lubricant in social settings. Marijuana comes from the hemp plant, *Cannabis sativa,* a plant cultivated for at least 5,000 years and found throughout the world. It is the world's fourth most widely used psychoactive drug (following caffeine, nicotine, and alcohol) and, by far, the most widely used illicit drug in the United States. The proportion of the population who are current users of marijuana peaked in 1979, then declined until 1993, with a resurgence since. Considering just high school seniors, 51 percent in 1979 said they had smoked marijuana in the past year, 22 percent said this in 1992, and 38 percent reported using it in 1999 (University of Michigan study, reported in U.S. Department of Education, 2001:161). Currently, about one-third of adults in the United States have used the drug, with only 3 percent current users.

The inhalation of marijuana produces a relaxing effect, increases the intensity of sense impressions, and provides a "high" akin to one produced by alcohol. Goode has described the most common effects by users:

> [E]uphoria, relaxation; a sense of one's mind wandering, a kind of stream of consciousness; a sensation that time is slowed down . . . an impairment of one's short-term memory; a feeling of ravenous hunger; a strong increase in the enjoyment of one's senses—food tastes better, music sounds richer, more exciting, touch becomes more sensuous, one's sexual orgasm becomes more intense; one feels far more inclined to find things amusing, silly, uproarious; moving about feels more sinuous, smoother, more graceful and sensuous; one feels a kind of "floating" sensation; there is a reduced and impaired ability to think logically, rationally, in a linear fashion; one finds it difficult or impossible to read well or at all; there is a kind of "eureka" feeling about ordinarily common and usually uninteresting experiences and insights. (Goode, 1973:10)

Marijuana is a widely misunderstood drug. Some people consider pot smokers to be dope fiends. Many consider marijuana addictive, asserting that it creates physiological dependence. Some researchers have argued that it causes lower levels of sex hormones to be produced in males and breaks up chromosomes, causing genetic problems for future generations. These are but a few major problems noted in the media and scientific journals. The current data on marijuana are inconsistent, however, on these and other alleged problems. For example, five research studies done in the 1970s reported that marijuana caused a loss of motivation and the ability to think straight; another five studies reported no such effect.

Although much remains to be learned about the effects of marijuana, three dangers are evident. Marijuana has a negative effect on the lungs (smokers get about four times as much tar in their lungs per puff as tobacco smokers); its use also increases dangers for people with damaged hearts. The third danger is arrest and a criminal record, the consequence of its use officially defined as criminal. On the positive side, we know that marijuana is not physiologically addictive; there is no evidence of a lethal dose; and it has been found to have positive effects for certain medical problems, such as migraine headaches, muscle spasms associated with epilepsy and multiple sclerosis, glaucoma, and asthma. Of special note is the successful use of marijuana to reduce or eliminate the nausea that accompanies chemotherapy treatments for cancer. It can also stimulate appetite in the chronically ill. Voters in Arizona, California, Colorado, Maine, Nevada, Oregon, Hawaii, and Washington have approved ballot initiatives allowing the use of medical marijuana. However, the U.S. Supreme Court ruled unanimously in 2001 that a federal law classifying marijuana as illegal has no exception for ill patients.

- **Psychedelics.** Also called hallucinogens, psychedelics produce sensory experiences that represent a different reality to the user. The person may react to trivial everyday objects as if they had great meaning. Emotions may be greatly intensified. Among the perceptual phenomena experienced by some is the feeling that one is looking at oneself from the outside. Hallucinogens occur naturally in the peyote cactus, some mushrooms, and certain fungi and other plants. Bad experiences with psychedelics include panic associated with loss of control, the common hallucination that spiders are crawling over the body, paranoia and delusions, and occasionally suicide. The psychedelic drug phencyclidine (PCP), also known as angel dust, is perhaps the most dangerous. This drug, which is relatively easy to manufacture, can cause psychotic reactions (hallucinations, combative or self-destructive impulses), loss of bowel and bladder control, slurred speech, and inability to walk. Taken in large quantities, it can induce seizures, coma, and death. There is no evidence that physical dependence develops for any of the hallucinogenic drugs. For some people, though, psychological dependence occurs.

  The drug "ecstacy" is a synthetic drug with stimulant and hallucinogenic effects. Users say that ecstacy produces a high for up to 6 hours with feelings of euphoria, empathy, and heightened senses. A 2000 survey by the University of Michigan estimates that 1.3 million students in grades 8 through 12 have tried ecstacy (reported in Ragavan, 2001). According to the federal government, the use of ecstasy is growing faster than any other illegal drug. One indicator of its exponential growth, U.S. customs officials seized 9.3 million pills in 2000, more than 20 times as much as in 1997 (Klam, 2001). Regular use can produce blurred vision, confusion, sleeplessness, depression, muscle cramping, fever, chills, hallucinations, and anxiety. With overdoses there can be loss of consciousness, seizures, heat stroke, and heart failure.

- **GHB (Gamma Hydroxy Buterate).** GHB is a central nervous system depressant. It is a colorless, odorless liquid that is mixed with alcoholic drinks or fruit juices. It relaxes or sedates the body, slowing breathing and the heart rate. Users feel euphoric, then sleepy. Overdose results in nausea, vomiting, drowsiness, and headache and can escalate to loss of consciousness. GHB has two qualities that make it a favorite date-rape drug: (1) it knocks out users and their short-term memory, and (2) it clears quickly from the body, so laboratory tests might not detect it (Leinwand, 2001).

- **Narcotics (Opiates).** Narcotics are powerful depressants that have a pronounced effect on the respiratory and central nervous systems. Medically, they are used very effectively to relieve pain, treat diarrhea (paregoric), and stop coughing (codeine). These drugs, which include opium and its derivatives, morphine, and heroin, also produce a euphoria. Many users describe the first "rush" as similar to sexual orgasm, followed by feelings of warmth, peacefulness, and increased self-esteem.

Opiates are highly addictive. Prolonged users experience severe withdrawal symptoms. It is dangerous for four reasons—each a result of the drug's illegal status, not of the drug itself. First, because the drug is not regulated, it can include harmful impurities and be of varying potency. As a result between 3,000 and 4,000 users die annually of heroin overdoses. Second, the sharing of needles is a major cause of hepatitis and, in recent years, HIV infection (the precursor of AIDS). Efforts to supply clean needles to the addict population (between 500,000 and 750,000 in the United States) are resisted by government officials because that would appear to condone, even promote, an illegal activity. The third danger associated with heroin is the high cost of purchasing the illegal drug. The users must spend much of their time finding funds to supply their habit. For men, finding funds typically means theft, and for women shoplifting or prostitution—all hazardous occupations. Fourth, possession of heroin is a criminal offense, leading to incarceration. Taken together, then, the criminal activities an addict turns to plus the complications of poor quality drugs and infection lead to a relatively high rate of deaths. But, as Charles McCaghy argues: "The danger of heroin stems not from the drug itself, but from the conditions that its illegality creates" (McCaghy, 1976:288).

Cocaine. Cocaine stimulates an area in the brain that regulates the sensation of pleasure, intensifying sexual highs, euphoria, alertness, and feelings of confidence. Fort and Cory have reported that one measure of the drug's appeal is seen in the willingness of laboratory animals to work extraordinarily hard to be rewarded with the drug. When given drug rewards for pushing levers, animals "will push levers up to 250 times in a row for caffeine, 4,000 times for heroin, and 10,000 times for cocaine" (Fort and Cory, 1975:39).

In 1999, some 6.2 percent of high school seniors had used cocaine in the past year and 2.6 percent had within the past 30 days (U.S. Department of Education, 2001). Repeated use of cocaine can produce paranoia, hallucinations, sleeplessness, tremors, weight loss, and depression. Because the drug is normally "snorted" (the powder is ingested through the nostrils), use can permanently destroy the mucous membranes and create breathing difficulties. Snorting cocaine draws the cocaine powder through the nasal passages, which allows it to be absorbed rapidly into the bloodstream and subsequently the brain. If the user desires a more potent dosage, cocaine can be injected in solution directly into the veins or chemically converted and smoked in the process called freebasing. Another variation is to mix cocaine with heroin, which combines a powerful stimulant with a potent depressant.

Crack is a smokable form of cocaine, created by mixing cocaine, baking soda, and water and heating them. This potent drug provides an almost instant rush, reaching the brain within eight seconds, with peak effects within a few minutes. Because crack's effects are more short-lived and more intense than powder cocaine, there is a greater urge toward repeated use (Currie, 1993:335). Crack, compared with powder cocaine, is cheaper and provides a quicker high.

Cocaine is not physically addictive, but psychological dependence is a problem for many users. Another problem is that cocaine use can lead to the use of sedatives (such as Quaaludes) to calm down after the high in an effort to quell the urge for more cocaine.

The United States is number one in the use of cocaine, consuming 70 percent of the world's output.

Legal But Dangerous Drugs

Nicotine. Nicotine is the active ingredient of tobacco. Because the vast majority of smokers smoke fifteen or more cigarettes a day, they are averaging at least one cigarette for each hour they are awake. In this way nicotine "is the only drug that humans use hour by hour, week after week, till death do them prematurely part" (Fort and Cory, 1975:41). Nicotine is a stimulant that raises blood pressure, increases the heart rate, dulls the appetite, and provides the user with a sense of alertness. As a stimulant, nicotine is responsible for a relatively high probability of heart disease and strokes among cigarette smokers. In addition to the nicotine, smokers inhale various coal tars, nitrogen dioxide, formaldehyde, and other ingredients that increase the chances of contracting lung cancer, throat cancer, emphysema, and bronchitis. According to the latest estimates, more than 400,000 Americans will die of tobacco-related causes (about 4 million worldwide), including 180,000 cardiovascular disease deaths, 120,000 lung cancer deaths, and 9,000 deaths from secondhand smoke. (See Figure 13.2 for tobacco deaths worldwide.) Put in its starkest terms: According to the Centers for Disease Control and Prevention (CDC), tobacco addiction kills more Americans than alcohol, cocaine, crack, heroin, homicide, suicide, fires, car accidents, and AIDS—combined (Ellerbee, 1995). Moreover, tobacco contributes to respiratory infections in babies, triggers new cases of asthma in previously unaffected children, and exacerbates symptoms in asthmatic children.

Nicotine is addictive:

> [D]ozens of studies have revealed nicotine to be at least as addictive as illegal drugs like cocaine and heroin. . . . 17 million adults try to quit smoking each year, but only 1 in 10 succeeds. . . . [S]mokers show all the physiological marks of the addict. Before the morning's first cigarette, the smoker has all the signs of withdrawal, including hair-trigger reflexes, a lack of concentration and altered brain waves. (Brownlee and Roberts, 1994:36)

The number of smokers has declined significantly. In 1965, 42 percent of adults age 18 and older smoked; by 1980 this had declined to 33 percent; and by 1998, 24.1 percent of American adults were regular smokers of tobacco (Cen-

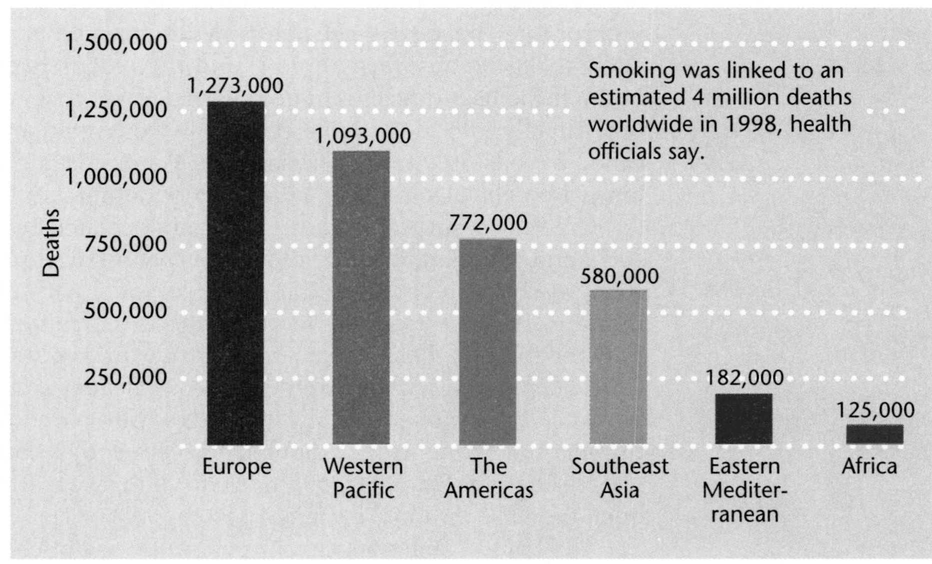

FIGURE 13.2
World Smoking-Related Deaths, by Region
Source: USA Today (January 25, 2000):1A.

ters for Disease Control and Prevention study, reported by Associated Press, 2000b). More men smoke than women but women are catching up. In 1964, 52 percent of men smoked, compared with 34 percent of women. In 2000, the proportion dropped for both sexes, with women having almost the same percentage as men (26 percent for adult men, compared to 22 percent of adult women). More teenage girls (nearly 30 percent) are smoking now than 10 years ago. Another interesting trend is that the proportion of teenagers who smoke, which had been declining since 1977, has increased recently. According to the CDC, "each day in America 6,000 teenagers light up their first cigarette; 3,000 teens enter the ranks of "regular smokers," meaning they've smoked at least one cigarette a day for a month; and 1,000 adults die prematurely as a direct result of a decision made in adolescence to take up smoking" (Smolowe, 1997:27).

Although the tobacco industry is huge (a $45 billion industry in the United States), it is faced with declining sales. The tobacco companies have responded in three ways. First, the tobacco companies have invested heavily in the federal, state, and local campaigns of politicians (mostly Republicans but some Democrats as well) in the hope of favorable legislation (regarding such issues as public smoking, selling through vending machines, reining in the Federal Drug Administration, and the extent of liability in impending law suits). The companies gave $4 million during the 1996 campaign and $2 million in "soft money" in the first half of 1997 to political parties ($1.6 million to Republican committees and $324,461 to Democrats) (Gullo, 1997). In addition, the tobacco industry spent more than $19 million on outside lobbyists in 1997, three times as much as in 1996 (Torry, 1998). In the 2000 election, the tobacco industry gave more than $8.4 million to candidates and political parties (more than 80 percent to Republican candidates and committees) (*USA Today,* 2001a).

The second strategy of the tobacco companies is to increase their advertising in the United States—from $2 billion in 1982 to $3.2 billion in 1989, $6 billion in 1996, and $8.24 billion in 1999 (Rubin, 2001). This advertising is aimed primarily at African Americans, Latinos, women, and youths. Third, the tobacco companies have increased advertising and sales overseas to compensate for declining domestic sales.

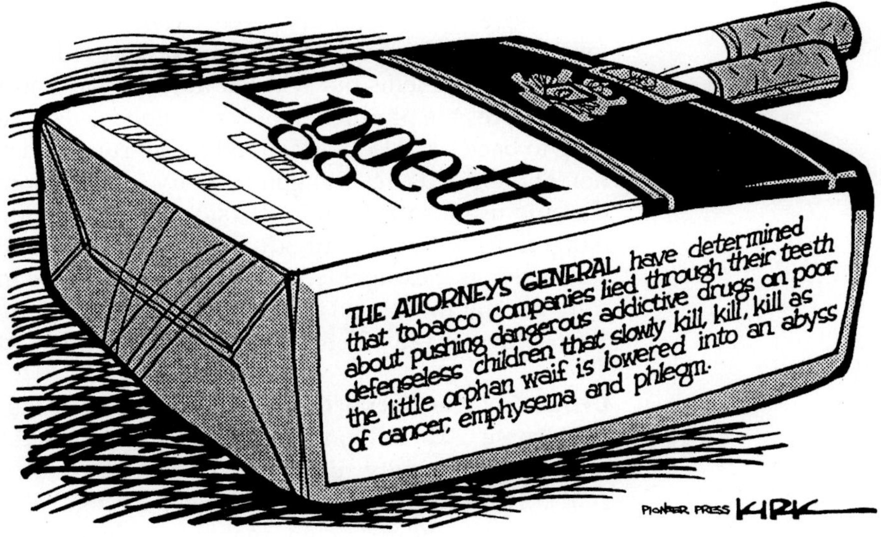

Kirk Anderson

- **Alcohol.** Alcohol is a relatively safe drug when used in moderation, but one of the most dangerous when abused. It is a depressant that directly affects the central nervous system. Alcohol slows brain activity and muscle reactions. Thus, it is a leading cause of accidents:

    - About four in ten traffic deaths occur in alcohol-related accidents. Automobile accidents involving intoxicated drivers are the leading cause of death among teenagers.
    - Alcoholics have a suicide rate six to fifteen times greater than the rate for the general population, and they die in fires ten times more frequently than nonalcoholics.
    - Approximately seven out of ten drowning victims had been drinking prior to their deaths.

    Alcohol consumption is related to other problems as well. Some examples:

    - About 3 million violent crimes occur each year in which victims perceive the offender to have been drinking at the time of offense (Greenfeld, 1998).
    - Among those criminals caught, if they used drugs prior to committing a crime, alcohol rather than illicit drugs was much more likely the drug of choice.
    - Alcohol abuse costs the United States $185 billion a year in workdays lost, drunken-driving accidents, and health care claims—*more than all illegal drugs combined* (Kalb, 2001).
    - There are intangible and unmeasurable expenses due to disrupted families, spouse and child abuse, desertion, and countless emotional problems that arise from drinking. Most significant, two-thirds of victims who suffered violence from an intimate (a current or former spouse, boyfriend, or girlfriend) reported that alcohol had been a factor (Greenfeld, 1998).
    - Among youth (high school and college), excessive drinking is related to vandalism, racist acts, homophobic violence, and sexual assault.

    Continued use of large quantities of alcohol can result in indigestion, ulcers, degeneration of the brain, and cirrhosis of the liver; 14,000 alcoholics die of cirrhosis of the liver each year. Malnutrition is often associated with prolonged use of alcohol; a pint of whiskey provides about half of a person's daily calorie requirements but without the necessary nutrients. Heavy consumption also reduces the production of white blood cells, so alcoholics have a low resistance to bacteria. Alcoholics, in addition, run the danger of permanent destruction of brain cells, resulting in memory loss and sometimes psychotic behavior. Chronic use also results in physiological addiction. Withdrawal can be very dangerous, with the individual experiencing convulsions and delirium. The conclusion is inescapable, then, that alcohol is the most dangerous drug physically for the individual and socially for society. In fact, alcohol claims about 100,000 lives a year, 25 times as many as all illegal drugs combined.

- **Drugs for the Social Control of Youth.** In the 12 months ending in June 2001 some 20.6 million prescriptions were used to treat ADHD (attention deficit/hyperactivity disorder), up from 11 million 5 years ago (K. Thomas, 2001). The symptoms for ADHD are inattentiveness, fidgetiness, not listening, being easily distracted, making careless mistakes, and excessive talking.

Stimulants such as Ritalin, Adderall, Concerta, and Dexedrine are prescribed to have the paradoxical effect of calming and focusing children who are chronically inattentive and hyperactive. These drugs stimulate the central nervous system, with many of the same pharmacological effects of cocaine. They affect the brain by enhancing the chemical dopamine, the neurotransmitter that plays a major role in cognition, attention, and inhibition For 65 percent of those who take the drug, their symptoms of ADHD are diminished with their behaviors more or less "normal," and for another 10 percent there is a substantial improvement in their behavior (Gladwell, 1999). Their side effects are nervousness, insomnia, and loss of appetite.

While these stimulants for children are often successful, their widespread use raises some important questions:

- The United States consumes 80 percent of the world's methylphenidate (the generic name for Ritalin). "Are American youngsters indeed suffering more behavioral illnesses, or have we as a society become less tolerant of disruptive behavior" (Shute, Locy, and Pasternak, 2000:47)? Does this mean that U.S. children are more prone to hyperactivity than children from other societies?
- Is hyperactivity the inevitable by-product of a societywide addiction to speed—to cellular phones, faxes, e-mail, overnight mail, ever-faster computers? And, what about the high-stimulus activities that saturate children's lives—video games, interactive television, hundreds of cable channels, and fast action with vivid violence movies (Gladwell, 1999)?
- There are five times as many boys as girls diagnosed with ADHD and subsequently medicated (Hart, 1999). Is the preponderance of boys diagnosed as hyperactive because adults find that boys are more difficult to control than girls?
- Why are these drugs used to calm and focus disproportionately prescribed for White middle-class and upper-class children, typically with two working parents who place high value on academic performance (Lang, 1997)?
- It is estimated that 3 to 5 percent of school-age children are medicated because their inattention threatens their success at school (Wingert, 2000). Are the schools and teachers promoting this also because it is successful at getting problem students to sit down, shut up, and pay attention, thus making classrooms less disruptive?
- Surely there are youngsters who need medication for serious hyperactivity. But is this wave of medicating millions of children simply because it makes life easier for the adults around them (Hart, 1999)?
- What is the role of the pharmaceutical companies in the rapid growth of medications for ADHD? This is a billion-dollar sector of the pharmaceutical market. Brand-name ads for ADHD drugs are appearing in women's magazines and on cable TV, breaking a 30-year-old agreement between nations and the pharmaceutical industry not to market controlled substances that have high potential for abuse (K. Thomas, 2001).
- What is the role of managed-care companies and insurers in promoting the medication of children for ADHD? These organizations are concerned with costs (see Chapter 17) and it is much cheaper to prescribe pills, thus avoiding referring children to more expensive mental health specialists (Bloom, 2000; Shute, Locy, and Pasternak, 2000).

- Ritalin and other stimulants prescribed for ADHD work on the brain much like cocaine does. Children using this drug are "wired" every day, raising concern over its long-term effects. Are we creating an entire generation (called by some the "Rx generation") with a "sweet tooth for cocaine"?

The widespread use of these stimulants leads to their abuse by adolescents and adults seeking pharmacological highs. Taken in larger amounts than prescribed and crushed and snorted, these drugs produce euphoria, greater energy and productivity, increased sexual appetite, and an overall feeling of being a lot smarter (K. Thomas, 2000b). As a result, the Drug Enforcement Agency says that drugs to treat ADHD rank among today's most stolen prescriptions and most abused drugs (K. Thomas, 2001). A study of 6,000 public school students in Massachusetts found that almost 13 percent of high school students and 4 percent of middle-school students had used Ritalin without a prescription (reported in Thomas, 2000b).

Drug Patterns by Class and Race

Drug use is not uniform throughout society. Intravenous drug users continue to be found predominantly among the inner-city poor. This practice places them at great risk of exposure to the AIDS virus from the sharing of needles. The common estimate is that about 40 percent of diagnosed AIDS cases were African Americans and Latinos, who constitute the overwhelming majority of intravenous drug users. One devastating consequence: Black babies are twenty-five times more likely to get AIDS than are White babies.

The disproportionate use of drugs by the poor is not limited to illicit drugs. The incidence of cigarette smoking is lower for Whites than for Blacks. This is not true for teenagers, however. In 1999 White high school students were twice as likely to have smoked in the past 30 days as African American high school students (38.6 percent compared to 19.7 percent, with Latino teens at about 34 percent) (Centers for Disease Control study, reported in McClam, 2000). For alcohol, young people age 18 to 25, 33 percent of Whites had consumed five or more drinks on the same occasion at least once in the past month, compared to 22 percent of Latinos and 13 percent of Blacks (U.S. Department of Health and Human Services, 1999:215). Among adults, however, smoking is inversely related to socioeconomic status (SES)—the lower the SES, the greater the incidence of cigarette smoking. Figure 13.3 shows that among women, the lower the educational attainment, the more likely to smoke.

For alcohol consumption, African Americans, especially African American men, have more alcohol-related problems than Whites (the information on alcohol and race in this section is taken from U.S. Department of Health and Human Services, 1991). Age is a significant variable, as Whites are more likely to drink than Blacks as youths, but between ages 30 and 39 the rate of heavy consumption rises sharply for Blacks, surpassing that for Whites. Gender, too, is relevant, as Black women are much more likely to be abstainers than White women. Income has an interesting effect—as income rises for Black men, rates of heavy drinking fall; while among White men, an increase in income is accompanied by an increase in heavy drinking.

Latino males are more likely to have problems related to alcohol abuse than African American or White males. Among Latino males, Mexican Americans

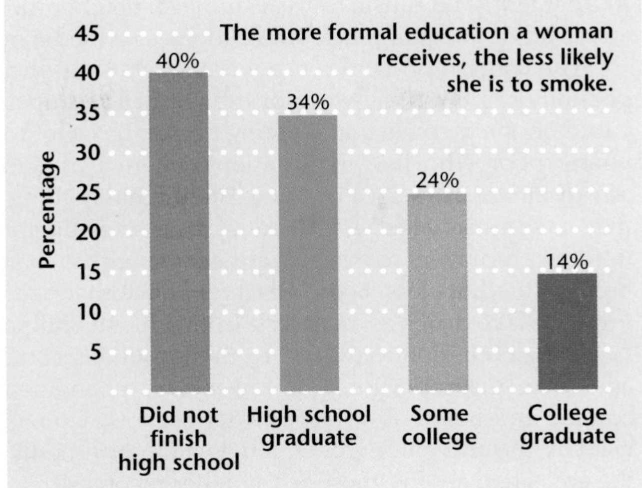

FIGURE 13.3

Women, Educational Level, and Smoking

Source: Marcy Mullins. 2001. *USA Today* (March 26):19A.

and Puerto Ricans drink more and have more alcohol-related problems than men in other Latino subgroups (Cubans and those from the countries of Central and South America and the Caribbean). Mexican American men have the highest rates of heavy drinking (defined as downing five or more drinks in one sitting at least five times a month), with 23 percent compared to 12 percent of White men and 15 percent of Black men. Another indicator of the seriousness of drinking: In Los Angeles, cirrhosis of the liver kills Mexican American men at double the rate of White and Black men (Nazario, 1999). By age, the pattern for Latino men is similar to that of Black men—heavy drinking increases during the thirties and continues into older ages. Latino women tend to abstain or drink infrequently.

Among Native Americans, alcohol abuse is a contributing factor in 40 percent of deaths (accidents, chronic liver disease, homicide, and suicide). The rate of fetal alcohol syndrome, a leading cause of mental retardation, is 6.1 per 1,000 for Native American mothers, compared to 2.2 per 1,000 in North America. This is despite the fact that Native American women drink considerably less than men. Alcohol use varies considerably from tribe to tribe. Some tribes have fewer drinking adults than found in the U.S. population, while others have many more drinking adults. Unlike the pattern for African Americans and Latinos, Native American youth in tribes where drinking is heavy tend to drink heavily.

Alcohol consumption patterns among Asian Americans show that they use and abuse alcohol less frequently than non-Asians. This holds for those with Chinese, Japanese, Filipino, and Korean heritage, although there are ethnic differences, with the Japanese and Filipinos the most likely to have heavy drinkers. Women drink less than men in all four groups. Combining gender, age, and socioeconomic status, among Asian Americans, the most likely to drink are men under age 45 who have higher social status.

In general, the poor are more inclined than the rich to use harmful substances. Why? The relative lack of education and therefore awareness of the dangers is one possibility. With respect to cigarettes and alcohol, another reason may arise from the tobacco and alcohol companies' special effort to target potential Black and Latino consumers for their products: They sponsor sports tournaments and music festivals in Black neighborhoods and purchase considerable advertising in Black publications and media outlets.

The connection between poverty and using illicit drugs is less clear. One possibility is the irrelevance of the antidrug campaigns, which are implicitly based on the premise that a young person has a lot to lose by using drugs. The young poor who live in situations where jobs and other opportunities for advancement are scarce or nonexistent have nothing to lose by using drugs—they have already lost. The threat of drug-screening programs now increasingly used by employers may constrain people with a chance for a job, but it has no hold on the hopeless. Some observers have theorized that ghetto dwellers are prone to take drugs as an escape from a harsh and painful reality.

This discussion may lead to the erroneous conclusion that drug use and abuse are disproportionately lower-class phenomena. This is true for crack cocaine and heroin, but not powder cocaine, which is much more commonly used by the affluent. Alcohol, too, is more commonly consumed by Whites, by the educated, and by those with higher incomes.

To offset the assumption that class is inversely related to alcohol abuse, consider drinking by college students. College students, mostly from privileged backgrounds, often are heavy, binge drinkers during their college years. A 1997 Harvard School of Public Health survey of 14,521 students at 116 colleges found that (1) 52 percent of the students "drank to get drunk" (up from 39 percent in 1993); (2) those who reported having been drunk three or more times within the last month increased from 22.9 percent in 1993 to 27.9 percent in 1997; and (3) four out of five members of fraternities and sororities qualified as "binge drinkers" (Hall, 1998). At many colleges and universities there is a very significant drinking subculture. At the University of Virginia, one of the finest public universities in the United States, there is a tradition for seniors to consume a fifth of liquor for the last home football game (a practice known as the "fourth-year fifth"). Each weekend at that school three to ten students drink

Alcohol is more commonly consumed by Whites, the educated, and those with higher incomes.

so much that they need medical treatment. Of the students who drink at the University of Virginia, 25 percent have been binge drinking three or more times in the previous 2 weeks (Winerip, 1998). Most interesting in terms of social class, a study from Columbia University's Center on Addiction and Substance Abuse found that students living in fraternities and sororities consumed an average of fifteen drinks per week each, three times as many as the average student. A survey of 25,400 students at 61 schools found that fraternity and sorority leaders drink more heavily than other students in Greek organizations. The study found that 74 percent of fraternity leaders reported having binged in the previous 2 weeks, compared with 58 percent of chapter members. Among sorority leaders, 55 percent had engaged in binge drinking in the previous 2 weeks, compared to 46 percent of the regular members (*Chronicle of Higher Education*, 1998).

In terms of race on campus, White males average the most, with nine drinks a week; African American women the least, with one drink a week (*U.S. News & World Report*, 1994). A survey of 40,000 students found that overall, White college students average 5.6 drinks a week, while African American students drank less than one-third that amount—1.8 drinks (*Denver Post*, 1994).

There are more than 2 million barbiturate and tranquilizer addicts in the United States, and they are generally middle- and upper-class Whites. Unlike the poor—who tend to use illicit drugs and, therefore, are hassled by the authorities and treated in prisons and public hospitals—the more affluent tend to use legal and prescription drugs and are treated by private physicians. Thus, their addiction is typically protected and hidden from public awareness.

Impact of Social Factors on Drug Use

There is a variation in the patterns of drug use and in the behavioral effects that are caused by social factors. For example, the use of distilled alcohol was unknown to Native Americans prior to its introduction by Europeans. Thus, they had no socially acceptable norms to define its proper use and how to behave under its influence. As a consequence, when they obtained the intoxicant, members of some tribes frequently became drunk and violent. In other tribes, where alcohol was accepted and defined as a way to express happiness, violence from drinking was unknown.

A common belief is that alcohol numbs people's social control so that they behave without inhibition. MacAndrew and Edgerton argue that, on the contrary, the degree of inhibition release depends on the culture of the society, not on the amount of alcohol consumed: "Persons learn about drunkenness what their societies impart to them, and comporting themselves in consonance with these understandings they become living confirmations of their society's teachings" (MacAndrew and Edgerton, 1969:172). In other words, the behavior expected of drunks varies from culture to culture, as does their actual behavior. Similarly, one learns from others what to experience from a drug. A person's first experience with heroin is likely to produce feelings of fear and sickness rather than pleasure. As McCaghy has put it:

> *The reason is that positive responses to the effects of heroin are neither automatic nor inherent in the chemical properties of the drug.* One's responses are learned. Most first experiences with heroin occur in the company of others who encourage a favorable interpretation of the drug's effects. This influence may counteract even the most distasteful initiation to heroin. (McCaghy, 1976:284)

So, too, with marijuana. Most users are introduced to marijuana and continue to use it in a group context. They learn from other users the proper techniques to maximize the drug's effects, how to perceive the effects and connect them with the drug, and, finally, how to enjoy the effects. Writing of this last stage, sociologist Howard Becker has said:

> [The user] must learn to enjoy the effects he has just learned to experience. Marijuana-produced sensations are not automatically or necessarily pleasurable. The taste for such experience is a socially acquired one, not different in kind from acquired tastes for oysters or dry martinis. The user feels dizzy, thirsty; his scalp tingles; he misjudges time and distance. Are these things pleasurable? He isn't sure. If he is to continue marijuana use, he must decide that they are. . . . In no case will use continue without a redefinition of the effects as enjoyable. This redefinition occurs, typically, in interaction with more experienced users who, in a number of ways, teach the novice to find pleasure in this experience which is at first so frightening. They may reassure him as to the temporary character of the unpleasant sensations and minimize their seriousness, at the same time calling attention to the more enjoyable aspects. . . .
>
> In short, what was once frightening and distasteful becomes, after a taste for it is built up, pleasant, desired, and sought after. Enjoyment is introduced by the favorable definition of the experience that one acquires from others. Without this, use will not continue, for marijuana will not be for the user an object he can use for pleasure. (Becker, 1963:53–56)

Finally, the new marijuana user must, with the help of the group, set aside his or her conception of morality and decide to continue consciously breaking the law. According to Becker, "A person will feel free to use marijuana to the degree that he comes to regard conventional conceptions of it as the uninformed views of outsiders and replaces those conceptions with the 'inside' view he has acquired through his experience with the drug in the company of other users" (Becker, 1963:78).

Medical and Social Pressures to Use Drugs

In recent times chemists have created numerous synthetic substances that have positive health consequences. Vaccines have been developed to fight diseases such as polio, mumps, smallpox, diphtheria, and measles. Many of these contagious diseases have been eliminated by the wonders of science. Similarly, antibiotics were created as cures for a number of infectious diseases. The public quickly accepted these drugs as beneficial.

In the early 1950s chemists made a breakthrough in drugs that treated mental disorders such as depression, insomnia, aggression, hyperactivity, and tension. These drugs (tranquilizers, barbiturates, and stimulants) have since been widely prescribed by doctors for these problems.

In the 1990s, pharmacology has added drugs to combat stage fright, impulsiveness, obsession, anxiety, impotence, and obesity. **Psychopharmacology,** the science of drugs that affect the mind, is on the verge of developing pills that will enrich memory, heighten concentration, enhance intelligence, and eliminate shyness or bad moods:

> Now the same scientific insights into the brain that led to the development of Prozac are raising the prospect of nothing less than made-to-order, off-the-shelf personalities. For good or ill, research that once mapped the frontiers of

> disease—identifying the brain chemistry involved in depression, paranoia and schizophrenia—is closing in on the chemistry of normal personality. As a result, researchers are on the verge of "chemical attempts to modify character," writes neuropsychiatrist Richard Restak. . . . "For the first time in human history," says Restak, "we will be in a position to design our own brain." (Begley, 1994:37)

Physicians and pharmaceutical companies have been instrumental in encouraging the use of drugs. But this encouragement is only part of the reason people in the United States buy drugs. Many people find life so stressful, boring, competitive, alienating, and frustrating that they seek drugs for a change in mood or to repress what they do not want to think about. Various pressures cause anxiety, stress, or other symptoms for some individuals. Doctors may prescribe "uppers" for stimulation or "downers" to help people relax. Those who reject reality may even seek to find inner meaning through hallucinogens. Others may find life so harsh that they seek the oblivion that certain drugs induce.

The pressure to succeed in competitive situations may also encourage some people to take drugs. Individuals who want to be especially alert or calm in order to do well may take a drug to accomplish their goal.

Sports presents an excellent example of drug use to enhance performance. Two types of drugs are used by athletes: **restorative drugs** (to heal a traumatized part of the body) and **additive drugs** (to improve performance). Amphetamines, human growth hormones, hormones such as androstenedione (the favorite of home run king Mark McGwire)—which is legal in baseball but banned in track and professional football—and anabolic steroids are the additive drugs commonly used by athletes. Amphetamines increase alertness, respiration rate, blood pressure, muscle tension, heart rate, and blood sugar. The user is literally "psyched up" by amphetamines. Moreover, these drugs have the capacity to abolish a sense of fatigue. Growth hormones increase body size and strength. Anabolic steroids are male hormones that aid in adding weight and muscle. If an athlete wants to be a world-class weightlifter, shot putter, or discus thrower, the pressures are great to use anabolic steroids: They make the user stronger, and many competitors use such drugs to get the edge on the competition. Football players, even in high school, use these drugs to gain weight and strength in order to be a "star" (various studies report that about 7 percent of high school boys and about 2 percent of high school girls take steroids).

The pressures to use drugs are unrelenting. They come from doctors, coaches, parents, teachers, peers, and advertising. People may learn to drink in families where social drinking is an integral part of meals, celebrations, and everyday relaxation. Peer groups are also important sources. As mentioned earlier, social groups are important for the entry of the individual into the world of illicit drug use. The person learns from others how to use the drug and how to interpret the drug's effects positively. A person may be part of a subculture (whether in college or in the ghetto) where drug experimentation and regular use are the norm. In situations such as cocktail parties guests are expected to drink alcoholic beverages as part of the social ritual. The hosts continually encourage their guests to drink more. Similarly, marijuana is the "social lubricant" at many social gatherings, and individuals are expected to participate. For people who want to impress others, the pressures to conform are enormous.

POLITICS OF DRUGS

Drugs are a social problem in U.S. society. Yet not all drugs are considered problems, nor are all people who take drugs. Some drugs are legal, and others are not. Some drugs caused problems once but are now considered safe; some that were not considered problems now are. Some drug use is labeled "abuse," but other use is simple use. These inconsistencies demonstrate two central points: (1) the subjective nature of social problems—what is or what is not considered a social problem depends on how other people interpret the phenomenon, and this interpretation varies by place, time, group, and situation; and (2) the politics of social problems—what is a social problem depends on the current law, which reflects the unequal power of pressure groups.

The importance of these two factors is seen vividly in the public's view of drugs and in the official laws governing their use. Ironically, the drugs most objected to and most strictly controlled are not those most dangerous to users and society. Marijuana and heroin, though illegal, are less dangerous than are barbiturates, alcohol, and nicotine, which can be legally obtained and used indiscriminately. To explain such irrationality, we must understand how drugs and their use came to be considered safe or illicit.

Historical Legality of Drugs

The definition of drug use and abuse is complicated in U.S. society because different patterns of use are acceptable for different people. Some religious groups forbid the use of any drugs, even for medicinal purposes. Others accept medicines but reject all forms of drugs, including caffeine, for recreational use. At the other extreme are groups that may use drugs in their religious rituals to expand the mind, the better to know the unknowable. Time also changes interpretation. Early in this century, for example, it was socially acceptable for men to smoke tobacco, but not for women. Then around 1950 or so it became socially acceptable for women to smoke tobacco. Now, increasingly, smokers of both sexes find their smoking unacceptable in public places.

Not only is there variance from group to group within society and from time to time, but there has also been virtually no consistency concerning the legality of drugs historically. The history of the acceptance or rejection of opiates (such as opium, morphine, and heroin) in the United States affords a useful example, for it parallels what happened to public attitudes toward other drugs.

Opiates were legal in the nineteenth-century United States and were widely used as painkillers in the Civil War, with many soldiers becoming addicted. Morphine was legally manufactured from imported opium, and opium poppies were legally grown in the United States. Opium was widely dispensed in countless pharmaceutical preparations.

The only nineteenth-century context in which opiates were declared illegal was one created by anti-Chinese sentiment. The Chinese, who were imported to the West Coast to provide cheap labor to build the railroads, brought opium with them. At first, their opium dens were tolerated. But as the cheap Chinese labor began to threaten the White labor market, there was agitation to punish the Chinese for their "evil" ways. San Francisco and several other West Coast cities passed ordinances around 1875 prohibiting opium dens. These laws were, as Morgan has noted, aimed at the Chinese, not the drug:

> We conclude that the first opium laws in California were not the result of a moral crusade against the drug itself. Instead, it represented a coercive action directed against a vice that was merely an appendage of the real menace—the Chinese—and not the Chinese per se, but the laboring "Chinamen" who threatened the economic security of the white working class. (Morgan, 1978:59)

The early 1900s were characterized as a period of reform. A number of individuals and groups agitated to legislate morals; the Eighteenth Amendment, which prohibited the sale and use of alcohol, was passed in 1919 as a result of pressure from these reform forces. These groups rallied against psychoactive drugs because they believed them to be sinful. They fought against "demon rum" and "demon weed" as well as other moral evils such as gambling and prostitution. They believed that they were doing God's will and that, if successful, they would provide a better way of life for everyone. Therefore, they lobbied vigorously to achieve appropriate legislation and enforcement of the laws to rid the country of these immoral influences. In Reasons's words:

> All of these evils violated the ethical and philosophical foundations of the religious and moral culture which dominated political power at that time. Narcotics use, like alcohol use, led to a lack of rationality and self-control which were the cornerstones of proper "WASP" behavior. (Reasons, 1974:388)

As a result of these reform efforts, Congress passed the Harrison Narcotics Act of 1914. This act was basically a tax law requiring people who dispensed opium products to pay a fee and keep records. The law was relatively mild. It did not prohibit the use of opium in patent medicines or even control its use. It did, however, establish a Narcotics Division in the Treasury Department (which eventually became the Bureau of Narcotics). This department assumed the task (which was not specified in the formal law) of eliminating drug addiction. Treasury agents harassed users, physicians, and pharmacists. The bureau launched a propaganda campaign to convince the public that there was a link between drug use and crime. Finally, the bureau took a number of carefully selected cases to court to broaden its powers. In all these endeavors the bureau was successful. The net result was that "what had been a medical problem, if a problem at all, had become a legal one; patients became criminals practically overnight" (McCaghy, 1976:292).

This point cannot be overemphasized: Prior to the Harrison Act, drug addicts were thought (by the public and government officials) to be sick and in need of individual help. They were believed to be enslaved and in need of being salvaged through the humanitarian efforts of others. But with various government actions (laws, court decisions, and propaganda) and the efforts of reformers, this image of addicts changed from a "medical" to a "criminal" problem. Reasons observes:

> The addict's image was being transformed rapidly from the "sick" and "repentant" deviant, to the "enemy" deviant. . . . Subsequently the addict would be viewed as the "enemy" deviant, indulging in drugs for his own pleasure in defiance of the values of those in power. Furthermore, he was increasingly perceived in criminal terms as a threat to the personal safety and moral well-being of "good citizens." While the early imagery was primarily one of a moral degenerate, increasing emphasis was being placed upon the user's affiliations with the criminal class. The user of the drugs became

> associated with the "dangerous classes" and was viewed as manifesting disrespect for the dominant mores and values of society. (Reasons, 1974:397)

Factors Influencing Drug Laws and Enforcement

The previous section shows how differently a drug can be viewed over time. Clearly, current policies regarding opium (most common in the form of heroin) are repressive, but alcohol and tobacco continue to be socially acceptable drugs. These differences, especially since the laws do not reflect the drugs' relative dangers to users, demonstrate that official drug policies are arbitrary and problematic. What, then, are the factors that affect the focus of our drug laws? We examine two factors: cultural reasons and interest groups.

Cultural Reasons. Drug laws and policies tend to reflect how people typically perceive drug use. Certain drugs have negative stereotypes, and others do not. These stereotypes may have been orchestrated by government or they may be the result of faulty research, propaganda of reformers, negative portrayals in the media, religious ideology, and so on. In the 1940s, for example, most people in the United States shared the assumption that marijuana smokers were "dope fiends." They believed that marijuana users were criminals, immoral, violent, and out of control. Until about 1965 public consensus supported strict enforcement of the marijuana laws. Marijuana was believed to be a dangerous drug associated with other forms of deviance, such as sexual promiscuity and crime. Even college students were virtually unanimous in their condemnation of marijuana smokers as deviants of the worst sort. But the social upheavals of the 1960s included experimentation with drugs and the questioning of society's mores. Rapid changes in attitudes and behavior occurred, especially among the young and college educated. Most significantly, the use of marijuana skyrocketed. In 1965, 18,815 people were arrested for violations of state and local marijuana laws; this number rose to 420,700 in 1973. By 2000 many millions of Americans used marijuana, making it the most widely accepted illegal indulgence since drinking during Prohibition.

Despite these changes in attitudes, public opinion still firmly opposes the legalization of marijuana. Moreover, most people still believe that marijuana is physically addictive and that its use leads to the use of hard drugs. Research has shown both notions to be false. Marijuana is not physically addictive; it does not cause people to use heroin or other, harder drugs. Despite the facts, however, the public generally accepts the negative stereotypes and thus fears the drug and supports strict enforcement.

Some drug use has been interpreted as a symbolic rejection of mainstream values, and in this situation the drug is condemned by those supporting the status quo. Drugs such as alcohol and nicotine do not have this connotation. Because marijuana use was closely associated with the youth protest of the 1960s, many construed it as a symbol of an alternative life-style—as rejection of the traditional values of hard work, success through competition, initiative, and materialism and as support for socialism, unpatriotic behavior, sexual promiscuity, and rejection of authority. As long as this view prevailed, punitive measures against marijuana users seemed justified to many if not most citizens.

Interest Groups. The approaches for controlling drug use have more to do with the power structure of society than with the inherent characteristics of the substance being controlled (Himmelstein, 1978). There is evidence that elites in complex societies ban the use of psychoactive drugs because they link them with subversion. And, in fact, dissident groups often use drug-induced experiences to affirm social solidarity in opposition to the powerful.* Himmelstein has provided examples of this phenomenon from a variety of periods:

> We find again and again that elites try to suppress drug use because they link it to subversion and that drugs actually are important elements in many oppositional movements. Egyptian pharaohs (c. 2500 B.C.) fought a continual battle against beer and wine use in the temples of Memphis, which were centers of political unrest. The time-honored image of the coffee house as a center of subversion goes back at least to the sixteenth-century Moslem world, where the death penalty was levied for visiting them. Peyote (in the Native American Church), marijuana (in the Jamaican Ras Tafari movement and of course in the 1960s in the U.S.), and alcohol (in the Afro-Brazilian movement) all have served as the foci for culturally and politically subversive movements. (Himmelstein, 1978:45)

The powerful in society also direct their repression at the drugs used primarily by minority groups, the poor, and criminals (Bonnie and Whitebread, 1974:13-31). Just as the early antiopium laws were aimed at Chinese workers, not at opium itself, so the reform movements aimed at prohibition of alcohol represented retaliation by the old middle class—rural, Protestant, native born—against the largely Catholic urban workers and immigrants who threatened their privileged status. Himmelstein notes:

> In this context, the movement against alcohol turned from reform to prohibition and from concern to moral indignation. Alcohol became a symbol of everything in the new society that threatened the old middle class, and Prohibition became a symbolic way for that class to reassert its cultural and political dominance. (Himmelstein, 1978:46)

This connection between drug laws and social class is also apparent in the enactment of laws against the opiates. Their change in status occurred as use of the drug shifted from the middle to lower class in the early 1900s (Duster, 1970:9–10). A final example of the relation between social class use and drug policy can be found in the current drive to liberalize marijuana laws. When marijuana was used primarily by the lower class (such as Mexican Americans and deviant groups), the laws against its use were extremely punitive. But in the 1960s, middle-class, White, affluent, college youth became the primary users. However much parents may have disagreed with their children's use of marijuana, they did not want them treated as criminals and stigmatized as drug users. The ludicrousness of the gap between the punishments for marijuana use and for alcohol use became readily apparent to the educated. As a result, White, affluent, and powerful people in most communities and states mounted a push to liberalize the laws.

Powerful economic interests promote drug laws favorable to themselves. For example, a significant part of U.S. agriculture and consumer industry is engaged (with government support) in the production and marketing of

*This is not to say that drugs are always used to unify resistance groups. As Himmelstein has shown, some resistance groups reject drug use entirely for two basic reasons. First, they reject drugs approved by society because they symbolize the majority's power. Second, radicals claim that drugs dull the revolutionary urge, destroy commitment, and undermine discipline.

nicotine and alcohol products. Even though it is well known that tobacco is harmful to users, the government will not ban its use because of the probable outcry from farmers, the states where tobacco is a major crop, and the tobacco manufacturers, wholesalers, retailers, transporters, and advertisers. Marijuana, on the other hand, is merchandised and sold illegally, so there is no legitimate economic interest pushing for its legalization.

Similarly, the pharmaceutical industry works diligently to dissuade Congress from further restricting amphetamines and other pills. In 1970, pushed by President Nixon, Congress passed the Comprehensive Drug Abuse Prevention and Control Act. Some forces tried to include amphetamines in the dangerous-drug category in that bill, but without success. The law declared marijuana possession a serious crime but did not do the same for amphetamines, despite irrefutable evidence that they are more dangerous to the user. This inconsistency led one observer to conclude: "The end result is a national policy which declares an all-out war on drugs which are not a source of corporate income" (Graham, 1972:14).

The illegal status of some drugs enables illicit economic interests to flourish. Underworld suppliers of drugs oppose changes in the law because legalization would seriously reduce their profits. They therefore promote restrictive legislation. The result is often a strange alliance between underworld economic interests and religious/moral interests seeking the same end—prohibition of the drug—but for opposite reasons. Thus, a member of Congress could safely satisfy religious zealots and organized crime alike by voting for stricter drug laws.

The law enforcement profession is another interest group that may use its influence to affect drug policy. If drugs and drug users are considered threats, then budgets to seize them will be increased. More arrests will be made, proving the necessity of enforcement and, not incidentally, the need for higher pay and more officers. Perhaps the best example of this syndrome is provided by the activity of the Narcotics Bureau, created by the Harrison Act of 1914. As mentioned earlier, the bureau was instrumental in changing the definition of opiate use from a "medical" activity to a "criminal" one. The bureau used a number of tactics to "prove" that its existence was necessary: It won court cases favorable to its antidrug stance; it vigorously used the media to propagate the "dope fiend" mythology; and it used statistics to incite the public or to prove its own effectiveness.

One result of these efforts was the passage of the Marijuana Tax Act of 1937. Although the arguments for enacting the law were based on moral grounds, some observers have suggested that it reflected the bureau's desire to increase its size and importance and that marijuana, which was an unregulated drug at the time, was a convenient tool to accomplish that goal. The head of the bureau, Harry J. Anslinger (who served in that post from 1930 to 1962), led an assault on marijuana in which he depicted the drug as an assassin of youth, leading to heroin addiction. Stories of "marijuana atrocities" by "dope fiends" were supplied to the media. The bureau even sponsored a movie, *Reefer Madness,* which portrayed marijuana users as people who would do anything to obtain the "killer weed." Anslinger's campaign culminated in the passage of the Marijuana Tax Act. There is evidence, however, that Anslinger's crusade was motivated not by the drug but because Congress had cut the bureau's budget in each of the preceding 4 years. Clearly, the bureau's attack on marijuana was not exclusively based on morality.

To summarize, the current drug laws are illogical. Their severity is not related to the danger the drugs pose to individuals and society. Rather, they reflect successful political lobbying by a variety of powerful interest groups, with the less powerful suffering the consequences.

U.S. OFFICIAL POLICY: A WAR ON DRUGS

The U.S. drug war is fought on two fronts: stopping the flow of drugs into the United States and using the criminal justice system to punish those who sell and use illegal drugs within the United States. The cost of this program is $40 billion (Becker, 2001). Many billions more are spent at the state level for law enforcement and prisons.

Stopping the supply of drugs into the country (**interdiction**) involves the use of customs agents at the borders inspecting the baggage of passengers and cargo from planes, trucks, and ships. It involves working with other countries (especially Colombia, Peru, Ecuador, Bolivia, and Mexico) to destroy the places where drugs are grown, manufactured, and processed and to destroy the transportation networks to the United States (by sea and air, and by land through Mexico). These efforts involve the State Department, the Treasury Department, the Coast Guard, various branches of the military, and the Central Intelligence Agency (CIA). These agencies train local soldiers and supply them with equipment (helicopters, radar, surveillance aircraft) and supplies (herbicides, guns, munitions). This means, of course, that the United States is involved in destroying the crops (opium poppy and coca) of local farmers. It means the involvement of the United States (through the CIA) in local politics, that is, siding with

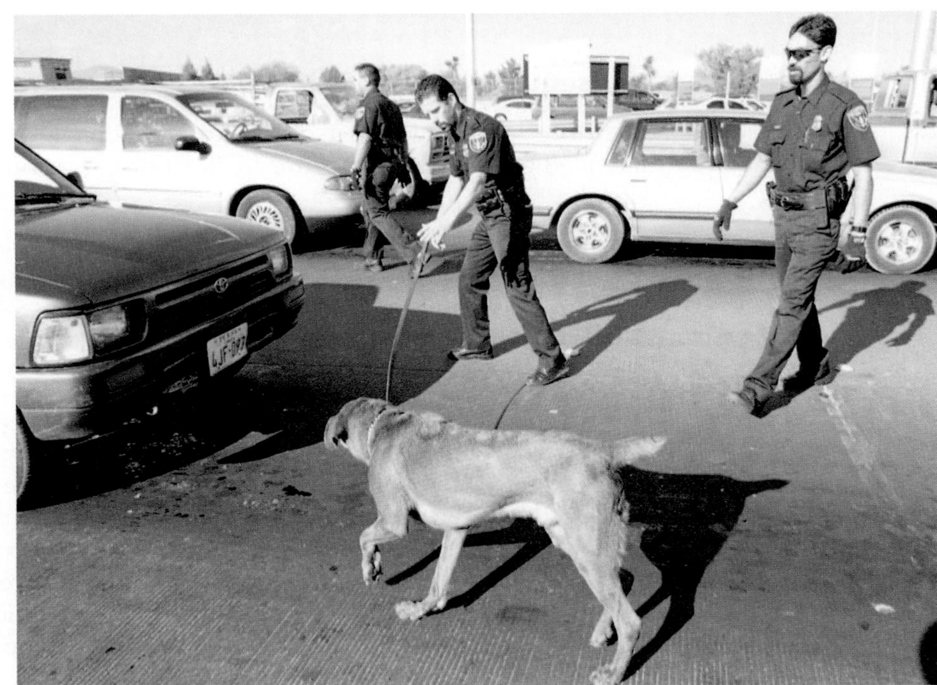

The government attempts to stop the supply of drugs at the border by inspecting the baggage of passengers and cargo from planes, trucks, and ships.

pro-U.S. factions against anti-U.S. factions. Or, involvement in civil wars, where rebels finance their operations with drugs in the fight against the established governments. It encourages violence, threats, and bribery as drug cartels use any means to keep their lucrative businesses flourishing.

The policy of interdiction clearly is a failure. Drugs are found by the U.S. Customs, sometimes large amounts. But massive amounts of drugs cross U.S. borders and enter an intricate distribution system within this country. Despite all of our efforts, we have not stopped the supply; we have only dented it and made the drugs that enter the United States more expensive. The drug policy of interdiction also fails because it has led to strained relations with drug-producing nations in South America. By fighting our battles on their soil, the United States is often viewed as the villain.

The second front in the war on drugs occurs within the United States. Beginning in the 1970s the courts became more punitive toward people selling or possessing illegal drugs. In New York State, for example, a law was passed in 1973 requiring a minimum sentences of 15 years to life for a first-time offender caught selling as little as 2 ounces or possessing 4 ounces of cocaine or herioin. The police, too, became more active in ferreting out buyers and sellers through the use of undercover agents, wiretaps, sting operations, and the like. As a result, the number of prisoners in the nation's jails and prisons for drug offenses grew from about 50,000 in 1980 to approximately 500,000 in 2000 (Nadelmann, 2001). This led to tremendous overcrowding of both the courts and the prisons (30 percent of all inmates), resulting in a huge and costly growth in the number and size of prisons (each new cell built costs about $80,000 and each new prisoner added costs about $25,000 annually). Again using New York State as an example, its mandatory sentencing laws have meant that in 20 years, $4 billion was spent building prison cells to lock up nonviolent drug offenders at an incarceration cost of $700 million annually (*New York Times*, 2000a, b).

Consequences of Official Drug Policies

The drug laws in the United States are irrational: They do not achieve their intended goals (reduce or eliminate illicit drug use) but, rather, have the opposite effect:

> With the exception of Prohibition, which was finally repealed, the approach has been unvaried. Pass a law; if that does not work make the sentences harsher, get more policemen, get better detection devices, loosen up the law to make arrests easier, and so on. Whatever you do, refuse to recognize that making some behaviors criminal does not prevent them. (McCaghy, 1976:300)

The drug laws are intended to deter crime by severely punishing the seller and user. There are three fundamental reasons this approach does not work as intended. First, by making drugs illegal and therefore dangerous to produce, transport, and sell, society pushes the cost to many times what it would be if they were legally available. Thus, heroin users, for example, are often forced into crime to sustain a high-cost habit. Crimes committed to produce money for drugs are typically nonviolent (pimping, prostitution, shoplifting, selling drugs, and burglary), but their cost is enormous. Suppose, for example, that there are 100,000 addicts in New York City with habits each costing $50 daily. If they each steal $300 worth of goods daily in order to get the $50 (a 6-to-1 ratio is about the way fencing works), the amount stolen in the city would be $30 million daily or $10.68 billion a year!

The necessity of criminal activity to supply an expensive drug habit has another consequence that runs counter to the intent of the law. The addict must devote much—if not all—of his or her time to securing the expensive drug, and this time spent impairs his or her ability to function relatively smoothly in society. As Hartjen has argued:

> When drugs are readily available, addiction apparently had minimal impact on the social functioning of addicts. Little if any serious impairment of marital, occupational, and other role-performances resulted. As long as addicts could secure the drug without difficulty, they were able, for the most part, to live reasonably normal, productive lives. (Hartjen, 1977:95)

The second reason that crime is encouraged by punitive drug laws is that someone has to supply the illicit goods. Legislation does not dry up demand, as was vividly shown during Prohibition. Organized crime thrives in this climate. Illegal drugs are, for the most part, imported, processed, and distributed by organized crime groups:

> Competing American gangs intimidate and assault, and sometimes murder, anyone who opposes them as they fight over the large illicit profits from drugs. This has helped to devastate many inner-city neighborhoods because poor blacks and Hispanics in their neighborhoods are the main foot soldiers in drug supply networks. (Becker, 2001:32).

Drug laws, then, have the indirect effect of providing organized crime with its most lucrative source of income.

A third source of crime caused by drug laws is police corruption. Black market activities by organized crime or other entrepreneurs are difficult without the cooperation of police officials or drug enforcement agents, so their assistance is often bought.

The corruption of police officials causes disrespect for the law, another consequence of the unenforceable drug laws. Realization of the arbitrariness of the drug laws (such as the fact that marijuana is illegal but alcohol is legal) is another source of widespread disrespect for the law. A third source of irreverence toward the law is the overzealousness of narcotics agents. In their efforts to capture drug law violators, agents have sometimes violated the constitutional rights of individuals (wiretapping, search and seizure without a warrant, entrapment, use of informants who are themselves addicts, and so on). All these abuses have contributed to an attitude of insolence on the part of many people toward agents of the law.

Criminal laws create crime and criminals. If there were no law regulating a behavior, then there would be no criminal. So it is with drug laws. Prior to 1914, heroin users were not criminals, nor were marijuana users before 1937. The drug laws, then, have created large numbers of criminals. By labeling and treating these people as criminals, the justice system creates further crime (secondary deviance). In other words, efforts at social control actually cause the persistence of the deviant behaviors they are designed to eliminate. Several interrelated processes are at work here. First, as noted earlier, the drug user is forced to rely on illegal and very expensive sources. This reliance typically forces the user into crime or interaction with the criminal fringes of society. Second, when processed by the criminal justice system, the individual is stigmatized, which makes reintegration into normal society very difficult. All these factors encourage those pejoratively labeled by society to join together in a deviant drug subculture. Hartjen has described the effects:

> Probably the most significant consequence of punitive drug policies has been the development of a drug subculture. When drugs were legal and available, it was unnecessary for addicts to associate with other addicts. But when legitimate sources of supply were closed, addicts had two alternatives: (1) either give up drugs or (2) find a new source of supply. For those not willing or able to kick the habit, the illegal nature of drug use led many addicts to seek out and join others of their kind facing similar difficulties. Thus, the emergence of the drug subculture. The subculture offered addicts two advantages. For one, drugs could be secured from other addicts, and contact with other addicts led to the sharing of information on various ways to secure drugs or the resources necessary to do so. At the same time, knowledge of new drugs and techniques to take them could be transmitted. With the growth of the drug subculture, all the elements characteristic of other deviant groups also began to appear. Addicts began to develop a sense of solidarity among themselves, an elaborate ideology justifying addiction, status rankings, and a philosophy that rejected "straight" or "square" society. And, as with other groups, the subculture actively began to recruit new members to its fold. (Hartjen, 1977:94–95)

Thus, official drug policies have been predicated on the assumption that punitive laws and rigorous enforcement were necessary to eradicate the menace of certain drugs. The policies, however, have had just the opposite effect. They have harmed the drug users in a variety of unnecessary ways; they have cost society untold billions of dollars in enforcement costs and have clogged courts and prisons; they have resulted in additional indirect and direct crime; and they have kept organized crime very profitable.

Is the Drug War Racist?

The official policy of the federal government is to punish the sellers and users of illicit drugs. The problem is that the laws and the punishment for their violation are unfair to African Americans and other racial minorities. Four facts buttress this allegation. First, the data show consistently that *while Whites are more likely to use illegal drugs, African Americans are four times more likely to be imprisoned for drug offenses.*

- In 1997 while just 13 percent of regular illegal drug users were Black, 62.7 percent of drug offenders sentenced to prison were Black (Lewis, 2000).
- Of felony drug defendants in state courts 37 percent are White while 61 percent are African Americans.
- Of White drug felons 32 percent are given probation or nonincarceration sentences in state courts, compared to 25 percent of Blacks (U.S. Department of Justice, 2000).
- Human Rights Watch reported that nearly twice as many Black men and women are imprisoned for drug offenses than are Whites, even though there are five times more White drug users than Black ones (reported in Holmes, 2000).

Second, federal drug enforcement has waged its war against crack cocaine almost exclusively in minority neighborhoods. This is ironic because three times

While Whites are more apt to use illegal drugs, African Americans are four times more likely than Whites to be arrested for drug offenses.

as many Whites as Blacks (and seven times as many Whites as Latinos) have used crack cocaine (National Institute on Drug Abuse, cited in Weikel, 1995):

> Whites are more likely than any other racial group to use crack cocaine, but about 96 percent of the crack defendants in federal court are nonwhite, according to national surveys and sentencing reports. Not a single white suspect was federally prosecuted in 17 states and many cities, including Denver, Boston, Chicago, Miami, Dallas, and L.A. The reason is that federal law enforcement has waged its war against crack almost exclusively in minority neighborhoods, exposing black and Latino offenders to the toughest drug penalties. (Weikel, 1995:1A)

Third, the laws differ in the severity of punishment if violated. Although powder cocaine and crack cocaine are the same drug, federal law treats them quite differently. For example, possession of 5 grams of crack (a teaspoon) gets a mandatory 5-year sentence, while it takes 100 times that amount of powder cocaine to get a comparable sentence. This unfair 100-to-1 ratio is racist because the defendants in crack cocaine cases are almost always Black (89 percent) and the defendants in powder cocaine cases are typically White (70 percent) (Flaherty and Biskupic, 1996).

As a final example of the racial double standard in the war on drugs, consider the disposition of those found guilty of drug violations. There is a strong tendency for the courts to administer medical treatment for White drug users and the criminal justice system for Black users. This is especially true when social class is added to the racial mix—affluent Whites compared to poor Blacks.

Alternatives

The nation's drug laws and policies, as we have seen, are counterproductive. They not only fail to accomplish their goals but in many respects also actually achieve the opposite results. The drug war creates criminals. Organized crime flourishes because of official drug policies. The criminalization of drugs encourages corruption within the criminal justice system and it reduces the freedoms guaranteed by the Constitution. As conducted, the war on drugs is unfair to racial minorities. It overburdens the courts and prisons, and, most significant, it does not work. As the *Progressive* editorialized:

> The war on drugs is a failure. It has not solved the problem of drug abuse in our society, and the costs—economic, political, social, international, and the public health—are exorbitant. To continue to wage this war (or to escalate it as some suggest) would only increase the costs. What's more, the war on drugs is based on a faulty assumption, an unrealistic goal: that we can attain a drug-free, zero tolerance society. We can't. (*Progressive,* 1999:10)

The United States has three alternatives concerning drug policy: (1) to continue to wage the war on drugs by enacting and enforcing criminal laws, (2) to legalize drugs and regulate them through licensing and taxation, and (3) to take a public health approach, with an emphasis on decriminalization. We have already considered the first option—the criminalization of drug use—so we concentrate here on the other alternatives.

Regulation of Trade or Use through Licensing and Taxation

Legalizing a drug but regulating its use, as is now the case with alcohol, tobacco, and prescription drugs, has some obvious benefits:

- It ensures the products' conformity to standards of purity and safety.
- It dries up the need for vast criminal networks that distribute drugs.
- It provides the government with revenues.
- Prison space and police activities would be reserved for the truly dangerous.

Most important, prohibition has not worked:

> [In 1920] there were probably fewer than 300,000 narcotics addicts in the whole country, [and] we decided to root them out. Today, after an eighty-year, trillion-dollar *jihad,* the total number of addicts is up around 4 million. Instead of decreasing the rate of addiction, we [by declaring war and criminalizing the activity], gave it a [huge] boost. (M. Gray, 1999:16)

Opponents argue that government regulation would actually condone the use of drugs. This apparent approval together with the easy availability and relatively low prices would promote experimentation and use of the drug, perhaps increasing the number of users. Politically, such a policy would be difficult if not impossible to implement. Opinion polls show that the public strongly opposes legalization and politicians do not want to seem "soft on drugs."

Under this regulation option, the biggest population to deal with would be the heroin addicts. These users are a special problem to themselves and society. Their habits are the most expensive, so of all drug users they are most likely to turn to crime. Their habit also requires almost full-time diligence in securing the drug; and being "strung out," they do not function normally in society. How, then, should the government deal with them? Hard-liners argue that they should be classified as criminals and incarcerated. Other people suggest that addicts could remain in society and be relatively productive if drugs were supplied to them cheaply, under government regulation and medical supervision.

This can be accomplished through **methadone maintenance,** which treats addicts as medical problems rather than criminal problems. Methadone is a heroin substitute that can be taken orally. It is just as addictive as heroin, but it is considered safer. Its effects last longer than heroin's, so that an addict needs a fix perhaps once a day rather than three or four times a day. Moreover, the drug does not make the user drowsy. The net effect is that a methadone user can easily continue to be a productive member of society without having to steal for his or her habit.

A variation of the methadone maintenance program is occurring in Baltimore (Shenk, 1999b). Here there is a methadone treatment option (cost of about $3,500 a year) and a 28-day inpatient program (cost of $2,900 for each patient). The city also runs a needle-exchange program to reduce the incidence of HIV/AIDS infection. The problem is that Baltimore has an estimated 60,000 addicts; it is spending over $30 million annually and needs another $35 million to meet the needs of those addicts wanting treatment. Additionally, former addicts need vocational training, family counseling, and other expensive services if the long-term goal of stability for these addicts and former addicts is to be met.

A strength of these plans is that addicts are not labeled as criminals. They are considered to have a medical, not a moral, problem. Equally important is that addicts remain participating members of the community.

Critics of methadone maintenance argue that such programs encourage wider use of hard drugs. They also assert that these plans will not be acceptable to most citizens, who will continue to label addicts as criminals and sinful. Liberals, while likely to approve of either plan over the current criminal model, foresee a danger in government control over an addict population dependent on it for drugs. Also, such programs attack the problem at the individual level (blaming the victim) and ignore the social and cultural sources of drug use.

Currie's (1993) summary of the research on methadone maintenance shows that this treatment, while not perfect, does have the positive effects of decriminalizing narcotics use, placing addicts under medical supervision, and returning many addicts to a productive life.

Noninterference

Libertarians argue that it is none of the government's business what drugs people put into their bodies. There should be no governmental interference in this private act. Thomas Szasz, for example, argues that all drugs, regardless of their danger, should be legalized:

> I favor free trade in drugs for the same reason the Founding Fathers favored free trade in ideas. In an open society, it is none of the government's business what idea a man puts into his mind; likewise, it should be none of the government's business what drug he puts into his body. (Szasz, 1972:75)

This view, however, does not excuse drug users from their behavior. According to Szasz:

> The right of self-medication should be hedged in by similar limits. Public intoxication, not only with alcohol but with any drug, should be an offense punishable by the criminal law. Furthermore, acts that may injure others—such as driving a car—should, when carried out in a drug-intoxicated state, be punished especially strictly and severely. The right to self-medication must thus entail unqualified responsibility for the effects of one's drug-intoxicated behavior on others. For unless we are willing to hold ourselves responsible for our own behavior, and hold others responsible for theirs, the liberty to use drugs (or to engage in other acts) degenerates into a license to hurt others. (Szasz, 1972:77)

Proponents of total **decriminalization (legalization) of drugs** argue that all societies throughout known history have had psychoactive drugs. Legislation and strict enforcement will not curb the tendency among many people to want to alter their consciousness artificially. Such acts should be neither penalized nor encouraged because it is none of the government's business what individuals do to themselves. (For the way that the Dutch handle marijuana, see the panel titled "Social Problems in Global Perspective.")

Critics suggest that decriminalization will encourage the spread of drug use. Drug use will spread because drugs will be readily available and because commercial interests will see potential profits in these formerly illicit drugs and will produce them and promote their use. Finally, and perhaps most significant, some argue that drug use is not an isolated act that affects only the user. In short, although many people believe that drug use is a "victimless vice," there is always a victim. As Nettler has argued:

> If our spouses wrong their bodies, we pay a price. If children harm themselves, their parents are victims. If parents are dissolute, their children are victims. If enough individuals harm themselves, then society is the victim. In

SOCIAL PROBLEMS IN GLOBAL PERSPECTIVE

DUTCH MARIJUANA POLICY

In the 1970s, the United States and some other countries reduced penalties for marijuana offenses. In some places criminal penalties for personal possession were eliminated altogether. A second wave of marijuana law reform is now occurring today in Europe and Australia. Leading the way, in the 1970s and today, is the Netherlands. Following the recommendations of two national commissions, the Dutch Parliament decriminalized cannabis possession and retail sale in 1976. Even before this date the police seldom made arrests for possession or small-volume sales. While not officially legalizing marijuana, the 1976 law allowed the Dutch government to create a set of guidelines under which coffee shops could sell marijuana and hashish without fear of criminal prosecution.

Guidelines for the coffee shops have changed somewhat over time and vary slightly from community to community. The basic rules in place today include a ban on advertising, a minimum purchase age of 18, and a 5-gram limit on individual transactions. The sale of any other illicit drug on the premises is strictly prohibited, and is grounds for immediate closure. Local government officials may limit the number of coffee shops concentrated in one area, and they can close an establishment if it creates a public nuisance. In the Netherlands, there are now over 1,000 coffee shops where adults can purchase marijuana and hashish to be used there or carried away for use later.

The decision of Dutch legislators to permit the regulated sale and use of cannabis was based on a number of practical considerations. By allowing marijuana to be sold indoors rather than on the streets, the Dutch sought to improve public order. By separating the retail market for marijuana from the retail market for "hard drugs," they sought to reduce the likelihood of marijuana users being exposed to heroin and cocaine. By providing a nondeviant environment in which cannabis could be consumed, they sought to diminish the drug's utility as a symbol of youthful rebellion. Dutch officials have little faith in the capacity of the criminal law to stop people from using marijuana. They fear that arresting and punishing marijuana users—particularly youthful marijuana users—will alienate them from society's mainstream institutions and values.

These principles of normalization also guide the Dutch approach to drug education and prevention. Programs are specifically designed to be low-key and minimalist, to avoid provoking young people's interest in drugs. There are no mass media campaigns against drugs, and school-based programs do not use scare

> brief, there can be victimless vice only when no one influences anyone. As long as someone pays a price for someone else's action, that action is not victimless. The prices paid can be offenses to one's taste or invasions of one's purse. The prices paid can be as varied as insults to eye, ear, and nose; to having to wend one's way on public streets through prostitutes; to having to pay taxes in support of rehabilitation centers for sick addicts; and so on. (Nettler, 1976:168)

What, then, is the answer to drug use? Probably some combination of these alternatives makes the most sense. Clearly, the arguments about the solution will continue to incite passion. There will be those who are concerned with the use of certain drugs and who feel that society must control such deviance. They insist on imposing their morals on others. At the other extreme are those who are more concerned with how the laws and their rigorous enforcement cause social problems. As the various segments in society continue the debate, legislation will be proposed and eventually passed. The astute observer should note the role of interest groups in what is decided and also who benefits and who loses by the decision reached.

tactics or moralistic "just say no" messages. Instead, in the context of general health education, young people in the Netherlands are given information about drugs and cautionary warnings about their potential dangers. In leaflets distributed through the coffee shops, current users of cannabis are advised to be "sensible and responsible."

This pragmatic cannabis policy has not resulted in an explosion of marijuana use. During the 1970s, marijuana use increased in the Netherlands, as it did in the United States. Today, as shown in the table, marijuana prevalence rates in the United States and the Netherlands are similar for most age groups. However, among young adolescents, marijuana use is lower in the Netherlands—about 7 percent compared to about 13 percent in the United States. A 1994 survey in the city of Amsterdam, where marijuana is more available than almost anywhere else in the world, found that the average age of initiation into cannabis use was twenty, compared to an average age of initiation in the United States of 16.3.

Percentage of People Who Have Ever Used Marijuana

	United States	*Netherlands*
Total population	31.11[1]	28.52[2]
Young adults	47.33[3]	45.54[4]
Older teens	38.25[5]	29.56[6]
Younger teens	13.57[7]	7.28[8]

Sources for data:

1. U.S. population, age 12 and older: National Household Survey on Drug Abuse: Population Estimates, 1994.
2. Amsterdam residents, age 12 and older: Sandwijk, J. P,. et al., *Licit and Illicit Drug Use in Amsterdam II,* 1994.
3. Age 18–34: See note 1 above.
4. Age 20–34: See note 2 above.
5. Twelfth graders, average of 1992, 1993, and 1994 data: The Monitoring the Future Study, 1975–1994.
6. Ages 16–19, average of data from 1994 Amsterdam survey: See note 2 above and 1992 national school-based survey by De Zwart, et al., *Key Data: Smoking, Drinking, Drug Use and Gambling among Pupils Aged 10 Years and Older,* Netherlands Institute on Alcohol and Drugs.
7. Eighth graders, average of 1992, 1993, and 1994 data: See note 5 above.
8. Age 12–15, average of 1994 Amsterdam data: See note 2 above and 1992 national data; see note 6 above.

Source: Lynn Zimmer and John P. Morgan. 1997. *Marijuana Myths/Marijuana Facts: A Review of the Scientific Evidence.* New York: Lindesmith Center, pp. 49–52.

To conclude, let us examine some of the insights of Elliott Currie, who has written perceptively about drugs in the United States:

- For addicts, "successful recovery has less to do with the chemistry of the drug itself or the particular modality of treatment than with the realistic possibilities for an alternative way of life" (Currie, 1993:237). These alternatives involve work, friendships, and family relations through which the addict develops a positive identity outside the drug culture.
- If we are to solve the drug problem, we must attack the conditions that breed it. "It is not accidental that the United States has both the developed world's worst drug problem and its worst violence, poverty, and social exclusion, together with its least adequate provision of health care, income support, and social services. Taking on the drug problem in an enduring way means tackling those social deficits head-on" (Currie, 1993:280–281). Or as he said in a later article: "We need a multilayered approach: we need better treatment, more harm-reduction programs, selective decriminalization, more creative adolescent prevention efforts and much more—all in the context of a broader 'strategy of inclusion' that would systematically tackle the misery and hopelessness that, as study after study shows, has bred the worst drug abuse in America and elsewhere. That strategy involves investing in, among other things, family support centers, apprenticeship programs, paid family leaves, high-quality childcare and a lot else" (Currie, 1999:18).

CHAPTER REVIEW

1. Some drugs in U.S. society are legal and others are not. The division is based not on their potential for harm to the users or society but on politics—the exercise of power by interest groups and the majority to legislate their views on others.
2. Most people in the United States take some drug on a regular basis. Those drugs considered legal are caffeine, alcohol, nicotine, tranquilizers, amphetamines, and barbiturates. Illegal drugs used by millions in U.S. society are marijuana, cocaine, inhalants, psychedelics, and heroin.
3. The prevailing culture, group norms, and social pressures strongly affect the patterns of drug use and their behavioral effects.
4. The pressure to use drugs may come from doctors, coaches, pharmaceutical firms, tobacco and alcohol companies, and one's friends and associates.
5. People in the United States seek and use drugs for a variety of reasons, ranging from medical necessity to desire for a change in mood because life is too boring, stressful, competitive, and frustrating.
6. The acceptability of certain drugs such as marijuana or heroin has varied historically. Opiates, once legal in the United States, became illegal for two reasons: (a) Members of the White working class on the West Coast felt threatened by cheap Chinese labor and sought coercive measures against those Chinese; and (b) religious groups interpreting opiate use as a moral evil mounted successful pressure. The result was the Harrison Narcotics Act of 1914, which made opiate use a criminal offense. Thus, behavior once considered a medical problem became a criminal problem.
7. Laws defining which drugs are legal and which are not reflect negative stereotypes held by the general public and efforts for control by interest groups (such as religious groups, the pharmaceutical industry, and organized crime) and law enforcement professionals. The result is that current drug laws are illogical. They are not related to the danger of the drugs but reflect the political interests of the powerful.
8. The drug war appears to be racist because of four patterns in the criminal justice system: (a) While Whites are more apt to use illegal drugs, Blacks are four times more likely to be arrested for drug offenses; (b) while Whites use crack more than Blacks, drug enforcement of crack occurs almost exclusively in Black neighbor-

hoods; (c) although crack cocaine and powder cocaine are basically the same, the government punishes the users and sellers of crack much more severely; and (d) the courts tend to administer medical treatment for White drug users and the criminal justice system for Black users.

9. Drug laws promote crime in at least four ways: (a) They create criminals by making possession and use of certain drugs illegal; (b) users often engage in criminal activity because the drugs, being illegal, are so expensive; (c) punitive drug laws encourage organized crime by making importation, processing, and distribution of illegal drugs extremely lucrative; and (d) people selling illicit drugs often corrupt the police.
10. Government can adopt three alternative policies toward drug use: (a) prohibition of trade and use through enforcement of criminal penalties (the current policy); (b) regulation through licensing and taxation; and (c) noninterference (ignoring drugs, because what people do to themselves is not the government's business).

KEY TERMS

Drug. Any substance that directly affects the brain or nervous system when ingested.

Social construction of drugs. Definitions concerning drugs and drug-related behaviors based on the meanings that people in groups have imputed to certain things and behaviors.

Ontological truth. A universal and undeniable reality.

Politics of drugs. The labeling of some drugs as licit and others as illicit depends on the definition of drugs by the most powerful interest groups, which are able to get their definitions incorporated into the law.

Psychoactive drug. Chemical that alters the perceptions and/or moods of people who take it.

Psychopharmacology. Science of drugs that affect the mind.

Restorative drug. Chemical that heals a traumatized part of the body.

Additive drug. Chemical that improves performance.

Interdiction. Public policy of stopping the flow of drugs into the United States by guarding the borders and by curtailing the creation, processing, and distributing of drugs in other countries.

Heroin maintenance. British approach to heroin addiction that treats addicts as sick rather than as criminal; thus, addicts are placed under the jurisdiction of physicians who administer drugs to their patients.

Methadone maintenance. Similar to heroin maintenance, this provides a heroin substitute (methadone) to addicts under medical supervision.

Decriminalization of drugs. Legalization of drugs.

WEBSITES FOR FURTHER REFERENCE

http://www.health.org/
This is the website for the National Clearinghouse for Alcohol and Drug Information (NCADI), a service of the Substance Abuse and Mental Health Services Administration. NCADI is the world's largest resource for current information and materials concerning substance abuse. This is "the nation's one-stop resource for the most current and comprehensive information about substance abuse prevention and treatment." NCADI is one of the largest federal clearinghouses, offering more than 500 items to the public, many of which are free of charge. This organization distributes the latest studies and surveys, guides, videocassettes, and other types of information and materials on substance abuse from various agencies, such as the U.S. Departments of Education and Labor, the Center for Substance Abuse Prevention, the Center for Substance Abuse Treatment, the National Institute on Alcohol Abuse and Alcoholism, and the National Institute on Drug Abuse.

http://www.drugsense.org
If you are concerned about the War on Drugs, explore DrugSense to become informed and active. DrugSense provides accurate information relevant to drug policy in order to heighten awareness of the extreme damage being caused to our nation and the world by our current flawed and failed War on Drugs. DrugSense aims to "inform the public of the existence of rational alternatives to the drug war, and to help organize citizens to bring about needed reforms."

http://www.acmed.org/
The International Association for Cannabis as Medicine (IACM) was founded in March 2000. It is a "scientific society advocating the improvement of the legal situa-

tion for the use of the hemp plant (Cannabis sativa L.) and its pharmacologically most important active compounds, the cannabinoids, for therapeutic applications through promotion of research and dissemination of information."

http://www.casacolumbia.org/
The National Center on Addiction and Substance Abuse at Columbia University exists to inform Americans of the economic and social costs of substance abuse and its impact on their lives, and assess what works in prevention, treatment, and law enforcement. This organization's mission is to "encourage every individual and institution to take responsibility to combat substance abuse and addiction," and to "remove the stigma of abuse and replace shame and despair with hope."

http://www.dare-america.com/
This is the official site of the Drug Abuse Resistance Education or D.A.R.E. program for kids. "Since its early beginnings, D.A.R.E. has always taken the antidrug, antiviolence message to the streets. Now D.A.R.E. has taken this powerful message to the biggest street in the world, the Information Superhighway." This site is not only for kids, however; there is also quite a bit of information on this website for educators.

http://www.drugfreeamerica.org/
The Partnership for a Drug-Free America is a nonprofit coalition of professionals from the communications industry whose mission is to help teens reject substance abuse. Through its national antidrug advertising campaign and other forms of media communication, The Partnership works to "decrease demand for drugs and other substances by changing societal attitudes which support, tolerate, or condone drug use."

http://www.usdoj.gov/dea/
The mission of the Drug Enforcement Administration (DEA) is to "enforce the controlled substances laws and regulations of the United States and bring to the criminal and civil justice system of the United States, or any other competent jurisdiction, those organizations and principal members of organizations involved in the growing, manufacture, or distribution of controlled substances appearing in or destined for illicit traffic in the United States; and to recommend and support nonenforcement programs aimed at reducing the availability of illicit controlled substances on the domestic and international markets."

PART FIVE
INSTITUTIONAL PROBLEMS

hen a man tells you that he got rich through hard work, ask him, "Whose?"

—Don Marquis

Work is central to the human experience. Societies are organized to allocate work in order to produce the goods and services needed by the society and its members for sustenance, clothing, shelter, defense, and even luxury. Work provides individuals with their social identity, economic resources, and social location. Work dominates their time and is a primary source of life's meaning because it constitutes their contributions to other people.

The world of work also has a dark side, however. The structure of work is a major source of social problems. Work is alienating for many people. The organization of work sometimes exploits, does harm to workers, and often dehumanizes them. The distribution of work and how it is rewarded are major sources of inequality in society.

This chapter focuses on the social problems generated by the social organization of work. The chapter is divided into four parts. The first part examines the problems common to the experience of the U.S. work world: the control of workers, alienated labor, the hazards in the workplace, the inequality generated by a segmented labor market and capitalist patriarchy, and unemployment. The second part of the chapter describes the structural transformation of the U.S. economy as it shifts from an industrial society to an information/service economy. The third part examines the job-related problems posed by the structural transformation of the society. And the final part focuses on the inequality generated by these massive structural changes in the economy.

Problems of Work

Work is a universal human activity. People everywhere engage in physical and mental activities that enhance the physical and social survival of themselves and others. Although people universally must work to meet their material needs, the way work is structured varies by society. This section examines the problems created from the way work is structured in U.S. society.

Control of Workers

With the advent of the Industrial Revolution more and more families left agrarian life, moved to cities, and worked in factories. Work in these factories was sometimes difficult, sometimes dangerous, often tedious, and usually boring. There was always the threat of lowered productivity and worker unrest under these adverse conditions. The factory owners and their managers used several tactics to counteract these potential problems and especially to maintain high productivity—scientific management, hierarchical control, technical control, and extortion.

Scientific management (also called *Taylorization,* after its founder, Frederick Taylor) came to the fore in U.S. industry around 1900. The emphasis was on breaking down work into very specialized tasks, the standardization of tools and procedures, and the speeding up of repetitive work. These efforts to increase worker efficiency and therefore to increase profits meant that workers developed a very limited range of skills. Instead of a wide knowledge of building cars or furniture, their knowledge was severely curtailed. This specialization had the effect of making the workers highly susceptible to automation and to being easily replaced by cheaper workers. But this scientific management approach also had a contradictory effect. In its attempt to increase efficiency by having workers do ever more compartmentalized tasks, it increased the repetition, boredom, and meaninglessness of work—hence, the strong tendency for workers to become alienated and restless. Consider the description by George Ritzer:

> [The assembly line clearly] offers a dehumanizing setting in which to work. Human beings, equipped with a wide array of skills and abilities, are asked to perform a limited number of highly simplified tasks over and over. Instead of expressing their human abilities on the job, people are forced to deny their humanity and act like robots. People cannot express themselves in their work. (Ritzer, 1996:26)

Closely related to scientific management is the use of bureaucracy to control workers. Work settings, whether in factories, offices, or corporations, are organized into bureaucratized hierarchies. In this hierarchy of authority (chain of command) each position in the chain gives orders to those below, taking responsibility for their actions and following orders from above. The hierarchical arrangement controls workers by holding out the possibility of advancement, with more prestigious job titles, higher wages, and greater benefits as one moves up the ladder. Those who hope to be upwardly mobile in the organization must become obedient rule followers who do not question authority.

Similarly, work organized along an assembly line permits maximum control over workers, "who must do certain tasks at specific points during the production process. It is immediately obvious when a worker fails to perform the required tasks" (Ritzer, 1996:25–26).

Workers are also controlled by management's use of technology to monitor and supervise them. Some businesses use lie detectors to assess worker loyalty. Psychological tests and drug tests (70 percent of major companies require employees to undergo urine tests for drugs) are used to screen applicants for work. E-mail and use of the Internet are monitored (Faltermayer, 2000). Telephone taps have been used to determine whether workers use company time for personal use. Closed-circuit television, two-way mirrors, and other devices have been used by management to determine whether workers are using their time most productively. The most common contemporary technology for worker control is the computer. The computer can count keystrokes, time phone calls, monitor frequency of errors, assess overall employee performance, and even issue warnings when the employee falls short of the ideal.

A final management tool to control workers is extortion. If workers become too militant in their demands for higher wages, safe working conditions, or benefits, management can threaten them with reprisals. In the past, owners threatened to hire cheaper labor (new immigrants, for example) or to use force to end a strike. Today, the most common and successful management tool is the threat to move the plant to a nonunion state or even outside the United States if the union does not reduce its demands or to replace the workers with robots or other forms of automation.

Alienation

Alienation refers to the separation of human beings from each other, from themselves, and from the products they create. In capitalism, according to Karl Marx, worker alienation occurs because the workers do not have any control over their labor, because they are manipulated by managers, because they tend to work in large, impersonal settings, and because they work at specialized tasks. Under these circumstances workers use only a fraction of their talents and have no pride in their own creativity and in the final product. Thus, we see that worker alienation is linked with unfulfilled personal satisfaction. As Blauner has described it:

> Alienation exists when workers are unable to control their immediate work processes, to develop a sense of purpose and function which connects their jobs to the overall organization of production, to belong to integrated industrial communities, and when they fail to become involved in the activity of work as a mode of personal self-expression. (Blauner, 1964:5)

Put another way, this time by philosopher Albert Camus: "Without work all life goes rotten. But when work is soulless, life stifles and dies" (quoted in Levitan and Johnson, 1982:63).

In the absence of satisfaction and personal fulfillment, work becomes meaningless. When this meaninglessness is coupled with management's efforts to control workers, the repetitious nature of the work, and the requirement of punching a time clock, many workers feel a profound resentment. This resentment may lead workers to join together in a union or other collective group to improve their working conditions. For many workers, though, the alienation remains at a personal level and is manifested by higher worker dissatisfaction, absenteeism, disruption in the workplace, and alcohol or other drug abuse on the job.

Alienation is not limited to manual workers. The work of white-collar workers such as salesclerks, secretaries, file clerks, bank tellers, and data entry clerks is mostly routine, repetitive, boring, and unchallenging. These workers, like assembly line workers, follow orders, do limited tasks, and have little sense of accomplishment.

Studs Terkel, in introducing his book *Working*, summarized the personal impact of alienating work:

> This book, being about work, is, by its very nature, about violence—to the spirit as well as to the body. It is about ulcers as well as accidents, about shouting matches as well as fistfights, about nervous breakdowns as well as kicking the dog around. It is, above all (or beneath all), about daily humiliations. To survive the day is triumph enough for the walking wounded among the great many of us.
>
> It is about a search, too, for daily meaning as well as daily bread, for recognition as well as for cash, for astonishment rather than torpor; in short, for a sort of life rather than a Monday through Friday sort of dying. Perhaps immortality, too, is part of the quest. To be remembered was the wish, spoken and unspoken, of the heroes and heroines of this book.
>
> For the many, there is a hardly concealed discontent. The blue-collar blues is no more bitterly sung than the white-collar moan. "I'm a machine," says the spotwelder. "I'm caged," says the steelworker. "A monkey can do what I do," says the receptionist. "I'm less than a farm implement," says the migrant worker. "I'm an object," says the high-fashion model. Blue collar and white call upon the identical phrase: "I'm a robot." (Terkel, 1975:xiii–xiv)

Dangerous Working Conditions

In a capitalist economy workers represent a cost to profit-seeking corporations. The lower that management can keep labor costs, the greater will be its profits. Historically, low labor costs meant that workers received low wages, had inferior or nonexistent fringe benefits such as health care and pensions, and worked in unhealthy conditions. Mines and factories were often extremely unsafe. The labor movement early in the 1900s gathered momentum because of the abuse experienced by workers.

After a long and sometimes violent struggle the unions were successful in raising wages for workers, adding fringe benefits, and making the conditions of work safer. But the owners were slow to change; and worker safety was, and continues to be, one of the most difficult areas. Many owners of mills, mines, and factories continue to consider the safety of their workers a low-priority item, presumably because of the high cost.

About 30 years ago, the federal government instituted the Occupational Safety and Health Administration (OSHA) to make the workplace safer. The result has been a 75 percent drop in workplace fatalities, despite resistance by the business community and weak enforcement by government. Even with this dramatic drop in worker deaths, the problem of worker safety remains.

> 6,000 workers die each year from workplace trauma, and estimates of 50,000 to 60,000 annual deaths from occupational disease almost surely understate the actual number of fatalities. Even less acknowledged are the millions of injuries that occur each year, leaving many victims with aching backs, bad knees, amputated fingers and other pains and disabilities that diminish quality of life for months, years, or often a lifetime. (*Multinational Monitor,* 2000:5)

Put another way, criminologist Jeffrey Reiman estimates that there are 31,218 occupational deaths from work injuries or diseases from exposure to carcinogens at work annually plus 3.6 million serious work injuries (Reiman, 2001:82).

Significant occupational dangers continue to plague workers, especially in certain jobs (see the "Voices" panel, p. 406). The dangers today are invisible contaminants such as nuclear radiation, chemical compounds, coal tars, dust, and asbestos fibers in the air. These dangers from invisible contaminants are increasing because the production of synthetic chemicals has increased so dramatically. The following examples describe the specific risks of continued exposure to dangerous chemicals in certain industries:

- Workers in the dyestuffs industry (working with aromatic hydrocarbons) have about thirty times the risk of the general population of dying from bladder cancer.
- About 10 percent of coal miners suffer from black lung, caused by years of breathing coal dust in areas with inadequate ventilation.
- Migrant farm workers have a life expectancy 30 years below the national average. This low rate is a consequence of living in poverty or near poverty and, most significant, of the exposure to herbicides and pesticides sprayed on the fields where they work.
- Workers in the semiconductor industry face special dangers from exposure to acids, gases, and solvents used in chip manufacturing. For example, ten of thirty-six semiconductor plants in California were cited by OSHA for health and safety shortfalls between 1993 and 1997. Similarly, the Environmental Protection Agency (EPA) found that some companies

VOICES

HEALTH DANGERS AT ZILOG

Zilog Corporation has a semiconductor factory in rural Idaho. The first signs of a problem occurred in 1993 when nearly 900 employee accident reports noted workers with blistered faces and bleeding from their mouths. Some coughed uncontrollably and vomited blood. Others blacked out. A few workers reported miscarriages.

- On June 25, 1993, Maria Ramos blacked out in the factory clean room. "When I opened my eyes my vision was very, very blurry. I couldn't see the clock. I had pain all through my joints. And my head just throbbed," she says.

  Two days later, working through pain, Ramos lost control of her bowels and soiled her uniform. She was told to work an extra hour to make up the time it took to change clothes.

  Ramos was diagnosed with breast cancer in November 1993. Recently released after another trip to the hospital, she says, "I have no proof that will relate my cancer to Zilog, it's only what I feel."
- In November 1994, former clean room worker Dottie Gudgel produced a bone sample of arsenic 30 times normal after undergoing hip replacement surgery. For years Gudgel cleaned poisonous arsenic residues from Zilog factory equipment. She says now, "I was on the company's side right up until I was diagnosed with arsenic in my bones."

The problems at Zilog were caused by negligence by the company and insufficient oversight by the federal government. According to internal company records and the reports of consultants, workers in the clean room at Zilog were exposed to poisonous chemicals from leaking, badly maintained equipment. Compounding the hazardous situation were faulty chemical monitors, inoperative alarms and an inadequate exhaust system.

Officials at Zilog compounded the problem by mistakenly telling the public that it stopped using a dangerous solvent associated with high miscarriage rates and damage to testes. Zilog also inaccurately reported its waste accumulations to regulators from 1992 to 1994. The company also hired an occupational medicine specialist who assured workers that the plant was safe.

Government agencies were lax in their monitoring of the Idaho Zilog plant. When workers complained to OSHA, the agency, overburdened by having only ten investigators to monitor the 65,000 companies in Idaho, ordered Zilog to investigate itself. At the state level, the Idaho Division of Environmental Quality hasn't inspected the Zilog plant since 1990.

Source: E. B. Smith. 1998. "The Zilog Mystery: What Made So Many Workers So Sick?" *USA Today* (January 13): 1B, 3B.

in this industry continued to use chemicals suspected of causing cancer and miscarriages, even though the vast majority of companies recognized the danger and changed to safer alternatives (Schmit, 1998).

- Pregnant operators of video display terminals have disproportionate numbers of miscarriages or babies with birth defects, apparently from exposure to nonionizing radiation.

The record of industry has often been one of ignoring the scientific data (the Manville Corporation, e.g., despite many studies documenting the dangers of exposure to asbestos, continued to manufacture and sell the product) or of stalling through court actions rather than making plants safer. Most important, some companies have not informed workers of the dangers.

This discussion raises some critical questions: Should profits supersede human life? Are owners guilty of murder if their decisions to minimize plant

Migrant farm workers have a life expectancy 30 years below the national average. This low rate is a consequence of living in poverty or near poverty and of the exposure to herbicides and pesticides sprayed on the fields where they work.

safety result in industrial deaths? Who is a greater threat, the thug in the streets or the executives in the suites? Jeffrey Reiman answers these questions:

> Is a person who kills another in a bar brawl a greater threat to society than a business executive who refuses to cut into his profits to make his plant a safe place to work? By any measure of death and suffering the latter is by far a greater danger than the former. Because he wishes his workers no harm, because he is only indirectly responsible for death and disability while pursuing legitimate economic goals, his acts are not called "crimes." Once we free our imagination from the blinders of the one-on-one model of crime, can there be any doubt that the criminal justice system does *not* protect us from the gravest threats to life and limb? It seeks to protect us when danger comes from a young lower-class male in the inner city. When a threat comes from an upper-class business executive in an office, the criminal justice system looks the other way. This is in the face of growing evidence that for every two American citizens murdered by thugs, more than three American workers are killed by the recklessness of their bosses and the indifference of their government. (Reiman, 2001:85)

Sweatshops

A **sweatshop** is a substandard work environment where workers are paid less than the minimum wage and are not paid overtime premiums, and where other labor laws are violated. Although sweatshops occur in various types of manufacturing, they occur most frequently in the garment industry, where the Department of Labor estimates that more than half of the 22,000 U.S. sewing businesses violate minimum wage and overtime regulations (Branigan, 1997).The government estimates that more than half of the garment shops in San Francisco violate labor laws, as do the more than 3,000 apparel sweatshops employing 50,000 workers in New York City (Echaveste and Nussbaum, 1994).

Garment sweatshops are also common in Los Angeles, El Paso, and Seattle. The workers in these places make clothes for such brands as Levi Strauss, Esprit, Casual Corner, the Limited, and the Gap and for such merchandisers as J. C. Penney, Sears, and Wal-Mart. The workers, mostly Latina and Asian immigrant women, are paid much below the minimum wage, receive no benefits, and work in crowded, unsafe, and stifling conditions.

U.S. corporations also sell products produced by workers in sweatshop conditions in other countries. Soccer balls are sewn together by child laborers in Pakistan. "Mattel makes tens of millions of Barbies a year in China, where young female Chinese workers who have migrated thousands of miles from home are alleged to earn less than the minimum wage of $1.99 a day" (Holstein, 1996:50). Many of Disney's products are make in Sri Lanka and Haiti—countries notorious for the lack of labor and human rights. *Multinational Monitor* rated Nike as one of the "Ten Worst Corporations of 1997" for paying its workers in Vietnam an average of 20 cents per hour, and by exposing its workers in one Vietnam plant to carcinogens that exceeded local legal standards by over 100 times (*Multinational Monitor*, 1997b).

Unions and Their Decline

Historically, labor unions have been extremely important in changing management–labor relations. Joining together, workers challenged owners to increase wages, add benefits, provide worker security, and promote safety in the workplace. Through the use of strikes, work slowdowns, public relations, and political lobbying, working conditions improved and union members, for the most part, prospered. In wages and benefits, union workers earn about 34 percent more than nonunion workers. Consider the following differences (from Hansen, 1998):

- Union women earn 40 percent more than nonunion women; African American union members earn 44 percent more than comparable nonunion members; and Latino unionists earn 53 percent more.
- Of union workers 85 percent have medical benefits, compared with 74 percent of nonunion workers.
- Of unionists 79 percent have defined-benefit retirement plans, which are federally insured with a guaranteed monthly payment, while only 44 percent of nonunion workers have such plans.
- Union workers have greater job stability, with more than 60 percent having worked for their current employers for at least 10 years, compared with only 30 percent of nonunion workers.

But unions have lost their power since about 1980, as membership declined from 34 percent of the nonagricultural labor force in 1955 to 13.5 percent in 2000 (Greenhouse, 2001a). With such small and dwindling numbers, labor unions are in danger of becoming irrelevant.

The reasons for the decline in union membership (and clout) are several. First, there was a direct assault against unions by Republican Presidents Reagan and Bush. Both of these administrations were unsympathetic with strikes and sometimes used federal leverage to weaken them. Similarly, their appointees to the post of Secretary of Labor and the National Labor Relations Board (NLRB) were probusiness rather than prolabor. Long delays in decision making at the NLRB and their antiunion rulings have resulted in management sometimes firing prounion workers with impunity. In effect, from 1981 on, the NLRB reversed its previous policies of protecting worker rights (Novak, 1991).

Second, public opinion has turned against unions because some of them are undemocratic, scandal ridden, and too zealous in their demands. Public opinion has also turned against organized labor because of a probusiness, procapitalist bias that increased during the era of supply-side economics that dominated the Reagan and Bush administrations and much of Congress during that time. That bias, although muted a bit, continued during the Clinton administration but was resurrected during George W. Bush's administration.

Third, businesses do all they can to block unions. Typically, companies are required to have a union vote if 30 percent of workers sign a petition. When such an election does occur, companies have won more than half the time, versus 28 percent in the early 1950s. The antiunion vote by workers is the result usually of an all-out assault by the company, including information arguing that unionization may lead to downsizing or even closing plants, "worker appreciation" days with free barbeque or pizza, and the selective firing of workers who are union activists (an illegal activity, but it happens in about one-fourth of the union drives, according to a commission study established by President Clinton) and other forms of intimidation (Jones, 1997b).

A major reason for the decline of union strength is the transformation of the economy (discussed later in this chapter). Manufacturing jobs, which are in decline, have historically been prounion while service jobs, which are increasing, have been typically nonunionized. Many businesses, faced with stiff competition from low-wage economies, have insisted on reducing wages and/or worker benefits or have said they would go bankrupt or move overseas themselves. The increased use of microchip technology threatens jobs with increased automation in the factory (robots to replace assembly line workers) and in the office (computers to displace typists and file clerks). Similarly, the advent of computers, modems, and fax machines has increased the number of workers who work at home as temporaries and part time. These workers are the least likely to join unions.

These forces have given the strong advantage to management. This trend has several negative consequences. First, faced with the threat of plants closing or moving to nonunion localities or to low-wage nations, unions have chosen, typically, to give back many of the gains they made during the 1960s and 1970s. Thus, workers have lost real wages and benefits. A second consequence of union decline is that the workplace may be less safe: Some of the most injury-prone industries, like cattle, chicken, turkey, and catfish processing and textiles, have clustered in right-to-work (i.e., nonunion) states across the South.

A major consequence of union decline is the further dwindling of the middle class. In the words of the late Albert Shanker, president of the American Federation of Teachers:

> [T]he union movement took a lot of workers who were relatively unskilled and turned them into middle class people who educated their children and supported the United States economy. Now, we've got businesses turning their employees into third-world workers. (Shanker, 1992b:E9)

Implied in this statement is a related consequence: If businesses turn their employees into Third World workers, then they will not be able to purchase enough goods and services to encourage economic growth and societywide prosperity. As Norman Birnbaum has said, "nations with strong unions and social contracts have the highest living standards" (Birnbaum, 1992:319):

> Another consequence is a weakened voice and political power for working people. Today, we need unions to raise money and raise hell as much as to raise wages. In politics, business is outspending labor 3 to 1, has captured the votes of Washington and sets the agenda for national debate—a debate that pits the far right against the moderate right and ignores everyone else. . . . Democracy doesn't work unless everyone has a say. Today, it's out of whack. (Gartner, 1995b:11A)

A final consequence points to a possible contradiction—the precipitous decline in unions may actually lead to labor's regeneration. As the unions decline, with workers poorly compensated and ever fearful of losing their jobs, with management becoming more arrogant and demanding, the situation may get bad enough that there will be a turnaround—a surge in union membership and worker militancy. This could lead not only to a stronger collective voice in the work arena but also in the nation's politics. Those nations with strong unionized labor (e.g., Canada, Germany, and Sweden) have a social democratic conception of society, which means universal health care, progressive income taxes, and more equitable government programs.

Of course, this scenario may not occur. Unions may continue to decline in size. The political influence of organized labor may continue to slide; a likely occurrence as business interests outspend organized labor by eleven to one in campaign contributions. The pay and benefits to workers may continue to erode, and workers will be fragmented rather than united.

Discrimination in the Workplace: Perpetuation of Inequality

Women and minorities have long been the objects of discrimination in U.S. industry. Currently (and we have progressed mightily), approximately 50,000 charges of discrimination by organizations are filed annually with the Equal Employment Opportunity Commission. The charges now and in the past have centered on hiring policies, seniority rights, restricted job placement, limited opportunities for advancement, and lower pay for equal work. A number of court suits (and those settled out of court) illustrate that discriminatory policies have been common among such major corporations as AT&T, General Motors, and Northwest Airlines and in such industries as banking and steel.

Two mechanisms operating in the U.S. economy perpetuate inequalities in the job market by social class, race, and gender—the segmented labor market and male dominance.

Segmented Labor Market. The capitalist economy is divided into two separate sectors that have different characteristics, different roles, and different rewards for laborers within each. This organization of the economy is called the **segmented labor market,** or the **dual labor market.** The primary sector is composed of large, bureaucratic organizations with relatively stable production and sales. Jobs within this sector require developed skills, are relatively well paid, occur in good working conditions, and are stable. Within this sector there are two types of jobs. The first type, those in the upper tier, are high-status professional and managerial jobs. The pay is very good for the highly educated people in these jobs. They have a high degree of personal autonomy and the jobs offer variety, creativity, and initiative. Upward mobility is likely for those

"How could we discriminate against minority employees... we don't even have any."

who are successful. The second type, the lower-tier jobs within the primary sector, are held by working-class people. The jobs are either white-collar clerical or blue-collar skilled and semiskilled. The jobs are repetitive and mobility is limited. The jobs are relatively secure because of unionization, although they are much more vulnerable than those in the upper tier.

The secondary economic sector is composed of marginal firms in which product demand is unstable. Jobs within this sector are characterized by poor working conditions, low wages, few opportunities for advancement, and little job security. Little education or skill is required to perform these tasks. Workers beginning in the secondary sector tend to get locked in because they lack the skills required in the primary sector and they usually have unstable work histories. A common interpretation of this problem is that secondary-sector workers are in these dead-end jobs because of their pathology—poor work history, lack of skills, and lack of motivation. Such an explanation, however, blames the victim. Poor work histories tend to be the result of unemployment caused by the production of marginal products and the lack of job security. Similarly, these workers have few, if any, incentives to learn new skills or to stay for long periods with an employer because of the structural barriers to upward mobility. And unlike workers in the primary sector, workers in the secondary sector are more likely to experience harsh and capricious work discipline from supervisors, primarily because there are no unions.

The significance of this dual labor market is threefold. First, placement in one of these segments corresponds with social class, which tends to be perpetuated from generation to generation. Second, employment in the secondary sector is often so inadequately paid that many full-time workers live in poverty, as noted in Chapter 7. And third, the existence of a dual labor market reinforces racial, ethnic, and gender divisions in the labor force. White males, while found in both segments, are overrepresented in the upper tier of the primary sector. White females and White ethnics tend to be clerks in the lower tier of the primary sector. Males and females of color are found disproportionately in the secondary sector. These findings explain why unemployment rates for

"IF WE PAY THEM STARVATION WAGES, WHY DO THEY NEED A LUNCH BREAK?"

African Americans and Latinos are consistently much higher than the rate for Whites. They explain the persistent wage differences found by race and gender. That is why there is a vast overrepresentation of people of color and women living in poverty. These facts are especially relevant as the workforce is increasingly composed of racial and ethnic minorities, most notably Latinos (see Figure 14.1).

- **Male Dominance at Work.** Closely tied to segmented labor markets is the dominance of men in work-related roles. This dominance is reflected in two ways—males tend to make the rules and enforce them, and males receive unequal (i.e., greater) rewards.

Current gender inequality results from a long history of patriarchal social relations where men have consciously kept women in subordinate roles at work and in the home. Men as workers consistently have acted in their own interests to retain power and to keep women either out of their occupations or in subordinate and poorly paid work roles. Historically, through their unions, males insisted that the higher-status and better-paying jobs be exclusively male. They lobbied legislatures to pass legislation supportive of male exclusiveness in occupations and in opposition to such equalization measures as minimum wages for women. Also, the male unions prevented women from gaining the skills that would lead them to equal-paying jobs. The National Typographical Union in 1854, for example, insisted not only that women be refused jobs as compositors but also that they not be taught the skills necessary to be a compositor (Hartmann, 1976).

Throughout U.S. history business owners have used gender inequality in the workplace to their advantage. Women were hired because they would work for less money than men, which made men all the more fearful of women in the workplace. Capitalists even used the threat of hiring lower-paid women to take the place of higher-paid men to keep the wages of both sexes down and to lessen labor militancy.

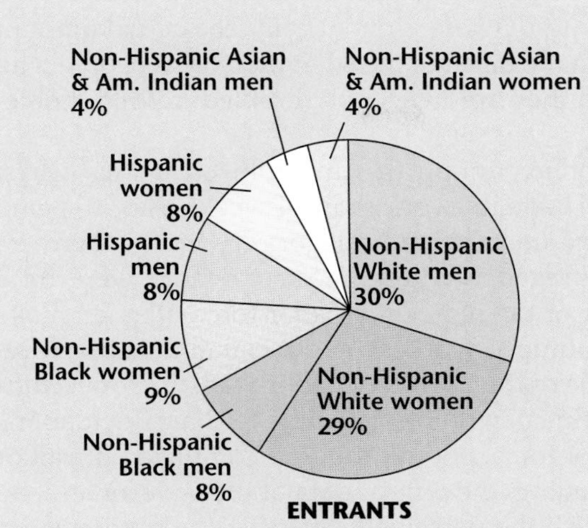

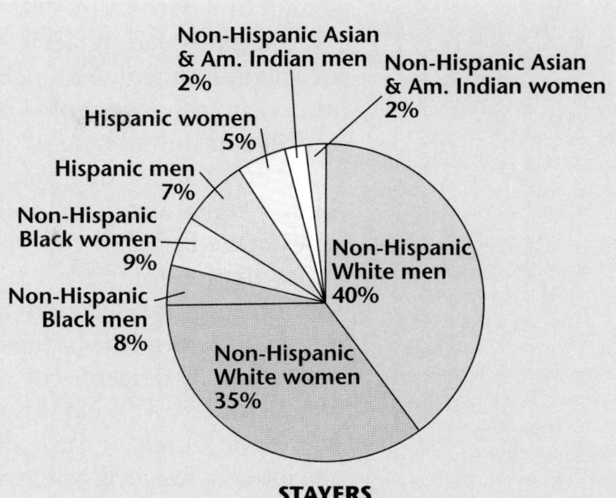

Between 1998 and 2008, about 42 million people are expected to enter the labor force. The composition of these new entrants differs significantly from the 112.5 million people who will remain in the labor force during this period. Those "stayers"—40% White male and 25 percent minority—will be joined by a group of new workers that is just 30 percent white male but 41 percent minority. About one-fourth of the entrants are expected to be Hispanic or Asian—two groups who make up one-seventh of today's labor force. (Women are expected to be 50 percent of the entrants, compared with 47 percent of the stayers.) These projected developments largely reflect the growth in racial and ethnic diversity in the total U.S. population, as well as the younger age structure of minority populations.

Assuming that these trends continue into 2025, the American labor force will become slightly more female (48 percent vs. 46 percent today) and noticeably more minority (32 percent vs. 26 percent today). The aging of the baby boom generation also will make the labor force older in 2025—40 percent of workers will be ages 45 and over, compared with 33 percent in 1998. The integration between the new workers and the current ones wil provide both opportunities and challenges for American businesses, as well as for the country as a whole.

FIGURE 14.1

Who's Entering the Labor Force?

Sources: H. N. Fullerton, Jr. 1999. "Labor Force Projections to 2008: Steady Growth and Changing Composition." *Monthly Labor Review* (November):19–32; H. N. Fullerton, Jr. 1999. "Labor Force Participation: 75 Years of Change, 1950–98 and 1998–2025." *Monthly Labor Review* (December):3–12; Population Reference Bureau. 2001. *2000 United States Population Data Sheet: The American Work Force.* Washington, DC: Population Reference Bureau.

In contemporary U.S. society men and women, with some exceptions, are accorded different, and unequal, positions in religious, government, school, work, and family activities. Looking only at work, women and men do different work both in the family and in the labor force. This division of labor between the sexes preserves the differential power, privilege, and prestige of men (see Chapter 9). Men are overrepresented in administrative and supervisory roles. Women are found disproportionately in jobs where they follow orders. Women are found, as just noted, more often than men in the secondary job market where jobs are menial, poorly paid, and with little or no benefits.

Unemployment

The Bureau of Labor Statistics supplies the official unemployment statistics. The official unemployment rate in the United States since 1980 has ranged from a high of 9 percent in 1982–1983 to a low of 3.9 percent in October 2000. These rates are misleading because they understate, dramatically, the actual amount of unemployment. Not included in the data are the 60 million or so people who are not in the labor force because they are in school, disabled, retired, homemakers, or not seeking work.

The data are distorted by undercounting the unemployed in two ways. First, people who have not actively sought work in the 4 weeks prior to being interviewed are not counted in the unemployed category. Typically, there are more than 1 million such **discouraged workers,** most of whom were once employed in the secondary sector of the segmented labor force. Women make up about two-thirds of these discouraged workers, and racial minorities represent about 30 percent. The rationale of the Bureau of Labor Statistics for excluding dispirited workers is that the function of the statistic is to chart fluctuations in the conditions of the active labor force, not to provide a complete portrait of the jobless. Regardless of the reasoning, the official data of the government, by undercounting joblessness, diminish the perceived severity of unemployment and therefore reduce the zeal to do anything about the problem. The extent to which the public perceives unemployment as a problem is further lessened by the counting as employed of anyone who had worked for as little as an hour for pay in the week before being interviewed. There are an estimated 4 million part-time workers who want to work full time (Carre and Tilly, 1998:22). Thus, people who subsist on odd jobs, temporary work, or minimal part-time work are counted as fully employed by the government. The point to remember when looking at the official unemployment statistics: "For every worker officially unemployed, at least one other worker is a 'discouraged worker' or an underemployed worker. If discouraged workers and those who work part-time who want to work full-time were included in the statistics, the real unemployment-underemployment rate would be almost double the official unemployment rate" (Feagin and Feagin, 1997:86).

Even the decidedly understated government figures on unemployment reveal that there are many millions of people who want to work but do not. In April 2001, for example, there were 6.4 million people officially out of work. If we add the 1 million or so discouraged workers and the people working part time who would rather work full time (more than 4 million), the percentage of the labor force experiencing total or partial unemployment would be about 9 percent, which is a huge surplus of labor.

Unemployment is commonly believed to be functional (i.e., have positive consequences) for society by reducing inflationary pressures. It is also kept relatively high by capitalists because high unemployment deflates wages and therefore increases profits. When there are unemployed people willing to work, workers will not make inordinate demands for higher wages for fear that they will be replaced by cheaper labor. Thus, even unionized labor becomes relatively docile when unemployment is high. Joe and Clairece Feagin have summarized the capitalist argument:

> The . . . unemployed are essential to the operation of the capitalist system because they put downward pressure on wages and provide a reserve labor force that can be drawn back into employment when profit and investment conditions require it. Not only the officially unemployed, but also other groups make up this reserve labor force: discouraged workers, part-time workers, newly arrived immigrant laborers. Workers who protest too hard in times of a glutted labor market will find themselves replaced by people from the great pool of the unemployed. (Feagin and Feagin, 1997:92)

Unemployment affects some groups more than others. This **reserve army of the unemployed** is disproportionately composed of people of color (Latinos, African Americans, Native Americans), teenagers, and residents in declining cities. Typically, the official unemployment rates for African Americans and Latinos are at least twice as high as the rate for Whites. In April 2001, when the overall unemployment rate was 4.5 percent, the White unemployment rate was 4 percent compared with the African American rate of 8.2 percent (Uchitelle, 2001). These proportions by race tend to be relatively constant whether the overall unemployment rate is high or low, whether the economy is in a boom or a slump. Thus, the labor market assigns people of color disproportionately not only to the low-paying jobs but also to jobs that are the most unstable, precisely the situation of the secondary sector in the segmented labor market.

An important consequence of the reserve army of the unemployed being composed primarily of racial minorities is that it inflames racial antipathies against them by people who hold unstable jobs. These job holders perceive their enemy as the people below them who will work for lower wages, rather than as the capitalists who oppose full employment and adequate wages for all people.

We have seen that the number of jobs is less than the number of workers because the government wants to keep inflation in check and because capitalists want to depress wages. Several compelling structural reasons maintain unemployment as well, as we discuss in the next section. But first, let us examine another factor that limits the number of jobs: demographics.

There are clear demographic reasons for the shortage of jobs now and for the near future. In the past 25 years or so an unusually large number of women entered the labor force, motivated by the necessity of supplementing family income and the need for self-fulfillment in nontraditional roles. About seven in ten married women with children work outside the home. The other demographic force behind unemployment pressures was the very large numbers of young people entering the job market during the 1970s. The baby-boom generation—those 10 million more babies born between 1946 and 1956 than in the previous 10 years—reached the job-seeking stage in the 1970s. These baby boomers increased the pressure for jobs and depressed the wages of people with jobs. The immense burden they put on jobs, wages, and promotions will affect jobs not only for those preceding them but also most notably for those following them. In the 1970s an astonishing 21 million new jobs were created. But because of the unprecedented number of women and young people entering the job market, the labor force grew by more than 24 million, leaving a shortfall of 3 million jobs.

But as important as these demographic trends are in explaining the unemployment problem, they are relatively minor when compared with the effects of the structural transformation that is occurring in the U.S. economy. This critical shift and the accompanying changes are the subjects of the remainder of the chapter.

Structural Transformation of the Economy

There have been two fundamental turning points in human history. The Neolithic agricultural revolution began about 8000 BC, marking the transition from nomadic pastoral life, where the animal and vegetable sources of food were hunted and gathered, to life in settlements based on agriculture. During this phase of human existence, cities were built; tools were created and used;

language, numbers, and other symbols became more sophisticated; and mining and metal working were developed.

The second fundamental change, the Industrial Revolution, began in Great Britain in the 1780s. With the application of steam power and later oil and electricity as energy sources for industry, mining, manufacturing, and transportation came fundamental changes to the economy, the relationship of people and work, family organization, and a transition from rural to urban life. In effect, societies are transformed with each surge in invention and technological growth. Peter F. Drucker describes the historical import of these changes:

> Every few hundred years in Western history there occurs a sharp transformation. We cross . . . a "divide." Within a few short decades, society rearranges itself—its worldview; its basic values; its social and political structure; its arts; its key institutions. Fifty years later, there is a new world. And the people born then cannot even imagine the world in which their grandparents lived and into which their own parents were born. We are currently living through such a transformation. (Drucker, 1993:1)

The United States is now in the midst of a new transformation, one fueled by new technologies and applications (e.g., superfast computers, the Internet as a distributor of information, goods, and services, fiber optics, biotechnology, the decoding of the human genome, and cell telephony). These amazing scientific breakthroughs have had and will continue to have immense implications for commerce, international trade, global politics, and at the individual level work opportunities (as some businesses thrive and others become outmoded). In Drucker's words:

> The next two or three decades are likely to see even greater technological change than has occurred in the decades since the emergence of the computer, and also even greater change in industry structures, in the economic landscape, and probably in the social landscape as well. (Drucker, 1999:54)

We are now in a new era, which is referred to as the **structural transformation of the economy.** Whereas employment throughout the Industrial Revolution showed ever greater domination by manufacturing, now employment has shifted toward service occupations and the collection, storage, and dissemination of information.

The present generation is in the midst of social and technological changes that are more far-reaching and are occurring faster than changes that occurred at any other time in human history. Several powerful forces converging in the United States are transforming its economy, redesigning and redistributing jobs, exacerbating inequality, reorganizing cities and regions, and profoundly affecting families and individuals. These forces are (1) technological breakthroughs in microelectronics, (2) the globalization of the economy, (3) capital flight, and (4) the shift from an economy based on the manufacture of goods to one based on information and services.

New Technologies Based on Microelectronics

The computer chip is the technology that is transforming the United States toward a service/information economy. Microelectronic-based systems of information allow for the storage, manipulation, and retrieval of data with speed and accuracy unknown just a few years ago. Information can be sent in microseconds via communications satellites throughout the world. Parallel processing with supercomputers gives machines the ability to reason and make judgments. Computer-aided design (CAD) permits engineers to design and modify an incredible array of products in three dimensions very quickly. Computer-aided manufacturing (CAM), or the industrial robot, is replacing conventional machines and workers.

Globalization of the Economy

Because of the size of the domestic market, the relative insulation of the Pacific and Atlantic Oceans, and superior technological expertise, the U.S. economy throughout most of this century has been relatively free from competitive pressures from abroad. This situation changed dramatically about 1970. The United States, once the world's industrial giant, employing 35 percent of the world's manufacturing workforce, has lost its premier status, now employing about 15 percent of the workforce in manufacturing. Many of the goods now used in the United States are produced in low-wage societies.

The shift to a global economy has been accelerated by the tearing down of tariff barriers. The North American Free Trade Agreement (NAFTA) and the General Agreement on Tariffs and Trade (GATT), both passed in 1994, are two examples of agreements that increased the flow of goods across national boundaries.

This trend has two related consequences for workers in the United States, at least in the short term. First, low-wage jobs in the United States are eliminated as U.S. companies move to low-wage countries and as goods are produced by low-wage employees in other countries, whether in U.S.-owned plants or not. Second, foreign competition means reduced profits to U.S. corporations. Their typical response has been to cut costs by demanding concessions from workers, laying them off, or encouraging early retirements. Many corporations in the hardest hit areas such as steel simply shut down plants, throwing thousands of employees out of work and the communities in which they were located into difficult dislocations. Another strategy by U.S. corporations was to compete as strongly as possible through massive investments in labor-saving devices, which, of course, does little to help workers. (For the dark side of global capitalism, see the "Social Problems in Global Perspective" panel, p. 418.)

Capital Flight

Private businesses, in their search for profit, make crucial investment decisions. The term **capital flight** refers to the investment choices that involve the movement of corporate monies from one investment to another. This movement takes several forms: investment in plants located overseas, plant relocation within the United States, and mergers. While these investment decisions may be positive for the recipients of the move, they also take away investment (disinvestment) from others (workers and their families, communities, and suppliers).

Overseas Locations for U.S. Firms. U.S. multinational corporations have invested heavily in production of their goods in foreign countries. Corporate capital is invested overseas because manufacturing overseas is profitable, mainly because of cheap and nonunionized labor and the relative lack of government regulations over their operations. The companies believe that these

SOCIAL PROBLEMS IN GLOBAL PERSPECTIVE

THE DARK SIDE OF GLOBAL CAPITALISM

Some have argued that the answer to many social problems is a global capitalistic economy with free markets. The argument is that in such an arena, people and societies will prosper. The counter argument is that modern capitalism creates and aggravates many troubling conditions, which is our focus. (The following is taken from Joe R. Feagin's presidential address to the American Sociological Association in 2000; Feagin, 2001.)

Many of the World's People Still Live in Misery

The global economy has meant a substantial transfer of wealth from the world's poor and working classes to the world's rich and affluent social classes. "Of the 6 billion people on earth, a large proportion live in or near poverty and destitution with 1.2 billion living on less than one dollar a day. . . . Today one-fifth of the world's people, those in the developed countries, garner 86 percent of the world's gross domestic product, with the bottom fifth garnering just one percent." (Feagin, 2001:2)

Working Families Are Exploited and Marginalized

Multinational corporations work for their own interests, which may mean destroying and discarding regions, countries, peoples, cultures, and natural environments.

- There are about 1 billion unemployed or underemployed workers around the world.
- Some 30 million people die from hunger annually in a world where agriculture produces more than enough food for all.
- "The real effects of expanding capitalism for a large proportion of the planet's inhabitants are not only greater inequality but also job restructuring, unsafe working conditions, low wages, underemployment or unemployment, loss of land, and forced migration." (Feagin, 2001:3)

Capitalism Imposes Huge Environmental Costs

The global capitalistic economy generates profits while causing environmental degradation. As noted in Chapter 4, the levels of greenhouse gases have grown significantly because of the increasing use of fossil fuels, deforestation, and industrial pollution. The resulting global warming changes rain patterns, destroys forests, causes social erosion, and spreads disease.

Global Capitalism Reinforces Other Injustice and Inequality

The persisting forms of discrimination and oppression such as racism, sexism, homophobia, ableism, and ageism are reinforced or exacerbated by the processes of modern capitalism.

Feagin predicts that the current difficult economic and environmental times will bring pressures to change capitalism.

> By the end of the twenty-first century, it is likely that there will be sustained and inexorable pressures to replace the social institutions associated with corporate capitalism and its supporting governments. Why? Because the latter will not have provided humanity with just and sustainable societies. (Feagin, 2001:4)

regulations—on pollution and worker safety, for instance—are excessive and expensive.

The main reason for overseas location, though, is greater profit from lower wages. For example, more than 1,100 U.S.-owned plants—owned by corporations such as Ford, General Motors, RCA, Zenith, and Westinghouse—are located in northern Mexico close to the U.S. border (these plants are called **maquiladoras**). The corporations are allowed to ship raw materials, components, equipment, and machinery to Mexico duty free. They are delivered to factories in Mexico and then assembled by low-wage workers. The finished products are then exported back to the United States, with duty paid only on the value added. Obviously, the corporations profit greatly from such an arrangement; U.S. workers do not.

- **Relocation of Businesses.** Corporate administrators may decide to move their business to another locality. Such decisions involve what is called plant migration or, more pejoratively, "runaway shops." The decision may be to move the plant to Mexico (as we have seen), to the Caribbean, to Central America (all baseballs for major league teams, e.g., are manufactured in Costa Rica), or to the Far East, where many U.S. plants involved in textiles, electronics assembly, and other labor-intensive industries are located.

  U.S. corporations are also moving some of their operations to other English-speaking countries such as Ireland, Barbados, Jamaica, the Philippines, and Singapore, where cheap labor performs such tasks as data entry for accounting, medical transcription, airline and hotel reservations, and telemarketing. For example, in 2000 Caltrex Petroleum Corporation moved its headquarters from Dallas to Singapore, shifted its website development to South Africa, and set up its accounting division in the Philippines.

  Capital is also moved within the United States as corporations shut down operations in one locality and start up elsewhere. Profit is the motivation for investment in a new place and disinvestment in another. Corporations move their plants into communities and regions where wages are lower, unions are weaker or nonexistent, and the business climate more receptive (i.e., there are lower taxes and greater government subsidies to the business community).

  Regardless of whether plants are moved within the United States or to foreign countries, there are consequences to individuals and communities. Plant closures are devastating. Workers in the affected plants are suddenly unemployed and so, too, may be many people in the affected communities whose jobs were directly and indirectly tied to that plant (such as transportation, supplies, and services). Real estate, banking, schools, and other businesses are adversely affected. The local governments can no longer provide the same level of services because the tax base has shrunk. The recipient "boom" communities benefit from the increase in jobs, greater tax revenues, and the image of growth and progress. The communities, however, often cannot meet the greater demand for new roads, sewage treatment, schools, hospitals, recreation facilities, and housing that the new plants engender.

- **Mergers and Takeovers.** Another type of capital flight occurs when corporations use their capital to purchase companies in related or unrelated enterprises rather than to expand and modernize their plants. In 1999 mergers amounted to $3.48 trillion (Valdmanis, 2000).

  This trend toward megamergers has at least three negative consequences: (1) It increases the centralization of capital, which reduces competition and raises prices for consumers; (2) as corporations become fewer and larger, they have increased power over workers, unions, and governments; and (3) mergers reduce the number of jobs. As an example of the last point, after Qwest merged with US West in 2000, the new entity cut 11,000 jobs and 1,800 contractor positions. Along with the downsizing of jobs, Qwest announced that former US West employees would now contribute to their medical, vision, and dental health plans rather than receive those benefits free as they had previously.

From Manufacturing to Knowledge-Based Services

In a special issue devoted to the twenty-first-century corporation, *Business Week* noted the profound transformation of corporations occurring now:

> For nearly all of its life, the modern corporation has made money by making things. It has done so by amassing fixed assets, organizing large workforces, and managing hierarchically. The 21st century corporation will do little of that. It will make money by producing knowledge created by talented people working with partners all over the world. So fundamental will the changes be that the corporation as we know it will likely exist only on the margins of the economy. . . .We are just in the beginning of the beginning. The 21st century is going to be hard on corporations, governments, and all the rest of us. But the changes the century will bring will be nothing short of astonishing. (*Business Week*, 2000:278)

The United States has an economy based on ideas rather than physical capital. By 2006 the government estimates that manufacturing jobs will account for just 12 percent of the labor force (McGinn and McCormick, 1999). Thus, the demand for workers shifts from physical labor to cognitive abilities. The best educated and trained will benefit with good jobs, benefits, and opportunities. The less educated with not benefit in such a climate. When workers had strong union industrialized jobs, their wages and benefits were enough for a middle-class life-style. Now, typically, their work provides the services that are poorly paid, and some have few if any benefits, working as clerks, cashiers, custodians, nurses aides, security guards, waiters, retail salespersons, and telemarketers. As a result, "high school grads' median weekly earnings are 43% less than those of college grads, far worse than the 28% gap in 1979" (Coy, 2000:79).

AGE OF DISCONTINUITY

Every new era poses new problems of adjustment, but this one differs from the agricultural and industrial eras. The earlier transformations were gradual enough for adaptation to take place over several decades, but conditions are significantly different now. The rate of change is phenomenal and unprecedented. In today's global economy, communication is instantaneous and capital is incredibly mobile. The types of work and the characteristics of the workforce in the United States are changing. These factors, which are discussed in this section, result in considerable discontinuity and disequilibrium, especially job loss.

Changing Nature of Jobs

Joseph Schumpeter (1950) described a process inherent to capitalism that he called "creative destruction." By this he meant that as the economic structure of capitalism mutates, some sectors will lose out while others gain. For example, in 1917 the largest U.S. corporation, with three times the assets of its nearest competitor, was U.S. Steel, employing 268,000 workers. Today U.S. Steel is worth about one-fifth what it was in 1917 and employs only 20,800 workers. Replacing U.S. Steel at the apex of the nation's corporate elite are companies such as Microsoft, Intel, and Merck. Today the largest employer in the United States is Wal-Mart. These facts illustrate how manufacturing, the backbone of the U.S. economy in the twentieth century, is no longer dominant. It has been replaced by the service sector and knowledge-based companies. In 1947 employment in the service sector of the economy reached 50 percent, and now it is about 80 percent. Whereas in the past people mostly worked at producing goods, now they tend to be doing work in offices, banking, insurance, retailing, health care, education, custodial work, restaurant work, security, and transportation.

The shift away from manufacturing to services and information/knowledge means that some sectors of the economy fade in importance or will even die out completely. These sectors are known as **sunset industries** (e.g., steel, tires, shoes, and textiles). Over 1,500 plants in these industries have closed permanently since 1975. And literally millions of blue-collar jobs, most of which were unionized with good pay and benefits, are lost and not replaced.

Many blue-collar jobs have also been lost to automation. Robots have replaced humans doing routine work such as picking fruit, shearing sheep, welding, painting, and scanning products for defects. Similarly, many white-collar jobs are being lost because of new technologies. The Internet, for example, allows people to make their own travel arrangements, reducing or eliminating the need for travel agents, or to buy and sell stocks making stock brokers unnecessary. Also, there is software that helps people do their tax returns without the need of a tax specialist. Within firms, computer programs take care of payrolls, control inventory, and delivery schedules reducing the need for accountants. Primarily because of voice mail, laser printers, and word processors, hundreds of thousands of secretarial and clerical jobs have been eliminated. To emphasize the force of creative destruction on jobs, Tom Peters, the esteemed expert on work, has estimated that 90 percent of white-collar jobs in the United States will be either destroyed or altered significantly in the next 10 to 15 years (Peters, 2000).

But while jobs have shrunk by the millions in the last two decades, many millions more have been created in **sunrise industries** (those industries characterized by increased output and employment). Such jobs are involved in the production of high-tech products (computers, software, medical instruments, bioengineering, robotics). Also, lower-end service jobs such as sales clerks, janitors, and security guards are plentiful.

The concept of work is also being reshaped. The Internet is revolutionizing how business is transacted. About 30 million American workers work in temporary, contracted, self-employed, leased, part-time and other "nonstandard" arrangements (Economic Policy Institute, reported in Cook, 2000). These **contingent workers** (i.e., employees who work part time, in temporary jobs, or as independent contractors) typically lack an explicit contract for ongoing

More and more employers are hiring contingent workers. This practice saves employers money in wages and in the benefits they tend not to provide to these workers.

employment and thus receive sporadic wages. They earn about 16 percent less than their counterparts who do the same work and only 5 percent have employer-provided health coverage, compared to four-fifths of their full-time counterparts (Jorgensen and Reimer, 2000).

This trend represents a dramatic change in work. Businesses argue that they need this arrangement for flexibility in a rapidly changing competitive economy. These growing numbers of workers are not tied to an employer, which makes them free to choose from available work options. There is a downside to this trend, however: About 60 percent of these nonstandard jobs are low quality, paying less than regular full-time jobs held by similar workers. Temps earn on average 40 percent less per hour than full-time workers. In short, this trend has meant the proliferation of marginal jobs, with employers now shifting the burden of fringe benefits to individual workers and their families.

About three-fourths of those working in contingent work arrangements are women, many of whom work out of their homes. Home-based work includes word processing, editing, accounting, and telemarketing. Employers contract women to do home-based work because money is saved—the employers pay only for work delivered, they avoid unions, and they do not pay benefits such as health insurance, paid leaves, and pensions.

Job Insecurity

Even during the economic boom of the late 1990s when the unemployment rate was the lowest in 30 years, about one-third of the nations 140 million workers feared losing their jobs (Leonhardt, 2000). African American workers are more economically insecure than White workers. The median African American family income in 1999 of $31,778 was only 60 percent of median White family income, and their rate of joblessness is consistently at least twice that of Whites. Women are much less secure than men. They earn less money (72 cents for every dollar a man made in 1999). They are easy targets when downsizing occurs because they usually have less seniority. More women than men are contingent workers, where they have no guarantees of work. And, almost six out of ten minimum wage workers are women, where benefits are virtually nonexistent.

Job insecurity is heightened by several factors mentioned earlier. Mergers reduce the number of jobs. Corporations downsize when profits decline. Workers can be displaced by robots. Corporations may decide to move their operations to other countries. Workers may find their expertise is no longer needed and they are not prepared for rapidly changing technology.

Downsizing, of course, has human costs. It puts people out of work and it threatens those who have not been downsized. The loss of income from unemployment makes the unemployed and their families vulnerable to unanticipated financial crises such as health problems, a fire or flood, or an automobile accident. These events may result in the loss of a home, bankruptcy, or inadequate health care. There are physical and emotional costs as well. There is evidence that when workers are involuntarily unemployed, they tend, when compared to the employed, to have more hypertension, high cholesterol, ulcers, respiratory diseases, and hyperallergic reactions. Similarly, they are more prone to headaches, upset stomachs, depression, anxiety, and aggression. In sum, the families of displaced workers experience considerable strain and are thus disproportionately characterized by illness, divorce, separation, physical abuse, and turmoil.

But can't these downsized workers quickly find another job? A 1996 Department of Labor study of displaced workers focused on displaced workers with jobs they had held for at least three years (the following is from Koretz, 1998a). The study found that 60 percent of the downsized were white-collar workers and 40 percent were blue-collar workers in goods-producing industries. The good news from the study was that 79 percent of the displaced workers had found work, 7 percent were unemployed, and 14 percent had dropped out of the labor force (the Department of Labor does not label these folks as officially unemployed). The least likely to be reemployed were displaced workers over age 54. The bad news is that downsizing tends to mean downward mobility. Of the 2.2 million full-time workers laid off in 1993 and 1994, only two-thirds had full-time jobs in 1996. Most significant, over half of this group were earning less than at their former jobs and over a third had pay cuts of 20 percent or more. Another sixth of former full-time workers were working part-time and/or as contingent workers.

Increased Workload

Americans work more hours per week than in any other country in the advanced industrialized world. The data in Figure 14.2 show, for example, that American workers spend the equivalent of three additional 40-hour work-weeks a year on the job compared with the Japanese. Some 8 million people had more than one job in 1997, more than double the number of multiple-job holders in 1965. Between 1977 and 1997 the average workweek increased from 43 to 47 hours with 37 percent of workers putting in 50 or more hours per week (Zuckerman, 2000a). *The State of Working America,* a study sponsored by the Economic Policy Institute (Mishel, Bernstein, and Schmitt, 2000), reports that from 1989 to 1998 the average number of work hours by all middle-income families increased by 246 hours to 3,885 (about 6 extra full-time weeks a year). Middle-income Latino families worked 4,050 hours, and African American middle-income families worked 4,278 hours per year, almost 500 hours per year more than White families. In effect, then, an average middle-income African American family needed over 12 more weeks of work than the average White family in order to reach and maintain a middle-income rank.

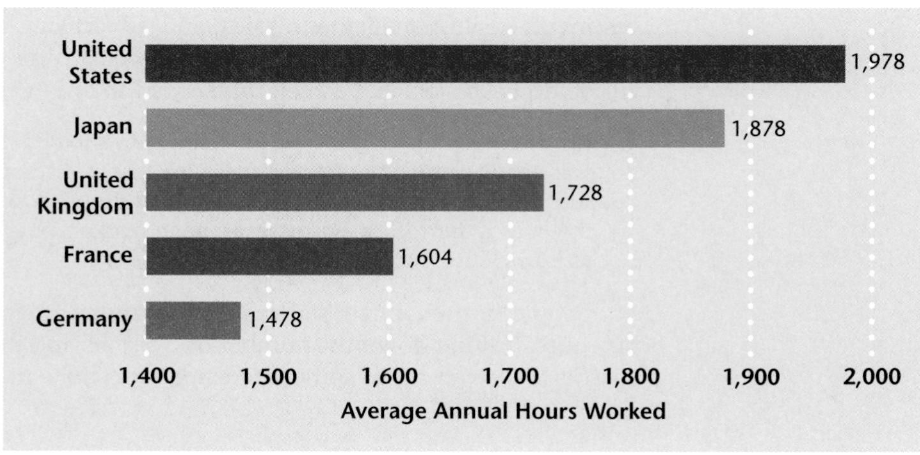

FIGURE 14.2

Average Hours Worked Annually in Selected Nations, 2000

Source: Greenhouse. 2001. International Labor Organization. http://www.nytimes.com/2000/09/01/national/01HOUR.html.

There are several possible reasons for U.S. workers increasing their workload. First, as noted in Chapter 2, the gap between the haves and the have-nots is widening, and this disparity creates incentives for employees to work harder. They assume that their increased work effort will pay off in pay hikes and promotions (Koretz, 2001). Second, the widening inequality gap results in relatively lower wages and net worth for the less than affluent, which, with the increased cost of housing and automobiles, makes working more a necessity. The third reason for the increased workload, and one articulated by labor unions, is that many businesses require their workers to work more in order to reduce the costs of adding more workers and their benefits.

Global Economy and Domestic Jobs

The profound transformation in the international economy is another factor making this era in history different from previous transition periods. For thousands of years caravans moved across the land and ships sailed with the winds and currents. People explored, conquered, and exploited other peoples and their resources, but the pace was slow and the interaction among different nations muted by time and space. Now, however, there is instant communication around the globe, and transportation anywhere is only a day away rather than 6 months or more.

These dramatic advances in communication and transportation have at least two important ramifications. First, technological advances now diffuse rapidly. During the Industrial Revolution technological change was quite slow (although rapid compared with change in previous epochs). The first steam-powered cotton mill in the United States, for example, began in 1847, 63 years after its adoption in Britain. Now technological breakthroughs in one country spread rapidly to other nations.

The second consequence of advances in transportation and communications is the enhanced mobility of capital. Money can be moved to any country in the world with a few keystrokes. Managers and key personnel can be moved by jet anywhere within 24 hours. Information moves almost instantaneously by television, satellite transmission, and e-mail. All of these enable capital to move, as never before, with speed heretofore unknown, anywhere in the world.

Corporations of almost any size now make plans regarding raw materials, workers, and markets across national boundaries. Corporations seek cheap labor, which means a transfer of jobs—millions of jobs—to other nations. Consider Nike, the sports shoe and apparel company: There are 8,000 U.S. employees involved in management, sales, and advertising and 75,000 mostly Asian employees who actually make the products. In the case of General Electric, 20,000 domestic jobs have been transferred to low-wage countries since 1985:

> [In 1990] the ratio of U.S.-based GE employees to non U.S.-based employees was about four to one—for every GE job that existed overseas, there were four here. By the end of 2000 that ratio had dropped to 1.15 to 1. What it gets down to is that GE has virtually as many workers outside the United States as it has here. (Fire, 2001:31)

People in the United States now buy more foreign goods than foreigners buy ours, driving down the number of U.S. jobs and the wages of U.S. workers. Arthur Macewan raises some interesting questions in this regard:

> My morning coffee came from Brazil. A GM subsidiary in Mexico produced the wiring system for my car. Three items in my medicine cabinet were produced in a German-owned plant in the United States. My son's new tape recorder is from Japan. My clothes arrive from ten or more different countries, produced mostly through subcontracting arrangements with large U.S. retailers. (Macewan, 1994:35)
>
> What difference does it make where my coffee came from or where the wiring system for my car was assembled? Does it matter to me whether my clothes come from Brazil, Bangladesh, or from a local factory? What about the Brazilian, Bangladeshi, and local workers? How are they affected by the international movement of goods? And does the nationality of the factory owners matter? Should I care whether a U.S., Japanese, German, or Brazilian owner profits from my purchases? (Macewan, 1994:8)

Demography and Jobs

Three population facts—declining overall growth, disproportionate growth by racial minorities, and much greater participation by women in the workforce—combine to make this time in economic history different from other stages. In this section we examine, briefly, each of these trends.

A major source of economic growth during the Industrial Revolution was rapid population growth in the technologically advanced countries. The provision of services, construction, and the like provided a significant source of employment, especially in the rapidly growing urban centers. Since about 1970, however, population growth (births minus deaths) has stabilized in some Western countries and actually declined in others. This trend provides a further impetus for corporations to seek markets and workers in other countries.

The second demographic trend making this era unique is that the fertility rate for Whites has declined significantly in the United States, but the rate for racial minorities has remained about the same. This imbalance, combined with

Nike is a multinational corporation with 8,000 U.S. employees involved in management, sales, and advertising and 75,000 mostly Asian employees who actually make the products.

the influx of legal and illegal immigrants, has led to the disproportionate growth of racial minorities and their continuing economic plight. Throughout U.S. history, racial minorities have been denied equality in education and jobs. They have been relegated to the semiskilled and unskilled jobs in agriculture, in the mines, in construction, in packing plants, and on the production line. This bias continues today, at a time when these jobs are declining and becoming obsolete, made unnecessary in a society increasingly committed to knowledge, high technology, and education. Immigrants are thus at a distinct disadvantage, more than at any time in history. So, too, are the racial minorities already here, who are locked into poverty by institutional racism, relegated to blighted neighborhoods with inferior services (especially education), and given fewer and fewer jobs.

The third major demographic trend contributing to the uniqueness of the present economic transformation is the entry of women into the workforce on a massive scale. In 1950, about one-third of women held jobs outside the home; now, more than two-thirds do, and the proportion is growing. This change is directly related to shifts in the economy, especially the expansion of the service sector. Two-thirds of the jobs created in the past decade have been filled by women. In fact, it is precisely this great increase in women's paid work that has been a primary factor in the rise of service jobs. These changes, combined with the economic requirements of families (high cost of housing, education, and the like), have made women's labor force participation a permanent phenomenon and have contributed to their greater autonomy.

Changing Economy, Demography, and the Future of Work

The demographic facts just described point to some important shifts as the United States moves into the twenty-first century. First, because the baby-boom generation, which swelled the labor force for the past two decades, is aging and is being replaced by the "baby-bust" generation, the supply of workers for good jobs will not meet the demand. Second, one in three new entrants to the labor force in 2000 was non-White. Third, about two-thirds of the new workers will be women. This is a profound shift from the recent past, when almost half of U.S. workers were White men.

When these trends are combined with technological changes, which are continually upgrading the work required for most jobs, the result is that the United States will be running out of workers with the job skills needed for the new millennium. In effect, there is a mismatch between an increasing number of people wanting jobs and the skills required for the new jobs.

These trends and their consequences present reasons for hope and despair. On the hopeful side, there will be room for people without privilege (minorities, women, and recent immigrants) for upward mobility, if they have the skills or demonstrate that they have the potential to obtain them. A second reason for hope is that the powerful people in government and business will realize that their past decisions to emphasize technology rather than the maximizing of human capital were wrong and must be rectified.

More and more the argument is advanced in the business community that the schools must do a better job of educating all students and that businesses must also work at retraining their workforce and at training new employees for the skills required for the new technology. Also, businesses will have to provide more benefits to workers with families (flexible work schedules, maternity leaves, provision of day care) in order to expand the pool of workers. Thus, there is a chance that class, race, and gender barriers to privilege will be removed, at least to some degree.

As these trends converge, however, there is also a strong negative potential. If history is a guide, the education and business communities will not educate the disadvantaged for highly skilled jobs. The children of the poor will continue to receive inferior educations. Many of them will see no hope in the mainstream of schools and jobs because the rewards are not there.

But this conventional argument misses the point. The problem is not a lack of education but a lack of jobs. Walda Katz-Fishman makes this point forcefully:

> Today the factory system of production with machine technology, that was the basis of the expansion of educational opportunities for the working class during the 20th century, no longer exists. The revolution in technology has transformed the production process. Human labor is being displaced permanently by electronically based automated production. Production line workers are being replaced by robots. Secretaries are being replaced by word processors. Technical designers and programmers are being replaced by software packages. Sales clerks are being replaced by uniform pricing code scanners. Low wage workers are being replaced by lower wage workers in the neocolonies. The largest number of jobs being created are those at minimum wage. Full-time jobs with benefits are being split into part-time jobs with no benefits. . . . As the masses of workers, i.e., "human capital," are replaced by forms of automated production, the capitalist system no longer needs to educate them. *It should thus be clear that the reason more and more working class youth are not getting good jobs with decent wages is not because they do not have a college degree. Rather, the reason they cannot get a college education is precisely because there are not enough good jobs that pay decent wages in our society to warrant the college education of the majority of the working class.* [Italics added.] (Katz-Fishman, 1990:23)

TRANSFORMATION OF THE ECONOMY AND THE BIFURCATION OF THE UNITED STATES

There are two contrasting views on the dramatic transformation of the economy. For some people, this change in the workforce from manufacturing work to information work has great positive potential. They argue, first, that it is a shift from a few huge industrial giants to many smaller technological and service-oriented firms, where innovation will lead to more rapid economic growth. Second, the shift from the old industries to those based on the microchip means a transfer from manual labor to mental labor. Cook argues that "if the old tool industries were an extension of the human hand and back, the new ones are an extension of the human brain and nervous system. The basic thrust of the technology is immaterial, and its productivity potential is enormous" (Cook, 1982:163). Third, as economist Robert J. Samuelson has argued, the expansion of the service sector is a sign of national health, not decay. For him, the shifting of labor from manufacturing to services indicates that fewer workers are needed to produce the goods we need, just as fewer agricultural workers today produce many times the products that it took so many farm workers to do several generations ago (Samuelson, 1984:61). Fourth, because of this trend, the United States is creating jobs at a rapid rate. And finally, jobs in the service category, when compared with those in the industrial category, are safer, cleaner, and less alienating. With machines to do society's dirty work, people will be freed to do the challenging and rewarding work.

Although there is some truth to these claims, the fundamental shift in the economy has clearly had negative effects for many workers. Technological changes, the global economy, and the shift from manufacturing to service jobs have reduced labor's bargaining power, lowered wages and workers' benefits in many sectors, and increased job insecurity. Thus, powerful forces are shifting the income distribution of people in the United States so that the middle class is declining and the gap between the haves and have-nots is expanding.

One reason for a declining middle class is the loss of jobs in the relatively well-paid industrial sector. The jobs being created in services, information, and high technology are at the extremes, with few in the middle. There are first-tier jobs in the primary sector with advancement potential, high pay, and prestige, such as in banking, finance, and engineering. These jobs require considerable education and specialized training. Jobs in the secondary sector of the services industry offer low pay, few benefits, low prestige, and no bridge to the first-tier jobs. These jobs as retail clerks, janitors, fast-food handlers, cashiers, home health aides, teacher aides, and child care providers, for example, require little training and not even a high school education. Workers who have lost their middle-income manufacturing jobs are not suited for the first-tier jobs in the service sector (if they found jobs, these pay on average 20 percent less than the jobs they lost). Neither are their children, unless they have graduated from college.

The first-tier jobs offer great opportunities, but the catch is that only about 20 percent of the jobs being created are for the engineers, executives, and other professionals in this category. Four out of five of the new jobs will be in the low-wage, low-prestige, alienating jobs. For people whose industrial jobs were terminated and replaced with these second-tier jobs, the differences in pay are significant.

The decline in manufacturing that traditionally generated middle-income, blue-collar occupations also has added to the numbers in poverty or near poverty. This category of the new poor of **displaced workers** is composed of laid-off workers who face never being reemployed at comparable-paying jobs because their training and skills have become obsolete. These people typically worked hard and steadily in hard-hat industries, but their skills and experience do not fit into the high-technology sector of manufacturing. Those older workers who were laid off are especially vulnerable because companies may not be willing to invest in their training.

Many communities have been devastated by the loss of companies employing thousands. When U.S. Steel or some other corporation closes its plants, permanently laying off thousands in a community, individuals and families suffer but so, too, do the communities, with declining real estate values, diminished retail sales, plummeting tax revenues, and severely reduced bank assets. Thus, the standard of living for entire communities is affected.

Finally, even workers who remain in the declining manufacturing industries will experience a decline in their standard of living. Given the triple threats of employers moving plants to the Sun Belt or overseas, heightened international competition, and more layoffs, the unions have tended to accept steep concessions to stem further job losses. Thus, the wages and benefits of industrial workers decline further, removing them from the middle-class lifestyle they once enjoyed.

In summary, the problems associated with work in U.S. society are structural in origin. The source is not in unmotivated or unwilling workers. To understand the work setting in our society, we must understand the nature of capitalism, where profit guides managerial decisions rather than the human consequences. And in looking at unemployment, we must recognize that the economy fails to produce enough jobs with living wages and adequate benefits for the workers to maintain a middle-class life-style. Finally, in examining this labor market, we must understand that the economy is undergoing a profound transformation. The next few generations will be caught in the nexus between one stage and another, and many will suffer because of the dislocations. So, too, will a society that refuses to plan but, rather, lets the marketplace dictate the choices of economic firms.

CHAPTER REVIEW

1. Societies are organized to allocate work in order to produce the goods and services required for survival. The way work is organized generates important social problems.
2. Owners and managers of firms and factories control workers in several ways: (a) through scientific management, (b) through bureaucracy, (c) by monitoring worker behavior, and (d) through extortion.
3. Blue-collar and white-collar workers in bureaucracies and factories are susceptible to alienation, which is the separation of human beings from each other, from themselves, and from the products they create. Specialized work in impersonal settings leads to dissatisfaction and meaninglessness.
4. A primary goal of business firms in a capitalist society is to reduce costs and thus increase profits. One way to reduce costs is not to provide adequately for worker safety.
5. Labor unions have declined in numbers and power. This has resulted in lower real wages and benefits, less safe work conditions, and a declining middle class.
6. Another work-related problem is discrimination, in which women and minorities have long received unfair treatment in jobs, pay, and opportunities for advancement. Two features of the U.S. economy promote these inequities: (a) the segmented labor market and (b) capitalist patriarchy.
7. The official government data on unemployment hide the actual amount by undercounting the unemployed in two ways: (a) people not actively seeking work (discouraged workers) are not counted; and (b) people who work at part-time jobs are counted as fully employed.
8. Unemployment has positive consequences for some people. Having a certain portion unemployed tends to keep inflation in check, according to some economists. Also, unemployment benefits capitalists by keeping wages down.
9. The economy of the United States is in the midst of a major structural transformation. This fundamental shift is the consequence of several powerful converging forces: (a) technological change, (b) the globalization of the economy, (c) capital flight, and (d) the shift from an industrial economy to a service/information economy.
10. These forces combine to create considerable discontinuity and disequilibrium in society. The trend toward robotics and other forms of superautomation reduces the jobs for the unskilled and semiskilled. This high-tech society, however, creates a need for workers skilled in communication, reasoning, mathematics, and computer programming. The proportion of workers traditionally found in these jobs (White males) is declining, while the proportion of new workers is increasingly non-White. Because non-Whites are disadvantaged economically and educationally, there is a skills mismatch. This skills gap offers the disadvantaged the potential of upward mobility if they, governments, schools, and businesses meet the challenge. If not, the gap between the advantaged and the disadvantaged will continue to widen.
11. Deindustrialization and the shift to a service economy have reduced the number of jobs providing a middle-class standard of living and have expanded the number of lower standard-of-living jobs. The result is a bifurcation of the labor force into the haves and the have-nots.

KEY TERMS

Scientific management. Efforts to increase worker efficiency by breaking down work into very specialized tasks, the standardization of tools and procedures, and the speeding up of repetitive work.

Alienation. Separation of human beings from each other, from themselves, and from the products they create.

Sweatshop. Substandard working environment where labor laws are violated.

Segmented labor market (dual labor market). Capitalist economy is divided into two distinct sectors—one in which production and working conditions are relatively stable and secure, the other composed of marginal firms in which working conditions, wages, and job security are low.

Discouraged workers. People who have not actively sought work for 4 weeks. These people are not counted as unemployed by the Bureau of Labor Statistics.

Reserve army of the unemployed. Unemployed people who want to work. Their presence tends to depress the wages of workers and keeps those workers from making demands on employers for fear of being replaced.

Structural transformation of the economy. Fundamental change of the economy resulting from several powerful contemporary forces: technological breakthroughs in microelectronics, the globalization of the economy, capital flight, and the shift from a manufacturing economy to one based on information and services.

Capital flight. Investment choices that involve the movement of corporate monies from one investment to another (investment overseas, plant relocation, and mergers).

Maquiladoras. U.S. manufacturing plants located across the border in Mexico.

Sunset industries. Industries declining in output and employment.

Sunrise industries. Industries characterized by increased output and employment.

Contingent employment. Employment arrangement where employees work as temporaries or independent contractors, freeing employers from paying fringe benefits.

Displaced workers. Unemployed workers who face never being employed at comparable paying jobs because their training and skills have become obsolete.

WEBSITES FOR FURTHER REFERENCE

http://www.prospect.org/archives/20/20blue.html
Barry Bluestone's "The Inequality Express": A report found in the American Prospect Online Magazine on economic restructuring and its impact on workers and their families.

http://www.isr.umich.edu/src/psid/
The Panel Study of Income Dynamics is a longitudinal survey of a representative sample of U.S. individuals and the families in which they reside. It has been ongoing since 1968. The data are collected annually, and the data files contain the full span of information collected over the course of the study. PSID data can be used for cross-sectional, longitudinal, and intergenerational analysis, and for studying both individuals and families.

http://epinet.org/
The Economic Policy Institute website provides information and data on various policy alternatives.

http://www.bls.gov/
The Bureau of Labor Statistics provides a comprehensive picture of the U.S. economy at any given moment in time. The Bureau of Labor Statistics is the principal fact-finding agency for the federal government in the broad field of labor economics and statistics.

http://utip.gov.utexas.edu/
The University of Texas Inequality Project is a small research group concerned with measuring and explaining movements of inequality in wages and earnings and patterns of industrial changes around the world.

http://198.108.159.119/index.htm
The W.E. Upjohn Institute for Employment Research is an independent, nonprofit research organization devoted to finding, evaluating, and promoting solutions to employment-related problems.

http://www.bls.gov/lau/home.htm
The Local Area Unemployment Statistics (LAUS) pro-

gram produces monthly and annual employment, unemployment, and labor force data for census regions and divisions, states, counties, metropolitan areas, and many cities, by place of residence.

http://www.ilo.org

The International Labour Organization (ILO) is a UN specialized agency which promotes social justice and human and labor rights. Its website provides information on the organization, its publications, upcoming meetings, labor standards and workers' rights, employment and labor market policies, social protection, and social dialog. Available at the site is the LABORSTA database, which contains annual time-series labor statistics for countries.

http://www.unions.org

The Union Resource Network (URN) is the most complete index of union websites on the Internet. URN provides union-made websites, hosting, and solidarity services. Currently, approximately 10% of all union websites in the world are hosted on the URN server.

http://www.thebird.org/strikes/

The Great Speckled Bird Strike Page provides updates on all worker strikes against corporations around the United States. Information on all current strikes is available. This page is hosted by *The Great Speckled Bird* (also known as *The Bird*), the "underground" liberal newspaper of Atlanta dating from the 1960s. Most of *The Bird*'s regular columnists maintain their own homepages and archived articles; they are linked directly from the site. *The Bird* also hosts the drive to establish a formal Liberal Party of the United States.

http://www.osha.gov/

The mission of the Department of Labor's Occupational Safety and Health Administration (OSHA) is to ensure safe and healthful workplaces in America. "Since the agency was created in 1971, workplace fatalities have been cut in half and occupational injury and illness rates have declined 40 percent. At the same time, U.S. employment has nearly doubled from 56 million workers at 3.5 million worksites to 105 million workers at nearly 6.9 million sites."

http://www.embassyofmexico.org/english/4/6/border2.htm

The Mexico–U.S. Relationship: This site provides a profile of the relationship between Mexico and the United States since the enactment of NAFTA. In addition, this site discusses the importance of the border between these two countries. "Due to both its geographical location as the first point of binational interaction, and to the intensity of exchange registered, the border has strategic importance for both countries."

15 Families

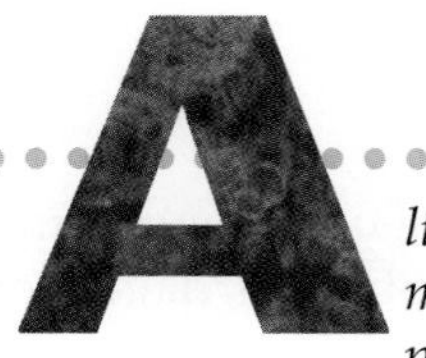

lthough it may seem overwhelming to see family problems as only one symptom of a much larger social crisis, it is in some ways encouraging. It means, for example, that people have not suddenly and inexplicably "gone bad." They are struggling with serious dilemmas and, though many make poor choices or cannot carry out their highest ideals, are generally trying to do their best. There is evidence that we can help families do better and that we can do so now.

—Stephanie Coontz

Family changes occurring in the last few decades have led some social analysts to conclude that the family is in serious trouble, that we have lost our "family values," and that the decline of the two-parent family is responsible for our worst social problems. Pundits and commentators tell us that today's family patterns are symptoms of decline and decay. This rhetoric has become so entrenched in our public discourse that in 1996 it even served as the rationale for dismantling the U.S. social welfare system (see Chapters 7 and 17).

The family is an easy target for those who blame social problems on bad people doing bad things. They assume that when the family fails, the rest of society fails. This view of the world is flawed in two fundamental respects. First, it reverses the relationship between family and society by treating families as the building blocks of society rather than as a reflection of social conditions. Second, it ignores the structural reasons for family breakdown and the profound changes occurring throughout the world. Even in very different societies, families and households are undergoing similar shifts as a result of global economic changes.

Some social problems have their locus in family settings. Although many of these problems are rooted in conditions outside the family—in social, economic, and demographic trends—they become family problems that affect growing numbers of children and adults. This chapter examines the family as a social institution and the social problems that have their locus in family life. The chapter is divided into five parts. The first section shows the gap between common images of the family and family life as it is actually experienced in this society. The remaining four sections examine representative family-based social problems: the economic disadvantages for the members of some families and how they are perpetuated, inadequate child care, divorce, and domestic violence.

THE MYTHICAL FAMILY IN THE UNITED STATES

There are a number of myths about families. These beliefs are bound up with nostalgia and cultural values concerning what is typical and true about families. The following beliefs, based on folk wisdom and common beliefs, are rarely challenged except by social scientists and family scholars.

1. *The myth of a stable and harmonious family of the past.* The common assumption is that families of the past were better than families of the present. They are believed to have been more stable, better adjusted, and happier. However, family historians have found that there is no golden age of the family. There have always been desertion by spouses, illegitimate children, and certainly spouse and child abuse. Divorce rates were lower and meant that many children were raised by single parents or stepparents. Although strong religious prohibitions kept divorce rates low, many "empty" marriages continued without love and happiness to bind them.

Historian Stephanie Coontz has reexamined our assumptions about family history. Her book *The Way We Never Were* (1992) explodes the myth that the family has recently "gone bad." The reality of past family life was quite different from the stereotype. Desertion by spouses, the presence of illegitimate children, and other conditions that are considered modern problems existed in the past. Part of the family nostalgia holds that there were three generations living under one roof or in close proximity. This image of the three-generational family is also false. Few examples of this "classical family of western nostalgia" (Goode, 1983:43) have been found by family historians.

2. *The myth of the family as a "haven in a heartless world"* (Lasch, 1977). This is the positive image of the family as a place of intimacy, love, and trust where individuals escaped the competition and dehumanizing forces in modern society. Of course, love, intimacy, and trust are the glue for many families, but this glorification of private life tends to mask the ugly side of some families, where emotional and physical aggression are commonplace, and where competition between spouses and among children sometimes destroys relationships. This myth ignores the harsh effects of economic conditions (e.g., poverty or near poverty, unemployment and underemployment, downward mobility or the threat of downward mobility). It ignores the social inequalities (racism, sexism, ageism, homophobia) that prevent certain kinds of people from experiencing the good things in life. And the idealized family view masks the inevitable problems that arise in intimate settings (tensions, anger, and even violence in some instances).

3. *The myth of the monolithic family form.* We get a consistent image of what the American family is supposed to look like from our politicians, from our ministers and priests, from children's literature, and from television. This image is of a White middle-class, heterosexual father as breadwinner, mother as homemaker, and children at home, living in a one-family house. This model, however, accounts for fewer than 10 percent of today's families. Women have joined the paid labor force in great numbers. A number of family forms are common: single-parent families (resulting either from unmarried parenthood or divorce), remarried couples, unmarried couples, stepfamilies, foster families, extended or multigenerational families, and the doubling up of two families within the same home (Ahlburg and De Vita, 1992:2). Half of marriages end in divorce, and half of all children will spend at least part of their childhood in a single-parent family (90 percent with their mothers).

4. *The myth of a unified family experience.* We assume that all family members experience family life in the same way. This image hides the diversity *within* families. The family is a gendered institution. Women and men experience marriage differently. There are gender differences in decision making, in household division of labor, and in forms of intimacy and sexuality. Similarly, divorce affects them differently. Remarriage patterns differ by gender, as well. Girls and boys experience their childhoods differently, as there are different expectations, different rules, and different punishments according to gender.

5. *The myth of family decline as the cause of social problems.* The rhetoric about family values argues that all family arrangements *different* from the two-parent, father-working, mother and children at home model are the sources of social problems. Fatherless families, or women working outside the home, are said to be the reasons for poverty, violence, drug addiction, and crime. Divorce, and unwed mothers, in this view are damaging children, destroying families, and tearing apart the fabric of society.

FAMILIES IN CONTEMPORARY U.S. SOCIETY: THE FAMILY IN CAPITALISM

Family arrangements in the United States are closely related to economic development. Industrialization moved the center of production from the domestic family unit to the workplace. Families became private domestic retreats set off from the rest of society. Men went off to earn a wage in factories and offices, while women remained in the home to nurture their children. From the rise of the industrial economy until World War II, capitalism operated within a simple framework. Employers assumed that most families included one main breadwinner—a male—and one adult working at home directing domestic work—a female; in short, jobs with wives. As a result, many men received the income intended to support a family.

The emergence of the private family with a breadwinner father and a homemaker mother was important, but economic conditions precluded this pattern for many families. As the nation's economy industrialized, wave after wave of immigrants filled the labor force. Through working for wages, entire families became an integral part of society. Immigrant families did not separate themselves into private units. Instead, they used extended family ties to adjust in the new society. Families were crucial in assisting their newly arrived kin and other members of their ethnic groups to adapt to the new society. Many immigrants came to the United States in family groupings, or they sent for families once they were established in cities. Kin assisted in locating jobs

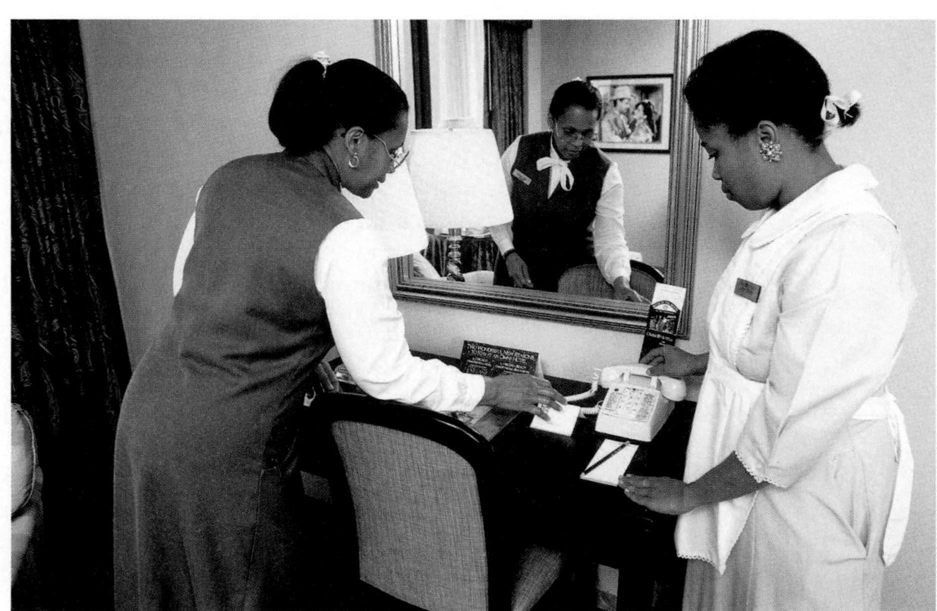

The "breadwinner-homemaker" pattern does not apply to people who lack the opportunities to earn a family wage.

and housing, and they provided other forms of support. Contrary to the typical portrayal of immigrants, their transplanted kinship and ethnic bonds did not disintegrate, but rather were maintained and regenerated in the new society (Early, 1983; Vecoli, 1964).

The developing capitalist economy did not provide equal opportunities for all people. Racial-ethnic people did not have the opportunity to become part of the industrial labor force. Instead, they labored in nonindustrial sectors of the economy. This often required family arrangements that were different from those in the dominant society.

The breadwinner–homemaker pattern never applied to immigrants and racial minorities because they were denied the opportunities to earn a family wage. So, many married women took jobs to make ends meet. Some women took in boarders or did piecework; some worked as maids in middle-class and upper-class homes; and some became wage workers in sweatshops, department stores, and offices. For these families, the support of the community and extended family members was crucial (Albelda, 1992:7).

Families have always varied with social conditions. What many uphold as the legitimate family is a product of *social structure*. From the original settlement of the American colonies through the midtwentieth century, families of European descent often received economic and social supports to establish and maintain families. Following World War II, the GI Bill, the National Defense Education Act, the expansion of the Federal Housing Authority and Veterans Administration loan subsidy programs, and government funding of new highways provided the means through which middle-class Whites were able to achieve the stable suburban family lives that became the ideal against which other families were judged (Coontz, 1992). These kinds of supports have rarely been available for people of color and, until quite recently, were actively denied them through various forms of housing and job discrimination. Family history makes it clear that social forces have always created many different family arrangements.

What we think of as "the family" is an ideal. It implies a private retreat set apart from society. This image masks the real relationship between families and the larger society. A better way of understanding how families are related to social institutions is to distinguish between families and households. A **family** is a construct of meanings and relationships; a **household** is a residential and economic unit (Osmond and Thorne, 1993:607; Rapp, 1982). To put it another way, a household is a residence group that carries out domestic functions, whereas a family is a kinship group (Holstein and Gubrium, 1999:31). A good example of the importance of distinguishing between family and household is the restructuring of family obligations and household composition after divorce (Ferree, 1991:107).

STRATIFICATION AND FAMILY LIFE: UNEQUAL LIFE CHANCES

In previous chapters we examined growing inequalities in the distribution of resources and rewards. These stratification hierarchies—class, race, and gender—are changing and reshuffling families and individuals. In this section, we examine the effects of social class on families in the United States. Of course, the social patterning of inequality occurs along many other dimensions including age, family characteristics, and place of residence (see Table 15.1).

TABLE 15.1

Persons and Families in Poverty by Selected Characteristics: 1998

Characteristics	*Below Poverty Percent*	*Characteristics*	*Below Poverty Percent*
People		*Families*	
Total	12.7	Total	10.0
Family Status		**Type of Family**	
In families	11.2	Married couple	5.3
Householder	10.0	White	5.0
Related children under 18	18.3	White, non-Hispanic	3.8
Related children under 6	20.6	Black	7.3
In unrelated subfamilies	19.9	Hispanic origin	15.7
Children under 18	50.5	Female householder, no husband present	29.9
Unrelated individuals	19.9	White	24.9
Male	17.0	White, non-Hispanic	20.7
Female	22.6	Black	40.8
Race		**Race**	
White	10.5	White	8.0
White, non-Hispanic	8.2	White, non-Hispanic	6.1
Black	26.1	Black	23.4
Asian and Pacific Islander	12.5	Asian and Facific Islander	11.0
Hispanic origin	25.6	Hispanic origin	15.7
Age			
Under 18 years	18.9		
18 to 24 years	16.6		
25 to 34 years	11.9		
35 to 44 years	9.1		
45 to 54 years	6.9		
55 to 59 years	9.2		
60 to 64 years	10.1		
65 years and over	10.5		
Nativity			
Native	12.1		
Foreign born	18.0		
Naturalized citizen	11.0		
Not a citizen	22.2		
Region			
Northeast	12.3		
Midwest	10.3		
South	13.7		
West	14.0		
Residence			
Inside metropolitan areas	12.3		
Inside central cities	18.5		
Outside central cities	8.7		
Outside metropolitan areas	14.4		

Source: U.S. Bureau of the Census. 2000. "Poverty in the United States: 1998." *Current Population Reports.* Series P60-207. Washington, DC: U.S. Government Printing Office, Table A, pp. vi, vii.

Families are embedded in a class hierarchy that is "pulling apart" to shrink the middle class while more families join the growing ranks of the rich or the poor (Usdansky, 1992). This movement creates great differences in family living and no longer guarantees that children's placement in the class system will follow that of their parents. Still, a family's location in the class system is the single most important determinant of family life.

Social and economic forces produce different family configurations. Households in different parts of the class structure have different connections with the outside economy and different ways of acquiring the necessities of life. They do so through inheritance, salaries, wages, welfare, or various involvements with the hidden economy, the illegal economy, or the irregular economy. Families with more secure resources conform more closely to the nuclear family ideal of self-support. In a stratified society, family structures differ because households vary systematically in their ability to hook into, accumulate, and transmit wealth, wages, or welfare (Rapp, 1982). This variation is closely related to the connections that households and families have with other social institutions. The social networks or relationships outside the family—at work, school, church, and voluntary associations—are the social forces that shape class and racial differences in family life.

The middle-class family form is one of the most idealized in our society. This form, composed of mother, father, and children in a self-supporting, freestanding unit, has long been most characteristic of middle-class and upper-middle-class families. Middle-class families of the twenty-first century are quite different from the employed father and homemaker mother that evolved with industrialization. Today, many families can sustain their class status only through the economic contributions of employed wives. Here, households are based on stable and secure resources provided by the occupations of adult women and men. Family "autonomy" is shaped by supportive forces in the larger society. When exceptional economic resources are called for, nonfamilial institutions usually are available in the form of better medical coverage, expense accounts, and credit at banks (Rapp, 1982:181).

These links with nonfamily institutions are precisely the ones that distinguish life in middle-class families from families in other economic groups. The strongest links are with the occupations of middle-class family members, especially those of the husband-father. Occupational roles greatly affect family roles and the quality of family life (Schneider and Smith, 1973). Occupations are part of the larger opportunity structure of society. Occupations that are highly valued and carry high income rewards are unevenly distributed. The amount of the paycheck determines how well a given household can acquire the resources needed for survival and perhaps for luxury. The job or occupation that is the source of the paycheck connects families with the opportunity structure in different ways.

In the working class, material resources depend on wages acquired in exchange for labor. When such hourly wages are insufficient or unstable, individuals in households must pool their resources with other people in the larger family network. The pooling of resources may involve exchanging babysitting, sharing meals, or lending money. Pooling represents an attempt to cope with the tenuous nature of connections between household and opportunity structures of society, and it requires that the boundaries of "the family" be expanded. This is one reason that the idealized nuclear family is impossible for many people to sustain. At the lower levels of the class hierarchy, people lack the material resources to form autonomous households.

The fluid boundaries of these families do not make them unstable. Instead, this family flexibility is a way of sustaining the limited resources that result from their place in the class hierarchy. Even the Black single-parent family, which has sometimes been criticized as being disorganized or even pathological, is often embedded in a network of sharing and support. Latino families also exhibit strong and persistent kinship bonds that provide socioeconomic and emotional support. In fact, most racial-ethnic families are characterized by the presence of extended kinship and a network of support spread across multiple households. Looking at how these families are influenced by larger social forces allows us to see that variation in family organization is a way of adapting to a society where racial stratification shapes family resources and family structures (Baca Zinn, 1990).

Most important, the differences in family boundaries arise from different kinds of linkages with institutions that are *consequences* of class position, not causes of that position. Lacking economic resources to purchase services from specialists outside the family, poor people turn to relatives and exchange these services. This family network then becomes a crucial institution in both the working class and the lower class.

Middle-class families with husbands (and perhaps wives) in careers have both economic resources and built-in ties with supportive institutions such as banks, credit unions, medical facilities, and voluntary associations. These ties are intrinsic to some occupations and to middle-class neighborhoods. They are structurally determined. Such institutional linkages strengthen the autonomy of middle-class families. Yet the middle class is shrinking, and many middle-class families are without middle-class incomes because of changes in the larger economy. Changes in family structure have also contributed to the lowering of family income. High divorce rates, for example, create many more family units with lower incomes.

Turning to the upper class, we find that family boundaries are more open than are those of the middle class, even though class boundaries are quite closed. Among the elite, family constitutes not only a nuclear family but also the extended family. The elite have multiple households (Rapp, 1982:182). Their day-to-day life exists within the larger context of a network of relatives (Dyer, 1979:209).

The institutional linkages of the elite are national in scope. Families in various sections of the country are connected by such institutions as boarding schools, exclusive colleges, exclusive clubs, and fashionable vacation resorts. In this way the elite remains intact, and the marriage market is restricted to a small (but national) market (Blumberg and Paul, 1975:69). Family life is privileged in every sense, as Stein, Richman, and Hannon report:

> Wealthy families can afford an elaborate support structure to take care of the details of everyday life. Persons can be hired to cook and prepare meals and do laundry and to care for the children. (Stein, Richman, and Hannon, 1977:9)

The vast economic holdings of these families allow them to have a high degree of control over the rewards and resources of society. They enjoy freedoms and choices not available to other families in society. These families maintain privileged access to **life chances** and life-styles.

Kinship ties, obligations, and interests are more extended in classes at the two extremes than they are in the middle (McKinley, 1964:22). In the upper extreme and toward the lower end of the class structure, kinship networks serve different functions. At both extremes they are institutions of resource management. The kin-based family form of the elite serves to preserve inherited wealth. It is intricately tied to other national institutions that control the wealth of society. The kin-based family form of the working and lower classes is a primary institution through which individuals participate in social life as they pool and exchange their limited resources to ensure survival. It is influenced by society's institutions, but it remains separate from them.

Structural Transformation and Family Life

In Chapter 14, we discussed the structural transformation of the economy. Given the magnitude of the economic transformation, we should not be surprised that families and individuals are profoundly affected by the global shifts now occurring.

As U.S. companies move production overseas, use new technology to replace workers, and engage in megamergers, jobs are lost and wages decline. Declining industries are those that historically provided high-earning positions for men. On the other hand, the new growth in the U.S. economy has been precisely in the sectors that are major employers of women. As the need for certain kinds of labor diminishes, more and more working-class and middle-class families are the victims of economic dislocation. Families are affected when they face economic and social marginalization and when family members are unemployed or underemployed. The modern economic system undermines "family values" (Thurow, 1995a:A11). (The following section is adapted from Baca Zinn and Eitzen, 2002:106–113.)

Economic changes have affected not only production workers but white-collar workers and managers as well. What does **downward mobility** mean for families? Katherine Newman describes the experience of the downwardly mobile middle class:

> They once "had it made" in American society, filling slots from affluent blue collar jobs to professional and managerial occupations. They have job skills, education, and decades of steady work experience. Many are, or were, home owners. Their marriages were (at least initially) intact. As a group they savored the American dream. They found a place higher up the ladder in this society and then, inexplicably, found their grip loosening and their status sliding. Some downwardly mobile middle-class families end up in poverty, but many do not. Usually they come to rest at a standard of living above the poverty level but far below the affluence they enjoyed in the past. They must, therefore, contend not only with financial hardship but with the psychological, social, and practical consequences of "falling from grace," of "losing their proper place" in the world. (Newman, 1988:8)

The personal consequences of "falling from grace" involve stigma, embarrassment, and guilt for those affected. Downward mobility is devastating in U.S. society, not only because of the loss in economic resources but also because self-worth is so closely connected to occupation. People in the United States tend to interpret loss of occupational status as the fault of the downwardly mobile.

Downward mobility also occurs within the stable working class, whose link with resource-granting opportunity structures has always been tenuous. Many downwardly mobile families find successful coping strategies to deal with their adverse situations. Some families develop a tighter bond to meet their common problems. Others find support from families in similar situations or from their kin networks. But for many families, downward mobility adds tensions that make family life especially difficult. Family members experience stress, marital tension, and depression. Newman has suggested that these conditions are normal given the persistent tensions generated by downward mobility. Many families experience some degree of these pathologies and yet somehow endure. But some families disintegrate under these pressures, with serious problems of physical brutality, incapacitating alcoholism, desertion, and even suicide (Newman, 1988:134–140).

Although families throughout the social structure are changing as a result of macroeconomic forces, the changes are most profound among the working class. Blue-collar workers have been hardest hit by the economic transformation. Their jobs have been eliminated by the millions because of the new technologies and competition from other lower-wage (much lower) economies. They have been disproportionately fired or periodically laid off. Sometimes their places of work have shut down entirely and moved to other societies. Their unions have lost strength (in numbers and clout). And their wages have declined.

The changing forms of the family are a major consequence of the economic transformation. In 1950, some 60 percent of U.S. households fit this pattern: an intact nuclear household composed of a male breadwinner, his full-time wife, and their dependent children. Although this family form was dominant in society, its prevalence varied by social class. Sociologist Judith Stacey (1990, 1991) calls this type of family the **modern family.** But this family form was disrupted by deindustrialization and the changes in women's work roles. Stacey found that working-class families, especially the women in them, created innovative ways to cope with economic uncertainty and domestic upheavals. In effect these women were and are the pioneers of emergent family forms. Stacey calls these new family forms **postmodern** because they do not fit the criteria for a "modern" family. Now there are divorce-extended families that include ex-spouses and their lovers, children, and friends. Households now expand and contract as adult children leave and then return home only to leave again. The

Postmodern families reflect diverse ways of coping with changes in society.

vast majority of these postmodern families have dual earners. Many now involve husbands in greater child care and domestic work than in earlier times. Kin networks have expanded to meet economic pressures. Parents now deal with their children's cohabitation, single and unwed parenthood, and divorce. The result is that fewer than 10 percent of households now conform to the "modern" family form. According to Stacey:

> No longer is there a single culturally dominant family pattern, like the modern one, to which the majority of Americans conform and most of the rest aspire. Instead, Americans today have crafted a multiplicity of family and household arrangements that we inhabit uneasily and reconstitute frequently in response to changing personal and occupational circumstances. (Stacey, 1991:19)

These "postmodern" family forms are new to working-class and middle-class families as they adjust to the structural transformation, *but they are not new to the poor*. The economic deprivation faced by the poor has always forced the poor to adapt in similar ways: single-parent families, relying on kin networks, sharing household costs, and multiple wage earners among family members.

Changing Composition of Households and Families

To understand current trends in family life, we must return to the distinction between households and families discussed earlier in this chapter. [The following is based on Ahlburg and De Vita (1992) and Bianchi and Casper (2000:8).] The U.S. Bureau of the Census defines a *household* as all persons who occupy a housing unit such as a house, apartment, or other residential unit. A household may consist of one person who lives alone or of several people who share a dwelling. A *family,* on the other hand, is two or more persons related by birth, marriage, or adoption who reside together. All families comprise households, but not all households are families under the Census Bureau's definition. Indeed the growth of the **nonfamily household** (i.e., persons who live alone or with unrelated individuals) is one of the most dramatic changes to occur during the past four decades, as shown in Figure 15.1. In 1969, 85 percent of households were family households. At the same time, nonfamily households have been on the rise. The fastest growth has been among persons living alone. The proportion of households with just one person doubled from 13 to 26 percent between 1960 and 2000 (Bianchi and Casper, 2000:8).

Nonfamily households are a diverse group. They may consist of elderly individuals who live alone, college-age youths who share an apartment, cohabiting couples, individuals who delay or forgo marriage, or those who are "between marriages" (Ahlburg and De Vita, 1992; Rawlings, 1995: 22).

Another dramatic shift in household composition between 1970 and 1995 was the decline in the percentage of households with children. (The following is based on Bianchi and Casper, 2000:8). Two-parent households with children dropped from 44 to 24 percent between 1960 and 2000. This downward trend reflects the decline in birthrates, the shift toward smaller families, and the extended period of time before young adults marry. During the next 15 years, the overall composition of households is projected to shift, with a decreasing proportion of family households with children and increasing proportions of family households with no children and people living alone (Day, 1996:11).

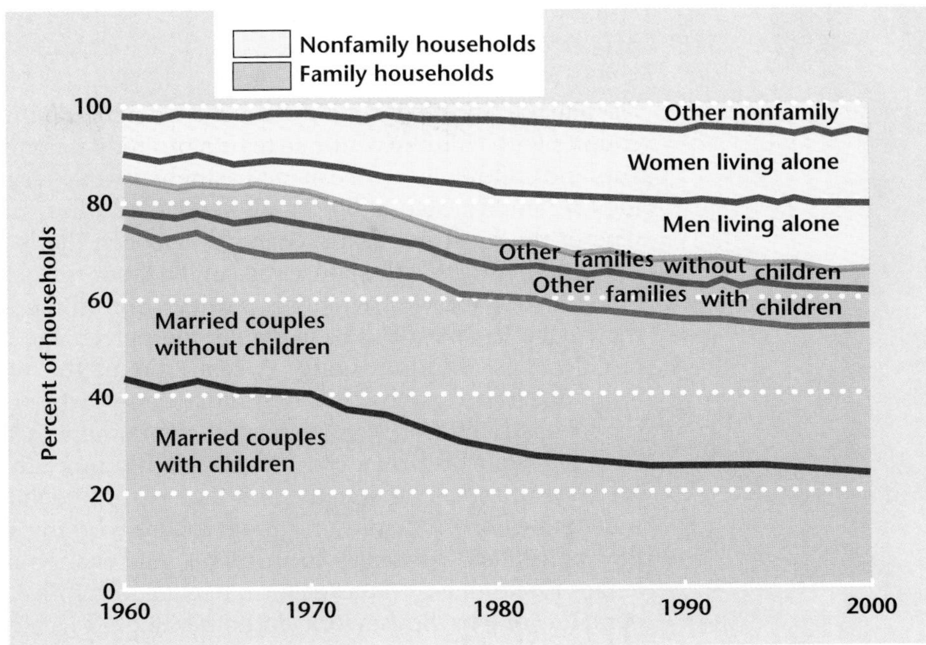

FIGURE 15.1

Trends in U.S. Households, 1960 to 2000

Source: S. M. Bianchi and L. M. Casper. 2000. "American Families." *Population Bulletin 55* (December):8.

However, household composition varies considerably among different segments of the population. Minorities are much more likely than Whites to live in households that include children. Over 40 percent of minority households in 1995 had at least one child under age 18 compared with 32 percent of White households. This difference arises primarily because minority populations tend to have younger age structure than the White population (i.e., greater share of minorities are in the prime child-bearing ages) and minorities tend to have higher fertility rates than Whites (De Vita, 1996:34).

Households headed by women account for a growing proportion of families over the past two decades. By 2000, single-mother families accounted for 22 percent of all families with children, up from 6 percent in 1950 (Bianchi and Casper, 2000:9). Many mothers are single by choice. New reproductive technologies and women's increased independence mean that husbands are less of a necessity. Still, 41 percent of single-mother households subsist below the poverty line (Eckel, 1999). In fact, the rise in single-parent households is one of the main factors, contributing to the growing proportion of children raised in poverty. Between 1973 and 1999 the percentage of U.S. children living in poverty expanded from 14 to 17 percent. Families headed by a single parent run a high risk of being poor because they lack the economic resources of dual-parent families. Furthermore, single-parent households are usually headed by women who are at great risk of economic hardship. The earnings gap found in all occupations makes female-headed households especially vulnerable (see Chapter 9). In 1997, the poverty rate for families maintained by women was 42.5 percent, six times the rate for married couples with children (Bianchi and Casper, 2000:28). This growing class of families has profound implications for our society as a whole.

PARENTS AND CHILDREN

Despite the overall decline in the proportion of families with children, married couples with children continue to be a prominent family pattern. However, parents and children now live in increasingly diverse settings, including intact biological families, stepfamilies and blended families, and single-parent families. One of the most important changes has been the increase in married-couple families in which both spouses are in the labor force, or **dual-worker families.** Since 1960, the rise of women's participation in the labor force has been dramatic (see Chapter 9). For example, the percentage of women in two-parent families with children under 6 years old in the workforce increased from around 19 percent in 1960 to almost two-thirds in 1999; for mothers with school-aged children, the percentage of mothers in the labor force increased from less than 40 percent in 1960 to slightly more than three-fourths in 1999. Most significant, 1987 was the first time that more than one-half of all mothers with babies one year old or younger were working or looking for work, and that percentage continues to increase. This change has produced great challenges for families. Whatever form they take, families with children must mesh demands of jobs, housework, and parenting, as well as find good child care.

Social Supports for Working Parents

Dual-earner families and single-parent families share a common problem—the lack of adequate social supports in the community and workplace to ease the strains of their dual roles of workers and parents. In general, U.S. society is unresponsive to the needs of working parents. Among the many problems facing working parents, two are critical: obtaining job-protected leaves for family emergencies, including birth, and finding satisfactory care for their children while they are at work. In both instances, the policies of the federal and state governments lag behind the child-support policies of other Western nations. (The following sections are adapted from Baca Zinn and Eitzen, 2002:484–487.)

Parental Leave. Some businesses provide generous parental leave policies for their employees so that parents can have children, remain at home for some time after the birth of children, or meet the emergency health needs of their families without losing their jobs, benefits, or wages. Other employers have less generous programs or no programs at all for their workers. Likewise, some states require maternity leaves while others do not.

In 1993, after 7 years of legislative efforts and two presidential vetoes, a federal policy concerning parental leaves was enacted. The **Family and Medical Leave Act of 1993** requires firms with more than 50 employees to provide their employees with unpaid maternity leaves of up to 12 weeks, guaranteed jobs (the same or an equivalent job after the leave), and the retention of job benefits during the leave.

Although this legislation is a progressive step, it is a relatively small step with two large problems. First, this policy does not cover 40 percent of the workers in the United States (those who work for businesses with fewer than 50 employees). Second, unpaid leave is a severe financial hardship for many parents. Almost all other industrialized countries provide new mothers and sometimes fathers with paid maternity leave (a range of 4 months to 1 year at

80 to 90 percent of normal pay). The two biggest competitors of the United States—Japan and Germany—each guarantee at least 3 months of paid leave, with additional unpaid leave if desired. Moreover, most of the other industrial countries offer parental leave to care for sick children (from 10 weeks to 3 years, usually with low or no pay).

In 1997 President Clinton granted federal employees up to 24 hours of unpaid leave each year for family matters and emergencies. At the same time he urged Congress to extend the same benefit to all workers by expanding the Family and Medical Leave Act.

Child Care. Probably the biggest problem facing working parents is finding accessible and acceptable child care. (The following is from Baca Zinn and Eitzen, 2002:485–487.) "Accessible" refers to cost, proximity, and compatibility with work schedules; "acceptable" refers to various dimensions of adequacy, such as sanitation, safety, stimulation, and caring supervision. Each of these variables is important, but the most immediate concerns are availability and cost. Child care is very expensive; it is the largest single work-related expense for working mothers (costing in most urban areas more to send a 4-year-old to child care than it does to pay public college tuition for a 19-year-old) (Folbre, 2000). This means, of course, that more affluent parents can take advantage of higher-quality facilities that emphasize child development and other learning opportunities. Those less well off are more likely to use child care facilities that are overcrowded, unlicensed, and perhaps even unhealthy.

Some parents may opt out of employment because they do not have the resources for adequate child care. Research also suggests that the lack of good child care often confines women to part-time or home-based work. The result is that inadequate child care traps many women in low-paying, dead-end work.

Availability of quality day care is often the biggest problem facing working parents.

The United States has no comprehensive child care system. This lack of a system differentiates us from the other industrialized nations. Currently the federal government is involved modestly in providing for child care through two programs. First, it permits the deduction of child care payments on income tax returns. This amounts to about a $4 billion tax credit, which is considerable. The problem, however, is that by being tied to taxes, it benefits the most affluent families and has negligible effects on the poor because they do not earn enough to take advantage of it. Second, the welfare legislation of 1996 included approximately $4 billion in new child care funds over 6 years. "But the new law forces so many parents into the work force that this increase falls far short of what is needed to meet the new demand for child care generated by the law, much less to ensure that vulnerable children receive good care" (Children's Defense Fund, 1997:38).

The government's less-than-adequate child care programs are fundamentally flawed in at least two respects. Foremost, they are underfunded. The amounts the federal government promised simply do not meet child care needs. The other problem is that they rely on the states to implement the programs and to match the federal grants if they are to receive the monies. The states, through their governors, legislatures, and social service bureaucracies, vary greatly in their enthusiasm for child care, their licensing and monitoring of child care programs, and the standards they set to ensure quality in child care. If history is a guide, then it is likely that many states will not commit the greater resources needed to receive the federal funds.

Aside from the issue of availability of good child care, there is the crucial question of the effects of child care on children. (The following is from Baca Zinn and Eitzen, 2002:326–328.) The common assumption is that a preschool child deprived of maximum interaction with his or her parents, especially the mother ("maternal deprivation"), will be harmed. Since this belief is widely accepted, many working parents feel guilty for their assumed neglect.

The relationship between child care and child development is complex, involving sources within the child (e.g., temperament and impairment), factors in the child's immediate environment (such as the quality of relationships with parents), and factors in the child's larger social environment (e.g., neighborhood and the broader culture). Although this complexity prevents us from gaining a full understanding of the relationships between child care and child development, the cumulative evidence from empirical studies does permit us to draw some conclusions [the following is from a thorough review of the research by a panel on child care of the National Research Council as reported by Hayes, Palmer, and Zaslow (1990:47–144) and Belsky (1991); for findings from other research, see Burchinal (1999)].

1. Young children need to develop enduring relationships with a limited number of specific individuals—relationships characterized by affection, reciprocal interaction, and responsiveness to the individualized cues of young children.
2. There is a normal tendency for children to form multiple, simultaneous attachments to caregivers.
3. Children can benefit from "multiple parenting" if it provides affection, warmth, responsiveness, and stimulation in the context of enduring relationships with a reasonably small number of caregivers (usually assumed to be five or fewer).

4. For children beginning child care after their first year in life, there is little indication of differences in the mother–child relationship. Children beginning full-time child care within the first year, however, have a greater risk of insecurity in their attachments to their mothers than children at home full time with their mothers.
5. Children reared in child care orient more strongly to peers and somewhat less strongly to adults than do their home-reared counterparts.
6. Child care does not negatively affect the cognitive development of middle-class children, and it has positive consequences for the intellectual development of low-income children (if the child care programs emphasize cognitive enrichment, as Head Start does).
7. The overall quality of child care (group size, caregiver/child ratio, caregiver training, and educational material available) is associated with children's cognitive and social development.
8. The children who experience quality care in their families and child care environments have the strongest development. Children from low-income families are the most likely to be found in lower-quality care settings; thus, they experience the double jeopardy from encountering stresses at home and stress in their care environments.

Thus, we conclude that child care under the right conditions can be a positive experience for children. Over three-fourths of preschoolers are cared for on a regular basis by someone other than the parent. Unfortunately, many of these children are in day care situations that do not meet the standards. A key problem is the hiring and retaining of high-quality, well-trained day care workers. The problem with most day care centers is that they are underfunded.

Single Parents and Their Children

More than one-fourth (27 percent) of all U.S. children live with just one parent, up from 12 percent in 1970. Half of all children spend some of their childhood in single-parent families (Children's Defense Fund, 1997:13) (see Figure 15.2a, p. 448). One in five children spends his or her entire childhood in a single-parent household (Demo and Cox, 2001). Over 80 percent of single-parent families are headed by a women. Single mothers, on average, spend a total of about 9 years raising children without a partner present (Bianchi and Casper, 2000:22). In 1999 over half of all African American children (51 percent) lived in mother-only families, compared with 27 percent of Latino children, 16 percent of White children, and 15 percent of Asian American children (AmeriStat, 2000) (see Figure 15.2b, p. 448).

The disproportionate number of single-parent families headed by a woman is a consequence first of the relatively high divorce rate and the strong tendency for divorced and separated women to have custody of the children. Second, there is the relatively high rate of never-married mothers. To counter the common myth, the facts indicate that two-thirds of unwed mothers are *not* teenagers.

The important question to answer concerning this trend is, What are the effects on children of living in mother-only families? Research has shown consistently that children from single-parent homes are more likely than children from intact families to have behavioral problems such as mental illness, drug abuse, and delinquency. McLanahan and Booth's (1991) review of the recent

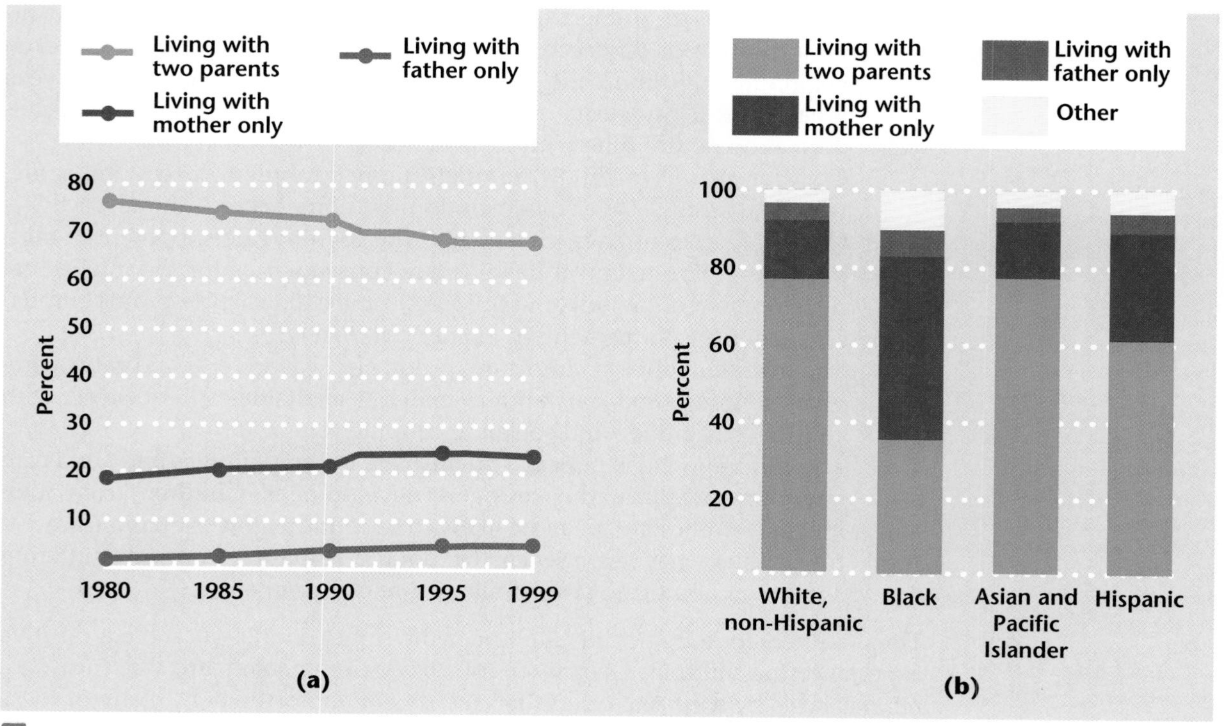

FIGURE 15.2

(a) Living Arrangements of Children, 1980 to 1999. (b) Living Arrangements of Children by Race/Ethnicity, 1999.
Source: Online. Available: http://ameristat.org/children/image3.html, 11/6/01.

research on children from mother-only families, compared to children from two-parent families, shows that:

- They have poorer academic achievement. This relationship is even more negative for boys than for girls.
- They are more likely to have higher absentee rates at school.
- They are more likely to drop out of school.
- They are more likely to marry early and to have children early, both in and out of marriage.
- If they marry, they are more likely to divorce.
- They are more likely to commit delinquent acts and to engage in drug and alcohol use.

Because over 80 percent of one-parent families are headed by a woman, the common explanation for the disproportionate pathologies found among the children of single parents has been that the absence of a male adult is detrimental to their development. The presence of both mothers and fathers contributes to the healthy development of the child (Marsiglio et al., 2001). Also, the absence of a spouse makes coping with parenting more difficult. Coping is difficult for any single parent—female or male—because of three common sources of strain: (1) responsibility overload, in which single parents make all the decisions and provide for all their family's needs; (2) task overload, in which the demands of work, housekeeping, and parenting can be overwhelming for one person; and (3) emotional overload, in which single parents must always be on call to provide the necessary emotional support. Clearly, when two people share these parental strains, it is more likely that the needs of the children will be met.

While the factors just described help to explain the behavioral differences between children from one-parent and two-parent homes, they sidestep the major reason—a fundamental difference in economic resources. As Andrew Cherlin has argued, "it seems likely that the most detrimental aspect of the absence of fathers from one-parent families headed by women is not the lack of a male presence *but the lack of a male income*" [Italics added.] (Cherlin, 1981:81). There is a strong likelihood that women raising children alone will be financially troubled. In 1999, for example, 28 percent of the children living in single-parent families headed by a women were poor, compared with 5 percent of children in two-parent families (U.S. Bureau of the Census, 2000a).

The reasons for a disproportionate number of mother-headed families that are poor are obvious. First, many single mothers are young and never married. They may have little education so that, if they work, they have poorly paid jobs. Second, many divorced or separated women have not been employed for years and find it difficult to re-enter the job market. Third, and more crucial, jobs for women, centered as they are in the bottom tier of the segmented job market, are poorly paid. Fourth, half of the men who owe child support do not pay all they owe, and a quarter of them do not pay anything; women who do receive child support find that the amount covers less than half the actual cost of raising a child.

Half of all children spend some of their childhood in single-parent families.

The economic plight of single-parent families is much worse for families of color. Women of color who head households have the same economic problems as White women who are in the same situation, plus the added burdens of institutional racism. In addition, they are less likely to be receiving child support (their husbands, unlike White husbands, are much more likely to be poor and unemployed), and they are more likely to have been high-school dropouts, further reducing their potential for earning a decent income.

The dominant stereotype of female-headed households sees them as Black and urban. When discussions about female-headed households focus on the decline of central cities and the growth of the urban underclass, we lose sight of the unique obstacles that 2 million rural female-headed households encounter. Rural female-headed households are as likely to be poor as female-headed households in central cities. In 1990, the poverty rate for rural female-headed households was 43.2 percent, as compared with 43.6 percent for central cities. (See the panel titled "Voices" about rural single mothers.)

The financial plight of female heads of households is sometimes alleviated in part by support from a kinship network. Relatives may provide child care, material goods, money, and emotional support. The kin network is an especially important source of emergency help for African Americans and Latinos. But for many, kin may not be near or helpful.

In sum, the social costs attributed to the children of single mothers are, in large part, the costs of poverty. The majority of single mothers are likely to have inadequate economic resources. This translates into huge negatives for single mothers and their children—differences in health care, diet, housing, neighborhood safety, and quality of schools.

Societal Response to Disadvantaged Children

As a nation, the United States has taken deliberate actions to reduce poverty among the elderly while simultaneously allowing childhood poverty to increase. (The following is adapted from Baca Zinn and Eitzen, 2002:479–481.) In 1970, the proportion of elderly in poverty was double the national average, yet by 1999 the poverty rate among the elderly was below the national average (9.7 percent compared to the national rate of 11.8 percent). The poverty rate for children under age 18 in 1970 was more than one-third lower than that for the elderly. By 1999, this situation had changed, with 17 percent of children under age 18 living in poverty (U.S. Bureau of the Census, 2000a) (see Figure 15.3, p. 452).

During the last 20 years, federal benefits to the elderly have risen from one-sixth of the federal budget to 30 percent (to about $300 billion annually). This increase occurred because federal policymakers created programs such as Medicare and Medicaid and because Social Security benefits were indexed to offset inflation. Conversely, however, these same decision makers did not provide adequately for needy families with children. The government actually reduced the programs targeted to benefit children (e.g., the children's share of Medicaid, Aid to Families with Dependent Children [AFDC], Head Start, food stamps, child nutrition, and federal aid to education).

Childhood poverty is especially acute for racial minorities. The bias against children in federal programs is heightened for minority children. Former senator Daniel Patrick Moynihan pointed out that there are two ways the federal government provides benefits to children in single-parent families. The first is Aid to Families with Dependent Children. The majority of the children receiv-

VOICES

POOR SINGLE MOTHERS AND THEIR CHILDREN IN RURAL AMERICA

Linda is a divorced mother of two children, ages 5 and 9. She is White and lives in a rural area in Michigan. She has a court order for child support, but has received nothing for the past 4 years. Linda is on AFDC (Aid to Families with Dependent Children) and is enrolled in a college program to become a registered nurse. She explains:

> Well, I was married ever since I was fifteen years old and I had no skills at all to work. I stayed home, took care of the family, and that was it. And then, when I split up from my husband—I'd only gone to the eighth grade—I got my high school diploma which took a long time because I had no high school credits—none at all.

The lives of single mothers in rural places are constrained in ways that differ from the experience of other single mothers. This panel discusses three ways in which the rural context structures inequalities to the disadvantage of female-headed households: welfare, transportation, and housing.

Rural women and children receiving AFDC generally receive lower benefits than urban women and their children. A recent study found that median annual AFDC benefits in 1993 were $3,361 per family in metropolitan counties, compared with $2,088 for nonmetropolitan county residents. An additional problem in rural places is the reluctance or unwillingness of many families to accept public assistance. Welfare use is highly stigmatized in rural communities, with many rural residents believing that welfare use is a sign of personal failure. Research finds that rural residents are less likely to make use of the services for which they are eligible and more likely to discontinue using welfare than their urban counterparts.

Transportation is perhaps the most serious dilemma poor rural women encounter. Social services are generally implemented with a single office serving an entire rural county. Women living in outer areas may need to travel 20 or more miles to a social service office. Furthermore, service sites are not necessarily centralized. Often women with multiple needs must criss-cross a county to access assistance for their families.

Opportunities for higher education are seldom available locally in rural communities. Transportation presents a problem for Linda because the college she attends is 50 miles away in an urban center. AFDC does not help her insure, maintain, or fuel her car. In a recent month the rear seal of her car failed and the exhaust system fell off. She tells how she is coping:

> Well, I'm just driving my car without the exhaust system and I just stop every once in a while and put some oil in it, and keep going, you know. What else? I've got to get there and back, and there's no money to fix it. And you pray every day that you're going to make it.

Linda lives in a mobile home in a village with no low-income housing. Rental housing is generally scarce and expensive in rural communities and differs in character from urban rental housing. Nearly all of the rental units in Linda's community are single-family dwellings; 56 percent of the rental units are trailers. Trailers tend to be dilapidated and are especially problematic in winter due to high heating costs and susceptibility to frozen or bursting water pipes. As a result of the double squeeze of expensive rural housing and low AFDC benefits, single mothers and their children sometimes go several weeks without a permanent address. Community officials occasionally find three families sharing a small substandard trailer.

Daily life is difficult for Linda and, she fears, monotonous for her children. She acknowledges that attending school, commuting, and studying leave her with less time for her children than she would like. Opportunities for family entertainment are very limited in her community, but she says she doesn't have the money anyway. Even a trip to the regional library, 15 miles away, is costly in terms of scarce commodities: time and gas money. Although Linda has taken out educational loans that she worries will take a lifetime to repay, she remains optimistic about the future. She says:

> My kids, they go to school and say, "My mommy is going to be a nurse." And you know, they're proud, too. They know what I'm trying to do.

Source: This essay was written expressly for *Social Problems* by Barbara A. Wells, Department of Sociology, Maryville College.

IGURE 15.3

Percent of Children in Poverty, 1975–1999

Source: Annie E. Casey Foundation. 2001. *2001 KIDS COUNT, Pocket Guide on America's Youth.* Washington, DC: Population Reference Bureau, p. 7.

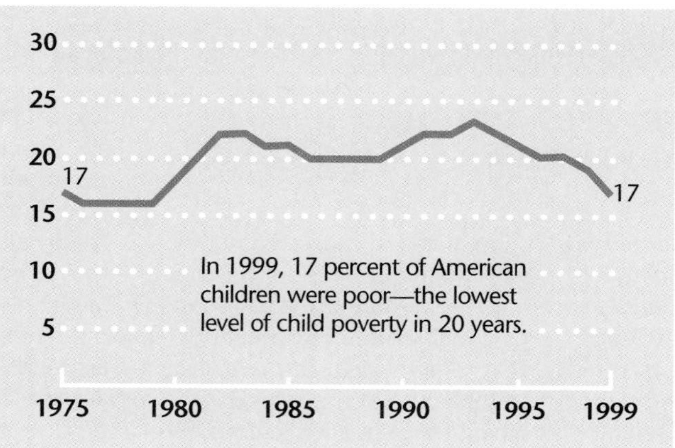

ing this type of aid are Black or Hispanic. Since 1970 the government has decreased the real benefits by 13 percent. The other form of assistance is Survivors Insurance (SI), which is part of Social Security. The majority of children receiving SI benefits are White, and these benefits have increased by 53 percent since 1970 (adjusted for inflation). Moynihan, writing 8 years before the 1996 welfare legislation, said:

> To those who say we don't care about children in our country, may I note that the average provision for children under SI has been rising five times as fast as average family income since 1970. We do care about some children. Majority children. It is minority children—not only but mostly—who are left behind. (Moynihan, 1988:5)

Another telling illustration is that while Congress in 1996 eliminated AFDC and severely cut food stamps and school nutrition programs for the poor, it did not cut cash and food programs for poor senior citizens.

The decisions to disproportionately help the elderly reflect the electoral power that the elderly have compared to the young. The elderly are organized, with several national organizations dedicated to political action that will benefit their interests. The American Association of Retired Persons (AARP), for example, is the nation's largest special-interest organization, with more than 40 million members. With the elderly making up 16 percent of the voting public (and much more in states such as Florida and Arizona, which have high concentrations of elderly people), politicians tend to pay attention to their special needs.

Children, on the other hand, have no electoral power and few advocates (an exception is the Children's Defense Fund). Their parents, especially those who are poor, are not organized. So, in a time of fiscal austerity the needs of children—prenatal care for poor women, nutritional and health care, day care, and better schools—are underfunded. The irony here is that the political right wing, which claims to be profamily, limits its political agenda to antiabortion legislation and court cases and ignores or fights governmental assistance to needy children and their struggling parents.

The argument here is not that the elderly and the young should compete for scarce resources and that one or the other should win. Rather, both age groups are dependents and are in need. The test of a civilization is the condition of its dependents. So far the United States has opted to care moderately well for one and not at all for the other.

DIVORCE

Most people in the United States marry, but not all marriages last forever; some eventually are dissolved. Recent divorce rates show that the chances of a first marriage in the United States ending in divorce are about one in two. Although the U.S. divorce rate is the world's highest, it is important to note that divorce rates have increased dramatically in most Western countries.

Many politicians, clergy members, editorial writers, and others have shown great concern over the current high rates of marital dissolution in the United States. Although the present divorce rate is historically near its peak, it has been declining slowly for the past 20 years. Divorce is not evenly distributed through the population but varies according to social and economic characteristics. The following are some generalizations about divorce in the United States:

- Half of all divorces occur during the first 7 years of marriage.
- The younger the age at marriage of the partners, the greater is the likelihood of divorce. Martin and Bumpass (1989) conclude that age at first marriage is the strongest predictor of divorce in the first 5 years of marriage. "Men and women who are under the age of 20 when they first marry are two to three times more likely to divorce than their counterparts who first marry in their twenties" (Price and McKenry, 1988:17).
- The lower the income, the greater the likelihood of divorce. In fact, poor two-parent families are twice as likely to dissolve as are two-parent families not in poverty. Thus, poverty is a major factor contributing to the breakup of families (Pear, 1993:A6).
- The higher the education for males, the lower the incidence of divorce. In contrast to males, a more complicated pattern is found for women. The highest rate of divorce is found among the least-educated women, followed by those with postgraduate degrees. The lowest rates were found for women with high school and college educations.
- The divorce patterns for Blacks and Hispanics differ significantly from those of Whites. From 1960 through the mid-1990s, African American divorce rates have been twice as great as those of Whites and Hispanics.
- About four out of every five people who obtain a divorce will remarry, with men more likely than women to do so.

Some of the many reasons for the increased divorce rate include: increased independence (social and financial) of women, economic restructuring that eliminates many jobs for men and makes women's employment necessary, women's inequality, greater tolerance of divorce by religious groups, and reform of divorce laws, especially the adoption of no-fault divorce in many states (i.e., one spouse no longer has to prove that the other was at fault in order to obtain a divorce). An important reason is the striking change in public attitudes toward divorce. Divorce is a difficult step and one that commands sympathy for the partners and children. But it is no longer considered a moral violation. Instead, divorce is generally accepted today as a possible solution for marital difficulties.

Consequences of Divorce

Divorce is an intensely personal event, and this intensity makes the breakup a painful experience, even when both parties want the marriage to end. In this section we review the personal side of divorce—the consequences for ex-wives and ex-husbands and for their children. (This section is adapted from Baca Zinn and Eitzen, 2002:393–398.)

"His" and "Her" Divorce. Both partners in a divorce are victims. Each is affected, in the typical case, by feelings of loneliness, anger, remorse, guilt, low self-esteem, depression, and failure. Although ex-spouses tend to share these negative feelings, the divorce experience differs for husband and wife in significant ways because of the structure of society and traditional gender inequality.

"His" Divorce. Ex-husbands have some major advantages and a few disadvantages over their ex-wives. On the positive side, they are almost always much better off financially. Typically, they were the major income producers for their families, and after the separation their incomes stay disproportionately with them. Bianchi, Bubaiya, and Kahn (1999) found, for example, that custodial mothers experienced a 36 percent decline in standard of living following separation, while noncustodial fathers experienced a 28 percent increase.

Another benefit that men have over women after divorce is greater freedom. If there are children, they usually live with the mother (about 85 percent), so most men are free from the constraints not only of marriage but also of child care. Thus, they are freer than ex-wives to date, travel, go to school, take up a hobby, or work at a second job. Especially significant is sexual freedom because males tend to have more money and leisure time.

The experience of ex-husbands on some counts, however, is more negative than that of ex-wives. Many divorced men, especially those from traditional marriages, experience initial difficulty in maintaining a household routine. They are more likely to eat erratically; sleep less; and have difficulty with shopping, cooking, laundry, and cleaning. And since ex-wives usually have legal custody of the children, ex-husbands are able to see their children only relatively rarely and at prescribed times. Thus, they may experience great loneliness because they have lost both wife and children.

The image of liberated ex-husbands as swinging bachelors does not fit many men. Some find dating difficult. They find that women in general have changed, or that they themselves have changed. Many men withdraw from relationships because of their fear of rejection. They may also be wary over concerns about AIDS or other sexually transmitted diseases.

"Her" Divorce. The benefits of divorce for women are few. To be sure, many ex-wives are relieved to have ended an onerous relationship, and some are even freed from a physically abusive one. Some are now liberated from a situation that stifled their educational and career goals. Of course, divorce also frees spouses to seek new and perhaps more fulfilling relationships.

For women, the negatives of divorce clearly outweigh the positives. In particular, women oriented toward traditional gender roles tend to feel helpless and experience a loss of identity associated with their husbands' statuses. Divorced mothers who retain sole custody of their children often feel overwhelmed by the demands of full-time parenting and economic survival. The emotional and schedule overloads that usually accompany solo parenting leave little time for personal pursuits. The result is that divorced women often experience personal and social isolation, especially the feeling of being locked into a child's world. Also, White women cope less well with divorce than do African American women (Price and McKenry, 1988:63). Presumably, this is because Black women have better social supports (extended family networks, friendship and church support networks) than do White women (Taylor et al., 1991:280–281).

Both ex-husbands and ex-wives tend to lose old friends. For the first 2 months or so after the divorce, married friends are supportive and spend time with each of the former mates. But these contacts soon decline because, as individuals, divorced people no longer fit into couple-oriented activities. This disassociation from marital friends is especially acute for women because their child-raising responsibilities tend to isolate them from adult interactions.

On the positive side, women tend to have stronger family and friendship networks than men. These networks provide support, explaining, in part, why women fare better emotionally than men after divorce (Faust and McKibben, 1999). Moreover, because most women receive custody of their children after divorce, they are more connected to their children than noncustodial fathers.

The biggest problem facing almost all divorced women is a dramatic decline in economic resources. Paul Amato, after examining the relevant research, concludes that "overall, mothers' postseparation standard of living [is] only about one half that of fathers" (Amato, 2001:1277). As Lenore Weitzman argues, for most women and children:

> [D]ivorce means precipitous downward mobility—both economically and socially. The reduction in income brings residential moves and inferior housing, drastically diminished or nonexistent funds for recreation and leisure and intense pressures due to inadequate time and money. Financial hardships in turn cause social dislocation and a loss of familiar networks for emotional support and social services, and intensify the psychological stress for women and children alike. On a societal level, divorce increases female and child poverty and creates an ever-widening gap between the economic well-being of divorced men on the one hand, and their children and former wives on the other. (Weitzman, 1985:323)

Divorce has drastic social and economic effects on women and their children. It is a major social problem created by institutions that perpetuate gender discrimination and by divorced fathers who do not contribute to the support of their children (Arendell, 1990).

Children and Divorce

Approximately 65 percent of divorcing couples have minor children, meaning that about 1 million children are involved in new divorces annually. This means that about two-fifths of children—one in three White children and two in three African American children by age 16—will experience the permanent disruption of their parents' marriage. Most of them will remain with their mothers and live in a fatherless home for at least 5 years. Most significant, many children of divorce effectively lose their fathers (Amato and Booth, 1996). "Ten years after a divorce, fathers will be entirely absent from the lives of almost two-thirds of these children" (Weissbourd, 1994:68). Some are twice cursed by the broken relationships of their parents. About one-third of White children and one-half of Black children whose mothers remarry will experience a second divorce before the children reach adulthood.

The crucial question is: What are the consequences of divorce on children? There is clearly the possibility of emotional scars from the period of family conflict and uncertainty prior to the breakup. Children will be affected by the permanency of divorce and the enforced separation from one of the parents. Most commonly, this is separation from their father.

There are the possible negative effects of being raised by a single parent who is overburdened by the demands of children, job, economics, and household maintenance. And there are the negative consequences that may result from the sharp decline in resources available to the family when the parents separate. The data are consistent: female-headed single-parent families, compared to two-parent families and to male-headed single-parent families, have much lower incomes. This severe decline in family resources for female-headed single-parent families produces a number of challenges for children's adjustment, often including moving to a different home and school, eliminating or greatly reducing the probability of a college education, and other alternations in life-styles. As a result of all of these possible outcomes of divorce, children may experience behavioral problems, decline in school performance, and other manifestations of maladjustment.

Summaries of the research on the consequences of divorce on children (Amato, 2001; Amato and Booth, 1997; Amato and Keith, 1991) reveal that children with divorced parents score lower than children with continuously married parents on measure of academic success, conduct, psychological adjustment, self-concept, and social competence. Although the differences between children from divorced and two-parent families were small, they were consistent. Research also finds that children are better off on a variety of outcomes if parents in high-conflict marriages divorced than if they remained married. But because only some divorces are preceded by a high level of conflict, "divorce probably helps fewer children than it hurts" (Amato, 2001:1278).

We must note that the long-term effects of divorce are difficult to measure. Does divorce actually cause the problems displayed by divorced children? Could it be that these troubled children are being raised by troubled parents who eventually divorce (Cherlin, 1999)? We simply cannot know, for example, how the children from a particular family would have fared if the parents had stayed together in a tension-filled household. Reviews of the studies on the effects of divorce on children find that "the 'large majority' of children of divorce . . . do not experience severe or long-term problems: Most do not drop out of school, get arrested, abuse drugs, or suffer long-term emotional distress" (Coontz, 1997:100; see Acock and Demo, 1994; Amato and Keith, 1991).

VIOLENCE IN U.S. FAMILIES

The family has two faces. It can be a haven from an uncaring, impersonal world, a place where love and security prevail. The family members can love each other, care for each other, and be accepting of each other. But there is also a dark side of the family. The family is a common context for violence in society. "People are more likely to be killed, physically assaulted, sexually victimized, hit, beat up, slapped, or spanked in their own homes by other family members than anywhere else, in our society" (Gelles, 1995:450). The intensity that characterizes intimate relationships can give way to conflict. Some families resolve the inevitable tensions that arise in the course of daily living, but in other families conflict gives way to violence.

Violence and the Social Organization of the Family

Although the family is based on love among its members, the way it is organized encourages conflict. First, the family, like all other social organizations, is a power system; that is, power is unequally distributed between parents and children and between spouses, with the male typically dominant. As we saw in Chapter 9, male dominance has been perpetuated by the legal system and religious teaching. Threats to male dominance are often resisted through violence. Parents have authority over their children. They feel they have the right to punish children to shape them in ways the parents consider important.

Unlike most organizations, in which activities and interests are relatively narrow, the family encompasses almost everything. Thus, there are more "events" over which a dispute can develop. Closely related to this phenomenon is the vast amount of time out of each day that family members spend interacting. This lengthy interaction increases the probability of disagreements, irritations, violations of privacy, and the like, which increase the risk of violence. Family privacy is another characteristic that enhances the likelihood of violence. The rule in our society that the home is private has two negative consequences. First, it insulates the family members from the protection that society could provide if a family member becomes too abusive. Second, the rule of privacy often prevents the victims of abuse from seeking outside help.

Spouse Abuse

The marriage license for many is a license to hit. Violence between husbands and wives in the form of beating, slapping, kicking, and throwing objects is relatively common in U.S. society as well as in countries around the world. (See the panel titled "Social Problems in Global Perspective.") That such violence

SOCIAL PROBLEMS IN GLOBAL PERSPECTIVE

WOMEN REPORTEDLY BEATEN BY THEIR SPOUSES

A recent report by the U.S. National Academy of Sciences calls violence against women a serious reproductive health problem. The consequences of violence against women include physical injuries, sexually transmitted diseases, unwanted pregnancies, unsafe abortions, and mental disorders such as depression and anxiety. The fear of domestic violence can make a woman unable to negotiate condom use or practice contraception if, for example, she fears accusations of infidelity.

Source: Population Today 26 (March 1998):6.

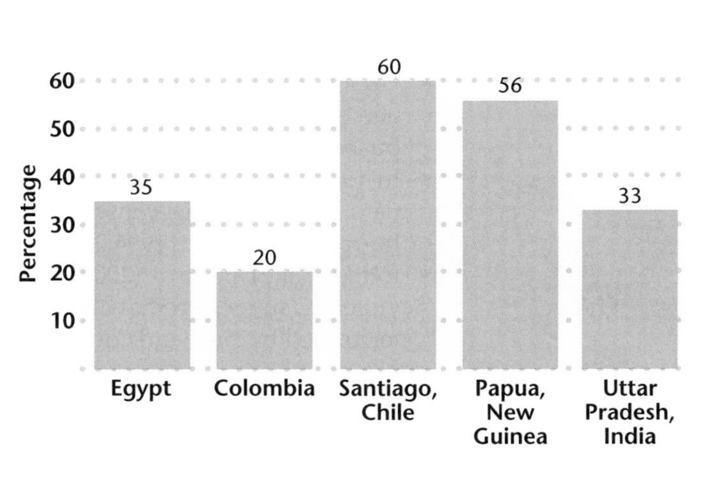

occurs between persons who supposedly joined together because of their mutual love is puzzling indeed. (This section is adapted from Baca Zinn and Eitzen, 2002:346–359.)

The discussion of spouse abuse here is limited in two ways. First, we are concerned with only physical violence. Thus, we do not consider verbal abuse and psychological forms of violence, although these are also cruel and coercive. Second, the discussion of spouse abuse focuses exclusively on the most common type—**wife abuse** by males. Violence directed by wives at husbands is much less likely to occur and is often the result of self-defense because of an abusive husband. The federal government's National Crime Victimization Survey for 1998 revealed that women are far more likely than men to be the victims of violence by intimate partners (Rennison and Welchans, 2000). We do not negate the existence of physical violence by wives, because it does occur; but since the frequency and severity are so much less than in husbands' attacks on wives, we will describe in detail only physical abuse of wives.

Incidence of Wife Abuse. As with other forms of family violence, the actual data on battered wives are impossible to obtain. First, the events generally take place in private with no witnesses other than family members. Second, battered women are often attended by physicians who treat their wounds without asking embarrassing questions or, if they know the cause, do not report the abuse to the authorities. Third, the victims, most commonly, lie about the causes of their injuries because of shame or fear. Lastly, many victims do not go to public agencies for help because they have often found these organizations to be unresponsive. This situation is especially true of the police and the courts, who typically feel that most domestic violence is a private affair and none of their business. Also, the situation often comes down to the wife's word against her husband's word, making prosecution difficult, if not impossible under existing laws.

Within the limitations of the data, the following are some estimates of the extent of wife abuse:

- Criminologist Jim Fyfe estimates that 25 to 45 percent of U.S. homicides stem from domestic fights (cited in Davis, 1994).
- The U.S. Department of Justice estimates that two-thirds of the 2.5 million annual female victims of violence are attacked by intimate friends or family (Bachman, 1994).
- Up to 15 million women have been abused at least once by a male partner. Every 12 seconds, a woman in the United States is beaten by her husband or lover (Peterson, 1994).
- In 1992 the U.S. Surgeon General ranked abuse by husbands and partners as the leading cause of injuries to women age 15 to 44 (cited in Ingrassia and Berk, 1994:26–27).
- Johnson and Ferraro (2001), after reviewing the research on domestic violence, suggested that about 2 million women in the United States are terrorized by husbands or other male partners.

Conditions That Favor Wife Abuse. Although the statistics on wife abuse are somewhat unreliable, we do have a more precise understanding about the conditions under which this phenomenon occurs. Foremost, although battered women are found in all social strata, they tend to be found primarily in families threatened by economic hardships. "Less income usually means more problems and fewer possibilities for solving them" (Chasin, 1997:80).

Unemployment is a very significant variable. Reviewing the research, Stephanie Coontz notes that the rise of family violence is nearly six times greater among people laid off from their jobs than among their employed peers, regardless of whether the perpetrators had a prior history of psychiatric disorder or alcohol abuse (Coontz, 1997:145).

The most common trait associated with wife abuse is the excessive use of alcohol. The problem with assuming a relationship between alcohol abuse and wife abuse is that the relationship is not causal but contributory. Put another way, stress may be the antecedent to both drinking and spouse abuse (Barnett, Miller-Perrin, and Perrin, 1997:198).

It is commonly believed that spouse abuse is transmitted across generations. That is, children learn to behave both by experiencing how others treat them and by observing how their parents treat each other. The assumption is that "children who grow up in families in which they witness interparental violence or experience child abuse are more likely to imitate or tolerate these behaviors than are children from nonviolent homes" (Stith et al., 2000:640). Research, however, finds only a weak relationship between growing up in an abusive family and becoming involved in a violent marital relationship. Thus, we conclude "that while growing up in a violent family may put one at risk for using violence as an adult, the relationship is far from absolute. The fact remains that most adults who grow up in violent homes do not become violent adults" (Stith et al., 2000:641).

A key determinant, then, is the dominance of males throughout society—in politics, the media, the economic system, the schools, and all other institutions—that makes women "inferior." The secondary status of women makes them subject to those with power. One response for men, when faced with threats to their dominance, is to use physical force. Thus, the reduction and eventual elimination of gender inequality throughout society will be a major step in solving the problem of wife beating.

Child Abuse and Neglect

Gelles and Straus have concluded that "with the exception of the police and the military, the family is perhaps the most violent social group, and the home the most violent social setting, in our society" (Gelles and Straus, 1979a:15). "A small child has more chance of being killed or severely injured by its parents than by anyone else. For children, the home is often the most dangerous place to be" (Collins and Coltrane, 1995:476–477). Of the various forms of family violence, violence by parents toward their children is the most prevalent. This problem is reviewed here, focusing on the definition, incidence, causes, and consequences of child abuse. (The following discussion is adapted from Baca Zinn and Eitzen, 2002:360–365.)

Definition. What is child abuse? The extreme cases of torture, scalding, beatings, and imprisonment are easy to place in this category. But there are problems in determining whether many other actions are abusive. For example, one definition of child abuse is violence "carried out with the intention of, or perceived as having the intention of, physically hurting the child" (Gelles and Straus, 1979b:336). This definition includes everything from spanking to murder. The problem is that spanking is used by nine in ten parents and is considered legitimate and acceptable behavior. At what point does appropriate punishment become excessive? This is an important question for which there is, as yet, no universally accepted answer. It is important for counselors, social workers, health practitioners, and the courts to agree on a definition because the consequences for children and parents are enormous. To have a definition that is too lax imperils the health and safety of children, and to have one that is too stringent jeopardizes parents who might incorrectly receive the label of "child abuser," have their children taken from them, and even be imprisoned.

Perhaps the most useful definition, focusing on violence, is that child abuse occurs when there is a nonaccidental physical injury requiring medical attention. But this definition omits the area of child neglect. This type of abuse involves a range of behaviors, including the inadequate feeding of a child or lack of provision of sanitary living conditions. These forms of neglect may be just as damaging to children, physically and mentally, as physical aggression. This type of problem is complicated, too, because the neglect may or may not be willful on the part of parents.

Given these problems with defining **child abuse,** we have chosen an all-inclusive definition: "The distinctive acts of violence and nonviolence and acts of omission and commission that place children at risk" (Gelles, 1976:136). We should not be misled, in using this broad definition, into thinking that all forms of child abuse and neglect are essentially alike, caused by the same sources, and subject to a uniform treatment (Gelles, 1976). We generalize about this problem, but the reader is warned that it is, like all social problems, very complex.

Incidence. The precise extent of child abuse and neglect is impossible to know, for two reasons. First, studies of the phenomena have not used uniform definitions; second, the issue is extremely sensitive to the people involved. To be the perpetrator or victim of child abuse is generally something for which people are stigmatized. Acts of violence and neglect are hidden from society because they occur in private. When asked by a survey researcher if they have ever physically abused their children, abusing parents will most likely deny such an act. Thus, many statistics are taken from police, teachers, social workers, and medical personnel who must assume that the children were victims of abuse. Obviously, such subjective observations are subject to error. As one illustration of the problem of subjectivity, we can note that the parents and children of the middle and upper classes are commonly viewed quite differently by authorities than are those from the lower classes. Trained personnel are more likely to assess a poor child with a black eye as a victim of child abuse than a child from a rich family. Also, of course, many cases of abuse and neglect are never seen by authorities. Official statistics, then, always underreport the actual incidence.

Given the problems with defining and determining the exact incidence of child abuse, probably the best estimate currently available on violence toward children is from a national study by Straus and Gelles conducted in 1985. They found for that year that (1) two-thirds of parents had used some form of violence toward their children, (2) about 2 percent of parents engaged in a violent act with a high probability of injuring the child, and (3) for those children who experienced beatings, it was repeated on average of once every 2 months.

The best official estimate found that in 1994 social service agencies received 3.14 million reports of child maltreatment (physical and sexual abuse or neglect), which translates into a rate of about 47 in every 1,000 children (Weise and Daro, 1995).

Causes. The reasons for the abuse and neglect of children by parents are complex and varied, involving personal, social, and cultural factors. The most commonly assumed cause for abusive behavior toward children is that the perpetrators are mentally ill. This assumption, however, is a myth that hinders the understanding of child abuse (Gelles, 1976:138). In the view of experts, only about 10 percent of maltreating parents have severe personality disorders or psychoses. This is not to say that personal factors are unimportant. Obviously, abusive parents let their aggressive feelings go too far. There are several possible reasons that they do. One important reason is that abused children have a higher probability of becoming abusive parents than do nonabused children. In short, violence tends to beget violence. Some caution is advised concerning this relationship, however. The evidence is that about 30 percent of physically abused children grow up to be abusive adults. Although this is much higher than the overall societal rate of between 2 and 3 percent, we must not ignore the fact that seven in ten abused children *do not* become abusive adults (Gelles, 1993:15).

A relatively common trait of abusing parents is chronic alcohol consumption. This activity reduces the normal restraints inhibiting aggression in the individual. Chronic alcoholism is also associated with a number of other factors that produce strain and disruption in stable family patterns—greater unemployment, poor health, low self-esteem, isolation, and preoccupation with self.

Finally, a caution from Gelles and Strauss; "When our explanations focus on 'kinds of people'—mentally disturbed, poor alcoholics, drug abusers, etc.—we blind ourselves to the structural properties of the family as a social institution that makes it our most violent institution with the exception of the military in time of war" (Gelles and Strauss, 1988:51).

The data from a number of studies indicate that child abuse is more likely to occur in families of low socioeconomic status. We must be careful in interpreting these data because wealthier families are simply better able to hide abuse (e.g., they go to private physicians who may be more reluctant to report signs of abuse in their "respectable" clients than are the doctors ministering to the poor in general hospitals). Nonetheless, the generalization is appropriate that children of the poor are more likely to be abuse victims (Gelles and Straus, 1979a:550). However, as Gelles reminds us:

> This conclusion . . . does not mean that domestic violence is confined to lower-class households. Investigators reporting the differential distribution of violence are frequently careful to point out that child abuse and spouse abuse can be found in families across the spectrum of socioeconomic status. (Gelles, 1990:115)

Unemployment is another condition associated with child abuse. This may lead to poverty, low self-esteem (because of being a failure in a success-oriented society), and depression. The unemployed are also homebound, increasing their interaction with children.

The lack of social supports is also related to child abuse. The research by Gelles and Straus found that the most violent parents had lived in the community less than 2 years; belonged to few, if any, community organizations; and had little contact with friends and relatives.

Men are much more likely than women to be the assailants in all forms of family violence except child abuse, where women are the perpetrators as often as men. Not only do women spend more time with children, but they are much more likely than men to be in stressful economic situations (to head households alone, to be in poverty, and to do less fulfilling and less economically rewarding work). Because she is the primary parent, a mother also feels more responsibility and guilt than does the father for the failures of her children. Given all these differential pressures on women, it is impressive that women commit only 50 percent of child abuse (Breines and Gordon, 1983:504).

Gertrude Williams (1980:597) has argued that there are some additional gender-related issues that promote child abuse by women. In her opinion, the primary reason for child abuse is the pronatalist bias in society. **Pronatalism** is the widespread belief that a woman's only fulfilling activity is motherhood. This ideology forces many women into a role that they may not want. They are also forced into the mother role by the lack of interesting and well-paid work options and by unwanted pregnancies from inadequate contraceptive methods and beliefs opposing abortion. Unwanted children born to a woman in a marginal economic situation are prime candidates for abuse and neglect.

Consequences. Many consequences of child abuse are obvious. About 1,200 children die annually from abuse. Hundreds of thousands endure physical injuries such as fractures, burns, internal damage, and neurological dysfunctions, which may lead to permanent damage or even death. The physical disabilities and/or mental anguish resulting from abuse may lead to problems with learning, speech, and acceptable behavior patterns for the victims. Psychological problems are another obvious consequence from the trauma of being abused by one's parents.

Parental abuse has also been found to be a fundamental reason for a child running away from home. Incest and other forms of child abuse have been found responsible for about half of runaways. Running away during childhood or adolescence generally has additional negative consequences—a higher incidence of malnutrition; health problems; being victims of assault; and criminal activity, especially prostitution, both male and female.

Adults who were mistreated as children have a greater tendency to be violent when compared with those who were not mistreated. As noted earlier, they are more prone to be child abusers themselves. "The rate of abuse in families where the parents were themselves abused as children is approximately six times higher than the rate in the general population" (Vandeven and Newberger, 1994:371).

Violence in the family presents the ultimate paradox—the physical abuse of loved ones in the most intimate of social relationships. The bonds between wife and husband, parent and child, and adult child and parent are based on love, yet for many people these bonds represent a trap in which they are victims of unspeakable abuses.

Although it is impossible to know the extent of battering that takes place in families, the problem these forms of violence represents is not trivial. The threat of violence in intimate relationships exists for all couples and for all parents and children. Violence in the family, however, is not only a problem at the microlevel of family units. It also represents an indictment of the macrolevel—society, its institutions, and the cultural norms that support violence.

The forms of intimate violence occur within a social context. This social context of intimate violence includes a patriarchal ideology that condones and maintains the power of men over women. The social context includes a media barrage with the consistent message that violence solves social problems. The social contexts includes an economy in which poverty, unemployment, and corporate downsizing jeopardize millions of families. The social context includes institutional sexism, institutional racism, and institutional heterosexuality, which make life more difficult for certain categories of people, especially limiting the possibilities for women, people of color, and lesbians and gays. In short, these social forces create the conditions that foster abuse in intimate relationships.

Although the existence of family violence is strongly affected by social forces, individuals acting singly, or with others, can and do shape, resist, and challenge the forces affecting their lives. Concerned citizens—abused women, feminists, and others—have worked through organizations to change the societal forces that encourage abuse. They have also worked to change laws and procedures to protect the victims of abuse.

CHAPTER REVIEW

1. The family is one of the most idealized of all of society's institutions. There are disparities between the common images of the family and real patterns of family life. New sociological research has given us a better understanding of the U.S. family in past and present.
2. Families are embedded in class and race hierarchies. This gives them different connections with institutions that can provide resources for family support. It also creates variation in household and family structure. Class and race are important determinants of the quality of family life.
3. The changing nature of work has a direct impact on the family life in several significant ways: (a) As the need for skilled labor has diminished, many blue-collar families have experienced unemployment or underemployment; (b) both spouses working outside the home has become an economic necessity for many families; and (c) some forms of work have moved into the home, with mixed consequences for women.
4. A major demographic trend since World War II has been the sharp rise in mothers with young children who work outside the home. Thus, a critical need has emerged in society for accessible and acceptable child care. In general, U.S. society has been unresponsive to this need.
5. About one-fourth of all households with children are single-parent families. In 80 percent of the cases these families are headed by a woman. Single-parent families have a number of unique problems, the most prominent being a lack of economic resources.
6. Seventeen percent of all children in the United States live in poverty.
7. The economic situation of children has worsened relative to the elderly.
8. The divorce rate in U.S. society is the highest in the world. The reasons for this high rate are the increased social and financial independence of women, increased affluence, greater tolerance of divorce by religious groups, no-fault divorce laws, and a more lenient public attitude toward divorce.
9. There are several important consequences of divorce: (a) Males and females experience divorce differently, with males having more advantages than females; (b) the economic resources (life chances) for children are reduced; and (c) the trauma for children is heightened for young children, for boys, for large families, and for children whose mother goes to work for the first time after divorce.
10. Researchers on family violence have concluded that the family is among the most violent social groups and that the home is among the most violent settings in U.S. society. The forms of domestic violence are wife beating, child abuse and neglect, incest, and elder abuse.

11. Wife beating is the most frequently occurring crime in the United States. This abuse is most common when husbands (a) are facing economic problems, (b) are underachievers, and (c) have grown up in violent families. What is most important is that wife beating occurs in a society that supports such violence. A key societal support of wife beating is male dominance.

KEY TERMS

Family. Social arrangements whereby people related by ancestry, marriage, or cohabitation live together, form an economic unit, and often raise children.

Household. Residential unit in which members share resources. These units vary in membership and composition. A household is not always a family (parents and children), and a family is not always a household (because it may be separate geographically).

Life chances. Opportunities throughout one's life cycle to live and to experience the good things in society.

Downward mobility. Movement to a lower social class.

Modern family. Nuclear family that emerged in response to the requirements of an urban, industrial society. It consisted of an intact nuclear household unit with a male breadwinner, full-time homemaker wife, and their dependent children.

Postmodern family. Multiplicity of family and household arrangements that has emerged as a result of a number of social factors, such as women in the labor force, divorce, remarriage, and cohabitation arrangements.

Nonfamily household. Persons who live alone or with unrelated individuals.

Dual-worker family. Family in which both spouses are in the labor force.

Family and Medical Leave Act of 1993. Federal law providing workers in establishments with more than 50 workers the right to unpaid job-protected leave for meeting family health needs.

Family values. Conservative phrase supporting the two-parent family. The implication is that all other family arrangements are the source of social problems.

Wife abuse. Use of physical force by a man against his intimate cohabiting partner.

Child abuse. Distinctive acts of violence and nonviolence and acts of omission and commission that place children at risk.

Pronatalism. Strong positive value a society places on having children.

WEBSITES FOR FURTHER REFERENCE

http://www.ncfr.org/

The National Council of Family Relations (NCFR) "provides a forum for family researchers, educators, and practitioners to share in the development and dissemination of knowledge about families and family relationships, establishes professional standards, and works to promote family well-being." The Council provides several sources and articles on topics related to marriage.

http://www.ins.usdoj.gov/graphics/aboutins/history/tools.html

The Immigration and Naturalization Service (INS) provides several historical research tools to help individuals search their family records. In addition, these tools provide a wealth of information for scholarly researchers. "INS history is the history of U.S. immigration since the 1890s. Agency records at the National Archives, many of them long ignored and forgotten, constitute a rich resource for social, ethnic, labor, intellectual, and legal historians, as well as all students of U.S. immigration policy."

http://www.bls.gov/nlsyouth.htm

The National Longitudinal Survey of Youth is a nationally representative sample of 12,686 young men and young women who where 14 to 22 years of age when they were first surveyed in 1979. Data collected during the yearly surveys of the NLSY chronicle important events in the lives of these youth, and provide researchers a unique opportunity to study in detail the life course experiences of a large group of young adults who can be considered representative of all American men and women born in the late 1950s and early 1960s.

http://www.childrensdefense.org/
The Children's Defense Fund exists to provide a strong and effective voice for all the children of America, who cannot vote, lobby, or speak out for themselves

http://www.childrennow.org/
Children Now is a nonpartisan, independent voice for children, working to translate the nation's commitment to children and families into action. Recognized nationally for its policy expertise and up-to-date information on the status of children, Children Now uses communications strategies to reach parents, lawmakers, citizens, business, media, and community leaders, creating attention and generating positive change on behalf of children.

http://www.childtrends.org/
Child Trends is a nonprofit, nonpartisan research organization that studies children, youth, and families through research, data collection, and data analysis.

http://www.ssc.wisc.edu/nsfh/home.htm
The National Survey of Families and Households includes interviews with 13,007 respondents from a national sample. The sample includes a main cross-section of 9,637 households, plus an oversampling of blacks, Puerto Ricans, Mexican Americans, single-parent families, families with stepchildren, cohabiting couples, and recently married persons.

http://www.contemporaryfamilies.org/
The Council on Contemporary Families (CCF) is a nonprofit organization founded in 1996 by a diverse group of family researchers, mental health and social work practitioners, and activists. CCF's goal is to enhance the national conversation about what contemporary families need and how these needs can best be met. "CCF believes that the public is asking for both more accurate information about the condition of America's families and for a more humane and sensitive discussion of the larger social, legal, cultural, and psychological issues that are often simplified under the rubric of 'family values.'" It is their purpose to achieve this goal through the dissemination of educational materials, media coverage, conferences, and seminars.

http://www.familiesandwork.org/
Families and Work Institute is a nonprofit organization that addresses the changing nature of work and family life. This institute is committed to finding "research-based strategies that foster mutually supportive connections among workplaces, families, and communities."

http://www.abanet.org/family/home.html
The Family Law Section of the American Bar Association was organized in 1958 to improve the administration of justice in the field of family law. Today, family law is a fast-growing, complex area with an interstate and at times international character. Well known but rapidly changing areas such as divorce, custody, adoption, alimony, and support are within the scope of the Section, as are emerging issues such as third-party parental rights, marital torts, federal and interstate legislation, mediation, and the complicated questions of paternity, perinatal drug addiction, bankruptcy to deprive divorcing spouses of property, and genetic engineering.

http://www.mincava.umn.edu/
The Minnesota Center Against Violence and Abuse (MINCAVA) seeks to provide a quick and easy-to-use access point to the extensive electronic resources on the topic of violence and abuse available through the Internet.

http://www.cavnet2.org/
The Communities Against Violence Network (CAVNET) is an international network of antiviolence experts and advocates. The website serves as a tool for disseminating new research information about violence and abuse, as well as providing tips for avoiding it.

http://www.stepfam.org/
The Stepfamily Association of America is a national organization dedicated to providing support and guidance to families with children from previous relationships . . . stepfamilies. This association's vision is that stepfamilies in the United States will be accepted, supported, and successful.

http://www.divorceonline.com/
Divorce Online, an electronic resource for people involved in, or facing the prospect of, divorce provides free articles and information on the financial, legal, psychological, real-estate, and other aspects of divorce. Additionally, the Professional Referral section of Divorce Online provides a listing of professional providers.

http://ameristat.org/
Ameristat.Org is a website developed by the Population Reference Bureau in partnership with the Social Science Data Analysis Network. It provides the latest statistics on marriage, family, children, fertility, foreign-born populations, income and poverty, and the elderly.

16 Education

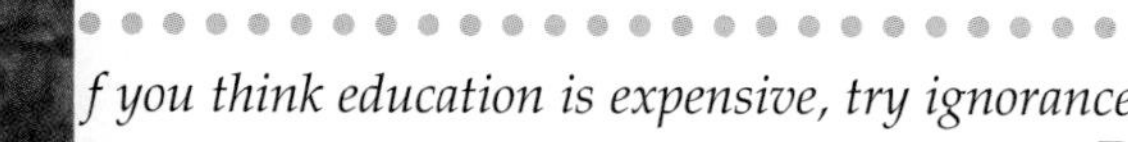

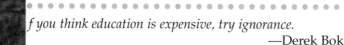

f you think education is expensive, try ignorance.

—Derek Bok

This chapter examines one of society's basic institutions—education. The chapter is divided into four sections. The first describes the characteristics of U.S. education. The second focuses on how corporate society reproduces itself through education—in particular, how the schools socialize youth in accordance with their class position and point them toward factory, service, bureaucratic, or leadership roles in the economy. The third section describes the current role of education in perpetuating inequality in society. The concluding section describes alternatives to eliminate the race and class biases in education.

CHARACTERISTICS OF EDUCATION IN THE UNITED STATES

Education as a Conserving Force

The formal system of education in U.S. society (and in all societies) is conservative because the avowed function of the schools is to teach newcomers the attitudes, values, roles, specialties, information, and training necessary for the maintenance of society. In other words, the special task of the schools is to preserve the culture, not to transform it. Thus, the schools indoctrinate their pupils in the culturally prescribed ways. Children are taught to be patriotic. They learn the myths of the superiority of their nation's heritage; they learn who are the heroes and who are the villains. Jules Henry has put it this way:

> Since education is always against some things and for others, it bears the burden of the cultural obsessions. While the Old Testament extols without cease the glory of the One God, it speaks with equal emphasis against the gods of the Philistines; while the children of the Dakota Indians learned loyalty to their own tribe, they learned to hate the Crow; and while our children are taught to love American democracy, they are taught contempt for the totalitarian regimes. (Henry, 1963: 285–286)

There is always an explicit or implicit assumption in U.S. schools that the American way is the only really right way. When this assumption is violated on the primary and secondary school level by the rare teacher who asks students to consider the viability of world government or who proposes a class on the teachings of Karl Marx or about world religions, then strong enough pressures usually occur from within the school (administrators, school board) or from without (parents, the American Legion, Daughters of the American Revolution, the Christian right) to quell the disturbance. As a consequence, creativity and a questioning attitude are curtailed in school, as Parenti points out forcefully:

> Among the institutions . . . , our educational system looms as one of the more influential purveyors of dominant values. From the earliest school years, children are taught to compete individually rather than work cooperatively for common goals and mutual benefit. Grade-school students are fed stories of their nation's exploits that might be more valued for their inspirational nationalism than for their historical accuracy. Students are instructed to believe in America's global virtue and moral superiority and to fear and to hold a rather uncritical view of American politico-economic institutions. One

> nationwide survey of 12,000 children (grades two to eight) found that most youngsters believe "the government and its representatives are wise, benevolent and infallible, that whatever the government does is for the best." The study found that teachers concentrate on the formal aspects of representative government and accord scant attention to the influences that wealthy, powerful groups exercise over political life. Teachers in primary and secondary schools who wish to introduce radical critiques of American politico-economic institutions do so often at the risk of jeopardizing their careers. High school students who attempt to sponsor unpopular speakers and explore controversial views in student newspapers have frequently been overruled by administrators and threatened with disciplinary action.
>
> School texts at the elementary, high-school, and even college levels seldom give more than passing mention to the history of labor struggle and the corporate exploitation of working people at home and abroad. Almost nothing is said of the struggles of Native Americans, indentured servants, small farmers, and Latino, Asian, and European immigrant labor. The history of resistance to slavery, racism, and U.S. expansionist wars is largely untaught in U.S. schools at any level. (Parenti, 1995b:35; see also Loewen, 1995)

Mass Education

People in the United States have a basic faith in education. This faith is based on the assumption that a democratic society requires an educated citizenry so that individuals can participate in the decisions of public policy. For this reason they not only provide education for all citizens but also compel children to remain in school at least until the eighth grade or until age 16 (although the law varies somewhat from state to state).

Who can quarrel with the belief that all children should be compelled to attend school, since it should be for their own good? After all, the greater the educational attainment, the greater is the likelihood of larger economic rewards and upward social mobility. However, to compel a child to attend school for 6

Children are taught to be patriotic as part of their cultural indoctrination.

hours a day, 5 days a week, 40 weeks a year, for at least 10 years, is quite a demand. The result is that many students are in school for the wrong reason. The motivation is compulsion, not interest in acquiring skills or curiosity about their world. This involuntary feature of U.S. schools is unfortunate because so many school problems are related to the lack of student interest.

As a result of the goal of and commitment to mass education, an increasing proportion of people have received a formal education. In 1960, for example, 41 percent of Americans age 25 and older had completed high school. This proportion increased to 67 percent in 1970 and 84 percent in 2000 (U.S. Bureau of the Census, cited in *Chronicle of Higher Education,* 2001:22).

Local Control of Education

Although the state and federal governments finance and control education in part, the bulk of the money and control for education comes from local communities. There is a general fear of centralization of education—into a statewide educational system or, even worse, federal control. Local school boards (and the communities themselves) jealously guard their autonomy. Because, as is commonly argued, local people know best the special needs of their children, local boards control allocation of monies, curricular content, and the rules for running the schools, as well as the hiring and firing of personnel.

There are several problems with this emphasis on local control. First, tax money from the local area traditionally finances the schools. Whether the tax base is strong or weak has a pronounced effect on the quality of education received (a point we return to later in this chapter). Second, local taxes are almost the only outlet for a taxpayers' revolt. Dissatisfaction with high taxes (federal, state, and local) on income, property, and purchases is often expressed at the local level in defeated school bonds and school tax levies. A current population trend—families with school-age children declined from 46 percent of the U.S. population in 1950 to 33 percent in 1999—increases the ever-greater likelihood of the defeat of school issues. Third, because the democratic ideal requires that schools be locally controlled, the ruling body (school board) should represent all segments of that community. Typically, however, the composition of school boards has overrepresented the business and professional sectors and overwhelmingly underrepresented blue-collar workers, the poor, and various minority groups. The result is a governing body that is typically conservative in outlook and unresponsive to the wishes of people unlike themselves.

Fourth, local control of education may mean that the religious views of the majority (or, at least, the majority of the school board) may intrude in public education. An explicit goal of the Christian Coalition, a conservative religious organization founded by Pat Robertson, is to win control of local school boards. Its agenda opposes globalism, restricts sex education to the promotion of family values, promotes school prayer and the teaching of biblical creationism in science classes, and censors books that denigrate Christian values (favorite targets are, for example, *Catcher in the Rye* by J. D. Salinger and John Steinbeck's *The Grapes of Wrath*).

The following are some examples by states and cities to install religious values in schools:

- In 1995, the Alabama Board of Education voted to insert a sticker in school biology textbooks that reads, in part: "This textbook discusses evolution, a controversial theory some scientists present as a scientific explanation for the origin of living things, such as plants, animals, and humans. No one was present when life first appeared on earth. Therefore, any statement about life's origins should be considered as theory, not fact" (quoted in Smolkin, 1999:2A,33A).

- In 1999, the Kansas Board of Education voted to delete virtually any mention of evolution from the state's science curriculum. As of 2000, twelve states do not use the word *evolution* in the public school science curricula (Marklein, 2000).
- Although the U.S. Supreme Court outlawed the posting of the Ten Commandments in public schools, numerous local school boards believe they can survive legal challenges if the commandments are posted in a display with other historical documents, such as the Magna Carta and the Declaration of Independence (Johnson, 2000).

A final problem with local control is the lack of curriculum standardization across the nation's 15,367 school districts and 50 states:

> Unlike virtually every other industrialized country, the United States has no national curriculum and no agency that supervises the development of classroom materials. *Each of the nation's 15,367 school districts is a kingdom unto itself*—with the power to decide what its students will be taught. [Italics added.] (Kantrowitz and Wingert, 1992:59)

Arguing for a common curriculum, Albert Shanker, the president of the American Federation of Teachers, states:

> A common curriculum means that there is agreement about what students ought to know and be able to do and, often, about the age and grade at

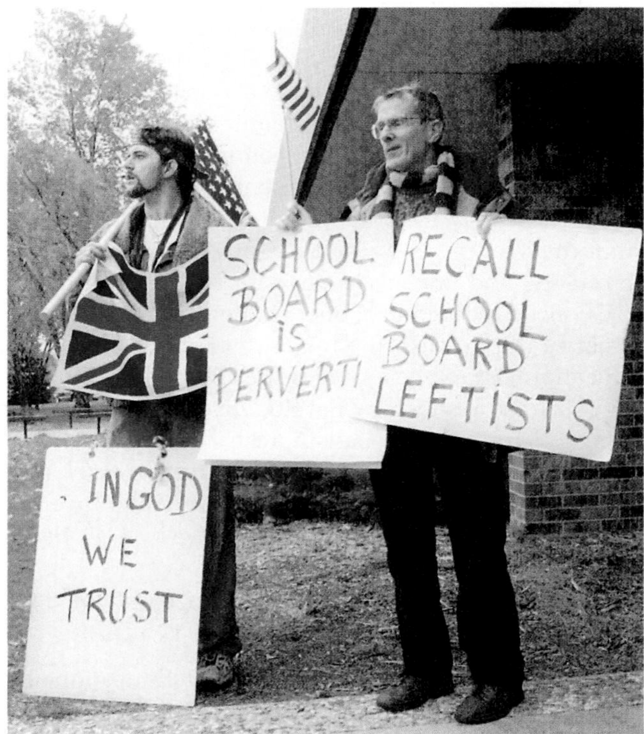

A goal of some conservative Christian groups is to place members on local school boards to oppose liberal ideas and to promote their version of "family" values.

> which they should be able to accomplish these goals. . . . In most countries with a common curriculum, linkage of curriculum, assessment and teacher education is tight. . . . In the U.S., we have no such agreement about curriculum—and there is little connection between what students are supposed to learn, the knowledge on which they are assessed, and what we expect our teachers to know. (Shanker, 1991:E7)

The lack of a common curriculum has at least two negative consequences. First, there is a wide variation in the preparation of students. Second, because families move on the average of once every 5 years (and the rate is probably higher for families with school-age children), there are large numbers of children each year who find the requirements of their new schools different, sometimes very different, from their previous schools.

The educational system in the United States is moving toward greater fragmentation rather than less. More and more parents are opting to send their children to private schools (about 12 percent) or to school them at home (about 2 percent). The number of children home schooled, for example, increased from 301,000 in 1990 to 850,000 in 1999 and, according to U.S. Department of Education, the number of home-schooled children is growing about 15 percent a year (Toppo, 2001; Winters, 2000). Taxpayer-funded charter schools are also growing rapidly. These schools are based on a hybrid "free-market" system in which educators, students, and parents choose a curriculum and educational philosophy free from the dictates of school boards and educational bureaucracies but financed publicly. In 2000 there were some 1,700 charter schools with Arizona having 351. Vouchers are another plan that splinters the educational system. This plan gives parents a stipulated amount of money per child that can be used to finance that child's education in any school, public or private. This plan sets up an educational "free market" where schools have to compete for students. This competition will, theoretically, improve schools because they must provide what parents want for their children, whether that be better discipline, emphasis on learning the fundamentals, religious instruction, focus on the arts, vocational training, or college preparation.

Each of these educational reforms that are underway have strengths and weaknesses (for a summary, see Gardner, 2000). Most important, they represent a trend that is rapidly dividing and subdividing the educational system. For many, this is viewed as a strength, representing the core American values of individualism and competition. Others see this trend as fragmenting further an already disaggregated educational system. Moreover, they see the charter and voucher systems as working against inclusiveness (Fuller, 2000), thereby increasing the gap between the "winners" and "losers" in U.S. society.

Competitive Nature of U.S. Education

Not surprisingly, schools in a highly competitive society are competitive. Competition extends to virtually all school activities. The compositions of athletic teams, cheerleading squads, pom-pon squads, debate teams, choruses, drill teams, bands, and dramatic play casts are almost always determined by competition among classmates. Grading in courses, too, is often based on the comparison of individuals (grading on a curve) rather than on measurement against a standard. To relieve boredom in the classroom, teachers often invent competitive games such as "spelling baseball" or "hangman." In all these cases the individual learns at least two lessons: (1) Your classmates are enemies, for if they succeed, they do so at your expense; and (2) you'd better not fail—fear of failure is the great motivator, not intellectual curiosity or love of knowledge.

"Sifting" and "Sorting" Function of Schools

Schools play a considerable part in choosing the youth who come to occupy the higher-status positions in society. Conversely, school performance also sorts out those who will occupy the lower rungs in the occupational-prestige ladder. Education is, therefore, a selection process. The sorting is done with respect to two different criteria: a child's ability and his or her social class background. Although the goal of education is to select on ability alone, ascribed social status (the status of one's family, race, and religion) has a pronounced effect on the degree of success in the educational system. The school is analogous to a conveyor belt, with people of all social classes getting on at the same time but leaving the belt in accordance with social class—the lower the class, the shorter the ride.

Preoccupation with Order and Control

Most administrators and teachers share a fundamental assumption that school is a collective experience requiring subordination of individual needs to those of the school. U.S. schools are characterized, then, by constraints on individual freedom. The school day is regimented by the dictates of the clock. Activities begin and cease on a timetable, not in accordance with the degree of interest shown or whether students have mastered the subject. Another indicator of order is the preoccupation with discipline (i.e., absence of unwarranted noise and movement, and concern with the following of orders).

In their quest for order, some schools also demand conformity in clothing and hairstyles. Dress codes are constraints on the freedom to dress as one pleases. School athletic teams also restrict freedom, and these restrictions are condoned by the school authorities. Conformity is also demanded in what to read, where to set the margins on word processors, and how to give the answers the teacher wants.

The many rules and regulations found in schools meet a number of expressed and implicit goals. The school authorities' belief in order is one reason for this dedication to rules. Teachers are rated not on their ability to get pupils to learn but, rather, on the degree to which their classrooms are quiet and orderly. The community also wants order.

The paradoxes listed here indicate the many profound dilemmas in U.S. education. They set the foundation for the remaining sections of this chapter, which deal with the crises facing education and with some alternative modes.

- Formal education encourages creativity but curbs the truly creative individual from being too disruptive to society.
- Formal education encourages the open mind but teaches dogma.
- Formal education has the goal of turning out mature students but does not give them the freedom essential to foster maturity.
- Formal education pays lip service to meeting individual needs of the students but in actuality encourages conformity at every turn.
- Formal education has the goal of allowing all students to reach their potential, yet it fosters kinds of competition that continually cause some people to be labeled as failures.

- Formal education is designed to allow people of the greatest talent to reach the top, but it systematically benefits certain categories of people regardless of their talent: the middle-and upper-class students who are White.

EDUCATION AND INEQUALITY

Education is presumed by many people to be the great equalizer in U.S. society —the process by which the disadvantaged get their chance to be upwardly mobile. The data in Figure 16.1 show, for example, that the higher the educational attainment, the higher the income. But these data do not in any way demonstrate equality of opportunity through education. They show clearly that African Americans and Latinos with the same educational attainment as Whites receive lower economic rewards at every educational level. These differences reflect discrimination in society, not just in schools. This section examines the ways that the schools help to perpetuate class and race inequities.

The evidence that educational performance is linked to socioeconomic background is clear and irrefutable (we include race/ethnicity along with economic status since they are highly correlated).

- There is a strong relationship between test scores in reading, writing, and mathematics and poverty (see Figure 16.2, p. 474, for an analysis of the Denver school district, which is representative of the correlation).
- Children in the poorest families are five times as likely as children in wealthier families to drop out of high school (Children's Defense Fund, 2001:62).
- College students whose families are in the top income quartile earn eight times as many bachelor's degrees by age 24 as students from the bottom quartile (Scott, 2001). Moreover, students from high-income families complete their college educations faster than students from low-income

FIGURE 16.1

Median Annual Income for Full-Time Workers by Educational Attainment for People 25 Years Old and Over by Race and Hispanic Origin: 2000

Source: U.S. Bureau of the Census. 2000. "Educational Attainment in the United States: March 2000. "*Current Population Reports.* Series P20-536. Washington, DC: U.S. Government Printing Office.

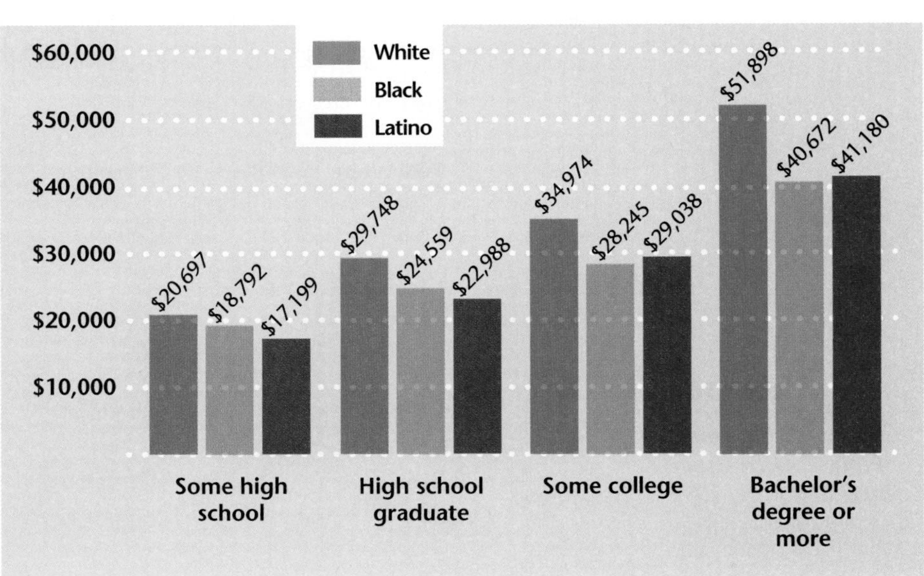

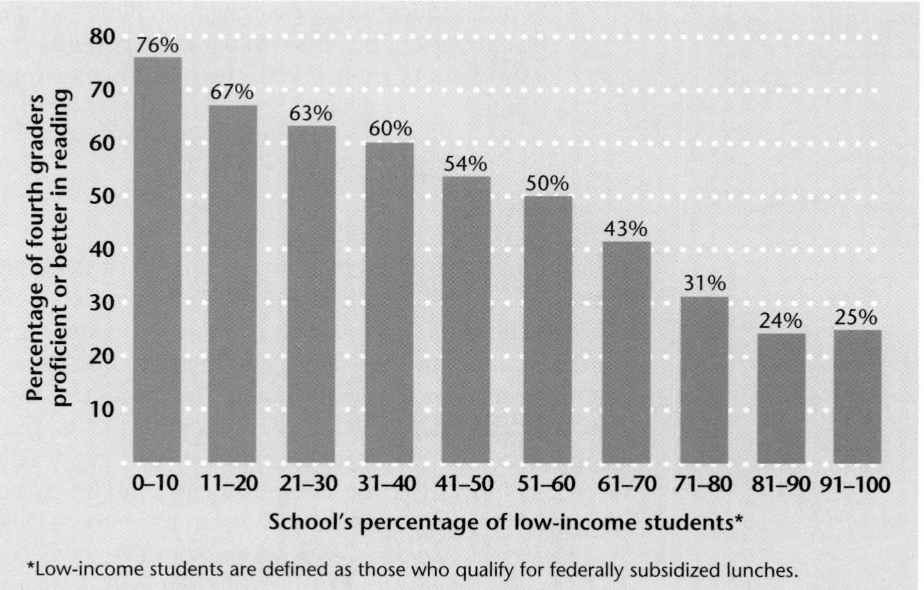

FIGURE 16.2

Poverty and Achievement in Denver Schools, 1999

Source: Denver Post (February 27, 2000):1A.

families (40 percent get a degree within 5 years, compared to only 6 percent of those from low-income families [Gay, 2000]).

- Achievement gaps in reading, writing, and mathematics persist between minority and White students (see Figure 16.3).
- African American, Latino, and Native American students lag behind their White peers in graduation rates and most other measures of student performance. Although the gap between test scores of African American and White students widened from 1990 to 1999 (Zernike, 2000), a longer range comparison shows that from 1971 to 1996 the Black–White reading gap shrank by almost half and the math gap by a third (Jencks and Phillips, 1998).
- African Americans and especially Latinos have much higher dropout rates than Whites (Henry, 2001a). As a result, in 1999, 84 percent of

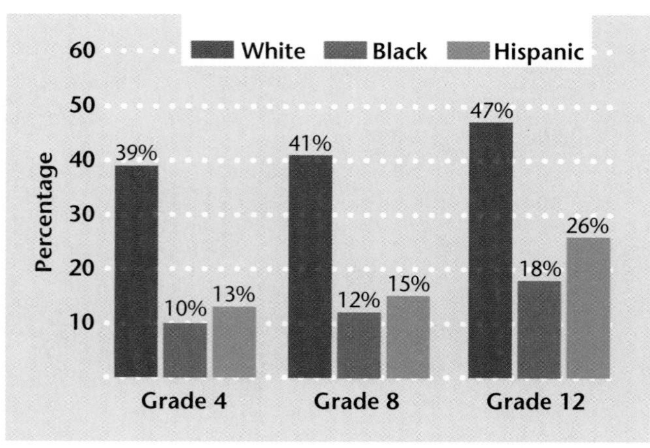

FIGURE 16.3

Reading Achievement Proficiency by Grade Level and Race, 1998

Source: USA Today (May 30, 2000):16A.

Whites age 25 and older had at least a high school diploma, compared to 77 percent of Blacks and 56 percent of Latinos (Armas, 2000b). Latinos, however, are not a homogenous category: among Latinos 25 and older, 23 percent of Cubans had a college degree (Whites had a 25 percent graduation rate), compared to 17 percent of Central and South Americans, 13 percent of Puerto Ricans, and 7 percent of Mexicans (Armas, 2001).

- Black, Latino, and Native American students are suspended or expelled in numbers disproportionate to those of Whites (Henry, 2000).

These social class and racial gaps in academic achievement are found in almost every school and district in the United States. On the surface these patterns reinforce the Social Darwinist assumptions that the affluent are successful because they are intelligent, and, conversely, the poor and minorities are at society's bottom because they do not have the requisite abilities to be successful. Similarly, dysfunctional families, unmotivated students, and the culture of poverty are believed by some to explain the academic achievement gap. We argue, to the contrary, that structural factors explain why the poor and minorities are disadvantaged in our supposedly meritocratic educational system. In effect, the educational system is stacked in favor of middle- and upper-class children and against children from the lowest classes.* At least four interrelated factors explain why the education system tends to reinforce the socioeconomic status differentials in the United States: finances, curriculum, segregation, and personnel. We examine the first three factors in the following sections. The next section discusses school finances.

Financing Public Education

Schools in the United States reflect the economic divide that exists in society:

> In America, the type of education provided, the way its funded and the content of the curriculum are local matters directed by local authorities. The result is easy to see. Across America one sees the extremes: from schools that resemble shining mansions on a hill to ramshackle, dilapidated structures. (Kamau, 2001:8I).

Approximately 86 percent of U.S. children attend public schools (12 percent attend private schools and about 2 percent are home schooled). These schools receive funds from three governmental sources—about 7 percent from the federal government, and depending on the allocation within each state, about 43 percent from the state, and 50 percent from property taxes in each district within the state. The result of this distribution is that schools are funded unequally in the United States, with public schools being more successful in educating children in middle-class communities but often failing children in poor neighborhoods.

*We have phrased the sentence to focus on the system, not the victims, contrary to the typical response, which is to focus on the **cultural deprivation** of the poor. That approach attacks the home and culture of poor people. It assumes that these people perform inadequately because they are handicapped by their culture. Observers cannot, however, make the value judgment that a culture is deprived. They can note only that their milieu does not prepare children to perform in schools geared for the middle class. In other words, children of the poor and/or minority groups are not nonverbal; they are very verbal, but not in the language of the middle class.

Kirk Anderson

Equal opportunity in education (at least measured by equal finances) has not been accomplished nationwide because wealthier states are able to pay much more per pupil than are poorer states. The top-spending states, for example, invest more than double the amount per pupil than those states spending the least. Because the federal government provides only about 7 percent of the money for public schools, equalization from state to state is impossible as long as education is funded primarily by state and local governments because both entities vary in wealth and commitment to public education.

The disparities in per-pupil expenditures within a given state are also great, largely because of the tradition of funding public schools through local property taxes. This procedure is discriminatory because rich school districts can spend more money than poor ones on each student—and at a lower taxing rate. Thus, suburban students are more advantaged than are students from the inner city; districts with business enterprises are favored over agricultural districts; and districts with natural resources are better able to provide for their children than are districts with few resources. In some states the disparity in spending for each pupil may be as much as three times more in affluent districts than in poor areas. In New York State, the poorest districts, mostly in the city, spend $2,800 per child less than the richest, mostly located in the suburbs, a finance gap of some $60,000 less per class (Symonds, 2001:76). This gap is even greater when one considers the monies raised in each district from bake sales and other fund raisers, soda machine contracts, and foundation contributions. In Colorado, for example, Pitkin County (the location of various affluent mountain communities) schools in 1999 raised an extra $2,194 per student compared to just $163 in Saguache County (an arid, rural area with a high concentration of poverty) (*Denver Post*, 2001).

There have been a number of court challenges to unequal funding within states with systems in several states judged unconstitutional. In 2001, for example, a New York court ruled that New York's funding system deprived students of the education guaranteed by the state constitution and violated federal civil rights laws because it disproportionately hurt minority students in New York

City schools (reported in Children's Defense Fund, 2001:64). Various schemes have been proposed to meet the objections of the courts, but inequities remain even in the more progressive states. Progressive plans to address financial inequities are fought by the affluent districts and their constituents because, they argue, their taxes should be spent on their children, not others.

Some have argued that the money spent per pupil in a district is not related to educational performance. Bob Chase, president of the National Education Association, argues the opposite, while acknowledging that money alone will not suffice:

> Money matters because books matter, small classes matter, and the one-on-one interactions between teacher and student matter. Generations of wealthy families who have sent their children to expensive private prep schools have long understood the importance of money in education. . . . The crucial point is this: You need money to create excellent schools. . . . (Chase, 1997:20)

Research shows that poor students and the schools serving them:

- Have one computer for every sixteen students, compared to one computer for every seven students in the affluent schools (Mendels, 2000).
- Have teachers that are underpaid relatively to their peers in affluent schools. In Los Angeles, for example, teachers with 5 years experience make $29,500, while teachers in nearby Beverly Hills with similar experience make $73,400 (Newton, 2000). The result is that affluent schools are more likely to retain their most experienced and highly qualified teachers, while poor districts will have trouble keeping excellent teachers.
- Are more likely than their more affluent peers to be taught by teachers who did not major in the subject area in which they teach.
- Are more likely to attend schools in need of repairs, renovations, and modernization.
- Are more likely to attend schools that lack some necessary classroom materials.
- Have higher pupil/teacher ratios.

Family Economic Resources

The average combined SAT (Scholastic Aptitude Test) scores for youth from families whose annual income was $70,000 or more is about 200 points higher than youth from families whose income is $10,000 less. By race, Whites score 100 points higher than African Americans on average (U.S. Department of Education, 2001). How are we to explain these differences on the SATs by income and race? Among the reasons are the benefits that come from economic privilege. Poor parents (disproportionately people of color), most without health insurance, are unable to afford prenatal care, which increases the risk of babies being born at low birth weight, a condition that may lead to learning disabilities. As these poor children age, they are less likely to receive adequate nutrition, decent medical care, and a safe and secure environment. These deficiencies increase the probability of their being less alert, less curious, and less able to interact effectively with their environment than are healthy children.

Poor children are more likely than the children of the affluent to attend schools with poor resources, which, as we have seen, means that they are less likely to receive an enriched educational experience. Similarly, most poor young people live in communities that have few opportunities to apply academic skills and build new ones because they are either not available or not accessible (libraries, planetariums, summer camps, zoos, nature preserves, museums). The lack of community resources is especially destructive during the summer months, the time when children doing least well in school (a group that is disproportionately poor) slide backward the farthest.

Children from poor families cannot afford private early development programs, which prepare children for school. They can be in Head Start, but these government programs only have funding for about one-third of those eligible.

The level of affluence also affects how long children will stay in school because schools, even public schools, are costly. There are school fees (many school districts, e.g., charge fees for participation in music, athletics, and drama), supplies, meals, transportation, and other costs of education. These financial demands pressure youngsters from poorer families to drop out of school prematurely to go to work. The children from the middle and upper classes, not constrained by financial difficulties, tend to stay in school longer, which means better jobs and pay in the long run:

> These children [dropouts]—most of them poor, Black or Hispanic—are America's educational underclass. While middle-class kids enjoy gleaming laboratories and computers, these children struggle in an educational Third World where supplies are shoddy, teachers are baffled by a barrage of different languages, and discrimination handicaps even the brightest and most willing child. From this classroom ghetto, it's a short journey to the world of adults trapped in joblessness and poverty. (Horn, 1987:66)

The affluent also give their children educational advantages such as home computers, travel experiences abroad and throughout the United States, visits to zoos, libraries, and various cultural activities, and summer camps to hone their skills and enrich their experiences in such activities as sports, music, writing, and computers. Another advantage available to the affluent is the hiring of tutors to help children having difficulty in school or to transform good students into outstanding ones. And parents may also send children to specialized tutorials such as computer schools:

> Consider FutureKids, the world's largest computer-school chain for children. The program, which costs up to $25 an hour, goes where the money is. There are 25 franchises in Los Angeles, but none in the inner city. (*Christian Science Monitor*, 1994:1)

Affluent parents may also use their privilege to get other advantages for their children. For example, in addition to spending money for their children to enroll in SAT preparation classes, they may get a psychologist's or medical doctor's recommendation for a youth to be identified as having a learning disability so that he or she would be given extra time to complete tests such as the SAT. The College Board reports that while only a tiny fraction—1.9 percent—of students nationwide are given special accommodations for taking the SAT, the percentage jumps fivefold for students from New England prep schools (exclusive private schools that send their students to elite colleges and universities). In contrast, at ten Los Angeles inner-city high schools, no students sought the time accommodation. This, despite the fact that learning disabilities are more frequently found in economically disadvantaged populations (Weiss, 2000).

The well-to-do often send their children to private schools (about 12 percent of U.S. children attend these schools). Parents offer several rationales for sending their children to private schools. Some do so for religious reasons. Another reason is that private schools, unlike public schools, are selective in whom they accept. Thus, parents can ensure that their children will interact with children similar to theirs in race (some private schools were expressly created so that White children could avoid attending integrated public schools) and social class. Similarly, private schools are much more likely than public schools to get rid of troublesome students (e.g., behavioral problems and low achievers), thereby providing an educational environment more conducive to learning and achievement. A final reason for attending private schools is that the most elite of them provide a demanding education and entry to the most elite universities, which, in turn, lead to placement in top positions in the professional and corporate occupational worlds.

The most exclusive and expensive private schools are boarding schools with tuition at the top-tier schools at $25,000 or more (S. G. Smith, 2001). Traditionally, these schools catered to the White, male, and rich students, with a smaller number serving female equivalents. The graduates of these schools attend the most prestigious universities, later to become, for the most part, lawyers, doctors, educators, investment bankers, and even presidents. For example, George W. Bush attended Andover as did his father, George H. W. Bush; John Kennedy graduated from Choate, as did Franklin D. Roosevelt from Groton. Three of the unsuccessful presidential candidates in 2000 attended boarding schools (Al Gore, St. Albans; John McCain, Episcopal; and Steve Forbes, Brooks). This old Establishment bias is breaking down somewhat as about one-third of students now receive some financial aid and schools with a national enrollment have about 20 percent minority students.

Obtaining a college degree is an important avenue to later success. In 1998, the average income of families headed by a high school graduate was $48,434, while a college degree lifted family income to $85,423, and a professional degree meant a family income of $101,670 (Reich, 2000c). The payoff in jobs and pay is directly related to the prestige of the college or university attended, and this depends primarily on one's family finances.

The cost of college is high and getting higher. Throughout the 1980s and 1990s, the cost of college rose at a rate more than twice the inflation rate. In 1999–2000, on average, the total annual expenses to attend a private school as a resident were $23,651 compared to $10,909 for a public school (Reisberg, 1999). The cost of room, board, fees, and tuition at the nation's most exclusive schools is about $35,000 for a single school year. The high costs, coupled with declining scholarship monies, preclude college attendance not only for the able poor but also increasingly for children of the working and lower middle classes. The ability to pay for college reinforces the class system in two ways. The lack of money shuts out the possibility of college for some students. For students who do attend college, money stratifies. The poorest, even those who are talented, are most likely to attend community colleges, which are the least expensive; these schools emphasize technical careers and are therefore limiting in terms of later success (around 45 percent of the nation's college students attended community colleges). Students with greater resources are likely to attend public universities. Finally, students with the greatest financial backing are the most likely to attend elite and prestigious private institutions. It is important to note that although talent is an important variable, it is money—not ability—that places college students in this stratified system. For example, students from upper-class families are given favorable ratings by admission committees at elite universities if they are children of alumni or children of big contributors to the university's fund-raising campaigns.

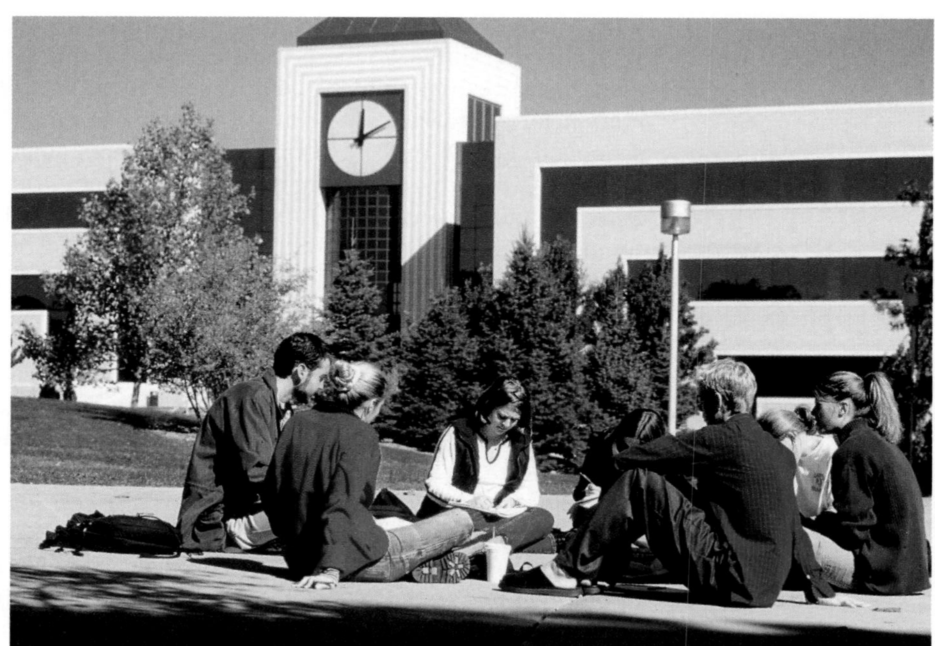

Racial minorities and children from poor families are underrepresented among college students.

Because racial minorities are much more likely than Whites to be poor or near poor, they are underrepresented in colleges and among college graduates. For example, for adults 25 years and older, 28 percent of Whites have a college degree, compared to 16 percent of African Americans, and 11 percent of Latinos (U.S. Department of Education, 2001:17). Moreover, racial minorities are more likely than Whites to attend community colleges and schools that are less funded, and they are more likely to leave college with greater debts than White students.

The disproportionately low number of college degrees earned by minorities is reflected in the relatively low number of students who attend and graduate from graduate school (see Table 16.1 by gender and race). This, of course, results in a low proportion of minorities in the various professions in the near

TABLE 16.1

Recipients of Doctorates from U.S. Universities by Gender and Race, 1990 and 1998

Characteristic	*1990 (%)*	*1998 (%)*
Male	63.7	58.0
Female	36.3	42.0
White	86.5	78.1
Black	3.8	5.1
Asian/Pacific Islander	4.9	8.8
Native American	0.4	0.6
Latino	3.1	4.2
Other/unknown	1.4	3.1

Source: National Science Foundation. 1998. "Survey of Earned Doctorates." Washington, DC future. Of special significance is their low representation among full-time faculty in higher education now and projected for the future.

Asian Americans, unlike other racial minorities in the United States, are more likely than Whites to attend college (55 percent of those age 18 to 24, compared to the U.S. average of 34 percent). This fact is misleading, however, because it hides the ethnic diversity within this social category. Figure 16.4 shows that five Asian groups are below the U.S. average, and it also shows a range in college attendance of 67 percent of Chinese young adults to only 26 percent of Laotian young adults. Most important, these differences reflect social class differences among these Asian subgroups.

Curriculum

U.S. schools are essentially middle or upper class. The written and spoken language in the schools, for example, is expected to be middle class. For children of the poor, however, English (at least middle-class English) may be a second language. English is clearly a second language for many Latino and Asian youngsters, making their success in U.S. schools especially problematic. Standardized tests often ask the student to determine how objects are similar. For students whose first language is Spanish, this task presents a problem. "Spanish, which separates words into masculine and feminine categories, tends to emphasize the differences between objects. This interferes with tasks that require the subject to describe how objects are similar" (Philippus, 1989:59). The schools, in general, have failed to recognize the special needs of these and other bilingual students, which results in their overall poor student performance.

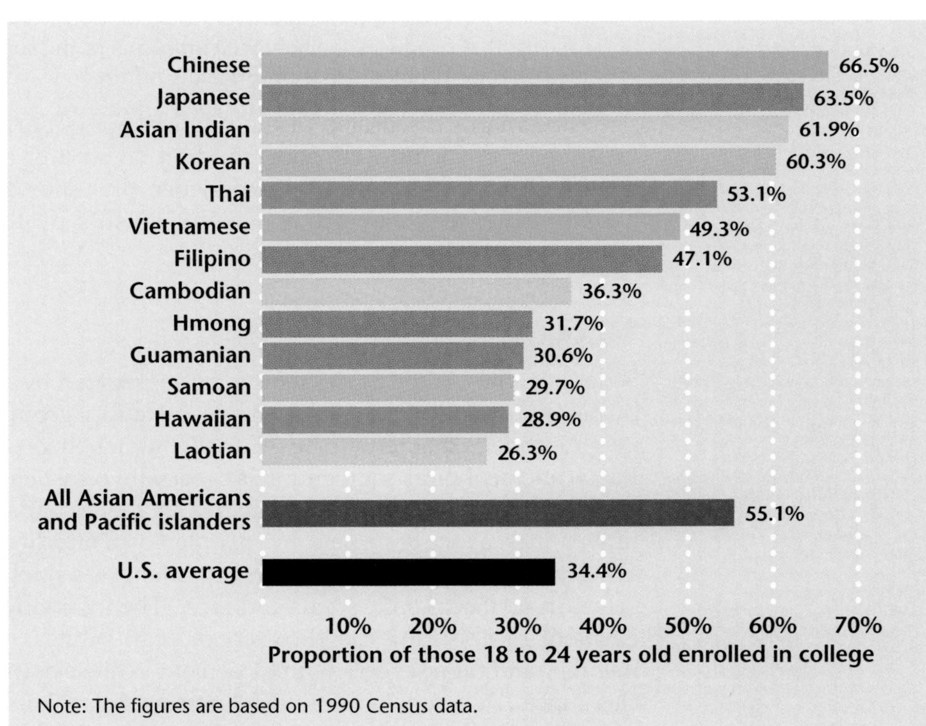

FIGURE 16.4

Asian Americans and Pacific Islanders and College Enrollment

Source: Chronicle of Higher Eucation (May 23, 1997):A38.

In these and other matters the curriculum of the schools does not accommodate the special needs of the poor. To the contrary, the schools assume that the language and behaviors of the poor are not only alien but also wrong—things to be changed. This assumption denigrates the ways of the poor and leads to loss of ego strength (a trait already in short supply for the poor in a middle-class world).

The curriculum also is not very germane to the poor child's world. What is the relevance of conjugating a verb when you are hungry? What is the relevance of being able to trace the path of how a bill becomes a law when your family and neighbors are powerless? Irrelevancy for the poor is also seen in the traditional children's primers, which picture middle-class surroundings and well-behaved blond children. There is little effort at any educational level to incorporate the experience of slum children in relation to realistic life situations of any kind. Schools also have a way of ignoring real-life problems and controversial issues. Schools are irrelevant if they disregard topics such as race relations, poverty, and the distribution of community power.

The typical teaching methods, placement tests, and curricula are inappropriate for children from poor families. This factor, along with the others mentioned earlier, results in failure for a large proportion of these youngsters. They perceive themselves (as do others in the system) as incompetents. As Silberman has put it:

> Students are not likely to develop self-respect if they are unable to master the reading, verbal, and computational skills that the schools are trying to teach. Children must have a sense of competence if they are to regard themselves as people of worth; the failure that minority-group children, in particular, experience from the beginning can only reinforce the sense of worthlessness that the dominant culture conveys in an almost infinite variety of ways, and so feed the self-hatred that prejudice and discrimination produce. Chronic failure makes self-discipline equally hard to come by; it is these children's failure to learn that produces the behavior problems of the slum school . . . and not the behavior problems that produce the failure to learn. (Silberman, 1970:67)

Silberman's discussion of the problems of minority group children can be broadened to include all poor children (who are, after all, also a minority group). The poor of all races experience prejudice and discrimination. They quickly learn that they are considered misfits by the middle class (teacher, administrator, citizen).

Segregation

Schools in the United States tend to be segregated by social class and race, both by neighborhood and, within schools, by ability grouping. Schools are based in neighborhoods that tend to be relatively homogeneous by socioeconomic status. Racial and economic segregation is especially prevalent at the elementary school level, carrying over to a lesser degree in the secondary schools. Colleges and universities, as we have seen, are peopled by a middle-and upper-class clientele. Thus, at every level, children tend to attend a school with children like themselves in socioeconomic status and race. (The following is from Orfield, 1999.) In terms of race, during the 1996 school year, Whites, on average, attended elementary and high schools with 81 percent White classmates (and 9 percent Black classmates, 7 percent Latinos, and 3 percent Asians). In contrast, Blacks and Latinos attend schools where slightly more than half the children are from their own racial group. At the extreme, 8 percent of U.S. schools were intensely segregated with between 90 and 100 percent Black and Latino students:

> Of these schools, 87% of the children were impoverished. In other words, the students in the segregated minority schools were 11 times more likely to be schools with concentrated poverty and 92% of white schools did not face this problem. This relationship is absolutely central to explaining the different educational experiences and outcomes of the schools. A great many of the educational characteristics of schools attributed to race are actually related to poverty. (Orfield, 1999:12)

Tracking and Teachers' Expectations

In 1954 the Supreme Court declared segregated schools unconstitutional. As we have seen, many schools remain at least partially segregated by social class and race because schools draw students from residential areas that are more or less homogeneous by class and race. Segregation is reinforced further by the tracking system within the schools. **Tracking** (also known as ability grouping) sorts students into different groups or classes according to their perceived intellectual ability and performance. The decision is based on grades and teachers' judgments but primarily through standardized tests. The result is that children from poor families and from ethnic minorities are overrepresented in the slow track, while children from advantaged backgrounds are disproportionately in the middle and upper tracks. The rationale for tracking is that it provides a better fit between the needs and capabilities of the student and the demands and opportunities of the curriculum. Slower students do not retard the progress of brighter ones, but teachers can adapt their teaching more efficiently to the level of the class if the students are relatively homogeneous in ability. The special problems of the different ability groups, from gifted to challenged, can be dealt with more easily when groups of students share the same or similar problems. The arguments are persuasive.

Although these benefits may be real, tracking is open to serious criticisms. First, students in lower tracks are discouraged from producing up to their potential. They tend to be given repetitive and unchallenging tasks. Students labeled as *low ability* tend to be taught a "dumbed down" curriculum. They are given low-level work that increases the gap between them and students in the higher tracks. Rather than seeing the remedial track as a way to get students up to speed, many "teachers see themselves as weeders, getting rid of the kids who can't make it, rather than nurturers trying to make all grow to their potential" (Rachlin, 1989:52).

Second, students in the upper track develop feelings of superiority, while those in the lower track tend to define themselves as inferior. As early as the second grade, students know where they stand on the smart or dumb continuum, and this knowledge profoundly affects their self-esteem. These psychological wounds can have devastating effects.

Third, the low-track students are tracked to fail. The negative labels, low teacher expectations, poor education resources (e.g., the highest track is much more likely to have access to computers and to have the most talented teachers), and because teachers typically do not want to teach these classes (there is a subtle labeling among teachers regarding who gets to teach what level) all lead to a high probability of failure among students assigned to the lowest track. Given all these negatives, it is not surprising that students who are discipline problems or who eventually drop out come disproportionately from the low track.

Fourth, the tracking system is closely linked to the stratification system—that is, students from low-income families are disproportionately placed in the lowest track, resulting in a reinforcement of the social class structure. Data from a nationwide study of 14,000 eighth-grade students in English classes reveal that this is true (see Table 16.2). Thus, U.S. schools deny equality of educational opportunity, which is contrary to the ideal of the school system as open and democratic.

Finally, and most telling, research calls into serious question whether tracking has educational value. Research at Johns Hopkins University found, for example, that "given the same curriculum in elementary and middle-grade schools, there is no difference in achievement between advanced students in a tracked school and students in the top third of a class made up of students with varying abilities" (Rachlin, 1989:52). The Carnegie Corporation, in a report assessing the state of middle-grade schools, advocated "abolishing tracking on the grounds that it discriminates against minorities, psychologically wounds those labeled slow, and doesn't work" (Rachlin, 1989:51).

The tracking system appears not to accomplish its educational goals, but it is powerful in its negative effects. There are four principal reasons this system stunts the success of students who are negatively labeled.

- **Stigma.** Assignment to a lower track carries a strong **stigma** (a label of social disgrace). Such students are labeled as intellectual inferiors. Their self-esteem wanes as they see how other people perceive them and behave toward them. Thus, individuals assigned to a track other than college prep perceive themselves as second class, unworthy, stupid, and in the way. Clearly, assignment to a low track is destructive to a student's self-concept.

- **Self-Fulfilling Prophecy.** A self-fulfilling prophecy (see Chapter 7) is an event that occurs because it is predicted and people alter their behavior to conform to the prediction. This effect is closely related to stigma. If placed in the college-prep track, students are likely to receive better instruction, have access

TABLE 16.2

Ability Grouping by Race and Class

	Percent in			
Category	*High Ability*	*Middle Ability*	*Low Ability*	*Mixed*
Race/Ethnicity				
Asian	40	37	16	7
White	32	40	14	15
Hispanic	18	42	29	12
Black	15	38	34	13
Native American	9	44	35	13
Socioeconomic Status				
Top one-fourth	39	39	14	8
Bottom one-fourth	13	36	37	14

Note: From a national study of 14,000 eighth-grade students in English classes.

Source: U.S. Department of Education, National Center for Educational Statistics. 1990. *National Education Longitudinal Study of 1988*. Washington, DC: U.S. Government Printing Office.

to better facilities, and be pushed more nearly to their capacity than are students assigned to other tracks. The reason is clear: The teachers and administration expect great things from the one group and lesser things from the other. Moreover, these expectations are fulfilled. Students in the higher track do better, and those in the lower track do not. These behaviors justify the greater expenditures of time, faculties, and experimental curricula for those in the higher track—thus perpetuating what Merton has called a "reign of error" (Merton, 1957:421–436).

An example comes from a controversial study by Rosenthal and Jacobson (1968). Although this study has been criticized for a number of methodological shortcomings, the findings are consistent with theories of interpersonal influence and with the labeling view of deviant behavior. In the spring of 1964, all students in an elementary school in San Francisco were given an IQ test. The following fall the teachers were given the names of children identified by the test as potential academic spurters, and five of these children were assigned to each classroom. The spurters were chosen by means of a table of random numbers. The only difference between the experimental group (those labeled as spurters) and the control group (the rest of the class) was in the imaginations of the teachers. At the end of the year all the children were again tested, and the children from whom the teachers expected greater intellectual gains showed such gains (in IQ and grades). Moreover, they were rated by their teachers as being more curious, interesting, happy, and more likely to succeed than were the children in the control group.

The implications of this example are clear. Teachers' expectations have a profound effect on students' performance. When students are overrated, they tend to overproduce; when they are underrated, they underachieve. The tracking system is a labeling process that affects the expectations of teachers (and fellow students and parents). The limits of these expectations are crucial in the educational process. Yet the self-fulfilling prophecy can work in a positive direction if teachers have an unshakable conviction that their students can learn. Concomitant with this belief, teachers should hold *themselves*, not the students, accountable if the latter should fail (Silberman, 1970:98). Used in this manner, the self-fulfilling prophecy can work to the benefit of all students.

Future Payoff. School is perceived as relevant for students going to college. Grades are a means of qualifying for college. For the non-college-bound student, however, school and grades are much less important for entry into a job. At most, students need a high school diploma, and grades really do not matter as long as one does not flunk out. Thus, non-college-bound students often develop negative attitudes toward school, grades, and teachers. These attitudes for students in the lower tracks are summed up by sociologist Arthur Stinchcombe:

> Rebellious behavior is largely a reaction to the school itself and to its promises, not a failure of the family or community. High school students can be motivated to conform by paying them in the realistic coin of future advantage. Except perhaps for pathological cases, any student can be motivated to conform if the school can realistically promise something valuable to him as a reward for working hard. But for a large part of the population, especially the adolescent who will enter the male working class or the female candidates for early marriage, the school has nothing to offer. . . . In order to secure conformity from students, a high school must articulate academic work with careers of students. (Quoted in Schafer, Olexa, and Polk, 1972:49)

As we have seen, being on the lower track has negative consequences. Lower-track students are more rebellious, both in school and out, and do not participate as much in school activities. Finally, what is being taught is often not relevant to their world. Thus, we are led to conclude that many of these students tend to feel that they are not only second-class citizens but perhaps even pariahs. What other interpretation is plausible in a system that disadvantages them, shuns them, and makes demands of them that are irrelevant?

Student Subculture. The reasons given previously suggest that a natural reaction of people in the lower track would be to band together in a **student subculture** that is antagonistic toward school. This subculture would quite naturally develop its own system of rewards, since those of the school are inaccessible.

These factors (stigma, negative self-fulfilling prophecy, low future payoff, and a contrary student subculture) show how the tracking system is at least partly responsible for the fact that students in the lower tracks tend to be low achievers, unmotivated, uninvolved in school activities, and more prone to break school rules and drop out of school. To segregate students either by ability or by future plans is detrimental to the students labeled as inferior. It is an elitist system that for the most part takes the children of the elite and educates them to take the elite positions in society. Conversely, children of the nonelite are trained to recapitulate the experiences of their parents. In a presumably democratic system that prides itself on providing avenues of upward social mobility, such a system borders on immorality (Oakes, 1985).

The conclusion is inescapable: Inequality in the educational system causes many people to fail in U.S. schools. This phenomenon is the fault of the schools, not of the children who fail. To focus on these victims is to divert attention from the inadequacies of the schools. The blame needs to be shifted:

> We are dealing, it would seem, not so much with culturally deprived children as with culturally depriving schools. And the task to be accomplished is not to revise, and amend, and repair deficient children but to alter and transform the atmosphere and operations of the schools to which we commit these children. Only by changing the nature of the educational experience can we change its product. (Ryan, 1976:60)

POSSIBILITIES FOR PROMOTING EQUALITY OF OPPORTUNITY

A fundamental tenet of U.S. society is that each individual, regardless of sex, race, ethnicity, religion, age, and social class, has the opportunity to be unequal on her or his own merits. In other words, the system must not impede individuals from reaching their potential and from gaining the unequal rewards of an unequal society. The data presented in this chapter show that U.S. schools tend to block the chances of minority and poor children in their quest to be successful in society. This section outlines several programs that schools and society could adopt to promote equality of opportunity for all children.

We must realize at the start that if the situation for poor and minority children is difficult now, it will worsen significantly if changes are not made. This assertion is based on three societal trends. The first, documented throughout this book, is that the gap between the affluent and poor is widening. Also, as the demographic mix of the nation continues to change, more and more children of color from relatively poor families are going and will go to our schools. Today about 20 percent of school children have a foreign-born parent (mostly Latino and Asian), a proportion that will likely increase. These poor and brown children of immigrants are disproportionately found in inner cities in increasingly segregated neighborhoods. With the poor and people of color clustered in cities, these local governments, faced with a declining tax base, will be less and less able to provide the services required of their citizens, including education. Similarly, certain regions—the Pacific Coast, the Southwest, and Florida—are especially affected by immigration, placing an extraordinary financial burden on those states and localities. And, we know this, the poorer and browner the children, the poorer the condition of their schools, the less the availability of certified teachers, and the fewer the financial resources, all of which lead to deficient academic performances (Smokes, 2000).

The second trend that will negatively affect the educational opportunities of minorities unless changes are made is that the number of minority students is increasing and will in the next decades make Whites the numerical minority (as they are today in many school districts). Moreover, racial and ethnic minorities are concentrated in poor states (the South and Southwest) and poor geographical regions (Appalachia, the Ozarks, along the Rio Grande, and in the Mississippi delta) and in poor sections of cities. This is significant because racial/ethnic minorities have higher rates of poverty than do the majority and have less stable family lives, more unemployment, and lower educational attainment than do the more fortunate majority. In effect, under current policies, children from minorities are disadvantaged economically and are at greater risk of educational failure. So, wherever these children are overrepresented, there will be disproportionately less local money to meet their educational needs (because of the lower tax base). Ironically, the poor require more money than the affluent to catch up, such as enriched preschool, after school programs, summer reading programs, and small classes, yet the richest school districts spend 56 percent more per student than the poorest do (Children's Defense Fund, 2001) (see the "Social Policy" panel, p. 488).

In addition to the rise in the proportion of racial minority students, there are several addition demographic trends that make reform difficult. One demographic trend negatively impacting education is the aging of society (see Chapter 5). As a greater proportion of the population no longer has children in school, there will be a greater reluctance on their part to vote for tax increases directed at education. Another population trend is for increased enrollments from the baby-boom echo—that is, the children of children of the disproportionately large baby-boom generation are in school or soon will be, swelling the numbers significantly. This means that more classrooms and teachers are needed. However, as new students are being added to the schools, many teachers are leaving for better paying jobs, resulting in a predicted national shortage of some 2.5 million teachers over the next decade (Wilgoren, 2000).

Reforming the Financing of Education. There must be a commitment to a free education for all students. Presumably, public education at the elementary and secondary levels is free, but this assumption is a fallacy, as discussed earlier. Although circumstances vary by district, typically children must pay for their supplies, textbooks, laboratory fees, locker rental, admission to plays and athletic events, insurance, transportation, meals, equipment for and participation in extracurricular activities, and the like. Some districts waive these costs

SOCIAL POLICY

A TEN-POINT EDUCATION AGENDA FOR EVERY CHILD

Too often lost amid rhetoric about education reform is this simple fact: education is about one thing only—**our children.** If America's public education system—the pillar of our democracy—is to be revitalized, it must be refocused exclusively on the well-being of **all** students. While appropriately ambitious, the following ten-point agenda for education reform is realistic, achievable, and absolutely essential. A deep sense of urgency is necessary to face this challenge of preparing a new generation of children for the future. This agenda puts children first in education policy by insisting that America:

1. **Operate from the premise that all children can learn and perform at high levels**—and thus focus every action in our education system from school board decisions down to teaching in the classroom on helping all children perform at high levels.
2. **Ensure that every child enters school ready to learn and ready to succeed**—and that requires access to safe, nurturing, quality early child development experiences and preschool opportunities.
3. **Set measurable and appropriate standards for success**—and hold everyone—administrators, teachers, parents, students, and communities, in that order—accountable for meeting those standards.
4. **Empower teachers and principals—working with parents—to make as many key education decisions as possible**—reduce the size of educational bureaucracies and change their role from one of direction to one of support because decisions made at the level closest to the students will best meet their needs.
5. **Invest in quality teaching**—by ensuring lifelong training and retraining, strengthening and renewing respect for the teaching profession, and compensating teachers commensurate with their ability and essential role in our society.
6. **Provide every child with facilities that support learning and state-of-the-art tools**—ranging from up-to-date text books (many school districts still don't have enough) to Internet access.
7. **Ensure adequate resources to make all of the above a reality**—but use those resources wisely and efficiently.
8. **Involve the entire community—especially parents—in this cause, ensuring that students receive the support and services they need to succeed in school**—that requires a coordinated effort by social service agencies, the business community, law enforcement officials, neighborhood groups, faith-based institutions, health care providers, and the full range of voluntary organizations that work with children along with educators.
9. **Engage the public in the school reform debate**—only with full participation by those who elect education decision-makers and pay taxes can child-centered reform succeed.
10. **Address every one of the above elements now**—in its entirety this agenda will succeed. Addressed in pieces, it will not.

Source: Children's Defense Fund. 2001. *The State of America's Children: Yearbook 2001*. Washington, DC: Children's Defense Fund, p. 65.

for poor families. But waivers do not occur uniformly across school districts, and the procedures for granting these waivers are often degrading (i.e., done in such a way that other people know who receives the handouts). These costs are regressive because they take a larger proportion of the poor family's budget, thereby increasing the pressure to withdraw the child from school, where he or she drains the family resources.

By making education absolutely free to all children, communities could reduce dropout rates among the poor. A program of greater scope would also provide a living allowance for each child from a poor family who stayed in school beyond the eighth grade. This program would be analogous to the GI Bill, which provided similar benefits to soldiers returning after World War II.

Special care must be given to provide these benefits, as did the GI Bill, without making their acceptance degrading.

Obtaining a college diploma is an important avenue to later success. The poor are severely disadvantaged by the U.S. system of higher education in two ways. First, their taxes help subsidize public higher education (typically, at least one-third of the average college student's costs are subsidized by states), yet—and this is the second way in which the poor are disadvantaged—their children are likely to find the costs of higher education prohibitive. These costs are high and rising faster than is inflation, making college attendance by children of the poor and even the not so poor more and more unlikely.

An important way to produce equal opportunity is to provide a free college education to all students who qualify. This means the elimination of tuition and fees and an allowance for books for everyone, plus grants and loans for students in need to pay for living expenses while attending college (see the "Social Policy" panel, p. 490, for an example of one state's efforts to provide a college education for all).

The federal government now provides about 7 percent of the monies for elementary and secondary education in the United States. The federal government should engage in four programs to promote equal opportunity for the disadvantaged. First, the government should provide national education standards, a national curriculum, and national tests. There are 40.7 million students, 15,387 school districts, and 83,000 schools in the United States. We must require that each school district and school, rather than acting on its own, meet specific standards for school achievement agreed to by a national consensus among educational leaders. The minimum result of this would be that students, whether growing up in Nebraska or New York, would learn the same basic materials at about the same time. This also means that as students move with their families from one locality to another, they would not be at a disadvantage because of the esoteric schooling they had received.

The second reform at the federal level would be to spend the federal monies unequally to equalize differences among the states. In effect, the federal government must take the money it receives in taxes, taking disproportionately from the wealthy states, and redistribute it to the poor states. Otherwise, the gap between the rich and poor states will be maintained.

The third effort at the federal level would be to encourage states to distribute their funds to eliminate or minimize disparities between rich and poor districts. This could be done by the federal government's withholding funds from states with discrepancies between their poor and rich districts that exceed federal guidelines. In such cases, the federal government could channel its monies directly to the poorer districts within the offending states.

Fourth, the federal government must increase its funding for programs such as Head Start and must continue such compensatory programs through at least kindergarten and first grade. At present the program is underfunded and many children who qualify are turned away.

Clearly, the federal government must reorder its priorities if poor and minority children are to be given a chance to succeed in school and later in society.

At the state level, monies must be equalized across the districts. Nationwide, the traditional property tax system of raising money for education locally is under assault. The supreme courts in various states are ruling in case after case that the states are failing the children in the poorer districts. In effect, they are saying that the state should collect monies from the rich districts and redis-

SOCIAL POLICY

GEORGIA'S SCHOLARSHIP PROGRAM FOR COLLEGE STUDENTS

Georgia has instituted a scholarship program for college students called HOPE (Helping Outstanding Pupils Educationally). Funded by the state lottery, HOPE pays 100 percent of tuition at Georgia state colleges or vocational or technical schools for all Georgia residents—regardless of income—who maintain a B average and are not already receiving federal aid (much of the following is taken from Jaffe, 1997; Firestone, 2001). There is also a $3,000 annual rebate given to state students who maintain a B average at private colleges located in Georgia. Nearly 118,000 students in 1997 qualified for HOPE grants, receiving scholarships totaling $125 million. Since the pioneering effort by Georgia, some thirteen states now have similar programs.

In an earlier era, state colleges were either low-tuition or tuition-free to in-state students. But beginning in the 1970s this changed as states began charging for tuition, and these costs have escalated, with the cost of tuition at a 4-year public university soaring 235 percent from 1980 to 1995 (a time when median household income rose only 82 percent). The HOPE plan counteracts this trend for higher tuition and thereby makes higher education more accessible to all segments of the Georgia population.

This ambitious plan provides a tuition-free education for students doing well academically in the state schools. This encourages Georgia students to go to school in their home state and, most important, it makes college more affordable for students from all backgrounds. This would appear to be especially beneficial to economically disadvantaged students.

The downside to HOPE is that the B average criterion will likely encourage grade inflation as many professors may opt to give undeserved B's rather than kill a scholarship. The necessity of B's will likely encourage some students to shun difficult courses or majors and to take lighter course loads. Most important, though, is that these grants from the state provide more assistance to the children of the privileged than for children of the poor. Critics argue that the primary goal of financial aid should be to make college available to the poor. The Georgia plan, however, does not accomplish this. Because the plan is available to all, regardless of wealth, children of the wealthy get an unneeded financial break. Children of the middle class and working class receive a financial boost, making a college education more possible. Children of the poor, however, are hindered by the provisions of HOPE, which stipulate that the scholarship will be reduced by whatever amount the student receives from the federal government. Poor students who receive federal Pell grants, then, may not receive any HOPE scholarship money. If they were allowed to retain the Pell grant and the HOPE grant, then the poor, who, by definition, do not have the economic resources to attend college, would have their tuition paid and have money for living expenses, making college a realistic option. But since Pell recipients offset what they might receive from HOPE grants, many qualified students, even with a seemingly enlightened program such as HOPE, do not attend college because of inadequate resources. The Georgia legislature faced with this question—should it give poor students the full HOPE tuition award so they could use the Pell grants for living expenses or should HOPE include affluent students—opted for the latter. The result, as Larry Gladieux, executive director of the College Board, said: "HOPE tips the balance of aid too much in favor of the privileged" (Jaffe, 1997:A13). Put another way, the HOPE scholarships "represent an enormous transfer of money—$1.2 billion since 1993—from lottery players, who tend to live in the poorest counties of the state, to 504,000 college students, who come from the wealthiest counties" (Firestone, 2001:3). As a consequence, the seemingly universality of the HOPE grants actually perpetuates the existing stratification system in Georgia.

tribute them to the poor districts. This, of course, is typically fought by the advantaged.

Finally, at the state and district levels, special efforts should be made to increase the racial/ethnic diversity of teachers. Now, about 90 percent of all public school teachers are White:

> The issues regarding the impact of minority teachers in the classroom are complex. Some advocates believe minority students should have minority teachers, but clearly not all can unless the number of minority students in teaching rises dramatically. Many agree that in the multi-cultural society of the U.S., it is beneficial for all students—regardless of race or ethnic heritage—to be exposed during their early educational careers to teachers and role models from a variety of racial, ethnic, and cultural backgrounds. (Griffith, Frase, and Ralph, 1989:16)

- **Universal Preschool Programs.** The most important variable affecting school performance is not race but socioeconomic status. Regardless of race, children from poor families tend to do less well in school than do children from families who are better off. Compensatory programs such as Head Start and Follow Through are predicated on the assumption that if children from lower-class homes are to succeed in middle-class schools, they must have special help to equalize their chances (see the "Social Policy" panel on helping disadvantaged youth).

  California has initiated an innovative program to eliminate the learning gap between middle-class and lower-class children. This program, for all youngsters from kindergarten through the third grade, aims at having every youngster reading and writing, computing, and excited about school by the

SOCIAL POLICY

WAYS TO HELP ECONOMICALLY DISADVANTAGED YOUNGSTERS

Sandra Feldman, president of the American Federation of Teachers, has called for a national commitment to narrow the achievement gap between poor and more economically advantaged children. Specifically she proposes (quoted in Henry, 2001a):

- Universal preschool for children as young as 3 to teach basic academic and social skills in preparation for kindergarten and the early elementary grades.
- Full-day kindergarten in every school district (only fifteen states offer full-day programs).
- Extend both the school day and school year for prekindergarten through twelfth grade in low-performing schools.
- Provide stimulating summer programs for poor prekindergarten children through twelfth graders.

Former secretary of labor under Clinton, Robert Reich, makes another proposal to help economically disadvantaged children. He proposes a plan designed to get more money to poor children and to break up concentrations of poor children in the same schools. His radical proposal (Reich, 2000d:56):

> Instead of giving poor kids less money per pupil than middle-income kids get, give them more. Per-pupil public expenditures now average between $6,000 and $7,000 a year. . . . So back up every child from America's poorest 20 percent of families with $10,000 to $12,000, and children from families in the next quintile with $8,000 to $10,000. At the same time, bust up the concentrations of poor kids in the same schools. Create incentives for them to disperse. Let any school that meets minimum standards compete to enroll these kids and receive the public money that goes with them. . . . Go a step further: Give children from families in the top 20 percent of income only $2,000 to $4,000 in public money each year (the families are of course free to top this off with their own money), and children from families in the next-to-highest quintile, $4,000 to $6,000. That way, schools in nearby wealthy suburban communities also will try to lure some of the poor kids their way in order to meet their budgets—perhaps sending out vans to collect them and drop them off.

time he or she is 8 years old. This goal is accomplished through parent involvement and individualized instruction. Using parent volunteers, paid aides, and teachers reduces the adult–pupil ratio to 1:10. Early results show that although all students benefit from this plan, children from schools in lower-class areas are gaining faster than are those in other schools. The plan is expensive, but administrators hope that the costs will be offset by great reductions in expenditures for remedial work for older students. The payoff for the children is enormous: The program allows them to be normal participants in school and to avoid the stigma of failure.

The problem with compensatory programs is that they blame the victim. The effort is to change the individual so that he or she will adapt to society. As noted in this and earlier chapters, these programs are based on the assumption that the individual is culturally deprived and needs extra help. By blaming the individual, well-meaning people direct attention away from the schools and society—the real sources of the problem. The two types of programs described next focus on the reformation of the school and society.

- **Reducing Class and School Size.** Schools can be restructured to meet the needs of students better. A beginning would be to reduce class size. A Tennessee study (Project Star) found that students in smaller classes tended to achieve higher grades, had better high school graduation rates, were more likely to attend college, and the gap between Black–White academic achievement narrowed by 38 percent (Herbert, 2001b). Not only small classes, but smaller schools are also beneficial, generating higher graduation rates, more participation, less alienation, and less violence. Yet three out of four teenagers today attend factorylike high schools with an enrollment of more than 1,000. Smaller schools and smaller classes create an intimacy that can improve performance. A study of Chicago's experiment with small schools in some of its poorest neighborhoods found that student attendance rises and dropout rates fall (reported in Symonds, 2001).

- **Attracting and Retaining Excellent Teachers.** Schools need to attract and retain excellent teachers. This means higher salaries, mentoring of new teachers, and paying teachers a bonus for teaching in difficult school situations.

> The single most important factor in raising academic performance in poor schools appears to be the presence of experienced, competent and caring teachers. Disadvantaged youths currently are taught by the least prepared and most transient instructors in the system. Devising incentives for recruiting and maintaining highly qualified teachers and for retraining existing staff in high-poverty schools should be the top priority of those serious about raising standards. (Orfield and Wald, 2000:40)

- **Extending the School Day and Year.** The United States devotes the shortest amount of time to teaching its children of any advanced nation. The 6-hour day and the 9-month calendar instituted to accommodate farm life have not changed since the nineteenth century.

> The summer break is especially harmful to minority and poor kids. They enter the first grade half a year behind upper-income children but fall 2.5 years behind by the end of the fifth grade, according to a [Johns Hopkins University study.] Almost all of this gap can be traced to summer vacations, when lower-income kids were treading water and upper-income kids were forging ahead. (Symonds, 2001:76)

- **Holding Educators Accountable.** Virtually every state has instituted statewide examinations in the past decade, linking the results to such things as grade promotion, high school graduation, and teacher and principal salaries. The cornerstone of President Bush's education plan is to have nationwide testing, mandating annual tests in grades 3 through 8, plus one in high school, with penalties for those schools that fail. The goals of this plan make sense. Nationwide norms for each grade are crucial. Tests are needed to assess the progress (or lack thereof) of students, teachers, and schools. There are problems, however. Do you punish schools from economically disadvantaged districts with children who are more proficient in a language other than English? When a school fails, do you punish or do you invest more resources (tutoring, after-school programs, summer school, smaller class size, modem-schools wired for the future)? A major problem with high-stakes testing is that it encourages teaching for the test (test strategies, facts, rote memorization) rather than creativity and understanding.

> Most curriculum experts recommend that students approach topics from a variety of perspectives, using all of their senses, over extended periods of time. Many high-stakes tests, however, rely upon multiple-choice questions, ask students to interpret isolated passages unrelated to larger themes or units, and require them to adhere to rigid writing formats that allow little room for deviation. . . . Learning to take reading and writing tests is not the same as learning to read and write. (Orfield and Wald, 2000:40)

The pressure on teachers and administrators that their schools score well may lead to cheating or to manipulate their rankings by exempting special education students and slow learners from taking the tests (*USA Today,* 1999c), or through the subtle encouragement of slow learners to drop out of school.

A final criticism of high-stakes testing is that research at the state level finds that tests attached to grade promotion and high school graduation lead to increased dropout rates, especially for minority students (Orfield and Wald, 2000).

These criticisms are valid and important, but to criticize them does not invalidate the need for standards and evaluation. The key is to heavily invest in poor children, beginning in preschool, and to enrich their school with meaningful experiences and talented, caring teachers. With such a commitment, over time all children can be held to the same standards and their schools held accountable

- **Reforming the Educational Philosophy of Schools.** The reforms listed above do not question the structure and philosophy of the educational system, which opponents argue essentially stifles children in attaining their potential. In the view of the critics, the system itself is wrong and the generator of many profound problems. These critics want to reconstruct the entire educational enterprise along very different lines. This demand for change is based on three related assumptions. The first is that the school is a microcosm of the larger society. Because society is too competitive, repressive, inhumane, materialistic, racist, and imperialist, so, too, are the schools. Changing society entails changing the schools. The second assumption of the radical critics of education is that the process of public education as it currently exists damages, thwarts, and stifles children. The schools somehow manage to suppress the natural curiosity of children. They begin with inquisitive children and mold them into acquisitive children with little desire to learn.

Third, the educational system is a product of society and hence shapes its products to meet the requirements of society. The present system is predicated on the needs of an industrial society in which citizens must follow orders, do assigned tasks in the appropriate order and time span, and not challenge the status quo. But these behaviors will not be appropriate for life in the near future or perhaps even the present. The future will likely require people who can cope with rapid turnover—changes in occupations, human relationships, and community ties. Moreover, the citizens of the future (present?) must be able to cope with a myriad of choices. Does an educational system built on order, a rigid time schedule, and the lecture method adequately prepare youngsters for life as it is and will be? The proponents of these and other alternatives are critical of U.S. education. They conclude that schools are failing not only children from the ghettos of large cities but also suburban and small-town youngsters. The schools fail because they treat children as miniature adults, because they treat children as a group rather than as individuals, because they stifle creativity, because they are repressive, and because they fail to allow children to reach their potential. This situation is not new, though. As Peter Drucker states:

> [T]oday's school does no poorer a job than it did yesterday; the school has simply done a terribly poor job all along. But what we tolerated in the past we no longer can tolerate. . . . The school has suddenly assumed such importance for the individual, for the community, for the economy and for society, that we cannot suffer the traditional, time-honored incompetence of the educational system. (Drucker, 1972:49)

This approach makes the revolutionary assumption that the success or failure of the child lies with the school, not the child. The child is innately curious. If she or he is apathetic, then it must be the fault of the school. Because the self-fulfilling prophecy is such a powerful factor, teachers should hold themselves, not their students, responsible if the students do not learn. Middle-class bias in all its forms (e.g., teacher expectations for behavior and class bias tests) must be eradicated from schools because it ensures the failure of the lower-class child.

Restructuring Society

The approaches to equality described previously focus on changing either individual students or the schools. But if equality of opportunity is truly the goal, education cannot accomplish it alone. The problem is not in the individual or in the school but in the structure of society. As Bowles has argued:

> [T]he burden of achieving equality of educational opportunity . . . cannot be borne by the educational system alone. The achievement of some degree of equality of opportunity depends in part on what we do in the educational system but also, to a very large degree, in what we do elsewhere in the economy, in the polity, and in the society as a whole. (Bowles, 1969:121)

Closing the achievement gap between advantaged and disadvantaged students cannot be accomplished without a societywide assault on racism and poverty. Christopher Jencks and his associates maintain that this assault requires fundamental changes in the system of societal rewards: a redistribution of wealth through equalizing occupational rewards, a minimum income for all members of society, and a reduction in the ability of parents to transmit their economic advantages and disadvantages to their offspring (Jencks et al., 1972). After a thorough investigation of inequality in our society, they concluded that inequality in the U.S. schools is not the major cause of economic stratification among adults. Poverty can be eliminated only through fundamental revisions in the economic and familial institutions. This is not to say that reform of the schools should be ignored. Efforts to improve our schools should parallel attempts to restructure the other institutions of society.

CHAPTER REVIEW

1. The system of education in the United States is characterized by (a) conservatism—the preservation of culture, roles, values, and training necessary for the maintenance of society, (b) belief in mass education, (c) local control, (d) competition, (e) reinforcement of the stratification system, and (f) preoccupation with order and control.
2. The belief that our society is meritocratic, with the most intelligent and talented at the top, is a myth. Education, instead of being the great equalizer, reinforces social inequality.
3. Schools perform a number of functions that maintain the prevailing social, political, and economic order: (a) socializing the young, (b) shaping personality traits to conform with the demand of the culture, (c) preparing for adult roles, and (d) providing employers with a disciplined and skilled labor force.
4. The curricula, testing, bureaucratic control, and emphasis on competition in schools reflect the social class structure of society by processing youth to fit into economic slots similar to those of their parents.
5. The schools are structured to aid in the perpetuation of social and economic differences in several ways: (a) by being financed principally through property taxes, (b) by providing curricula that are irrelevant to the poor, and (c) by tracking according to presumed level of ability.
6. The tracking system is closely correlated with social class; students from low-income families are disproportionately placed in the lowest track. Tracking thwarts the equality of educational opportunity for the poor by generating four effects: (a) a stigma, which lowers self-esteem, (b) the self-fulfilling prophecy, (c) a perception of school as having no future payoff, and (d) a negative student subculture.
7. Equality of educational opportunity must begin with the reform of educational finance in order to equalize the budgets of schools regardless of the wealth of individual districts.
8. The federal government could promote equality of opportunity by (a) providing national educational standards, a national curriculum, and national tests; (b) distributing money unequally to the states according to need; (c) encouraging states to minimize economic disparities among their school districts; and (d) increasing funding for Head Start and other compensatory programs.
9. Compensatory programs have achieved some success in narrowing the gap between children of the poor and of the affluent. The problem with these programs is that they blame the children for not measuring up to society's standards. Thus, this approach diverts attention away from the schools and society—the real sources of the problem.
10. To promote equality of opportunity and excellence in the public schools requires: (a) the reform of how schools are financed, (b) providing universal preschool programs, (c) reducing class and school size, (d) attracting and retaining excellent teachers, (e) extending the school year, (f) holding educators responsible for their students' outcomes, and (g) changing the philosophy of schools.
11. The restructuring of schools will not meet the goal of equality of educational opportunity, radical critics argue, unless the society is also restructured. This change requires a society-wide assault on racism and poverty and a redistribution of wealth to reduce the inequalities that result from economic advantage.

KEY TERMS

Cultural deprivation. Erroneous assumption that some groups (e.g., the poor) are handicapped by a so-called inferior culture.

Tracking. Ability grouping in schools.

Stigma. Powerful negative social label that affects a person's social identity and self-concept.

Student subculture. Members of the disadvantaged band together in a group with values and behaviors antagonistic toward school.

WEBSITES FOR FURTHER REFERENCE

http://www.uscharterschools.org

U.S. Charter Schools.Org is an online learning community designed to serve and support the United States' charter schools and to educate others about them.

http://www.rethinkingschools.org/

Fifteen years ago, a group of Milwaukee-area teachers had a vision. They wanted not only to improve education in their own classrooms and schools, but to help shape reform throughout the public school system in the United States. Today that vision is embodied in Rethinking Schools. Rethinking Schools began as a local effort to address problems such as basal readers, standardized testing, and textbook-dominated curriculum. Since its founding in 1986, it has grown into a nationally prominent publisher of educational materials, with subscribers in all 50 states, all 10 Canadian provinces, and many other countries.

http://www.americatakingaction.com/

America Taking Action is a national network of school websites linking kids and communities across America. The network has been created entirely by involved parents, teachers and community leaders as a public service, with no financial backing or influence. The goals of the network are to connect schools nationwide by providing a network of free school websites; providing numerous resources for teachers, students, and parents; fostering communication between teachers, students, and parents; and providing funding for education.

http://www.aihec.org/

The mission of American Indian Higher Education Consortium (AIHEC) is to maintain commonly held standards of quality in American Indian education; support the development of new tribally controlled colleges; promote and assist in the development of legislation to support American Indian higher education; and encourage greater participation by American Indians in the development of higher education policy.

http://www.hacu.com/

The mission of Hispanic Association of Colleges & Universities (HACU) is to promote the development of member colleges and universities; to improve access to and the quality of post-secondary educational opportunities for Hispanic students; and to meet the needs of business, industry, and government through the development and sharing of resources, information, and expertise.

http://www.nafeo.org/

National Association for Equal Opportunity in Higher Education (NAFEO) is the national umbrella and public policy advocacy organization for 118 of the nation's historically and predominantly Black colleges and universities. Its mission is to champion the interests of Historically Black Colleges and Universities (HBCUs) through the executive, legislative, regulatory, and judicial branches of federal and state government.

http://www.nhsa.org/

The National Head Start Association (NHSA) is a private not-for-profit membership organization representing more than 923,000 children, upwards of 180,000 staff, and more than 2,400 Head Start programs in America. NHSA provides a national forum for the continued enhancement of Head Start services for poor children ages 0 through 5, and their families. It is the only national organization dedicated exclusively to the concerns of the Head Start community.

http://www.nea.org/

NEA is America's oldest and largest organization committed to advancing the cause of public education. Founded in 1857 in Philadelphia and now headquartered in Washington, D.C., NEA proudly claims more than 2.5 million members who work at every level of education, from preschool to university graduate programs. NEA has affiliates in every state, as well as in over 13,000 local communities across the United States.

http://www.ed.gov/

U. S. Department of Education's "award-winning site is designed to help pursue the President's initiatives, including *No Child Left Behind,* and advance our mission as a Department—to ensure equal access to education and to promote educational excellence for all Americans."

Health and Health Care Delivery

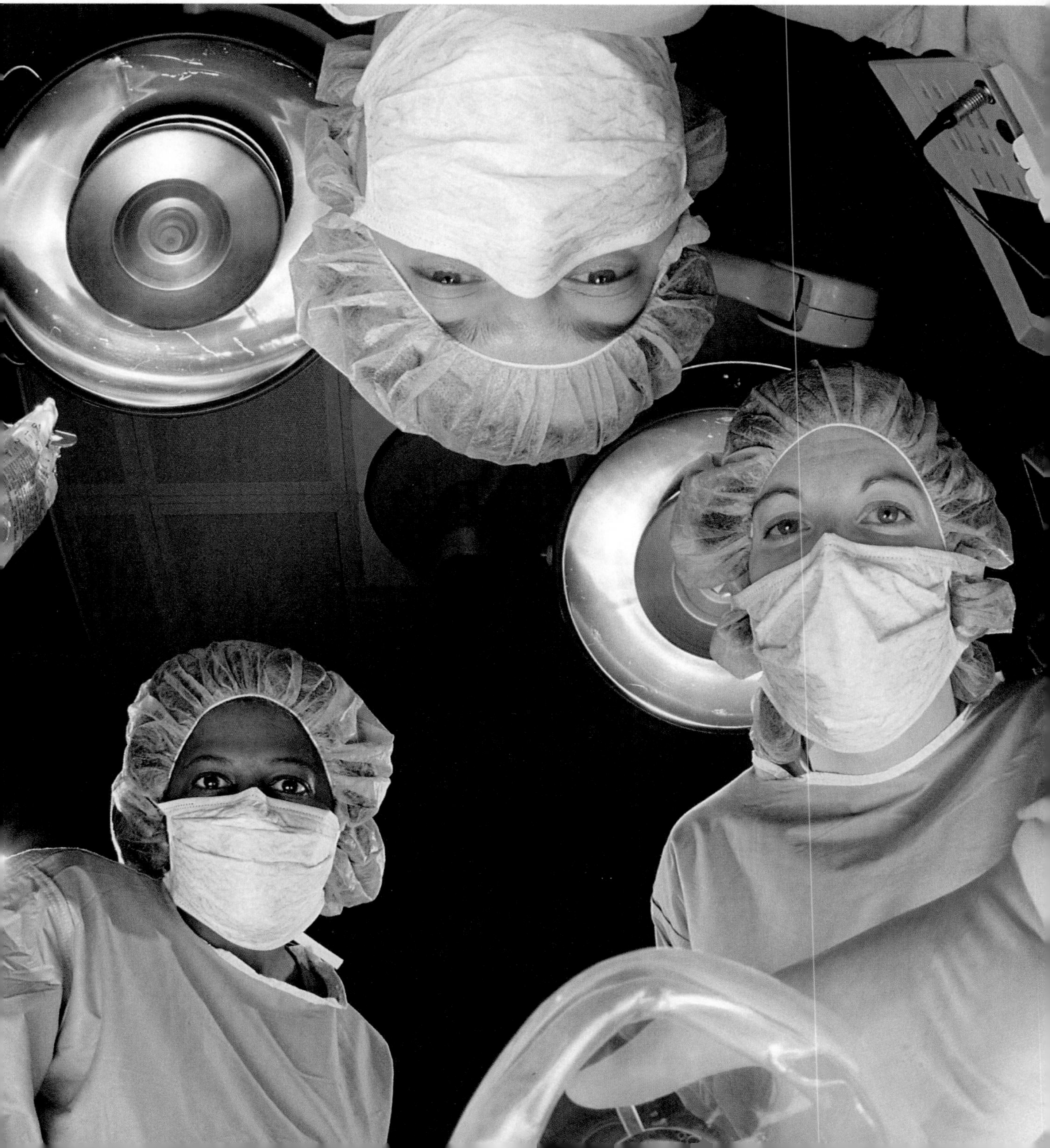

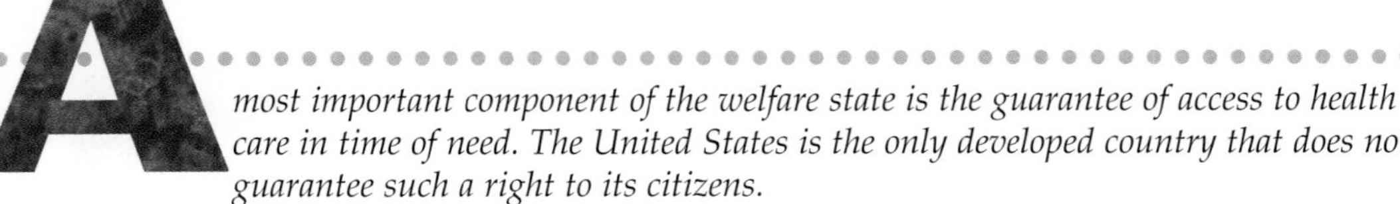

A most important component of the welfare state is the guarantee of access to health care in time of need. The United States is the only developed country that does not guarantee such a right to its citizens.

—Vicente Navarro

The lower you are in a social hierarchy, the worse your health and the shorter your life are likely to be.

—Alejandro Reuss

The day has come when somebody has to do in the hospital business what McDonald's has done in the fast-food business and what Wal-Mart has done in the retailing business.

—Richard Rainwater

In 2000 health care costs in the United States rose to a record $1.2 trillion. It is estimated that overall health care spending will more than double to $2.6 trillion by 2010, in part because drug costs are projected to rise on average 12.6 percent every year (McQueen, 2001a). The United States spends more for health care, both in amount spent per capita and percentage of gross national product, than any other industrialized nation. The nation's health care system is also the most technologically sophisticated with the best-trained practitioners. But according to the World Health Organization (WHO) the health system of the United States is ranked thirty-seventh among the world's 191 countries (see Table 17.1).

TABLE 17.1

World Health Organization Ranking of Health Care Systems

Country	*Overall Performance Rating*	*Total Private and Public Health Spending (as % of GDP)*	*Total Health Spending Per Person (US$)*	*Public Health Spending (as % of Total Health Spending*	*Expected Healthy Life Span (years)*	*Infant Mortality (per 1,000 live births)*
France	1	9.8	$2,369	76.9	73.1	4.7
Italy	2	9.3	1,855	57.1	72.7	6.2
Spain	7	8.0	1,071	70.6	72.8	5.0
Japan	10	7.1	2,373	80.2	74.5	3.6
Norway	11	6.5	2,283	82.0	71.7	4.0
Netherlands	17	8.8	2,041	70.7	72.0	5.2
United Kingdom	18	5.8	1,303	96.9	71.7	5.7
Sweden	23	9.2	2,456	78.0	73.0	3.6
Germany	25	10.5	2,713	77.5	70.4	4.7
Canada	30	8.6	1,783	72.0	72.0	5.5
Australia	32	7.8	1,730	72.0	73.2	5.0
United States	37	13.7	4,187	44.1	70.0	7.2

Source: World Health Organization. 1997. "Infant Mortality Data from Organization for Economic Co-operation and Development." *World Health Report 2000*. Online. Available: www.oecd.org/els/health/software/fad02.htm.

> WHO ranked health system output on five indicators: the population's overall health, health inequalities, how well the system performs, how well people of varying income levels are served, and how costs are distributed. On the basis of those indicators, the USA ranked 15th in the world. . . . But the USA's health system dropped to 37th overall because of its inefficiency. In other words, for the amount of money spent on health care—$3,700 per capita—Americans should be even healthier. (Rubin, 2000:10D)

The inefficiency of the U.S. health care system is the topic of this chapter. With the United States spending 50 percent more per capita on health care than any other country, it seems reasonable to expect that Americans would be the healthiest people on Earth. But there are major problems with the health care system in the U.S. Some of these are (Baxandall, 2001):

- Of Americans 16 percent are not covered by health insurance.
- The poor lack access to basic care.
- The system rations health care by ability to pay and by refusing to cover certain treatments.
- "Profit drives the U.S. system, and what is most profitable for hospitals, insurance companies, or drug companies is not most effective at producing good health" (Baxandall, 2001:40).

The problem is that health care in the United States is rationed on the basis of ability to pay; that is, the system is superb for people who can afford it and falls woefully short for those who cannot. For the affluent, the best physicians, surgeons, hospital care, and the latest technology are available. Among the impoverished and near poor, however, approximately 42 million people are uninsured, which means that they are essentially left outside the health care system. Another 50 million are underinsured, which leaves them exposed to large financial risks or excludes coverage for certain medical problems. In short, the health delivery system in the United States and the health of people in the country are maldistributed.

The three sections of this chapter examine health and inequality from several vantage points: (1) unequal access to health care, looking at the U.S. health care system by class, race, and gender; (2) the social organization of health care delivery; and (3) the examination of some alternatives to the present system of health care and health care delivery.

UNEQUAL ACCESS TO HEALTH CARE

In examining the structure of a society and any of its institutions, the analyst of social problems asks, Who benefits and who suffers from the way it is organized? When health care delivery is the focus, the answer to this question is clear: Glaring inequities result in some categories of people being less healthy than others. Our examination of this structural inequity focuses on the three fundamental structures of inequality: class, race, and gender, which are key determinants of health (i.e., the distribution of health and disease) and health care delivery (i.e., the distribution of treatment). These structures of inequality make a difference, not surprisingly, with the advantaged being advantaged and the disadvantaged being disadvantaged.

> Whether or not you are healthy, or can be healthy, depends on lots of factors beyond your control. Do you have access to nutritious food and good

> medical care? That depends on whether you can afford them. Are you able to minimize your stress level? That depends on your working conditions. Is your neighborhood free of environmental hazards? That depends on the color of your skin. In other words, your health depends on where you fit into the larger, and how your society—or any society—fits into the global economic scheme. (*Dollars and Sense,* 2001:2)

Social Class

Economic disadvantage is closely associated with health disadvantages. Put another way: "How people live, get sick, and die depends not only on their race and gender, but primarily on the class to which they belong" (Navarro, 1991:2). The poor are more likely than the affluent to suffer from certain forms of cancer (cancers of the lung, cervix, and esophagus), hypertension, low birth weight, hearing loss, diabetes, and infectious diseases (especially influenza and tuberculosis). The well-to-do live longer, and when stricken with a disease, they are more likely to survive than are the poor. For example, women with family incomes below $10,000 are more than three times as likely to die of heart disease, compared to those with family incomes above $25,000 (Reuss, 2001). Using education as an indicator of social class, men with less than 12 years of education are more than twice as likely to die of heart disease, and more than three times as likely to die as a result of injury, compared to those with 13 or more years of education (Reuss, 2001).

The physical health of poor people is more likely to be impaired than is the health of the more well-to-do because of differences in diet, life-style (e.g., the lower the social class, the more likely to smoke), sanitation, shelter, exposure to environmental hazards (e.g., air pollution, lead, untreated water), work conditions, and medical treatment. Child health, for example, varies by family income. As family income increases, the percentage of children in good health increases. In 1997, for example, about 68 percent of children in families living in poverty were in very good or excellent health, compared with 86 percent of children in families living at or above the poverty line (Federal Interagency Forum on Child and Family Statistics, 2000:25). Table 17.2 compares the health outcomes for poor and nonpoor children.

An obvious health advantage of the affluent is access to health-promoting and health-protecting resources and, when needed, access to medical services, typically paid for, at least in part, with health insurance. But the United States does not have universal health insurance as do Canada and the nations of Western Europe and Scandinavia. Health insurance in the United States is typically tied to employment, with employers and employees splitting the cost. Structural changes in the U.S. economy (see Chapter 14)—the shift of employment from manufacturing to services, the rise in contingent and part-time employment, and the decline in union membership—have resulted in a decline in employment-related health insurance coverage. And the lower the prestige and the lower the wages in the job, the less likely the pay will include a health benefits package.

Currently, about 42 million Americans, mostly the poor and the near poor younger than age 65, have no medical insurance, including more than 11 million children (15.5 percent of all children) and an estimated 500,000 pregnant women (see Table 17.3, p. 502). The working poor are the hardest hit because the restrictive eligibility requirements for Medicaid eliminate them from the

TABLE 17.2

Poor Outcomes for Poor Children

Outcome	*Poor Children's Risk Relative to Nonpoor Children*
Health	
Death in childhood	1.5 to 3 times more likely
Stunted growth	2.7 times more likely
Iron deficiency in preschool years	3 to 4 times more likely
Partial or complete deafness	1.5 to 2 times more likely
Partial or complete blindness	1.2 to 1.8 times more likely
Serious physical or mental disabilities	About 2 times more likely
Fatal accidental injuries	2 to 3 times more likely
Pneumonia	1.6 times more likely
Education	
Average IQ score at age 5	9 points lower
Average achievement scores at age 3 and above	11 to 25 percentiles lower
Learning disabilities	1.3 times more likely
Placement in special education	2 or 3 percentage points more likely
Below-usual grade for child's age	2 percentage points more likely for each year of childhood spent in poverty
Dropping out between ages 16 and 24	2 times more likely than middle-income youths; 11 times more likely than wealthy youths

Source: Children's Defense Fund. 1998. *The State of America's Children: Yearbook 1998*. Washington, D.C.: Children's Defense Fund, 1998, p. xiv. Copyright 1998 by the Children's Defense Fund. Used with permission.

program because, although poor, they earn too much money to qualify, resulting in nearly half of poor people who worked full time being uninsured.

The uninsured, of course, cannot afford the costs for physicians, dentists (130 million Americans do not have dental insurance), and hospitals, so they often do without. Poor pregnant women (26 percent of women of child-bearing age have no maternity coverage), as a result, often do not receive prenatal and postnatal health care. The consequences are a high maternal death rate (typically from hemorrhage and infection) and a relatively high **infant mortality rate,** which is the number of deaths per 1,000 live births. In 1997, the U.S. infant mortality rate was 7.2 infant deaths per 1,000 live births. Although this was an all-time low for the United States, the rate still was significantly higher than in most advanced industrial societies (Japan, e.g., has a rate of 3.6).

Ironically, when the uninsured go to a doctor, they pay more for services than the more well-to-do insured patients. The reason is that health insurance companies insist on discounts. The result is that a doctor may charge $25 for a routine exam insured by a group insurance plan but charge $175 for the same exam for a person without insurance.

> "It's horribly ironic," said Paul Menzel, a professor of philosophy at Pacific Lutheran University in Tacoma, Washington. The care of the poor once was supported by the wealthy and the insured, but now the opposite is

TABLE 17.3

The Medically Uninsured, 1999

Characteristics	*Percent Who Are Uninsured*
Total	42.6 million (15.5%)
Age	
Under 18	13.9%
18–24	29.0
25–34	23.2
35–44	16.5
45–64	13.8
65 and older	1.3
Race/ethnicity	
Whites	11.0
Asian Americans	20.8
African Americans	21.1
Latinos	33.0
Household income	
$75,000 or more	8.3
Less than $25,000	24.1
Immigrant status	
Low-income immigrant children	46.0
Low-income native-born children	20.0

Sources: U.S. News and World Report (October 9, 2000):12; Ralph Nader. 2001. "What about the Uninsured?" *Progressive Populist* (August 1):9; Mimi Hall. 2000. "Insurance Blanket Covers More People." *USA Today* (September 29):8A; Abby Scher. 2001. "Access Denied: Immigrants and Health Care." *Dollars and Sense* No. 235 (May/June):8.

happening, he said. "It is the people who are most provided for, not the people who are least provided for, who get the benefit of cost-shifting," Professor Menzel said. (Kolata, 2001:1–2)

There are two government health programs—**Medicare** for the elderly and **Medicaid** for the very poor. Virtually all the elderly population have at least some health care coverage through Medicare. The same is not true for the poor who are not covered by insurance and should be covered by Medicaid. Medicaid is funded jointly by the federal government and each state. Each state administers its version of Medicaid with few federal guidelines. Thus, Medicaid varies from state to state in quality, eligibility of patients, coverage, and the adequacy of fees for the services of physicians and hospitals. The consequence of this policy is to make obtaining Medicaid services a function of the state one lives in, rather than level of poverty or need.

Millions of poor people in the United States are treated under Medicaid, but there are serious problems with this program. Many physicians refuse to treat Medicaid patients (because the government does not reimburse them enough for their services), resulting in delayed medical attention, and then typically in hospital emergency rooms, where such patients cannot be turned away. This overburdens hospitals and postpones treatment as patients often must wait many hours before being seen by a physician. Often the examination is superficial and the treatment careless because the attending physicians are overwhelmed by the numbers of patients.

Even when the poor do go to physicians and clinics, they are more likely than the more affluent to receive inferior services. This results from several factors. First, the poor often are served by understaffed clinics and public hospitals, which means that their visits often require long waits and hurried attention by overworked health practitioners. Second, there are disproportionately fewer physicians in poor urban and poor rural areas than in affluent urban and suburban areas (a consequence of physicians' tending to cluster where their practices will be the most lucrative). For instance, in affluent Beverly Hills there is one doctor for every 150 residents, but in the poor areas of East Los Angeles there is one doctor for every 3,500 residents (Lundberg, 2000:55). Third, the inferior service that the poor tend to receive is a consequence of their relative passivity in the patient–physician relationship.

The common belief is that the poor are accountable for their health deficiencies. Their lack of education and knowledge may lead to poor health practices (diet, exercise, preventive health care). They may, for example, be unaware of the dangers of lead in old paint where their children play, or may not know that excessive sodium in diets is a major contributor to hypertension. The poor, from this perspective, have cultural norms that differ from the majority. Their life-style is less likely than the life-style of the more affluent to include proper exercise for a healthy heart. Their diets are more likely to contain relatively high amounts of fat. They are more likely to smoke cigarettes and to abuse drugs. The children of the poor, for instance, are more likely than the children of the affluent to be born addicted to crack and to be victims of fetal alcohol syndrome.

The essence of this argument is that the problems of ill health that beset the poor disproportionately are a consequence of their different life-style. In short, this line of reasoning blames the poor for their failure to follow healthier life-styles.

This approach, however, ignores the fundamental realities of social class. Williams (1990), in his comprehensive review of the social science literature on socioeconomic status and health, argues that privilege in the social stratification system translates both directly and indirectly into better health in several major ways.

First, the privileged live in home, neighborhood, and work environments that are less stressful. The economically disadvantaged, on the other hand, are more subject to the stresses (and resulting ill health) from high crime rates, financial insecurity, marital instability, death of loved ones, exposure to unhealthy work conditions where they are exposed to hazardous risks and toxic substances, and exposure to pollution and toxic wastes in their neighborhoods. Poor workers are more likely than the nonpoor to be in jobs with low job security. The poor have more stress and hypertension (high blood pressure) because of living in crowded conditions and worrying about having enough resources for food, utilities, and rent. The poor also may not have adequate heat, ventilation, and sanitation, which means that they are more susceptible to infectious and parasitic diseases.

Second, the privileged have more knowledge of positive health habits (adequate sleep, refraining from smoking, drinking moderately, maintaining normal weight, physical exercise, and monitoring cholesterol and blood pressure levels) and the resources to implement them.

Third, the children of privilege have healthier environments in the crucial first 5 years of life. Many adults from disadvantaged backgrounds suffer throughout their lives because of an unhealthy environment in their formative years.

Fourth, the privileged have better access to and make better use of the health care system (the primary subject of this chapter). Early intervention at the onset of a disease and medical management of a chronic illness affect both the survival rates and the quality of life. The fewer the economic resources, the less likely a person will receive preventive care and early treatment. This is because medicine in U.S. society is a market commodity and thus is dispensed unequally to the people who can afford it.

Physicians and private hospitals treat people who can afford their services, often leaving aside those who cannot. This practice is called **patient dumping.** For-profit hospitals either turn away patients who cannot afford their services or they tend to switch them to public hospitals as soon as possible or they keep the poor away by not providing the services they most require (e.g., an emergency room). These practices help the hospital's bottom line but they do not help the poor who need specialized care. Also, patient dumping decreases the quality of care at public hospitals because it increases overcrowding and increases the demand on the limited resources of public hospitals. The practice of patient dumping also indirectly increases the profits of private hospitals by increasing the desire of many of the affluent to choose them over public hospitals. The rationale is provided by Lekachman:

> One of the tribulations of hospitalization is the sort of people one meets. In the next bed may restlessly toss someone of the wrong color, occupation, life style or income. Privatization promises better company. Treatment in a strategically located Humana hospital warrants continuation in sickness as in health of safe, middle-class suburban life. Your fellow patients fit snugly into your own class niche. Their education, jobs, income, and opinions are just like those you encounter in your car pool or on the commuter train. Critics of corporate hospitals justifiably complain that they cream the population, consigning difficult people and their complicated ailments to public and voluntary units. Of course. The critics have identified the major attraction of private hospitals to those creamed. Who prefers skimmed milk to cream? (Lekachman, 1987:303)

As strong as the case is for providing equal access to medical care to all people, it is not the most fruitful approach to correcting the differences in health by socioeconomic class. The answer, most fundamentally, is to reduce the inequalities of class (and race and gender) that perpetuate poor health among the disadvantaged. According to Williams:

> [T]he available evidence suggests . . . that equality in the health care delivery system [while a legitimate and desired goal] will not eliminate inequality in health status . . . if the inequalities remain in the fundamental reward structures of society. The point here is neither that changes in health care delivery will make no difference nor that the determinants of inequality are static. What is implied is that inequality will persist in a variety of social indicators as long as the basic reward structures remain unequal. (Williams, 1990:95)

Race

Non-White people in the United States are disproportionately poor (e.g., about one in four Latinos and African Americans are below the poverty line). This fact combined with racial discrimination leads to unfavorable patterns of health and health care delivery for them. Let us examine some of these health differences by race.

- **Life Expectancy.** Perhaps the best illustration of the difference that race makes on health is in life expectancy. The 1996 data reveal that the difference between White males and Black males was 7.7 years, and the difference between White females and Black females was 5.4 years. The discrepancy is even wider for Native Americans, who have the poorest health of any racial category in the United States, with a life expectancy 10 years below that of the nation as a whole.

- **Infant Mortality.** The rate of infant mortality in the United States reveals striking differences by race. According to the National Center for Health Statistics, the infant mortality rate for Whites in 1998 was 6.0 deaths per 1,000 births, while the rate for Black babies was more than twice as high at 13.7 per 1,000 live births. Among Latinos the rate ranged from 5.5 for infants of Cuban origin to 7.9 for Puerto Ricans, a difference explained in large part by social class differences. The same relationship is found among Asians with infant mortality rates ranging from 3.1 for infants of Chinese origin to 5.8 for Filipinos (Federal Interagency Forum on Child and Family Statistics, 2000:29). Since 1970 the rate has been halved for Whites and Blacks, but obviously the gap between Whites and Blacks remains, and the evidence is that this gap is no longer narrowing. Most significant, in the racial ghettos of some of the nation's inner cities the infant mortality rate is as high as that of some of the poorest Third World countries. A 1990 study, reported in the *New England Journal of Medicine,* for example, found that Black men in Harlem had a 40 percent chance of living to age 65, while men from Bangladesh had a 55 percent chance of reaching that age (Gamble, 1994).

- **Maternal Mortality.** Statistics reveal that the death rate of African American women (18.6 per 100,000 deliveries) due to complications during birth is more than triple the rate for White mothers (Centers for Disease Control and Prevention, reported in Rubin, 1998). A major reason for this racial disparity is that Black women are less likely to receive prenatal care.

- **Prenatal Care.** In 1998 there was a substantial racial disparity in early prenatal care, with 85 percent of White mothers receiving it, compared to 74 percent of Latino mothers, 73 percent of African American mothers, and 69 percent of Native American mothers. More than twice as many African American mothers and Native American mothers as White mothers initiated care during the third trimester or received no prenatal care (Children's Defense Fund, 2001:34).

- **Low Birth Weight.** Low birth weight is closely related to two factors: mothers not receiving adequate prenatal care and prospective mothers smoking during pregnancy. In 1998 African American children were twice as likely to be born with a low birth weight (less than 5 pounds, 8 ounces) as were White children and Latino children (Children's Defense Fund, 2001:34). These proportions by race have remained about the same since 1960.

- **Heart Disease.** Heart disease in all its forms is the nation's leading cause of death. The evidence is that Black men are twice as likely as White men to die

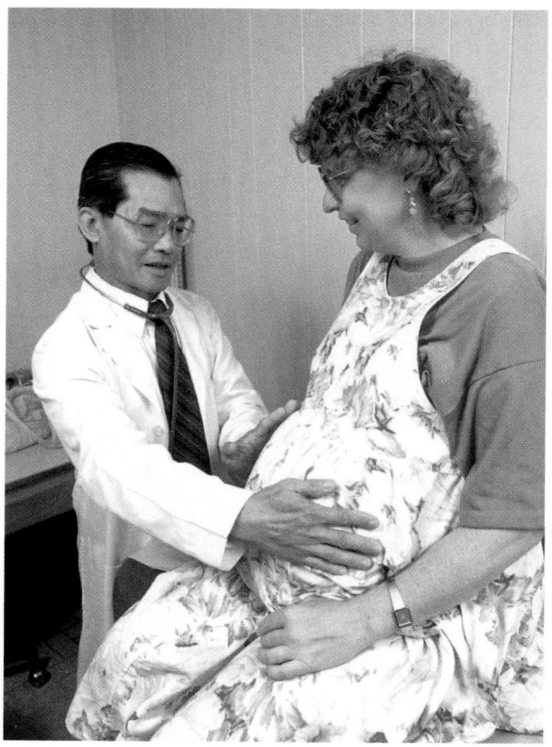

African American and Latina mothers-to-be are twice as likely as White pregnant women to not *receive prenatal care.*

from heart disease before the age of 65. Overall, the national death rate for African American men is 841 per 100,000 compared to 666 White men. Latino men and Asian men, on the other hand, have rates lower than White men—432 and 372 per 100,000 respectively (Centers for Disease Control and Prevention, reported in Sternberg, 2001).

- **Cancer.** The death rate from cancer is about three and one-half times greater for Black males than for White males. The rate for Black women is also higher than it is for White women. The problem, generally, is that African Americans (and Latinos) are more likely to be diagnosed with cancer in its later stages, making survival less likely. This, of course, is not because of race per se but because of the greater likelihood of African Americans and Latinos to be poor and without adequate medical insurance.

  The cancer rate is higher for African Americans than Whites for all cancers except stomach cancer and breast cancer. The latter anomaly may be explained by the apparent fact that the younger a mother is at the birth of her first child, the lower the breast cancer risk, and Black women tend to have children at younger ages. Once cancer is detected in both Blacks and Whites, Whites have a much higher survival rate. Latinos have the lowest incidence of breast cancer, but their chances of survival are not as good as Whites. Overall, Asian American women are much less likely than White or Black women to develop breast cancer, and their 5-year survival rate is the best. However, for cervical cancer, the rate for Vietnamese Americans is 5.7 times that of Whites and 7.5 times that of Japanese Americans, according to the National Cancer Institute (reported in Pascual, 2000). The apparent reason for this extraordinary high rate for Vietnamese Americans is their very low early screening rates; because most of them are recent immigrants, they may be unfamiliar with the concept of preventive care or they are too poor to visit a doctor. Related to this last point, the 1996 welfare reform passed by Congress barred recent immigrants from receiving federally funded Medicaid until they had been in the country for 5 years (Scher, 2001) and, as stated, many Vietnamese Americans are recent immigrants.

- **Vision Problems.** More than 9 million people in the United States have visual impairment, caused usually by glaucoma, diabetes, and retinal diseases. African American adults are nearly twice as likely as Whites to be legally blind or vision impaired, according to a study in the *Archives of Ophthalmology* (Goldfarb, 1990). African Americans are six times more likely to have glaucoma than are Whites and four times more likely to be blinded by it. These high glaucoma rates for Blacks are attributable to their relative lack of access to medical care and their high rate of high hypertension (Atkins, 1991). Latinos are more likely than Whites to be blind, primarily because of complications from diabetes, a disease they are three times more likely than Whites to have (Altman, 1991).

- **Communicable Diseases.** The diseases especially found among the poor (e.g., influenza, pneumonia, and tuberculosis) are disproportionately found among non-Whites because they are disproportionately poor. Tuberculosis occurs fourteen times more frequently among African Americans than Whites, and it is four times more likely to occur among Hispanics than Whites. Native Americans are four times more likely to die from tuberculosis and dysentery than are non-Native Americans.

  Cultural or life-style differences offer some explanations. This blaming-the-victim approach argues that racial minorities do not take proper care of themselves. Their diets tend to be high in fat, sugar, and salt. They are more likely to smoke (a fact not lost on the tobacco companies as they target their products and advertising to African Americans and Latinos). They are less likely than members of the majority to exercise. Thus, Blacks, for example, have a high incidence of obesity, hypertension, and heart disease.

  But even though life-style differences among the races account for some variations in health, other factors are more important. Economic factors explain much of the variation. Minority racial and ethnic groups are disproportionately poor. This means that many of them must live in rat-infested neighborhoods, where they are exposed to diseases carried by these vermin. Their neighborhoods also have high concentrations of lead (in the paint and plumbing), which exposes their children to many health dangers, including brain damage. Living in poverty also means living in inadequate shelter, where exposure to the cold leads to complications such as bronchitis and pneumonia. Living in overcrowded situations leads to the spread of communicable diseases. A low income means reliance on a diet of cheap, fattening, nonnutritious food.

  Living in poverty also results in the disruption of social networks and in heightened fears and anxieties caused by arson, drug abuse, and violent crime. Regarding this last point, Blacks are nearly six times more likely than Whites to be murdered, are almost twice as likely to be robbed, and are raped at a rate nearly double that of Whites.

  The poor also are less likely to receive adequate medical attention. Many, as noted, do not have medical insurance, and being poor they cannot afford medical care on a regular, preventive basis. The absence of insurance coverage is related to race: 33 percent of all Latinos in 1999 were without private or public health insurance, compared with 21 percent of African Americans and 11 percent of Whites (Nader, 2001b). Recent immigrants are denied Medicaid until they have been in this country for 5 years. Thus, they delay going to the physician, dentist, or hospital until the health problem is too serious to ignore. This may mean that the problem is too advanced for a cure.

But even when African Americans and Latinos seek medical attention, they often are given less attention than Whites. For example, a study of an emergency room in an Atlanta hospital found that Black patients with a broken arm or leg were less likely to be given pain medication than White patients with similar injuries and complaints of pain. A similar study in Los Angeles found that Latino patients received pain medication less often than White patients (reported in *USA Today,* 1999a).

The poor in general, and African Americans and other racial minorities in particular, are much more likely than Whites to rely on emergency room and hospital outpatient departments than on a family physician. The two most important reasons for this are that they cannot afford a family physician, and, if they could afford one, physicians are in short supply where the poor live. Most of the uninsured live in areas that have inadequate medical care, including a shortage of primary-care physicians. When these underserved areas are compared to adequately served areas, the underserved have tuberculosis rates five times higher, hepatitis rates twice as high, and an immunizable disease rate of 30.5 (per 100,000) compared to 0.7 (Keen, 1993).

There are four negative outcomes from this for racial minorities. First, they do not meet regularly with a physician who is familiar with their health history. Second, the number of hospitals in the poor sections of cities and where rural poverty is prevalent is declining. Third, the federal cutbacks during the 1980s and 1990s resulted in decreased medical attention for the poor. And fourth, even when health services are accessible, racial minorities may face racial discrimination in attempting to obtain care.

Thus, a major reason for the high death rate of African Americans from cancer is, as the American Cancer Society has noted, because they often do not have access to quality health care. But the link may be stronger than that—when Blacks (and other racial minorities) have access to good medical care, they do not receive the same treatment as do Whites, a consequence of economics, and possibly discrimination. Racial minorities (and women), for example, wait longer for liver transplants than Whites (Fallik, 1998). Similarly, fewer African Americans undergo bypass surgery or angioplasty, resulting in their reduced heart disease survival (Levy, 1997).

Poverty and its attendant problems are exacerbated by the social inequalities associated with race. Being African American, Latino, or Native American means for many people to be considered inferior, even to be despised. Thus, hierarchy and its attendant discrimination creates tensions and stresses. African Americans have higher blood pressure than do Whites. Is the reason genetic or social in origin? Sociologist Joe Feagin and his colleagues conducted focus groups on discrimination's costs with African Americans in California, Michigan, and Florida. He found that a common report from these African Americans is that bottling up stress and rage stemming from discrimination leads, from their considered perspective, to such health problems as stomach problems, chest pains, hypertension, and depression (Feagin, 1997:15).

African Americans, especially those with low income, have higher hypertension (high blood pressure) rates than the more well-to-do. This is partially the result of a poor diet. But it also is reasonable to assume that the stress associated with hypertension results from blocked social mobility, anger over perceived and real injustices, fear of crime, and being treated as a social inferior.

Gender

The health of women and the health care they receive reflect primarily their status in society and only secondarily their physiological differences from men. Women do have significant health advantages over men; for example, their life expectancy exceeds that of males by about 7 years. These advantages begin in the womb, where female fetuses have a 10 percent higher survival rate than do male fetuses. These advantages continue after birth and throughout the life cycle as male death rates exceed female death rates at all ages. Women are less likely than men to die from the leading causes of death, including heart disease, cancer, accidents, suicide, and homicide (the only exception is death from diabetes).

There are both biological and social reasons for some of the health advantages that women have over men. During early childhood girls have biological benefits over boys, as exhibited by their greater resistance to infectious and chronic diseases. As adults, women in the past were more protected than were men, at least until menopause, especially from heart disease and hypertension, because of the hormone estrogen.

More important, though, than the biological differences between the sexes are the significant social differences that also account for gender differences in health. The adolescent and young adult male gender role includes being assertive and daring. This accounts for the greater likelihood of males being in automobile accidents (five out of seven victims of traffic accidents are men), driving while drunk, and using more alcohol (men are three times as likely to be alcoholics), illegal drugs, and cigarettes (recently, however, the number of women who smoke is increasing, so that the difference between men and women is converging). Males also are more likely than females to work at risky jobs (including military combat).

The female gender role is more conducive to good health in several ways. Women are expected to be more knowledgeable about health matters and thus to be more aware of changes in their bodies than are men. Women are also more likely to see a physician or be admitted into a hospital than are men (traditional men tend to see this behavior in males as a sign of weakness).

That women receive more health care than men appears to be more than just a manifestation of gender roles. The evidence is that women, despite their greater longevity, are sick more often than men. As examples, women have fifty bouts with flu for every thirty-seven that men have; women are bedridden 35 percent more days than men are; women are fifteen times more likely to have autoimmune thyroid disease and nine times more likely to have lupus; and women visit doctors more often for anemia, constipation, gallstones, arthritis, and bronchitis (Painter, 1992).

Women on average are less likely than men to have medical insurance. This disadvantage is strongest for women between ages 45 and 64 (before they qualify for Medicare) and especially for African American and Latina women in this age category (about 35 percent of women compared with two-thirds of men). This is because women are more often employed in part-time work, work at low-wage jobs, and work for small businesses. Also, insurance coverage for women stops under their husbands' policies when they are widowed or divorced. As a result, millions of women are too poor to buy health insurance but earn too much to get public aid.

Whether one has health insurance or not is literally a matter of life and death. Using the example of breast cancer, researchers have found that uninsured women are less likely to receive cancer-screening services than are women with private insurance, that they are less likely to have their breast cancer adequately evaluated, and they are less likely to have their breast cancer aggressively treated. As a consequence, they are less likely than insured women to survive the 54- to 89-month period after initial diagnosis (Weiss, 1997:31).

Women face two major health risks. One is child bearing, which can be unhealthy, even deadly, for mothers. The other health risk is a consequence of traditional gender roles. Because women in U.S. society are evaluated by their physical appearance, they are much more likely than men to suffer from anorexia nervosa and bulimia (conditions that result when individuals take extraordinary measures to lose weight). Women are also much more likely than men to risk surgery for cosmetic reasons (tummy tucks, liposuction, breast implants or reduction, and face lifts), which may have negative health effects. Since 1963, when the first breast implant operation was performed, about 2 million U.S. women have used this procedure (80 percent for cosmetic reasons and 20 percent for reconstruction after surgery for breast cancer). This operation, while usually successful, can have side effects such as scarring, firmness of the implant, leakage, and a loss of sensation. There is also the question of the long-term safety of silicon in the body.

The advantage women have over men in mortality rates is overshadowed by the advantages men receive from the medical profession. First, the medical schools and the medical profession are dominated by males. Women in medicine are vastly overrepresented in the nurturant, supportive, underpaid, and relatively powerless roles of nurse and aide.

Second, until 1990, when the government confirmed that women had been intentionally left out of federally funded medical research, much medical research has excluded women as subjects. For example, the major study on whether taking daily doses of aspirin can reduce the risk of a heart attack used 22,071 subjects—all men. In most cases, a drug proved effective in men is also effective for women. But the differences in hormone proportions and the menstrual cycle can be important. In the aspirin study, it would have been useful to determine whether taking aspirin prevents heart attacks in premenopausal women, in only postmenopausal women, or not in any women. Another study used 12,866 male subjects to explore the links between heart disease and high cholesterol, lack of exercise, and smoking. By excluding women from the study, the medical profession has no clear scientific proof whether the linkages among these variables found for men also occur for women (Purvis, 1990).

The National Women's Health Resource Center has noted that other major health studies have overlooked women. As in the aspirin and heart disease study, research using only male subjects has studied diet, exercise, and cholesterol; Type A behavior and heart disease; and alcohol and blood pressure (Silberner, 1990). Since 1990 the representation of women in research studies has increased but only slightly. A review of studies published from 1991 to 2000 found women were 25 percent of the subjects in heart-related research, up from 20 percent in research from 1966 to 1990 (reported in Tanner, 2001).

Third, research appears to put women's health priorities second to men's. For example, the National Institutes of Health has spent much less of its research budget on women's health care issues than men's issues. Perhaps this explains why medical research has yet to come up with an acceptable, safe, and effective male contraceptive. This deficiency has meant that women have had to bear the responsibilities and health risks of contraception. This oversight in medical research is gradually being rectified. Recent research has uncovered genes linked to hereditary breast cancer, made advances in the prevention of osteoporosis, and created drugs to fight ovarian cancer (Shalala, 1997).

Fourth, female patients interacting with male physicians encounter a number of sexist practices. These include paternalistic attitudes; insensitivity toward the special problems of women surrounding the menstrual cycle, childbirth (see the panel titled "Voices," pp. 512–513), and menopause; siding with husbands who were leery of vasectomies and performing, rather, tubal ligations on wives, even though the cost and medical risk were much greater; and requiring more specific tests for men than for women during diagnostic examinations. Another example of male physicians' insensitivity to women often occurs during an unwanted pregnancy. Many male physicians often consider women's interests secondary to fetal survival.

Fifth, women are discriminated against in the treatment they receive or do not receive. Three examples make this point. A study reported in the *New England Journal of Medicine* found that Blacks and women with chest pains were 40 percent less likely to get a common test for heart disease than Whites or men (reported in Fackelmann, 1999). The American Heart Association found that men were twice as likely as women to receive newer, life-saving treatments for heart attacks such as clot-busting drugs or angioplasty (Altman, 1991). Another study found that among cancer patients under age 50, women were twice as likely as men the same age to receive less potent pain medication for the pain they suffer (Snider, Healy, and Miller, 1992).

Class, Race, and Gender: Who Wins and Who Loses in the Battle Against HIV/AIDS?

Twenty years after the killer AIDS (acquired immune deficiency syndrome) epidemic began, the worldwide toll was 22 million people, and 438,000 Americans had died of the disease. In the United States, AIDS deaths have been reduced dramatically by the use of expensive protease inhibitors and other drugs. But there are 40,000 new cases of HIV infection (the forerunner of AIDS) each year. No one knows how long individuals taking these drugs will survive, or whether the virus will mutate, or become resistant to the drugs (Herbert, 2001c).

Within the United States, there are approximately 900,000 people with HIV. If they can afford the expensive drugs, they will likely survive, while those who are unable to purchase the drugs will eventually have AIDS and die. Managed-care programs (medical insurance providers such as health maintenance organizations) typically have annual limits for the reimbursement of drug purchases, usually no more than $3,000 annually. The federal government provides some funds to the states to help the uninsured with their medical problems, but the

VOICES

DOES THE DOCTOR'S GENDER MATTER?

[A] female OB or a female nurse can sympathize a little more with what you are going through than a male, . . . [Male attendants] could possibly watch their wives go through it but they don't know what it's like exactly.

—Tricia, White mother of two

I wanted to be sure to be heard, and I know with medicine, being a child of a physician, I just [know] at times that women's concerns can be seen as over-reactive, exaggerating, unfounded concerns.

—Tonya, African American mother of one

You know, when I said to her, "Gee, this really hurts over here," she could relate to it. With a guy, it was kind of like, "It's all just in your mind." She really could relate to everything. And her personality was wonderful, and she had a great bedside manner. She listened to your questions.

—Jill, White mother of two

These women's comments exemplify many others' feelings about women as doctors.* A 1996 study of women's childbirth experiences in a mid-Atlantic state found that the gender of the doctor did affect many women's reproductive experiences. Eight (or 42 percent) out of nineteen interviewees specifically chose female doctors. Some explained that they had had prior bad experiences with male OB-GYN's or intimates, and thus had switched to female doctors at some point. Other women specifically wanted a doctor who should be "more caring," hinting that feelings and emotions during pregnancy and childbirth were important. Others explained that they wanted to be on more "equal footing" with their attendant.

Vicki, a mother of two from England, recounted her experience with a male OB-GYN:

> Yeah, he basically gave me no information. When I asked him about birth courses, you know, . . . he told me to go to the birthing course at the hospital. And [the class] was mostly on drugs, it was very strange. And he patted me on the head and said, "I'll handle it, don't you worry about a thing." And I didn't like that, and I didn't want any part of it [the second time].

The authoritative medical knowledge that this doctor held

*All names of women have been changed to ensure confidentiality.

states vary widely in their generosity toward those with HIV/AIDS. Some states have opted to do nothing for these people while other states offer limited financial assistance.

In 1996, for the first time since the epidemic began in the United States, the number of people diagnosed with AIDS declined from the previous year's numbers. This was a direct result of these new drugs halting HIV from becoming AIDS. But because the new drugs go only to those who can afford them, and to a fortunate few who are poor but live in states with generous assistance, the drop in AIDS was not across the board but rather benefited those with racial privilege. The new cases of AIDS dropped 13 percent among Whites, but rose 19 percent among heterosexual Black men and 12 percent among heterosexual Black women (Meyer, 1997).

Since then the epidemic has increased again. Especially hard hit are minority men and women (see Figure 17.1, p. 514):

> AIDS is the leading cause of death for African Americans between the ages of 25 and 44. While Blacks are just 13 percent of the U.S. population, more than half of all new HIV infections occur among Blacks. Blacks are 10 times more

supposedly gave him the right to withhold certain types of information from Vicki, leaving her with little knowledge of what would happen during birth. He assumed that Vicki would be comfortable simply allowing him to "handle it." The desire to be heard and informed is also evident in this next woman's response:

> Just from the different experiences I've had, [female doctors will] sit down and listen to you more, they'll understand your concerns, or they'll answer questions you might not have thought of that they've known . . . just in general, they seem more, not more caring or sympathetic, just open to other ideas, instead of being a leader person. (Heidi, White, mother of three)

The mere fact that female doctors often have had their own birthing experiences was an additional reason to choose them, for experience was equated with greater competency, knowledge, and understanding of the birth process. Thus, female doctors brought comfort for many women on many levels. Stephanie, a White mother of two, stated: "You have a lot going on, you know, they're prodding and poking you and I just felt—because I'm a modest person—I just knew that I would be more comfortable with a female [doctor]." Rachel, a White mother of one, stated that she "would be more comfortable [asking a] myriad of questions with a woman. I felt that I could get a little bit more of an insight especially because Dr. [name] had had children as well." And Natasha, another White mother of one, suggested that she was not comfortable "talking about this kind of stuff to begin with, so I have a hard time talking about this stuff even with a woman. I probably would have been red in the face the whole time talking to a man."

In contrast to the situations explained here, women who received prenatal care from male doctors did not necessarily "choose" the gender of their doctor. Of those who had male doctors, only 3 out of 11 (approximately 25 percent) stated that the gender of their doctor mattered to them. Thus, we can assume that the rest of the women interviewed simply followed a pre-established model for birth (perhaps going to doctors that relatives or friends recommended), which included birth in a hospital setting with a male doctor in charge. If gender did matter to a woman, then she was more likely to seek out a female doctor.

Source: This essay was written expressly for *Social Problems* by Heather E. Dillaway. 2000. Department of Sociology, Michigan State University.

> likely than Whites to be diagnosed with AIDS, and 10 times more likely to die from it. . . . Black women are becoming infected at a frightening rate. They account for 64 percent of all new infections among women in the U.S. One in every 160 Black women is believed to be infected with HIV. By comparison, one in 250 White men is infected, and one in 3,000 White women. (Herbert, 2001a)

The trends are especially troubling for women. While AIDS rates remain lower among women than men, women now account for a fourth of all newly diagnosed cases, double the percentage from 10 years ago. This growth is largely the disproportionate spread of the disease among heterosexual African American women, particularly in the South:

> Researchers say that in many ways the epidemic in the South more closely resembles the situation of the developing world [see Chapter 3] than of the rest of the country. Joblessness, substance abuse, teenage pregnancy, sexually transmitted diseases, inadequate schools, minimal access to health care and entrenched poverty all conspire to thwart the progress that has been made among other high-risk groups, particularly gay men. (Sack, 2001:2)

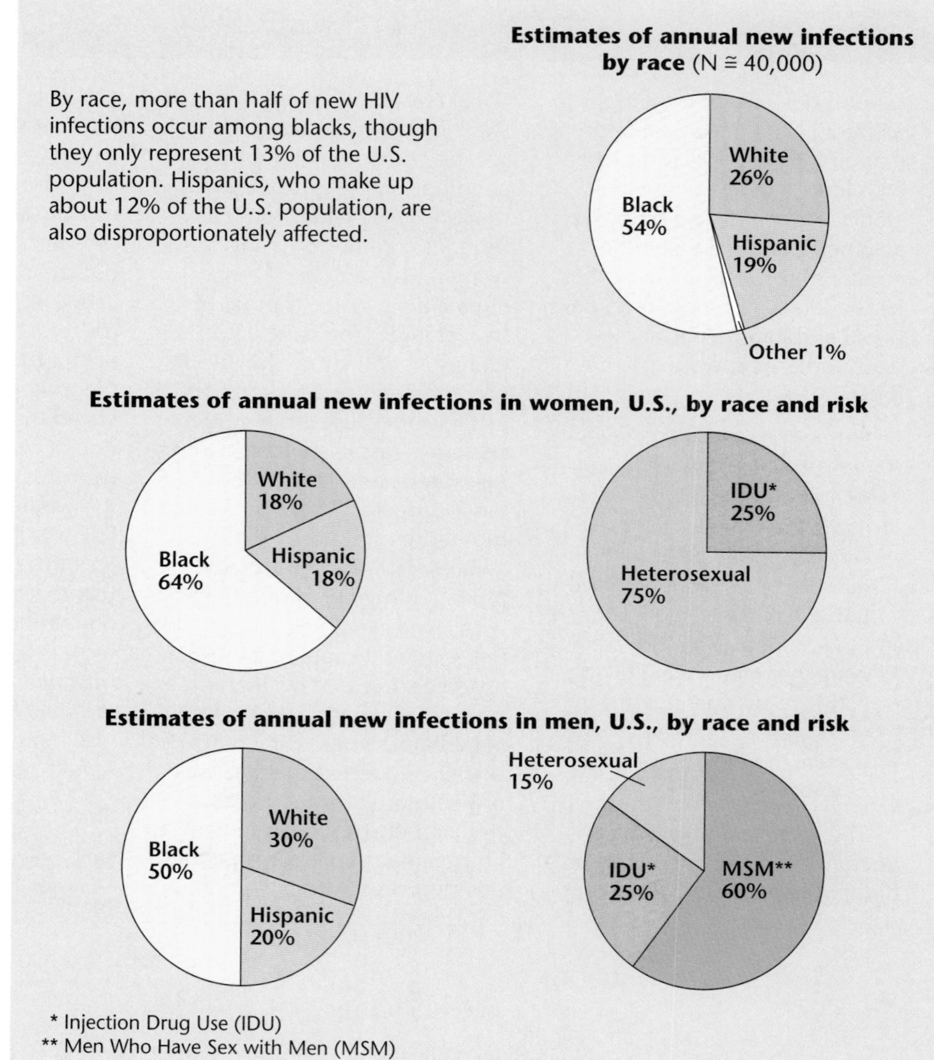

FIGURE 17.1

The HIV Epidemic by Race and Gender, December 2000

Source: Centers for Disease Control and Prevention. 2001. *HIV/AIDS Update.* Washington, DC: Department of Health and Human Services.

CHANGING SOCIAL ORGANIZATION OF HEALTH CARE DELIVERY

The United States spends over $1.2 trillion on health care, much more than any other nation. The private sector (businesses providing benefits for their employees) pays about one-fourth of the total U.S. health bill, governments (federal, state, and local) pay two-fifths (using tax dollars), and individuals pay about one-third, either through direct payments of patients or through private insurance premiums. The previous section considered the government programs for the elderly (Medicare) and the poor (Medicaid) and those left out (the uninsured). This section considers (1) the health care system for the majority of U.S. residents—those covered by insurance programs, (2) the dramatic transformation in this system within the past few years from physician-centered care

Within the United States, there are approximately 900,000 people with HIV. If they can afford the expensive drugs, they will likely survive, while those who are unable to purchase the drugs will eventually have AIDS and die.

to managed care, and (3) in a related shift, the move from nonprofit hospitals to for-profit hospitals.

Health insurance in the United States is tied to employment. Most employers in the private sector negotiate with insurance companies or with medical plans to provide health insurance for their employees, usually with the costs shared by the employers and employees. Until recently, the typical situation for a sick employee (or that of a family member) was to go to a physician or a hospital, and the insurance would pay all or part of the resulting bill.

Fee-for-Service System

The prevailing system was that the cost of the health services was determined by the people who provided the services—physicians, therapists, hospitals, clinics, and laboratories—with little outside interference. Physicians, for example, were, for the most part, independent, fee-for-service entrepreneurs. Patients had little power to complain or go elsewhere because physicians and hospitals have so much more knowledge and power and because fees tend to be relatively standardized within a community or region. This meant, in effect, that health providers were able to increase their profits because there were few incentives to control consumer costs and few controls to limit abuses. For example, the more that physicians had their patients visit them for checkups and treatments, the more money they made. Also, patients could not purchase prescription drugs without the physician's prescription. This permitted a physician to see dozens of patients a day for the normal office call fee in order to write the prescription. Also, in some cases, the physician shared in the profits with the pharmacist. The result is that the average physician's income in the United States is about double that of physicians in Canada and Germany and about three times what physicians make in Japan and the United Kingdom (Rasell, 1993).

Just as with physicians, hospitals are more profitable the more tests are performed on patients and the longer the patients stay. Probably most treatments by physicians and tests by hospitals are necessary, but the profit-enhancing system encouraged the likelihood of such abuses as excessive inpatient care and unnecessary tests.

This problem of increasing costs was exacerbated by the rise of the third-party system of funding—payments by insurance companies or by the government (Medicare and Medicaid). Medicare and Medicaid were organized so that physicians and hospitals were reimbursed for their costs. This practice encouraged hospitals, nursing homes, and physicians to order excessive and, therefore, more expensive treatment. The irony is that about one-fourth of the people in the United States still do not receive enough medical care (especially the working poor, who often are excluded because they do not qualify for Medicaid); and some people receive more care than is sometimes necessary.

Typically, consumers paid only about one-third of physician's fees and about one-tenth of hospital bills. The remainder was paid by insurance or government programs. This third-party system encouraged high health costs in two ways, depending on the source of payment. Health insurance limits payments to inpatient care by physicians and to hospital-related expenses, both of which inflated expenses by encouraging these activities even when they may not have been needed.

Especially costly was the incentive (for the profit of physicians and hospitals) to use a variety of laboratory tests, elaborate and expensive technology for diagnostic tests (e.g., computerized tomography—CT scanners—or magnetic resonance imaging—MRI machines), and elaborate new surgeries such as heart bypass and organ and bone-marrow transplants. Even though these procedures are sometimes successful, they are usually very expensive. Tim Wise has summarized the problem:

> Under fee-for-service, hospitals and physicians have been paid on a cost-plus basis, much like defense contractors. They set their fees to cover costs and guarantee a profit, then send the bill to the insurer. Private insurers guarantee payment, build in their own profit margins, and pass the costs on in higher premiums. Neither the provider nor the insurer has much incentive to hold down costs. (Wise, 1989:6)

Shift to Managed Care

Under the fee-for-service system, health costs in the United States rose rapidly, typically at least twice the inflation rate. This ever-spiraling cost has resulted in a shift away from fee-for-service to managed care.

Shocked by double-digit medical inflation, major corporations have used several strategies to fight the high cost of medical care for their employees. One strategy is to reduce the number of employees who are eligible (downsizing the actual number of employees, hiring temporary workers or independent contractors). The second tactic is to switch from traditional insurance plans to **health maintenance organizations (HMOs).** Because employers pay HMOs a flat fee, these organizations have a huge incentive to control costs. Then they can pass some of these savings to employers. A third approach is for employers not to provide health care benefits for their workers. Our focus here is on the trend to health maintenance organizations, which have grown dramatically so that about two thirds of Americans in 2000 were members (see Figure 17.2).

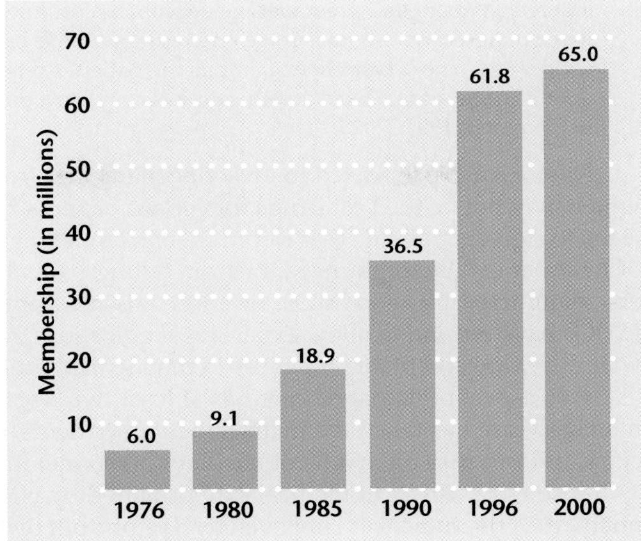

FIGURE 17.2

HMOs Are Growing

Sources: USA Today (July 13, 1998):12A; "The Growing Pains of Managed Care." *New York Times* (August 5, 2001). Online. Available: nytimes.com/2001/08/05/opinion/05SUN2.html.

The shift has been dramatic. "In less than a decade, managed care has turned the system upside down, from one in which payments tempted doctors to do too much, to a system in which payments tempt them to do too little" (Brink and Shute, 1997:60).

Managed care, as found in the typical HMO, works this way. Members pay a set fee (as much as $5,000 a year), which is supplemented by their employer. The HMO contracts with selected physicians and hospitals that furnish a comprehensive set of health care services to enrolled members. The members go to the doctors and hospitals in their plan as needed. The HMO monitors the patients, doctors, and hospitals to keep costs at a minimum.

Companies have been attracted to managed care because it limits costs. Individuals, too, have found that HMOs save them money ($1,000 or $2,000 less per year than a standard health insurance policy, in which the insured pays a monthly premium plus 20 to 30 percent of the charges). This is the good news about the transformation in health care delivery.

However, there is a downside to this dramatic shift, due almost exclusively to the profit motive. Foremost, there is now the danger that physicians are no longer the patient's advocate. HMOs reward doctors by the number of patients they see, by their prescribing remedies that cost less than the norm, and by penalizing them for prescribing remedies that cost more than the norm (in essence, this makes the doctor's income contingent on how much care is withheld).

The pressure to limit care to cut costs is often overt and structured into doctors' contractual arrangements with HMOs. "At U.S. Healthcare and other for-profits, each doctor is given a certain amount of money for each patient every month, to take care of that person and 'keep them healthy.' This is called capitation," explains Susan Steigerwalt, a high blood pressure specialist in Detroit who is former president of Physicians for a National Health Program.

> But if you refer your patients to specialists more often than what the company considers to be acceptable, or if your patient goes to the emergency room more than they think is acceptable, then a portion of the money that they pay you is withheld. Conversely . . . if your patients don't go to the

> emergency room and your average per month cost for specialty care is low, you'll receive a bonus at the end of the year. We call it "fee-for-non-service" . . . The bottom line . . . it pits the patient's interests against the doctor's. She adds, "Even an ethical physician has a difficult time." (cited in Slaughter, 1997:22–23)

Doctors are encouraged to prescribe medicines from lists of cheaper drugs, which may not be the best drugs for certain patients. Some HMOs force physicians to sign agreements that forbid them from telling patients about the range of treatments they might need, or from telling patients how they (the doctors) are reimbursed by the HMOs. In effect this has sometimes meant that some HMOs have refused to allow expensive medications, tests, and treatments even when they are acceptable practices in the medical profession.

This aspect of managed care has at least two negative consequences. First, managed care has taken the management of patients' health away from physicians and put it in the hands of ancillary personnel in corporate headquarters. "Almost every aspect of medical care provided by HMOs is second guessed—not by the government . . . not even by doctors, but by the bean counters" (Gorman, 1998:23). Thus, physicians in HMO networks no longer have the freedom to practice what they believe is the best medicine for their patients. A second casualty is damage to the doctor–patient relationship. "Today's medical market displaces patients and caregivers from center stage, elbowing aside the human relationships and cultural crux of care" (Woolhandler and Himmelstein, 1997:6).

In their zeal to cut costs, some HMOs have instituted such practices as limiting new mothers to no more than 24 hours in the hospital after giving birth, doing mastectomies without any hospitalization, and the like. Similarly, HMOs often refuse to pay for the emergency room bill of patients who did not receive preapproval as required by the rules of the HMOs (the following is from *USA Today,* 1998a). Knowing this, many may be deterred from seeking urgently needed care. Also, since the preapproval of emergency care requires that ailments often be diagnosed over the phone by a managed-care gatekeeper, who is not necessarily a physician, the result may be misdiagnosis. For example, there often is little difference between the pains of indigestion and those that signal a heart attack; flulike symptoms may actually be meningitis. These unhealthy practices have been curtailed as various states have forced HMOs to modify their sometimes inhumane practices. Most states, for example, now prohibit health plans from denying a new mother two days in the hospital.

In a profit-oriented health system, it makes sense to maximize the number of insured who are healthy and to restrict the number who are sick. In other words, the sickest patient is a cost center to be avoided (the following is from Hilzenrath, 1998). HMOs can accomplish this by **medlining** (the practice in health care of avoiding the sick, similar to the practice of redlining, the practice in lending and insurance of avoiding deteriorating neighborhoods or racial minority neighborhoods). One medlining strategy is to not have physicians who treat severe conditions (e.g., cardiologists) in the network. Similarly, when building clinics or recruiting doctors, the HMO can limit exposure to the chronically sick by seeking those in affluent locales, where the incidence of AIDS and tuberculosis, for example, is low. By having gaps in coverage, certain unhealthy populations can be omitted from the plan, increasing profits. For instance, a plan that does not pay for the devices that diabetes patients use to monitor blood sugar will attract fewer diabetics than plans that do pay for these required materials.

Kirk Anderson

Historically, one of the strengths of HMOs is that they emphasize preventive medicine. Patients are, theoretically, given annual checkups, screening for early warning signs of high blood pressure, cervical cancer (Pap smear test), prostate cancer (PSA test), heart disease (irregular heartbeat, high cholesterol), diabetes (blood test), and breast cancer (mammogram). Armed with the information from these tests, weight, and other measures, patients are then counseled about diet, exercise, pharmaceutical interventions, and other preventive measures. These preventive measures, it is argued, make sense for HMOs because it will save them money if patients remain healthy. In practice, however, the emphasis on prevention varies from HMO to HMO (the following is from *USA Today,* 1998a). In 1997 the National Committee for Quality Assurance (NCQA), a nonprofit organization of employers, consumers, and health care providers, reported huge gaps in the prevention efforts by managed care. They found, for example, that while vaccinating children can produce a ten-to-one economic return, on average, managed care provided complete immunizations to only two-thirds of eligible patients. The worst plans immunized only 20 percent of the children in their plans. Similarly, the class of drugs known as beta blockers protect heart attack victims from future heart attacks. But NCQA found that while the best managed-care plans provided such care to all eligible patients, others did no better than 15 percent. So, too, with prenatal care, where the best plans took care of all eligible patients, but the worst plans took care of only 40 percent. The main reason for this inconsistency is that the decision makers in some HMOs have decided that it is not in their financial interest to provide preventive health maintenance because HMO patients switch plans often (in California, 20 percent change plans at least once a year), which means that HMOs do not have a long-term interest in their patients.

HMOs also have been found to use less-practiced surgeons for their patients to keep their costs down and profits up (the following is from a study by Feldman and Scharfstein, reported in McNamee, 1998). Research has shown that for physicians and hospitals alike, surgeons who perform a particular procedure the most tend to deliver better results. Examining breast, colorectal, and gynecological cancer operations in Massachusetts in 1995, Sarah Feldman and

David Scharfstein found that nonelderly patients with traditional fee-for-service insurance tended to go to surgeons who were the most experienced in these specialized surgeries and to have them done in hospitals where these surgeries were commonly performed, much more so than patients enrolled in the state's six largest managed-care plans. The researchers speculate that "managed care plans tend to contract with less specialized hospitals, where the plans can get bigger discounts, leading in turn to use of lower-volume surgeons" (McNamee, 1998:20).

Shift from Private to For-Profit Hospitals

The corporate takeover of health care includes the ownership of hospitals. Traditionally, hospitals in the United States have been nonprofit organizations run by churches, universities, and municipalities. Since the mid-1960s, however, private profit-oriented hospitals and hospital chains have emerged, and they are growing rapidly. "According to Public Citizen, 447 community hospitals were objects of mergers or acquisitions in 1995, and 58 nonprofit hospitals converted to for-profit status in that year alone" (Cahill, 1997:14). These mergers, plus the explosive growth of outpatient centers, have resulted in a downsizing of hospital beds and the number of hospitals.

In addition to downsizing in the hospital industry, there has been a simultaneous process of concentration of ownership. "In other words, while the total number of hospitals and beds has been declining for several years, those that remain are falling under the control of fewer and fewer corporate owners" (Weiss, 1997:68). For example, Columbia/HCA Healthcare Corporation, the world's largest for-profit hospital chain, owned in 1997 some 350 hospitals (10 percent of the nation's hospitals), 133 outpatient diagnostic and surgery centers, and hundreds of nursing homes, home care units, blood centers, and psychiatric facilities. Its worth in 1997 was $20.2 billion, employing 285,000 people and operating in 38 states (*USA Today*, 1997a; Cahill, 1997). Columbia's strategy has been to purchase nonprofit hospitals, creating quasi-monopolies. They then slash basic services and increase the price of services to boost profits. Richard E. Rainwater, a co-founder of Columbia, calls this strategy for hospital empire building "the Wal-Mart approach to health care" (Weiss, 1997:68).

For-profit hospitals are established to maximize profits and they usually do. Thomas Frist, for example, invested $125,000 along with a similar amount by Richard Rainwater to form Columbia in 1987; in 1996 his stake in the company was valued at $350 million (Ginsburg, 1996). A number of strategies are employed by the for-profit hospitals to optimize profits. They avoid low-income areas by locating in states and neighborhoods with well-insured populations. Often they build hospitals without emergency rooms, neonatal intensive units, or burn units because such facilities often lose money. For-profit hospitals have a special interest in minimizing their care for emergency patients because they attract Medicaid and charity cases, and federal law requires that hospitals must care for all emergencies even if the patients have no insurance. Thus, hospitals without emergency rooms or with inadequate emergency facilities can

> dump tens of thousands of patients a year on the doorsteps of public hospitals. That is, they may minimally "stabilize" poor patients who show up at the ER, but as soon as possible they transport them to a public hospital to avoid having to provide more extensive treatment for little or no reimbursement. (Weiss, 1997:72)

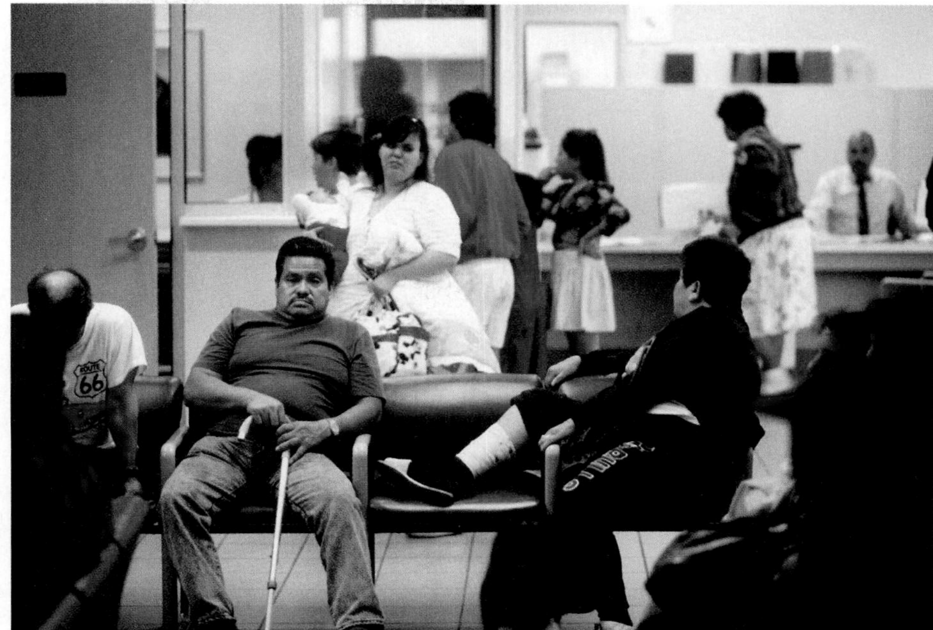

For-profit hospitals have a special interest in minimizing *their care for emergency patients because they attract Medicaid and charity cases, and federal law requires that hospitals must care for all emergencies even if patients have no insurance.*

In Lee County, Florida, for example, state officials found that in 1994 the public hospital provided $13.1 million in "charity/uncompensated care." The total for the three hospitals in that county owned by Columbia/HCA Healthcare, on the other hand, only provided slightly more than $1 million to those who could not pay for services (Ginsburg, 1996:20).

Another strategy to increase profits is to purchase all of the nonprofit hospitals in an area, creating a monopoly—and with a monopoly comes higher prices for services. Still other organizations purchase hospitals that are nonunion, which allows them to keep salaries and wages relatively low. They can also skimp on the quality of supplies, the level of cleanliness, and the level of staffing (Ginsburg, 1996). Thus, as hospitals have become increasingly owned by private profit-seeking interests, the cost of medical care has increased.

To summarize this section on the transformation of the health care delivery system in the United States, consider this quote from Carl Ginsburg, which criticizes the shift to for-profit hospitals but is applicable to what has happened in the managed-care industry as well:

> Making fat profits on hospitals at the expense of the poor and the sick may not be a prison offense in this country. What is a crime is the galloping privatization of the nation's health resources and the rise of a competitive health care system that has less and less to do with health and access to care and *everything to do with money*. [Italics added.] (Ginsburg, 1996:22)

TOWARD A BETTER HEALTH CARE SYSTEM: SOME ALTERNATIVES

The United States, as we have stated, spends much more for health care, both in total dollars and as a percentage of its gross national product, than any other nation. Overall, we do not get a very good return on this investment. All major indicators of national health show that other nations are getting more for their health dollars than is the United States. The reason for the relatively high rates in infant mortality and low rates for longevity is that so many people in the United States do not receive adequate care because they cannot afford it. At the other end of the resource hierarchy, however, the U.S. health care system is superb, with all the wonders of high-technology medicine and the most qualified (and expensive) physicians available. At present the U.S. health care system is rationed according to ability to pay (either from one's own resources or through one's insurance).

The U.S. system of health care—medical insurance financed individually or jointly through employers, Medicare for the old, and Medicaid for the poor—desperately needs reform. Medicare does not work because it still leaves the elderly paying almost one-fourth of their incomes for uncovered services. Medicaid covers slightly less than half of the poor and leaves out the near poor. Forty-two million people are uninsured and many millions more are underinsured. And managed care, which has become the dominant source of health care, is inefficient and so profit-oriented that patient needs are not always met. Given this gloomy health climate, are there reforms that could improve health care in the United States?

This section examines some alternatives to the present system of health care in the United States. These alternatives are (by increasing scale of difficulty to attain) (1) reforms within the health care system, (2) alternative national health insurance plans, and (3) societal changes that indirectly affect the health of its citizens.

Reforms within the Medical Community

A number of reforms within the medical community could spread the benefits of health care to more people and also could reduce costs. These reforms require changes in philosophy at the governmental and personal levels about where to concentrate resources, decisions by medical schools and medical associations, better oversight by the government, insurance companies, and the medical profession over medical practices, and changes in philosophy by the government and insurance companies on which medical activities are appropriate and which are not. The following list is not comprehensive, but it is a start:

- Spend more money on basic medicine and less, much less, on heroic medicine. As Richard Lamm has pointed out, "we keep people alive for whom there is no happy outcome, yet we do not vaccinate kids" (Lamm, 1989b:59).
- Society needs more accessible physicians. This means two things: (1) Colleges of medicine must train more physicians who practice family medicine, pediatrics, and internal medicine and fewer specialists (only 10 percent of U.S. physicians are general practitioners, compared with 50 percent of the physicians in Canada); and (2) the number of physicians and other health care practitioners should be redistributed so that they work in appropriate numbers in rural areas and in inner cities. Such a redistribution can be accomplished by giving health care workers incentives to work in underserviced areas.
- Spend more money on preventive medicine. Currently, insurance programs, managed care, and government health programs emphasize treating people who are sick rather than trying to keep them healthy.

HMOs were intended to accomplish this with periodic health examinations and emphasis on wellness programs and preventive care. Unfortunately, many HMOs have neglected preventive medicine as a short-term way to increase profits.

- There needs to be government oversight over HMOs and other managed-care systems and for-profit hospitals to ensure that the practices employed are appropriate medically.
- There needs to be federal control over the medical industry, rather than the piecemeal, state-by-state system of regulations. The "Patients Bill of Rights," passed by Congress in 2001, is a good beginning.

National Health Insurance

The United States is the only developed country that does not have universal, government-paid medical programs for residents. Rather, the United States distributes health care by the ability to pay. Medical insurance is obtained usually through employment. This system leaves the uninsured and the underinsured—who are disproportionately non-White, women, and children—with inadequate health care. The results are a relatively high infant mortality rate, a higher rate of disability for youth, a greater likelihood of premature death and lingering illnesses for adults, and, in general, a poorer quality of life.

In addition, as noted repeatedly in this chapter, there are a number of abuses in the current system, such as the physician's income being contingent on how much care is withheld, not providing for the poor in emergency rooms, avoiding the insurance coverage of people who are sick or likely to get sick, and the like. The for-profit system that prevails in the United States lacks a social mission; it is more responsive to Wall Street than to Main Street. Economist Robert Kuttner says this:

> The only way to cut through this mess is, of course, to have universal health insurance. All insurance is a kind of cross-subsidy. The young, who on average need little care, subsidize the old. The well subsidize the sick.
>
> With a universal system, there is no private insurance industry spending billions of dollars trying to target the well and avoid the sick, because everyone is in the same system. There is no worry about "portability" when you change jobs, because everyone is in the same system. And there are no problems choosing your preferred doctor or hospital, because everyone is in the same system. (Kuttner, 1998b:27)

Most advocates of universal health insurance argue for a **single-payer plan** (a tax-supported program, such as exists in Canada, Sweden, Norway, Denmark, and Japan, in which the government is the sole insurer). This plan would serve all citizens at lower cost; Canada spends 10 percent of its gross domestic product (GDP) on health care, compared to 14 percent in the United States. It would be more efficient not only in serving everyone but in less bureaucracy and paper work (overhead is less than 10 percent in Canada, while it exceeds 25 percent in the United States) (Coddington and Fischer, 2001). (For a progressive health care plan at the state level, see the "Social Policy" panel, p. 524.) Such a plan, however, is vigorously opposed by the American Medical Association (AMA), the nation's largest association of physicians with approximately 300,000 members. This association has always resisted a national, comprehensive medical insurance program because it does not want government intrud-

SOCIAL POLICY

THE PROGRESSIVE HEALTH CARE SYSTEM IN VERMONT

The array of health benefits provided to its citizens by Vermont is unmatched by any other state (the following is from Rosenbaum, 2000). The provisions:

- The state guarantees free medical and dental care to every resident age 18 and younger from a family with income below $50,000 (this covers 55,000 of the state's 145,000 children).
- Adults with income below 150 percent of the federal poverty line (a single adult making less than $12,500 and a family of four making less than $25,500) are entitled to medical coverage for a nominal fee.
- Drug coverage to the elderly and people with disabilities for $3 a month.
- Health insurance companies are required to sell policies to residents who request one and must provide them at the same cost to all customers, regardless of their age or medical history.

This plan, implemented gradually, has the support of a Democratic governor (and a former physician), state legislators from both parties, doctors, and the public. Says John Bloomer, Jr., a Republican leader in the state's senate: "Generally speaking, it's a bipartisan goal to expand health care access and affordability" (quoted in Rosenbaum, 2000:11A).

ing into the professional lives of physicians. Its position is that even though the U.S. health care system needs improvement, it basically works. The AMA's answer is to force more employers to provide health insurance and to expand Medicaid coverage for the poor. The single-payer model is also opposed by the health insurance and for-profit hospital industries for obvious reasons—since they would become obsolete.

There are more than 200 health-related political action committees (PACs) representing the AMA and other physician organizations, for-profit hospitals, HMOs, insurance companies, and pharmaceutical firms that contribute money to congressional candidates. When President Clinton tried to modify the health care system during his first term, more than 650 groups spent more than $100 million over a 15-month period to influence the legislation (Seelye, 1994). The congressional recipients receiving the largest amounts from PACs were members of key committees considering health legislation. In essence, this money was spent to block or minimize health care reform. As Tom Goodwin, public affairs director of the Federation of American Health Systems, which represents some 1,400 for-profit hospitals, said, "We spend our money on those members . . . most interested in maintaining the current system" (Kemper and Novak, 1992:9).

Societal Changes

The Canadian system or some variation of a national and universal health insurance is a must if the United States is to be a more just society.

More than this is necessary, however, if we are to have a more healthy society. The United States must cooperate with other nations to make the fragile environment safer and healthier. This commitment to the environment must also be shared by the U.S. business community and all people. Also, the business community, monitored by the government, must provide work environments safe from hazards such as toxic chemicals, polluted air, and risky work conditions.

Moreover, there should be educational campaigns against eating unhealthful foods (e.g., fats, sugars, and chemical additives) and against using dangerous drugs (i.e., illegal as well as legal drugs). The effort to reduce smoking, for example, has had dramatic and positive effects. Most important, though, if U.S. society is committed to the better health of its people, would be the elimination of poverty.

We have seen that poverty is directly related to higher rates of illness and to higher mortality rates. These are the results of poor diets; living in overcrowded rooms in dilapidated, ill-heated housing; and living in unsanitary conditions. The quality of the health of poor people is also diminished because of the greater likelihood of having to live and work where pollution and danger are most likely to prevail. The point is that even if there were a universal health program in which the poor received adequate medical attention, the existence of poverty would still make the poor more prone to illness and disease. Thus, a commitment to a society in which all members have the right to an appropriate health standard requires both universal health care and the elimination of poverty. At a minimum this means that all people should be brought above the poverty line. This action would improve the health (and other aspects of well-being) for the millions of poor people who are disproportionately African American, Latino, and Native American and who are disproportionately single women and children. The important issue is whether the people of the United States will make such a commitment. Obviously, it is a matter of priority, and so far the nation has given the health and welfare of its poorest citizens a low priority.

CHAPTER REVIEW

1. The U.S. health care system is rationed according to ability to pay for services. For people who can afford it, the United States provides the most advanced medical technology and the best trained medical personnel in the world. For those who cannot (about one-fourth of the population), medical care is poor in quality and quantity.
2. Economic disadvantage is closely related to health disadvantages. The poor are much more likely than the affluent to die in infancy, to suffer from certain diseases, and as adults to die sooner. They are less likely to receive medical attention because of being uninsured (42 million) or underinsured (50 million), and when they do receive medical care, to receive inferior service.
3. The most commonly held explanation for the strong relationship between social class and health is that the poor are responsible for their disproportionate ill health because of ignorance or neglect. This approach blames the victim because it ignores the primary role that privilege plays in health and the lack of privilege in poor health. The fundamental solution for reducing socioeconomic differences in health is to reduce the inequalities in society that perpetuate poor health among the disadvantaged.
4. Race is also related to health, with non-Whites disadvantaged by a combination of economic disadvantage and racial discrimination.
5. Health and ill health are also related to gender differences. Women have health advantages over men because of their physical differences and differing gender expectations. Women are placed at risk, however, by child-bearing, the greater likelihood of unnecessary surgery such as hysterectomies, the relative lack of medical research using women as subjects, and the still common sexist practices by physicians, who are predominantly male.
6. AIDS, once a death sentence, can now be controlled for the most part by combinations of very expensive drugs. Those with HIV (the pre-

cusor to AIDS) who are most likely to die from AIDS are the poor in the developing nations and the poor in the United States who live in states that do not subsidize the expensive treatments. While the number of new cases of AIDS has dropped appreciably among Whites in the United States, it has risen substantially among heterosexual African American men and women.

7. In the past decade there has been a major transformation in the delivery of health care in the United States. The system has shifted from a fee-for-service system where those providing the services determined the cost, which was paid by patients and insurance companies, to managed-care systems. In the new system, members pay a fixed fee and their medical needs are provided by the HMO or other form of managed care.
8. The downside to managed care is that the object of the providers is to limit costs and maximize profits. Thus, doctors in the plan are rewarded for keeping costs down and penalized for excessive costs. The management of patients' health now has shifted in many ways from the physician to policies formed at corporate headquarters. Another problem is that HMOs try to attract healthy people into the membership, while limiting those with the most health risks.
9. Similar problems occur with the shift from private to for-profit hospitals. Again, the profit motive often works against the health of patients. Most prominent are the efforts not to provide care to charity cases, to develop monopolies and then raise prices, and to skimp on personnel and services.
10. One solution to the problems in the health field is to institute reforms within the medical community. A more extreme solution—and one opposed by the majority of physicians—is a national, comprehensive health care program. The United States is the only industrialized nation in the Western world without such a program. The Canadian health care system provides an interesting model that some people have suggested should be used in the United States. Their system, which is universally applied to all residents, is more efficient, is less costly, and has better medical results than the current U.S. model.
11. A national health program with the goal of bringing all residents up to a minimum acceptable standard not only must include a universal health program but also must eliminate the worst of poverty, because poverty itself is a major contributor to ill health.

KEY TERMS

Infant mortality rate. Number of deaths per 1,000 live births.

Medicare. Government program that provides partial coverage of medical costs primarily for people over age 65.

Medicaid. Government health program for the poor.

Patient dumping. Practice by physicians and private hospitals of treating only patients who can afford their services.

Health maintenance organization (HMO). Health program in which members pay a fixed annual fee in return for all necessary health services.

Medlining. Practice of managed-care companies of limiting the number of patients with health problems and maximizing the number of healthy patients.

Single-payer plan. Tax-supported health program in which the government is the sole insurer.

WEBSITES FOR FURTHER REFERENCE

http://www.cdc.gov/

The Centers for Disease Control and Prevention (CDC) is recognized as the lead federal agency for protecting the health and safety of people—at home and abroad, providing credible information to enhance health decisions, and promoting health through strong partnerships. CDC serves as the national focus for developing and applying disease prevention and control, environmental health, and health promotion and education activities designed to improve the health of the people of the United States.

http://www.jstor.org/journals/00221465.html
The *Journal of Health and Social Behavior* (JHSB) publishes articles that apply sociological concepts and methods to the understanding of health, illness, and medicine in their social context.

http://www.os.dhhs.gov/
The Department of Health and Human Services (HHS) is the United States government's principal agency for protecting the health of all Americans and providing essential human services, especially for those who are least able to help themselves. The Department includes more than 300 programs, covering a wide spectrum of activities. Some highlights include: medical and social science research, preventing outbreak of infectious disease, assuring food and drug safety, Medicare (health insurance for elderly and disabled Americans) and Medicaid (health insurance for low-income people), financial assistance and services for low-income families, improving maternal and infant health, Head Start (pre-school education and services), preventing child abuse and domestic violence, substance abuse treatment and prevention, services for older Americans, and comprehensive health services for Native Americans.

http://ncvhs.hhs.gov/
The National Committee on Vital and Health Statistics (NCVHS) serves as the statutory public advisory body to the Secretary of Health and Human Services in the area of health data and statistics. In that capacity, the Committee provides advice and assistance to the Department and serves as a forum for interaction with interested private sector groups on a variety of key health data issues.

http://www.omhrc.gov/
The Office of Minority Health (OMH) was created by the U.S. Department of Health and Human Services (HHS) in 1985 as a result of the *Report of the Secretary's Task Force on Black and Minority Health*. Under the direction of the Deputy Assistant Secretary for Minority Health, OMH advises the Secretary and the Office of Public Health and Science (OPHS) on public health issues affecting American Indians and Alaska Natives, Asian Americans, Native Hawaiians and other Pacific Islanders, Blacks/African Americans, and Hispanics/Latinos. The mission of OMH is to "improve the health of racial and ethnic populations through the development of effective health policies and programs that help to eliminate disparities in health."

http://www.natmed.org/Frameset_home_non.htm
The National Medical Association promotes "the collective interests of physicians and patients of African descent." "We carry out this mission by serving as the collective voice of physicians of African descent and a leading force for parity in medicine, elimination of health disparities, and promotion of optimal health."

http://www.nih.gov/
Begun as a one-room Laboratory of Hygiene in 1887, the National Institutes of Health today is one of the world's foremost medical research centers, and the federal focal point for medical research in the United States. Simply described, "the goal of NIH research is to acquire new knowledge to help prevent, detect, diagnose, and treat disease and disability, from the rarest genetic disorder to the common cold."

http://www.uic.edu/orgs/sds/
The Society for Disability Studies is a nonprofit scientific and educational organization established to promote interdisciplinary research on humanistic and social scientific aspects of disability and chronic illness. Its membership includes social scientists, scholars in the humanities, and disability rights advocates concerned with the problems of disabled people in society.

http://www.who.int/home-page/
The website of the World Health Organization (WHO). Current information about health status and health problems around the world can be accessed from this website.

www.ashastd.org
The American Social Health Association is recognized by the public, patients, providers, and policymakers for developing and delivering accurate, medically reliable information about sexually transmitted diseases (STDs). Public and college health clinics across the U.S. order ASHA educational pamphlets and books to give to clients and students. Community-based organizations depend on ASHA, as well, to help communicate about risk, transmission, prevention, testing, and treatment.

http://www.managedcaremag.com/
The online home of *Managed Care* magazine. "A guide for managed care executives and physicians covering capitation, compensation, disease management, NCQA accreditation and HEDIS®, contracting, ethics, practice management, formulary development, and other health insurance issues."

http://www.opensecrets.org/news/mcare/
The Center for Responsive Politics is a nonpartisan, nonprofit research group based in Washington, D.C. that tracks money in politics and its effect on elections and public policy. This center hosts a website, called OpenSecrets.Org, that researches issues that citizens want to know more about—researching managed care and HMOs. "The health insurance industry has been transformed in recent years with the rise of managed care networks and health maintenance organizations (HMOs). Though such companies have been touted for bringing affordable health coverage to a wide range of consumers, they have been criticized for cutting costs by limiting treatment options and patient choice.

Doctors and patients increasingly have asked Congress to regulate the managed care industry by giving patients new rights, the foremost of which is the ability to sue their health plans. Such proposals, however, have faltered in recent years, as lawmakers battled over how to protect patients without further driving up already expensive health care costs."

http://www.ama-assn.org/special/hiv/hivhome.htm

The HIV/AIDS Resource Center was created and is updated by the *Journal of the American Medical Association (JAMA)*. The JAMA HIV/AIDS Resource Center is designed as a resource for physicians and other health professionals, but can also be accessed by the lay public.

http://sis.nlm.nih.gov/

Want to know more about HIV/AIDS and other pressing health issues? The Specialized Information Services (SIS) Division of the National Library of Medicine (NLM) is responsible for information resources and services in toxicology, environmental health, chemistry, HIV/AIDS, and specialized topics in minority health.

http://www.unaids.org/

The Joint UN Programme on HIV/AIDS. As the leading advocate for worldwide action against HIV/AIDS, the global mission of UNAIDS is to lead, strengthen, and support an expanded response to the epidemic that will: prevent the spread of HIV; provide care and support for those infected and affected by the disease; reduce the vulnerability of individuals and communities to HIV/AIDS; and alleviate the socioeconomic and human impact of the epidemic.

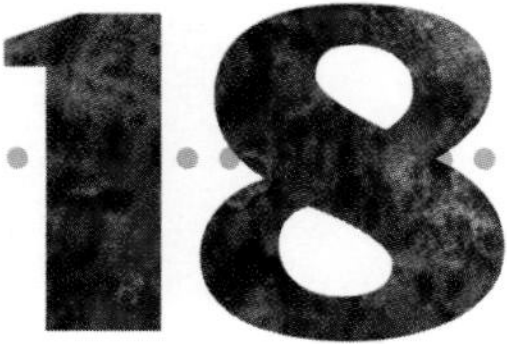

National Security in the Twenty-First Century

This is the end: the end of an era, the era of our invulnerability. . . . Today our leaders tell us an aerial shield will deflect all enemy attacks aimed at our shores. It is a comforting thought, reinforced by our abiding faith in technology and our history of fighting wars on the soil of others. But all that has now been revealed as a fantasy. Like a person riding in an armor-plated car who is felled by a virus, we have been attacked from within—by hostile terrorists commanding our own commercial airliners carrying Americans on their daily journeys across our vast land.

—Ronald Steel

I am ready to die for Islam. If I am killed there will be 100 bin Ladens.

—Osama bin Laden (in a letter after the bombings in New York and Washington)

We cannot win a war on terrorism. . . . Terrorism is a methodology, and a methodology cannot be vanquished. . . . Moreover, the threat of terrorism cannot be conquered. For as long as the war continues—and beyond that—the United States will be vulnerable to terrorism; no military action is going to alter that reality.

—David Corn

On the morning of September 11, 2001, four commercial planes left East Coast airports loaded with passengers and fuel for cross-country flights. These flights were taken over by hijackers who piloted the planes to new destinations and the course of history was changed. The first plane left Boston for Los Angeles but headed instead for New York City where it rammed into the World Trade Center's north tower setting its upper floors ablaze. Fifteen minutes later a second plane, scheduled for Boston to Los Angeles, steered into the south tower of the World Trade Center. Within the next hour both towers, each 110 stories high, melted from the intense heat and collapsed. A third plane departed from Washington D.C. for Los Angeles but turned around and plunged into the Pentagon. The fourth plane left Newark for San Francisco, changed direction, but, presumably because of heroic passengers attacking the hijackers, failed in its mission, crashing instead in rural Pennsylvania. Thus, within 2 hours or so these four planes commandeered by terrorists in synchronized suicide missions had attacked two symbols of the United States—the World Trade Center, the hub of U.S. capitalism, and the Pentagon, the headquarters of the world's greatest military, killing in the process 3,000 people, about the same number of Americans who died at Pearl Harbor. "Not since the Civil War have we seen as much bloodshed on our soil. Never in our history did so many innocents perish on a single day" (Gergen, 2001c:60). There was also a huge toll in psychological trauma:

> By rough estimates, at least 40,000 people—survivors, witnesses, emergency workers—suffered serious psychological trauma during the attack on the Trade Center. Countless others will experience weeks of grief, shock, fear, and even despair as they replay the televised images in their minds. Eventually, most of us will put the experience behind us. Most, but not all. Past experience suggests that a third or more of the people touched directly by this event will develop post-traumatic stress disorder (PTSD). For those people, every day will be Sept. 11. (Cowley, 2001:50)

With this attack on the United States, a state of war was established, but this was to be a war like no other. Throughout history wars have been fought between political entities over land and resources, but the terrorists do not represent a nation and they are not intent on occupying the United States. Moreover, unlike conventional wars, the terrorists do not have battleships and airfields to be targeted. Instead they are a loose band of terrorists organized in cells in thirty-four countries, conspiring to kill their enemies by unconventional means. These terrorists located around the globe do not wear uniforms but rather live in their host countries as students or workers, just as other residents. Combat will include the use of conventional force but also will include invading the enemy's cyberspace, diplomacy to secure cooperation against money laundering, and customs officials stopping suspicious persons at U.S. borders (Rumsfeld, 2001). In this new warfare, the combatants will not know victory. "There's no land to seize, no government to topple, no surrender that will bring closure" (Parrish, 2001:2). If the leaders are identified, will their deaths signal victory? No, others will take their place. Finally, great advantages in military technology, as demonstrated by the successful attacks on the World Trade Center and Pentagon, do not make a nation invulnerable. Terrorists can terrorize in many ways. If a nation meets the challenge against one form of terrorism (e.g., perfect airport security), then other forms of terrorism will emerge making defense unsure, if not impossible. A fortress society in this new era is not the answer for national security.

This chapter begins with a description of the current defense establishment, followed by the broad outlines of the challenges to the United States by the new terrorism, including a recent history of terrorist attacks against the United States, the organizations of terror, why the United States and its citizens are targeted by the terrorists, the many weapons that terrorists might use, the consequences of the new terrorism for the United States and its citizens, and the strategies to neutralize terrorist networks

U.S. MILITARY ESTABLISHMENT

Nation states organize to defend their borders, protect their national interests, and shield their citizens and businesses abroad. These national security efforts include armies, military bases, intelligence (spy) networks, and embassies/consulates. National security in the United States is organized and administered by the president, the departments of state and defense, the National Security Council, the Joint Chiefs of Staff (representing the branches of the military), the Central Intelligence Agency, Congress, and, more recently, the Office of Homeland Security. Huge expenditures fuel this defense apparatus.

Military might has been the typical security strategy of nations. Since World War II the United States, for example, has spent more than $15 trillion dollars (adjusted for inflation) on defense, including $5.5 trillion on the nuclear arms race. This enormous military expense was based on a foreign policy dominated by fear of the Soviet Union, containing communism, and the importance of spreading the U.S. way of life. Similarly, the foreign policy of the Soviet Union was determined by its fear of the United States and an ideology that justified expansion of the communist way of life throughout the world. As a result both sides lined up allies, with the Soviet Union sometimes using force to keep its allies in line, and the communist party in charge of the various satellite nations sending arms and other forms of aid. Both sides engaged in covert activities to gain access to the other's secrets and to manipulate circumstances in other countries so that the leaders favorable to them would gain and retain power. Both the United States and the Soviet Union engaged in an expensive arms race to defend themselves, to strike first if necessary, and to scare the other side into not attacking first. As a result, each side built up an arsenal of nuclear and conventional weapons capable of destroying the other many times over. The activities of each side in this momentous struggle for world supremacy caused the other to fear them all the more, thus presenting the rationale for further military expenditures, the development of new and more devastating weapons, deployment of troops and missiles around the world to protect their interests, and covert activities. Each side perceived the other as the ultimate enemy—as untrustworthy, uncompromising, ruthless, expansionary ideologues bent on winning the **Cold War** (the tension and arms race between the United States and the Soviet Union at whatever cost).

The Cold War ended for a number of reasons, including: (1) The hugely expensive arms race had detrimental effects on the economies of both nations, causing enormous debt, the relative neglect of social services domestically, and in the Soviet Union a major disregard of its agricultural and consumer goods production. (2) Dissidents gained power in the various Soviet republics and in the Soviet-dominated countries, resulting in the demise of totalitarian regimes and the rise of some form of democracy. (3) Both sides lost credibility at home because of internal Cold War tactics, which included secret police activities, the erosion of civil liberties, secrecy, and lying. (4) Both sides were seen as opportunistic rather than idealistic. In the case of the United States, a cost of the Cold War was a loss of credibility as to its guiding principle, since it supported dictatorships and repressive regimes if the ruling elite was anticommunist. (5) Both sides found that long, protracted military involvements in foreign countries (e.g., the United States in Vietnam and the Soviet Union in Afghanistan) weakened internal support for the ruling elites.

The world has changed with the end of the Cold War. The United States no longer has a superpower rival. A few nations are potential enemies (Iraq, Iran, Libya, North Korea, and Cuba), but together they spend a small fraction on their militaries, compared to what the United States spends. The world's nuclear stockpile is decreasing.

While communism is no longer a threat, potential threats to the world's (and United States) security remain: China, with one-fourth of the world's population, has nuclear weapons; India, the second most populous nation, has tested nuclear weapons, as has its enemy and neighbor Pakistan; nine other nations have nuclear weapons, with other nations soon to join the "nuclear club," and many nations have chemical weapons of mass destruction; rogue nations terrorize their neighbors; civil wars erupt sporadically around the globe; terrorist acts by political and religious zealots endanger innocents, and repressive governments abuse the civil rights of their citizens; and famine and disease ravage the poorest nations. Thus, while the fears of the Cold War have receded, smaller but nonetheless important worries persist.

But terrorist networks now pose a bigger threat to the national security of the United States than rogue nation states. Moreover, if the U.S. response to terrorism by Islamic fundamentalists is perceived by the 1.2 billion Muslims worldwide as too extreme, there is the potential for 18 percent of the world to be united against it.

What will be the role of the United States in the uncharted and uncertain waters of this new era? The military establishment is organized to deal with the last war, not the new terrorism. Even after the events of September 11, 2001, the Pentagon and the political leadership in Washington were still bent on establishing a missile defense system that will protect from missile attacks by rogue nations (2 weeks after the terrorist attack with our own planes, Congress allocated $8.3 billion for the missile shield program, an increase of $3 billion over the previous year).

Before turning our attention to the new terrorism and our response to it, let us examine the military establishment, by answering two questions: (1) How big is the military? (2) What does a post–Cold War era mean for the military?

How Big Is the U.S. Military?

U.S. leaders preside over a global military apparatus of a magnitude never before seen in human history. In 2001 this military behemoth included (Kelly, 2001; Korb, 2001; Langewiesche, 2001; Zuckerman, 2001):

- An active duty military force of 1.4 million, including 260,000 troops deployed overseas in military bases in thirty-five foreign countries. There are 1.3 million members of the National Guard and reserves, and 672,000 civilians who are directly on the military payroll.
- A worldwide satellite network providing constant intelligence and surveillance.
- A vast array of equipment including 250,000 ground vehicles, 15,000 aircraft, about 150 satellites, and more than 1,000 oceangoing vessels.
- A navy with a fleet larger in total tonnage and firepower than all the other navies of the world combined, consisting of missile cruisers,

The U.S. military force includes 1.4 million active duty personnel, 15,000 aircraft, and 1,000 oceangoing vessels.

nuclear submarines, nuclear aircraft carriers, destroyers, and spy ships that sail every ocean and make port on every continent.
- An air force that controls the skies. U.S. bomber squadrons and long-range missiles can reach any target, carrying enough explosive force to destroy entire countries.
- A nuclear arsenal of 5,400 warheads loaded on intercontinental ballistic missiles at land and sea; 1,750 nuclear bombs and cruise missiles that can be launched from the B-2 and B-52 bombers; and 1,670 "tactical" nuclear weapons (Barry and Thomas, 2001). In contrast to the U.S. nuclear arsenal, Russia has 6,400 deployed warheads, China 300, Israel 200, India 50, and Pakistan 25 (*Time,* 2001a).
- U.S. rapid deployment forces have a firepower in conventional weaponry vastly superior to any other nation's.

The U.S. emphasis on sophisticated technology and military hardware, while necessary, perhaps, for the wars of the twentieth century, did not prevent terrorists armed only with knives and the knowledge of how to avoid detection in airports and how to pilot large aircraft from a successful attack on the United States on September 11, 2001.

What Is the Cost of Maintaining U.S. Superiority in Military Might?

The United States, the most powerful nation on Earth, outspends all other nations on defense. In fact, the United States spends more than the *combined* total of the next seven military powers (Zuckerman, 2001). The United States alone accounts for *36 percent of the world's military expenditures.* (See the panel "Social Problems in Global Perspective" for the proportion of gross national product various nations spend on defense.) The United States and its allies account for *65 percent of the world's total military expenditures.* The total combined defense expenditures in 1999 of potential enemies (Iran, Iraq, Libya, North Korea, Cuba, and Syria) was $13.8 billion, or about *4 percent of the U.S. defense budget* (Korb, 2001).

> In 1985, at the height of the Reagan [military] build-up, the United States and the Soviet Union spent equal amounts on defense; now Russia spends only one-sixth of what the United States spends. If one adds in the spending of U.S. allies, the picture becomes even more favorable to the United States. Our NATO allies spend three times more on defense than Russia. Israel spends as much as Iraq and Iran combined. South Korea spends nine times more on defense than North Korea. And Japan spends more on defense than China (Korb, 2001:10).

In keeping with the U.S. tradition of outspending all other nations for defense President Bush proposed a military budget of $334 billion for fiscal year 2002. There are at least three reasons given by the government for defense spending at its current high level. First, the Soviet threat, while low at present, may surface in the future. The military in Russia may take over its government (the largest of the former Soviet republics) and, with its nuclear arsenal, become a real threat to the United States.

Second, the leadership of both U.S. political parties believes that we need to be so strong that no one would dare challenge us militarily. While other nations may have more people (e.g., China and India), they do not have the United States' sophisticated weaponry, weapons delivery systems, and nuclear

SOCIAL PROBLEMS IN GLOBAL PERSPECTIVE

DEFENSE EXPENDITURES

Of the advanced societies, the United States spends a disproportionate amount of its gross domestic product (GDP) on defense. Why? Is it necessary? Do the other nations spend less of their GDP because they rely on the U.S. defense system to protect them? If so, is this fair? The following table provides the comparative data:

Defense Expenditures for Selected Nations, Fiscal Year 1999–2000

Country	*Percent of GDP Spent on Defense*	*Country*	*Percent of GDP Spent on Defense*
Australia	1.9	Iran	2.9
Austria	1.2	Ireland	0.9
Brazil	1.9	Italy	1.7
Canada	1.2	Japan	0.9
China	1.2	Mexico	1.0
Denmark	1.7	Norway	2.1
Finland	2.0	Sweden	2.1
France	2.9	United Kingdom	2.7
Germany	1.5	United States	3.2

Source: The World Factbook 2000. 2001. Washington, DC: Central Intelligence Agency.

stockpile. The United States chooses to retain this superiority because its leaders believe there is "peace through strength." Thus, our defense policy "embraces a uniquely high standard for defense sufficiency: the maintenance of U.S. military superiority over all current and potential rivals" (Conetta and Knight, 1998:38). While this strategy held for the most part during the Cold War years, the raids on the World Trade Center and the Pentagon showed that this rationale does not hold for the terrorism that we confront in the twenty-first century.

Third, the world, even without the Soviet threat, is an unsafe place, where terrorism and aggression occur and must be confronted and curtailed. Several nations, including regimes with expansionist agendas and hated enemies, have nuclear weapons, limited delivery systems, and chemical and biological agents of mass destruction. In such an uncertain world the United States must be ever vigilant, keeping its military superiority. For example, President Bush has proposed a new plan (actually similar to President Reagan's "Star Wars" plan) for a national missile defense shield that would intercept ballistic missiles aimed at the United States at a cost of as much as $1 trillion over 20 years or so. Although the threat is not immediate, advocates of this plan argue that hostile nations are boosting their long-range arsenals placing the United States at risk. The missile shield would deter them from attacking the United States. Critics argue that the strength of the United States is so overwhelming and no nation would attempt

By Mike Smith. *Las Vegas Sun*. United Features Syndicate.

a missile strike, even without a missile shield. This costly program is unnecessary and only a boon to defense contractors. Moreover, this missile shield, it is argued, is destabilizing, causing other nations to fear the intentions of the United States and bringing on a costly arms race. The biggest problem, of course, is that a workable missile defense system has not been invented yet. Is there a system possible that would be able to detect armed missiles from hundreds of dummy missiles and destroy every one of them?

Finally, given the events of September 11, 2001, we clearly recognize that a missile shield will not defend against terrorist attacks by suicide bombers or other terrorist strategies. The defense requirements have changed. The irony is that the terrorists with few resources converted the superior technology of the United States into a lethal instrument against the United States. Thus, the militarily weak are actually on an equal footing with the militarily powerful (Pryce-Jones, 2001). With the end of the Cold War, American insecurity no longer comes from a superpower rival. As the *New York Times* editorialized:

> Increasingly, it comes from a range of smaller, militarily weaker countries and international terrorists. . . . all three services need to adjust their equipment purchases to the needs of mobile, long-distance 21st-century warfare. Their budgets are badly distorted by commitments to expensive weapons designed for the cold war. . . . Americans are ready to rebuild the nation's security. The Pentagon must see to it that military spending goes to the right places. (*New York Times,* 2001a:1–2)

In other words, the high-cost military organization of the United States, while spectacular in its lethal capabilities, is predicated on fighting the wars of the twentieth century rather than the wars of the twenty-first century.

> It is probably the most effective conventional-war fighting force in history. But the basic assumptions, the culture, of the military-intelligence complex seem suddenly anachronistic. The nexus of national-defense and intelligence agencies may be as unsuited for a long-term offensive anti-terrorist campaign as they were unprepared to defend New York and Washington against the aerial attacks of September 11th. (Klein, 2001:44)

TERRORISM

The U.S. Department of Defense defines **terrorism** as "the unlawful use of force or violence against persons or property to intimidate or coerce a government, the civilian population or any segment thereof, in furtherance of political or social objectives" (quoted in LeVine, 2001:1). The goal may vary: Terrorists may seek to take over a government (e.g., the government of the Shah of Iran was overthrown by Muslim fundamentalists), political change (the Irish Republican Army bombings to remove the British from Northern Ireland), revenge (Palestinian suicide bombers, in response to Israeli expansion into their territory, killing innocent Israelis, and then the Israelis retaliating with air strikes against the Palestinians), or expressing anger against a government (Timothy McVeigh detonating a bomb at the Oklahoma City federal building as a reprisal for FBI actions against the Branch Davidians at Waco, Texas).

Most of the remainder of this chapter is devoted to international terrorism, but let us begin with a brief account of the internal terrorist threat—attacks by Americans on Americans.

Domestic Terrorism

We typically think of terrorism as deadly acts committed by foreigners, usually Islamic fundamentalists from the Middle East. Thus, when a bomb destroyed the federal building in Oklahoma City in 1995, killing 168, the immediate suspects were Muslim extremists. But Timothy McVeigh and Terry Nichols, two American ex-military men, were convicted. (McVeigh received the death penalty for detonating the bomb and was executed in 2001; Nichols was sentenced to life imprisonment for his involvement in planning the bombing.) As extreme as the Oklahoma City bombing was, the act of detonating a bomb to harm Americans is not unusual, since there are about 2,000 bombings annually within the United States.

Foreigners acting alone or as agents of their government killing Americans is relatively easy to understand, but Americans killing Americans is more difficult to comprehend. The history of the United States, however, is full of examples of various dissident groups that have used violence against their neighbors to achieve their aims. Colonists, farmers, settlers, Native Americans, immigrants, slaves, slaveholders, laborers, strike breakers, anarchists, vigilantes, the Ku Klux Klan and other White supremacist organizations, antiwar protesters, and prolife extremists have gone outside the law to accomplish their ends. Just in recent years, various extremists have bombed the federal building in Oklahoma City, more than 40 women's clinics, African American churches primarily in the South, Jewish synagogues and Islamic mosques throughout the United States, various government offices, including, for example, the U.S. Bureau of Land Management office in Reno and the Forest Service office in Carson City,

The worst case of domestic terrorism occurred in 1995 when a bomb detonated by Timothy McVeigh destroyed the federal building in Oklahoma City, killing 168 people.

Nevada, and the 1996 Olympic games in Atlanta (still unsolved). In addition to bombings, there have been acts of arson, beatings, killings, and letters/packages with bombs or anthrax addressed to political targets.

Extreme actions by the government have persuaded some individuals to become part of what is known as the Patriot movement. Just as when the government acted in what the radical left believed were outrageous ways during the Vietnam War (i.e., the war itself but also acts of "official violence" such as the killing of Kent State students by the National Guard), the radical right today finds some acts indefensible. Two recent events rallied the Patriots in a common fear of the government's arbitrary aggression against its citizens. In 1992 the Bureau of Alcohol, Tobacco, and Firearms (ATF) attacked Randy Weaver, a White supremacist in Idaho, for gun violations. In the process Weaver's wife and son were killed by ATF snipers. The second event was the 1993 assault by ATF on David Koresh and the Branch Davidians near Waco, Texas. This siege, again over guns violations, ended with the deaths of 86 men, women, and children. Those in the Patriot movement interpreted these acts as government run amok, using its power to take away the liberties individuals are granted by the Constitution (Frankel, 1997). Thus, the membership in this movement "far from thinking itself outside the law, believes it is the critical force making for a restoration of the Constitution" (Wills, 1995:52). (See the "Voices" panel for a letter from Timothy McVeigh, airing his grievances with the United States.)

In 2000, the Southern Poverty Law Center estimated that there were 217 active domestic Patriot militia groups (*SPLC Report,* 2000). Moreover, there

VOICES

A LETTER FROM TIMOTHY McVEIGH

Three years before he ignited a bomb that destroyed the federal building in Oklahoma City, killing 168 people, Timothy McVeigh wrote a letter to his hometown newspaper, the Lockport (N.Y.) *Union-Sun & Journal,* listing his concerns about the government.

> Crime is out of control. Criminals have no fear of punishment. Prisons are overcrowded so they know they will not be imprisoned long. . . .
>
> Taxes are a joke. Regardless of what a political candidate "promises," they will increase taxes. More taxes are always the answer to government mismanagement. . . .
>
> The "American Dream" of the middle class has all but disappeared, substituted with people struggling just to buy next week's groceries. Heaven forbid the car breaks down! . . .
>
> Politicians are out of control. Their yearly salaries are more than an average person will see in a lifetime. They have been entrusted with the power to regulate their own salaries, and have grossly violated that trust to live in their own luxury. . . .
>
> Who is to blame for the mess? At a point when the world has seen communism falter as an imperfect system to manage people, democracy seems to be headed down the same road. No one is seeing the "big" picture. . . .
>
> What is it going to take to open up the eyes of our elected officials? AMERICA IS IN SERIOUS DECLINE.
>
> We have no proverbial tea to dump; should we instead sink a ship full of Japanese imports? Is a Civil War imminent? Do we have to shed blood to reform the current system? I hope it doesn't come to that. But it might.

were 602 hate groups operating in 48 states (none in Rhode Island and Vermont), and 366 active hate-group websites on the Internet (*SPLC Report,* 2001). The antigovernment militia movement has lost some momentum since the Oklahoma City bombing but the hate groups are growing. Morris Dees, cofounder of the Southern Poverty Law Center, and Mark Potok, editor of that organization's *Intelligence Report,* speculate on the future of American terrorism, given these current contradictory trends:

> Are we safer now that the militia movement has faded? Probably not. The radical fringe's willingness to resort to violence has long been with us. In the 1970's and 1980's, for instance, the anti-Semitic Posse Comitatus raged through the Midwest. In the late 1980's and early 1990's, neo-Nazi skinhead groups grew, and they were responsible for a series of murders around the country. Today's "hate groups"—smaller, more Nazified, more revolutionary—are perhaps even more dangerous than some of the groups in the militia movement. So while the particular movement that spawned Timothy McVeigh is dwindling, the threat of domestic terrorism remains very much alive. (Dees and Potok, 2001:wk15)

A serious policy question is how to deal with the potential threat of domestic terrorism. Should agents of the government infiltrate extremist groups? Should the FBI use wiretaps, intercept e-mails, and obtain phone logs, bank records, and other personal information on suspects without warrants? There are at least three problems with these tactics. First, this would reduce the civil liberties for all. Morris Dees, head of the Southern Poverty Law Center, says that such tactics run the danger that the government might "trample on the rights of people with controversial views to organize and express those views" (Shanahan and Benson, 1995:48A). Second, since the government has abused such powers in the past, this would increase the likelihood of future government abuses. During the 40 years after World War II, for example, the FBI was given broad powers to combat communism within the United States. It abused these powers by spying on civil rights organizations, the National Organization of Women, and the John Birch Society, to name a few. It even tried to discredit Martin Luther King, Jr., as a communist. What are the guarantees that such abuses would not happen again? The third problem is that any efforts by the government to increase its surveillance of the militias and other right-wing groups, infiltrate their groups, and examine their personal records would justify the paranoia held by many about the government. Thus, these extra efforts by the government would increase citizen resistance and probably increase membership in extremist organizations and, perhaps, even the amount of terrorist activity.

Clearly, the government must walk a fine line in dealing with potential domestic terrorist organizations. The government cannot be intimidated by them, nor can it come down too hard on them before the fact (i.e., before terrorist acts).

To conclude this section, we need to remind ourselves of two facts concerning political radicals. First, it is important to note that to harbor radical views on the right or the left is not wrong, immoral, or un-American. Indeed, extreme political views are part of the American tradition. However, there is a national security concern when extremist views involve violence.

Second, it is wrong to consider all the new revolutionaries as "crackpots." "This 'crackpot' theory is not an accurate picture of everyone in the militia movement: it dismisses out of hand every political grievance they have, and it denies the social roots of the militia movement" (Berlet and Lyons, 1995:24). The government has abused its power on many occasions. The livelihoods of many are threatened, sometimes by government policies. These grievances go unresolved, and those affected have a sense that no one is listening to them.

But the immediate terrorist threat to the United States has international origins, and it is to that threat that we now turn.

Recent Acts of International Terrorism on the United States

The United States and its citizens have been targeted by various foreign terrorist organizations. We concentrate here on the present threat of terrorism from Islamic radicals. A chronology of recent terrorists acts directed at the United States by Muslim terroristists includes the following:

- In 1983 Shiite Muslim suicide bombers destroyed U.S. Marine and French paratrooper barracks in Lebanon, killing 299, including 241 Americans.
- In 1988 terrorists linked to Libya bombed a Pan Am 747 headed for the United States over Lockerbie, Scotland, killing 270 passengers and residents of the town.
- In 1993 a truck bomb was detonated in the garage of the World Trade Center, killing 6 and injuring more than 1,000.
- In 1995 the Army training headquarters in Riyadh, Saudi Arabia, was bombed, killing 5 Americans and wounding 31.
- In 1996, 19 U.S. soldiers were killed and 372 Americans injured by an attack on military housing in Dhahran, Saudi Arabia.

- In 1998 car bombs exploded outside U.S. embassies in Tanzania and Kenya, killing 224 people, including 12 Americans.
- In 2000 the *U.S.S. Cole* was attacked in a Yemen harbor by suicide bombers in a small boat, killing 17 sailors.
- September 2001, hijacked planes rammed into both towers of the World Trade Center and the Pentagon, killing about 3,000.

Why Is the United States the Target of Terrorists?

Terrorists engage in nefarious acts because they are convinced of the righteousness of their cause, which is embedded in real or imagined grievances. They believe that these grievances provide legitimate reasons for their hatred and thus the actions they take are morally correct. Timothy McVeigh believed that the government was wrong in its aggressive killing of people at Ruby Ridge and Waco. He was so convinced that he had the moral high ground that he blew up the federal building in Oklahoma, even justifying the deaths of innocents as "collateral damage" and with no remorse. Similarly, the attacks on the United States by terrorists from the Middle East are believed by them as legitimate and part of *jihad* (a struggle or holy war) against the forces of evil.

To understand the motives of the terrorists, we must listen to their grievances against the United States. We must understand the attack as a consequence of history and policy. "The perpetrators were motivated by political, cultural, and ideological concerns forged over years" (Corn, 2001:1). To establish context does not justify or excuse their actions or suggest that the United States deserved to be attacked but to understand the social context of those actions and the animosity many Muslims hold toward the United States. In short, the listing of U.S. crimes "is not to justify terrorism, but to understand the terrain that breeds terrorism and terrorists" (Albert and Shalom, 2001:6). We concentrate here on the hatred directed at the United States by some in the twenty-two nations of the Arab world.

They Hate Us for What We Do. Saudi Arabia's Prince Alwaleed bin talal bin Abbdulaziz Alsaud is a multibillionaire with huge investments in U.S. companies. He is clearly pro-American, but following the terrorist attacks in September 2001, he said: "America has to understand the roots of investment in the Arab world and the Muslim world" (quoted in Rossant, 2001b:64). There are a number of reasons why the United States is hated by many in the Muslim world. Different groups within that world focus on one or more of the perceived failings of the United States. Foremost among the reasons is unwavering and generous economic and military support of Israel by the United States. The territory between the Mediterranean Sea and the Jordan River has been called Palestine since the time of the Old Testament (the following material is from Ackerman, 2001). It was conquered by the Arabs in the seventh century and by 1887 was 95 percent Arab. The British ruled the area as a protectorate beginning in 1920. This encouraged Zionists (Jews who believed that Palestine was the Jewish homeland) to migrate there, increasing the Jewish population sevenfold by 1947. That year, the United Nations created the nation of Israel, seeking to partition the land into Israel for the Jews and Palestine for the Moslems. The Arabs rejected the plan and a war ensued, driving more than 700,000 Arabs off their land and into refugee camps. In 1967 after another Arab-Israeli war, more land—the West Bank and Gaza Strip—came under Israeli occupation. Decades later, many Arabs continue to live without a homeland, living in Israel where they are repressed and dispossessed. The result is that the Palestinians and their supporters have a strong sense of injustice, mixed with rage and despair over their being dominated by Israel and indirectly by the United States. Israel has been aggressive in the region, leading to counterattacks and reprisals. Sometimes the attacked and sometimes the attacker, terrorist acts occur as all sides practice a continuous "eye for an eye" strategy of vengeance. Many in the Islamic world are also incensed that Israel controls Jerusalem's Islamic holy places (Jerusalem is the third holiest city in Islam). The United States is seen, rightly, as Israel's benefactor and protector. Moreover, since the Israeli military power is supplied by the United States, whenever Israel attacks Muslims, it does so with planes made in the United States and with bullets and missiles made in the United States.

U.S. policy in the Mideast is not consistent with its stated principles of promoting fairness, democracy, and freedom.

> In the Middle East. . . the United States supports Israeli oppression of Palestinians, providing the military, economic, and diplomatic backing that makes that oppression possible. It condemns conquest when it is done in Iraq, but not when done by Israel. It has bolstered authoritarian regimes (such as Saudi Arabia) that have provided mammoth oil profits and has helped overthrow regimes (such as Iran in the early 1950s) that challenged those profits. When terrorist acts were committed by U.S. friends such as the Israeli-supervised massacres in the Sabra and Shatilla refugee camps in Lebanon, no U.S. sanctions were imposed. But about the U.S. imposed sanctions on Iraq, leading to the deaths of hundreds of thousands of innocent children, Secretary of State Madeleine Albright could only say that she thought it was worth it. When the U.S. went to war against Iraq, it targeted civilian infrastructure. When Iran and Iraq fought a bloody war, the United States surreptitiously aided both sides. (Albert and Shalom, 2001:5)

The United States also maintains a military presence in the Middle East, especially with military bases in Saudi Arabia, where the U.S. Air Force has about 5,000 personnel. This is seen as an abomination for it defiles the land that was the birthplace of the prophet Muhammad and of Islam.

- **They Hate Us for Who We Are.** The World Trade Center and the Pentagon were not random targets. They were symbols of the economic success and undisputed military might of the United States. The United States is resented for its power and envied for its wealth. For the most part, the Arab countries are poor, with the masses virtually destitute. For example, Pakistan, which is not the poorest of the Arab nations, has an annual per capita income of $460, with a 30 percent unemployment rate (Cox, 2001). U.S. multinationals such as Procter & Gamble, Bristol-Myers Squibb, American Express, and Citigroup are located in Pakistan, which is interpreted by some as the U.S. exploiting cheap labor and Pakistan's natural resources. The hunger, disease, and misery associated with poverty is widespread in most of these countries. The United States, then, is resented for its wealth, much of which is perceived as the result of exploiting Third World countries. When the various grievances against the United States are added to the ever-widening disparity between the wealthy and poor nations, the resulting mix is volatile, especially among the destitute and marginalized.

The Muslim extremists see Western culture, led by the United States, as an "imperialist acid eating away at Muslim virtue and values" (Woodward,

2001:68). This Western secularism is an infidel power spreading its permissive, secular culture through television, movies, and advertising worldwide.

> At its most extreme, groups such as bin Laden's Al Qaeda network or the underground al Gamma al-Islamiyya, responsible for the murder of 58 tourists in Egypt in 1997, view America as the infidel power that is spreading its permissive, secular culture, the Great Satan that pollutes the world with its pornographic cinema, its alcohol, and its equal treatment of women. (Rossant, 2001a:47)

The radical fundamentalists want to install a feudal society where Islamic principles would govern every aspect of personal and social behavior, as they believe life was for Muhammed in the seventh century. The rigid rules imposed by the Taliban in Afghanistan provide the model, where there is a strict (and, many Muslims would say, a distorted) interpretation of the Koran (see the "A Closer Look" panel entitled "Religion and Extremism"). Under Taliban rule the laws demanded that adult males must pray five times a day, wear turbans, and have beards at least fist length and forbid having birds as pets, flying kites,

A CLOSER LOOK

RELIGION AND EXTREMISM

Most Islamic religious scholars believe that the Islamic fundamentalists have distorted Islamic teachings. In 1998, bin Laden issued a *fatwa* (a religious ruling) declaring that it is the "individual duty of every Muslim to kill the Americans and their allies—civilians and military . . . in any country in which it is possible" (quoted in Sheler, 2001:56). When issued by a recognized Muslim cleric, a *fatwa,* is deemed an authoritative document, though not necessarily binding on all Muslims. Bin Laden, however, having no formal theological training, is not a Muslim cleric. In fact, he is widely denounced by mainstream Islamic scholars, so his *fatwa* is not credible. Moreover, bin Laden's religious ideology is the opposite of traditional Islamic doctrine. Magnus Ranstorp, an expert on Islamic fundamentalism at the University of St. Andrews in Scotland, says that "the *fatwa*'s call for the killing of civilians is strictly prohibited by Islamic law" (quoted in Sheler, 2001:57). "It [the slaughter of thousands of civilians in the World Trade Center and the Pentagon] violates the very foundations of Islamic law," says Imam Yahya Hendi, Muslim chaplain at Georgetown University (quoted in Woodward, 2001:67). In addition, the heavenly promise to suicide terrorists that a bevy of virgins awaits Muslim martyrs in paradise is not found in the Koran, says Azizah al-Hibri, professor of law at the University of Richmond (quoted in Grossman, 2001b:6D).

Karen Armstrong, an expert on comparative religions, notes that during the twentieth century, the militant fundamentalism found in Islam has also

> erupted in every major religion as a rebellion against modernity. Every fundamentalist movement I have studied in Judaism, Christianity, and Islam is convinced that liberal, secular society is determined to wipe out religion. Fighting, as they imagine, a battle for survival, fundamentalists often feel justified in ignoring the more compassionate principles of their faith. But in amplifying the more aggressive passages that exist in all our scriptures, they distort the tradition. (Armstrong, 2001:48)

Extremists in any religion can and have twisted the principles of their faith to justify their terrorist acts, as have militant Israelis killing Palestinians or militant Protestants killing Catholics in Northern Ireland. Some recent examples from Christianity in the United States include (Armstrong, 2001; Lilla, 2001): Christians who bomb abortion clinics or attempt to assassinate doctors who perform abortions, and Christians who mix religion with White Supremacy in hate organizations such as various neo-Nazi groups, and the Ku Klux Klan. In both instances, leaders use selective passages from the Bible to support their aggressive behaviors.

painting one's nails, creating drawings or photographs of living things, or inviting a foreigner to tea (Power, 1998). Most significant, there was gender apartheid. Under Taliban law, the windows of a woman's house must be painted black. She may leave the house only if accompanied by a close male relative and then dressed in a head-to-toe garment—a burqa—with only a tiny mesh-covered opening for vision. Women could not work outside the home and girls were banned from attending school. If the Taliban government had the model for what an Islamic society should be, then the United States, which promotes materialism, individualism, and democracy, and where sex is openly used to sell products, is surely the land of evil. This portrayal of the United States as a kind of Sodom and Gomorrah is a very powerful mobilizing message among those facing a hopeless future (Hale and Walt, 2001).

Organization of International Terror

The terrorist acts listed earlier are thought to be the work of Muslim extremist groups located in various nations of the Middle East and Africa, such as Afghanistan, Sudan, Libya, and Lebanon. Although there are several organizations such as Hizbollah and Hamas (see Table 18.1) that use terrorism as a means to secure their goals, the one most linked to attacks on the United States is al Qaeda, the organization of Osama bin Laden. Al Qaeda runs military camps mostly in Afghanistan where recruits are schooled in the use of explosives and other weapons, strategies, and a radical version of Islam that preaches death to its enemies. Al Qaeda has an estimated 5,000 members organized in cells in at least thirty-five countries (see Figure 18.1, p. 546). The cell structure works this way:

- Secrecy and security are essential and cells are usually small. For terrorist actions, al Qaeda cells apparently are split into planning and execution phases.
- Members of one cell do not necessarily know members of another.
- Communications between cells are usually made secretively, sometimes by using dead drops.
- Cells may remain inactive for years, or engage only in fundraising or peaceful Islamic activities. A cell may suddenly be called into action.
- Sympathizers are recruited to perform low-level logistical tasks (DeYoung and Dobbs, 2001:21)

Information from captured documents and testimony from an al Qaeda defector reveals an organization with bin Laden and a consultive council at the top, with committees to handle business enterprises, military training, and religious policy (DeYoung and Dobbs, 2001). Al Qaeda is part of a larger cluster of terrorist groups in which bin Laden shares leadership. That group—The World Islamic Front for the Struggle Against the Jews and Crusaders—serves as an umbrella organization covering several radical Islamic movements. According to Bruce Hoffman, Director of RAND Corporation's Washington office and an expert on Middle East terrorism: "He's [bin Laden] been singularly successful in unifying the diverse strands of terrorism in the Middle East and weaving them into a more formidable whole than it's ever been. This is the first truly 'terrorist internationale.' Others have had pretentions, but he's the first to be able to do it. It's money, charisma, being in the right place at the right time—they all play a role, but fundamentally, it's vision" (quoted in Watson, Marshall, and Drogin, 2001:3AA).

TABLE 18.1
Islamic Terrorist Organizations

The U.S. State Department keeps a list of terrorist organizations that threaten the security of American citizens or the national security of the United States. Many of these organizations have ties to one another and to nations that back terror. Among the 29 groups named in the State Department's list, released in April 2001, the following Islamic organizations were included (the following is from <www.state.gov/s/ct/rls/lpgtrpt/2000/index.cfm?docid=2450>):

Abu Sayyaf Group (Philippines)	Engages in terrorism to promote an independent Islamic state in part of the Philippines.
Armed Islamic Group (Algeria)	Seeks to overthrow the secular Algerian regime and replace it with an Islamic state.
Al Gama'a al-Islamiyya (Egypt)	It seeks to overthrow the Egyptian government and replace it with an Islamic state.
HAMAS (Palestine)	Pursues the establishment of an Islamic Palestinian state in place of Israel.
Harakat ul-Mujahidin (Pakistan)	Linked to bin Laden, this group has called for attacks on U.S. and Western interests.
Hizbollah (Lebanon)	Strongly anti-West and anti-Israel, this group opposes Middle East peace negotiations.
Islamic Movement of Uzbekistan	Goal is the establishment of an Islamic state in Uzbekistan.
Al Jihad (Egypt)	A close partner to bin Laden's al Qaeda organization, it seeks the overthrow of the Egyptian government and the establishment of an Islamic state.
Kach and Kahane Chai (Israel)	The goal is to restore the biblical state of Israel.
Mujahedin-e Khalq Organization (Iran)	Seeks to counter what is perceived as excessive Western influence in Iran.
The Palestine Islamic Jihad	Committed to the creation of an Islamic Palestinian state and the destruction of Israel.
al Qaeda (Afghanistan)	Established by bin Laden in the late 1980s. Its goal is to establish a pan-Islamic Caliphate throughout the world by working with allied Islamic groups to overthrow regimes it deems "non-Islamic" and expelling Westerners and non-Muslims from Muslim countries.

The goals of al Qaeda are clear from the terrorist actions carried out by its members and the pronouncements by bin Laden. A sample of his revealing statements include:

- In 1996 bin Laden denounced the "occupation" of the Arab Holy Land by "American crusader forces," which he described as the latest and greatest aggression against the Islamic world since the death of the prophet Muhammad in 632 (Dobbs, 2001:15).
- Under the signature of bin Laden and other leaders of militant Islamic groups, the Declaration of the World Islamic Front for Jihad Against the Jews and Crusaders, declared the *fatwa,* or ruling, which holds that: "To kill Americans and their allies, both civil and military, is an individual duty of every Muslim who is able, in any country where this is possible, until the Aqsa Mosque in Jerusalem and the Haram Mosque in Mecca

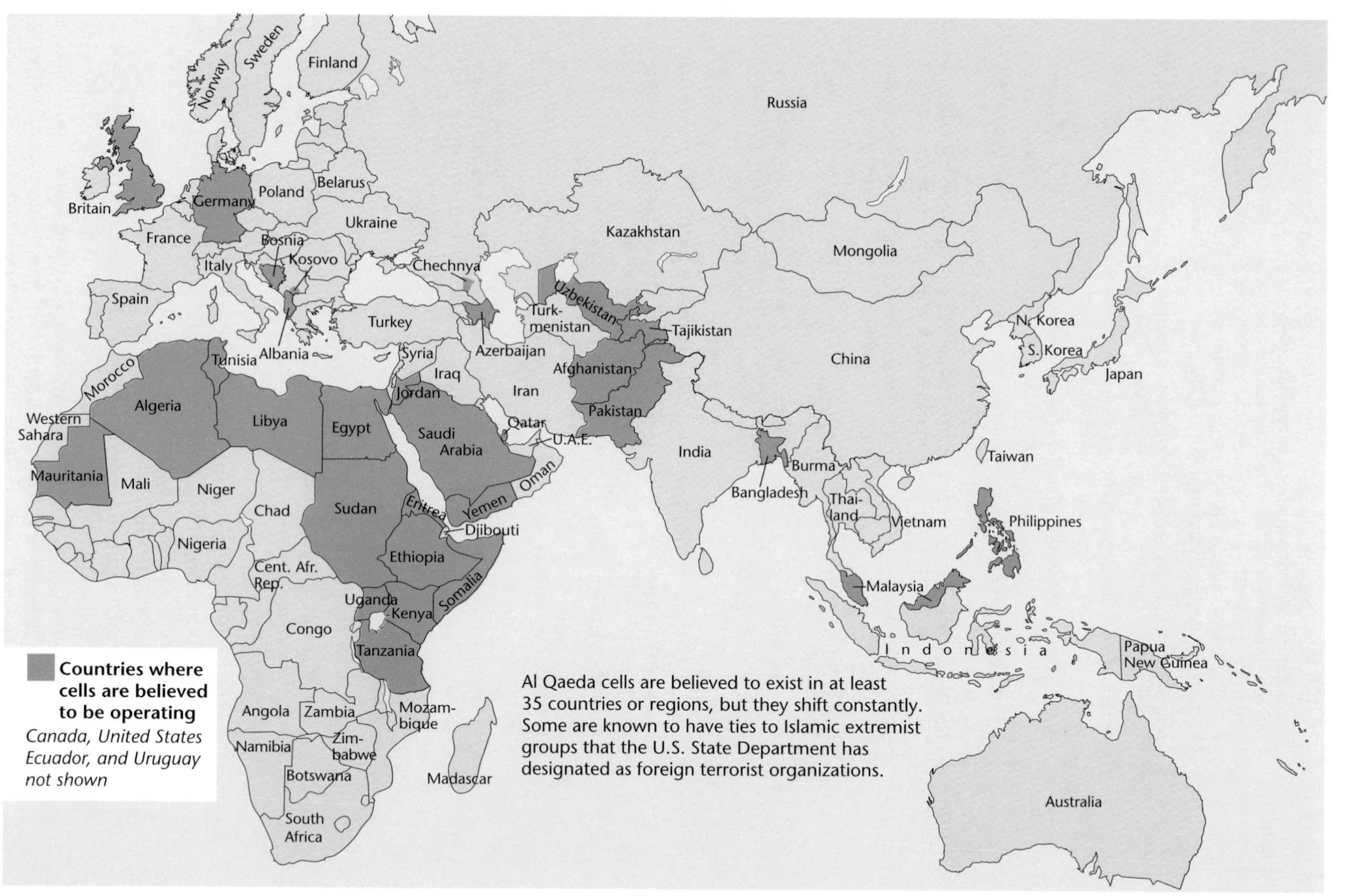

FIGURE 18.1

Location of Al Qaeda Cells Worldwide

Source: The Washington Post National Weekly Edition (September 24–30, 2001), p. 21.

are freed from their grip and until their armies, shattered and broken-winged, incapable of threatening any Muslim. . . . By God's leave, we call on every Muslim who believes in God and hopes for reward to obey God's command to kill the Americans and plunder their possessions wherever he finds them and whenever he can. Likewise we call on the Muslim ulema and leaders and youth and soldiers to launch attacks against the armies of the American devils and against those who are allied with them from among the helpers of Satan" (quoted in Lewis, 2001b:5B).

- "Terrorism can be commendable, and it can be reprehensible. The terrorism we practice is of the commendable kind for it is directed at the tyrants and the aggressors and the enemies of Allah" (a statement to journalist John Miller in 1998, cited in *Time,* 2001b:58).

Warnings

These inflammatory statements were ominous warnings, as were those various terrorist acts directed at the United States but in foreign lands. Moreover, the United States was warned of an attack by its officials. In July of 1999 Secretary of Defense William S. Cohen predicted a terrorist attack on U.S. soil: "In the past year, dozens of threats to use chemical or biological weapons in the United States have turned out to be hoaxes. Someday they will be real" (quoted in Klein, 2001:45). In June 2000 a National Commission on Terrorism report noted "today's terrorists seek to inflict mass casualties, and they are attempting to do so both overseas and on American soil" (quoted in *USA Today*, 2001c:23A). This was followed in February 2001 when a bipartisan group chaired by former Senators Gary Hart and Warren Rudman ended their report with this scary conclusion: "A direct attack against American citizens on American soil is likely. Americans will likely die . . . possibly in large numbers" (quoted in McPhee, 2001:22A). That prescient report also said that military superiority is not enough to protect against weapons of mass disruption, which could target air-traffic controllers or the Internet. These reports by highly placed officials were ignored by the media and the government. Apparently, in the words of former U.S. ambassador Gail Schoettler, "in our overwhelming military and economic superiority, we [had] become complacent, and even arrogant" (Schoettler, 2001:4E).

Actual and Potential Terrorist Weapons

The attacks on the World Trade Center and the Pentagon revealed the vulnerability of the United States. The threat of international terrorism is heightened by globalization. **Globalization** "is the process of growing international activity in many areas that is creating ever-closer ties, enhanced interdependence, and greater opportunity and vulnerability for all" (Flanagan, Frost, and Kugler, 2001:7).

> The central features of globalization are the rapidly growing and uneven cross-border flows of goods, services, people, money, technology, information, ideas, culture, crime, and weapons. Owing to globalization, international and transnational activity is growing exponentially, and the rate of change is accelerating almost everywhere, often faster than governments and institutions can respond. (Flanagan, Frost, and Kugler, 2001:8)

While for many globalization is a hopeful trend, it has a dark side, including the exploitation of Third World economies and their workers, and the loss of jobs in the United States. For our purposes here, globalization means that as the nations become increasingly connected, they are increasingly vulnerable to terrorist attacks by individuals and organizations. The United States, in particular, is relatively unprotected from terrorist attacks because it is a mobile, open society with porous borders that are difficult to police. For example, on an average day in 2000, U.S. Customs processed (Aston, 2001:48):

- 1.3 million people
- 348,000 private vehicles
- 38,000 trucks and railcars
- 16,000 containers on 600 ships
- 2,600 aircraft

Every year 18.5 million containers arrive in the United States by truck, railcar, and sea. With current personnel and technology it is impossible for the United States to secure its borders by searching carefully each of these containers. Consider, for example, the 16,000 containers measuring roughly 8 feet by 40 feet, weighing over 40 tons, that are unloaded at U.S. docks every day:

> According to U.S. Coast Guard Academy teacher Stephen Flynn, it would take five customs inspectors three hours to thoroughly inspect each one of these containers. But these containers must move swiftly, to meet the just-in-time requirements of their customers. If each container were really inspected, the whole global economy would seize up. The upshot, Flynn said, is that customs officials in Long Beach [where they receive about 1,000,000 containers each year] clear one container every 20 seconds—in other words, virtually without inspection.
>
> Now let's assume that one of these containers holds a biological weapon, loaded in Pakistan by a bin Laden agent with ties to a plausible shipping company, and destined for, say, Baltimore. That container would be zipped through Long Beach, loaded on a train and be halfway across the country—in Chicago's transshipment yards, for instance—when that weapon was activated. (Longworth, 2001:Section 2:8)

Modern technology, like globalization, is a double-edged sword, providing efficiency, power, and wonder to our lives but at the same time can be used against us (Levy, 2001). The terrorists use of corporate-owned aircraft filled with fuel as guided missiles illustrates how technology can be turned against its owners. A highly technical society provides a huge array of targets for terrorists. For example, the United States has 60,000 chemical plants and 103 nuclear power plants that could be sabotaged. So, too could hydroelectric dams, power grids, oil refineries, oil and natural gas pipe lines, railroad tracks, bridges, airports, water treatment plants, and factories. In essence, "the more powerful our tools are, the more dangerous they are when turned against us. For centuries we've accepted that. It's simply the downside of tech" (Levy, 2001:65). Let us take a brief look at the ways terrorists use technology to disrupt society and destroy lives.

- **Cyberterrorism.** Computers, software, and the Internet, for example, are fantastic tools for communication, coordinating tasks, and facilitating business transactions. But the dense thicket of connections that comprise communications and other activities can be shut down by clever computer experts. This form of **cyberterrorism** could be used to, for example, halt the movement of oil and natural gas transported through pipe lines, confuse or shut down the air-traffic control system, steal classified information from businesses or governments, disrupt 911 emergency calls in a region, transfer money and other assets from one account to another, divert water flows from irrigation to flooding low-lying areas, and spill sewage into reservoirs.* Of special significance this "information warfare" could be used to dismantle the U.S. military's 2.5 million computers. In 2001, it was reported that a group of computer hackers had been breaking into the top-secret files on Pentagon war-planning systems for over 3 years. Known as the "Moonlight Maze" group, the hackers have eluded the FBI, the CIA and the National Security Agency, despite the biggest cyberprobe ever (Swartz, 2001):

> An adversary could use [computer viruses] to launch a digital blitzkrieg against the United States. It might send a worm [a program that reproduces itself and causes networks to overload] to shut down the electric grid in Chicago and air-traffic-control operations in Atlanta, a logic bomb to open the floodgates of the Hoover Dam and a sniffer to gain access to the funds-transfer networks of the Federal Reserve. (Stone, 2001:2A)

The government has been lax in its attempts to counter cyberterrorism:

> The U.S. government spends only $1.8 billion a year to protect our webs, which, the F.B.I. will tell you, are already under daily hack by cyberterrorists. Meanwhile we are considering spending $100 billion on a missile shield to defend our walls from missiles that terrorists don't yet possess and may never use. It will probably take a cyberattack that causes real chaos for us to see that our big threat is not a mushroom cloud but the I.T. cloud [the complex web of fiber-optic cables and routers], and that threat will come up the web, not over a wall. (Friedman, 2001b:2)

- **Nuclear Weapons.** The technology for making nuclear weapons is widely known. The trick is to obtain fissionable material such as enriched uranium, make a bomb, and transport it to the targeted site. The fissionable material could be purchased or stolen from a nation such as North Korea, Iraq, Libya, Pakistan, or some of the states of the former Soviet Union. Transporting the bomb, which would weigh several hundred pounds, could be accomplished by private plane or private boat, just as drugs are smuggled into the United States. Another method would be to store the bomb in a container, then ship by commercial shipping, and detonate by remote control in the U.S. harbor of destination.

A more likely scenario is radiational terrorism (an attack on a nuclear power plant using conventional weapons or taking over a nuclear power plant and triggering a meltdown of its reactor core). If such an assault were successful, it could release more radiation than Chernobyl (an accident in a Soviet nuclear plant that resulted in 30,000 deaths, and incredible damage to livestock and agriculture). A 1982 study found, for example, that a reactor catastrophe near New York would cause 50,000 deaths and $314 billion in damage (Vergano, 2001).

*The vulnerability of our connected world is illustrated by the "Love Bug" computer virus, devised by two Filipino techies in 1999. Their virus "melted down roughly 10 million computers and $10 billion in data on several continents in 24 hours" (Friedman, 2000:7B).

- **Biological and Chemical Warfare.** Infectious (biological) or toxic (chemical) weapons are invisible and deadly.* The chemical weapons include cyanide, mustard gas, nerve gas, phosgene, organophosphate, sarin, and soman, and biological weapons include typhus, anthrax, the Ebola virus, smallpox, botulism, salmonella, *E. coli,* and bubonic plague. The object would be to sicken and kill people and even to destroy livestock and crops ("agricultural terrorism"). These weapons are relatively cheap to create and easy to inflict on an enemy. As for delivery systems, they can be deployed with a missile, through the mail, or via aerosol sprays, carried by the wind or by migratory birds, or flushed into a sewage system:

> A small cloud of bacteria or viruses could easily and silently infect tens of thousands of people, triggering fatal outbreaks of anthrax, smallpox, pneumonic plague or any of a dozen other deadly diseases. And victims infected with contagious ailments could pass the microbes to thousands of others before doctors even figured out what was going on. . . . "The events of New York and Washington were tragedies beyond what anyone had previously imagined, but the potential of biological terrorism is far greater in terms of loss of life and disruption," says Michael Osterholm, director of the University of Minnesota's Center for Infectious Disease Research and Policy. "It would be less graphic—no flames and explosions—but much more insidious. Anyone with a cough would be a weapon." (Weiss, 2001:39)

Consequences of the New Terrorism for the United States

The attacks of September 11, 2001, and subsequent events have had profound effects on the United States and its residents. The immediate effects were the loss of thousands of lives and the destruction of property. Ease of travel has been replaced by delays and security searches. The social fabric of society, based on social order and an implicit trust of others, has, for many, been replaced by fear of and alienation from those perceived as "others." Fear itself is a consequence of terrorism:

> The thing we most have to fear now is not more terrorism, but the terror it brings—paralyzing fear that saps our ability to think clearly, to decide carefully, to live normal lives: to travel, to shop, dance, joke or laugh. To hope. This is precisely why they call it terrorism. The purpose of an attack is not so much to destroy property or kill, but to instill fear and poison the psyche. (Ropeik, 2001:15A)

But a shared national tragedy and a common foe (not a country this time but a cause mobilized against the United States) also can bring national unity and purpose, as was evidenced by the civic and patriotic spirit evident throughout the United States. There are exceptions to this civic "pulling together" as Arab Americans and Muslims have been attacked, a topic to which we return shortly.

Let us examine other consequences, under these categories: changes in the military, economic repercussions, racial/ethnic profiling, the differences that social class position makes, and the loss of liberties in a free society.

*"Bioterrorism is not new. Fourteenth-Century barbarians tossed plague-infected corpses over the walls of fortified cities to spread the deadly infection among their enemies. In 1763, the English at Fort Pitt, Pa., gave smallpox-laden blankets to the Indians who had been loyal to the French. And, as recently as the mid-1990s, U.N. weapons inspectors discovered that Iraq had stockpiled warheads containing anthrax spores and the toxin that causes botulism" (Weiss, 2001:39).

- **Changes in the Military.** There are two major consequences for the military. First, the real threat of terrorism and the retaliation against terrorist networks have resulted in larger budgets for the military. Complacency has been replaced by resolve, beginning with a more generous backing of the military establishment—a budget for fiscal 2002 of $343 billion, up from about $300 billion. Fighting terrorism at home and abroad will mean that defense spending will likely consume a greater share of gross domestic product.

  The second consequence for the military is the realization that the military, organized to fight the Cold War, must be reorganized to meet the challenges of terrorism. This requires different strategies, technologies, and methods of intelligence gathering. It also means closing obsolete bases and the careful allocation of resources, not the traditional spending resulting from the cozy relationships among the Pentagon, Congress, defense corporations, and unions.

- **Economic Changes.** The economic costs of the terrorist attacks are enormous. First, the attacks of September 11, 2001, occurred when the economy was already slumping. The attacks created new uncertainties, driving consumer confidence, corporate profits, and the stock market down. As a result some 200,000 jobs were lost in the first month after the attacks. Some sectors of the economy were especially hard hit, especially those related to travel (the airlines, aircraft building, e.g., Boeing will deliver 100 fewer planes in 2002 than previously predicted, hotels, resorts, travel agents). Similarly, the economies of certain cities that depend heavily on tourism and conventions were impacted severely (Las Vegas, Honolulu, Miami, Orlando, San Francisco, and New Orleans). New York City will lose an estimated $105 billion over 2 years because of the loss of the World Trade Center, higher unemployment, the loss of tax revenues, the cost of cleanup and rebuilding the city's infrastructure, and the many fewer tourists visiting the city (Stashenko, 2001).

  There are some positives for the economy as well. Some businesses benefit from the threat of terrorism, such as those that manufacture guns and gas masks. Similarly, those companies involved in new surveillance technologies will benefit. One company, Visionics, a leader in biometrics, a method of identifying people by scanning and quantifying their unique characteristics, believes that every major airport will need at least 300 of their devices (the price of this stock more than tripled in the first week after the terrorist attack). Companies engaged in providing the Pentagon with new military technologies will benefit, as will those corporations that provide businesses and public places with safety devices. The government has provided aid to New York City to help clean up the rubble and rebuild, which provides money and jobs for the companies providing the services.

- **Race and Ethnicity Matters.** In times of crisis, Americans have tended to be intolerant of racial and ethnic minorities who were believed to support its enemies. In 1798, Congress fearful of a foreign conspiracy, enacted the Alien and Sedition Acts, which made it a federal crime to criticize the government, resulting in the expulsion of some immigrants. Ulysses S. Grant sought to expel Jews from Southern states. During World War II Japanese Americans were interned by the government, with the support of the Supreme Court, for their assumed allegiance to Japan. Now with the terrorist attacks on the United States being waged by Muslims, Americans who look Arab or who attend the 3,000 Islamic centers, mosques, and prayer locations are sometimes victims of **hate crimes,**

Kirk Anderson

defined as "crimes that are motivated by hate include words or actions intended to harm or intimidate an individual because of his or her perceived membership in or association with a particular group" (Craig and Waldo, 1996:113; see also Green, McFalls, and Smith, 2001). Some receive death threats. Some have been beaten and even killed. Mosques and Muslim schools have been vandalized and fire bombed. Arab children in junior high and high school are often victims of harassment, threats, and violence by their classmates.

In Chapter 12 we noted the problem of racial profiling as it pertained to the penchant for the police and other authorities to assume criminal behavior of African Americans. Now this is a problem for the 6 million to 7 million Muslims in this country. They are watched more closely than other Americans, searched more carefully and more often than other Americans especially in airports (e.g., in the first weeks after the attacks, pilots in four instances removed passengers off planes because they looked too Middle Eastern). Now FWM (flying while Muslim) has been added to DWB (driving while Black) for racial/ethnic profilers.

Racial profiling extends to the site of the World Trade Center, where Black, Latino, and dark-skinned people engaged in the cleanup are monitored more closely than Whites (Benjamin, 2001). They are detained more and asked more questions as they go through the various checkpoints. Leaving the site, they are searched more than White workers, as the guards are suspicious of their looting of the premises.

If gender is combined with ethnicity, we find that Islamic women are more vulnerable to harassment than Islamic men because of the conspicuous religious and cultural clothing they wear. Islamic men are more likely to escape harassment because their clothing is usually indistinguishable from typical men's clothing in U.S. society.

- **Social Class Differences.** In the fallout from the initial terrorist attack in 2001, there were several examples of the working and lower classes being disadvantaged more than the privileged. First, within 10 days of the bombing, Congress gave the U.S. airlines a $15 billion bailout. Not included in this package were: (1) any government demands to lower the compensation of airline executives; and (2) any compensation for the 100,000 airline employees who were suddenly laid off with no notice or severance pay.

  Second, it is estimated that about 100,000 low-wage service workers (clerks, restaurant workers, janitors, hotel maids) in New York City will lose their jobs directly as a result of the disaster (Reich, 2001b). Most have no health insurance. Most will not even qualify for unemployment insurance because they have not worked long enough in the same job or they work part-time or do contract work.

  Third, in 1996, as noted in Chapter 7, the government passed welfare reform that moved many from welfare to work and reduced the safety net. Now with the economic recession and massive layoffs, life will be especially difficult for those who have been laid off from low-skilled jobs. Many have used up the 5-year lifetime limit on welfare and no longer qualify for aid. Many do not qualify for unemployment insurance, which depends on the policies of the various states. In Nevada, for instance, where layoffs are common because of fewer visitors to Las Vegas, a jobless person has to earn $5,600 in a 3-month period to qualify for the average unemployment benefit. That is more than twice what a woman leaving welfare typically earns (DeParle, 2001).

  Fourth, the government, faced with a much larger military budget and reduced government revenues because of the economic recession, will likely reduce expenditures for social programs. This will increase the already huge gap between the affluent and the poor and working poor even more. State governments will also feel the pinch of reduced income from taxes, increasing the likelihood of lowering expenditures for social programs to aid the less fortunate.

  Finally, the federal government is faced with trying to stimulate a faltering economy. As this is being written, President Bush has proposed a stimulus package worth $75 billion that: (1) permanently abolishes the corporate alternate minimum tax, which forces companies that can mask their profits with deductions to pay at least some taxes, and (2) accelerates the income tax reductions passed by Congress in 2001. The *New York Times* in an editorial (2001b) stated that these proposals are too corporate friendly and overwhelmingly favor high-income Americans.

- **Erosion of Civil Liberties.** The threat of terrorism is real and it presents U.S. society and its citizens with a dilemma—security versus civil liberties. Security is problematic in the new political environment. Terrorists can cross the borders into the United States rather easily. Some terrorists, called "sleepers," live in the United States, raising children, working at jobs, and acting like ordinary citizens. To the degree that there are "sleepers," law enforcers may have no choice but to treat everybody like a suspect, which means the government surveillance of all types is justified (France and Green, 2001). Some of the antiterrorism possibilities are:

  - The imposition of a national electronic identification card, with computer chips that would contain fingerprints, facial characteristics, the pattern of the eyes, and other detailed information. These could be programmed to permit or limit access to buildings or areas. They could track someone's location, financial transactions, and criminal history (Glaberson, 2001).

- Increased surveillance of public places.
- The use of surveillance technology to monitor e-mail traffic and to record the websites visited by individuals. The FBI, for example, has a tool called "Carnivore" that monitors everyone who uses the same Internet service provider that the suspect uses—whether they are under investigation or not.
- Holding suspects without filing charges.
- Detaining undocumented immigrants indefinitely and without appeal.
- Easing the rules of wiretapping so that suspects could be monitored easily and quickly and for long periods..
- Expansion of the right to search and seize as needed, without cumbersome legal technicalities.

Proponents argue that the dangers are serious, and these and other security measures are needed to make the nation secure by making it easier to identify, prevent, and punish terrorists. Giving up privacy is a small price to pay for safety in a hostile world.

Critics, on the other hand, argue that these measures go too far in expanding government's abilities to intrude on citizens' lives, thereby weakening individual rights. Citizens have guarantees from the Constitution that protect them from government surveillance, reading the mail, and listening to phone conversations of its citizens—in short, Americans have the right to privacy and freedom from unreasonable search and seizure. Moreover, there is a high probability that the invasion of privacy will not be randomly distributed, but more likely will be directed at noncitizens, Muslims, and people who look "Middle Eastern."

There is a fine line between what is needed for security and protecting the freedoms that characterize the United States. If we stray too far toward restricted freedoms, we end up, ironically, terrorizing ourselves. Another irony is that President Bush declared on the night of the assault on the World Trade Center and Pentagon that "America is the brightest beacon for freedom in the world and that no one will keep that light from shining," yet the domestic antiterrorism actions proposed by the government will "darken that very beacon of freedom by making a new attack on our own people's already-endangered civil liberties" (Hightower, 2001:1).

Strategies to Combat the New Terrorism

The strategies employed against terrorism will not resemble those used during the Cold War. It is not a matter of military strength. A missile shield is not the answer. The enemy is not a nation or a cluster of allied nations. This time it is different. How, then, do we address the problem of terrorism by a relatively small, militarily weak, shadowy network of people and groups, willing to blow themselves up for a cause greater than they are? Although terrorism is possible from many sources, we concentrate here on ways to neutralize the current threat from Islamic extremists. What follows are some ideas from which to develop strategies organized around lessons that we know:

- **Lesson 1: Military Might Alone Does Not Make a Nation Secure.** Overwhelming military and economic superiority did not protect the United States from nineteen men who hijacked four planes with plastic knives, turning them into guided missiles. "They used our high-tech, well fueled aircraft as their bombs and our open society as their opportunity" (Schoettler, 2001:4E).

- **Lesson 2: Vengeance Is Self-Defeating.** Responding to attacks with similar attacks ("an eye for an eye and a tooth for a tooth") may make the combatants feel better, but it just fuels existing hatreds that extends from generation to generation and a never-ending violence. The history of the Israeli–Palestinian conflict where car bombs planted by Palestinians bring air attacks by the Israeli government provides ample proof, as does the ongoing conflict between Protestants and Catholics in Northern Ireland. The response to attacks must be limited to seeking justice, not revenge.

- **Lesson 3: Terrorists Seek a Savage Response to Win Sympathy for and Converts to Their Cause.** A noted military scholar, Sir Michael Howard of Oxford University, traced examples of terrorism over the last 130 years, concluding that one of the principal aims of terrorists has always been to provoke savage acts of retaliation to win sympathy for their cause (cited in B. Lewis, 2001). If the United States uses its military might, perhaps even nuclear weapons, it would be self-defeating, polarizing the world into Islam versus Christianity. If the United States wreaks a holocaust in Arab countries such as Afghanistan or Iraq or Syria or Pakistan, then bin Laden or whomever replaces him will have accomplished his goal of bringing most of the world's 1.2 billion Muslims together in a *jihad* against the West.

- **Lesson 4: The Best Way to Deal with Terrorism Is to Address Its Root Causes.** The United States should take seriously the grievances of the Muslim peoples in this region. "We now have a historical opportunity to reflect on our responsibility, to listen to these enemies for the first time, and to create a more peaceful world. While this may sound like idealistic rhetoric, it is much more mature, hardheaded, and achievable than thinking we can stop violence with violence" (Franklin, 2001:46A). First, the Israeli–Palestinian conflict must be resolved. While ensuring security for Israel, a Palestinian state must be established, with a multinational peacekeeping force placed between the two countries. Further, this Palestinian homeland must be provided ample aid to bolster its economy, provide jobs for its people, and provide the necessary infrastructure (housing, schools, irrigation systems, roads, sewage treatment, and the like).

  Second, U.S. troops and bases must be removed from Saudi Arabia, Egypt, Oman, and other Arab states in the region, thus eliminating the U.S. military, the symbol of domination, from the cradle of Islam.

  Third, this part of the world has a few very rich people, a small middle class, and a huge population of very poor people. Needed is a "Marshall Plan" stretching from the Strait of Gibralter to the Indonesian archipelago, where the vast majority suffer from poverty, hunger, disease, and hopelessness. This arc of poverty across many countries is the setting where the seeds of terrorism flourish, where impoverished young men accept the role of suicide bombers as a way to replace their dismal existence with paradise (see the "Social Problems in Global Perspective" panel "Donating Sons to Jihad," p. 556). If the affluent West provided investment, aid, technical assistance, and technology to these countries, then their people and their economies will thrive and the attractive-

SOCIAL PROBLEMS IN GLOBAL PERSPECTIVE

DONATING SONS TO JIHAD

Westerners have difficulty in understanding why young male Islamic militants are willing to die for their religion and why their parents not only accept but encourage such behavior. They may strap explosives to their bodies to die in suicide missions or they die in battle doing "God's will." The following description by Jessica Stern provides the rationale:

> What happens to families whose children become martyrs? Most of the mothers I interviewed said they were happy to have donated their sons to jihad because their sons could help them in the next life—the "real life."
>
> Syed Qurban Hussain, the father of a martyr, said, "Whoever gives his life in the way of Allah lives forever and earns a place in heaven for 70 members of his family, to be selected by the martyr."
>
> Families of martyrs become celebrities after their children die. "Everyone treats me with more respect now that I have a martyred son," Hussain added. "And when there is a martyr in the village, it encourages more children to join the jihad. It raises the spirit of the entire village."
>
> Foundations have been set up to help the families of martyrs. For example, the Shuhda-e-Islam Foundation, founded by Jamaat i Islami, claims to have disseminated 13 million rupees in Pakistan since 1995.
>
> One family I visited lived on a street lined with open sewers. But the house, which is made of unpainted concrete, was partly paid for by the foundation. It is a large improvement over their earlier home, a mud hut. After son Zafar Iqbal died in Kashmir, the foundation helped pay the family's substantial debts, and it helped Habeeb Iqbal, the martyr's father, to start a business. He now owns two shops in the village.
>
> When Zafar Iqbal died, 8,000 people attended his funeral in Kashmir, his mother told me. "God is helping us out a lot," she said, pointing to her home and smiling. They also plan to donate their youngest "to God," her husband added, pointing to their 10-year-old son.
>
> After completing fifth grade in a government school, the boy will study in a madrisa full time to prepare himself mentally and physically for jihad. I asked the boy what he wants to do when he grows up. "Be a mujahed [a boy who courts death in the name of God]," he said.

Source: J. Stern. 2001. "Meeting with the Muj." *Bulletin of the Atomic Scientists 57* (January/February):45.

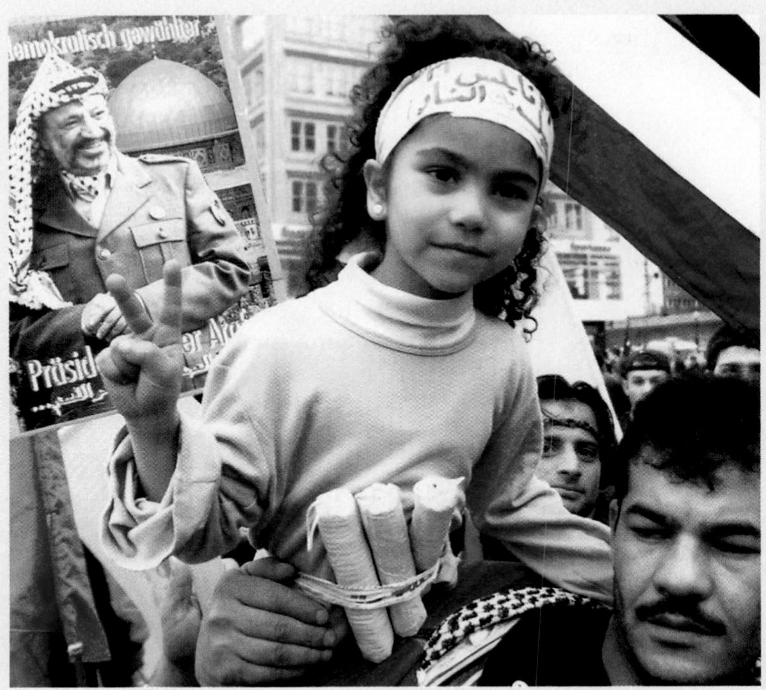

Not only are sons raised by some Islamic militants to be martyrs, so too are young girls.

A CLOSER LOOK

THE CASE FOR PEACE

If we want to be effective in a long-term struggle against terror, we need a strategy to marginalize the terrorists by making it much harder for them to appeal to legitimate anger at the U.S. Imagine if the bin Ladens and other haters of the world had to recruit people against the U.S. at a time when:

1) the U.S. was using its economic resources to end world hunger and redistribute the wealth of the planet so that everyone had enough.

2) The U.S. was the leading voice championing an ethos of generosity and caring for others, leading the world in ecological responsibility, social justice and openhearted treatment of minorities, and rewarding people and corporations for social responsibility.

3) The U.S. was restructuring its internal life so that all social practices, corporations and institutions were being judged not only on whether they maximized profit but also to the extent that they maximized love and caring, sensitivity and an approach to the universe based on awe and wonder at the grandeur of creation. Imagine a new Social Responsibility Amendment to the U.S. Constitution that would make a corporation's ability to operate in the U.S. dependent on its ability to prove a history of social responsibility both in the U.S. and around the world.

If the U.S. uses this moment to develop this kind of "New Bottom Line," we will do far more to create safety for ourselves and our children than bombing Afghanistan will achieve. The ordinary citizens, fire fighters and police who risked (and in many instances lost) their lives to help others survive on Sept. 11 demonstrate a possibility that our culture has often rendered invisible: we could build a world based on generosity, mutual caring and spiritual wisdom. If we want a world of peace and justice, we need to be more peaceful and more just.

Source: Michael Lerner. 2001. "The Case for Peace," *Time* (October 1):77.

ness of the terrorist cause is significantly diminished—and the safety of the world enhanced appreciably. While the cost will be high, the economies of the United States, Europe, and Japan produce more than $20 trillion annually, making it possible to fund such a project that is ultimately a win/win proposition (*Nation,* 2001c). The United States must adapt to a shrinking world, which makes all nations more interdependent. This means that unless the United States finds a way to help those left behind in the Third World, it is in trouble. Case in point: "While the global economy has grown at an average of 2.3 percent a year for the past three decades, the gap between the best-off and worst-off countries (as measured in per capital gross national product) is 10 times wider now than 30 years ago" (Reich, 2001a:48). This widening gap is a large part of the problem. The United States ignores this lesson at its peril. (See "A Closer Look" panel for a further argument that the United States must share its resources if it wants a lasting peace.)

- **Lesson 5: The United States Cannot Fight Terrorism Alone.** The affluent nations need to construct a coalition that works together to fund and implement the "Marshall Plan" for the Third World. The United States also needs other countries for shared intelligence, to cut off terrorists funding, as well as their help to stop potential terrorists and to apprehend the perpetrators of terrorism.

  Foremost, though, the battle against Islamic extremists can only be won if Islamic clerics and other Muslim leaders convince the Muslim people that their extremist ideology is contrary to the principles of Islam, which means they must condemn terrorist leaders who sabotage Islam. If successful, this would diminish the numbers of militants, restrict their activities, and bring stability in the Arab countries fearful of radical takeover. Combining this with a Middle Eastern "Marshall Plan" would secure a more peaceful world.

CHAPTER REVIEW

1. Military might, to be second to none in power, is the principle guiding national security in the United States. The Cold War with the Soviet Union, which ended about 1990, was very costly to both sides (huge debt for the United States, resulting in the neglect of basic services to the disadvantaged; and the breakup of the Soviet Union).
2. The United States is the world's greatest military power. This power does not come cheap—36 percent of the world's military expenditures are spent by the United States, with only 5 percent of the world's population. One-fourth of the federal budget is for defense.
3. Domestic terrorism (Americans killing Americans) has occurred throughout U.S. history. The current threat comes from the Patriot movement in reaction to government actions that in their view violate fundamental liberties granted by the Constitution.
4. The United States and its citizens have been targets of Islamic radicals for the past 20 years or so. The United States is a target because of its policies, especially its total political, military, and economic support of Israel, and its military presence in the Middle East, especially Saudi Arabia, the cradle of Islam. The United States is also resented for its power and envied for its wealth. Finally, the United States is viewed by some as an infidel power spreading its permissive, secular culture into the Muslim world, eroding traditional Muslim values.
5. The new terrorists use modern technology as weapons to disrupt the United States and destroy lives. This includes the disruption of computer networks and the Internet (cyberterrorism), the use of nuclear weapons, as well as biological and chemical warfare.
6. Among the consequences resulting from terrorist attacks are: (a) an increase in military spending, (b) the reorganization of the military from "Cold Warriors" to combating terrorism, (c) a weakening of an already fragile economy, (d) discrimination (racial profiling, hate crimes) directed at Arab Americans and Muslims, (e) the working and lower classes being disadvantaged more than the privileged, and (f) the erosion of civil liberties for greater security.
7. To combat the new terrorism the United States needs to construct strategies and policies based on an understanding of history and the roots of the new terrorism. These lessons are: (a) military might alone does not make a nation secure, (b) vengeance is self-defeating, (c) terrorists seek a savage response to win sympathy and recruits for their cause, and (d) the United States cannot fight terrorism alone; it needs other nations including leaders in the Islamic world.

KEY TERMS

Cold War. The tension and arms spiral between the United States and the Soviet Union from World War II until 1990.

Terrorism. Unlawful use of force or violence against persons or property to intimidate or coerce a government, the civilian population, or any segment thereof, to further political or social objectives.

Terrorist acts. Violent acts by religious or political zealots to achieve their aims.

Globalization. Process of growing international activity in many areas that is creating ever-closer ties, enhanced interdependence, and greater opportunity and vulnerability for all.

Cyberterrorism. Use of computers to disrupt communication, transportation, and commercial activities.

Hate crimes. Crimes intended to harm or intimidate an individual because of his or her perceived membership in or association with a particular group.

WEBSITES FOR FURTHER REFERENCE

http://www.nap.edu/terror/index.html?do_se46
This website of the National Academies Press features a collection of resources on terrorism and security issues. Individuals can search for information from 26 recent publications from the National Academies about the science and policy issues surrounding terrorism and security. All reports and analyses can be read online free.

http://www.terrorism.com/index.shtml
The Terrorism Research Center is dedicated to informing the public of the phenomena of terrorism and information warfare. This site features essays and thought pieces on current issues, as well as links to other terrorism documents, research, and resources.

http://www.fbi.gov
The Federal Bureau of Investigation (FBI) is the principal investigative arm of the United States Department of Justice (DOJ). Title 28, United States Code (U.S. Code), Section 533, which authorizes the Attorney General to "appoint officials to detect . . . crimes against the United States," and other federal statutes give the FBI the authority and responsibility to investigate specific crimes. Currently, the FBI has investigative jurisdiction over violations of more than 200 categories of federal crimes. Information obtained through an FBI investigation is presented to the appropriate U.S. Attorney or DOJ official, who decides if prosecution or other action is warranted. Top priority has been assigned to the five areas that affect society the most: counterterrorism, drugs/organized crime, foreign counterintelligence, violent crimes, and white-collar crimes.

http://www.vvmf.org
As the founders of The Wall, the Vietnam Veterans Memorial Fund works to preserve the legacy of the Vietnam Veterans Memorial and to educate current and future generations about the enduring lessons of the Vietnam War on American society. In doing so, the Memorial Fund serves as a resource to individuals, schools, colleges, and community organizations seeking information about the Memorial and the role it has played in the remembrance of those who served in the Vietnam War. The Memorial Fund also develops educational resources and sponsors projects that foster the understanding, healing, and reconciliation of Americans.

http://www.rawa.org
Revolutionary Association for the Women of Afghanistan (RAWA) was established in Kabul, Afghanistan, in 1977 as an independent political/social organization of Afghan women fighting for human rights and for social justice in Afghanistan.

http://www.debka.com
DEBKA*file* is a self-supporting Internet publication devoted to independent investigative reporting and forward analysis in the fields of international terrorism, intelligence, international conflicts, Islam, military affairs, security, and politics. DEBKA*file* is published seven days a week in English and Hebrew, with additional language sites planned. This website includes specific regional information on national and international security issues around the world.

http://www.foreignaffairs.org/home/terrorism.asp
Foreign Affairs Magazine, published by the prestigious U.S. Council on Foreign Relations, makes available previously published articles that contribute to an understanding of the tragic attacks on New York and Washington. Several of the essays analyze the nature of contemporary terrorism and the capabilities of the United States to combat it. Other essays provide the Middle Eastern and radical Islamic contexts for so much recent terrorism, including, apparently, the attacks on the World Trade Center and the Pentagon.

http://www.eiu.com/
The Economist Intelligence Unit is the world's leading provider of country intelligence. Its mission is to "help executives make better business decisions by providing up-to-date, reliable and impartial analysis on worldwide market trends and business strategies. . . . We continuously assess and forecast political, economic and business conditions in almost 200 countries, and provide insight into how companies are responding."

http://www.defenselink.mil/
Official website of the U.S. Department of Defense. The latest news on the United States' foreign affairs and involvement, Pentagon information, and information on the various branches of the military can be accessed through this site. Special DoD reports and publications as well as photos are also available.

http://www.aclu.org/
The American Civil Liberties Union is the nation's foremost advocate of individual rights: "litigating, legislating, and educating the public on a broad array of issues affecting individual freedom in the United States."

PART SIX
SOLUTIONS

19 Progressive Plan to Solve Society's Social Problems

*ociety has a moral obligation, which includes taking government action when necessary, to meet basic human needs and pursue justice in economic life.*

—National Conference of Catholic Bishops

In his 1989 inaugural address, President Bush said, "We have more will than wallet" to deal with social problems. Today we have the wallet but, evidently, not the will.

—Marilyn Moon and Joanne Silberner

Social problems are social. That is, they are human arrangements, created and sustained by people (this chapter is taken from Eitzen, 1996; Eitzen and Leedham, 2001:3–12; Eitzen and Baca Zinn, 2001, Chapter 18; and Baca Zinn and Eitzen, 2002, Chapter 13). The politicoeconomic system of a society, from which social problems emanate, does not simply evolve from random events and aimless choices. The powerful in societies craft policies to accomplish certain ends within the context of historical events, budgetary constraints, and the like. Addressing the issue of inequality, Fischer and his colleagues say:

> The answer to the question of why societies vary in their structure of rewards is . . . political. . . . By loosening markets or regulating them, by providing services to all citizens or rationing them according to income, by subsidizing some groups more than others, societies, through their politics, build their ladders [the height and breadth of the rungs of the stratification system]. To be sure, historical and external constraints deny full freedom of action, but a substantial freedom of action remains. . . . In a democracy, this means that the inequality that Americans have is, in significant measure, the historical result of policy choices Americans—or, at least, Americans' representatives—have made. In the United States, the result is a society that is distinctly unequal. Our ladder is, by the standards of affluent democracies and even by the standards of recent American history, unusually extended and narrow—and becoming more so. (Fischer et al., 1996:8)

In other words, America's level of inequality, which is greater than found in any of the Western democracies, is by design (Fischer et al., 1996:125).

Social policy is about design, about setting goals and determining the means to achieve them. Do we want to regulate and protect more, as the well-developed welfare states do, or should we do less? Should we create and invest in policies and programs that protect citizens from poverty, unemployment, and medical inattention, or should the market economy sort people into winners, players, and losers based on their abilities, efforts, and the luck or misfortune of the families into which they were born and raised? In the past decade, decision makers in the United States have opted to reduce drastically the welfare system (e.g., elimination of Aid to Families with Dependent Children [AFDC], reduced monies for food stamps) while the taxes on the affluent have been reduced significantly and subsidies such as the tax exemption on the interest and taxes paid on housing have been retained. And, when faced with what to do with the budget surplus generated from a booming economy, Congress and state legislatures have rejected subsidies to low-income families for child care, medical care, and job training. Similarly, the boards of corporations, faced with major profit gains and increased productivity during most of the 1990s and even during the economic downturn of 2000 and 2001, have opted to reward their executives with ever more generous salaries and stock options.

Meanwhile, these same corporations have downsized their workforces, reduced entry-level wages, hired more temporary and contingent workers, and reduced health and other benefits to employees. Thus, the combined acts of federal and state governments and corporations have increased the gap between the top one-fifth ("the fortunate fifth") and those in the bottom one-fifth of the income/wealth distribution. The resulting inequality gap is a major source of social problems.

The important sociological point is that if societies are designed, and some of the arrangements result in social problems, *they can be changed to reduce or eliminate those problems.* In other words, the design can be changed.

Such change is not easy, though. Social arrangements can be tradition bound and often imbued with religious approval (also, by the way, a social construction), which impedes efforts at change. The status quo is defined as natural, and those who challenge it are seen as "impractical, ridiculous, crazy, dangerous and/or immoral. By definition, the conventional wisdom of the day is widely accepted, continually reiterated and regarded not as ideology but as reality itself" (Willis, 1998:19). But change is possible. In the words of progressive Senator Paul Wellstone:

> It's the power that won the eight-hour day, women's right to choose, civil rights laws, and the end of the Vietnam War. Grassroots movements brought about these and most great changes that have advanced the people of this country. *People organized, protested, educated one another, kept up the pressure, and held their ideals high.* [In doing so] the collected voices of concerned and committed Americans spoke clearly and loudly enough to be heard over those who resisted change. (Wellstone, 1998b:1)

As the New Party (a progressive alternative to the Republican and Democratic parties) says: "Ordinary people can do extraordinary things if they are organized" (*New Party News,* 1997:12).

SOCIOLOGY, SOCIAL PROBLEMS, AND SOCIAL CHANGE

This textbook is a sociological introduction to the understanding of social problems, their sources, and their consequences. Let us look more closely at the discipline of sociology and make explicit what has been implicit throughout this book.

Sociological Paradox: Structure and Agency

Throughout the discussion in this book, we have emphasized the power of social context and the social forces that so strongly affect human behavior (the following is from Eitzen and Baca Zinn, 2001:525–526). As sociologist Peter Berger says:

> Society not only controls our movements, but shapes our identity, our thoughts and our emotions. The structures of society become the structures of our own consciousness. Society does not stop at the surface of our skins. Society penetrates us as much as it envelops us. (Berger, 1963:121)

This **deterministic view** is too strong, however. While society constrains what we do, it does not determine what we do (Giddens, 1991:863). While society and its structures are powerful, the members of society are not totally controlled. We are not passive members. We can take control of the conditions of our own lives. Human beings cope with, adapt to, and change social structures to meet their needs. Individuals, acting alone or with others, can shape, resist, challenge, and sometimes change the social organizations and social institutions that impinge on them. These actions constitute **human agency.**

The paradox of sociology—the power of society over its members versus the power of social actors to change society—has several important meanings and implications. Foremost, society is not a rigid, static entity composed of robots. People in interaction are the architects of society in an ongoing project. That is, society is created, sustained, and changed by people.

Second, the social forms that people create often take on a sacred quality—the sanctity of tradition—that constrains behavior in socially prescribed ways. The sociological insight is, to restate the previous point, that what many consider sacred and unchangeable is a social construction and can therefore be reconstructed.

A third implication is that since social structures are created and sustained by people, they are imperfect. There are positive and negative consequences of the way people have organized. Many are content with the status quo because they benefit from it. Others accept it even though they are disadvantaged by it. But there are also those who seek change to improve it or, perhaps, to transform it into something completely different. They are the agents of change.

In sum, the essence of agency is that individuals through collective action are capable of changing the structure of society and even the course of history. But while agency is important, we should not forget the power of the structures that subordinate people, making change difficult or, at times, impossible.

Sociological Dilemma: Recognition and Rejection

Sociologists wish to be taken seriously by those in power. We are experts on social life. We have answers, not all by any means, but many, nonetheless, based on empirical research. But society's governmental and corporate leaders rarely seek sociological expertise in tackling social problems. Repeatedly, for example, sociologists have pointed out to political deaf ears that it "costs less to educate people than to leave them untrained. It costs less to provide prenatal care than to care for underweight babies. It costs less to house people than to build prisons to warehouse them" (Jackson, 1998a:20). It costs less and is more effective to deal with children before they get into trouble than to ignore them and put them in the criminal justice system after they have become disheartened and alienated because they have no hope of conventional success. But this understanding goes unheeded as budgets for Head Start–type programs dry up and budgets for prisons escalate.

Sociologists Barbara Risman and Donald Tomaskovic-Devey convey this dilemma of having helpful knowledge but being marginal in our effectiveness as public intellectuals:

> One of the wonderful things about being sociologists is knowing that collectively we have something powerful to contribute to the understanding of most, probably all, problems faced by society. One of the most frustrating things about being sociologists is how rarely we see sociological knowledge guiding the social choices and strategies of others. This happens at all levels, from the construction of global warming policy, to campaign finance reform,

to affirmative action in our own universities, to couples struggling to create egalitarian relationships. (Risman and Tomaskovic-Devey, 1998:vii)

Why is this the case? Why are sociologists rejected by those in power? Several related reasons combine to make sociologists marginal (the following is from Risman and Tomaskovic-Devey, 1998, and Eitzen and Baca Zinn, 1998b: 8–9). Foremost, the sociological perspective is subversive. That is, sociology undermines everything because it questions all social arrangements, whether religious, political, economic, or familial. Such an approach is threatening to those in power. As Risman and Tomaskovic-Devey say: "Our insights, regardless of how intellectually and empirically powerful they might be, are not always welcomed by the privileged" (1998:vii). But it is not just the powerful elites who are threatened; it is those who are powerful because they are in the majority by virtue of their social class position, their race/ethnicity, their gender, or their sexual orientation. Sociology unmasks the institutional classism, racism, sexism, and homophobia that is present in the "normal" and "accepted" ways that social structures work to discriminate against the powerless and keep them "in their place."

The message of sociologists is rejected by many because it challenges the core of society's dominant ideology. The economy of the United States is capitalism. This system has its strengths but it also leads to many social problems, as has been amply shown throughout this book.

Related to capitalism is the emphasis in U.S. society on individualism. Unlike Canada, the Scandinavian countries, and the nations of Western Europe, the United States focuses more on individual achievement and competition, letting the losers fend mostly for themselves. In essence, we say for the most part, you are on your own; get an education; get a job; take care of yourself and your family; and you are not obligated to take care of others. Thus, government programs to help the economically disadvantaged are minimal. The governments of the other Western democracies have a different philosophy. They are much more inclined to provide for the common good (e.g., generous welfare programs to lift people out of poverty; universal health insurance; more public resources for parks, orchestras, and mass transit). Sociologists are quick to point out the difference between the United States and its peers, noting that while the United States is the wealthiest country, it has the highest proportion of people living in poverty, the highest proportion of children growing up in poverty, and the most unequal income and wealth distributions (Frank and Cook, 1995; Lipset, 1996). Thus, the individualism that pervades U.S. society has a severe downside, leading to serious social problems. But because the individualist ideology is a core belief of most Americans, any criticism of it is viewed with alarm, as being un-American. Thus, sociologists, when they examine and report what they see as the consequences of public policy, which has as its foundation the emphasis on individualism, are moved to the margins of public discourse about social problems.

We are confident that many of the readers of this book have found the sociological examination of social problems uncomfortable. Perhaps you have found it subversive because it questions the underlying assumptions about U.S. society. Even though this critical approach may be uncomfortable to many people, it is necessary for the understanding of human social arrangements and for finding solutions to social problems. Thus, we ask that you think sociologically: (1) to view social arrangements critically and (2) to view social problems as emanating from social structure, not bad people. In essence, we ask that you overcome the societal bias against sociology by adopting the sociological perspective as you consider what society should do about its social problems.

PROGRESSIVE PRINCIPLES TO GUIDE PUBLIC POLICY

This book has focused on the structural basis for social problems. These problems are formidable, but not insolvable. We can do something about them. This effort to change problematic social arrangements is the essence of human agency.

What, then, do we do to solve social problems? The first step must be to determine the facts. This requires that we challenge the myths that often guide public opinion and policymakers. Providing the facts and demythologizing social life have been major goals of this book.

The second step is to establish, as a society, the principles that will guide public policy. This, we realize, is politically impossible at the moment for at least two reasons. Foremost, underlying many of the problems in the United States is the power of money over the decision-making process. Politicians of both political parties, locally and nationally, receive donations from special interests whether they be individual corporations or unions or teachers or physicians or insurance companies. Implicit in these contributions is a *quid pro quo:* The money is for the politician's past or anticipated favorable governmental actions. The problem, of course, is that the powerful use this mechanism to retain power, and the relatively powerless (e.g., single mothers, the homeless, renters, children, the working poor, recent immigrants, and contingent workers) are left with no effective political voice. This is not democracy; it is a **plutocracy** (a government where the wealthy class rules). Representative Bernie Sanders of Vermont says:

> [T]he basic reason that neither major political party stands up for the average American is that both parties are heavily indebted to their wealthy contributors. The richest one-quarter of one percent of Americans make 80 percent of the political contributions and corporations outspend labor by a margin of 10–1. (Sanders, 1998b:1)

Until campaign finance is straightened out, no significant change is possible. It can be fixed by eliminating "soft money" (see Chapter 2), limiting the funds received to a very small amount per contributor, having the television and radio networks provide free and equal time to candidates (this could be accomplished by the government granting broadcasting licenses only to those entities that provide free time to candidates). Most important, the public must demand campaign finance reform and accept nothing less.

The second stumbling block to change is that, currently, majorities in the federal and state legislatures are political conservatives. This means that the power wielders (often in both major parties) stand for the status quo, market solutions to social problems, and reducing government.

Assuming that the bias of money in politics and the political power of the conservative right can be overcome—dubious assumptions at best—let us propose some principles that we believe ought to guide public policy in order to reduce or eliminate major social problems that plague U.S. society.

1. *A call for policies and behaviors that enhance our moral obligation to our neighbors (broadly defined) and their children, to those unlike us as well as those similar to us, and to future generations.* This principle runs counter to our societal celebration of individualism. But, we argue, the emphasis on individualism over community leads to exacerbated inequality; the tolerance of inferior housing, schools, and services for "others"; and public policies that are punitive to the economically disadvantaged. Moreover, exaggerated individualism is the antithesis of cooperation and solidarity—the requirements of community.

What happens when the gap between the rich and the poor widens? This phenomenon of income inequality has implications for democracy, crime, and civil unrest. As economist Lester Thurow has asked:

> How much inequality can a democracy take? The income gap is eroding the social contract. If the promise of a higher standard of living is limited to a few at the top, the rest of the citizenry, as history shows, is likely to grow disaffected, or worse. (Thurow, 1995b:78)

Similarly, sociologist Todd Gitlin's reading of history leads him to conclude that "[g]rowing inequality erodes social solidarity" (Gitlin, 1995:225).

The welfare states of Canada, Europe, and Scandinavia have comprehensive social supports for their peoples. They provide universal health care insurance systems. They have a much more ample minimum wage than does the United States. They provide generous pensions and nursing home care for the elderly. They have paid maternity (and in some cases paternity) leave. Education is free through college. These benefits are costly, with income, inheritance, and sales taxes considerably higher than in the United States. The tradeoff is that poverty is rare and the population feels relatively safe from crime and from the insecurities over income, illness, and old age. Most important, there is a large middle class with a much stronger feeling of community and social solidarity than is found in the United States.

In sharp contrast, the United States has the highest poverty rate by far among the industrialized countries, a withering bond among those of different social classes, a growing racial divide, and an alarming move toward a two-tiered society. Should we move further toward an extreme bipolar society, the following is likely to occur:

> If you had a million dollars, where would you want to live, Switzerland or the Philippines? Think about all the extra costs, monetary and otherwise, if you chose a vastly unequal country like the Philippines. Maybe you'd pay less in taxes, but you'd wind up shuttling between little fenced-in enclaves. You'd have private security guards. You'd socialize only in private clubs. You'd visit only private parks and beaches. Your kids would go to private schools. They'd study in private libraries. (quoted in Carville, 1996:87)

The United States is not the Philippines, but we are already seeing a dramatic rise in private schooling and home schooling and in the number of walled and gated affluent neighborhood enclaves on the one hand and ever greater segregation of the poor and especially poor racial minorities in deteriorating neighborhoods and inferior schools on the other. Personal safety is more and more problematic as violent crime rates increase among the young and disaffected. Finally, democracy is on the wane as more and more people opt out of the electoral process, presumably because, among other things, they are alienated and their choice among politicians is limited to those whose interests favor the wealthy, not the economically disadvantaged.

Courtesy of Kirk Anderson

There is a flaw in the individualistic credo. We cannot go it alone entirely—our fate depends on others. Thus, it is in our individual interest to have a collective interest. As sociologist Alan Wolfe, discussing the Scandinavian countries, has put it:

> The strength of the welfare state—indeed, the accomplishment that makes the welfare state the great success story of modern liberal democracy—is the recognition that the living conditions of people who are strangers to us are nonetheless our business. (Wolfe, 1989:133)

2. Acceptance of the first principle leads to the second: *A call for government programs that provide for people who cannot provide for themselves.* This is a call to bring all members of society up to a minimum standard of dignity. At a minimum, this includes universal health insurance, jobs, a living wage that places one above the poverty line, and guaranteed and adequate pensions.

This position is opposite the direction of President George W. Bush, Congress, and the state legislatures, whose stance is to reduce rather than expand the already constricted U.S. welfare safety net. The ideological consensus among the Republicans, the New Democrats, and various pressure groups has two related propositions. First, government subsidies exacerbate social problems rather than solve them. Second, individuals who fail are to blame for their failure. Ironically, these propositions are assumed by the powerful to hold for individuals but *not for corporations*.

Since the 1930s, the United States has had a social safety net of AFDC, food stamps, Head Start, subsidized housing, and the like to help those in need. Conservatives see this safety net as the problem since they believe that it destroys incentives to work and encourages poor single mothers to have children. They argue, then, that welfare is the problem and that social problems will get worse if we are more generous to the poor. By this logic, if we spend less on welfare, we save money, government is reduced, and the lot of the poor improves. Thus, since about 1970 the federal government has gradually reduced or eliminated welfare programs. Has this dismantling of a relatively meager welfare program helped the poor? Has it made society safer?

From the progressive position, the poor have fared badly "because of an erosion of their labor market opportunities, not because of an erosion of their work ethic" (Danziger and Gottschalk, 1995:4).

3. Acceptance of these principles leads to a third: *A special commitment to children, all children, and to implement this commitment with viable, universal programs.* In sociologist Jay Belsky's words:

> The time has come for this nation to regard child care as an infrastructure issue and make the same kind of investment in it that we talk about making in our bridges and roads and that we initially made in these vital transportation systems. We need to recognize that, in the same way that the massive capital investment in transportation and communication systems resulted in huge capital gains that we continue even to this day to realize, investment in child care can bring with it comparable long-term benefits. To gain insight into the costs, specifically foregone opportunity costs of not endeavoring to improve child care and increase options for families, imagine for a moment an America with the automobile but without paved roads. (Belsky, 1990:11)

Such a commitment to children involves providing prenatal and postnatal medical care, childhood immunization, protection from exposure to toxic chemicals, adequate nutrition, the elimination of child poverty, access to preschool and after-school programs, safe neighborhoods, and equally financed schools.

Jonathan Kozol, the longtime children's advocate, speaking on behalf of these children, said this:

> "Conservatives," [Kozol] said, "now demand that poor children prove their worthiness before aid can be considered while liberals wring their hands and capitulate to the ethos of our time." In New York's South Bronx, as many as 25 percent of children are born HIV-positive while the nation's richest neighborhoods in Manhattan, a 12-minute bus ride away, look on and do nothing. Across the country, the story is the same everywhere.
>
> [Kozol] noted that the nation balks at spending $6,000 a year to educate poor children while it unhesitatingly spends $60,000 a year to incarcerate them when their hopelessness leads to crime. "What honorable Judeo-Christian society would pay 10 times as much to punish a child as to educate him? The neglect of America's children," argued Kozol, "is nothing less than collective sin." (Quoted in Judson, 1997:2A)

Kozol's term "collective sin" is important for our consideration since the neglect of children is not just a matter of the neglect of individual parents, as it sometimes is, but much more important *it is a matter of society's neglect.* As a society, the United States could eliminate poverty, provide universal health insurance, and ensure that all children receive preschool training. But as a society, we continue to look the other way (see the panel titled "Looking toward the Future" for a situation where we might make collective efforts to provide for all children).

4. *A call to redistribute societal resources to lift those urban and rural areas that are economically disadvantaged.* Some areas of the nation are especially at risk. There are many pockets of rural poverty, such as Appalachia and the Mississippi Delta, where jobs are few and poorly paid and poverty rates are many

LOOKING TOWARD THE FUTURE

THE CHILDSWAP SOCIETY: A Fable

Consider the following fable provided by Sandra Feldman, president of the American Federation of Teachers. In this pretend society there is a national child lottery held every four years. Every child's name was put in—there were no exceptions—and children were randomly redistributed to new parents, who raised them for the next four years. Babies were not part of this lottery. Parents got to keep their newborn children until the next lottery, but then they became part of the national childswap. The cycle was broken every third swap and kids were sent back to their original parents until the next lottery. So by the time you were considered an adult, at age 26, the most time you could have spent with your birth parents was 10 years. The other 16 were simply a matter of chance.

Maybe one of your new parents would be the head of a gigantic multinational company and the most powerful person in the country or the president of a famous university. Or you might find yourself the child of a family living in a public housing project or migrant labor camp. . . . People in the childswap society took the lottery for granted. They didn't try to hide their children or send them away to other countries; childswapping was simply a part of their culture. And one thing the lottery did was to make the whole society very conscientious about how things were arranged for kids. After all, you never knew where your own child would end up after the next lottery, so in a very real sense everyone's child was—or could be—yours. As a result, children growing up under this system got everything they needed to thrive, both physically and intellectually, and the society itself was harmonious.

What if someone wrote a story about what American society in the late 20th century takes for granted in the arrangements for its children? We might not want to admit it, but don't we take for granted that some kids are going to have much better lives than others? Of course. We take for granted that some will get the best medical treatment and others will be able to get little or none. We take for granted that some kids will go to beautiful, well-cared-for schools with top-notch curriculums, excellent libraries, and computers for every child and others will go to schools where there are not enough desks and textbooks to go around—wretched places where even the toilets don't work.

We take for granted that teachers in wealthy suburban schools will be better paid and better trained than those in inner city or rural schools. We take for granted, in so many ways, that the children whom the lottery of birth has made the most needy will get the least. "After all," we say to ourselves, "it's up to each family to look after its own. If some parents can't give their children what they need to thrive, that's their problem."

Obviously I'm not suggesting that the United States adopt a childswap system. The idea makes me cringe, and, anyway, it's just a fable. But I like to imagine what would happen if we did. We'd start with political figures and their children and grandchildren, with governors and mayors and other leaders. What do you suppose would happen when they saw that their children would have the same chance as the sons and daughters of poor people—no more and no less? What would happen to our schools and healthcare system—and our shameful national indifference to children who are not ours? I bet we'd quickly find a way to set things straight and make sure all children had an equal chance to thrive.

Source: Excerpted from Sandra Feldman. 1998. "The Childswap Society." *New York Times* (January):wk7.

times higher than the national average. These areas need federal assistance for schools, job training, and infrastructure. They need government subsidies through tax rebates to encourage businesses to locate there and hire local workers (the subsidies to be received when company performance conditions—jobs, pay, benefits to workers—are met).

There are extraordinary numbers of recent immigrants in California, Texas, and Florida who are poor and have special needs such as job training. Those people need jobs, shelter, food, and services such as education and health care. Those states especially affected by immigration need help from the federal government to supply assistance to the immigrants. At present, immigration is a federal policy, but the states are left with the financial responsibility (as mentioned in Chapter 5). This results in either the immigrants not receiving the necessary assistance or the states stretching their welfare budgets too thin for the immigrant and nonimmigrant poor. Clearly, these states need federal assistance to meet the special needs of recent immigrants.

The other important area of neglect is the declining central cities, where 80 million people, including 20 million children, live (this section is dependent on Rogers, 1998). As noted in Chapter 6, the central cities have been abandoned by the middle classes, who have moved to the suburbs, and by corporations that have moved their businesses (and jobs) to the suburbs, to other parts of the country, or out of the country. The tax base in the cities has eroded, leaving declining transit systems, parks, and services, most notably schools. This erosion contributes to cutbacks in services and more flight to the suburbs. The high unemployment and continued job flight leads to despair, hopelessness, drug and alcohol abuse, and crime, further justifying the decisions of businesses and families to leave.

Policies of the federal government are partly responsible for urban decay:

> We have spent trillions building non-metro roads, but nowhere near that on metro ones or mass transit. Federal annual funding for mass transit has never been more than a fifth of highway funding, and state ratios are even more unbalanced. The overwhelming share of federal and state economic development funding also goes to non-metro sites—more highways, sprawl-supporting infrastructure, exurban tax credits and low-interest loans for new development. Similarly, the deliberate siting of military bases and other government facilities outside cities or more developed regions remains a deliberate national policy. (Rogers, 1998:14)

The federal government can reverse these antiurban policies, thus helping to revitalize the cities. To date, there is no will by the politicians to do so. These politicians choose to ignore the human and economic costs of this neglect.

5. *Although some social policies should be made and administered at the local level, others must be largely financed, organized, and administered by the federal government*. This principle is based on the assumption that some issues are national in scope and require uniform standards (e.g., nutrition guidelines, immunization timetables, preschool goals, the certification of teachers, and health care guarantees). Other policies such as reducing poverty require the massive infusion of money and compensatory programs, coupled with centralized planning. This principle runs counter to the current mood of Congress, which wants to return most programs to the states.

While dismantling the welfare system, the strategy has been to cut funds and move the programs from the federal level to the states (called **devolution**). This devolution trend has the effect of making benefits very uneven, as some states are relatively generous while others are much less so. The distinguished historian Arthur Schlesinger, Jr., has said this about the role of the federal government vis-à-vis the state governments:

> It is a delusion to say that, because state government is closer to the people, it is more responsive to their needs and concerns. Historically it is national government that has served as the protector of the powerless. It is national gov-

> ernment that affirmed the Bill of Rights against local vigilantism and preserved natural resources against local greed. The national government has civilized industry, secured the rights of labor organizations, improved income for the farmer, and provided a decent living for the old. Above all, the national government has vindicated racial justice against local bigotry. Had the states' rights creed prevailed, the U.S. would still have slavery. And historically the national government has been more honest and efficient than state and local governments. . . . As for bureaucracy, duplication, and waste, will there be more or less if a single federal agency is to be replaced by fifty separate state agencies? (Shanker, 1995:E7)

IS A PROGRESSIVE SOCIAL POLICY POSSIBLE?

Three questions remain: (1) Why should we adopt a progressive social agenda? (2) How do we pay for these programs? (3) Is there any hope to enact progressive solutions to social problems?

Should a Progressive Plan Be Adopted by U.S. Society?

Why should we adopt a progressive plan to deal with our social problems? Foremost, these are serious problems, and market solutions will not alleviate them. We are convinced that public policy based on abandoning the powerless exacerbates social problems. To name two such problems: present market-based strategies are leading to ever greater inequality and a further erosion of the social compact.

A second reason to favor progressive solutions has to do with domestic security (see Chapter 18). We ignore the problems of poverty, wealth inequality, and a rationed health care system at our own peril. If we continue on the present path of ignoring these problems or reducing or eliminating programs to deal with them, we will be less secure and we will have more problem people that require greater control—and at an ever greater social and economic cost.

The final argument for a progressive attack on social problems is an ethical one. We need, in our view, to have a moral obligation to others. We need to restore a moral commitment to the safety net. We should take the moral high ground, as Jonathan Kozol has argued: "There is something ethically embarrassing about resting a national agenda on the basis of sheer greed. It's more important in the long run, more true to the American character at its best, to lodge the argument in terms of simple justice" (quoted in Nore, 1991:36).

Or consider this moral warning from an unlikely source, the very conservative British Chancellor of the Exchequer Kenneth Clarke, who explained his resistance to calls for a minimalist state: "This is a modern state. It is not the fifties. . . not southeast Asia. I believe in North American free-market economics, but I do not wish to see [here] the dereliction and decay of American cities and the absolute poverty of the American poor" (*The Nation*, 1996:5).

Financing the Progressive Agenda

There are several sources of additional funds. The first is to reduce defense spending. We are the world's mightiest nation by far and there no longer is a Soviet threat, yet we maintain a defense budget of $334 billion (fiscal year 2002) that is more than is spent by all of our allies combined.

A second source of funds would be to reduce or eliminate corporate welfare and subsidies to the wealthy. At the moment, corporations receive more than $100 billion in direct subsidies and tax breaks. The wealthiest Americans pay lower tax rates and have more tax loopholes than found in any other modern nation. Annually we have about $400 billion in "tax expenditures" (i.e., money that is legally allowed to escape taxation). The economically advantaged receive most of these tax advantages.

A third source of funds is spending the budget surplus on social programs. But Congress with the urging of President Bush in 2001 provided a tax rebate and a 10-year plan to reduce tax rates by over $1 trillion. The argument was that surplus funds should be returned to the taxpayers. Progressives argued to the contrary, that these monies should help pay for various aspects of the physical infrastructure (repairing or replacing aging bridges and water systems, providing better transportation systems, replacing crumbling school buildings), and social infrastructure (e.g., universal health care, adequate pensions, a living wage, free education through college, and subsidized day care).

Finally, we should increase tax revenues. Totaling federal, state, and local taxes equals 30 percent of the gross domestic product. This is the lowest rate of any industrialized nation. In comparison, the English pay 36 percent, Germans and Canadians pay 37 percent, the French pay 44 percent, and at the high end the Swedes pay 56 percent (Gartner, 1995a). In addition, we should enact a truly progressive income tax. "As the biggest 'winners' in the economy since the 1970s, the top third or so of income earners could easily pay proportionately more income tax" (Skocpol, 2000:162).

Is There Any Hope of Instituting a Social Agenda Based on Progressive Principles?

The final issue, and, of course, the crucial issue, is: Is there any hope of mounting a successful progressive program? At first the negative side seems overwhelming. We have already mentioned several formidable obstacles: (1) the widely held belief in individualism as the core of American ideology, (2) political conservatives dominant the executive and legislative branches at the federal and state levels, and (3) the two major parties are financed by big money. There are at least three other barriers to progressive change. The first is the massive multitrillion dollar debt, which is viewed by politicians of both parties as a giant weight on government that makes it difficult to fund existing programs, let alone institute new ones. Similarly, the tax cut over 10 years passed by Congress in 2001 puts a damper on spending because it limits revenues to the federal government.

Another major obstacle is the present weakness of the union movement in the United States. Each of the generous welfare states of Canada, Scandinavia, and Western Europe has a heavily unionized workforce. Unions use their collective power to work for pensions, universal health care, worker safety, a strong minimum wage, and other benefits to workers and their families. This condition is not present in the United States, as unions have declined significantly in membership since the 1960s to only 14 percent of all workers in 1997.

The final barrier to progressive change is that those who will benefit most from progressive social policies (the poor, the working poor, racial minorities, inhabitants of the inner cities) are the least likely to vote. For example, the

Republicans, fresh from their victories in the 1994 congressional elections—where they became the majority in each house of Congress and won a number of governorships—claimed a mandate for their Contract with America (a vision precisely opposite from the progressive view). Most political pundits agreed that they had such a mandate, but did they? Only 38 percent of the electorate voted in 1994 and only 52 percent of that three-eighths, or 19.8 percent of the public, voted for Republicans. Those who voted were disproportionately White, relatively affluent, and suburban. What about the poor and the near poor, racial minorities, blue-collar laborers, and city dwellers who chose not to vote? Why did they not vote? What is the source of their alienation? Was it because neither political party speaks to their needs? Is it because there is little difference between Republicans and Democrats, both of whom direct their attention to the White, affluent suburban voters?

> [A]n increasing majority of those eligible to vote find that no one represents them. This, in turn, has created a crisis, a public estrangement from civic life, that seriously threatens our democracy. (*In These Times*, 1998:3)

Given these obstacles to progressive change, is there a possibility that the progressives might eventually prevail? Although this is unlikely in the near term, there are some plausible arguments for this optimistic view. First, the current crop of Republicans may take what they consider a mandate and go too far with it, thereby alienating substantial portions of the citizenry. Kevin Phillips (1995), an avowed conservative and Republican, has analyzed three historical periods (1855–1860, 1896, and 1968–1972) when Republicans captured a national watershed election. He notes patterns that are relevant for the 1994 Republican takeover of both houses of Congress:

> After winning these critical elections with middle-class nationalism and economic themes, the GOP invariably redirected itself toward tax cuts, laissez-faire, and ennoblement of entrepreneurs, speculators, and financial markets. Concentration of wealth and incomes surged. . . . [The Republican Party today] doesn't want to debate wealth and income polarization. It's even less anxious to discuss the role of bank, corporate, and currency bailouts and Wall Street socialism. But this new brand of redistributionism and collectivism is central to the squeeze on the middle class and favoritism toward the rich. (Phillips, 1995:18)

We must remind ourselves, however, that there is no guarantee that if the Republicans go too far, the pendulum will swing in the opposite and more progressive direction. This can occur, but so, too, can the situation steadily worsen.

Again looking at lessons from history (Dionne, 1996; Weisberg, 1996), a little more than 100 years ago the Progressive movement began as a reaction to unchecked capitalism, the robber barons, economic exploitation, and political corruption. Out of the Progressive Era came an activist government that addressed problems of the workplace by instituting workplace safety regulations, prohibiting child labor, mandating the 8-hour workday, and providing disability compensation. The government broke up business monopolies, established a national parks system, and gave women the vote.

During the depths of the Great Depression, President Roosevelt and Congress passed sweeping social programs including Social Security, unemployment insurance, AFDC, and massive public building projects that provided jobs, wages, and physical infrastructure (bridges, dams, roads, parks, schools, gymnasiums, libraries, rural electrification, and water conservation).

Following World War II and lasting for about three decades, society became more inclusive with the racial integration of the armed forces, sports, and workplaces. Despite significant opposition, civil rights protections, including the right of all citizens to vote, were mandated by the law. After World War II Congress opened up college education to all social classes by passing the GI Bill, which made a college education a reality for millions of returning veterans of all class and racial backgrounds.

In short, there are times in U.S. history when progressive steps were taken. Former Secretary of Labor Robert Reich summarizes:

> Nations are not passive victims of economic forces. Citizens can, if they so choose, assert their mutual obligations to extend beyond their economic usefulness to one another and act accordingly. Throughout our history the United States has periodically asserted the public's interest when market outcomes threatened social peace—curbing the power of great trusts, establishing pure food and drug laws, implementing a progressive federal income tax, imposing a forty-hour workweek, barring child labor, creating a system of social security, expanding public schooling and access to higher education, extending health care to the elderly and so forth. We effected part of this explicitly through laws, regulations, and court rulings, and partly through social norms and expectations about how we wanted our people to live and work productively together. In short, this nation developed and refined a strong social compact that gave force to the simple proposition that prosperity could include almost everyone. The puzzle is why we seem to have stopped. (Reich, 1998:12)

If today's conservatives go too far and the marketplace replaces the welfare state completely, then it may lead to a further unraveling of social solidarity and a less secure society. In short, it may lead to a search for new answers—perhaps a new progressive era, just as it did 110 years ago.

Two necessary conditions for progressive social policies to prevail are a strong union movement and a class-based labor party or Social Democratic party. While the labor movement has been moribund for two decades or so in the United States, there is some evidence that it is undergoing a shift toward more organizing and more ambitious and aggressive approaches against hostile employers and unfriendly laws. If the momentum accelerates, then there is hope for a labor renaissance and an organized push for progressive social policies (Moberg, 1996).

A new progressive era will work only if a class-based party emerges. In particular, progressive leaders need to articulate a vision, a sense of direction, that builds a sense of community. Our future, we must recognize, depends on the welfare of all in the community in which we live, and the society of which we are a part, not just our own accumulated wealth.

The alternative vision that we have proposed may seem very radical. We do not think so. Most of the suggestions are found in one form or another in each of the Western social democracies except the United States. Can we learn from them? Should we learn from them? Can we afford them? Can we afford not to adopt them?

HUMAN AGENCY: SOCIAL CHANGE FROM THE BOTTOM UP

Sociologists know that social problems emanate from social structure. That is why the progressive agenda, which aims at changing social structure, makes sense. The progressive agenda that we have proposed is aimed at societal changes, at macro solutions. But what can we do as individuals in families, at work, in our churches, and in our communities, to bring about changes to solve social problems? What can we do to make a difference—to be agents of social change?

We begin with the premise, already stated, that individuals can make a difference through collective action. Individuals need to join with others who share their goals to have any hope of success. Sociologists Kenneth Kammeyer, Geroge Ritzer, and Norman Yetman show the importance of collective actions for individuals to be effective agents of change:

> As individuals, we are limited in our ability to make the societal changes we would like. There are massive social forces that make change difficult; these forces include the goverment, large and powerful organizations, and the prevailing values, norms, and attitudes. As individuals protesting to officials, we have minimal power. As individuals standing against the tide of public opinion, we have little hope of exerting influence. As individuals confronting a corporate structure, we are doomed to frustration and failure. But if we combine with others who share our convictions, organize ourselves, and map out a course of actions, we may be able to bring about numerous and significant changes in the social order. Through participation in a social movement, we can break through the social constraints that overwhelm us as individuals. (Kammeyer, Ritzer, and Yetman, 1997:632–633)

Individuals Protesting and Organizing for Change

Throughout U.S. history, individuals have organized to change elements of society that they deemed unethical, unjust, racist, sexist, or oppressive. Harlan Cleveland put it this way:

> The tidal waves of social change of our lifetimes—evironmental sensitivity, civil rights for all races, the enhanced status of women, recognition of the rights of consumers and small investors—were not generated by the established leaders in government, business, labor, religion, or higher education. They boiled up from people (and new leaders) who had not previously been heard from. (Cleveland, 1992:16)

Let us examine briefly two representative movements.

Racial Minorities. Although collective efforts by African Americans for freedom and justice have occurred throughout their history in the United States, a major shift to bring justice to Blacks occurred in 1955. An African American woman, Rosa Parks, was jailed in Montgomery, Alabama, for not giving her seat on a bus to a White man, as was the custom fortified by the law. As a result of this courageuos act, the Black community in Montgomery mobilized to bring down the segregated public busing system. A leader emerged, a young local minister, Martin Luther King, Jr., who inspired Blacks to use nonviolent

Under the leadership of Martin Luther King, Jr., African Americans and other civil rights supporters mobilized to desegregate public facilities in the South.

resistance to overthrow their oppressors and their unfair laws and practices. The Blacks boycotted the transportation system for 381 days, walking to work or using a car-pooling network. The city eventually abolished segregation in public transportation—a clear case of agency, as the powerless successfully changed an unfair system through their collective power.

Under the leadership of Reverend King, African Americans and White sympathizers mobilized to desegregate other public facilities. There were sit-ins in restaurants, waiting rooms, and churches, and wade-ins at public beaches. Economic boycotts were organized. Court cases were initiated. Brave students became the first African Americans to integrated schools. And there were protest marches to publicize grievances. These efforts were violently resisted by Whites. King and others were jailed. Demonstrators were abused verbally and physically. There were lynchings, bombings, drive-by shootings, and other forms of intimidation to keep Blacks "in their place," especially to keep them from registering to vote.

King's movement was bent on tearing down the segregationist norms and practices and substituting new ones. To a limited but nonetheless significant extent, the movement succeeded. Schools were desegregated with the help of federal troops. The 1964 Civil Rights Bill banned discrimination in public facilities, education, employment, and any organization receiving government funds. The 1965 Voting Rights Act prohibited the use of literacy and similar tests to screen voting applicants and allowed federal examiners to monitor elections.

But while civil rights battles have been won, the war for racial equality is still being fought in legislatures, in the courts, in school districts, and in neighborhoods. As before, individuals and groups are taking agency seriously, working to change institutional racism in all its forms.

- **Workers.** Early in the nineteenth century, U.S. workers were nonunionized. As a result, work conditions were often unsafe, work was poorly paid, and child labor was commonplace. Eventually, despite the aggressive opposition of business owners, workers formed unions. With unionization, workers were no longer alone in their bargaining with management. Collectively, workers had power to demand and receive higher wages and benefits and safer working conditions or they would strike or boycott the products of the company. Their unions are engaged politically, lobbying for social legislation and working for the election of candidates sympathetic to the cause of workers. Unquestionably, unions have improved the conditions of U.S. workers.

By the 1990s unions had lost much of their power. Union membership has declined significantly. The result has been a worsening of conditions for workers—declining wages and benefits, increasing job insecurity, and the tendency of management to hire temporary workers. In this climate, the Teamsters in 1997 conducted a strike against United Parcel Service (UPS; a company that at the time employed 340,000 workers worldwide and delivered 80 percent of all packages shipped by ground in the United States) (the following is from Brecher, 1998). Although better working conditions and wages were part of the Teamsters' demands, the major point of contention was that UPS hired too many part-time workers who were paid much less than full-time workers. The Teamsters wanted UPS to make many of the part-timers into full-time positions. Because this issue was an important one for labor, the AFL-CIO supported the Teamsters with loans of $10 million a week and promoted solidarity rallies in a number of cities. Faced with this opposition and the loss of $30 million a day in profits because of the strike, UPS accepted a settlement that created 10,000 new full-time jobs, promoted a minimum of 10,000 part-timers to full-time status, and granted full-timers a raise of 15 percent over 5 years and part-timers a raise of 37 percent, to reduce the wage differential. "It's a big win not only for the union but for labor," said Robert Ridley, a 44-year-old UPS driver in Austin, Texas. "This was labor against corporate American" (Brecher, 1998:27). And labor, composed of individual working women and men with power gained collectively, won.

In sum, society's structural arrangements are not inevitable. Individuals converging across lines of race, ethnicity, gender, and sexual orientation can work at the grass-roots level organizing opposition, educating the public, demonstrating to promote a cause, electing allied candidates, using the courts, or employing other tactics to transform society. Human beings are the agents of change if they choose to be. The choice is ours.

Frances Fox Piven, the eminent social scientist, in writing about the need for social change to solve our current social problems, says:

> No one has ever successfully predicted the movements when ordinary people find their footing, discover new capacities for solidarity and power and new visions of the possible. Still, the development of American democracy depended on the perennial emergence of popular revolt in the past, and it does once again. (Piven, 1996:67)

CHAPTER REVIEW

1. The politicoeconomic system of a society, from which social problems emanate, is the result of historical events and conscious choices by political elites.
2. Social policy is about the way society should be designed—setting goals and determining the means to achieve them. If societies are designed, and some of the arrangements result in social

problems, they can be changed to reduce or eliminate those problems.

3. The sociological paradox involves two opposing forces affecting human behavior. On the one hand, social forces constrain what we do. But while societies and its structures are powerful, people are not totally controlled. They shape, resist, challenge, and sometimes change the social organizations and social institutions that impinge on them. These actions constitute human agency.
4. Sociologists, as the experts on social life, have answers to many social problems based on empirical research, but society's governmental and corporate leaders rarely seek their advice. Sociologists tend to be rejected by those in power because their perspective is subversive and they challenge the core of society's dominant ideology.
5. We propose five progressive principles to guide public policy: (a) policies and behaviors that enhance our moral obligation to others; (b) government provision of benefits to people who cannot provide for themselves; (c) a special commitment to all children to ensure health, safety, preparation for school, and equal funding for schools; (d) a redistribution of jobs and resources to economically troubled rural and urban locations; and (e) addressing many problems with federal money, standards, and administration.
6. A progressive agenda is needed because (a) it would reverse the current trend toward greater inequality, (b) it would make society more secure, and (c) it would promote social justice.
7. A progressive agenda, while expensive, could be financed by reducing the military budget, eliminating corporate welfare and subsidies to the wealthy, using the budget surplus for social programs, and increasing tax revenues.
8. Despite many obstacles, there are several possibilities for progressive change. The conservatives who control government could go too far with their market-based strategies, thereby alienating many who would resist. Historically, there have been progressive periods (the Progressive Era of the 1890s, the Great Depression, the 30 years following World War II) where social programs were instituted, corporate power thwarted, and inclusive policies implemented.
9. Social change can occur from the bottom up—from individuals acting collectively with a plan and mobilizing for action. Throughout U.S. history, individuals sharing a vision have organized to change elements of society. Case studies of this are presented using racial minorities and workers.

KEY TERMS

Deterministic view. Belief that some variable controls social life.

Human agency. Individuals acting alone or with others shape, resist, challenge, and sometimes change the social organizations and the social institutions that impinge on them.

Plutocracy. Government where the wealthy class rules.

Devolution. Process of shifting federal programs to the states.

WEBSITES FOR FURTHER REFERENCE

http://www.forbetterlife.org
The Foundation for a Better Life is a 501(c)(3) nonprofit organization. The programs and projects of the Foundation are noncommercial and are solely humanitarian endeavors. The mission of The Foundation for a Better Life, through various media efforts, is to "encourage adherence to a set of quality values through personal accountability and by raising the level of expectations of performance of all individuals regardless of religion or race." The Foundation for a Better Life creates public service campaigns to communicate the values that make a difference in our communities—values such as honesty, caring, optimism, hard work, and helping others. These messages, communicated utilizing television, theaters, billboards, radio, Internet, etc., model the benefits of a life lived by positive values. "These seemingly small examples of individuals living values-based lives may not change the world, but collectively they will make a difference. And in the process help make the world a better place for everyone."

http://www.igc.org/nonviolence/
Nonviolence International (NI) assists individuals, organizations, and governments striving to utilize nonviolent methods to bring about changes reflecting the values of justice and human development on personal, social, economic, and political levels. NI is committed to "educating the public about nonviolent action and to reducing the use of violence worldwide."

http://www.communitychange.org
Center for Community Change (CCC) helps poor people to improve their communities and change policies and institutions that affect their lives by developing their own strong organizations.

http://www.ccsd.ca/
The Canadian Council on Social Development (CCSD) is one of Canada's most authoritative voices promoting better social and economic security for all Canadians. A national, self-supporting, nonprofit organization, the CCSD's main product is information and its main activity is research, focusing on concerns such as income security, employment, poverty, child welfare, pensions, and government social policies.

http://www.homenetww.org.uk/
"Millions of workers, most of them women, carry out different forms of paid employment in their homes. But because they work behind closed doors, their work is invisible and rarely recognized." Since the 1970s there have been organizations working with homebased workers to make them visible and to fight for recognition of their rights and for improvement of their living and working conditions. HomeNet is an international membership association that has lobbied internationally for policies on street vendors, global trade and investment policies, social protection, and organization of women in the informal economy and their representation in policymaking. HomeNET has members in over 25 countries and publishes a newsletter that reaches organizations in over 130 countries.

http://www.groots.org/
GROOTS is an international movement "giving voice and power to grassroots women's initiatives for eradication of poverty, through policy change and development partnerships." GROOTS shares resources, information, and experiences to inject a grassroots women's perspective in national and international policy arenas.

http://www.commoncause.org/
Common Cause is a nonprofit, nonpartisan citizen's lobbying organization promoting open, honest and accountable government. Supported by the dues and contributions of over 200,000 members in every state across the nation, Common Cause represents the "unified voice of the people against corruption in government and big money special interests."

http://www.citizen.org/
Public Citizen is a national, nonprofit consumer advocacy organization founded by Ralph Nader in 1971 to represent consumer interests in Congress, the executive branch, and the courts. Its goal is to fight for openness and democratic accountability in government; for the right of consumers to seek redress in the courts; for clean, safe, and sustainable energy sources; for social and economic justice in trade policies; for strong health, safety, and environmental protections; and for safe, effective, and affordable prescription drugs and health care.

http://www.bettercampaigns.org/
The Alliance for Better Campaigns is a public interest group that seeks to "improve elections by promoting campaigns in which the most useful information reaches the greatest number of citizens in the most engaging way."

http://www.berkshire.net/~ifas/activist/
The Electronic Activist is a service of the Institute for First Amendment Studies, a 501(c)(3) research and educational organization focusing on the separation of church and state. Its database currently contains contact information for U.S. senators and representatives, governors, and some state legislatures. You can view all legislators' webpages as well as e-mail all legislators from this page.

http://wlo.org/
Women Leaders Online: Women Organizing for Change. "We're mostly women, but also some men . . . Asian, black, Latina, Native American, and white . . . young, middle-aged, and old . . . atheist, Catholic, Jewish, Protestant, Muslim, and Wiccan . . . straight, lesbian, bi, and trans . . . doctors, lawyers, homemakers, students, professors, engineers, web designers, journalists, businesswomen, nurses, teachers, union members, elected officials, and retirees. We're everyone who believes in equality for women. Join us today!"

http://www.amnestyusa.org/
Founded in 1961, Amnesty International is a Nobel-Prize-winning grassroots activist organization with over one million members worldwide. Amnesty International USA (AIUSA) is the U.S. section of this international human rights movement. Amnesty is committed to "freeing all prisoners of conscience; ensuring fair and prompt trials for political prisoners; abolishing the death penalty, torture, and other cruel treatment of prisoners; and ending extrajudicial executions and 'disappearances.'"

http://www.mathematica-mpr.com/
Mathematica Policy Research, Inc. is a leader in policy research and analysis. It was founded in 1968 to

conduct the first major social policy research experiment in the United States. Since then, it has conducted some of the most important evaluations of policies and programs in health care, welfare, education, nutrition, employment, and early childhood development.

http://www.cfpa.org/
Founded in 1976, the Center for Policy Alternatives (CPA) is the nation's leading nonpartisan progressive public policy and leadership development center, serving state legislators, state policy organizations, and state grassroots leaders.

Bibliography

Academe. 2001. Bulletin of the American Association of University Professors. Vol. 87 (March/April).

Acker, Joan. 1992. "Gendered Institutions: From Sex Roles to Gendered Institutions." *Contemporary Sociology* 21 (September):565–568.

Ackerman, Seth. 2001. "Losing Ground." *Harper's Magazine* 303 (December):88.

Ahlburg, Dennis A., and Carol J. De Vita. 1992. "New Realities of the American Family." *Population Bulletin* 47 (August): entire issue.

Albelda, Randy. 1992. "Whose Values, Which Families?" *Dollars & Sense* 182 (December):6–9.

Albelda, Randy, and Chris Tilly. 1997. *Glass Ceilings and Bottomless Pits: Women's Work, Women's Poverty*. Boston: South End Press.

Albert, Michael, and Stephen R. Shalom. 2001. "September 11 and Its Aftermath." *Z Magazine* 14 (October):2–8.

Albinak, Paige. 1998. "Gender Gap on Nightly Beats." *Broadcasting and Cable* 128 (February 9):32

Allen, Walter R., and Angie Y. Chung. 2000. "Your Blues Ain't Like My Blues: Race, Ethnicity and Social Inequality in America." *Contemporary Sociology* 29 (November):796–805.

Alster, Norm. 2000. "Are Old PCs Poisoning Us?" *Business Week* (June 12):78,80.

Altman, Lawrence K. 1991. "Study Finds a Gender Gap in the Treatment of Heart Attacks." *New York Times* (April 13):A12.

Amato, Ivan. 1999. "Can We Make Garbage Disappear?" *Time* (November 8):115–117.

Amato, Paul R. 2001. "The Consequences of Divorce for Adults and Children." In Robert M. Milardo (Ed.), *Understanding Families Into the New Millennium: A Decade in Review*. Minneapolis: National Council on Family Relations, pp. 1269–1287.

Amato, Paul R., and Alan Booth. 1996. "A Prospective Study of Divorce and Parent–Child Relationships." *Journal of Marriage and the Family* 58 (May):356–365.

Amato, Paul R., and Alan Booth. 1997. *A Generation at Risk: Growing Up in an Era of Family Upheaval*. Cambridge, MA: Harvard University Press.

Amato, Paul R., and Bruce Keith. 1991. "Parental Divorce and Well-Being of Children: A Meta-Analysis." *Psychological Bulletin* 110:26–46.

American Association of University Women. 1992. "How Schools Shortchange Girls." Executive Summary. *AAUW Report*. Washington, DC: American Association of University Women Educational Foundation.

American Federation of Teachers. 2000. "Maybe It's Something in the Perrier?" *AFT on Campus* (April):2.

AmeriStat. 2000. "Children: Two-Parent Families on the Decline." Online. Available: www.AmeriStat.org/children/TwoParentFamiliesDecline.html.

Amole, Gene. 1999. "A Current Portrait of the Global Village." *Rocky Mountain News* (July 25):5A.

Amott, Teresa. 1993. *Caught in the Crisis: Women and the U.S. Economy Today*. New York: Monthly Review Press.

Andersen, Margaret L. 1997. *Thinking about Women*, 4th ed. Boston: Allyn & Bacon.

Andersen, Margaret L. 2000. *Thinking about Women*, 5th ed. Boston: Allyn & Bacon.

Andersen, Margaret L. In press. "Diversity without Oppression: Race, Ethnicity, and Power." In Mary Kenyatta and Robert Tai (Eds.), *Critical Ethnicity: Countering the Waves of Identity Politics*. Lanham, MD: Rowman & Littlefield.

Andersen, Margaret L., and Patricia Hill Collins. 1998. "Conceptualizing Race, Class, and Gender." In Margaret L. Andersen and Patricia Hill Collins (Eds.), *Race, Class and Gender: An Anthology*, 3rd ed. Belmont, CA: Wadsworth, pp. 67–87.

Andersen, Margaret L., and Patricia Hill Collins (Eds.). 2001. *Race, Class, and Gender: An Anthology*, 4th ed. Belmont, CA: Wadsworth.

Anderson, Curt. 1997. "Study: By 2025, Food Will Lag Production." Associated Press (December 1).

Angier, Natalie. 1993. "Bias against Gay People: Hatred of a Special Kind." *New York Times* (December 26):4E.

Angier, Natalie. 2000. "Scientists: DNA Shows Humans Are All One Race." *Denver Post* (August 22):2A,5A.

Annan, Kofi A. 2001. "We Can Beat AIDS." *New York Times* (June 25). Online. Available: http://www.nytimes.com/2001/06/25/opinion/25ANNA.html.

Aponte, Robert. 1991. "Urban Hispanic Poverty: Disaggregations and Explanations." *Social Problems* 38 (4): 516–528.

Arellano, Kristi. 2000. "Minority Group Finds Disparities in Mortgage Lending." *Denver Post* (September 29):2C.

Arendell, Terry. 1990. "Divorce: A Woman's Issue." In Christopher Carlson (Ed.), *Perspectives on the Family: History, Class, and Feminism*. Belmont, CA: Wadsworth, pp. 460–478.

Armas, Genaro C. 2000a. "Foreign-Born Population in U. S. Passes 28.3 Million." Associated Press (January 3).

Armas, Genaro C. 2000b. "Number of High School Grads Rises." Associated Press (September 15).

Armas, Genaro C. 2000c. "More Americans Getting Diplomas, Census Estimates." Associated Press (December 19).

Armas, Genaro C. 2001. "Report Finds Hispanic Adults Lagging in Education." Associated Press (March 6).

Armstrong, Karen. 2001. "The True, Peaceful Face of Islam." *Time* (October 1):48.

Associated Press. 1997. "Klanwatch Study Reports a 6% Rise in Extremist Groups Since 1995." (March 6).

Associated Press. 1999. "Priest, Nun Told to End Ministry to Gays." (July 14).

Associated Press. 2000. "Adult Smoking Steady at 1 in 4." (October 6).

Associated Press. 2001a. "Report: Blacks Searched More Often." (June 1).

Associated Press. 2001b. "Computer Screens a Bane to Landfills." (August 13).

Aston, Adam. 2001. "Pandora's Cargo Boxes." *Business Week* (October 22):47–48.

Atkins, Elizabeth. 1991. "U.S. Blacks More Likely to Contract Glaucoma." *Fort Collins Coloradoan* (December 8):E4.

Atkins, Gary L. 1989. "Lesbians and Gays: Forced March in the Military." *Nation* (January 2):16–18.

Ayers, Ed. 1999. "Will We Still Eat Meat?" *Time* (November 6):106–107.

Baca Zinn, Maxine. 1990. "Family, Feminism and Race in America." *Gender and Society* 14 (March):62–86.

Baca Zinn, Maxine, and Bonnie Thornton Dill. 1994. "Difference and Domination." In Maxine Baca Zinn and Bonnie Thornton Dill (Eds.), *Women of Color in U.S. Society*. Philadelphia: Temple University Press, pp. 3–12.

Baca Zinn, Maxine, and Bonnie Thornton Dill. 1996. "Theorizing Difference from Multicultural Feminism." *Feminist Studies* 22 (Summer):1–11.

Baca Zinn, Maxine, and D. Stanley Eitzen. 1993. "The Demographic Transformation and the Sociological Enterprise." *American Sociologist* 24 (Summer):5–12.

Baca Zinn, Maxine, and D. Stanley Eitzen. 1999. *Diversity in Families*, 5th ed. New York: Longman.

Baca Zinn, Maxine, and D. Stanley Eitzen. 2002. *Diversity in Families*, 6th ed. Boston: Allyn & Bacon.

Baca Zinn, Maxine, Pierrette Hondagneu-Sotelo, and Michael A. Messner. 2000. "Sex and Gender through the Prism of Difference." In Maxine Baca Zinn, Pierrette Hondagneu-Sotelo, and Michael A. Messner (Eds.), *Through the Prism of Difference: A Sex and Gender Reader,* 2nd ed. Boston: Allyn & Bacon, pp. 1–8.

Baca Zinn, Maxine, and Angela Y. H. Pok. 2002. "Tradition and Transition in Mexican-Origin Families." In Ronald L. Taylor (Ed.), *Minority Families in the United States: A Multicultural Perspective*. Upper Saddle River, NJ: Prentice-Hall.

Bachman, Ronet. 1994. *Violence against Women: A National Crime Victimization Survey Report*. Washington, DC: U.S. Department of Justice. NCJ-145325.

Bales, Kevin. 1999. *Disposable People: New Slavery in the Global Economy*. Berkeley: University of California Press.

Bales, Kevin. 2000. *New Slavery: A Reference Book*. Santa Barbara, CA: ABC-CLIO.

Balswick, Jack, with James Lincoln Collier. 1976. "Why Husbands Can't Say 'I Love You.'" In Deborah S. David and Robert Brannon (Eds.), *The Forty-Nine Percent Majority*. Reading, MA: Addison-Wesley, pp. 58–59.

Balswick, Jack, and Charles Peck. 1971. "The Inexpressive Male: A Tragedy of American Society." *Family Coordinator* 20:363–368.

Banfield, Edward C. 1977. *The Unheavenly City Revisited*. Boston: Little, Brown.

Bannon, Lisa. 2000. "Gender-Specific Toy Marketing Irks Some." *Wall Street Journal* (February 17):7D.

Barber, Benjamin R. 1992. "Jihad vs. McWorld." *Atlantic Monthly* 269 (March):53–63.

Barlett, Donald L., and James B. Steele. 2000. "Soaked by Congress. *Time* (May 15):64–75.

Barlett, Donald L., and James B. Steele. 2001. "How the Little Guy Gets Crunched." *Time* (February 7):40–43.

Barlow, Dudley. 1999. "AAUW Gender Equity: Scholarship or Partisanship?" *Education Digest* 64 (March):45–60.

Barnes, Colin, Geof Mercer, and Tom Shakespeare. 1999. *Exploring Disability: A Sociological Introduction*. Malden, MA: Blackwell Publishers.

Barnett, Ola W., Cindy L. Miller-Perrin, and Robin D. Perrin. 1997. *Family Violence Across the Lifespan*. Thousand Oaks, CA: Sage.

Barrera, Mario. 1979. *Race and Class in the Southwest: A Theory of Racial Inequality*. Notre Dame, IN: University of Notre Dame Press.

Barrett, M. J. 1993. "The Newest Minority." *Atlantic Monthly* 272 (July):22–25.

Barrington, Linda. 2000. *Does a Rising Tide Lift All Boats?* Research Report 1271-00-RR. New York: The Conference Board.

Barry, John, and Evan Thomas. 2001. "Dropping the Bomb." *Newsweek* (June 25):28–30.

Barry, Skip. 1998a. "City Families Face Housing Squeeze." *Dollars & Sense* 215 (January/February):32–36.

Barten, Patty. 1999. "Your Next Job." *Newsweek* (February 1):43–45.

Barton, Len. 1996. "Sociology and Disability: Some Emerging Issues." In Len Barton (Ed.), *Disability and Society: Emerging Issues and Insights*. London: Longman, pp. 3–17.

Basow, Susan. 1996. "Gender Stereotypes and Roles." In Karen E. Rosenblum and Toni-Michelle Travis (Eds.), *The Meaning of Difference*. New York: McGraw-Hill, pp. 81–96.

Bates, Eric. 1999. "The Shame of Our Nursing Homes." *Nation* (March 29):11–19.

Baumann, Marty. 1994. "Progress Mixed for World's Women." *USA Today* (June 21):8A.

Baxandall, Phineas. 2001. "Spending #1, Performance #37: How U.S. Health Care Stacks Up Internationally." *Dollars & Sense,* No. 235 (May/June):38–40.

Bayles, Fred. 2001. "Civil Unions Blur at Vermont's State Line." *USA Today* (July 11):3A.

Beck, Allen J. 2000. "Prisoners in 1999." *Bureau of Justice Statistics Bulletin* (NCJ 183476) (August).

Beck, Allen J. 2001. "Prison and Jail Inmates at Midyear 2000." *Bureau of Justice Statistics Bulletin* (NCJ 185989) (March).

Beck, Joan. 1995. "Preschool Can Help Close the Poverty Gap." *Denver Post* (January 19):7B.

Beck, Melinda. 1990. "The Goal: A Nurse in Each Nursing Home." *Newsweek* (October 8):77–78.

Becker, Gary S. 2001. "It's Time to Give Up the War on Drugs." *Business Week* (September 17):32.

Becker, Howard S. 1963. *The Outsiders: Studies in the Sociology of Deviance*. New York: Free Press.

Becker, Howard S. 1967. "Whose Side Are We On?" *Social Problems* 14 (Winter):239–247.

Begley, Sharon. 1994. "One Pill Makes You Larger, One Pill Makes You Small. . . ." *Newsweek* (February 7):36–40.

Begley, Sharon. 2001. "AIDS at 20." *Newsweek* (June 11):35–37.

Beirne, Piers, and James Messerschmidt. 1995. *Criminology*, 2nd ed. Orlando, FL: Harcourt Brace.

Bell, Alan P., and Martin S. Weinberg. 1978. *Homosexual Ties: A Study of Human Diversity*. New York: Simon & Schuster.

Belluck, Pam. 1997. "Hispanic Lawsuit Cracks Housing Bias." *Denver Post* (August 8):2A.

Belsky, Jay. 1990. "Infant Day Care, Child Development, and Family Policy." *Society* (July/August):10–12.

Belsky, Jay. 1991. "Parental and Nonparental Child Care and Children's Socioemotional Development." In Alan Booth (Ed.), *Contemporary Families: Looking Forward, Looking Back.* Minneapolis, MN: National Council on Family Relations, pp. 122–140.

Benac, Nancy. 2001. "Executed Usually Poor, Uneducated." Associated Press (May 8).

Bender, William, and Margaret Smith. 1997. "Population, Food, and Nutrition." *Population Bulletin* 51 (February): entire issue.

Benedetto, Richard. 2001. "President Asks Mayors to Back Faith-Based Plan." *USA Today* (June 26):11A.

Bengtson, Vern L., Gerardo Marti, and Robert E. L. Roberts. 1991. "Age-Group Relationships: Generational Equity and Inequity." In Karl Pillemer and Kathleen McCartney (Eds.), *Parent–Child Relations Throughout Life.* Hillsdale, NJ: Erlbaum, pp. 253–278.

Bengtson, Vern L., Carolyn Rosenthal, and Linda Burton. 1990. "Families and Aging: Diversity and Heterogeneity." In Robert H. Binstock and Linda K. George (Eds.), *Handbook of Aging and Social Sciences,* 3rd ed. San Diego, CA: Academic Press, pp. 263–287.

Benjamin, Playthell. 2001. "Even in the Ruins, Race Matters." *AlterNet* (October 11). Online. Available: www.alternet.org/story.html?StoryID=11693.

Benokraitis, Nijole, and Joe R. Feagin. 1974. "Institutional Racism: A Review and Critical Assessment of the Literature." Paper presented at the American Sociological Association, Montreal, Canada, August.

Benokraitis, Nijole, and Joe R. Feagin. 1995. *Modern Sexism.* 2nd ed. Upper Saddle River, NJ: Prentice-Hall.

Berenson, Alex. 1996. "Quickie Lenders Popular." *Denver Post* (July 4):1C.

Berger, Peter. 1963. *Invitation to Sociology: A Humanistic Perspective.* Garden City, NY: Doubleday Anchor Books.

Berlet, Chip, and Matthew N. Lyons. 1995. "Militia Nation." *Progressive* 59 (June):22–25.

Berlow, Alan. 2001. "The Broken Machinery of Death." *American Prospect* (July 30):16–17.

Berube, Michael. 1998. "Pressing the Claim." In S. Linton (Ed.), *Claiming Disability: Knowledge and Identity.* New York: New York University Press, pp. viii–xi.

Bianchi, Suzanne. 1995. "Changing Economic Roles of Women and Men." In Reynolds Farley (Ed.), *State of the Union: America in the 1990s,* Vol. 1. New York: Russell Sage Foundation, pp. 107–154.

Bianchi, Suzanne M.,. L. Bubaiya, and J. R. Kahn. 1999. "The Gender Gap in the Economic Well-Being of Nonresident Fathers and Custodial Mothers." *Demography* 36:195–203.

Bianchi, Suzanne M., and Lynn M. Casper. 2000. "American Families." *Population Bulletin* 55 (December): entire issue.

Bianchi, Suzanne M., and Daphene Spain. 1996. "Women, Work, and Family in America." *Population Bulletin* 51 (December): entire issue.

Biema, David. 1995. "Bury My Heart in Committee." *Time* (September 18):48–51.

Birnbaum, Norman. 1992. "One Cheer for Clinton." *Nation* (September 28):318–320.

Black, Dan, Gary Gates, Set Sanders, and Lowell Taylor. 2000. "Demographics of the Gay and Lesbian Population in the United States." *Demography* 37 (May): 139–154.

Blauner, Robert. 1964. *Alienation and Freedom.* Chicago: University of Chicago Press.

Blauner, Robert. 1972. *Racial Oppression in America.* New York: Harper & Row.

Bloch, Hannah. 1998. "Tracking Nuclear Weapons." *Time* (May 25):38–42.

Block, Pamela, Fabricio Balcazar, and Christopher Keys. 2001. "From Pathology to Power: Rethinking Race, Poverty, and Disability." *Journal of Disability Policy Studies* 12 (Summer):18–27,39.

Bloom, Amy. 2000. "Generation Rx." *New York Times* (March 12). Online. Available: http://www.nytimes.com.library/library/magazine/home/2000/03/12mag-kidsdrugs.html.

Blumberg, Paul M., and P. W. Paul. 1975. "Continuities and Discontinuities in Upper-Class Marriage." *Journal of Marriage and the Family* 37 (February):63–78.

Blumstein, Alfred, and Richard Rosenfeld. 1998. "Assessing the Recent Ups and Downs in U.S. Homicide Rates." In "Crime's Decline—Why?" *National Institute of Justice Journal,* No. 237 (October):9–11.

Blumstein, Philip, and Pepper Schwartz. 1983. *American Couples: Money, Work, Sex.* New York: Morrow.

Bok, Derek. 1993. *The Cost of Talent: How Executives and Professionals Are Paid and How It Affects America.* New York: Free Press.

Bonacich, Edna. 1992. "Inequality in America: The Failure of the American System for People of Color." In Margaret L. Andersen and Patricia Hill Collins (Eds.), *Race, Class, and Gender.* Belmont, CA: Wadsworth, pp. 96–109.

Bonilla-Silva, Eduardo. 1996. "Rethinking Racism: Toward a Structural Interpretation." *American Sociological Review* 62 (June):465–480.

Bonnie, Richard J., and Charles Whitebread II. 1974. *The Marijuana Conviction.* Charlottesville, VA: University Press of Virginia, pp. 13–31.

Borosage, Robert L. 2001. "Forked-Tongue Budget." *Nation* (April 30):4–5.

Bouvier, Leon F., and Lindsey Grant. 1994. *How Many Americans: Population, Immigration and the Environment.* San Francisco: Sierra Club Books.

Bowles, Samuel. 1969. "Toward Equality of Educational Opportunity." *Harvard Educational Review.* Cambridge, MA: Harvard University Press.

Boyd, Robert. 1996. "Biologists Reject Notion of Race." *Denver Post* (October 20):37A.

Braile, Robert. 2000. "Report: Earth's in Bad Shape." *Denver Post* (January 16):16A.

Branigan, William. 1997. "Sweatshops Are Back." *Washington Post National Weekly Edition* (February 24):6–7.

Brasher, Philip. 2000. "Hunger in America Declines 24 Percent Since '95." Associated Press (September 9).

Brecher, Jeremy. 1998. "American Labor on the Eve of the Millennium: The Implications of the UPS Strike." *Z Magazine* 11 (October):25–28.

Breines, Wini, and Linda Gordon. 1983. "The New Scholarship on Family Violence." *Signs* 8 (Spring): 490–531.

Briggs, David. 1995. "Women's Gains Fall Short in Pulpit." *Denver Post* (May 5):2A.

Briggs, David. 1997. "Bishops Tell Parents Not to Reject Gay Children." *Boston Globe* (October 1):1A.

Brink, Susan, and Nancy Shute. 1997. "Are HMOs the Right Prescription?" *U.S. News & World Report* (October 13):60–67.

Briscoe, D. 1999. "Faltering Pledge Leaves 275M Kids Uneducated." Associated Press (March 27).

Brisenden, S. 1986. "Independent Living and the Medical Model of Disability." *Disability, Handicap and Society* 1 (2):173–178.

Brockerhoff, Martin P. 2000. "An Urbanizing World." *Population Bulletin* 55 (September): entire issue.

Brogan, Pamela. 1994. "Gender Pay Gap Runs Deep in Congress, Study Finds." *Denver Post* (February 26):17A.

Bronfenbrenner, Urie, Peter McClelland, Elaine Wethington, Phyllis Moen, and Stephen J. Ceci. 1996. *The State of Americans.* New York: Free Press.

Brown, Lester R. 1995. "Nature's Limits." In Lester R. Brown, et al. (Eds.), *State of the World 1995.* New York: W. W. Norton, pp. 3–20.

Brown, Lester R. 2001. "Eradicating Hunger: A Growing Challenge." In Lester R. Brown, et al. (Eds.), *State of the World 2001.* New York: W. W. Norton, pp. 43–62.

Brown, Lester R., Michael Renner, and Christopher Flavin. 1998. *Vital Signs 1998: The Environmental Trends That Are Shaping Our Future.* Washington, DC: Worldwatch Institute.

Brown, Lester R., et al. 1999. *State of the World 1999.* New York: W. W. Norton.

Brownlee, Shannon, and Steven V. Roberts. 1994. "Should Cigarettes Be Outlawed?" *U.S. News & World Report* (April 18):32–38.

Brownworth, Victoria A. 1989. "Stonewall + 20." *Nation* (July 3):5–6.

Bullard, Robert D. 2000. *Dumping in Dixie: Race, Class, and Environmental Quality,* 3rd ed. Boulder, CO: Westview Press.

Burchinal, Margaret R. 1999. "Child Care Experiences and Developmental Outcomes." *Annals* 563 (May):73–97.

Buriel, Raymond and Terri De Ment. 1997. "Immigration and Sociocultural Change in Mexican, Chinese, and Vietnamese American Families." In Alan Booth, Ann C. Crouter, and Nancy Landale (Eds.), *Immigration and the Family.* Mahwah, NJ: Erlbaum, pp. 165–200.

Burnett, Bob. 2001. "Publisher's Notes." *In These Times* (February 19):1.

Burns, Haywood. 1973. "Black People and the Tyranny of American Law." *Annals* 407 (May):156–166.

Burtless, Gary, Tom Corbett, and Wendell Primus. 1997. *Improving the Measurement of American Poverty.* Washington, DC: Brookings.

Business Week. 2000. "Global Capitalism." (November 6):278.

Business Week. 2001. "The 21st Century Corporation." (August 28):278.

Cagan, Joanna, and Neil deMause. 1998. "A Tale of Two Cities." *Nation* (August 10):24.

Cahill, Sean. 1997. "The Wal-Mart of Hospitals." *In These Times* (March 3):14–16.

Campbell, Frances A., and Craig T. Ramey. 1994. "Effects of Early Intervention on Intellectual and Academic Achievement: A Follow-Up Study of Children from Low-Income Families." *Child Development* 65 (April):684–698.

Campenni, C. Estelle. 1999. "Gender Stereotyping of Children's Toys: A Comparison of Parents and Nonparents." *Sex Roles* 40($^1/_2$):121–138.

Caplan, Nathan, and Stephen D. Nelson. 1974. "Who's to Blame?" *Psychology Today* 8 (November):99–104.

Carman, Diane. 2001. "Gay Teens Need Our Support." *Denver Post* (March 22):1B.

Carmichael, Stokely, and Charles V. Hamilton. 1967. *Black Power: The Politics of Liberation in America.* New York: Random House.

Carre, Francoise, and Chris Tilly. 1998. "Part-Time and Temporary Work." *Dollars & Sense* 215 (January/ February):22–25.

Carter, Michael J., and Susan Boslego Carter. 1981. "Women Get a Ticket to Ride after the Gravy Train Has Left the Station." *Feminist Studies* 7:477–504.

Carville, James. 1996. *We're Right, They're Wrong: A Handbook for Spirited Progressives.* New York: Random House.

Cassidy, John. 1997. "The Melting Pot Myth." *New Yorker* (July 14):40–43.

Celis, William. 1993. "Colleges Battle Culture and Poverty to Swell Hispanic Enrollments." *New York Times* (February 23):B6.

Chafel, Judith A. 1997. "Societal Images of Poverty." *Youth and Society* 28 (June):432–463.

Chafetz, Janet Saltzman. 1997. "Feminist Theory and Sociology: Underutilized Contributions for Mainstream Theory." *Annual Review of Sociology* 23: 97–120.

Chambliss, William. 1978. *On the Take.* Bloomington, IN: Indiana University Press.

Chase, Bob. 1997. "All Children Are Equal But Some Children Are More Equal Than Others." *Washington Post National Weekly Edition* (April 28):20.

Chasin, Barbara H. 1997. *Inequality and Violence in the United States.* Atlantic Highlands, NJ: Humanities Press.

Cherlin, Andrew. 1981. *Marriage, Divorce, Remarriage.* Cambridge, MA: Harvard University Press.

Cherlin, Andrew. 1999. "Going to Extremes: Family Structure, Children's Well-Being and Social Science." *Demography* 36 (November):421–428.

Chideya, Farai. 1999. "A Nation of Minorities: America in 2050." *Civil Rights Digest* 4 (Fall):35–41.

Children's Defense Fund. 1990. *The Adolescent and Young Adult Fact Book.* Washington, DC: Children's Defense Fund.

Children's Defense Fund. 1995. *The State of America's Children: Yearbook 1995.* Washington, DC: Children's Defense Fund.

Children's Defense Fund. 1997. *The State of America's Children: Yearbook 1997.* Washington, DC: Children's Defense Fund.

Children's Defense Fund. 1998. *The State of America's Children: Yearbook 1998.* Washington, DC: Children's Defense Fund.

Children's Defense Fund. 2000. *The State of America's Children.* Washington, DC: Children's Defense Fund.

Children's Defense Fund. 2001. *The State of America's Children: Yearbook 2001.* Washington, DC: Children's Defense Fund.

Christian Science Monitor. 1994. "Will Computers in Schools Make the Poor Poorer?" (February 25):1.

Chronicle of Higher Education. 1998. "Note Book." (January 9):A55.

Chronicle of Higher Education. 1999. "A 'Gay Gene'? Perhaps Not." (April 30):A21.

Chronicle of Higher Education. 200l. "Almanac Issue." (August 31): entire issue.

Clark, Roger, Rachel Lennon, and Leanna Morris. 1993. "Of Caldecotts and Kings: Gendered Images in Recent Children's Books by Black and Non-Black Illustrators," *Gender & Society* 7 (2):227–245.

Clausen, Jan. 1996. *Beyond Gay or Straight: Understanding Sexual Orientation.* Philadelphia: Chelsea House.

Cleveland, Harlan. 1992. "The Age of People Power." *Futurist* 26 (January/February):14–18.

Clifford, Lee. 2001. "Fortune 500." *Fortune* (April 16):101–103.

Clifford, Mark, and Manjeet Kripalani. 2001. "Different Countries, Adjoining Cubicles." *Business Week* (August 28):182–184.

Clymer, Adam. 1992. "Spending in Congressional Races Is Up in a Topsy-Turvy Year." *New York Times* (August 9):16.

Coddington, Dean C., and Elizabeth Fischer. 2001. "Myth: Managed Care More Efficient Than Medicine." *Rocky Mountain News* (March 6):2G.

Cohn, Bob. 1992. "Discrimination: The Limits of the Law." *Newsweek* (September 14):38–39.

Cole, David. 1994. "Five Myths about Immigration." *Nation* (October 17):410–412.

Cole, David. 1999. "The Color of Justice." *Nation* (October 11):12–15.

Cole, Wendy, and Christine Gorman. 1993. "The Shrinking Ten Percent." *Time* (April 26):27–29.

Collins, Chris. 1998. "Hispanic Kids Less Likely to Be Enrolled in Medicaid." *USA Today* (April 27):3A.

Collins, Chuck. 1999. "The Wealth Gap Widens." *Dollars & Sense,* No. 225 (September/October):12–13.

Collins, Chuck, Betsy Leondar-Wright, and Holly Sklar. 1999. *Shifting Fortunes: The Perils of the Growing American Wealth Gap.* Boston: United for a Fair Economy.

Collins, Chuck, and Felice Yeskel. 2000. *Economic Apartheid in America: A Primer on Economic Inequality and Insecurity.* New York: New Press.

Collins, Patricia Hill. 1990. *Black Feminist Thought.* Cambridge, MA: Unwin Hyman.

Collins, Patricia Hill. 1997. "Comment on Heckman's 'Truth and Method: Feminist Standpoint Theory Revisited': Where's the Power?" *Signs* 22 (2):375–381.

Collins, Randall, and Scott Coltrane. 1995. *Sociology of Marriage and the Family,* 4th ed. Chicago: Nelson-Hall.

Conetta, Carl, and Charles Knight. 1998. "Inventing Threats." *Bulletin of the Atomic Scientists* 54 (March/April):32–38.

Conley, Dalton. 2001. "The Black–White Wealth Gap." *Nation* (March 26):20–22.

Connell, Robert W. 1992. "A Very Straight Gay: Masculinity, Homosexual Experience, and the Dynamics of Gender," *American Sociological Review* 57:735–751.

Constable, Pamela. 1999. "India's Clock Just Keeps on Ticking." *Washington Post National Weekly Edition.* (August 30):16.

Contemporary Sociology. 1995. "Symposium: The Bell Curve." Vol. 24 (March):149–161.

Cook, Christopher D. 2000. "Temps Demand a New Deal." *Nation* (March 27):13–20.

Cook, James. 1982. "The Molting of America." *Forbes* (November 22):161–167.

Coontz, Stephanie. 1992. *The Way We Never Were.* New York: Basic Books.

Coontz, Stephanie. 1994. "The Welfare Discussion We Really Need." *Christian Science Monitor* (December 29):19.

Coontz, Stephanie. 1997. *The Way We Really Are.* New York: Basic Books.

Cooper, Mark, Peter Rosset, and Julia Bryson. 1999. "Warning! Corporate Meat and Poultry May Be Hazardous to Workers, Farmers, the Environment, and Your Health." In Douglas H. Boucher (Ed.), *The Paradox of Plenty: Hunger in a Bountiful World.* Oakland, CA: Food First Books, pp. 155–163.

Corbet, Barry. 2000a. "Your Fears, My Realities." *Denver Post* (August 13):11B.

Corbet, Barry. 2000b. "Disabled Could Be King-Makers." *Denver Post* (September 27):9B.

Corn, David. 2001. "Going to Extremes." *AlterNet* (September 14). Online. Available: www.alternet.org/ story.html?StoryID=11505.

Cose, Ellis. 2000. "Facts Support Inequity Beliefs." *USA Today* (May 4):17A.

Cowley, Geoffrey. 2001. "After the Trauma." *Newsweek* (October 1):50–52.

Cox, James. 2001. "Pakistan's Loyalty May Rest on Its Economy." *USA Today* (October 5):1B–2B.

Cox, Meki. 1998. "Philly Cheats on Crime Rate." *Denver Post* (December 9):18A.

Coy, Peter. 2000. "The Creative Economy." *Business Week* (August 28):76–82.

Crabb, Peter, and Dawn Bielawski. 1994. "The Social Representation of Material Culture and Gender in Children's Books," *Sex Roles* 30 (1/2):69–79.

Craig, K. M., and C. R. Waldo. 1996. "So What's a Hate Crime Anyway?" *Law and Human Behavior* 20 (2):113–129.

Crenson, Matt. 2001. "Global Impact of U.S. Lifestyle Raises Concerns." Associated Press (January 14).

Crews, Kimberly. 1996. "A Look at the Trends Shaping African Americans' Future." *Population Today* 21 (February):1–2.

Crews, Kimberly A., and Cheryl Lynn Stauffer. 1997. *World Population and the Environment.* Washington, DC: Population Reference Bureau.

Crooks, Louise. 1991. "Women and Pensions." *Vital Speeches of the Day* 57 (February 15):283–285.

Crooks, Robert, and Karla Baur. 1987. *Our Sexuality,* 3rd ed. Menlo Park, CA: Benjamin Cummings.

Cross, Merry. 1994. "Abuse." In L. Keith (Ed.), *Mustn't Grumble.* London: Women's Press.

Crossette, Barbara. 1999. "At 1 Billion India Losing As It Gains." *Denver Post* (August 5):2A.

Crystal, Stephen, and Dennis Shea. 1990. "Cumulative Advantage, Cumulative Disadvantage, and Inequality among Elderly People." *Gerontologist* 30 (August): 437–443.

Cunningham, Shea. 1994. "Farm Workers in the '90s." *Food First Action Alert* 16 (Fall):1–4.

Curran, Daniel J., and Claire M. Renzetti. 2000. *Social Problems: Society in Crisis,* 5th ed. Boston: Allyn & Bacon.

Currie, Elliott. 1985. *Confronting Crime: An American Challenge.* New York: Pantheon.

Currie, Elliott. 1993. *Reckoning: Drugs, the Cities, and the American Future.* New York: Hill & Wang.

Currie, Elliott. 1998. *Crime and Punishment in America: Why the Solutions to America's Most Stubborn Social Crisis Have Not Worked—and What Will.* New York: Metropolitan Books.

Currie, Elliott. 1999. "Yes, Treatment, But . . ." *Nation* (September 20):18–19.

Curtin, Dave. 2001. "Report Blasts Teacher Prep." *Denver Post* (February 3):1B.

Danziger, Sheldon, and Peter Gottschalk. 1995. *America Unequal*. New York: Russell Sage Foundation.

Darder, Antonia, and Rodolfo D. Torrez. 1998. "Introduction: Latinos and Society: Culture, Politics, and Class." In Antonia Darder and Rodolfo D. Torrez (Eds.), *The Latino Studies Reader*. New York: Blackwell, pp. 3–26.

David, Deborah S., and Robert Brannon. 1980. "The Male Sex Role." In Arlene S. Skolnick and Jerome H. Skolnick (Eds.), *Family in Transition*, 3rd ed. Boston: Little, Brown.

Davidson, Nicholas. 1990. "Life without Father: America's Greatest Social Catastrophe." *Policy Review* 51 (Winter):40–44.

Davis, Laurel R. 2000. Personal communication.

Davis, Robert. 1994. "Abuse Knows No Social Boundaries." *USA Today* (June 20):3A.

Dawson, John M., and Patrick A. Langan. 1994. "Murder in Families." *Bureau of Justice Statistics Special Report* (July):1–4.

Day, Jennifer Cheesman. 1996. "Projects of the Number of Households and Families in the United States: 1995 to 2010." *Current Population Reports*. Series P25-1129. Washington, DC: U.S. Government Printing Office.

Dees, Morris, and Mark Potok. 2001. "The Future of American Terrorism." *New York Times* (June 10):WK15.

Deibel, Mary. 2000. "CEOs Pay Hikes Far Outpace Workers." *Rocky Mountain News* (September 3):G1.

DeKeseredy, Walter S., and Martin D. Schwartz. 1996. *Contemporary Criminology*. Belmont, CA: Wadsworth.

Delgado, Richard, and David Yun. 1997. "The Lessons of Loving vs. Virginia." *Rocky Mountain News* (June 2):57A.

del Pinal, Jorge, and Audrey Singer. 1997. "Generations of Diversity: Latinos in the United States." *Population Bulletin* 52 (October): entire issue.

Demo, David H., and Martha J. Cox. 2001. "Families with Young Children: A Review of Research in the 1990s." In Robert M. Milardo (Ed.), *Understanding Families in the New Millennium*. Minneapolis: National Council on Family Relations, pp. 95–114.

Denver Post. 1994. "Blacks Less Apt to Drink in College." (September 14):18A.

Denver Post. 2001. "The Haves and the Have-Nots." (June 17):6D.

DeParle, Jason. 2001. "A Mass of Newly Laid-Off Workers Will Put Social Safety Net to the Test." *New York Times* (October 8). Online. Available: www.nytimes.com/2001/10/08/national/08LAYO.html.

Dervarics, Charles. 2000. "Health Experts Make Case for Environmental Justice." *Population Today* 28 (May/June):1,4.

De Vita, Carol J. 1996. "The United States at Mid-Decade." *Population Bulletin* 50 (March): entire issue.

De Young, Karen, and Michael Dobbs. 2001. "The Architect of New Global Terrorism." *Washington Post National Weekly Edition* (September 24–30):20–21.

Diamond, David. 1997. "Behind Closed Gates." *USA Weekend* (January 31):4–5.

Dibble, Ursula, and Murray S. Straus. 1980. "Some Social Structure Determinants of Inconsistency between Attitudes and Behavior: The Case of Family Violence." *Journal of Marriage and the Family* 42 (February):71–80.

di Leonardo, Micaela. 1992. "Boyz on the Hood." *Nation* (August 17/24):178–186.

Dill, Bonnie Thornton, Lynn Weber Cannon, and Reeve Vanneman. 1987. "Race, Gender, and Occupational Segregation." In *Pay Equity: An Issue of Race, Ethnicity, and Sex*. Washington, DC: National Committee on Pay Equity.

Dill, Bonnie Thornton, Maxine Baca Zinn, and Sandra Patton. 1993. "Feminism, Race, and the Politics of Family Values." *Report from the Institute for Philosophy and Public Policy*. University of Maryland, Vol. 13 (Fall).

Dionne, E. J., Jr. 1996. *They Only Look Dead: Why Progressives Will Dominate the Next Political Era*. New York: Simon & Schuster.

Dobbs, Michael. 2000. "Terrorists Beware." *Washington Post National Weekly Edition* (April 10):8–9.

Dobbs, Michael. 2001. "Bin Laden: A Master Impresario." *Washington Post National Weekly Edition* (September 17–23):15.

Dollars & Sense. 2001. "Here's to Our Health." No. 235 (May/June):2.

Domhoff, G. William. 1978. *The Powers That Be: Processes of Ruling Class Domination in America*. New York: Random House.

Donziger, Steven R. (Ed.). 1996. *The Real War on Crime: The Report of the National Criminal Justice Commission*. New York: Harper Perennial.

Dorning, Mike. 1992. "Upgrading Infrastructure Linked to Rebuilding U.S. Productivity." *Chicago Tribune* (September 27):1C,4C.

Doyle, Jack, and Paul T. Schindler. 1974. "The Incoherent Society." Paper presented at the American Sociological Association, Montreal, Canada, August 25–29.

Dreier, Peter. 1992. "Bush to Cities: Drop Dead." *Progressive* 56 (July):20–23.

Dreier, Peter. 2000. "Sprawl's Invisible Hand." *Nation* (February 21):6–7.

Dreier, Peter, and John Atlas. 1994. "Reforming the Mansion Subsidy." *Nation* (May 2):592–595.

Dreier, Peter, and John Atlas. 1995. "Housing Policy's Moment of Truth." *American Prospect* 22 (Summer):68–77.

Drozdiak, William. 2000. "Demand Strains Supply." *Washington Post National Weekly Edition* (November 27):20.

Drucker, Peter F. 1972. "School around the Bend." *Psychology Today* 6 (June):49.

Drucker, Peter F. 1993. *Post-Capitalist Society*. New York: HarperCollins.

Drucker, Peter F. 1999. "Beyond the Information Revolution." *Atlantic Monthly* 284 (October):47–57.

Drummond, Tammerlin. 2001. "The Marrying Kind." *Time* (May 14):52.

Duberman, Martin. 1993. *Stonewall*. New York: Dutton.

Duncan, Margaret Carlisle. 2001. "The Sociology of Ability and Disability in Physical Activity." *Sociology of Sport Journal* 18(1):1–4.

Dunn, Dana. 1996. "Gender and Earnings." In Paula J. Dubeck and Kathryn Borman (Eds.), *Women and Work: A Handbook*. New York: Garland, pp. 61–63.

Durkheim, Emile. 1960. *The Division of Labor in Society*. (George Simpson, Trans.). Glencoe, IL: Free Press.

Durning, Alan B. 1990. "Ending Poverty." In Lester R. Brown et. al. (Eds.), *State of the World 1990*. New York: W. W. Norton, pp. 135–153.

Duster, Troy. 1970. *The Legislation of Morality: Law, Drugs, and Moral Judgment*. New York: Free Press.

Dyer, Everett. 1979. *The American Family: Variety and Change*. New York: McGraw-Hill.

Early, Frances H. 1983. "The French-Canadian Family Economy and Standard of Living in Lowell, Massachusetts, 1870." In Michael Gordon (Ed.), *The American Family in Social Historical Perspective*, 3rd ed. New York: St. Martin's Press, pp. 482–503.

Easterbrook, Gregg. 1999. "Overpopulation Is No Problem—in the Long Run." *New Republic* (October 11):22–28.

Ebony. 1995. "Amazing Grace: 50 Years of the Black Church." Vol. 50 (April):87–96.

Echaveste, Maria, and Karen Nussbaum. 1994. "96 Cents an Hour: The Sweatshop Is Reborn." *New York Times* (March 6):F13.

Eckel, Sahah. 1999. "Single Mothers, Many Faces." *American Demographics* 21 (May):63–66.

Economic Policy Institute. 2000. "The Myth of Economic Mobility." Online. Available: http://www.epinet.org/books/siva2000/graph.htm.

Economist. 1992. "Pull Together?" (May 9):25, 28.

Economist. 1993. "The Other America" (July 10):17–18.

Edelman, Peter. 2001. "The Question Now Isn't Just Poverty. For Many, It Is Survival." *Washington Spectator* 27 (August 1):1–3.

Edmondson, Brad. 1996. "Work Slowdown." *American Demographics* 18 (March):4–7.

Edwards, Richard C., Michael Reich, and Thomas E. Weisskopf. 1978. "Sexism." In R. C. Edwards, M. Reich, and T. E. Weisskopf (Eds.), *The Capitalist System*, 2nd ed. Upper Saddle River, NJ: Prentice-Hall, pp. 331–341.

Ehrenreich, Barbara. 1991. "Welfare: A White Secret." *Time* (December 16):84.

Ehrlich, Paul R., Gretchen C. Daily, Scott C. Daily, Norman Myers, and James Salzman. 1997. "No Middle Way on the Environment." *Atlantic Monthly* 280 (December):98–104.

Ehrlich, Paul R., and Anne H. Ehrlich. 1972. *Population/Resources/Environment: Issues in Human Ecology*, 2nd ed. San Francisco: Freeman.

Ehrlich, Paul R., and Anne H. Ehrlich. 1988. "Population, Plenty, and Poverty." *National Geographic* 174 (December):914–945.

Ehrlich, Paul R., and Anne H. Ehrlich. 1990. *The Population Explosion*. New York: Simon & Schuster Touchstone.

Eisler, Peter. 2000. "Toxic Exposure Kept Secret." *USA Today* (September 6):1A–2A,15A–18A.

Eisenstein, Zillah. 1979. "Developing a Theory of Capitalist Patriarchy and Socialist Feminism." In Zillah Eisenstein (Ed.), *Capitalist Patriarchy and the Case for Socialist Feminism*. New York: Monthly Review Press, pp. 5–40.

Eitzen, D. Stanley. 1984. "Teaching Social Problems: Implications of the Objectivist-Subjectivist Debate." *Society for the Study of Social Problems Newsletter* 16 (Fall):10–12.

Eitzen, D. Stanley. 1993. "National Security: Children, Crime, and Cities." *Vital Speeches of the Day* 59 (March 1):315–316.

Eitzen, D. Stanley. 1996. "Dismantling the Welfare State." *Vital Speeches of the Day* 62 (June 15):532– 536.

Eitzen, D. Stanley, and Maxine Baca Zinn (Eds.). 1989a. *The Reshaping of America*. Upper Saddle River, NJ: Prentice-Hall.

Eitzen, D. Stanley, and Maxine Baca Zinn. 1989b. "The De-Athleticization of Women: The Naming and Gender Marking of Collegiate Sport Teams." *Sociology of Sport Journal* 6:362–370.

Eitzen, D. Stanley and Maxine Baca Zinn. 1998a. *In Conflict and Order: Understanding Society*, 8th ed. Boston: Allyn & Bacon.

Eitzen, D. Stanley, and Maxine Baca Zinn. 1998b. "The Shrinking Welfare State: The New Welfare Legislation and Families." Paper presented at the annual meeting of the American Sociological Association, San Francisco, CA, August 21–25.

Eitzen, D. Stanley, and Maxine Baca Zinn. 2001. *In Conflict and Order: Understanding Society*, 9th ed. Boston: Allyn & Bacon.

Eitzen, D. Stanley and Craig S. Leedham. 1998. "U.S. Social Problems in Comparative Perspective." In D. Stanley Eitzen and Craig S. Leedham (Eds.), *Solutions to Social Problems: Lessons from Other Societies*. Boston: Allyn & Bacon, pp. 3–12.

Eitzen, D. Stanley and Craig S. Leedham (Eds.). 2001. *Solutions to Social Problems: Lessons from Other Societies*, 2nd ed. Boston: Allyn & Bacon.

Eitzen, D. Stanley, and George H. Sage. 1997. *Sociology of North American Sport*, 6th ed. Dubuque, IA: Wm. C. Brown.

Eitzen, D. Stanley, and George H. Sage. 2003. *Sociology of American Sport*, 7th ed. St. Louis: McGraw Hill.

Eitzen, D. Stanley, and Kelly Eitzen Smith (Eds.). 1993. *Experiencing Poverty: Voices from the Bottom*. Belmont, CA: Wadsworth.

Ellerbee, Linda. 1995. "A Wrong I Taught My Children." *Rocky Mountain News* (February 4):43A.

Elliott, Michael. 1994/1995. "Forward to the Past." *Newsweek* (December 26/January 2):130–133.

El Nasser, Haya. 1999. "Urban Experts Pick Top Factors Influencing Future." *USA Today* (September 27):4A.

El Nasser, Haya. 2001a. "Immigration Helped Restore Cities." *USA Today* (March 19):3A.

El Nasser, Haya. 2001b. "Census Analysis Shows Birth of 'Boomburgs.'" *USA Today* (June 22):1A,11A.

Employment Research Foundation. 1988. *A Shift in Military Spending in American Cities*. Washington, DC: Employment Research Foundation/U.S. Conference of Mayors.

Epstein, Cynthia Fuchs. 1970. *Woman's Place*. Berkeley, CA: University of California Press.

Erikson, Kai T. 1962. "Notes on the Sociology of Deviance." *Social Problems* 9 (Spring):307–314.

Erikson, Kai T. 1966. *Wayward Puritans: A Study in the Sociology of Deviance*. New York: Wiley.

Espiritu, Yen Le. 1996. "Asian American Panethnicity." In Karen E. Rosenblum and Toni-Michelle Travis (Eds.), *The Meaning of Difference*. New York: McGraw-Hill, pp. 51–61.

Estrada, Richard. 1998. "Schools' Greatest Problem Is Growth." *Rocky Mountain News* (February 8):5B.

Evans, David. 1993. "We Arm the World." *In These Times* (November 15):14–18.

Fackelmann, Kathleen. 1999. "Does Unequal Treatment Really Have Roots in Racism?" *USA Today* (September 16):10D.

Fall Colors. 2000. "How Diverse is the 1999–2000 TV Season's Prime Time Lineup?" *Children Now*. (January). Oakland, CA.

Fallik, Dawn. 1998. "Minorities, Women Wait Longer for Liver Transplants." Associated Press (March 5).

Faltermayer, Charlotte. 2000. "Cyberveillance." *Time* (August 14):B22–B25.

Faludi, Susan. 1991. *Backlash: The Undeclared War against Women*. New York: Crown.

Farrell, Greg. 2000. "Employee Theft Grows for Retailers." *USA Today* (November 10):B2.

Faust, Kimberly A., and Jerome N. McKibben. 1999. In Marvin Sussman, Suzanne K. Steinmetz, and Gary W. Peterson (Eds.), *Handbook of Marriage and the Family,* 2nd ed., New York: Plenum Press, pp. 475–499.

Fausto-Sterling, Anne. 1992. *Myths of Gender: Biological Theories about Women and Men*. New York: Basic Books.

Feagin, Joe R. 1997. "Death by Discrimination?" *Society for the Study of Social Problems Newsletter* 28 (Winter):15–16.

Feagin, Joe R. 2000. Racist America. New York: Routledge.

Feagin, Joe R. 2001. "Social Justice and Sociology: Agendas for the Twenty-First Century." *American Sociological Review* 66 (February):1–20.

Feagin, Joe R., and Clairece Booher Feagin. 1994. *Social Problems: A Critical Power-Conflict Perspective,* 4th ed. Upper Saddle River, NJ: Prentice-Hall.

Feagin, Joe R., and Clairece Booher Feagin. 1997. *Social Problems: A Critical Power-Conflict Perspective,* 5th ed. Upper Saddle River, NJ: Prentice-Hall.

Feagin, Joe, and Melvin P. Sikes. 1994. *Living with Racism: The Black Middle-Class Experience*. Boston: Beacon Press.

Federal Bureau of Investigation. 2000. *Uniform Crime Reports*. Washington, DC: U.S. Government Printing Office. Published annually.

Federal Interagency Forum on Child and Family Statistics. 2000. *America's Children: Key National Indicators of Well-Being 2000*. Washington, DC: U.S. Government Printing Office.

Feldman, Sandra. 1998. "The Childswap Society." *New York Times* (January 4):WK7.

Ferree, Myra Marx. 1991. "Feminism and Family Research." In Alan Booth (Ed.), *Contemporary Families: Looking Forward, Looking Back*. Minneapolis, MN: National Council on Family Relations, pp. 103–121.

Findlay, Steven. 1998. "Study: Care Costs Seniors Dearly." *USA Today* (March 3):3A.

Fire, Ed. 2001. "Resisting the Goliath." *Multinational Monitor* 22 (July/August):31–33.

Firestone, David. 2001. "Free-Tuition Program Transforms the University of Georgia." *New York Times* (February 4). Online. Available: http://www.nytimes.com/2001/02/04/national/04HOPE.html.

Fischer, Claude S., Michael Hout, Martin Sanchez Jankowski, Samuel R. Lucas, Ann Swidler, and Kim Voss. 1996. *Inequality by Design: Cracking the Bell Curve Myth*. Princeton, NJ: Princeton University Press.

Fischer, Joannie Schrof. 2000. "Facing Facts About the AIDS Pandemic." *U.S. News & World Report* (July 24):24.

Fishman, Pamela M. 1978. "Interaction: The Work Women Do." *Social Problems* 25 (April):397–406.

Flaherty, Mary Pat, and Joan Biskupic. 1996. "The Racial Divide of Crack vs. Powder Cocaine Penalties." *Washington Post National Weekly Edition* (October 21):10–11.

Flanagan, Stephen J., Ellen L. Frost, and Richard L. Kugler. 2001. *Challenge of the Global Century: Report of the Project on Globalization and National Security*. Washington, DC: Institute for National Strategic Studies, National Defense University.

Fletcher, Michael A. 1998. "All Fighting for a Piece of the Dream: Immigration Has Transformed the Racial Dynamic of South Central Los Angeles." *Washington Post National Weekly Edition* (May 18):8–9.

Flynt, Wayne. 1996. "Rural Poverty in America." *National Forum* 76 (Summer):32–34.

Folbre, Nancy. 1985. "The Pauperization of Motherhood: Patriarchy and Social Policy in the U.S." *Review of Radical Political Economics* 16(4).

Folbre, Nancy. 1995. *The New Field Guide to the U.S. Economy*. New York: New Press.

Folbre, Nancy. 2000. "Universal Childcare: It's Time." *Nation* (July 3):21–23.

Folbre, Nancy, James Heintz, and the Center for Popular Economics. 2000. *The Ultimate Field Guide to the U.S. Economy*. New York: New Press.

Foner, Eric. 1996. "Plessy Is Not Passe." *Nation* (June 3):6.

Forbes. 1998a. "The Forbes 500s." (April 20):246–456.

Forbes. 1998b. "The International 500." (July 27):116–178.

Forbes. 1998c. "The 100 Largest U.S. Multinationals." (July 27):162–164.

Forbes. 1998d. "The World's 200 Working Rich." (July 6):190–252.

Forbes. 2000. "The 400 Richest People in America." (October 9):117–128.

Fort, Joel, and Christopher T. Cory. 1975. *American Drugstore: A (Alcohol) to V (Valium)*. Boston: Little, Brown.

Fost, Dan. 1991. "American Indians in the Nineties." *American Demographics* 13 (December):26–34.

Fowlkes, Martha R. 1994. "Single Worlds and Homosexual Lifestyles: Patterns of Sexuality and Intimacy." In Alice S. Rossi (Ed.), *Sexuality across the Life Course*. Chicago: University of Chicago Press, pp. 151–184.

Fox, James Alan. 1996. "The Calm before the Juvenile Crime Storm?" *Population Today* 24 (September):4–5.

France, David. 2000. "Slavery's New Face." *Newsweek* (December 18):61–65.

France, Mike, and Heather Green. 2001. *Business Week* (October 1):50.

Frank, Robert H. 2001. "Traffic and Tax Cuts." *New York Times* (May 11). Online. Available: http://www.nytimes.com/2001/05/11/opinion/11FRAN.html.

Frank, Robert H., and Philip J. Cook. 1995. *The Winner-Take-All Society*. New York: Free Press.

Frankel, Glenn. 1997. "A Most Un-American Act." *Washington Post National Weekly Edition* (June 9):29.

Frankenberg, Ruth. 1993. *The Social Construction of Whiteness: White Women, Race Matters*. Minneapolis, MN: University of Minnesota Press.

Franklin, Jeffrey. 2001. "Logic of 'Holy War' on Terror Morally Evil." *Rocky Mountain News* (September 28):46A.

Freedman, Alex M. 1993. "Peddling Dreams: A Marketing Giant Uses Its Sales Prowess to Profit from Poverty." *Wall Street Journal* (September 22):A1, A12.

Freeman, Jo. 1979. "The Women's Liberation Movement: Its Origins, Organizations, Activities, and Ideas." In J. Freeman (Ed.), *Women: A Feminist Perspective,* 2nd ed. Palo Alto, CA: Mayfield, pp. 557–574.

Freiberg, Peter. 1987a. "The March on Washington." *Advocate* (November 10):11–22.

Frey, William H. 1999. "'New Sun Belt' Metros and Suburbs Are Magnets for Retirees." *Population Today* 27 (October):1–3.

Friedman, Lawrence. 1993. *Crime and Punishment in American History*. New York: Basic Books.

Friedman, Milton. 1978. *The Economics of Freedom*. Cleveland, OH: Standard Oil Company.

Friedman, Thomas L. 2000. "Threats to U.S. Security Come from Many Places." *Denver Post* (February 14):4–6.

Friedman, Thomas L. 2001a. "Who's Crazy Here?" *New*

York Times (May 15). Online. Available: http://www.nytimes.com/2001/05/15/opinion/15FRIE.html.

Friedman, Thomas L. 2001b. "Digital Defense." *New York Times* (July 27). Online. Available: http://www.nytimes.com/2001/07/27/opinion/27FRIE.html.

Fuller, Bruce (Ed.). 2000. *Inside Charter Schools: The Paradox of Radical Decentralization*. Cambridge, MA: Harvard University Press.

Furstenberg, Frank F., Jr. 1988. "Child Care after Divorce and Remarriage." In E. M. Hetherington and J. Arasteh (Eds.), *The Impact of Divorce, Single Parenting and Stepparenting on Children*. Hillsdale, NJ: Erlbaum, pp. 245–261.

Gamble, Vanessa. 1994. "The Politics of Health: Race Blindness in D.C.?" *Dissent* 41 (Spring):200–203.

Gannett News Service. 1992. "Huge Gap in Funds for Children Seen from State to State." (March 6).

Gans, Herbert J. 1990. "Second Generation Decline." *Ethnic Racial Studies* 15:173–192.

Gardner, Gary, and Brian Halweil. 2000. "Escaping Hunger, Escaping Excess." *World Watch* 13 (July/ August):25–35.

Gardner, Howard. 2000. "Paroxysms of Choice." *New York Review of Books* (October 19):44–49.

Gartner, Michael. 1995a. "Raise Taxes, Cut Defense Spending." *USA Today* (May 30):11A.

Gartner, Michael. 1995b. "Unions Can Still Speak for the Little Guy." *USA Today* (June 20):11A.

Gates, Gary J. 2001. "Domestic Partner Benefits Won't Break the Bank." *Population Today* 29 (April):1,4.

Gavzer, Bernard. 1999. "Take Out the Trash, and Put It . . . Where?" *Parade Magazine* (June 13):4–6.

Gay, Lance. 2000. "Rising Costs Boost College Dropout Rate." Scripps Howard News Service (February 11).

Geewax, Marilyn. 1999. "One Planet, But Two Worlds." *Rocky Mountain News* (July 27):31A.

Geiger, H. Jack. 1990. "Generation of Poison and Lies." *New York Times* (August 5):E19.

Gelbard, Alene, Carl Haub, and Mary M. Kent. 1999. "World Population Beyond Six Billion." *Population Bulletin* 54 (March): entire issue.

Gelles, Richard J. 1976. "Demythologizing Child Abuse." *Family Coordinator* 25 (April).

Gelles, Richard J. 1990. "Domestic Violence and Child Abuse." In Neil Alan Weiner, Margaret A. Zahn, and Rita J. Sagi (Eds.), *Violence: Patterns, Causes, and Public Policy*. San Diego, CA: Harcourt, Brace.

Gelles, Richard J. 1993. "Family Violence." In Robert L. Hampton, Thomas P. Gullota, Gerald R. Adams, Earl H. Potter, and Roger P. Weissberg (Eds.), *Family Violence: Prevention and Treatment*. Newbury Park, CA: Sage.

Gelles, Richard J. 1995. *Contemporary Families: A Sociological View*. Thousand Oaks, CA: Sage.

Gelles, Richard J., and Murray A. Straus. 1979a. "Determinants of Violence in the Family." In Wesley R. Burr, Reuben Hill, F. Ivan Nye, and Ira L. Reiss (Eds.), *Contemporary Theories about the Family*. Vol. 1. New York: Free Press, pp. 549–581.

Gelles, Richard J., and Murray A. Straus. 1979b. "Domestic Violence and Sexual Abuse of Children." In Alan Booth (Ed.), *Contemporary Families: Looking Forward, Looking Back*. Minneapolis, MN: National Council on Family Relations, pp. 327–340.

Gelles, Richard J., and Murray A. Straus. 1988. *Intimate Violence*. New York: Simon & Schuster.

GenderGap.Com. "Election 2000—Women Candidates." Online. Available: http://www.gendergap.com/elections/election2000/wmn2000.htm.

Gergen, David. 2000. "Averting Our Eyes." *U.S. News & World Report* (September 25):76.

Gergen, David. 2001a. "Bush as Global Steward." *U.S. News & World Report* (February 5):64.

Gergen, David. 2001b. "Listen, Learn—Change." *U.S. News & World Report* (May 14):68.

Gergen, David. 2001c. "It's Not Can We, But Will We?" *U.S. News & World Report* (September 24):60.

Gerschick, Thomas J., and Adam Stephen Miller. 2001. "Coming to Terms: Masculinity and Physical Disability." In Michael S. Kimmel and Michael A. Messner (Eds.), *Men's Lives*, 5th ed. Boston: Allyn & Bacon, pp. 313–326.

Giddens, Anthony. 1991. *Introduction to Sociology*. New York: W. W. Norton.

Giele, Janet Z. 1988. "Gender and Sex Roles." In Neil J. Smelser (Ed.), *Handbook of Sociology*. Newbury Park, CA: Sage, pp. 291–323.

Gilman, Richard. 1971. "Where Did It All Go Wrong?" *Life* (August 13):40–55.

Gilson, Stephen French, and Elizabeth Depoy. 2000. "Multiculturalism and Disability: A Critical Perspective." *Disability and Society* 15 (March):207–218.

Ginsburg, Carl. 1996. "The Patient as Profit Center: Hospital Inc. Comes to Town." *Nation* (November 18):18–22.

Giroux, Henry A. 1996. "Beating Up on Kids." *Z Magazine* 9 (July/August):14–17.

Gitlin, Todd. 1995. *The Twilight of Common Dreams*. New York: Henry Holt.

Glaberson, William. 2001. "Technology's Role to Grow in a New World of Security." *New York Times* (September 18). Online. Available: www.nytimes.com/2001/09/18/national/18RULE.html.

Gladwell, Malcolm. 1999. "Running from Ritalin." *New Yorker* (February 5):80–84.

Glassman, James K. 1997. "Corporate Welfare in the Sky." *U.S. News & World Report* (July 28):49.

Glazer, Nathan. 1996. "The Hard Questions: Life in the City." *New Republic* (August 19):37.

Gleick, Elizabeth. 1995. "Rich Justice, Poor Justice." *Time* (June 19):40–47.

Goffman, Irving. 1963. *Stigma: Notes on the Management of Spoiled Identity*. Englewood Cliffs, NJ: Prentice-Hall.

Goldberg, Carey. 1998. "Acceptance of Gays Increases." *Rocky Mountain News* (May 31):40A.

Goldfarb, Bruce. 1990. "Eye Problems More Likely among Blacks." *USA Today* (February 7):1.

Goliber, Thomas J. 1997. "Population and Reproductive Health in Sub-Saharan Africa." *Population Bulletin* 52 (December): entire issue.

Goode, Erica. 1999. "For Good Health It Helps to Be Rich and Important." *New York Times* (June 1):1E.

Goode, William J. 1973. *The Drug Phenomenon: Social Aspects of Drug Taking*. Indianapolis, IN: Bobbs-Merrill.

Goode, William J. 1983. "World Devolution in Family Patterns. In Arlene Skolnick and Jerome Skolnick (Eds.), *Family in Transition*, 4th ed. Boston: Little, Brown, pp. 43–52.

Goodgame, Dan. 1993. "Welfare for the Well-Off." *Time* (February 22):36–38.

Goozner, Merrill. 2000. "The Price Isn't Right." *American Prospect* (September 11):25–29.

Gordon, Beth Omansky, and Karen E. Rosenblum. 2001.

"Bring Disability into the Sociological Frame: A Comparison of Disability with Race, Sex, and Sexual Orientation Statuses." *Disability and Society* 16 (January):5–19.

Gorman, Christine. 1998. "Playing the HMO Game." *Time* (July 13):22–28.

Gould, Meredith. 1979. "Statutory Oppressions: An Overview of Legalized Homophobia." In Martin P. Levine (Ed.), *Gay Men: The Sociology of Male Homosexuality*. New York: Harper & Row, pp. 51–67.

Gould, Stephen Jay. 1994. "Curveball." *New Yorker* (November 28):139–149.

Graham, James M. 1972. "Amphetamine Politics on Capital Hill." *Transaction* 9 (January):14.

Graham, Stephen. 2001. "Germany Gives Gay Couples Legal Status." *USA Today* (August 2):10A.

Gray, Charles. 1999. "Corporate Goliaths: Sizing Up Corporations and Governments." *Multinational Monitor* 20 (June):26–27.

Gray, Mike. 1999. "Perils of Prohibition." *Nation* (September 20):16–18.

Green, Donald P., Laurence H. McFalls, and Jennifer K. Smith. 2001. "Hate Crime: An Emergent Research Agenda." *Annual Review of Sociology* 27:479–504.

Greenfeld, Lawrence A. 1998. *Alcohol and Crime*. Washington, DC: U.S. Department of Justice.

Greenfeld, Lawrence A., and Steven K. Smith. 1999. "American Indians and Crime." *Bureau of Justice Statistics* (NCJ 173386) (February).

Greenfeld, Lawrence A., and Tracy L. Snell. 1999. "Women Offenders." *Bureau of Justice Studies Special Report* (NCJ 175688) (December).

Greenhouse, Steven. 2001a. "Unions Hit Lowest Point in 6 Decades." *New York Times* (January 21). Online. Available: http://www.nytimes.com/2001/01/21/national/21LABO.html.

Greenhouse, Steven. 2001b. "Report Shows Americans Have More 'Labor Days.'" *New York Times* (September 1). Online. Available: http://www.nytimes.com/2001/09/01/national 01HOUR.html.

Greider, William. 1994. "Why the Mighty GE Can't Strike Out." *Rolling Stone* (April 21):36.

Greim, Lisa. 1998. "Working Women Protest Pay Gap." *Rocky Mountain News* (April 4):1B.

Griffith, Jeanne E., Mary J. Frase, and John H. Ralph. 1989. "American Education: The Challenge of Change." *Population Bulletin* 44 (December): entire issue.

Grossman, Cathy Lynn. 2001a. "Protestants Face Annual Sexual Divide." *USA Today* (June 6):D1–D2.

Grossman, Cathy Lynn. 2001b. "Faith Fights Terror's Image." *USA Today* (September 24):6D.

Grzywinski, Ronald. 1991. "The New Old-Fashioned Banking." *Harvard Business Review* (May/June): 87–88.

Gugliotta, Guy. 2001. "Still Skeptical: Three Mile Island and Chernobyl Left Americans Dreading Nuclear Power." *Washington Post National Weekly Edition* (June 18):18–19.

Gullo, Karen. 1997. "Tobacco Interests Ply Both Parties to Tune of $2 Million." *Denver Post* (August 13):12A.

Guttman, Monika. 1996. "The New Pot Culture." *USA Weekend* (February 16–18):4–7.

Hafner, Katie. 1998. "Girl Games: Plenty and Pink." *New York Times* (September 10):8G.

Hagan, Frank E. 1994. *Introduction to Criminology*, 3rd ed. Chicago: Nelson-Hall.

Hagan, John. 1994. *Crime and Disrepute*. Thousand Oaks, CA: Pine Forge Press.

Hagedorn, John. 1998. *People and Folks: Gangs, Crime and the Underclass in a Rustbelt City*, 2nd ed. Chicago: Lake View Press.

Hahn, Harlan. 1986. "Public Support for Rehabilitation Programs: The Analysis of U.S. Disability Policy." *Handicap and Society* 1 (2):121–138.

Hahn, Harlan. 1988. "The Politics of Physical Difference: Disability and Discrimination." *Journal of Social Issues* 44:39–47.

Hale, Ellen, and Vivienne Walt. 2001. "Extremists' Hatred of U.S. Has Varied Roots." *USA Today* (September 19):1A,4A.

Hall, Carl T. 1998. "Campuses Drowning in Booze." *Rocky Mountain News* (September 12):59A.

Hall, M. Ann. 1985. "Knowledge and Gender: Epistemological Questions in the Social Analysis of Sport." *Sociology of Sport Journal* 2:25–42.

Hampson, Rick. 2001. "1990s Boom Reminiscent of 1890s." *USA Today* (April 2):3A.

Hanchette, John. 1998. "War Averted, But Bioterrorism Still Big Problem." Gannett News Service (February 27).

Hanna, William J., and Elizabeth Rogovsky. 1991. "Women with Disabilities: Two Handicaps Plus." *Disability, Handicap and Society* 6(1):55–56.

Hansen, James. 1998. "Organized Labor Just as Relevant in Robust Times." *Rocky Mountain News* (December 13):5B.

Harjo, Susan Shown. 1996. "Now and Then: Native Peoples in the United States." *Dissent* 43 (Summer):58–60.

Harper's Magazine. 2001. "Harper's Index." Vol. 302 (April):7.

Harrington, Michael. 1963. *The Other America: Poverty in the United States*. Baltimore: Penguin Books.

Harrington, Michael. 1965. *The Accidental Century*. Baltimore: Penguin Books.

Harrington, Michael. 1968. "The Urgent Case for Social Investment." *Saturday Review* (November 23):34.

Harrington, Michael. 1979. "Social Retreat and Economic Stagnation." *Dissent* 26 (Spring):131–134.

Harrington, Michael. 1984. *The New American Poverty*. New York: Holt, Rinehart & Winston.

Harris, Kathleen Mullan. 1996. "The Reforms Will Hurt, Not Help, Poor Women and Children." *Chronicle of Higher Education* (October 4):B7.

Harris, Roderick J., and Claudette Bennett. 1995. "Racial and Ethnic Diversity." In Reynolds Farley (Ed.), *The State of the Union: America in the 1990s*, Vol. 2. New York: Russell Sage, pp. 141–210.

Harry, Joseph. 1983. "Gay Male and Lesbian Relationships." In Eleanor D. Macklin and Roger H. Rubin (Eds.), *Contemporary Families and Alternative Lifestyles*. Beverly Hills, CA: Sage, pp. 216–234.

Hart, Betsy. 1999. "Parents Hooking 'Hyperactive' Kids." *Rocky Mountain News* (June 4):60A.

Hartjen, Clayton A. 1977. *Possible Trouble: An Analysis of Social Problems*. New York: Praeger.

Hartjen, Clayton A. 1978. *Crime and Criminalization*, 2nd ed. New York: Praeger.

Hartmann, Heidi I. 1976. "Capitalism, Patriarchy, and Job Segregation by Sex." *Signs* 1 (Spring):137–169.

Harwood, Richard. 1997. "America's Unchecked Epidemic." *Washington Post National Weekly Edition* (December 8):27.

Havemann, Judith. 1998. "The Long Line for Housing." *Washington Post National Weekly Edition* (June 22):34.

Hayes, Cherly D., John L. Palmer, and Martha J. Zaslow

(Eds.). 1990. *Who Cares for America's Children? Child Care Policy for the 1990s*. Washington, DC: National Academy Press.

Hazen, Don. 2001. "Secrets of the Chemical Industry Exposed." *Progressive Populist* (April 15):1,12–13.

Heilbroner, Robert L. 1974. *An Inquiry into the Human Prospect*. New York: W. W. Norton.

Heiman, Diane, and Phyllis Bookspan. 1992. "Word on the Street: Bias There, Too." *Rocky Mountain News* (July 28):30.

Henle, Robert J. 1994. "The Role of Women in Catholic Parish Life." *American* 171 (September):6–7.

Henry, Jules. 1963. *Culture against Man*. New York: Random House/Vintage.

Henry, Tamara. 2000. "Report: Education Not Equal Yet." *USA Today* (March 1):1A.

Henry, Tamara. 2001a. "Study: Latinas Shortchanged by U.S. Schools." *USA Today* (January 25):8D.

Henry, Tamara. 2001b. "Teachers Union Calls for Universal Preschool." *USA Today* (July 12):9D.

Henry, William A., III. 1990. "Beyond the Melting Pot." *Time* (April 9):28–35.

Henslin, James M., and Larry T. Reynolds (Eds.). 1976. *Social Problems in American Society*, 2nd ed. Boston: Holbrook Press.

Henwood, Doug. 1999. "Debts Everywhere." *Nation* (July 19):12.

Henwood, Doug. 2001. "Wealth Report." *Nation* (April 9):8.

Herbert, Bob. 2000. "The Danger Point." *New York Times* (July 6). Online. Available: http://www.nytimes.com/library/opinion/herbert/070600herb.html.

Herbert, Bob. 2001a. "The Quiet Scourge." *New York Times* (January 11). Online. Available: http://www.nytimes.com/2001/03/12/opinion/11HERB.html.

Herbert, Bob. 2001b. "Fewer Students, Greater Gains." *New York Times* (March 12). Online. Available: http://www.nytimes.com/2001/03/12/opinion/12HERB.html.

Herbert, Bob. 2001c. "It Hasn't Gone Away." *New York Times* (May 31). Online. Available: http://www.nytimes.com/2001/05/31/opinion/31HERB.html.

Herman, Edward S. 1994. "The New Racist Onslaught." *Z Magazine* 7 (December):24–26.

Herman, Edward S. 1996. "America the Meritocracy." *Z Magazine* 9 (July/August):34–39.

Herrnstein, Richard. 1971. "I.Q." *Atlantic* 228 (September):43–64.

Herrnstein, Richard J. 1973. *I.Q. in the Meritocracy*. Boston: Little, Brown.

Herrnstein, Richard J., and Charles Murray. 1994. *The Bell Curve: Intelligence and Class Structure in American Life*. New York: Free Press.

Hershey, Laura. 2000. "Choosing Disability." In Estelle Disch (Ed.), *Reconstructing Gender: A Multicultural Anthology*, 2nd ed., Mountain View, CA: Mayfield, pp. 556–563.

Herz, Diane E., and Barbara H. Wootton. 1996. "Women in the Workforce: An Overview." In Cynthia Costello and Barbara Kivimae Krimgold (Eds.), *The American Woman. 1996–1997*, New York: W. W. Norton, pp. 44–78.

Hess, Beth B., Elizabeth W. Markson, and Peter J. Stein. 1988. *Sociology*, 3rd ed. New York: Macmillan.

Higginbotham, Elizabeth. 1994. "Black Professional Women: Job Ceilings and Employment Sectors." In Maxine Baca Zinn and Bonnie Thornton Dill (Eds.), *Women of Color in U.S. Society*. Philadelphia: Temple University Press, pp. 113–131.

Hightower, Jim. 1997. "Class War." *Dollars & Sense* 214 (November/December):7.

Hightower, Jim. 2001. "Stand Up for Your Democracy." *AlterNet* (September 19). Online. Available: www.alternet.org/story.html?StoryID=11537.

Hill, M. 1994. "Getting Things Right." *Community Care Inside* 31 (March):7.

Hilzenrath, David S. 1998. "Showing the Sickest Patients the Door." *Washington Post National Weekly Edition*. (February 2):30.

Himmelstein, Jerome L. 1978. "Drug Politics Theory: Analysis and Critique." *Journal of Drug Issues* 8 (Winter):37–52.

Hinden, Stan. 2001. "Some Snags in the Safety Net." *Washington Post National Weekly Edition* (May 28):18.

Hoagland, Jim. 1997. "Crisis-Managing in a Fog." *Washington Post National Weekly Edition* (December 1):5–6.

Hogendoorn, E. J. 1997. "A Chemical Weapons Atlas." *Bulletin of the Atomic Scientists* 53 (September/October):35–39.

Holden, Karen C., and Pamela J. Smock. 1991. "The Economic Costs of Marital Dissolution: Why Do Women Bear a Disproportionate Cost." *Annual Review of Sociology* 17:51–78.

Hole, Judith, and Ellen Levine. 1979. "The First Feminists." In Jo Freeman (Ed.), *Women: A Feminist Perspective*. Palo Alto, CA: Mayfield.

Holmes, Steven A. 2000. "Race Analysis Cites Disparity in Sentencing for Narcotics." *New York Times* (June 8). Online. Available: http://www.nytimes.com/library/national/060800race-prison.html.

Holstein, William J. 1996. "Santa's Sweatshop." *U.S. News & World Report* (December 16):50–56.

Holstein, William J. 2000. "Take My Personal Computer—Please." *U.S. News & World Report* (June 5):51.

Holstein, James A., and Jay Gubrium. 1999. "What Is Family? Further Thoughts on a Social Constructionist Approach." *Marriage and Family Review* 28 (3/4):3–20.

Horn, Miriam. 1987. "The Burgeoning Educational Underclass." *U.S. News & World Report* (May 18):66–67.

Hosenball, Mark, and Evan Thomas. 2001. "Danger: Terror Ahead." *Newsweek* (February 19):32–35.

Hudson, Mike. 1996. "Cashing in on Poverty." *Nation* (May 20):11–14.

Human Rights Watch. 2001. "Hatred in the Hallways: Violence and Discrimination Against Lesbian, Gay, Bisexual, and Transgender Students in U.S. Schools. Online. Available: http://www.hrw.org/reports/2001/uslgbt.

Hunt, Albert R., and Alan Murray. 1999. "Hazardous Waste." *Smart Money* (September):89–90.

Hutchins, Robert M. 1976. "Is Democracy Possible?" *Center Magazine* 9 (January/February):2–6.

Idle, Tracey, Eileen Wood, and Serge Desmarais. 1993. "Gender Role Socialization in Toy Play Situations: Mothers and Fathers with Their Sons and Daughters." *Sex Roles* 28 (11/12):679–691.

Ingrassia, Michelle, and Melinda Berk. 1994. "Patterns of Abuse." *Newsweek* (July 4):26–33.

Institute for Research on Poverty. 1998. "Revising the Poverty Measure." *Focus* 19 (Spring): entire issue.

Intelligence Report. 2001. "Reevaluating the Net." The Southern Poverty Law Center (Summer), Issue 102:54–55.

Inter-Parliamentary Union (IPU). 2001. National Parliaments Database. (July 1). Online. Available: www.ipu.org/wmn-e/classif.htm.

In These Times. 1997. "The Military Budget Boondoggle." (June 16):2

In These Times. 1998. "Let's Get Back to Basics." (October 18):3.

Ireland, Doug. 2000. "Gay-Baiting in the Military Under 'Don't Ask, Don't Tell.'" *Nation* (July 10):11–16.

ISR Newsletter. 1982. "Why Do Women Earn Less?" Ann Arbor, MI: University of Michigan, Institute for Social Research, Spring/Summer.

Ivins, Molly. 2000. "Capitalism Gets a Really Bad Name." *Progressive Populist* (May 15):22–23.

Jackson, Derrick Z. 2001. "Gas Hogs Rise in the Bush Era." *Rocky Mountain News* (March 4):5B.

Jackson, Janine. 2000. "A Right, Not a Favor: Coverage of Disability Act Misses Historical Shift." Online. Available: http://www.fair.org/extra-0011/ada.html.

Jackson, Jesse. 1998a. "The Coming Collision." *Progressive Populist* 4 (August):19–20.

Jackson, Jesse. 1998b. "Leave No One Behind: A Call to Action in Appalachia." *Liberal Opinion Week* (September 28):3.

Jackson, Jesse. 1998c. "Market Rules and New Democracy." *Progressive Populist* 4 (June):19.

Jackson, Jesse. 2001. "Talking the Talk about the Poor." *Progressive Populist* (July 1):19.

Jackson, Kenneth T. 1985. *Crabgrass Frontier: The Suburbanization of the United States*. New York: Oxford University Press.

Jackson, Kenneth T. 1996. "America's Rush to Suburbia." *New York Times* (June 9):E15.

Jackson, Maggie. 1999. "Minority Women Report Obstacles." *Denver Rocky Mountain News* (July 14):6B.

Jaffe, Greg. 1997. "Georgia's Scholarships Are Open to Everyone, and That's the Problem." *Wall Street Journal* (June 2):A1, 13.

Jencks, Christopher, and Meredith Phillips. 1998. "America's Next Achievement Test." *American Prospect*, No. 40 (September/October):44–53.

Jencks, Christopher, et al. 1972. *Inequality: A Reassessment of the Effect of Family and Schooling in America*. New York: Basic Books.

Jensen, Arthur R. 1969. "How Much Can We Boost IQ and Scholastic Achievement?" *Harvard Educational Review* 39 (Winter):1–123.

Jensen, Arthur R. 1980. *Bias in Mental Testing*. New York: Free Press.

Jensen, Holger. 2001. "U.S. Keeps Its Place as Global Leader—in International Arms Sales." *Rocky Mountain News* (August 25):5A.

Jeter, Jon. 2000. "A Tarnished Land Legacy." *Washington Post National Weekly Edition* (February 28):14–15.

Johnson, Dirk. 2000. "Commandments Find Way into Schools." *Rocky Mountain News* (February 27):68A.

Johnson, Michael P., and Kathleen J. Ferraro. 2001. "Research on Domestic Violence in the 1990s: Making Distinctions." In R. M. Milardo (Ed.), *Understanding Families Into the New Millennium: A Decade in Review*, Minneapolis: National Council on Family Relations, pp. 167–182.

Johnston, David Cay. 1999. "Gap between Rich and Poor Found Substantially Wider." *New York Times* (September 5):16.

Jones, Barry. 1990. *Sleepers Wake! Technology and the Future of Work*, rev. ed. New York: Oxford University Press.

Jones, Del. 1997a. "Domestic Partner Benefits on Rise." *USA Today* (October 14):8B.

Jones, Del. 1997b. "Firms Fighting, Winning to Keep Unions at Bay." *USA Today* (September 19):1B–2B.

Jones, Rachel L. 1996. "Hispanic Children Biggest Minority." *Denver Post* (July 2):A1–A11.

Jorgensen, Helene, and Hans Reimer. 2000. "Permatemps." *American Prospect* (August 14):38–40.

Judson, David. 1997. "Neglect of Kids 'No Less Than Collective Sin.'" Gannett News Service (June).

Kalb, Claudia. 2001. "Can This Pill Stop You from Hitting the Bottle?" *Newsweek* (February 12):48–51.

Kalet, Hank. 2000. "Unequal Justice." *Progressive Populist* (June 1):14.

Kamau, Pius. 2001. "Education Funding Unfair." *Denver Post* (April 8):8I.

Kammeyer, Kenneth C. W., George Ritzer, and Norman R. Yetman. 1997. *Sociology*, 7th ed. Boston: Allyn & Bacon.

Kanter, Rosabeth Moss. 1977. *Men and Women of the Corporation*. New York: Basic Books.

Kantrowitz, Barbara, and Pat Wingert. 1992. "One Nation, One Curriculum?" *Newsweek* (April 6):59–60.

Kasinitz, Philip, and Jan Rosenberg. 1996. "Missing the Connection: Social Isolation and Employment on the Brooklyn Waterfront." *Social Problems* 43 (2):180–190.

Katz, Bruce, and Jennifer Bradley. 1999. "Divided We Sprawl." *Atlantic Monthly* (December):26–42.

Katz-Fishman, Wanda. 1990. "Higher Education in Crisis: The American Dream Denied." *Society for the Study of Social Problems Newsletter* 21 (Fall):22–23.

Kay, Jane Holtz. 1997. *Asphalt Nation: How the Automobile Took Over America and How We Can Take It Back*. New York: Crown.

Kay, Jane Holtz. 1998. "Paving America First." *Nation* (July 27):7.

Keegan, Patricia. 1989. "Playing Favorites." *New York Times Magazine* (August 6):A26.

Keen, Judy. 1993. "In Cities, Health Care Is Second to Jobs, Housing." *USA Today* (July 7):A9.

Keen, Sam. 1991. *Fire in the Belly: On Being a Man*. New York: Bantam Books.

Kelly, Michael. 2001. "77 North Washington Streeet." *Atlantic Monthly* 288 (October):8.

Kemper, Vicki, and Viveca Novak. 1992. "What's Blocking Health Care Reform?" *Common Cause Magazine* 18 (January/February):8–13, 25.

Kendall, Diana. 2001. *Sociology*, 3rd ed. Belmont, CA: Wadsworth.

Kennedy, David. 1996. "Can We Still Afford to Be a Nation of Immigrants?" *Atlantic Monthly* (November):51–80.

Kent, Mary M., Kelvin M. Pollard, John Haaga, and Mark Mather. 2001. "First Glimpses from the 2000 U.S. Census." *Population Bulletin* 56 (June): entire issue.

Kibria, Nazli. 1997. "The Concept of 'Bicultural Families' and Its Implications for Research on Immigrant and Ethnic Families." In Alan Booth, Ann C. Crouter, and Nancy Landale (Eds.), *Immigration and the Family*. Mahwah, NJ: Erlbaum, pp. 205–210.

Kim, Marlene. 1998. "Are the Working Poor Lazy?" *Challenge* 41 (May/June):85–99.

Kimmel, Michael. 1992. "Reading Men, Masculinity, and Publishing." *Contemporary Sociology* 21 (March): 162–171.

Kimmel, Michael S., and Michael A. Messner. 1998. *Men's Lives,* 4th ed. Boston: Allyn & Bacon.

King, Ledyard. 2000. "A Fight to Die Without Poverty." *USA Today* (October 19):12D.

Kirkland, Richard I., Jr. 1992. "What We Can Do Now." *Fortune* (June 1):41–48.

Kirksey, Jim. 2001. "Activist Decries Impact on Disabled." *Denver Post* (February 22):49A.

Klam, Matthew. 2001. "Experiencing Ecstasy." *New York Times Magazine* (January 21). Online. Available: http://www.nytimes.com/library/magazine/home/20010121mag-ecstacy.html.

Klare, Michael T. 1994. "Armed and Dangerous." *In These Times* (June 13):14–19.

Klein, Joe. 2001. "Closework: Why We Couldn't See What Was Right in Front of Us." *New Yorker* (October 1):44–53.

Knowles, Louis L., and Kenneth Prewitt (Eds.). 1965. *Institutional Racism in America.* Upper Saddle River, NJ: Prentice-Hall.

Kochanek, Kenneth D., Betty L. Smith, and Robert N. Anderson. 2001. "Deaths: Preliminary Data for 1999," National Center for Health Statistics, *National Vital Statistics Report,* Vol. 49, No. 3. (June). Hyattsville, MD.

Kocieniewski, David, and Robert Hanley. 2000. "Racial Profiling Routine, New Jersey Finds." *New York Times* (November 28). Online. Available: http://www.nytimes.com/2001/11/28/nyregion/28TROOMet.html.

Kolata, Gina. 2001. "Medical Fees Are Often Higher for Patients without Insurance." *New York Times* (April 2). Online. Available: http://www.nytimes.com/2001/04/02/national/02INSU.html.

Korb, Lawrence J. 2001. "10 Myths about the Defense Budget." *In These Times* (April 2):10–12.

Koretz, Gene. 1998a. "Downsizing's Painful Effects." *Business Week* (April 13):23.

Koretz, Gene. 1998b. "Wanted: Black Entrepreneurs." *Business Week* (December 14):26.

Koretz, Gene. 2001. "Why Americans Work So Hard." *Business Week* (June 11):34.

Kosberg, Jordan I. 1976. "Differences in Proprietary Institutions Caring for Affluent and Nonaffluent Elderly." In Cary S. Hart and Barbara B. Manard (Eds.), *Aging in America.* Port Washington, NY: Alfred.

Kotkin, Joel. 1997. "Rebuilding Blocks." *Washington Post National Weekly Edition* (April 28):21–22.

Kozol, Jonathan. 1991. *Savage Inequalities: Children in America's Schools.* New York: Crown.

Krauss, Clifford. 1994. "Women Doing Crime, Women Doing Time." *New York Times* (July 3):3E.

Kroeger, Brook. 1994. "The Road Less Rewarded." *Working Woman* (July):50–55.

Kuttner, Robert. 1998. "Toward Universal Coverage." *Washington Post National Weekly Edition* (July 20):27.

Labell, Linda S. 1979. "Wife Abuse: A Sociological Study of Battered Women and Their Mates." *Victimology* 4 (2):258–267.

Lacayo, Richard. 1998. "The New Gay Struggle." *Time* (October 26):32–36.

Lacayo, Richard. 2000. "The Rain of Dollars." *Time* (August 14):36–37.

Ladner, Joyce A. 1971. *Tomorrow's Tomorrow.* New York: Doubleday.

Lamberth, John. 1998. "DWB Is Not a Crime." *Washington Post National Weekly Edition* (August 24):23.

Lamm, Richard. 1989. "U.S. Must Cure Health-Care Ills." *Rocky Mountain News* (July 23):59.

Landers, Ann. 1996. "Culture Dictates Marriage between a Man/a Woman." *Denver Post* (July 26):12D.

Lang, John. 1997. "Ritalin: Helpful or Harmful?" *Rocky Mountain News* (June 9):3A, 38A.

Langewiesche, William. 2001. "Peace Is Hell." *Atlantic Monthly* 288 (October):51–80.

Langlois, Judith H., and A. Chris Downs. 1980. "Mothers, Fathers, and Peers as Socialization Agents of Sex-Typed Play Behaviors in Young Children." *Child Development* 57:1237–1247.

Lappe, Frances Moore. 1999. "Like Driving a Cadillac." In Douglas H. Boucher (Ed.), *The Paradox of Plenty: Hunger in a Bountiful World.* Oakland, CA: First Food Books, pp. 103–126.

Lappe, Frances Moore, and Joseph Collins. 1979. *Food First: The Myth of Scarcity.* New York: Ballantine Books.

Lappe, Frances Moore, and Joseph Collins. 1986. *World Hunger: Twelve Myths.* New York: Grove Press.

Lasch, Christopher. 1977. *Haven in a Heartless World: The Family Besieged.* New York: Basic Books.

Laumann, Edward O., John H. Gagnon, and Stuart Michaels. 1994. *The Social Organization of Sexuality: Sexual Practices in the United States.* Chicago: University of Chicago Press.

Layton, Lyndsey. 2000. "Leaving the Driving to Someone Else." *Washington Post National Weekly Edition* (May 8):29.

Layton, Lyndsey. 2001. "And, You Don't Have to Look for Parking." *Washington Post National Weekly Edition* (April 23):34.

Lazare, Daniel. 2001. *America's Undeclared War: What's Killing Our Cities and How We Can Stop It.* New York: Harcourt.

Lee, Jean H. 2001. "World Population May Grow by Half Over Next 50 Years." Associated Press (February 28).

Lee, Sharon M. 1998. "Asian Americans: Diverse and Growing." *Population Bulletin* 53 (June):entire issue.

Leen, Jeff. 1998. "A Shot in the Dark on Drug Use." *Washington Post National Weekly Edition* (January 12):32–33.

Lefkowitz, Bernard. 1998. *Our Guys.* New York: Random House Vintage.

Leinwand, Donna. 1999. "Debate Rages on Remedies for Women's Pay Gap." *Denver Post* (October 11):15A.

Leinwand, Donna. 2001. "The Lowdown on the Hippest Highs." *USA Today* (August 28):6D–7D.

Lekachman, Robert. 1979. "The Specter of Full Employment." In Jerome H. Skolnick and Elliott Currie (Eds.), *Crisis in American Institutions,* 4th ed. Boston: Little, Brown, pp. 50–58.

Lekachman, Robert. 1987. "The Craze for 'Privatization.'" *Dissent* 34 (Summer):302–307.

Leland, John. 2000. "Shades of Gay." *Newsweek* (March 20):46–49.

Lemann, Nicholas. 1986. "The Origins of the Underclass." Parts 1 and 2. *Atlantic Monthly* (June):31–55; (July):54–68.

Lemert, Edwin M. 1967. *Human Deviance, Social Problems and Social Control.* Upper Saddle River, NJ: Prentice-Hall.

Leonard, Arthur S. 1990. "Gay/Lesbian Rights: Report from the Legal Front." *Nation* (July 2):12–15.

Leonard, Mary. 1997. "Abortion: 25 Years after Roe v. Wade,

Middleground in Battlefield." *Boston Globe* (December 14):1F, 3F.

Leonhardt, David. 2000. "Lingering Job Worries Amid a Sea of Plenty." *New York Times*. Online. Available: http://www.nytimes.com/library/tech/yr/mo/bizrtech/articles/ 29worry.html.

Lerner, Michael. 2001. "The Case for Peace." *Time* (October 1):77.

Leslie, Jacques. 2000. "Running Dry: What Happens When the World No Longer Has Enough Fresh Water?" *Harper's Magazine* 301 (July):37–52.

LeVay, Simon. 1991. "A Difference in Hypothalamic Structure between Heterosexual and Homosexual Men." *Science* 253:1034–1037.

Lever, Janet. 1976. "Sex Differences in the Games Children Play." *Social Problems* 23 (April):478–487.

LeVine, Mark. 2001. "10 Things to Know about Terrorism." *AlterNet* (October 4). Online. Available: www.alternet.org/story.html?StoryID=11647.

Levine, Martin P. 1979. "Employment Discrimination against Gay Men." *International Review of Modern Sociology* 9 (July–December):151–163.

Levitan, Sar A., and Clifford M. Johnson. 1982. *Second Thoughts on Work*. Kalamazoo, MI: W. E. Upjohn Institute for Employment Research.

Levy, Doug. 1997. "Blacks Receive Less Aggressive Heart Treatment." *USA Today* (February 13):1D.

Levy, Steven. 2001. "Tech's Double-Edged Sword." *Newsweek* (September 24):65.

Lewin, Tamar. 1998. "How Boys Lost Out to Girl Power," *New York Times* (December 13):3D.

Lewin, Tamar. 2001. "Disabled Patients Win Sweeping Changes from H.M.O." *New York Times* (April 13). Online. Available: http://www.nytimes.com/2001/04/13/national/13DISA.html.

Lewis, Anthony. 2000. "Breaking Silence on Failed Drug War." *Rocky Mountain News* (August 1):33A.

Lewis, Anthony. 2001. "To Thine Own Self Be True." *New York Times* (September 22). Online. Available: http://www.nytimes.com/2001/09/22/opinion/22LEWI.html.

Lewis, Bernard. 2001. "Understanding bin Laden." *Rocky Mountain News* (September 22):4B–5B.

Lewis, Michael. 1972. "There's No Unisex in the Nursery." *Psychology Today* 5 (May):54–57.

Liazos, Alexander. 1972. "The Poverty of the Sociology of Deviance: Nuts, Sluts, and Perverts." *Social Problems* 20 (Summer):103–120.

Liazos, Alexander. 1982. *People First: An Introduction to Social Problems*. Boston: Allyn & Bacon.

Lichtenberg, Judith. 1992. "Racism in the Head, Racism in the World." *Report from the Institute for Philosophy and Public Policy*. University of Maryland, Vol. 12 (Spring/Summer):3–5.

Liebow, Elliot. 1967. *Tally's Corner*. Boston: Little, Brown.

Lilla, Mark. 2001. "Extremism's Theological Roots." *New York Times* (October 7). Online. Available: http://www.nytimes.com/2001/10/07/opinion/07LILL.html.

Linden, Eugene. 2000. "Condition Critical." *Time* (April 30):18–24.

Linton, Simi. 1998. *Claiming Disability: Knowledge and Identity*. New York: New York University Press.

Lipset, Seymour Martin. 1996. *American Exceptionalism: A Double-Edged Sword*. New York: W. W. Norton.

Livernash, Robert, and Eric Rodenburg. 1998. "Population Change, Resources, and the Environment." *Population Bulletin* 53 (March): entire issue.

Llewellyn, A., and K. Hogan. 2000. "The Use and Abuse of Modes of Disability." *Disability and Society* 15 (January):157–165.

Lockheed, Marlaine. 1985. "Sex Equity in the Classroom Organization and Climate." In Susan S. Klein (Ed.), *Handbook for Achieving Sex Equity through Education*. Baltimore: Johns Hopkins University Press, pp. 189–217.

Locy, Toni. 2000. "Violent Crime Rate Lowest Since 1978." *USA Today* (October 16):3A.

Loewen, James W. 1995. *Lies My Teacher Told Me: Everything Your American History Textbook Got Wrong*. New York: Touchstone.

Long, Gary T., and Faye E. Sulton. 1987. "Contributions from Social Psychology." In Louis Diamant (Ed.), *Male and Female Homosexuality: Psychological Approaches*. Washington, DC: Hemisphere Publications, pp. 221–237.

Longman, Phillip J. 1999. "The World Turns Gray." *U.S. News & World Report* (March 1):30–39.

Longman, Phillip J. 2001. "American Gridlock." *U.S. News & World Report* (May 28):16–22.

Longworth, R. C. 2001. "The Seeds of Terror Thrive in Poor Ground." *Chicago Tribune* (September 30):Section 2:1,8.

Lorber, Judith. 1994. *Paradoxes of Gender*. New Haven, CT: Yale University Press.

Lott, Juanita Tamayo, and Judy C. Felt. 1991. "Studying the Pan Asian Community." *Population Today* 19 (April 1):6–8.

Love, Alice Ann. 1998. "Gender Wage Gap Shrinks Slightly." *USA Today* (June 10):1A.

Lowenstein, Thomas K. 2001. "Collateral Damage." *American Prospect* (January 1–15):33–36.

Lucal, Betsy. 1996. "Oppression and Privilege: Toward a Relational Conceptualization of Race." *Teaching Sociology* 24 (July):245–255.

Lundberg, George D. 2000. *Severed Trust: Why American Medicine Hasn't Been Fixed*. New York: Basic Books.

Lutz, Wolfgang. 1994. "The Future of World Population." *Population Bulletin* 49 (June): entire issue.

MacAndrew, Craig, and Robert Edgerton. 1969. *Drunken Comportment: A Social Explanation*. Chicago: Aldine.

Macewan, Arthur. 1994. "Markets Unbound: The Heavy Price of Globalization." *Dollars & Sense* 195 (September/October):8–9,35–37.

Macewan, Arthur. 2001. "Ask Dr. Dollar." *Dollars & Sense*, No. 233 (January/February):40.

Mach, Henry Jay. 1987. "Shrink, Shrank, Shrunk: The Stormy Relationship between Gays and Mental Health Experts." *Advocate* (October 13):43–49.

Madeley, John. 1999. *Big Business, Poor Peoples: The Impact of Transnational Corporations on the World's Poor*. London: Zed Books.

Magnet, Myron (Ed.). 2000. *The Millennial City: A New Urban Paradigm for 21st Century America*. Chicago: Ivan R. Dee.

Maharidge, Dale. 1998. "The Sleeping Giant Awakes." *Mother Jones* 23 (January/February):57–61.

Mairs, Nancy. 1992. "On Being a Cripple." In L. McDowell and R. Pringle (Eds.), *Defining Women*. Cambridge: Polity.

Males, Mike. 1994. "The Real Generational Gap." *In These Times* (February 7):18–19.

Mark, Jason. 1998. "Who's in the Driver's Seat? Industry,

Government, and the Car of the Future." *Dollars & Sense* 218 (July/August):16–19,40.

Marklein, Mary Beth. 2000. "19 States Get a Bad Grade for Their Teaching of Evolution." *USA Today* (September 27):11D.

Marquis, Christopher. 2001. "Military's Ouster of Gays Rose 17 Percent Last Year." *New York Times* (June 2). Online. Available: http://www.nytimes.com/2001/06/02/national1092GAYS.html.

Marsiglio, William, Paul Amato, Ronald D. Day, and Michael E. Lamb. 2001. "Scholarship on Fatherhood in the 1990s and Beyond." In Robert M. Milardo (Ed.), *Understanding Families into the New Millennium: A Decade in Review*. Minneapolis: National Council on Family Relations, pp. 392–410.

Martin, Patricia Yancey. 1998. "Reflections: Gender and Organizations." In Kristen A. Myers, Cynthia D. Anderson, and Barbara J. Risman (Eds.), *Feminist Foundations: Toward Transforming Sociology*. Thousand Oaks, CA: Sage, pp. 322–325.

Martin, Philip, and Elizabeth Midgley. 1999. "Immigration to the United States." *Population Bulletin* 54 (June): entire issue.

Martin, Teresa Castro, and Larry L. Bumpass. 1989. "Recent Trends in Marital Disruption." *Demography* 26:37–51.

Maschinot, Beth. 1995. "Behind the Curve." *In These Times* (February 6):31–34.

Maslow, Abraham H. 1954. *Motivation and Personality*. New York: Harper & Row.

Massachusetts Department of Education. 2000. *1999 Massachusetts Youth Risk Behavior Survey*. Boston. On-line. Available: http://www.doe.mass.edu/lss/ yrbs99.

Massey, Douglas. 1993. "Latino Poverty Research: An Agenda for the 1990s." *Items*, The Social Science Research Council, Vol. 47 (March):7–11.

Massey, Douglas. 1996a. "Concentrating Poverty Breeds Violence." *Population Today* 24 (June/July):5.

Massey, Douglas. 1996b. "The Age of Extremes: Concentrated Affluence and Poverty in the Twenty-First Century." *Demography* 33 (November):395–412.

Massey, Douglas, and Nancy Denton. 1993. *American Apartheid: Segregation and the Making of the Underclass*. Cambridge, MA: Harvard University Press.

Mauer, Marc, and Tracy Huling. 1995. *Young Black Americans and the Criminal Justice System, Five Years Later*. Washington, DC: Sentencing Project.

McAdoo, John. 1988. "Changing Perspectives on the Role of the Black Father." In P. Bronstein and C. P. Cowan (Eds.), *Fatherhood Today, Men's Changing Role in the Family*. New York: John Wiley, pp. 79–92.

McCaghy, Charles H. 1976. *Deviant Behavior: Crime, Conflict, and Interest Groups*. New York: Macmillan.

McChesney, Robert W. 1999a. "The Big Media Game Has Fewer and Fewer Players." *Progressive* 63 (November):20–24.

McChesney, Robert W. 1999b. "Rich Media, Poor Democracy." *In These Times* (November 14):15–17.

McClam, Erin. 2000. "Less Teens Smoked in '99, CDC Says." Associated Press (August 25).

McGinn, Daniel. 2001. "Screeching to a Halt." *Newsweek* (October 1):54–56.

McGinn, Daniel, and John McCormick. 1999. "Your Next Job." *Newsweek* (February 1):43–45.

McIntosh, Pegg. 1992. "White Privilege and Male Privilege." In Margaret L. Andersen and Patricia Hill Collins (Eds.), *Race, Class, and Gender*. Belmont, CA: Wadsworth, pp. 70–81.

McIntyre, Robert S. 2000. "Return of the Corporate Freeloaders." *American Prospect* (November 20):12.

McIntyre, Robert S. 2001. "On Tax Cuts, Loopholes and Avoidance." *Multinational Monitor* 22 (June):24–29.

McKibben, Bill. 1998. "A Special Moment in History." *Atlantic Monthly* 281 (May):55–78.

McKinley, Donald Gilbert. 1964. *Social Class and Family Life*. Glencoe, IL: Free Press.

McLanahan, Sara and Karen Booth. 1991. "Mother Only Families." In Alan Booth (Ed.), *Contemporary Families: Looking Forward, Looking Back*. Minneapolis: National Council of Family Relations, pp. 405–428.

McLanahan, Sara, and Lynne Casper. 1995. "Growing Diversity and Inequality in the American Family." In Reynolds Farley (Ed.), *The State of the Union, America in the 1990s*. Vol. 2. New York: Russell Sage Foundation, pp. 1–45.

McNamee, Mike. 1998. "Are HMO Users Shortchanged?" *Business Week* (August 10):20.

McPhee, Mike. 2001. "Hart: Media Ignored Terror Study." *Denver Post* (September 19):22A.

McQueen, Anjetta. 2001a. "Health Care Costs Could Double to $2.6 Trillion by 2010." Associated Press (March 12).

McQueen, Anjetta. 2001b. "Abuse Leaps in Nursing Homes." Associated Press (July 31).

Meacham, Jon. 1995. "Defiance in the Sun Belt." *Newsweek* (April 24):33.

Means, Marianne. 1996. "Blatant Bigotry in Name of Christ." *Rocky Mountain News* (June 15):56A.

Meddis, Sam Vincent. 1993a. "In Twin Cities, A Tale of Two Standards." *USA Today* (July 26):6A.

Memmott, Mark. 2001. "Report: Poor Nations Need Help with Debts." *USA Today* (April 30):3B.

Mendels, Pamela. 2000. "Crumbling Schools Have Trouble Getting Online." *New York Times* (February 23). Online. Available: http://www.nytimes.com/library/tech/yr/mo/cyber/education/23education. html.

Merton, Robert K. 1957. *Social Theory and Social Structure*, 2nd ed. Glencoe, IL: Free Press.

Messina-Boyer, Chris. 1999. "Women Minority Network Reporters Still Struggling with Visibility." *Media Report to Women: Covering All the Issues Concerning Women and Media* 27 (2):1–3.

Messner, Michael A. 1992. *Power at Play: Sports and the Problem of Masculinity*. Boston: Beacon.

Messner, Michael A. 1996. "Studying Up on Sex." *Sociology of Sport Journal* 13:221–237.

Meyer, Tara. 1997. "New AIDS Cases Show Dramatic Decline." Associated Press (September 19).

Meyerson, Harold. 1998. "Why Liberalism Fled the City . . . and How It Might Come Back." *American Prospect* 37 (March/ April):46–55.

Milchen, Jeff, and Jonathan Power. 2001. "Why Is Killing for Capital Not a Capital Crime?" *Progressive Populist* (July 15):9.

Miles, Robert. 1989. *Racism*. New York: Tavistock.

Miles, Rosalind. 1988. *A Women's History of the World*. London: Joseph.

Miller, Casey, and Kate Swift. 1980. *The Handbook of Nonsexist Writing*. New York: Lippincott and Crowell.

Miller, David. 1991. "A Vision of Market Socialism." *Dissent* 38 (Summer):406–414.

Miller, Jerome G. 1996. *Search and Destroy: African-American Males in the Criminal Justice System*. New York: Cambridge University Press.

Miller, Juanita E. 2000. "The Working Poor." Ohio State University Extension Fact Sheet. Online. Available: http://www. ag.ohio-state.edu/ohioline/hyg-fact/5000/5703.html.

Mills, C. Wright. 1962. In Irving Louis Horowitz (Ed.), *Power, Politics, and People: The Collected Essays of C. Wright Mills*. New York: Ballantine Books, pp. 395–402.

Miringoff, Marc, and Marque-Luisa Miringoff. 1999. *The Social Health of the Nation*. New York: Oxford University Press.

Mishel, Lawrence, Jared Bernstein, and John Schmitt. 1998. "A Boom for Whom? The State of Working America 1998–99." *Progressive Populist* 4 (October):1,12–13.

Mishel, Lawence, Jared Bernstein, and John Schmitt. 2000. *The State of Working America: 2000/2001*. Ithaca, NY: Cornell University Press.

Mitchell, Alanna. 1997. "Census Reveals Changing Face." *Toronto Globe and Mail* (November 5):1A,10A.

Mitchell, Linda M., and Amy Buchele-Ash. 2000. "Abuse and Neglect of Individuals with Disabilities." *Journal of Disability Policy Studies* 10(2): 225–243.

Moberg, David. 1995. "Cutting Corporate Aid." *In These Times* (April 17):24–25.

Moberg, David. 1996. "The New Union Label." *Nation* (April 1):11–19.

Moberg, David. 2001. "Bush's Energy Deficiency." *In These Times* (June 11):14–15.

Mokhiber, Russell. 1999. "Crime Wave! The Top 100 Corporate Criminals of the 1990s." *Multinational Monitor* (July/August):9–29.

Mokhiber, Russell, and Robert Weissman. 1999. "The 100 Corporate Criminals." *Progressive Populist* 5 (October):20.

Monthly Forum for Women in Higher Education. 1995. "Women College Presidents." *Monthly Forum for Women in Higher Education* 1 (December):9.

Moon, Marilyn, and Joanna Silberner. 1998. "What About Health Care for the Uninsured?" *Washington Post National Weekly Edition* (July 6):26.

Moore, Joan W., and Raquel Pinderhughes (Eds.). 1994. *In the Barrios: Latinos and the Underclass Debate*. New York: Russell Sage Foundation.

Morales, Edward. 1990. "Ethnic Minority Families and Minority Gays and Lesbians." In Fredrick W. Bozett and Marvin B. Sussman (Eds.), *Homosexuality and Family Relations*. New York: Harrington Park Press, pp. 217–239.

Morgan, Patricia A. 1978. "The Legislation of Drug Law: Economic Crisis and Social Control." *Journal of Drug Issues* 8 (Winter):53–62.

Morganthau, Tom. 1995. "The View from the Far Right." *Newsweek* (May 1):36–39.

Morin, Richard. 1998. "Income Gap Quickly Begets Geographical Chasm." *Denver Post* (January 29):25A, 26A.

Morris, Jenny. 1991. *Pride against Prejudice*. London: Women's Press.

Moynihan, Daniel P. 1988. "Our Poorest Citizens—Children." *Focus* 11 (Spring):5–6.

Multinational Monitor. 1997a. "The Great Digital Giveaway." Vol. 18 (May):5.

Multinational Monitor. 1997b. "Nike: Swooshes and Sweatshops." Vol. 18 (December):13–14.

Multinational Monitor. 2000. "What Is Society Willing to Spend on Human Beings?" Vol. 21 (November):5.

Multinational Monitor. 2001. "The Case Against GE." Vol. 22 (July/August): entire issue.

Murdoch, William M. 1980. *The Poverty of Nations: The Political Economy of Hunger and Population*. Baltimore: Johns Hopkins University Press.

Murdoch, William M. 1981. "Hungry Millions in World That Could Feed All." *Los Angeles Times* (October 18):part 1, p. 3.

Murdock, Joyce, and Deb Price. 2001. *Courting Justice: Gay Men and Lesbians v. the Supreme Court*. New York: Basic Books.

Murphy, Cait. 2000. "Are the Rich Cleaning Up?" *Fortune* (September 4):252–262.

Murphy, Robert F. 1990. *The Body Silent*. New York: W. W. Norton.

Murphy, Robert F. 1995. "Encounters: The Body Silent in America." In B. Instad and S. Reynolds White (Eds.), *Disability and Culture*. Berkeley, CA: University of California Press, pp. 140–157.

Murray, Charles. 1984. *Losing Ground*. New York: Basic Books.

Muwakkil, Salim. 1994. "Dangerous Curve." *In These Times* (November 28):22–24.

Muwakkil, Salim. 1998a. "Movin' on Apart." *In These Times* (March 22):11–12.

Muwakkil, Salim. 1998b. "Real Minority, Media Majority: TV News Needs to Root Out Stereotypes about Blacks and Crime." *In These Times* (June 28):18–19.

Mydans, Seth. 1991. "Vote in a 'Melting Pot' of Los Angeles May Be Mirror of California's Future." *New York Times* (June 2):16.

Myrdal, Gunnar. 1944. *An American Dilemma*. New York: Pantheon Books.

Nadelman, Ethan A. 2001. "An Unwinnable War on Drugs." *New York Times* (April 26). Online. Available: http://www.nytimes.com/2001/04/26/opinion/26NADE.html.

Nader, Ralph. 1970, 1977. Speeches at Colorado State University in May 1970 and November 1977.

Nader, Ralph. 2001a. "Corporate Welfare Spoils." *Nation* (May 7):7,26.

Nader, Ralph. 2001b. "What About the Uninsured?" *Progressive Populist* (August 1):9.

Nakashima, Ellen. 2000. "Student Loan Default Rate Plummets to 6.9 Percent." *Denver Post* (October 2):12A.

Naples, Nancy A. 1998. "Women's Community Activism and Feminist Action Research." In Nancy A. Naples (Ed.), *Community Activism and Feminist Politics*. New York: Routledge, pp. 1–27.

Nation. 1996. "In Fact. . . ." (January 1):5.

Nation. 2001a. "Flunking the Tests." (July 9):4.

Nation. 2001b. "Energy Imperialism." (July 23):5.

Nation. 2001c. "Hitting Terrorism's Roots." (October 22):3.

National Center on Elder Abuse. 1998. *National Elder Abuse Incidence Study*. Washington, DC: American Public Health Services Association.

National Council of LaRaza. 1999. "The Mainstreaming of Hate: A Report on Latinos and Harassment, Hate Violence, and Law Enforcement Abuse in the '90s." (July). Washington, DC.

Natural Resources Defense Council, the Union of Concerned Scientists, and the U.S. Public Interest Research

Group. 1999. "Carbon Kingpins: The Changing Face of the Greenhouse Gas Industries." *Multinational Monitor* 20 (June): 9–14.

Navarro, Vicente. 1991. "Class and Race: Life and Death Situations." *Monthly Review* 43 (September):1–13.

Nazario, Sonia. 1999. "Mexican-American Society Begins to Face Alcohol's Toll." *Denver Post* (April 24):38A.

Neergaard, Lauran. 2000. "Alzheimer's Alarm Sounded." Associated Press (July 10).

Neilson, Joyce McCarl. 1990. *Sex and Gender in Society,* 2nd ed. Prospect Heights, IL: Waveland Press.

Nelson, Lars-Erik. 1994. "Ending Corporate Welfare: A Worthy Goal." *Denver Post* (November 29):9B.

Nelson, Mariah Burton. 1999. "Learning What 'Team' Really Means," *Newsweek* (July 19):55.

Nesbitt, Paula J. 1996. "Women Clergy." In Paula J. Dubeck and Kathryn Borman (Eds.), *Women and Work: A Handbook.* New York: Garland Publishing, pp. 181–184.

Nettler, Gwynn. 1976. *Social Concerns.* New York: McGraw-Hill.

Neubeck, Kenneth J., and Davita Silfen Glalsberg. 1996. *Sociology: A Critical Approach.* New York: McGraw-Hill.

Neugarten, Bernice L. 1980. "Grow Old along with Me! The Best Is Yet to Be." In Beth Hess (Ed.), *Growing Old in America.* New Brunswick, NJ: Transaction Books, pp. 180–197.

Newman, Cathy. 2000. "Race Divides the Fortunes of Older Americans." *Denver Post* (August 10):3A.

Newman, Katherine. 1996. "Working Poor, Working Hard." *Nation* (July 29/August 5):20–23.

Newman, Katherine S. 1988. *Falling from Grace: The Experience of Downward Mobility in the American Middle Class.* New York: Free Press.

New Party News. 1997. "New Party Principles." Vol. 6 (Fall):12.

News Report. 1989. "Slow Economy, Discrimination Block Opportunity for Blacks." (August/September):2–6.

Newsweek. 1997. "A Nation of Drivers." (August 11):15.

Newton, Christopher. 2000. "A Gap in Compensation." Associated Press (June 3).

New York Times. 2000a. "Drug Laws That Destroy Lives." (May 24). Online. Available: http://www. nytimes. com/yr/mo/day/editorial/24wed1.html.

New York Times. 2000b. "Drug Laws that Misfired." (June 5). Online. Available: http://www.nytimes.com/yr/mo/day/editorial/05mon1.html.

New York Times. 2000c. "Modern-Day Slavery." (September 9). Online. Available: http://www.nytimes.com/2000/09/09/opinion/09SAT2.html.

New York Times. 2000d. "Expanding Debt Relief." (October 1). Online. Available: http://www.nytimes.com/2000/10/01/opinion/01SUN3.html.

New York Times. 2000e. "A Fix for the Broadcast Giveaway." (October 11). Online. Available: http://nytimes.com/2000/10/11/opinion/ 11WED2.html.

New York Times. 2001a. "Remaking the Military." (September 30). Online. Available: http://www.nytimes.com/2001/09/30/opinion/30SUN1.html.

New York Times. 2001b. "A Flawed Stimulus Plan." (October 6). Online. Available: http://www.nytimes.com/2001/10/06/opinion/06SAT2.html.

Noguera, Pedro A., and Antivi Akom. 2000. "Disparities Demystified." *Nation* (June 5):29–31.

Nore, Gordon W. E. 1991. "An Interview with Jonathan Kozol." *Progressive* 55 (December):34–36.

Norwegian Parliament. 1991. "Human Rights." Oslo, Norway: The Royal Ministry of Foreign Affairs.

Novak, Viveca. 1991. "Why Workers Can't Win." *Common Cause Magazine* 17 (July/August):28–32.

Oakes, Jeannie. 1985. *Keeping Track: How Schools Structure Inequality.* New Haven: Yale University Press.

Obeidallah, Dawn A., Susan A. McHale, and Ranier K. Silbereisen. 1996. "Gender Role Socialization and Adolescents' Reports of Depression: Why Some Girls and Not Others?" *Journal of Youth and Adolescence* 25 (6):775–785.

O'Donnell, Jayne. 2000. "Suffering in Silence." *USA Today* (April 3):1B–2B.

O'Hare, William P. 1992. "America's Minorities: The Demographics of Diversity." *Population Bulletin* 47 (December): entire issue.

O'Hare, William P. 1993. "Diversity Trend: More Minorities Looking Less Alike." *Population Today* 21 (April):1–2.

O'Hare, William P. 1996. "A New Look at Poverty in America." *Population Bulletin* 51 (September): entire issue.

O'Hare, William P. 1998. "Managing Multiple Race Data." *American Demographics* (April):1–4.

O'Kelly, Charlotte. 1980. *Women and Men in Society.* New York: Van Nostrand.

Oliver, Mike. 1996a. *Understanding Disability: From Theory to Practice.* New York: St. Martin's Press.

Oliver, Mike. 1996b. "A Sociology of Disability or a Disablist Sociology?" In Len Barton (Ed.), *Disability and Society: Emerging Issues and Insights.* New York: Longman, pp. 18–42.

Oliver, Melvin L., and Thomas M. Shapiro. 1995. *Black Wealth/White Wealth: A New Perspective on Racial Equality.* New York: Routledge.

Omi, Michael, and Howard Winant. 1986. *Racial Formation in the United States.* London: Routledge & Kegan Paul.

Omi, Michael, and Howard Winant. 1994. *Racial Formation in the United States,* 2nd ed. New York: Routledge & Kegan Paul.

Orenstein, J. B. 2001. "America's Hospital Emergency." *Washington Post National Weekly Edition* (April 30):21.

Orfield, Gary. 1999. "The Resegregation of Our Nation's Schools." *Civil Rights Journal* 4 (Fall):8–12.

Orfield, Gary, and Johanna Wald. 2000. "Testing, Testing." *Nation* (June 5):38–40.

Ortner, Sherry B. 1974. "Is Female to Male as Nature Is to Culture?" In Michelle Zimbalist Rosaldo and Louise Lamphere (Eds.), *Woman, Culture, and Society.* Stanford, CA: Stanford University Press. pp. 66–88.

Osmond, Marie Withers, and Barrie Thorne. 1993. "Feminist Theories: The Social Construction of Gender in Families and Society." In P. G. Boss, W. J. Doherty, R. LaRossa, W. R. Schumm, and S. K. Steinmetz (Eds.), *Sourcebook of Family Theories and Methods: A Contextual Approach.* New York: Plenum Press, pp. 591–623.

Outtz, Janice Hamilton. 1995. "Higher Education and the New Demographic Reality." *Educational Record* 76 (Spring/Summer):65–69.

Painter, Kim. 1992. "NIH Offers 'Promise' to Women." *USA Today* (September 22):A1.

Parenti, Michael. 1978. *Power and the Powerless,* 2nd ed. New York: St. Martin's Press.

Parenti, Michael. 1980. *Democracy for the Few,* 3rd ed. New York: St. Martin's Press.

Parenti, Michael. 1983. *Democracy for the Few,* 4th ed. New York: St. Martin's Press.

Parenti, Michael. 1988. *Democracy for the Few,* 5th ed. New York: St. Martin's Press.

Parenti, Michael. 1995a. *Against Empire.* San Francisco: City Lights Books.

Parenti, Michael. 1995b. *Democracy for the Few,* 6th ed. New York: St. Martin's Press.

Parker, Laura. 2001. "U.S. Hispanics' Youth Assures More Growth." *USA Today* (May 10):3A.

Parlee, Mary Brown. 1979. "Conversational Politics." *Psychology Today* 12 (May):48–56.

Parrish, Geov. 2001. "Fanning the Flames of Terrorism." *AlterNet* (September 20). Online. Available: www.alternet.org/story.html?StoryID=11547.

Pascale, Celine-Marie. 1995. "Normalizing Poverty." *Z Magazine* 8 (June):38–42.

Pascual, Cathy. 2000. "Cervical Cancer's Ethnic Tie." *Denver Post* (October 14):33A.

Patton, Cindy. 1985. *Sex and Germs: The Politics of AIDS.* Boston: South End press.

Paulson, Michael. 2000. "More Women Embracing the Study of Jewish Faith." *Boston Globe* (March 13):1B,5B.

Pear, Robert. 1993. "Poverty Is Cited as Divorce Factor." *New York Times.* (January 15):A6.

Pear, Robert. 2001. "Spending on Prescription Drugs Increase by Almost 19 Percent." *New York Times* (May 8). Online. Available: http://www.nytimes.com/2001/05/08/national/08DRUG.html.

Pearce, Diana. 1978. "The Feminization of Poverty: Women, Work, and Welfare." *Urban Change Review* 2 (February):24–36.

Pearl, Arthur. 1977. "Public Policy or Crime: Which Is Worse?" *Social Policy* 7 (January/February):47–54.

Pedersen, Daniel, Vern E. Smith, and Jerry Adler. 1999. "Sprawling, Sprawling. . . ." *Newsweek* (July 19):24–27.

Pelka, Fred. 1997. *The Disability Rights Movement.* Santa Barbara, CA: ABC-CLIO.

Pellow, David N. 2000. "Environmental Inequality Formation." *American Behavioral Scientist* 43 (January):581–601.

Peplau, Letitia Ann. 1981. "What Homosexuals Want." *Psychology Today* 15 (March):28–38.

Peters, Peter J. 1992. *Intolerance of, Discrimination against, and the Death Penalty for Homosexuals as Prescribed in the Bible.* LaPorte, CO: Scriptures for America.

Peters, Tom. 2000. "What Will We Do for Work?" *Time* (May 22):68–71.

Peterson, Karen S. 1994. "Abused Women: Afraid to Stay, Afraid to Leave." *USA Today* (January 18):D6.

Peterson, Linda, and Elaine Enarson. 1974. "Blaming the Victim in the Sociology of Women: On the Misuse of the Concept of Socialization." Paper presented at the Pacific Sociological Association, San Jose, CA, March.

Peterson, Peter. 1999. "The Global Aging Crisis." *Denver Post* (February 7):1J–2J.

Peterson, Richard R. 1996. "A Re-Evaluation of the Economic Consequences of Divorce." *American Sociological Review* 61 (June):528–536.

Peyser, Marc. 1999. "Home of the Gray." *Newsweek* (March 1):50–53.

Philippus, M. J. 1989. "Hispanics Fail Tests Because Tests Fail Them." *Rocky Mountain News* (June 15):59.

Phillips, Kevin. 1995. "Today's 'Gingrichomics' Echoes GOP Eras of Old." *Christian Science Monitor* (December 22):18.

Pillemer, Karl A. 1993. "Abuse Is Caused by the Deviance and Dependence of Abusive Caregivers." In Richard J. Gelles and Donileen R. Loseke (Eds.), *Current Controversies on Family Violence.* Newbury Park, CA: Sage, pp. 237–249.

Pitt, Leon. 1996. "Chicago Children among Poorest: Poverty Rate Ranked 2nd Worst in National Study." *Chicago Sun-Times* (December 11):7.

Piven, Frances Fox. 1996. "Welfare and the Transformation of Electoral Politics." *Dissent* 43 (Fall):61–67.

Piven, Frances Fox, and Richard A. Cloward. 1971. *Regulating the Poor.* New York: Random House.

Pleck, Joseph H. 1981. "Prisoners of Manliness." *Psychology Today* 15 (September):68–83.

Pollak, Richard. 2001. "Is GE Mightier than the Hudson?" *Nation* (May 28):11–18.

Pollard, Kelvin M. and William P. O'Hare. 1999. "America's Racial and Ethnic Minorities," *Population Bulletin,* Vol. 54, No. 3 (September). Washington, DC: Population Reference Bureau.

Pollitt, Katha. 2001. "Childcare Scare." *Nation* (May 14):10.

Pomeroy, W. 1965. "Why We Tolerate Lesbians." *Sexology* (May):652–654.

Population Reference Bureau. 1998. *1998 World Population Data Sheet.* Washington, DC: Population Reference Bureau.

Population Reference Bureau. 1999. "America's Diversity: on the Edge of Two Centuries." *Reports on America* 1 (May): entire issue.

Population Reference Bureau. 2000. "Largest Group Ever Now Entering Adulthood." *Population Today* 28 (August/September):8.

Population Today. 1998a. "Census Race and Ethnic Categories Retooled." Vol. 26 (January):4.

Population Today. 1998b. "More Babies Facing Health Risks Identified." Vol. 26 (March):5.

Population Today. 2000. "Unequal Justice in U.S. Courts, Prisons." Vol. 28 (July):5.

Population Today. 2001. "Median Net Worth of U.S. Households by Race and Ethnicity." Vol. 29 (April):4.

Portes, Alejandro, and Min Zhou. 1993. "The New Second Generation: Segmented Assimilation and Its Variants." *Annals of the American Academy of Political and Social Science* 530:74–96.

Postel, Sandra. 1994. "Carry Capacity: Earth's Bottom Line." *Challenge* 37 (March/April):4–12.

Potok, Mark. 2000. "The Year in Hate." *Phi Kappa Phi Journal* 80 (Spring):32–36.

Power, Carla. 1998. "When Women Are the Enemy." *Newsweek* (August 3):37–38.

Prell, Ed. 1995. "What's Happening to America?" *New Priorities Voice* (Spring):1–2.

Press, Eyal, and Jennifer Washburn. 2000. "Neglect for Sale." *American Prospect* (May 8):22–29.

Price, Sharon J., and Patrick C. McKenry. 1988. *Divorce.* Beverly Hills, CA: Sage.

Priest, Dana. 1998. "The Impact of the 'Don't Ask, Don't Tell' Policy." *Washington Post National Weekly Edition* (February 1):35.

Progressive. 1980. "Out of the Bottle." Vol. 44 (August):8.

Progressive. 1999. "A Sane Drug Policy." Vol. 63 (October):8–10.

Pryce-Jones, David. 2001. "Why They Hate Us." *National Review* 53 (October 1):8.

Purdum, Todd S. 2000. "Shift in the Mix Alters the Face of California." *New York Times* (July 4). Online. Available: http://www.nytimes.com/library/national/070400calatin.html.

Pursell, Carroll W., Jr. (Ed.). 1972. *The Military Industrial Complex*. New York: Harper & Row.

Purvis, Andrew. 1990. "Research for Men Only." *Time* (March 5):59–60.

Putnam, Robert D. 2000. *Bowling Alone: The Collapse and Revival of American Community*. New York: Simon and Schuster.

Quinney, Richard. 1970. *The Social Reality of Crime.* Boston: Little, Brown.

Rachlin, Jill. 1989. "The Label That Sticks." *U.S. News & World Report* (July 3):51–52.

Ragavan, Chitra. 2001. "Cracking Down on Ecstasy." *U.S. News & World Report* (February 5):14–17.

Rainwater, Lee, and Timothy M. Smeeding. 1995. "Doing Poorly: The Real Income of American Children in Comparative Perspective." Working Paper No. 127, Luxembourg Income Study, Maxwell School of Citizenship and Public Affairs. Syracuse, NY: Syracuse University.

Rapp, Rayna. 1982. "Family and Class in Contemporary America." In Barrie Thorne and Marilyn Yalom (Eds.), *Rethinking the Family: Some Feminist Questions*. New York: Longman, pp. 168–187.

Rasell, Edie. 1993. "A Bad Bargain: Why U.S. Health Care Costs So Much and Covers So Few." *Dollars & Sense* 186 (May):6–8, 21.

Rawlings, Steve. 1995. "Households and Families," *Population Profile of the United States: 1995. Current Population Reports,* Series P1-23-189:28.

Reasons, Charles. 1974. "The Politics of Drugs: An Inquiry in the Sociology of Social Problems." *Sociological Quarterly* 15 (Summer):381–404.

Reed, Adolph, Jr. 1990. "The Underclass as Myth and Symbol: The Poverty of Discourse about Poverty." *Radical America* 24 (January/March):21–40.

Reed, Adolph, Jr. 1994. "Looking Backward." *Nation* (November 28):654–662.

Reeves, Richard. 1988. "The Developing New Politics of a Rapidly Aging America." *Denver Post* (December 18):3H.

Reich, Robert B. 1998. "Broken Faith: Why We Need to Renew the Social Compact." *Nation* (February 16):11–17.

Reich, Robert B. 2000a. "The Great Divide." *American Prospect* (May 8):56.

Reich, Robert B. 2000b. "What's the Difference?" *American Prospect* (August 28):64.

Reich, Robert B. 2000c. "How Selective Colleges Heighten Inequality." *Chronicle of Higher Education* (September 15):B7–B10.

Reich, Robert B. 2000d. "The Liverwurst Solution." *American Prospect* (November 6):56.

Reich, Robert B. 2001a. "A Proper Global Agenda." *American Prospect* (September 24):48.

Reich, Robert B. 2001b. "A Stimulus Right Now, Aimed at Lower-Wage Workers." AlterNet (October 1). On-line. Available:www.alternet.org/story.html?StoryID=11611.

Reiman, Jeffrey H. 2001. *The Rich Get Richer and the Poor Get Prison: Ideology, Class, and Criminal Justice,* 6th ed. Boston: Allyn & Bacon.

Reisberg, Leo. 1999. "Average Tuition and Fees at College Rose Less Than 5% This Year." *Chronicle of Higher Education* (October 15):A52.

Renner, Michael. 1995. "Budgeting for Disarmament." In Lester R. Brown et al. (Eds.), *State of the World.* New York: W. W. Norton, pp. 1150–1169.

Rennison, Callie Mare, and Sarah Wechans. 2000. "Intimate Partner Violence." *Bureau of Justice Statistics* (NCJ 178247).

Renzetti, Claire M., and Daniel J. Curran. 1999. *Women, Men, and Society,* 4th ed. Boston: Allyn & Bacon.

Reskin, Barbara, and Irene Padavic. 1994. *Women and Men at Work.* Thousand Oaks, CA: Pine Forge Press.

Reskin, Barbara F., and Patricia A. Roos. 1990. *Job Queues, Gender Queues*. Philadelphia: Temple University Press.

Reuss, Alejandro. 2001. "Cause of Death: Inequality." *Dollars & Sense,* No. 235 (May/June):10–12.

Richardson, Laurel Walum. 1981. *The Dynamics of Sex and Gender,* 2nd ed. Boston: Houghton Mifflin.

Riche, Martha Farnsworth. 2000. "America's Diversity and Growth: Signposts for the 21st Century." *Population Bulletin* 55 (June): entire issue.

Richmond, Julius B. 1994. "Give Children an Earlier Head Start." *USA Today* (April 12):13A.

Richmond-Abbott, Marie. 1992. *Masculine and Feminine: Sex Roles over the Life Cycle,* 2nd ed. New York: McGraw-Hill.

Risen, James. 2000. "Secrets of History: The CIA in Iran." *New York Times* (April 16). Online. Available: http://www.nytimes.com/library/world/mideast/041600iran-cia- index.html.

Risman, Barbara J. 1998. *Gender Vertigo*. New Haven, CT: Yale University Press.

Risman, Barbara J., and Donald Tomaskovic-Devey. 1998. "Editors Note." *Contemporary Sociology* 27 (March):vii–viii.

Ritter, John. 2000. "Gay Students Stake Their Ground." *USA Today* (January 18):1A–2A.

Ritzer, George. 1996. *The McDonaldization of Society,* rev. ed. Thousand Oaks, CA: Pine Forge Press.

Robinson, Simon, and Nancy Palus. 2001. "An Awful Human Trade." *Time* (April 30):40–41.

Rocky Mountain News. 1992. "Vatican: There Is No 'Right' to Be Gay." (July 24):3.

Roeder, David. 1997. "Study: '95 Mortgage Loans to Low-Income Groups Slip." *Chicago Sun-Times* (February 13):56.

Rogers, Joel. 1998. "Turning to the Cities: A Metropolitian Agenda." *In These Times* (October 18):14–17.

Rogers, Susan Carol. 1978. "Women's Place: A Critical Review of Anthropological Theory." *Comparative Studies in Society and History* 20 (1):123–162.

Romero, Mary. 1997. "Introduction." In Mary Romero, Pierrette Hondagneu-Sotelo, and Vilma Ortiz (Eds.), *Challenging Fronteras: Structuring Latina and Latino Lives in the U.S.* New York: Routledge, pp. xii–xix.

Ronai, Carol Rambo, Barbara A. Zsembik, and Joe R. Feagin. 1997. "Introduction." In Carol Rambo Ronai, Barbara A. Zsembik, and Joe R. Feagin (Eds.), *Everyday Sexism in the Third Millennium*. New York: Routledge, pp. 1–11.

Ropeik, David. 2001. "Conquer Terrorists" Most Powerful Weapon: Fear." *USA Today* (September 27):15A.

Rosaldo, Michelle Zimbalist. 1974. "Women, Culture, and Society: A Theoretical Overview." In Michelle Zimbalist Rosaldo and L. Lamphere (Eds.), *Woman, Culture, and Society*. Stanford, CA: Stanford University Press, pp. 17–42.

Rosaldo, Michelle Zimbalist. 1980. "The Use and Abuse of Anthropology." *Signs* 5 (Spring):389–417.

Rosenbaum, David E. 2000. "Universal Health Care Working in Vermont." *Denver Post* (June 18):2A,11A.

Rosenbaum, David E. 2001. "Ruling on Disability Rights Is a Blow, Advocates Say." *New York Times* (February 22). Online. Available: http://www.nytimes.com/2001/02/22/national/22REAC.html.

Rosenberg, Eric, and Stewart M. Powell. 2000. "Military Finds Widespread Harassment of Gays." *Rocky Mountain News* (March 25):41A.

Rosenblum, Karen D., and Toni-Michelle C. Travis. 1996. "Introduction." In Karen E. Rosenblum and Toni-Michelle C. Travis (Eds.), *The Meaning of Difference*. New York: McGraw-Hill, pp. 1–34.

Rosenthal, Robert, and Lenore Jacobson. 1968. *Pygmalion in the Classroom: Teacher Expectations and Pupils' Intellectual Development*. New York: Holt, Rinehart & Winston.

Ross, Ellen, and Rayna Rapp. 1983. "Sex and Society: A Research Note from Social History and Anthropology." In Ann Snitow, Christine Stansell, and Sharon Thompson (Eds.), *Power of Desire: The Politics of Sexuality*. New York: Monthly Review Press, pp. 51–73.

Rossant, John. 2001a. "The Roots of Resentment." *Business Week* (October 1):46–47.

Rossant, John. 2001b. "A Prince with Divided Loyalties." *Business Week* (October 15):64.

Rubenstein, Ed. 1995. "The Economics of Crime." *Vital Speeches of the Day* 62 (October 15):19–21.

Rubin, Rita. 1998. "Maternal Mortality Too High." *USA Today* (May 19):8D.

Rubin, Rita. 2000. "WHO's Assessment: U.S. Health System Is Inefficient." *USA Today* (June 21):10D.

Rubin, Rita. 2001. "Female Smoking Deaths Double." *USA Today* (March 28):1A.

Rumsfeld, Donald H. 2001. "A New Kind of War." *New York Times* (September 27). Online. Available: http://www.nytimes.com/2001/09/27/opinion/ 27RUMS.html.

Russell, Marta. 1998. *Beyond Ramps: Disability at the End of the Social Contract*. Monroe, ME: Common Courage Press.

Russell, Marta. 2000. "The Political Economy of Disablement." *Dollars & Sense*, No. 231 (September/ October):13–15,48–49.

Russell, Stephen T., and Kara Joyner. 1998. "Adolescent Sexual Orientation and Suicide Risk." Paper presented at the meetings of the American Sociological Association, San Francisco (August).

Ryan, Joanna. 1972. "IQ—The Illusion of Objectivity." In Ken Richardson and David Spears (Eds.), *Race and Intelligence*. Baltimore: Penguin.

Ryan, William. 1970. "Is Banfield Serious?" *Social Policy* 1 (November/December):74–76.

Ryan, William. 1972. "Postscript: A Call to Action." *Social Policy* 3 (May/June):54.

Ryan, William. 1976. *Blaming the Victim*, rev. ed. New York: Random House (Vintage).

Sack, Kevin. 2001. "AIDS Epidemic Takes Toll on Black Women." *New York Times* (July 3). Online. Available: http://www.nytimes.com/2001/07/03/health/03AIDS.html.

Sacks, Karen. 1974. "Engels Revisited: Women, the Organization of Production, and Private Property." In Michelle Zimbalist Rosaldo and Louise Lamphere (Eds.), *Woman, Culture, and Society*. Stanford, CA: Stanford University Press, pp. 207–222.

Sadker, Myra, and David Sadker. 1994. *Failing at Fairness. How America's Schools Cheat Girls*. New York: Scribner.

Salvatore, Nick. 1992. "The Decline of Labor." *Dissent* 39 (Winter):86–92.

Samuelson, Robert J. 1984. "We're Not a National Laundromat." *Newsweek* (July 9):61.

Sandefur, Gary D. 1990. "Census Volume on the American Indian." *Social Science Research Council Items* 44 (June/September):37–40.

Sanders, Bernard. 1994. "Whither American Democracy." *Los Angeles Times* (January 16):Bl.

Sanders, Bernard. 1998a. "The International Monetary Fund Is Hurting You." *Z Magazine* 11 (July/August):94–96.

Sanders, Bernard. 1998b. "A Modest Success for Campaign Finance Reform." *Sanders Scoop*. Sanders for Congress newsletter. (Fall):1–2.

Sanders, Bernard. 2000. "The 'Booming' Economy." *Sanders Scoop*. Sanders for Congress newsletter (Spring):3.

Sapiro, Virginia. 1999. *Women in American Society*, 4th ed. Mountain View, CA: Mayfield.

Sarasohn, David. 1997. "Hunger on Main St." *Nation* (December 8):13–18.

Schafer, Walter E., Carol Olexa, and Kenneth Polk. 1972. "Programmed for Social Class." In Kenneth Polk and Walter E. Schafer (Eds.), *Schools and Delinquency*. Upper Saddle River, NJ: Prentice-Hall.

Scher, Abby. 2000. "Corporate Welfare: Pork for All." *Dollars & Sense*, No. 229 (May/June):11.

Scher, Abby. 2001. "Access Denied: Immigrants and Health Care." *Dollars & Sense*, No. 235 (May/June):8.

Schlosser, Eric. 2001. *Fast Food Nation: The Dark Side of the All-American Meal*. Boston: Houghton Mifflin.

Schmit, Julie. 1998. "Dirty Secrets: Exposing the Dark Side of a 'Clean' Industry." *USA Today* (January 12):1B,2B.

Schmitt, Eric. 2001. "Analysis of Census Finds Segregation Along with Diversity." *New York Times* (April 4). Online. Available: http://www.nytimes.com/2001/04/04/national/04CENS.html.

Schmoke, Kurt L. 1992. "Foreword." In S. Staley (Ed.), *Drug Policy and the Decline of American Cities*. New Brunswick, NJ: Transaction Publishers, pp. xiii–xvi.

Schneider, David M., and Raymond T. Smith. 1973. *Class Differences and Sex Roles in American Family and Kinship Structure*. Upper Saddle River, NJ: Prentice-Hall.

Schoettler, Gail. 2000. "You Can't Buy Human Decency." *Denver Post* (October 1):2L.

Schoettler, Gail. 2001. "Learning from Tragedy." *Denver Post* (September 16):4E.

Schorr, Lisbeth B., with Daniel Schorr. 1988. *Within Our Reach: Breaking the Cycle of Disadvantage*. New York: Doubleday Anchor Press.

Schouten, Fredreka, and Carl Weiser. 1999. "Local Lawmakers Leaning on Lobbyists." *USA Today* (November 16):11A.

Schumpeter, Joseph. 1950. *Capitalism, Socialism, and Democracy*, 3rd ed. New York: Harpers.

Schur, Edwin. 1971. *Labeling Deviant Behavior: Its Sociological Implications*. New York: Harper & Row.

Schur, Edwin. 1973. *Radical Nonintervention: Rethinking the Delinquency Problem*. Upper Saddle River, NJ: Prentice-Hall.

Schur, Edwin M. 1965. *Crimes without Victims*. Upper Saddle River, NJ: Prentice-Hall.

Schwarz, John E., and Thomas J. Volgy. 1993. "Above the Poverty Line—But Poor." *Nation* (February 15):191–192.

Scotch, Richard K. 1989. "Politics and Policy in the History of the Disability Rights Movement." *Millbank Quarterly* 67, Suppl. 2, Pt. 2:380–400.

Scott, Katherine Hutt. 2001. "Factors Conspire to Keep Poor Students Out of College." *USA Today* (March 5):8D.

Seelye, Katharine Q. 1994. "Lobbyists Are the Loudest in the Health Care Debate." *New York Times* (August 16):A1,A10.

Seltzer, Judith. 1994. "Consequences of Marital Dissolution for Children." *Annual Review of Sociology* 20:235–266.

Sen, Amartya. 1999. *Development as Freedom.* New York: Knopf.

Sen, Amartya. 2000. "Population and Gender Equity." *Nation* (July 24):16–18.

Shakespeare, Tom. 1996. "Power and Prejudice: Issues of Gender, Sexuality, and Disability." In Len Barton (Ed.), *Disability and Society: Emerging Issues and Insights,* New York: Longman, pp. 191–214.

Shalala, Donna E. 1997. "Great Strides for Women." *USA Today* (August 19):12A.

Shanahan, Michael, and Miles Benson. 1995. "Civil Liberties Threatened by Bombing." *Rocky Mountain News* (April 28):48A.

Shanker, Albert. 1990. "The French System of Child Care: A Welcome for Every Child." *New York Times* (November 11):E7.

Shanker, Albert. 1991. "Dumbing Down America." *New York Times* (January 27):E7.

Shanker, Albert. 1992a. "Children in Crisis." *New York Times* (February 16):E9.

Shanker, Albert. 1992b. "How Far Have We Come?" *New York Times* (August 16):E9.

Shanker, Albert. 1995. "In Defense of Government." *New York Times* (November 5):E7.

Shapiro, Isaac, and Robert Greenstein. 1999. "The Widening Income Gulf." Center on Budget and Policy Priorities. Online. Available: http://www.cbpp.org/9-4-99tax-rep.htm.

Shapiro, Joseph P. 1995. "An Epidemic of Fear and Loathing." *U.S. News & World Report* (May 8):37–44.

Shapiro, Judith. 1981. "Anthropology and the Study of Gender." In Elizabeth Langland and Walter Gove (Eds.), A *Feminist Perspective in the Academy.* Chicago: University of Chicago Press, pp. 110–129.

Sharma, O. P. 2001. "2001 Census Results Mixed for India's Women and Girls." *Population Today* 29 (May/June):1–3.

Sharn, Lori. 1997. "Clergy Still Tough Career for Women." *USA Today* (July 7):1A,2A.

Sheed, Wilfrid. 1996. "Gay in the Eyes of God." *Time* (May 27):44.

Shelden, Randall G. 2001. *Controlling the Dangerous Classes: A Critical Introduction to the History of Criminal Justice.* Boston: Allyn & Bacon.

Sheler, Jeffrey L. 2001. "Of Faith, Fear, and Fanatics." *U.S. News & World Report* (September 24):56–57.

Shenk, Joshua Wolf. 1999a. "America's Altered States." *Harper's Magazine* 298 (May):38–52.

Shenk, Joshua Wolf. 1999b. "An Old City Seeks a New Model: Baltimore Moves Toward 'Medicalization.'" *Nation* (September 20):22–28.

Shiller, Brendan. 1997. "Loop to Get $300 Million Subsidy." *Streetwise* (February 16):8.

Shreve, Anita. 1984. "The Working Mother as Role Model." *New York Times Magazine* (September 9):43.

Shuit, Douglas P. 1995. "Filling the Void." *Los Angeles Times* (July 27): B2.

Shute, Nancy, Toni Locy, and Douglas Pasternak. 2000. "The Perils of Pills." *U.S. News & World Report* (March 6):45–50.

Sidel, Ruth. 1994. *Battling Bias.* New York: Penguin Books.

Sidel, Ruth. 1996. *Keeping Women and Children Last: America's War on the Poor.* Baltimore: Penguin.

Silberman, Charles E. 1970. *Crisis in the Classroom.* New York: Random House.

Silberner, Joanne. 1990. "Health: Another Gender Gap." *U.S. News & World Report* (September 24):54–55.

Silvers, Anita. 1998. "Formal Justice." In Anita Silvers, David Wasserman, and Mary B. Mahowald (Eds.), *Disability, Difference, Discrimination.* Lanham, MD: Rowman & Littlefield, pp. 13–145.

Silvers, Anita, David Wasserman, and Mary B. Mahowald. 1998. *Disability, Difference, Discrimination Perspectives on Justice in Bioethics and Public Policy.* Lanham, MD: Rowman & Littlefield.

Silverstein, Charles. 1981. *Man to Man: Gay Couples in America.* New York: Morrow.

Simon, David R., and D. Stanley Eitzen. 1993. *Elite Deviance,* 4th ed. Boston: Allyn & Bacon.

Simon, Rita J., Angela J. Scanlan, and Pamela Madell. 1993. "Rabbis and Ministers: Women of the Book and Cloth." *Sociology of Religion* 54 (1):115–122.

Simon, Roger. 1998. "From Cover Story to Urban Initiative: Clinton's Youth Plan." *Chicago Tribune* (July 22):15.

Sklar, Holly. 1992. "Reaffirmative Action." *Z Magazine* 5 (May/June):9–15.

Sklar, Holly. 1995. *Chaos or Community: Seeking Solutions, Not Scapegoats for Bad Economics.* Boston: South End Press.

Sklar, Holly. 1997. "Imagine a Country." *Z Magazine* 10 (July/August):65–71.

Sklar, Holly. 2001. "CEO Ponzi Scheme." Online. Available: http://www.inequality.org/ceopayedit2.html.

Skocpol, Theda. 2000. *The Missing Middle: Working Families and the Future of American Social Policy.* New York: W. W. Norton.

Skolnick, Arlene S. 1997. "Family Trouble: Arlene Skolnick Responds," *American Prospect,* No. 33 (July/ August):16.

Skolnick, Jerome. 1966. *The Politics of Protest.* New York: Ballantine Books.

Skolnick, Jerome. 1994. "Wild Pitch: 'Three Strikes, You're Out' and Other Bad Calls on Crime." *American Prospect* 17 (Spring):30–37.

Skolnick, Jerome, and Elliott Currie. 1973. "Introduction: Approaches to Social Problems." In Jerome Skolnick and Elliott Currie (Eds.), *Crisis in American Institutions,* 2nd ed. Boston: Little, Brown, pp. 1–17.

Slaughter, Jane. 1997. "Doctors Unite: Corporate Medicine and the Surprising Trend of Doctor Unionization." *Multinational Monitor* 18 (November):22–24.

Smeeding, Timothy M., and Peter Gottschalk. 1998. "Cross-National Income Inequality: How Great It Is and What Can We Learn From It?" *Focus.* University of Wisconsin-Madison Institute for Research on Poverty, Vol. 19 (Summer/Fall):15–19.

Smith, Elliot Blair. 2001. "Migrants Flex Muscles Back Home in Mexico." *USA Today* (June 28):9A.

Smith, Stephen G. 2001. "Boarding Schools." *U.S. News & World Report* (May 14):38–42.

Smokes, Saundra. 2000. "Fix Disparities among Our Schools." *USA Today* (April 28):17A.

Smolkin, Rachel. 1999. "Creationist Strategy Evolving." *Rocky Mountain News* (August 14):2A,33A.

Smolowe, Jill. 1997. "Sorry Pardner: Big Tobacco Fesses Up." *Time* (June 30):25–29.

Snider, Mike, Michelle Healy, and Leslie Miller. 1992. "Women Likely to Get Less Pain Medication." *USA Today* (July 27):D6.

Snipp, Matthew. 1996. "The First Americans: American Indians." In Silvia Pedraza and Ruben G. Rumbaut (Eds.), *Origins and Destinies: Immigration, Race, and Ethnicity in America.* Belmont, CA: Wadsworth, pp. 390–403.

Sociologists for Women in Society. 1986. *Facts about Pay Equity* (April): entire issue.

Solow, Robert M. 2000. "Welfare: The Cheapest Country." *New York Review of Books* (March 23):20–24.

South Shore Bank. 1998. *Development Deposits.* Pamphlet. Chicago: South Shore Bank.

Spain, Daphne, and Suzanne M. Bianche. 1996. *Balancing Act.* New York: Russell Sage Foundation.

Spector, Malcolm, and John I. Kitsuse. 1987. *Constructing Social Problems.* Hawthorne, NY: Aldine de Gruyter.

Spector, Michael. 1998. "Birthrate Drop Spurs Fear." *Rocky Mountain News* (July 12):40A.

Spielman, Fran. 1997. "Privatization Creates Poverty, Study Finds." *Chicago Sun-Times* (February 26):18.

SPLC Report. 1998. "Intelligence Project Documents Big Growth in Hate Groups." Vol. 28. Southern Poverty Law Center (March): entire issue.

SPLC Report. 1999. "Crime Study: Violent Crime Hit Native Americans Hardest." (Spring):1.

SPLC Report. 2000. "'Patriot' Movement on the Wane." Vol. 30. Southern Poverty Law Center (June):3.

SPLC Report. 2001. "Hate Group Numbers Rise." Vol. 31. Southern Poverty Law Center (May):3.

St. Clair, Jeffrey. 2001. "Dumps 'R Us." *In These Times* (February 19):8.

Stacey, Judith. 1990. *Brave New Families: Stories of Domestic Upheaval in Late Twentieth-Century America.* New York: Basic Books.

Stacey, Judith. 1991. "Backward toward the Postmodern Family: Reflections on Gender, Kinship, and Class in the Silicon Valley." In Alan Wolfe (Ed.), *America at Century's End.* Berkeley, CA: University of California Press, pp. 17–34.

Stack, Carol B. 1990. "Different Voices, Different Visions: Gender, Culture, and Moral Reasoning." In Faye Ginsburg and Anna Lowenhaupt Tsing (Eds.), *Uncertain Terms: Negotiating Gender in American Culture*. Boston: Beacon Press, pp. 19–27.

Staples, Robert. 1982. *Black Masculinity: The Black Male Role in American Society*. San Francisco: Black Scholar Press.

Stashenko, Joel. 2001. "Cost of Trade Center Loss May Reach $105 Billion." *Denver Post* (October 5):21A.

Steel, Ronald. 2001. "The Weak at War with the Strong." *New York Times* (September 14). Online. Available: http://www.nytimes.com/2001/09/14/opinion/14STEE.html.

Stein, Peter J., Judith Richman, and Natalie Hannon. 1977. *The Family: Functions, Conflicts, and Symbols.* Reading, MA: Addison-Wesley.

Steinberg, Jacques. 1994. "U.S. Social Well-Being Is Rated Lowest Since Study Began in 1970." *New York Times,* "Themes of the Times" (Fall):4.

Steinberg, Jacques. 2001. "Gains Found for the Poor in Rigorous Preschool." *New York Times* (May 9). On-line. Available: http://www.nytimes.com/2001/05/09/national/09SCHO.html.

Steinhauer, Jennifer. 2001. "AIDS Altered the Fabric of New York in Ways Subtle and Vast." *New York Times* (June 4). Online. Available: http://www.nytimes.com/2001/06/04/health/04AIDS.html.

Steinmetz, Suzanne K. 1977/1978. "The Battered Husband Syndrome." *Victimology* 2 (3/4):449–509.

Steinmetz, Suzanne K. 1978. "Battered Parents." *Society* 15 (July/August):54–55.

Sternberg, Steve. 1998. "Scientists Disturbed by Slow Pace." *USA Today* (July 23):1D, 2D.

Sternberg, Steve. 2001. "Race, Locale Raise Men's Heart Risk." *USA Today* (June 18):1D.

Stevens, William K. 1989. "Racial Differences Found in Kind of Medical Care Americans Get." *New York Times* (January 13):1,C18.

Stith, Sandra M., Karen H. Rosen, Kimberly A. Middleton, Amy L. Busch, Kirsten Lundeberg, and Russell P. Carleton. 2000. "The Intergenerational Transmission of Spouse Abuse: A Meta-Analysis." *Journal of Marriage and the Family* 62 (August):640–654.

Stolberg, Sheryl Gay. 1997. "The Better Half Got the Worse End." *New York Times* (July 20):E1, E4.

Stolberg, Sheryl Gay. 2001a. "After Two Centuries, Washington Is Losing Its Only Public Hospital." *New York Times* (May 7). Online. Available: http://www.nytimes.com/2001/05/07/health/07HOSP.html.

Stolberg, Sheryl Gay. 2001b. "AIDS: U.S. at 'End of the Beginning' of Epidemic." *Denver Post* (June 3):14A.

Stone, Andrea. 2001. "Cyberspace Is the Next Battlefield." *USA Today* (June 19):1A–2A.

Stone, Christopher. 1999. "Race, Crime, and the Administration of Justice." *National Institute of Justice* (April):26–32.

Stone, Lawrence. 1985. "Sex in the West: The Strange History of Human Sexuality." *New Republic* (July 8):25–37.

Straus, Murray A., and Richard J. Gelles. 1985. "Societal Change and Change in Family Violence from 1975 to 1985 as Revealed by Two National Surveys." Paper presented at the American Society of Criminology, San Diego, CA, November. Published by the Family Violence Research Program, University of New Hampshire, Durham.

Straus, Murray A., Richard Gelles, and Suzanne K. Steinmetz. 1980. *Behind Closed Doors: Violence in the American Family.* New York: Anchor Books.

Street, Paul. 2001a. "Race, Prison, and Poverty." *Z Magazine* 14 (May):25–31.

Street, Paul. 2001b. "Free to be Poor." *Z Magazine* 14 (June):25–29.

Swartz, Jon. 2001. "Experts Fear Cyberspace Could Be Terrorists' Next Target." *USA Today* (October 9):1B–2B.

Swedish Institute. 1993. "General Facts on Sweden." Fact Sheets on Sweden (December 5):2.

Sykes, Gresham M., and Francis T. Cullen. 1992. *Criminology,* 2nd ed. Orlando, FL: Harcourt Brace Jovanovich.

Symonds, William C. 2001. "How to Fix America's Schools." *Business Week* (March 19):67–80.

Szasz, Thomas S. 1970. *The Manufacture of Madness.* New York: Delta Books.

Szasz, Thomas S. 1972. "The Ethics of Addiction." *Harper's Magazine* (April):74–79.

Szasz, Thomas S. 1975. *Ceremonial Chemistry: The Ritual Persecution of Drugs, Addicts, and Pushers*. Garden City, NY: Doubleday/Anchor.

Takaki, Ronald. 1993. *A Different Mirror: A History of Multicultural America*. Boston: Little, Brown.

Tannen, Deborah. 1990. *You Just Don't Understand: Women and Men in Conversation*. New York: Ballantine Books.

Tannen, Deborah. 1991. "Teachers' Classroom Strategies Should Recognize That Men and Women Use Language Differently." *Chronicle of Higher Education* 37 (40):B3.

Tanner, Lindsey. 2001. "Cardiac Studies Not Representative." *USA Today* (August 8):7D.

Taub, Diane E., and Patricia L. Fanflick. 2000. "The Inclusion of Disability in Introductory Sociology Textbooks." *Teaching Sociology* 28 (January):12–23.

Taylor, Robert Joseph, Linda M. Chatters, M. Belinda Tucker, and Edith Lewis. 1991. "Developments in Research on Black Families." In Alan Booth, (Ed.), *Contemporary Families: Looking Forward, Looking Back*. Minneapolis, MN: Naitonal Council on Family Relations, pp. 275–296.

Temple, Raston. 2000. "Oil Won't Solve Energy 'Crisis.'" *USA Today* (December 22):9A.

Terkel, Studs. 1975. *Working: People Talk about What They Do All Day and How They Feel about What They Do*. New York: Avon Books.

Thomas, Evan, and Michael Hirsh. 2000. "The Future of Terror." *Newsweek* (January 10):35–37.

Thomas, Jo. 2001. "Painful Steps in the Evolution of a Group Home." *New York Times* (April 10). Online. Available: http://www.nytimes.com/2001/04/10/national/10MENT.html.

Thomas, Karen. 2000a. "Parents Pressured to Put Kids on Drugs." *USA Today* (August 8):1D.

Thomas, Karen. 2000b. "Stealing, Dealing and Ritalin." *USA Today* (November 27):1D–2D.

Thomas, Karen. 2001. "Back to School for ADHD Drugs." *USA Today* (August 28):1D–2D.

Thompson, Larry. 1995. "Search for a Gay Gene." *Time* (June 12):61–62.

Thompson, Mark. 1998. "Shining a Light on Abuse." *Time* (August 3):42–43.

Thorne, Barrie. 1993. *Gender Play: Girls and Boys in School*. New Brunswick, NJ: Rutgers University Press.

Thornton, Russell. 1996. "North American Indians and the Demography of Contact." In Silvia Pedraza and Ruben Rumbaut (Eds.), *Origins and Destinies: Immigration, Race, and Ethnicity in America*. Belmont, CA: Wadsworth, pp. 43–50.

Thurow, Lester C. 1995a. "Companies Merge; Families Break Up." *New York Times* (September 3):A11.

Thurow, Lester C. 1995b. "Why Their World Might Crumble." *New York Times Magazine* (November 19):78–79.

Tienda, Marta, and Susan Simonelli. 2001. "Hispanic Students Are Missing from Diversity Debates." *Chronicle of Higher Education* (June 1):A16.

Time. 2001a. "Where the Bombs Are." (May 14):26.

Time. 2001b. "Sayings of Osama." (September 24):58.

Timmer, Doug A. 1991. "Drug War: The State in the Inner-City." Paper presented to the joint meeting of the Law and Society Association and the Research Committee on the Sociology of Law of the International Sociological Association, University of Amsterdam, the Netherlands, June.

Timmer, Doug A., D. Stanley Eitzen, and Kathryn D. Talley. 1994. *Paths to Homelessness: Extreme Poverty and the Urban Housing Crisis*. Boulder, CO: Westview Press.

Tingus, Steven. 2000. "Telethon Broadcasts the Wrong Message." *Denver Post* (September 4):10B.

Tivnan, Edward. 1987. "Homosexuals and the Churches." *New York Times Magazine* (October 11):84–91.

Tolan, Sandy. 2001. "Despair Feeds Hatred, Extremism." *USA Today* (September 20):13A.

Toppo, Greg. 2001. "850,000 Kids Are Being Taught at Home." *USA Today* (August 6):5D.

Torry, Saundra. 1998. "Building a Valhalla for Lobbyists." *Washington Post National Weekly Edition* (March 23):32.

Townsend, Johnny. 1996. "Murder Is a Family Value." *Z Magazine* 9 (June):11–12.

Trafford, Abigail. 1982. "New Health Hazard: Being Out of Work." *U.S. News & World Report* (June 14):81–82.

Tullock, S. (Ed.). 1993. *The Reader's Digest Oxford Wordfinder*. Oxford: Clarendon Press.

Turner, Jonathan H. 1977. *Social Problems in America*. New York: Harper & Row.

Uchitelle, Louis. 2001. "U.S. Jobless Rate Rose to 4.5% in April." *New York Times* (May 5). Online. Available: http://www.nytimes.com/2001/05/05/business05ECON. html.

Union of the Physically Impaired against Segregation. (UPIAS). 1976. *Fundamental Principles of Disability*. London: UPIAS.

Unnithan, N. Prabha. 1994. "The Processing of Homicide Cases with Child Victims: Systemic and Situational Contingencies." *Journal of Criminal Justice* 22(1):41–50.

USA Today. 1989. "Kids' Health: The Obstacles." (March 3):1.

USA Today. 1996a. "Smoke and Mirrors Can't Cure Fast-Failing Medicare." (June 6):12A.

USA Today. 1997a. "Scandal Exposes Virtues, Sins of For-Profit Hospitals." (August 12):14A.

USA Today. 1997b. "Schools Need Answers to Rising Dropout Rates." (October 14):14A.

USA Today. 1998a. "HMOs Tout Prevention, But Not All Take It Seriously." (August 11):10A.

USA Today. 1998b. "Raising Retirement Age a Poor Solution to Social Security Woes." (July 29):10A.

USA Today. 1999a. "A Small But Useful Start on Providing Long-Term Care." (January 5):16A.

USA Today. 1999b. "One-Size-Fits All Won't Control Urban Sprawl." (May 12):14A.

USA Today. 1999c. "Pressure to Boost Scores Leads Schools to Exclude Weaker Kids." (September 7):16A.

USA Today. 2001a. "Bush's Stealth Tactics Threaten Anti-Smoking Gains." (June 1):15A.

USA Today. 2001b. "America's Terrorist Enemies Have Bases Worldwide." (September 19):4A.

USA Today. 2001c. "Intelligence Fails." (September 21):23A.

USA Today. 2002. "Gender Equity: Suit Unfairly Attacks Effort to Boost Women's Sports." (January 21):10A.

Usborne, David. 1998. "Klan: The Next Generation." *Mexico City Times* (June 15):5.

U.S. Bureau of the Census. 1993a. *We the American . . . Asians*. Washington, DC: U.S. Government Printing Office.

U.S. Bureau of the Census. 1993b. *We the American . . . For-*

eign Born. Washington, DC: U.S. Government Printing Office.

U.S. Bureau of the Census. 1997. *Statistical Abstract of the United States: 1997*. Washington, DC: U.S. Government Printing Office.

U. S. Bureau of the Census. 2000a. "Poverty in the United States 1999." *Current Population Reports*. Series P60-210. Washington, DC: U.S. Government Printing Office.

U.S. Bureau of the Census. 2000b. "The Asian and Pacific Islander Population in the United States, 1999." *Current Population Reports*. Series P20-529. Washington, DC: U.S. Government Printing Office.

U.S. Bureau of the Census. 2000c. "Educational Attainment in the United States: March 2000." *Current Population Reports*. Series P-20-536. Washington, DC: U.S. Government Printing Office.

U.S. Bureau of the Census. 2000d. *Statistical Abstract of the U.S. 2000*, 120th ed. Washington, DC: U. S. Government Printing Office.

U.S. Bureau of the Census. 2001a. "Population Profile of the United States 1999." *Current Population Reports*. Series P23-205. Washington, DC: U.S. Government Printing Office.

U.S. Bureau of the Census. 2001b. "The Foreign-Born Population in the U.S." *Current Population Reports*. Series P20-534. Washington, DC: U.S. Government Printing Office.

U.S. Bureau of the Census. 2001c. "Overview of Race and Hispanic Origin: Census 2000 Brief." *Current Population Reports* (March). Washington, DC: U.S. Government Printing Office.

U.S. Bureau of the Census. 2001d. "The Hispanic Population in the U.S.: March 2000." *Current Population Reports*. Series P20-535. Washington, DC: U.S. Government Printing Office.

Usdansky, Margaret L. 1992. "Middle Class 'Pulling Apart' to Rich, Poor." *USA Today* (February 20):A1.

U.S. Department of Education. 2001. *Digest of Education Statistics 2000*. NCES 2001-034. Washington, DC: U.S. Government Printing Office.

U.S. Department of Health and Human Services. 1991. "Research on the Prevention of Alcohol-Related Problems among Ethnic Minorities." (June). Washington, DC: U.S. Government Printing Office.

U.S. Department of Health and Human Services (DHHS). 1999. *Health, United States 1999*. DHSS publication 99-1232. Washington, DC: DHHS.

U.S. Department of Justice. Published annually. *Uniform Crime Reports*. Washington, DC.

U.S. Department of Justice. Published annually. *National Crime Survey*. Washington, DC.

U.S. Department of Justice. 1998. "Prison and Jail Inmates at Midyear 1997." Bureau of Justice Statistics Bulletin, NCJ 167247 (January).

U.S. Department of Justice. 2000. "State Court Sentencing of Convicted Felons." *Bureau of Justice Statistics*.

U.S. Department of Labor. 1965. *The Negro Family: The Case for National Action*. Washington, DC: U.S. Government Printing Office.

U.S. Department of Labor, Bureau of Labor Statistics. 1999. *Employment and Earnings*. Washington, DC: Division of Labor Statistics.

U.S. Department of Labor, Bureau of Labor Statistics. 2001. *Employment and Earnings 2001*. Washington, DC: Division of Labor Statistics.

U.S. Department of Labor, Women's Bureau. 1997a. *Nontraditional Occupations for Employed Women in 1997*. Washington, DC: U.S. Government Printing Office.

U.S. Department of Labor, Women's Bureau. 1997b. *20 Leading Occupations of Employed Women*. Washington, DC: U.S. Government Printing Office.

U.S. Department of Labor, Women's Bureau. 2000a. *20 Leading Occupations of Employed Women, 2000 Annual Averages*. Washington, DC: U.S. Government Printing Office.

U.S. Department of Labor, Women's Bureau. 2000b. *Nontraditional Occupations for Women in 2000*. Washington, DC: U.S. Government Printing Office.

U.S. Department of Labor, Women's Bureau. 2000c. *20 Facts on Women Workers*. Washington, DC: Division of Labor Statistics.

U.S. Department of Labor, Women's Bureau. Bureau of Labor Statistics. *Nontraditional Occupations for Women in 2000*. Online. Available: http://www.dol.gov.wb/public/wb-pubs/nontra2000.htm.

U.S. News & World Report. 1994. "Campus Drinking: Who, Why, and How Much." (June 20):21.

U.S. Senate Committee on Governmental Affairs. 1978. *Interlocking Directorates among the Major United States Corporations*. Washington, DC: U.S. Government Printing Office.

Valdmanis, Thor. 2000. "Big Merger Wave Appears to Be Winding Down to a Trickle." *USA Today* (January 2):2B.

Valian, Virginia. 1998. "Running in Place." Sciences 38 (January/February):18–23.

Vandeven, Andrea M., and Eli H. Newberger. 1994. "Child Abuse." *Annual Review of Public Health* 15:367–379.

Vasey, S. 1992. "A Response to Liz Crow." *Coalition* (September):42–44.

Vecoli, Rudolph J. 1964. "Contadini in Chicago: A Critique of the Uprooted." *Journal of American History* 51:405–417.

Verdin, Tom. 2000. "Minorities in the Majority." Associated Press (August 31).

Vergano, Dan. 2001. "Chances of a Nuclear Attack Rated 'Very Low.'" *USA Today* (September 24):6A.

Vogel, Jennifer. 1994. "A Poor Excuse: If You Don't Have Money, It's Your Own Damn Fault." *Utne Reader* 62 (March/April):30–32.

Volti, Rudi. 1995. *Society and Technological Change*, 3rd ed. New York: St. Martin's Press.

Waldman, Steven. 1990. "The Stingy Politics of Head Start." *Newsweek*, Special Issue on Education (Fall/Winter):78–79.

Waldrop, Judith. 1990. "You'll Know It's the 21st Century When . . ." *American Demographics* 13 (December):23–27.

Waldrop, Judith, and Thomas Exter. 1991. "The Legacy of the 1980s." *American Demographics* (March):32–38.

Wali, Alakka. 1992. "Multiculturalism: An Anthropological Perspective." *Report from the Institute for Philosophy and Public Policy*, University of Maryland, Vol. 23 (Spring/Summer):6–8.

Walley, Dean. n.d. *What Boys Can Be*. Kansas City: Hallmark.

Walley, Dean. n.d. *What Girls Can Be*. Kansas City: Hallmark.

Walter, Norbert. 2001. "Gobbling Energy and Wasting It, Too." *New York Times* (June 13). Online. Available: http://www.nytimes.com/2001/06/13/opinion/13WALT.html.

Waters, Mary C. 1996. "Optional Ethnicities: For Whites Only?" In Silvia Pedraza and Ruben G. Rumbaut (Eds.),

Origins and Destinies: Immigration, Race, and Ethnicity in America. Belmont, CA: Wadsworth, pp. 444–454.

Watson, Paul, Tyler Marshall, and Bob Drogin. 2001. "Bin Laden's Hate for America Has Its Roots in Iraq." *Denver Post* (September 16):3AA.

Watson, Traci. 2001. "U.N. Study: Global Warming Is Evident Now." *USA Today* (February 19):5A.

Wattenberg, Ben. 2001. "The Big News in Birth Data Doesn't Concern Only Teens." *Rocky Mountain News* (May 11):50A.

Weaver, Peter. 2000. "Going Hungry: It Still Happens." *AARP Bulletin* 41 (June):9–11.

Webb, Tom. 1994. "Farmers' Chemicals Deadly, Study Says." *Denver Post* (October 19):8A.

Weber, Lynn. 2001. *Understanding Race, Class, Gender, and Sexuality: A Conceptual Framework*. New York: McGraw-Hill.

Weikel, Dan. 1995. "Crack War Waged by Race." *Denver Post* (May 21):1A,7A.

Weisberg, Jacob. 1996. *In Defense of Government*. New York: Scribner.

Weiss, Kenneth R. 2000. "More Rich Kids Get to Take Extra Time on SAT." *Denver Post* (January 9):2A.

Weiss, Lawrence D. 1997. *Private Medicine and Public Health: Profit, Politics, and Prejudice in the American Health Care Enterprise*. Boulder, CO: Westview Press.

Weiss, Rick. 2001. "Medieval Warfare in Modern Times." *Washington Post National Weekly Edition* (September 24):39.

Weissbourd, Richard. 1994. "Divided Families, Whole Children." *American Prospect* 18 (Summer):66–72.

Weissman, Robert. 1998. "Staggering Inequality." *Multinational Monitor* 19 (September):28–29.

Weitzman, Lenore J. 1985. *The Divorce Revolution: The Unexpected Social and Economic Consequences for Women and Children in America*. New York: Free Press.

Weitzman, Lenore J., Deborah Eifler, Elizabeth Hokada, and Catherine Ross. 1972. "Sex-Role Socialization in Picture Books for Preschool Children." *American Journal of Sociology* 77 (May):1125–1150.

Weller, Robert. 1998. "Gay 'Conversion' Therapy Decried." *Denver Post* (December 12):6A.

Wellman, David T. 1977. *Portraits of White Racism*, 2nd ed. Cambridge: Cambridge University Press.

Wellstone, Paul. 1998a. "The People's Trust Fund." *Nation* (July 27/August 3):4–5.

Wellstone, Paul. 1998b. "A Time for Change." On the Road with Paul Wellstone. *Newsletter*. (Summer):1–2.

Werner, Erica. 2001. "Some See 'Minority' as an Outdated Term in No-Majority California." *Denver Post* (May 8):5A.

Wertheimer, Fred. 1996. "The Dirtiest Election Ever." *Washington Post National Weekly Edition* (November 11): 29–30.

West, Candace, and Don Zimmerman. 1987. "Doing Gender." *Gender & Society* 1:125–151.

Wharton, Tony. 1998. "Expect Hurricanes Because of Gays, Pat Robertson Says." *Denver Post* (June 10):14A.

Wheeler, David L. 1992. "Studies Tying Homosexuality to Genes Draw Criticism from Researchers." *Chronicle of Higher Education* (February 5):A1–A2, A9.

Wickham, DeWayne. 2001. "Baltimore Is Facing a Bleak Future." *Coloradoan* (June 11):A6.

Wilgoren, Jodi. 1999. "Police Profiling Debate: Acting on Experience or on Bias." *New York Times* (April 9): 1,5.

Wilgoren, Jodi. 2000. "As U.S. Debate Intensifies, Pay for Teachers Rises 3%." *New York Times* (July 5). Online. Available: http://www.nytimes.com/library/national/070500salary-edu.html.

Will, George. 1991. "A Plan to Pull Poor Up and Out." *Rocky Mountain News* (March 24):115.

Williams, David R. 1990. "Socioeconomic Differentials in Health: A Review and Redirection." *Social Psychology Quarterly* 53 (June):81–99.

Williams, David R. 1996. "The Health of the African American Population." In Silvia Pedraza and Ruben G. Rumbaut (Eds.), *Origins and Destinies: Immigration, Race, and Ethnicity in America*. Belmont, CA: Wadsworth, pp. 404–416.

Williams, Gertrude. 1980. "Toward the Eradication of Child Abuse and Neglect at Home." In Gertrude Williams and John Money (Eds.), *Traumatic Abuse and the Neglect of Children at Home*. Baltimore: Johns Hopkins University Press, pp. 588–605.

Williams, J. Allen, JoEtta A. Vernon, Martha C. Williams, and Karen Malecha. 1987. "Sex Role Socialization in Picture Books: An Update." *Social Science Quarterly* 68 (March):148–156.

Williams, Juan. 1994. "The New Segregation." *Modern Maturity* 37 (April/May):24–33.

Williamson, Theresa. 2000. "Minorities Pay Higher Interest, Group Says." *Chicago Sun-Times* (November 1):71,74.

Williamson, Thad. 2000. "The Real Y2K Crisis: Global Economic Inequality." *Dollars & Sense*, No. 227 (January/February):42.

Willis, Ellen. 1998. "We Need a Radical Left." *Nation* (June 29):18–21.

Wills, Garry. 1995. "The New Revolutionaries." *New York Review* (August 10):50–55.

Wilson, E. O. 2000. "Vanishing Before Our Eyes." *Time* (April/May):29–34.

Wilson, William J. 1987. *The Truly Disadvantaged: The Inner City, the Underclass, and Public Policy*. Chicago. University of Chicago Press.

Wilson, William J. 1996. *When Work Disappears: The World of the New Urban Poor.* New York: Knopf.

Wilson, William J., and Andrew J. Cherlin. 2001. "The Real Test of Welfare Reform Still Lies Ahead." *New York Times* (July 13). Online. Available: http://www.nytimes.com/2001/07/13/opinion/13WILS. html.

Winant, Howard. 1994. *Racial Conditions: Politics, Theory, Comparisons.* Minneapolis, MN: University of Minnesota Press.

Winant, Howard. 1997. "Behind Blue Eyes: Whiteness and Contemporary U.S. Racial Politics." In Michelle Fine, Lois Weis, Linda C. Powell, and L. Mun Wong (Eds.), *Off White: Readings on Race, Power, and Society.* New York: Routledge, pp. 40–53.

Winerip, Michael. 1998. "Binge Nights: The Emergency on Campus." *New York Times,* "Educational Life" (January 4):29–31, 42.

Wingert, Pat. 2000. "No More 'Afternoon Nasties'" *Newsweek* (December 4):59.

Winters, Rebecca. 2000. "From Homeless to Harvard." *Time* (September 11):55.

Wise, Tim. 1989. "Radical Surgery." *Dollars & Sense* 150 (October):6–9.

Witt, Susan. 1997. "Parental Influence on Children's Socialization to Gender Roles." *Adolescence* 32 (126): 253–259.

Wolf, Rosalie S. 2000. "The Nature and Scope of Elder Abuse." *Generations* 24 (Summer):6–12.

Wolfe, Alan. 1989. *Whose Keeper? Social Science and Moral Obligation*. Berkeley, CA: University of California Press.

Wolff, Edward N. 1995. *Top Heavy: A Study of the Increasing Inequality of Wealth in America*. New York: Twentieth Century Fund Press.

Wolff, Edward N. 2001. "The Rich Get Richer. . . and Why the Poor Don't." *American Prospect* (February 12):15–17.

Woodward, Kenneth L. 2001. "A Peaceful Faith, a Fanatic Few." *Newsweek* (September 24):67–68.

Woolhandler, Steffie, and David Himmelstein. 1997. "For Patients, Not Profits." *Nation* (December 22):6–7.

Wyly, Elvin K., Norman J. Glickman, and Michael L. Lahr. 1998. "A Top 10 List of Things to Know about American Cities." *Cityscape: A Journal of Policy Development and Research* 3 (3):7–32.

Yetman, Norman R. 1991. "Introduction." In Norman R. Yetman (Ed.), *Majority and Minority: The Dynamics of Race and Ethnicity in American Life*. Boston: Allyn & Bacon, pp. 1–29.

Zagorin, Adam. 2000. "Are We Over a Barrel?" *Time* (December 18):B6,B11.

Zajac, Brian. 2000. "Global Giants: The Largest 100 U.S. Multinationals." *Forbes* (July 24):335–338.

Zaldivar, R. A. 1997. "Men Still Rare in Women's Work." *Denver Post* (February 2):19A.

Zeitlin, Maurice, Kenneth G. Lutterman, and James W. Russell. 1977. "Death in Vietnam: Class, Poverty, and the Risks of War." In Maurice Zeitlin (Ed.), *American Society, Inc.*, 2nd ed. Chicago: Rand McNally, pp. 143–155.

Zepezauer, Mark, and Arthur Naiman. 1996. *Take the Rich Off Welfare*. Tucson, AZ: Odonian Press.

Zernike, Kate. 2000. "Gap Widens Again on Tests Given to Blacks and Whites." *New York Times* (August 25). Online. Available: http://www.nytimes.com/library/national/082500race-tests-edu.html.

Zhou, Min. 1997. "Growing Up American: The Challenge Confronting Immigrant Children and Children of Immigrants." *Annual Review of Sociology* 23:63–95.

Zikmund, Barbara Brown, Adair T. Lummis, and Patricia Mei Yin Chang. 1998. *Clergy Women: An Uphill Calling*. Louisville, KY: Westminster John Knox Press.

Zimmer, Lynn, and John P. Morgan. 1997. *Marijuana Myths/Marijuana Facts: A Review of the Scientific Evidence*. New York: Lindesmith Center.

Zimmerman, Tim, Susan V. Lawrence, and Brian Palmer. 1996. *U.S. News & World Report* (September 9):36–39.

Z Magazine. 2000. "For Justice and Against Prison." Vol. 13 (March):4.

Zuckerman, Mortimer B. 2000a. "Whistling While We Work." *U.S. News & World Report* (January 24):72.

Zuckerman, Mortimer B. 2000b. "A Bit of Straight Talk." *U.S. News & World Report* (October 2):76.

Zuckerman, Mortimer B. 2001. "Rethinking the Next War." *U.S. News & World Report* (March 5):64.

Zwerling, L. Steven. 1995. "Commentary: Redefining One-Third of a Nation." *Educational Record* 76 (Spring/Summer):19–21.

Name Index

Subject Index

Photo Credits, *continued from copyright page*
Chapter 3: p. 53, © Reuters/Pat Hamilton/Archive Photos/Getty Images; p. 68, © AFP/CORBIS; p. 74, © William F. Campbell/TimePix.
Chapter 4: p. 79, © Science Photo Library/Photo Researchers, Inc.; p. 83, © Van Bucher/Photo Researchers, Inc.; p. 86, © Andrew Lichtenstein/The Image Works; p. 94, AP/Wide World Photos.
Chapter 5: p. 112, © Rudi Von Briel/PhotoEdit; p. 118, © Felicia Martinez/PhotoEdit; p. 119, © A. Ramey/PhotoEdit; p. 140, © Wally McNamee/CORBIS.
Chapter 6: p. 143, © Miro Vintoniv/Stock Boston; p. 148, © David Wells/The Image Works; p. 157, © Dennis MacDonald/PhotoEdit.
Chapter 7: p. 179, © Attal Serge/CORBIS Sygma; p. 186, © Jeff Greenberg/PhotoEdit; p. 195, © Michael Newman/PhotoEdit.
Chapter 8: p. 214, © Jeff Greenberg/PhotoEdit; p. 222, © Morton Beebe/CORBIS; p. 225, AP/Wide World Photos; p. 232, © Will Hart/PhotoEdit; p. 238. AP/Wide World Photos.
Chapter 9: p. 242, © Bill Bachmann/The Image Works; p. 251, © Michelle Bridwell/PhotoEdit; p. 253, © Mary Kate Denny/PhotoEdit; p. 271, © Michelle Bridwell/PhotoEdit.
Chapter 10: p. 279, © Pizzoli Alberto/CORBIS Sygma; p. 290, © Alex Wong/Newsmakers/Getty Images; p. 297, © James Wilson/Woodfin Camp & Associates.
Chapter 11: p. 305, AP/Wide World Photos; p. 307, © Nita Winter/The Image Works; p. 313, AP/Wide World Photos; p. 323, © Mark Richards/PhotoEdit.
Chapter 12: p. 332, © A. Ramey/Woodfin Camp & Associates; p. 339, © Joe Raedle/Newsmakers/Getty Images; p. 349, AP/Wide World Photos; p. 354, © A. Ramey/PhotoEdit.
Chapter 13: p. 368, © Michael L. Abramson/Woodfin Camp & Associates; p. 380, © Mark Richards/PhotoEdit; p. 389, © Bobbie DeHerrera/Getty Images; p. 393, © Cont/Jose Azel/Woodfin Camp & Associates.
Chapter 14: p. 401, © James Nielsen/Getty Images; p. 407, © Chuck Nacke/Woodfin Camp & Associates; p. 421, © Michael Newman/PhotoEdit; p. 425, AP/Wide World Photos.
Chapter 15: p. 432, © Darren Modricker/CORBIS; p. 435, © Richard Pasley/Stock Boston; p. 441, © Michael Newman/PhotoEdit; p. 445, © Elena Rooraid/PhotoEdit; p. 449, © Katherine McGlynn/The Image Works.
Chapter 16: p. 466, © Peter Byron/PhotoEdit; p. 468, © Michael Newman/PhotoEdit; p. 470, AP/Wide World Photos; p. 480, © Paul Solomon/Woodfin Camp & Associates.
Chapter 17: p. 497, © Charles Gupton/Stock Boston; p. 506, © Bob Daemmrich/The Image Works; p. 515, © A. Ramey/PhotoEdit; p. 521, © Mark Richards/PhotoEdit.
Chapter 18: p. 529, © Greg Martin/CORBIS Sygma; p. 533, Photo by James A. Farrally/U.S. Navy/Getty Images; p. 538, AP/Wide World Photos; p. 556, AP/Wide World Photos.
Chapter 19: p. 560, © Paul Conklin/PhotoEdit; p. 576, AP/Wide World Photos.

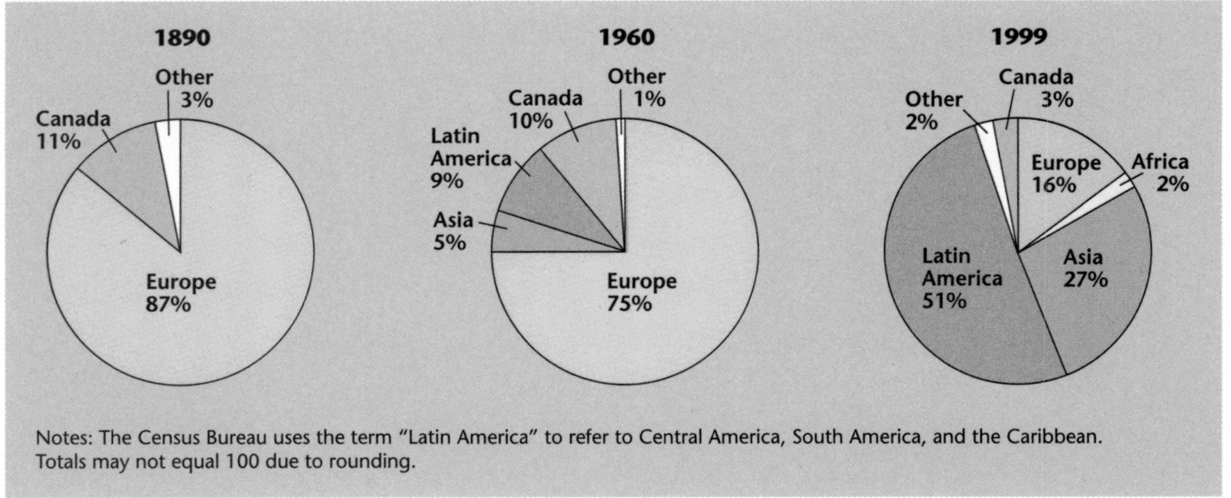

Composition of the U.S. Foreign-Born Population, by Regions or Country of Birth

Source: Foreign-Born Population. June 30, 2001. Online. Available: http://ameristat.org.

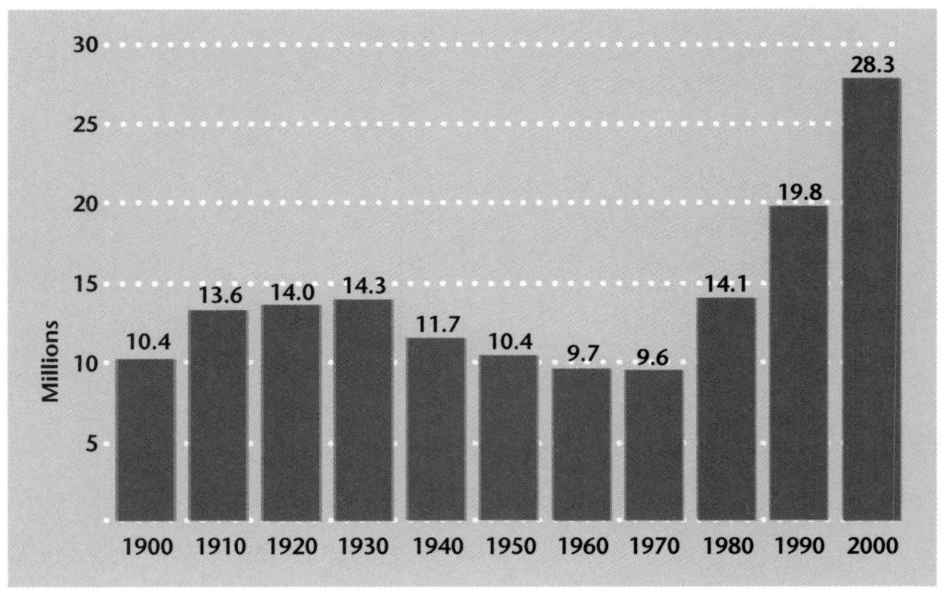

Foreign-Born Population: 1900 to 2000 (millions)

Sources: U.S. Bureau of the Census. 1993. *We the Americans . . . Foreign Born.* (September):2; G. C. Armas. 2000. "Foreign-Born Population in U.S. Passes 28.3," Associated Press (January 3).